BIOLOGICAL KNOWLEDGE DISCOVERY HANDBOOK

Wiley Series on

Bioinformatics: Computational Techniques and Engineering

A complete list of the titles in this series appears at the end of this volume.

BIOLOGICAL KNOWLEDGE DISCOVERY HANDBOOK
Preprocessing, Mining, and Postprocessing of Biological Data

Edited by

MOURAD ELLOUMI
Laboratory of Technologies of Information and Communication and Electrical Engineering (LaTICE) and University of Tunis-El Manar, Tunisia

ALBERT Y. ZOMAYA
The University of Sydney

Cover Design: Michael Rutkowski
Cover Image: ©iStockphoto/cosmin 4000

Published by John Wiley & Sons, Inc., Hoboken, New Jersey.
Published simultaneously in Canada.

For general information on our other products and services or for technical support, please contact our Customer Care Department within the United States at (800) 762-2974, outside the United States at (317) 572-3993 or fax (317) 572-4002.

Wiley also publishes its books in a variety of electronic formats. Some content that appears in print may not be available in electronic formats. For more information about Wiley products, visit our web site at www.wiley.com.

Library of Congress Cataloging-in-Publication Data:

Elloumi, Mourad.
  Biological knowledge discovery handbook : preprocessing, mining, and postprocessing of biological data / Mourad Elloumi, Albert Y. Zomaya.
    pages cm. – (Wiley series in bioinformatics; 23)
  ISBN 978-1-118-13273-9 (hardback)
  1. Bioinformatics. 2. Computational biology. 3. Data mining. I. Zomaya, Albert Y. II. Title.
    QH324.2.E45 2012
    572.80285–dc23

                                                                    2012042379
Printed in the United States of America

10 9 8 7 6 5 4 3 2 1

To my family for their patience and support.

Mourad Elloumi

To my mother for her many sacrifices over the years.

Albert Y. Zomaya

CONTENTS

PART B: BIOLOGICAL DATA MODELING

PART C: BIOLOGICAL FEATURE EXTRACTION

PART D: BIOLOGICAL FEATURE SELECTION

SECTION II   BIOLOGICAL DATA MINING

PART E: REGRESSION ANALYSIS OF BIOLOGICAL DATA

PART F: BIOLOGICAL DATA CLUSTERING

SECTION III   BIOLOGICAL DATA POSTPROCESSING

PART K: BIOLOGICAL KNOWLEDGE INTEGRATION AND VISUALIZATION

PREFACE

With the massive developments in molecular biology during the last few decades, we are witnessing an exponential growth of both the volume and the complexity of biological data. For example, the Human Genome Project provided the sequence of the 3 billion DNA bases that constitute the human genome. Consequently, we are provided too with the sequences of about 100,000 proteins. Therefore, we are entering the postgenomic era: After having focused so many efforts on the accumulation of data, we now must to focus as much effort, and even more, on the analysis of the data. Analyzing this huge volume of data is a challenging task not only because of its complexity and its multiple and numerous correlated factors but also because of the continuous evolution of our understanding of the biological mechanisms. Classical approaches of biological data analysis are no longer efficient and produce only a very limited amount of information, compared to the numerous and complex biological mechanisms under study. From here comes the necessity to use computer tools and develop new in silico high-performance approaches to support us in the analysis of biological data and, hence, to help us in our understanding of the correlations that exist between, on one hand, structures and functional patterns of biological sequences and, on the other hand, genetic and biochemical mechanisms. *Knowledge discovery and data mining* (KDD) are a response to these new trends.

Knowledge discovery is a field where we combine techniques from algorithmics, soft computing, machine learning, knowledge management, artificial intelligence, mathematics, statistics, and databases to deal with the theoretical and practical issues of extracting *knowledge*, that is, new concepts or concept relationships, hidden in volumes of raw data. The knowledge discovery process is made up of three main phases: *data preprocessing*, *data processing*, also called *data mining*, and *data postprocessing*. Knowledge discovery offers the capacity to automate complex search and data analysis tasks. We distinguish two types of knowledge discovery systems: *verification systems* and *discovery* ones. Verification systems are limited to verifying the user's hypothesis, while discovery ones autonomously predict and explain new knowledge. Biological knowledge discovery process should take into account both the characteristics of the biological data and the general requirements of the knowledge discovery process.

Data mining is the main phase in the knowledge discovery process. It consists of extracting nuggets of information, that is, pertinent patterns, pattern correlations, and estimations or rules, hidden in huge bodies of data. The extracted information will be used in the verification of the hypothesis or the prediction and explanation of knowledge. Biological data mining aims at extracting motifs, functional sites, or clustering/classification rules from biological sequences.

Biological KDD are complementary to laboratory experimentation and help to speed up and deepen research in modern molecular biology. They promise to bring us new insights into the growing volumes of biological data.

This book is a survey of the most recent developments on techniques and approaches in the field of biological KDD. It presents the results of the latest investigations in this field. The techniques and approaches presented deal with the most important and/or the newest topics encountered in this field. Some of these techniques and approaches represent improvements of old ones while others are completely new. Most of the other books on biological KDD either lack technical depth or focus on specific topics. This book is the first overview on techniques and approaches in biological KDD with both a broad coverage of this field and enough depth to be of practical use to professionals. The biological KDD techniques and approaches presented here combine sound theory with truly practical applications in molecular biology. This book will be extremely valuable and fruitful for people interested in the growing field of biological KDD, to discover both the fundamentals behind biological KDD techniques and approaches, and the applications of these techniques and approaches in this field. It can also serve as a reference for courses on bioinformatics and biological KDD. So, this book is designed not only for practitioners and professional researchers in computer science, life science, and mathematics but also for graduate students and young researchers looking for promising directions in their work. It will certainly point them to new techniques and approaches that may be the key to new and important discoveries in molecular biology.

This book is organized into 11 parts: Biological Data Management, Biological Data Modeling, Biological Feature Extraction, Biological Feature Selection, Regression Analysis of Biological Data, Biological Data Clustering, Biological Data Classification, Association Rules Learning from Biological Data, Text Mining and Application to Biological Data, High-Performance Computing for Biological Data Mining, and Biological Knowledge Integration and Visualization. The 48 chapters that make up the 11 parts were carefully selected to provide a wide scope with minimal overlap between the chapters so as to reduce duplication. Each contributor was asked that his or her chapter should cover review material as well as current developments. In addition, the authors chosen are leaders in their respective fields.

Mourad Elloumi and Albert Y. Zomaya

CONTRIBUTORS

Jad Abbass, Faculty of Science, Engineering and Computing, Kingston University, London, United Kingdom and Department of Computer Science and Mathematics, Lebanese American University, Beirut, Lebanon

Muhammad Abulaish, Center of Excellence in Information Assurance, King Saud University, Riyadh, Saudi Arabia and Department of Computer Science, Jamia Millia Islamia (A Central University), New Delhi, India

Syed Toufeeq Ahmed, Vanderbilt University Medical Center, Nashville, Tennessee

Shiva Akbari-Birgani, Laboratory of Systems Biology and Bioinformatics, Institute of Biochemistry and Biophysics, University of Tehran, Tehran, Iran

Ali Al Mazari, School of Information Technologies, The University of Sydney, Sydney, Australia

Mohamed Al Sayed Issa, Computers and Systems Department, Faculty of Engineering, Zagazig University, Egypt

Yazdan Asgari, Laboratory of Systems Biology and Bioinformatics, Institute of Biochemistry and Biophysics, University of Tehran, Tehran, Iran

Wassim Ayadi, Laboratory of Technologies of Information and Communication and Electrical Engineering (LaTICE) and LERIA, University of Angers, Angers, France

Haider Banka, Department of Computer Science and Engineering, Indian School of Mines, Dhanbad, India

Laure Berti-Équille, Institut de Recherche pour le Développement, Montpellier, France

Gianluca Bontempi, Machine Learning Group, Computer Science Department, Université Libre de Bruxelles, Brussels, Belgium

Nigel P. Brown, BioQuant, University of Heidelberg, Heidelberg, Germany

Giulia Bruno, Dipartimento di Ingegneria Gestionale e della Produzione, Politecnico di Torino, Torino, Italy

David Campos, DETI/IEETA, University of Aveiro, Aveiro, Portugal

Jessica Andrea Carballido, Laboratorio de Investigación y Desarrollo en Computación Científica (LIDeCC), Dept. Computer Science and Engineering, Universidad Nacional del Sur, Bahía Blanca, Argentina

Luciano Cascione, Department of Clinical and Molecular Biomedicine, University of Catania, Italy

Ümit V. Çatalyürek, Department of Biomedical Informatics, The Ohio State University, Columbus, Ohio

Carlo Cattani, Department of Mathematics, University of Salerno, Fisciano (SA), Italy

Meghana Chitale, Department of Computer Science, Purdue University, West Lafayette, Indiana

Young-Rae Cho, Department of Computer Science, Baylor University, Waco, Texas

Kwok Pui Choi, Department of Statistics and Applied Probability, National University of Singapore, Singapore

Matteo Comin, Department of Information Engineering, University of Padova, Padova, Italy

Francesca Cordero, Department of Computer Science, University of Torino, Turin, Italy

Suresh Dara, Department of Computer Science and Engineering, Indian School of Mines, Dhanbad, India

Bhaskar DasGupta, Department of Computer Science, University of Illinois at Chicago, Chicago, Illinois

Hasan Davulcu, Department of Computer Science and Engineering, Ira A. Fulton Engineering, Arizona State University, Tempe, Arizona

Mourad Elloumi, Laboratory of Technologies of Information and Communication and Electrical Engineering (LaTICE) and University of Tunis-El Manar, Tunisia

Juan Esquivel-Rodríguez, Department of Computer Science, Purdue University, West Lafayette, Indiana

Alfredo Ferro, Department of Clinical and Molecular Biomedicine, University of Catania, Italy

Alessandro Fiori, Dipartimento di Automatica e Informatica, Politecnico di Torino, Torino, Italy

Adelaide Valente Freitas, DMat/CIDMA, University of Aveiro, Portugal

Terry Gaasterland, Scripps Genome Center, University of California San Diego, San Diego, California

Cristian Andrés Gallo, Laboratorio de Investigación y Desarrollo en Computación Científica (LIDeCC), Dept. Computer Science and Engineering, Universidad Nacional del Sur, Bahía Blanca, Argentina

Roger J. Garsia, Department of Clinical Immunology, Royal Prince Alfred Hospital, Sydney, Australia

Raffaele Giancarlo, Department of Mathematics and Informatics, University of Palermo, Palermo, Italy

Rosalba Giugno, Department of Clinical and Molecular Biomedicine, University of Catania, Italy

Jin-Kao Hao, LERIA, University of Angers, Angers, France

Ayat Hatem, Department of Biomedical Informatics, The Ohio State University, Columbus, Ohio

Heiko Horn, Department of Disease Systems Biology, The Novo Nordisk Foundation Center for Protein Research, Faculty of Health Sciences, University of Copenhagen, Copenhagen, Denmark

Ting Hu, Computational Genetics Laboratory, Geisel School of Medicine, Dartmouth College, Lebanon, New Hampshire

Kun Huang, Department of Biomedical Informatics, The Ohio State University, Columbus, Ohio

Zina M. Ibrahim, Social Genetic and Developmental Psychiatry Centre, King's College London, London, United Kingdom

Dino Ienco, Institut de Recherche en Sciences et Technologies pour l'Environnement, Montpellier, France

Costas S. Iliopoulos, Department of Informatics, King's College London, Strand, London, United Kingdom and Digital Ecosystems & Business Intelligence Institute, Curtin University, Centre for Stringology & Applications, Perth, Australia

Jahiruddin, Department of Computer Science, Jamia Millia Islamia (A Central University), New Delhi, India

Laetitia Jourdan, INRIA Lille Nord Europe, Villeneuve d'Ascq, France

Lakshmi Kaligounder, Department of Computer Science, University of Illinois at Chicago, Chicago, Illinois

Radha Krishna Murthy Karuturi, Computational and Mathematical Biology, Genome Institute of Singapore, Singapore

Khairul A. Kasmiran, School of Information Technologies, The University of Sydney, Sydney, Australia

Ioannis Kavakiotis, Department of Informatics, Aristotle University of Thessaloniki, Thessaloniki, Greece

Kamer Kaya, Department of Biomedical Informatics, The Ohio State University, Columbus, Ohio

Catharina Maria Keet, School of Computer Science, University of KwaZulu-Natal, Durban, South Africa

Daisuke Kihara, Department of Computer Science, Purdue University, West Lafayette, Indiana and Department of Biological Sciences, Purdue University, West Lafayette, Indiana

Gaurav Kumar, Department of Chemistry and Biomolecular Sciences and ARC Centre of Excellence in Bioinformatics, Macquarie University, Sydney, Australia

Chee Keong Kwoh, School of Computer Engineering, Nanyang Technological University, Singapore

Giuseppe Lancia, Department of Mathematics and Informatics, University of Udine, Udine, Italy

Hee-Jin Lee, Department of Computer Science, Korea Advanced Institute of Science and Technology, Daejeon, South Korea

Juntao Li, Computational and Mathematical Biology, Genome Institute of Singapore, Singapore and Department of Statistics and Applied Probability, National University of Singapore, Singapore

Wentian Li, Robert S. Boas Center for Genomics and Human Genetics, Feinstein Institute for Medical Research, North Shore LIJ Health Systems, Manhasset, New York

Yehua Li, Department of Statistics and Statistical Laboratory, Iowa State University, Ames, Iowa

Charles Lindsey, StataCorp, College Station, Texas

Giosué Lo Bosco, Department of Mathematics and Informatics, University of Palermo, Palermo, Italy and I.E.ME.S.T., Istituto Euro Mediterraneo di Scienza e Tecnologia, Palermo, Italy

Nashat Mansour, Department of Computer Science and Mathematics, Lebanese American University, Beirut, Lebanon

Ali Masoudi-Nejad, Laboratory of Systems Biology and Bioinformatics, Institute of Biochemistry and Biophysics, University of Tehran, Tehran, Iran

Sérgio Matos, DETI/IEETA, University of Aveiro, Aveiro, Portugal

Patrick E. Meyer, Machine Learning Group, Computer Science Department, Université Libre de Bruxelles, Brussels, Belgium

Debahuti Mishra, Institute of Technical Education and Research, Siksha O Anusandhan University, Bhubaneswar, Odisha, India

Sashikala Mishra, Institute of Technical Education and Research, Siksha O Anusandhan University, Bhubaneswar, Odisha, India

Ahmed Mokaddem, Laboratory of Technologies of Information and Communication and Electrical Engineering (LaTICE) and University of Tunis-El Manar, El Manar, Tunisia

Kartick Chandra Mondal, Laboratory I3S, University of Nice Sophia-Antipolis, Sophia-Antipolis, France

Jason H. Moore, Computational Genetics Laboratory, Geisel School of Medicine, Dartmouth College, Lebanon, New Hampshire

Fouzia Moussouni, Université de Rennes 1, Rennes, France

Mohamed Nadif, LIPADE, University of Paris-Descartes, Paris, France

Radhika Nair, Department of Computer Science and Engineering, Ira A. Fulton Engineering, Arizona State University, Tempe, Arizona

Jean-Christophe Nebel, Faculty of Science, Engineering and Computing, Kingston University, London, United Kingdom

Alioune Ngom, School of Computer Science, University of Windsor, Windsor, Ontario, Canada

Thuy Diem Nguyen, School of Computer Engineering, Nanyang Technological University, Singapore

Oleg Okun, SMARTTECCO, Stockholm, Sweden

José Luis Oliveira, DETI/IEETA, University of Aveiro, Portugal

Hatice Gülçin Özer, Department of Biomedical Informatics, The Ohio State University, Columbus, Ohio

Evangelos Pafilis, Institute of Marine Biology Biotechnology and Aquaculture, Hellenic Centre for Marine Research, Heraklion, Crete, Greece

Jong C. Park, Department of Computer Science, Korea Advanced Institute of Science and Technology, Daejeon, South Korea

Nicolas Pasquier, Laboratory I3S, University of Nice Sophia-Antipolis, Sophia-Antipolis, France

Chintan Patel, Department of Computer Science and Engineering, Ira A. Fulton Engineering, Arizona State University, Tempe, Arizona

Yudi Pawitan, Department of Medical Epidemiology and Biostatistics, Karolinska Institute, Stockholm, Sweden

Ruggero G. Pensa, Department of Computer Science, University of Torino, Turin, Italy

Giuseppe Pigola, IGA Technology Services, Udine, Italy

Luca Pinello, Department of Biostatistics, Harvard School of Public Health, Boston, Massachusetts; Department of Biostatistics and Computational Biology, Dana-Farber Cancer Institute, Boston, Massachusetts; and I.E.ME.S.T., Istituto Euro Mediterraneo di Scienza e Tecnologia, Palermo, Italy

Solon P. Pissis, Department of Informatics, King's College London, Strand, London, United Kingdom

Alberto Policriti, Department of Mathematics and Informatics and Institute of Applied Genomics, University of Udine, Udine, Italy

Ignacio Ponzoni, Laboratorio de Investigación y Desarrollo en Computación Científica (LIDeCC), Dept. Computer Science and Engineering, Universidad Nacional del Sur, Bahía Blanca, Argentina and Planta Piloto de Ingeniería Química (PLAPIQUI) CONICET, Bahía Blanca, Argentina

Alfredo Pulvirenti, Department of Clinical and Molecular Biomedicine, University of Catania, Italy

Shoba Ranganathan, Department of Chemistry and Biomolecular Sciences and ARC Centre of Excellence in Bioinformatics, Macquarie University, Sydney, Australia

Hendrik Rohn, Leibniz Institute of Plant Genetics and Crop Plant Research (IPK), Gatersleben, Germany

Haifa Ben Saber, Laboratory of Technologies of Information and Communication and Electrical Engineering (LaTICE) and University of Tunis, Tunisia

Lee Sael, Department of Computer Science, Purdue University, West Lafayette, Indiana and Department of Biological Sciences, Purdue University, West Lafayette, Indiana

Ali Salehzadeh-Yazdi, Laboratory of Systems Biology and Bioinformatics, Institute of Biochemistry and Biophysics, University of Tehran, Tehran, Iran

Rodrigo Santamaría, Department of Computer Science and Automation, University of Salamanca, Salamanca, Spain

Bertil Schmidt, Institut für Informatik, Johannes Gutenberg University, Mainz, Germany

Falk Schreiber, Leibniz Institute of Plant Genetics and Crop Plant Research (IPK), Gatersleben, Germany and Institute of Computer Science, Martin Luther University Halle-Wittenberg, Halle, Germany

Khedidja Seridi, INRIA Lille Nord Europe, Villeneuve d'Aseq, France

Kailash Shaw, Department of CSE, Gandhi Engineering College, Bhubaneswar, Odisha, India

Simon J. Sheather, Department of Statistics, Texas A&M University, College Station, Texas

Stephen A. Smith, Department of Ecology and Evolutionary Biology, University of Michigan, Ann Arbor, Michigan

Junilda Spirollari, Department of Computer Science, New Jersey Institute of Technology, Newark, NJ

Alexandros Stamatakis, Scientific Computing Group, Heidelberg Institute for Theoretical Studies, Heidelberg, Germany

El-Ghazali Talbi, INRIA Lille Nord Europe, Villeneuve d'Ascq, France

Kean Ming Tan, Department of Statistics, Purdue University, West Lafayette, Indiana

Xin Lu Tan, Department of Statistics, Purdue University, West Lafayette, Indiana

Bahar Taneri, Department of Biological Sciences, Eastern Mediterranean University, Famagusta, North Cyprus and Institute for Public Health Genomics, Cluster of Genetics and Cell Biology, Faculty of Health, Medicine and Life Sciences, Maastricht University, The Netherlands

Mingjie Tang, Department of Computer Science, Purdue University, West Lafayette, Indiana

Ahmed Y. Tawfik, Information Systems Department, French University of Egypt, El-Shorouk, Egypt

Sukru Tikves, Department of Computer Science and Engineering, Ira A. Fulton Engineering, Arizona State University, Tempe, Arizona

George Tzanis, Department of Informatics, Aristotle University of Thessaloniki, Thessaloniki, Greece

Filippo Utro, Computational Genomics Group, IBM T.J. Watson Research Center, Yorktown Heights, New York

Davide Verzotto, Department of Information Engineering, University of Padova, Padova, Italy

Francesco Vezzi, Department of Mathematics and Informatics and Institute of Applied Genomics, University of Udine, Udine, Italy

Alessia Visconti, Department of Computer Science, University of Torino, Turin, Italy

Ioannis Vlahavas, Department of Informatics, Aristotle University of Thessaloniki, Thessaloniki, Greece

Jason T. L. Wang, Department of Computer Science, New Jersey Institute of Technology, Newark, NJ

Penghao Wang, School of Mathematics and Statistics, The University of Sydney, Sydney, Australia

Dongrong Wen, Department of Computer Science, New Jersey Institute of Technology, Newark, NJ

Pengyi Yang, School of Information Technologies, University of Sydney, Sydney, Australia

Jean Yee-Hwa Yang, School of Mathematics and Statistics, University of Sydney, Sydney, Australia

Yaning Yang, Department of Statistics and Finance, University of Science and Technology of China, Hefei, China

Zejun Zheng, Singapore Institute for Clinical Sciences, Singapore

Ling Zhong, Department of Computer Science, New Jersey Institute of Technology, Newark, NJ

Bing B. Zhou, School of Information Technologies, University of Sydney, Sydney, Australia

Albert Y. Zomaya, School of Information Technologies, University of Sydney, Sydney, Australia

BIOLOGICAL DATA PREPROCESSING

PART A

BIOLOGICAL DATA MANAGEMENT

CHAPTER 1

GENOME AND TRANSCRIPTOME SEQUENCE DATABASES FOR DISCOVERY, STORAGE, AND REPRESENTATION OF ALTERNATIVE SPLICING EVENTS

BAHAR TANERI[1,2] and TERRY GAASTERLAND[3]
[1]Department of Biological Sciences, Eastern Mediterranean University, Famagusta, North Cyprus
[2]Institute for Public Health Genomics, Cluster of Genetics and Cell Biology, Faculty of Health, Medicine and Life Sciences, Maastricht University, The Netherlands
[3]Scripps Genome Center, University of California San Diego, San Diego, California

1.1 INTRODUCTION

Transcription is a critical cellular process through which the RNA molecules specify which proteins are expressed from the genome within a given cell. DNA is transcribed into RNA and RNA transcripts are then translated into proteins, which carry out numerous functions within cells. Prior to protein synthesis, RNA transcripts undergo several modifications including 5′ capping, 3′ polyadenylation, and splicing [1]. Premature messenger RNA (pre-mRNA) processing determines the mature mRNA's stability, its localization within the cell, and its interaction with other molecules [2]. In addition to constitutive splicing, the majority of eukaryotic genes undergo alternative splicing and therefore code for proteins with diverse structures and functions.

In this chapter, we describe the process of RNA splicing and focus on RNA alternative splicing. As described in detail below, splicing removes noncoding introns from the pre-mRNA and ligates the coding exonic sequences to produce the mRNA transcript. Alternative splicing is a cellular process by which several different combinations of exon–intron architectures are achieved with different mRNA products from the same gene. This process generates several mRNAs with different sequences from a single gene by making use of alternative splice sites of exons and introns. This process is critical in eukaryotic gene expression and plays a pivotal role in increasing the complexity and coding potential of genomes. Since alternative splicing presents an enormous source of diversity and greatly

Biological Knowledge Discovery Handbook: Preprocessing, Mining, and Postprocessing of Biological Data, First Edition. Edited by Mourad Elloumi and Albert Y. Zomaya.
© 2014 John Wiley & Sons, Inc. Published 2014 by John Wiley & Sons, Inc.

elevates the coding capacity of various genomes [3–5], we devote this chapter to this cellular phenomenon, which is widespread across eukaryotic genomes.

In particular we explain the databases for Alternative Splicing Queries (dbASQ), a computational pipeline we used to generate alternative splicing databases for genome and transcriptome sequences of various organisms. dbASQ enables the use of genome and transcriptome sequence data of any given organism for database development. Alternative splicing databases generated via dbASQ not only store the sequence data but also facilitate the detection and visualization of alternative splicing events for each gene in each genome analyzed. Data mining of the alternative splicing databases, generated using the dbASQ system, enables further analysis of this cellular process, providing biological answers to novel scientific questions.

In this chapter we provide a general overview of the widespread cellular phenomenon alternative splicing. We take a computational approach in answering biological questions with regard to alternative splicing. In this chapter you will find a general introduction to splicing and alternative splicing along with their mechanism and regulation. We briefly discuss the evolution and conservation of alternative splicing. Mainly, we describe the computational tools used in generating alternative splicing databases. We explain the content and the utility of alternative splicing databases for five different eukaryotic organisms: human, mouse, rat, frutifly, and soil worm. We cover genomic and transcriptomic sequence analyses and data mining from alternative splicing databases in general.

1.2 SPLICING

A typical mammalian gene is a multiexon gene separated by introns. Exons are relatively short, about 145 nucleotides, and are interrupted by much longer introns of about 3300 nucleotides [6, 7]. In humans, the average number of exons per protein coding gene is 8.8 [7]. Both introns and exons of a protein-coding gene are transcribed into a pre-mRNA molecule [1]. Approximately 90% of the pre-mRNA molecule is composed of the introns and these are removed before translation. Before the mRNA molecule transcribed from the gene can be translated into a protein molecule, there are several processes that need to take place. While in total an average protein-coding gene in human is about 27,000 bp in the genome and in the pre-mRNA molecule, the processed mRNA contains only about 1300 coding nucleotides and 1000 nucleotides in the untranslated regions (UTRs) and polyadenylation (poly A) tail. The removal of introns and ligation of exons are referred to as the splicing process or the RNA splicing process [1, 7]. Splicing takes place in the nucleus. Final products of splicing which are the ligated exonic sequences are ready for translation and are exported out of the nucleus [1].

1.2.1 Mechanism of Splicing

Simply, splicing refers to removal of intervening sequences from the pre-mRNA molecule and ligation of the exonic sequences. Each single splicing event removes one intron and ligates two exons. This process takes place via two steps of chemical reactions [1]. As shown in Figure 1.1, within the intronic sequence there is a particular adenine nucleotide which attacks the 5′ intronic splice site. A covalent bond is formed between the 5′ splice site of the intron and the adenine nucleotide releasing the exon upstream of the intron. In the second chemical reaction, the free 3′-OH group at the 3′ end of the upstream exon ligates with the 5′ end of the downstream exon. In this process, the intronic sequence, which contains an RNA loop, is released.

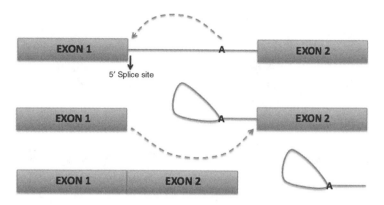

FIGURE 1.1 Illustration of two chemical reactions needed for one splicing reaction (A: adenine nucleotide at branch point of intron).

1.2.2 Regulation of Splicing

There are many *cis*-acting and *trans*-acting factors involved in splicing. The network of these factors facilitates splicing through exon definition and intron definition. Exon definition occurs early in splicing and involves interactions recognizing the exonic 5′ splice site and 3′ splice site, whereas for intron definition initial interactions take place across the intron for the recognition of 5′ and 3′ splice sites of the intron [8]. Splicing is regulated by a dynamic combinatorial network of RNA and protein molecules. Spliceosome, the splicing machinery, is a very complex system and is composed of five small nuclear RNAs (snRNAs), termed U1, U2, U4, U5, and U6 [1]. These are short RNA sequences of about 200 nucleotides long. In addition to the snRNAs, about 100 proteins are parts of the spliceosome. Assembly of snRNAs with the proteins forms small nuclear ribonucleoprotein complexes (snRNPs), which precisely bind to splice sites on the pre-mRNA to facilitate splicing [9]. Figure 1.2 shows the main steps of spliceosome assembly in the cell. Initially the 5′ intronic splice site interacts with U1. Then U2 interacts with the branch point. Next, U1 is replaced by the U4/U6, U5 complex, which then interacts with the U2, initiating intronic lariat formation. It is thought that the complex molecular content and assembly of the spliceosome are due to the need for highly accurate splicing in order to prevent formation of malfunctional or nonfunctional protein molecules.

In addition to the complex splicing machinery in the cell, specific sequence signals are needed for realization of splicing. There are four main sequence signals on the pre-mRNA molecule which play important roles in splicing. As shown in Figure 1.3, these are the 5′ splice site (exon–intron junction at the 5′ end of the intron), 3′ splice site (exon–intron junction at the 3′ end of the intron, the branch point (specific sequence slightly upstream of the 3′ splice site), and the polypyrimidine tract (between the branch point and the 3′ splice site). These sequences facilitate the two transesterification reactions involved in intron removal and exon ligation.

However, these sequences are not sufficient for alternative splice site selection. There are multiple other sequence signals involved in alternative splicing. There are several types of *cis*-acting regulatory sequences for splicing within the RNA molecule termed *enhancers* and *silencers*, which stimulate or suppress splicing, respectively. Exonic splicing enhancers (ESEs), exonic splicing silencers (ESSs), intronic splicing enhancers (ISEs), and intronic splicing silencers (ISSs) are among the *cis*-acting splicing regulatory sequences.

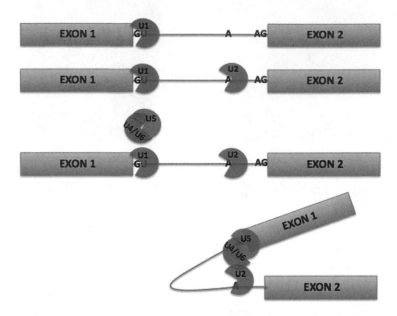

FIGURE 1.2 Spliceosome assembly (U1, U2, U4, U5, U6: snRNAs; GU: guanine and uracil nucleotides forming 5′ splice site signal; AG: adenine and guanine nucleotides forming 3′ splice site signal).

Here, we provide an example of ESE regulatory function. ESEs act as binding sites for regulatory RNA binding proteins (RBPs), particularly as binding sites for SR proteins (proteins rich in serine–arginine). SR proteins have two RNA recognition motifs (RRMs) and one arginine–serine rich domain (RS domain). SR proteins bind to RNA sequence motifs via their RRM domains [10], and they recruit the spliceosome to the splice site via their RS domain. By this process the SR proteins enable exon definition [6]. SR proteins recruit the basal splicing machinery to the RNA; therefore they are required for both constitutive and alternative splicing. Figure 1.4 illustrates SR protein binding to ESEs on the RNA molecule. In addition, SR proteins work as inhibitors of splicing inhibitory proteins binding to ESS sites close to ESEs, where SRs are bound (Figure 1.4). Many exons contain ESEs, which overall have varying sequences [8].

Though less well understood than ESEs, ESSs are known negative regulators of splicing. They interact with repressor heterogeneous nuclear ribonucleoproteins (hnRNPs) to silence splicing [11]. Certain *trans*-acting splicing regulatory proteins could bind to ESS sequences causing exon skipping [12]. Similarly, intronic sequences can act both as enhancers and silencers of splicing events. Certain intronic sequences function as ISEs and can enhance

FIGURE 1.3 Splicing signals on pre-mRNA molecule (GU: guanine and uracil nucleotides forming 5′ splice site signal; AG: adenine and guanine nucleotides forming 3′ splice site signal; A: adenine nucleotide at branch point of intron; polypyrimidine tract: pyrimidine-rich short sequence close to 3′ splice site).

FIGURE 1.4 SR protein binding on pre-mRNA: SR inhibition of splicing inhibitory protein.

the splicing of their upstream exon [8]. Certain ISSs could signal for repressor protein binding. For example, specifically YCAY motifs, where Y denotes a pyrimidine (U or C), signal for NOVA binding (a neuron-specific splicing regulatory protein). These particular sequences can act as ISSs depending on their location within the pre-mRNA molecule [13]. ISSs are further discussed in Section 1.3.3.

1.3 ALTERNATIVE SPLICING

1.3.1 Introduction to Alternative Splicing

Alternative splicing is a widespread phenomenon across and within the eukaryotic genomes. Of the estimated 25,000 protein-coding genes in human, ~90% are predicted to be alternatively spliced [14]. The impact of alternative splicing is widespread on the eukaryotic organisms' gene expression in general [5]. Earlier studies have shown that the majority of the immune system and the nervous system genes exhibit alternative splicing [15]. We have previously shown that the majority of mouse *transcription factors* are alternatively spliced, leading to protein domain architecture changes [16]. Below, we detail different types of alternative splicing and the mechanism and regulation of this cellular process. We mention the evolution and conservation of alternative splicing across different genomes.

- *Types of Alternative Splicing* Alternative splicing of the pre mRNA molecule can occur in several different ways. Figure 1.5 shows different types of alternative splicing events which include the presence and absence of cassette exons, mutually exclusive exons, intron retention, and various forms of length variation. A given RNA transcript can contain multiple different types of alternative splicing.

- *Examples of Widespread Presence of Alternative Splicing in Eukaryotic Genes* Alternative splicing is a well-documented, widespread phenomenon across the eukaryotic genomes. Here, we provide two interesting examples of alternatively spliced genes, one from *Drosophila melanogaster* and the other from the human genome. One of the most interesting examples of alternative splicing involves the Down syndrome cell adhesion molecule (Dscam) gene of *D. melanogaster*. There are 95 cassette exons in this gene and a total of 38,016 different RNA transcripts can potentially be generated from this gene through differential use of the exon–intron structure [5, 17]. The Dscam example illustrates the enormous coding-changing capacity of alternative splicing and its influence on the variation of gene expression within and across cells [5]. The *KCNMA 1* human gene presents another interesting case of alternative splicing. This gene exhibits both cassette exons and exons with length variation at 5′ and 3′ ends. These alternative exons generate over 500 different RNA transcripts [5].

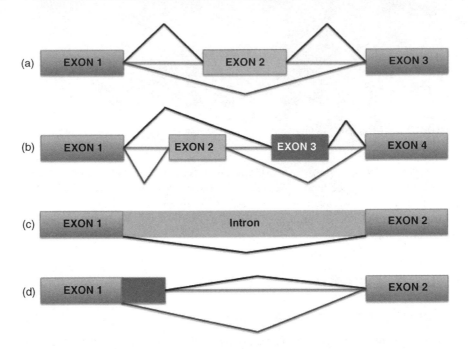

FIGURE 1.5 Types of alternative splicing: (a) cassette exon, present or absent in its entirety or from RNA transcript; (b) mutually exclusive exons, only one present in any given RNA transcript; (c) intron retention; (d) length-variant exon, nucleotide length variation possible on both 5′ and 3′ ends or on either end (only use of alternative 5′ splice site shown, use of alternative 3′ splice site not shown).

1.3.2 Mechanism of Alternative Splicing

Mainly the mechanism of alternative splicing involves interaction of *cis*-acting and *trans*-acting splicing factors. Recruitment of the splicing machinery to the correct splice sites, blocking of certain splice sites, and enhancing the use of other splice sites all contribute to this process [5]. Furthermore, RNA splicing and transcription are temporally and spatially coordinated. As the pre-mRNA is transcribed, splicing starts to take place [2]. Alternative splicing co-occurs with transcription and may be dependent on the promoter region of the gene. Different promoters might recruit different amounts of SR proteins. Or different promoters might recruit fast- or slow-acting RNA polymerases, which changes the course of splicing. Slow-acting promoters present more chance for exon inclusion and fast-acting ones promote exon exclusion [18]. Furthermore, epigenetics plays a role in the process of alternative splicing. The dynamic chromatin structure, which affects transcription, is also implicated in alternative splicing [19]. In addition, it has been shown that histone modification takes place differentially in the areas with constitutive exons compared to those with alternative exons [20, 21].

1.3.3 Regulation of Alternative Splicing

Alternative splicing is a tissue-specific, developmental stage and/or physiological condition dependent [5, 22] and is regulated in this manner. Complex interactions between *cis* regulatory sequences and *trans* regulatory factors of RNA binding proteins lead to a tissue-specific, cell-specific, developmental stage and physiological condition–dependent

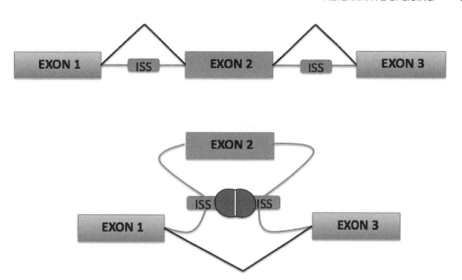

FIGURE 1.6 ISS-based exon exclusion (black structure: regulatory protein).

regulation of splicing [23–26]. An example of *cis*-acting regulation is the ISS-based alternative exon exclusion. Inclusion of an alternative exon depends on several factors, including the affinity and the concentrations of positive and negative regulators of splicing. ISSs flank the alternative exons on both sides and could bind the negative regulators of splicing. Protein–protein interaction among these negative regulators results in alternative exon skipping [6]. Figure 1.6 shows ISS regulation leading to exon exclusion from the mRNA.

- *Splicing Regulatory Proteins* Splicing regulatory proteins which control tissue-specific alternative splicing are expressed in certain cell types [24]. Most such well-known splicing factors are neuron-specific Nova1 and Nova2 proteins [27]. Importantly, splicing could be regulated by different isoforms of a splicing factor [28]. Here, we provide a partial list of splicing regulatory proteins: polypyrimidine tract binding (PTB) protein [29], various SR proteins [30–32], various hnRNPs [33–36], ASF/SF2 [37], transformer-2 (tra-2) [38], Sam68 [39], CELF [40], muscleblind-like (MBNL) [41], Hu [42], Fox-1 and Fox-2 [43], and sex-lethal [44]. Long and Caceres [31] provide an extensive review of SR proteins and SR protein–related regulators of splicing and alternative splicing.

- *Tissue-Specific Isoform Expression* It is well established that alternative splicing is a tissue-specific cellular process. Since an increased number of alternatively spliced isoforms has been shown to be expressed in the brain of mammals [45], we choose to illustrate the tissue specificity of alternative splicing by discussing a case of neuron-specific regulation of this process. Several *trans*-acting regulatory factors for splicing are proteins providing tissue-specific regulation of alternative splicing. Nova1 and Nova2 proteins are the first tissue-specific splicing regulators identified in vertebrates [46]. Nova proteins are neuron-specific regulators of alternative splicing. The *cis* regulatory elements to which Nova proteins bind have been identified as YCAY clusters, where Y denotes either U or C, within the sequence of the pre-mRNA [13]. Nova proteins can promote or prevent exon inclusion in their target RNAs, depending on where they bind in relation to exon–intron architecture of the RNA molecule. When Nova binds within exonic YCAY clusters, exon is skipped, whereas intronic binding of Nova enhances exon inclusion. Nova promotes removal of introns containing YCAY clusters and those introns close to YCAY clusters [13]. Ule et al. [13] define a genomewide map of *cis* regulatory elements of neuron-specific alternative splicing regulatory protein Nova. They combine bioinformatics with CLIP technology which stands for cross-linking and immunoprecipitation and splicing microarrays to identify target exons of Nova. Spliceosome assembly is differentially altered by Nova binding to different locations of *cis*-acting elements within the genome. Nova regulated exons are enriched in YCAY clusters (on average ~28 nucleotides) near the splice junctions. This is well conserved among human and mouse alternative exons regulated by Nova [13].

1.3.4   Evolution and Conservation of Splicing and Alternative Splicing

The RNA splicing process is thought to have originated from Group II introns with autocatalytic function [47, 48]. Evolutionary advantages of splicing and alternative splicing stem from various exon–intron rearrangements, which would allow for emergence of new proteins with different functions [1]. The basic splicing machinery and alternative splicing are evolutionarily conserved across species [47, 49–51]. Bioinformatic analyses have shown that alternative exons and their flanking introns are conserved to higher levels than constitutive exons [52, 53]. When compared across species, alternative exons and their splice sites are conserved indicating their functional roles [54, 55]. Similar sequence characteristics of alternative splicing events across different species indicate that these events are functionally significant. Mouse and human genes are highly conserved. About 80% of the mouse genes have human orthologs. The Mouse Genome Sequencing Consortium 2002 indicated that more than 90% of the human and mouse genomes are within conserved syntenic regions. Cross-species analyses between these two species with whole-genome sequence alignments revealed the conserved splicing events [50].

1.4   ALTERNATIVE SPLICING DATABASES

1.4.1   Genomic and Transcriptomic Sequence Analyses

In the genome era, availability of genomic sequences and the wide range of transcript sequence data enabled detailed bioinformatic analyses of alternative splicing. Multiple-sequence alignment approaches have been widely used within and across species in order to detect alternative exons and other alternative splicing events within transcriptomes [56–60]. In this section, we provide a brief overview of various alternative splicing databases and we focus on describing alternative splicing databases developed using the dbASQ system and a wide range of genome and transcriptome sequence data. The databases described here identify, classify, compute, and store alternative splicing events. In addition, they answer biological queries about current and novel splice variants within various genomes.

1.4.2   Literature Overview of Various Alternative Splicing Databases

Over the last decade, utilizing bioinformatics tools, various computational analyses of alternative splicing, and data generation in this field have been accelerated. Mainly storage and

TABLE 1.1   Alternative Splicing Databases

Alternative SDBs	Description	Reference
ASPicDB	Database of annotated transcript and protein variants generated by alternative splicing	[61]
TassDB2	Comprehensive database of subtle alternative splicing events	[62]
H-DBAS	Human transcriptome database for alternative splicing	[63]
ASTD	Alternative splicing and transcript diversity database	[64]
AS-ALPS	Database for analyzing effects of alternative splicing on protein structure, interaction, and network in human and mouse	[65]
ASMD	Alternative Splicing Mutation Database	[66]
ProSAS	Database for analyzing alternative splicing in context of protein structures	[67]
Fast DB	Analysis of regulation of expression and function of human alternative splicing variants	[68]
EuSplice	Analysis of splice signals and alternative splicing in eukaryotic genes	[69]
SpliceMiner	Database implementation of the National Center for Biotechnology Information (NCBI) Evidence Viewer for microarray splice-variant analysis	[70]
ECgene	Provides functional annotation for alternatively spliced genes	[71]
ASAP II	Analysis and comparative genomics of alternative splicing in 15 animal species	[72]
HOLLYWOOD	Comparative relational database of alternative splicing	[73]
ASD	Bioinformatics resource on alternative splicing	[74]
MAASE	Alternative splicing database designed for supporting splicing microarray applications	[75]
ASHESdb	Database of exon skipping	[76]
AVATAR	Database for genomewide alternative splicing event detection	[77]
DEDB	Database of *D. melanogaster* exons in splicing graph form	[78]
ASG	Database of splicing graphs for human genes	[79]
EASED	Extended alternatively spliced expressed sequence tag (EST) database	[80]
PASDB	Plant alternative splicing database	[81]
ProSplicer	Database of putative alterantive splicing information	[82]
AsMamDB	Alternative splice database of mammals	[83]
SpliceDB	Database of canonical and noncanonical mammalian splice sites	[84]
ASDB	Database of alternatively spliced genes	[85]

representation of sequence data enabled collection of alternative splicing data in the form of databases. Table 1.1 provides a comprehensive list of alternative splicing databases and a literature source for the database. (This list is exhaustive but may not be complete at the time of publication.) In the next section we detail the generation and utility of five specific alternative splicing databases generally called splicing databases (SDBs) built using the computational pipeline system dbASQ.

It should be noted that, in addition to alternative splicing databases, various computational tools and platforms such as AspAlt [86] and SpliceCenter [87] have been developed to analyze alternative splicing across various genomes. Another example is by Suyama et al. [88], who focus on conserved regulatory motifs of alternative splicing. We will not be providing an exhaustive list for such computational tools and platforms as this is out of the scope of this chapter.

1.4.3 SDBs

- *dbASQ—Computational Pipeline for Construction of SDBs*   SDBs were built using a computational pipeline referred to as the dbASQ system. This system is based on the AutoDB system previously reported by Zavolan et al. [89]. Figure 1.7 illustrates the dbASQ computational pipeline used for the development of SDBs. Input transcripts are obtained from UniGene and are aligned to the University of California at Santa Cruz (UCSC) genomes using BLAT [90] and SIM4 [91]. dbASQ filters each transcript based on the following two criteria. Each transcript has to have at least 75% identity to the genome. Transcripts with lower sequence identities are not included in the final versions of the databases. Each exon of the transcripts that pass the initial filter is individually screened for sequence identitiy to the genome. Each exon of a matching transcript has to have at least 95% identity to the genome. Transcripts which have one or more exons with lower sequence identity are not included in the final versions of the databases. In addition, transcripts which have only one exon are not included given that there are no splice sites in such transcripts. The remaining transcripts are clustered together (Figure 1.7). Each group of transcripts that map to a certain locus in the genome is termed a splice cluster. Each individual splice cluster is further filtered by dbASQ based on the number of transcripts it contains. A given splice cluster has to

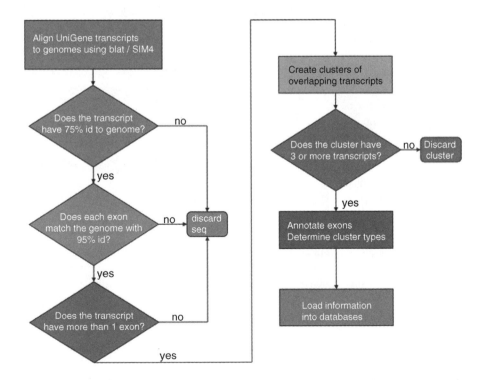

FIGURE 1.7   dbASQ computational pipeline for database construction.

contain at least three transcripts to be included in the final version of the database. Splice clusters with less than three transcripts are not included (Figure 1.7). After transcripts and clusters are filtered, transcript sequence data are loaded to the databases using PostgreSQL-7.4.

- *Database Terminology—Genomic Exons and Other Database Terms*   To carry out the alternative splicing analyses using the SDBs, we defined several terms unique to our databases and our analyses. Some of these terms have been introduced by Taneri et al. [16] and are defined as follows. A *transcript* is a sequence transcribed as pre-mRNA from the genomic DNA sequence and processed into mature mRNA. A *splice cluster* is a set of overlapping transcripts that map to the same genomic region. If a splice cluster contains differently spliced transcripts, it is termed a *variant cluster*. An *invariant cluster* contains no variant transcripts. An *exon* is a continuous sequence of a transcript that is mapped to the genome sequence. To facilitate the alternative splicing analysis, in this study we define a unique notion called the *genomic exon*. This notion is novel to our analysis and differentiates SDBs from already existing alternative splicing databases. A *genomic exon* is an uninterrupted genomic region aligned to one or more overlapping transcript exons. Based on the genomic exon notion, here we define an *intron* as the genomic region located between two neighboring genomic exons. The genomic exon map of any given splice cluster contains all the genomic exons and the introns of that particular cluster. Identification and labeling of any alternative exon in any given splice cluster rely on the genomic exon map of that particular cluster. A *constitutive exon* is an exon that is present in all transcripts of a given splice cluster, and its genomic coordinates match or are contained within the corresponding genomic exon. In a variant cluster, a *cassette* exon is present in some transcripts and is absent from others. In previous studies, these exons have been termed *cryptic*, *facultative*, or *skipped*. A *length-invariant* exon has the same splice donor and acceptor sites in all transcripts in which it is present. *Length-variant* exons have alternative 5′ or 3′ splice sites or both; therefore they are called *5′ variant*, *3′ variant*, or *5′, 3′ variant*, respectively. Importantly, the coordinates of a genomic exon for a length-variant exon reflect the outermost splice sites. An exon can be both cassette and length variant. A *variant exon* is either cassette or length variant or both. Genomic exons to which at least portions of protein-coding regions are projected are called *coding exons*. *Joined genomic exons* (JGEs) are concatenations of all genomic exon sequences without the intronic sequences within a given splice cluster. JGEs are designed to facilitate the homology analyses.

- *Data Tables of SDBs*   SDBs created using dbASQ contain six different data tables. Data schema of SDBs are shown in Table 1.2. These tables are called Cluster Table, Clone Table, Clone Exon Table, Clone Intron Table, Cds Table, and Genomic Exon Table. Cluster Table contains cluster identification numbers (İDs), chromosome IDs, and information on cluster types as variant and invariant. Clone Table contains transcript IDs, cluster IDs, chromosome IDs, clone lenghts, data sources of transcripts, their libraries and annotations, transcript sequences, and the number of exons of each transcript. Both Cluster Table and the Clone Table contain information on genomic orientation and about the beginnings and ends of genomic coordinates of transcripts. Clone Exon Table contains exon IDs, clone IDs, exon numbers, chromosome IDs, orientation, begining and end coordinates of transcripts, transcript sequences, chromosome sequences, 5′ and 3′ splice junction sites, variation types of alternative exons,

TABLE 1.2 Data Schema of SDBs

Cluster Table	Clone Table	Clone Exon Table		Clone Intron Table	Cds Table	Genomic Exon Table
Cluster id	Clone id	Exon id	Cassette	Intron id	Clone id	Cluster exon
Chr id	Cluster id	Clone id	Cassette initial	Clone id	Chr id	Cluster id
Orientation	Data source	Exon no	Cassette internal	Intron no	Orientation	Exon no
Chr begin	Chr id	Cluster exon	Cassette terminal	Chr id	Chr beg	Chr id
Chr end	Orientation	Chr id	Variation 5′ end	Orientation	Chr end	Orientation
Variant	Chr begin	Orientation	Variation 3′ end	Position clone	Clone beg	Chr beg
	Chr end	Clone begin	Splice site 5′ end	Chr beg	Clone end	Chr end
	Clone length	Clone end	Map 5′ end	Chr end	Data source	Chr length
	No exons	Clone seq	Splice site 3′ end	Splice site 5′	Synonyms	Variant
	Sequence	Chr beg	Map 3′ end	Splice site 3′		Chr seq
	Library	Chr end	Problem exon	Data source		Cassette
	Annotation	Chr seq	Data source	Synonyms		Cassette initial
	Synonyms	Splice junction 5′ site	Synonyms			Cassette internal
		Splice junction 3′ site				Cassette terminal
						Variation 5′ end
						Variation 3′ end

and data sources of transcripts. Clone Intron Table contains intron IDs, intron numbers, clone IDs, chromosome IDs, orientation, data sources of transcripts. Cds Table contains clone IDs, chromosome IDs, orientation, begining and end coordinates of chromosomes, beginning and end coordinates of transcripts, and data sources of transcritps. Genomic Exon Table contains exon numbers, cluster IDs, chromosome IDs, orientaiton, and exon types (Table 1.2).

- *Construction of SDBs for Five Eukaryotic Organisms* Using the dbASQ system, we have constructed five relational databases for the *Homo sapiens* (human), *Mus musculus* (mouse), *Rattus norvegicus* (rat), *D. melanogaster* (fruitfly), and *Caenorhabditis elegans* (soil worm) transcriptomes and genomes, called HumanSDB3, MouSDB5, RatSDB2, DmelSDB5, and CeleganSDB5, respectively. These databases contain expressed sequences precisely mapped to the genomic sequences using methods described above. UCSC genome builds hg17, mm5, rn3, dm2, and ce2 were used as input genome sequences for human, mouse, rat, fruitfly, and soil worm, respectively. UniGene database version numbers 173, 139, and 134 were used as input transcript sequences for human, mouse, and rat, respectively. For *D. melanogaster* and *C. elegans*, the full-length transcript nucleotide sequences were downloaded via Entrez query. The query limited results only to mRNA molecules and excluded expressed sequence tags (ESTs), sequence-tagged sites (STSs), genome sequence survey (GSSs), third-party annotation (TPA), working drafts, and patents. In addition, ESTs were downloaded from dbEST entries for the organisms of choice. All sequence sets were initially localized within genomes using BLAT [90]. The BLAT suite was installed from jksrc444 dated July 15, 2002. SIM4 was then used to generate a more refined alignment of the top 10% of BLAT matches [91]. SIM4 transcript genome alignments were included in the final splicing databases if they satisfied the criteria described above, including at least 75% transcript genome identity, at least 95% exon genome identity, and presence of at least two exons in the transcript. The SIM4 alignment provided exon splice sites. Following the SIM4 alignment, software developed by our group was used to cluster the transcripts, compute genomic exons, and determine the variation classification for each exon, each transcript, and each locus. Database schemas represent genomic positions of transcribed subsequences with indications of variation types.

- *Web Access to SDBs*   Online access to the PostgreSQL-7.4 SDBs is provided via dbASQ website at the Scripps Genome Center (SGC). HumanSDB3, MouSDB5, RatSDB2, DmelSDB5, and CeleganSDB5 web pages are dynamically generated by PHP scripts, deployed on the Apache-2.0 webserver. PostgreSQL database connections are carried out via built-in PHP database functions. Each SDB has been supplemented by additional tables that provide faster online access to the SDB statistical analyses described above. General information about splice clusters and individual chromosomes are also provided. When a particular splice cluster is accessed for the first time through a Web interface, graphical cluster maps are generated as PNG files by either PHP scripts or a Perl script using GD library. Graphical splice cluster files display positions of color coded genomic exons and individual transcripts from this cluster with projections of their exons onto the genomic map. Graphical files are cached for faster subsequent access to the splice cluster. SDBs can be browsed for individual chromosomes or for lists of splice clusters. Gene annotation keywords, splice cluster IDs, GenBank accession numbers, UniGene IDs, chromosome numbers, and variation status of the splice clusters can be used as search parameters. Pairs of orthologous and potentially orthologous human, mouse, and rat splice clusters can be identified using any of the following parameters: keyword, gene symbol, splicing cluster ID, GeneBank accession number, and UniGene cluster ID. If a particular splice cluster pairwise comparison is requested, a PHP script generates a graphical map with lines that connect homologous genomic exons. Pairwise cluster maps are cached to facilitate faster subsequent access to a given homologous splice cluster pair. Figures 1.8–1.12 show Web interfaces for human, mouse, rat, fruitfly, and soil worm clusters and demonstrate search options.

- *Database Statistics for HumanSDB3, MouSDB5, RatSDB2, DmelSDB5, and CeleganSDB5*   Using the SDBs created by the dbASQ pipeline, various alternative splicing queries can be answered. Initially, we looked at the overall presence of alternative splicing in the genomes of the various organisms. In this section we report the numbers of input and mapped transcripts, numbers of variant exons, and numbers of variant gene clusters across the five individual databases. Table 1.3 shows the distribution of variant versus invariant clusters within each genome. As defined above, variant clusters denote those genes displaying alternative splicing and invariant clusters are genes for which alternative splicing was not detected given the available transcript data at the time of database generation. As seen in Table 1.3, in mammalian organisms we detect widespread presence of alternative splicing.

Scripps Genome Center   Database of Splicing Variants

| HumanSDB3 homepage | Help | Browse Database | Search Database | Database Statistics | Compare Species | Exit |

Database of Splicing Variants. HumanSDB3

HumanSDB3 homepage.

You are connected to PostgreSQL database on host **emmy**.

This database is a result of the collaborative effort between The Rockefeller University Laboratory of Computational Genomics and Scripps Institution of Oceanography's Scripps Genome Center.

It was built using the automated sequence analysis pipeline combining several open-source software packages. Please see Help for further information.

What You Can Do:	How You Will Do That:
Browse Database	Browse alternatively or constitutively spliced transcripts using graphical interface to the PostgreSQL database.
Search Database	Search HumanSDB3 using graphical interface to the PostgreSQL database or directly through SQL queries.
View HumanSDB3 statistics	View HumanSDB3 statistics, e.g. number of found genes (clusters), number of genomic exons, number of used transcripts, size of genome, etc.
View Help	View help file for more information about Automated Splicing Database

(a)

Scripps Genome Center   Database of Splicing Variants

| HumanSDB3 homepage | Help | Browse Database | Search Database | Database Statistics | Compare Species |

Database of Splicing Variants HumanSDB3

Click on the chromosome ID below to browse HumanSDB3.

Chromosome	Number of Clusters	Invariant Clusters	Variant Clusters
chr1	2033	654	1379
chr10	847	285	562
chr10_random	1	1	0
chr11	1110	374	736
chr12	1082	379	703
chr13	370	136	234
chr13_random	4	3	1
chr14	663	239	424
chr15	659	209	450
chr15_random	4	2	2
chr16	899	280	619
chr16_random	3	1	2
chr17	1145	371	774
chr17_random	30	13	17
chr18	327	137	190
chr19	1317	442	875
chr19_random	7	5	2
chr1_random	49	15	34
chr2	1389	495	894
chr20	582	213	369
chr21	237	90	147
chr22	495	168	327
chr22_random	1	1	0

(b)

FIGURE 1.8   Web interface for HumanSDB3: (a) homepage; (b) browse database option; (c) search database option (example search by gene symbol *BRCA*); (d) variant cluster display (example variant cluster of *BRCA2* gene).

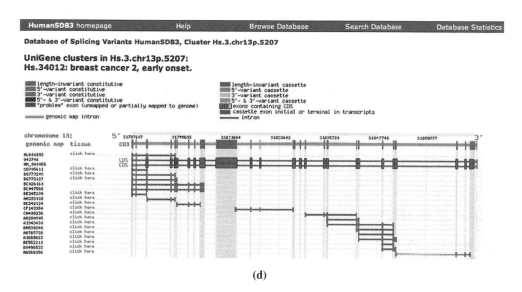

FIGURE 1.8 *(Continued)*

Due to stringent mapping criteria in dbASQ, only 26–53% of input transcripts contributed to the computation of variant exons and types of variation in the five genomes analyzed. Even so, the proportion of variant genes, or splice clusters, was found to be 58% for rat genome, 74% for mouse genome, and 81% for human genome. *Drosophila melanogaster* and *C. elegans* exhibit 35 and 23% alternative splicing in their respective transcriptomes (Table 1.3). Queries to databases produced by the dbASQ system for a number of organisms, including human, mouse, and rat, demonstrate that alternative splicing is a general phenomenon and the frequency of observation of variant splicing is directly correlated to the number of expressed sequences available per gene structure. The proportion of variant splice clusters increased proportionally to the number of mapped transcripts per cluster. We have detected that the number of input transcripts is correlated with the percentage of alternative splicing detected for the organism. As shown in Table 1.4, the higher the number of input transcripts, the more alternative splicing detected for any analyzed genome. Percent variation is correlated with the number of input transcripts and with the average number of transcripts per cluster (data not shown).

Next, we have analyzed alternative and constitutive exons within these five genomes. Table 1.5 shows the results. Of all exons in human, 43% are alternatively spliced, indicating a great number in variation. In mouse, 36% of all exons are alternatively spliced. In rat compared to human and mouse, the input transcript numbers were much less, and hence the determined alternative splicing was lower, reflecting the 17% alternative exons in rat. Similarly the fruitfly and the soil worm contain 15 and 7% alternative exons, respectively (Table 1.5).

An overwhelming majority of the alternative exons in all five genomes analyzed are cassette exons. As defined above, cassette exons are those found in some transcripts and

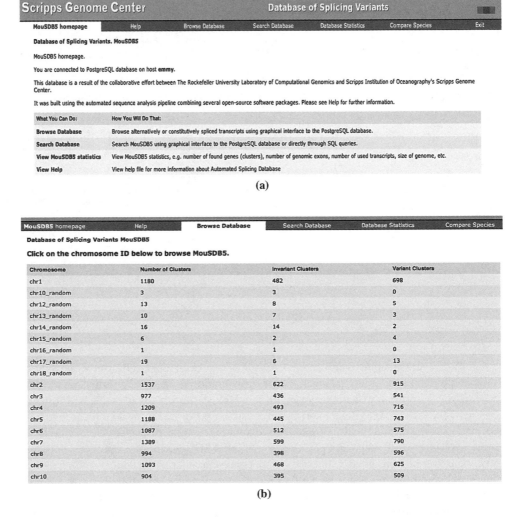

FIGURE 1.9   Web interface for MouSDB5: (a) homepage; (b) browse database option; (c) search database option (search with annotation "splicing factor" reveals 25 clusters, 10 of which are shown); (d) variant cluster display (example variant cluster of splicing factor 3a, subunit 2, partial view).

MouSDB5 homepage   Help   Browse Database   Search Database   Database Statistics   Compare Species

Database of Splicing Variants MouSDB5

QUERY: "SELECT mesh_annotation,chromosome_id,cluster_id,variant,orientation,chr_beg,chr_end FROM cluster WHERE mesh_annotation ILIKE '%splicing factor%' LIMIT 100"
retrieved 25 records:

Showing page 1: records 1-20 out of 25

Show page: 1

##	Annotation	Chromosome	Strand	Beginning	End	Cluster ID	Type	Number of Exons	Number of Clones
1	Mm.2478: splicing factor, arginine/serine-rich 4 (SRp75)	chr4	p	130122624	130141095	Mm.5.chr4p.12862	invariant	3	5
2	Mm.210352: splicing factor, arginine/serine-rich 10 (transformer 2	chr16	n	22079932	22100201	Mm.5.chr16n.7278	variant	10	335
3	Mm.262677: splicing factor 3a, subunit 2	chr10	p	80706621	80713455	Mm.5.chr10p.1823	variant	9	26
4	Mm.20913: splicing factor, arginine/serine-rich 16 (suppressor-of-	chr7_random	n	7080663	7303941	Mm.5.chr7_randomn.17100	variant	20	78
5	Mm.25779: splicing factor 3a, subunit 3	chr4_random	p	43601240	43602310	Mm.5.chr4_randomp.13293	invariant	2	10
6	Mm.196532: splicing factor 3b, subunit 2	chr19	n	5048751	5083925	Mm.5.chr19n.9427	variant	22	538
7	Mm.2478: splicing factor, arginine/serine-rich 4 (SRp75)	chr4	p	130141157	130150687	Mm.5.chr4p.12861	invariant	4	16
8	Mm.25779: splicing factor 3a, subunit 3	chrUn_random	p	65156228	65168513	Mm.5.chrUn_randomp.19457	variant	12	122
9	Mm.43331: splicing factor, arginine/serine-rich 5 (SRp40, HRS)	chr12	p	76212547	76295828	Mm.5.chr12p.4138	variant	7	451
10	Mm.335761: Transcribed sequence with weak similarity to protein sp:P23246	chr4	n	41860719	41865442	Mm.5.chr4n.12588	variant	7	24

(c)

MouSDB5 homepage   Help   Browse Database   Search Database   Database Statistics

Database of Splicing Variants MouSDB5, Cluster Mm.5.chr10p.1823

UniGene clusters in Mm.5.chr10p.1823:
Mm.262677: splicing factor 3a, subunit 2.

length-invariant constitutive
5'-variant constitutive
3'-variant constitutive
5'- & 3'-variant constitutive
"problem" exon (unmapped or partially mapped to genome)

genomic map intron

length-invariant cassette
5'-variant cassette
3'-variant cassette
5'- & 3'-variant cassette
exons containing CDS
cassette exon initial or terminal in transcripts
intron

(d)

FIGURE 1.9   (*Continued*)

completely absent from other transcript sequences transcribed from the same gene. Table 1.6 shows alternative exon analysis of cassette exons. Significantly, we report that the majority of alternative exons (over half of the alternative exons) in all five transcriptomes are cassette exons. In human 75%, in mouse 70%, in rat 70%, in frutifly 59%, and in soil worm 56% of all alternative exons are of cassette type. These findings indicate the functional importance of cassette exons in elevating the number alternative splicing events of eukaryotic genomes. The remaining alternative exons are of constitutive length-variant type. Table 1.7 shows alternative exon analysis of length-variant exons. In all five genomes, the majority of the

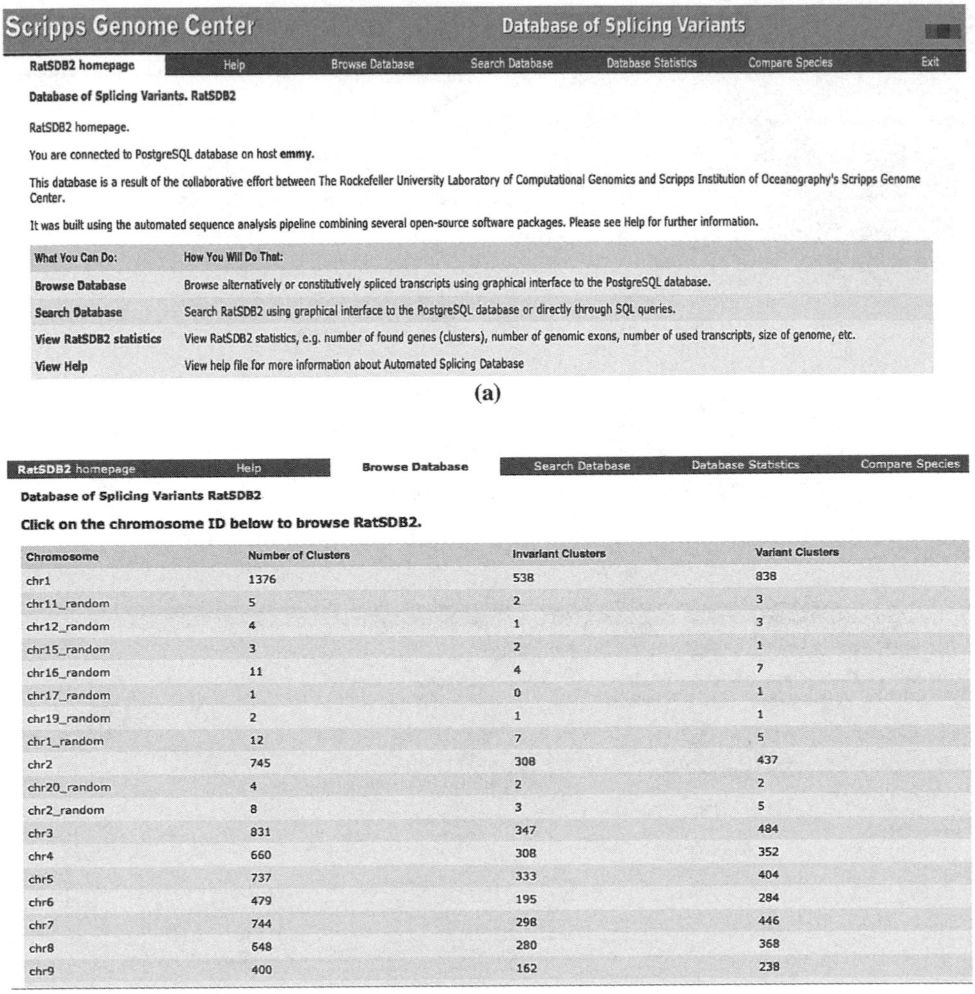

Chromosome	Number of Clusters	Invariant Clusters	Variant Clusters
chr1	1376	538	838
chr11_random	5	2	3
chr12_random	4	1	3
chr15_random	3	2	1
chr16_random	11	4	7
chr17_random	1	0	1
chr19_random	2	1	1
chr1_random	12	7	5
chr2	745	308	437
chr20_random	4	2	2
chr2_random	8	3	5
chr3	831	347	484
chr4	660	308	352
chr5	737	333	404
chr6	479	195	284
chr7	744	298	446
chr8	648	280	368
chr9	400	162	238

(b)

FIGURE 1.10 Web interface for RatSDB2: (a) homepage; (b) browse database option (partial image); (c) search database option (search with annotation "transcription factor" reveals 100 clusters, 10 of which are shown); (d) variant cluster display (example variant cluster of transcription factor 1).

constitutive length-variant exons show variation on both 5′ and 3′ ends, whereas exons variant on their 5′ end only and those variant on their 3′ end only tend to be much higher in numbers and equally distributed (Table 1.7).

1.5 DATA MINING FROM ALTERNATIVE SPLICING DATABASES

1.5.1 Implementation of dbASQ and Utility of SDBs

dbASQ provides a tool for both computational and experimental biologists to develop and utilize alternative spicing databases. Availability of a generic tool like dbASQ enables easy

RatSDB2 homepage   Help   Browse Database   Search Database   Database Statistics   Compare Species

Database of Splicing Variants RatSDB2

QUERY: "SELECT mesh_annotation,chromosome_id,cluster_id,variant,orientation,chr_beg,chr_end FROM cluster WHERE mesh_annotation ILIKE '%transcription factor%' LIMIT 100"
retrieved 100 records:

Showing page 1: records 1-20 out of 100

Show page: 1 2 3 4 5

##	Annotation	Chromosome	Strand	Beginning	End	Cluster ID	Type	Number of Exons	Number of Clones
1	Rn.10536: pancreas specific transcription factor, 1a	chr17	p	93505522	93507376	Rn.2.chr17p.4602	invariant	2	3
2	Rn.6179: NK2 transcription factor related, locus 5 (Drosophila)	chr10	p	16607232	16610005	Rn.2.chr10p.1763	invariant	2	5
3	Rn.21091: LOC365486 similar to HMG-box transcription factor TCF4E	chr1	p	262420982	262435947	Rn.2.chr1p.711	variant	5	3
4	Rn.30005: BarH-class homeodomain transcription factor	chr14	p	3888149	3893041	Rn.2.chr14p.3769	invariant	3	3
5	Rn.44609: Sp1 transcription factor	chr7	p	141243710	141265408	Rn.2.chr7p.9168	invariant	4	3
6	Rn.40259: LOC362286 similar to Death associated transcription factor 1	chr3	n	169668489	169689086	Rn.2.chr3n.6443	invariant	14	3
7	Rn.3181: LOC362579 similar to Y box transcription factor	chr5	n	139864401	139881074	Rn.2.chr5n.8107	invariant	8	44
8	Rn.18770: LOC307474 similar to transcription elongation regulator 1;	chr18	p	35752159	35812591	Rn.2.chr18p.4959	variant	25	19
9	Rn.84872: general transcription factor II I repeat domain-containing 1	chr12	p	23181243	23289343	Rn.2.chr12p.2742	variant	32	17
10	Rn.10445: POU domain, class 1, transcription factor 1	chr11	p	2959378	2980547	Rn.2.chr11p.2639	variant	6	9

(c)

RatSDB2 homepage   Help   Browse Database   Search Database   Database Statistics

Database of Splicing Variants RatSDB2, Cluster Rn.2.chr11p.2639

UniGene clusters in Rn.2.chr11p.2639:
Rn.10445: POU domain, class 1, transcription factor 1.

(d)

FIGURE 1.10   (*Continued*)

access to alternative splicing data by biologists and contributes greatly to the studies in this field either on a single-gene level or on an entire-genome level. In addition to the studies done on human, mouse, rat, fruifly, and soil worm, dbASQ can be implemented for other genomes. Further, as detailed below, the available SDBs can be used to answer several alternative splicing queries. Previously, we used the SDBs to identify the alternatively spliced tissue-specific mouse transcription factors and to assess the impact of cassette exons on the protein domain architecture of this particular group of proteins [16]. In addition, in a later comparative study we used SDBs to identify species-specific alternative exons in human, mouse, and rat genomes and to further identify previously unannotated alternative exons in these three genomes [92]. Here, we provide an example illustrating the utility of the SDBs on initial and terminal exon variation. Several such bio(medical) queries could be answered through SDBs.

Scripps Genome Center   **Database of Splicing Variants**

| DmelSDB5 homepage | Help | Browse Database | Search Database | Database Statistics | Compare Species | Exit |

Database of Splicing Variants. DmelSDB5

DmelSDB5 homepage.

You are connected to PostgreSQL database on host **emmy**.

This database is a result of the collaborative effort between The Rockefeller University Laboratory of Computational Genomics and Scripps Institution of Oceanography's Scripps Genome Center.

It was built using the automated sequence analysis pipeline combining several open-source software packages. Please see Help for further information.

What You Can Do:	How You Will Do That:
Browse Database	Browse alternatively or constitutively spliced transcripts using graphical interface to the PostgreSQL database.
Search Database	Search DmelSDB5 using graphical interface to the PostgreSQL database or directly through SQL queries.
View DmelSDB5 statistics	View DmelSDB5 statistics, e.g. number of found genes (clusters), number of genomic exons, number of used transcripts, size of genome, etc.
View Help	View help file for more information about Automated Splicing Database

(a)

Database of Splicing Variants DmelSDB5

Click on the chromosome ID below to browse DmelSDB5.

Chromosome	Number of Clusters	Invariant Clusters	Variant Clusters
chr2L	1553	1044	509
chr2R	1729	1157	572
chr2h	33	14	19
chr3L	1659	1074	585
chr3R	2137	1398	739
chr3h	26	10	16
chr4	79	25	54
chr4h	6	4	2
chrM	2	0	2
chrU	39	19	20
chrX	1388	897	491
chrXh	14	5	9

(b)

FIGURE 1.11   Web interface for DmelSDB5: (a) homepage; (b) browse database option; (c) search database option (example search by annotation DSCAM); (d) variant cluster display (variant cluster of DSCAM, partial view).

1.5.2 Identification of Transcript-Initial and Transcript-Terminal Variation

Transcript-terminal cassette exons are at either the $5'$ or the $3'$ end of the transcript mapping to intronic regions. A novel finding using SDBs is the observation that transcript-terminal cassette (TTC) and transcript-initial cassette (TIC) exons occur in a large proportion of variant splice clusters, indicating that alternative promotion and alternative termination of transcription are closely correlated with alternative splicing of internal exons. Queries reveal

Database of Splicing Variants DmelSDB5.

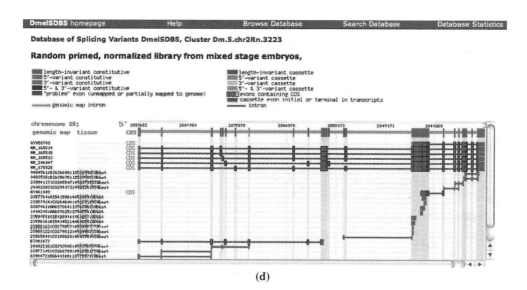

(c)

(d)

FIGURE 1.11   (*Continued*)

that variant use of initial and terminal exons rarely occurs without variant use of internal splice sites. This observation is made possible only by the design of the schema of dbASQ, where the schema explicitly represent internal variant exons versus initial and terminal variant exons. Using human, mouse, and rat databases, we quantitatively demonstrate that variation which leads to alternate initiation or termination of transcription occur rarely without internal alternative exons. Interestingly, just 6–7% of variant splice clusters had only TIC or TTC variant exons, with no internal splice variation. Further studies on TIC and TTCs will reveal properties of these exons in comparison to the properties of internal variant exons in terms of frame preservation, nucleotide length, and conservation across transcriptomes.

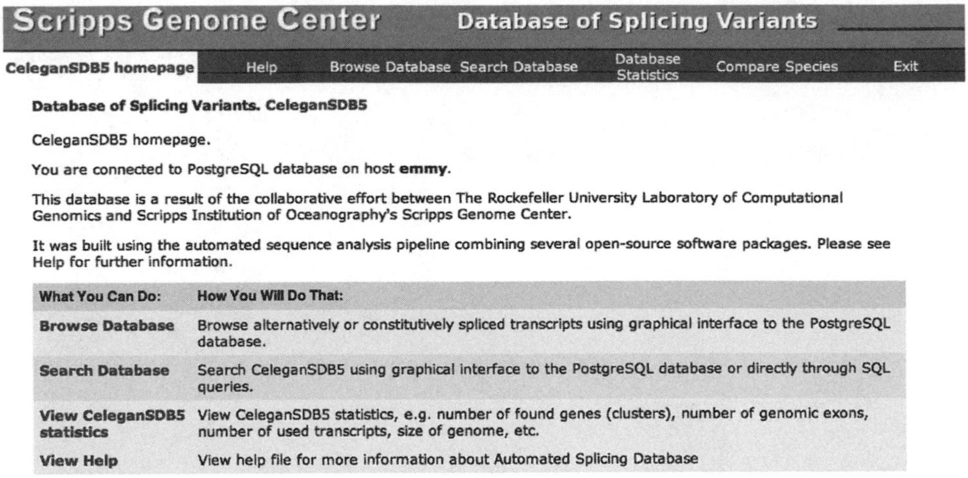

(a)

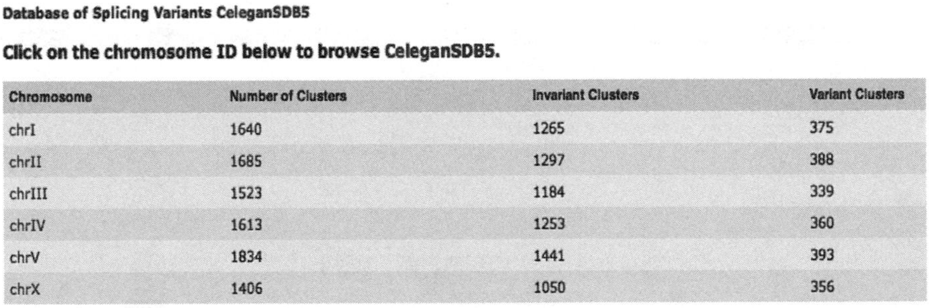

(b)

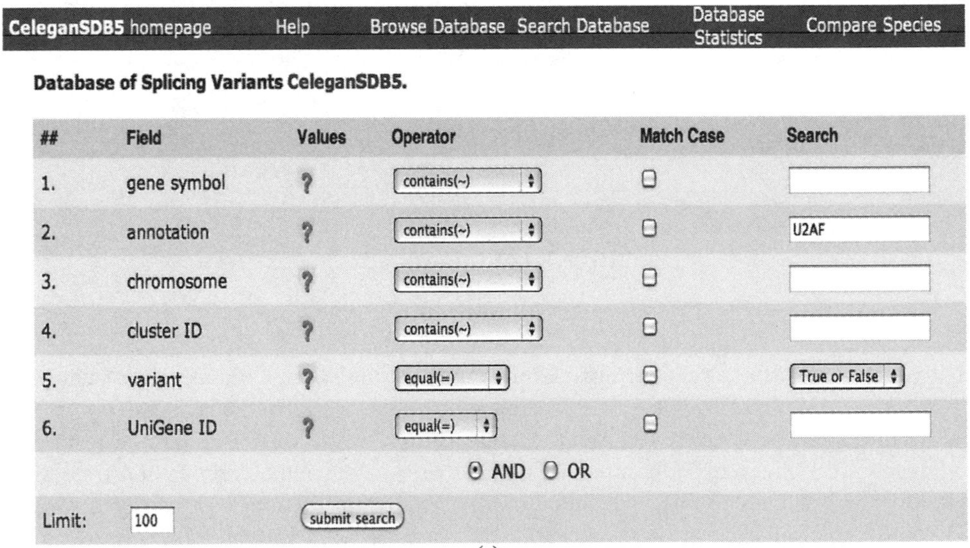

(c)

FIGURE 1.12   Web interface for CeleganSDB5: (a) homepage; (b) browse database option; (c) search database option (example search by annotation U2AF); (d) variant cluster display (cluster of U2AF).

Database of Splicing Variants CeleganSDB5, Cluster Ce.5.chrIIIn.4032

Caenorhabditis elegans U2AF splicing factor (55.4 kD) (uaf-1) complete mRNA.

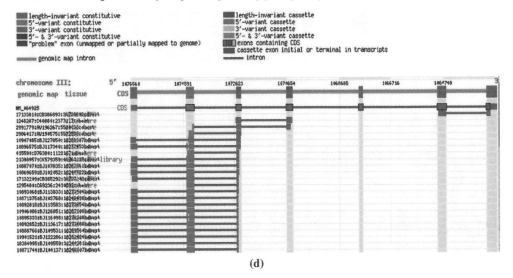

(d)

FIGURE 1.12 *(Continued)*

TABLE 1.3   SDB Cluster Analysis

Organism	Database	Total Number of Clusters	Total Number of Invariant Clusters	Total Number of Variant Clusters	Percentage of Variant Clusters
Human (*H. sapiens*)	HumanSDB3	20,707	3,881	16,826	81
Mouse (*M. musculus*)	MouSDB5	20,090	5,221	14,869	74
Rat (*R. norvegicus*)	RatSDB2	11,330	4,721	6,609	58
Fruitfly (*D. melanogaster*)	DmelSDB5	8,665	5,647	3,018	35
Soil worm (*C. elegans*)	CeleganSDB5	9,701	7,490	2,211	23

TABLE 1.4   Correlation of Input Transcript Numbers and Presence of Alternative Splicing

Organism	Database	Number of Input Transcripts	Number of Rejected Transcripts	Percentage of Rejected Transcripts	Number of Mapped Transcripts	Percentage of Mapped Transcripts
Human (*H. sapiens*)	HumanSDB3	4,635,471	3,175,505	69	1,459,966	31
Mouse (*M. musculus*)	MouSDB5	3,322,164	2,172,506	65	1,149,658	35
Rat (*R. norvegicus*)	RatSDB2	552,436	409,605	74	142,831	26
Fruitfly (*D. melanogaster*)	DmelSDB5	418,039	197,580	47	220,459	53
Soil worm (*C. elegans*)	CeleganSDB5	329,189	192,634	59	136,555	41

TABLE 1.5   SDB Exon Analysis

Organism	Database	Total Number of Exons	Total Number of Constitutive Length- Invariant Exons	Total Number of Alternative Exons	Percentage of Alternative Exons
Human (*H. sapiens*)	HumanSDB3	241,824	137,150	104,674	43
Mouse (*M. musculus*)	MouSDB5	216,432	143,780	72,652	36
Rat (*R. norvegicus*)	RatSDB2	143,095	118,595	24,500	17
Fruitfly (*D. melanogaster*)	DmelSDB5	47,403	40,257	7,146	15
Soil worm (*C. elegans*)	CeleganSDB5	72,984	68,136	4,848	7

TABLE 1.6   Alternative Exon Analysis of Cassette Exons

Organism	Database	Total Number of Alternative Exons	Total Number of Cassette Exons	Percentage of Cassette Exons
Human (*H. sapiens*)	HumanSDB3	104,674	78,146	75
Mouse (*M. musculus*)	MouSDB5	72,652	51,163	70
Rat (*R. norvegicus*)	RatSDB2	24,500	16,893	70
Fruitfly (*D. melanogaster*)	DmelSDB5	746	4,197	59
Soil worm (*C. elegans*)	CeleganSDB5	4,848	2,719	56

ACKNOWLEDGMENTS

The authors acknowledge Lee Edsall, Alexey Novoradovsky, and Ben Snyder for their technical contributions.

WEB RESOURCES

dbASQ—SDBs: `http://www.emmy.ucsd.edu/sdb.php`.

dbEST: `http://www.ncbi.nlm.nih.gov/dbEST`.

CeleganSDB5 homepage: `http://emmy.ucsd.edu/sdb.php?db=CeleganSDB5`.

DmelSDB5 homepage: `http://emmy.ucsd.edu/sdb.php?db=DmelSDB5`.

Entrez: `http://www.ncbi.nlm.nih.gov/Entrez`.

HumanSDB3 homepage: `http://emmy.ucsd.edu/sdb.php?db=HumanSDB3`.

MouSDB5 homepage: `http://emmy.ucsd.edu/sdb.php?db=MouSDB3`.

RatSDB2 homepage: `http://emmy.ucsd.edu/sdb.php?db=RatSDB2`.

UCSC Genomes: `http://hgdownload.cse.ucsc.edu/goldenPath/`.

UniGene: `ftp://ftp.ncbi.nlm.nih.gov/repository/UniGene/`.

TABLE 1.7 Alternative Exon Analysis of Length-Variant Exons

Organism	Database	Total Number of Alternative Exons	Total Number of Constitutive Length-Variant Exons	Total Number of Constitutive Length-Variant Exons (5′ and 3′)	Total Number of Constitutive Length-Variant Exons (5′)	Total Number of Constitutive Length-Variant Exons (3′)
Human (*H. sapiens*)	HumanSDB3	104,674	26,528	1,978 (8%)	12,761 (48%)	11,789 (44%)
Mouse (*M. musculus*)	MouSDB5	72,652	21,489	1,140 (5%)	10,721 (50%)	9,628 (45%)
Rat (*R. norvegicus*)	RatSDB2	24,500	7,607	215 (3%)	3,864 (51%)	3,528 (46%)
Fruitfly (*D. melanogaster*)	DmelSDB5	7,146	2,949	51 (2%)	1,414 (48%)	1,484 (50%)
Soil worm (*C. elegans*)	CeleganSDB5	4,848	2,129	46 (3%)	1,031 (48%)	1,052 (49%)

REFERENCES

1. B. Alberts, A. Johnson, J. Lewis, M. Raff, K. Roberts, and P. Walter. *Molecular Biology of the Cell*, 5th ed. Garland Science, New York, 2007.

2. P. Cramer, A. Srebrow, S. Kadener, S. Werbajh, M. de la Mata, G. Melen, G. Nogues, and A. R. Kornblihtt. Coordination between transcription and pre-mRNA processing. *FEBS Lett.*, 498:179–182, 2001.

3. D. L. Black. Protein diversity from alternative splicing: A challenge for bioinformatics and postgenome biology. *Cell*, 103:367–370, 2000.

4. D. Brett, H. Popisil, J. Valcarel, J. Reich, and P. Bork. Alternative splicing and genome complexity. *Nature Genet.*, 1:29–30, 2002.

5. T. W. Nilsen and B. R. Graveley. Expansion of the eukaryotic proteome by alternative splicing. *Nature*, 463(7280):457–463, 2010.

6. L. Cartegni, S. L. Chew, and A. R. Krainer. Listening to silence and understanding nonsense: Exonic mutations that affect splicing. *Nat. Rev. Genet.*, 3(4):285–298, 2002.

7. J. Tazi, N. Bakkour, and S. Stamm. Alternative splicing and disease. *Biochim Biophys Acta.*, 1792(1):14–26, 2009.

8. Z. Wang and C. B. Burge. Splicing regulation: From a parts list of regulatory elements to an integrated splicing code. *RNA*, 14(5):802–813, 2008.

9. M. S. Jurica and M. J. Morre. Pre-mRNA Splicing: Awash in a sea of proteins. *Mol. Cell*, 12:5–14, 2003.

10. X. Ma and F. He. Advances in the study of SR protein family. *Genomics Proteomics Bioinformatics*, 1(1):2–8, 2003.

11. Z. Wang, M. E. Rolish, G. Yeo, V. Tung, M. Mawson, and C. B. Burge. Systematic identification and analysis of exonic splicing silencers. *Cell*, 119(6):831–845, 2004.

12. J. M. Izquierdo, N. Majós, S. Bonnal, C. Martínez, R. Castelo, R. Guigó, D. Bilbao, and J. Valcárcel. Regulation of Fas alternative splicing by antagonistic effects of TIA-1 and PTB on exon definition. *Mol. Cell.*, 19(4):475–484, 2005.

13. J. Ule, G. Stefani, A. Mele, M. Ruggiu, X. Wang, B. Taneri, T. Gaasterland, B. J. Blencowe, and R. B. Darnell. An RNA map predicting Nova-dependent splicing regulation. *Nature*, 444(7119):580–586, 2006.

14. Q. Pan, O. Shai, L. J. Lee, B. J. Frey, and B. J. Blencowe. Deep surveying of alternative splicing complexity in the human transcriptome by high-throughput sequencing. *Nat. Genet.*, 40(12):1413–1415, 2008.

15. B. Modrek and C. Lee. A genomic view of alternative splicing. *Nat. Genet.*, 30(1):13–19, 2002.

16. B. Taneri, B. Snyder, A. Novoradovsky, and T. Gaasterland. Alternative splicing of mouse transcription factors affects their DNA-binding domain architecture and is tissue specific. *Genome Biol.*, 5(10):R75, 2004.

17. A. M. Celotto and B. R. Graveley. Alternative splicing of the Drosophila Dscam pre-mRNA is both temporally and spatially regulated. *Genetics*, 159(2):599–608, 2001.

18. J. F. Cáceres and A. R. Kornblihtt. Alternative splicing: Multiple control mechanisms and involvement in human disease. *Trends Genet.*, 18(4):186–193, 2002.

19. M. Alló, V. Buggiano, J. P. Fededa, E. Petrillo, I. Schor, M. de la Mata, E. Agirre, M. Plass, E. Eyras, S. A. Elela, R. Klinck, B. Chabot, and A. R. Kornblihtt. Control of alternative splicing through siRNA-mediated transcriptional gene silencing. *Nat. Struct. Mol. Biol.*, 16(7):717–724, 2009.

20. S. Schwartz, E. Meshorer, and G. Ast. Chromatin organization marks exon-intron structure. *Nat. Struct. Mol. Biol.*, 16(9):990–995, 2009.

21. R. F. Luco, M. Allo, I. E. Schor, A. R. Kornblihtt, and T. Misteli. Epigenetics in alternative pre-mRNA splicing. *Cell*, 144(1):16–26, 2011.

22. B. R. Graveley. Alternative splicing: Increasing diversity in the proteomic world. *Trends Genet.*, 17(2):100–107, 2001.

23. A. J. Lopez. Alternative splicing of pre-mRNA: Developmental consequences and mechanisms of regulation. *Annu. Rev. Genet.*, 32:279–305, 1998.

24. D. L. Black and P. J. Grabowski. Alternative pre-mRNA splicing and neuronal function. *Prog. Mol. Subcell. Biol.*, 31:187–216, 2003.

25. Z. Z. Tang, S. Zheng, J. Nikolic, and D. L. Black. Developmental control of CaV1.2 L-type calcium channel splicing by Fox proteins. *Mol. Cell. Biol.*, 29(17):4757–4765, 2009.

26. B. R. Graveley, A. N. Brooks, J. W. Carlson, M. O. Duff, J. M. Landolin, L. Yang, C. G. Artieri, M. J. van Baren, N. Boley, B. W. Booth, J. B. Brown, L. Cherbas, C. A. Davis, A. Dobin, R. Li, W. Lin, J. H. Malone, N. R. Mattiuzzo, D. Miller, D. Sturgill, B. B. Tuch, C. Zaleski, D. Zhang, M. Blanchette, S. Dudoit, B. Eads, R. E. Green, A. Hammonds, L. Jiang, P. Kapranov, L. Langton, N. Perrimon, J. E. Sandler, K. H. Wan, A. Willingham, Y. Zhang, Y. Zou, J. Andrews, P. J. Bickel, S. E. Brenner, M. R. Brent, P. Cherbas, T. R. Gingeras, R. A. Hoskins, T. C. Kaufman, B. Oliver, and S. E. Celniker. The developmental transcriptome of *Drosophila melanogaster*. *Nature*, 471(7339):473–479, 2011.

27. N. Jelen, J. Ule, M. Zivin, and R. B. Darnell. Evolution of Nova-dependent splicing regulation in the brain. *PLoS Genet.*, 3(10):1838–1847, 2007.

28. T. R. Pacheco, A. Q. Gomes, N. L. Barbosa-Morais, V. Benes, W. Ansorge, M. Wollerton, C. W. Smith, J. Valcárcel, and M. Carmo-Fonseca. Diversity of vertebrate splicing factor U2AF35: Identification of alternatively spliced U2AF1 mRNAS. *J. Biol. Chem.*, Jun 25; 279(26):27039–27049, 2004.

29. K. Sawicka, M. Bushell, K. A. Spriggs, and A. E. Willis. Polypyrimidine-tract-binding protein: A multifunctional RNA-binding protein. *Biochem. Soc. Trans.*, 36(Pt. 4):641–647, 2008.

30. P. J. Shepard and K. J. Hertel. The SR protein family. *Genome Biol.*, 10(10):242, 2009.

31. J. C. Long and J. F. Caceres. The SR protein family of splicing factors: Master regulators of gene expression. *Biochem J.*, 417(1):15–27, 2009.

32. S. Cho, A. Hoang, S. Chakrabarti, N. Huynh, D. B. Huang, and G. Ghosh. The SRSF1 linker induces semi-conservative ESE binding by cooperating with the RRMs. *Nucleic Acids Res.*, 39(21):9413–9421, 2011. doi: 10.1093/nar/gkr663.

33. E. Buratti and F. E. Baralle. The multiple roles of TDP-43 in pre-mRNA processing and gene expression regulation. *RNA Biol.*, 7(4):420–429, 2010.

34. C. W. Lee, I. T. Chen, P. H. Chou, H. Y. Hung, and K. H. Wang. Heterogeneous nuclear ribonucleoprotein hrp36 acts as an alternative splicing repressor in *Litopenaeus vannamei* Dscam. *Dev. Comp. Immunol.*, 36(1):10–20, 2012. doi:10.1016/j.dci.2011.05.006.

35. X. Tang, V. D. Kane, D. M. Morré, and D. J. Morré. hnRNP F directs formation of an exon 4 minus variant of tumor-associated NADH oxidase (ENOX2). *Mol. Cell. Biochem.*, 357(1–2): 55–63, 2011. doi:10.1007/s11010-011-0875-5.

36. L. B. Motta-Mena, S. A. Smith, M. J. Mallory, J. Jackson, J. Wang, and K. W. Lynch. A disease-associated polymorphism alters splicing of the human CD45 phosphatase gene by disrupting combinatorial repression by heterogeneous nuclear ribonucleoproteins (hnRNPs). *J. Biol. Chem.*, 286(22):20043–20053, 2011.

37. T. A. Cooper. Alternative splicing regulation impacts heart development. *Cell*, 120(1):1–2, 2005.

38. N. Benderska, K. Becker, J. A. Girault, C. M. Becker, A. Andreadis, and S. Stamm. DARPP-32 binds to tra2-beta1 and influences alternative splicing. *Biochim. Biophys. Acta*. 1799(5–6):448–453, 2010.

39. M. P. Paronetto, M. Cappellari, R. Busà, S. Pedrotti, R. Vitali, C. Comstock, T. Hyslop, K. E. Knudsen, and C. Sette. Alternative splicing of the cyclin D1 proto-oncogene is regulated by the RNA-binding protein Sam68. *Cancer Res.*, 70(1):229–239, 2010.

40. A. Kalsotra, X. Xiao, A. J. Ward, J. C. Castle, J. M. Johnson, C. B. Burge, and T. A. Cooper. A postnatal switch of CELF and MBNL proteins reprograms alternative splicing in the developing heart. *Proc Natl. Acad. Sci.*, 105(51):20333–20338, 2008.

41. K. S. Lee, Y. Cao, H. E. Witwicka, S. Tom, S. J. Tapscott, and E. H. Wang. RNA-binding protein Muscleblind-like 3 (MBNL3) disrupts myocyte enhancer factor 2 (Mef2) {beta}-exon splicing. *J. Biol. Chem.*, 285(44):33779–33787, 2010.

42. H. J. Okano and R. B. Darnell. A hierarchy of Hu RNA binding proteins in developing and adult neurons. *J. Neurosci.*, 17(9):3024–3037, 1997.

43. C. Zhang, Z. Zhang, J. Castle, S. Sun, J. Johnson, A. R. Krainer, and M. Q. Zhang. Defining the regulatory network of the tissue-specific splicing factors Fox-1 and Fox-2. *Genes Dev.*, 22(18):2550–2563, 2008.

44. M. J. Lallena, K. J. Chalmers, S. Llamazares, A. I. Lamond, and J. Valcárcel. Splicing regulation at the second catalytic step by Sex-lethal involves 3′ splice site recognition by SPF45. *Cell* 109(3):285–296, 2002.

45. D. D. Licatalosi and R. B. Darnell. RNA processing and its regulation: Global insights into biological networks. *Nat. Rev. Genet.* 11(1):75–87, 2010.

46. R. B. Darnell. Developing global insight into RNA regulation. *Cold Spring Harb. Symp. Quant. Biol.*, 71:321–327, 2006.

47. G. Ast. How did alternative splicing evolve? *Nat. Rev. Genet.*, 5(10):773–782, 2004.

48. H. Keren, G. Lev-Maor, and G. Ast. Alternative splicing and evolution: Diversification, exon definition and function. *Nat. Rev. Genet.*, 11(5):345–355, 2010.

49. G. W. Yeo, E. L. Van Nostrand, and T. Y. Liang. Discovery and analysis of evolutionarily conserved intronic splicing regulatory elements. *PLoS Genet.*, May 25;3(5):e85, 2007.

50. T. A. Thanaraj, F. Clark, and J. Muilu. Conservation of human alternative splice events in mouse. *Nucleic Acids Res.*, May 15;31(10):2544–2552, 2003.

51. J. M. Mudge, A. Frankish, J. Fernandez-Banet, T. Alioto, T. Derrien, C. Howald, A. Reymond, R. Guigo, T. Hubbard, and J. Harrow. The origins, evolution and functional potential of alternative splicing in vertebrates. *Mol. Biol. Evol.*, 28(10):2949–2959, 2011. doi:10.1093/molbev/msr127.

52. C. W. Sugnet, W. J. Kent, M. Ares, Jr., and D. Haussler. Transcriptome and genome conservation of alternative splicing events in humans and mice. *Pac. Symp. Biocomput.*, 66–77, 2004.

53. A. Resch, Y. Xing, A. Alekseyenko, B. Modrek, and C. Lee. Evidence for a subpopulation of conserved alternative splicing events under selection pressure for protein reading frame preservation. *Nucleic Acids Res.*, 32(4):1261–1269, 2004.

54. R. Sorek and G. Ast. Intronic sequences flanking alternatively spliced exons are conserved between human and mouse. *Genome Res.*, 13(7):1631–1637, 2003.

55. I. Carmel, S. Tal, I. Vig, and G. Ast. Comparative analysis detects dependencies among the 5′ splice-site positions. *RNA*, 10(5):828–840, 2004.

56. C. Grasso, B. Modrek, Y. Xing, and C. Lee. Genome-wide detection of alternative splicing in expressed sequences using partial order multiple sequence alignment graphs. *Pac. Symp. Biocomput.*, 29–41, 2004.

57. Y. Xing, A. Resch, and C. Lee. The multiassembly problem: Reconstructing multiple transcript isoforms from EST fragment mixtures. *Genome Res.*, 14(3):426–441, 2004.

58. H. Sakai and O. Maruyama. Extensive search for discriminative features of alternative splicing. *Pac. Symp. Biocomput.*, 54–65, 2004.

59. N. Kim and C. Lee. Bioinformatics detection of alternative splicing. *Methods Mol. Biol.*, 452:179–197, 2008.

60. H. Lu, L. Lin, S. Sato, Y. Xing, and C. J. Lee. Predicting functional alternative splicing by measuring RNA selection pressure from multigenome alignments. *PLoS Comput. Biol.*, 5(12):e1000608, 2009.

61. P. L. Martelli, M. D'Antonio, P. Bonizzoni, T. Castrignanò, A. M. D'Erchia, P. D'Onorio De Meo, P. Fariselli, M. Finelli, F. Licciulli, M. Mangiulli, F. Mignone, G. Pavesi, E. Picardi, R. Rizzi, I. Rossi, A. Valletti, A. Zauli, F. Zambelli, R. Casadio, and G. Pesole. ASPicDB: A database of annotated transcript and protein variants generated by alternative splicing. *Nucleic Acids Res.*, 39(Database issue):D80–85, 2011.

62. R. Sinha, T. Lenser, N. Jahn, U. Gausmann, S. Friedel, K. Szafranski, K. Huse, P. Rosenstiel, J. Hampe, S. Schuster, M. Hiller, R. Backofen, and M. Platzer. TassDB2—A comprehensive database of subtle alternative splicing events. *BMC Bioinformatics*, 11:216, 2010.

63. J. Takeda, Y. Suzuki, R. Sakate, Y. Sato, T. Gojobori, T. Imanishi, and S. Sugano. H-DBAS: Human-transcriptome database for alternative splicing: Update 2010. *Nucleic Acids Res.*, 38(Database issue):D86–90, 2010.

64. G. Koscielny, V. Le Texier, C. Gopalakrishnan, V. Kumanduri, J. J. Riethoven, F. Nardone, E. Stanley, C. Fallsehr, O. Hofmann, M. Kull, E. Harrington, S. Boué, E. Eyras, M. Plass, F. Lopez, W. Ritchie, V. Moucadel, T. Ara, H. Pospisil, A. Herrmann, J. G. Reich, R. Guigó, P. Bork, M. K. Doeberitz, J. Vilo, W. Hide, R. Apweiler, T. A. Thanaraj, and D. Gautheret ASTD: The Alternative Splicing and Transcript Diversity database. *Genomics*, 93(3):213–220, 2009.

65. M. Shionyu, A. Yamaguchi, K. Shinoda, K. Takahashi, and M. Go. AS-ALPS: A database for analyzing the effects of alternative splicing on protcin structure, interaction and network in human and mouse. *Nucleic Acids Res.*, 37(Databasc issuc):D305–309, 2009.

66. J. M. Bechtel, P. Rajesh, I. Ilikchyan, Y. Deng, P. K. Mishra, Q. Wang, X. Wu, K. A. Afonin, W. E. Grose, Y. Wang, S. Khuder, and A. Fedorov. The Alternative Splicing Mutation Database: A hub for investigations of alternative splicing using mutational evidence. *BMC Res. Notes*, 1:3, 2008.

67. F. Birzele, R. Küffner, F. Meier, F. Oefinger, C. Potthast, and R. Zimmer. ProSAS: A database for analyzing alternative splicing in the context of protein structures. *Nucleic Acids Res.*, 36(Database issue):D63–68, 2008.

68. P. de la Grange, M. Dutertre, M. Correa, and D. Auboeuf. A new advance in alternative splicing databases: From catalogue to detailed analysis of regulation of expression and function of human alternative splicing variants. *BMC Bioinformatics*, 8:180, 2007.

69. A. Bhasi, R. V. Pandey, S. P. Utharasamy, and P. Senapathy. EuSplice: A unified resource for the analysis of splice signals and alternative splicing in eukaryotic genes. *Bioinformatics*, 15;23(14):1815–1823. 2007.

70. A. B. Khan, M. C. Ryan, H. Liu, B. R. Zeeberg, D. C. Jamison, and J. N. Weinstein. SpliceMiner: A high-throughput database implementation of the NCBI Evidence Viewer for microarray splice variant analysis. *BMC Bioinformatics*, 8:75, 2007.

71. Y. Lee, Y. Lee, B. Kim, Y. Shin, S. Nam, P. Kim, N. Kim, W. H. Chung, J. Kim, and S. Lee. ECgene: An alternative splicing database update. *Nucleic Acids Res.*, 35(Database issue):D99–103, 2007.

72. N. Kim, A. V. Alekseyenko, M. Roy, and C. Lee. The ASAP II database: Analysis and comparative genomics of alternative splicing in 15 animal species. *Nucleic Acids Res.*, 35(Database issue):D93–98, 2007.

73. D. Holste, G. Huo, V. Tung, and C. B. Burge. HOLLYWOOD: A comparative relational database of alternative splicing. *Nucleic Acids Res.*, 34(Database issue):D56–62, 2006.

74. S. Stamm, J. J. Riethoven, V. Le Texier, C. Gopalakrishnan, V. Kumanduri, Y. Tang, N. L. Barbosa-Morais, and T. A. Thanaraj. ASD: A bioinformatics resource on alternative splicing. *Nucleic Acids Res.*, 34(Database issue):D46–55, 2006.

75. C. L. Zheng, Y. S. Kwon, H. R. Li, K. Zhang, G. Coutinho-Mansfield, C. Yang, T. M. Nair, M. Gribskov, and X. D. Fu. MAASE: An alternative splicing database designed for supporting splicing microarray applications. *RNA*, 11(12):1767–1776, 2005.

76. M. K. Sakharkar, B. S. Perumal, Y. P. Lim, L. P. Chern, Y. Yu, and P. Kangueane. Alternatively spliced human genes by exon skipping—A database (ASHESdb). *In Silico Biol.*, 5(3):221–225, 2005.

77. F. R. Hsu, H. Y. Chang, Y. L. Lin, Y. T. Tsai, H. L. Peng, Y. T. Chen, C. Y. Cheng, M. Y. Shih, C. H. Liu, and C. F. Chen. AVATAR: A database for genome-wide alternative splicing event detection using large scale ESTs and mRNAs. *Bioinformation*, 1(1):16–18, 2005.

78. B. T. Lee, T. W. Tan, and S. Ranganathan. DEDB: A database of *Drosophila melanogaster* exons in splicing graph form. *BMC Bioinformatics*, 5:189, 2004.

79. J. Leipzig, P. Pevzner, and S. Heber. The Alternative Splicing Gallery (ASG): Bridging the gap between genome and transcriptome. *Nucleic Acids Res.*, 32(13):3977–3983, 2004.

80. H. Pospisil, A. Herrmann, R. H. Bortfeldt, and J. G. Reich. EASED: Extended Alternatively Spliced EST Database. *Nucleic Acids Res.*, 32(Database issue):D70–74, 2004.

81. Y. Zhou, C. Zhou, L. Ye, J. Dong, H. Xu, L. Cai, L. Zhang, and L. Wei. Database and analyses of known alternatively spliced genes in plants. *Genomics*, 82(6):584–595, 2003.

82. H. D. Huang, J. T. Horng, C. C. Lee, and B. J. Liu. ProSplicer: A database of putative alternative splicing information derived from protein, mRNA and expressed sequence tag sequence data. *Genome Biol.*, 4(4):R29, 2003.

83. H. Ji, Q. Zhou, F. Wen, H. Xia, X. Lu, and Y. Li. AsMamDB: An alternative splice database of mammals. *Nucleic Acids Res.*, 29(1):260–263, 2001.

84. M. Burset, I. A. Seledtsov, and V. V. Solovyev. SpliceDB: Database of canonical and non-canonical mammalian splice sites. *Nucleic Acids Res.*, 29(1):255–259, 2001.

85. I. Dralyuk, M. Brudno, M. S. Gelfand, M. Zorn, and I. Dubchak. ASDB: Database of alternatively spliced genes. *Nucleic Acids Res.*, 28(1):296–297, 2000.

86. A. Bhasi, P. Philip, V. T. Sreedharan, and P. Senapathy. AspAlt: A tool for inter-database, inter-genomic and user-specific comparative analysis of alternative transcription and alternative splicing in 46 eukaryotes. *Genomics*, 94(1):48–54, 2009.

87. M. C. Ryan, B. R. Zeeberg, N. J. Caplen, J. A. Cleland, A. B. Kahn, H. Liu, and J. N. Weinstein. SpliceCenter: A suite of web-based bioinformatic applications for evaluating the impact of alternative splicing on RT-PCR, RNAi, microarray, and peptide-based studies. *BMC Bioinformatics*, July 18;9:313, 2008.

88. M. Suyama, E. D. Harrington, S. Vinokourova, M. von Knebel Doeberitz, O. Ohara, and P. Bork. A network of conserved co-occurring motifs for the regulation of alternative splicing. *Nucleic Acids Res.*, 38(22):7916–7926, 2010.

89. M. Zavolan, E. van Nimwegen, and T. Gaasterland. Splice variation in mouse full-length cDNAs identified by mapping to the mouse genome. *Genome Res.*, 12(9):1377–1385, 2002.

90. W. J. Kent. BLAT—the BLAST like alignment tool. *Genome Res.*, 12:656–664, 2002.

91. L. Florea et al. A computer program for aligning a cDNA sequence with a genomic DNA sequence. *Genome Res.*, 8:967–974, 1998.

92. B. Taneri, A. Novoradovsky, and T. Gaasterland. Identification of shadow exons: Mining for alternative exons in human, mouse and rat comparative databases. DEXA 2009, IEEE-Xplore, 20th International Workshop on Database and Expert Systems Application, 2009, pp. 208–212.

CHAPTER 2

CLEANING, INTEGRATING, AND WAREHOUSING GENOMIC DATA FROM BIOMEDICAL RESOURCES

FOUZIA MOUSSOUNI[1] and LAURE BERTI-ÉQUILLE[2]
[1]Université de Rennes 1, Rennes, France
[2]Institut de Recherche pour le Développement, Montpellier, France

2.1 INTRODUCTION

Four biotechnological advances have been accomplished in the last decade: (i) sequencing of whole genomes giving rise to the discovery of thousands of genes, (ii) functional genomics using high-throughput DNA microarrays to measure the expression of each of these genes in multiple physiological and environmental conditions, (iii) scaling of proteins using Proteome to map all the proteins produced by a genome, and (iv) the dynamics of these genes and proteins in a network of interactions that gives life to any biological activity and phenotype. These major breakthroughs resulted in the massive collection of data in the field of life sciences. Considerable efforts have been made to sort, curate, and integrate every relevant piece of information from multiple information sources in order to understand complex biological phenomena.

Biomedical researchers spend a phenomenal time to search data across heterogeneous and distributed resources. Biomedical data are indeed available in several public data banks: banks for genomic data (DNA, RNA) like Ensembl, banks for proteins (polypeptides and structures) such as SWISS-PROT, generalist data banks such as GenBank, EMBL (European Molecular Biology Laboratory), and DDBJ (DNA DataBank of Japan). Other specialized databases exist today to describe specific aspects of a biological entity, including structural data of proteins [Protein Data Bank (PDB)], phenotype data Online Mendelian Inheritance in Man (OMIM), gene interactions Kyoto Encyclopedia of Genes and Genomes (KEGG), and gene expression data (ArrayExpress). Advances in communication technologies enabled these databases to be worldwide accessible by scientists via the Web. This has promoted the desire to share and integrate the data they contain, for connecting each biological aspect to another, for example, gene sequence to biological functions, gene to partners, gene to cell, tissue and body locations, and signal transductions to phenotypes and diseases. However, semantic heterogeneity has been a major obstacle to the interoperability of these databases,

Biological Knowledge Discovery Handbook: Preprocessing, Mining, and Postprocessing of Biological Data,
First Edition. Edited by Mourad Elloumi and Albert Y. Zomaya.
© 2014 John Wiley & Sons, Inc. Published 2014 by John Wiley & Sons, Inc.

moving to semantic scale the structuring efforts of biomedical information. Since then, interoperability (i.e., the linking of distributed and heterogeneous information items) has become a major problem in bioinformatics. Besides, biological data integration is still error prone and difficult to achieve without human intervention.

Despite these barriers, the last decade has been an explosion of data integration approaches and solutions to help life sciences researchers to interpret their results and test and generate new hypothesis. In high-throughput bio technologies like DNA-Chips, data warehouse solutions encountered great success because of the constant need to locally store the delivered gene expression data and confront and enrich them with data extracted from other sources to conduct multiple novel analyses.

Life sciences data sources are supplied by researchers as well as accessed by them to interpret results and generate new hypotheses. However, in the case of insufficient mechanisms for characterizing the quality of the data, such as truthfulness, accuracy, redundancy, inconsistency, completeness, and freshness, data are considered a "representation" of reality. Many imperfections in the data are not detected or corrected before integration and analysis. In this context, tremendous amount of data warehouse projects integrate data from various heterogeneous sources, having different degrees of quality and trust. Most of the time, the data are neither rigorously chosen nor carefully controlled for data quality. Data preparation and data quality metadata are recommended but still insufficiently exploited for ensuring quality and validating the results of information retrieval or data-mining techniques [1].

Most online life sciences data banks are riddled with errors that result from many factors. The three major sources of data quality problems are the following:

- *Heterogeneity of Data Sources* Public molecular databases [GenBank, SWISS-PROT, DDBJ, EMBL, Protein Information Resource (PIR), among others] are large and complex artifacts. They integrate data from multiple sources and transform the data using various programs, scripts, and manual annotation procedures that are neither traced nor documented and reproducible and change over time. Extensive duplication, repeated submissions of the sequences to the same or different databases, and cross-updating of databases accelerate the propagation of errors within and across the main online data banks.

- *Free-Ruled Data Annotation* Biological data come from journal literature and direct author submissions unpublished sources. There are usually no content restrictions for the submitters or collaborators to present their data to the data banks, even allowing claim patents, copyrights, or other intellectual property rights in all or a portion of the data with little assessment of the information content validity. Data entry errors can be easily introduced due to the lack of standardized nomenclature and variations in naming conventions (synonyms, homonyms, and abbreviations). In addition, information content may have different interpretations.

- *Instrumentation/Experimental Errors* The tools driving current automated, high-throughput sequencing systems are not error-free. 1% error rate in the sequencing may have tremendous consequences. Due to the unlimited information feature of coding and origin in genomic sequence data, researchers of molecular biology have to extract relevant data when performing an analysis and addressing specific research. Any data problem or error in the symbol sequences and repetitions may cause misleading and wrong data analysis results or misinterpretations.

- *Inadequacy of Data Quality Control Mechanisms and Scalability Issues*   Since the data sizes of major public data banks have been increasing exponentially [e.g., Gen-Bank contains approximately 152,599,230,112 bases in 165,740,164 sequence records in the traditional GenBank divisions and 453,829,752,320 bases in 112,488,036 sequence records in the Whole Genome Shotgun (WGS) division as of June 2013], manual data curation still predominates, despite its high cost and obvious problems of scalability [2]. Systematic approaches to data checking and cleaning are lacking [3].

A wide range of data quality problems may emerge at any time during a data life cycle (i.e., data acquisition, assembly, transformation, extraction, integration, storage, internal manipulation, etc.) from primary raw experiment databases to large public data banks and specialized laboratory information management systems (LIMSs). Careful data cleaning and data preparation are necessary prerequisites to any process of knowledge discovery from integrated biological data.

In this chapter, we review the literature on data integration in the life sciences with a particular focus on the approaches that have been proposed to handle biological data quality problems (Section 2.2). We propose a classification of data quality problems in biomedical resources and present some of preprocessing solutions that can be practically implemented before any data-mining task (Section 2.3). Based on our previous work on data cleaning, integration, and warehousing of biomedical data, we present the lessons we have learned and the approaches implemented in practice (Section 2.4). Finally, we conclude with some challenging research directions for biomedical data preprocessing and integration (Section 2.5).

2.2 RELATED WORK

The first-generation data integration systems for the life sciences were based on flat file indexing (e.g., SRS, DBGet, Entrez, Atlas), multi-database query languages (Kleisli, OPM, P/FDM), and federated databases (DiscoveryLink, BioMediator, caGRID). Recent systems are now mediation systems (or mediators) that consist in connecting fully autonomous distributed heterogeneous data sources [4]. Mediators do not assume that integrated sources will all be relational databases. Instead, integrated resources can be various database systems (relation, object relational, object, XML, etc.), flat files, and so on. The integration component of mediation is in charge of (1) providing a global view of integrated resources to the user, (2) proving the user with a query language to query integrated resources, (3) executing the query by collecting needed data from each integrated resource, and (4) returning the result to the user. For the user, the system provides a single view of the integrated data as it was a single database. Several mediation systems have been designed for domain-specific integration of biomolecular data, providing nonmaterialized views of biological data sources. They include:

- BioKleisli [5, 6] and its extensions K2 [7] and Pizzkell/Kleisli (also known as Discovery Hub [8])
- Multidatabase system based on the object protocol model (OPM) [9] to design object views [10] and its Object-Web Wrapper [11]
- DiscoveryLink [12]
- P/FDM [13, 14]
- TAMBIS [15]

Indeed, mediation systems often offer an internal query language that allows the integration of (new) resources (data and tools) in addition to a user's query language that is used by biologists to access, analyze, and visualize the data. Existing mediation approaches rely on traditional database query languages (e.g., SQL, OQL). As an example of ontology-based integration, TAMBIS [15] is primarily concerned with overcoming semantic heterogeneity through the use of ontologies. It provides users an ontology-driven browsing interface. Thus it restricts the extent to which sources can be exploited for scientific discovery.

To summarize, these systems have made many inroads into the task of data integration from diverse biological data sources. They all rely on significant programming resources to adjust to specific scientific tasks. They are also difficult to maintain and provide users a query language that requires programming ability (such as SQL, OQL, Daplex, etc.) and significantly limit the query capabilities.

However, none of the existing systems allow the management of data quality metadata and none of them offer the flexibility of customization for ETL (extract–transform–Load) or data preprocessing tasks [16]. These functionalities may be partially covered by emerging scientific work flow management systems [17–20] emphasizing data provenance as a critical dimension of biological knowledge discovery [21].

2.3 TYPOLOGY OF DATA QUALITY PROBLEMS IN BIOMEDICAL RESOURCES

We can classify data quality problems that occur in biomedical resources as follows:

- *Redundancy* Redundant or duplicated data are mainly caused by oversubmission. This category is due to overlapping annotations and replication of identical sequence information; for example, the same sequence can be submitted to different databases or submitted several times to the same database by different groups and/or the protein sequence may be translated from the duplicate nucleotide sequence and several records may contain fragmented or overlapping sequences with more or less complete sequences. The redundancy problem often comes along with partial incompleteness of records and more generally is caused by the evolving nature of knowledge. Extensive redundancy is caused by records containing fragmented or overlapping sequences with more complete sequences in other records (see Example 2.1).

Example 2.1 *Redundancy* Consider two records describing the same biological entity, GI:11692004 and GI:11692006, respectively, from the National Center for Biotechnology Information (NCBI) nucleotide data bank presented in Figure 2.1. The only difference between the two records relies on the sequence length. The record GI:11692006 provides additional irrelevant bases "a."

- *Incompleteness* Paradoxically, oversubmission does not prevent submission of incomplete records and fragmented information from one record to another with potentially overlapping or conflicting data.
- *Inconsistency* Multiple database records of the same nucleotide or protein sequences contain inconsistent or conflicting feature annotations. This category includes data entry errors, misspelling errors, misannotations of sequence functions, different expert interpretations, and inference of features or annotation transfer based on best

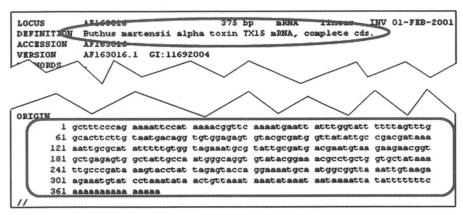

http://www.ncbi.nlm.nih.gov/entrez/viewer.fcgi?db=nucleotide&val=11692004

http://www.ncbi.nlm.nih.gov/entrez/viewer.fcgi?db=nucleotide&val=11692006

FIGURE 2.1   Two redundant records with uninformative sequence portions.

matches of low sequence similarity. Problematic data may lack domain consistency, such as contaminated data existing in a coding region due to unsure reasons or outdated, missing, and discrepant annotations compared with other databanks. Various inconsistencies may occur:

(a) *Syntax Errors*   Syntax errors are violations of syntactic constraints on particular format/fields of the data bank record.

(b) *Semantic Errors*   Semantic errors contain data field discrepancy, invalid data content identified either by the data bank flat file format or other NCBI specifications, for example, invalid MedLine or PubMed number or invalid reference number. Another type of error is the misuse of fields when data content does not correspond to the field usage (see Example 2.2).

(c) *Naming Ambiguities*   The manifestation of synonyms, homonyms, and abbreviations results in information ambiguities which cause problems in biological entity identification and keyword searching. For example, BMK stands for big map kinase, B-cell/myeloid kinase, bovine midkine, and Bradykinin-potentiating peptide. The scorpion neurotoxin BmK-X precursor has a permutation of synonyms. It is also known as BmKX, BmK10, BmK-M10, Bmk M10, neurotoxin M10, alpha-neurotoxin TX9, and BmKalphaTx9.

(d) *Undersized/Oversized Fields*   Sequences with meaningless content can be found in protein records queried using Entrez to the major protein or translated nucleotide databases: These are protein sequences shorter than four residues and sequences shorter than six bases. The undersized fields may alter the entity identification: for example, "M" is the synonym of the protein ACTM_HELTB (record GI:1703137) but "M" also corresponds to 1,389,441 records on the NCBI protein database.

(e) *Cross-Annotations with Conflicting Values*   Multiple database records of the same nucleotide or protein sequences may contain conflicting feature annotations, data entry errors, misannotation of sequence functions, different expert interpretations, and inference of features or annotation transfer based on best matches of low sequence similarity (see Example 2.2).

(f) *Putative Information*   Functional annotation sometimes involves searching for the highest matching annotated sequence in the database. Features are then extrapolated from the most similar known searched sequences. In some cases, even the highest matching sequence from database search may have weak sequence similarities and therefore does not share similar functions as the query sequence. "Blind" inference can cause erroneous functional assignment.

Example 2.2 *Inconsistency*   Consider the bibliographic reference provided in the record GenBank: AF139840.1 presented in Figure 2.2. This record and sequence information has been directly submitted to GenBank and does not correspond to a peer-reviewed publication *stricto sensu*.

- *Irrelevancy*   Less meaningful, nonsense, or irrelevant data may exist in a free-text field of annotation or description (e.g., coding region) which may intervene with the target analysis. Some values of finer granularity may be concatenated and automatically imported into a data field of coarser granularity. These values are so-called misfielded (see Example 2.3).

  (a) *Uninformative Features or Data*   A profuse percentage of the unknown residues ("X") or unknown bases ("N") can reduce the complexity of the sequence and thus the information content of the sequence.

```
REFERENCE    1  (bases 1 to 687)
  AUTHORS    Direct Submission.
  TITLE      A long terminal repeat(LTR)of the human endogenous retrovirus ERV-9
             is located in the 5' end of the human beta globin gene locus
             control region(LCR)
  JOURNAL    Unpublished
REFERENCE    2  (bases 1 to 687)
  AUTHORS    Kutlar,F., Leithner,C., Zeng,S. and Tuan,D.
  TITLE      Direct Submission
  JOURNAL    Submitted (31-MAR-1999) Hematology/Oncology, Hemoglobin Laboratory,
             Medical College of Georgia, 15 th St. AC-1000, Augusta, GA 30912,
             USA
```

FIGURE 2.2   Example of misuse of the bibliographic references field.

(b) *Contaminated Data*   Introns and exons must be nonoverlapping except in cases of alternative splicing. But in some erroneous records, nucleotide sequences have overlapping intron/exon regions and some sequences may be contaminated with vectors commonly used for the cloning.

Example 2.3 *Irrelevancy*   Consider the following Definition field of the protein record AAB25735.1 (`http://www.ncbi.nlm.nih.gov/protein/AAB25735.1`): It includes the species, the sequence length, and so on. These additional information items are irrelevant and misfielded.

```
DEFINITION neurotoxin, NTX [Naja naja=Formosan cobra,
ssp. atra, venom, Peptide, 62 aa]
```

- *Obsolescence*   Instead of checking existing records related to the biological entity of interest and updating one of them, users may prefer to submit a new record. This not only may increase the interrecord redundancy and overlaps in the databank but also has two consequences: (1) increase the difficulty in achieving entity resolution and correctly group together the records that may be truly related to the same biological entity and (2) keep out-of-date records with misleading or no longer valid knowledge elements.

Table 2.1 summarizes potential intrarecord data quality problems into categories and the fields they can affect in a traditional record content.

Since redundancy can be observed from a group of records, it can be classified as an interrecord data quality problem. In Table 2.2, we present the existing solutions for consolidating data at both the intra- and interrecord levels. These solutions are based on integrity [22], format and constraint checking, comparative analysis, and duplicate detection depending on the type of data quality problem.

2.4   CLEANING, INTEGRATING, AND WAREHOUSING BIOMEDICAL DATA

The aim of this section is to report on our experience during the design of GEDAW, the Gene Expression Data Warehouse [23] and the implementation of the biomedical data integration process in the presence of syntactic and semantic conflicts. We will point out the lessons learned from data preprocessing and propose the different but complementary solutions adopted for quality-aware data integration.

2.4.1   Lessons Learned from Integrating and Warehousing Biomedical Data on Liver Genes and Diseases

Liver diseases, including those from infectious, alcoholic, metabolic, toxic, and vascular etiology, are a major public health problem. They are frequently complicated by the occurrence of acute liver failure or the development of cirrhosis and liver cancer, which shorten life expectancy. Molecular mechanisms involved in the occurrence of these diseases and their complications are still not well known. Ongoing research focuses on identifying new relative molecular mechanisms leading to new diagnostic and therapeutic tools.

One way to study liver diseases and correlated complications is the use of DNA-Chips technology for high-throughputs transcriptome study. Using this technology, thousands

TABLE 2.1 Categorization of Potential Intrarecord Data Quality Problems

Categories	Data Quality Problems	Global Identifier	Definition	Taxonomy	References	Cross-Links	Feature Annotations	Raw Data
					Record Fields			
Inconsistency	Typo/misspelling		X		X			X
	Format violation		X		X		X	X
	Ambiguous naming (homonyms, synonyms, abbreviations)		X	X	X		X	X
	Misfielded values		X		X		X	X
	Undersized/oversized field		X				X	X
	Measurement error, contaminated data					X	X	X
	Syntax errors and format violations		X	X	X	X	X	X
Irrelevancy	Putative information		X				X	X
	Uninformative data		X		X		X	X
Incompleteness	Incomplete data/default values		X	X	X	X	X	X
Obsolescence	Out-of-date data	X	X		X	X	X	X

42

TABLE 2.2 Practical Solutions to Biological Data Quality Problems

Categories	Data Quality Problems	Attribute-Based Solutions	Intrarecord Solutions	Interrecord Solutions
Inconsistency	Typo/misspelling	Dictionary look-up	Constraint checking	Duplicate detection
	Ambiguous naming (homonyms. synonyms, abbreviations)	Dictionary look-up	Entity resolution	Duplicate detection
	Misfielded values	Integrity constraints	Constraint checking	Duplicate detection
	Format violation	Integrity constraints	Formatting ETL	Schema remapping
	Undersized/oversized field	Integrity constraints	Size checking	Comparative analysis
	Measurement error, contaminated data	Vector screening, sequence structure parser	Constraint checking	Comparative analysis
	Syntax errors and format violations	Format checking	Format checking	Format checking
Irrelevancy	Putative information	Keywords search	—	Comparative analysis
	Uninformative data	Constraint checking	Constraint checking	Comparative analysis
Incompleteness	Incomplete data/default values	Constraint checking	Constraint checking	Comparative analysis
Obsolescence	Out-of-date data	Constraint checking	Constraint checking	Comparative analysis

of genes can be studied simultaneously in order to find out the subset of genes that are abnormally expressed in injured tissues, which delivers new knowledge on gene networks and regulation mechanisms.

However, the data generated on gene expression are massive and involve difficulties in their management and analysis. Furthermore, for the interpretation of a single gene expression measurement, the biologist has to consider the available knowledge about this gene in different data banks, including its chromosomal location, relative sequences with promoters, molecular function and classification, biological processes, gene interactions, expressions in other physiopathological situations, clinical follow-ups, and an increasingly important bibliography.

The GEDAW developed at the National Medical Research Institute (INSERM) stores data on genes expressed in the liver during iron overload and liver pathologies. Relevant information from public data banks, DNA-Chips home experiments, and medical records have been integrated, stored, and managed in GEDAW to globally analyze the delivered gene expression measurements.

GEDAW is aimed at the in silico study of liver pathologies by using expression levels of genes in different physiological situations enriched with annotations extracted from a variety of scientific data sources, ontologies, and standards in the life sciences and medicine. In GenBank, each record, usually associated to a gene, describes the genomic sequence with several annotations and is identified by a unique accession number. It may also be retrieved by keywords (cf. Figure 2.5 later in the chapter). Annotations may include the description of the genomic sequence: function, size, species for which it has been determined, related scientific publications, and a description of the regions constituting the sequence [codon start, codon stop, introns, exons, open reading frame (ORF), etc.].

However, designing a single global data warehouse schema that integrates syntactically and semantically many heterogeneous life sciences data sources is a challenging task. Only structured and semistructured data sources were used to integrate GEDAW using a global-as-view (GAV) schema-mapping approach and a rule-based transformation process from a given source schema to the global schema of the data warehouse (cf. Figure 2.3). As an almost hands-off integration method, this technique is quite advanced at this time, compared to previous developed warehouses like [24] for which yeast data were completely flat.

Figure 2.3 gives a synthesized class diagram of GEDAW and some correspondence with the GenBank document type definition (DTD) (e.g., Seqdes_title and Molinfo values were extracted and transformed and migrated to other description attributes of the class Gene in the GEDAW global scheme).

The GEDAW system presented in [23] allows massive import of biological and medical data into an object-oriented data warehouse that supports transcriptome analyses specific to the human liver. It focuses on the relevant genomic, biological, and medical resources that have been used to build GEDAW. The integration process of the full sequence annotations of the genes expressed was performed by parsing and cleaning the corresponding XML description in GenBank, transforming the recorded genomic items to persistent objects, and storing them in the warehouse. This process is almost systematic because another aspect related to the conciliation of duplicate records has been added. Elements formalizing expertise rules for mapping such data were given. This ongoing work is still a difficult problem in information integration in life sciences and has not yet satisfied answers by classical solutions proposed in existing mediation systems. For strong analysis on expressed genes and to correlate expression profiles to liver biology and pathological phenotype, a second annotation method has been added to the integration process.

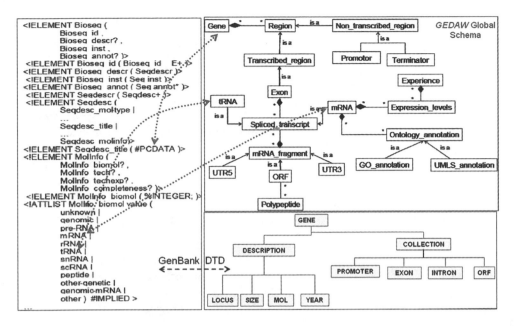

FIGURE 2.3   Mapping GenBank DTD to GEDAW.

2.4.2 Data Quality-Aware Solutions

Different input data sources have been considered during the building of GEDAW: (i) GenBank for the genomic features of the genes, (ii) annotations of genes in biomedical ontologies and terminologies (such as UMLS, MeSH, and GO), and (iii) gene expression measurements generated in different physiological conditions.

Because of the amount of gene expression data (more than two thousand measures per experiment and a hundred experiments per gene), the use of schema integration in our case that is, the replication of the source schema in the warehouse, would highly burden the data warehouse.

By using a GAV mapping approach to integrate one data source at a time (cf. Figure 2.3 for GenBank), we have minimized as much as possible the problem of identification of equivalent attributes. The problem of equivalent instance identification is still too complex to address. This is due to the general redundancy in the occurrence of a biological entity even within one data source. As we pointed out in Section 2.3, biological data banks may have inconsistent values of equivalent attributes referring to the same real-world object. For example, in GenBank, there are more than 10 data forms associated to the same human *HFE* gene, a central gene associated to iron uptake! Obviously the same segment could be a clone, a marker, or a genomic sequence.

This is mainly due to the fact that life sciences researchers can submit any biological information to public data banks with more or less formalized submission protocols that usually do not include name standardization or data quality controls. Erroneous data may be easily entered and cross-referenced. Even if some tools propose clusters of records (like LocusLink for GenBank, more recently called EntryGene) to identify a same biological concept across different biological data banks for being semantically related, biologists still must validate the correctness of these clusters and resolve interpretation of differences between records.

Entity resolution and record linkage are required in this situation. The problem is augmented and made more complex due to the high level of expertise and knowledge required (i.e., difficult to formalize because it is related to many different subdisciplines of biology, chemistry, pharmacology, and medical sciences). After the step of biological entity resolution, data are scrubbed and transformed to fit the global data warehouse schema with the appropriate standardized format for values, so that the data meet all the validation rules that have been decided upon by the warehouse designer. Problems that can arise during this step include null or missing data, violations of data type, nonuniform value formats, and invalid data.

2.4.3   Biological Entity Resolution and Record Linkage

As the first preprocessing step for data integration, the process of entity identification, resolution, and record linkage has to be performed using a sequence of increasingly sophisticated linkage techniques, described in the following, and also additional knowledge bases, ontologies, and thesaurus (such as UMLS Metathesaurus and MeSH-SR vocabulary), each operating on the set of records that were left unlinked in the previous phase:

Linkage based on exact key matching: that is, based on gene names and cross-referenced accession numbers [e.g., between a gene from the HUGO Gene Nomenclature Committee (HGNC) and a protein in SWISS-PROT]

Linkage based on nearly exact key matching (i.e., based on all the synonyms of a term and all the identifiers of a gene or gene product in HGNC, the UMLS Metathesaurus, and MeSH-SR and in the cluster of records proposed by EntryGene)

Probabilistic linkage based on the full set of comparable attributes (i.e., based on the search for information about a gene or a gene product: the set of concepts related to this gene in the Gene Ontology [Molecular Function (F), Biological Process (P), and Cellular Component (C)] and the set of concepts related to the gene in UMLS and MedLine abstracts (including chemicals and drugs, anatomy, and disorders):

Search for erroneous links (false positives)

Analysis of residual data and final results for biological entity resolution

As an example, consider data related to *Ceruloplasmin*, a gene expressed mainly in the liver and involved in iron metabolism through its ferroxidase activity, which is dependent of the copper charge of the protein. A related disease, called Aceruloplasminemia, is a genetic disease responsible for iron overload [25]. The level of plasmatic ceruloplasmin is modulated during various chronic liver diseases [26].

As shown in Figure 2.4, a first phase of linkage based on a search for *Ceruloplasmin* in the GOA[19] database and HGNC provides related terms and returns the corresponding accession numbers in GeneEntry (1356) or SWISS-PROT, approved gene name (*Ceruloplasmin ferroxidase*), and gene symbol (*CP*). The accession number can then be used to find information in external sources.

Another search for the term on Gene Ontology returns the set of concepts of each of the categories F, P, and C. From the UMLS context, terms associated to *Ceruloplasmin* in the Metathesaurus and terms that co-occur with *Ceruloplasmin* in MedLine are extracted and MedLine abstracts are made accessible.

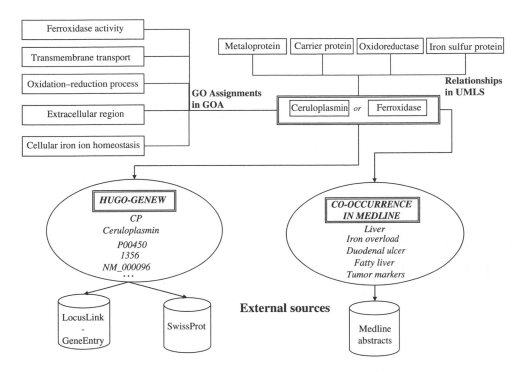

FIGURE 2.4   Entity resolution and record linkage of *Ceruloplasmin* gene.

Indeed, in our experience, combining medical and molecular biology knowledge provides valuable information about genes; for example, *Ceruloplasmin* is involved in molecular functions such as iron transport mediation and has relationships to diseases like Iron overload and duodenal ulcer. It can be used to support various tasks to cluster genes according to their properties. Moreover, integration is required for better understanding of disease–molecular data relationships. All these functionalities are presented with more detail in [27].

2.4.3.1 *Biomedical Data Scrubbing and Conflict Resolution*
In order to define an appropriate data aggregation of all the available information items resulting from the previous step of biological entity resolution, data conflicts have to be resolved using rules for mapping the source records and conciliating different values recorded for the same concept.

Mapping rules have been defined to allow data exchange from public data banks to GEDAW. Apart from experimental data, public information items are automatically extracted by scripts using the DTD of the data source translated into the GEDAW conceptual data model.

Three categories of mapping rules were proposed for GEDAW: (1) structural mapping rules, (2) semantic mapping rules, and (3) cognitive mapping rules according to the different knowledge levels involved in the biological interpretation of data.

Structural mapping rules are defined at the schema level according to the GEDAW model by identifying the existing correspondence with relevant DTD elements; for example, in Figure 2.3, the Seqdesc_title element in GenBank DTD is used to extract the attribute Name of the gene and the MolInfo_biomol value to determine the type of molecule.

Semantic and *cognitive mapping rules* are used for data unification at the instance level: Several rules may use available tools for determining analogies between homologous data (such as sequence alignment). The result of the BLAST algorithm (Basic Local Alignment Search Tool) implemented as a set of similarity search programs allows as to match two genomic sequences.

The nomenclature provided by the entity resolution and record linkage phase described in the previous section is also often used to reconcile duplicate records based on several ontologies. For instance, UMLS ontology covers the whole biomedical domain and Gene Ontology^{TM} focuses on genomics, as well as additional terminologies. HGNC also provides solutions to resolve synonymy conflicts.

More semantic mapping rules are built using this information during the integration process. For example, the Gene-ID is used to cluster submitted sequences (DNA, mRNA, and proteins) associated to the same gene with cross-referenced records in GeneEntry databank and the official gene name along with its aliases to relate different gene name appearances in the literature. These aliases are also stored in the data warehouse and used to tackle the mixed or split citation problems similar to those studied by [28] in digital libraries.

Example 2.4 Three distinct records are obtained from the nucleotide data bank Gen-Bank by querying the DNA sequence for the human gene *HFE* as partially presented in Figures 2.5–2.7:

- A first record **1** identified by the accession number AF204869 describes a partial gene sequence (size 3043) of the *HFE* gene with no annotation but one relevant and fundamental information item about the position of the promoter region at [1..3043] in the misc_feature field which cannot be found in the other records.
- A second record **2** identified by the accession number AF184234 describes a partial sequence (size 772) of the protein precursor of *HFE* gene with a detailed but incomplete annotation.
- The third record **3** identified by the accession number Z92910 describes the complete gene sequence (size 12146) of the *HFE* gene with a complete annotation.

We need to integrate this information and evaluate the quality of these three records because they are complementary regarding the biological topic of interest (i.e., *HFE* human gene). The first record has a relevant data item that the other records do not have, the second record overlaps the third one regarding the gene sequence but provide more detailed annotations, and the third record is complete regarding the gene sequence. This example shows the main quality criteria we use: completeness, relevancy, and detail level of annotation.

In this example, using the BLAST algorithm to determine the sequence alignment between the two sequences of records **2** and **3** shows 100% of alignment. This indicates that the sequences in both records **2** and **3** are perfectly identical and can be merged. The detailed annotation of record **2** can be concatenated with the more complete annotation of record **3** in the data warehouse.

Several cognitive mapping rules may be used in this example to reconcile data such as the position offset: in record **3** the fourth exon is located at position 6494 and in record **2** this same exon is located at the relative position 130; thus, using overlapping information that identifies the same entities, we can deduce the position offset and use the following cognitive rule:

```
record(AF18423)/exon[number >=4]/position = record(Z92910)/
exon[number >=4]/position - 6364
```

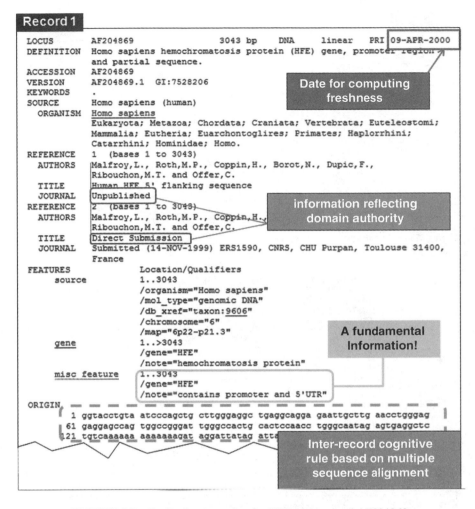

FIGURE 2.5   GenBank screen shot for *HFE* gene: record AF204869.

2.4.3.2 *Database Profiling and Data Quality Metrics*   Several information quality dimensions with their related metrics can be defined, computed, and associated as metadata to the data extracted from biological data banks. These metadata can be very useful for data integration and knowledge pre- and postfiltering. We have categorized them as follows (cf. Table 2.3):

- Bioknowledge-based quality metadata such as originality and domain authority of the authors who submitted the sequence
- Schema-based quality metadata such as local and global completeness, level of details, and intra- and interrecord redundancy
- Contextual quality metadata such as freshness and consolidation degree

2.4.4   Ontology-Based Approaches

The semantic Web anticipates the use of ontologies to facilitate data sharing over the Web, and ontologies are proposed as a solution to reconcile and attain heterogeneity between

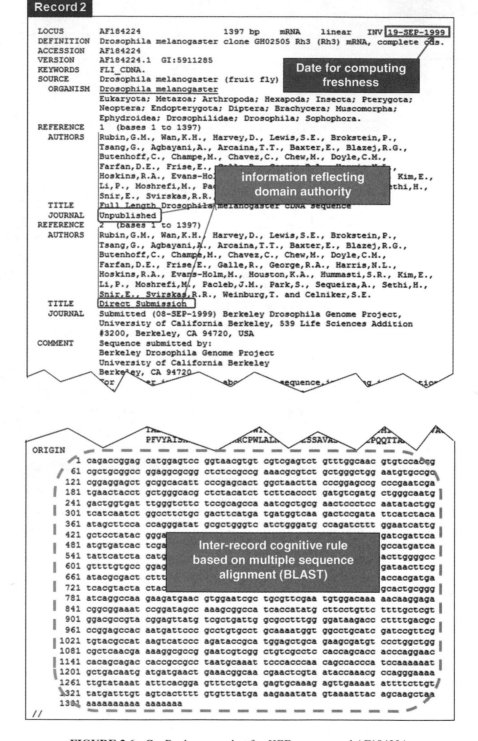

FIGURE 2.6   GenBank screen shot for *HFE* gene: record AF184224.

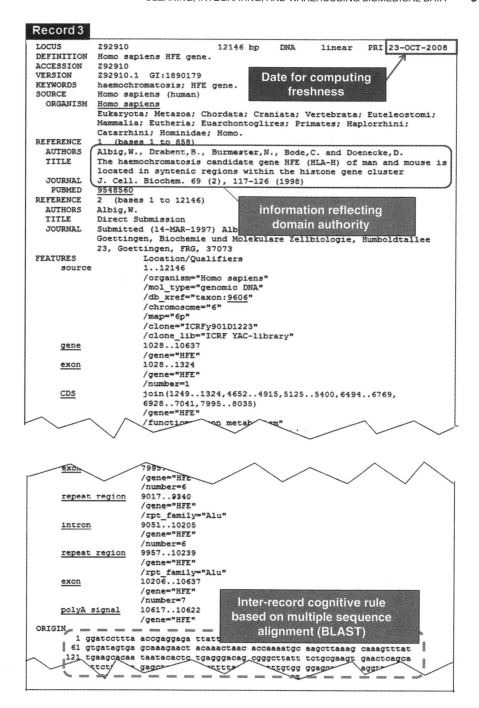

FIGURE 2.7   GenBank screen shot for *HFE* gene: record Z92910.

TABLE 2.3 Computing Data Quality Metadata for Documenting Biomedical Sources before Integration

Category	Quality Criterion	Target	Definition
Bioknowledge-based quality criteria	Originality	Data items and subitems per record	Considering a set of records related to the same bioentity (i.e., entity identification resolved), the originality of a data (sub-) item in a record set is defined by its occurrence frequency and its variability based on the normalized standard deviation of the edit distance between the considered strings.
	Domain authority	Record	Domain authority is a grade in [0,1] that is computed depending on the status of the reference (*published, submitted, unpublished*), the number of referenced submissions of the authors in the record and the user-grade defined on the journal, and authors' reputations of the most recent reference of these authors.
Schema-based quality criteria	Local completeness	Record	Local completeness is defined by the fraction of the number of items and subitems with nonnull values on the total number of items and subitems in the local data source schema (DTD).
	Global completeness	Record	Global completeness is defined by the fraction of the number of items and subitems with nonnull values provided by a source on the total number of items and subitems in the global schema of the data warehouse.
	Level of detail	Data items and subitems per record	Level of detail is the number of subitems per item described with nonnull values by a local source normalized by the total of possible subitems in the data source schema.
	Intrarecord redundancy	Record	Intrarecord redundancy is defined by the fraction of items and subitems in the record that are approximately the same based on the edit or q-grams distance functions or other semantic and cognitive rules.
	Interrecord redundancy	Record set of same bioentity	Interrecord redundancy is defined by the fraction of items and subitems in the record set that are approximately the same based on edit or q-grams distance functions, BLAST or other sequence alignment techniques, or other cognitive rules.
Contextual quality criteria	Freshness	Record	Freshness is defined by the difference between the current date and the publication date of the record.
	Consolidation degree	Data items and subitems per record	Consolidation degree is defined by the number of interrecord redundancies and overlaps.

data sources as much as possible. As a result, the use of ontologies for semantic-driven data integration to build multiple data warehouses that combine and analyze different sorts of data is promising.

Two major events have urged the development of ontologies in life sciences: (i) strong emergence of large volumes of data represented heterogeneously in multiple data sources and (ii) increasing motivation to worldwide sharing of these data on the Web.

Following the publication of the genome sequences and their various annotations, the use of bio-ontologies became essential to deal with the heterogeneity of data and sources. Bio-ontologies helped to unify different definitions, improve data quality, and promote data sharing and exchange [29–31].

Paradoxically, it is the medical informatics community that first developed strategies to facilitate and improve access to biomedical knowledge using ontologies. Thus, the NLM (National Library of Medicine) has developed the Unified Medical Language System (UMLS), a rich knowledge base qualified as a medical ontology of more than one million concepts and developed by the unification of 60 biomedical terminologies [32].

Thus, previous achievements on ontologies in the medical domain had a direct impact on the bioinformatics community. Understanding functional genomic data being one of the challenges of modern medicine, the two communities have combined their efforts in the development of bio-ontologies.

While Gene Ontology has rapidly become the leading ontology in functional genomics, other ontologies have emerged as a response to the constant need to formalize the fields of life and health sciences. Consequently, the Open Biological and Biomedical Ontologies (OBO) Foundry archives a collection of bio-ontologies in a standard format. Strong community involvement was crucial to avoid redundancy as much as possible and ensure that only single ontologies for each area are in the public domain.

As shown in Table 2.4, the OBO Foundry supports various domain knowledge of life and health sciences and includes Gene Ontology, Pathway Ontology, Disease Ontology, Systems Biology Ontology, and Chemical Entities of Biological Interest (CHEBI) Ontology [33].

Shared ontologies are used to reconcile data conflicts as much as possible. Various standards in life sciences have been developed to provide domain knowledge to be used for semantically driven integration of information from different sources.

Unfortunately, the one way that was massively used to integrate life science data using ontologies is through annotation of the multiple sorts of data in genomics (gene sequences and proteins) using the common vocabulary carried by these ontologies. But the great success of this approach has led to proliferation of bio-ontologies that again has created obstacles to data integration. In some ways, the OBO Foundry Consortium has emerged to overcome this problem [33].

More ideally, the aim of such ontologies in the context of data integration would be of granting a model of biological concepts that can be used to form a semantic framework for querying the heterogeneous life sciences sources or for systematizing annotation of experimental results. As an example, the TaO ontology (TAMBIS ontology), which describes a wide range of life sciences concepts and their relationships, provided such a framework. Rather than placing biodata in integrated data warehouses, the TAMBIS project provided a single and transparent access point for life sciences information through the use of a mediating ontology [15]. Queries are written in terms of TaO ontology concepts and converted to queries to appropriate sources.

More recently, there are an extraordinary number of bioinformatics applications [34] based on ontology as a background domain knowledge and a unified model against life

TABLE 2.4 OBO Foundry Ontologies (April 2007)

Ontology	Scope	URL	Custodians
Mature Ontologies Undergoing Incremental Reform			
Cell Ontology (CL)	Cell types from prokaryotic to mammalian	`http://obofoundry.org/cgi-bin/detail.cgi?cell`	Michael Ashburner Jonathan Bard, Oliver Hofmann, Sue Rhee
Gene Ontology (GO)	Attributes of gene products in all organisms	`http://www.geneontology.org`	Gene Ontology Consortium
Foundational Model of Anatomy (FMA)	Structure of mammalian and in particular human body	`http://fma.biostr.washington.edu`	J. L. V. Mejino, Jr., Cornelius Rosse
Zebrafish Anatomical Ontology (ZAO)	Anatomical structures in *Danio rerio*	`http://zfin.org/zf.info/anatomy/dict/sum.html`	Melissa Haendel, Monte Westerfield
Mature Ontologies Still in Need of Through Review			
Chemical entities of Biological Interest (ChEBI)	Molecular entities which are products of nature or synthetic products used to intervene in processes of living organisms	`http://www.ebi.ac.uk/chebi`	Paula Dematos, Rafael Alcantara
Disease Ontology (DO)	Types of human disease	`http://diseaseontology.sf.net`	Rex Chisholm
Plant Ontology (PO)	Flowering plant structure, growth and development stages	`http://plantontology.org`	Plant Ontology Consortium
Sequence Ontology (SO)	Features and properties of nuclic acid sequences	`http://www/sequenceontology.org`	Karen Eilbeck
Ontologies for Which Early Versions Exist			
Ontology for Clinical Investigations (OCI)	Clinical trails and related clinical studies	`http://www.bioontology.org/wiki/index.php/CTO:Main.Page`	OCI Working Group
Common Anatomy Reference Ontology (CARO)	Anatomical structure in all organisms	`http://obofoundry.org/cgi-bin/detail.cgi?caro`	Fabian Neuhaus, Melissa Haendel, David Sutherland
Environment Ontology	Habitats and associated spatial regions and sites	`http://www.obofoundry.org/cgi-bin/detail.cgi?id=envo`	Norman Morrison, Dawn Field
Ontology for Biomedical Investigations (OBI)	Design, protocol, instrumentation, and analysis applied in biomedical investigations	`http://obi.sf.net`	OBI Working Group
Phenotypic Quality Ontology (PATO)	Qualities of biomedical entities	`http://www.phenotypeontology.org`	Michael Ashburner, Suzanna Lewis, Georgios Gkoutos
Protein Ontology (PRO)	Protein types and modifications classified on basis of evolutionary relationships	`http://pir.georgetown.edu/pro`	Protein Ontology Consortium
Relation Ontology (RO)	Relations in biomedical ontologies	`http://obofoundry.org/ro`	Barry Smith, Chris Mungall
RNA Ontology (RnaO)	RNA three-dimensional structures, sequence alignments, and interactions	`http://roc.bgsu.edu/`	RNA Ontology Consortium

Sciences resources to remediate data annotation, data integration, and data heterogeneity [35]. However, ontology development and maintenance are time consuming and require constant investment from expert curators. Open collaborative platforms enable the wider scientific community to become involved in developing and maintaining them but raise concerns regarding the quality and correctness of the information added [36].

2.5 CONCLUSIONS AND PERSPECTIVES

Many data sources in the biomedical domain are renowned for containing data of poor quality. This is due to the experimental nature of the field, the quickly changing knowledge landscape, the high redundancies in experiments performed often leading to contradicting results, and the difficulties in properly describing the results of an experiment in a domain as complex as molecular biology. Furthermore, it has often been observed that data quality problems multiply when data of low quality are integrated and reused for annotation.

Based on our past experience of building the biomedical data warehouse GEDAW (Gene Expression Data Warehouse) that stores all the relevant information on genes expressed in the liver during iron overload and liver pathologies (i.e., records extracted from public data banks, data generated from DNA-Chips home experiments, data collected in hospitals and clinical institutions as medical records), we presented some lessons learned, data quality issues in this context, and solutions proposed for quality-aware integrating and warehousing our biomedical data. In this chapter, we gave an overview of data quality problems and solutions relevant to any preprocessing approach and also elements for data quality awareness for the complex processes of integrating and warehousing biomedical data.

With regard to the limits of any data warehousing approach, it is relevant to generate quality metadata at the preprocessing and preintegration stage as long as the whole data integration process (from the original data sources into the destination data warehousing system) stays feasible automatically and with a reasonable performance. Generally the final data filtering task has to be performed by the expert on the delivered annotations or data analysis before their storage in the warehouse by using multiple data quality criteria, for instance the authoritativeness of the information source and the credibility of the authors of the submitted record.

Quality in the results of data mining and knowledge discovery from biomedical resources critically depends on the preparation and quality of analyzed data sets. Indeed, biomedical data-mining processes and applications require various forms of data preparation, correction, and consolidation, combining complex data transformation operations and cleaning techniques, because the data input to the mining algorithms is assumed to conform to "nice" data distributions, containing no missing, inconsistent, or incorrect values. This leaves a large gap between the available "dirty" data and the available machinery to process and analyze the data for discovering added-value knowledge and decision making in life sciences.

The aspects of measuring data quality and detecting hot spots of poor quality constitute very challenging research directions for the bioinformatics community. These include analyzing contradicting values in the case of duplicate entries and detecting hard-to-catch errors. Such erroneous data may look perfectly legitimate. Yet, if we examine the values in conjunction with other attribute values, the data appear questionable. Detecting such dubious values is a major problem in data cleaning, but it becomes much harder in complex domains such as life sciences.

WEB RESOURCES

ArrayExpress Database: `http://www.ebi.ac.uk/arrayexpress/`.

DBGet retrieval system: `http://www.genome.jp/dbget/`.

DDBJ (DNA Data Bank of country-regionplaceJapan): `http://www.ddbj.nig.ac.jp/`.

EMBL (European Molecular Biology Laboratory Databank): `http://www.ebi.ac.uk/embl/`.

Ensembl Genome Browser: `http://www.ensembl.org/index.html`.

Entrez Search Engine: `http://www.ncbi.nlm.nih.gov/Entrez/`.

GENATLAS (Gene Atlas): `http://www.genatlas.org/`.

GenBank Genetic Sequence Database: `http://www.ncbi.nlm.nih.gov/genbank/`.

Gene Ontology^{TM} (GO): `http://www.ontologos.org/IFF/Ontologies/Gene.html`.

GOA (Gene Ontology Database): `http://www.geneontology.org/GO.database.shtml`.

HGNC (Human Gene Nomenclature Database): `http://www.genenames.org/`.

KEGG (Kyoto Encyclopedia of Genes and Genomes): `http://www.genome.jp/kegg/pathway.html`.

LocusLink (superceded by Entrez Gene): `http://www.ncbi.nlm.nih.gov/LocusLink`.

MedLine Database, PubMed Access: `http://www.ncbi.nlm.nih.gov/entrez/query.fcgi?db=PubMed`.

MeSH (Medical Subject Headings): `http://www.nlm.nih.gov/mesh/MBrowser.html`.

NCBI Record AF204869: `http://www.ncbi.nlm.nih.gov/nuccore/af204869`.

NCBI Record AF184224: `http://www.ncbi.nlm.nih.gov/nuccore/af184224`.

NCBI Record Z95910: `http://www.ncbi.nlm.nih.gov/nuccore/z92910`.

OBO Foundry Paper: `http://www.obofoundry.org/`.

OMIM (the Online Mendelian Inheritance in Man): `http://www.ncbi.nlm.nih.gov/omim`.

PDB (the Protein Data Base): `http://www.pdb.org/pdb/home/home.do`.

SRS Browser: `http://srs.ebi.ac.uk/`.

SWISS-PROT Database: `http://www.expasy.org/sprot`.

UMLS (Unified Medical Language System®): `http://www.nlm.nih.gov/research/umls/`.

REFERENCES

1. L. Berti-Équille and F. Moussouni. Quality-Aware Integration and Warehousing of Genomic Data. In *Proceedings of the 10th International Conference on Information Quality (ICIQ'05)*, Massachusetts Institute of Technology, Cambridge, MA, November 2005, pp. 442–454.

2. W. A. Baumgartner, Jr., K. B. Cohen, L. M. Fox, G. Acquaah-Mensah, and L. Hunter. Manual curation is not sufficient for annotation of genomic databases. *Bioinformatics*, 23(13):i41, 2007.

3. P. Buneman, J. Cheney, W.-C. Tan, and S. Vansummeren. Curated databases. In *Proceedings of the Twenty-Seventh ACM SIGMOD-SIGACT-SIGART Symposium on Principles of Database Systems (PODS'08)*, Vancouver, BC, Canada, June 9–11, 2008, pp. 1–12.

4. A. M. Jenkinson, M. Albrecht, E. Birney, H. Blankenburg, T. Down, R. D. Finn, H. Hermjakob, T. J. P. Hubbard, R. C. Jimenez, P. Jones, A. Kähäri, E. Kulesha, J. R. Macías, G. A. Reeves, and A. Prlic. Integrating biological data: The Distributed Annotation System. *BMC Bioinformatics*, 9(Suppl. 8):S3, 2008.

5. S. B. Davidson, G. C. Overton, V. Tannen, and L. Wong. BioKleisli: A digital library for biomedical researchers. *Int. J. Digit. Libr.*, 1(1):36–53, 1997.

6. P. Buneman, J. Crabtree, S. Davidson, V. Tannen, and L. Wong. *BioKleisli: BioInformatics*. Kluwer Academic, Dordrecht, 1998.

7. S. Davidson, J. Crabtree, B. Brunk, J. Schug, V. Tannen, C. Overton, and C. Stoeckert. K2/Kleisli and GUS: Experiments in integrated access to genomic data sources. *IBM Syst. J.*, 40(2):512–531, 2001.

8. L. Wong. Kleisli, its exchange format, supporting tools, and an application protein interaction extraction. *Proc. of the IEEE International Symposium on Bio-Informatics and Biomedical Engineering (BIBE)*, IEEE Press, Washington DC, 2000.

9. I.A. Chen and V.M. Markowitz. An overview of the object-protocol model (OPM) and OPM data management tools. *Inform. Syst.*, 20(5):393–418, 1995.

10. I.A. Chen, A.S. Kosky, V.M. Markowitz, and E. Szeto. Constructing and maintaining scientific database views. In *Proceedings of the Ninth International Conference on Scientific and Statistical Database Management (SSDBM'97)*, IEEE Computer Society, Washington, DC, 1997, pp. 237–248.

11. Z. Lacroix. Biological data integration: Wrapping data and tools. *IEEE Trans. Inf. Technol. Biomed.*, 6(2):123–128, 2002.

12. L. Haas, P. Kodali, J. Rice, P. Schwarz, and W. Swope. Integrating life sciences data—With a little garlic. In *IEEE International Symposium on Bio-Informatics and Biomedical Engineering (BIBE)*, IEEE Press, Washington, DC, 2000.

13. G. Kemp, C. Robertson, and P. Gray. Efficient access to biological databases using CORBA. *CCP11 Newslett.*, 3.1(7), 1990.

14. G. Kemp, N. Angelopoulos, and P. Gray. A schema-based approach to building a bioinformatics database federation. *IEEE International Symposium on Bio-Informatics and Biomedical Engineering (BIBE)*, Washington, DC, 2000.

15. P. Baker, A. Brass, S. Bechhofer, C. Goble, N. Paton, and R. Stevens. TAMBIS: Transparent access to multiple bioinformatics information sources. An overview. *Proc. Sixth Int. Conf. Intell. Syst. Mol. Biol.* 1998.

16. H. Müller and F. Naumann. Data quality in genome databases. In *Proceedings of the Eighth International Conference on Information Quality (IQ'03)*, Cambridge, MA, USA, November 7–9, 2003, pp. 269–284.

17. A. Ailamaki, V. Kantere, and D. Dash. Managing scientific data. *Commun. ACM*, 53(6):68–78, 2010.

18. P. Missier, N. Paton, and P. Li. Workflows for information integration in the life sciences. *Lecture Notes Comput. Sci.*, 6585/2011:215–225, 2011.

19. S. C. Boulakia and U. Leser. Search, adapt, and reuse: The future of scientific workflows. *SIGMOD Rec.*, 40(2):6–16, 2011.

20. Z. G. Ives. Data integration and exchange for scientific collaboration. In *Proceedings of Data Integration in the Life Sciences, 6th International Workshop (DILS'09)*, Manchester, UK, July 20–22, 2009, *Lecture Notes in Computer Science*, Springer, 2009, pp. 1–4.

21. S. Cohen-Boulakia and W.C. Tan. Provenance in scientific databases. In *Encyclopedia of Database Systems*, 2009.

22. M. Gertz. Managing data quality and integrity in federated databases. In *Proceedings of the IFIP TC11 Working Group 11.5, Second Working Conference on Integrity and Internal Control in Information Systems: Bridging Business Requirements and Research Results, Conference,* Warrenton, Virginia, USA, November 19–20, 1998, Kluwer, 1998, pp. 211–230.

23. E. Guérin, G. Marquet, A. Burgun, O. Loréal, L. Berti-Équille, U. Leser and F. Moussouni. Integrating and warehousing liver gene expression data and related biomedical resources in GEDAW. *Proc. Int. Workshop Data Integrat. Life Sci., Lecture Notes in Bioinformatics,* 3615:158–174, 2005.

24. N. W. Paton, S. Khan, A. Hayes, F. Moussouni, A. Brass, K. Eilbeck, C. A. Goble, S. Hubbard, and S. G. Oliver. Conceptual modelling on genomic information. *Bioinformatics J.,* 16(6):548–558, 2000.

25. O. Loréal, B. Turlin, C. Pigeon, A. Moisan, M. Ropert, P. Morice, Y. Gandon, A.M. Jouanolle, M. Vérin, R.C. Hider, K. Yoshida, and P. Brissot. Aceruloplasminemia: New clinical, pathophysiological and therapeutic insights. *J. Hepatol.,* 36(6):851–856, 2002.

26. F. Laine, M. Ropert, C. L. Lan, O. Loreal, E. Bellissant, C. Jard, M. Pouchard, A. Le Treut, and P. Brissot. Serum ceruloplasmin and ferroxidase activity are decreased in HFE C282Y homozygote male iron-overloaded patients. *J. Hepatol.,* 36(1):60–65, 2002.

27. E. Guérin, G. Marquet, J. Chabalier, M.B. Troadec, C. Guguen-Guillouzo, O. Loréal, A. Burgun, and F. Moussouni. Combining biomedical knowledge and transcriptomic data to extract new knowledge on genes. *J. Integr. Bioinformatics,* 3(2), 2006, available online.

28. D. Lee, B.-W. Von, J. Kang, and S. Park. Effective and scalable solutions for mixed and split citation problems in digital libraries. In *Proceedings of IQIS'05, 2nd International Workshop on Information Quality in Information Systems,* ACM, New York, NY, 2005, pp. 69–76.

29. M. Brochhausen, A.D. Spear, C. Cocos, G. Weiler, L. Martín, A. Anguita, H. Stenzhorn, E. Daskalaki, F. Schera, U. Schwarz, S. Sfakianakis, S. Kiefer, M. Dörr, N. Graf and M. Tsiknakis. The ACGT master ontology and its applications: Towards an ontology-driven cancer research and management system. *J. Biomed. Inform.,* 44(1):8–25, 2011.

30. G. Marquet, A. Burgun, F. Moussouni, E. Guérin, F. Le Duff, and O. Loréal. BioMeKe: An ontology-based biomedical knowledge extraction system devoted to transcriptome analysis. *J. Studies Health Technol. Informatics,* 95:80–85, 2003.

31. J. Mercadé, A. Espinosa, J.E. Adsuara, R. Adrados, J. Segura, and T. Maes. Orymold: Ontology based gene expression data integration and analysis tool applied to rice. *BMC Bioinformatics,* 10:158, 2009.

32. O. Bodenreider. The Unified Medical Language System (UMLS): Integrating biomedical terminology. *Nucleic Acids Res.,* 32 (Database issue):D267–270, 2004.

33. B. Smith, et al.. The OBO Foundry: coordinated evolution of ontologies to support biomedical data integration. *Nat. Biotechnol.,* 25:1251–1255, 2007.

34. E.Z. Erson and M.C. Çavuşoğlu. Design of a framework for modeling, integration and simulation of physiological models. In *2010 Annual International Conference of the IEEE Engineering in Medicine and Biology Society (EMBC),* August 31-September 4, 2010, pp. 1485–1489.

35. Z. Lacroix, R. Cartik, P. Mork, R. Rifaieh, M. Wilkinson, J. Freire, and S. Cohen-Boulakia. Biological resource discovery. *Encyclopedia of Database Systems,* Springer, 2009, 220–223.

36. R. Hoehndorf, J. Bacher, M. Backhaus, S.E. Gregorio, Jr., F. Loebe, K. Prüfer, A. Uciteli, J. Visagie, H. Herre, and J. Kelso. BOWiki: An ontology-based wiki for annotation of data and integration of knowledge in biology. *BMC Bioinformatics,* May 6(10 Suppl 5):S5, 2009.

CHAPTER 3

CLEANSING OF MASS SPECTROMETRY DATA FOR PROTEIN IDENTIFICATION AND QUANTIFICATION

PENGHAO WANG[1] and ALBERT Y. ZOMAYA[2]
[1]School of Mathematics and Statistics, University of Sydney, Sydney, Australia
[2]School of Information Technologies, University of Sydney, Sydney, Australia

3.1 INTRODUCTION

With the sequencings of genomes of most of organisms, there has been increasing interest in the analysis and understanding of proteins. Proteins are essential parts of organisms and participate in virtually every process within cells. Large-scale protein analysis plays a crucial role in biological and medical sciences. Most of the current protein research is not limited to understanding the structures and functions of specific proteins but targets studies of thousands of proteins, even the entire proteome [1], including the modifications made to a particular set of proteins produced by an organism [2]. Currently, proteomics research utilizes mass spectrometry as a technology platform to identify protein compositions and quantify protein expressions within a sample. Mass spectrometry (MS) technology provides a high-throughput and high-precision means to identify thousands of proteins simultaneously. Using tandem MS-based technologies (MS/MS), even higher sensitivity and specificity can be achieved, leading to more accurate protein identification [3]. Coupled with recent advances in isotope labeling and tagging methodologies [4], tandem MS provides a powerful means to study the relative expression level of proteins at the proteomics level. In MS-based proteomics studies, the protein mixture is often purified and digested by enzymes such as trypsin. The sample is then injected to one- or two-dimensional liquid chromatography (LC) and captured by a mass spectrometer by the mass-to-charge ratio (m/z) of the generated peptide and peptide fragment ions. Figure 3.1 presents a snapshot of the procedure of MS-based proteomics experiments. MS experiments produce huge amounts of data, and it is typical that one experiment generates more than 40 billion raw spectra. However, it is a very challenging task to infer the proteins from the observed spectra [5].

Protein identification is commonly accomplished by comparing the observed spectra with theoretical spectra generated in silico from a given protein database [6–9], or with an annotated spectral library [10, 11]. When the database-based searching is performed, due

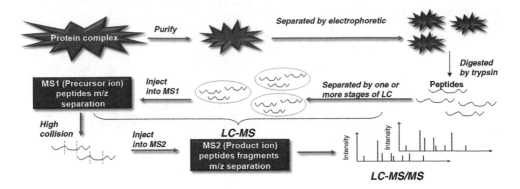

FIGURE 3.1 Brief overview of experimental procedure of MS proteomics.

to the presence of various noise, machine artifacts, isotopic interences, random variation of the peptide fragmentation, the deficiencies of the search algorithm and scoring metrics, the incompleteness of the protein database, and the ambiguity of peptide to protein assignment [12], protein identification suffers high false discovery rates (FDRs) and only a fraction of the highest scored peptide-to-spectrum matches are typically correct and only about 50% of the proteins can be identified [13–16]. As a result, how to improve the quality of protein identification plays a critical role in MS-based proteomics research.

There are two different approaches to improve the results of protein identification. The first approach is to preprocess the MS raw spectra data prior to the protein identification process. The second approach is to filter the incorrect protein identification after the database searching–based protein identification is completed. Figure 3.2 presents an example on the two approaches to improve the protein identification. In this chapter, we will examine the effectiveness of existing methods of the aforementioned two approaches, demonstrate

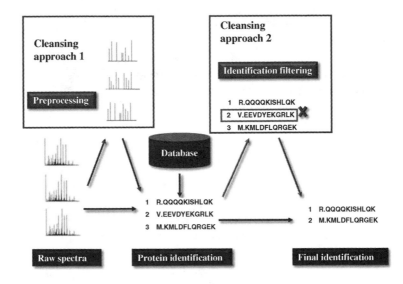

FIGURE 3.2 Two approaches to cleanse MS data for protein identification.

the limitations, and finally present our new methods in both categories: a new preprocessing approach and a new identification filtering approach for improving the protein identification.

3.2 PREPROCESSING APPROACH FOR IMPROVING PROTEIN IDENTIFICATION

3.2.1 Existing Approaches

The first approach, spectra preprocessing, involves accurately identifying and locating peak-shaped signals within raw precursor MS and tandem MS spectra while removing various noise and spurious signals. These peak-shaped signals theoretically correspond to the presence of specific peptide or peptide fragment ions produced by fragmenting and ionizing peptides of the sample. As mass spectra are usually tempered with a number of interferences, including electrical and chemical noise, machine artifacts, sample contamination, and many others, accurately cleansing the spectra without compromising real signals is very difficult. To improve the accuracy of the downstream protein identification process, spectra preprocessing must address several problems at the same time: denoising, baseline removal, peak detection, and peak intensity estimation. Based on different utilized MS ionization technologies, there are a number of possibilities of charge states for peptides, which vary from spectrum to spectrum. When performing protein identification, the traditional approach is to search the spectrum multiple times for each possible charge state. Such an approach increases the identification computation severalfold and is prone to produce incorrect identification [17]. Therefore, preprocessing the spectra before the protein identification also involves estimating the correct peptide charge state.

Whether spectra are efficiently and accurately preprocessed can have great impact over the downstream protein identification and quantification analyses [18, 19]. All existing protein identification methods depend on the quality of the peak information used as input to their algorithms. There are a number of preprocessing methods, and they may be roughly classified into three categories [20]: (1) intensity-based approach, (2) empirical modeling–based approach, and (3) wavelet-based approach.

The intensity-based approach is by far the one used most. The intensity approach uses a very simple algorithm: It applies certain hard or soft thresholds to filter weak signals, leaving the most intensive peaks. Methods that utilize such an approach include mzWiff [21] provided by the Trans-Proteomic Pipeline (TPP), wiff2dta [22], and InSpecT [23]. A number of protein identification engines, for example, OMSSA [9] and X!Tandem [8], apply a similar intensity-based thresholding method before initiating the protein identification algorithm. Intensity-based methods can be improved by using predefined mass-to-charge ratio (m/z) intervals as introduced in MaxQuant [24]. These are the most commonly used methods and their main advantages are simplicity and computational speed. However, it is very common that low-abundance signals dominate the MS spectra and some real peptide fragment signals are not much stronger than specific noise. Thus, the limitation of these intensity-based methods is that they often fail to detect real peptide fragment signals and lead to a significant decrease in the number of correct protein identifications. On the other hand, the intensity-based approach cannot efficiently remove noise from the spectra, and this may significantly increase the false discovery rates in protein identification. In order to reduce the FDR, some methods apply certain noise filters before applying the intensity-based peak identification. For example, MEND [25] uses a matched filter as the starting point (it also applies other techniques), PROcess [26] uses a moving-average filter, mzMine [27] uses a Savitzky-Golay filter, and LIMPIC [28] uses a Kaiser window filter. Compared with simple intensity-based methods, these methods can better control the FDR in protein identification. Unfortunately, these noise filters may cause distortion of the spectra and it is often hard to tell whether all the noise has been successfully filtered or whether a significant proportion remains in the spectra [20].

The empirical modeling–based preprocessing approach tries to distinguish the real peptide and peptide fragment signals from noise using additional information other than signal intensity. There are a number of empirical modeling–based methods that have been developed, for example, the methods described by Gras et al. [29], Genztel et al. [30], Qu et al. [31], Randolph and Yasui [32], and Lange et al. [33]. Because peptide and peptide fragment signals have characteristic shapes and patterns that depend on the utilized MS instruments, using an empirical peak-shaped model provides a powerful means to identify real signals from white and colored noise. It is very desirable that these methods present solid peak models for preprocessing the spectra. However, most of the peak models use empirical peak width as the matching criterion to reduce false discovery rate in protein identification. In real-life applications, such a static approach may become impractical because usually peaks have complex patterns, and various interferences such as isotope overlaps can make the peak width estimation difficult. Therefore, the peak shape and width usually cannot be directly estimated and depend on a number of factors. In addition, the width and height of real peaks can vary significantly across different spectra and even within the same spectrum [20]. For instance, within a single spectrum peaks in the high-m/z regions are usually slightly wider and much lower in amplitude compared to ones in the low-m/z regions. Therefore, empirical and static peak models tend to produce highly variable and unreliable results in real applications [34]. There have been some efforts incorporating more information into the empirical peak models, for example, the methods described by Gras et al. [29]. Nevertheless, these methods find it very difficult in preprocessing complex fragmentation and peak patterns of tandem MS spectra to improve the protein identification.

Wavelet-based spectra preprocessing methods may be divided into two categories: discrete-wavelet (DWT) methods and continuous-wavelet (CWT) methods. Due to the frequency low-pass nature and the convenient reverse construction of discrete and diagonal wavelets, DWT methods are generally used directly as noise filters (Figure 3.3 presents an example of the DWT process). Then an intensity-based algorithm is followed after the noise is filtered by DWT. For example, the Cromwell method [35] applies such an approach: The peaks arc identified after filtering the noise by Daubechies family wavelets. The CWT approach is very different from its DWT counterpart. The CWT wavelet can be formulated as

$$C(a, b) = \int_R s(t)\psi_{a,b}(t), \quad \psi_{a,b} = \frac{1}{\sqrt{a}}\psi\left(\frac{t-b}{a}\right) \qquad a \in R^+ - \{0\} \quad b \in R \qquad (3.1)$$

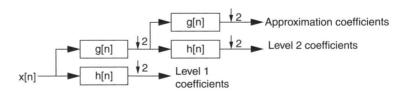

FIGURE 3.3   Process of computing DWT. Here "↓ 2" means down sampling by 2, $h[n]$ is a high-pass filter, and $g[n]$ is a low-pass filter.

where $s(t)$ is the signal, a is the scaling factor, b is the translation factor, $\psi a, b(t)$ is the scaled and translated mother wavelet, and C is the wavelet coefficient. CWT methods have several advantages compared with DWT methods. The CWT is not limited as a noise filter and can be utilized for several procedures of spectra preprocessing. One major advantage is that with CWT it is possible to identify peptide and peptide fragment signals without explicitly removing disturbing artifacts. Under the continuous-wavelet framework, the baseline, noise, and real signals can be efficiently separated by their different frequency ranges. A well-designed CWT method, which respects the specific characteristics of peptide signals, renders additional noise filters unnecessary, as noise filtering is spontaneously achieved by wavelets. Therefore, the procedure for a traditional five-step spectra preprocessing procedure can be simplified into three steps with CWT methods, where noise removal, baseline removal, and peak identification are achieved simultaneously. The CWT generates a redundant and information-rich two-dimensional (2D) wavelet coefficient space, and the peak shape and characteristics are easier to identify within this 2D coefficient space. This provides many opportunities in modeling the peptide and peptide fragment signals. Du et al. [34] first described a method (MassSpecWavelet) which directly utilizes the CWT coefficient matrix generated from the spectrum to identify peaks. By using an empirical range of scaled wavelets, the method can detect peaks with a lower false-positive rate and better signal-to-noise ratio (SNR). The disadvantages of this method are the arbitrary selection of a large range of wavelet scales and the inability to select the most relevant ones. Such a static model may perform well in a specific situation; however, it may become difficult when wavelets are incorrectly selected and this may significantly increase false positives. Thus it is desirable to have a good algorithm to correctly determine the best matching wavelets as the peak model.

3.2.2 New Dynamic Wavelet-Based Spectra Preprocessing Method

We have developed a new dynamic continuous wavelet-based spectra preprocessing method for improving the protein identification to address the shortcomings found in existing preprocessing methods. A detailed description of this method can be found in [20]. Compared with existing spectra preprocessing methods, the new method has several advantages. First, it supports a wide array of instruments and it dynamically adjusts the peak model to achieve better performance. The new method detects the real peptide and peptide fragment signals in the 2D continuous-wavelet coefficient domain, and this enables the new method to utilise additional information regarding peak shape more efficiently. Second, it is one of the few methods that incorporates an efficient algorithm to estimate the peptide charge. The incorporated charge state estimation algorithm applies an isotope wavelet model by extending the work described previously [36]. By this new algorithm, the peptide charge state can be accurately estimated even for the spectra produced by the low-precision MS instruments, where existing charge state estimation methods fail. Built within the wavelet framework, the new charge state estimation algorithm is seamlessly integrated with the preprocessing method. Third, our new dynamic spectra preprocessing method supports standard formats in the community and is designed as an integrated component of a complete data analysis work flow. This greatly facilitates large-scale protein analyses.

Our new method first transforms the spectra into continuous-wavelet coefficients, and the coefficients reflect the pattern matching between the signal s and the mother wavelet $\psi a, b(t)$ as given in Equation (3.1). The CWT technique provides a convenient and flexible analytical advantage because it provides freedom in the choice of mother wavelets and the parameters of the mother wavelets to be transformed. By using different wavelets and parameters, the daughter wavelet $\psi a, b(t)$ can therefore provide a dynamic peak model without the need for extra nonlinear curve fitting. To accurately model the real peptide and peptide fragment peaks, the daughter wavelets should locally resemble the real signal. Gaussian family wavelets have been proven to be very effective in modeling MS peak signals [33] since the peaks in tandem MS spectra are not strongly asymmetric. Our new method uses the Marr wavelet, which is proportional to the second derivative of the Gaussian wavelet function. The Marr wavelet can be formulated as

$$\psi(t) = \frac{1}{\sqrt{2\pi}a^3}\left(1 - \frac{t^2}{a^2}\right)\exp\left(\frac{-t^2}{2a^2}\right) \tag{3.2}$$

Since the resolution of a mass spectrometer only depends on the instrument, our method applies a linear model to the relationship between peak width and m/z. Depending on the peak width and the spectrum m/z region, the underlying peak model is dynamically adjusted in a data-driven fashion.

In the wavelet coefficient domain, a local maximum will correspond to the position of a peak centroid and the coefficient becomes larger when the daughter wavelet more closely resembles the peak. Linking the local maxima of wavelet coefficients across the applied daughter wavelets, the peaks can be accurately identified. We developed a new model to estimate the distribution of the amplitude of the coefficient maxima across different wavelet parameters; therefore, the best matched daughter wavelets will be assigned more weight in the processing of identifying peaks. Details of this process can be found in [20].

The last procedure of our new spectra preprocessing method is peptide charge state estimation. Charge state estimation is achieved by estimating the isotope peak intervals at the precursor MS spectra. Due to the precision and complicated nature of the spectra, direct estimation is difficult. Therefore, we adopted an isotope wavelet to model the isotope signal distributions, which can be formulated as

$$\psi(t, \lambda, \mu) = \theta(t)\frac{\sin(2\pi\mu t/m_n)\,\exp(-\lambda)\lambda^{\mu t}}{\Gamma(\mu t + 1)} \tag{3.3}$$

where θ denotes the Heaviside function and m_n is the mass of a neutron and thus the characteristic distance between two subsequent single-charged isotopic peaks; μ represents the charge state and therefore stretches or squeezes the pattern accordingly; and $\lambda = \lambda(m)$ is a low-rank polynomial variable describing the mean mass signal. Equation (3.3) may be interpreted as an oscillating sine wave with frequency adapted to the isotopic pattern and the amplitude following a continuous analog of a Poisson distribution. Note that the wavelet as denoted in Equation (3.3) is different from the traditional definition of a wavelet because it averages to zero. Therefore, we subtract the resulting mean of the isotope wavelet to fulfil the requirement. After the isotope wavelet transform, the monotopic peak centroids will be detected, and thus the peptide charge state can be estimated based on the interval between the monotopic peak centroids.

3.3   IDENTIFICATION FILTERING APPROACH FOR IMPROVING PROTEIN IDENTIFICATION

3.3.1   Existing Approaches

The second approach to improve protein identification is through filtering incorrect identification after the database search protein identification process is completed. Such an approach is based on the estimation of false discovery rates in the obtained protein identification from a utilized identification engine. There arc a number of methods for filtering identifications, and they may be broadly classified into two categories [3]: the Bayesian approach and the target–decoy approach. The Bayesian approach tries to estimate the probability of each reported protein identification being correct based on the identification score distribution of a given protein identification algorithm. Some of the Bayesian methods are based on empirical Bayesian estimation, for example, the method proposed by Keller et al. [37], and other methods are based on nonparametric Bayesian estimation, for example, the method introduced by Zhang et al. [38]. The Bayesian methods usually use a number of learning features obtained from the list of protein identification reported by an identification engine and combine a linear discriminant analysis (LDA) or an expectation–maximization (EM) model to estimate the probability that each identification is correct. These methods usually assume that the discriminate scores of the protein identification follow a mixture of a Gaussian distribution and a gamma distribution representing incorrect and correct identifications, respectively. By fitting the mixture model using the EM algorithm, it produces a posterior probability for an identification being correct. Recently there have been efforts in extending the Bayesian approach to incorporate more flexible models (e.g., variable-component-mixture model) [39] and other database search identification engines [40].

For this study, we focus on the second identification filtering approach, the target–decoy approach. This approach involves generating a "decoy" database from the target protein database and uses it as the "null incorrect distribution" for estimating the correctness of protein identification [41]. Since any identification from the decoy database is definitely incorrect, the false discovery rates in the protein identification can thus be estimated by using the total number of identifications and the number of incorrect identifications from the decoy database. There are also methods that attempt to integrate the above two categories, for example, the semisupervised method proposed by Choi and Nesvizhskii [42]. The decoy database is usually obtained by reversing the protein sequences in a protein database (the target database) as initially introduced by Moore et al. [39] and further extended by Elias and Gygi [41]. The target–decoy approach is based on two assumptions. First, no or very few peptide sequences are in common between the target and thc decoy database. Second, the likelihood of obtaining an incorrect identification from the target database is equal to the likelihood of obtaining an incorrect identification from the decoy database. The first assumption can be easily validated and checked; however, the second assumption is usually quite problematic and has become an issue for the target–decoy filtering approach.

How to generate a decoy database is crucial for the target–decoy approach. The widely used approach, generating a decoy database by reversing the protein sequences in the target database, has been demonstrated to produce systematic bias [42, 43]. The major reason is due to the sequence properties, such as the sequence similarity inherent in the protein database. A typical example is given in Figure 3.4. As demonstrated, there are a number of proteins

---

Q05639 FIKNMITGTSQADCAVLIVAAGVGEFEAGISKNGQTREHALLAYTLGVKQ ... Compared protein
P68104 FIKNMITGTSQADCAVLIVAAGVGEFEAGISKNGQTREHALLAYTLGVKQ ... Identities=427/461(92%)
Q5VTE0 FIKNMITGTSQADCAVLIVAAGVGEFEAGISKNGQTREHALLAYTLGVKQ ... Identities=425/461(92%)
Q9Y450 FIPNMITGAAQADVAVLVVDASRGEFEAGFETGGQTREHGLLVRSLGVTQ ... Identities=173/440(39%)
P15170 FVPNMIGGASQADLAVLVISARKGEFETGFEKGGQTREHAMLAKTAGVKH ... Identities=165/443(37%)

FIGURE 3.4 Protein Q05649 and its sequence. Note that several proteins share high similarity with it in the database.

that share very high sequence similarity with protein Q05639, and some of the proteins have similarity over 90%. This intrinsic characteristic in the protein database significantly influences the likelihood of obtaining incorrect protein identification. However, the reversed sequence of Q05639 protein, as the typical decoy database, has no highly similar proteins. As a result, it is much more likely to obtain incorrect identification of Q05639 from the similar proteins in the target database than from the corresponding reversed decoy database. We refer to this situation as *unequal matching bias*. This problem in the target–decoy strategy has been reported [44], even if the ubiquity and the magnitude of this effect have not been fully evaluated.

Several methods have been proposed to address this problem. Some methods involve a more sophisticated FDR estimation measurement which explicitly takes various biases into account. For example, Kall et al. [45] described a q-value statistic for multiple testing correction in the target–decoy filtering approach. Kim et al. [46] proposed a generating function to independently assess the reliability of each identified protein and integrated it to the target–decoy approach [47]. However, instead of addressing the prerequisite unequal matching bias of the target–decoy approach, these methods apply an ad hoc bias correction approach. Therefore, it is very desirable to have efficient methods to alleviate the bias of the target–decoy filtering approach which can better represent the distribution of protein identification.

3.3.2 New Target-Decoy Approach for Improving Protein Identification

We have developed a novel substitution-based target–decoy method for improving protein identification. For each protein in the target database, we generate the corresponding decoy protein by applying amino acid substitution at each of the amino acid sites. This involves a predefined substitution probability p and a substitution matrix M. For each amino acid of a protein in the target database, the substitution probability p is defined as the likelihood of substitution occurring at this amino acid site. The actual substitution is then defined by the substitution matrix, such as BLOSUM [48]. The substitution matrix M is the normalized BLOSUM62 matrix, where the substitution values of each amino acid to the other 20 amino acids in BLOSUM62 are normalized so they add up to unity. For a given amino acid site in a protein, when a substitution process occurs, a randomized procedure is applied where an amino acid with a higher substitution score will have a better chance to be selected to replace the current amino acid site. Our method is described by pseudocode in Algorithm 3.1.

ALGORITHM 3.1 Substitution-Based Target–Decoy Algorithm

```
 1: Input: target base T, probability p, substitution matrix M
 2: Output: decoy base D
 3: for each protein sequence in T do
 4:    use s to record current sequence;
 5:    for each amino acid in s do
 6:       if p fulfilled then
 7:          substitute current amino acid based on M;
 8:       end if
 9:       add the substituted sequence s′ to D;
10:    end for
11: end for
12: return D;
```

While the chance of substitution of each site is determined by p, the individual replacement of an amino acid site is independently determined by the substitution matrix if the substitution happens. This allows different types of substitution matrices to be applied.

The substitution probability p plays a key role in the decoy database construction. The larger the value of p, the more diverse the decoy sequences are compared to the corresponding original target sequences. In order to obtain the optimal value of p, we introduce the criterion given in Equation (3.4). The function sums the square of the normalized ratios of the number of false positive identifications (FPIs) between the target database and the decoy database under different thresholds of a search algorithm:

$$\text{FDR}(p) = \sum_c \sqrt{\left(1 - \frac{\max(F_t^c, F_d^c(p))}{\min(F_t^c, F_d^c(p))}\right)^2} \tag{3.4}$$

where $\max(x)$ and $\min(x)$ give the maximum and minimum values of the two inputs, respectively; F_t^c represents the number of incorrect identifications in the target database under the threshold c; and $F_d^c(p)$ represents the number of incorrect identification in the decoy database under the same threshold and the substitution probability p.

The substitution probability p should present the minimum difference of the number of incorrect identifications to the target database. To evaluate the effect of p and obtain the optimal value, we perform extensive experiments. The experimental procedure is summarized below and an overview is given in Figure 3.5:

Step 1: Create a substitution decoy database from the target database with a specified value of p.

Step 2: Combine the control protein sequences with the decoy database.

Step 3: Apply a separate search against the target database and decoy database and calculate the number of incorrect identifications from these two databases.

Step 4: Minimize the number of incorrect identifications from these two databases by adjusting the value of p and repeating the above steps.

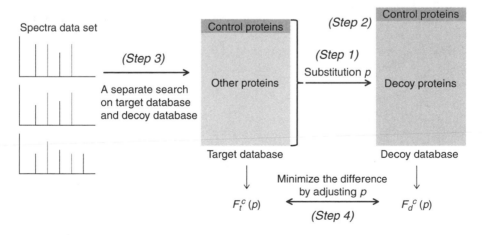

FIGURE 3.5 Schematic representation of work flow for constructing substitution-based decoy database.

3.4 EVALUATION RESULTS

3.4.1 Evaluation of New Proprocessing Method

Our new spectra preprocessing method has been extensively evaluated on several publicly available MS data sets, and the method has been shown to outperform other methods [20]. Here we present more evaluation results on in-house data sets generated at the Sydney University Proteome Research Unit.

3.4.1.1 Evaluation Data Set   The data sets consist of four human samples which were mixed and diluted at the same concentration. The samples were digested using trypsin overnight at room temperature. The samples were separated by two stages of liquid chromatography (LC) and injected into the QSTAR^{TM} time-of-flight mass spectrometer for analysis. The mass spectrometer was configured to scan tandem MS spectra for the most intensive precursor ions.

3.4.1.2 Evaluation Strategy   We compared our method with two widely used algorithms. The first is the intensity-based approach mzWiff offered by the Trans-Proteomic-Pipeline (TPP). This algorithm was chosen because, to our knowledge, it is the most used tandem MS preprocessing algorithm. The second one is the commercial software Analyst^{TM} provided by ABI for the QSTAR mass spectrometer. Proprietary software normally involves sophisticated algorithm design optimized for the supporting instrument. Thus it should produce very reliable results. After spectra preprocessing, X!Tandem [8] is used to perform protein identification. The default search parameters are used and searches are conducted against the SWISS-PROT human database. The performance of the compared preprocessing algorithms is evaluated by comparing the peptide and protein identification results. The performance is evaluated by three key criteria: (1) the number of protein identifications, (2) the confidence in the protein identification, and (3) the signal-to-noise ratio of the spectra.

Figure 3.6 presents the evaluation results on the number of protein identifications, and it clearly demonstrates that our new method performs significantly better compared to the other methods. Using our in-house MS data set, our method identifies approximately 30% more unique proteins for a given false-positive rate compared to the proprietary software and the commonly used intensity-based approach. This indicates that the spectra processed by our method are of much higher quality, greatly facilitating the successful identification of the proteins from the tandem MS spectra. It is interesting to see that the commercial software performs only slightly better than the intensity-based approach mzWiff. This is especially the case on samples 2 and 3. This may be because, when processed by the intensity-based approach, the spectra are much bigger than the ones generated by the commercial software, where many correct signals were removed by the commercial software.

When evaluating the preprocessing methods by the criterion of the protein identification confidence, we first reversed the identification score and then compared the mean scores for the identified proteins. Figure 3.7 presents our evaluation results. The results demonstrate that our new preprocessing method is able to significantly increase the confidence for protein identification, and up to 20% improvement can be achieved compared with the intensity-based approach. The commercial software seems to perform better with this criterion than it does in terms of how many protein identifications can be obtained. This indicates that the

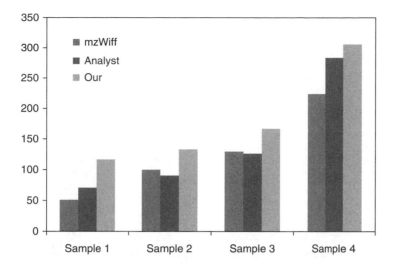

FIGURE 3.6 Evaluation results on number of correct protein identifications after spectra were preprocessed using compared preprocessing methods at same FDR.

commercial software might be "too aggressive" in removing spurious peaks and noise; on the other hand, the intensity-based approach is not very effective in removing the noise and artifacts in the spectra.

The SNR of preprocessed spectra can be estimated by comparing the file size of the peak lists giving rise to similar numbers of identified proteins. mzWiff can reduce the information in the raw spectrum significantly. As Figure 3.8 demonstrates, this can be reduced by up to

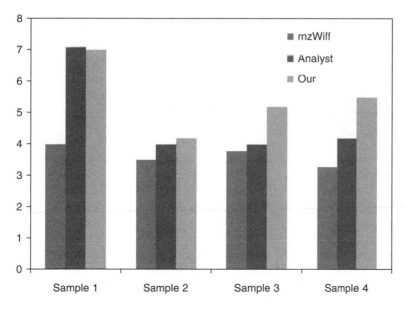

FIGURE 3.7 Evaluation results of confidence of protein identification after spectra were preprocessed using compared preprocessing methods at same FDR. The y axis presents the reversed scores.

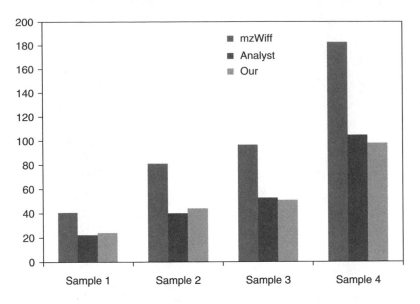

FIGURE 3.8 Evaluation results of SNR of preprocessed spectra.

another 40% by the commercial software and our wavelet-based method. This significant reduction of file size is achieved without compromising the real peptide and peptide fragment signals. This indicates that the proprietary algorithm and the wavelet method achieve much better SNR compared to the intensity-based mzWiff. It seems that our new wavelet method performs similarly to the commercial software when compared by the obtained file sizes. However, the Analyst software reduces the number and the confidence of the identified proteins. This demonstrates that the wavelet achieves better SNR than the commercial software, and this may greatly improve the reliability of the downstream analysis. A better SNR has two benefits. First, because MS experiments generate huge volumes of spectra data, peak lists with higher SNRs require less storage space and make spectra transfer more convenient. Second, higher SNRs and smaller file sizes result in a significant increase in the computational speed of downstream analysis.

3.4.2 Evaluation of New Identification Filtering Method

3.4.2.1 Evaluation Data Sets To evaluate the performance of our new substitution-based target–decoy protein identification filtering method, we used two publicly available data sets. (1) The first data set is generated by the Seattle Proteome Centre (SPC) and is thus termed "Seattle" spectra data set. The Seattle spectra data set is a protein mixture analyzed by the ABI 4700 spectrometer. The data set contains 18 control proteins (proteins that are known beforehand) derived from multiple organisms (bovine, *Escherichia coli*, *Bacillus licheniformis*, rabbit, horse, and chicken) with 15 possible contaminants; details provided in [49]. (2) The second is the Aurum data set [43]. Aurum is a public, open library of MS and MS/MS spectra generated on an ABI 4700 matrix-assisted laser desorption/ionization (MALDI) tandem time of flight (TOF/TOF) from known purified and trypsin-digested protein samples. The acquisition procedure utilizes a work flow used for gel-purified proteins. To our knowledge, Aurum is one of few large, publicly available MS and MS/MS reference

TABLE 3.1   **Summary of Two Reference Data Sets**

Data Set	Control Proteins	Contaminations	Species
Seattle	18	15	Multiple species
Aurum	246	100	*Homo sapiens*

data sets where the raw spectra are provided and the identity of the proteins is known in advance of the analysis. A summary of these two benchmark data sets is given in Table 3.1. The corresponding target database for searching the Seattle data set is the SWISS-PROT sequence library while the corresponding target database for searching the Aurum data set is the human-specific protein sequences extracted from the SWISS-PROT sequence library.

3.4.2.2 Evaluation Strategy   We use X!Tandem as the search algorithm for our evaluation. The reported expectation values (E values) of the search algorithm are used as thresholds to calculate the number of incorrect identifications, the number of true identifications, and the corresponding FDRs. We examine the E-value thresholds ranging from 0.001 to 0.1 with an interval of 0.001 to assess the performance of each decoy database. Note that we only consider peptides that are uniquely assigned to a single protein (unique peptide). Therefore, we avoid the peptide-sharing problem [12], and every incorrect peptide identification is exclusively an incorrect identification at the protein level. The identification results are averaged across different thresholds. For FDR estimation comparison, we concatenated the target and the decoy database and used the combined database to perform identification. The estimated FDR using different decoy databases can be compared with the gold standard FDR (GS-FDR) in the target database. The GS-FDR in this case is calculated by counting the incorrect identification and the correct identification from the target database alone using the reference data set with control protein compositions. The closer the estimated FDR to the GS-FDR, the better the method is. We also evaluate whether the decoy databases satisfy the assumption that incorrect identifications from the target database and the decoy database are equally likely to be selected. This is done by removing the control protein sequences in the target database and reapplying the concatenated search. Because the amino acid replacement is based on a random substitution procedure, with the same value of p the generated decoy database is different every time. Therefore, we create five replicates of decoy databases for the Seattle and Aurum data sets, respectively.

   The performance of target–decoy protein identification filtering methods depends on the decoy database. If the decoy database is able to more accurately model the incorrect protein identifications obtained by an identification engine, it will produce more accurate estimation of the FDR in protein identifications, thus leading to better protein identification results. Therefore, the validity and the usefulness of a decoy database can be verified by comparing the estimated FDR with the GS-FDR. Figure 3.9 shows the GS-FDRs of the target database and the estimated FDRs (denoted as E-FDR). The reverse decoy database and the substitution decoy database of $p = 0.1$ are used under the searching threshold from 0.001 to 0.1 with an interval of 0.001. We present results from five independent generations of the substitution decoy databases for the Aurum and Seattle data sets that account for the random substitution procedure. It is clear that substitution-based decoy databases provide a much better FDR estimation, while the reverse decoy databases highly underestimate the GS-FDRs.

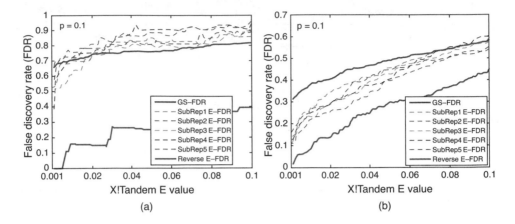

FIGURE 3.9 Comparison of estimated FDRs with GS-FDRs. For the estimated FDRs, the spectra from (a) Seattle data set and (b) Aurum data set are searched against the concatenated databases of target and different decoy databases, respectively. For the GS-FDRs, the spectra from these two data sets are searched against the corresponding target databases alone.

When removing the known protein sequences of the reference data sets from the target database, any match from the target database is a wrong identification. The spectra are searched against the concatenated database of the target database with the reverse decoy database, substitution decoy database, and decoy database created using PTTRNFNDR [50], respectively. In this way, the overall equal likelihood of obtaining incorrect identification can be evaluated by counting the number of identifications from the target database and the decoy databases. Figure 3.10 gives the results using the Seattle and Aurum data sets under the threshold ranging from 0.001 to 0.1 with an interval of 0.001. The results indicate that the number of incorrect identifications obtained from the reverse decoy databases greatly deviates from those obtained from the target databases. The decoy databases created by PTTRNFNDR only give marginal improvement because sequence similarity cannot be efficiently modeled and captured by PTTRNFNDR. In contrast, the substitution decoy databases show much closer number of incorrect identifications to the target databases, thus, largely retaining the equal-likelihood assumption.

3.5 CONCLUSION

Due to numerous factors, protein identification from mass spectrometry data is a very challenging and error-prone process. Even if there have been several available protein identification methods, existing protein identification methods face two serious problems. The first problem is low protein identification coverage: It is typical that only 50% of the proteins can be successfully identified using existing protein identification methods. The second problem is the high false discovery rates in protein identification. Usually a fraction of the reported protein identifications are correct and even the top-ranking identifications by existing protein identification methods may be incorrect. The problem is even worse since very small overlap can be found among multiple protein identification engines. Given the crucial role of protein identification in the proteomics research, it is imperative to have

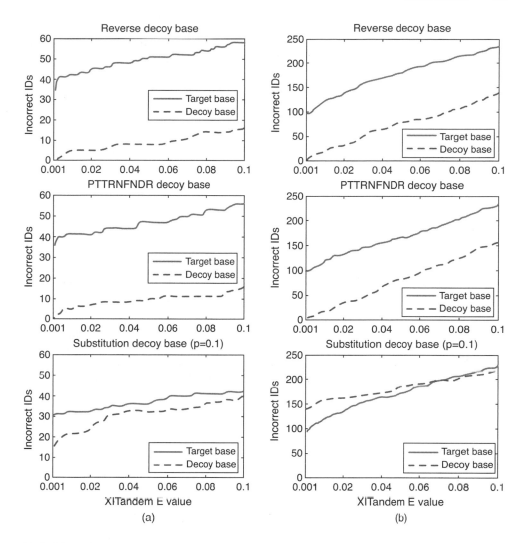

FIGURE 3.10 Number of incorrect identifications from each decoy database and target database with known protein sequences removed. The spectra from (a) Seattle data set and (b) Aurum data set are searched against the concatenated databases of target and different decoy databases, respectively.

efficient methods to improve the protein identification results. In this chapter, we proposed that there are two possible approaches to improve the protein identification results. The first approach is to preprocess the MS spectra before the spectra are given to search engines for protein identification; the second approach is to filter the incorrect protein identifications after the database search identification process is completed. We have described two new methods in each category.

As demonstrated by our new spectra preprocessing method, the preprocessing approach has a great impact on protein identification. Based on our evaluation on public benchmark data sets and in-house data sets, our new preprocessing method can increase protein identification coverage by a maximum of 30% compared with the traditional intensity-based approach. This demonstrates the necessity and significance of preprocessing MS spectra before performing protein identification. Unfortunately, spectra preprocessing has been largely overlooked, and it is quite common that preprocessing is entirely missing from the protein analysis work flow. Our study indicates that even applying a simplistic hard threshold of intensity to preprocess the spectra will make a big difference in the downstream analyses and may significantly increase the number of proteins that can be correctly identified. The performance of our new wavelet-based method also demonstrates the advantage of wavelet analysis for preprocessing MS spectra. Since the real peptide and peptide fragment signals can be effectively separated from various interferences in the wavelet coefficient domain, the wavelet provides a powerful way to identify peaks. In addition, the continuous wavelet analysis is able to further expand the MS spectra into 2D spaces, therefore greatly facilitating the peak modeling.

In this study, we demonstrated that the mostly used target–decoy protein identification filtering approach deviates from one of its two theoretical assumptions and tends to produce serious bias. We have demonstrated this contributes largely to the similarity present in the protein sequence database. With the traditional approach, more than 50% of the incorrect protein identifications cannot be filtered and this seriously undermines the analysis and may push one to make incorrect biological hypotheses. Our new substitution-based target–decoy protein identification filtering method can greatly alleviate this problem. The evaluation study has shown that our method can be applied to a wide range of MS instruments and increases the accuracy in identification filtering by around 20%.

Our study demonstrates that spectra preprocessing and identification filtering are very effective approaches to improve protein identification. These two approaches can significantly increase protein identification coverage and protein identification accuracy. We strongly recommend that these approaches be performed in any MS proteomics analysis.

REFERENCES

1. M. Wilkins et al. From proteins to proteomes: Large scale protein identification by two-dimensional electrophoresis and amino acid analysis. *Nat. Biotechnol.*, 14(1):61–65, 1996.

2. A. Belle et al. Quantification of protein half-lives in the budding yeast proteome, *PNAS*, 103(35):13004–13009, 2006.

3. A. I. Nesvizhskii et al. Analysis and validation of proteomic data generated by tandem mass spectrometry. *Nat. Methods*, 4(10):787–797, 2007.

4. S. E. Ong and M. Mann. Mass spectrometry–based proteomics turns quantitative. *Nat. Chem. Biol.*, 1(5):252–262, 2005.

5. J. Colinge and K. Bennett. Introduction to computational proteomics. *PLoS Computat. Biol.*, 3(7):e114, 2007.

6. J. K. Eng et al. An approach to correlate tandem mass spectral data of peptides with amino acid sequences in a protein database. *J. Am. Soc. Mass Spectrom.*, 5(11):976–989, 1994.

7. D. N. Perkins et al. Probability-based protein identification by searching sequence databases using mass spectrometry data. *Electrophoresis*, 20(18):3551–3567, 1999.

8. R. Craig and R. C. Beavis. TANDEM: Matching proteins with tandem mass spectra. *Bioinformatics*, 20(9):1466–1467, 2004.

9. L. Y. Geer et al. Open mass spectrometry search algorithm. *J. Prot. Res.*, 3(5):958–964, 2004.

10. R. Craig et al. Using annotated peptide mass spectrum libraries for protein identification. *J. Prot. Res.*, 5(8):1843–1849, 2006.

11. H. Lam et al. Development and validation of a spectral library searching method for peptide identification from MS/MS. *Proteomics*, 7(5):655–667, 2007.

12. A. I. Nesvizhskii and R. Aebersold. Interpretation of shotgun proteomic data: The protein inference problem. *Mol. Cell. Prot.*, 4(10):1419–1440, 2005.

13. D. C. Comrad et al. Evaluation of algorithms for protein identification from sequence databases using mass spectrometry data. *Proteomics*, 4(3):619–628, 2004.

14. L. McHugh and J. W. Arthur. Computational methods for protein identification from mass spectrometry data. *PLoS Comput. Biol.*, 4(2):e12, 2008.

15. J. Samuelsson et al. Modular, scriptable and automated analysis tools for high-throughput peptide mass fingerprinting. *Bioinformatics*, 20(18):3628–3635, 2004.

16. J. W. H. Wong et al. msmsEval: Tandem mass spectral quality assignment for high-throughput proteomics. *BMC Bioinformatics*, 8(1):51, 2007.

17. D. L. Tabb et al. Determination of peptide and protein ion charge states by Fourier transformation of isotope-resolved mass spectra. *J. Am. Soc. Mass Spectrom.*, 17(7):903–915, 2006.

18. S. E. Ong et al. Mass spectrometric–based approaches in quantitative proteomics. *Methods*, 2:124–130, 2003.

19. W. Yu et al. Statistical methods in proteomics. In *Springer Handbook of Engineering Statistics*. 1st ed. Springer, 2006, pp. 623–638.

20. P. Wang et al. A dynamic wavelet-based algorithm for pre-processing tandem mass spectrometry data. *Bioinformatics*, 26(18):2242–2249, 2010.

21. P. Pedrioli et al. A common open representation of mass spectrometry data and its application to proteomics research. *Nat. Biotechnol.*, 22:1459–1466, 2004.

22. A. M. Boehm et al. Extractor for ESI quadrupole TOF tandem MS data enabled for high throughput batch processing. *BMC Bioinformatics*, 5:162, 2004.

23. S. Tanner et al. InsPecT: Identification of posttransiationally modified peptides from tandem mass spectra. *Anal. Chem.*, 77:4626–4639, 2005.

24. J. Cox and M. Mann. MaxQuant enables high peptide identification rates, individualized p.p.b.-range mass accuracies and proteome-wide protein quantification. *Nat. Biotechnol.*, 26:1367–1372, 2008.

25. V. Andreev et al. A universal denoising and peak picking algorithm for LC-MS based on matched filtration in the chromatographic time domain. *Anal Chem.* 75(22):6314–6326, 2003.

26. X. Li et al. SELDI-TOF mass spectrometry protein data. In *Bioinformatics and Computational Biology Solutions Using R and Bioconductor*. 1st ed. Springer, 2005, pp. 91–109.

27. M. Katajamaa et al. MZmine: Toolbox for processing and visualization of mass spectrometry based molecular profile data. *Bioinformatics*, 22:634–636, 2006.

28. D. Mantini et al. LIMPIC: A computational method for the separation of protein MALDITOF-MS signals from noise. *BMC Bioinformatics*, 8:101, 2007.

29. S. Gras et al. Modeling peptide mass fingerprinting data using the atomic composition of peptides. *Electrophoresis*, 20(18):3527–3534, 1999.

30. M. Gentzel et al. Preprocessing of tandem mass spectrometric data to support automatic protein identification. *Proteomics*, 3:1597–1610, 2003.

31. Y. Qu et al. Data reduction using a discrete wavelet transform in discriminant analysis of very high dimensionality data. *Biometrics*, 59:143–151, 2003.

32. T. W. Randolph and Y. Yasui. Multiscale processing of mass spectrometry data. *Biometrics*, 63:589–597, 2006.

33. E. Lange et al. High-accuracy peak picking of proteomics data using wavelet techniques. *Pac. Symp. Biocomput.*, 243–254, 2006.

34. P. Du et al. Improved peak detection in mass spectrum by incorporating continuous wavelet transform-based pattern matching. *Bioinformatics*, 22:2059–2065, 2006.

35. K. R. Coombes et al. Improved peak detection and quantification of mass spectrometry data acquired from surface-enhanced laser desorption and ionization by denoising spectra with the undecimated discrete wavelet transform. *Proteomics*, 5:4107–4117, 2005.

36. R. Hussong et al. Highly accelerated feature detection in proteomics data sets using modern graphics processing units. *Bioinformatics*, 25(15):1937–1943, 2009.

37. A. Keller et al. Empirical statistical model to estimate the accuracy of peptide identifications made by MS/MS and database search. *Anal. Chem.*, 74(20):5383–5392, 2002.

38. J. Zhang et al. Bayesian nonparametric model for the validation of peptide identification in shotgun proteomics. *Mol. Cell. Prot.*, 8(3):547–557, 2009.

39. R. E. Moore et al. Qscore: An algorithm for evaluating SEQUEST database search results. *J. Am. Soc. Mass Spectrom.*, 13(4):378–386, 2002.

40. H. Choi and A. I. Nesvizhskii. False discovery rates and related statistical concepts in mass spectrometry-based proteomics. *J. Prot. Res.*, 7(1):47–50, 2008.

41. J. Elias and S. Gygi. Target-decoy search strategy for increased confidence in large-scale protein identifications by mass spectrometry. *Nat. Methods*, 4(3):207–214, 2007.

42. H. Choi and A. I. Nesvizhskii. Semisupervised model-based validation of peptide identifications in mass spectrometry-based proteomics. *J. Prot. Res.*, 7(1):254–265, 2008.

43. J. A. Falkner et al. Validated MALDI-TOF/TOF mass spectra for protein standards. *J. Am. Soc. Mass Spectrom.*, 18(5):850–855, 2007.

44. J. Elias and S. Gygi. Target-decoy search strategy for mass spectrometry-based proteomics. *Methods Mol. Biol.*, 604:55–71, 2010.

45. L. Kall et al. Assigning significance to peptides identified by tandem mass spectrometry using decoy databases. *J. Prot. Res.*, 7(1):29–34, 2007.

46. S. Kim et al. Spectral probabilities and generating functions of tandem mass spectra: A strike against decoy databases. *J. Prot. Res.*, 7(8):3354–3363, 2008.

47. N. Gupta and P. A. Pevzner. False discovery rates of protein identifications: A strike against the two-peptide rule. *J. Prot. Res.*, 8(9):4173–4181, 2009.

48. S. Henikoff and J. G. Henikoff. Amino acid substitution matrices from protein blocks. *Proc. Nat. Acad. Sci.*, 89(22):10915–10919, 1992.

49. J. Klimek et al. The standard protein mix database: A diverse dataset to assist in the production of improved peptide and protein identification software tools. *J. Prot. Res.*, 7(1):96–103, 2008.

50. J. Feng et al. Probability-based pattern recognition and statistical framework for randomization: Modeling tandem mass spectrum/peptide sequence false match frequencies. *Bioinformatics*, 23(17):2210–2217, 2007.

CHAPTER 4

FILTERING PROTEIN–PROTEIN INTERACTIONS BY INTEGRATION OF ONTOLOGY DATA

YOUNG-RAE CHO

Department of Computer Science, Baylor University, Waco, Texas

4.1 INTRODUCTION

Proteins interact with each other for biochemical stability and functionality, building protein complexes as larger functional units. Protein–protein interactions (PPIs) therefore play a key role in biological processes within a cell. Recently, high-throughput experimental techniques, such as the yeast two-hybrid system [10, 13, 18, 44], mass spectrometry [9, 12], and synthetic lethality screening [43], have made remarkable advances in identifying PPIs on a genome wide scale, collectively referred to as the interactome. Since the evidence interactions provides insights into the underlying mechanisms of biological processes, the availability of a large amount of PPI data has introduced a new paradigm towards functional characterization of proteins on a system level [17, 28].

Over the past few years, systematic analysis of the interactome by theoretical and empirical studies has been in the spotlight in the field of bioinformatics [38, 45, 51]. In particular, a wide range of computational approaches have been applied to the protein interaction networks for functional knowledge discovery, for instance, function prediction of uncharacterized genes or proteins [7, 8, 33], functional module detection [21, 34, 35], and signaling pathway identification [4, 32]. Although the automated methods are scalable and robust, their accuracy is limited because of unreliability of interaction data. The PPIs generated by large-scale high-throughput technologies include a significantly large number of false positives, that is, a large fraction of the putative interactions detected must be considered spurious because they cannot be confirmed to occur in vivo [30, 36, 47]. Filtering PPI data is thus a critical preprocessing step when handling interactomes. The erroneous interaction data can be curated by other resources which are used to judge the level of functional associations of interacting protein pairs, such as gene expression profiles [2, 15].

A recent study [14] has suggested the integration of Gene Ontology (GO) data to assess the validity of PPIs through measuring semantic similarity of interacting proteins. GO [42] is a repository of biological ontologies and annotations of genes and gene products.

Biological Knowledge Discovery Handbook: Preprocessing, Mining, and Postprocessing of Biological Data,
First Edition. Edited by Mourad Elloumi and Albert Y. Zomaya.
© 2014 John Wiley & Sons, Inc. Published 2014 by John Wiley & Sons, Inc.

Although the annotation data on GO are created by the published evidence resulting from mostly unreliable high-throughput experiments, they are frequently used as a benchmark for functional characterization because of their comprehensive information.

Functional similarity between proteins can be quantified by semantic similarity, a function that returns a numerical value reflecting closeness in meaning between two ontological terms annotating the proteins [20]. Since an interaction of a protein pair is interpreted as their strong functional association, one can measure the reliability of PPIs using semantic similarity: Proteins with higher semantic similarity are more likely to interact with each other than those with low semantic similarity. Therefore, absent of true information identifying which proteins actually interact, semantic similarity can be an indirect indicator of such interactions.

In this chapter, we assess the reliability of PPIs determined experimentally and computationally as a preprocessing step of analyzing the PPIs. The chapter is organized as follows. In Section 4.2, we discuss the general background of GO and semantic similarity measures. The performance of existing semantic similarity measures is analyzed in terms of functional consistency, including the combinations of the measures which achieve improved performance over the previous methods. In Section 4.3, we show the experimental results of identifying false-positive PPIs in current *Saccharomyces cerevisiae* PPI databases when the selected semantic similarity measures are applied.

4.2   EVALUATION OF SEMANTIC SIMILARITY

An *ontology* is a formal way of representing knowledge which is described by concepts and their relationships [3]. In the field of bioinformatics, the ontologies are used to capture domain knowledge within complex biological data [39]. For example, the use of ontologies has been proposed to measure similarity between entries in a biological data resource, called "semantic similarity" [20]. In this section, we discuss the general background of GO, which provides complete ontologies in the domain of bioinformatics. We also survey existing semantic similarity measures for the application of assessing functional similarity between genes or proteins.

4.2.1   Gene Ontology

As a collaborative effort to specify bio-ontologies, GO addresses the need for consistent descriptions of genes and gene products across species [41]. It provides a collection of well-defined biological concepts, called *GO terms*, spanning three domains: biological processes, molecular functions, and cellular components. GO is structured as a *directed acyclic graph* (DAG) by specifying general-to-specific relationships between terms such as "is-a" and "part-of." An example of the GO structure is illustrated by Figure 4.1. Five GO terms as nodes are linked with directed edges having parent-to-child relationships. For instance, GO:Node3 has two parent GO terms, GO:Node1 and GO:Node2.

As another important feature, GO maintains annotations for genes and gene products to their most specific GO terms. In Figure 4.1, gene *g2* is annotated to GO:Node2, and two genes, *g4* and *g5*, are annotated to GO:Node3. These are called *direct annotations*. Because of the general-to-specific relationships in the ontology structure, a gene that is annotated to a specific term is also annotated to all its parent terms on the paths toward the root. Since *g4* and *g5* are annotated to GO:Node3, they are also annotated to GO:Node2, GO:Node1,

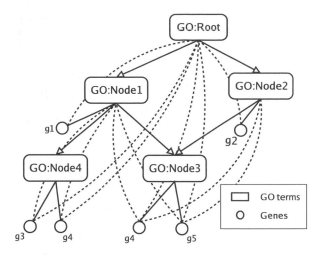

FIGURE 4.1 Example of GO structure having five GO terms and its annotation for five genes from *g*1 to *g*5. Solid lines between genes and GO terms indicate direct annotations and dotted lines indicate inferred annotations.

and GO:Root. These are called *inferred annotations*. Considering both direct and inferred annotations, we can quantify the specificity of a GO term by the proportion of the number of annotated genes on the term to the total number of annotated genes in the ontology. Suppose G_i and G_j are the sets of genes annotated to the GO terms t_i and t_j, respectively, and t_i is a parent term of t_j. The size of G_i, $|G_i|$, is always greater than or equal to $|G_j|$.

Note that a gene can be annotated to multiple GO terms. In Figure 4.1, gene *g4* is annotated to both GO:Node3 and GO:Node4. Suppose a gene x is annotated to m different GO terms. Then $G_i(x)$ denotes a set of genes annotated to the GO term t_i whose annotation includes x, where $1 \leq i \leq m$. In the same way, suppose n different GO terms have the annotations including both x and y, where $n \leq m$. Then $G_j(x, y)$ denotes a set of genes annotated to the GO term G_j whose annotation includes both x and y, where $1 \leq j \leq n$. The minimum size of $G_i(x)$, $\min_i |G_i(x)|$, is then less than or equal to $\min_j |G_j(x, y)|$.

4.2.2 Survey of Semantic Similarity Measures

Semantic similarity measures are the functions computing the level of similarity in meaning between terms within an ontology. A variety of semantic similarity measures have been proposed previously [24, 26, 48]. They can be grouped into four broad categories: *path length–based methods* (or called *edge-based methods*), *information content–based methods* (or called *annotation-based methods*), *common term–based methods* (or called *node-based methods*), and *hybrid methods*. Path length–based methods calculate the path length between terms in an ontology as their similarity. Information content–based methods use an information-theoretic measure based on the notion of term likelihood to assign higher values to terms that have higher specificity. Common term–based methods consider the number of shared ancestor terms in an ontology to assign a similarity value. Hybrid methods incorporate aspects of two different categories. The semantic similarity measures in these four categories are summarized in Table 4.1.

TABLE 4.1   Summary of Semantic Similarity Measures in Four Categories

Category/Method	Description
Path length (edge based)	
Path length	Path length between two terms
Normalized path length	Normalized path length between two terms with depth of GO
Depth to SCA [11]	Depth of SCA of two terms
Normalized depth to SCA [50]	Normalized depth of SCA with average depth of two terms
Information content	
Resnik [27]	Information content of SCA of two terms
Lin [19]	Normalized Resnik method with information contents of two terms
Jiang and Conrath [16]	Sum of differences of information contents between SCA and two terms
Common terms (node based)	
Term overlap (TO) [23]	Number of common ancestors of two terms
NTO [23]	Normalized TO method with smaller set of ancestors of two terms
simUI / DTO [11]	Normalized direct TO method with union set of ancestors of two terms
Hybrid methods	
Wang [49]	Combined method of TO with normalized depth
simGIC [25]	Combined method of simUI with information contents
IntelliGO [5]	Combined method of information content with normalized depth

Note: SCA denotes the most *specific common ancestor* of two terms of interest in GO.

4.2.2.1 Path Length–Based Methods (Edge-Based Methods)   Path length–
based methods calculate semantic similarity by measuring the shortest path length between
two terms. The path length can be normalized with the maximum depth of the ontology,
which represents the longest path length out of all shortest paths from the root to leaf nodes:

$$\text{sim}_{\text{Path}}(C_1, C_2) = -\log\left(\frac{\text{len}(C_1, C_2)}{2 \cdot \text{depth}}\right) \tag{4.1}$$

where $\text{len}(C_1, C_2)$ is the shortest path length between two terms C_1 and C_2 in an ontology.
The semantic similarity is also measured by the depth to the SCA of two terms, that is,
the shortest path length from the root to the SCA [11]. The longer the path length to the
SCA of the two terms, the more similar they are in meaning. The depth to the SCA can be
normalized with the average depth to the terms [50]. This normalized measure is used to
adjust the similarity distorted through the depths of the terms of interest:

$$\text{sim}_{\text{wu}}(C_1, C_2) = \frac{2 \cdot \text{len}(C_{\text{root}}, C_{\text{sca}})}{\text{len}(C_{\text{sca}}, C_1) + \text{len}(C_{\text{sca}}, C_2) + 2 \cdot \text{len}(C_{\text{root}}, C_{\text{sca}})} \tag{4.2}$$

where C_{root} denotes the root term and C_{sca} is the most specific common ancestor term of
C_1 and C_2.

To compute functional similarity between two proteins, we take into consideration semantic similarity between pairwise combinations of the terms having direct annotations of the proteins. These path length–based methods are applicable to the ontology in which each edge between two terms represents the same quantity of specificity. However, according to published results, new terms are added resulting in complex relationships between terms which lead to inconsistent specificity of edges in GO. Therefore, path length–based methods are not suitable for measuring semantic similarity from GO.

4.2.2.2 *Information Content–Based Methods (Annotation-Based Methods)*

Self-information in information theory is a measure of the information content associated with the outcome of a random variable. The amount of self-information contained in a probabilistic event c depends on the probability $P(c)$ of the event. More specifically, the smaller the probability of the event, the larger the self-information to be received when the event indeed occurs. The information content of a term C in an ontology is then defined as the negative log likelihood of C, $-\log P(C)$. In the application to GO, the likelihood of a term $P(C)$ can be calculated by the ratio of the number of annotated genes on the term C to the total number of annotated genes in the ontology.

The information content-based semantic similarity is measured by the commonality of two terms; the more common the information the two terms share, the more similar they are. Resnik [27] used the information content of the SCA that subsumes two terms C_1 and C_2:

$$\text{sim}_{\text{Resnik}}(C_1, C_2) = -\log P(C_{\text{sca}}) \tag{4.3}$$

Lin [19] considered not only commonality but a difference between terms by normalizing the Resnik semantic similarity measure with the average of the individual information content of C_1 and C_2:

$$\text{sim}_{\text{Lin}}(C_1, C_2) = \frac{2 \log P(C_{\text{sca}})}{\log P(C_1) + \log P(C_2)} \tag{4.4}$$

Jiang and Conrath [16] used the differences of information content between C_1 and C_{sca} and between C_2 and C_{sca} to measure the semantic distance between C_1 and C_2:

$$\text{dist}_{\text{Jiang}}(C_1, C_2) = 2 \log P(C_{\text{sca}}) - \log P(C_1) - \log P(C_2) \tag{4.5}$$

The semantic similarity between C_1 and C_2 is then calculated by the inverse of their semantic distance:

$$\text{sim}_{\text{Jiang}}(C_1, C_2) = \frac{1}{1 + \text{dist}_{\text{Jiang}}(C_1, C_2)} \tag{4.6}$$

Note that all methods in the path length–based and information content–based categories measure semantic similarity between two GO terms. We however aim at quantifying functional similarity between two proteins which might be annotated to multiple GO terms. We therefore apply three different ways of aggregating semantic similarity values between pairwise combinations of the terms having annotations of the two proteins. Suppose S_1 and S_2 are the sets of GO terms having direct annotations of protein g_1 and protein g_2, respectively. At first, in order to compute functional similarity between two proteins g_1 and g_2, we can select the maximum semantic similarity value among all similarity values of term pairs from S_1 and S_2:

$$\text{sim}_{\text{MAX}}(g_1, g_2) = \max_{C_1 \in S_1, C_2 \in S_2} \text{sim}(C_1, C_2) \tag{4.7}$$

Next, the average sematic similarity value of all possible pairwise combinations of the terms from S_1 and S_2 can be used as the functional similarity of g_1 and g_2:

$$\text{sim}_{\text{AVG}}(g_1, g_2) = \frac{1}{|S_1||S_2|} \sum_{C_1 \in S_1, C_2 \in S_2} \text{sim}(C_1, C_2) \tag{4.8}$$

Finally, by combining the two methods above, the *best-match average* (BMA) approach computes the average of all pairwise best matches [40]:

$$\text{sim}_{\text{BMA}}(g_1, g_2) = \frac{\sum_{C_1 \in S_1} \max_{C_2 \in S_2} \text{sim}(C_1, C_2) + \sum_{C_2 \in S_2} \max_{C_1 \in S_1} \text{sim}(C_1, C_2)}{|S_1| + |S_2|} \tag{4.9}$$

4.2.2.3 *Common Term–Based Methods (Node-Based Methods)* Common term–based methods calculate semantic similarity by measuring the overlap between two sets of terms, not between two terms. The methods in this category are therefore applied directly to estimating functional similarity between two annotating proteins. The more common the GO terms to which the proteins g_1 and g_2 are annotated, the higher the functional similarity they have:

$$\text{sim}_{\text{TO}}(g_1, g_2) = |S_1 \cap S_2| \tag{4.10}$$

The TO method uses the sets of GO terms having both direct and inferred annotations of g_1 and g_2 as S_1 and S_2, respectively. These approaches can be normalized with the union of the two sets of GO terms [11] or with the smaller of them [23]:

$$\text{sim}_{\text{UI}}(g_1, g_2) = \frac{|S_1 \cap S_2|}{|S_1 \cup S_2|} \tag{4.11}$$

$$\text{sim}_{\text{NTO}}(g_1, g_2) = \frac{|S_1 \cap S_2|}{\min(|S_1|, |S_2|)} \tag{4.12}$$

The DTO measure uses S_1 and S_2 in Equation (4.11) as the sets of GO terms having only direct annotations of g_1 and g_2, respectively.

4.2.2.4 *Hybrid Methods* Hybrid methods combine the approaches from different categories to compute semantic similarity. For example, Wang et al. [49] proposed a semantic similarity measure that integrates the NTO with the concept of the normalized depth to the most specific terms in an ontology. IntelliGO [5] is a vector representation model that combines the normalized depth with information contents as weights. However, as discussed, the path length–based approaches do not fit in the GO applications because of complex relationships between terms.

SimGIC [25] integrates the information-theoretic measures with term overlaps. It calculates the sum of information contents in the intersection of S_a and S_b divided by the sum of information contents in their union:

$$\text{sim}_{\text{GIC}}(g_1, g_2) = \frac{\sum_{C_a \in S_1 \cap S_2} \log\ P(C_a)}{\sum_{C_b \in S_1 \cup S_2} \log\ P(C_b)} \qquad (4.13)$$

where $P(C)$ is the likelihood of the term C, that is, the ratio of the number of annotated genes on the term C to the total number of annotated genes in the ontology.

As another way of integrating the measures from two different categories, we can apply a linear combination. For example, we can combine the Resnik information content–based method with the DTO method in common term–based approaches such as

$$\text{sim}_{\text{LC}}(g_1, g_2) = \alpha\ \text{sim}_{\text{Resnik-MAX}}(g_1, g_2) + (1 - \alpha)\ \text{sim}_{\text{DTO}}(g_1, g_2) \qquad (4.14)$$

where α is a weighting parameter used to assign relative weight to the contributions from both similarity measures. This *linear combination* (LC) method takes advantage of two orthogonal sources of information: direct annotation term information and the information content of the most specific common term. By considering two distinct sources of information, a more accurate picture of semantic similarity is attained.

4.2.3   Correlation with Functional Categorizations

To compare the performance of the semantic similarity measures, we assessed the general correlation with functional consistency. We downloaded the genome wide PPI data set of *Saccharomyces cerevisiae* from the BioGRID database [37] and selected 10,000 interacting protein pairs uniformly at random. The semantic similarity scores were calculated for each pair using all methods in Table 4.1.

As a reference ground-truth data set, we used manually curated MIPS functional categorizations (FunCat) [29]. Since the MIPS functional categories are hierarchically distributed, we extracted the functional descriptions and their annotations on the third level from the root of the hierarchy. We then computed functional consistency from the FunCat data by taking the number of shared functions for a protein pair divided by the size of the union of their function sets (i.e., the jaccard index). Pearson correlation is then calculated between each semantic similarity score and the functional consistency.

Table 4.2 lists the Pearson correlation results for the tested semantic similarity measures. We found that the combined methods in the hybrid category, such as simGIC and LC, achieved high correlation with the functional consistency. In particular, the LC method of DTO and Resnik-MAX using an α weighting of 0.15 shows the best correlation (indicated in boldface).

Figure 4.2 graphically shows the correlation between the semantic similarity from various measures and the functional consistency. The semantic similarity values for each method were binned and the average functional consistency taken for each bin. As can be seen, three measures, simGIC, LC, and DTO, show fairly positive correlation with functional consistency from the MIPS functional categorizations because their plots are close to the diagonal line.

TABLE 4.2   Correlation Scores between Semantic Similarity and Functional Consistency from MIPS Functional Categorizations

Semantic Similarity Measures	Pearson Correlation
Resnik-MAX	0.3774
Resnik-BMA	0.5286
Lin-MAX	0.2448
Lin-BMA	0.5162
DTO	0.7683
NTO	0.6726
simGIC	0.7703
LC ($\alpha = 0.10$)	0.7733
LC ($\alpha = 0.15$)	**0.7742**
LC ($\alpha = 0.25$)	0.7715
LC ($\alpha = 0.50$)	0.7215
LC ($\alpha = 0.75$)	0.5815

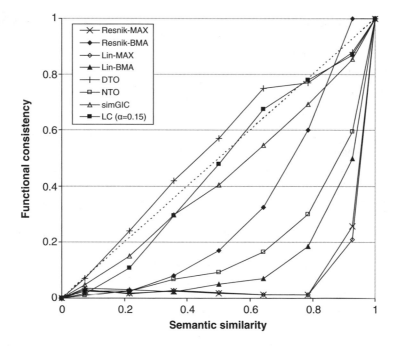

FIGURE 4.2   Correlation plots between semantic similarity from various measures and functional consistency.

4.3   IDENTIFICATION OF FALSE PROTEIN–PROTEIN INTERACTION DATA

The genomewide PPI data of several model organisms are publicly available in a number of open databases, for example, BioGRID [37], IntAct [1], MINT [6], MIPS [22], STRING [46], and DIP [31]. Because they were mostly generated by high-throughput experimental methods, it is generally assumed that they contain a significant number of false positives. The false-positive interactions can be identified by evaluating how dissimilar each interacting protein pair is semantically. In this section, we discuss classification methods to identify the false positives from a PPI data set and evaluate their accuracy.

4.3.1 Classification Method

To test false-positive identification, we calculated semantic similarity using the measures discussed previously for 10,000 PPIs randomly selected from the BioGRID database. These similarity values were then subjected to a variable threshold. When the value exceeds the threshold, the semantic similarity method classifies the PPI as a true (positive) interaction. Otherwise, it is classified as a false (negative) interaction. All methods were implemented for 100 different thresholds ranging from 0.0 to 0.99.

In addition to the semantic similarity classifiers, we created an additional "voting" scheme of the combined hybrid method, which only outputs a positive classification when the Resnik-MAX measure exceeds the threshold and the DTO value is above the median DTO value for the data set. Mathematically, the voting classifier is defined as follows:

$$C(g_1, g_2) = (\text{sim}_{\text{Resnik-MAX}}(g_1, g_2) > \theta) \wedge (\text{sim}_{\text{DTO}}(g_1, g_2) > \beta) \tag{4.15}$$

where θ is the threshold parameter and β is the median DTO semantic similarity value of the data set. The output of $C(g_1, g_2)$ is restricted to the set $\{0, 1\}$ (binary output), due to the nature of logical conjunction. This method was developed to further reduce the number of false-positive identifications over most threshold values.

To compare the performance of false-positive identification, we used as ground truth any nonempty intersection of functions for two interacting proteins within the MIPS functional categorizations. When the protein pair share at least one functional categorization, they are assumed to interact with each other. Accuracy was then calculated as the number of correct classifications divided by the total number of classifications.

4.3.2 Accuracy of PPI Classification

Of the 10,000 PPIs assessed, a majority of them (5554) are expected to be false interactions as measured by the MIPS ground truth data set. These interacting protein pairs have no shared functional categorizations and therefore are labeled as negative examples. Table 4.3 shows the classification accuracy for the tested semantic similarity classifiers.

The most accurate method for PPI classification is the LC classifier of DTO and Resnik-MAX measures using an α value of 0.90, which achieves a maximum accuracy of 0.82 over the data set (indicated in bold). Equally important is the area under the curve, which gives an indication of how accurate the various methods are over all thresholds. The combined voting method achieves the largest area under the curve, with a value of 0.76 (also in bold). In addition to this result, it also achieves the second best maximum accuracy, behind the LC classifier with $\alpha = 0.90$ and $\alpha = 0.75$. The combined hybrid methods collectively achieve the best performance on the classification task, with the voting method performing well for almost all thresholds.

Lin's method has the worst performance on the classification task, with the lowest maximum accuracy of all methods tested. DTO appears to trade good performance over many thresholds (area under the curve) for maximum classification accuracy, as does NTO. The simGIC measure achieves fairly good performance, with the second best area-under-the-curve performance. Since it is also a hybrid method combining the information contents

TABLE 4.3 Classification Accuracy for Semantic Similarity Classifiers

Classifier	Maximum Accuracy	Area Under Curve
Resnik-MAX	0.8087	0.5348
Resnik-BMA	0.7671	0.5989
Lin-MAX	0.6478	0.4970
Lin-BMA	0.7528	0.5686
DTO	0.7573	0.6519
NTO	0.7636	0.6348
simGIC	0.7892	0.6689
LC ($\alpha = 0.10$)	0.7670	0.6393
LC ($\alpha = 0.15$)	0.7723	0.6336
LC ($\alpha = 0.25$)	0.7810	0.6221
LC ($\alpha = 0.50$)	0.8020	0.5932
LC ($\alpha = 0.75$)	0.8135	0.5643
LC ($\alpha = 0.90$)	**0.8163**	0.5469
Voting	0.8114	**0.7606**

with term overlaps, similar to the combined method that achieves the best performance, this provides additional evidence for the performance advantages of using common term–based methods in combination with information content–based methods.

Figure 4.3 shows the classification accuracy results for DTO, Resnik-MAX, and the combined voting classifiers. Different from the DTO and Resnik-MAX measures, the voting classifier is able to achieve high classification accuracy across all threshold values. By forcing both subclassifiers to agree on a positive classification, false positives are avoided, leading to higher accuracy given the large percentage of negatively labeled instances in the data set.

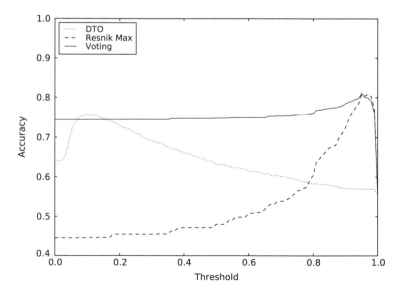

FIGURE 4.3 Accuracy of PPI classification over all thresholds for Resnik-MAX, DTO, and the combined voting classifier.

TABLE 4.4   Experimental System Types and Proportions of False Positives in
S. cerevisiae **PPI Data Set**

Experimental System	Number of False Positives	% of Total
Negative Genetic	67,723	0.47
Affinity Capture-MS	21,027	0.15
Positive Genetic	12,078	0.08
Synthetic Growth Defect	11,025	0.08
Synthetic Lethality	6,390	0.04
Two-hybrid	4,847	0.03
Biochemical Activity	4,015	0.03
Affinity Capture-RNA	3,461	0.02
PCA	2,897	0.02
Phenotypic Enhancement	2,485	0.02
Phenotypic Suppression	2,385	0.02
Affinity Capture-Western	1,578	0.01
Synthetic Rescue	1,403	0.01
Dosage Rescue	1,396	0.01
Others	1,967	0.01

4.3.3 Reliability of PPI Data

We extend the classification task to assess the reliability of current PPI data. Using the most accurate parameters for the LC classifier of DTO and Resnik-MAX measures ($\alpha = 0.90$, threshold $= 0.88$), we classified all *S. cerevisiae* PPIs in the BioGRID database. As a preprocessing step, we excluded those that lacked corresponding gene annotations within the GO annotation data of *S. cerevisiae*. This resulted in a total of 247,048 interactions, of which 144,677 (58.6%) were classified as false-positive interactions.

The PPIs in the BioGRID database have been determined by several different experimental systems. Among the experimental systems, Negative Genetic (0.47%) and Affinity-Capture-MS (0.15%) were the most prevalent in generating false positives. False interactions were most likely to result from genetic experiment types (73%) and high-throughput methods (90%). Table 4.4 displays an ordered ranking of the experimental systems responsible for the majority of false-positive data.

Using the combined semantic similarity classifier, we are able to discover potential false positives existing in PPI data repositories and automate the process of filtering PPI data sets. Given a high accuracy of classification when calibrated against manually curated functional categorization data from the MIPS database (roughly 0.82% accuracy), it is likely that many of the false-positive interactions identified by the classifier indeed represent spurious PPIs. Table 4.5 lists a random sampling of 20 negatively classified PPIs having a zero semantic similarity value as measured by the combined hybrid classifier, which are therefore likely to represent false-positive interactions.

4.4 CONCLUSION

PPIs are crucial resources for functional knowledge discovery. However, as an innate feature, the PPI data sets include an extremely large number of false positives. Our results indicate that more than 50% of current *S. cerevisiae* PPI data are false positives, determined by

TABLE 4.5 Selected PPIs with Zero-Valued Semantic Similarity (Likely False PPIs)

Protein A	Protein B	Experimental System
YDR124W	YOR158W	Affinity Capture-MS
YGL122C	YJL107C	Affinity Capture-RNA
YGL122C	YML118W	Affinity Capture-RNA
YJR059W	YER010C	Biochemical Activity
YNL307C	YBR225W	Biochemical Activity
YHR082C	YML083C	Biochemical Activity
YMR216C	OK/SW-cl.3	Biochemical Activity
YOL090W	YGL081W	Negative Genetic
YEL051W	YKL098W	Negative Genetic
YBL015W	YDL118W	Negative Genetic
YDL074C	YMR206W	Negative Genetic
YHR167W	YDR249C	Negative Genetic
YPR078C	YDR488C	Negative Genetic
YGR012W	YLR053C	Negative Genetic
YDR542W	YKL109W	Negative Genetic
YCR091W	YJL147C	Negative Genetic
YNL197C	YOL036W	Negative Genetic
YOR043W	YGR161C	Negative Genetic
YDR388W	YJR083C	Protein-peptide
YMR186W	YER039C-A	Synthetic Growth Defect

mostly high-throughput experimental systems. Identifying the false-positive interactions is thus a critical preprocessing step for accurate analysis of PPIs. The work presented in this chapter focuses on using the ontology structures and annotations from GO to automatically prune false positives from the PPI data sets.

Several semantic similarity methods were assessed for their correlation to manually curated MIPS functional categorizations. A combined hybrid method was presented that demonstrates performance gains over existing methods. This method takes into account both the maximum information content of the most specific common ancestor as well as information provided by overlap of directly annotated terms in the GO for a pair of genes. Although the individual method, in isolation, is less accurate for classification, it can improve the performance when combined in a majority vote fashion. An additional "voting" variant was also developed that achieves the best overall classification accuracy over a variety of selection thresholds. It was motivated by the idea that two somewhat accurate classifiers can be more accurate when combined in a suitable manner.

REFERENCES

1. B. Aranda et al. The IntAct molecular interaction database in 2010. *Nucleic Acids Res.*, 38:D525–D531, 2010.

2. J. S. Bader, A. Chaudhuri, J. M. Rothberg, and J. Chant. Gaining confidence in high-throughput protein interaction networks. *Nat. Biotechnol.*, 22(1):78–85, 2004.

3. J. B. L. Bard and S. Y. Rhee. Ontologies in biology: Design, applications and future challenges. *Nat. Rev. Genet.*, 5:213–222, 2004.

4. G. Bebek and J. Yang. PathFinder: Mining signal transduction pathway segments from protein-protein interaction networks. *BMC Bioinformatics*, 8:335, 2007.

5. S. Benabderrahmane, M. Smail-Tabbone, O. Poch, A. Napoli, and M.-D. Devignes. IntelliGO: A new vector-based semantic similarity measure including annotation origin. *BMC Bioinformatics*, 11:588, 2010.

6. A. Ceol, A. Chatr-aryamontri, L. Licata, D. Peluso, L. Briganti, L. Perfetto, L. Castagnoli, and G. Cesareni. MINT: The molecular interaction database: 2009 update. *Nucleic Acids Res.*, 38:D532–D539, 2010.

7. X. Chen, M. Liu, and R. Ward. Protein function assignment through mining cross-species protein-protein interactions. *PLoS One*, 3(2):e1562, 2008.

8. Y.-R. Cho and A. Zhang. Predicting function by frequent functional association pattern mining in protein interaction networks. *IEEE Trans. Inform. Technol. Biomed. (TITB)*, 14(1):30–36, 2010.

9. A.-C. Gavin et al. Functional organization of the yeast proteome by systematic analysis of protein complexes. *Nature*, 415:141–147, 2002.

10. L. Giot et al. A protein interaction map of *Drosophila melanogaster*. *Science*, 302:1727–1736, 2003.

11. X. Guo, R. Liu, C. D. Shriver, H. Hu, and M. N. Liebman. Assessing semantic similarity measures for the characterization of human regulatory pathways. *Bioinformatics*, 22(8):967–973, 2006.

12. Y. Ho et al. Systematic identification of protein complexes in *Saccharomyces cerevisiae* by mass spectrometry. *Nature*, 415:180–183, 2002.

13. T. Ito, T. Chiba, R. Ozawa, M. Yoshida, M. Hattori, and Y. Sakaki. A comprehensive two-hybrid analysis to explore the yeast protein interactome. *Proc. Natl. Acad. Sci. USA*, 98(8):4569–4574, 2001.

14. S. Jain and G. D. Bader. An improved method for scoring protein-protein interactions using semantic similarity within the gene ontology. *BMC Bioinformatics*, 11:562, 2010.

15. R. Jansen, D. Greenbaum, and M. Gerstein. Relating whole-genome expression data with protein-protein interactions. *Genome Res.*, 12:37–46, 2002.

16. J. J. Jiang and D. W. Conrath. Semantic similarity based on corpus statistics and lexical taxonomy. In *Proceedings of 10th International Conference on Research in Computational Linguistics*, 1997.

17. R. Kelley and T. Ideker. Systematic interpretation of genetic interactions using protein networks. *Nat. Biotechnol.*, 23(5):561–566, 2005.

18. S. Li et al. A map of the interactome network of the metazoan *C. elegans*. *Science*, 303:540–543, 2004.

19. D. Lin. An information-theoretic definition of similarity. In *Proceedings of 15th International Conference on Machine Learning (ICML)*, 1998, pp. 296–304.

20. P. W. Lord, R. D. Stevens, A. Brass, and C. A. Goble. Investigating semantic similarity measures across the Gene Ontology: The relationship between sequence and annotation. *Bioinformatics*, 19(10):1275–1283, 2003.

21. F. Luo, Y. Yang, C.-F. Chen, R. Chang, J. Zhou, and R. H. Scheuermann. Modular organization of protein interaction networks. *Bioinformatics*, 23(2):207–214, 2007.

22. H. W. Mewes, et al. MIPS: Analysis and annotation of genome information in 2007. *Nucleic Acids Res.*, 36:D196–D201, 2008.

23. M. Mistry and P. Pavlidis. Gene Ontology term overlap as a measure of gene functional similarity. *BMC Bioinformatics*, 9:327, 2008.

24. T. Pedersen, S. V. S. Pakhomov, S. Patwardhan, and C. G. Chute. Measures of semantic similarity and relatedness in the biomedical domain. *J. Biomed. Informatics*, 40:288–299, 2007.

25. C. Pesquita, D. Faria, H. Bastos, A. E. N. Ferreira, A. O. Falcao, and F. M. Couto, Metrics for GO based protein semantic similarity: A systematic evaluation. *BMC Bioinformatics*, 9(Suppl 5):S4, 2008.

26. C. Pesquita, D. Faria, A. O. Falcao, P. Lord, and F. M. Couto. Semantic similarity in biomedical ontologies. *PLoS Computat. Biol.*, 5(7):e1000443, 2009.

27. P. Resnik. Using information content to evaluate semantic similarity in a taxonomy. In *Proceedings of 14th International Joint Conference on Artificial Intelligence*, 1995, pp. 448–453.

28. J.-F. Rual, et al. Towards a proteome-scale map of the human protein-protein interaction network. *Nature*, 437:1173–1178, 2005.

29. A. Ruepp, A. Zollner, D. Maier, K. Albermann, J. Hani, M. Mokrejs, I. Tetko, U. Guldener, G. Mannhaupt, M. Munsterkotter, and H. W. Mewes. The FunCat: A functional annotation scheme for systematic classification of proteins from whole genomes. *Nucleic Acids Res.*, 32(18): 5539–5545, 2004.

30. L. Salwinski and D. Eisenberg. Computational methods of analysis of protein-protein interactions. *Curr. Opin. Struct. Biol.*, 13:377–382, 2003.

31. L. Salwinski, C. S. Miller, A. J. Smith, F. K. Pettit, J. U. Bowie, and D. Eisenberg. The database of interacting proteins: 2004 update. *Nucleic Acids Res.*, 32:D449–D451, 2004.

32. J. Scott, T. Ideker, R. M. Karp, and R. Sharan. Efficient algorithms for detecting signaling pathways in protein interaction networks. *J. Computat. Biol.*, 13(2):133–144, 2006.

33. R. Sharan, I. Ulitsky, and R. Shamir. Network-based prediction of protein function. *Mol. Syst. Biol.*, 3:88, 2007.

34. J. Song and M. Singh. How and when should interactome-derived clusters be used to predict functional modules and protein function? *Bioinformatics*, 25(23):3143–3150, 2009.

35. V. Spirin and L. A. Mirny. Protein complexes and functional modules in molecular networks. *Proc. Natl. Acad. Sci. USA*, 100(21):12123–12128, 2003.

36. E. Sprinzak, S. Sattath, and H. Margalit. How reliable are experimental protein-protein interaction data? *J. Mol. Biol.*, 327:919–923, 2003.

37. C. Stark, et al. The BioGRID interaction database: 2011 update. *Nucleic Acids Res.*, 39: D698–D704, 2011.

38. U. Stelzl, et al. A human protein-protein interaction network: A resource for annotating the proteome. *Cell*, 122:957–968, 2005.

39. R. Stevens, C. A. Goble, and S. Bechhofer. Ontology-based knowledge representation for bioinformatics. *Brief. Bioinformatics*, 1(4):398–414, 2000.

40. Y. Tao, L. Sam, J. Li, C. Friedman, and Y. A. Lussier. Information theory applied to the sparse gene ontology annotation network to predict novel gene function. *Bioinformatics*, 23:i529–i538, 2007.

41. The Gene Ontology Consortium. Gene Ontology: Tool for the unification of biology. *Nat. Genet.*, 25:25–29, 2000.

42. The Gene Ontology Consortium. The Gene Ontology in 2010: Extensions and refinements. *Nucleic Acids Res.*, 38:D331–D335, 2010.

43. A. H. Y. Tong, et al. Global mapping of the yeast genetic interaction network. *Science*, 303: 808–813, 2004.

44. P. Uetz et al. A comprehensive analysis of protein-protein interactions in *Saccharomyces cerevisiae*. *Nature*, 403:623–627, 2000.

45. K. Venkatesan, et al. An empirical framework for binary interactome mapping. *Nat. Method*, 6(1):83–90, 2009.

46. C. von Mering, L. J. Jensen, M. Kuhn, S. Chaffron, T. Doerks, B. Kruger, B. Snel, and P. Bork. STRING7-recent developments in the integration and prediction of protein interactions. *Nucleic Acids Res.*, 35:D358–D362, 2007.

47. C. von Mering, R. Krause, B. Snel, M. Cornell, S. G. Oliver, S. Fields, and P. Bork. Comparative assessment of large-scale data sets of protein-protein interactions. *Nature*, 417:399–403, 2002.

48. J. Wang, X. Zhou, J. Zhu, C. Zhou, and Z. Guo. Revealing and avoiding bias in semantic similarity scores for protein pairs. *BMC Bioinformatics*, 11:290, 2010.

49. J. Z. Wang, Z. Du, R. Payattakool, P. S. Yu, and C.-F. Chen. A new method to measure the semantic similarity of GO terms. *Bioinformatics*, 23(10), 2007.

50. Z. Wu and M. Palmer. Verb semantics and lexical selection. In *Proceedings of 32th Annual Meeting of the Association for Computational Linguistics*, 1994, pp. 133–138.

51. H. Yu, et al. High-quality binary protein interaction map of the yeast interactome network. *Science*, 322:104–110, 2008.

PART B

BIOLOGICAL DATA MODELING

CHAPTER 5

COMPLEXITY AND SYMMETRIES IN DNA SEQUENCES

CARLO CATTANI

Department of Mathematics, University of Salerno, Fisciano (SA), Italy

5.1 INTRODUCTION

From a biological point of view the DNA (a deoxyribonucleic acid) sequence can be roughly described as a double-strand helix of paired-up chemical bases (nucleotides). The order of nucleotides along the sequence determines the information for chemical reactions and biological activity. In fact, DNA contains the whole set of instructions necessary for the life of each individual. Nucleotides or nucleic acids are adenine (A), cytosine (C), guanine (G), and thymine (T); they all are made by a combination of phosphate group, a sugar, and a nitrogen base.

From a mathematical point a view the DNA sequence is a symbolic sequence of four symbols {A, C, G, T} with alternating empty spaces (no coding regions). When this sequence is converted into a digital sequence, it can be studied as a numerical signal [35, 60, 66], and in some recent papers many results were obtained about its multifractality [5, 9, 11, 19, 20, 41, 42] and its influence on DNA [8, 47–49, 58], the existence of long-range correlation [4, 7, 10, 12, 13, 24, 43, 45, 46, 53, 61–63, 67, 69], and the information content and measure of its complexity [1, 21, 22, 29, 44, 50, 56, 57, 68]. Almost all papers on these topics are aimed at detecting the existence of regular patterns in the genomic signal [3, 6, 23, 27, 28, 30, 33, 34, 37, 39, 51, 54], thus speculating on a possible functional meaning.

In order to get some information from a DNA sequence, the first step is to convert the symbolic sequence into a numerical sequence to be analyzed by classical methods of signal analysis based on classical statistical parameter such as variance and deviation or non-classical ones such as complexity, entropy, fractal dimension, and long-range dependence. However, as we shall see, these sequences look very much like some random sequences, from which it seems to be quite impossible to single out any single correlation (see, e.g., [24] and references therein). In other words, at first glance, any DNA sequence is characterized by the same values of global parameters which characterize any other kind of random sequence, thus raising some doubts about the existence of correlation among bases. We will see that apparently DNA looks like a random sequence, and probably this can be explained

Biological Knowledge Discovery Handbook: Preprocessing, Mining, and Postprocessing of Biological Data,
First Edition. Edited by Mourad Elloumi and Albert Y. Zomaya.

by the fact that we should look more carefully at the close neighbors of each base while, instead, global parameters take into account some long-distance influence.

A very expedient method to analyze the influence of close base pairs (bp), by focusing on local average and jumps, is to compute the short (or window) wavelet transform [14–18, 20]. It will be shown that wavelet [2, 4, 6, 16, 26] analysis is able to offer a more detailed and localized analysis so that we can single out symmetries and regular distribution on the wavelet coefficients [19, 20, 55, 59]. The analysis of wavelet coefficients will show that DNA sequences and random sequences have, more or less, the same wavelet coefficients; however, if we analyze by wavelets the walks, on DNA compared with random walks, we can see that there exists some differences. In other words, it is possible to characterize a DNA sequence through the wavelet coefficients of its DNA walks. In particular, simulations will be given for bacteria and archaea DNA, which apparently look very close to random sequences.

Previous researchers have studied various sequences of DNA, such as leukemia variants, influenza virus A (H1N1) variant, mammalian variants, and a fungus [17–22]) provided by the National Center for Biotechnology Information [52]. In all these papers it was observed that DNA has to fulfill not only some chemical steady state given by the chemical ligands but also some symmetrical distribution of nucleotide along the sequence. In other words, base pairs have to be placed exactly in some positions. In the following we will take into consideration some complete sequences of DNA concerning the following (aerobic/anaerobic) bacteria/fungi/archaea:

b1 *Mycoplasma putrefaciens* KS1 chromosome, complete genome. DNA, circular, length 832,603 bp, [52], accession NC 015946. Lineage: Bacteria; Tenericutes; Mollicutes; Mycoplasmatales; Mycoplasmataceae; Mycoplasma; *M. putrefaciens*; *M putrefaciens* KS1.

b2 *Mortierella verticillata*, mitochondrion, complete genome. Double-stranded DNA (dsDNA), circular, length 58,745 bp, [52], accession NC 006838. Lineage: Eukaryota; Opisthokonta; Fungi; *Fungi incertae sedis*; basal fungal lineages; Mucoromycotina; Mortierellales; Mortierellaceae; *Mortierella*; *M. verticillata*.

b3 *Blattabacterium* sp. (*Periplaneta americana*) str. BPLAN, complete genome. DNA, circular, length 636,994 nt, [52], accession NC 013418. Lineage: Bacteria; Bacteroidetes/Chlorobi group; Bacteroidetes; Flavobacteria; Flavobacteriales; Blattabacteriaceae; *Blattabacterium*; *Blattabacterium* sp. (*P. americana*); *Blattabacterium* sp. (*P. americana*) str. BPLAN.

h1 *Aeropyrum pernix* K1, complete genome. DNA, circular, 1,669,696 bp, [52], accession BA000002.3. Lineage: Archaea; Crenarchaeota; Thermoprotei; Desulfurococcales; Desulfurococcaceae; *Aeropyrum*; *A. pernix*; *A. pernix* K1. This organism, which was the first strictly aerobic hyperthermophilic archaeon sequenced, was isolated from sulfuric gases in Kodakara-Jima Island, Japan, in 1993.

h2 *Acidianus hospitalis* W1, complete genome. DNA, circular, 2,137,654 bp, [52], accession CP002535. Lineage: Archaea; Crenarchaeota; Thermoprotei; Sulfolobales; Sulfolobaceae; *Acidianus*; *A. hospitalis*; *A. hospitalis* W1.

h3 *Acidilobus saccharovorans* 345-15. Complete genome. DNA, circular, 2,137,654 bp, [52], accession CP001742.1. Lineage: Archaea; Crenarchaeota; Thermoprotei; Acidilobales; Acidilobaceae; *Acidilobus*; *A. saccharovorans*; *A. saccharovorans* 345-15. Anaerobic bacteria found in hot springs.

According to previous results, it will be shown that, as any other living organisms, these elementary organisms have DNA walks with fractal shape. The most important result, given in the following, is to show that anaerobic organisms, which should be understood as the most elementary in the first step of life, have the same symmetries on wavelet coefficients as more evolved organisms. In other words, life has to fulfill some constrained distribution of nucleotides in order to give rise to an organism, even at the most elementary step.

This chapter is organized as follows. Section 5.2 gives some remarks on archaea, and a preliminary analysis of DNA based on the indicator matrix is given in Section 5.3 together with some elementary approach to a fractal estimate of DNA sequences. Global parameters for a measure of complexity, such as entropy and fractal dimension, are discussed in Section 5.4.

A DNA complex representation and DNA (complex) walks are presented in Sections 5.5 and 5.6 respectively. It is proved that DNA complex walks are fractals, and they are compared with walks on pseudo random and deterministic complex sequences. Section 5.6 deals with wavelet analysis and shows the existence of symmetries in wavelet coefficients.

5.2 ARCHAEA

Archaea are a group of single-cell microorganisms having no cell nucleus or any other membrane-bound organelles within their cells. They are very similar to bacteria, due to the same size and shape (apart from a few exceptions) and the generally similar cell structure, but cell composition and organization set the archaea apart. However, for this reason they were initially wrongly named archaeabacteria, but this classification is now regarded as outdated. In fact, it has been observed that both the evolutionary history of archaea and their biochemistry has significant differences with regard to other forms of life. For this reason there are three phylogenetically distinct branches of evolutionary descent: archaea, bacteria, and eukaryotes.

Archaea [38, 65] exist in a broad range of habitats, and as a major part of global ecosystems may contribute up to 20% of Earth's biomass. The first examples of archaea were discovered in some environments with extreme life conditions and for this reason they were considered extremophiles [38, 40]. Indeed, some archaea survive to high temperatures, often above 100° C, as found in geysers, black smokers, and oil wells. Other common habitats include very cold habitats and highly saline, acidic, or alkaline water. However, archaea include some mesophiles living in mild conditions.

As a consequence of their extreme habitat, archaea are classified as:

   (i) Halophiles, living in hypersaline environments with a very high concentration of salt
  (ii) Thermophiles, living and growing in extremely hot environments that would kill most other organisms, with optimal temperature between 60 and 108°C
 (iii) Alkaliphiles, thriving in alkaline environments with a pH of 9–11
 (iv) Acidophiles, surviving in very acidic conditions

Beyond this coarse classification there are many more phyla because the vast majority of archaea have never been studied in the laboratory and their classification is continuously updated. Almost all archaea are very close to bacteria, but their biochemistry differs, significantly for example, their reliance on ether lipids in their cell membranes. More-over, archaea get their energy from a large number sources (sugars, ammonia, metal ions, hydrogen gas, sunlight, carbon) compared with the energy taken by eukaryotes.

Archaea were initially discovered in extreme environments but were subsequently found in almost all habitats so they are now recognized as the major part of life on Earth. It has also been recognized that the archaeal lineage may be the most ancient on Earth, so archaea and eukaryotes represent lines of descent that diverged early on from an ancestral colony of organisms. As we will see in the following, archaea DNA is much closer to random sequences than bacteria DNA (and other eukaryotes [17, 19–22]). It seems likely that their evolution started from the ancestral colony of an organism whose DNA followed by randomly combined sequences. It will be shown that more evolved organisms tend to assume a more organized distribution of nucleotides by increasing the distinctions from a random sequence.

5.3 PATTERNS ON INDICATOR MATRIX

The DNA of each living organism of a given species is a sequence of a specific number of base pairs (bp). Each base pair is defined on the four nucleotides:

$$A = \text{adenine} \qquad C = \text{cytosine} \qquad G = \text{guanine} \qquad T = \text{thymine}$$

The base pairs are distributed along a double helix with two opposite strands where opposite nucleotides fulfill the ligand rules of base pairs:

$$A \longleftrightarrow T \qquad C \longleftrightarrow G$$

where A and G are purines and C and T are pyrimidines.

In each DNA sequence some subsequences have special meaning, the most significant being triplets of adjacent bases called *codons*. Since the bases are 4, there are $4^3 = 64$ possible codons. Each codon synthesizes a specific amino acid, so that a sequence of codons defines a protein. Proteins are made from a set of 20 different amino acids and the amino acids are made by codons. There are only 20 amino acids; therefore, the correspondence codons to amino acids is many to one (see Table 5.1).

Let

$$\mathcal{A} \stackrel{\text{def}}{=} \{A, C, G, T\} \tag{5.1}$$

be the finite set (alphabet) of nucleotides and $x \in \mathcal{A}$ any member of the alphabet. A DNA sequence is the finite symbolic sequence

$$\mathcal{S} = \mathbb{N} \times \mathcal{A}$$

so that

$$\mathcal{S} \stackrel{\text{def}}{=} \{x_h\}_{h=1,\dots,N} \qquad N < \infty$$

where

$$x_h \stackrel{\text{def}}{=} (h, x) = x(h) \qquad (h = 1, 2, \dots, N; \ x \in \mathcal{A}) \tag{5.2}$$

with the nucleotide x at the position h.

TABLE 5.1 Correspondence of Codons to Amino Acids

	Amino Acid	Codon
1	M = methionine	ATG
2	E = glutamic acid	GAA, GAG
3	Q = glutamine	CAA, CAG
4	D = aspartic acid	GAT, GAC
5	R = arginine	CGT, CGC, CGA, CGG, AGA, AGG
6	T = threonine	ACT, ACC, ACA, ACG
7	N = asparagine	AAT, AAC
8	H = histidine	CAT, CAC
9	V = valine	GTT, GTC, GTA, GTG
10	G = glycine	GGT, GGC, GGA, GGG
11	L = leucine	TTA, TTG, CTT, CTC, CTA, CTG
12	S = serine	TCT, TCC, TCA, TCG, AGT, AGC
13	P = proline	CCT, CCC, CCA, CCG
14	F = phenylalanine	TTT, TTC
15	I = isoleucine	ATT, ATC, ATA
16	C = cysteine	TGT, TGC
17	A = alanine	GCT, GCC, GCA, GCG
18	K = lysine	AAA, AAG
19	Y = thyroxine	TAT, TAC
20	W = tryptophan	TGG
	Stop	TAA, TAG, TGA

In general, we can define an ℓ-length alphabet as follows: Let the ℓ-length DNA word defined by the ℓ-combination of the four nucleotides (5.1). For each fixed length ℓ there are 4^ℓ words; however, not all of them can be considered, from a biological point of view, as independent instances (see, e.g., Table 5.1). For this we define the ℓ-length alphabet as the set of ℓ-length independent words

$$\mathcal{A}_\ell \stackrel{\text{def}}{=} \{a_1, a_2, \ldots, a_{M_\ell}\} \qquad M_\ell \stackrel{\text{def}}{=} |\mathcal{A}_\ell| \leq 4^\ell$$

where $|\mathcal{A}_\ell|$ is the cardinality of the set $\mathcal{A}_\ell$ and

$$\ell \stackrel{\text{def}}{=} \text{length}(a_j) \qquad (j = 1, \ldots, M)$$

For instance, with $\ell = 1$, the alphabet is $\mathcal{A}_1 = \mathcal{A} = \{A, C, G, T\}$, and with $\ell = 3$ the alphabet is given by the 20 amino acids

$$\mathcal{A}_3 = \{M, E, Q, D, R, T, N, H, V, G, L, S, P, F, I, C, A, K, Y, W\}$$

each amino acid being represented by a three-length word of Table 5.1.

Let $\mathcal{S}_N$ be an N-length ordered sequence of nucleotides $\{A, C, G, T\}$ and $\mathcal{A}_\ell$ the chosen alphabet, a DNA sequence of words is the finite symbolic sequence

$$\mathcal{D}_\ell(S_N) = \mathbb{N} \times \mathcal{A}_\ell$$

so that

$$\mathcal{D}_\ell(S_N) \stackrel{\text{def}}{=} \{x_h\}_{h=1,\ldots,N} \qquad (x \in \mathcal{A}_\ell; \; N < \infty)$$

where

$$x_h \stackrel{\text{def}}{=} (h, x) \qquad (h = 1, 2, \ldots, N; \; x \in \mathcal{A}_\ell) \tag{5.3}$$

with the word x at the position h.

A simple way to measure the complexity of a sequence is to analyze the information content in the words of the sequence. In doing so, we need to define the probability distribution of words. The simplest probability distribution can be defined on $\mathcal{A}_1$ as explained in the following section.

5.3.1 Indicator Matrix

The two-dimensional (2D) indicator function, based on the one-dimensional (1D)-definition given in [61], is the map

$$u : \mathcal{S} \times \mathcal{S} \to \{0, 1\}$$

such that

$$u(x_h, \; x_k) \stackrel{\text{def}}{=} \begin{cases} 1 & \text{if} \quad x_h = x_k \\ 0 & \text{if} \quad x_h \neq x_k \end{cases} \qquad (x_h \in \mathcal{S}, \; x_k \in \mathcal{S}) \tag{5.4}$$

where

$$u(x_h, \; x_k) = u(x_k, \; x_h) \qquad u(x_h, \; x_h) = 1$$

According to (5.4), the indicator of an N-length sequence can be easily represented by the $N \times N$ sparse symmetric matrix of binary values $\{0, 1\}$ which results from the indicator matrix (see also [19–21])

$$u_{hk} \stackrel{\text{def}}{=} u(x_h, \; x_k) \qquad (x_h \in \mathcal{S}, \; x_k \in \mathcal{S}; h, k = 1, \ldots, N)$$

being, explicitly,

$\vdots$		$\vdots$	$\vdots$	$\vdots$	$\vdots$	$\vdots$	$\vdots$	$\vdots$	$\vdots$	$\vdots$	$\vdots$	$\cdot\cdot\cdot$
G		0	1	0	0	0	0	0	0	0	1	...
C		0	0	0	1	0	0	0	0	1	0	...
A		1	0	0	0	1	0	1	1	0	0	...
A		1	0	0	0	1	0	1	1	0	0	...
T		0	0	1	0	0	1	0	0	0	0	...
A		0	0	0	0	1	0	0	1	0	0	...
C		0	0	0	1	0	0	0	0	1	0	...
T		0	0	1	0	0	1	0	0	0	0	...
G		0	1	0	0	0	0	0	0	0	1	...
A		1	0	0	0	1	0	0	1	0	0	...
u_{hk}		A	G	T	C	A	T	A	A	C	G	...

This squared matrix can be plotted in two dimensions by putting a black dot when $u_{hk} = 1$ and a white spot when $u_{hk} = 0$ (Figure 5.1), thus giving rise to the 2D dot plot, which is a special case of the *recurrence plot* [28].

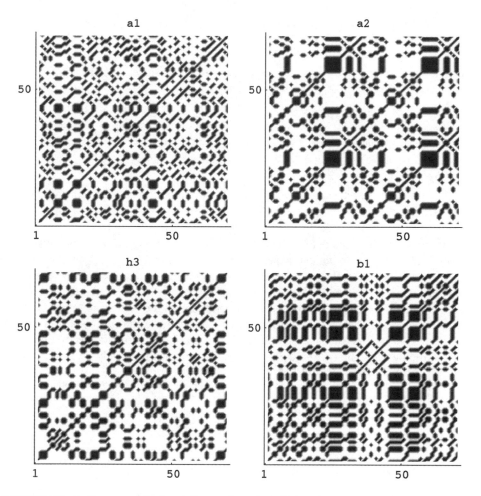

FIGURE 5.1 Indicator matrix for: (a1) pseudorandom 70-length sequence; (a2) pseudoperiodic 70-length sequence with period $\pi = 35$; (b1) 70-length DNA sequence of *Mycoplasma* KS1 bacteria; (h3) 70-length DNA sequence of *Acidilobus* archaea.

5.3.2 Test Sequences

In the following, in order to single out the main features of biological sequences, we will compare the DNA sequence with some test sequences:

1. The pseudorandom N-length sequence of nucleotides is the sequence $\{\mathcal{R}_i\}_{i=1,\ldots,N}^{\ell}$ where r_i is a symbol randomly chosen in the alphabet $\mathcal{A}_\ell$, for example, $\ell = 1$:

$$\{A, C, A, G, T, A, T, G, G, A, T, T, A, C, C, G, \ldots\}$$

2. The pseudoperiodic N-sequence of nucleotides with period π is the direct sum of a given π-length pseudorandom sequence such that $N = k\pi$, $k \in \mathbb{N}$, and $\mathcal{R}_i = \mathcal{R}_{i+\pi}$, for example,

$$\{A, C, A, G, A, C, A, G, A, C, A, G, A, C, A, G, \ldots\} \qquad (\pi = 4)$$

When $\pi = 1$, we have a pseudorandom sequence.

If we plot the indicator matrix of some bacteria and compare it with a pseudorandom sequence, we can see that (Figure 5.1):

1. There are some motifs which are repeated at different scales, such as in a fractal.
2. Empty spaces are more distributed than filled spaces in the sense that the matrix u_{hk} is a sparse matrix (having more 0's than 1's).
3. It seems that there are some square like islands where black spots are more concentrated; these islands show the persistence of a nucleotide (Figure 5.1, a2 and b1).
4. Pseudoperiodic sequences show the persistence of nucleotides along straight lines (Figure 5.1, a2).
5. The dot plot of archaea is very similar to the dot plot of a random sequence (Figure 5.1, a1 and h3).

Note that analysis of the dot plot shows that DNA sequences of a living organism look very similar (Figure 5.1) to random sequences built on the alphabet (5.1). However, the more primitive the sequence is, the more randomly distributed the nucleotides are. It seems that, as a consequence of the evolution, nucleotides move from a disordered aggregation toward a more organized structure. The organized sequence shows the increasing organization by the growing surface of islands in the dot plot. We can conjecture about the evolution that the challenge for self-organization might follow from random permutations of a primitive disordered sequence so that the organization (i.e., the complexity) is only the result of many arbitrary permutations of randomness.

5.4   MEASURE OF COMPLEXITY AND INFORMATION

Let $\mathcal{S}_N$ be an N-length ordered sequence of nucleotides and

$$p_x(h) \qquad x \in \mathcal{A}_1 = \{A, C, G, T\}$$

be the probability to find the nucleotide x at the position h, $1 \leq h \leq N$. According to (5.4), we define

$$a_h \stackrel{\text{def}}{=} \sum_{j=1}^{h} u_{Aj} \qquad c_h \stackrel{\text{def}}{=} \sum_{j=1}^{h} u_{Cj}$$

$$g_h \stackrel{\text{def}}{=} \sum_{j=1}^{h} u_{Gj} \qquad t_h \stackrel{\text{def}}{=} \sum_{j=1}^{h} u_{Tj} \qquad (1 \leq h \leq N)$$

as the number of nucleotides in the h-length segment of $\mathcal{S}_N$, so that

$$a_h + c_h + g_h + t_h = h \tag{5.5}$$

The corresponding frequencies are

$$\nu_x(h) \stackrel{\text{def}}{=} \frac{1}{h} \sum_{j=1}^{h} u_{xj} \qquad x \in A_1 \qquad (1 \leq h \leq N) \tag{5.6}$$

We can assume that for large sequences

$$p_x(h) \cong \nu_x(h) \tag{5.7}$$

Although the investigated organisms show some different distribution of frequencies, they all tend to some constant values (Figure 5.2), and the random sequence of nucleotides tends to an asymptotic value. However, it can be seen that this asymptotic value of the random sequence is underestimated compared with the biological sequences (Figure 5.2).

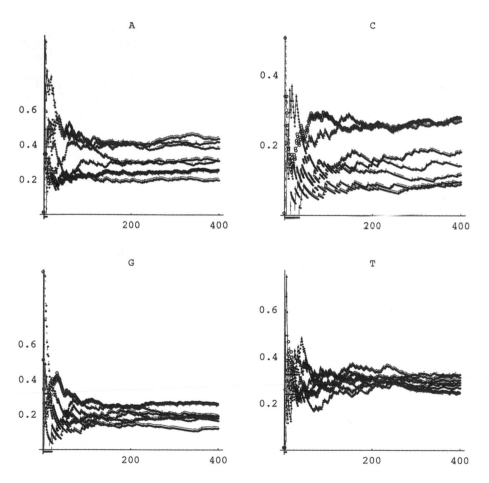

FIGURE 5.2 Frequency distribution (5.6) for bacteria b1, b2, b3; archaea h1, h2 h3; and random sequences (in bold).

5.4.1 Complexity

The existence of repeating motifs, periodicity, and patchiness [31, 32, 36] can be considered as a simple pattern to be easily found in each sequence, while nonrepetitiveness or singular behavior is taken as a characteristic feature of complexity. In order to have a measure of complexity, for an n-lenght sequence, it has been proposed [9] that

$$K = \log \Omega^{1/n}$$

with

$$\Omega = \frac{n!}{a_n! c_n! g_n! t_n!}$$

By using a sliding n-window [9] over the full DNA sequence, one can visualize the increasing complexity of the sequence (Figure 5.3).

This parameter tends to the asymptotic constant value (Figure 5.3)

$$K \cong 1.3$$

because the more nucleotides we add, the faster the information grows to a maximum value. We can see that at least in the initial stage there are some differences between pseudorandom sequences, primitive bacteria, and more evolved bacteria.

It is interesting to note that the archaea *Acidilobus* is closer to the pseudorandom sequence than to the pseudoperiodic one, so it seems that the nucleotide distributions in primitive biosequences are more likely random than pseudodeterministic. Moreover, the evolution reduces the complexity of the sequence as seen in *Mycoplasma* (Figure 5.3).

In Table 5.2 the complexity of the first 100-length segment of the DNA sequence is computed.

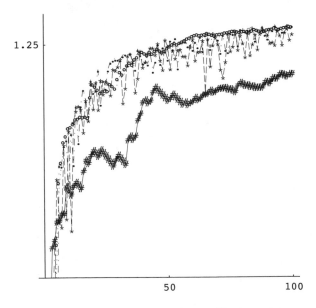

FIGURE 5.3 Complexity for the 100 bp of *M. putrefaciens* (#), *A. saccharovorans* (o), pseudorandom sequence (·), and pseudoperiodic sequence (∗).

TABLE 5.2 Complexity

Mycoplasma p. 1.151						
Mortierella v. —	—	—	—	1.285		
Blattabacterium —	1.197					
A. pernix —	—	1.212				
A. hospitalis —	—	—	1.231			
Acidilobus s. —	—	—	—	—	—	1.296
Pseudorandom —	—	—	—	—	1.295	

5.4.2 Fractal Dimension

The frequency distribution implies a corresponding frequency of correlation in the correlation matrix and in particular in the dot plot. By the box-counting algorithm [10, 11] it is possible to give a measure of the fractal dimension by computing the number of black dots in a square with increasing length which randomly cover the dot plot.

The fractal dimension is the average of the number $p(n)$ of 1's in the randomly taken $n \times n$ minors of the $N \times N$ correlation matrix u_{hk} or equivalently the number $p(n)$ of black dots in the randomly taken $n \times n$ squares over the dot plot:

$$D = \frac{1}{2N} \sum_{n=2}^{N} \frac{\log p(n)}{\log n}$$

Some interesting values can be observed in Table 5.3 where the fractal dimension on the first 100-length segment of the sequence is computed with an approximation up to 10^{-3}:

If we compare the fractal dimensions of the bacteria with the pseudorandom and pseudoperiodic sequences, we can see that the fractal dimension of nucleotide distribution ranges, for all variants, in the interval 1.28–1.30. However, those sequences which look more random (see, e.g., Figure 5.3) have more higher fractal dimension.

5.4.3 Entropy

In order to measure the heterogeneity of data, the entropy function has been considered and it gives a measure of the information content [1, 29, 50, 56, 57, 68]. In other words, we can roughly say that less information means larger uncertainty, and vice versa, more information leads to a more deterministic model. If we consider the DNA as a sequence of symbols carrying chemical–functional information, then it is interesting to investigate the information content in each sequence and for each alphabet defined on it.

TABLE 5.3 Fractal Dimensions

Mycoplasma p. 1.283							
Mortierella v. —	—	—	—	—	1.296		
Blattabacterium —	—	1.287					
A. pernix —	—	—	1.288				
A. hospitalis —	—	—	—	1.290			
Acidilobus s. —	—	—	—	—	—	1.297	
Pseudorandom —	—	—	—	—	—	—	1.298
Pseudoperiodic —	1.285						

As a measure of the information distribution we consider the normalized Shannon entropy [56, 68], which is defined, for a distribution over the alphabet $\mathcal{A}_\ell$, as

$$H(n) = -\frac{1}{\log \ell} \sum_{x \in \mathcal{A}_\ell} p_x(n) \times \begin{cases} \log p_x(n) & \text{if} \quad p_x(n) \neq 0 \\ 0 & \text{if} \quad p_x(n) = 0 \end{cases} \qquad (5.8)$$

where, for large sequences, $p_x(n)$ is given by (5.6) and (5.7):

$$p_x(n) = \frac{1}{n} \sum_{i=1}^{n} u_{xi} \qquad (x \in \mathcal{A}_\ell, \ 1 \leq n \leq N)$$

Since $\sum_{x \in \mathcal{A}_\ell} p_x(n) = 1 \ \forall n$ the main values of this function are as follows:

1. If $p_x(n) = 1$, $p_{x'}(n) = 0$ $(x \neq x' \in \mathcal{A}_\ell)$, then $H(n) = 0$. This happens when the information is concentrated in only one symbol.
2. If

$$p_x(n) = p_{x'}(n) = \frac{1}{\ell}$$

   then

$$H(n) = 1$$

   In this case the information is equally distributed over all symbols.
3. Assume

$$0 \leq H(n) \leq 1$$

   In general, the information content is distributed over the range [0, 1]

Therefore, entropy is a positive function ranging in the interval [0, 1]; the minimum value is obtained when the distribution is concentrated on a single symbol, while the maximum value is obtained when all symbols are equally distributed.

In particular, for higher values of n, according to the frequency definition of probability, entropy tends to the constant value 1 (see Figure 5.4) for both nucleotides and amino acids. However, the entropy plot of Figure 5.4 looks very similar to the complexity plot in Figure 5.3. In fact, it can be easily seen that:

TABLE 5.4 Shannon Entropy

M. putrefaciens	0.877					
M. verticillata	—		—	—	0.976	
Blattabacterium	—	0.911				
A. pernix	—	—	0.922			
A. hospitalis	—	—	—	0.937		
A. saccharovorans	—	—	—	—	—	0.984
Pseudorandom	—	—	—	—	—	0.984

Theorem 5.1 The entropy H and the measure of complexity K differ for a factor.

Proof In fact,

$$K = \frac{\log n! - \log a_n! - \log c_n! - \log g_n! - \log t_n!}{n}$$

$$= -\frac{\log a_n! + \log c_n! + \log g_n! + \log t_n!}{n} + \frac{\log n!}{n}$$

On the other hand,

$$H = -\frac{v_A(n)\log_2 v_A(n) + v_C(n)\log_2 v_C(n) + v_G(n)\log_2 v_G(n) + v_T(n)\log_2 v_T(n)}{\log 4}$$

that is,

$$H = -\left[\frac{a_n}{n}\log_2\frac{a_n}{n} + \frac{c_n}{n}\log_2\frac{c_n}{n} + \frac{g_n}{n}\log_2\frac{g_n}{n} + \frac{t_n}{n}\log_2\frac{t_n}{n}\right]\Big/\log 4$$

$$= -\left[a_n\log_2\frac{a_n}{n} + c_n\log_2\frac{c_n}{n} + g_n\log_2\frac{g_n}{n} + t_n\log_2\frac{t_n}{n}\right]\Big/(n\log 4)$$

$$= -\left[a_n\log_2 a_n + c_n\log_2 c_n + g_n\log_2 g_n + t_n\log_2 t_n\right.$$

$$\left. -\frac{a_n + c_n + g_n + t_n}{n\log 4}\log_2 n\right]$$

$$= -\frac{\log_2 a_n^{a_n} + \log_2 c_n^{c_n} + \log_2 g_n^{g_n} + \log_2 t_n^{t_n}}{n\log 4} + \frac{\log_2 n}{\log 4}$$

The proof follows from the equivalent behavior of the two functions x^x and $x!$ (it can also be easily seen by the equivalence of their corresponding Taylor series). ∎

In Table 5.4 the entropy computed on the first 100-length segment of the DNA sequences is given. It is interesting to compare it with Tables 5.2 and 5.3 to see that the same order is preserved.

As a consequence, in order to study the complexity of a sequence, we can equivalently use either the simple complexity parameter K or the Shannon entropy H (see, e.g., Figure 5.4).

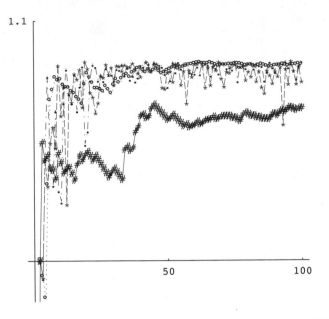

FIGURE 5.4 Entropy for first 100 bp of *M. putrefaciens* (#), *A. saccharovorans* (o), pseudorandom sequence (·), and pseudoperiodic sequence (∗).

5.5 COMPLEX ROOT REPRESENTATION OF DNA WORDS

The complex (digital) representation of a DNA sequence of words is the map of the symbolic sequence of words into a set of complex numbers and is defined as

$$\mathcal{D}_\ell(S_N) \xrightarrow{\rho} \mathbb{C}$$

such that for each $x_h \in \mathcal{D}_\ell(S_N)$ it is $\rho(x_h) \in \mathbb{C}$.

The complex root representation of the sequence S_N is the sequence $\mathcal{D}_\ell(S_N)$ of complex numbers $\{y_h\}_{h=1,\dots,N}$ defined as

$$y_h = \rho(x_h) \stackrel{\text{def}}{=} e^{2\pi i(j-1)/|\mathcal{A}_\ell|} \qquad (j = 1, \dots, |\mathcal{A}_\ell|, \; h = 1, \dots, N) \qquad (5.9)$$

with $i = \sqrt{-1}$ the imaginary unit. There follows that, independently of the alphabet,

$$|y_h| = |e^{2\pi i(j-1)/|\mathcal{A}_\ell|}| = 1 \qquad (\forall \ell; \; h = 1, \dots, N)$$

being all complex roots of the unit located on the unit circle of the complex plane $\mathbb{C}^1$.

For instance, with $\mathcal{A}_1 = \{A, C, G, T\}$, the cardinality of the alphabet is $|\mathcal{A}_1| = 4$ and

$$\begin{aligned}
\rho(A) &= e^{0/4} = 1 & j &= 1 \\
\rho(C) &= e^{\pi i/2} = i & j &= 2 \\
\rho(G) &= e^{\pi i} = -1 & j &= 3 \\
\rho(T) &= e^{\pi i 3/2} = -i & j &= 4
\end{aligned}$$

Analogously, with $\mathcal{A}_3 = \{M, E, \ldots, W\}$, $|\mathcal{A}_3| = 20$ and

$$\rho(M) = e^{0/20} = 1 \qquad\qquad\qquad j = 1$$

$$\rho(E) = e^{\pi i/10} = \tfrac{1}{4}\left[\sqrt{2(5+\sqrt{5})} + i(\sqrt{5}-1)\right] \qquad j = 2$$

$$\rho(Q) = e^{\pi i/5} = \tfrac{1}{4}\left[1 + \sqrt{5} + i\sqrt{2(5-\sqrt{5})}\right] \qquad j = 3$$

$$\vdots \qquad\qquad\qquad\qquad\qquad \vdots$$

$$\rho(W) = e^{\pi i 19/10} = \tfrac{1}{4}\left[\sqrt{2(5+\sqrt{5})} - i(\sqrt{5}-1)\right] \qquad j = 20$$

Therefore the DNA sequence

$$\{A,\ T,\ G,\ C,\ G, C,\ A,\ A, C,\ G,\ A,\ C,\ C,\ G,\ C, \ldots\}$$

is represented in the $\mathcal{A}_1$ alphabet by the complex sequence

$$\{1,\ -i,\ -1,\ i,\ -1,\ i,\ 1,\ 1,\ i,\ -1,\ 1,\ i,\ i,\ -1,\ i, \ldots\}$$

and in the $\mathcal{A}_3$ alphabet

$$\{M,\ R,\ N,\ D,\ R, \ldots\}$$

by

$$\{1,\ e^{\frac{2}{3}\pi i},\ e^{\frac{3}{5}\pi i},\ e^{\frac{3}{10}\pi i},\ e^{\frac{2}{3}\pi i}, \ldots\}$$

so that the representation is a map $\mathcal{S} \to \mathbb{C}^1$ and the time series

$$\mathbf{Y}_N \overset{\text{def}}{=} \mathcal{D}_1(\mathcal{S}_N) = \{y_h\}_{h-1,\ldots,N}$$

is a sequence of complex numbers

$$y_h = \xi_h + \eta_h i \qquad \xi_h = \Re(y_h) \qquad \eta_h = \Im(y_h)$$

with y_h given by (5.9).

5.5.1 Pseudorandom Sequence on Unit Circle

A pseudorandom (white-noise) complex sequence belonging to the unit circle can be defined as

$$R_n \overset{\text{def}}{=} (-1)^{r_n} i^{s_n} \tag{5.10}$$

with r_n, s_2, random values in the set $\{0, \mathbb{N}\}$ and it looks like

$$\{-1, i, 1, 1, -i, i, -1, -i, i, 1, -i, i, -1, i, 1, -i, -i, -i, -1, \ldots\}$$

Like the complex representation of DNA, each random complex value belongs to the unit circle since it is $|R_n| = 1$.

5.6   DNA WALKS

A DNA walk on the complex sequence $\mathbf{Y}_N$ is defined as the series $\mathbf{Z}_N = \{z_n\}_{n=1,\ldots,N}$,

$$z_n \stackrel{\text{def}}{=} \sum_{k=1,\ldots,n} y_k \qquad n = 1, \ldots, N \tag{5.11}$$

which is the cumulative sum on the DNA sequence representation

$$\left\{ y_1 \, , y_1 + y_2 \, , \ldots, \sum_{s=1}^{n} y_s, \ldots, \sum_{s=1}^{N} y_s \right\}$$

So the DNA walk is the complex values signal $\{Z_n\}_{n=0,\ldots,N-1}$ with

$$z_n = (a_n - g_n) + (t_n - c_n)i \tag{5.12}$$

where the coefficients a_n, g_n, t_n, c_n given by (5.4) fulfill the condition (5.5).

The DNA walk (DNA series) on a complex cardinal representation is a complex series as well. If we map the points

$$P_n = (\Re\left[z_n\right], \qquad \Im\left[z_n\right]) = (a_n - g_n, t_n - c_n) \qquad n = 0, \ldots, N - 1$$

whose coordinates are the real and the imaginary coefficients of each term of the DNA walk sequence, we obtain a cluster showing the existence of some patches or some kind of self-similarity (Figure 5.5) typical of fractals.

An alternative definition of random walk can be defined on the log series: The DNA walk on the complex sequence $\mathbf{Y}_N$ is defined as the series $\mathbf{Z}_N = \{z_n\}_{n=1,\ldots,N}$,

$$w_n \stackrel{\text{def}}{=} \sum_{k=1,\ldots,n} \log y_k \qquad n = 1, \ldots, N \tag{5.13}$$

which is equivalent to

$$w_n \stackrel{\text{def}}{=} \log \prod_{k=1,\ldots,n} y_k \qquad n = 1, \ldots, N \tag{5.14}$$

which is the cumulative product on the DNA sequence representation:

$$\left\{ y_1, y_1 y_2, \ldots, \prod_{s=1}^{n} y_s, \ldots, \prod_{s=1}^{N} y_s \right\}$$

5.6.1   Walks on Pseudorandom and Deterministic Complex Sequences

The random walk on the pseudorandom sequence is defined as

$$\sum_{n=1}^{\infty} (-1)^{r_n} i^{s_n}$$

A deterministic (periodic) sequence can be defined by assigning a given rule to the distribution of nucleotide, for example,

$$x_h = A \qquad x_{1+h} = C \qquad x_{2+h} = G \qquad x_{3+h} = T \qquad (h \in \mathbb{N})$$

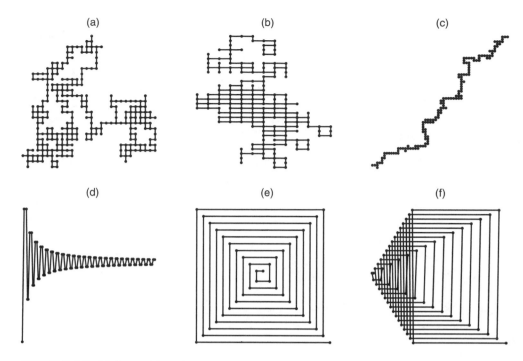

FIGURE 5.5 Walks on (a) random sequence, (b) *A. saccharovorans*, (c) *Mycoplasma*, and deterministic sequences (d) Equation (5.15), (e) Equation (5.16), (f) Equation (5.17).

More easily a deterministic walk can be defined directly on the complex representation (Figure 5.5d)

$$\sum_{n-1}^{\infty} z_n \stackrel{\text{def}}{=} \sum_{n-1}^{\infty}(-i)^n \sin\frac{\pi}{n} + 1 \tag{5.15}$$

or, more similar to a DNA sequence (Figure 5.5e),

$$\sum_{n=1}^{\infty} z_n \stackrel{\text{def}}{=} \sum_{n=1}^{\infty} i^n \tag{5.16}$$

and (Figure 5.5f)

$$\sum_{n=1}^{\infty} z_n \stackrel{\text{def}}{=} \sum_{n=1}^{\infty} i^n n + 1 \tag{5.17}$$

If we compare the DNA walks with walks on pseudorandom and deterministic sequences, it can be seen (Figure 5.5) that the fractal shape of a DNA walk (Figures 5.5c and 5.6) is completely different from corresponding walks on deterministic sequences. However, primitive archaea such as h3 (Figure 5.5b) are very similar to the random sequence (Figure 5.5a).

If we compare the DNA walks, we can also see some differences between bacteria and archaea (Figure 5.6). In particular, archaea seem to grow less than other bacteria (with the exception of b2). This difference can be emphasized by the absolute value of the DNA walk: $|z_n|$ (see Figure 5.7).

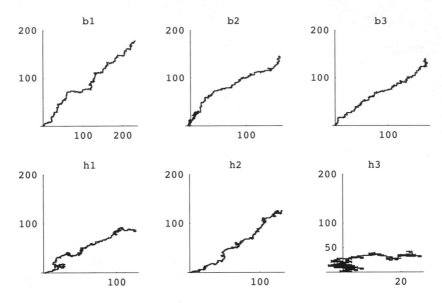

FIGURE 5.6 Walks on first 200 nucleotides: (b1) *M. putrefaciens*, (b2) *M. verticillata*, (b3) *Blattabacterium*, (h1) *A. pernix*, (h2) *A. hospitalis*, (h3) *A. saccharovorans*.

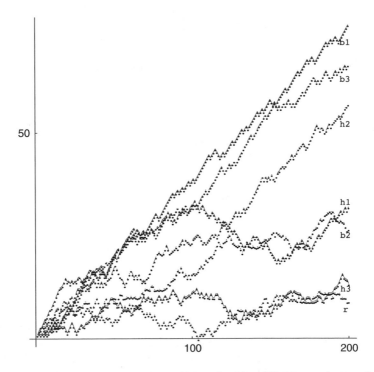

FIGURE 5.7 Absolute value of walks on first 200 nucleotides: (b1) *M. putrefaciens*, (b2) *M. verti-cillata*, (b3) *Blattabacterium*, (h1) *A. pernix*, (h2) *A. hospitalis*, (h3) *A. saccharovorans*, (r) random walk.

5.6.2 Variance

For a given sequence $\{Y_0,\ Y_1,\ldots,\ Y_{N-1}\}$ the variance is

$$\sigma^2 \stackrel{\text{def}}{=} \frac{1}{N}\sum_{i=0}^{N-1}Y_i^2 - \left(\frac{1}{N}\sum_{i=0}^{N-1}Y_i\right)^2 \tag{5.18}$$

and the variance at the distance $N-k$ is

$$\sigma_k^2 \stackrel{\text{def}}{=} \frac{1}{N-k}\sum_{i=0}^{N-k-1}Y_i^2 - \left(\frac{1}{N-k}\sum_{i=0}^{N-k-1}Y_i\right)^2 \tag{5.19}$$

From the variance the standard deviation follows immediately:

$$\sigma = \sqrt{\sigma^2} \tag{5.20}$$

It can be seen that the variance for the first 500 nucleotides of bacteria/archaea DNA sequences increases more slowly than the variance of the pseudorandom sequence (see Figure 5.8).

The autocorrelation at the distance $k(k=0,\ldots,N-1)$ is the sequence (see, e.g., [10])

$$c_k \stackrel{\text{def}}{=} \frac{1}{\sigma^2}\left(\frac{1}{N-k}\sum_{i=0}^{N-k-1}Y_iY_{i+k} - \frac{1}{(N-k)^2}\sum_{i=0}^{N-k-1}Y_i\sum_{i=0}^{N-k-1}Y_{i+k}\right) \tag{5.21}$$

with $k=0,\ldots,N-1$.

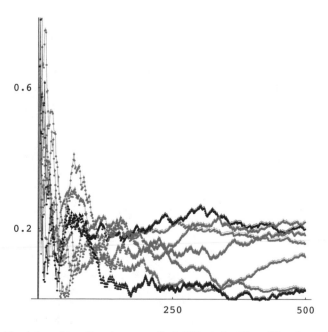

FIGURE 5.8 Absolute value of variance on first 500 nucleotides: *Blattabacterium* (black, upper line), pseudorandom sequence (black, lower line), and remaining intermediate gray lines for *M. putrefaciens, M. verticillata, A. pernix, A. hospitalis, A. saccharovorans.*

A simplified definition of correlation in the fragment $F - N$ has been given [27] as follows:

$$c_k \overset{\text{def}}{=} \sum_{i=F}^{N-1-k} \frac{1}{N - F - k} u_{x_i}(x_{i+1+k})$$

with the indicator given by (5.4).

5.7 WAVELET ANALYSIS

Wavelet analysis is a powerful method extensively applied to the analysis of biological signals [4, 6, 45, 69] aiming to single out the most significant parameters of complexity and heterogeneity in a time series and, in particular, in a DNA sequence. The main idea is that when the linear sequence of DNA nucleotides is converted into a time series, the time series can be treated as any other signals and undergo to the various methods of wavelet analysis of time series. Wavelet analysis is one of the most powerful methods for time series analysis [26, 55, 64] due to the localization property of wavelets, compared, for example, with Fourier methods [25]. Heterogeneity is due to the fact that in some fragments of DNA there exists a higher concentration of nucleotides C, G with poor distribution of A, T while, other fragments are more rich in A, T and poor in C, G. However, it is not clear if this heterogeneity has some functional meaning. It is expected that the distribution of nucleotides should follow some rules not yet discovered. In the following we will see that by the wavelet analysis we can find a conjecture about the distribution of nucleic acid.

5.7.1 Haar Wavelet Basis

The *Haar scaling function* $\varphi(x)$ is the characteristic function on $[0, 1]$; its family of translated and dilated scaling functions is defined as

$$\varphi_k^n(x) \overset{\text{def}}{=} 2^{n/2}\varphi(2^n x - k) \qquad (0 \le n,\ 0 \le k \le 2^n - 1)$$

$$\varphi(2^n x - k) = \begin{cases} 1 & x \in \Omega_k^n \\ 0 & x \notin \Omega_k^n \end{cases} \qquad \Omega_k^n \overset{\text{def}}{=} \left[\frac{k}{2^n}, \frac{k+1}{2^n} \right) \qquad (5.22)$$

The *Haar wavelet* family $\{\psi_k^n(x)\}$ is the orthonormal basis for the $L^2(\mathbb{R})$ functions [26]:

$$\psi_k^n(x) \overset{\text{def}}{=} 2^{n/2}\psi(2^n x - k) \qquad\qquad ||\psi_k^n(x)||_{L^2} = 1$$

$$\psi(2^n x - k) \overset{\text{def}}{=} \begin{cases} -1 & x \in \left[\dfrac{k}{2^n}, \dfrac{k+\frac{1}{2}}{2^n} \right) \\[2ex] 1 & x \in \left[\dfrac{k+\frac{1}{2}}{2^n}, \dfrac{k+1}{2^n} \right) \\[2ex] 0 & \text{elsewhere} \end{cases} \qquad (0 \le n,\ 0 \le k \le 2^n - 1) \qquad (5.23)$$

5.7.2 Discrete Haar Wavelet Transform

Let $\mathbf{Y} \equiv \{Y_i\}$ ($i = 0, \ldots, 2^M - 1$, $2^M = N < \infty$, $M \in \mathbb{N}$) be a real and square summable time series $\mathbf{Y} \in \mathbb{K}^N \subset \ell^2$ (where $\mathbb{K}$ is a real field) sampled at the *dyadic points* $x_i = i/(2^M - 1)$ in the interval restricted, for convenience and without restriction, to $\Omega = [0, 1]$. The *discrete Haar wavelet transform* is the $N \times N$ matrix $\mathcal{W}^N : \mathbb{K}^N \subset \ell^2 \to \mathbb{K}^N \subset \ell^2$ which maps the vector $\mathbf{Y}$ into the vector of *wavelet coefficients* $\boldsymbol{\beta}_N = \{\alpha, \ \beta_k^n\}$:

$$\mathcal{W}_N \mathbf{Y} = \boldsymbol{\beta}_N$$
$$\boldsymbol{\beta}_N \overset{\text{def}}{=} \{\alpha, \beta_0^0, \ldots, \beta_{2^{M-1}-1}^{M-1}\} \tag{5.24}$$
$$\mathbf{Y} \overset{\text{def}}{=} \{Y_0, \ Y_1, \ldots, \ Y_{N-1}\} \qquad (2^M = N)$$

Let the direct sum of matrices A, B be defined as

$$A \oplus B = \begin{pmatrix} A & \mathbf{0} \\ \mathbf{0} & B \end{pmatrix}$$

$\mathbf{0}$ being the matrix of zero elements. The $N \times N$ matrix $\mathcal{W}_N$ can be computed by the recursive product [14, 15]

$$\mathcal{W}_N \overset{\text{def}}{=} \prod_{k=1}^{M} \left[(P_{2^k} \oplus I_{2^M - 2^k})(H_{2^k} \oplus I_{2^M - 2^k}) \right] \qquad N = 2^M \tag{5.25}$$

of the direct sum of some elementary matrices (see, e.g., [19]).
For example, with $N = 4$, $M = 2$, it is [19]

$$\mathcal{W}_4 = \prod_{k=1,2} \left[(P_{2^k} \oplus I_{4-2^k})(H_{2^k} \oplus I_{4-2^k}) \right]$$
$$= [(P_2 \oplus I_2)(H_2 \oplus I_2)]_{k=1} \, [(P_4 \oplus I_0)(H_4 \oplus I_0)]_{k-2}$$

that is,

$$\mathcal{W}_4 = \begin{pmatrix} \frac{1}{2} & \frac{1}{2} & \frac{1}{2} & \frac{1}{2} \\ -\frac{1}{2} & -\frac{1}{2} & \frac{1}{2} & \frac{1}{2} \\ -\frac{1}{\sqrt{2}} & \frac{1}{\sqrt{2}} & 0 & 0 \\ 0 & 0 & -\frac{1}{\sqrt{2}} & \frac{1}{\sqrt{2}} \end{pmatrix} \tag{5.26}$$

5.7.3 Haar Wavelet Coefficients and Statistical Parameters

From Equation (5.24) with $M = 2$, $N = 4$, by explicit computation, we have

$$\alpha = \tfrac{1}{4}(Y_0 + Y_1 + Y_2 + Y_3)$$

and [17–19]

$$\beta_0^0 = \frac{1}{2}(Y_2 - Y_0 + Y_3 - Y_1)$$

$$\beta_0^1 = \frac{1}{\sqrt{2}}(Y_0 - Y_1)$$

$$\beta_1^1 = \frac{1}{\sqrt{2}}(Y_3 - Y_2)$$

When the wavelet coefficients are given, the above equations can be solved with respect to the original data. With $M = 2$, $N = 4$, we have, for example,

$$Y_0 = \alpha - \frac{\beta_0^0 + \sqrt{2}\beta_0^1}{2} \qquad Y_1 = \alpha - \frac{\beta_0^0 - \sqrt{2}\beta_0^1}{2}$$

$$Y_2 = \alpha + \frac{\beta_0^0 - \sqrt{2}\beta_1^1}{2} \qquad Y_3 = \alpha + \frac{\beta_0^0 + \sqrt{2}\beta_1^1}{2}.$$

Thus the first wavelet coefficient α represents the average value of the sequence and the other coefficients β the finite differences. The wavelet coefficients β, also called details coefficients, are strictly connected with the first-order properties of the discrete-time series.

5.7.4 Hurst Exponent

Concerning the variance, from definition (5.18), in terms of wavelet coefficients, we obtain by direct computation the expression

$$\sigma^2 = \frac{1}{N} \sum_{n=0}^{M-1} \sum_{k=0}^{2^n-1} \left(\beta_k^n\right)^2 \qquad (N = 2^M). \tag{5.27}$$

It has been observed [7] that for scale-invariant functions the standard deviation (5.20) as a function of the scale n is

$$\sigma(2^n) = \sigma(2^0)2^{n(H-1)} \tag{5.28}$$

where H is the Hurst exponent. So in a log-log plot

$$\log_2 \sigma(2^n) = n(H - 1)\log_2 \sigma(2^0)$$

we obtain a straight line whose slope gives an estimate of H.

The Hurst exponent, in terms of wavelet coefficients, can be evaluated by the following [19]:

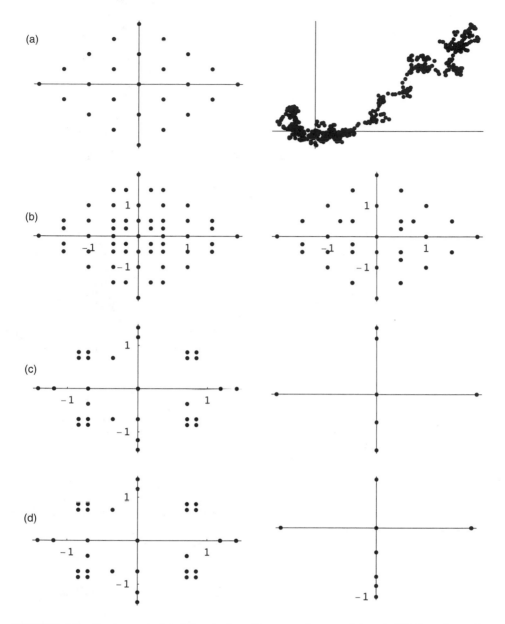

FIGURE 5.9 Cluster analysis of fourth short Haar wavelet transform of 4000-length random sequence (left) and its 2000-length random walk (right): (a) (α, α^*); (b) $(\beta_0^0, \beta_0^{*0})$; (c) $(\beta_0^1, \beta_0^{*1})$; (d) $(\beta_1^1, \beta_1^{*1})$.

Theorem 5.2 The Hurst exponent is given in terms of wavelet coefficients by

$$
H = \frac{1}{2} + \begin{cases} \dfrac{1}{n}\log_2 \left| \dfrac{\left[\sum_{k=0}^{2^n-1}(\beta_k^n)^2\right]^{1/2}}{\beta_0^0} \right| & \text{if} \quad \sum_{k=0}^{2^n-1}(\beta_k^n)^2 \neq 0 \\[4mm] 0 & \text{if} \quad \sum_{k=0}^{2^n-1}(\beta_k^n)^2 = 0 \end{cases} \tag{5.29}
$$

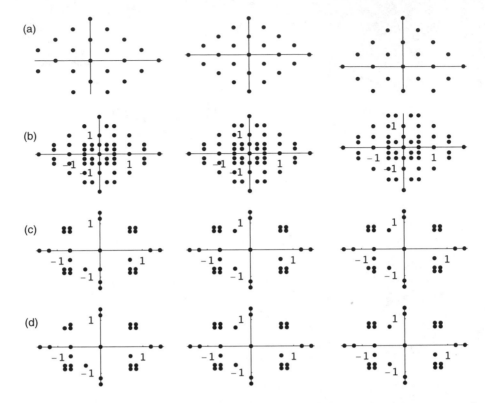

FIGURE 5.10 Cluster analysis of fourth short Haar wavelet transform of complex representation for first 4000 nucleotides of (from left to right) (b1) *M. putrefaciens*; (b2) *M. verticillata*; (b3) *Blattabacterium* in planes: (a) (α, α^*); (b) $\left(\beta_0^0, \beta_0^{*0}\right)$; (c) $\left(\beta_0^1, \beta_0^{*1}\right)$; (d) $\left(\beta_1^1, \beta_1^{*1}\right)$.

Proof The proof is given in [19]. ∎

However, since the detail coefficients are very small, compared with β_0^0, this parameter does not change too much for the bacteria/archaea and random sequence, being (more or less) about 0.51 ± 0.01.

5.8 ALGORITHM OF SHORT HAAR DISCRETE WAVELET TRANSFORM

In order to reduce the computational complexity of the wavelet transform (5.24), (5.25), the sequence **Y** can be sliced into subsequences and the wavelet transform is applied to each slice. With the reduced Haar transform [17–19] it is possible to reduce the number of basis functions and the computational complexity.

Let the set $\mathbf{Y} = \{Y_i\}_{i=0,\ldots,N-1}$ of N data segmented into $\sigma = N/p$ $(1 \leq \sigma \leq N)$ segments of $p = 2^m$ data:

$$\mathbf{Y} = \{Y_i\}_{i=0,\ldots,N-1} = \bigoplus_{s=0}^{\sigma-1} \mathbf{Y}^s \qquad \mathbf{Y}^s \equiv \{Y_{sp}, Y_{sp+1}, \ldots, Y_{sp+p-1}\}$$

$$(s = 0, \ldots, N-p; \ 1 \leq p \leq N)$$

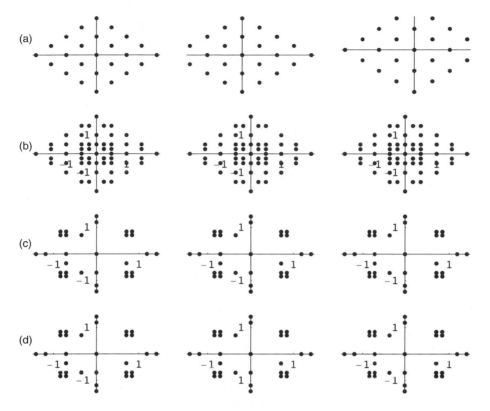

FIGURE 5.11 Cluster analysis of fourth short Haar wavelet transform of complex representation for first 4000 nucleotides of (from left to right) (h1) *Aeropyrum*; (h2) *Acidianus*; (h3) *A. saccharovorans* in planes: (a) (α, α^*); (b) $\left(\beta_0^0, \beta_0^{*0}\right)$; (c) $\left(\beta_0^1, \beta_0^{*1}\right)$; (d) $\left(\beta_1^1, \beta_1^{*1}\right)$.

The p-parameter short (reduced or windowed) discrete Haar wavelet transform $\mathcal{W}^{p,\sigma}\mathbf{Y}$ of $\mathbf{Y}$ is defined as

$$\mathcal{W}^{p,\sigma} \equiv \bigoplus_{s=0}^{\sigma-1} \mathcal{W}^p \qquad \mathbf{Y} = \bigoplus_{s=0}^{\sigma-1} \mathbf{Y}^s$$

$$\mathcal{W}^{p,\sigma}\mathbf{Y} = \left(\bigoplus_{s=0}^{\sigma-1} \mathcal{W}^p\right) \qquad \mathbf{Y} = \left(\bigoplus_{s=0}^{\sigma-1} \mathcal{W}^p \mathbf{Y}^s\right)$$

$$\mathcal{W}^{2^m}\mathbf{Y}^s = \left\{\alpha_0^{0(s)}, \ \beta_0^{0(s)}, \ \beta_0^{1(s)}, \ \beta_1^{1(s)}, \dots, \beta_{2^{m-1}-1}^{m-1(s)}\right\} \qquad (2^m = p)$$

For example, the reduced wavelet transform $\mathcal{W}^{4,2}$ is given as

$$\mathcal{W}^{4,2} = \mathcal{W}^4 \oplus \mathcal{W}^4$$

that is,

$$
\mathcal{W}^{4,2} =
\begin{pmatrix}
\frac{1}{2} & \frac{1}{2} & \frac{1}{2} & \frac{1}{2} & 0 & 0 & 0 & 0 \\[6pt]
-\frac{1}{2} & -\frac{1}{2} & \frac{1}{2} & \frac{1}{2} & 0 & 0 & 0 & 0 \\[6pt]
-\frac{1}{\sqrt{2}} & \frac{1}{\sqrt{2}} & 0 & 0 & 0 & 0 & 0 & 0 \\[6pt]
0 & 0 & -\frac{1}{\sqrt{2}} & \frac{1}{\sqrt{2}} & 0 & 0 & 0 & 0 \\[6pt]
0 & 0 & 0 & 0 & \frac{1}{2} & \frac{1}{2} & \frac{1}{2} & \frac{1}{2} \\[6pt]
0 & 0 & 0 & 0 & -\frac{1}{2} & -\frac{1}{2} & \frac{1}{2} & \frac{1}{2} \\[6pt]
0 & 0 & 0 & 0 & -\frac{1}{\sqrt{2}} & \frac{1}{\sqrt{2}} & 0 & 0 \\[6pt]
0 & 0 & 0 & 0 & 0 & 0 & -\frac{1}{\sqrt{2}} & \frac{1}{\sqrt{2}}
\end{pmatrix}
\tag{5.30}
$$

5.8.1 Clusters of Wavelet Coefficients

For the ($N = 2^M$)-length complex vector $\mathbf{Y}$ the wavelet transform is applied to the real part $\mathcal{W}^N \Re(\mathbf{Y})$ and to the imaginary part $\mathcal{W}^N \Im(\mathbf{Y})$ and gives a cluster of N points in the product of 2D space.

$$
\prod_{i=1}^{N} \mathbb{R}_i^2 : (\alpha, \alpha^*) \times \left(\beta_0^0, \beta^*{}_0^0\right) \times \left(\beta_0^1, \beta^*{}_0^1\right) \times \cdots \times \left(\beta_{2^{M-1}-1}^{M-1}, \beta^*{}_{2^{M-1}-1}^{M-1}\right)
$$

where the star denotes the wavelet coefficients of $\Im(\mathbf{Y})$. By using, instead, the p-parameter short Haar wavelet transform, we can analyze the cluster of points

$$
\left(\mathcal{W}^p \Re(\mathbf{Y}^s), \mathcal{W}^p \Im(\mathbf{Y}^s)\right) \quad s = 0, \ldots, \sigma = N/p
$$

in the $2p$-dimensional space $\mathbb{R}^p \times \mathbb{R}^p$, that is,

$$
(\alpha, \alpha^*), \left(\beta_0^0, \beta^*{}_0^0\right), \ldots, \left(\beta_{2^{p-1}-1}^{p-1}, \beta^*{}_{2^{p-1}-1}^{p-1}\right)
$$

For the complex sequence $\{y_k\}_{k=0,\ldots,N-1} = \{\xi_k + i\,\eta_k\}_{k=0,\ldots,N-1}$, we can consider the correlations (if any) between the wavelet coefficients of the real part $\{\xi_k\}_{k=0,\ldots,N-1}$ against the imaginary coefficients $\{\eta_k\}_{k=0,\ldots,N-1}$. This has been summarized as the cluster algorithm [19].

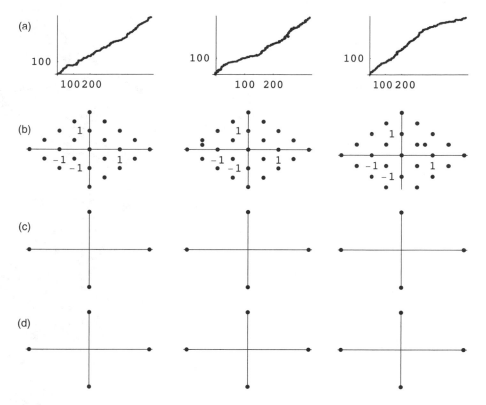

FIGURE 5.12   Cluster analysis of fourth short Haar wavelet transform of complex representation for DNA walk on first 2000 nucleotides of (from left to right) (b1) *M. putrefaciens*; (b2) *M. verticillata*; (b3) *Blattabacterium* in planes: (a) (α, α^*); (b) $\left(\beta_0^0, \beta_0^{*0}\right)$; (c) $\left(\beta_0^1, \beta_0^{*1}\right)$; (d) $\left(\beta_1^1, \beta_1^{*1}\right)$.

This algorithm enables us to construct clusters of wavelet coefficients and to study the correlation between the real and imaginary coefficients of the DNA representation and DNA walk, as given in the following section.

5.8.2 Cluster Analysis of Wavelet Coefficients of Complex DNA Representation

Let us first compute the clusters of wavelet coefficients for the random sequence (5.10). As can be seen, the wavelet coefficients for both the sequence and its series range in some discrete set of values (see Figure 5.9).

The cluster algorithm applied to the complex representation sequence shows that the values of the wavelet coefficients belong to some discrete finite sets (Figure 5.9).

For each complex DNA representation there are two sets of wavelet coefficients which correspond to the real and complex coefficients of the complex values of (5.11) and (5.12). However, even if the real and complex coefficients of the DNA walk show some nonlinear patterns (Figure 5.9a, right) the detail coefficients range in some discrete sets of values, in the sense that they jump from one value to another (see, e.g., Figure 5.9).

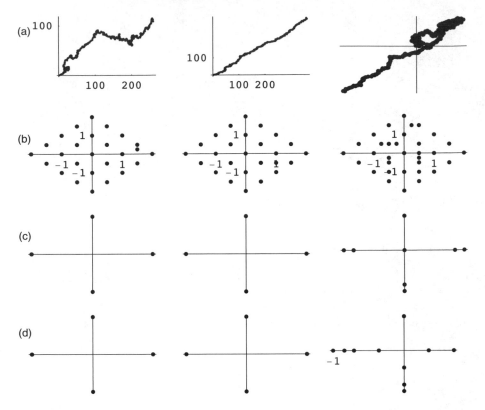

FIGURE 5.13   Cluster analysis of fourth short Haar wavelet transform of complex representation for DNA walk on first 2000 nucleotides of (from left to right) (h1) *Aeropyrum*; (h2) *Acidianus*; (h3) *A. saccharovorans* in planes: (a) (α, α^*); (b) $(\beta_0^0, \beta^{*0}_0)$; (c) $(\beta_0^1, \beta^{*1}_0)$; (d) $(\beta_1^1, \beta^{*1}_1)$.

If we compare the clusters of pseudorandom sequence (Figure 5.9, left) with the clusters of DNA sequences (Figures 5.10 and 5.11), we can see that the set of wavelet coefficients range in the same sets of values. In other words, there is no way to recognize a pseudorandom sequence from a DNA sequence.

Moreover, it should be noted that all wavelet coefficients are distributed on symmetric grids (Figures 5.9–5.11). Even if the DNA representation looks like the pseudorandom sequence (5.10), the wavelet (detail) coefficients are quantized and symmetrically distributed.

Some very small differences can be detected in the comparison of random walks [Figures 5.9 (right column) and 5.12 and 5.13]. It can be seen that the smoother is the walk, the smaller is the variability of detail coefficients. In particular, note that the coefficient β_0^0 (Figures 5.9b, 5.12b, and 5.13b) shows that when the sequence is closer to the random sequence, there appear some more spots. Less spots seem to refer to more evolved sequences. Also the finer structures of the detail coefficients β_0^1, β_1^1 tell us that the random walk (and DNA walks close to it as the h3 sequence) has more spots in the phase plane.

Figure 5.14 gives the wavelet coefficients of some sequences obtained by comparing the differences (discrete derivative) of the original sequence. Also here we can see some symmetries; however, random sequences show a higher variability.

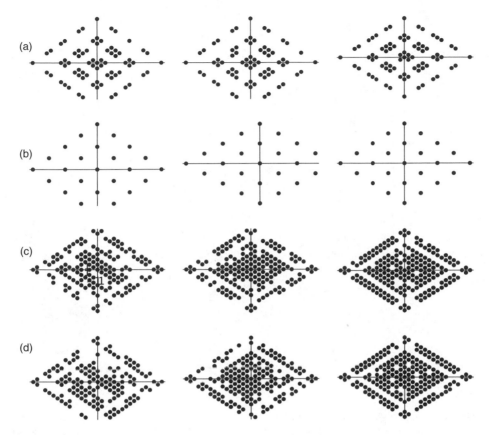

FIGURE 5.14 Cluster analysis of fourth short Haar wavelet transform of derivatives of 2000-length sequence of (from left to right) (b1) *M. putrefaciens*; (h3) *A. saccharovorans*; (rr) pseudorandom sequence in planes: (a) (α, α^*); (b) $\left(\beta_0^0, \beta^{*0}_0\right)$; (c) $\left(\beta_0^1, \beta^{*1}_0\right)$; (d) $\left(\beta_1^1, \beta^{*1}_1\right)$.

We can say that the distribution of nucleotides is done in a such a way that:

(a) Any random permutation of the DNA sequence increases the number of detail coefficients (see Figure 5.15).

(b) Since the wavelet coefficients are computed on a four-length window, nucleotides are correlated on a short range in the sense that when the first nucleotide is given the following three nucleotides have to be chosen in a such a way that the number of detail coefficients is the least (compared with random sequences)

Thus we conjecture that when the first nucleotide in a DNA sequence is chosen the following three nucleotides cannot be arbitrarily given since they have to be selected in a such a way that the number of wavelet coefficients is the minimum.

5.9 CONCLUSIONS

In this chapter the complexity of DNA symbolic sequences has been investigated. In particular, the main global parameters, such as complexity, fractal dimension, and entropy,

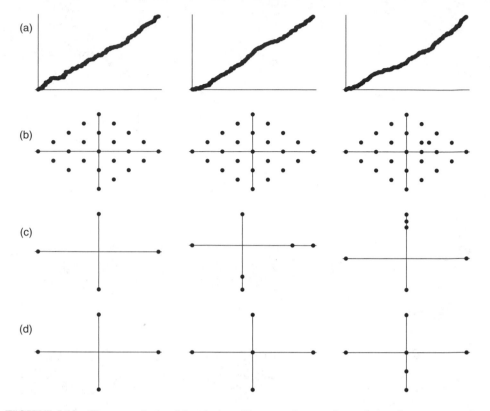

FIGURE 5.15 Cluster analysis of fourth short Haar wavelet transform of complex representation for DNA walk on first 2000 nucleotides of (from left to right) (b1) *M. putrefaciens*; (r1) random permutation of b1; (r2) random permutation of b1 in planes: (a) (α, α^*); (b) $(\beta_0^0, \beta_0^{*0})$; (c) $(\beta_0^1, \beta_0^{*1})$; (d) $(\beta_1^1, \beta_1^{*1})$.

have been explicitly computed and compared for some sequences of bacteria, archaea and pseudorandom sequences. It has been observed that they all agree in a classification of complexity for the sequences from the random sequence and archaea toward the more evolved (from a biological point of view) sequences of bacteria. However, in order to draw some conclusion from these parameters one has to compare many different sequences. On the other hand, some archaea are very similar to random sequences. By using wavelet analysis on the walks on DNA and random walks, it has been observed that, as expressed in the final conjecture, the number of wavelet coefficients for DNA is the minimum, thus making it possible to recognize a DNA sequence without any comparison with other sequences. This seems to be an intrinsic parameter to be used for DNA classification. It has been also noted that DNA sequences and random sequences look very similar, only the analysis of the DNA walks and random walks make it possible to single out the living organism from a chaotic assembly of nucleotides. From the analysis of these DNA sequences we can also conjecture that the evolution from a biological point of view could be the result of random permutations from a primitive random sequence. There is a sequence of random permutations until a steady state is reached. As a steady state of the nucleotide distribution is taken the sequence where the number of wavelet coefficients has reached the minimum value.

REFERENCES

1. P. R. Aldrich, R. K. Horsley, and S. M. Turcic. Symmetry in the language of gene expression: A survey of gene promoter networks in multiple bacterial species and non-σ regulons. *Symmetry*, 3:1–20, 2011.

2. M. Altaiski, O. Mornev, and R. Polozov. Wavelet analysis of DNA sequence. *Genet. Anal.*, 12:165–168, 1996.

3. D. Anastassiou. Frequency-domain analysis of biomolecular sequence. *Bioinformatics*, 16(12):1073–1081, 2000.

4. A. Arneado, E. Bacry, P. V. Graves, and J. F. Muzy. Characterizing long-range correlations in DNA sequences from wavelet analysis. *Phys. Rev. Lett.*, 74:3293–3296, 1995.

5. A. Arneado, Y. D'Aubenton-Carafa, E. Bacry, P. V. Graves, J. F. Muzy, and C. Thermes. Wavelet based fractal analysis of DNA sequences? *Phys. D*, 96:291–320, 1996.

6. A. Arneado, Y. D'Aubenton-Carafa, B. Audit, E. Bacry, J. F. Muzy, and C. Thermes. What can we learn with wavelets about DNA sequences? *Phys. A*, 249:439–448, 1998.

7. B. Audit, C. Vaillant, A. Arneodo, Y. d'Aubenton-Carafa, and C. Thermes. Long range correlations between DNA bending sites: Relation to the structure and dynamics of nucleosomes. *J. Mol. Biol.*, 316:903–918, 2002.

8. Bai-Lin Hao. Fractals from genomes-exact solutions of a biology inspired problem. *Phys. A*, 282:225–246, 2000.

9. J. A. Berger, S. K. Mitra, M. Carli, and A. Neri. Visualization and analysis of DNA sequences using DNA walks. *J. Franklin Inst.*, 341:37–53, 2004.

10. P. Bernaola-Galván, R. Román-Roldán, and J. L. Oliver. Compositional segmentation and long-range fractal correlations in DNA sequences. *Phys. Rev. E*, 55(5):5181–5189, 1996.

11. C. L. Berthelsen, J. A. Glazier, and M. H. Skolnick. Global fractal dimension of human DNA sequences treated as pseudorandom walks. *Phys. Rev. A*, 45(12):8902–8913, 1992.

12. B. Borstnik, D. Pumpernik, and D. Lukman. Analysis of apparent $1/f^\alpha$ spectrum in DNA sequences. *Europhys Lett.*, 23:389–394, 1993.

13. S. V. Buldyrev, A. L. Goldberger, A. L. Havlin, C.-K. Peng, M. Simons, F. Sciortino, and H. E. Stanley. Long-range fractal correlations in DNA. *Phys. Rev. E*, 51:5084–5091, 1995.

14. C. Cattani. Haar wavelet based technique for sharp jumps classification. *Math. Comput. Model.*, 39:255–279, 2004.

15. C. Cattani. Haar wavelets based technique in evolution problems. *Proc. Estonian Acad. Sci. Phys. Math.*, 53(1):45–63, 2004.

16. C. Cattani and J. J. Rushchitsky. Wavelet and wave analysis as applied to materials with micro or nanostructure, series on advances in mathematics for applied sciences. *World Sci. Singapore*, 74, 2007.

17. C. Cattani. Complex representation of DNA sequences. In *Communications in Computer and Information Science, Proceedings of the "Bioinformatics Research and Development Second International Conference (BIRD 2008)* Vienna, Austria, July 7–9, 2008, M. Elloumi et al. (Eds). Springer-Verlag, Berlin and Heidelberg, CCIS 13, 2008 pp. 528–537.

18. C. Cattani. Harmonic wavelet approximation of random, fractal and high frequency signals. *Telecommun. Syst.*, 43(3–4):207–217, 2010.

19. C. Cattani. Wavelet algorithms for DNA analysis. In *Algorithms in Computational Molecular Biology: Techniques, Approaches and Applications*, Wiley Series in Bioinformatics, M. Elloumi and A. Y. Zomaya (Eds.). Wiley, Hoboken, NJ, 2010, pp. 799–842.

20. C. Cattani. Fractals and hidden symmetries in DNA. *Math. Prob. Eng.*, 2010:1–31, 2010.

21. C. Cattani and G. Pierro. Complexity on acute myeloid leukemia mRNA transcript variant. *Math. Prob. Eng.*, 2011:1–16, 2011.

22. C. Cattani, G. Pierro, and G. Altieri, Entropy and multi-fractality for the myeloma multiple TET 2 gene. *Math. Prob. Eng.*, 2011:1–17, 2011.

23. E. A. Cheever, D. B. Searls, W. Karanaratne, and G. C. Overton. Using signal processing techniques for DNA sequence comparison. *Proc. 15th Annu. Northeast Bioeng. Conf.*, 15:173–174, 1989.

24. P. D. Cristea. Large scale features in DNA genomic signals. *Signal Process.*, 83:871–888, 2003.

25. E. Coward. Equivalence of two fourier methods for biological sequences. *J. Math. Biol.*, 36:64–70, 1997.

26. I. Daubechies. *Ten Lectures on Wavelets*. SIAM, Philadelphia, PA, 1992.

27. G. Dodin, P. Vandergheynst, P. Levoir, C. Cordier, and L. Marcourt. Fourier and wavelet transform analysis, a tool for visualizing regular patterns in DNA sequences. *J. Theor. Biol.*, 206:323–326, 2000.

28. J. P. Eckmann, S. O. Kamphorst, and D. Ruelle. Recurrence plots of dynamical systems. *Europhys. Lett.*, 5:973–977, 1987.

29. R. Ferrer-i-Cancho and N. Forns. The self-organization of genomes. *Complexity*, 15:34–36, 2010.

30. J. P. Fitch and B. Sokhansanj. Genomic engineering: Moving beyond DNA sequence to function. *Proc. IEEE*, 88(12):1949–1971, 2000.

31. M. A. Gates. Simpler DNA sequence representations. *Nature*, 316:219, July 18, 1985.

32. M. A. Gates. A simple way to look at DNA. *J. Theor. Biol.*, 119(3):319–328, 1986.

33. H. Gee. A journey into the genome: What's there. *Nature*, 12, February 2001.

34. K. Hu, P. Ch. Ivanov, Z. Chen, P. Carpena, and H. E. Stanley. Effect of trends on detrended fluctuation analysis. *Phys. Rev. E*, 64:011114, 2001.

35. X.-Y. Jiang, D. Lavenier, and S. S.-T. Yau, Coding region prediction based on a universal DNA sequence representation method. *J. Computat. Biol.*, 15(10):1237–1256, 2008.

36. E. Hamori and J. Ruskin. H curves, a novel method of representation of nucleotide series especially suited for long DNA sequences. *J. Biol. Chem.*, 258(2):1318–1327, 1983.

37. H. Herzel, E. N. Trifonov, O. Weiss, and I. Grosse. Interpreting correlations in biosequences. *Phys. A*, 249:449–459, 1998.

38. J. L. Howland. *The Surprising Archaea*. Oxford University Press, New York, 2000.

39. S. Karlin and V. Brendel. Patchiness and correlations in DNA sequence. *Science*, 259:677–680, 1993.

40. M. T. Madigan and B. L. Marrs. Extremophiles. *Sci. Am.*, 4:82–87, 1997.

41. M. Li. Fractal time series—A tutorial review. *Math. Prob. Eng.*, 2010:1–26, 2010.

42. M. Li and J.-Y. Li. On the predictability of long-range dependent series. *Math. Prob. Eng.*, 2010:1–9, 2010.

43. M. Li and S. C. Lim. Power spectrum of generalized Cauchy process. *Telecommun. Syst.*, 43(3–4):219–222, 2010.

44. W. Li. The complexity of DNA: The measure of compositional heterogenity in DNA sequence and measures of complexity. *Complexity*, 3:33–37, 1997.

45. W. Li. The study of correlation structures of DNA sequences: A critical review. *Comput. Chem.*, 21(4):257–271, 1997.

46. W. Li and K. Kaneko. Long-range correlations and partial $1/f^\alpha$ spectrum in a noncoding DNA sequence. *Europhys. Lett.*, 17:655–660, 1992.

47. J. G. McNally and D. Mazza. Fractal geometry in the nucleus. *EMBO J.*, 29:2–3, 2010.

48. K. Metze, I. Lorand-Metze, N. J. Leite, and R. L. Adam. Goodness-of-fit of the fractal dimension as a prognostic factor. *Cell. Oncol.*, 31:503–504, 2009.

49. K. Metze. Fractal dimension of chromatin and cancer prognosis. *Epigenomics*, 2(5):601–604, 2010.

50. T. Misteli. Self-organization in the genome. *Proc. Natl. Acad. Sci. USA*, 106:6885–6886, 2009.

51. K. B. Murray, D. Gorse, and J. M. Thornton. Wavelet transform for the characterization and detection of repeating motifs. *JMB, J. Mol. Biol.*, 316:341–363, 2002.

52. National Center for Biotechnology Information. `http://www.ncbi.nml.nih.gov/GenBank`; Genome Browser, `http://genome.ucsc.edu`; European Informatics Institute, `http://www.ebi.ac.uk`; Ensembl, `http://www.ensembl.org`.

53. C.-K. Peng, S. V. Buldryev, A. L. Goldberg, S. Havlin, F. Sciortino, M. Simons and H. E. Stanley. Long-range correlatins in nucleotide sequences. *Nature*, 356:168–170, 1992.

54. C.-K. Peng, S. V. Buldryev, S. Havlin, M. Simons, H. E. Stanley and A. L. Goldberg. Mosaic organization of DNA nucleotides. *Phys. Rev. E*, 49:1685–1689, 1994.

55. D. B. Percival and A.T. Walden. *Wavelet Methods for Time Series Analysis.* Cambridge University Press, 2000.

56. C. E. Shannon. A mathematical theory of communication. *Bell Syst. Tech. J.*, 27:379–423, 623–656, 1948.

57. R. V. Solé. Genome size, self-organization and DNA's dark matter. *Complexity*, 16:20–23, 2010.

58. M. Takahashi. A fractal model of chromosomes and chromosomal DNA replication. *J. Theor. Biol.*, 141:117–136, 1989.

59. A. A. Tsonis, P. Kumar, J. B. Elsner, and P. A. Tsonis. Wavelet analysis of DNA sequences. *Phys. Rev. E*, 53:1828–1834, 1996.

60. P. P. Vaidyanathan and B.-J. Yoon. The role of signal-processing concepts in genomics and proteomics. *J. Franklin Inst.*, 341:111–135, 2004.

61. R. F. Voss. Evolution of long-range fractal correlations and $1/f$ noise in DNA base sequences. *Phys. Rev. Lett.*, 68(25):3805–3808, 1992.

62. R. F. Voss. Long-range fractal correlations in DNA introns and exons. *Fractals*, 2:1–6, 1992.

63. O. Weiss and H. Herzel. Correlations in protein sequences and property codes. *J. Theor. Biol.*, 190:341–353, 1998.

64. G. Wornell. *Signal Processing with Fractals: A Wavelet-Based Approach*. Prentice-Hall, Englewood Cliffs, NJ, 1996.

65. C. R. Woese and G. E. Fox. Phylogenetic structure of the prokaryotic domain: The primary kingdoms. *Proc. Natl. Acad. Sci.*, 74:5088–5090, 1977.

66. S. S.-T. Yau, J. Wang, A. Niknejad, C. Lu, N. Jin, and Y.-K. Ho. DNA sequence representation without degeneracy. *Nucleid Acids Res.*, 31:3078–3080, 2003.

67. Z. G. Yu, W. W. Anh, and B. Wang. Correlation property of length sequences based on global structure of the complex genome. *Phys. Rev. E*, 63:011903, 2001.

68. R. M. Yulmetyev, N. A. Emelyanova, and F. M. Gafarov. Dynamical shannon entropy and information Tsallis entropy in complex systems. *Phys. A*, 341:649–676, 2004.

69. M. Zhang. Exploratory analysis of long genomic DNA sequences using the wavelet transform: Examples using polyomavirus genomes. *Genome Sequencing Anal. Conf.*, VI:72–85, 1995.

CHAPTER 6

ONTOLOGY-DRIVEN FORMAL CONCEPTUAL DATA MODELING FOR BIOLOGICAL DATA ANALYSIS

CATHARINA MARIA KEET

School of Computer Science, University of KwaZulu-Natal, Durban, South Africa

6.1 INTRODUCTION

Biological data modeling serves many purposes, and many approaches exist that are used in this endeavor. The main topics of advanced conceptual data modeling for database and object-oriented software development to support biological data analysis are included in Figure 6.1, which extends the traditional "waterfall" software development methodology depicted in bold in Figure 6.2. The scope of this chapter is to provide an overview of the ontological and logical aspects of conceptual data modeling tailored to molecular biology and biological knowledge discovery.

Many databases and software applications have been and are being developed in bioinformatics, which, following good computing methodologies, are—or should have been—developed in stages, going from requirements analysis ("what should the envisioned software do?") and conceptual analysis ("what data should it be able to manage?") to design-level code and then to the actual implementation. It is well known that omitting the conceptual analysis stage by going straight to coding or scripting just adds to the pile of one-off (bioinformatics) tools that have more bugs and are much less, or not at all, maintainable and interoperable. Conversely, availing of a proper software development methodology with a representation at the conceptual layer has been shown to result in mitigation, avoidance, and/or solving such issues and therewith contributed to a software infrastructure that enabled more sophisticated biological data analysis and knowledge discovery [15, 24, 48, 54, 58, 59, 63]. The output of the conceptual analysis stage for software development is a conceptual data model, normally represented in a language such as Extended Entity-Relationship (EER) for relational databases [18], the Unified Modeling Language (UML) for object-oriented software [52], or Object-Role Modeling (ORM) for either one [30], which have been used also for software development in bioinformatics (e.g., [11, 15, 21, 34, 54, 58]). These languages are not equivalent; one language may be better for biological data modeling than another [34], and modelers tend to prefer one graphical language over

Biological Knowledge Discovery Handbook: Preprocessing, Mining, and Postprocessing of Biological Data,
First Edition. Edited by Mourad Elloumi and Albert Y. Zomaya.

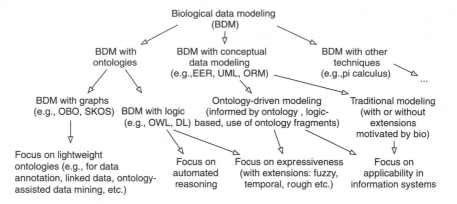

FIGURE 6.1   Informal overview of the main subtopics in Biological Data Modeling with ontologies and conceptual data modeling and several usage scenarios.

another. So, assessing the expressiveness of those languages and the associated quality of the conceptual data models are of vital importance to ascertain their suitability for biological data modeling. This has been investigated as a component of *ontology-driven conceptual data modeling* to create ontology-driven information systems [25], where an ontology is positioned as an *application-independent* formal representation of (our understanding of) a piece of reality and a conceptual data model as an *implementation-independent* representation that is tailored to the application scenario. For instance, one can make more precise the representation of UML's aggregation association or part–whole relation by availing of advances in ontology (philosophy) and making them applicable to conceptual data modeling [3, 29, 41]; one can then use scientific arguments and explain why, for example, a protein chain's Residue's Coordinates are not part of the residue [11] but an attribute that describes its location and distinguish between spatial containment and structural parthood [41]. Moreover, only if the data are stored and managed correctly can one achieve

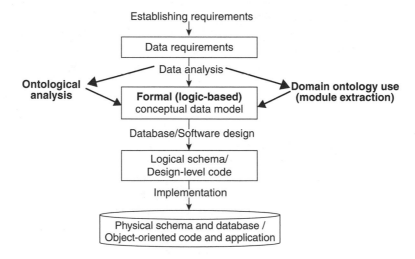

FIGURE 6.2   Waterfall methodology, augmented with ontological analysis considering aspects from Ontology, Artificial Intelligence (knowledge representation), and ontologies depicted in boldface.

the most comprehensive and reliable discovery of biological knowledge. An ontology also can be used to generate multiple conceptual data models [20, 32, 61], which improves their quality and ensures interoperability between them. Both scenarios require a formal, logic-based, foundation of a conceptual data modeling language to foster precision, accuracy, adequate coverage of the subject domain semantics, and implementability. A benefit of the logic foundations is that a conceptual data model then can be subjected to automated reasoning services, such as consistency checking and deriving implicit constraints [1, 9, 16, 22, 38, 56], thereby improving its quality further and, hence, preventing software bugs. In addition, automated reasoning can be used as a tool for biological knowledge discovery [39, 63].

Thus, a necessary first step is to fix a formalization for the main conceptual data modeling languages, thereby differentiating between human–computer interaction issues and the real language expressiveness, hence clearing up part of the argument regarding suitability of a particular conceptual data modeling language for biology. Moreover, this enables not only assessing but also extending the real modeling features of the languages and laying the basis for applications of automated reasoning. The here proposed formalization into one formal common conceptual data modeling language—called $\mathcal{CM}_{com}$, based on the $\mathcal{DLR}_{ifd}$ description logic language—captures most of ORM and all of UML Class Diagram and EER language features. Conceptual data models are then improved upon with extensions coming from Ontology and ontologies in the form of modeling guidelines to improve the quality of conceptual data models, and extensions to the representation language, therewith solving certain outstanding modeling issues. This will be illustrated by markedly enriching the representation of, among others, catalytic reactions, transforming entities, and pathway information. Thanks to the formal foundation, automated reasoning services can be used conventionally and unconventionally to find (derive) implicit knowledge and be used in in silico hypothesis testing, thereby contributing to biological knowledge discovery. To this end, a class classification and three main query scenarios will be introduced and illustrated.

The remainder of this chapter introduces $\mathcal{CM}_{com}$ (Section 6.2), ontological and language extensions to represent more complex knowledge more precisely (Section 6.3), and how automated reasoning can benefit biological knowledge discovery (Section 6.4). We conclude in Section 6.5.

6.2 DESCRIPTION LOGICS FOR CONCEPTUAL DATA MODELING

Description logics (DL) languages are decidable fragments of first-order logic and are used for logic-based knowledge representation. They have been shown useful for reasoning both over conceptual models like entity relationship (ER) and UML [6, 9, 16] and ontology languages such as OWL [50]. All DL languages have *concepts* (classes) and *roles* (relationships, n-ary predicates with $n \geq 2$) and have several constructs, therewith giving greater or lesser expressivity to the language and efficiency of reasoning over the logical theory. DL knowledge bases are composed of the *Terminological Box* (TBox), which contains axioms at the concept level, and the *Assertional Box* (ABox) that contains assertions about instances; refer to [6] for details.

We first introduce $\mathcal{DLR}$ [12], which was developed to provide a formal characterization of conceptual data modeling languages to enable automated reasoning over them, to use it as unifying paradigm for database integration through integrating their respective conceptual data models [16], and to compare conceptual data modeling languages [36]. The basic

TABLE 6.1   Semantics of $\mathcal{DLR}$ and $\mathcal{DLR}_{ifd}$

$\mathsf{T}_n^{\mathcal{I}} \subseteq (\Delta^{\mathcal{I}})^n$	$A^{\mathcal{I}} \subseteq \Delta^{\mathcal{I}}$
$\mathbf{P}^{\mathcal{I}} \subseteq \mathsf{T}_n^{\mathcal{I}}$	$(\neg C)^{\mathcal{I}} = \Delta^{\mathcal{I}} \setminus C^{\mathcal{I}}$
$(\neg \mathbf{R})^{\mathcal{I}} = \mathsf{T}_n^{\mathcal{I}} \setminus \mathbf{R}^{\mathcal{I}}$	$(C_1 \sqcap C_2)^{\mathcal{I}} = C_1^{\mathcal{I}} \cap C_2^{\mathcal{I}}$
$(\mathbf{R}_1 \sqcap \mathbf{R}_2)^{\mathcal{I}} = \mathbf{R}_1^{\mathcal{I}} \cap \mathbf{R}_2^{\mathcal{I}}$	$(\$i/n : C)^{\mathcal{I}} = \{(d_1, \ldots, d_n) \in \mathsf{T}_n^{\mathcal{I}} \mid d_i \in C^{\mathcal{I}}\}$
$\mathsf{T}_1^{\mathcal{I}} = \Delta^{\mathcal{I}}$	$(\exists[\$i]\mathbf{R})^{\mathcal{I}} = \{d \in \Delta^{\mathcal{I}} \mid \exists(d_1, \ldots, d_n) \in \mathbf{R}^{\mathcal{I}}.d_i = d\}$
	$(\leq k[\$i]\mathbf{R})^{\mathcal{I}} = \{d \in \Delta^{\mathcal{I}} \mid |\{(d_1, \ldots, d_n) \in \mathbf{R}_1^{\mathcal{I}} \mid d_i = d\}| \leq k\}$

elements of $\mathcal{DLR}$ are atomic relations (**P**) and atomic concepts A, which allows construction of arbitrary relationships (arity ≥ 2) and concepts according to the following syntax:

$$\mathbf{R} \longrightarrow \mathsf{T}_n | \mathbf{P} | (\$i/n : C) | \neg \mathbf{R} | \mathbf{R}_1 \sqcap \mathbf{R}_2$$

$$C \longrightarrow \mathsf{T}_1 | A | \neg C | C_1 \sqcap C_2 | \exists[\$i]\mathbf{R} | \leq k[\$i]\mathbf{R}$$

where i denotes a component of a relation; if components are not named, then integer numbers between 1 and $n_{\max}$ are used, where n is the arity of the relation and k is a nonnegative integer for cardinality constraints. Only relations of the same arity can be combined to form expressions of type $\mathbf{R}_1 \sqcap \mathbf{R}_2$ and $i \leq n$. The model-theoretic semantics of $\mathcal{DLR}$ is specified through the usual notion of an *interpretation*, where $\mathcal{I} = (\Delta^{\mathcal{I}}, \cdot^{\mathcal{I}})$ and the interpretation function $\cdot^{\mathcal{I}}$ assigns to each concept C a subset $C^{\mathcal{I}}$ of domain $\Delta^{\mathcal{I}}$ and assigns to each n-ary $\mathbf{R}$ a subset $\mathbf{R}^{\mathcal{I}}$ of $(\Delta^{\mathcal{I}})^n$ such that the conditions are satisfied following Table 6.1.

A *knowledge base* is a finite set $\mathcal{KB}$ of $\mathcal{DLR}$ (or $\mathcal{DLR}_{ifd}$) axioms of the form $C_1 \sqsubseteq C_2$ and $R_1 \sqsubseteq R_2$. An interpretation $\mathcal{I}$ *satisfies* $C_1 \sqsubseteq C_2$ ($R_1 \sqsubseteq R_2$) if and only if the interpretation of C_1 (R_1) is included in the interpretation of C_2 (R_2), that is, $C_1^{\mathcal{I}} \subseteq C_2^{\mathcal{I}}$ ($R_1^{\mathcal{I}} \subseteq R_2^{\mathcal{I}}$). Here T_1 denotes the interpretation domain; T_n for $n \geq 1$ denotes a subset of the n-cartesian product of the domain, which covers all introduced n-ary relations. The "$(\$i/n : C)$" denotes all tuples in T_n that have an instance of C as their ith component. The following abbreviations hold: $C_1 \sqcup C_2$ for $\neg(\neg C_1 \sqcap \neg C_2)$, $C_1 \Rightarrow C_2$ for $\neg C_1 \sqcup C_2$, $(\geq k[i]R)$ for $\neg(\leq k - 1[i]R)$, $\exists[i]R$ for $(\geq 1[i]R)$, $\forall[i]R$ for $\neg\exists[i]\neg R$, $R_1 \sqcup R_2$ for $\neg(\neg R_1 \sqcap \neg R_2)$, and $(i : C)$ for $(i/n : C)$ when n is clear from the context. Note that a qualified role $\exists P.C$ is represented in $\mathcal{DLR}_{ifd}$ as $\exists[\$1](P \sqcap (\$2/2 : C))$, its inverse, $\exists P^-.C$, as $\exists[\$2](P \sqcap (\$1/2 : C))$, likewise for universal quantification ($\forall P.C$ as $\neg\exists[\$1](P \sqcap (\$2/2 : \neg C))$) and its inverse $\forall P^-.C$ as $\neg\exists[\$2](P \sqcap (\$1/2 : \neg C))$ [12].

There are four extensions to $\mathcal{DLR}$. The most relevant in the current scope are $\mathcal{DLR}_{ifd}$ [13], because it can capture most or all of the common conceptual modeling language features, and $\mathcal{DLR}_{US}$, because it has an expressive temporal extension. $\mathcal{DLR}_{ifd}$ has two additional constructs compared to $\mathcal{DLR}$. It has *i*dentification assertions on a concept C, which have the form (**id** $C[i_1]R_1, \ldots, [i_h]R_h$), where each R_j is a relation and each i_j denotes one component of R_j. This is useful for external uniqueness in ORM, weak entity types in ER, and objectification. It also caters for nonunary $f$unctional $d$ependency assertions on a relationship R, which have the form (**fd** R $i_1, \ldots, i_h \rightarrow j$), where $h \geq 2$, and $i_1, \ldots, i_h, j$ denote components of R, which are useful primarily for UML's methods and ORM's derived-and-stored fact types. Observe that there is no change in semantic rules because the algorithm for the extensions is checked against a (generalized) ABox [13]. $\mathcal{DLR}_{US}$ has the $\mathcal{U}$ntil and $\mathcal{S}$ince operators for temporal ontologies and EER conceptual data models ($\mathcal{ER}_{VT}$) [2, 5], which has been used for modeling essential parthood [3], relation migration [42]. Generally, temporal extensions are very useful to represent constraints in molecular biology, such as formally characterizing that some enzymatic reaction happens only *after* another, *precedes* it, or happens *concurrently*.

6.2.1 Generic Common Conceptual Data Model $\mathcal{CM}_{com}$

Given the $\mathcal{DLR}_{ifd}$ syntax and semantics, we now can define the $\mathcal{CM}_{com}$ conceptual data modeling language; that is, given a particular conceptual data model in the generic conceptual data modeling language $\mathcal{CM}_{com}$, there is an equi-satisfiable $\mathcal{DLR}_{ifd}$ knowledge base. The formalization adopted here is based on previous presentations [1, 13, 17, 36], with two principal extensions so as make better use of the "ifd" features of $\mathcal{DLR}_{ifd}$ that have not been addressed in those earlier works. These are the representation of weak entity types, UML's (hardly used) subassociation end and ORM's subroles, role exclusion, and disjunctive mandatory roles, which were hitherto used only for the more recent ORM2-to-$\mathcal{DLR}_{ifd}$ mapping [38]. Given that they are not harmful at all to UML and (E)ER, and UML CASE tool features are moving in this direction, they are included in $\mathcal{CM}_{com}$. Also, refinements with respect to [36] are made concerning cardinality on relationships and on attributes and disjointness of classes and of relations, and more precise constraints are added on components of a relationship. We introduce the $\mathcal{CM}_{com}$ syntax in Definition 6.1, illustrate it with an example by mapping several elements of the syntax to graphical elements of EER, UML, and ORM2, proceed to the semantics in Definition 6.2, and then show the mapping from $\mathcal{CM}_{com}$ to $\mathcal{DLR}_{ifd}$ in Definition 6.3.

Definition 6.1 *Conceptual Data Model $\mathcal{CM}_{com}$ Syntax*   A $\mathcal{CM}_{com}$ conceptual data model is a tuple $\Sigma = (\mathcal{L}, \text{REL}, \text{ATT}, \text{CARD}_R, \text{CARD}_A, \text{ISA}_C, \text{ISA}_R, \text{ISA}_U, \text{DISJ}_C,$ $\text{COVER}_C, \text{DISJ}_R, \text{KEY}, \text{EXTK}, \text{FD}, \text{OBJ}, \text{REX}, \text{RDM})$ such that:

1. $\mathcal{L}$ is a finite alphabet partitioned into the sets $\mathcal{C}$ (*class* symbols), $\mathcal{A}$ (*attribute* symbols), $\mathcal{R}$ (*relationship* symbols), $\mathcal{U}$ (*role* symbols), and $\mathcal{D}$ (*domain* symbols); the tuple $(\mathcal{C}, \mathcal{A}, \mathcal{R}, \mathcal{U}, \mathcal{D})$ is the *signature* of the conceptual model Σ.

2. ATT is a function that maps a class symbol in $\mathcal{C}$ to an $\mathcal{A}$-labeled tuple over $\mathcal{D}$, ATT : $\mathcal{A} \mapsto \mathcal{D}$, so that $\text{ATT}(C) = \{A_1 : D_1, \ldots, A_h : D_h\}$, where h a nonnegative integer.

3. REL is a function that maps a relationship symbol in $\mathcal{R}$ to an $\mathcal{U}$-labeled tuple over $\mathcal{C}$, $\text{REL}(R) = \{U_1 : C_1, \ldots, U_k : C_k\}$, k is the *arity* of R, and if $(U_i, C_i) \in \text{REL}(R)$, then $\text{PLAYER}(R, U_i) = C_i$ and $\text{ROLE}(R, C_i) = U_i$. The signature of the relation is $\sigma_R = \langle \mathcal{U}, \mathcal{C}, \text{PLAYER}, \text{ROLE}\rangle$, where for all $U_i \in \mathcal{U}$, $C_i \in \mathcal{C}$, if $\sharp U \geq \sharp C$, then for each u_i, c_i, REL(R), we have $\text{PLAYER}(R, U_i) = C_i$ and $\text{ROLE}(R, C_i) = U_i$, and if $\sharp U > \sharp C$, then $\text{PLAYER}(R, U_i) = C_i$, $\text{PLAYER}(R, U_{i+1}) = C_i$ and $\text{ROLE}(R, C_i) = U_i, U_{i+1}$.

4. CARD_R is a function $\text{CARD}_R : \mathcal{C} \times \mathcal{R} \times \mathcal{U} \mapsto \mathbb{N} \times (\mathbb{N} \cup \{\infty\})$ denoting cardinality constraints. We denote with $\text{CMIN}(C, R, U)$ and $\text{CMAX}(C, R, U)$ the first and second components of CARD_R.

5. CARD_A is a function $\text{CARD}_A : \mathcal{C} \times \mathcal{A} \mapsto \mathbb{N} \times (\mathbb{N} \cup \{\infty\})$ denoting multiplicity constraints for attributes. We denote with $\text{CMIN}(C, A)$ and $\text{CMAX}(C, A)$ the first and second components of CARD_A, and $\text{CARD}_A(C, A)$ may be defined only if $(A, D) \in \text{ATT}(C)$ for some $D \in \mathcal{D}$.

6. ISA_C is a binary relationship $\text{ISA}_C \subseteq \mathcal{C} \times \mathcal{C}$.

7. ISA_R is a binary relationship $\text{ISA}_R \subseteq \mathcal{R} \times \mathcal{R}$. ISA_R between relationships is restricted to relationships with the same signature, that is, given an $R_1 \subseteq R_2$, then $\sigma_{R_1} = \sigma_{R_2}$, and $\text{PLAYER}(R_1, U_i) \subseteq \text{PLAYER}(R_2, U_i)$.

8. ISA_U is a binary relationship $\text{ISA}_U \subseteq \mathcal{U} \times \mathcal{U}$. ISA_U between roles of relationships is restricted to relationships with the same signature, that is, given an $R_1 \subseteq R_2$, then $\sigma_{R_1} = \sigma_{R_2}$, and $\text{ROLE}(R_1, C_i) \subseteq \text{ROLE}(R_2, C_i)$.

9. DISJ_C, COVER_C are binary relationships over $2^{\mathcal{C}} \times \mathcal{C}$, describing disjointness and covering partitions, respectively, over a group of ISA that share the same superclass.

10. DISJ_R is a binary relationship over $2^{\mathcal{R}} \times \mathcal{R}$, describing disjointness over a group of relations.

11. KEY is a function, $\text{KEY} : \mathcal{C} \mapsto \mathcal{A}$, that maps a class symbol in $\mathcal{C}$ to its key attribute and $A \in \mathcal{A}$ is an attribute already defined in $\text{ATT}(C)$, that is, $\text{KEY}(C)$ may be defined only if $(A, D) \in \text{ATT}(C)$ for some $D \in \mathcal{D}$.

12. EXTK is called an identification assertion/external uniqueness/weak entity type, which is a function that maps a class to a set of relation–role pairs or attributes, $\text{EXTK} : \mathcal{C} \mapsto 2^{2^{(\mathcal{R} \times \mathcal{U}) \cup \mathcal{A}}}$, where $R \in \mathcal{R}$, $\text{REL}(R)$ so that $\text{PLAYER}(R, U) = C$ (with $C \in \mathcal{C}$) and for any participating $A \in \mathcal{A}$ such that $(A, D) \in \text{ATT}(C)$ for some $D \in \mathcal{D}$.

13. FD is a functional dependency assertion on a relation, $\text{FD} : \mathcal{R} \mapsto 2^{2^{\mathcal{U}}} \times \mathcal{U}$, where $U_1, \ldots, U_i, U_j \in \mathcal{U}$ denote components of $R \in \mathcal{R}$; $\text{FD}(R)$ may be defined only if $\text{ROLE}(R, C_i) \in \text{REL}(R)$ and $i \geq 2$.

14. OBJ is an objectification function that maps an n-ary relation symbol $R \in \mathcal{R}$ to n binary relations $r_1, \ldots r_n \in \mathcal{R}$ over $\mathcal{C}$, that is, $\text{OBJ} : \mathcal{R} \mapsto \mathcal{C}$. Whenever $\text{OBJ}(R) = R'$ with $R' \in \mathcal{C}$, $\text{ROLE}(R, C_i) = U_i$ and, with ROBJ denoting the relationification of the role, $\text{ROBJ}(U_i) = r_i$, where r_i is a new binary relation, $\text{REL}(r_i) = \{u_1 : R', u_2 : C_i\}$, $2 \leq i \leq n$, and $\text{EXTK}(R') = \{u_1[r_1], \ldots, u_1[r_n]\}$, and $\text{CMAX}(C, r_i, u_1) = 1$.

15. REX, RDM are binary relations over $2^{\mathcal{U}} \times \mathcal{U}$, describing disjointness partitions over a group of roles $\mathcal{U}$ of relations in $\mathcal{R}$ of the same arity to which $\mathcal{C}$ participates.

Thus, the explicit new features in $\mathcal{CM}_{com}$ compared to previous DL-focused definitions of conceptual modeling languages are ISA_U, DISJ_R, EXTK, FD, OBJ, REX, and RDM, which thereby introduces also the distinction between "simple" keys (KEY) and other keys like external uniqueness and natural keys (EXTK) and FDs for UML methods and ORM's derived and derived-and-stored fact types.

One can map the $\mathcal{CM}_{com}$ syntax to any set of icons or fixed-syntax pseudo-natural language as long as the relation between the $\mathcal{CM}_{com}$ syntax and icons or pseudonatural language has been specified. Put differently, with $\mathcal{CM}_{com}$ the mappings between the conceptual data modeling languages can be from one syntax (and semantics) to many graphical and textual representations instead of developing and maintaining $m : n$ mappings between the various graphical languages. The following example demonstrates the principal mechanism for $\mathcal{CM}_{com}$ syntax and icons in UML Class Diagram, EER, and ORM2 notation.

Example 6.1 *Graphical Syntaxes for $\mathcal{CM}_{com}$*   Figure 6.3 depicts a UML, an EER, and an ORM2 diagram. The mappings from $\mathcal{CM}_{com}$ syntax to these graphics are:

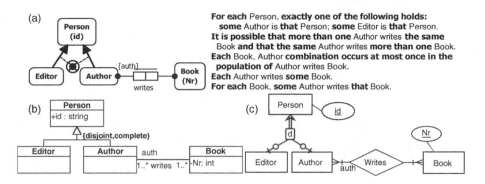

For each Person, **exactly one of the following holds:**
  some Author is **that** Person; **some** Editor is **that** Person.
It is possible that more than one Author writes **the same**
  Book **and that the same** Author writes **more than one** Book.
Each Book, Author **combination occurs at most once in the**
  population of Author writes Book.
Each Author writes **some** Book.
For each Book, **some** Author writes **that** Book.

FIGURE 6.3 Examples of graphical syntaxes for $\mathcal{CM}_{com}$ with (a) ORM2 diagram drawn in NORMA that also provides pseudonatural language renderings, (b) UML class diagram drawn in VP-UML, and (c) EER diagram drawn with SmartDraw.

Author ISA Person   *(directed arrow in UML, EER, ORM2)*
CARD (Author, Writes, auth) = (1,*n*)
                    (1..* in UML, craw's feet and line in EER, blob and line in ORM2)
KEY (Person) = id   *(underlined* id *in EER,* (id) *in ORM2)*
{Author, Editor} DISJ Person
                    ({disjoint} in UML, encircled d *in EER, encircled* X *in ORM2)*
{Author, Editor} COVER Person
                    ({complete} in UML, open shaft arrow in EER, encircled blob in ORM2)

Looking back at $\mathcal{DLR}_{ifd}$ in the introduction of this section and ahead to the demonstration that $\mathcal{CM}_{com}$ has an equi-satisfiable knowledge base (Definition 6.3), the equivalent representation in $\mathcal{DLR}_{ifd}$ is as follows:

Author $\sqsubseteq$ Person   (subsumption)
Author $\sqsubseteq$ $\exists$[auth]writes   (at least one)
Person $\sqsubseteq$ $\exists^{=1}$[From]id, $\top$ $\sqsubseteq$ $\exists^{<1}$[To](id $\sqcap$ [From]:Person)   (key)
Author $\sqsubseteq$ $\neg$Editor   (disjoint)
Person $\sqsubseteq$ Author $\sqcup$ Editor   (covering)

One also can map the syntax to pseudonatural language; for example, for the ISA and NORMA's verbalization pattern *Each ... is an instance of ...* one obtains for Author ISA Person a domain expert readable surface rendering of *Each Author is an instance of Person*; the others are shown in Figure 6.3a.   ◇

The model-theoretic semantics associated with $\mathcal{CM}_{com}$ is as follows.

Definition 6.2 $\mathcal{CM}_{com}$ ***Semantics*** Let Σ be a $\mathcal{CM}_{com}$ conceptual data model. An *interpretation* for the conceptual model Σ is a tuple $\mathcal{I} = (\Delta^{\mathcal{I}} \cup \Delta_D^{\mathcal{I}}, \cdot^{\mathcal{I}})$ such that:

- $\Delta^{\mathcal{I}}$ is a nonempty set of abstract objects disjoint from $\Delta_D^{\mathcal{I}}$;
- $\Delta_D^{\mathcal{I}} = \bigcup_{D_i \in \mathcal{D}} \Delta_{D_i}^{\mathcal{I}}$ is the set of basic domain values used in Σ; and
- $\mathcal{I}$ is a function that maps:

(a) Every basic domain symbol $D \in \mathcal{D}$ into a set $D^{\mathcal{I}} = \Delta_{D_i}^{\mathcal{I}}$.

(b) Every class $C \in \mathcal{C}$ to a set $C^{\mathcal{I}} \subseteq \Delta^{\mathcal{I}}$.

(c) Every relationship $R \in \mathcal{R}$ to a set $R^{\mathcal{I}}$ of $\mathcal{U}$-labeled tuples over $\Delta^{\mathcal{I}}$, that is, let R be an n-ary relationship connecting the classes $C_1, \ldots, C_n$, $\text{REL}(R) = \{U_1 : C_1, \ldots, U_n : C_n\}$, then $r \in R^{\mathcal{I}} \to (r = \{U_1 : o_1, \ldots, U_n : o_n\} \wedge \forall i \in \{1, \ldots, n\} . o_i \in C_i^{\mathcal{I}})$.

(d) Every attribute $A \in \mathcal{A}$ to a set $A^{\mathcal{I}} \subseteq \Delta^{\mathcal{I}} \times \Delta_D^{\mathcal{I}}$ such that, for each $C \in \mathcal{C}$, if $\text{ATT}(C) = \{A_1 : D_1, \ldots, A_h : D_h\}$, then $o \in C^{\mathcal{I}} \to (\forall i \in \{1, \ldots, h\}, \exists a_i . \langle o, a_i \rangle \in A_i^{\mathcal{I}} \wedge \forall a_i . \langle o, a_i \rangle \in A_i^{\mathcal{I}} \to a_i \in \Delta_{D_i}^{\mathcal{I}})$.

$\mathcal{I}$ is a *legal database state* or *legal application software state* if it satisfies all of the constraints expressed in the conceptual data model:

- For each $C_1, C_2 \in \mathcal{C}$: if $C_1 \text{ ISA}_C C_2$, then $C_1^{\mathcal{I}} \subseteq C_2^{\mathcal{I}}$.

- For each $R_1, R_2 \in \mathcal{R}$: if $R_1 \text{ ISA}_R R_2$, then $R_1^{\mathcal{I}} \subseteq R_2^{\mathcal{I}}$.

- For each $U_1, U_2 \in \mathcal{U}$, $R_1, R_2 \in \mathcal{R}$, $\text{REL}(R_1) = \{U_1 : o_1, \ldots, U_n : o_n\}$, $\text{REL}(R_2) = \{U_1 : o_1, \ldots, U_m : o_m\}$, $m = n$, $R_1 \neq R_2$: if $U_1 \text{ ISA}_U U_2$, then $U_1^{\mathcal{I}} \subseteq U_2^{\mathcal{I}}$.

- For each $R \in \mathcal{R}$ with $\text{REL}(R) = \{U_1 : C_1, \ldots, U_k : C_k\}$: all instances of R are of the form $\{U_1 : o_1, \ldots, U_k : o_k\}$ where $o_i \in C_i^{\mathcal{I}}$, $U_i \in U_i^{\mathcal{I}}$, and $1 \leq i \leq k$.

- For each cardinality constraint $\text{CARD}_R(C, R, U)$, then $o \in C^{\mathcal{I}} \to \text{CMIN}(C, R, U) \leq \#\{r \in R^{\mathcal{I}} \mid r[U] = o\} \leq \text{CMAX}(C, R, U)$.

- For each multiplicity constraint $\text{CARD}_A(C, A)$, then $o \in C^{\mathcal{I}} \to \text{CMIN}(C, A) \leq \#\{(o, a) \in A^{\mathcal{I}}\} \leq \text{CMAX}(C, A)$.

- For all $C, C_1, \ldots, C_n \in \mathcal{C}$: if $\{C_1, \ldots, C_n\} \text{ DISJ}_C C$, then $\forall i \in \{1, \ldots, n\} . C_i \text{ ISA}_C C \wedge \forall j \in \{1, \ldots, n\}, j \neq i . C_i^{\mathcal{I}} \cap C_j^{\mathcal{I}} = \emptyset$.

- For all $R_1, \ldots, R_n \in \mathcal{R}$: if $\{R_1, \ldots, R_n\} \text{DISJ}_R$ then $\forall i \in \{1, \ldots, n\} . R_i^{\mathcal{I}} \cap R_j^{\mathcal{I}} = \emptyset$.

- For all $C, C_1, \ldots, C_n \in \mathcal{C}$: if $\{C_1, \ldots, C_n\} \text{ COVER}_C C$, then $\forall i \in \{1, \ldots, n\} . C_i \text{ ISA}_C C \wedge C^{\mathcal{I}} = \bigcup_{i=1}^{n} C_i^{\mathcal{I}}$.

- For each $C \in \mathcal{C}$, $A \in \mathcal{A}$ such that $\text{KEY}(C) = A$, then A is an attribute and $\forall a \in \Delta_D^{\mathcal{I}} . \#\{o \in C^{\mathcal{I}} \mid \langle o, a \rangle \in A^{\mathcal{I}}\} \leq 1$.

- For each $C \in \mathcal{C}$, $R_h \in \mathcal{R}$, $h \geq 1$, $\text{REL}(R_h) = \{U : C, U_1 : C_1, \ldots, U_k : C_k\}$, $k \geq 1$, $k + 1$ the arity of R_h, such that $\text{EXTK}(C) = \{[U_1]R_1, \ldots, [U_h]R_h\}$, then for all $o_a, o_b \in C^{\mathcal{I}}$ and for all $t_1, s_1 \in R_1^{\mathcal{I}}, \ldots, t_h, s_h \in R_h^{\mathcal{I}}$ we have that:

$$
\left.
\begin{aligned}
o_a &= t_1[U_1] = \cdots = t_h[U_h] \\
o_b &= s_1[U_1] = \cdots = s_h[U_h] \\
t_j[U] &= s_j[U] \quad \text{for } j \in \{1, \ldots, h\} \text{ and for } U \neq j
\end{aligned}
\right\} \quad \text{implies } o_a = o_b
$$

where o_a is an instance of C that is the U_jth component of a tuple t_j of R_j for $j \in \{1, \ldots, h\}$ and o_b is an instance of C that is the U_jth component of a tuple s_j of R_j for $j \in \{1, \ldots, h\}$, and for each j, t_j agrees with s_j in all components different from U_j; then o_a and o_b are the same object.

- For each $R \in \mathcal{R}$, $U_i, U_j \in \mathcal{U}$ for $i \geq 2$, $i \neq j$, $\text{REL}(R) = \{U_1 : C_1, \ldots, U_i : C_i, U_j : C_j\}$, $\text{FD}(R) = \langle U_1, \ldots, U_i \to U_j \rangle$, then for all $t, s \in R^{\mathcal{I}}$, we have that $t[U_1] = s[U_1], \ldots, t[U_i] = s[U_i]$ implies $t_j = s_j$.

- For each $R, r_1, \ldots, r_n \in \mathcal{R}$, $R', C_1, \ldots, C_n \in \mathcal{C}$, $U_1, \ldots, U_n, u_{s1}, \ldots, u_{sn}$, $u_{t1}, \ldots, u_{tn} \in \mathcal{U}$, REL$(R) = \{U_1 : C_1, \ldots, U_n : C_n\}$, OBJ$(R) = R'$, ROBJ$(U_i) = r_i$, REL$(r_i) = \{u_{s1} : R', u_{t1} : C_i\}$, $2 \leq i \leq n$, EXTK$(R') = \{u_{s1}[r_1], \ldots, u_{sn}[r_n]\}$, CARD$(R', r_i, u_{si}) = (1, 1)$, CARD$(C_i, r_i, u_{ti}) = (0, 1)$, REL, CARD, and EXTK interpreted as above, then $\forall i \in \{2, \ldots, n\} . \{U_i, u_{si}, u_{ti} \in U^{\mathcal{I}} \wedge r, r_i \in R^{\mathcal{I}} \wedge o_i, r' \in C^{\mathcal{I}} \mid u_{si} \in U^{\mathcal{I}} \to \text{PLAYER}(R, U) = r' \wedge u_{ti} \in U^{\mathcal{I}} \to \text{PLAYER}(R, U) = o_i\}$.

- For each $U_i \in \mathcal{U}$, $i \geq 2$, $R_i \in \mathcal{R}$, each R_i has the same arity m (with $m \geq 2$), $C_j \in \mathcal{C}$ with $2 \leq j \leq i(m-1) + 1$, and REL$(R_i) = \{U_i : C_i, \ldots U_m : C_m\}$ (and, thus, $R_i \in R_i^{\mathcal{I}}$ and $o_j \in C_j^{\mathcal{I}}$), if $\{U_1, U_2, \ldots U_{i-1}\}$ REX U_i, then
$\forall i \in \{1, \ldots, i\} . o_j \in C_j^{\mathcal{I}} \to \text{CMIN}(o_j, r_i, u_i) \leq 1 \wedge u_i \neq u_1 \wedge \cdots \wedge u_i \neq u_{i-1}$ where $u_i \in U_i^{\mathcal{I}}, r_i \in R_i^{\mathcal{I}}$.

- For each $U_i \in \mathcal{U}$, $i \geq 2$, $R_i \in \mathcal{R}$, each R_i has the same arity m (with $m \geq 2$), $C_j \in \mathcal{C}$ with $2 \leq j \leq i(m-1) + 1$, and REL$(R_i) = \{U_i : C_i, \ldots U_m : C_m\}$, if $\{U_1, U_2, \ldots U_{i-1}\}$ RDM U_i, then $\forall i \in \{1, \ldots, n\} . o_j \in C_j^{\mathcal{I}} \to \text{CMIN}(o_j, r_i, u_i) \geq 1$ where $u_i \in U_i^{\mathcal{I}}, r_i \in R_i^{\mathcal{I}}$.

We summarize how $\mathcal{DLR}_{ifd}$ can capture conceptual models expressed in $\mathcal{CM}_{com}$, following the same approach as [1, 36] and extended with the new features.

Definition 6.3 *Mapping $\mathcal{CM}_{com}$ into $\mathcal{DLR}_{ifd}$* Let $\Sigma = (\mathcal{L}, \text{REL}, \text{ATT}, \text{CARD}_R, \text{CARD}_A,$ ISA$_C$, ISA$_R$, ISA$_U$, DISJ$_C$, COVER$_C$, DISJ$_R$, KEY, EXTK, FD, OBJ, REX, RDM) be a $\mathcal{CM}_{com}$ conceptual data model. The $\mathcal{DLR}_{ifd}$ knowledge base, $\mathcal{K}$, mapping Σ is as follows.

- For each $A \in \mathcal{A}$, then $A \sqsubseteq \text{From} \sqcap \text{To} \sqcap \top \in \mathcal{K}$;
- If C_1 ISA$_C$ $C_2 \in \Sigma$, then $C_1 \sqsubseteq C_2 \in \mathcal{K}$;
- If R_1 ISA$_R$ $R_2 \in \Sigma$, then $R_1 \sqsubseteq R_2 \in \mathcal{K}$;
- If U_1 ISA$_U$ $U_2 \in \Sigma$, then $\mathcal{K}$ contains: $[U_1]R_1 \sqsubseteq [U_2]R_2$; $R_1 \sqsubseteq \neg R_2$;
- If REL$(R) = \{U_1 : C_1, \ldots, U_k : C_k\} \in \Sigma$, then $R \sqsubseteq U_1 : C_1 \sqcap \cdots \sqcap U_k : C_k \in \mathcal{K}$;
- If ATT$(C) = \{A_1 : D_1, \ldots, A_h : D_h\} \in \Sigma$, then $C \sqsubseteq \exists[\text{From}]A_1 \sqcap \cdots \sqcap \exists[\text{From}]A_h \sqcap \forall[\text{From}](A_1 \to \text{To} : D_1) \sqcap \cdots \sqcap \forall[\text{From}](A_h \to \text{To} : D_h) \in \mathcal{K}$;
- If CARD$_C(C, R, U) = (m, n) \in \Sigma$, then $C \sqsubseteq \exists^{\geq m}[U]R \sqcap \exists^{\leq n}[U]R \in \mathcal{K}$;
- If CARD$_A(C, A) = (m, n) \in \Sigma$, then $C \sqsubseteq \exists^{\geq m}[U]R \sqcap \exists^{\leq n}[U]R \in \mathcal{K}$;
- If $\{C_1, \ldots, C_n\}$ DISJ$_C$ $C \in \Sigma$, then $\mathcal{K}$ contains $C_1 \sqsubseteq C \sqcap \neg C_2 \sqcap \cdots \sqcap \neg C_n, C_2 \sqsubseteq C \sqcap \neg C_3 \sqcap \cdots \sqcap \neg C_n, \ldots, C_n \sqsubseteq C$;
- If $\{R_1, ..., R_n\}$DISJ$_R \in \Sigma$, then $\mathcal{K}$ contains $R_1 \sqsubseteq \neg R_2 \sqcap \cdots \sqcap \neg R_n, R_2 \sqsubseteq \neg R_3 \sqcap \cdots \sqcap \neg R_n, \ldots, R_{n-1} \sqsubseteq \neg R_n$;
- If $\{C_1, \ldots, C_n\}$ COVER$_C$ $C \in \Sigma$, then $\mathcal{K}$ contains $C_1 \sqsubseteq C, \ldots, C_n \sqsubseteq C$; $C \sqsubseteq C_1 \sqcup \cdots \sqcup C_n$;
- If KEY$(C) = A \in \Sigma$, then $\mathcal{K}$ contains $C \sqsubseteq \exists^{=1}[\text{From}]A$; $\top \sqsubseteq \exists^{\leq 1}[\text{To}](A \sqcap [\text{From}] : C)$;
- If EXTK$(C) = \{[U_1]R, \ldots, [U_h]R_h\} \in \Sigma$, then $\mathcal{K}$ contains $(\textbf{id } C [U_1]R_1, \ldots, [U_h]R_h)$;
- If FD$(R) = \langle U_1, \ldots, U_i \to j \rangle \in \Sigma$, then $\mathcal{K}$ contains $(\textbf{fd } R U_1, \ldots, U_i \to j)$;

- If $\text{OBJ}(R) = R'$, then $\mathcal{K}$ contains $(\textbf{\textit{id}}\ R'\ [u_{s1}]r_1, \ldots, [u_{sn}]r_n)$;

$R' \sqsubseteq \exists [u_{s1}]r_1 \sqcap (\leq 1[u_{s1}]r_1) \sqcap \forall [u_{s1}](r_1 \Rightarrow (u_{t1} : C_1)) \sqcap$

$\exists [u_{s2}]r_2 \sqcap (\leq 1[u_{s2}]r_2) \sqcap \forall [u_{s2}](r_2 \Rightarrow (u_{t2} : C_2)) \sqcap$

$\vdots$

$\exists [u_{sn}]r_n \sqcap (\leq 1[u_{sn}]r_n) \sqcap \forall [u_{sn}](r_n \Rightarrow (u_{tn} : C_n))$

- If $\{U_1, U_2, \ldots, U_{i-1}\}$ REX $U_i \in \Sigma$, then $\mathcal{K}$ contains $C \sqsubseteq (\exists^{\leq 1}[U_1]R_1 \sqcup \cdots \sqcup \exists^{\leq 1}[U_i]R_i)$; $[U_1]R_1 \sqsubseteq \neg[U_2]R_2 \sqcap \cdots \sqcap \neg[U_{i-1}]R_{i-1}$, $[U_2]R_2 \sqsubseteq \neg[U_3]R_3 \sqcap \cdots \sqcap \neg[U_{i-1}]R_{i-1}, \ldots, [U_{i-1}]R_{i-1} \sqsubseteq \neg[U_i]R_i$;

- If $\{U_1, U_2, \ldots, U_{i-1}\}$ RDM $U_i \in \Sigma$, then $\mathcal{K}$ contains $C \sqsubseteq (\exists^{\geq 1}[U_1]R_1 \sqcup \cdots \sqcup \exists^{\geq 1}[U_i]R_i)$; $[U_1]R_1 \sqsubseteq \neg[U_2]R_2 \sqcap \cdots \sqcap \neg[U_{i-1}]R_{i-1}$, $[U_2]R_2 \sqsubseteq \neg[U_3]R_3 \sqcap \cdots \sqcap \neg[U_{i-1}]R_{i-1}, \ldots, [U_{i-1}]R_{i-1} \sqsubseteq \neg[U_i]R_i$

Thus, $\mathcal{CM}_{com}$ has an equi-satisfiable $\mathcal{DLR}_{ifd}$ knowledge base and therewith we can avail of the nice computational properties of $\mathcal{DLR}_{ifd}$ [9, 13]. One could have chosen another expressive DL language as a formal foundation, such as OWL 2 DL [50] with a corresponding mapping to a $\mathcal{CM}'_{com}$. However, such a $\mathcal{CM}'_{com}$ would have REL restricted to binaries, it would not have EXTK, FD, OBJ, REX, and RDM, but it would have gained the option to represent transitivity, reflexivity, irreflexivity, asymmetry, and symmetry. Those gains with the relational properties, however, are useful only to formalize ORM's ring constraints and come at the cost of 2NExpTime complexity in concept and theory satisfiability ($\mathcal{DLR}_{ifd}$ is in ExpTime). There are always trade-offs in a formalization, and the priority here is being able to deal with the core features of conceptual data modeling languages before extending one's horizon. As we shall see in Section 6.2.2, $\mathcal{CM}_{com}$ is the greatest common denominator by capturing most or all features of EER, UML Class Diagrams, and ORM.

6.2.2 EER, UML, and ORM in Terms of $\mathcal{CM}_{com}$

With the formal apparatus in place, we now can consider definitions of EER, UML, and ORM 2 in terms of $\mathcal{CM}_{com}$. The rationale for the exact combination of constraints has been explained and discussed in detail elsewhere [36] (e.g., regarding UML's OCL [55], aggregation [41], and identification [40]). The "−" in "$_{ORM2^-}$" is due to, mainly, ORM's undecidability due to constraints over k roles over an n-ary relation, $n \geq 3$, and $k < n$ [38], and the unknown computational complexity of antisymmetry (the fine-grained arguments are beyond the current scope). The important point here is to have basic definitions so as to focus on language features and the ontology-driven aspects.

Definition 6.4 $\mathcal{CM}_{EER}$ A $\mathcal{CM}_{EER}$ conceptual data model is a tuple

$$\Sigma = (\mathcal{L}, \text{REL}, \text{ATT}, \text{CARD}_R, \text{ISA}_C, \text{DISJ}_C, \text{COVER}_C, \text{KEY}, \text{EXTK})$$

adhering to $\mathcal{CM}_{com}$ syntax and semantics.

Definition 6.5 $\mathcal{CM}_{UML}$ A $\mathcal{CM}_{UML}$ conceptual data model is a tuple

$$\Sigma = (\mathcal{L}, \text{REL}, \text{ATT}, \text{CARD}_R, \text{ISA}_C, \text{ISA}_R, \text{DISJ}_C, \text{COVER}_C, \text{EXTK}, \text{FD}, \text{OBJ}, \text{PW})$$

adhering to $\mathcal{CM}_{com}$ syntax and semantics, except for the aggregation association PW, with syntax PW $= \{U_1 : C_1, U_2 : C_2\}$, that has no defined semantics.

Definition 6.6 A $\mathcal{CM}_{ORM2-}$ conceptual data model is a tuple

$$\Sigma = (\mathcal{L}, \text{REL}, \text{ATT}, \text{CARD}_R, \text{CARD}_A, \text{ISA}_C, \text{ISA}_R, \text{ISA}_U, \text{DISJ}_C, \text{COVER}_C, \text{KEY}, \text{EXTK},$$
$$\text{FD}, \text{OBJ}, \text{DISJ}_R, \text{REX}, \text{RDM})$$

adhering to $\mathcal{CM}_{com}$ syntax and semantics.

There is a notable difference between $\mathcal{CM}_{EER}$, $\mathcal{CM}_{UML}$, and $\mathcal{CM}_{ORM}2^-$. Although it is possible to include ISA$_U$ for UML's association ends in $\mathcal{CM}_{UML}$ and interpret the Object Management Group (OMG) standard [52] liberally on keys (KEY and EXTK; see [40] for a discussion) and attributes (by modeling them external to the class so that one can use CARD$_A$), this is yet to be refined in the standard and implemented in the CASE tools. From a human–computer interaction (HCI) perspective, a less expressive language may be pleasing for a novice modeler, but it is worth noting that extensions have been deemed necessary [34] and were proposed for EER to address better the requirements of molecular biologists [21] (discussed in Section 6.3). Here we illustrate two modeling aspects—role exclusion and ternaries—and their solutions with $\mathcal{CM}_{com}$.

Example 6.2 *Modeling Features in the Graphical and Formal Languages*   Let us take Kazic's complaint on not being able to represent thymidine phosphorylase binding with thymidine or phosphate [33]. This requires an exclusion constraint over roles (REX), which is possible to represent with ORM and $\mathcal{CM}_{ORM2-}$, as demonstrated in Figure 6.4a, but not in the EER or UML graphical syntax. Formally, we have {bindsT, bindsP} REX binds in $\mathcal{CM}_{com}$, and thus the $\mathcal{DLR}_{ifd}$ knowledge base $\mathcal{K}$ contains

```
ThymidinePhosphorylase ⊑ (∃≤1[bindsT]binds₁ ⊔ ∃≤1[bindsP]binds₂),
[bindsT]binds₁ ⊑ ¬[bindsP]binds₂
```

Clearly, the formal foundation now underpinning EER and UML with $\mathcal{CM}_{EER}$ and $\mathcal{CM}_{UML}$ permits one to add such constraints to the respective graphical language.

The widely noted OWL shortcoming of n-ary relationships with $n \geq 3$ can be handled easily in $\mathcal{CM}_{com}$, because we can with $\mathcal{DLR}_{ifd}$. Figure 6.4b depicts a ternary for recording epidemiological data on the path of infection of particular HIV subtypes from Donor to Recipient, which is represented in $\mathcal{CM}_{com}$ as REL (HIVtransmission) = {object:HIVsubtype, from:Donor, to:Recipient}, where object, from and to are the roles played by the objects (not depicted in Figure 6.4b). The corresponding translations into $\mathcal{DLR}_{ifd}$ is

```
HIVtransmission ⊑ [object]HIVsubtype ⊓ [from]Donor ⊓ [to]
Recipient                                                            ◇
```

Such differences in both graphical syntax and the underlying formalization are being investigated [1, 9, 16, 36, 38, 55] and proof-of-concept implementations exist [22, 56]. What they have in common is the use of a *decidable* logic language so as to guarantee that the reasoning services terminate. We will look at several reasoning scenarios in Section 6.4.1.

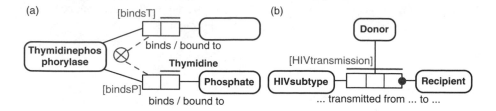

FIGURE 6.4   ORM2 examples: (a) role exclusion, which cannot be represented in standard UML and EER; (b) ternary relation, which cannot be represented fully in OWL.

6.3 EXTENSIONS

The need for extensions of conceptual data modeling languages clearly depends on which language one chooses to extend because each one differs in expressiveness, as we have seen in the previous section. In addition to the expressiveness within $\mathcal{DLR}_{ifd}$—say, adding KEY or ISA$_U$ to $\mathcal{CM}_{UML}$ (hence, to UML)—one can add features to the language that go beyond $\mathcal{DLR}_{ifd}$ or even beyond first-order predicate logic. Such extensions are motivated by the identification of *what* to represent and *how* in order to better capture the subject domain semantics. We shall look first at the former, which concerns incorporating notions of Ontology that generally require extensions to the language, which will be addressed afterward.

6.3.1 Ontology-Driven Modeling

The case for ontology-driven conceptual data modeling is described in some detail in [26, 27]: notions from philosophy can be used to solve modeling issues, improve conceptual data models, and provide explanations why one representation of a piece of information is better than another. Methodologically, this can be done by (i) providing a solution to a recurring modeling problem, (ii) using an ontology to generate several conceptual data models (preliminary solutions are described in [20, 32, 61]), and (iii) integrating (a section of) an ontology into the conceptual data model that subsequently is converted into data in the database; they were depicted in boldface with respect to the traditional waterfall methodology of database and software development in Figure 6.2. The first two options are young fields of research, whereas the third option is used widely in bioinformatics databases, where, for example, the Kyoto Encyclopedia of Genes and Genomes (KEGG) [44] or the Gene Ontology (GO) [24] are used for annotation of gene products, thereby linking primary and boutique databases, such as Uniprot [62] and the Horizontal Gene Transfer DataBase (HGT-DB) [23].

Option (i) considers (re-)usable components of foundational ontologies such as the Descriptive Ontology for Linguistic and Cognitive Engineering (DOLCE) [49], Basic Formal Ontology (BFO) [10], or General Formal Ontology (GFO) [31], being the high-level categories and generic relationships, such as the distinction between endurants and perdurants, and relationships like parthood, participation, and dependency. It provides modeling guidance and informs and refines language features, such as relational properties like transitivity, positionalism of relations, and identification mechanisms. In all cases, it offers answers how to best represent some piece of information and provides justifications why. The most prominent results of ontology-driven modeling to solve a recurring modeling issue is that of part–whole relations [3, 4, 29, 35, 41]. These refinements deal both with clarifying the different types of part–whole relations and how the entities participate in the relation. The part–whole relations can be structured in a hierarchy [41], which, in turn, contributes to correct usage and deductions in the conceptual data model and, if linked to data, enhances capabilities for information retrieval.

Example 6.3 *Ontology-Driven Conceptual Data Modeling: Parthood* A cell nucleus is spatially *contained in* an eukaryotic cell, but not a structural part of it, whereas the region occupied by the nucleus is a proper part of the region occupied by the eukaryotic cell it contains (proper parthood implies proper containment, but not vice versa). A cell receptor is a *structural part of* a cell wall's lipid bilayer but not a proper part because part of the receptor is external to it.

Let REL (hasStructuralPart) = {whole:3-Chlorobenzoate, part: Benzene} and hasStructuralPart ISA$_R$ hasPart, then a query "retrieve all molecules that hasPart some Benzene" will have in the query answer 3-Chlorobenzoate despite it not being represented explicitly: it is inferred thanks to the ISA$_R$ assertion. A query "retrieve all molecules that hasStructuralPart some Benzene" will *not* return enzyme–substrate complexes involving benzene rings where the benzene ring is spatially contained in the "hole" or lock of the receptor in the receptor–ligand interaction; hence, with a differentiation between parthood and containment (among others), the query answer will not contain false positives or noisy information.   ◇

In addition to refining particular relationships, there are guidelines from Ontology and AI to design a good taxonomy, such as using ideas from the OntoClean method [28]. OntoClean relies on metalevel properties, such as rigidity, and the foundational ontologies help in identifying the nature of the class or relationship under consideration. For instance, Protein has the property of being rigid (each individual object that is member of a Protein class is a protein for its entire existence), whereas Enzyme is antirigid (each individual enzyme is not necessarily always an enzyme), and an antirigid class cannot subsume a rigid one. Hence, one should *not* have Protein ISA$_C$ Enzyme in the model; instead it should have Enzyme ISA$_C$ Protein. Digging deeper, we see that the essential property of an enzyme is to catalyze a reaction, which is the *function* or *role* that the molecule performs, and it may be that at some point in time that protein still exists but is somehow defective in its functioning as an enzyme. Similarly, one might encounter Tetanospasmin ISA$_C$ Zinc-Endopeptidase and Zinc-Endopeptidase ISA$_C$ Toxin in a conceptual data model: tetanospasmin is indeed a zinc-endopeptidase and a toxin produced by *Clostridium tetani*, but it only has the role of being a toxin in humans, as *C. tetani* uses the enzyme in its natural functioning of the cell. A solution pattern to better model this type of information is provided by a foundational ontology: One creates a hierarchy for rigid properties and one for antirigid ones that, in turn, *inhere in* or *depend on* the rigid ones, thereby distinguishing between what it structurally *is* and what it functionally *does*, which leads to an assertion like REL (inheresIn) = {role:Enzyme, bearer:Protein}. Fortunately, one does not have to start from scratch anymore with such analyses in the subject domain of molecular biology, as several ontologies exist that take this approach (e.g., BioTop [8]), which can be used in the way as outlined in option (ii) in the introduction of this section. Overall, this will result in better conceptual data models, which is illustrated in the next example for catalytic reactions.

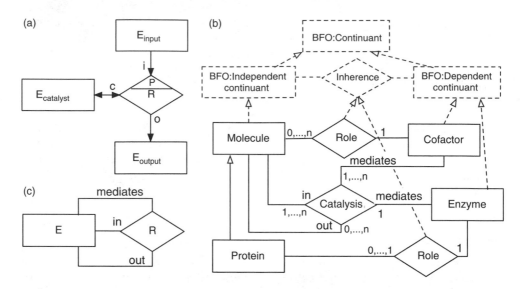

FIGURE 6.5   Static aspects of modeling single processes (catalytic reactions) in EER: (a) Elmasri et al.'s [21] proposal, with input, output, and catalyst molecules; (b) essential roles played; (c) example of a more refined representation of catalysis, informed by ontology, where the dashed entities and subsumption relationships are a fragment of BFO.

Example 6.4 *Ontology-Driven Conceptual Data Modeling: Catalysis*   Catalysis has three principal participants: molecule(s) in and out and the enzyme that catalyzes the reaction. Elmasri et al. [21] proposes a "process relationship" in EER to represent the static (atemporal) aspects of chemical processes, which is depicted in Figure 6.5a, which can be scaled up trivially to multiple inputs, outputs, and/or catalysts. However, the three entities are all molecules and, more importantly, some molecule can be both an `Einput` and an `Eoutput` in different reactions or the `Eoutput` molecule is also the `Ecatalyst` (autocatalytic reaction). Modeling the molecule's roles in a certain situation as different entity types results in duplication of data, which in turn leads to inconsistencies or "dirty" data in the database or application. The minimalist approach that avoids these problems is shown in Figure 6.5b, but it is unsatisfactory due to its lack of detail. To really solve it, we use a foundational ontology for modeling guidance and the BFO [10] and Relation Ontology [60] in particular. Then, the molecule's structural characteristics—like being a Protein consisting of amino acids— are distinguished from the role it plays—like Enzyme—and matched with entity types in BFO: `Protein` ISA$_C$ `Molecule`, `Molecule` ISA$_C$ `Object`, and `Enzyme` ISA$_C$ `Role`, which are related through a refinement of the RO `inherence` relation such that `role` ISA$_R$ `inherence`, REL(`role`) = {`role`:`Enzyme`, bearer: `Protein`}, and CARD (`Enzyme`,`role`,`role`) = 1..1. `Object`'s superclass in BFO is `Independent-Continuant` (`IC`), and `Role`'s superclasses are `RealizableEntity`, `SpecificallyDependentContinuant`, and `DependentContinuant` and, more generally with respect to the RO, REL(`inherence`) = {`role`:`DC`,bearer:`IC`}. Practically in the conceptual data model, the two branches from the BFO hierarchy can be added in whole or in abbreviated form, which is indicated with the dashed lines and rectangles in Figure 6.5c. This conceptual model fragment already solves the problem of data duplication that would occur with a database based on the conceptual model from Figure 6.5a and facilitates querying such that the query answer will have less noisy results (see also Examples 6.3 and 6.6). ◇

6.3.2 More Expressive Languages

Multiple extensions to conceptual data modeling languages exist, of which the most interesting one from a molecular biology perspective is the temporal dimension, that is, to have a means to specify unambiguously what changes, how, and under which conditions. This can be an object instantiating different classes at different points in time (called *object migration*), attributes that hold for a specific duration, or the relation between objects change (*relation migration*). For instance, each immune system cell Macrophage must have been an instance of Monocyte beforehand, that is, it "dynamically evolved" (DEV$^-$) [37], the value for DNA's attribute hasFoldingState changes to unfolded only for the duration that it is being transcribed, and the enzyme inheres in the molecule that is also a substrate in an autocatalytic reaction, so the interaction "dynamically extends" (RDEX) [42] to autoCatalysis, where RDEX can be defined using a temporal interpretation [42]:

$$ R \, \text{Rdex} \, R' \text{ if and only if } \langle o_1, o_2 \rangle \in R^{\mathcal{I}(t)} \rightarrow \exists t' > t \quad \langle o_1, o_2 \rangle \in R'^{\mathcal{I}(t')} \qquad (6.1) $$

where R, R' are relationships, $t, t' \in \mathcal{T}_p$ and $\mathcal{T}_p$ is a set of time points, and $\cdot^{\mathcal{I}}(t)$ is the interpretation function for a given snapshot of the state of affairs at that time. An elegant extension to $\mathcal{CM}_{com}$ can handle this (introduced below), so that the conceptual data model contains assertions such as REL (role) = {bearer:RNAmolecule, role: Ribozyme} and REL (autoCatalysis) = {substrate:RNAmolecule , catalyst: Ribozyme} and such that role RDEX autoCatalysis holds. Another typical challenge is how to represent metabolic pathways or genetics' Central Dogma with its part processes in a specific sequence.

To cater for the representation of this kind of information, the first questions to answer are: Which fundamental aspects involving time have to be represented, which language features does it require, and can it be done in a conceptual data model in such a way that it can be stored by the software and the consistency checked? Extant proposals include adding an ordered bag to EER to represent a notion of sequence of events [21] and using UML's sequence and activity diagrams (to model SARS-CoV infection) [58] that can represent processual information, although the UML diagrams have no formal foundation. Both proposals, however, do not let one represent concurrent reactions, detect inconsistencies (e.g., contain a cycle where there should not be one), or derive implicit information about such dynamic information. To be able to do so, one has to be able to represent the reactions as *n*-ary relationships, which can be represented in $\mathcal{CM}_{com}$, and formalize notions such as "precedes", "during" and similar natural language terms, which requires a language extension. For instance, we have to include somehow that "a immediately precedes b" means that we have not only (a, t) and (b, t') but also for each time point that $\neg \exists t''.t < t'' < t'$ and $t \neq t'$, where $t, t', t'' \in \mathcal{T}_p$. One can formalize "a during b" and the other 11 Allen temporal relations using the same approach. MADS [53] for spatiotemporal conceptual data modeling is fairly comprehensive, though its inclusion of temporal knowledge representation has been extended informed by a $\mathcal{DLR}_{US}$ foundation that also has a mapping to the temporally extended EER, called $\mathcal{ER}_{VT}$ [5]. $\mathcal{DLR}_{US}$ is in the same DL family as $\mathcal{DLR}_{ifd}$, but it does not have the "ifd" features—hence, compared to $\mathcal{CM}_{com}$, it will not have EXTK, FD, and OBJ—and instead has temporal classes, relationships, attributes, and evolution constraints to specify what changes and how. Let us briefly illustrate this for temporal classes. A fragment of the $\mathcal{DLR}_{\mathcal{US}}$ syntax is:

$$C \rightarrow \top \mid \bot \mid A \mid \neg C \mid C_1 \sqcap C_2 \mid C_1 \sqcup C_2 \mid \exists^{\leq k}[U_j]R \mid$$
$$\Diamond^+ C \mid \Diamond^- C \mid \Box^+ C \mid \Box^- C \mid \oplus C \mid \ominus C \mid C_1 \, \mathcal{U} \, C_2 \mid C_1 \, \mathcal{S} \, C_2$$

where the first line is the same as what we have seen for $\mathcal{DLR}$ and the second line introduces the temporal operators. The semantics of these operators are as follows. First, the $\mathcal{U}$ntil and $\mathcal{S}$ince operators, where $(u, v) = \{w \in \mathcal{T} \mid u < w < v\}$:

$$(C_1 \, \mathcal{U} \, C_2)^{\mathcal{I}(t)} = \left\{ d \in \top^{\mathcal{I}(t)} \mid \exists v > t \,.\, (d \in C_2^{\mathcal{I}(v)} \wedge \forall w \in (t, v) \,.\, d \in C_1^{\mathcal{I}(w)}) \right\}$$
$$(C_1 \, \mathcal{S} \, C_2)^{\mathcal{I}(t)} = \left\{ d \in \top^{\mathcal{I}(t)} \mid \exists v < t \,.\, (d \in C_2^{\mathcal{I}(v)} \wedge \forall w \in (v, t) \,.\, d \in C_1^{\mathcal{I}(w)}) \right\}$$

Second, $\mathcal{U}$ and $\mathcal{S}$ together with $\bot$ and $\top$ suffice to define the other ones: the temporal operator $\Diamond^+$ (some time in the future) as $\Diamond^+ C \equiv \top \, \mathcal{U} \, C$, $\oplus$ (at the next moment) as $\oplus C \equiv \bot \, \mathcal{U} \, C$, and likewise for their past counterparts $\Diamond^-$ (some time in the past) as $\Diamond^- C \equiv \top \, \mathcal{S} \, C$ and $\ominus$ (at the previous moment) as $\ominus C \equiv \bot \, \mathcal{S} \, C$. The operators $\Box^+$ (always in the future) and $\Box^-$ (always in the past) are the duals of $\Diamond^+$ and $\Diamond^-$ (some time in the past), respectively, that is, $\Box^+ C \equiv \neg \Diamond^+ \neg C$ and $\Box^- C \equiv \neg \Diamond^- \neg C$, and, finally, the operators $\Diamond^*$ (at some moment) and its dual $\Box^*$ (at all moments) can be defined as $\Diamond^* C \equiv C \sqcup \Diamond^+ C \sqcup \Diamond^- C$ and $\Box^* C \equiv C \sqcap \Box^+ C \sqcap \Box^- C$, respectively. This is similar for relationships in $\mathcal{DLR}_{\mathcal{US}}$. Then, we can perform the same procedure as for $\mathcal{CM}_{com}$: generate a fixed textual version for $\mathcal{CM}_{com}^-$+temporal extension, $^t\mathcal{CM}$ (alike Definition 6.1), declare a mapping from $^t\mathcal{CM}$ to a graphical syntax for the temporal operators, fix the semantics (alike Definition 6.2), and declare a mapping (alike Definition 6.3) to show that for each $^t\mathcal{CM}$ there is an equi-satisfiable $\mathcal{DLR}_{\mathcal{US}}$ knowledge base. This has been done already for EER without EXTK, FD, and OBJ [5] (named $\mathcal{ER}_{VT}$), which we shall not repeat here, but illustrate with the aforementioned examples. The "RDEX" of the aforementioned assertion `role RDEX autoCatalysis` can be added to the language's syntax (to a Definition 6.1' for $^t\mathcal{CM}$), the semantics as in Equation 6.1 aded to a Definition 6.2', and a mapping into $\mathcal{DLR}_{\mathcal{US}}$ as $R \sqsubseteq \Diamond^+ R'$ added to a Definition 6.3'. The dynamic evolution constraint for classes is represented syntactically as C DEV C', has a semantics of $o \in C^{\mathcal{I}(t)} \rightarrow \exists t' > t, o \in C^{\mathcal{I}(t')}$, and is mapped into $\mathcal{DLR}_{\mathcal{US}}$ as $C \sqsubseteq \Diamond^+ (C' \sqcap \neg C)$. We now also can distinguish between the "a precedes b", that is, a at holds at *some time* before b, $\Diamond^-$, and "a immediately precedes b," $\ominus$. This extension is particularly useful in molecular biology for modeling (and, as we will see later, checking consistency of) metabolic and biosynthetic pathways, which is illustrated in the next example.

Example 6.5 *Language Extensions: Temporal*   We can use the DEV evolution constraint to represent formally a meaningful relation between aforementioned Monocyte and Macrophage: In the normal course of things, each monocyte transforms into a macrophage, but such a cell is never both at the same time, and hence, the conceptual data model has `Monocyte DEV Macrophage` (i.e., `Monocyte` $\sqsubseteq \Diamond^+$ `(Macrophage` $\sqcap \neg$ `Monocyte)` in the $\mathcal{DLR}_{\mathcal{US}}$ knowledge base); it is trivial to model this the other way around with DEV$^-$ (that each macrophage must have been a monocyte earlier).

Let us now consider SARS viral infection events [58] that informally asserts that first the virus binds to the receptor, then either the membranes fuse or the virus detaches from the cell, and the virus enters the cell only after membrane fusion. Informed by a foundational ontology, one can create either a hierarchy of processes (`Binds ISA`$_C$ `Process` etc.)

and such that each process has participants (REL (hasParticipant) = {process: Binds, participant: Virus} and REL (has-Participant) = {process: Binds, participant: CellReceptor} etc.) or a more compact representation by creating relationships REL (binds) = {binder: Virus, bindsTo: Cell-Receptor} and likewise for REL (membraneFusion), REL (detach), and REL (viralEntry). As it does not matter which option we choose thanks to having temporal operators on both classes and relations in $\mathcal{DLR}_{\mathcal{US}}$, let us take the second option. Then, given the subject domain semantics, ViralEntry $\sqsubseteq \Diamond^-$ Binds must hold ("for each viral entry, it must have been bound some time before"), but not the converse (Binds $\sqsubseteq \Diamond^+$ ViralEntry) because the virus may detach. Regarding instances and tuple migration in a scenario of, say, simulations or processing annotations of video about cell processes, then the intention to add a migration from ⟨virus1, cell1⟩ ∈ viralEntry to ⟨virus1, cell1⟩ ∈ membraneFusion should result in a violation of the integrity constraint suggested by the subject domain knowledge of the database. This cannot be guaranteed in software based on plain UML, EER, or ORM but can with the additional temporal extension; hence, it ensures that the data represent events in reality more precisely with less errors. ◇

Besides temporality, one can add, among others, fuzzy, rough, or probabilistic features (e.g., fuzzy $\mathcal{DLR}$ [47]), which offer further options for creative modeling. For instance, $\mathcal{DLR}_{\mathcal{US}}$ has been shown to be useful to define the notions of *essential* and *immutable* parts [3], the fuzzy extension can cope with inclusion of a concept like Small Molecule that has no clear cutoff point for the actual size, and probabilistic knowledge can be used to represent "default" and "typical" cases [45]. The trade-off, however, is that while the additional features are great for modeling biological knowledge more precisely, it negatively affects automated reasoning services and scalability of the information systems—and it is exactly the automated reasoning services that contribute to in silico biological knowledge discovery.

6.4 AUTOMATED REASONING AND BIOLOGICAL KNOWLEDGE DISCOVERY

In this section, we briefly describe how various automated reasoning services and sophisticated querying can be used in the domain expert's "toolbox" for biological knowledge discovery.

6.4.1 Exploiting Automated Reasoning Services

A major advantage of the formal foundation for the conceptual data modeling languages with $\mathcal{DLR}_{ifd}$ is its decidability and, hence, the guarantee that the reasoning services that can be deployed for in silico biological knowledge discovery will terminate; more precisely, $\mathcal{DLR}_{ifd}$ is ExpTime-complete and so is $\mathcal{CM}_{com}$. As a basis, we can use so-called standard reasoning services for checking diagram and class consistency, class subsumption reasoning, and certain other implicit consequences. We describe them here briefly in terms of DL:

- *Conceptual Data Model Consistency* The whole conceptual data model Σ is consistent if it admits an instantiation, that is, all classes in $\mathcal{C}$ can be populated without violating any of the constraints; formally in $\mathcal{DLR}_{ifd}$: $\Sigma \nvDash \top \sqsubseteq \bot$.

- *Class Consistency* A class $C \in \mathcal{C}$ is consistent if Σ admits an instantiation in which the class has a nonempty set of instances; formally: $\Sigma \nvDash C \sqsubseteq \bot$.
- *Class Subsumption* A class C_1 subsumes a class C_2 (i.e., C_2 ISA C_1 in Σ) if Σ implies that C_1 is a generalization of C_2 (or all instances of C_2 are also instances of C_1), with $C_1, C_2 \in \mathcal{C}$; formally: $\Sigma \models C_2 \sqsubseteq C_1$.

Berardi et al. [9] also include refinement of multiplicities and typing for UML Class Diagrams, which means that the interaction of properties of several related classes may result in stricter multiplicities or typing than has been specified explicitly in Σ, and this service can be applied to $\mathcal{CM}_{com}$ as well. In addition, we can avail of two more reasoning services commonly used with DL knowledge bases, but only if one somehow combines the conceptual data model Σ with the instances in the software application or database. These services are *instance classification*—is a a member of C in Σ? that is, $\Sigma \models C(a)$—and *instance retrieval*, meaning to compute all individuals a such that $C(a)$ is satisfied by every interpretation of Σ (i.e., $\{a \mid \Sigma \models C(a)\}$).

A notable achievement in biological data discovery using automated reasoning has been the classification of protein phosphatases [63], where a novel protein phosphatase was discovered. It has also been used for finding suitable molecules in rubber manufacturing that matched the criteria (i.e., chosen attributes) [7], whose approach can be employed also in pharmainformatics when looking for drug candidates. For instance, to search for potential antibiotics by using criteria for the desired molecule such as "has as part a β-lactam ring" and "is water-soluble" and that also "function as enzyme inhibitor." Automated reasoning is illustrated in the next example with enzymes, proteins, substrate, and cofactors.

Example 6.6 *Reasoning over Ontology-Driven Conceptual Data Model*   Let us take a ontology-enhanced sample UML diagram about enzymes, as shown in Figure 6.6, that is both formalized in $\mathcal{CM}_{com}$ (with REL(inheresIn) = {role: Enzyme, bearer: Protein}, CARD(Enzyme, Protein, inheresIn) = (1, n), etc.) and the enzymes, proteins, substrates, and cofactors are extracted from one or more ontologies—that is, they are ontology modules adapted for conceptual data modeling (see Section 6.3.1 and Figure 6.1)—such as the PRO protein ontology [51] and Biopax [19]. Class subsumption reasoning reorders the classes in the taxonomy according to the properties they have; for example, for E2, we have not only REL(inheresIn) = {role:E2, bearer: Protein} but also REL(hasSubstrate) = {actor:E2, actee: S2}, that is, one more property than Enzyme, and hence, all instances of E2 must also be instances of Enzyme in all possible models and therefore E2 ISAEnzyme holds. E5 does

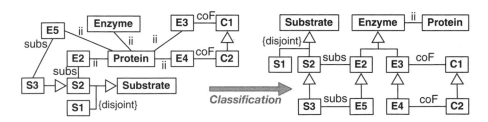

FIGURE 6.6   Sample $\mathcal{CM}_{\text{UML}}$ before (left) and after (right) classification (multiplicity not drawn); associations: (ii) inheres in; (subs): has substrate; (coF) has cofactor.

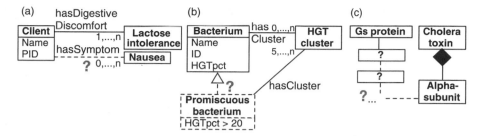

FIGURE 6.7 Graphical depiction of three query patterns to find "new" classes or relationships supported by data: (a) correlation; (b) hypothesis about existence of subclass PromiscuousBacterium; (c) path query to check whether Gs protein somehow relates to alpha-subunit of CholeraToxin.

not have more properties, but S3 ISA S2 and therefore E5 ISA E2. If the diagram would have had CARD (E3, C1, coF) = (1, 1) and CARD(E4, C2, coF) = (1, n), then it would have deduced CARD(E4, C2, coF) = (1, 1) as refined cardinality to comply with the inherited constraint. Now, if we add the hasSubstrate association to E3, then several things can happen, depending on the substrate: (i) if REL (hasSubstrate) = {actor:E3, actee:S2}, then the reasoner will deduce E3 ISA E2; (ii) if REL (hasSub- strate) = {actor:E3, actee:S3}, then E3 ISA E5; and (iii) if REL (hasSubstrate) = {actor:E3, actee:S1}, then E3 ISA Enzyme (because {S1, S2} DISJ$_c$ Substrate).

Querying is a form of reasoning, too, which can be done over the conceptual data model itself, over a database, or their combination [14, 15]. For instance, an automated reasoner evaluates "retrieve all enzymes that have C1 as coFactor" by traversing the tree from Enzyme down to all classes that have an association coFactor with C1 as class at the other end. In the case of the conceptual data model depicted in Figure 6.6, it will return E3, E4 as the answer: E3 because it is directly related and E4 because each C2 is also a C1. ◇

6.4.2 Finding New Relationships and Classes by Using Instances

Combining conceptual data models and the data in the information system is challenging and, to the best of our knowledge, no end-user usable implementations have been realized for the scenarios described in this section. The idea is that instances will justify information represented in the conceptual data model and the model is used for analyzing instances so that the requirements are essentially those for a knowledge base (TBox and Abox) and in particular scalability of reasoning over a conceptual data model in the presence of large amounts of data stored in a database (see, e.g., [14, 46] for preliminary results). Focusing on the advantages this option offers, there are three patterns for discovering implicit knowledge in standard knowledge bases [43]. For brevity, let lowercase letters denote instances of their respective classes in the conceptual data model. Then we have:

(i) "For each $X(x)$, $Y(y)$, $R(r)$, $R(X, Y)$, does there exist a $Z(z)$, $S(s)$ such that there exists ≥ 1 x and $s(x, z)$?" This is a query for the "known unknown" Z.

(ii) "For each $X(x)$, $Y(y)$, $R(r)$, $R(X, Y)$ in the data store, does there exist an $s(x, z)$ and an $t(x, a)$ where $Z(z)$, $S(s)$, $A(a)$, $T(t)$ hold?" This tests the hypothesis that there may be a quaternary relationship among A, X, Y, and Z instead of three binaries or perhaps a subtype X' that satisfies the conditions.

(iii) A path query (arbitrary relatedness): "For each $X(x)$, return any $r_1, \ldots, r_n$, their type of role, and the concepts $Y_1, \ldots, Y_n$ they are related to."

The first pattern is illustrated in Figure 6.7a in the setting of electronic health records where X = Client, S = has symptom, and Z = Nausea, thereby querying if patients suffering from lactose intolerance have the symptom of being nauseous.

The aim in the third pattern is to find type-level knowledge where the query answer also includes the class to which the instance(s) belong. This still can be tractable if one considers only classes directly related to X, but exploring the search space of sequences of conjunctive queries of arbitrary length is unrealistic. Restricted queries have been examined regarding discovering the relationships between Histone code, DNA sequence, and Gene expression regulation [57]; an example is depicted in Figure 6.7c, where one queries for a path that connects the G_s protein to the α-subunit only.

An unconstrained type (ii) query leads to a combinatorial explosion, which can be contained by requiring that the user select several classes and relationships when composing the query, therewith keeping a degree of knowledge discovery; for example, to find the type (species) of a plant specimen and to refine a classification of enzymes by adding properties. This type of query is not yet supported by standard DL and OWL reasoners, but some cues to implement this can be gleaned from database reverse engineering, whose algorithms detect concepts, relations, and mandatory and uniqueness constraints from the table definitions and data in the tables. A variation on this theme is to consider also incomplete information with rough sets, which has been shown to be useful in hypothesis testing [39]. For instance, it is known that some bacteria transfer more genes horizontally than others do ('promiscuous bacteria'), but is it not clear what the characteristics are and who has them. One may hypothesize that promiscuous bacteria have, say, >20% of their genes that are predicted to be horizontally acquired and have ≥5 clusters of horizontally transferred genes (see Figure 6.7b): In $\mathcal{CM}_{com}$, we have ATT(PromiscuousBacterium) = {HGTpct : $\text{Real}_{>20}$}, REL(hasClusters) = {org: PromiscuousBacterium, geneclust:HGTCluster}, and the constraint CARD (Pro-miscuousBacterium, HGTCluster, hasCluster) = 5..n. The data retrieved will be a set of bacteria of which some have the same values for the chosen properties, yet they are assumed to be distinct bacteria. Where possible, one can add new properties in successive steps to find the right combination of properties and thereby have discovered the means to indeed distinguish the bacteria. Any potentially useful intermediate combinations of properties can be easily included in the conceptual data model and be subjected to automated classification, as was illustrated in Example 6.6.

6.5   CONCLUSIONS AND OUTLOOK

Ontology-driven formal conceptual data modeling brings rigor to database and software development in the form of ontological guidance and use of ontologies to represent information more accurately, therewith resulting in a better quality conceptual data model and hence better software. The formal foundation ensures precision in representation of the semantics of the subject domain and enables automated reasoning over conceptual data models, which not only detects inconsistencies and derives implicit information and thereby contributes to the quality of conceptual data models, but also can be used in biological knowledge discovery processes. The latter include services such as consistency checking, class and instance classification, and querying. To substantiate these advantages, we presented a formal foundation for UML, EER, and ORM, being $\mathcal{CM}_{com}$, which has an equi-satisfiable $\mathcal{DLR}_{ifd}$ knowledge base. Ontological guidance to motivate better modeling choices was illustrated with a refinement for representing catalytic reactions. There are many language features and extensions thereof. We demonstrated that several that claimed to be "non-representable" biological knowledge actually can be represented in $\mathcal{CM}_{com}$ (hence, also in $\mathcal{DLR}_{ifd}$), such as constraints among relationships, and that for other requirements language extensions do exist that can give formal semantics to, among others, temporal knowledge. The latter was demonstrated with transforming entities and related processes in a cascade of interactions of viral infection. Automated reasoning services were illustrated for taxonomic classification, and three different query patterns to find new type-level information were described.

Ontology-driven formal conceptual data modeling is still a relatively young field, and many more usage scenarios are yet to be investigated fully, such as handling incomplete information in hypothesis testing [39], how OntoClean [28] ideas can be incorporated in conceptual data modeling methodologies, and developing a formal link between ontologies and conceptual data models. Development of CASE tools with both a unifying formalism—be this $\mathcal{CM}_{com}$ or another language—and an integrated automated reasoner is necessary as well, not just with one language interface [22] but with multiple graphical syntaxes. Temporal reasoning beyond $\mathcal{ER}_{VT}$ and its $\mathcal{DLR}_{US}$ foundation, principally either as extension to UML Class Diagrams or as formalization of sequence and activity diagrams, also may yield useful results for biological knowledge discovery.

REFERENCES

1. A. Artale, D. Calvanese, R. Kontchakov, V. Ryzhikov, and M. Zakharyaschev. Reasoning over extended ER models. In C. Parent, K.-D. Schewe, V. C. Storcy, and B. Thalheim (Eds.), *Proceedings of the 26th International Conference on Conceptual Modeling (ER'07)*, Auckland, New Zealand, November 5–9, 2007, *Lecture Notes in Computer Science*, Vol. 4801. Springer, 2007, pp. 277–292.

2. A. Artale, E. Franconi, F. Wolter, and M. Zakharyaschev. A temporal description logic for reasoning about conceptual schemas and queries. In S. Flesca, S. Greco, N. Leone, and G. Ianni (Eds.), *Proceedings of the 8th Joint European Conference on Logics in Artificial Intelligence (JELIA-02)*, *Lecture Notes in Artificial Intelligence*, Vol. 2424. Springer Verlag, 2002, pp. 98–110.

3. A. Artale, N. Guarino, and C. M. Keet. Formalising temporal constraints on part-whole relations. In G. Brewka and J. Lang (Eds.), *11th International Conference on Principles of Knowledge Representation and Reasoning (KR'08)*, Sydney, Australia, September 16–19, 2008. AAAI Press, Washington, DC, 2008, pp. 673–683.

4. A. Artale and C. M. Keet. Essential, mandatory, and shared parts in conceptual data models. In T. Halpin, H. Proper, and J. Krogstie (Eds.), *Innovations in Information Systems Modeling: Methods and Best Practices*, Advances in Database Research Series. IGI Global, 2008, pp. 17–52.

5. A. Artale, C. Parent, and S. Spaccapietra. Evolving objects in temporal information systems. *Ann. Math. AI*, 50(1–2):5–38, 2007.

6. F. Baader, D. Calvanese, D. L. McGuinness, D. Nardi, and P. F. Patel-Schneider (Eds.), *The Description Logics Handbook—Theory and Applications*, 2nd ed. Cambridge University Press, 2008.

7. S. Bandini and A. Mosca. Mereological knowledge representation for the chemical formulation. In *2nd Workshop on Formal Ontologies Meets Industry 2006 (FOMI2006)*, Trento, Italy, December 2006, pp. 55–69.

8. E. Beisswanger, S. Schulz, H. Stenzhorn, and U. Hahn. BioTop: An upper domain ontology for the life sciences—a description of its current structure, contents, and interfaces to OBO ontologies. *Appl. Ontol.*, 3(4):205–212, 2008.

9. D. Berardi, D. Calvanese, and G. De Giacomo. Reasoning on UML class diagrams. *AI*, 168(1–2):70–118, 2005.

10. BFO. Basic formal ontology. `http://www.ifomis.org/bfo`, accessed August 2010.

11. E. Bornberg-Bauer and N. Paton. Conceptual data modelling for bioinformatics. *Brief. Bioinformatics*, 3(2):166–180, 2002.

12. D. Calvanese and G. De Giacomo. Expressive description logics. In *The DL Handbook: Theory, Implementation and Applications*. Cambridge University Press, 2003, pp. 178–218.

13. D. Calvanese, G. De Giacomo, and M. Lenzerini. Identification constraints and functional dependencies in description logics. In B. Nebel (Ed.), *Proceedings of the 17th International Joint Conference on Artificial Intelligence (IJCAI'01)*, Seattle, Washington, USA, August 4–10, 2001, Vol. 1. Morgan Kaufmann, 2001, pp. 155–160.

14. D. Calvanese, G. D. Giacomo, D. Lembo, M. Lenzerini, A. Poggi, M. Rodríguez-Muro, and R. Rosati. Ontologies and databases: The DL-Lite approach. In S. Tessaris and E. Franconi (Eds.), *Semantic Technologies for Informations Systems: 5th International Reasoning Web Summer School (RW'09)*, Brixen-Bressanone, Italy, August 30–September 4, 2009, *Lecture Notes in Computer Science*, Vol. 5689. Springer, 2009, pp. 255–356.

15. D. Calvanese, C. M. Keet, W. Nutt, M. Rodríguez-Muro, and G. Stefanoni. Web-based graphical querying of databases through an ontology: The WONDER system. In S. Y. Shin, S. Ossowski, M. Schumacher, M. J. Palakal, and Chih-Cheng Hung (Eds.), *Proceedings of ACM Symposium on Applied Computing (ACM SAC'10)*, Sierre, Switzerland, March 22–26, 2010, ACM, 2010, pp. 1389–1396.

16. D. Calvanese, M. Lenzerini, and D. Nardi. Description logics for conceptual data modeling. In *Logics for Databases and Information Systems*. Kluwer, Amsterdam, 1998.

17. D. Calvanese, M. Lenzerini, and D. Nardi. Unifying class-based representation formalisms. *J. AI Res.*, 11:199–240, 1999.

18. P. P. Chen. The entity-relationship model—Toward a unified view of data. *ACM Trans. Database Syst.*, 1(1):9–36, 1976.

19. E. Demir et al. The BioPAX community standard for pathway data sharing. *Nat. Biotechnol.*, 28(9):935–942, 2010.

20. H. El-Ghalayini, M. Odeh, R. McClatchey, and D. Arnold. Deriving conceptual data models from domain ontologies for bioinformatics. In *2nd Conference on Information and Communication Technologies (ICTTA'06)*, Damascus, Syria, April 24–28, 2006, IEEE Computer Society, 2006, pp. 3562–3567.

21. R. Elmasri, F. Ji, and J. Fu. Modeling biomedical data. In J. Chen, E. Amandeep, and S. Sidhu (Eds.), *Biological Database Modeling*. Artech House, 2007, Chapter 3.

22. P. R. Fillottrani, E. Franconi, and S. Tessaris. The ICOM 3.0 intelligent conceptual modelling tool and methodology. *Semantic Web J.*, 3(3):293–306, 2012.

23. S. Garcia-Vallvé, E. Guzman, M. Montero, and A. Romeu. HGT-DB: A database of putative horizontally transferred genes in prokaryotic complete genomes. *Nucleic Acids Res.*, 31(1):187–189, 2003.

24. Gene Ontology Consortium. Gene Ontology: Tool for the unification of biology. *Nat. Genet.*, 25:25–29, 2000.

25. N. Guarino. Formal ontology and information systems. In *Proceedings of Formal Ontology in Information Systems (FOIS'98)*. IOS Press, Amsterdam, 1998.

26. N. Guarino. The ontological level: Revisiting 30 years of knowledge representation. In A. Borgida et al. (Eds.), *MylopoulosFestschrift, Lecture Notes in Computer Science*, Vol. 5600. Springer, Heidelberg, 2009, pp. 52–67.

27. N. Guarino and G. Guizzardi. In the defense of ontological foundations for conceptual modeling. *Scand. J. Inform. Syst.*, 18(1), debate forum, 9p, 2006.

28. N. Guarino and C. Welty. An overview of OntoClean. In S. Staab and R. Studer (Eds.), *Handbook on Ontologies*. Springer, Heidelberg, 2004, pp. 151–159.

29. G. Guizzardi. Ontological foundations for structural conceptual models, PhD thesis. University of Twente, The Netherlands, Telematica Instituut Fundamental Research Series No. 15, 2005.

30. T. Halpin and T. Morgan. *Information Modeling and Relational Databases*, 2nd ed. Morgan Kaufmann, San Mateo, CA, 2008.

31. H. Herre and B. Heller. Semantic foundations of medical information systems based on top-level ontologies. *Knowledge-Based Syst.*, 19:107–115, 2006.

32. M. Jarrar, J. Demy, and R. Meersman. On using conceptual data modeling for ontology engineering. *J. Data Semantics: Special Issue on Best Papers from the ER/ODBASE/COOPIS 2002 Conferences*, 1(1):185–207, 2003.

33. T. Kazic. Putting semantics into the semantic web: How well can it capture biology? *Proc. Pacific Symp. Biocomput.*, 11:140–151, 2006.

34. C. M. Keet. Biological data and conceptual modelling methods. *J. Conceptual Modeling*, 29, October 2003. Available: http://www.inconcept.com/jcm.

35. C. M. Keet. Part-whole relations in object-role models. In R. Meersman et al. (Eds.), *2nd International Workshop on Object-Role Modelling (ORM 2006), OTM Workshops 2006*, Montpellier, France, Nov. 2–3, 2006, *Lecture Notes in Computer Science*, Vol. 4278. Springer-Verlag, Berlin, 2006, pp. 1116–1127.

36. C. M. Keet. A formal comparison of conceptual data modeling languages. In *13th International Workshop on Exploring Modeling Methods in Systems Analysis and Design (EMMSAD'08)*, June 16–17, 2008, Montpellier, France, *CEUR-WS*, Vol. 337, pp. 25–39, 2008.

37. C. M. Keet. Constraints for representing transforming entities in bio-ontologies. In R. Serra and R. Cucchiara (Eds.), *11th Congress of the Italian Association for Artificial Intelligence (AI*IA 2009), Lecture Notes in Artificial Intelligence*, Vol. 5883. Springer, Bologna, Italy, 2009, pp. 11–20.

38. C. M. Keet. Mapping the object-role modeling language ORM2 into description logic language $\mathcal{DLR}_{ifd}$. Technical Report arXiv:cs.LO/0702089v2, KRDB Research Centre, Free University of Bozen-Bolzano, Italy, April 2009.

39. C. M. Keet. Ontology engineering with rough concepts and instances. In P. Cimiano and H. Pinto (Eds.), *17th International Conference on Knowledge Engineering and Knowledge Management (EKAW'10)*, October 11–15, 2010, Lisbon, Portugal, *Lecture Notes in Computer Science*, Vol. 6317. Springer, Heidelberg, 2010, pp. 507–517.

40. C. M. Keet. Enhancing identification mechanisms in UML class diagrams with meaningful keys. In *Proceeding of the SAICSIT Annual Research Conference 2011 (SAICSIT'11)*, ACM Conference Proceedings, 2011, Cape Town, South Africa, October 3–5, 2011, pp. 283–286.

41. C. M. Keet and A. Artale. Representing and reasoning over a taxonomy of part-whole relations. *Appl. Ontol.—Special Issue on Ontological Foundations for Conceptual Modeling*, 3(1–2):91–110, 2008.

42. C. M. Keet and A. Artale. A basic characterization of relation migration. In R. Meersman et al. (Eds.), *OTM Workshops, 6th International Workshop on Fact-Oriented Modeling (ORM'10)*, October 27–29, 2010, Hersonissou, Crete, Greece, *Lecture Notes in Computer Science*, Vol. 6428. Springer, 2010, pp. 484–493.

43. C. M. Keet, M. Roos, and M. S. Marshall. A survey of requirements for automated reasoning services for bio-ontologies in OWL. In *Proceedings of the 3rd Workshop on OWL: Experiences and Directions (OWLED 2007)*, June 6–7, 2007, Innsbruck, Austria, CEUR-WS, Vol. 258, 2007.

44. KEGG. Kyoto Encyclopedia of Genes and Genomes. Available: `http://www.genome.jp/kegg/`.

45. T. Lukasiewicz and U. Straccia. Managing uncertainty and vagueness in description logics for the semantic web. *J. Web Semantics*, 6(4):291–308, 2008.

46. C. Lutz, D. Toman, and F. Wolter. Conjunctive query answering in the description logic EL using a relational database system. In *Proceedings of the 21st International Joint Conference on Artificial Intelligence (IJCAI'09)*. AAAI Press, Washington, DC, 2009.

47. Z. Ma, F. Zhang, L. Yan, and J. Cheng. Representing and reasoning on fuzzy UML models: A description logic approach. *Expert Syst. Appl.*, 38(3):2536–2549, 2011.

48. J. S. Madin, S. Bowers, M. P. Schildhauer, and M. B. Jones. Advancing ecological research with ontologies. *Trends Ecol. Evol.*, 23(3):159–168, 2008.

49. C. Masolo, S. Borgo, A. Gangemi, N. Guarino, and A. Oltramari. Ontology library. WonderWeb Deliverable D18 (vers. 1.0)., 2003. Available: `http://wonderweb.semanticweb.org`.

50. B. Motik, P. F. Patel-Schneider, and B. Parsia. OWL 2 web ontology language structural specification and functional-style syntax. W3c recommendation, W3C, 27 Oct. 2009. Available: `http://www.w3.org/TR/owl2-syntax/`.

51. D. A. Natale et al. The Protein Ontology: A structured representation of protein forms and complexes. *Nucleic Acids Res.*, 39(Database issue):D539–D545, 2011.

52. Object Management Group. Superstructure specification. Standard 2.3, Object Management Group, May 2010. Available: `http://www.omg.org/spec/UML/2.3/`.

53. C. Parent, S. Spaccapietra, and E. Zimányi. *Conceptual Modeling for Traditional and Spatio-Temporal Applications—The MADS Approach*. Springer Verlag, Berlin and Heidelberg, 2006.

54. O. Pastor, A. M. Levin, J. C. Casamayor, M. Celma, L. E. Eraso, M. J. Villanueva, and M. Perez-Alonso. Enforcing conceptual modeling to improve the understanding of human genome. In *Fourth International Conference on Research Challenges in Information Science (RCIS'10)*, Nice, France, 19–21 May 2010. IEEE Computer Society, 2010, pp. 85–92.

55. A. Queralt and E. Teniente. Reasoning on UML class diagrams with OCL constraints. In D. Embley, A. Olivé, and S. Ram (Eds.), *Proceedings of ER'06, Lecture Notes in Computer Science*, Vol. 4215. Springer-Verlag, Heidelberg, 2006, pp. 497–512.

56. A. Queralt and E. Teniente. Decidable reasoning in UML schemas with constraints. In Z. Bellahsene and M. Léonard (Eds.), *CAiSE, Lecture Notes in Computer Science*, Springer, Heidelberg, 2008, pp. 281–295.

57. M. Roos, H. Rauwerda, M. Marshall, L. Post, M. Inda, C. Henkel, and T. Breit. Towards a virtual laboratory for integrative bioinformatics research. In C. M. Keet and E. Franconi (Eds.), *CSBio Reader: Extended Abstracts of CS & IT with/for Biology Seminar Series 2005*. Free University of Bozen-Bolzano, Bolzano, Italy, 2005, pp. 18–25.

58. D. Shegogue and W. J. Zheng. Object-oriented biological system integration: A SARS coronavirus example. *Bioinformatics*, 21(10):2502–2509, 2005.

59. B. Smith, M. Ashburner, C. Rosse, J. Bard, W. Bug, W. Ceusters, L. Goldberg, K. Eilbeck, A. Ireland, C. Mungall, T. OBI Consortium, N. Leontis, A. Rocca-Serra, A. Ruttenberg, S.-A. Sansone, M. Shah, P. Whetzel, and S. Lewis. The OBO Foundry: Coordinated evolution of ontologies to support biomedical data integration. *Nat. Biotechnol.*, 25(11):1251–1255, 2007.

60. B. Smith, W. Ceusters, B. Klagges, J. Köhler, A. Kumar, J. Lomax, C. Mungall, F. Neuhaus, A. L. Rector, and C. Rosse. Relations in biomedical ontologies. *Genome Biol.*, 6:R46, 2005.

61. V. Sugumaran and V. C. Storey. The role of domain ontologies in database design: An ontology management and conceptual modeling environment. *ACM Trans. Database Syst.*, 31(3):1064–1094, 2006.

62. The UniProt Consortium. Ongoing and future developments at the universal protein resource. *Nucleic Acids Res.*, 39:D214–D219, 2011.

63. K. Wolstencroft, R. Stevens, and V. Haarslev. Applying OWL reasoning to genomic data. In C. Baker and H. Cheung (Eds.), *Semantic Web: Revolutionizing Knowledge Discovery in the Life Sciences*, Springer, New York, 2007, pp. 225–248.

CHAPTER 7

BIOLOGICAL DATA INTEGRATION USING NETWORK MODELS

GAURAV KUMAR and SHOBA RANGANATHAN

Department of Chemistry and Biomolecular Sciences and ARC Centre of Excellence in Bioinformatics, Macquarie University, Sydney, Australia

7.1 INTRODUCTION

The advent of global genomic sequencing efforts has inspired biological studies to discover gene functionality in the genomes of various model organisms. The study of individual genes and gene products, that is, proteins, has proved to be very successful in elucidating fundamental biological principles. It is possible to also address many unanswered fundamental biological questions with the development of high-throughput technology to carry out miniature biochemical assays on a massive scale. This technological development allowed researchers to integrate diverse data sets to provide a more comprehensive understanding of biological mechanisms, as most biological processes consist of complex networks of interconnected components or modules. Advances in genomic and proteomic techniques have helped to elucidate the relationship between genes and proteins in various cellular interactions, such as signal transduction pathways and protein–DNA and protein–gene interactions to decipher cellular complexity. Based on the integration of biological knowledge, such analyses are known collectively as systems biology [1]. For the statistician and computational biologist, systems biology brings many interesting and challenging problems to combine information from relatively heterogeneous data sources from multiple experiments for meta-analysis at the level of cellular systems [2].

Understanding the genetic basis of disease is another major challenge in today's medicine. Discovering the molecular basis of disease will be crucial to improve diagnosis and treatment. Therefore, an integrated genomic effort is required using tools from statistics, computer science, and molecular biology. Hence, systems biology focuses on the networks of complex biological processes hidden in large amounts of experimental data. Biological knowledge has to be synthesized from various biological studies. Enormous amounts of biological data have been generated and stored in various public and private databases. In this chapter, we explore the utility of various data sources as resources to facilitate the integration-driven knowledge synthesis using a network-based model system. Our aim is

Biological Knowledge Discovery Handbook: Preprocessing, Mining, and Postprocessing of Biological Data,
First Edition. Edited by Mourad Elloumi and Albert Y. Zomaya.
© 2014 John Wiley & Sons, Inc. Published 2014 by John Wiley & Sons, Inc.

to demonstrate the utility of network models to understand protein function, genetic interaction, and their importance in gene association to various human disease conditions.

7.1.1 Data Sources

To incorporate the heterogeneous results of high-throughput experiments and computation-based predictions, methods of data integration have been widely used to provide efficient visualization and analysis of proteomic and genetic interactions. Integration methods help to reduce the complexity at the cell's system level, while databases provide efficient data storage and retrieval capabilities. A large variety of biomolecular databases exist, differing in their aim, coverage, and search capabilities. Diversity and redundancy are reflected in a large variety of the interaction databases as high-throughput data are routinely generated along with the results of computation-based prediction methods. Interaction data are usually obtained by direct submission from experimentalists, by literature mining (curation), or by applying computational methods. In this section, we highlight the importance of specific data resources.

7.1.1.1 Gene and Protein Interaction Databases The recent success in decoding genomes of model organisms has made it possible to identify the function of genes, the detection of protein–DNA binding motifs, and the determination of gene regulation. Unlike the genome, which is the stable feature of an organism, the proteome varies with the stage of development, with the tissue type, and in response to the environment of an organism. Among the many features of proteins, their interaction within the cell is a key aspect of their efficacy in carrying out their biological and molecular functions. These protein interactions are very useful to understand gene regulatory networks, biochemical pathways, and protein complex formation, as proteins do not function in isolation. Table 7.1 contains a detailed list of gene and protein interaction databases, covering a range of data types, organisms, and protein and/or gene functional association.

The metabolic pathway databases historically started with KEGG and the largest category of data sources, while protein interaction databases such as DIP, HPRD, IntAct, and MINT are a source of experimental and curated information. Some of the databases are limited to a specific organism, such as DroID for the fruit fly, *Drosophila melanogaster*, and Hp-DPI for *Helicobacter pylori*. Databases relevant to disease include the HCPIN for cancer and HIV-1 Interaction for AIDS.

7.1.1.2 Gene Ontology Gene Ontology (GO) is a taxonomic description of relationships between genes and proteins inside the cell. The information about a gene or a protein in a specific context is described as annotation. Therefore, the Gene Ontology Annotation (GOA) refers to hierarchical description of biological terms in a directed acyclic graph (DAG). The GO database (http://www.geneontology.org) is the source of a structured vocabulary, annotating genes and proteins with respect to three major cellular aspects, as described below [3]:

1. Biological processes (BPs) in which proteins are involved together as a team to achieve a common goal, for example, signaling pathways
2. Molecular function (MF) in which proteins are described in terms of their biochemical activities, such as "kinases" or "hydrolases"
3. Cellular components (CCs) to define the localization of the gene product, that is, the protein, within the eukaryotic cell

TABLE 7.1   Comprehensive List of Databases

Database	Purpose and Scope	URL
BioCyc	Metabolic pathway	`http://biocyc.org/`
BioGrid	Metabolic pathway	`http://www.thebiogrid.org/`
BOND	Metabolic pathway	`http://bond.unleashed-informatics.com/`
DIP	Protein–protein interaction	`http://dip.doe-mbi.ucla.edu/dip/`
DroID	Comprehensive *Drosophila* Interaction Database	`http://www.droidb.org/`
HCPIN	Human Cancer Pathway Protein Interaction Network	`http://nesg.org:9090/HCPIN/`
HIV-1 Interaction	HIV-1 Human Protein Interaction Database	`http://www.ncbi.nlm.nih.gov/RefSeq/HIVInteractions/`
Hp-DPI	*Helicobacter pylori* Database of Protein Interactions	`http://dpi.nhri.org.tw/protein/hp/ORF/`
HPRD	Protein–protein interaction	`http://www.hprd.org/`
I2D	Interologous Interaction Database	`http://ophid.utoronto.ca/`
IBIS	Inferred Biomolecular Interaction Server	`http://www.ncbi.nlm.nih.gov/Structure/ibis/ibis.cgi`
ICBS	Inter-Chain Beta-Sheet	`http://contact14.ics.uci.edu/`
IntAct	Protein–protein interaction	`http://www.ebi.ac.uk/intact/`
KDBI	Kinetic Data of Biomolecular Interaction	`http://contact14.ics.uci.edu/`
KEGG	Kyoto Encyclopedia of Gene and Genome	`http://www.genome.jp/kegg/`
MINT	Protein–protein interaction	`http://mint.bio.uniroma2.it/mint/`
MIPS	Protein–protein interaction	`http://mips.gsf.de/`
MPIDB	Microbial Interaction Data Base	`http://www.jcvi.org/mpidb/`
NetPro	Protein–protein and protein–small molecules interaction database	`http://www.molecularconnections.com/home/en/home/products/NetPro`
PDZBase	Protein–protein interaction database specifically for interactions involving PDZ domain	`http://icb.med.cornell.edu/services/pdz/start`
REACTOME	Pathway database	`http://www.reactome.org/ReactomeGWT/entrypoint.html`
PID	Pathway Interaction Database	`http://pid.nci.nih.gov/`
POINT	Comprehensive Protein–Protein Interaction Database	`http://point.bioinformatics.tw/`
PRIME	PRotein Interaction and Molecular Information DatabasE	`http://prime.ontology.ims.u-tokyo.ac.jp:8081/`
SPiD	Subtilis Protein Interaction Database	`http://genome.jouy.inra.fr/cgi-bin/spid/`
TargetMine	Database for Candidate Gene Prioritisation	`http://targetmine.nibio.go.jp`

The annotation of a gene or protein features the threefold collection (BP, MF, and CC) arranged in a DAG, known collectively as its ontology. The terms in each ontology are arranged in a pattern of highest generality (the root node of DAG) to increased specificity (the leaf nodes of DAG). The root nodes for the BP, MF, and CC DAGs are GO:0008150, GO:0003674, and GO:0005575, respectively. The relationship between parent nodes and their descendants in each of the three ontologies of the GO data set is defined by "is-a" or "part-of" relationship. Relationships which describe a GO term as a subclass or subtype of the parent GO term are indicative of the is-a relationship; for example, if X is-a Y, then X is a subclass of Y. The part-of relationship indicates that the descendant GO term is actually a component of the parent GO term, that is, it suggests a partial ownership relation. All parent–child relationships in the GO are expected to follow the true-path rule, mandating that the hierarchical structure of the GO holds from any term to its top-level parent. The true-path rule must apply for all is-a or part-of relationships. It is possible to have many annotations for a given gene or protein and thus belong to multiple paths in the ontology. GO also has evidence codes to support the inference of annotation and is designed to be species independent.

With the increasing number of genome-sequencing projects, there is an urgent need for the consistent description of genes and proteins derived from various data sources. This has led to the development of methodology for measuring the semantic similarity of GO terms for functional gene–protein associations. There are different methods for calculating the semantic similarities between the GO terms. Jiang et al. [4] used the information content (IC) of nodes in the DAG ontology for measuring the semantic similarity between GO terms. The IC of a GO term, g can be quantified by

$$\mathrm{IC}(g) = \log^{-1} P(g) \tag{7.1}$$

where $P(g)$ is the probability of encountering an instance of the GO term, g. In the hierarchical setup, the node probability increases as it moves up in the DAG ontology, while its information content decreases. Therefore, the probability is 1 for the root node of ontology and its information content is 0. The semantic similarity between two GO terms is defined by

$$\mathrm{sim}(g_1, g_2) = \frac{1}{\mathrm{IC}(g_1) + \mathrm{IC}(g_2) - 2 \cdot \mathrm{Share}(g_1, g_2)} \tag{7.2}$$

where $\mathrm{Share}(g_1, g_2)$ is defined as the information content of their most informative common ancestor:

$$\mathrm{Share}(g_1, g_2) = \max\{\mathrm{IC}(a) | a \in \mathrm{CommonAncestors}(g_1, g_2)\} \tag{7.3}$$

Lin et al. [5] extended this idea to define the semantic similarity between g_1 and g_2 as the IC of their most informative common ancestor over their IC:

$$\mathrm{Sim_{Lim}}(g_1, g_2) = \frac{2 \cdot \mathrm{Share}(g_1, g_2)}{\mathrm{IC}(g_1) + \mathrm{IC}(g_2)} \tag{7.4}$$

The method of Resnik et al. [6] measures semantic similarity by taking the IC of their most informative common ancestor. According to this method, the IC is quantified as the negative of its likelihood, that is, $-\log(p(g))$. Thus, the higher in the ontology a GO term appears, the lower its IC, and the semantic similarity between two GO terms in a DAG is the minimum subsumer. When multiple inheritances are present between g_1 and g_2, the minimum path needs to be considered for measuring the probability as the minimum subsumer,

$$p_{\text{ms}}(g_1, g_2) = \min_{c \in (g_1, g_2)} \{p(g)\} \tag{7.5}$$

The similarity score between g_1 and g_2 is then defined by

$$\text{Sim}(g_1, g_2) = -\log p_{\text{ms}}(g_1, g_2) \tag{7.6}$$

Sevilla et al. [7] suggested that the limitation of the Jiang and Lin methods are due to the semantic similarity of GO terms being closer to the root of the GO ontology, compared to the lower nodes and thus providing an erroneous semantic measure at different levels of the GO hierarchy, whereas Resnik's method ignores the IC in the structure of the ontology to concentrate on the IC of common ancestors. To overcome these shortcomings, Wang et al. [8] measured the semantic similarity based on the overall contribution of all the terms in the DAG ontology. Thus, the semantic similarity between g_1 and g_2 is defined by

$$S_{\text{GO}}(g_1, g_2) = \frac{\sum_{t \in Tg_1 \cap Tg_2} [S_{g_1}(t) + S_{g_2}(t)]}{\text{SV}(g_1) + \text{SV}(g_2)} \tag{7.7}$$

where $S_{g_1}(t)$ and $S_{g_2}(t)$ are the *S-values* of the GO term t related to terms S_{g_1} and S_{g_2}, respectively. A GO term g can be represented by

$$\text{DAG}g = (g, T_g, E_g) \tag{7.8}$$

where T_g is the set of GO terms in *DAGg*, including the term g and all its ancestral terms in a *DAGg*. The S value for GO term t related to term g, $S_g(t)$, is defined by

$$S_g(g) = 1$$
$$S_g(t) = \max\{w_e \cdot S_g(t') | t' \in \text{children}(t)\} \quad \text{if } t \neq g \tag{7.9}$$

where w_e is the semantic contribution factor for edge $e \in E_g$ linking term t with its child term t' and has a value between $0 < w_e < 1$. SV(g) is the overall S value for all terms in *DAGg*, defined by

$$\text{SV}(g) = \sum_{t \in T_g} S_g(t) \tag{7.10}$$

In addition to the methods described here, a detailed overview of other semantic measurements on the GO is available from Pesquita et al. [9].

GO is widely used for content analysis in the gene enrichment process. In such analyses, statistical testing can be used to identify those GO categories and subgraphs with unusual gene counts across the gene list. Standard statistical testing under the null hypothesis assumes that each gene has equal probability of being detected as a differential expressed gene. Under this assumption, the number of genes associated with a GO category that overlaps with the set of differentially expressed genes follows a hypergeometric distribution. This distribution is often presented using the analogy of drawing balls from an urn without replacement. Let the total number of balls in the urn be N and assume the ball come in two colors, white and black. The probability of taking out white balls in L sequential draws with a random outcome X is defined by

$$P(X = k | N, Nc, L) = \frac{\binom{Nc}{k}\binom{N - Nc}{L - k}}{\binom{N}{L}} \tag{7.11}$$

where N is the total number of balls and N_c is the number of white balls. In this model, the objects being selected are genes or proteins annotated with a specific GO term. This model can be extended to the multivariate distribution of GO counts, as detailed by Shaw [10].

One can use the above statistics to see the commonality of gene and protein interactions and identify those GO paths which are significant in all the three GO categories. GO-based statistical analysis is useful for genome-scale experiments as it allows the combined analysis of gene lists or protein interactions differing mainly in size, experimental platform, or organisms. GO-based data analysis provides solutions at the level of biological function to address biologically important questions.

7.1.1.3 Gene Expression
Organisms contain information on how to develop their form and structure and the tools responsible for carrying out all their organism-specific biological processes. This information is encoded in their genes. With the development of cDNA microarray or DNA-Chip technology, it is possible to monitor hundreds or thousands of genes simultaneously and provide information for identifying genes as well as the changes in their activities. Therefore, microarray technology is well suited for analyzing chronic diseases associated of even an autoimmune or inflammatory nature [11].

The availability of inexpensive microarrays makes it possible to elucidate the network of genomic regulation masked by large amounts of biological data. The general technique to assign the functional association among genes is known as clustering and is based on the pairwise similarity or dissimilarity between genes and choosing an appropriate distance measure to link groups of genes. Distance measures for unsupervised clustering are based on Euclidean distance, CityplaceManhattan distance, Pearson correlation, and Spearman correlation. Correlation-based distance is normally the preferred option, as biologists are interested in grouping genes with similar changes in expression levels across conditions, irrespective of whether their average expression level is high or low. However, the Pearson correlation-based distance measure is more useful, as it alleviates the difficulty of associating gene pairs which are negatively associated with each other. After distance calculation, data points (genes) are forced into the nested subset or hierarchy. Thus, hierarchical clustering generates a tree where the length of the branch denotes the distance measure. Eisen et al. [12] were the first to apply hierarchical clustering to yeast genes in *Sacchromyces cerevisiae*. This clustering method is useful but falls short as the size and complexity of the data increase with more advanced organisms. Statistically, it is established that grouping based on pairwise distance reflects local decisions based on the bottom-up approach. Subsequently, the attention was shifted to partitioning clustering algorithms for gene association from the expression profile to minimize the heterogeneity of the cluster (intercluster distance) while maximizing their separation (intracluster distance) [13]. To address the statistical problems associated with hierarchical clustering, Tamayo et al. [14] used a partitioning clustering algorithm based on self-organizing maps (SOMs) to cluster genes based on the expression data, developing the computer package GENECLUSTER to produce and display SOMs from gene expression data. placeCityButte et al. [15] introduced an integrated network approach known as the "relevance network" for the functional association between pairs of genes. They measured the RNA expression levels in cancer cell lines with and without anticancer agents, allowing them to measure the baseline expression levels in cell lines for the presence of growth inhibitors. Their network technique, that is, the *relevance network*, then finds correlation across separate biological measures such as RNA expression and susceptibility to anticancer agents and calculates the minimum spuriously high correlation coefficient by calculating the entropy by

$$H = \sum_{x=1}^{10} p(x) \log_2[p(x)] \tag{7.12}$$

where $p(x)$ is the probability value with decile x of the feature. They then calculated the similarity of features in a pairwise manner after removing the lowest entropy. The rate of similarity is defined by

$$\hat{r} = \frac{r}{\text{abs}(r)} r^2 \tag{7.13}$$

where r^2 is the sample correlation coefficient and abs is the absolute value function. Relevance networks display nodes with varying degrees of cross-connectivity and distinguish true biological association from noise in the gene network.

Subramanian et al. [16] developed the Gene Set Enrichment Analysis (GSEA) to evaluate microarray data to rank genes for the characterization of the phenotypic class based on prior biological knowledge, such as biological pathways, chromosomal location (i.e., cytogenetic band), or GO category. They calculated the enrichment score (ES) as follows:

1. They rank the order of N genes in the expression data set D to form list $L = \{g_1, \ldots, g_N\}$ according to the correlation $r(g_j) = r_j$ based on their expression profile. Then they evaluate the fraction of genes in S(hits) weighted according to the expression correlation and the fraction of genes not in S(misses) up to a given position i in L,

$$P_{\text{hit}}(S, i) = \sum_{g_j \in S, j \leq i} \frac{|r_j|^p}{N_R} \quad \text{where } N_R = \sum_{g_j \in S} |r_j|^p \tag{7.14}$$

and

$$P_{\text{miss}}(S, i) = \sum_{g_j \notin S, j \leq i} \frac{1}{N - N_H} \tag{7.15}$$

2. The maximum deviation from $P_{\text{hit}} - P_{\text{miss}}$ is taken as the ES. For a randomly distributed S, ES(S) will be relatively small, but if it is concentrated at the top or bottom of the list or otherwise nonrandomly distributed, then ES(S) will be correspondingly high. When $p = 0$, ES(S) is reduced to standard Kolmogorov–Smirnov statistics. The genes in S are weighted by their expression correlation and normalized by the sum of the correlation over all the genes in S for $p = 1$.

TABLE 7.2   Gene Expression Databases

Database	Scope	URL
ArrayExpress	Database of Gene Expression and other microarry data	`http://www.ebi.ac.uk/arrayexpress/`
CIBX	Center for Information Biology Gene Expression database	`http://cibex.nig.ac.jp/index.jsp`
DRAGON	Database Referencing of Array Gene Online	`http://pevsnerlab.kennedy krieger.org/dragon.htm`
GEO	Gene Expression Omnibus	`http://www.ncbi.nlm.nih.gov/geo/`
GXD	Gene Expression Database	`http://www.informatics.jax.org/mgihome/GXD/aboutGXD.shtml`
HuGE	Human Gene Expression index	`http://www.biotechnology center.org/hio/`
IST	*In silico* Transcriptomics	`http://ist.genesapiens.org`
Oncomine	Compendium of cancer transcriptomic profiles	`www.oncomine.org`
PLEXdb	PLant EXpression Database	`http://www.plexdb.org/`
SMD	Stanford Microarray Database	`http://smd.stanford.edu/`

Table 7.2 contains the gene expression databases which are a publically available free resource for the study of gene expression and for testing new analysis methods.

7.1.1.4 *Protein Domain Interaction Databases*

Protein crystallographic structures suggest that the *domain* is the fundamental unit of protein and folds independently in the polypeptide chain. A large protein chain often shows signs of having evolved by joining the preexisting domains in new combinations. Thus, "domain shuffling" is an important event, as proteins are the structural and functional units, carrying out diverse biological processes inside the cell. Often interaction between domains is specific and has a well-defined binding surface, as the presence of certain domains in proteins facilitates the propensity for such interaction. The CBM database is developed to highlight domain interactions at atomic resolution [17].

Protein interactions observed in high-throughput experiments provide evidence for predicting domain interactions. The InterDom database [18] collects evidence for domain interaction using information from protein-protein interaction (PPI) data sources and scores the reliability of prediction based on the experimental evidence available for each interaction, while DIAM uses the phylogenetic profile of Pfam domains to create a domain interaction map [19].

It has been shown that domain fusion events can be used to establish the functional association between proteins [20]. The graph-based network model of protein domains suggests that the highly connected domains in eukaryotes evolved recently to support inter- and intracellular signaling events [21]. The availability of protein crystal structures deposited in PDB provides an opportunity to understand the characteristics of interacting surfaces in protein complex formation and domain interaction. PIBASE uses the structural classification of protein sequences present in SCOP and CATH to determine the domain interface, physical PPI, and structural and functional properties [22], whereas MOD-BASE contains three-dimensional (3D) structures to predict interacting protein partners and models putative interacting domain interfaces [23]. 3DID contains domain–domain and domain–peptide interactions by exploiting 3D structures [24], while iPfam has been developed for the visualization of protein interactions using the 3D structure at the domains and amino acid resolution [25].

7.1.2 Issues with Data Integration from Multiple Sources

In silico methods use experimental observations to infer interaction among genes and proteins. Data mining approaches help to integrate large datasets of experimental observations. However, the reliability and coverage of such interactions are questionable as it is difficult to estimate true interactions observed in experimental data, which are generated under various laboratory conditions and contain high error rates [26]. Moreover, large-scale assays are biased toward interactions between abundant proteins. Nonetheless, it is possible to study the interactions of genes and proteins under the assumption that evolution has left interaction-related imprints on the corresponding sequence, protein family and genome organization [27]. Gene expression analysis by Eisen et al. [12] suggested that biological function can be assigned to genes based on the knowledge of the functions of other genes in the cluster. It is generally believed that interacting protein pairs are more likely to be coexpressed as first shown by Spellman et al. [28] in the yeast cell cycle gene expression data. Huh et al. [29] studied protein localization data which suggests interacting protein pairs are more likely to occupy the same subcellular compartments, whereas Kumar and Ranganathan [30] have shown the statistical significance of a metabolic network in addition to a PPI network for studying the subcellular localization of human proteins. Therefore, both gene expression and subcellular localization of proteins can be used to assess the reliability of true interactions in the protein interaction data set.

7.2 BIOLOGICAL NETWORK MODELS

There are several experimental methods for identifying PPIs, but no experimental method exists to detect all PPIs. Furthermore, each experimental approach has generated a significant number of false-positive and false-negative interactions. For example, the yeast-two-hybrid (Y2H) systems generate false positives due to accidental activation of reporter genes and self-activating "bait" proteins. False-negative interactions are reported in this system as interaction is prevented due to the misfolding of fusion proteins and masking of interaction by the use of full-length proteins [31]. Moreover, "bait" and "prey" proteins are overexpressed in the nucleus, so that their interactions may not be physiologically relevant, while some interactions involving membrane proteins are undetectable [32] by the experimental approaches used. Therefore, computational methods have been developed to combine different high-throughput experimental data sets, with the majority of effort focused toward developing methods based on sequence similarity and graph-based learning techniques, trained on features of the known set of protein or gene interactions. Chacko and Ranganathan [33] have recently reviewed graph theory in bioinformatics while networks in biology have been reviewed by Kumar et al. [34]. In this section, we will briefly review the major computational methodologies available for predicting protein and gene interactions.

7.2.1 Sequence-Based Approach to Predict Interactions and Functional Links between Proteins

Sequence-based protein interaction is based on the evolutionary hypothesis (refer to Section 7.1.2), with the simplest model assuming that these interaction-related fingerprints

are the result of coevolution of interacting protein pairs due to their functional association. Based on the coevolution hypothesis, Pellegrini et al. [35] showed the presence of
functional linkage between proteins associated in biochemical pathways and in structural
protein complexes inside the cell. Functional linkage between two proteins, A and B, in
a given genome is defined by finding homologues in other genomes and comparing their
phylogenetic profiles, that is, the presence or absence of genes in different species. If the
presence of homologues is the same for both proteins A and B, then there is a functional
linkage under the hypothesis that proteins evolve in a correlated fashion. The sequence-
based method is extended to gene fusion events in genomes to show interactions between
proteins and in protein complex formation [36]. Molecular evolution suggests that gene
fusion events are advantageous in genomes, as they decrease the load of regulation inside
the cell for a particular biological process. Similar functional linkage between two separate
proteins A and B in one organism was established by observing the fusion of A and B as a
single protein in other species. The fused protein is known as the Rosetta stone sequence
[20]. Pazos et al. [37] predicted PPT by comparing the evolutionary distance between protein sequences. Here, the evolutionary distance was calculated as the average value of the
amino acid residue similarity. Their "mirror tree" method does not require the presence of
fully sequenced genomes as compared to the phylogenetic profile method. Overbeek et al.
[38] showed the importance of gene clusters in bacterial genomes to highlight the functional
coupling of genes and their regulation in the biochemical and signal transduction pathways.

7.2.2 Graph-Theoretic and Probabilistic-Based Protein Interaction Network Models

The availability of multiple sources of genomewide data provides complementary views
to single genomes and highlights the need for algorithms to unify these views. Integration
methods beyond direct experimental measurement of protein interaction will assist in improving the quality of experimental data, while using available sources of information, with
different weights for different data sources to capture global information. Balasubramaniam
et al. [39] used graph-based edge permutation and node label statistical testing to show the
importance of GO-derived and mRNA expression data for protein functional prediction in
the yeast genome.

Deng et al. [40] used an integrated approach to predict protein function using a Markov
random-field (MRF) method in the interaction networks. Their integrated approach includes
separate networks containing protein pairwise relationships, such as gene expression correlation profile and genetic interactions, and domain architecture as an individual protein
feature. The algorithmic details of MRF-based data integration using network models are
available from Deng et al. [40]. Letovsky and Kasif [41] proposed the MRF-based belief
propagation algorithm for the functional assignment of proteins in the PPI network. Leone
et al. [42] have developed a message-parsing algorithm known as belief propagation (BP)
for the rapid analysis of complex protein interaction networks. Jansen et al. [43] used the
Bayesian network approach for predicting protein function in the yeast genome. In their integrated approach, protein interaction data from high-throughput assays along with genomic
features such as expression data, GO biological process, and data on protein essentiality
were considered. Similar to the yeast genome, Rhodes et al. [44] used the Bayesian network to predict human PPIs, using an integrated approach to combine functional genomic
data. Genomic information such as interaction between the orthologues of human proteins,

gene expression profiles, GO molecular function, and shared enriched protein domains was considered.

Kondor and Lafferty [45] suggested the use of a diffusion kernel method to define similarity between protein pairs in an interaction network. Lanckriet et al. [46] extended the kernel-based method for protein function prediction using an SVM (support vector machine) approach. Combining different information sources as the linear combination of the kernel matrix, their method was applied to classify membrane and ribosomal proteins. Lee et al. [47] used a kernel-based method to understand protein function based on information on all neighboring proteins in the interaction network. They developed a kernel logistic regression (KLR) model to include protein domains, protein complexes, and gene expression information as separate networks.

7.2.3 Models in Genetic Interaction Networks

Genetic interaction between pairs of functionally related genes is defined by comparing the phenotypes of mutated gene pairs (i.e., double mutation) with that of the single mutation in either of the genes in the pair. Interactions among genes are classified as positive or negative interactions, depending on the difference in the phenotypes due to double mutants compared to single mutants. Genetic interaction is said to be positive if the phenotypes of the double mutants are significantly better than expected from the single mutants; otherwise the interaction is said to be negative [48]. There are two strategies for measuring genetic interactions in the yeast genome. The first is to use synthetic genetic arrays (SGAs) and similar high-density arrays of double mutants by mating pairs from an available set of single mutants [49]. The second approach provides an alternative to SGA, taking advantage of the sequence barcode embedded in a set of yeast deletion mutants to measure the relative growth rate in a population of double mutants by hybridization to an anti-barcode microarray [49]. Costanzo et al. [50] constructed the genetic interaction map for ~75% of *S. cerevisiae* genes using SGA. Their genetic landscape suggests that highly connected genes (hubs) are associated with several fundamental physiological and evolutionary properties. Moreover, hubs influence multiple phenotypic traits and are multifunctional in nature.

Biologists frequently encounter the problem of selecting candidate genes from the list of hundreds of genes in genetic studies such as cytogenetic, linkage, and GWASs (genomewide association studies) to identify chromosomal regions associated with a disease or a phenotype of interest. They usually rank candidate genes by matching their information across multiple data sources. A number of methods are currently available for gene prioritization. Aerts et al. [51] developed the Endeavour method for gene prioritization using an integrative approach by collating information from GO, microarray expression, EST expression, protein domains, PPIs, biological pathways, *cis* regulatory modules, transcriptional motifs, sequence similarity, and published literature. Similarly, Franke et al. [52] used a Bayesian classifier for integrating data from diverse sources into a gene network to rank genes associated with the human diseases. Köhler et al. [53] developed GeneWandered for prioritization using random-walk analysis that defines similarities in PPI networks. Their method assumes that global network similarity measures capture relationships between genes based on the shortest paths. These gene prioritization methods are of limited use where little is known about the molecular mechanism of the phenotype. To overcome this limitation, Nitsch et al. [54] assess candidate genes by considering the level of differential expression of the gene neighborhood under the assumption that candidate genes will tend to be surrounded by strongly differentially expressed neighbors. In their gene network, multiple paths between genes were considered using the Laplacian exponential diffusion kernel method. Candidate genes were ranked by considering the differential expression of neighbors as weights for distance function.

7.3 NETWORK MODELS IN UNDERSTANDING DISEASE

To understand the molecular mechanisms of human disease conditions, we require a data-mining approach aimed at modeling the functional relationships between genes and/or proteins as complex independent networks [55]. Moreover, extracting new biological insights from the high-throughput genomic studies of human diseases is challenging and limited by the difficulties in recognizing and evaluating relevant biological processes from enormous quantities of experimental data.

7.3.1 Interactome Network for Disease Prediction

Calvano et al. [56] studied the inflammatory response to bacterial endotoxin in the human interaction network using a leukocyte gene expression profile. They observed significant changes in interaction among genes as the inflammation progresses with time. Initial progression of inflammation showed changes in the expression of cytokines and chemokines followed by the nuclear factor k/relA family of transcription factors. In the later stage of inflammation, they found a decrease in the expression for genes involved in the mitochondrial energy production, protein synthesis, and protein degradation. They considered the biological pathways in their network as significant only if the statistical likelihood of the highly connected genes is greater than 4 (P value < 0.0001) as calculated from the equation

$$\text{Score} = -\log_{10}\left(1 - \sum_{i=0}^{f-1} \frac{C(G, i)C(N - G, s - i)}{C(N, s)}\right) \tag{7.16}$$

where N is the number of genes in the gene network with G focus genes, while for the pathway of s genes, f are focus genes and $C(n, k)$ is the binomial coefficient.

Lim et al. [57] studied ataxias and disorders of Purkinje cell degeneration using the protein interaction network. GO term enrichment analysis of their network suggests that proteins are enriched for biological processes: transcriptional regulation, RNA splicing, ubiquitination and cell cycles; cellular components: nucleus, proteasome complex, spliceosome complex, and nuclear membrane; and molecular functions: transcription factor binding, transcription cofactor activity, DNA binding, and kinase inhibitor activity. The authors also demonstrated the utility of network analysis in uncovering novel ataxia-causing genes and genetic modifiers for ataxia.

GWAS has shown that genetic variation in the nucleotides of DNA sequences underlines disease risk in human. However, molecular mechanisms underlying the disease conditions are poorly characterized. Heining et al. [58] used a network approach to understand the molecular mechanism underlying the autoimmune disease T1D (type 1 diabetes). They created the interferon regulatory factor 7 (IRF7)–driven inflammatory network (IDIN) by integrating transcription factor–driven gene networks of rat stains and their regulatory loci with that of the human gene expression and GWAS to identify genes, networks, and pathways for the human disease. Their study suggests that the IDIN genes contribute to T1D risk. These genes are also responsible for the innate viral response pathway and macrophages in the etiology of T1D.

7.3.2 Network Perturbation Due to Pathogens

Infectious diseases cause millions of deaths each year. Billions of dollars are spent annually toward the understanding of host–pathogen infection and to identify potential targets for drug discovery and clinical treatments. An important aspect in understanding the mechanism of parasite infection is how it infects the host. Protein interaction networks help in uncovering the complex mechanism of infection as interactions of host surface proteins with the pathogen initiate communication and play a vital role in pathogenesis. Here, we review briefly the analysis of host–pathogen protein interaction networks.

LaCount et al. [59] used the Y2H approach to screen protein interactions in the intraerythocytic stage of *Plasmodium falciparum*, the stage responsible for the pathogenesis of malaria in humans. They showed enrichment of the protein set involved in chromatin modification, transcriptional regulation, mRNA stability, and ubiquitination. These enriched protein sets have similar expression patterns, protein domains, and GO annotation. Suthram et al. [60] used the malaria parasite *P. falciparum* to compare and contrast the differences in the interaction patterns with those of eukaryotes such as *S. cerevisiae*, *Caenorhabditis elegans*, *D. melanogaster*, and *H. pylori*. Their finding suggests the conservation of network modules for endocytosis and chromatin remodeling. They also made an observation in their studies that the conservation of specific groups of related genes does not necessarily imply the conservation of interactions among their encoded proteins. Chassey et al. [61] created "infection" networks by integrating HCV (hepatitis C virus) proteins with those of the human interactome to study cellular interaction and signaling pathways related to viral biology and pathogenesis. Their network analysis suggests that HCV targets signaling pathways such as insulin, Jas/STAT, and TGFβ. Moreover, structural HCV proteins such as CORE, NS3, and NS5A are highly connected proteins in the infection network.

Analysis of virus–human protein interinteraction networks has revealed that host interactors tend to be enriched in proteins that are highly connected in the cellular networks. These hub proteins are thought to be essential for the normal cell functioning and during pathogenesis [62] and could serve as targets for drug design.

7.3.3 Network View of Cancer

Cancer is a disease that arises due to the genomic instability such as mutation, copy number variation, methylation, and changes in the expression pattern of genes. It is also caused by viral oncogenes (cancer genes) from simian virus 40, human papilloma virus, and adenovirus. Vogelstein and Levin [63] first suggested the use of a network approach to understand the biochemical rewiring of tumor suppressor gene *p53* in human. Thus, a deeper understanding of cancer molecular mechanisms needs modeling of functional interrelationships between genes and/or proteins as complex interdependent networks. In this section, we summarize integrative network modeling in recent cancer studies.

Pujana et al. [64] used an integrated approach to create a breast cancer–associated gene network (BCN) around four genes: *BRCA1*, *BRCA2*, *ATM*, and *CHECK2*. Their BCN data have been combined with that of the gene expression and orthologues found in other species to generate potential functional relationships between cancer genes/proteins inside the network. This analysis suggests a new gene, *HMMR*, to be associated with a higher risk of breast cancer. Chuang et al. [65] carried out a network analysis for the classification of breast cancer metastasis by integrating protein interaction networks and gene expression profiles and identified the protein functional relationships in pathways associated with the progression of cancer. placeCityTaylor et al. [66] showed the changes in global network modularity of the human interactome to characterize breast cancer prognosis. Their analysis on a cohort of sporadic, nonfamilial breast cancer patients suggests significant differences in the average Pearson correlation coefficient of hub proteins and their interacting partners in patients who were disease free after extended follow-up and those who died of disease. They classified hubs into inter- and intramodular types based on the coexpression correlation with its interacting partners. Shiraishi et al. [67] studied the bistable switches consisting of proteins/genes in complex networks to analyze disease progression in lung cancer and in hepatitis virus infections. The bistable switch converts a continuous input signal into discontinuous ON or OFF response and plays a very important role in information processing and decision making in various cellular interactions. The authors suggested the possibility of novel drug–target candidates for controlling disease progression using these signal processing switches.

Mukherjee et al. [68] proposed a probabilistic model based on a simple Boolean function to account for the stochastic variation observed in noisy biological data and showed its usefulness in the study of signaling pathways associated with cancer biology. Nagaraj and Reverter [69] applied the above method for candidate gene prioritization in colorectal cancer using 13 binarized Boolean variables. They showed that novel candidate genes are secreted proteins (FXYD1, GUCA2B, REG3A), kinases (CDC42BPB, EPHB3, TRPM6), and transcription factors (CDK8, MEF2C, ZIC2). Kim et al. [70] developed a method known as extreme-value association (EVA) to detect the biological mechanism of invasiveness in various forms of cancer. Their method identified the genes *COL11A1*, *INHBA*, and *THB2* associated with high specificity and invasiveness during the progression of cancer.

Network studies of disease genes confirm the importance of nonrandom gene association for particular phenotypes, functions, and progression of disease [71, 72]. Moreover, combining the gene expression profile to infer hot spots within the protein–gene interaction network has a huge potential for disease prediction.

7.4 FUTURE CHALLENGES

Biological data are regularly generated and stored in public databases. However, the absence of systematic statistical methods make it very difficult to reliably remove noisy data as biological data are known to contain false-positive and false-negative errors. Therefore, an important issue is the reliable integration of noisy data. Moreover, the future of DNA sequencing and whole-genome transcript profiling has both opportunities and challenges for data management as the cost of such technologies continues to decrease. Low sequencing cost provides an enormous opportunity to integrate genomic data at the gene and mRNA levels to model cellular complexity.

Although genes are encoded by the linear series of nucleotide bases, the genome of an organism interacts with histones (proteins) to form distinct 3D structures, that is, chromatin. Under such structural constraints, the histone code hypothesis suggests that multiple histone modifications such as acetylations and methylations act in a combinatorial fashion to specify distinct chromatin states [73]. Theoretical modeling of chromatin states to understand the dynamics of gene regulation is the next challenge to be addressed. Moreover, our understanding of gene regulation is limited, as genes are tightly regulated by regions distant from promoters, such as regulatory elements, insulators, and boundary elements [74]. ChIP-based methods [75] have a promising future for understanding the dynamic interplay between regulatory regions and the gene-coding regions, allowing our understanding of mechanisms governing gene regulation in disease states [76]. It has been suggested that the regulatory network of DNA binding proteins and gene regulatory elements can provide unique targets for therapeutic applications [77]. Cellular control happens not only at the gene level but also at the level of RNA sequences. CLIP-seq methods are used to decode microRNA–target and protein–RNA interaction maps [78].

Besides data integration, another critical challenge in computational biology is to develop methods and tools for analyzing, interpreting, and visualizing genomic data to underline the functioning of biological systems.

ACKNOWLEDGMENT

Gaurav Kumar acknowledges the award of a Macquarie University Research Scholarship (MQRES). This work was supported by the award of the ARC Centre of Excellence in Bioinformatics grant (CE0348221) to Shoba Ranganathan.

REFERENCES

1. T. Ideker, T. Galitski, and L. Hood. A new approach to decoding life: Systems biology. *Annu. Rev. Genomics Hum. Genet.* 2:343–372, 2001.

2. S. L. Normand. Meta-analysis: Formulating, evaluating, combining, and reporting. *Stat. Med.*, 18(3):321–359, 1999.

3. M. Ashburner, et al. Gene ontology: Tool for the unification of biology. The Gene Ontology Consortium. *Nat Genet.*, 25(1):25–29, 2000.

4. J. J. Liang and D. W. Conrath. Semantic similarity based on corpus statistics and lexical taxonomy. In *Proceedings of ROCLING X (1997) International Conference on Computational Linguistics*, Academic Sinica, Taipei, Taiwan, 1997, pp. 19–33.

5. D. Lin. An information-theoretic definition of similarity. In Jude W. Shavlik (Ed.), *Proceedings of the Fifteenth International Conference on Machine Learning (ICML'98)*, Madison, Wisconsin, USA, July 24–27, 1998, Morgan Kaufmann, San Francisco, CA, 1998, pp. 296–304.

6. R. Resnik. Semantic similarity in a taxonomy: An information-based measure and its application to problems of ambiguity in natural language. *J. AI Res.*, 11:95–130, 1999.

7. J. L. Sevilla, V. Segura, A. Podhorski, E. Guruceaga, J. M. Mato, L. A. Martinez-Cruz, F. J. Corrales, and A. Rubio. Correlation between gene expression and GO semantic similarity. *IEEE/ACM Trans. Comput. Biol. Bioinformatics*, 2(4):330–338, 2005.

8. J. Z. Wang, Z. Du, R. Payattakool, P. S. Yu, and C. F. Chen. A new method to measure the semantic similarity of GO terms. *Bioinformatics*, 23(10):1274–1281, 2007.

9. C. Pesquita, D. Faria, A. O. Falcao, P. Lord, and F. M. Couto. Semantic similarity in biomedical ontologies. *PLoS Comput. Biol.*, 5(7):e1000443, 2009.

10. C. A. Shaw. Gene ontology-based meta-analysis of genome-scale experiments. In D. R. Goldstein and R. Guerra (Eds.), *Meta-Analysis and Combining Information in Genetics and Genomics*, Chapman and Hall/CRC, 2009, pp. 175–197.

11. R. A. Heller, M. Schena, A. Chai, D. Shalon, T. Bedilion, J. Gilmore, D. E. Woolley, and R. W. Davis. Discovery and analysis of inflammatory disease-related genes using cDNA microarrays. *Proc. Natl. Acad. Sci. USA*, 94(6):2150–2155, 1997.

12. M. B. Eisen, P. T. Spellman, P. O. Brown, and D. Botstein. Cluster analysis and display of genome-wide expression patterns. *Proc. Natl. Acad. Sci. USA*, 95(25):14863–14868, 1998.

13. J. Rahnenfuhrer. Clustering algorithms and other exploratory methods for microarray data analysis. *Methods Inf. Med.*, 44(3):444–448, 2005.

14. P. Tamayo, D. Slonim, J. Mesirov, Q. Zhu, S. Kitareewan, E. Dmitrovsky, E. S. Lander, and T. R. Golub. Interpreting patterns of gene expression with self-organizing maps: Methods and application to hematopoietic differentiation. *Proc. Natl. Acad. Sci. USA*, 96(6):2907–2912, 1999.

15. A. J. Butte, P. Tamayo, D. Slonim, T. R. Golub, and I. S. Kohane. Discovering functional relationships between RNA expression and chemotherapeutic susceptibility using relevance networks. *Proc. Nat. Acad. Sci. USA*, 97(22):12182–12186, 2000.

16. A. Subramanian, et al. Gene set enrichment analysis: A knowledge-based approach for interpreting genome-wide expression profiles. *Proc. Natl. Acad. Sci. USA*, 102(43):15545–15550, 2005.

17. B. A. Shoemaker, A. R. Panchenko, and S. H. Bryant. Finding biologically relevant protein domain interactions: Conserved binding mode analysis. *Protein Sci.*, 15(2):352–361, 2006.

18. S. K. Ng, Z. Zhang, S. H. Tan, and K. Lin. InterDom: A database of putative interacting protein domains for validating predicted protein interactions and complexes. *Nucleic Acids Res.*, 31(1):251–254, 2003.

19. P. Pagel, M. Oesterheld, V. Stumpflen, and D. Frishman. The DIMA web resource—Exploring the protein domain network. *Bioinformatics*, 22(8):997–998, 2006.

20. E. M. Marcotte, M. Pellegrini, H. L. Ng, D. W. Rice, T. O. Yeates, and D. Eisenberg. Detecting protein function and protein-protein interactions from genome sequences. *Science*, 285(5428):751–753, 1999.

21. S. Wuchty. Scale-free behavior in protein domain networks. *Mol. Biol. Evol.* 18(9):1694–1702, 2001.

22. F. P. Davis and A. Sali. PIBASE: A comprehensive database of structurally defined protein interfaces. *Bioinformatics*, 21(9):1901–1907, 2005.

23. U. Pieper, et al. MODBASE, a database of annotated comparative protein structure models, and associated resources. *Nucleic Acids Res.*, 32(Database issue):D217–222, 2004.

24. A. Stein, A. Ceol, and P. Aloy. 3did: Identification and classification of domain-based interactions of known three-dimensional structure. *Nucleic Acids Res.*, 39(Database issue):D718–723, 2011.

25. R. D. Finn, M. Marshall, and A. Bateman. iPfam: Visualization of protein-protein interactions in PDB at domain and amino acid resolutions. *Bioinformatics*, 21(3):410–412, 2005.

26. G. T. Hart, A. K. Ramani, and E. M. Marcotte. How complete are current yeast and human protein-interaction networks? *Genome Biol.*, 7(11):120, 2006.

27. F. Pazos and A. Valencia. Protein co-evolution, co-adaptation and interactions. *EMBO J.*, 27(20):2648–2655, 2008.

28. P. T. Spellman, G. Sherlock, M. Q. Zhang, V. R. Iyer, K. Anders, M. B. Eisen, P. O. Brown, D. Botstein, and B. Futcher. Comprehensive identification of cell cycle-regulated genes of the yeast *Saccharomyces cerevisiae* by microarray hybridization. *Mol. Biol. Cell.*, 9(12):3273–3297, 1998.

29. W. K. Huh, J. V. Falvo, L. C. Gerke, A. S. Carroll, R. W. Howson, J. S. Weissman, and E. K. O'Shea. Global analysis of protein localization in budding yeast. *Nature*, 425(6959):686–691, 2003.

30. G. Kumar and S. Ranganathan. Network analysis of human protein location. *BMC Bioinformatics*, 11(Suppl. 7):S9, 2010.

31. T. Ito, T. Chiba, R. Ozawa, M. Yoshida, M. Hattori, and Y. Sakaki. A comprehensive two-hybrid analysis to explore the yeast protein interactome. *Proc. Natl. Acad. Sci. USA*, 98(8):4569–4574, 2001.

32. C. von Mering, R. Krause, B. Snel, M. Cornell, S. G. Oliver, S. Fields, and P. Bork. Comparative assessment of large-scale data sets of protein-protein interactions. *Nature*, 417(6887):399–403, 2002.

33. E. Chacko and S. Ranganathan. *Graphs in Bioinformatics; Algorithms in Computational Molecular Biology: Techniques, Approaches and Applications.* Wiley, Hoboken, NJ, 2011.

34. G. Kumar, A. P. Cootes, and S. Ranganathan. *Untangling Biological Networks Using Bioinformatics: Algorithms in Computational Molecular Biology: Techniques, Approaches and Applications.* Wiley, Hoboken, NJ, 2011.

35. M. Pellegrini, E. M. Marcotte, M. J. Thompson, D. Eisenberg, and T. O. Yeates. Assigning protein functions by comparative genome analysis: Protein phylogenetic profiles. *Proc. Natl. Acad. Sci. USA*, 96(8):4285–4288, 1999.

36. A. J. Enright and C. A. Ouzounis. Functional associations of proteins in entire genomes by means of exhaustive detection of gene fusions. *Genome Biol.*, 2(9):341–347, 2001.

37. F. Pazos and A. Valencia. Similarity of phylogenetic trees as indicator of protein-protein interaction. *Protein Eng.*, 14(9):609–614, 2001.

38. R. Overbeek, M. Fonstein, M. D'Souza, G. D. Pusch, and N. Maltsev. The use of gene clusters to infer functional coupling. *Proc. Natl. Acad. Sci. USA*, 96(6):2896–2901, 1999.

39. R. Balasubramanian, T. LaFramboise, D. Scholtens, and R. Gentleman. A graph-theoretic approach to testing associations between disparate sources of functional genomics data. *Bioinformatics*, 20(18):3353–3362, 2004.

40. M. Deng, T. Chen, and F. Sun. An integrated probabilistic model for functional prediction of proteins. *J. Comput. Biol.*, 11(2–3):463–475, 2004.

41. S. Letovsky and S. Kasif. Predicting protein function from protein/protein interaction data: A probabilistic approach. *Bioinformatics*, 19(Suppl 1):i197–204, 2003.

42. M. Leone and A. Pagnani. Predicting protein functions with message passing algorithms. *Bioinformatics*, 21(2):239–247, 2005.

43. R. Jansen, H. Yu, D. Greenbaum, Y. Kluger, N. J. Krogan, S. Chung, A. Emili, M. Snyder, J. F. Greenblatt, and M. Gerstein. A Bayesian networks approach for predicting protein-protein interactions from genomic data. *Science*, 302(5644):449–453, 2003.

44. D. R. Rhodes, S. A. Tomlins, S. Varambally, V. Mahavisno, T. Barrette, S. Kalyana-Sundaram, D. Ghosh, A. Pandey, and A. M. Chinnaiyan. Probabilistic model of the human protein-protein interaction network. *Nat. Biotechnol.*, 23(8):951–959, 2005.

45. R. I. Kondor and J. D. Lafferty. Diffusion kernels on graphs and other discrete input spaces. In C. Sammut and A. G. Hoffmann (Eds.), *Machine Learning: Proceedings of the Nineteenth International Conference (ICML'02)*, University of New South Wales, Sydney, Australia, July 8–12, 2002, Morgan Kaufmann, San Francisco, CA, 2002, pp. 315–322.

46. G. R. Lanckriet, T. De Bie, N. Cristianini, M. I. Jordan, and W. S. Noble. A statistical framework for genomic data fusion. *Bioinformatics*, 20(16):2626–2635, 2004.

47. H. Lee, Z. Tu, M. Deng, F. Sun, and T. Chen. Diffusion kernel-based logistic regression models for protein function prediction. *OMICS*, 10(1):40–55, 2006.

48. R. Mani, R. P. St Onge, J. Lt. Hartman, G. Giaever, and F. P. Roth. Defining genetic interaction. *Proc. Natl. Acad. Sci. USA*, 105(9):3461–3466, 2008.

49. C. Boone, H. Bussey, and B. J. Andrews. Exploring genetic interactions and networks with yeast. *Nat. Rev. Genet.*, 8(6):437–449, 2007.

50. M. Costanzo, et al. The genetic landscape of a cell. *Science*, 327(5964):425–431, 2010.

51. S. Aerts, et al. Gene prioritization through genomic data fusion. *Nat. Biotechnol.*, 24(5):537–544, 2006.

52. L. Franke, H. van Bakel, L. Fokkens, E. D. de Jong, M. Egmont-Petersen, and C. Wijmenga. Reconstruction of a functional human gene network, with an application for prioritizing positional candidate genes. *Am. J. Hum. Genet.*, 78(6):1011–1025, 2006.

53. S. Kohler, S. Bauer, D. Horn, and P. N. Robinson. Walking the interactome for prioritization of candidate disease genes. *Am. J. Hum. Genet.*, 82(4):949–958, 2008.

54. D. Nitsch, L. C. Tranchevent, B. Thienpont, L. Thorrez, H. Van Esch, K. Devriendt, and Y. Moreau. Network analysis of differential expression for the identification of disease-causing genes. *PLoS One*, 4(5):e5526, 2009.

55. I. G. Khalil and C. Hill. Systems biology for cancer. *Curr. Opin. Oncol.*, 17(1):44–48, 2005.

56. S. E. Calvano, et al. A network-based analysis of systemic inflammation in humans. *Nature*, 437(7061):1032–1037, 2005.

57. J. Lim, et al. A protein-protein interaction network for human inherited ataxias and disorders of Purkinje cell degeneration. *Cell*, 125(4):801–814, 2006.

58. M. Heinig, et al. A trans-acting locus regulates an anti-viral expression network and type 1 diabetes risk. *Nature*, 467(7314):460–464, 2010.

59. D. J. LaCount, et al. A protein interaction network of the malaria parasite *Plasmodium falciparum*. *Nature*, 438(7064):103–107, 2005.

60. S. Suthram, T. Sittler, and T. Ideker. The *Plasmodium* protein network diverges from those of other eukaryotes. *Nature*, 438(7064):108–112, 2005.

61. B. de Chassey, et al. Hepatitis C virus infection protein network. *Mol. Syst. Biol.*, 4:230, 2008.

62. M. D. Dyer, T. M. Murali, and B. W. Sobral. The landscape of human proteins interacting with viruses and other pathogens. *PLoS Pathog.*, 4(2):e32, 2008.

63. B. Vogelstein, D. Lane, and A. J. Levine. Surfing the p53 network. *Nature*, 408(6810):307–310, 2000.

64. M. A. Pujana, et al. Network modeling links breast cancer susceptibility and centrosome dysfunction. *Nat. Genet.*, 39(11):1338–1349, 2007.

65. H. Y. Chuang, E. Lee, Y. T. Liu, D. Lee, and T. Ideker. Network-based classification of breast cancer metastasis. *Mol. Syst. Biol.* 3:140, 2007.

66. I. W. Taylor, R. Linding, D. Warde-Farley, Y. Liu, C. Pesquita, D. Faria, S. Bull, T. Pawson, Q. Morris, and J. L. Wrana. Dynamic modularity in protein interaction networks predicts breast cancer outcome. *Nat. Biotechnol.*, 27(2):199–204, 2009.

67. T. Shiraishi, S. Matsuyama, and H. Kitano. Large-scale analysis of network bistability for human cancers. *PLoS Comput. Biol.*, 6(7):e1000851, 2010.

68. S. Mukherjee, S. Pelech, R. M. Neve, W. L. Kuo, S. Ziyad, P. T. Spellman, J. W. Gray, and T. P. Speed. Sparse combinatorial inference with an application in cancer biology. *Bioinformatics*, 25(2):265–271, 2009.

69. S. H. Nagaraj and A. Reverter. A Boolean-based systems biology approach to predict novel genes associated with cancer: Application to colorectal cancer. *BMC Syst. Biol.*, 5:35, 2011.

70. H. Kim, J. Watkinson, V. Varadan, and D. Anastassiou. Multi-cancer computational analysis reveals invasion-associated variant of desmoplastic reaction involving INHBA, THBS2 and COL11A1. *BMC Med. Genomics*, 3:51, 2010.

71. S. Wachi, K. Yoneda, and R. Wu. Interactome-transcriptome analysis reveals the high centrality of genes differentially expressed in lung cancer tissues. *Bioinformatics*, 21(23):4205–4208, 2005.

72. K. I. Goh, M. E. Cusick, D. Valle, B. Childs, M. Vidal, and A. L. Barabasi. The human disease network. *Proc. Natl. Acad. Sci. USA*, 104(21):8685–8690, 2007.

73. Z. Wang, et al. Combinatorial patterns of histone acetylations and methylations in the human genome. *Nat. Genet.*, 40(7):897–903, 2008.

74. A. C. Bell, A. G. West, and G. Felsenfeld. Insulators and boundaries: Versatile regulatory elements in the eukaryotic. *Science*, 291(5503):447–450, 2001.

75. M. J. Fullwood and Y. Ruan. ChIP-based methods for the identification of long-range chromatin interactions. *J. Cell. Biochem.*, 107(1):30–39, 2009.

76. G. A. Maston, S. K. Evans, and M. R. Green. Transcriptional regulatory elements in the human genome. *Annu. Rev. Genomics Hum. Genet.*, 7:29–59, 2006.

77. M. J. Fullwood, et al. An oestrogen-receptor-alpha-bound human chromatin interactome. *Nature*, 462(7269):58–64, 2009.

78. J. H. Yang, J. H. Li, P. Shao, H. Zhou, Y. Q. Chen, and L. H. Qu. starBase: A database for exploring microRNA-mRNA interaction maps from Argonaute CLIP-Seq and Degradome-Seq data. *Nucleic Acids Res.*, 39(Database issue):D202–209, 2011.

CHAPTER 8

NETWORK MODELING OF STATISTICAL EPISTASIS

TING HU and JASON H. MOORE

Computational Genetics Laboratory, Geisel School of Medicine,
Dartmouth College, Lebanon, New Hampshire

8.1 INTRODUCTION

Epistasis is recognized as ubiquitous in the genetic architecture of complex traits such as human disease susceptibility. Quantifying interaction effects among multiple loci throughout the human genome has become the major focus of current research for understanding the complex relationship between genetic variation and phenotypic traits [12, 13, 38, 39]. This task is challenging due to the fact that enumerating all possible combinations of genetic variants in a data set of moderate size is computationally infeasible. Thus, efficient tools are needed to overcome the statistical and computational difficulties of detecting genetic interactions.

The goal of this chapter is to introduce the new method of modeling statistical epistasis using networks. Networks allow for a structured representation of a set of entities and links that describe their relationships and provide a well-suited framework for epistasis studies. In addition, the classic graph theory [51] and rapidly developing network science [41] constitute a powerful tool to facilitate modeling epistasis using networks. We first discuss epistasis and the challenges in detecting it. Next, we introduce some fundamental definitions of networks and topological properties that are useful for epistasis modeling. We highlight two newly proposed network-based approaches to characterizing statistical epistasis and discuss their major findings and advances.

8.2 EPISTASIS AND DETECTION

In recent years, experimental studies in model systems and statistical studies in human populations both have shown unequivocally that nonadditive effects of genetic variation on complex traits are pervasive. The interactions between different genes on a biological

Biological Knowledge Discovery Handbook: Preprocessing, Mining, and Postprocessing of Biological Data,
First Edition. Edited by Mourad Elloumi and Albert Y. Zomaya.
© 2014 John Wiley & Sons, Inc. Published 2014 by John Wiley & Sons, Inc.

trait, that is, one gene masks the effect of one or more other genes, are generally defined as *epistasis* [6, 31, 46, 50]. Epistasis is discussed in the literature in two different forms. At the individual level, *biological epistasis* is observed as the phenotypic impact of physical interactions among proteins and other biomolecules, while *statistical epistasis* is observed at the population level as the nonadditive mathematical relationship among multiple genetic variants [12, 32, 42]. In this chapter, we focus on the latter, that is, statistical epistasis. Epistasis explains partially the nonlinearity of the relationship between genotype and phenotype in genetic studies. It should be recognized as a fundamental component of genetic architecture when studying the association between genotype and complex phenotypic traits, such as common human diseases [13, 31, 32].

Although the biological mechanism that forms epistasis is not clearly understood yet, it could be explained from an evolutionary point of view by canalization. The concept of *canalization* was proposed in the fields of developmental and evolutionary biology [18, 19, 48]. Canalization describes the ability of complex evolutionary systems to stabilize their phenotypic traits against genetic and environmental variations. It is an evolved underlying network, where multiple genetic factors jointly modify one phenotypic outcome, to keep a system intact in the face of mutational perturbations. These ideas are supported by both analytical studies on how mutational robustness results in epistatic effects on phenotype and subsequently facilitates phenotypic adaptation [17] and experimental studies on identifying epistatic interactions in yeast metabolism networks [45]. It is suggested that human systems evolve against negative mutational effects via increasing redundancy and robustness, and thus the resulting dependencies among genes lead to epistasis [32, 37].

Two reasons attribute to the statistical and computational challenge in detecting epistasis, especially in the era of genomewide association studies (GWAS) [20–22, 33, 38, 49]. First, it must process a vast amount of data sufficient to support the large number of hypotheses involved in modeling interactions, even when considering only pairwise interactions [21, 33, 36]. Second, the exhaustive evaluation of all possible combinations of genetic variants would require expensive computation. That is, when studying k-way interaction among n variables, the computational cost is of the order of n^k, which is exponential in k. Thus, the current computational power that we have does not allow us to do that for even not-so-large values of k [11, 13, 33, 38].

Several techniques have been proposed to reduce the computational complexity of detecting epistasis in high-dimensional data sets. Preselection of genetic variants for epistasis screening has become one of the most common strategies since usually not all variables are relevant. Most pruning methods prioritize main effects in that they select genetic markers based on the strength or statistical significance of their main effects on phenotypic traits. However, this strategy may fail in finding gene–gene interactions when the underlying genotype–phenotype association is pure epistatic [15, 46]. In other words, it has the risk of discarding important genetic variants involved in high-order interactions without the presence of significant or high main effects.

An alternative pruning method is to use synergistic interaction strength instead of main effect. This strategy prioritizes variable pairs showing relatively strong or significant two-locus interactions. Information-theoretic measures are usually used to quantify this pairwise synergistic interaction [1, 8, 9, 30, 34, 35]. In information-theoretic terms, the main and interaction effects correspond to the so-called *mutual information* and *information gain* [14]. Specifically, $I(A; C)$ denotes the mutual information of variable A's genotype and C, usually the class variable with status *case* or *control* in population-based disease association studies.

Intuitively, $I(A; C)$ is the reduction in the uncertainty of the class C due to knowledge about variable A's genotype. Its precise definition is

$$I(A; C) = H(C) - H(C|A) \tag{8.1}$$

where $H(C)$ is the *entropy* of C, that is, the measure of the uncertainty of class C, and $H(C|A)$ is the *conditional entropy* of C given knowledge of A. Entropy and conditional entropy are defined by

$$H(C) = \sum_c p(c) \, \log \frac{1}{p(c)} \qquad H(C|A) = \sum_{a,c} p(a, c) \, \log \frac{1}{p(c|a)} \tag{8.2}$$

where $p(c)$ is the probability that an individual has class c, $p(a, c)$ is that of having genotype a and class c, and $p(c|a)$ is that of having class c given the occurrence of genotype a. Mutual information $I(A; C)$ takes only nonnegative values. If the class C is independent of a variable A's genotype, $I(A; C) = 0$, that is, variable A does not predict the disease status. If a correlation exists between the class C and variable A, $I(A; C) > 0$, that is, variable A has a main effect and predicts some of the disease status. Larger values of $I(A; C)$ indicate stronger correlations between A and C. Given the pair of variables A and B, its synergistic interaction strength is the information gain $IG(A; B; C)$, where

$$IG(A; B; C) = I(A, B; C) - I(A; C) - I(B; C) \tag{8.3}$$

As such, $IG(A; B; C)$ is the reduction in the uncertainty, or the information gained, about the class C from the genotypes of variables A and B considered together minus that from each of these variables considered separately. In brief, $IG(A; B; C)$ measures the amount of synergistic influence variables A and B have on class C. A higher value indicates a stronger synergistic interaction. Note that $IG(A; B; C)$ can take nonpositive values. A negative value indicates that the genotypes of two variables tend to vary together (redundant information), while a value of zero indicates either that the genotypes of the two variables are independent or, more likely, that they interact with a mixture of synergy and redundancy. The synergistic part of the mix tends to make the information gain positive while the redundant part lowers the information gain.

Prioritizing pairwise interactions reduces the risk of overlooking important genetic variants that are only involved in genetic interactions and suggests a more powerful strategy to detect epistasis [52]. However, most existing approaches attempt to identify best models consisting of several variables and thus ignore the broader gene–gene interaction landscape. Network science has emerged as a particularly intuitive and promising approach to exploring the entire pairwise interaction space and, thus, the underlying genetic architecture of complex phenotypic traits. A network is generally defined as a collection of vertices joined in pairs by edges and is often used to represent and study complex interaction systems [41, 47]. It allows for a structured representation of entities and their relationships, which provides a well-suited framework for the study of epistasis.

8.3 NETWORK

A graph is an abstraction of the interconnection relationship among entities and is used in many disciplines. It has found applications to represent natural and artificial networks, such as the Internet, World Wide Web, telephone networks, science literature citation,

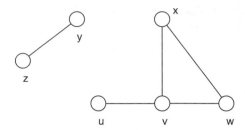

FIGURE 8.1   Example of undirected graph.

social networks, epidemiology networks, neural networks, and biochemical networks, just to name a few. In this section, we start with fundamental terminology in graph theory and then introduce some more notions relevant to using networks for epistasis research. Interested readers are referred to the monograph of West [51] for other details.

8.3.1   Fundamental Definitions

We denote a graph by $G = (V, E)$, where V is the set of *vertices* (or *nodes*) and E is the set of *edges* (or *links*). Two vertices u and v are joined by an edge $e = \{u, v\} \in E$ if they are related. Here, we say that u and v are "adjacent" to each other, that is, neighbors. In addition, we say that edge e is "incident" on u (and v) and that u and v are the *endpoints* of e. For example, the graph in Figure 8.1 has six vertices and five edges.

When the order of the vertex pair (or the direction of the link) is unimportant, we say G is an *undirected graph*. For example, the network of acquaintance can be represented using an undirected graph. Otherwise, if the directionality of an edge is important, it is called a *directed graph*. The pages and hyperlinks on the Web is an example of a very large directed graph. As a convention, when we say graph, we mean undirected graph unless otherwise specified. Edges in the form of $\{v, v\}$ are called *self-loops*. If there are multiple instances of $\{u, v\} \in E$, they are called *multiedges*. A *simple graph* is an undirected graph without self-loops or multiedges. The illustration in Figure 8.1 is a simple undirected graph. Edges in a directed graph are called *arcs*. In a directed graph, arcs (u, v) and (v, u) $(u \neq v)$ are *parallel arcs*. A simple directed graph allows parallel arcs but not self-loops. A graph is a *multigraph* if it is not simple, be it directed or undirected.

Given vertex v in an undirected graph, its *degree* is defined as the number of edges that are incident on it, denoted $\delta(v)$. In other words, the degree of a vertex is the number of its neighbors. For example, in Figure 8.1, $\delta(v) = 3$. Similarly, for v in a directed graph, its *out-degree* (respectively *in-degree*) is defined as the number of arcs going out of (respectively coming into) the node, denoted $\delta^+(v)$ [respectively $\delta^-(v)$]. Given a vertex v in an undirected graph, we use $N(v)$ to denote its *neighborhood*, that is, $\{u \in V | \{v, u\} \in E\}$. For the case of directed graph, we use $N^+(v)$ [respectively $N^-(v)$] to denoted its *out-neighborhood* (respectively *in-neighborhood*), that is, $\{u \in V | (v, u) \in E\}$ (respectively $\{u \in V | (u, v) \in E\}$).

A *path* in an undirected graph is a sequence $p = v_0 v_1 v_2 \cdots v_l$ where $\{v_{i-1}, v_i\} \in E$ ($i = 1, 2, \ldots, l$). Here, l is the *length* of p. If no vertex appears more than once in the sequence, we say that p is a *simple* path. If $v_1 = v_l$, the sequence is called a *cycle*, that is, a "closed" path. Here, the length of the cycle is $l - 1$. Likewise, a cycle is simple if no two vertices in the sequence other than v_0 and v_l are identical. For instance, $uvxw$ is a simple path and $xvwx$ is a simple cycle. Both path and cycle can be defined for directed graphs, and the only difference is that all consecutive edges in the sequence are directed from v_{i-1} to v_i. When there is no cycle in a graph, we say the graph is *acyclic*. For example, it is useful to use directed acyclic graph (DAG) to represent a partial order.

In an undirected graph, if there is a path p connecting u to v and its length is the least among all paths from u to v, we say that p is a *shortest path* from u to v and that its length is the *distance* from u to v, denoted $d(u, v)$. In the example of Figure 8.1, $d(u, x) = 2$. Apparently, $d(u, v) = d(v, u)$ in undirected graphs. In contrast, this is not true in a directed graph. In reality, the fact that there exists a path from u to v in a directed graph does not imply that there exists a path from v to u, or vice versa. In either a directed or an undirected graph, if there is a path from u to v, we say that v is *reachable* or *connected* from u. The *diameter* is meaningful for a finite undirected connected graph $G = (V, E)$, defined as $D_G = \max_{u,v \in V} d(u, v)$. For unconnected or infinite graphs, we write $D_G = \infty$.

A graph can also be represented by an *adjacency matrix*, and it is a powerful tool for computation in graphs. Given a graph $G = (V, E)$, its adjacency matrix $\mathbf{A}$ is an $n \times n$ matrix, where $n = |V|$, that is, the number of vertices in the graph, and the element $a_{i,j}$ is the number of arcs from vertex i to vertex j. As special cases, the adjacency matrix of an undirected graph is symmetric, and that of a simple graph is a 0–1 matrix with all diagonal elements equal to zero. For example, the adjacency matrix of the graph in Figure 8.1 is

$$
\begin{array}{c c}
 & \begin{array}{cccccc} u & v & w & x & y & z \end{array} \\
\begin{array}{c} u \\ v \\ w \\ x \\ y \\ z \end{array} &
\left(\begin{array}{cccccc}
0 & 1 & 0 & 0 & 0 & 0 \\
1 & 0 & 1 & 1 & 0 & 0 \\
0 & 1 & 0 & 1 & 0 & 0 \\
0 & 1 & 1 & 0 & 0 & 0 \\
0 & 0 & 0 & 0 & 0 & 1 \\
0 & 0 & 0 & 0 & 1 & 0
\end{array} \right)
\end{array}
$$

8.3.2   Notions on Connectivity

The connectivity of a graph can be measured in various ways. In graph theory, we call an undirected graph $G = (V, E)$ a *connected graph* if all of its vertices are connected to each other. Given a maximal subset $S \subseteq V$, we say that S and all edges with both endpoints in S form a *connected component* of G if every two vertices in S are connected to each other. Apparently, a connected graph has exactly one connected component. The example graph in Figure 8.1 has two connected components, one with four vertices and the other with two. For the case of a directed graph, it needs to have all vertices reachable from one to another to be a *strongly connected graph*. Similarly, we say a maximal subset $S \subseteq V$ and all arcs with both endpoints in S form a *strongly connected component* if every two vertices can reach each other in both directions.

There are an array of metrics to measure the robustness of a connected graph $G = (V, E)$, and we list a few examples below. Note that some of these metrics are microscopic and do not even require that the graph should be connected:

- G is said to be k connected ($k \geq 1$) if it remains connected after removing any $k - 1$ vertices. When $k = 1$, this notion degenerates to the original definition of connectivity.

Likewise, a graph is k-edge connected ($k \geq 1$) if it is still connected after removing any $k - 1$ edges. These metrics are useful to measure the resilience of a network against node or link outages.

- If the edges in G are somewhat evenly distributed, the ratio $|E|/D_G$ reflects the richness of the edges, where $|E|$ is the number of edges in G and D_G is the diameter of G.
- For a large network, it is not unlikely that a portion is not connected to the rest of the network. Thus, the size of the largest connected component relative to the entire network measures what portion of the network can be considered connected.
- A clustering coefficient measures how transitive connections in a graph are. It is defined as the fraction of paths of length 2 in the network that are closed. Here, given a simple path $v_0 v_1 v_2$, it is "closed" if $\{v_0, v_2\} \in E$. The clustering coefficient of vertex v, in a local sense, is the number of pairs of its neighbors that are adjacent divided by the total number of neighbor pairs of v.

8.3.3 Vertex Centrality

When studying a network, it is often useful to measure the contribution of individual nodes to the network. There have been a number of such metrics from social network analysis. Intuitively, the more neighbors a node has, the more influence it may have in the network. This assumes that all neighbors are considered equally important. Here, we introduce a number of such *centrality* measurements of graphs. Consider graph $G = (V, E)$ and its adjacency matrix $\mathbf{A}$.

1. *Degree Centrality* The degree centrality of a vertex is simply its degree. Apparently, all neighbors are treated equally in this case. Formally, if we use $\mathbf{1}$ to denote column vector $\{1, 1, 1, \ldots, 1\}$, the degree centrality of the vertices in the graph is vector $\mathbf{A1}$.
2. *Eigenvector Centrality* It would make sense to give a greater weight to a more important neighbor when calculating the centrality of a vertex. Specifically, the centrality of a vertex is proportional to the sum of the centrality of its neighbors. Hence, if the centrality of the vertices of the network is denoted a positive real column vector $\mathbf{x}$, it should satisfy

$$\mathbf{Ax} = c\mathbf{x}$$

for some constant c. That is, the relative values of the centrality across the network does not change after the incorporation of the neighbors' centrality. It turns out that the eigenvector centrality is always proportional to the leading eigenvector of $\mathbf{A}$. Note that the eigenvector centrality can also be defined iteratively from an "initial guess." In this case, after a sufficiently number of iterations, the centrality thus defined always converges to the same leading eigenvector of $\mathbf{A}$. As a result, the eigenvector centrality of a vertex is large either because it has a large number of neighbors or because it has "important" neighbors or both.
3. *Katz Centrality* An issue with eigenvector centrality is that some vertices in a directed graph may not have any centrality even if they do have nonzero in-degrees, for example, those in a strongly connected component that does not have any arc coming into the component. This would be problematic because their eigenvector centrality is all zero. Katz centrality addresses this issue by giving each vertex a small

amount of centrality "for free." That is, when written in matrix form, the centrality of vertices in the network is

$$\mathbf{x} = \alpha \mathbf{A} \mathbf{x} + \beta \mathbf{1}$$

where α and β are positive constants to govern the balance between the eigenvector term and the constant term. When α dominates, Katz centrality degenerates to eigenvector centrality; while β dominates, it becomes degree centrality.

4. *PageRank* In Katz centrality, if a vertex has a large number of out-neighbors, it has the capability of transferring its centrality to all of them. However, it would be more reasonable for these neighbors to share this endowment rather than inheriting it. PageRank is devised for this purpose,

$$\mathbf{x} = (\mathbf{I} - \alpha \mathbf{A} \mathbf{D}^{-1})^{-1} \mathbf{1} = \mathbf{D}(\mathbf{D} - \alpha \mathbf{A})^{-1} \mathbf{1}$$

where $\mathbf{D}$ is the diagonal matrix with elements $D_{ii} = \max(d_i^+, 1)$. PageRank is proved very effective and is the centerpiece of Google Web ranking technology.

8.3.4 Degree Distributions

The vertex degree is a microscopic metric in a network, but when studied collectively, its distribution across the network constitutes a good vehicle to characterize the network structure. The degree distribution $P(k)$ of a network is defined as the fraction of vertices in the network with degree k. That is, if n_k of the n vertices in the network have degree k, we have $P(k) = n_k/n$. In our example in Figure 8.1, we have $P_0 = 0$, $P_1 = \frac{3}{6}$, $P_2 = \frac{2}{6}$, and $P_3 = \frac{1}{6}$. The degree distribution does not capture all information of the network. There are obviously multiple networks that have the exact same degree distribution. Nevertheless, it is very effective in describing how vertices are connected to others given that it is relatively inexpensive to collect such information even in a very large network.

Apparently, depending on the nature of the network, different types of networks may have fairly different node distributions. For many large real-world networks, the majority of the vertices have a typical degree around a certain constant, while those with near-zero or very high degrees are much rarer. If we plot the degree distribution of such networks, we see that there is a peak not very far from the y axis and to the right of it there is very long tail in the x-axis direction. When the degree degrades at the rate of a power function $P(k) = c \times k^{-\gamma}$ (as apposed to exponential), that is, having a "long tail," we say that the vertex degree distribution follows a *power law* and that the network is a *scale-free* network.

8.3.5 Networks for Epistasis Studies

Networks can be used to characterize interactions at all levels of organization in biology from the molecular level with metabolic [25, 43], protein–protein interaction [24], and genetic regulatory networks [5] to the macroscopic level with food webs [29]. In epistasis studies, most existing network models are used to represent biological interactions and dependencies using gene expression and regulation data [2, 10, 44]. For statistical epistasis, networks have the potential to systematically infer the statistical dependencies between genetic variants and the underlying genetic architecture that can predict the phenotypic status. However, its power is yet to be fully exploited in the literature. Two example studies in this category are the gene association interaction network (GAIN) by McKinney et al.

[30] and our statistical epistasis networks (SEN) [23]. We will summarize these studies in the following two sections.

8.4   GENE-ASSOCIATION INTERACTION NETWORK

McKinney et al. [30] developed a phenotype-specific GAIN to visualize and interpret synergistic interactions between pairs of single-nucleotide polymorphisms (SNPs). They first ranked SNPs using their evaporative cooling (EC) feature selection approach that combines a main-effect score from Relief-F [27] and an interaction effect score from Random Forest [7]. Then a network was built using a filtered subset of SNPs with the highest EC rankings. In this network, each node represents a SNP and each edge linking a pair of SNPs represents the interaction between them. The information-theoretic measure $IG(A; B; C)$ was assigned to SNP pairs to describe the strength of their interaction, and a cutoff of $IG(A; B; C)$ was used to include only edges with relatively high strength into the network. In this network, the vertex degree centrality (PageRank centrality in their later work [16]) was then used to determine the importance of SNPs predicting the phenotypic outcome. That is, a SNP with a high centrality was regarded crucial related to a phenotypic trait.

In the framework of GAIN, it was the first time that networks were used to provide a broader picture of statistical genetic interactions and to identify important variants involved in those interactions. However, networks were used more as an interpretation and visualization tool rather than for systematic analyses. In addition, the computational overhead of using multiple methods to measure main and interaction effects and the threshold selection for pruning and building a network added another layer of complexity to this approach. Hence, alternative methods are imperative that can fully take advantage of systematic network analyses to show the global picture of statistical genetic interactions and, thus, to reveal the underlying genetic architecture of complex phenotypic traits.

8.5   STATISTICAL EPISTASIS NETWORKS

In [23], we proposed to infer genetic interaction networks that are not dependent on statistical main effects. Using a large population-based bladder cancer data set, we first ranked all possible pairwise interactions between SNPs according to their relative strength and subsequently built and analyzed SEN including only those interactions whose strength exceeds a theoretically derived threshold. Hence, the approach we applied distinguishes itself from existing ones in the following ways: (1) We qualified the strength of all pairwise interactions identifiable in the complete data set rather than a subset of high main-effect SNPs; (2) we organized our genetic network around the strongest pairwise interactions rather than around the strongest main effects; (3) we analyzed network topologies to systematically identify the network that best captured the genetic architecture inherent in the data; and (4) in contrast to many existing techniques that aim at identifying a classification model consisting of a subset of susceptibility SNPs, our epistasis network captured a global landscape of gene–gene interactions through exhaustively enumerating all possible pairwise interactions.

8.5.1   Network Construction and Analysis

SEN was used to characterize the space of pairwise interactions among 1422 SNPs spanning nearly 500 cancer susceptibility genes in a large population-based bladder cancer study consisting of 491 cases and 791 controls. More details on this data set are available in [3, 26].

In the networks, each vertex corresponds to a SNP, and we used v_A to denote the vertex corresponding to SNP A. An edge linking a pair of vertices, for instance, v_A and v_B, corresponds to an interaction between SNPs A and B. We first assigned a weight to each SNP and each pair of SNPs to quantify how much of the disease status the corresponding SNP and SNP pair genotypes explain. These weights correspond to the mutual information $I(A; C)$ and information gain $IG(A; B; C)$, where C is the class variable with status case or control. We then built a series of statistical epistasis networks by incrementally adding edges. These networks were denoted by G_t, where edges between SNPs were added only if their pair weights were greater than or equal to a threshold t. The threshold t varied between 0 and the maximum pair weight estimated based on the data. The networks G_t grew as the threshold t decreased. For $t_1 < t_2$, G_{t_1} contained all the edges and vertices of G_{t_2}.

Our analysis method relied on comparisons between the real data set and its derivatives generated by permutation testing. We generated 1000 permuted data sets by randomly shuffling the disease status of the 1282 samples 1000 times. This removed all the real biological signals that indicate the association between genotype and phenotype such that null networks were built from those permuted data sets and were used to determine the statistical significance of network properties observed from the real data.

8.5.2 Observations

In general, with the same decreasing threshold t, G_t built from the real data were found having more edges and connected vertices than the null networks built using permuted data. In addition, the largest connected component of G_t emerged earlier and grew faster then null networks. Figure 8.2 shows the percentage of vertices included in the largest connected

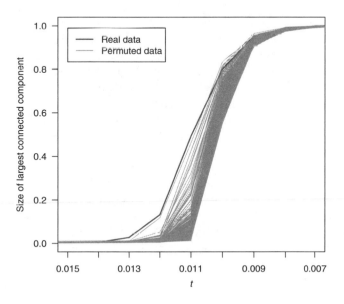

FIGURE 8.2 Size of largest connected component as function of threshold t [23]. Results from both the real data networks and null networks are shown.

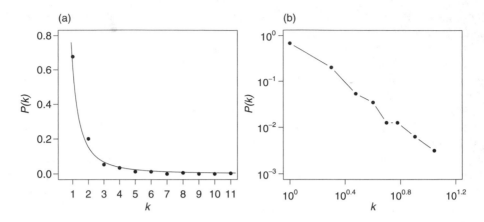

FIGURE 8.3   Vertex degree distribution of the network $G_{0.013}$ [23]. (a) Dots are observed data points and the curve is its best power-fitting curve $P(k) = 0.615 \times k^{-2.01}$ using least squares. (b) Degree distribution of $G_{0.013}$ plotted on a log–log scale.

component as a function of t for both the real data set and 1000 permuted data sets. The largest connected component emerged at a certain step and eventually included all vertices in the networks. The threshold $t = 0.013$ appeared to be of particular interest where the largest connected component started to form in the real data network while the null networks lagged one or two steps behind.

We further examined the degree distributions of G_t for varying t and found that $G_{0.013}$ had a unique approximately power law degree distribution. This property disappeared for $t < 0.013$ when more edges were added to the network due to chance rather than real biological significance, and their vertex degrees were found following a Poisson distribution, a typical property for networks built by randomly connecting vertices. Figure 8.3a shows the degree distribution of G_t and its best power-fitting curve $P(k) = 0.615 \times k^{-2.01}$. When a power law distribution is plotted at a log–log scale, it appears as a straight line (Figure 8.3b). Although power law degree distribution is usually only applied to very large networks [41], at least two to three magnitudes larger than that considered here, the network $G_{0.013}$ nevertheless was found approximately scale free, and it was the unique topology absent in both real data networks with other thresholds and all null networks.

The network $G_{0.013}$ had 319 vertices, 255 edges, and 79 connected components. The largest connected component of $G_{0.013}$ had 39 vertices. This was a unique observation that a component of this size was never found in any of the null networks using the same threshold 0.013. The graph of the largest connected component in $G_{0.013}$ (Figure 8.4) drew some interesting observations. First, similar to biological pathways, it showed very few cycles. Second, the network had a few vertices with degrees that were much higher than the average, while the majority of vertices connected directly to only one other vertex. Finally, vertices with high degrees or connected with wide edges were not necessarily of large size. That is, high main-effect SNPs do not necessarily have high centrality.

8.5.3   Implications

Through an exhaustive enumeration of all possible pairwise interactions and network topological analyses, our network approach was able to identify a statistically significant large

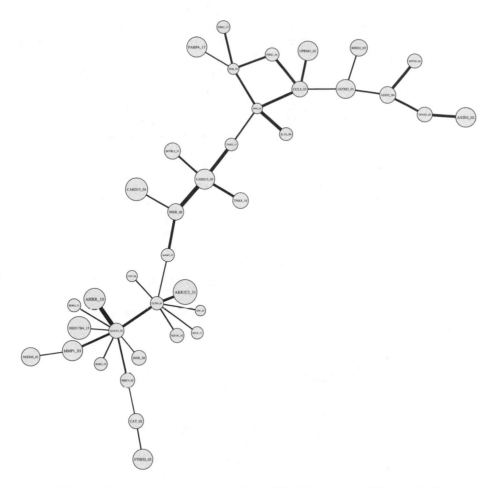

FIGURE 8.4 Largest connected component of $G_{0.013}$ [23]. Each vertex is labeled with the name of its corresponding SNP. The size of a vertex is proportional to its main effect and the width of an edge is proportional to the strength of the interaction between the two SNPs it joins. The length of an edge is for deployment purpose only.

connected structure embedded in the bladder cancer data. More interestingly, the derived network $G_{0.013}$ is approximately scale free.

Scale-free networks permeate natural and social sciences [4, 28, 40]. The most well-known scale-free networks are the backbone of the Internet and social networks. In biology, scale-free topologies have been found in metabolic networks [25], protein–protein interaction networks [24], and gene regulatory networks [5]. Those various scale-free networks share an intriguing property: The value of γ in the degree distributions $P(k) = c \times k^{-\gamma}$ mostly satisfies $2 \leq \gamma \leq 3$ [4], which is also the case for $G_{0.013}$ ($\gamma = 2.01$). As more scale-free networks are being discovered in a variety of fields, a question remains: How can systems as fundamentally different as the cell and the Internet have a similar architecture and obey the same laws [4]?

Scale-free networks typically have many vertices with low degrees and a few vertices with high degrees, also known as *hubs* [41]. This essentially differentiates scale-free networks from random networks where the majority of vertices have average degrees. The probability $P(k)$ of degree k in the Poisson distribution decreases exponentially as k increases, and thus random networks are very unlikely to have hubs with degrees much larger than the average. The existence of hubs in a scale-free network implies strong robustness against failures. Because random vertex removal is very unlikely to affect hubs, the connectivity of the network most likely remains intact. In biological networks, this robustness translates into the resilience of organisms to intrinsic and environmental perturbations. For instance, in protein–protein interaction networks [24], most proteins interact with only one or two other proteins but a few are able to interact to a large number. Such hub proteins are rarely affected by mutations and organisms can remain functional under most perturbations. The simultaneous emergence of scale-free topologies in many biological networks suggests that evolution has favored such a structure in natural systems. Moreover, it suggests that the robustness of natural systems does not only result from inherent genetic redundancy but also, and maybe more importantly, from the topological organization of entities and interactions [24].

Although our epistasis network is developed based on statistical rather than real biochemical interactions, it is encouraging to observe similar topologies between biological and statistical networks. More importantly, its scale-free topology well supported the evolution perspective of epistasis and indicated the complex and robust genetic architecture of bladder cancer.

8.6   CONCLUDING REMARKS

In this chapter, we introduced the new epistasis modeling approach of using networks. Fundamental definitions in graph theory were summarized. In particular, we discussed network properties, including network connectivity, vertex centrality, and degree distribution, that are mostly relevant to and can potentially benefit epistasis studies. Furthermore, we summarized two studies that used networks to model statistical epistasis. The gene association interaction network [30] was able to visualize a broader picture of synergistic interactions between SNP markers that were prioritized using data-mining techniques and to further identify important SNPs interacting with a large number of others in association with a phenotypic trait. Statistical epistasis networks [23] used the power of network topological analysis to systematically identify a significant network structure through exhaustive enumeration of all possible pairwise interactions in a bladder cancer data set. The derived network showed interesting properties including a large connected component and an approximately scale-free topology. It is believed to capture the important aspects of bladder cancer that have never been discovered previously. Both studies suggested the network-structured and robust nature of the genetic architecture of complex traits and showed the effectiveness and potential of using networks as a modeling tool for statistical epistasis.

Network science is a very useful tool to model entities and their interactions and has been successfully applied to study numerous complex real-world systems. Meanwhile, as the nonlinearity and complexity of genotype–phenotype mapping have been revealed by modern genetics studies, epistasis has become the center of the research for understanding the genetic architecture of complex traits such as common human diseases. Network science opens up a very promising research direction for modeling epistasis. We expect more future applications of networks in this field, especially in the era of GWAS due to the fact that the network is capable of efficiently and systematically analyzing high-throughput data.

ACKNOWLEDGMENT

This work was supported by the National Institute of Health USA grants AI59694, LM009012, and LM010098.

REFERENCES

1. D. Anastassiou. Computational analysis of the synergy among multiple interacting genes. *Mol. Syst. Biol.*, 3:83, 2007.

2. A. Andrei and C. Kendziorski. An efficient method for identifying statistical interactors in gene association networks. *Biostatistics*, 10(4):706–718, 2009.

3. A. S. Andrew, H. H. Nelson, K. T. Kelsey, J. H. Moore, A. C. Meng, D. P. Casella, T. D. Tosteson, A. R. Schned, and M. R. Karagas. Concordance of multiple analytical approaches demonstrates a complex relationship between DNA repair gene SNPs, smoking and bladder cancer susceptibility. *Carcinogenesis*, 27(5):1030–1037, 2006.

4. A.-L. Barabasi and E. Bonabeau. Scale-free networks. *Sci. Am.*, 5:50–59, 2003.

5. A.-L. Barabasi and Z. N. Oltvai. Network biology: Understanding the cell's functional organization. *Nat. Rev. Genet.*, 5:101–113, 2004.

6. W. Bateson. *Mendel's Principles of Heredity*. Cambridge University Press, Cambridge, UK, 1909.

7. L. Breiman. Random forest. *Machine Learning*, 45:5–32, 2001.

8. P. Chanda, L. Sucheston, A. Zhang, D. Brazeau, J. L. Freudenheim, C. Ambrosone, and M. Ramanathan. AMBIENCE: A novel approach and efficient algorithm for identifying informative genetic and environmental associations with complex phenotypes. *Genetics*, 180:1191–1210, 2008.

9. P. Chanda, L. Sucheston, A. Zhang, and M. Ramanathan. The interaction index, a novel information-theoretic metric for prioritizing interacting genetic variations and environmental factors. *Eur. J. Hum. Genet.*, 17:1274–1286, 2009.

10. J.-H. Chu, S. T. Weiss, V. J. Carey, and B. A. Raby. A graphical model approach for inferring large-scale networks integrating gene expression and genetic polymorphism. *BMC Syst. Biol.*, 3:55, 2009.

11. A. G. Clark, E. Boerwinkle, J. Hixson, and C. F. Sing. Determinants of the success of whole-genome association testing. *Genome Res.*, 15:1463–1467, 2005.

12. H. J. Cordell. Epistasis: What it means, what it doesn't mean, and statistical methods to detect it in humans. *Hum. Mol. Genet.*, 11(20):2463–2468, 2002.

13. H. J. Cordell. Detecting gene-gene interactions that underlie human diseases. *Nat. Rev. Genet.*, 10(6):392–404, 2009.

14. T. M. Cover and J. A. Thomas. *Elements of Information Theory*, 2nd ed., Wiley, Hoboken, NJ, 2006.

15. R. Culverhouse, B. K. Suarez, J. Lin, and T. Reich. A perspective on epistasis: Limits of models displaying no main effect. *Am. J. Hum. Genet.*, 70:461–471, 2002.

16. N. A. Davis, J. E. Crowe, Jr., N. M. Pajewski, and B. A. McKinney. Surfing a genetic association interaction network to identify modulators of antibody response to smallpox vaccine. *Genes Immun.*, 11:630–636, 2010.

17. J. A. Draghi, T. L. Parsons, G. P. Wagner, and J. B. Plotkin. Mutational robustness can facilitate adaptation. *Nature*, 463:353–355, 2010.

18. G. Gibson. Decanalization and the origin of complex disease. *Nat. Rev. Genet.*, 10:134–140, 2009.

19. G. Gibson and G. P. Wagner. Canalization in evolutionary genetics: A stabilizing theory? *BioEssays*, 22:372–380, 2000.

20. J. Hardy and A. Singleton. Genome-wide association studies and human disease. *N. Engl. J. Med.*, 360(17):1759–1768, 2009.

21. J. N. Hirschhorn. Genomewide association studies—illuminating biologic pathways. *N. Engl. J. Med.*, 360(17):1699–1701, 2009.

22. J. N. Hirschhorn and M. J. Daly. Genome-wide association studies for common diseases and complex traits. *Nat. Rev. Genet.*, 6(2):95–108, 2005.

23. T. Hu, N. A. Sinnott-Armstrong, J. W. Kiralis, A. S. Andrew, M. R. Karagas, and J. H. Moore. Characterizing genetic interactions in human disease association studies using statistical epistasis networks. *BMC Bioinformatics*, 12:364, 2011.

24. H. Jeong, S. P. Mason, A. L. Barabasi, and Z. N. Oltvai. Lethality and centrality in protein networks. *Nature*, 411:41–42, 2001.

25. H. Jeong, B. Tombor, R. Albert, Z. N. Oltvai, and A. L. Barabasi. The large-scale organization of metabolic networks. *Nature*, 407:651–654, 2000.

26. M. R. Karagas, T. D. Tosteson, J. Blum, J. S. Morris, J. A. Baron, and B. Klaue. Design of an epidemiologic study of drinking water arsenic exposure and skin and bladder cancer risk in a U.S. population. *Environ. Health Perspect.*, 106(4):1047–1050, 1998.

27. I. Kononenko. Estimating attributes: Analysis and extensions of Relief. In *Lecture Notes in Computer Science*, Vol. 784, Springer, Berlin, Germany, 1994, pp. 171–182.

28. L. Li, D. Alderson, J. C. Doyle, and W. Willinger. Towards a theory of scale-free graphs: Definition, properties, and implications. *Internet Math.*, 2(4):431–523, 2005.

29. N. D. Martinez. Constant connectance in community food webs. *Am. Soc. Naturalists*, 140(6):1208–1218, 1992.

30. B. A. McKinney, J. E. Crowe, J. Guo, and D. Tian. Capturing the spectrum of interaction effects in genetic association studies by simulated evaporative cooling network analysis. *PLoS Genet.*, 5(3):e1000432, 2009.

31. J. H. Moore. The ubiquitous nature of epistasis in determining susceptibility to common human diseases. *Hum. Hered.*, 56:73–82, 2003.

32. J. H. Moore. A global view of epistasis. *Nat. Genet.*, 37(1):13–14, 2005.

33. J. H. Moore, F. W. Asselbergs, and S. M. Williams. Bioinformatics challenges for genome-wide association studies. *Bioinformatics*, 26(4):445–455, 2010.

34. J. H. Moore, N. Barney, C.-T. Tsai, F.-T. Chiang, J. Gui, and B. C. White. Symbolic modeling of epistasis. *Hum. Hered.*, 63(2):120–133, 2007.

35. J. H. Moore, J. C. Gilbert, C.-T. Tsai, F.-T. Chiang, T. Holden, N. Barney, and B. C. White. A flexible computational framework for detecting, characterizing, and interpreting statistical patterns of epistasis in genetic studies of human disease susceptibility. *J. Theor. Biol.*, 241(2): 252–261, 2006.

36. J. H. Moore and M. D. Ritchie. The challenges of whole-genome approaches to common diseases. *J. Am. Med. Assoc.*, 291(13):1642–1643, 2004.

37. J. H. Moore and S. M. Williams. Traversing the conceptual divide between biological and statistical epistasis: Systems biology and a more modern synthesis. *BioEssays*, 27(6):637–646, 2005.

38. J. H. Moore and S. M. Williams. Epistasis and its implications for personal genetics. *Am. J. Hum. Genet.*, 85(3):309–320, 2009.

39. S. K. Musani, D. Shriner, N. Liu, R. Feng, C. S. Coffey, N. Yi, H. K. Tiwari, and D. B. Allison. Detection of gene-gene interactions in genome-wide sssociation studies of human population data. *Hum. Hered.*, 63:67–84, 2007.

40. M. E. J. Newman. Power laws, Pareto distributions and Zipf's law. *Contemp. Phys.*, 46(5): 323–351, 2005.

41. M. E. J. Newman. *Networks: An Introduction*. Oxford University Press, Oxford, UK, 2010.

42. P. C. Phillips. The language of gene interaction. *Genetics*, 149:1167–1171, 1998.

43. E. Ravasz, A. L. Somera, D. A. Mongru, Z. N. Oltvai, and A. L. Barabasi. Hierarchical organization of modularity in metabolic networks. *Science*, 297:1551–1555, 2002.

44. J. Schafer and K. Strimmer. An empirical Bayes approach to inferring large-scale gene association. *Bioinformatics*, 21(6):754–764, 2005.

45. D. Segre, A. DeLuna, G. M. Church, and R. Kishony. Modular epistasis in yeast metabolism. *Nat. Genet.*, 37(1):77–83, 2005.

46. K. V. Steen. Travelling the world of gene-gene interactions. *Brief. Bioinformatics*, 13(1):1–19, 2012.

47. S. H. Strogatz. Exploring complex networks. *Nature*, 410:268–276, 2001.

48. C. H. Waddington. Canalization of development and the inheritance of acquired characters. *Nature*, 150(3811):563–565, 1942.

49. W. Y. S. Wang, B. J. Barratt, D. G. Clayton, and J. A. Todd. Genome-wide association studies: Theoretical and practical concerns. *Nat. Rev. Genet.*, 6(2):109–118, 2005.

50. X. Wang, R. C. Elston, and X. Zhu. The meaning of interaction. *Hum. Hered.*, 70:269–277, 2010.

51. D. B. West. *Introduction to Graph Theory*, 2nd ed., Prentice Hall, Englewood Cliffs, NJ, 2001.

52. W. Wongseree, A. Assawamakin, T. Piroonratana, S. Sinsomros, C. Limwongse, and N. Chaiyaratana. Detecting purely epistatic multi-locus interactions by an omnibus permutation test on ensembles of two-locus analyses. *BMC Bioinformatics*, 10:294, 2009.

CHAPTER 9

GRAPHICAL MODELS FOR PROTEIN FUNCTION AND STRUCTURE PREDICTION

MINGJIE TANG,[1,†] KEAN MING TAN,[2,†] XIN LU TAN,[2] LEE SAEL,[1,3]
MEGHANA CHITALE,[1] JUAN ESQUIVEL-RODRÍGUEZ,[1]
and DAISUKE KIHARA[1,3]

[1]Department of Computer Science, Purdue University, West Lafayette, Indiana
[2]Department of Statistics, Purdue University, West Lafayette, Indiana
[3]Department of Biological Sciences, Purdue University, West Lafayette, Indiana

9.1 INTRODUCTION

One of the central aims of bioinformatics is to reveal hidden structures of biological entities and systems, such as protein/gene sequences, protein structures, and interactions, in order to understand how they are constructed and related to each other. Unveiling structures and relationships will also enable prediction and classification of unknown data. For this task, various machine learning techniques have been introduced in the bioinformatics field. In fact, the two-decade history of bioinformatics can be viewed, in one sense, as the history of adopting and applying new algorithms to biological data. The role of predictive and classification algorithms in bioinformatics will only become more important as the number and types of data increase.

In the early 1990s, *dynamic programming* (DP) was successfully applied to protein and DNA sequence alignment [1, 2]. Pairwise sequence alignment tools later evolved into tools for sequence database search [3–5]. Computational sequence alignment and database search tools have revolutionized biological studies. Nowadays sequence alignment and sequence database searches are routinely used in every molecular biology laboratory for obtaining clues for gene function and functional sites. DP has been further applied for RNA secondary-structure prediction [6], protein three-dimensional (3D) structure comparison [7, 8], and protein 3D structure prediction [9–11]. In the late 1990s, the hidden Markov model (HMM) became very popular partly due to the publication of a seminal book, *Biological Sequence Analysis: Probabilistic Models of Proteins and Nucleic Acids* [12]. HMM can handle a

---

†These two authors have equal contribution.

variance of biological sequences and structures in a probabilistic fashion and thus allows more sensitive searches of similarities in proteins. HMM has been widely applied for protein secondary-structure prediction [13, 14], transmembrane region prediction [15, 16], and 3D structure prediction [17, 18]. The artificial neural network (NN) [19] is another example that was widely applied in various prediction and classification problems in bioinformatics [20–22]. The support vector machine (SVM), which was introduced in the field around the beginning of this century, has gradually taken over the NN in various prediction methods [23–25]. Of course, DP, HMM, NN, and SVM are only a few examples among many others [26–30] of successfully applied machine learning techniques in bioinformatics.

In this chapter, we review bioinformatics applications of two emerging graphical models, the *Markov random field* (MRF) and the *conditional random field* (CRF). The main advantage of these two methods is that they can represent dependencies of variables using graphs. Since many biological data can be described as graphs, both methods have gained increasing attention in the bioinformatics community. We first briefly describe the MRF and the CRF in comparison with the HMM. What follows are applications of the two graphical models, focusing on gene prediction, protein function prediction, and protein structure prediction. These applications benefit from the graphical models by being able to represent dependencies between graph nodes, which contributed to improvement of prediction accuracy.

9.2 GRAPHICAL MODELS

A graphical model is able to represent complex joint distributions of a large number of variables compactly using a set of local relationships specified by a graph. It provides us a convenient way to understand and express complicated joint distributions. Each node in the graph represents a random variable and nodes are connected by edges, which describe the dependency between the variables.

In this section, we will discuss some basics of the graphical model. First, we discuss the directed graphical model, that is, the edges of the graphs have a particular directionality indicated by arrows (Bayesian networks or belief networks). Then, we proceed to undirected graphical models such as MRFs and CRFs. In the following section, we mainly consider the supervised learning process. For the set of variables (X, Y), X represents the input variables that are observed, and Y is the output variable which we want to predict.

9.2.1 Directed Graphical Model

A directed graph G is a set of vertices and edges $G(V, E)$ where $V = \{V_i\}$ is a set of nodes and $E = \{(V_i, V_j)\}$ is a set of edges with directions from V_i to V_j. We assume G is acyclic. Each V_i represents a random variable. Each node V_i has a set of parent nodes V_{parents}. The structure of the graph defines the conditional independence relationship among the random variables. The joint probability of all variables V can be calculated as the product of the conditional probability of each variables conditioned on its parents as presented in the following equation

$$\Pr(V) = \prod_{V_i \subset V} \Pr(V_i | V_{\text{parents}}) \tag{9.1}$$

The most widely used directed graphical model is the Naive Bayes model [31] (Figure 9.1). It predicts a single class variable y given a vector of features $x = (x_1, x_2, \ldots, x_n)$. For example, if all the features have discrete binary values $\{0, 1\}$, then a general distribution over x corresponds to a table of 2^n numbers of possible combinations of features for

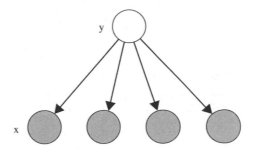

FIGURE 9.1 Naive Bayes model.

each class. Since the dimension of the number of possible combinations of features increases significantly as n becomes large, modeling $\Pr(X)$ will suffer from the curse of dimensionality. However, the conditional independence property in the graphical model enables us to get the joint distributions easily.

The naive Bayes has the conditional independence assumption that every attribute x_i is conditionally independent of other attributes x_j on the class label. The formula for the naive Bayes model and the graphical representation follows:

$$\Pr(x_1, x_2, \ldots, x_n, y) = \Pr(y) \prod_{i=1}^{n} \Pr(x_i | y) \tag{9.2}$$

The conditional independence assumption is one of the basic ideas of a graphical model because it can reduce the number of parameters to be estimated. The conditional independence is usually called D-separation for the joint distribution in a graph model [32].

9.2.2 Undirected Model (Markov Random Field)

An undirected graphical model can also be represented by $G = (V, E)$, except that the edges in E are undirected. The widely used undirected graph model is the MRF. The MRF allows one to incorporate local contextual constraints in labeling problems in a principled manner and is applied in vision, bioinformatics, and many other fields. It uses a concept called the Markov blanket of a node, which assumes that the node is conditionally independent from all the other nodes but conditioned only on the set of neighboring nodes [33]. By the conditionally independent property in the MRF, the joint probability for graph nodes (variables) is factorized. For example, we consider two nodes X_i, X_j in the graph, and they are not directly connected by edges in the graph (Figure 9.2). Then the conditional distribution for X_i and X_j would be illustrated by

$$\Pr(x_i, x_j | \sim \{x_i, x_j\}) = \Pr(x_i | \sim \{x_i, x_j\}) \Pr(x_j | \sim \{x_i, x_j\} \tag{9.3}$$

where $\sim \{x_i, x_j\}$ is the set of nodes in the graph with the node $\{x_i, x_j\}$ removed. By this conditional independence property, we can represent the joint distribution in terms of cliques in the graph. A clique is a fully connected graph where every node has links to all the other nodes in the graph. The size of the clique can vary from binary to the entire graph in consideration. We can also define an undirected graphical model as the set of all distributions:

$$\Pr(x, y) = \frac{1}{z} \prod_A \psi_A(X_A, Y_A) \tag{9.4}$$

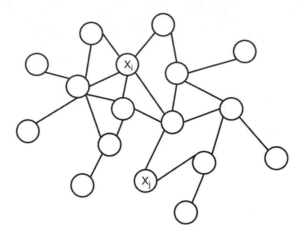

FIGURE 9.2   Markov random field.

where ψ_A is the potential function defined on the clique A in the graph and Z is a normalized factor defined by

$$Z = \sum_{X,Y} \prod_A \psi_A(X_A, Y_A) \tag{9.5}$$

where Z ensures that the distribution $\text{Pr}(x, y)$ is correctly normalized. The normalization constant is one of the major limitations of the undirected graphs. For example, suppose we have a model with M discrete nodes each of which has K states. Evaluation of the normalization term involves summing over the K_M state, which is exponential with the size of the model. The model parameter is learned from the potential functions ψ [34]. The potential function ψ takes positive values. Traditionally, we express the potential function, which is strictly positive as exponentials, so that

$$\psi = \exp[-E(X, Y)] \tag{9.6}$$

where $E(X, Y)$ is called an energy function and the exponential representation is called the *Boltzmann distribution.* The joint distribution is defined as the product of potentials, and so the total energy is obtained by adding the energies of each of the maximal cliques.

9.2.3 Discriminative versus Generative Model

In the framework of supervised learning, a new test data set can be classified using either a generative model or a discriminative model [35, 36] (Figure 9.3).

9.2.3.1 *Generative Model*   The first step in constructing a generative model is to find the prior distribution $\text{Pr}(Y_k)$ and the likelihood function or conditional distribution $\text{Pr}(X|Y_k)$ for every k, where k is the possible classes for the label. To predict the label for a new observation X, we need to calculate the conditional probability of a particular class Y_k given the observation X. This can be obtained using the Bayes rule:

$$\text{Pr}(Y_k|X) = \frac{\text{Pr}(Y_k)\,\text{Pr}(X|Y_k)}{\text{Pr}(X)} \tag{9.7}$$

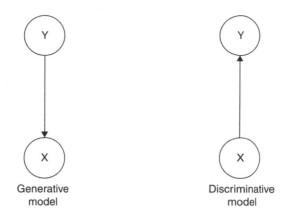

FIGURE 9.3   Graph representation of generative model and discriminative model.

where $\Pr(X)$ is a normalizing constant and is obtained by marginalizing Y for $\Pr(X, Y)$. Then, we can assign our output to the class that yields the highest posterior probability given an observation and make a decision by using a user-specified cost function. This is a generative model because we explicitly model the distribution of the observation, X.

9.2.3.2 *Discriminative Model*   A generative model such as the naive Bayes, HMM, and MRF computes the joint distributions $\Pr(X, Y)$. However, the difficulty lies primarily in computing $\Pr(X)$, especially when X is in high dimension and when most of the features are correlated. As we addressed in the naive Bayes model, we assume that features are conditionally independent given the class label. However, this assumption may hurt the performance of the generative model on a general application as compared to a discriminative model such as the logistic regression model [35].

For sequential data such as gene or protein structure, a generative model like HMM has the assumption that Y_i only depends on feature X_i. However, since some of the features might be missing in the training data, it is therefore necessary to explore and use X_i,'s neighbors' information. The generative model fails to capture this information. Moreover, usually the purpose of a model is to predict Y rather than modeling the distribution $\Pr(X)$. Hence, computing the joint distribution for X and Y would not be necessary to infer the posterior probability of Y.

A discriminative model builds a function that maps variable X directly to one decision boundary described by a posterior probability $\Pr(Y|X)$. The discriminative model does not need to make strict independence assumptions on the observations, and it is able to choose features in an arbitrary way. Also, the transition probability between labels may depend not only on the current observation but also on past and future observations.

9.2.4 Sequential Model

Classical classifiers such as naive Bayes and logistic regression predict only a single class of variable given an observation. These models fail when it comes to prediction of a label sequence given an observation sequence because both models assume that the predicted labels are independent from each other. It is called structure prediction or a sequential model because of the topological structure of input and output data. In bioinformatics,

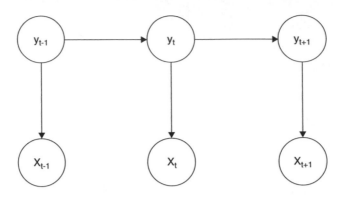

FIGURE 9.4   Hidden Markov model.

DNA sequences, protein sequences, and protein 3D structures are typical structure data. Two widely developed graph models, the HMM and the CRF, will be discussed in the following sections.

9.2.4.1 *Hidden Markov Model* The HMM [37] has been used extensively in various scientific fields for segmenting and predicting label sequences for a given observation sequence. In Figure 9.4, X is the observed sequence and Y is the label sequence, which is sometimes called the hidden state. The subscript t indicates the position of the label and the observation sequence. The arrows between hidden states represent the translation possibility $\Pr(y_t|y_{t-1})$, and the arrow between a hidden state and an observation represents the emission possibility $\Pr(x_t|y_t)$. There are three assumptions made in the HMM:

1. *Markov Assumption* The current state (label) is only dependent on the previous state. This means that each state y_t is independent from all other states, $y_1, y_2, \ldots, y_{t-2}$ given its previous state y_{t-1}.
2. *Stationary Assumption* The state transition probability is independent of the actual position at which the transition takes place.
3. *Independence Assumption* The current input x_t is statistically independent from the previous output x_{t-1} given the current state y_t.

In addition, each observation x_t depends only on the current state y_t. Based on these assumptions, we then have Equation (9.8) as the joint probability:

$$\Pr(Y, X) = \prod_{t=1} \Pr(y_t|y_{t-1})\Pr(x_t|y_t) \tag{9.8}$$

Here, $\Pr(x_t|y_t)$ is the transition matrix of our observation and $\Pr(y_t|y_{t-1})$ is the state transition matrix.

There are three fundamental questions in the HMM [37].

1. How do we estimate the parameters?
2. Which HMM is most probably used to generate the given sequence? This is also called the evaluation process.
3. Given an observation sequence, what is the most likely label sequence which has generated the observation sequence?

The HMM is a supervised learning method. In other words, given a set of training data sets, we have to optimize the parameters (transition and confusion matrices). We can consider the HMM model as an extension of the mixture Gaussian model by introducing the transition matrix between different hidden states. To optimize parameters, the expectation–maximization (EM) algorithm has been used extensively during the past decades [34]. As for the second question, one can use the forward algorithm to calculate the probability of an observation sequence [37]. The third question is to predict the label sequence for a new observation based on the learned parameters. In this case, we want to find label sequence Y^* that maximizes the conditional probability of the label sequence given an observation sequence:

$$y^* = \arg \max_Y \Pr(y|x) \tag{9.9}$$

The above equation is obtained using the Bayes rule [Equation (9.7)]. The probability $\Pr(X)$ does not depend on Y, so we can drop it. Now, the objective is to find the maximum of $\Pr(X, Y)$. Using a naive approach, we can list all the possible label sequences and see which one has the highest posterior probability. The time complexity is $O(S^T)$, where S is the number of possible labels and T is the total number of states in the sequence. But this task can be performed efficiently using a dynamic programming technique known as the Viterbi algorithm [37].

9.2.4.2 *Weakness of Hidden Markov Model*

As mentioned before, HMM is a generative model. It models the joint distributions of both observation sequences and label sequences. However, in most cases, our interest lies primarily in predicting a label sequence given an observation sequence.

In addition, the HMM assumes that each observation x_t is only dependent on its label y_t, and, hence, is incapable of modeling multiple features from the observation. However, in real-world applications, observation sequences tend to be dependent and are best represented in terms of multiple interacting features and long-range dependencies between observation elements.

9.2.5 Maximum-Entropy Markov Models and Label Bias Problem

Maximum-entropy Markov models (MEMMs) is a form of conditional model used to label sequential data given an observation (Figure 9.5). While the HMM is a generative model,

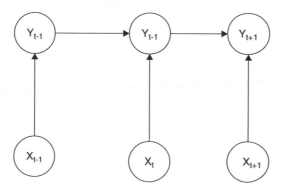

FIGURE 9.5 Maximum-entropy Markov models.

the MEMM is a discriminative model. Hence, the MEMM does not need to model the joint distributions of both observation and label sequences. Also, unlike the HMM, the MEMM is able to model multiple features from the observation using the function f_k in Equation (9.10). The MEMM had been applied to various fields for labeling sequential data. These include but are not limited to part-of-speech (POS) tagging and segmentation of text document problems [38].

$$\Pr(y_t|y_{t-1}, x_t) = \frac{1}{Z(x_t, y_{t-1})} \exp\left(\sum_{k=1}^{K} \lambda_k f_k(x_t, y_t, y_{t-1})\right) \tag{9.10}$$

Equation (9.10) is the state observation transition function using in the MEMM for time $(t-1)$ to t. This equation provides the probability of current state y_t given the previous state y_{t-1} and observation x_t. Computation of the likelihood of the whole state sequence involves multiplying the above probability of each of the time points together. Here, f_k is the kth feature function and λ_k is the weight assigned to f_k.

Although the MEMM has the advantageous characteristics over the HMM, the MEMM has an undesirable property called the label bias problem [39]. This is due to the per-state normalization at each transition. Hence, the model will tend to favor the label with fewer outgoing transitions. The details about the label bias problem can be found in a paper by Lafferty et al. [39]. More information on the MEMM can be found in a paper by McCallum et al. [38]. The conditional random field was proposed to solve the label bias problem and also inherit all the good properties of the MEMM.

9.2.6 Conditional Random Field

The CRF was first proposed by Lafferty et al. [39] in the context of segmentation and labeling of text sequences. The CRF models the posterior distribution $p(Y|X)$ directly. Because the CRF is a undirected graph model (Figure 9.6), it does not have arrows between the observation and hidden state as in the HMM. It has been proven to be very effective in many applications with structured outputs, such as information extraction, image processing, and parsing [40–42]. The CRF is able to model the conditional probability of a label sequence with nonindependent and interacting features of the observation sequence due to its conditional nature.

Since the CRF does not have the assumption for the distribution of the inputs $P(X)$ and finds the decision boundary directly, it can be regarded as an extension of logistic regression

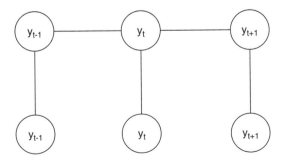

FIGURE 9.6 Conditional random field.

to model sequential data. The relationship among the CRF, logistic regression, and naive Bayesian model can be found in some previous works [35, 36].

Formally, we define $G = (V, E)$ as an undirected graph such that $Y = (Y_u)_{u \in V}$, and Y is indexed by the vertices of G. The couple (X, Y) is said to be a conditional random field if, when conditioned on X, the random variable y_t obeys the Markov property with respect to the graph: $\Pr(y_t | y_{S-\{t\}}, X) = \Pr(y_t | y_{Nt}, X)$, where $S \backslash \{t\}$ is the set of all the nodes in the graph except the node t and N_t is the set of neighbors of node t in G [39]. The conditional distribution for Y given X is

$$\Pr(Y|X) = \frac{1}{Z} \sum_{t \in \text{Nodes}} \exp\left[\sigma(y_t|X) + \theta(y_t, y_{ng}|X)\right] \tag{9.11}$$

where t is a node in the graph G and $\sigma(y_t|X)$ is an association potential function that reflects the feature X that has an influence on the label y_t. It can be a logistic regression model, a Bayesian model, a SVM, or a kernel regression model. The second term $\theta(y_t, y_{ng}|X)$ is the *association potential function* between y_t and its neighbors y_{ng}. These neighborhood nodes y_{ng} can be nodes in a clique of the graph in which the size of the clique can be arbitrary. The association potential function shows the influence among related predicted labels. The potential functions defined in Equation (9.11) transform the traditional logistic regression that fits a single scalar to fitting and labeling sequential data. Therefore, the CRF is similar to the logistic regression for classification where y is now sequential data, which can be discrete or continuous. The variable Z is the normalization factor given by

$$Z = \sum_{Y} \sum_{t \in \text{Nodes}} \exp\left[\sigma(y_t|X) + \theta(y_t, y_{ng}|X)\right] \tag{9.12}$$

So far we defined the graph as a linear chain in Figure 9.6. However, the structure of the graph G can be arbitrary provided that the conditional independence in the label sequences is correctly modeled. However, due to the high computational cost for training a general CRF model, the most widely used graph structure is the linear chain CRF as shown in Figure 9.6. The maximum clique among the label sequence is then a pairwise clique. From Equation (9.2), the joint distribution over the labels Y given the observation sequence X can be written as

$$\Pr(Y|X) = \frac{1}{Z(x)} \exp\left(\sum_{c \subset C} \sum_{k=1}^{K} \left[\lambda_k f_k(y_{t-1}, y_t, X) + \mu_k g_k(y_t, X)\right]\right) \tag{9.13}$$

Here f_k corresponds to θ and g_k corresponds to σ in Equation (9.11). Since the loss function [Equation (9.13)] is convex, it will always give us the global maximum if we optimize the function [39]. In the remainder of this chapter, Equation (9.13) is simplified by substituting the feature functions $f_k(y_{t-1}, y_t, X)$ and $g_k(y_t, X)$ to $f_k(X, i, y_{t-1}, y_t)$. Therefore, we obtain the equation

$$\Pr(Y|X) = \frac{1}{Z(X)} \prod_{t} \exp\left(\sum_{k=1}^{K} \lambda_k f_k(X, t, y_{t-1}, y_t)\right) \tag{9.14}$$

While the MEMM normalizes the probability on a per-state basis, the CRF normalizes the probability over the whole sequence. Hence, the MEMM will tend to be biased toward states with fewer outgoing transitions (the label bias problem). To the extreme, the MEMM will ignore the observation if there is only one single outgoing transition [39].

We note that every HMM can always be written as a special instance of the linear chain CRF. We define a single feature function for each of $\Pr(y_t|y_{t-1})$ and $\Pr(x_t|y_t)$ as

$$f_k(y_{t-1}, y_t, x) = \begin{cases} 1 & \text{if } x_{t-1} = y' \text{ and } y_t = y \\ 0 & \text{otherwise} \end{cases} \tag{9.15}$$

$$g_k(y_t, x) = \begin{cases} 1 & \text{if } y_t = y' \text{ and } x_t = x \\ 0 & \text{otherwise} \end{cases} \tag{9.16}$$

Here, the parameters λ_k and μ_k corresponding to these features are equivalent to the logarithms of the HMM transition and emission probabilities $\Pr(y_t|y_{t-1})$ and $\Pr(x_t|y_t)$. However, the CRF is a more general model because it allows arbitrary dependencies on the observation sequence. In general, a feature function can be any mapping $F_j : X \times Y \to R$.

Often, feature functions are just binary indicators (absence/not). For example, let us consider a simple DNA functional site model by considering motifs using the CRF. Because the CRF modeling is a supervised learning process, we use training data of DNA sequences with sequence patterns X and its related label Y. In order to capture the dependencies on the observation sequence patterns in one sequence, we can define one of feature functions as

$$f_1(y_{t-1}, y_t, x) = \begin{cases} 1 & \text{if } x_t = \text{CGCC}, y_t = \text{motif 1} \\ 0 & \text{otherwise} \end{cases} \tag{9.17}$$

$$f_2(y_{t-1}, y_t, x) = \begin{cases} 1 & \text{if } x_t = \text{TATA}, y_t = \text{motif 2}, y_{t-1} = \text{motif 1} \\ 0 & \text{otherwise} \end{cases} \tag{9.18}$$

For the feature functions f_1 and f_2, the corresponding weights λ_1, λ_2 reflect the probability for the observed sequence patterns and related sequence label. For example, whenever the CRF sees the sequence TATA, it will prefer to label the state as motif 1 because we observe TATA with a higher weight for motif 1.

9.2.6.1 *Parameter Estimation*   Maximum-likelihood estimation is widely used to learn the parameters in the CRF. Maximum-likelihood estimation chooses values of the parameters such that the logarithm of the likelihood, known as the log likelihood, is maximized [39]. The log likelihood for the CRF can be written as

$$l(\lambda) = \sum_{i=1}^{N} \log \Pr(y^{(i)}|x^{(i)}) \tag{9.19}$$

where N is the number of training sequences and λ is the vector of the parameters. Since typically there are thousands of parameters used in a CRF model, the CRF may be overfitted to the training data set. To avoid overfitting, a regularization factor is usually added to the log likelihood. Substituting Equation (9.13) into Equation (9.19) and adding a Gaussian regularization, we obtain the expression

$$l(\lambda) = \sum_{i=1}^{N} \sum_{t=1}^{T} \sum_{k=1}^{K} \lambda_k f_k\left(y_t^i, y_{t-1}^i, x_t^i\right) - \sum_{i=1}^{N} \log Z(X^i) - \sum_{k=1}^{K} \frac{\lambda_k^2}{2\sigma^2} \tag{9.20}$$

Note that the subscript i denotes the ith data samples, t is the position in a data, and k is the kth feature function. In order to maximize the log-likelihood function [Equation (9.20)], we differentiate the log-likelihood function with respect to the parameter λ_k, which yields

$$\frac{\partial l(\lambda)}{\partial \lambda_k} = \sum_{i=1}^{N} \sum_{t=1}^{T} f_k\left(y_t^i, y_{t-1}^i, x_t^i\right) - \sum_{i=1}^{N} \sum_{t=1}^{T} \sum_{y,y'} f_k\left(y, y', x_t^i\right) P\left(y, y'|x^{(i)}\right) - \sum_{k=1}^{K} \frac{\lambda_k}{\sigma^2} \quad (9.21)$$

Because Equation (9.21) does not have closed-form solutions, we cannot obtain the λ_k value by simply setting Equation (9.21) equal to zero. Thus, we need to take a different strategy to obtain the parameter values. For example, Lafferty et al. used the gradient ascent approach [39]:

$$\lambda^{n+1} = \lambda^n + \alpha \nabla \quad (9.22)$$

where α is the scaling factor and ∇ is the first deviant of the log-likelihood function [Equation (9.21)] for λ. However, the conventional approach requires too many iterations to be practical. The quasi-Newton method converges much faster than the original approach based on iterative scaling [36, 43]:

$$\lambda^{n+1} = \lambda^n - H^{-1} \nabla \quad (9.23)$$

where H is the Hessian matrix whose elements comprise the second derivatives of $l(\lambda)$ with respect to the components of λ. Other parameter learning methods can be found in some tutorials [36, 43].

9.2.6.2 Inference

Given the learned model, we are interested in labeling an unseen instance given an observation sequence and computing the marginal distribution. This is essentially the same as the HMM inference problem, because both of them aimed to find the maximal posterior possibility label sequence. In order to find the most probable label for a given observation sequence, we can use the Viterbi algorithm similar to the HMM. There are two major approaches to compute the marginal probability or the conditional probability: the exact inference and approximate inference methods.

The elimination algorithm is the basic method for the exact inference. The main idea is to efficiently marginalize out all the irrelevant variables using factored representation of the joint probability distribution. Forward–backward algorithms such as those used for the HMM can be applied to the linear chain CRF as well. The algorithm is further described in detail in papers by Hoefel and Elkan [44] and Lafferty et al. [39].

The computational complexity of the exact inference algorithms increases exponentially when the size of the cliques are very large. Hence, approximation methods are preferred in many practical applications. These approximation methods include the sampling method [45], the variation methods [46], or the loopy belief propagation [47]. A very efficient approach for high-dimensional data is the Markov chain Monte Carlo, including Gibbs sampling and Metropolis–Hastings sampling [48, 49]. The loopy belief propagation applies the original belief propagation algorithm to graphs even when they contain loops [50].

9.2.6.3 Conditional Random Field versus Markov Random Field

Kumar and Hebert [41] compared two major differences between the CRF and the original MRF framework. First, in the conditional random fields, the association potential function at any state is a function of all the observations X while in the MRF (with the assumption of conditional independence of the data) the association potential is a function of data only at that state X_t. Second, the interaction potential for each pair of nodes in MRFs is a function of only labels, while in the conditional models it is a function of labels as well as all the observations X. The interaction among labels in MRFs is modeled by the term $P(Y)$, which can be seen as a prior under the Bayesian framework. However, these label interactions do not depend on the observed data X. This difference plays a central role in modeling arbitrary interactions in sequential data. Above all, the MRF and HMM belong to the generative model which is based on modeling the joint distributions $\Pr(X, Y)$, while the CRF is a extension of the discriminative model such as the maximum-entropy model (usually regarded as logistic regression). The discriminative model is based on modeling the conditional distribution $\Pr(Y|X)$ directly.

9.2.6.4 *General Conditional Random Field*   In the previous sections, we have mainly discussed the learning and inference steps for the linear chain CRF. However, those methods can also be extended to general graphs by considering the long-range dependencies over labels. Several researchers have recently demonstrated that certain CRF graph structures are useful for handling special applications. For example, the Skip-Chain CRF takes into account the probabilistic dependencies between long-distance mentions for information extraction [51]. Liu et al. [52] extended the linear chain CRF to predict a type of protein structure [52]. In addition, several researchers modified the original CRF and proposed to integrate other techniques, for example, the Bayesian CRF [53], the boosting [54], and the neural network [55]. Other research directions include development of the semisupervised learning CRF in order to deal with insufficient training label data. Some recent developments of the semisupervised learning methods can be found in recent papers [56, 57].

9.2.7 Summary of Models and Available Resources

Each model has its strengths and drawbacks and one needs to examine which model (or if any model) is suitable for a particular problem. In Table 9.1, we summarize the pros and cons of the models discussed above.

There are several useful information sources and software for the MRF and CRF. For the MRF, some books, such as *Markov Random Field Modeling in Image Analysis* [58] and *Image Processing: Dealing with Texture* [59], provide details of the method. In addition, we provide a list of resources on the Internet we found useful (Table 9.2).

9.3 APPLICATIONS

In this section, we discuss some applications of the MRF and CRF on gene prediction, protein function prediction, and protein structure prediction.

9.3.1 Gene Prediction Using Conditional Random Fields

One of the first steps in gene analysis is to determine the coding regions given DNA sequences, which is called the gene prediction problem or the gene-finding problem. Generally gene prediction considers prediction of protein-coding genes, which are the sections of DNA that are translated to produce proteins [60]. According to the central dogma of molecular biology in eukaryotes, a DNA sequence first undergoes a transcription process

TABLE 9.1   Summary of Models

	Pros	Cons
Generative model	Based on the joint distribution, it is easy to calculate the posterior distribution.	Does not need to generate the joint distributions for variables when it comes to making a prediction.
Discriminative model	Do not need to model the joint distributions of the features and variables. It is able to calculate the posterior possibility directly. It just needs to estimate the parameters of the model rather than the whole distributions of data. The model has been extended to different ways by new regulation function, kernel methods, and others.	Could not compute the joint distribution of variables and features.
Naive Bayes model	Although this classifier has a strong assumption of independence of features, this model has been successfully applied in many applications.	Because the feature independence assumption is not promised in most of the applications, this classifier is not always suitable for such data.
Markov random field	Widely used in the computation vision and bioinformatics for modeling data naturally modeled as a graph.	It has the same drawback of generative model and the computation cost is high in most of cases, especially when the size of cliques gets larger.
Hidden Markov model	Suitable and applied for many sequential data, for example, in the bioinformatics, natural language processing, and computation visions.	It assumes that features are independent with each other and often difficult to model (train parameters) distant dependency of hidden states.
Maximum-entropy Markov models	It is proposed to handle the drawbacks of HMM.	Has the label bias problem.
Logistic/linear regression	Do not have assumption of feature independence and can handle nonlinear relation between features.	It does not model dependency between labels.
Conditional random field	It successfully deals with the drawbacks of HMM (assumption of independence of features) and MEMM (the label bias problem). Recently successfully applied in bioinformatics domain.	It still faces the problem of size of training data as the logistic regression. The available software package of CRF is hard to run on different data sets.

in which intergenic regions of the sequence are removed to produce premessenger RNAs (pre-mRNAs). A pre-mRNA is subject to gene splicing, where introns are removed producing a messenger RNA (mRNA). Finally, a mRNA is translated into a protein (amino acid) sequence, where identification of the coding region and *untranslated regions* (UTRs) is involved [61]. Thus, in most gene predictions, the aim is to accurately predict the

TABLE 9.2   Online Resources for MRF and CRF

Title and Web Site	Contents and Comments
Tutorials and Lectures	
Introduction to MRF and its application on computation vision `https://engineering.purdue.edu/~bouman/ece641/mrf_tutorial/`	Basic examples of graph model and the related source code will be useful to understand the graph model.
Collection for CRF `http://www.inference.phy.cam.ac.uk/hmw26/crf/`	Links to tutorials, papers, and software for CRF.
Video tutorial for CRF (Charles Elkan) `http://videolectures.net/cikm08_elkan_llmacrf/`	Basic tutorial for beginner to understand logistic regression model and CRF.
Software	
MRF source code collection `http://www.cs.cmu.edu/~cil/v-source.html`	It provides the collection of software on computation vision based on MRF.
MRF minimization `http://vision.middlebury.edu/MRF/code/`	It provides several benchmark software packages to compare MRF application on image segmentation and photomontage problems.
Collection of CRF program `http://www.cs.ubc.ca/~murphyk/Software/CRF/crf.html`	This website includes several 1D CRF model implementation packages.
Mallet-CRF `http://crf.sourceforge.net/`	Graphical Models in Mallet (GRMM) developed by the UMASS research group supports arbitrary factor graphs, which subsume Markov random fields, Bayesian networks, and conditional random fields.
CRFsuite `http://www.chokkan.org/software/crfsuite/`	Written in C++ and implemented in Windows 32, Linux platform.
CRF++ `http://crfpp.sourceforge.net/`	CRF++ is an open-source implementation of conditional random fields (CRFs) for segmenting/labeling sequential data.

intergenic regions, exons, introns, and UTRs of the target DNA sequence to determine the protein-coding regions in the DNA sequence.

In gene prediction, variants of the CRF, including the semi-Markov CRF–based method, was found to outperform many generative models (e.g., HMM-based methods) [62–65].

In a generative model such as the HMM, the joint probability of the observed sequence **x** and hidden gene structure y is modeled. The joint probability and the parameter θ that is chosen to maximize the joint probability in the training data set are used to predict the genes by selecting the path of hidden labels **y** that maximize the joint probability given a new sequence **x**. To improve gene prediction accuracy, one approach is to incorporate additional information that can come from a multiple-sequence alignment and/or experiential data such as the express sequence tag (EST) alignment information [66]. Unlike the generative models that need to model the relationship between the different types of information, which can quickly become too complex, CRF models can treat different types of information as features without modeling the dependency between the features making leverage of different sources of information possible [62]. Below we describe four variants of the CRF-based gene prediction method.

Culotta et al. first applied the linear chain CRF model in gene prediction and showed that multiple features can be incorporated in the gene prediction [60]. In their model, a base in the DNA sequence is classified as a coding region, an intron, or an intergenic region. To incorporate restrictions in the model, a finite-state machine model is used between label nodes (**y**): the starting state, three coding states, and three intron states. Edges between the states model the restrictions. Coding regions must start with the three bases ATG (in the case of human genes) and end with TAA, TGA, or TAG. The features that they use include (1) 11 base features that incorporate the statistics of amino acid sequences by examining the identity of the previous five bases from the current base position in the given DNA sequence; (2) four histogram features which measure the frequencies of the base conjunctions and disjunctions in a sliding window of size 5; and (3) five homology features, such as the number of hits obtained through a BLAST sequence database search. Here, we will not discuss their CRF model since they used the typical CRF setting, which we extensively described in earlier sections.

Bernal et al. developed an ab initio gene prediction method based on the semi-Markov CRF CRAIG (CRF-based ab initio Genefinder) [63]. An ab initio gene prediction method only considers the information that comes directly from the target DNA sequence and does not use homology information (multiple-sequence alignment). Although ab initio methods have generally a lower accuracy than methods that use homology information, ab initio methods are useful when no homology information is found. CRAIG also uses a finite-state machine to model the gene structure states (**y**): the initial state, the end state, the intergenic state, the start state of a coding region, the end state of a coding region, three exon states, and six intron states. The state machine of eukaryotic genes is shown in Figure 9.7. Instead of associating each label y_j to each base x_j, GRAIG associates DNA sequence **x** to the labeled segment of sequence **s** by relaxing the requirements of the Markov property (semi-Markov property). The gene prediction, given a target sequence **x**, finds the best scoring segmentation where the score, which is analogous to conditional probability $\Pr(y|\mathbf{x})$ in the typical CRF model, is defined as (Equation 2 in the original paper)

$$S_w(\mathbf{x}, \mathbf{s}) = \sum_{j=1}^{Q} w_j \cdot f(s_j, \text{lab}(s_{j-1}), \mathbf{x}) \tag{9.24}$$

That is, DNA sequence $\mathbf{x} = x_1, \ldots, x_p$ is associated with the likely sequence segments $\mathbf{s} = s_1, \ldots, s_Q$, where each segment has information of a starting position $\text{pos}(s_j) = p_j$, a length of segment $\text{len}(s_j) = l_j$, and a state label $\text{lab}(s_j) = y_j$, that is, $s_j = \langle p_j, l_j, y_j \rangle$.

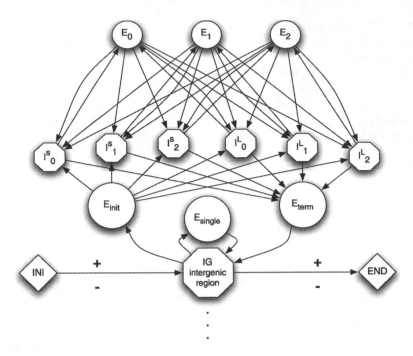

FIGURE 9.7 State machine of eukaryotic genes. The states represent the genomic regions and the directed edges between the states represent the biological signals. The short introns are denoted by I^S and long introns are denoted by I^L. States for exons start with E with subdivision of type of exons in subscript. (Reprinted with permission from [63].)

Each segment is described with a set of features that are computed from the current segment, the label of a previous segment, and the input sequence around the start position of the segment. The complete list of 19 features, such as length and sequence patterns of each state, can be found in Tables 6 and 7 of the original paper by Bernal et al. [63]. The weights of the features are learned using an online approach, where iteratively updating the weights as the input sequences is done one by one. Inference for a sequence $\mathbf{x}$ is computed with a variant of the Viterbi algorithm, which finds the label $\mathbf{s}$ that maximizes Equation (9.24).

Conrad is another semi-Markov CRF-based de novo gene prediction method [62, 67]. De novo methods use multiple-sequence alignments of the input DNA sequence. Conrad, like CRAIG, uses labeled segments S, that is, instead of associating a label to each bases in a sequence, a label $\mathbf{s}$ is represented as a segment of DNA sequence, $s_i = (t_i, u_i, v_i)$, where t_i is the start position, u_i is the end position, and v_i is the label of the segment. Each segment is assumed to only interact with its immediate neighbors such that feature sum F_j can be written as the sum of the Q number of local features f_j:

$$F_j(\mathbf{x}, \mathbf{s}) = \sum_{i=1}^{Q} f_j(v_{i-1}, t_i, u_i, v_i, \mathbf{x}) \tag{9.25}$$

Conrad combines the probabilistic features that are adopted from phylogenetic generalized HMM (GHMM) models [68], which are done by converting the GHMM model to an equivalent semi-Markov CRF model, with additional nonprobabilistic binary features. The components of the probabilistic features include (1) five reference features that model the nucleotide compositions of homologues sequences; (2) three length features that model the length distributions of introns, exons, and intergenic regions; (3) a transition feature that measures the frequencies of types of transitions; (4) eight boundary features; and (5) five phylogenetic features that come from data of multiple species. Nonprobabilistic features, or discriminative features, used include (1) six *gap features* which reflect insertion or deletion patterns that come from a multiple-sequence alignment; (2) three *footprint features* for each aligned sequence which give information of the position at which each sequence is aligned; and (3) nine EST features that come from EST alignments. Two methods are used to train the weights of the features: the condition maximum likelihood (CML) and the maximum expected accuracy (MEA). The CML indirectly optimizes the accuracy by maximizing the likelihood of correct segments over the training data set, whereas the MEA tries to directly optimize the accuracy of the inferred segment. The CML finds the weight $w_{CML} = \arg_w \max[\log(Pr_w(\mathbf{y}^0, \mathbf{x}^0)]$ on the training data $(\mathbf{y}^0, \mathbf{x}^0)$ by computing the gradient using dynamic programming. The MEA optimizes the weights using an objective function A, which is defined as the expected value of the similarity function S of the distribution of segments define by the SMCRF:

$$S(\mathbf{y}, \mathbf{y}^0, \mathbf{x}^0) = \sum_{i=1}^{n} s(y_{j-1}, y_i, y_i^0, \mathbf{x}^0, i)$$
$$A(\mathbf{w}) = E_w(S(\mathbf{y}, \mathbf{y}^0, \mathbf{x}^0)). \tag{9.26}$$

and the weights $w_{MEA} = \arg_w \max[A(w)]$ are obtained by computing a gradient-based function optimizer.

The last method, CONTRAST [65], is another de novo gene prediction method that uses the CRF model. CONTRAST is composed of local and global components. For the local components, boundaries of coding regions are learned using SVMs. The global components are composed of the gene structure that integrates the boundary information learned by SVM with additional features from multiple-alignment results. The gene structure of CONTRAST consists of one intergenic node, three starting-exon nodes, three single-exon nodes, three internal exon nodes, three terminal exon nodes, and three intron nodes. The constraints are posed with directed edges between the nodes. CONTRAST uses nonprobabilistic binary features that are categorized as (1) label transition features; (2) sequence-based features including features based on target sequence, a multiple alignment, and EST alignments; and (3) coding region boundary features that come from outputs of the SVM classifier using alignment information. The weights of the features are optimized using a gradient-based optimization algorithm and the RPROP algorithm [69]. The score of a labeling is computed as $\mathbf{w} \cdot \mathbf{F}(\mathbf{x}, \mathbf{y})$ where $\mathbf{F}(\mathbf{x}, \mathbf{y}) = \sum f(y_{i-1}, y_i, i, \mathbf{x})$. CONTRAST takes a slightly different approach of training the weights and predicting the labels as compared with traditional CRF models. In prediction, selected labels maximize the weighted difference between the expected number of true-positive and false-positive coding region boundary predictions, which can be computed using the forward and backward algorithms. The weight learning is done by optimizing the expected boundary accuracy in the training set, which is done using the gradient–based optimization algorithm.

9.3.2 Protein Function Prediction Using Markov Random Fields

The large growth in high-throughput genomic and proteomic data has spurred the need for advanced computational function prediction methods that can elucidate protein function by using this system-level information [70–74]. In this section we describe the computational methods that provide insight into functional annotations of proteins using the MRF.

Traditionally protein function is predicted using sequence information only [3, 75, 76]. In recent years high-throughput experimental technologies have provided us with rich information sources, such as protein–protein interaction (PPI) data, microarray expression data, and synthetic lethality of genes. These new information sources provide the context of the whole genome to study the function of proteins. Using these various features, machine learning approaches have been used to infer the function of new proteins. Deng et al. [77, 78] first proposed the use of the MRF for modeling the probability that a protein has a certain function by capturing the local dependency of protein function on its neighbors in the PPI network. They make use of the "guilt-by-association" rule in the neighborhood of a protein and apply the local Markov property that the function of a protein is independent of all the other proteins given its neighbors in the PPI network.

9.3.2.1 Markov Random Field for Function Prediction   Deng et al. [78] defined a Gibbs distribution over the PPI network of yeast, which was obtained from the Munich Information Center for Protein Sequences (MIPS) database [79]. They considered only one annotation category at a time and provided the probability that an unknown protein in the network has that function of interest F using the MRF. Given a PPI network with N proteins as nodes, out of which $P_1, \ldots, P_n$ are the n unannotated proteins and $P_{n+1}, \ldots, P_{n+m}$ are the m proteins whose annotation is known. The random variable X_i will be 1 if the ith protein has the annotation category F, else it will be zero. Thus, we obtain a vector X consisting of labeling $X_1 = \lambda_1, \ldots, X_n = \lambda_n$ and $X_{n+1} = \mu_{n+1}, \ldots, X_{n+m} = \mu_{n+m}$. Figure 9.8 shows the structure of the MRF. Let π be the fraction of proteins having annotation F. Let O_{ij} be 1 if there is interaction between proteins i and j, otherwise it is 0, and Nei(i) be the proteins interacting directly with P_i in the PPI network. Since interacting proteins are more likely to have the same function as noninteracting ones, they define the potential function $U(x)$ as

$$U(x) = -\alpha N_1 - \beta N_{10} - \gamma N_{11} - N_{00} \tag{9.27}$$

where N_1 is the number of nodes having functional annotation F, N_{11} is the number of interacting pairs where both partners have annotation F, N_{10} is the number of interacting pairs in the network where one interacting partner has F and the other does not have F, N_{00} is the number of interacting pairs in the network where both the interacting partners do not have F as their annotation and α is defined as $\log[\pi/(1-\pi)]$. With the general MRF theory we can write the global Gibbs distribution [Equation (9.28)] using the potential function $U(x)$ where $Z(\Theta)$ is the partition function and $\Theta = \{\alpha, \beta, \gamma\}$:

$$\Pr(X|\theta) = \frac{1}{Z(\theta)} \exp[-U(x)] \tag{9.28}$$

To predict the unknown labels $(X_1, \ldots, X_n)$, we need samples from the posterior distribution $\Pr(X_1, \ldots, X_n | X_{n+1}, \ldots, X_{n+m})$. These samples can be obtained by applying

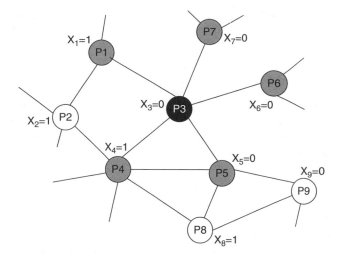

FIGURE 9.8 Markov random field based on PPI network. Shown is a PPI network with nodes as proteins and edges showing interactions between them. The MRF structure used by Deng et al. is based on the random variable X corresponding to each protein, which takes values one or zero depending on whether the protein has the annotation under consideration or not. The network also contains nodes whose X_i value is not known and thus will be predicted using the MRF framework. The node P_3 is shown in black and its neighbors, for example, Nei(P_3), are shown in gray. The edge $P_1 P_2$ is counted as N_{11}, the edge $P_1 P_3$ is counted as N_{10}, and the edge $P_3 P_5$ is counted as N_{00}.

the Gibbs sampling strategy where the samples from the conditional distribution in Equation (9.29) approximate the samples from the joint distribution:

$$
\begin{aligned}
\Pr(X_i = 1 | X_{[-i]}, \theta) &= \frac{\Pr\left((X_i = 1, X_{[-i]})\,|\theta\right)}{\Pr\left((X_i = 1, X_{[-i]})\,|\theta\right) + \Pr\left((X_i = 0, X_{[-i]})\,|\theta\right)} \\
&= \frac{\exp\left[\alpha + (\beta - 1)\,M_0^{(i)} + (\gamma - \beta)\,M_1^{(i)}\right]}{1 + \exp\left[\alpha + (\beta - 1)\,M_0^{(i)} + (\gamma - \beta)\,M_1^{(i)}\right]}
\end{aligned}
\tag{9.29}
$$

Here $X_{[-i]} = (X_1, \ldots, X_{i-1}, X_{i+1}, \ldots, X_{n+m})$ and $M_{(i)}^0$, $M_{(i)}^1$ are the number of interacting partners of protein $\Pr_i$ having label 0 and 1, respectively. Assuming that the parameters Θ are obtained using the method described in the next part, it first sets initial X_i labels using the probability π. The labels are then updated repeatedly from the ones in the previous stage for a burn-in period using Equation (9.29). Then, according to Gibbs, sampling the labels X_i obtained in the lag period approximates the probability of observing function F in protein P_i.

Since the partition function Z in Equation (9.28) is the function of Θ, it is difficult to use maximum-likelihood estimation. Hence they used the quasi-likelihood method to estimate the parameter Θ. This method is based on the standard linear logistic regression model and treats all observations independently. They obtained the logistic model [Equation (9.30)] by simplifying Equation (9.29) and the parameters were estimated using the subnetwork of known proteins:

$$\log \frac{\Pr(X_i = 1 | X_{[-i]}, \theta)}{1.0 - \Pr(X_i = 1 | X_{[-i]}, \theta)} = \alpha + (\beta - 1) M_0^{(i)} + (\gamma - \beta) M_1^{(i)} \tag{9.30}$$

Overall the method proposed by Deng et al. is novel because it applies the Markov property of the local functional dependence of the protein on its neighborhood to the PPI networks. They compared the performance of this method with the neighbor counting and the chi-square method in terms of receiver operating characteristic (ROC) curves. It was observed that for a given specificity their method was more sensitive than others. Also, they have observed that the sensitivity of the method increased when the unknown proteins have more interacting partners. Even though the method improves over the existing network-based prediction methods, there are some limitations, for example, the method treats the functions independently of each other and processes one function at a time. There are relationships across the functional categories of the Gene Ontology [80] used here that can change the probabilities of a particular protein having annotations of interest.

In the next example, Letovsky and Kasif [81] use the MRF model based on the same idea as Deng et al. that the graph neighbors are more likely to share the same annotations as opposed to the nonneighbors in the graph. They use the binomial model to describe the neighborhood function to quantify the probability of a node having a particular annotation given the annotations of its neighbors. Similar to Deng et al.'s method, this method also considers a separate MRF for each annotation label, and term dependencies are not explicitly considered. For each protein P_i a variable $L_{i,t}$ is defined which is 1 or 0 depending on whether protein P_i has label t or not. Using the Bayes rule [Equation (9.31)], they computed the label probability $\Pr(L_{i,t} = 1 | N_i, K_{i,t})$ that protein i has label t given that it has N_i neighbors and $K_{i,t}$ out of those neighbors are annotated with the label t. Subscripts are excluded in later descriptions of this equation:

$$\Pr(L_{i,t} | N_i, K_{i,t}) = \frac{\Pr(K_{i,t} | L_{i,t}, N_i) \cdot \Pr(L_{i,t})}{\Pr(K_{i,t} | N_i)} \tag{9.31}$$

where $f = \Pr(L)$ is computed as the frequency of term t in the network and $\bar{f}$ is given by $1 - f$. The main distinction of this model as compared with the previous method by Deng et al. [Equation (9.29)] is that it computes $\Pr(K | L, N)$ based on the binomial distribution $\text{Bin}(N, K, \Pr_1)$. The idea behind this is that if labels are randomly assigned they will follow a binomial distribution where $\Pr_1$ is the probability that an interacting partner is labeled with t given that the protein is labeled with t. Similarly, $\Pr(K | L, N)$ is the probability of observing the given number of neighbors with label t given that the protein does not have label t. It is given by $\text{Bin}(N, K, \Pr_0)$ where $\Pr_0$ is the probability that an interacting partner is labeled with t given that the protein is not labeled with t. Thus we have $P(K | N) = f \cdot P(K | L, N) + \bar{f} \cdot P(K | \bar{L}, N)$, which in turn simplifies Equation (9.31) and gives the probability of protein i having label t as shown in the equation.

$$\Pr(L | N, K) = \frac{\lambda}{1 + \lambda} \quad \text{where} \quad \lambda = \frac{f \cdot \Pr_1^K \cdot \Pr_1^{N-k}}{\bar{f} \cdot \Pr_0^K \cdot \Pr_0^{N-k}} \tag{9.32}$$

With the MRF framework based on the neighborhood conditional probability function defined in Equation (9.32), Letovsky and Kasif [81] used heuristic belief propagation to label unannotated proteins. Initially the proteins are assigned a label based on f; then in the first step using Equation (9.32) label probabilities are estimated for unlabeled nodes. Then in the second step the adjusted probabilities in the first step are used, and to avoid invalid self-reinforcement, they apply a threshold of 0.8 to select and label nodes. Then these two steps are repeated until no more labels can be assigned. The GRID database [82] has been used for PPI data, and SGD [80] yeast Gene Ontology (GO) annotations have been used as labels. The data set consisted of 4692 labeled and 2573 unlabeled proteins. With a specific jackknife procedure they have observed that the method has 98.6% precision and 21% recall when a threshold of 0.8 was used for probability.

Deng et al. [78] did not consider unannotated proteins for which the label is unknown when training the regression model for parameter estimation. Instead, Kourmpetis et al. [83] have used the same model and applied the adaptive Markov chain Monte Carlo (MCMC) to draw samples from the joint posterior of X, Θ. They have shown that, when compared for 90 GO terms, their method gives area-under-the curve (AUC) value 0.8195 as compared with Deng et al. (0.7578) [78] and Letovsky et al. (0.7867) [81]. Kourmpetis et al. used the MRF model with the same potential function [83] as Deng and colleagues and initialized the parameters Θ and labels X using quasi-likelihood estimation and Gibbs sampling, respectively. Then, in the given iteration t the parameters are updated using a differential evolution Markov chain, a type of adaptive MCMC, conditioned on current labels, and the labels X^t conditioned on the current parameters Θ^t for unannotated nodes are updated by using Gibbs sampling. They repeated this procedure until convergence. When comparing the methods they mentioned that both Deng et al. [78] and Kourmpetis et al. [83] could estimate the intercept parameter α well, but the interaction parameters $\beta - 1$ and $\gamma - \beta$ in Equation (9.30) were better estimated by Kourmpetis et al. and led to the better performance.

9.3.2.2 Integrating Multiple Data Sources

After developing the MRF model based on PPI data, Deng et al. have further developed an integrated model that can incorporate information from PPI networks, expression profiles of genes, protein complex data, and domain information by weighing different data sources to compute the posterior probability that a protein has a particular function [84]. Here we will describe how the potential function described in Equation (9.27) is modified to take multiple data sources into account. The prior probability π_i that a protein P_i has a function of interest (i.e., $X_i = 1$) is different for each protein and is computed based on the protein complex data shown in Equation (9.33). If the protein belongs to multiple complexes, the maximum prior from any complex is used:

$$\pi_i = \Pr(X_i = 1|\text{Complex}) = \frac{\text{Proteins having the function within complex}}{\text{Known proteins within complex}} \quad (9.33)$$

Now to integrate the pairwise associations between proteins obtained from multiple sources, they converted each association into a network Net_i. For the expression data they connected proteins having expression correlation above a fixed threshold, and for a genetic interaction network they connected interacting genes based on mutation analysis data. Assuming that there are L such networks, they write the network parameters from Equation (9.27) for each network l as $(N_{10}^{(l)}, N_{11}^{(l)}, N_{00}^{(l)})$. The potential function after incorporating multiple data sources is shown in Equation (9.34) with α_i defined as $\log[\pi_i/(1 - \pi_i)]$ and parameters

$\beta_l, \gamma_l, 1 \le l \le L$. The joint probability distribution over all networks is given by Equation (9.35).

$$U(x) = -\sum_{i=1}^{n+m} x_i \alpha_i - \sum_{l=1}^{L} \left(\beta_l N_{10}^{(l)} + \gamma_l N_{11}^{(l)} + N_{00}^{(l)} \right) \qquad (9.34)$$

$$\Pr\{\text{labeling, networks}\} = \frac{1}{Z(\theta)} \exp[-U(x)] \qquad (9.35)$$

To include the dependency of the protein's function on the domain composition (a protein can consist of multiple functional regions called domains), they considered a set of domains $D_1, \ldots, D_M$ for each protein. Now P_i has domain composition d_i given by $(d_{i1}, d_{i2}, \ldots, d_{iM})$, where d_{ij} is 1 if the domain j is present in the protein P_i and 0 otherwise. Probabilities $\Pr_{1m}$ and $\Pr_{0m}$ are conditional on $d_m = 1$ (i.e., the protein has the domain d_m) given that the protein has or has not the given function, respectively. They considered all domains to be independent and gave the probability of the protein having the domain structure d given the function of interest as shown in Equation (9.36). Similarly, the probability that the protein has the domain structure d given it does not have the function is shown in Equation (9.37).

$$\Pr_1(d) = \prod_{m=1}^{M} \Pr_{1m}^{dm} (1 - \Pr_{1m})^{1-dm} \qquad (9.36)$$

$$\Pr_0(d) = \prod_{m=1}^{M} \Pr_{0m}^{dm} (1 - \Pr_{0m})^{1-dm} \qquad (9.37)$$

where M is the total number of domains in consideration. Based on the given label assignment, the probability of domain features is obtained as per Equation (9.38), which is used to modify the joint probability distribution shown in Equation (9.39) to describe the MRF based on multiple data sources:

$$\Pr\{\text{domain features}|\text{labeling}\} = \prod_{i:Xi=1} \Pr_1(d_i) \cdot \prod_{i:Xi=0} \Pr_0(d_i) \qquad (9.38)$$

$$\Pr\{\text{labeling networks domain features}\} = \Pr\{\text{labeling networks}\}$$
$$\cdot \Pr\{\text{domain features}|\text{labeling}\} \qquad (9.39)$$

In Equation (9.38), X_i is 1 or 0 depending on whether the protein P_i has the function of interest or not. Equation (9.38) expresses the probability of the domain features of all the proteins given the presence or absence of the function of interest. The first term on the right-hand side of Equation (9.39) comes from the MRF [Equation (9.35) and the second term is Equation (9.38)].

To estimate the parameters Θ [all α's, β's, and γ's in Equation (9.34)] they used the quasi-likelihood method, the same as the one described before in this section, and Gibbs sampling was used to assign functional labels to unknown proteins. To gauge the improvement in prediction accuracy, they computed the precision and recall curve of the method using just the PPI data and also with different data sources integrated. For a precision value of 57%, using only PPI data obtained the recall of 57%, which was increased to 87% when all the data sources were used together.

9.3.3   Application to Protein Tertiary Structure Prediction

Protein tertiary structure prediction remains one of the most challenging tasks in bioinformatics. Graphical models have not been applied much in this area, but there are a few of notable works. We discuss three applications of the MRF and CRF below.

9.3.3.1   Side-Chain Prediction and Free-Energy Estimation   The native structure of a protein has the minimum free energy among the alternative conformations, which is defined as $G = E - TS$, where E represents the enthalpy of the system, T represents the temperature, and S denotes the entropy of the system. Thus, the aim of structure prediction of a protein is to find the structure for the protein sequence that has the minimum free energy. However, computation of the entropy is a costly process mainly because the entropy calculation requires exploring a large number of alternative conformations of the protein that make the solution infeasible.

Kamisetty et al. [85] applied the MRF to compute the free energy of protein side-chain conformations. A protein structure is represented as a set of three-dimensional atomic coordinates of the backbone atoms X_b and side-chain conformations X_s, $X = \{X_b, X_s\}$. The distribution of the conformations can be expressed as the probability of the side-chain conformations (rotamers) with respect to the backbone structure:

$$\Pr(X = x|\Theta) = \Pr(X_b = x_b)\,\Pr(X_s = x_s|X_b, \Theta) \qquad (9.40)$$

When the backbone structure X_b is fixed, we only take the latter term into account. Assume Θ represents all the model parameters. The left panel in Figure 9.9 shows the MRF for a part of a protein structure where atoms are connected by edges if they are closer than a certain predefined distance whose actual value can vary depending on the application. When the backbone structure is fixed, the MRF represents the probability distribution of the side-chain rotamers given the backbone. To compute the probability of a particular structure, a factor graph was defined to express the relationship between different atoms. The factor graph expresses the functional form of the probability distribution (Figure 9.9). Interactions are

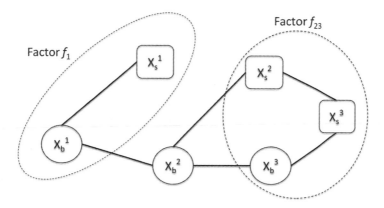

FIGURE 9.9   A factor graph from a backbone and side-chain representation is created by grouping pairwise interactions. The conjunction of all the interactions is equivalent to the functional form of the probability distribution.

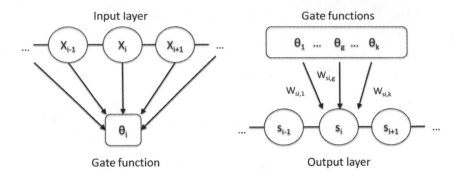

FIGURE 9.10   Conditional neural field for protein tertiary-structure prediction. The input layer x represents the sequence profile and the predicted secondary structure of q query protein and the output layer codes the angle distribution of each position.

restricted only to pairwise interactions (side chain to side chain, backbone to backbone, and side chain to backbone). In the factor graph those interactions are expressed as a series of local relationships that allow the translation from a standard backbone and side-chain representation (see Figure 9.10).

For example, simpler factors like f_1 can represent the relation between both backbone and side-chain atoms labeled x_1 (ψ_2 terms will be explained in the following paragraph). More complex relations such as f_{23} can denote backbone–backbone and side chain–side chain interactions between x_2 and x_3 (ψ_1 and ψ_3 terms, explained next). Each factor encodes the relationship between side-chain atoms by computing the pairwise potentials functions for each type of interaction:

$$\psi_1\left(X_s^{i_p}, X_s^{j_q}\right) = \exp\left(- E(x_s^{i_p}, x_s^{j_q})/k_B T\right)$$
$$\psi_2\left(X_s^{i_p}, X_b^{j}\right) = \exp\left(- E(x_s^{i_p}, x_b^{j})/k_B T\right) \qquad (9.41)$$
$$\psi_3\left(X_b^{i}, X_b^{j}\right) = 1$$

All atoms in the model are numbered. Let i and j denote the number assigned to two atoms that have some form of interaction either directly through the backbone or by side-chain interactions and i_p and j_q denote rotamers p and q of residues i and j. The first equation expresses the potential function of two rotamers p in residue i and q in residue j while the second equation specifies the potential function of the rotamer p of the residue i and the backbone residue j. The third function is set to 1 because we assume that the backbone is fixed. These equations model the probability according to the Boltzmann distribution, where E defines the interaction energy between two elements using a linear approximation to the repulsive van der Waals force. Also, T is temperature and k_B is the Boltzmann constant. In terms of potential functions, the probability of a side chain given a backbone can be expressed as

$$\Pr(X_s|X_b) = \frac{1}{Z} \prod_{c \in C(G)} \psi_c(x_1, x_2) \qquad (9.42)$$

Using the factors group, Equation (9.42) can be restated as

$$\Pr(x_s) = \frac{1}{Z} \prod_{f_a \in F} f_a\left(x_s^a\right) \tag{9.43}$$

The MRF model can be used to estimate the probability of a particular side-chain conformation. In addition, it can also be used to estimate the free-energy. As described before, the complexity of the free-energy computation comes from the large number of possible states. The way to solve this problem is to break up the factor graph into region R, which contains several factors f_R and variables x_R that can be used to compute the free energy of each region via estimates of marginal probabilities. Once the region-based estimates are computed, they can be added to produce an overall estimation. The model has been used to calculate entropy estimates that can help determine native structures from incorrect ones. The authors tested their model using 48 immunoglobin-related data sets, each containing an average of 35 decoys per data set. The native structure was ranked at the top in 42 of 48 data sets.

9.3.3.2 CRF Model for Protein Threading

The threading is a protein structure prediction method aimed at identifying protein structures that fit a query protein sequence from a database of protein structure templates [9, 10]. It employs a scoring function to evaluate fitness between the query sequence and a template structure which typically combines a scoring term for assessing protein sequence similarity and several terms for scoring amino acid propensity for structural environments in the template, such as the secondary structure or exposure/burial status. Using the scoring function, the query sequence is aligned with all templates in the database which are then sorted by score to identify the most well fitting template for the sequence. This problem can be modeled using the CRF [86].

In an alignment of the query sequence and a template structure, each alignment position will be assigned a label that represents a state from the set $X = \{M, I_s, I_t\}$, where M indicates that the position aligns a residue in the sequence with one in the template (matching state), I_s indicates that an insertion event occurs in the target sequence, and I_t represents an insertion in the template. The scoring function evaluates states in the alignment. For a target s and a template t, an alignment $a = \{a_1, a_2, \ldots, a_L\}$ denotes a particular assignment of labels, where each $a_i \in X$. The conditional probability of alignment a given the target and the template protein is defined as

$$\Pr_\Theta(a|s, t) = \frac{\exp\left(\sum_{i=1}^{L} F(a, s, t, i)\right)}{Z(s, t)} \tag{9.44}$$

where $\Theta = (\lambda_1, \lambda_2, \ldots, \lambda_p)$ are the model parameters and Z is a normalization factor, taking into account all possible alignments over s and t:

$$Z(s, t) = \sum_a \exp\left(\sum_{i=1}^{L_a} F(a, s, t, i)\right) \tag{9.45}$$

where F stands for the combination of features at a particular position i in the alignment. Its functional form is as follows:

$$F(a, s, t, i) = \sum_k \lambda_k e_k(a_{i-1}, a_i, s, t) + \sum_l \lambda_l v_l(a_i, s, t) \tag{9.46}$$

Both functions e and v represent feature functions that model two types of relations. The feature function e models an edge feature, the state transition between $i - 1$ and i, which depends on the features at these two positions. The second feature function, v, a label feature, models the relation between the state assigned to i and the features of the residue at the position. Note that both feature functions can be nonlinear, making the model richer in terms of the complexity of relations that can be modeled. In the CRF by Peng and Xu, predicted solvent accessibility, PSIPRED secondary structures, and PSI-BLAST sequence profiles were used as feature terms. The model is trained using the gradient tree boosting technique. Instead of visualizing function F as a linear combination of conventional terms, we can think about F being a linear combination of regression trees. The main advantage of this approach is that more complex features can be introduced and only the important ones emerge as part of the result. In their study, they chose 30 protein pairs from the PDB for training and 40 for validation, with an average size of 200 residues and sequence identity of less than 30% between them. They showed that their alignment accuracy improves with respect to existing methods, CONTRAlign and SP3/SP5, by at least 5%, being able to correctly align around 75% of the residues exactly and about 90% if a four-offset success criterion was used. They were also able to improve or get similar results in fold recognition, with respect to existing methods like RAPTOR and HHpred. The improvement is not as significant in some cases, but they show considerable increase at the superfamily level (around 10% of correctly identified residues).

9.3.3.3 Ab Initio Protein Structure Prediction

Xu et al. further developed an ab initio protein structure prediction method that employs CRF combined with the neural network [87]. The proposed framework was named the conditional neural field. The proposed method expresses the main-chain conformation as a distribution of angles at each residue position and represents nonlinear relations between features and the main-chain angles using the neural network.

A tertiary structure of the main chain of a protein can be uniquely determined by specifying a (hinge) angle θ at each residue at position i which is formed by positions $i - 1, i$, and $i + 1$ and τ, a pseudo–dihedral angle calculated from positions $i - 2, i - 1, i$, and $i + 1$. The conformations of residues in a protein can be expressed as a probability distribution of those angles. The probability distribution of the unit vector of each pair of angles (θ, τ) for a residue position can be modeled using the Fisher–Bingham (FB5) distribution. The probability density function FB5 is given by

$$f(u) = \frac{1}{c(\kappa, \beta)} \exp\left\{ \kappa\gamma_1 \cdot u + \beta \left[(\gamma_2 \cdot u)^2 - (\gamma_3 \cdot u)^2 \right] \right\} \qquad (9.47)$$

where u is a unit vector variable of the angles, the function c is a normalizing constant, κ determines the concentration of the angle distribution, and β is the ellipticity of the equal-probability contours. The γ values define the mean direction and the major axes. Using Equation (9.47), a protein main-chain structure can be modeled as a series of FB5 distributions, each determining likely directions that can be taken in order to place the next backbone residue. In order to limit the number of possible FB5 distributions that can be used at each position, 100 representative distributions were selected from a nonredundant protein set they analyzed. Once 1 out of the 100 distributions is assigned to a particular residue, concrete values of θ and τ can be sampled.

The FB5 distribution of angles was considered as a "label" and the probability of having each distribution for each position in a query protein sequence was estimated using the CRF. Two features were considered in the potential function of the CRF, namely, PSI-BLAST sequence profile and predicted secondary structure. In the conditional neural field, a hidden layer of nonlinear combinations was introduced (Figure 9.10). The hidden layers use a gate function $G_\theta(x) = 1/[1 + \exp(-\theta^T x)]$, with θ the parameter vector and x the feature vector.

The probability of a label assignment S (of FB5 distributions) given a sequence profile M and its secondary structure X was calculated as

$$\Pr_\Lambda(S|M, X) = \frac{\exp\left[\sum_{i=1}^N F(S, M, X, i)\right]}{Z(M, X)} \tag{9.48}$$

where $\Lambda = \{\lambda_1, \lambda_2, \ldots, \lambda_p\}$ are model parameters and the function Z is a normalization factor. The function F consists of first- and second-order feature functions (e_1, e_2) that describe the neighbor dependencies as well as a label feature function v that represents a linear combination of K gate functions with parameters w and f. The concrete form F for the features at position i is given by

$$F(S, M, X, i) = e_1(s_{i-1}, s_i) + e_2(s_{i-1}, s_i, s_{i+1}) + \sum_{j=i-w}^{i+w} v(s_{i-1}, s_i, M_j, X_j) \tag{9.49}$$

where

$$v(s_{i-1}, s_i, X, M) = \sum_{g=1}^K w_{s_{i-1}, s_i, g} G_{\theta_g}(f(X, M, i)) \tag{9.50}$$

This represents a linear combination of a series of gate functions G.

The benchmark study was performed on a set of about 3000 nonredundant proteins. Although they did not compare their results against other existing methods, they reported that there was an improvement with respect to their previous CRF-only method [88], showing that the introduction of the neural field layer contributed to better predictions. Additionally, the authors participated in the Critical Assessment of techniques for protein Structure Prediction in 2010 (CASP8) [89] to test their performance at the blind prediction competition. Their team was ranked notably high among the participants in CASP8. There was an average improvement of 10% in terms of TM-score/GDT-TS as compared with the CRF-only method.

9.4 SUMMARY

In this chapter, we introduced graphical models focusing on the Markov random field and the conditional random field. The latter half of this chapter was used to describe the recent applications of the graphical models in three important problems in bioinformatics, gene finding, protein function prediction, and protein structure prediction. We expect to see an increasing number of applications in coming years, especially in the protein structure prediction, since this area is not yet much explored by the graphical models, and moreover, the current applications have already produced promising results. As more complex biological data become available that are suitable to represent using networks, these graphical models has become more important and useful in the bioinformatics field.

ACKNOWLEDGMENTS

This work was supported in part by the National Institute of General Medical Sciences of the National Institutes of Health (R01GM075004) and the National Science Foundation (DMS0800568, EF0850009, IIS0915801).

REFERENCES

1. S. B. Needleman and C. D. Wunsch. A general method applicable to the search for similarities in the amino acid sequence of two proteins. *J. Mol. Biol.*, 48:443–453, 1970.

2. T. F. Smith and M. S. Waterman. Identification of common molecular subsequences. *J. Mol. Biol.*, 147:195–197, 1981.

3. S. F. Altschul, W. Gish, W. Miller, E. W. Myers, and D. J. Lipman. Basic local alignment search tool. *J. Mol. Biol.*, 215:403–410, 1990.

4. S. F. Altschul, T. L. Madden, A. A. Schaffer, J. Zhang, Z. Zhang, W. Miller, and D. J. Lipman. Gapped BLAST and PSI-BLAST: A new generation of protein database search programs. *Nucleic Acids Res.*, 25:3389–3402, 1997.

5. W. R. Pearson and D. J. Lipman. Improved tools for biological sequence comparison. *Proc. Natl. Acad. Sci. USA*, 85:2444–2448, 1988.

6. R. Nussinov and A. B. Jacobson. Fast algorithm for predicting the secondary structure of single-stranded RNA. *Proc. Natl. Acad. Sci USA*, 77:6309–6313, 1980.

7. C. A. Orengo and W. R. Taylor. SSAP: Sequential structure alignment program for protein structure comparison. *Methods Enzymol.*, 266:617–635, 1996.

8. I. N. Shindyalov and P. E. Bourne. Protein structure alignment by incremental combinatorial extension (CE) of the optimal path. *Protein Eng.*, 11:739–747, 1998.

9. H. Chen and D. Kihara. Effect of using suboptimal alignments in template-based protein structure prediction. *Proteins*, 79:315–334, 2011.

10. J. Skolnick and D. Kihara. Defrosting the frozen approximation: PROSPECTOR—A new approach to threading. *Proteins*, 42:319–331, 2001.

11. Y. Matsuo and K. Nishikawa. Protein structural similarities predicted by a sequence-structure compatibility method. *Protein Sci.*, 3:2055–2063, 1994.

12. R. Durbin, S. R. Eddy, A. Krogh, and G. Mitchison. *Biological Sequence Analysis: Probabilistic Models of Proteins and Nucleic Acids*. Cambridge University Press, Cambridge, 1998.

13. K. Asai, S. Hayamizu, and K. Handa. Prediction of protein secondary structure by the hidden Markov model. *Comput. Appl. Biosci.*, 9:141–146, 1993.

14. P. Lio, N. Goldman, J. L. Thorne, and D. T. Jones III. PASSML: Combining evolutionary inference and protein secondary structure prediction. *Bioinformatics*, 14:726–733, 1998.

15. A. Krogh, B. Larsson, G. von Heijne, and E. L. Sonnhammer. Predicting transmembrane protein topology with a hidden Markov model: Application to complete genomes. *J. Mol. Biol.* 305: 567–80, 2001.

16. E. L. Sonnhammer, H. G. von, and A. Krogh. A hidden Markov model for predicting transmembrane helices in protein sequences. *Proc. Int. Conf. Intell. Syst. Mol. Biol.*, 6:175–182, 1998.

17. R. Karchin, M. Cline, Y. Mandel-Gutfreund, and K. Karplus. Hidden Markov models that use predicted local structure for fold recognition: Alphabets of backbone geometry. *Proteins*, 51: 504–14, 2003.

18. A. Hildebrand, M. Remmert, A. Biegert, and J. Soding. Fast and accurate automatic structure prediction with HHpred. *Proteins*, 77 (Suppl. 9):128–132, 2009.

19. C. M. Bishop. *Neural Networks for Pattern Recognition*. Oxford University Press, Oxford, UK, 1995.

20. D. T. Jones. Protein secondary structure prediction based on position-specific scoring matrices. *J. Mol. Biol.*, 292:195–202, 1999.

21. B. Rost, P. Fariselli, and R. Casadio. Topology prediction for helical transmembrane proteins at 86% accuracy. *Protein Sci.*, 5:1704–1718, 1996.

22. P. Fariselli, F. Pazos, A. Valencia, and R. Casadio. Prediction of protein–protein interaction sites in heterocomplexes with neural networks. *Eur. J Biochem.*, 269:1356–1361, 2002.

23. A. J. Bordner and A. A. Gorin. Protein docking using surface matching and supervised machine learning. *Proteins*, 68:488–502, 2007.

24. J. Guo, H. Chen, Z. Sun, and Y. Lin. A novel method for protein secondary structure prediction using dual-layer SVM and profiles. *Proteins* 54:738–743, 2004.

25. S. Hirose, K. Shimizu, S. Kanai, Y. Kuroda, and T. Noguchi. POODLE-L: A two-level SVM prediction system for reliably predicting long disordered regions. *Bioinformatics*, 23:2046–2053, 2007.

26. P. Larranaga, B. Calvo, R. Santana, C. Bielza, J. Galdiano, I. Inza, J. A. Lozano, R. Armananzas, G. Santafe, A. Perez, and V. Robles. Machine learning in bioinformatics. *Brief. Bioinformatics*, 7:86–112, 2006.

27. A. L. Tarca, V. J. Carey, X. W. Chen, R. Romero, and S. Draghici. Machine learning and its applications to biology. *PLoS Comput. Biol.*, 3:e116, 2007.

28. Y. Saeys, I. Inza, and P. Larranaga. A review of feature selection techniques in bioinformatics. *Bioinformatics*, 23:2507–2517, 2007.

29. C. J. Needham, J. R. Bradford, A. J. Bulpitt, and D. R. Westhead. A primer on learning in Bayesian networks for computational biology. *PLoS Comput. Biol.*, 3:e129, 2007.

30. D. Che, Q. Liu, K. Rasheed, and X. Tao. Decision tree and ensemble learning algorithms with their applications in bioinformatics. *Adv. Exp. Med. Biol.*, 696:191–199, 2011.

31. N. Friedman, D. Geiger, and M. Goldszmidt. Bayesian network classifiers. *Machine Learning*, 29:131–163, 1997.

32. J. Pearl. *Probabilistic Reasoning in Intelligent Systems: Networks of Plausible Inference*. Morgan Kaufmann, San Francisco, CA, 1988.

33. M. I. Jordan. *Learning in Graphical Models*. MIT Press, Cambridge, MA, 1998.

34. C. M. Bishop. *Pattern Recognition and Machine Learning*. Springer, Secaucus, NJ, 2006.

35. A. L. Ng and M. I. Jordan. On discriminative vs. generative classifiers: A comparison of logistic regression and Naive Bayes. *Adv. Neural Inform. Process. Syst. (NIPS)*, 14, 2002.

36. C. Sutton and A. McCallum. An Introduction to conditional random fields. *Found. Trends Mach. Learn.*, 4:267–373, 2011.

37. L. R. Rabiner. A tutorial on hidden Markov models and selected applications in speech recognition. *Proc. IEEE*, 77:257–286, 1989.

38. A. McCallum, D. Freitag, and F. Pereira. Maximum entropy Markov models for information extraction and segmentation. *International Conference on Machine Learning*, San Francisco, CA, 2000, pp. 591–598.

39. J. Lafferty, A. McCallum, and F. Pereira. Conditional random fields: Probabilistic models for segmenting and labeling sequence data. *Proceedings of the 18th International Conference on Machine Learning*, San Francisco, CA, 2001, pp. 282–289.

40. F. Sha and F. Pereira. Shallow parsing with conditional random fields. *Proceedings of the 2003 Conference of the North American Chapter of the Association for Computational Linguistics on Human Language*, Edmonton, Canada, 2003, pp. 213–220.

41. S. Kumar and M. Hebert. Discriminative random fields: A discriminative framework for contextual interaction in classification. Paper presented at the IEEE International Conference on Computer Vision, Nice, France, 2003, pp. 1150–1157.

42. B. Wellner, A. McCallum, F. Peng, and M. Hay. An integrated, conditional model of information extraction and coreference with application to citation matching. Paper presented at the Conference on Uncertainty in Artificial Intelligence (UAI), Arlington, Virginia, 2004, pp. 593–601.

43. S. V. N. Vishwanathan, N. N. Schraudolph, M.W. Schmidt, and P. Kevin. Accelerated training of conditional random fields with stochastic gradient methods. Paper presented at the International Conference on Machine Learning, New York, NY, 2006, pp. 969–976.

44. G. Hoefel and C. Elkan. Learning a two-stage SVM/CRF sequence classifier. In *Proceedings of the 17th ACM Conference on Information and Knowledge Management (CIKM'08)*, Napa Valley, California, October 26–30, 2008.

45. K. P. Murphy, Y. Weiss, and M. I. Jordan. Loopy belief propagation for approximate inference: An empirical study. In *Proceedings of Uncertainty in Artificial Inteligence*, San Francisco, CA, 1999, pp. 467–475.

46. E. P. Xing, M. I. Jordan, and S. Russell. A generalized mean field algorithm for variational inference in exponential families. Paper presented at the Conference on Uncertainty in Artificial Intelligence (UAI), San Francisco, CA, 2003, pp. 583–591.

47. C. Sutton and T. Minka. Local training and belief propagation. MSR-TR-2006-121, 1-10. Microsoft, Seattle, WA, 2006.

48. P. J. Green. Reversible jump Markov chain Monte Carlo computation and Bayesian model determination. *Biometrika*, 82:711–732, 1995.

49. M. Welling and G. E. Hington. A new learning algorithm for mean field Boltzmann machines. In *Proceedings of the International Conference on Artificial Neural Networks*, Lausanne, Switzerland, 2002, pp. 351–357.

50. J. Yedidia, W. T. Freeman, and Y. Weiss. Advances in neural information processing systems. *Adv. Neural Inform. Process. Syst.*, 13:689–695, 2000.

51. C. Sutton and A. McCallum. Collective segmentation and labeling of distant entities in information extraction. UMass-TR-04-49, 1-8. University of Massachusetts, Amherst, 2004.

52. Y. Liu, J. Carbonell, P. Weigele, and V. Gopalakrishnan. Protein fold recognition using segmentation conditional random fields (SCRFs). *J. Comput. Biol.*, Barbados, 13:394–406, 2006.

53. Y. Qi, M. Szummer, and T. Minka. Bayesian conditional random fields. Paper presented at the Conference on Artificial Intelligence and Statistics, Barbados, 2005.

54. A. Torralba, W. T. MurFreeman, and K. P. Murphy. Using the forest to see the trees: A graphical model relating features, objects and scenes. *Commun. ACM*, 53:107–114, 2010.

55. X. He, R. S. Zemel, and M. A. Carreira-Perpinan. Multiscale conditional random fields for image labeling. Paper presented at IEEE International Conference on Computer Vision and Pattern Recognition, Washington DC, 2004, pp. 695–702.

56. P. Liang, M. I. Jordan, and D. Klein. Learning from measurements in exponential families. Paper presented at the International Conference on Machine Learning, Montreal, Canada, 2009, pp. 641–648.

57. Y. Grandvalet and Y. Bengio. Semi-supervised learning by entropy minimization. *Adv. Neural Inform. Process. Syst.*, 17:529–536, 2005.

58. S. Z. Li. *Markov Random Field Modeling in Image Analysis*. Springer, London, UK, 2009.

59. M. Petrou and P. G. Sevilla. *Image Processing: Dealing with Texture*. Wiley, Hoboken, NJ, 2006.

60. A. Culotta, D. Kulp, and A. McCallum. Gene prediction with conditional random fields. UM-CS-2005-028. University of Massachusetts, Amherst, 2005.

61. C. Mathé, M.-F. Sagot, T. Schiex, and P. Rouzé. SURVEY AND SUMMARY: Current methods of gene prediction, their strengths and weaknesses. *Nucleic Acids Res.* 2002, 30:4103–4117.

62. D. DeCaprio, J. P. Vinson, M. D. Pearson, P. Montgomery, M. Doherty, and J. E. Galagan. Conrad: Gene prediction using conditional random fields. *Genome Res.*, 17:1389–1398, 2007.

63. A. Bernal, K. Crammer, A. Hatzigeorgiou, and F. Pereira. Global discriminative learning for higher-accuracy computational gene prediction. *PLoS Comput. Biol.*, 3:e54, 2007.

64. M. K. Doherty. Gene prediction with conditional random fields. UM-CS-2005-028. University of Massachusetts, Amherst, 2007.

65. S. S. Gross, C. B. Do, M. Sirota, and S. Batzoglou. CONTRAST: A discriminative, phylogeny-free approach to multiple informant de novo gene prediction. *Genome Biol.*, 8:R269, 2007.

66. C. Wei and M. R. Brent. Using ESTs to improve the accuracy of de novo gene prediction. *BMC Bioinformatics*, 7:327, 2006.

67. J. P. Vinson, D. DeCaprio, M. D. Pearson, S. Luoma, and J. E. Galagan. Comparative gene prediction using conditional random fields. *Adv. Neural Inform. Process. Syst.*, 19:1441–1448, 2007.

68. R. H. Brown, S. S. Gross, and M. R. Brent. Begin at the beginning: predicting genes with 5′ UTRs. *Genome Res.*, 15:742–747, 2005.

69. M. Riedmiller and H. Braun. A direct adaptive method for faster backpropagation learning: The RPROP algorithm. *IEEE Int. Conf. Neural Networks*, 1:586–591, 1993.

70. R. Sharan, I. Ulitsky, and R. Shamir. Network-based prediction of protein function. *Mol. Syst. Biol.*, 3:88, 2007.

71. T. Hawkins, M. Chitale, S. Luban, and D. Kihara. PFP: Automated prediction of gene ontology functional annotations with confidence scores using protein sequence data. *Proteins*, 74:566–582, 2009.

72. X. M. Zhao, L. Chen, and K. Aihara. Protein function prediction with high-throughput data. *Amino Acids*, 35:517–530, 2008.

73. A. Vazquez, A. Flammini, A. Maritan, and A. Vespignani. Global protein function prediction from protein-protein interaction networks. *Nat. Biotechnol.*, 21:697–700, 2003.

74. D. Kihara. *Protein Function Prediction for Omics Era*. Springer, London, 2011.

75. M. Chitale, T. Hawkins, and D. Kihara. Automated prediction of protein function from sequence. In J. Bujnicki (Ed.), *Prediction of Protein Strucutre, Functions, and Interactions*. Wiley, Hoboken, NJ, 2009.

76. M. Chitale, T. Hawkins, C. Park, and D. Kihara. ESG: Extended similarity group method for automated protein function prediction. *Bioinformatics*, 25:1739–1745, 2009.

77. M. Deng, T. Chen, and F. Sun. An integrated probabilistic model for functional prediction of proteins. *J. Comput. Biol.*, 11:463–475, 2004.

78. M. Deng, K. Zhang, S. Mehta, T. Chen, and F. Sun. Prediction of protein function using protein-protein interaction data. *J. Comput. Biol.*, 10:947–960, 2003.

79. H. W. Mewes, D. Frishman, U. Guldener, G. Mannhaupt, K. Mayer, M. Mokrejs, B. Morgenstern, M. Munsterkotter, S. Rudd, and B. Weil. MIPS: A database for genomes and protein sequences. *Nucleic Acids Res.*, 30:31–34, 2002.

80. M. A. Harris, et al. The Gene Ontology (GO) database and informatics resource. *Nucleic Acids Res.*, 32:D258–D261, 2004.

81. S. Letovsky and S. Kasif. Predicting protein function from protein/protein interaction data: A probabilistic approach. *Bioinformatics*, 19 (Suppl. 1):i197–i204, 2003.

82. C. Stark, B. J. Breitkreutz, A. Chatr-Aryamontri, L. Boucher, R. Oughtred, M. S. Livstone, J. Nixon, A. K. Van, X. Wang, X. Shi, T. Reguly, J. M. Rust, A. Winter, K. Dolinski, and M. Tyers. The BioGRID Interaction Database: 2011 update. *Nucleic Acids Res.*, 39:D698–D704, 2011.

83. Y. A. Kourmpetis, A. D. van Dijk, M. C. Bink, R. C. van Ham, and C. J. ter Braak. Bayesian Markov random field analysis for protein function prediction based on network data. *PLoS ONE*, 5:e9293, 2010.

84. M. Deng, Z. Tu, F. Sun, and T. Chen. Mapping Gene Ontology to proteins based on protein-protein interaction data. *Bioinformatics*, 20:895–902, 2004.

85. H. Kamisetty, E. P. Xing, and C. J. Langmead. Free energy estimates of all-atom protein structures using generalized belief propagation. *J. Comput. Biol.*, 15:755–766, 2008.

86. J. Peng and J. Xu. Boosting protein threading accuracy. *Lect. Notes Comput. Sci.*, 5541:31, 2009.

87. F. Zhao, J. Peng, and J. Xu. Fragment-free approach to protein folding using conditional neural fields. *Bioinformatics*, 26:i310–i317, 2010.

88. F. Zhao, S. Li, B. W. Sterner, and J. Xu. Discriminative learning for protein conformation sampling. *Proteins*, 73:228–240, 2008.

89. J. Moult, K. Fidelis, A. Kryshtafovych, B. Rost, and A. Tramontano. Critical assessment of methods of protein structure prediction—Round VIII. *Proteins*, 77 (Suppl. 9):1–4, 2009.

PART C

BIOLOGICAL FEATURE EXTRACTION

CHAPTER 10

ALGORITHMS AND DATA STRUCTURES FOR NEXT-GENERATION SEQUENCES*

FRANCESCO VEZZI,[1,2] GIUSEPPE LANCIA,[1] and ALBERTO POLICRITI[1,2]
[1]Department of Mathematics and Informatics, University of Udine, Udine, Italy
[2]Institute of Applied Genomics, Udine, Italy

The first genome was sequenced in 1975 [87] and from this first success sequencing technologies have significantly improved, with a strong acceleration in the last few years. Today these technologies allow us to read (huge amounts of) contiguous DNA stretches and are the key to reconstructing the genome sequence of a new species, of an individual within a population, or to studying the levels of expressions of single cell lines. Even though a number of different applications use sequencing data today, the "highest" sequencing goal is always the reconstruction of the complete genome sequence. The success in determining the first human genome sequence has encouraged many groups to tackle the problem of reconstructing the codebook of others species, including microbial, mammalian, and plant genomes.

Despite such efforts in sequencing new organisms, most species in the biosphere have not been sequenced yet. There are many reason for this, but the two main causes are the costs of a sequencing project and the difficulties in building a reliable assembly.

Until few years ago, Sanger sequencing was the only unquestioned available technology. This method has been used in order to produce many complete genomes of microbes, vertebrates (e.g., human [96]), and plants (e.g., grapevine [37]). Roughly speaking, in order to sequence an organisms, it is necessary to *extract* the DNA, *break* it into small fragments, and *read* their tips. As a final result one obtains a set of sequences, usually named *reads*, that may be assembled in order to reconstruct the original genome sequence or searched within a database of an already reconstructed genome. Reads are randomly sampled along the DNA sequence, so in order to be sure that each base in the genome is present in at least one read we have to oversample the genome. Given a set of reads, the sum of all the read lengths divided by the genome length is the *coverage*. If the ratio between the overall length of the reads and the genome length is C, then we say that the genome has been sequenced with *depth of coverage C* or C times ($C\times$).

---

*Sequencing technologies are rapidly changing: every month new instruments and tools appear making this field one of the most dynamic ones. Therefore, readers have to keep in mind that this chapter was written and revised during the third quarter of 2011.

Biological Knowledge Discovery Handbook: Preprocessing, Mining, and Postprocessing of Biological Data,
First Edition. Edited by Mourad Elloumi and Albert Y. Zomaya.

One of the first and most important (practical) algorithmic insights in genome assembly (see [96]) was the observation that using reads coming from the two ends of a single sequence, named the *paired reads* of an *insert** of known estimated length, the overall down-line process of assembly was greatly simplified.

Recently, new sequencing methods have emerged [59]. In particular, the commercially available technologies include pyrosequencing (454 [1]), sequencing by synthesis (Illumina [3]), and sequencing by ligation (SOLiD [2]). Compared to the traditional Sanger method, these technologies function with significantly lower production costs and much higher throughput. These advances have significantly reduced the cost of several applications having sequencing or *resequencing* as an intermediate step.

The computationally significant aspect of these new technologies is that the reads produced are much shorter than traditional Sanger reads. At the actual state, Illumina HiSeq 2000, the latest Illumina instrument available on the market, is able to produce reads of length 150 bp and generates more than 200 billion of output data per run, Solid 4 System produces paired reads of length 50 bp, while Roche 454 GS FLX Titanium has the lowest throughput but it is able to produce single reads of length 400 bp and paired reads of length 200 bp. Other technologies are now approaching (Polonator, Helicos BioSciences, Pacific BioSciences, and Oxford Nanopore Technologies[66]) promising higher throughput and lower costs.

At the beginning of the new-generation sequencing (NGS) era, as a consequence of the extremely short lengths of both reads and inserts, NGS data have been used mainly in (several) *resequencing* projects [9, 23, 42, 102]. A resequencing project is based on the availability of a reference sequence (usually a fairly complete genome sequence) against which short sequences can be aligned, using a *short-read aligner* [48, 52, 71, 81]. Resequencing projects allow the reconstruction of the genetic information in similar organisms and the identification of differences among individuals of the same species. The most important such differences are single-nucleotide polymorphisms (SNPs) [53, 90], copy number variation (CNV) [17, 18, 32], and insertion/deletion events (*indels*) [62]. Despite the short length of reads, but encouraged by technology improvements, many groups have started to use NGS data in order to reconstruct new genomes from scratch. De novo assembly is in general a difficult problem and is made even more difficult not only by short read lengths [69] but also from the problem of having reliable sequencing and distribution error models. Many tools have been proposed (see, e.g., Velvet [104], ALLPATHS [56], and ABySS [92], to mention just a few of the available ones) but the results achievable to date are far from those of the Sanger-era assemblers (PCAP [34]).

The unbridled spread of second-generation sequencing machines has been accompanied by a (natural) effort toward producing computational instruments capable of analyzing the large amounts of newly available data. The aim of this chapter is to present and (comparatively) discuss the data structures that have been proposed in the context of NGS data processing. In particular, we will concentrate our attention on two widely studied areas: data structures for *alignment* and de novo assembly.

The chapter is divided into two main sections. In the first we will classify algorithms and data structures specifically designed for the alignment of short nucleotide sequences produced by NGS instruments against a database. We will propose a division into categories

*The name "insert" is used since the sequence providing the reads is inserted in a bacterial's genome to be reproduced in a sufficient number of copies.

and describe some of the most successful tools proposed so far. In the second part we will deal with de novo assembly. De novo assembly is a computationally challenging problem with NP-complete versions easily obtainable from its real-world definition. In this part we will classify the different de novo strategies and describe available tools. Moreover we will focus our attention on the limits of the currently most used tools, discussing when such limits can be traced back to data structures employed and when, instead, they are a direct consequence of the kind of data processed.

10.1 ALIGNERS

One of the main applications of string matching is computational biology. A DNA sequence can be seen as a string over the alphabet $\Sigma = \{A, C, G, T\}$. Given a reference genome sequence, we are interested in searching (*aligning*) different sequences (*reads*) of various lengths. When aligning such reads against another DNA sequence, we must consider both errors due to the sequencer and intrinsic errors due to the variability between individuals of the same species. For these reasons, all the programs aligning reads against a reference sequence must deal (at least) with mismatches [5, 41].

As a general rule, tools used to align Sanger reads (see [5]) are not suitable—that is, are not efficient enough—to align next-generation sequencer output due, essentially, to the sheer amount of data to handle. (The advent of next-generation sequencers moved the bottleneck from data production to data analysis.) Therefore, in order to keep the pace with data production, new algorithms and data structures have been proposed in the last years.

String matching can be divided into two main areas: exact string matching and approximate string matching. When doing approximate string matching, we need to employ a distance metric between strings. The most commonly used metrics are the *edit distance* (or Levenshtein distance) [47] and the *Hamming distance* [29].

Approximate string matching at distance k under the edit metric is called the *k-difference problem*, while under the Hamming metric, it is called the *k-mismatch problem*. In many practical applications like short-sequence alignment, we are interested in finding the *best* occurrence of the pattern with at most k mismatches. We will refer to this as the *best-k-difference/mismatch problem*. Recently, a flurry of papers presenting new indexing algorithms to solve this problem have appeared [46, 50, 51] (see Table 10.1 for a partial list of available NGS aligners). While all the aligners allow to specify constraints on the Hamming distance, only some of them allow to use also the edit distance. All aligners designed for NGS use some form of index to speed up the search phase.

Aligners usually build an index over the text, but some solutions that index only the reads or both are available. According to [49], we can cluster existing alignment algorithms into two main classes: algorithms based on hash tables and algorithms based on suffix-based data structures. A third category is formed by algorithms based on merge sorting but, to the best of our knowledge, the only available solution that belongs to this category is [57].

Hash-based aligners build a dictionary of the reference and then use this dictionary to search the query sequences. On the other hand, the suffix-based methods rely on the construction of a suffix/prefix trie structure over the reference. Aligners normally follow a multistep procedure to accurately map sequences. During a first *filtering* phase, heuristics techniques are used to quickly identify a small set of positions in the reference sequence where a read's best alignment is most likely to occur. Once this small subset of locations is computed, more accurate and usually slower alignment procedures are used.

TABLE 10.1   Examples of Available NGS Aligners

Name	Algorithm	Indels	Author	Year
AGILE	Hash	Yes	Misra et al.	2010
BWA-SW	FM	Yes	Li and Durbin	2010
LASTZ	Hash	Yes	Unpublished	2010
BFAST	SA/Hash	Yes	Homer et al.	2009
BOAT	Hash reads	Yes	Zhao et al.	2009
CLC-bio	Unknown	Yes	Commercial	
GASST	Hash	Yes	Rizk and Lavenier	2010
SSAHA2	Hash	Yes	Ning et al.	2001
ZOOM	Hash reads	Yes	Lin et al.	2008
BOWTIE	FM index	No	Langmead et al.	2009
BRAT	Hash	No	Harris et al.	2010
BWA	FM index	Yes	Li and Durbin	2009
ELAND	Hash	No	Commercial	
Galign	Hash	Yes	Shaham	2009
GEM	FM index	Yes	Unpublished	
GenomeMapper	Hash	Yes	Schneeberger et al.	2009
GSNAP	Hash	Yes	Wu and Nacu	2010
KARMA		Yes	Unpublished	
MAQ	Hash reads	No	Li et al.	2008
MOM	Hash	No	Dohm et al.	2008
MrFAST	Hash	Yes	Alkan et al.	2009
MrsFAST	Hash	Yes	Hach et al.	2010
PASS	Hash	Yes	Campagna et al.	2009
PatMaN	Index reads	Yes	Prüfer et al.	2008
PerM	Hash	No	Chen et al.	2009
RazerS	Hash	Yes	Weese	2009
RMAP	Hash reads	No	Smith et al.	2008
segemehl	SA	Yes	Unpublished	
SeqMap	Hash	No	Hui and Wong	2008
SHRiMP2	Hash	Yes	Matei et al.	2011
SOAP	Hash	No	Li et al.	2008
SOAP2	FM index	Yes	Li et al.	2009
CloudBurst	Hash/MapReduce	Yes	Schatz	2009
CrossBow	FM index/MapReduce	No	Langmead et al.	2009
GNUMAP	Hash/MPI	Yes	Clement	2010
Myrialign	GPU based	—	Unpublished	
NovoAlign	Hash/MPI	Yes	Krawitz et al.	2010
pBWA	FM-index/MPI	Yes	Unpublished	

Note: For each we specify the used indexing method and whether they align with or without indels. The four groups represent aligners designed for long reads, short/long reads, short reads only, and distributed architectures.

Usually a small portion of the read is searched through the data structure (hash as well as prefix trie) in order to isolate regions candidate to be an alignment. Only on these regions is a more accurate alignment performed. This procedure is usually named *seed and extend*. The seed (which usually corresponds to the first part of the read) is searched in an almost exact way allowing only a few number of mismatches.

One of the first and most basic hash-based aligners is BLAST [5]. BLAST basically searches the reference for perfect matches of the query of length 11. Once these exact seeds are identified, the search is refined by a Smith–Waterman alignment [26, 94]. Hash-based aligners for NGS refined and improved this basic seed-and-extend schema. Basic seeding has been substituted by *spaced seed* (SOAP [52], MAQ [50], and ZOOM [54], to mention a few) and *q-gram* (SHRiMP [19, 86], and RazerS [100], among the others). Another aligner (rNA [81]) uses a mismatch-aware hash function that is able to identify seeds at a predefined Hamming distance, exploiting an improved version of the Karp and Rabin algorithm [40]. Moreover, several improvements over the standard seed-and-extend schema concern the extend phase: In [86] a *vectorized* version of the Smith–Waterman algorithm is used to gain speed from the SSE2 CPU instructions implemented in the latest x86 CPUs.

Suffix-based aligners implement one of the many available indexes, for example, suffix trees [7], suffix arrays [58], and FM indexes [22]. In the NGS context, FM indexes are the most widely used due to their principal characteristic: (theoretically optimal) compressibility. Several of the short-read alignment programs (BOWTIE, BWA, and SOAP2, among others) are based on the Barrows–Wheeler transformation [14]. These methods usually use the FM indexes [22] that allow the efficient construction of a suffix array [58] with the further advantage that it can be compressed. The FM index retains the suffix array's potential for rapid searches with the great advantage that the index often is smaller than the text. Suffix-based aligners use heuristic similar to the one implemented in the hash based aligners: The index is used to search for exact matches that will be used as anchors for further extensions.

All the aligners are able to fruitfully exploit multiple core architectures. However, it is worth mentioning that there is a particular class of aligners that can use many machines in parallel. These *distributed* aligners can run over clusters or clouds of computers using, among others, frameworks for distributed computation like MPI [27] and MapReduce [20].

10.1.1 Hash-Based Aligners

Hash-based aligners preprocess the reference text and/or the query reads in order to obtain a dictionary that allows to search a read r in (expected) time proportional to $O(|r|)$. Basic hash-based aligners simply search for exact occurrences of seeds inside the text. As shown in [16] and later in [55] seeding with nonconsecutive matches improves sensitivity. A *spaced seed* is a seed of length l where matches are required in only k fixed positions. A spaced seed is usually represented by a string of 0's and 1's typically called a *template*. For example, the template 111010010100110111, requiring 11 matches at the 1 positions, is 55% more sensitive than BLAST when aligning two sequences allowing 70% similarity, which by default uses a seed with 11 consecutive matches. Usually we refer to the total number of 1's as the *weight* of the seed.

Seeds are usually searched allowing a small number of mismatches. If the read r must be aligned with at most k mismatches against the reference sequence, then there is at least one (consecutive) substring of length $\lfloor |r|/(k+1) \rfloor$ that occurs without errors (this is a simple consequence of the pigeonhole principle). With this clue in mind one can build a hash table of all l-mers with $l = \lfloor |r|/(k+1) \rfloor$ and use a seed-and-extend strategy. RMAP [93] uses this simple strategy. The main drawback of this technique is that, for practical values of $|r|$ and k, the seed length is so small that too many false positives are produced in the first phase, causing a long and inefficient extension phase. As a consequence, the vast majority of seed and spaced-seed approaches allow a small number of mismatches even in the seed. Moreover, the seed size is usually decided during the preprocessing stage. Allowing k mismatches in a seed means that $\binom{2k}{k}$ different templates are required (all the layouts that allow at most k mismatches). This number is exponential in k and therefore the method can become quickly inefficient. In [54] different spaced seeds are used at several designated read positions in order to find all possible occurrences of a read without losing occurrences. In particular, the ZOOM aligner [54], given the read length m and the maximum allowed Hamming distance k, tries to design the minimum number of spaced seeds of weight w to achieve full sensitivity. Other aligners (like SOAP [52] and MAQ [50]) use as seed the fist l bases of the read (the most reliable part of Illumina data sequences) allowing a limited number (usually two) of mismatches. In order to align a 32-bp read, RMAP [93] uses three templates of weight 10, MAQ requires six templates of weight 26, while ZOOM requires five seeds of length 14.

Seed and spaced-seed techniques do not allow gaps (indels) within the seed. Seed-based algorithms usually postpone the indel search to the extension phase, aligning the remaining part of the read with a Smith–Waterman-like algorithm. SHRiMP [86], its successor [19], and RazerS [100] build a hash table that embeds the indels thanks to q-grams. The q-gram concept (string of length q) was introduced in [82]: This method generalizes the basic principle of the seed method applying again the pigeonhole principle. The key observation is that if a read r of length $|r|$ occurs in the reference text with at most k differences (both mismatches and gaps), then at least $(|r| + 1 - (k + 1)q)$ of the q-grams in r occur in a window of size at most $|r|$ in the text. The main difference between seed- and q-gram-based methods is the fact that the former searches one long template while the latter searches for multiple short seeds in a restricted region. Anyway, both strategies are based on fast look-up tables.

The idea to use multiple seeds, without employing q-grams, is used in SSAHA2 [71]: This technique is used to speed up alignments of relatively long reads (e.g., 454 reads) where it is reasonable to require that two or more seeds fall in a small window of the reference.

In [81] the hash-based aligner rNA (randomized numerical aligner) is presented. The peculiarity of this tool lies in the fact that seeds are searched with errors by using a special kind of hash function. A read r is divided into $b = |r|/l$ nonoverlapping blocks and all seeds are used in the seeding phase, allowing $(k + 1)/b$ errors for each seed. This is possible, as said, due to an error-aware hash function. The starting point is the algorithm proposed by Karp and Rabin in [40], able to solve the exact string matching problem with average complexity $O(|T| + |P|)$ with T and P the text and the pattern being searched, respectively. When a string of length m over the alphabet Σ is encoded as a base-$|\Sigma|$ number, for practical values of m the numbers to be manipulated are too large to fit into a memory word. The simple and effective countermeasure proposed by Rabin and Karp is to use a large prime p and to work with numbers modulo p: A simple example of what today are called *fingerprints*. Every text position with the same pattern fingerprint is a possible starting point of an exact match. Policriti et al. [81] extend this approach to alignment with mismatches by computing the fingerprints using a Mersenne prime number q and precomputing the set $\mathcal{Z}$ of fingerprints in the Hamming sphere centered on (fingerprint of) the pattern. The rNA stores the fingerprints of the text in a hash table and operates only on those positions of the reference that have a fingerprint at the Hamming distance less than the user-defined threshold (i.e., the radius of the Hamming sphere). The choice of q guarantees a small size $\mathcal{Z}$, which in turn speeds up the whole process.

10.1.2 Prefix-Based Aligners

Algorithms that fall in this category are based on clever representations of a common data structure: the suffix/prefix trie. These representations (suffix trees [95, 101], directed acyclic

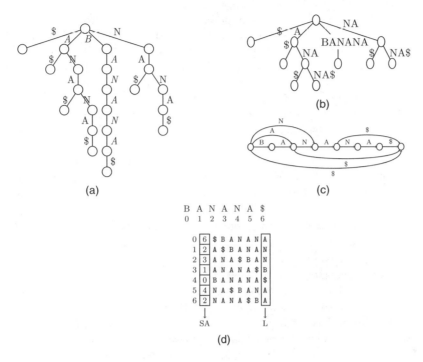

FIGURE 10.1 Suffix-based structure for string BANANA$. A suffix trie, a suffix tree, a DAWG generated through compression of the suffix trie (compressing in the same way the suffix tree would have generated a CDAWG), the suffix array, and the BWT transformation.

word graphs, or DAWGs [10], compressed DAWGs [11, 36], suffix arrays [39, 58], enhanced suffix arrays [4], and FM index [22]) have the advantage over hash-based algorithms that during the alignment phase identical copies of a substring in the reference need to be scanned only once. For example, in a suffix tree, identical substrings collapse on a single path, while in a suffix array they are stored in contiguous entries. Figure 10.1 represents the suffix trie, the suffix tree, the DAWG, the suffix array, and the BWT of the string "BANANA".

A *suffix trie*, or simply a *trie*, is a data structure that stores all the suffixes of a string. In particular, a trie for a text T could be constructed by simply inserting all its suffixes in an empty keyword tree [28]. A trie for a string T of length n over the alphabet Σ is a rooted tree with branching factor at most $|\Sigma|$ and with exactly n leaves numbered from 1 to n. In a suffix trie each internal node represents a unique substring of T; for this reason each edge is labeled with a nonempty character of T. Two edges leaving the same node cannot be labeled with the same character. For any leaf i, the concatenation of the edge labels on the path from the root to leaf i exactly spells the suffix of x starting at position i. A problem arises if a suffix j of T occurs also as a prefix of another suffix i. To avoid such a situation, the special character $\$ \notin \Sigma$ is usually added at the end of T. In order to boost the search, each node representing the string ay has a *suffix link* that leads to the node representing the substring y. This way, the time needed to determine if a query r has an exact occurrence using a trie is $O(|r|)$. The drawback of a trielike data structure is the fact that a string T needs space equal to $O(|T|^2)$, making this data structure useless for the vast majority of applications in bioinformatics.

A *suffix tree* is a more space efficient representation of a trie. In order to preserve space, unary paths (i.e., stretches of nodes with out degree 1) are compressed into a single node. Only the first character of the unary path needs to be stored. It can be shown that such a tree has only $O(|T|)$ internal nodes. First McGreight [61] and later Ukkonen [95] showed that this structure can be constructed in time $O(|T|)$. Later improvements [65] showed the possibility of representing a suffix tree in space proportional to $|T| \log_2 |T| + O(|T|)$ bits. However, despite this, most space-efficient implementations of bioinformatics, tools require 12–17 bytes per nucleotide, making the suffix tree impractical for indexing large genomes (e.g., the human one).

DAWGs and their compressed version (CDAWG) are deterministic automata able to recognize all the substrings of a string T. Similar to what happens in suffix trees, a node in a DAWG represents a substring of the text, but in this case each node is augmented with *failure* links (i.e., information to deal with the paths that are not present in the text). Leaves do not need to be distinguishable; therefore less space is necessary retaining, however, all the suffix tree's abilities. Despite this reduction, the known implementations are, again, not capable of scaling to large genomes.

The common disadvantages of previous solutions are the amount of memory required to actually represent the trie like data structures and the lack of memory locality of graphs in general. Suffix arrays have been proposed with the ambition to solve both problems. A suffix array for a string T is basically a sorted list of all the suffixes of T. As for suffix trees, in this case it is also useful to append a \$ to T. A suffix array can be built in time $O(|T|)$ and can be used to search a pattern r in time $O(|r| \log |T|)$ using a simple dichotomic search. In its basic representation this data structure requires 4 bytes per character (i.e., 4 bytes to represent a 32-bit pointer to the text). This advantage in space is limited by the presence of a $\log |T|$ factor in the search time. The suffix array, however, can be coupled with the two other arrays containing the information about the *longest common prefix (lcp)* that is an implicit representation of the suffix links. In this way a query time of $O(|r| + \log |T|)$ can be achieved without compromising the space efficiency. In [4] a clever representation of the suffix array and the lcp information is presented that allows a query time of $O(|r|)$ and uses 6.25 bytes per nucleotide.

Ferragina and Manzini [22] obtained a major improvement on memory with their FM index, a data structure based on the Burrows–Wheeler transform (BWT) [14]. The BWT inputs a text T and returns a reversible permutation of the text characters which gives a new string that is "easy to compress." In order to build the transformation for a text T, a \$ is appended at the end of T (for the same reason already seen with suffix trees and suffix arrays); then a "conceptual" matrix $\mathcal{M}$ is created whose rows are the lexicographically ordered cyclic shifts of $T\$$. The *transformed* string L returned is the last column of $\mathcal{M}$. Ferragina and Manzini [22] showed that there is a strong connection between the suffix array of T and the string L. In particular, given the suffix array S of T, $L[i] = \$$ if $S[i] = 0$; otherwise $L[i] = T[S[i] - 1]$. Hon [31] showed how it is possible to build the BWT of the human genome using no more than 1 GB of RAM.

Ferragina and Manzini showed how the BWT of T coupled with some other array can be used to efficiently search for a pattern P in T using the *backward-search* algorithm [22] in time $O(|P|)$. The backward-search algorithm is based on the observation that a pattern P that occurs in T induces an interval in the suffix array S.

In order to quickly compute this interval, two functions need to be precomputed: $C(a)$, returning the number of symbols in T that are lexicographically smaller than $a \in \Sigma$, and $O(a, i)$, returning the number of occurrences of a in $L[0, i]$.

$\underline{R}(P)$ and $\overline{R}(P)$ return the minimum and maximum indexes, respectively, of the suffix array S storing indexes corresponding to suffixes whose prefix is P. More formally:

- $\underline{R}(P) = \min\{k : P \text{ is a prefix of } T[S[k]..|T| - 1]\}$
- $\overline{R}(P) = \max\{k : P \text{ is a prefix of } T[S[k]..|T| - 1]\}$

Given a pattern P, the interval $[\underline{R}(P), \overline{R}(P)]$ is the suffix array interval and it stores all the occurrences of P into T. This information tells us all the positions at which the pattern occurs within the text T.

In [22] it is proven that if P occurs in T as a substring, then, for each character a,

- $\underline{R}(aP) = C(a) + O(a, O(\underline{R}(P) - 1) - 1) + 1$
- $\overline{R}(aP) = C(a) + O(a, O(\overline{R}(P)))$

and $\underline{R}(aP) \leq \overline{R}(aP)$ if and only if aP is a substring of T. This way, by iteratively computing $\underline{R}$ and $\overline{R}$ from the last character of P to the first, it is possible to find all the occurrences of P in T in time $O(|P|)$.

Ferragina and Manzini showed how it is possible to compress L without significantly increasing the search time. Without compression an FM index requires 2 bytes per character, but more sophisticated implementation require only 0.5 byte per character, allowing to store the entire human genome in 2 GB.

All the described data structures are well suited for exact string matching but do not scale well when (many) mismatches are allowed—for a compendium on data structures for inexact string matching refer to [70]. Therefore, in real-life applications, a seed-and-extend technique is often used. Usually the first l bases of the read are searched throughout the prefixlike index in order to identify the positions that have to be extended.

10.1.3 Distributed Architectures

All "practically oriented" aligners allow parallel execution in order to align the huge amount of data produced by NGS. This feature, coupled with the sophisticated algorithms presented above, makes it possible to align reads at a very high rate. Nevertheless, the increasing data production is moving several groups toward the implementation of distributed aligners (a road already successfully followed by de novo assemblers [92]). Despite being a topic worth mentioning, this solution does not propose new algorithms and data structures but simply aims at increasing the alignment throughput. Therefore we have decided to give just a brief description of some of the available solutions.

Two commonly used frameworks for distributed computation are MPI [27] and MapReduce [20]. The former is an API (*application programming interface*) specification that allows processes to communicate. The different processes can be on the same machines or on different machines (usually called *nodes*) connected through a communication channel (e.g., Ethernet and Infiniband). MapReduce is a framework that allows and simplifies distribution of independent, and hence parallelizable, operations. It mainly operates in two steps: During the Map step a master node partitions the input into smaller subsets and distributes those to worker nodes that, after processing data, return the results to the master node. In the Reduce step the master collects the results and combines them (for a review see [89]).

pBWA [74] is a parallel implementation of the popular software BWA [48]. It was developed by modifying BWA source code with the OpenMPI C library. mrNA (unpublished) is the MPI version of rNA aligner [81]. mrNA is different from the vast majority of distributed aligners for the fact that not only is the alignment phase distributed but also the indexing happens on different nodes.

Crossbow [45] is a Hadopp-based [6] (Hadoop is the open-source MapReduce's implementation) aligner and SNP-caller. Crossbow [45] uses Bowtie [46] to align reads and SOAPsnp [51] to find SNPs. Myrna [44] is designed for transcriptome differential expression analysis. Like Crossbow it uses the Hadoop interface. CloudBurst [88] is a parallel read-mapping algorithm and is able to obtain the same results of RMAP [93] but, due to the Hadoop framework, it is able to align large data sets within a reasonable amount of time.

10.2 ASSEMBLERS

The large volume of ongoing research in the field of sequence assembly makes it difficult to keep the pace with all the different available assembly techniques and their implementations. A common feature to existing assemblers is that they represent the reads by using (implicitly or explicitly) some type of graph data structure. In [64] de novo assemblers are divided into three main categories based on the core algorithm used: greedy graph approach (Greedy), overlap/layout/consensus (OLC) and de Bruijn graph (DBG). Table 10.2 contains a list of available assemblers and a short description for each of them.

The Greedy assemblers, usually called *seed-and-extend* assemblers, apply one basic operation: Given any read or contig, extends it by adding more reads or contigs [64]. This basic operation is repeated until no further extension is possible. At each extension step the highest scoring overlap is used to proceed. Despite all the heuristics and refined implementations of such a technique, greedy assemblers fail in reconstructing even short repeats and are not able to manage the large amount of reads to be dealt with while assembling a plant or a mammalian genome.

The OLC approach has demonstrated its capabilities in the Sanger Sequecing Projects. Assemblers like ARACHNE [8] and PCAP [34] implement this strategy. OLC assemblers represent the reads in an overlap graph (also named a *string graph* [67]) in which reads are nodes while an overlap between two strings of length k is represented by an edge of weight k. As suggested by their name, OLC assemblers go through three distinct phases: During the overlap phase an all-against-all comparison between reads is performed in order to build the overlap graph. In fact, a full all-against-all comparison is always avoided and fast and efficient approximated algorithms have been proposed to speed up this phase. The overlap graph is then used to generate a layout from which, during the consesus phase, a multiple-sequence alignment (MSA) is performed and the output is generated. Even though tools based on this approach have demonstrated their capabilities with Sanger sequencing data, they are not easy to extend to cope with short reads for two main reasons: First, the use of short reads forces the minimum overlap between reads to be so small that the number of overlaps occurring by chance becomes too high. Second, as a consequence of the extremely high amount of reads, the overlap phase becomes an overwhelming computational bottleneck.

DBG assemblers are the most successful type of assemblers for short-read sequences. A DBG is a graph in which the nodes are k-mers and there is an edge connecting two nodes a and b if and only if the $k - 1$ suffix of the k-mer a is identical to the $k - 1$ prefix of the k-mer b. Given a set of reads, the DBG is constructed by dividing all the reads in all possible

TABLE 10.2 Available Assemblers

Name	Algorithm	Author	Year
Arachne WGA	OLC	Batzoglou et al.	2002/2003
Celera WGA Assembler	OLC	Myers et al.	2004/2008
Minimus (AMOS)	OLC	Sommer et al.	2007
Newbler	OLC	454/Roche	2009
EDENA	OLC	Hernandez et al.	2008
FM-assebler	OLC	Durbin et al.	2010
MIRA, miraEST	OLC	Chevreux	1998/2008
PE-Assembler	OLC	Pramila et al.	2010
SUTTA	B&B	Narzisi et al.	2009/2010
TIGR	Greedy	TIGR	1995/2003
Phusion	Greedy	Mullikin et al.	2003
Phrap	Greedy	Green	2002/2008
CAP3, PCAP	Greedy	Huang et al.	1999/2005
Euler	DBG	Pevzner et al.	2001/2006
Euler-SR	DBG	Chaisson et al.	2008
Velvet	DBG	Zerbino et al.	2007/2009
ALLPATHS	DBG	Butler et al.	2008
Ray	DBG		2010
ABySS	DBG	Simpson et al.	2008/2009
SOAPdenovo	DBG	Ruiqiang et al.	2009
SHARCGS	Prefix tree	Dohm et al.	2007
SSAKE	Prefix tree	Warren et al.	2007
VCAKE	Prefix tree	Jeck et al.	2007
QSRA	Prefix tree	Douglas et al.	2009
Sequencher	—	Gene Codes Corporation	2007
SeqMan NGen	—	DNASTAR	2008
Staden gap4 package	—	Staden et al.	1991/2008
NextGENe	—	Softgenetics	2008
CLC Genomics Workbench	—	CLC bio	2008/2009
CodonCode Aligner	—	CodonCode Corporation	2003/2009

Note: The first four categories are divided on the base of the algorithm used (OLC, Greedy, DBG, and Prefix Tree). The last category is a noncomplete list of proprietary solutions.

k-mers, associating k-mers to nodes, and then connecting nodes. This construction has the double advantage that no overlap has to be computed and the amount of memory needed is proportional to the number of distinct k-mers and not to the number of distinct reads (the number of distinct k-mers belonging to the reads directly depends on the number of distinct k-mers of the genome being sequenced). In order to extract contigs from this graph one has to find an Eulerian tour or, at least, solve a Chinese postman problem. For a complete review about DBGs and the implementations of different tools, refer to [64].

As noticed in [73], the assembly programs are all based on a small number of algorithms, and they differ from each other in the details of how they deal with errors, inconsistencies, and ambiguities. Most of the published papers describing individual tools include a comparison with other already published assemblers, usually showing an improvement of their results. These observations, together with the large number of available solutions and available tools, demonstrate on the one hand how much this area is brisk and on the other hand that there is not a widely accepted tool/solution.

Significant efforts have been done in order to formalize and study the theoretical de novo assembly problem. In [69] Pop and Nagarajan showed that different assembly formulations are NP complete but under certain assumptions the problem becomes easy to solve. The main message resulting from the analysis is that the reduction of the de novo assembly problem to the shortest common super string problem (SCSP) is definitely not realistic and, probably, not even useful.

10.2.1 Greedy Assemblers: Seed and Extend

Greedy assemblers repeatedly pick up a *seed* (can be either a read or a previously assembled contig) and *extend* it using other reads. This is done through the computation of all, or almost all, the overlaps between the seed's tips and all the available reads. The reads used for the extension are the ones with the highest alignment score. It is clear that the seed-and-extend assemblers' key feature is the capability to quickly compute all the alignment scores. Usually this goal is achieved using hashing schemata or quick look-up tables in order to obtain at least all the perfect matches. Most of the solutions described in the following sections are variants of the general schemata. Often solutions differ from one another only for the heuristic implemented. The main drawback of seed-and-extend assemblers is their incapability to distinguish and correctly assemble repetitive regions. Each seed is independent from the others and therefore no global information is available. Despite this problem, several seed-and-extend assemblers have been proposed. A common heuristic is to use such solutions to obtain long reads (i.e., Sanger-like sequences) and use those sequences as input to a Sanger-based assembler.

10.2.1.1 SSAKE SSAKE [99] was the first short-read assembler proposed. It is designed for Illumina reads but, more recently, it has been adapted to use also for long Sanger reads. SSAKE populates a hash table that has as keys the sequences present in the multi-FASTA given as input and as values the multiplicity of each sequence. At the same time a tree is used to memorize the first 11 bases of each read. Once all sequences are read and stored, the reads are sorted by decreasing the number of occurrences. This information is used to understand the read coverage and to identify reads containing low copy sequences that are candidate to contain errors. Each unassembled read r_i is used in turn to start an assembly. SSAKE uses the prefix tree to progressively compute perfect alignments of length k.

The extension phase halts when there are no more reads to extend or when a k-mer matches the 5' end of more than one sequence read. This is done in order to minimize sequence misassemblies. A more flexible halting strategy consists in stopping the extension when the retrieved k-mer is smaller than a user-set minimum word length. Recently [98] SSAKE has been extended to use paired read information, Sanger reads, and imperfectly matching reads.

10.2.1.2 SHARCGS SHARCGS [21] is a DNA assembly program designed for de novo assembly of 25- to 40-mer input fragments and deep sequence coverage. The assembly strategy is similar to the one described for SSAKE with two more features: a pre- and a postprocessing phase.

In the preprocessing phase, SHARCGS discards reads that are likely to contain errors. These reads are identified by requiring a minimum number of exact matches in other reads and requiring a minimum quality value if available. SHARCGS performs three times this filtering phase, each time requiring a different stringency setting in order to generate three different filtered sets. Then in a SSAKE-like way it assembles every set independently. The postprocessing phase consists in merging the contigs obtained by running the algorithm with weak, medium and, strong filter parameters settings.

10.2.1.3 VCAKE   The aim of VCAKE [38] is to assemble millions of small nucleotide reads even in the presence of sequencing errors. The main improvement proposed by VCAKE is the ability to deal with imperfect matches during contig extension. In particular, VCAKE uses the same prefix tree implemented by SSAKE, but it allows one mismatch during the extension phase.

VCAKE has been further used in two hybrid pipelines: In [84] VCAKE and Newbler are used together in order to assemble a mixture of Illumina and 454 reads, while in [25] a VCAKE is combined with Newbler and Celera Assembler.

10.2.1.4 QSRA   QSRA [13] is built directly upon the SSAKE algorithm. QSRA creates a hash table and a prefix trie. Each hash entry stores a pair composed by the actual DNA sequence and the number of occurrences of the read. The prefix trie contains the unassembled reads as well as their reverse complements, all indexed by the first 11 bases. In a SSAKE/VCAKE similar fashion, QSRA starts the extension phase, finding all the reads which exactly match the end of the seed (the "growing" contig) for at least u bases (where u is a user-defined parameter) using the prefix trie. If the number of matches is less than a user-defined threshold but the quality values are available, QSRA will extend the growing contig as long as a minimum user-defined q-value score m is met.

10.2.1.5 SHORTY   SHORTY [33] is a de novo assembler targeted to the assembling sequences produced by Solid sequencers. It takes in input deep coverage of solid reads ($100\times$) and a small set of seed sequences. These seeds can be obtained from a set of Sanger sequences or even by assembling the short reads with another short-read assembler like abyss or velvet.

All the reads are stored in a compact trie that allows quick access and fast searches. After that all the seeds are processed once per time. For each seed we extract from the set of reads those which belong to the seed together with the paired reads that are outside the seed sequence. From the seed sequence and from the overlap information coming from the reads it is possible to generate contigs. SHORTY reiterates this step as long as it is possible to extend the contigs. At this point all the contigs generated from the seed are considered together for further processing to generate larger contigs. The last step uses again the paired-read information in order to create scaffolds.

10.2.2 Overlap–Layout–Consensus Assemblers

Assemblers based on the OLC approach have to calculate all the overlaps between the reads and use this information together with the coverage depth to reconstruct the original sequence. If available, the assembler can use the paired-read information.

OLC assemblers build an overlap graph [67]. The first mandatory step is the computation of the overlaps between reads. This step involves an all-against-all pairwise read comparison. Usually, for efficiency issues, the programs precompute the k-mer content among all reads and compute only the overlaps between reads that share a predefined number of k-mers. This kind of overlap computation is particularly sensitive to three parameters: the k-mer size, the minimum overlap length, and the percentage of identity required for an overlap. Larger parameter values are likely to produce more reliable but shorter contigs and at a higher computational cost. On the other hand, lower values can greatly reduce the computational needs, but at the price of producing too many misassemblies.

Once the read overlaps are computed, the overlap graph obtained is usually simplified in order to obtain an approximate read layout. This is done by identifying particularly problematic subgraphs in order to reduce the complexity.

The last step consists in performing MSAs in order to construct a precise layout and the consensus sequence. Again, this step is approximated by progressive pairwise alignments between reads believed to be close to one another, since no efficient method to compute optimal MSA is known [97].

OLC assemblers have been the unquestioned assemblers for more than 10 years. The advent of next-generation sequencing machines characterized by new error schemata and by ultrashort read lengths seemed to declare the end of an era. Nevertheless, some assemblers based on OLC have been proposed even to assemble short Illumina reads. Moreover, encouraged by the longer read lengths, some valuable assemblers designed for 454 reads have appeared.

10.2.2.1 *EDENA*

EDENA (Exact de novo Assembler) [30] is an assembler dedicated to process the millions of very short reads produced by the Illumina genome analyzer. In order to improve the assembly of very short sequences, it adds exact matching and detection of spurious reads. EDENA utilizes only exact matches for two main reasons: (i) allowing approximate matches increases the number of spurious overlaps and (ii) approximate matching is dramatically slower than exact matching. EDENA starts by removing from the data set all the reads that contain ambiguous characters or that are redundant and, meanwhile, it creates a prefix tree. After all overlaps of minimal size h are computed, the overlap graph is constructed. In order to calculate all the overlaps between reads, EDENA constructs a suffix array and loads all the overlaps in a bidirected graph structure, where for each read r_i there is a vertex v_i and two vertices v_i and v_j connected by a bidirected edge if r_i and r_j overlap. Each edge is labeled with the lenght of the corresponding overlap. Obviously, as in all OLC assemblers, the minimum overlap size is a crucial parameter for the assembly success.

The graph produced contains, in general, a large amount of branching paths hindering the construction of long contigs. EDENA executes a graph-cleaning step by removing *transitive* edges (an edge $v_1 \rightarrow v_3$ in the presence of a path $v_1 \rightarrow v_2 \rightarrow v_3$ is dubbed transitive and can be removed), short dead-end paths (a branching path of short length), and bubbles (two paths starting and ending on the same node and containing similar sequences). Short dead ends and bubbles are a consequence of sequencing errors (reads with errors in the last bases) and clonal polymorphism (in particular SNPs), respectively.

10.2.2.2 *SGA*

OLC assemblers do not scale well to large data sets composed by short reads, and hence EDENA cannot be used in practical scenarios. Other OLC assemblers are suited for 454-based projects that are characterized by longer (and more expensive) reads and low coverages (this second feature is partially a consequence of the first one).

In order to compute (almost) all possible alignments between reads, usually an index is built which represents all the reads. The large number of reads does not allow the use of standard data structures like suffix trees and suffix arrays. In [91] this problem is overcome by SGA, an OLC-based assembler suited for Illumina reads that uses the FM index [22]. In particular, SGA is able to build the overlap graph in time proportional to $O(N)$, with N the total length of all the reads.

SGA builds the FM index for the set of reads $\mathcal{R}$ using a variant of the Ko-Aluru [43] algorithm for the suffix array construction. The FM index of the set of the reversed reads is also computed. At this point, using the *backward-search* algorithm [22] the overlaps between read tips can be easily and quickly computed. In order to gain more speed, SGA can directly compute only nontransitive edges and therefore directly compute the simplified and reduced version of the string graph.

Despite the many details and technicalities presented in [91], SGA is the proof of how advanced data structures and algorithms proposed and adopted for string alignment are of primary importance in de novo assembly.

10.2.2.3 *Newbler*
Newbler [60] is the proprietary de novo assembler of 454 Life Science Corporation [60]. Newbler assembles the reads in "flow space." In this format, a read is represented as a sequence of signals whose strength is proportional to the number of direct repeats of that nucleotide at that position in the read. This is done in order to avoid the introduction of errors with an early base space conversion that can be postponed until the computation of the MSA.

Newbler implements a double OLC strategy and it is divided into three modules: overlapper, unitigger, and multialigner.

The overlapper performs a complete all-against-all fragment comparison to identify all possible overlaps between fragments. In order to assess the similarity between reads, it directly compares the *flowgrams* of each pair of reads. To increase efficiency, the overlapper uses a hashing indexing method to quickly identify fragments that might be considered as potential overlap candidates.

Based on the overlaps computed by the overlapper module, the unitigger groups the reads into *unitigs*. These unitigs are a sort of trusted contigs uncontested by reads external to the unitig. Unitigs are constructed from consistent chains of maximal depth overlaps (i.e., pairs of reads whose maximal overlaps are with each other).

Finally, the multialigner takes all the reads that compose the unitigs and aligns all the read signals in order to obtain the real unitig sequence.

The unitigs generated this way are sent through a contig optimization process composed by three steps. In the first one, an all-against-all comparison is performed and overlapping unitigs are joined. After this comparison, performed in nucleotide space, Newbler tries to identify repeat region boundaries based on where contig sequences diverge from a common region. Contigs are broken at those boundaries. In the second optimization step, the contigs produced during the fist step are used for a "restitching" operation: Reads that span two contig ends are used to join those contigs. The third and final optimization step is a quality-check step performed by aligning all the reads against the contigs and discarding contigs with low coverage.

As a last step, the consensus is recomputed, this time using the flowspace, in order to gain more precision and accuracy.

10.2.2.4 *CABOG*
CABOG [63] assembler is a revised version of Celera Assembler [68] designed for 454 reads. CABOG, like Newbler, parses the native SFF files produced by 454 machines. Like Celera Assembler it is divided into independent modules.

The *overlapped-based trimming* phase trims reads and identifies possible spurs and chimers (reads that join discontinuous genomic loci) by computing local alignments for all pairs of reads.

In the *anchors-and-overlaps* phase, CABOG uses exact-match seeds to detect possibly overlapping reads and builds the overlap graph. In order to speed up this phase, exact-match seeds are used to quickly identify overlapping reads. In order to avoid the use of k-mers containing sequencing errors or highly repeated regions, k-mers that occur in a single copy or with a number of copies larger than a precomputed threshold are not used in this phase.

Using the computed alignments, CABOG can build the overlapping graph G. In this phase a drastic and lossy data reduction is performed. The graph G is reduced to the *best overlapping graph* (BOG) by keeping for each node (i.e., each read) only the best edge (i.e., the longest overlap). Moreover, all cycles are eliminated by deleting a randomly chosen edge. The BOG is therefore acyclic, but paths in the BOG can still converge due to overlaps that are not mutually best for both reads involved.

CABOG sorts the reads by score, where the score of a read is defined as the number of other reads reachable from it in the BOG. Starting from the highest scoring reads, it follows the paths in the BOG to construct *unitigs* (trusted contigs). Unitigs that span intersections in the BOG are broken. Further unitig splitting is performed using paired-read information.

Once unitigs are computed and simplified, the *contig*, *scaffold* and, *consensus* steps of the Celera Assembler are performed.

10.2.3 DBG-Based Assemblers

The DBGs owe their success to their embedded capability of representing the myriad of reads produced by NGS in a reasonable amount of space. The DBG assemblers were first proposed in Sanger sequencing [35] based on a proposal for assembling using the old sequencing-by-hybridization technique [75].

The DBG approach is commonly also known as the *k-mer graph* approach and the *Eulerian* approach [78]. In a DBG, the nodes represent k-mers. Two nodes are connected by an oriented edge if the the k-mers that they represent overlap for $k - 1$ characters. The DBG approach starts with the counterintuitive step of reducing short reads in even shorter sequences (i.e., k-mers). In this way reads are represented by paths in the graph. The main advantage of this technique is that every k-mer is represented only one time despite the number of its occurrences. In an ideal setting with error-free reads and uniform coverage, the k-mer graph would be a DBG and an assembly would be represented by an Eulerian path, that is, a path that traverses each edge exactly once. It is clear that in real-life situations, where the reads contain errors and coverage is not uniform, the assembly procedure is slightly more complicated.

In this context, the assembly is a byproduct of the graph construction. Despite different implementations and heuristics, the graph construction relies on a hash table that tracks all the k-mers represented in the reads. While in theory the memory used is not dependent on the size of the input but only by the different number of k-mers, in practical situations (mammalian and plant genome-sequencing projects) the amount of memory required is still the main bottleneck. In order to overcome this problem, distributed assemblers have been proposed in the literature [85, 92].

Several factors are analyzed in [64] that complicate the application of k-mer graphs to sequence assembly (see Figure 10.2 for a graphical representation of the most common problems). First, DNA is double stranded. Different implementations have been proposed to

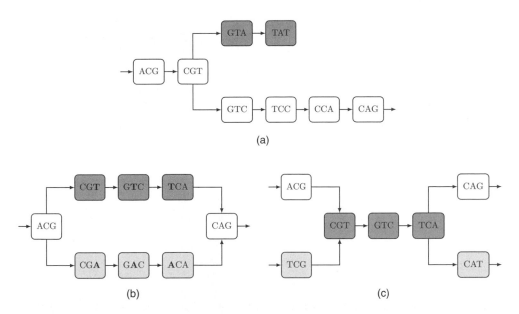

(a)

(b)   (c)

FIGURE 10.2   Three main sources of errors in DBG. (a) Spurs: If a read contains a single error a branching path is open. (b) Bulge/bubble: A single-nucleotide polymorphism causes a branching path that will soon converge. (c) Fray rope: A repeat causes two or more paths to converge in a single node and proceeds together until the end of the repeat.

handle reverse-forward overlaps. A second problem is the identification and reconstruction of complex repeated structures present in real genomes. Repeats longer than k introduce complexity in the graph and as a direct consequence complicate the assembly task. Repeats collapse in a single path inside the graph, with the consequence that many paths can converge inside a repeat and then diverge. Assemblers usually use reads to understand what the right path is (they search for read-coherent paths) and in a similar way they use paired-read information. The last problem is represented by sequencing errors. DBG-based assemblers use several strategies to cope with errors. Some assemblers preprocess the reads in order to remove errors by discarding/correcting reads containing low-quality bases or lowly represented k-mers. They discard those paths in the graph which are not supported by a high number of reads. Another technique consists in converting paths into sequences and using sequence alignment to collapse nearly identical paths.

10.2.3.1 *EULER-SR*   EULER was the first assembler to implement the DBG approach. The first version of EULER was suited for Sanger reads [78–80]. Despite the advantages of the method, it met only with marginal success. With the advent of next-generation sequencing and the need of processing large amounts of reads, EULER was adapted first to handle 454 GS20 reads [77] and, soon after, also the Illumina reads [72, 76].

The first step implemented by EULER is a correction phase. EULER identifies erroneous base calls looking for low-frequency k-mers. This filter is called *spectral alignment* [80]. A *spectrum* T is a collection of l-tuples. A string s is called a *T-string* if all its l-tuples belong to T. Given a collection of strings $S = \{s_1, \ldots, s_n\}$ from a sequencing project and an integer l, the spectrum of S is S_l (the set of all l-tuples from the reads $s_1, \ldots, s_n$ and $\overline{s_1}, \ldots, \overline{s_n}$, where $\overline{s_i}$ is the reverse complement read of s_i). Given S, Δ, and l, EULER introduces up to

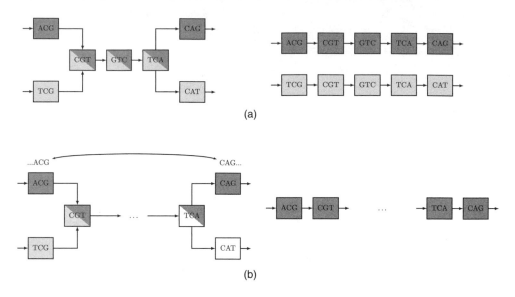

FIGURE 10.3   Read tracking: two commonly used techniques to resolve repeats. (a) Repeat resolution via read tracking: following the read paths small repetitions can be easily resolved. (b) Repeat resolution via paired reads: longer repeats can be resolved through paired reads.

Δ corrections in each read in S in order to minimize $|S_l|$. The idea is that reads that contain errors contains low-frequency k-mers. Instead of simply discarding these reads, EULER tries to correct them.

By reducing the total number of k-mers, the correction reduces the number of nodes in the graph and hence its complexity. This correction step can mask true polymorphism or delete valid k-mers belonging to low-coverage areas. OLC assemblers have an analogous base call correction step that uses overlaps rather than k-mers. EULER spectral alignment is able to cope only with mismatches and not with insertions or deletions.

EULER builds the k-mer graph or DBG from the set of filtered and corrected reads. The main drawback of this approach is that, since the basic units on which the graph is defined are k-mers rather than reads, the information about the original reads may become difficult to retrieve. EULER overcomes this problem by threading the reads through the graph. This implementation allows to easily resolve paths in the presence of repeats that are spanned by a read, as shown in Figure 10.3a. By tracking reads on the graph, we can resolve repeats of size between k and the read length.

In order to resolve repeats longer than the read length, EULER extends the described approach to paired reads. Paired ends that span a repeat provide the evidence to join one path that enters the repeat to one path that exits the repeat (see Figure 10.3b). In other words, EULER considers a paired read as a read with some missing characters in the middle. Moreover, EULER can use the insert size information in order to better distinguish between paths.

After this threading phase, EULER performs some graph simplification at regions with low coverage or high coverage. First, EULER removes spurs, that is, short branching paths that are likely due to sequencing errors. If quality information is available, EULER uses it to improve the assembly. Many of the platforms produce reads with low-quality values at the $3'$ ends. For this reason, EULER trusts more read prefixes than read suffixes.

The k-mer size parameter is a critical parameter when working with DBGs. A small k reduces the number of nodes and can result in an oversimplification of the graph (consider the case of $k=1$). On the other hand, a large k can yield a graph with too many nodes that is likely to produce a fragmented assembly (consider the case of k equal to the read lengths). EULER solves this problem by constructing two k-mer graphs with different values of k. EULER detects the edges present in the smaller k graph that are missing in the larger k graph. The idea is then to use a large k in order to resolve the gaps and later fill in the gaps by using the edges coming from the smaller k graph.

10.2.3.2 *VELVET*

VELVET [103, 104] is probably the most cited de novo assembler for short reads. It has been used in several projects, including the apple scab genome project [83].

The first step of the algorithm consists in the construction of the DBG. VELVET starts by hashing all the reads according to a user-predefined k-mer length. The value of k is bounded from above by the length of the reads and it must be odd (so that a k-mer cannot be its own reverse complement). This way VELVET builds a "roadmap," that is, the information that allows each read to be rewritten as a set of k-mers combined with overlaps of previously scanned reads. A second database is constructed, recording for each read the set of its original k-mers which are overlapped by subsequent reads. Once the graph is constructed, the reads can be traced through it by using the roadmap information.

VELVET does not make any read filtering step. However, it performs several graph simplification steps in order to remove from the graph the paths that are likely to be introduced by sequencing errors. In particular, VELVET identifies two common graph layouts that are likely to be a consequence of sequencing errors: *tips* and *bubbles*. A *tip* (sometimes called a *spur*) is a chain of nodes that is disconnected on one end (see Figure 10.2a) while *bubbles* (sometimes called *bulges*) are paths starting and ending on the same nodes and containing similar sequences (see Figure 10.2b). Tips are usually a consequence of reads with errors in the last bases, while bubbles can be caused either by SNPs or by sequencing errors.

VELVET performs several graph simplification steps in order to reduce the impact of such structures and to improve the final result. The first simplification step consists in merging all the *chains* (i.e., sequences of nodes with only one ingoing edge and only one outgoing edge). Subsequently, VELVET identifies tips shorter than $2k$ and removes them. The removal of those structures has only a local effect and does not cause disconnection of the graph. "Bubbles" are removed using the tour bus algorithm [104]: VELVET detects bubbles through a Dijkstra-like breadth-first search.

A fourth graph simplification aims at removing erroneous connection in the graph (i.e., edges that connect sequences that belong to different genomic loci). Erroneous graph connections do not associate to easily recognizable subgraphs and therefore are more difficult to detect. VELVET uses a coverage cutoff to remove connections with a coverage depth under a user-defined threshold. This threshold together with the k-mer length is one of the most important VELVET's parameters.

VELVET uses paired information to resolve complex and long repeats. In [104] the scaffolding phase is done through the "breadcrumb" algorithm. This algorithm was inspired by SHORTY [33]. It localizes on the graph simple paths (contigs) connected by paired reads. Using the long contigs as anchors, VELVET tries to fill the gap between them with short contigs. More recent versions of VELVET [103] use a more sophisticated algorithm, called *Pebble*. Pebble starts by identifying unique nodes (i.e., contigs) with the only help of the contig coverage values, using a statistic derived from the A-statistic. Pebble tries to connect the unique nodes identified previously but using the paired-end information. For each unique node, it estimates the distances from that node by exploiting the given insert length distribution. The complete set of estimated internode distances is called the *primary scaffold*. At this point, the algorithm tries to close the gap between contigs by finding a path that is consistent with the layout. In [103] also the "rock band" algorithm is introduced. This module exploits long (i.e., Sanger-like) reads to connect the nodes of the graph after the error correction phase. The main idea is that if all the long reads which exit from a node go consistently to another unique node and vice versa, then the two nodes can be safely merged.

10.2.3.3 *ALLPATHS*   ALLPATHS [15, 24, 56] is a whole-genome shotgun assembler that can generate high-quality assemblies from short reads. Assemblies are presented in graph form that retain ambiguities, such as those arising from polymorphisms, thereby providing information that has been absent from previous genome assemblies.

Like EULER, ALLPATHS uses a read-correcting preprocessor similar to EULER's spectral alignment. ALLPATHS identifies putatively correct (*trusted*) k-mer in the reads based on quality scores and on the k-mer frequencies. These trusted k-mers are used to correct the entire set of reads.

A second preprocessing step is implemented by ALLPATHS in order to create *unipaths*, that is, maximal unbranched sequences in the k-mer graph. Unipaths are constructed by building a compact searchable data structure by indexing the k-mers in order to avoid the computation of all the overlaps.

The first graph operation is the spur erosion, named *unitig graph shaving*. This operation aims at removing short branching paths that are usually caused by sequencing errors. Once this operation terminates, a subset of unipaths are elected to be *seeds*. *Seeds* are the unipaths around which ALLPATHS constructs the assembly. A seed is a long unipath characterized by a low copy number (ideally one). The idea is to extend the seed's neighborhood in order to join more than one unipath together with the help of paired-read information.

ALLPATHS partitions the graph in order to resolve genomic repeats by assembling regions that are locally nonrepetitive. Partitions are assembled separately and in parallel. At the end, ALLPATHS *glues* the local graphs by iteratively joining subgraphs that have long end-to-end overlapping stretches. ALLPATHS heuristically removes spurs, small disconnected components, and paths not spanned by paired reads.

The latest available version of ALLPATHS [24] is designed for Illumina reads of length 100. In particular, ALLPATHS requires two different kinds of paired reads: *fragment library* and *jumping library*. A fragment library is a library with a short insert separation, less than twice the read length, so that the reads may overlap (e.g., 100-bp Illumina reads taken from 180-bp inserts). A jumping library has a longer separation, typically in the 3–10-Kbp range. Additionally, ALLPATHS also supports *long jumping libraries*. A jumping library is considered to be long if the insert size is larger than 20 Kbp. These libraries are optional and used only to improve scaffolding in mammalian-sized genomes. Typically, long jump coverage of less than $1\times$ is sufficient to significantly improve scaffolding.

The latest available ALLPATHS version [24] is able to accurately assemble the human genome and to achieve a result close to Sanger sequencing assembly.

10.2.3.4 *ABySS*   ABySS [92] is a de novo sequence assembler designed for short reads. The single-processor version is useful for assembling genomes up to 40–50 Mbases in size.

The parallel version is implemented using MPI communication messages [27] and is capable of assembling larger genomes.

The assembly is performed in two major steps. First, without using the paired-end information, contigs are extended until either they cannot be unambiguously extended or they come to a blunt end due to a lack of coverage. In the second step, the paired-end information is used to resolve ambiguities and to merge contigs. In the second stage, mate-pair information is used to extend contigs by resolving ambiguities in contig overlaps.

ABySS constructs a DBG in a way similar to VELVET and EULER. As already explained for both algorithms, ABySS performs an error correction phase on the graph. In order to handle read errors, ABySS implements a strategy correspondig to a combination of EDENA, VELVET, and EULER-SR algorithms.

The advantage of ABySS is its capability of assembling large genomes due to the MPI parallel version. The construction of the DBG can be performed in a distributed way. Another, more recent, assembler able to exploit several nodes in a cluster is RAY [12].

REFERENCES

1. www.454.com.

2. www.appliedbiosystems.com.

3. www.illumina.com.

4. M. I. Abouelhoda, S. Kurtz, and E. Ohlebusch. Replacing suffix trees with enhanced suffix arrays. *J. Discrete Algorithms*, 2(1):53–86, 2004.

5. S. F. Altschul, et al. Gapped BLAST and PSI-BLAST: A new generation of protein database search programs. *Nucleic Acids Res.*, 25(17):3389–3402, 1997.

6. Apache Hadopp: http://hadoop.apache.org/.

7. A. Apostolico. The myriad virtues of sub-word trees. *Combinatorics on Words*, 112:85–96, 1985.

8. S. Batzoglou, et al. Arachne: A whole-genome shotgun assembler. *Genome Res.*, 12(1):177–189, Jan. 2002.

9. D. R. Bentley, et al. Accurate whole human genome sequencing using reversible terminator chemistry. *Nature*, 456(7218):53–9, Nov. 2008.

10. A. Blumer, et al. The smallest automation recognizing the subwords of a text. *Theor. Comput. Sci.*, 40:31–55, 1985.

11. A. Blumer, et al. Complete inverted files for efficient text retrieval and analysis. *J. ACM*, 34(3):578–595, July 1987.

12. S. Boisvert, F. Laviolette, and J. Corbeil. Ray: Simultaneous assembly of reads from a mix of high-throughput sequencing technologies. *J. Comput. Biol.*, 17(11):1519–1533, Nov. 2010.

13. D. W. Bryant, W. K. Wong, and T. C. Mockler. Qsra: A quality-value guided de novo short read assembler. *BMC Bioinformatics*, 10:69, 2009.

14. M. Burrows and D. J. Wheeler. A block-sorting lossless data compression algorithm. 1994. http://www.hpl.hp.com/techreports/Compaq-DEC/SRC-RR-124.pdf.

15. J. Butler, et al. Allpaths: De novo assembly of whole-genome shotgun microreads. *Genome Res.*, 18(5):810–820, May 2008.

16. A. Califano and I. Rigoutsos. Flash: A fast look-up algorithm for string homology. In *Proceedings of the 1st International Conference on Intelligent Systems for Molecular Biology*, AAAI Press, New York, NY, 1993, pp. 56–64.

17. P. J. Campbell, et al. Identification of somatically acquired rearrangements in cancer using genome-wide massively parallel paired-end sequencing. *Nat. Genet.*, 40(6):722–729, June 2008.

18. K. Chen, et al. Breakdancer: An algorithm for high-resolution mapping of genomic structural variation. *Nat. Methods*, 6(9):677–681, 2009.

19. M. David, et al. SHRiMP2: Sensitive yet practical short read mapping. *Bioinformatics* (Oxford, England), 27(7):1011–1012, Apr. 2011.

20. J. Dean and S. Ghemawat. MapReduce: Simplified data processing on large clusters. *Commun. ACM*, 51(1):107–113, 2008.

21. J. C. Dohm, C. Lottaz, T. Borodina, and H. Himmelbauer. Sharcgs, a fast and highly accurate short-read assembly algorithm for de novo genomic sequencing. *Genome Res*, 17(11):1697–1706, Nov. 2007.

22. P. Ferragina and G. Manzini. Opportunistic data structures with applications. In *Proceedings of the 41st Annual Symposium on Foundations of Computer Science (FOCS '00)*, IEEE Computer Society, Washington, DC, 2000, p. 390.

23. A. Fujimoto, et al. Whole-genome sequencing and comprehensive variant analysis of a Japanese individual using massively parallel sequencing. *Nat. Genet.*, 42(11):931–936, Nov. 2010.

24. S. Gnerre, et al. High-quality draft assemblies of mammalian genomes from massively parallel sequence data. *Proc. Natl. Acad. Sci. USA*, 108(4):1513–1518, 2011.

25. S. M. D. Goldberg, et al. A sanger/pyrosequencing hybrid approach for the generation of high-quality draft assemblies of marine microbial genomes. *Proc. Nat. Acad. Sci. USA*, 103(30):11240–11245, July 2006.

26. O. Gotoh. An improved algorithm for matching biological sequences. *J. Mol. Bio.*, 162(3): 705–708, Dec. 1982.

27. W. Gropp, E. Lusk, and A. Skjellum. Using MPI: Portable parallel programming with the message passing interface. 1999.

28. D. Gusfield. *Algorithms on Strings, Trees, and Sequences: Computer Science and Computational Biology*. Cambridge University Press, New York, NY, 1997, pp. 94–116.

29. R. W. Hamming. Error detecting and error correcting codes. *Bell Syst. Tech. J.*, 29(2):147–160, 1950.

30. D. Hernandez, et al. De novo bacterial genome sequencing: Millions of very short reads assembled on a desktop computer. *Genome*, 18:802–809, 2008.

31. W. K. Hon, et al. A space and time efficient algorithm for constructing compressed suffix arrays. *Algorithmica*, 48(1):23–36, Mar. 2007.

32. F. Hormozdiari, et al. Next-generation variationhunter: Combinatorial algorithms for transposon insertion discovery. *Bioinformatics*, 26(12):i350–i357, June 2010.

33. M. S. Hossain, N. Azimi, and S. Skiena. Crystallizing short-read assemblies around seeds. *BMC Bioinformatics*, 10 (Suppl. 1):S16, 2009.

34. X. Huang, J. Wang, S. Aluru, S. P. Yang, and L. Hillier. Pcap: A whole-genome assembly program. *Genome Res.*, 13(9):2164–2170, 2003.

35. R. M. Idury and M. S. Waterman. A new algorithm for dna sequence assembly. *J. Comput. Biol.*, 2(2):291–306, 1995.

36. S. Inenaga, et al. On-line construction of compact directed acyclic word graphs. In *Discrete Applied Mathematics*, Vol. 146, Springer, 2001, pp. 169–180.

37. O. Jaillon, et al. The grapevine genome sequence suggests ancestral hexaploidization in major angiosperm phyla. *Nature*, 449(7161):463–467, Sept. 2007.

38. W. R. Jeck, et al. Extending assembly of short dna sequences to handle error. *Bioinformatics*, 23(21):2942–2944, Nov. 2007.

39. J. Kärkkäinen, P. Sanders, and S. Burkhardt. Simple linear work suffix array construction. In *Automata, Languages and Programming, 30th International Colloquium, ICALP 2003, Lecture Notes in Computer Science*, Vol. 2719, Springer, 2003, pp. 943–955.

40. R. Karp and M. Rabin. Efficient randomized pattern-matching algorithms. *IBM J. Res. Develop.*, 31(2):249–260, 1987.

41. W. J. Kent. BLAT—The BLAST-like Alignment Tool. *Genome Res.*, 12(4):656–664, 2002.

42. J. I. Kim, et al. A highly annotated whole-genome sequence of a Korean individual. *Nature*, 460(7258):1011–1015, Aug. 2009.

43. P. Ko and S. Aluru. Space efficient linear time construction of suffix arrays. *J. Discrete Algorithms*, 3(2–4):143–156, June 2005.

44. B. Langmead, K. D. Hansen, and J. T. Leek. Cloud-scale RNA-sequencing differential expression analysis with Myrna. *Genome Biol.*, 11(8):R83, Jan. 2010.

45. B. Langmead, M. C. Schatz, J. Lin, M. Pop, and S. L. Salzberg. Searching for SNPs with cloud computing. *Genome Biol.*, 10(11):R134, Jan. 2009.

46. B. Langmead, C. Trapnell, M. Pop, and S. Salzberg. Ultrafast and memory-efficient alignment of short DNA sequences to the human genome. *Genome Biol.*, 10(3):R25, 2009.

47. Vladimir I. Levenshtein. Binary codes capable of correcting deletions, insertions, and reversals. *Sov. Phys. Doklady*, 10(8):707–710, 1966.

48. H. Li and R. Durbin. Fast and accurate short read alignment with Burrows-Wheeler transform. *Bioinformatics*, 25(14):1754–1760, 2009.

49. H. Li and R. Durbin. Fast and accurate long-read alignment with Burrows-Wheeler transform. *Bioinformatics*, 26(5):589, 2010.

50. H. Li, J. Ruan, and R. Durbin. Mapping short dna sequencing reads and calling variants using mapping quality scores. *Genome Res.*, 18(11):1851, 2008.

51. R. Li, Y. Li, X. Fang, H. Yang, J. Wang, and K. Kristiansen. Snp detection for massively parallel whole-genome resequencing. *Genome Res.*, 19(6):1124–1132, May 2009.

52. R. Li, Y. Li, K. Kristiansen, and J. Wang. Soap: Short oligonucleotide alignment program. *Bioinformatics* (Oxford, England), 24(5):713–714, Mar. 2008.

53. R. Li, et al. Soap2: An improved ultrafast tool for short read alignment. *Bioinformatics* (Oxford, England), 25(15):1966–1967, Aug. 2009.

54. H. Lin, Z. Zhang, M. Q. Zhang, B. Ma, and M. Li. ZOOM! Zillions of oligos mapped. *Bioinformatics* (Oxford, England), 24(21):2431–2437, Nov. 2008.

55. B. Ma, J. Tromp, and M. Li. Patternhunter: Faster and more sensitive homology search. *Bioinformatics* (Oxford, England), 18(3):440–445, Mar. 2002.

56. I. Maccallum, et al. Allpaths 2: small genomes assembled accurately and with high continuity from short paired reads. *Genome Biol.*, 10(10):R103, 2009.

57. N. Malhis, Y. S. N. Butterfield, M. Ester, and S. J. M. Jones. Slider—Maximum use of probability information for alignment of short sequence reads and snp detection. *Bioinformatics (Oxford, England)*, 25(1):6–13, Jan. 2009.

58. U. Manber and G. Myers. Suffix arrays: a new method for on-line string searches. In *Proceedings of the First Annual ACM-SIAM Symposium on Discrete Algorithms (SODA '90)*, San Francisco, California, USA, Society for Industrial and Applied Mathematics, Philadelphia, PA, 1990, pp. 319–327.

59. E. R. Mardis. The impact of next-generation sequencing technology on genetics. *Trends Genet.*, 24(3):133–141, Mar. 2008.

60. M. Margulies, et al. Genome sequencing in microfabricated high-density picolitre reactors. *Nature*, 437(7057):376–380, Sept. 2005.

61. E. McGreight. A space-economical suffix tree construction algorithm. *J. ACM*, 23:262–272, 1976.

62. P. Medvedev, M. Stanciu, and M. Brudno. Computational methods for discovering structural variation with next-generation sequencing. *Nat. Methods*, 6(11, Suppl.):S13–S20, Nov. 2009.

63. J. R. Miller, et al. Aggressive assembly of pyrosequencing reads with mates. *Bioinformatics*, 24(24):2818–2824, Dec. 2008.

64. J. R. Miller, S. Koren, and G. Sutton. Assembly algorithms for next-generation sequencing data. *Genomics*, 95(6):315–327, June 2010.

65. I. Munro, V. Raman, and S. S. Rao. Space efficient suffix trees. *J. Algorithm.*, 39(2):205–222, 2001.

66. D. J. Munroe and T. J. R. Harris. Third-generation sequencing fireworks at marco island. *Nat. Biotechnol.*, 28(5):426–428, May 2010.

67. E. W. Myers. The fragment assembly string graph. *Bioinformatics* (Oxford, England), 21 (Suppl 2):ii79–85, Sept. 2005.

68. E. W. Myers, et al. A whole-genome assembly of drosophila. *Science*, 287(5461):2196–2204, Mar. 2000.

69. N. Nagarajan and M. Pop. Parametric complexity of sequence assembly: Theory and applications to next generation sequencing. *J. Comput. Biol.*, 16(7):897–908, July 2009.

70. G. Navarro. A guided tour to approximate string matching. *ACM Comput. Surv.*, 33(1):31–88, Mar. 2001.

71. Z. Ning, A. J. Cox, and J. C. Mullikin. Ssaha: A fast search method for large dna databases. *Genome Res.*, 11(10):1725–1729, Oct. 2001.

72. A. P. Pavel and J. C. Mark. Short read fragment assembly of bacterial genomes. *Genome Res.*, 18(2):324–330, Feb. 2008.

73. K. Paszkiewicz and D. J. Studholme. De novo assembly of short sequence reads. *Brief. Bioinform.*, 11(5):457–472, 2010.

74. pBWA. Pbwa—Parallel burrows-wheeler aligner. Unpublished. `http://pbwa.source-forge.net/`.

75. P. A. Pevzner. 1-Tuple dna sequencing: Computer analysis. *J. Biomol. Struct. Dyn.*, 7(1):63–73, Aug. 1989.

76. P. A. Pevzner, M. J. Chaisson, and D. Brinza. De novo fragment assembly with short mate-paired reads: Does the read length matter? *Genome Res.*, 19(2):336–346, Feb. 2009.

77. P. A. Pevzner, P. A. Pevzner, H. Tang, and G. Tesler. De novo repeat classification and fragment assembly. *Genome Res.*, 14(9):1786–1796, Sept. 2004.

78. P. A. Pevzner and H. Tang. Fragment assembly with double-barreled data. *Bioinformatics*, 17(Suppl. 1):S225–233, June 2001.

79. P. A. Pevzner, H. Tang, and M. Chaisson. Fragment assembly with short reads. *Bioinformatics*, 20:2069–2074, 2004.

80. P. A. Pevzner, H. Tang, and M. S. Waterman. An Eulerian path approach to dna fragment assembly. *Proc. Natl. Acad. Sci. USA*, 98(17):9748–9753, Aug. 2001.

81. A. Policriti, A. Tomescu, and F. Vezzi. A randomized numerical aligner (rNA). In A.-H. Dediu, H. Fernau, and C. Martín-Vide (Eds.), *Language and Automata Theory and Applications. Lecture Notes in Computer Science*, Vol. 6031, Springer, Heidelberg, 2010, pp. 512–523.

82. K. R. Rasmussen, J. Stoye, and E. W. Myers. Efficient q-gram filters for finding all-matches over a given length. *J. Computat. Biol.*, 13:296–308, 2005.

83. D. J. Rees, L. H. Husselmann, and J. M. Celton. De novo genome sequencing of the apple scab (venturia inaequalis) genome, using illumina sequencing technology. Paper presented at the Plant & Animal Genomes XVII Conference. San Diego, CA, Abstract.

84. J. A. Reinhardt, et al. De novo assembly using low-coverage short read sequence data from the rice pathogen *Pseudomonas syringae* pv. oryzae. *Genome Res.*, 19(2):294–305, Feb. 2009.

85. S. Rodrigue, et al. Unlocking short read sequencing for metagenomics. *PLoS ONE*, 5(7):e11840, July 2010.

86. S. M. Rumble, P. Lacroute, A. V. Dalca, M. Fiume, A. Sidow, and M. Brudno. SHRiMP: Accurate mapping of short color-space reads. *PLoS Comput. Biol.*, 5(5):e1000386, 2009.

87. F. Sanger and A. R. Coulson. A rapid method for determining sequences in dna by primed synthesis with dna polymerase. *J. Mol. Biol.*, 94(3):441-448, May 1975.

88. M. C. Schatz. Cloudburst: Highly sensitive read mapping with mapreduce. *Bioinformatics (Oxford, England)*, 25(11):1363–1369, June 2009.

89. M. C. Schatz, A. L. Delcher, and S. L. Salzberg. Assembly of large genomes using second-generation sequencing. *Genome Res.*, 20(9):1165–1173, Sept. 2010.

90. Y. Shen, et al. A snp discovery method to assess variant allele probability from next-generation resequencing data. *Genome Res.*, 20(2):273–280, Mar. 2010.

91. J. T. Simpson and R. Durbin. Efficient construction of an assembly string graph using the fm-index. *Bioinformatics*, 26(12):i367–i373, June 2010.

92. J. T. Simpson, et al. Abyss: A parallel assembler for short read sequence data. *Genome Res.*, 19(6):1117–1123, June 2009.

93. A. D. Smith, Z. Xuan, and M. Q. Zhang. Using quality scores and longer reads improves accuracy of solexa read mapping. *BMC Bioinformatics*, 9:128, Jan. 2008.

94. T. F. Smith and M. S. Waterman. Identification of common molecular subsequences. *J. Mol. Biol.*, 147(1):195–197, Mar. 1981.

95. E. Ukkonen. On-line construction of suffix trees. *Algorithmica*, 14(3):249–260, 1995.

96. J. C. Venter, et al. The sequence of the human genome. *Science*, 291(5507):1304–1351, Feb. 2001.

97. L. Wang and T. Jiang. On the complexity of multiple sequence alignment. *J. Computat. Biol. J. Computat. Mole. Cell Biol.*, 1(4):337–348, Jan. 1994.

98. R. L. Warren. SSAKE 3.0 improved speed, accuracy and contiguity. Paper presented at the Pacific Symposium, 2007, pp. 570–570.

99. R. L. Warren, G. G. Sutton, S. J. M. Jones, and R. A. Holt. Assembling millions of short dna sequences using ssake. *Bioinformatics*, 23(4):500–501, Feb. 2007.

100. D. Weese, A. K. Emde, T. Rausch, A. Döring, and K. Reinert. Razers a fast read mapping with sensitivity control. *Genome Res.*, 19(9):1646, 2009.

101. P. Weiner. Linear pattern matching algorithms. In *Proceedings of the 14th IEEE Symposium on Switching and Automa Theory*, 1973, pp. 1–11.

102. D. A. Wheeler, M. Srinivasan, M. Egholm, Y. Shen, and L. Chen. The complete genome of an individual by massively parallel dna sequencing. *Nature*, 452(7189):872–876, Apr. 2008.

103. D. R. Zerbino. Genome assembly and comparison using de Bruijn graphs. PhD thesis, 2009.

104. D. R. Zerbino and E. Birney. Velvet: Algorithms for de novo short read assembly using De Bruijn graphs. *Genome Res.*, 18(5):821–829, May 2008.

CHAPTER 11

ALGORITHMS FOR NEXT-GENERATION SEQUENCING DATA

COSTAS S. ILIOPOULOS[1,2] and SOLON P. PISSIS[1]

[1]Department of Informatics, King's College London, Strand, London, United Kingdom
[2]Digital Ecosystems & Business Intelligence Institute, Curtin University, Centre for Stringology & Applications, Perth, Australia

11.1 INTRODUCTION

DNA sequencing includes several methods and technologies that are used for determining the exact order of the nucleotide bases—adenine, guanine, cytosine, and thymine—in a DNA macromolecule.

Sequencing technology has come a long way since the time when traditional sequencing techniques required many laboratories around the world to cooperate for years in order to sequence the human genome for the first time. The traditional sequencing methods, developed in the mid 1970s, had been the workhorse technology for DNA sequencing for almost 30 years. In 1977, Fred Sanger and Alan R. Coulson published two methodological papers on the rapid determination of DNA sequence [44, 46], which would go on to revolutionize biology, as a whole, by providing a tool for analyzing complete genes and later entire genomes. The method greatly improved earlier DNA-sequencing techniques developed by Maxam and Gilbert [34], published in the same year, and Sanger and Coulson's own *plus-and-minus* method, published two years earlier [45].

With the paramount goal of analyzing the human genome, the throughput demand of DNA sequencing increased by an unexpected magnitude, leading to new developments. Laboratory automation and process parallelization resulted in the foundation of factorylike companies, called sequencing centers, that accommodate hundreds of DNA-sequencing instruments. However, even the successful completion of the two antagonistic human genome projects did not satisfy biologists' hunger for even higher sequencing throughput and, especially, a more economical sequencing technology. The speed, accuracy, efficiency, and cost-effectiveness of sequencing technology have been improving since.

The first signs of what might transform the sequencing market arrived in 2005 with the milestone publication of the sequencing-by-synthesis (SBS) technology, developed by

454 Life Sciences [33], and the multiplex polony sequencing protocol of George Church's laboratory [49]. The SBS technology, which uses pyrosequencing for read-out, originally started with producing short sequences (reads) of length 100 base pairs (bp), which after 16 months on the market had increased to 250 bp. Recent advances have raised the mark again to more than 500 bp, drawing near today's Sanger sequencing read length of ~ 750 bp.

Apart from read length, the number of sequencing reads that can be produced in a single instrument run for a given cost is another important aspect. These concerns have been addressed by 454's competitors, whose systems produce up to 10-fold more reads at the cost of a much shorter read length of 150 bp or fewer. Today, three commercial *next-generation* sequencing systems are available: Roche's (454) Genome Sequencer FLX system, marketed by Roche Applied Sciences, Illumina's Solexa IIx sequencer, and, most recently, Applied Biosystem's SOLiD system. Additional competitors, which are believed to be ready to enter the market within one year, are the *third-generation*, also called *next-next-generation*, sequencing systems based on single-molecule analysis and developed by VisiGen and Helicos.

The impact that these next-generation sequencing innovations will have on clinical genetics will certainly be crucial. The low-scale, targeted gene/mutation analysis that currently dominates the clinical genetics field will ultimately be replaced by large-scale sequencing of entire disease gene pathways and networks, especially for the so-called complex disorders [40, 41, 51]. Eventually, the perceived clinical benefit of whole-genome sequencing will outweigh the cost of the procedure, allowing for these tests to be performed on a routine basis for diagnostic purposes, or perhaps in the form of a screening program, that could be used to guide personalized medical treatments throughout the lifetime of the individual [57].

The goal of producing large amounts of sequencing data, in the form of short reads, from closely related organisms is driving the application known as *resequencing*, which deals with the data in different ways than de novo assemblies of genomes. In resequencing, the assembly is directed by a reference sequence and demands much less *coverage* (8–12 times)—each base in the final sequence is present, on average, in 8–12 reads—than assembling genomes de novo (25–70 times). It requires the existence of a high-quality genome of some representative of the species (the reference), while the sequencing technology is used to sequence reads from the genome of another representative (the donor). If it were attainable to assemble the donor's genome from the reads, finding the differences between the two genomes would be relatively straightforward. However, de novo assembly of the human genome from next-generation sequencing reads can only produce short fragments, called contigs [35], as the presence of repeats makes it difficult or impossible to assemble longer fragments. Instead, the reads are compared to the reference sequence, and variants are identified via analysis of the aligned (mapped) reads. One study using this approach sequenced 10 mammalian mitochondrial genomes [16], thus enabling population–genetic studies based on complete mitochondrial genomes rather than just short sequence intervals. However, attempts to directly assemble short reads from simpler genomes have begun [50], and a first attempt for human assembly has also been recently reported [31].

The fundamental first step in the discovery of variants in the genome of the donor is the mapping of reads to a reference sequence. Mapping so many short reads to such a long reference sequence is a very challenging task that cannot be adequately carried out by traditional alignment programs like BLAST [1], FASTA [42], or BLAT [24]. Hence, recently, a broad array of short-read alignment programs has been published to address this task, placing emphasis on different aspects of the challenge.

A first generation of short-read alignment programs made use of hash table–based methods. The first efficient program developed was ELAND [7], which was integrated in Illumina's Solexa data processing package. ELAND indexes reads of length 20–32 bp and allows up to two mismatches in the alignment. SOAP [29] indexes the reference and allows either a certain number of mismatches or one continuous gap of length ranging from one to three. The gap could be inserted either in the read or in the reference sequence. SeqMap [21] indexes the reads and offers more flexibility in the alignment. It allows up to five mixed substitutions, deletions, and insertions. MAQ [28] indexes the reads, but it does not support gapped alignment for single-end reads. However, it is the first short-read alignment program that evaluates the reliability of mapping by assigning each individual alignment a quality score, which measures the probability that the true alignment is not the one found. In addition, it fully utilizes the mate-pair information of paired reads to correct wrong alignments, to add confidence to correct alignments, and to accurately map a read to repetitive sequences if its mate is confidently aligned.

The current second-generation short-read alignment programs make use of Burrows–Wheeler transform (BWT) [4] to create a permanent index of the reference sequence, which may be reused across alignment runs, and are able to achieve very good speed and memory efficiency. Bowtie [26] indexes the reference sequence using a scheme based on BWT and FM index. It uses the exact string-matching algorithm of Ferragina and Manzini [11] for searching in the FM index. It also introduces two extensions of the approximate string-matching problem allowing sequencing errors and genetic variations: a quality-aware backtracking algorithm that allows mismatches and favors high-quality alignments and *double indexing*, a strategy to avoid backtracking. It also follows a policy similar to MAQ's by allowing a small number of mismatches within the high-quality end of each read and places an upper limit on the sum of the quality scores at mismatched positions in the alignment. BWA [27], the successor of MAQ, uses backward search [11, 32] with BWT and is able to effectively mimic the top-down traversal on the prefix trie of the genome with a relatively small memory footprint [25] and to count the number of exact hits of a string in linear time regardless of the size of the genome. For inexact search, BWA samples from the implicit prefix trie the distinct substrings that are less than k edit distance from the query read. Because exact repeats are collapsed on one path on the prefix trie, it does not need to align the reads against each copy of the repeat. SOAP2 [30], a significantly improved version of SOAP, uses BWT compression to index the reference sequence instead of indexing the reference sequence in main memory. It determines an exact match by constructing a hash table to accelerate searching for the location of a read in the BWT reference index. For example, for a 13-mer on the hash, the reference index would be partitioned into 2^{26} blocks, and very few search interactions are sufficient to identify the exact location inside the block. For inexact alignment—mismatches, deletions, and insertions—the well-known strategy of *partitioning into exact matches* (cf. [39]) is applied.

This chapter presents new algorithmic methods for next-generation sequencing data. In particular, the focus of this chapter is on the application of resequencing. In Section 11.2, we present the basic definitions and notations that are used throughout the chapter. In Section 11.3, we present REad ALigner (REAL), an efficient, sensitive, and accurate short-read alignment program for mapping millions of short reads to a genome. In Section 11.4, we present cREAL, a simple extension of REAL, specifically designed for mapping millions of short reads to a genome with circular structure. In Section 11.5, we present DynMap, an efficient, sensitive, and accurate short-read alignment program for mapping millions of short reads to multiple closely related genomes. Finally, we briefly conclude in Section 11.6.

11.2 DEFINITIONS AND NOTATIONS

An *alphabet* Σ is a finite nonempty set whose elements are called *letters*. A *string* on an alphabet Σ is a finite, possibly empty, sequence of elements of Σ. The zero-letter sequence is called the *empty string*, and is denoted by ε. The set of all the strings on the alphabet Σ is denoted by Σ^*. The set of all the strings on the alphabet Σ except the empty string ε is denoted by Σ^+. A string x of length m is represented by $x[0, \ldots, m-1]$, where $x[i] \in \Sigma$ for $0 \leq i < m$. The length of a string x is denoted by $|x|$. A string x is a *factor* of a string y if there exist two strings u and v such that $y = uxv$. It is a *prefix* of x if u is empty and a *suffix* of x if v is empty. We use $C(x)$ to denote the *circular string* formed from string x by concatenating $x[0]$ at the right of $x[|x| - 1]$, thus turning x into a string that has neither a leftmost nor a rightmost position.

Let x be a nonempty string and y be a string. We say that there is an *occurrence* of x in y, or more simply that x *occurs* in y, when x is a factor of y. Every occurrence of x can be characterized by a position in y. Thus, we say that an occurrence of x *starts* at position i in y when $y[i, \ldots, i + |x| - 1] = x$.

The Hamming distance δ_H is defined only for strings of the same length. For two strings x and y, $\delta_H(x, y)$ is the number of positions in which the two strings differ. Let x be a nonempty string and y be a string. We say that x occurs in y with at most k mismatches if there exists a factor of y, say w, such that $\delta_H(x, w) \leq k$.

11.3 REAL: A READ ALIGNER FOR MAPPING SHORT READS TO A GENOME

In this section, we present REad ALigner (REAL), an efficient, sensitive, and accurate short-read alignment program, for mapping millions of short reads to a genome.

REAL adopts strategies that resemble the ones presented in [2] and [3] for exact and approximate string matching, respectively. It preprocesses the reference sequence first, based on the length of the reads, by using two-bits-per-base encoding of the DNA alphabet, word-level operations, and radix sort to create an index of the reference sequence in main memory. Then, it converts each read to a unique arithmetic value using two-bits-per-base encoding of the DNA alphabet, and the well-known strategy of *partitioning into exact matches* [39], binary search, and word-level operations are applied for the mapping.

We denote the produced short reads by the set $\{p_1, p_2, \ldots, p_r\}$, typically $r > 10^6$, and we call them *patterns*. The length m of each pattern, produced by Illumina's Solexa sequencer, is currently typically between 25 and 150 bp long. We denote the reference sequence of length n, typically $n > 10^6$, by t, and we call it *text*.

We formally define the problem of mapping millions of short reads to a reference sequence as follows.

Problem 11.1 *Mapping Short Reads*   Find whether the pattern $p_i = p_i[0, \ldots, m-1]$ for all $1 \leq i \leq r$, with $p_i \in \Sigma^+$, $\Sigma = \{A,C,G,T\}$, occurs, with at most k mismatches, in text $t = t[0, \ldots, n-1]$ with $t \in \Sigma^+$.

11.3.1 Algorithm

We make use of word-level operations to preprocess the text t by transforming each factor of length m of t into a *signature*. We get the signature $\sigma(x)$, where $\sigma : \Sigma^+ \rightarrow \mathbb{Z}^+$, of a

TABLE 11.1   Two-Bits-per-Base Encoding of DNA Alphabet $\Sigma = \{A,C,G,T\}$

Letter	Binary
A	00
C	01
G	10
T	11

nonempty string x by transforming x to a unique arithmetic value using two-bits-per-base encoding of the DNA alphabet $\Sigma = \{A,C,G,T\}$ (see Table 11.1).

Example 11.1   The signature $\sigma(x)$ of string $x = $ AGCAT is 0010010011.

We consider approximate string matching by the strategy of partitioning into exact matches. Let the nonempty string x be a pattern and the nonempty string y be the text. We want to find occurrences of x in y with at most k mismatches. Partitioning into exact matches works as follows.

We partition x into a set $\{x_0, \ldots, x_{q-1}\}$ of $q > k$ fragments such that $x_i \in \Sigma^+$ for all $0 \leq i < q$ and construct lists X_i containing the positions of occurrences of x_i. For each of the possibilities of choosing $q - k$ of the q fragments, we merge the respective lists of positions using the respective position offsets. This provides us with $\binom{q}{q-k}$ candidate position lists. The union X of these merged lists is a superset of the positions of occurrences of x in y with at most k mismatches. We obtain the list of occurrences of x in y by filtering X using an online algorithm for testing if the candidate positions designate occurrences with at most k mismatches.

Example 11.2   Consider searching for a pattern x in text y with at most one mismatch. We partition x into three fragments: x_0, x_1, and x_2. We have to consider three pairs of fragments: (x_0, x_1), (x_1, x_2), and (x_0, x_2). The first two combinations are easily found using an index for y; that is, we need only to search for the patterns $x_0 x_1$ and $x_1 x_2$. The third requires merging of lists in the conventional scheme.

Hence, we obtain the following auxiliary lemma.

Lemma 11.1   Given a set $\{x_0, \ldots, x_{q-1}\}$ of q fragments such that $x_i \in \Sigma^+$ for all $0 \leq i < q$ of a partitioned nonempty string x and the maximum number of allowed mismatches $k < q$, any of the k mismatches cannot exist, at the same time, in at least $q - k$ fragments of x.

Proof   Immediate from the pigeonhole principle, if n items are put into m pigeonholes, with $n > m$, then at least one pigeonhole must contain more than one item.   ∎

Without loss of generality, we require that

$$q - k = k \quad \text{and} \quad \left\lceil \frac{m \log |\Sigma|}{q - k} \right\rceil \leq w$$

where w is the size of the computer word. We partition $\sigma(x)$, viewed as binary, into a set $\{\sigma(x_0), \sigma(x_1), \ldots, \sigma(x_{q-1})\}$ of $q > k$ fragments, such that $\sigma(x_i) \in \mathbb{Z}^+$ for all $0 \leq i < q$.

We denote by $C_j(\sigma(x)) = \{\sigma(x_{a_0}), \sigma(x_{a_1}), \ldots, \sigma(x_{a_{q-k-1}})\}$, such that $a_0 < a_1 < \cdots < a_{q-k-1}$, the $\binom{q}{q-k}$ possible combinations of $q - k$ fragments of $\{\sigma(x_0), \sigma(x_1), \ldots, \sigma(x_{q-1})\}$ such that if

$$C_{j+1}(\sigma(x)) = \{\sigma(x_{b_0}), \sigma(x_{b_1}), \ldots, \sigma(x_{b_{q-k-1}})\}$$

then

$$\sum_{i=0}^{q-k-1} a_i \leq \sum_{i=0}^{q-k-1} b_i \quad \text{for all } 0 \leq j < \binom{q}{q-k} - 1$$

We denote by $D_j(\sigma(x)) = \{\sigma(x_{a_1}), \sigma(x_{a_1}), \ldots, \sigma(x_{a_{k-1}})\}$, such that $a_0 < a_1 < \cdots < a_{k-1}$, the $\binom{q}{q-k}$ possible combinations of the remaining k fragments of $\{\sigma(x_0), \sigma(x_1), \ldots, \sigma(x_{q-1})\}$ such that if

$$D_{j+1}(\sigma(x)) = \{\sigma(x_{b_0}), \sigma(x_{b_1}), \ldots, \sigma(x_{b_{k-1}})\}$$

then

$$\sum_{i=0}^{k-1} a_i \leq \sum_{i=0}^{k-1} b_i \quad \text{for all } 0 \leq j < \binom{q}{q-k} - 1$$

Example 11.3 Let the string $x = $ ACCGATCA, $q = 4$, and $k = 2$. If we partition $\sigma(x) = 0001011000110100$ into a set $\{0001, 0110, 0011, 0100\}$ of $q = 4$, then $C_0 = \{0001, 0110\}$, $D_0 = \{0001, 0110\}$, $C_1 = \{0001, 0011\}$, $D_1 = \{0001, 0011\}$, $C_2 = \{0001, 0100\}$, $D_2 = \{0001, 0100\}$, $C_3 = \{0110, 0011\}$, $D_3 = \{0110, 0011\}$, $C_4 = \{0110, 0100\}$, $D_4 = \{0110, 0100\}$, $C_5 = \{0011, 0100\}$, and $D_5 = \{0011, 0100\}$.

Our aim is to preprocess t and construct a set of lists X_j for all $0 \leq j < \binom{q}{q-k}$. Each X_j holds tuples $e^j = (u, s, \text{NF})$, where $e^j \cdot u$ represents the starting position of a factor x of t, $e^j \cdot s$ represents the concatenated signatures of the fragments in $C_j(\sigma(x))$, and $e^j \cdot \text{NF}$ is a pointer to tuple $e^l = (u, s, \text{NF})$ in X_l, where $e^l \cdot s$ represent the remaining concatenated signatures of the fragments in $D_l(\sigma(x))$.

We define the following operations:

- $f(q, k, j)$: an operation that, given integers q, k, and j, returns an integer l such that if

$$C_j(\sigma(x)) = \{\sigma(x_{a_0}), \sigma(x_{a_1}), \ldots, \sigma(x_{a_{q-k-1}})\}$$

and

$$D_l(\sigma(x)) = \{\sigma(x_{b_0}), \sigma(x_{b_1}), \ldots, \sigma(x_{b_{k-1}})\}$$

then

$$C_j(\sigma(x)) \cup D_l(\sigma(x)) = \{\sigma(x_0), \sigma(x_1), \ldots, \sigma(x_{q-1})\}$$

for some partitioned signature $\sigma(x)$, viewed as binary, of a string x.

- $\text{conc}(C)$: an operation that, given a set $C = \{\sigma(x_0), \sigma(x_1), \ldots, \sigma(x_{q-1})\}$ of q fragments, such that $\sigma(x_i) \in \mathbb{Z}^+$ for all $0 \leq i < q$ of a partitioned signature $\sigma(x)$ viewed as binary of a string x returns $\sigma(x)$.

- bs(X, $\sigma(x)$): a binary-search operation that, given a sorted list X of tuples and a signature $\sigma(x)$ of a string x as the key, returns a set $\{e_{a_0}, e_{a_1}, \ldots, e_{a_{v-1}}\}$ of tuples from X such that $e_{a_i} \cdot s = \sigma(x)$ for all $0 \le i < v$.
- bitop($\sigma(x)$, $\sigma(y)$): a word-level operation that, given two signatures $\sigma(x)$ and $\sigma(y)$ of two strings x and y, respectively such that $|x| = |y|$ and $\lceil \log |\Sigma| \rceil |x| \le w$, returns $\delta_H(x, y)$ in constant time.

Example 11.4 Let the string $x = $ ACCGATCA, $q = 4$, $k = 2$, and $j = 0$. Then $f(q, k, j) = 5$ since, given the set $\{0001, 0110, 0011, 0100\}$ of $q = 4$ fragments of $\sigma(x) = 0001011000110100$ and $C_0 = \{0001, 0110\}$ and $D_5 = \{0011, 0100\}$, it holds that

$$C_0 \cup D_5 = \{0001, 0110, 0011, 0100\}$$

Example 11.5 Let the string $x = $ ACCGATCA, $q = 4$, and $k = 2$. Then $C_0 = \{0001, 0110\}$ and conc(C_0) $= 00010110$.

Example 11.6 Let $q = 4$, $k = 2$, $|\Sigma| = 4$, and $w = 64$. Then

$$m \le \frac{w(q - k)}{\log |\Sigma|} = 64$$

An outline of the proposed algorithm for solving Problem 11.1 follows.

(i) *Creating Lists* We partition t into a set $\{t_0, t_1, \ldots, t_{n-m}\}$ of factors by using the sliding-window mechanism such that $t_i = t[i, \ldots, i + m - 1]$ for all $0 \le i \le n - m$ and compute $\sigma(t_i)$. Then we compute $C_j(\sigma(t_i))$, $l = f(q, k, j)$, and $D_l(\sigma(t_i))$ for all $0 \le j < \binom{q}{q-k}/2$ and add the tuples $e^j = (i, \text{conc}(C_j(\sigma(t_i))), \text{NF})$ and $e^l = (i, \text{conc}(D_l(\sigma(t_i))), \text{NF})$ to the lists X_j and X_l, respectively. As a result, we construct a set of $\binom{q}{q-k}$ lists (see Figure 11.1).

(ii) *Sorting Lists* We use radix sort to sort X_j for all $0 \le j < \binom{q}{q-k}$ by the element s—the signature—of the tuples in X_j, ensuring that, in the case that we swap tuples, we preserve that $e^j \cdot \text{NF}$ still points to e^l, and $e^l \cdot \text{NF}$ still points to e^j (see Figure 11.2).

(iii) *Mapping* Assume that we have a query pattern p of length m. We compute $\sigma(p)$, $C_j(\sigma(p))$, $l = f(q, k, j)$, and $D_l(\sigma(p))$ for all $0 \le j < \binom{q}{q-k}$. Then we perform the binary-search operation bs(X_j, conc($C_j(\sigma(p))$)), which returns a set of tuples $\{e^j_{a_0}, e^j_{a_1}, \ldots, e^j_{a_{v-1}}\}$.

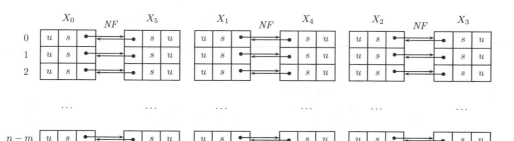

FIGURE 11.1 List X_j for all $0 \le j < \binom{q}{q-k}$ for $q = 4$ and $k = 2$ after step (i).

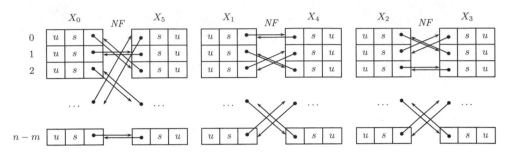

FIGURE 11.2 List X_j for all $0 \leq j < \binom{q}{q-k}$ for $q = 4$ and $k = 2$ after step (ii).

If there exists $e^l_{a_i}$—notice that $e^j_{a_i} \cdot NF$ points to $e^l_{a_i}$—for some $0 \leq i < v$, such that $\text{bitop}(\text{conc}(D_l(\sigma(p))), e^l_{a_i} \cdot s) \leq k$, then p occurs in t with at most k mismatches.

In practice, for long patterns (e.g., $m > 48$) it is not sufficient to choose $q = 4$ and $k = 2$. In the case that

$$\left\lceil \frac{m \log |\Sigma|}{q - k} \right\rceil > w$$

$k > 2$ is usually required. We apply the strategy of *seed and extend*, that is, we apply step (i), with $q = 4$ and $k' = 2$, only for a prefix $m' < m$, which we call *seed*, such that

$$\left\lceil \frac{m' \log |\Sigma|}{q - k'} \right\rceil \leq w$$

In step (iii), as soon as a match is located, with at most k' mismatches, it is extended to the right to complete the alignment. Hence we allow at most k' mismatches in the seed of length m' and the rest in the suffix of length $m - m'$ of the pattern.

Complexities By using the sliding-window mechanism, we read $t[0, \ldots, n - 1]$ from left to right, computing the signature $\sigma(t_i)$ of each factor of length m of t, $t_i = t[i, \ldots, i + m - 1]$, for all $0 \leq i \leq n - m$ and adding the tuples to the list X_j for all $0 \leq j < \binom{q}{q-k}$ in time $\Theta\left(\binom{q}{q-k}\right)$. As soon as we compute $\sigma(t_0)$, then each $\sigma(t_i)$ for all $1 \leq i \leq n - m$ can be retrieved in constant time using word-level operations, resulting in a total of $\Theta\left(\binom{q}{q-k}n\right)$ for step (i).

In step (ii), the time required for sorting the list X_j for all $0 \leq j < \binom{q}{q-k}$ using radix sort is $\Theta\left(\binom{q}{q-k}n\right)$. Maintaining the pointers of the tuples is of no extra cost.

According to Lemma 11.1, step (iii) runs in time $\mathcal{O}\left(rv\binom{q}{q-k} \log n\right)$, where r is the number of the patterns and v is the maximum number of factors of length m of t which contain fragments that are exactly matched with the corresponding fragments of a given pattern. The $\binom{q}{q-k} \log n$ factor is for the binary-search operation on list X_j for all $0 \leq j < \binom{q}{q-k}$.

Hence, overall, the proposed algorithm requires time $\mathcal{O}\left(\binom{q}{q-k}(n + rv \log n)\right)$, which is $\mathcal{O}\left(\binom{q}{q-k}(n + r \log n)\right)$, in practice, since $v \ll n$.

The list X_j for all $0 \leq j < \binom{q}{q-k}$ consists of exactly $n - m + 1$ tuples. Hence the space required is $\Theta\left(\binom{q}{q-k}n\right)$ for keeping the lists in memory.

11.3.2 Experimental Results

REAL was implemented in the C_{++} programming language and was developed under the GNU/Linux operating system. The program is implemented in such a way that it does not necessarily load the whole reference sequence in main memory. Instead, it loads blocks of the reference sequence depending on the size of the physical memory of the individual machine. Concerning the storage used for indexing, no additional hard disk space is necessary, as the program does not store the index of the reference sequence. The program takes as input arguments a file with the reference sequence in FASTA format, and a file with the short reads either in FASTA or in FASTQ format, and then produces a tab-delimited text file with the hits as output.

Successful alignments are scored using log odds scores (cf. [12]) based on the frequencies with which the occurring mismatches are actually observed in nature (cf. [48]). The score matrix is computed at the start-up of the program based on the sequence similarity level, the composition bias of the sequences, the mutation-type bias (transitions vs. transversions), and the difference in G's and C's ability to mutate compared to A's and T's. The log-odds scores are defined as $S_{ij} = \log(P_{ij}/P_i P_j)$, where P_{ij} is the target/observed frequency of base i becoming base j and is calculated from the given mutation biases. The denominator $P_i P_j$ is the probability of the event occurring by chance based on the background frequencies of the two bases involved and depends on the given base composition of the sequence. The log-odds scores are combined with base quality scores as proposed by [17].

The experiments were conducted on a desktop PC using a single core of a 2.40-GHz Intel Xeon E7340 CPU and 8 GB of main memory running the GNU/Linux operating system. REAL is distributed under the GNU General Public License (GPL). The implementation is available at a website [43] that maintains the source code and the documentation.

To evaluate the performance of REAL, we compared its performance to the respective performance of SOAP2 (v2.20) and Bowtie (v0.2.17), which are, up to date, two of the most popular short-read alignment programs. In each case, effort was made to make the programs run in as much a similar way as possible, so that the efficiency, sensitivity, and accuracy comparisons are fair. Thus, SOAP2 and Bowtie were always given the modifier $-l$ <INT> to adjust the length of the seed to be equal to the one of REAL. The programs were set to report only the best—nonrepetitive—hits; otherwise the reported hits of SOAP2 would be chosen at random between equal hits. In SOAP2, this was achieved with the use of $-M$ 4 $-r$ 0 modifiers and in Bowtie with the use of $-best$. Furthermore, since Bowtie makes use of the corresponding quality scores of the reads in FASTQ format while SOAP2 does not, two versions of REAL were used; one with the modifier $-q$ 0, to ignore the quality scores, and one with $-q$ 1, to make use of the quality scores.

As a reference, we used the human chromosome 6 (166,880,988 bp), *Homo sapiens* (human), Build 37.2, obtained from the NCBI [38]. The short reads were obtained by simulating 25,000,000 64-bp-long single-end reads from the same sequence. As it is demonstrated by the results in Table 11.2, REAL was able to complete the assignment much faster than SOAP2 and Bowtie. REAL $-q$ 0 finished in 26 min 43 s, SOAP2 in 33 min 35 s, REAL $-q$ 1 in 31 min 54 s, and Bowtie in 56 min 46 s. In terms of sensitivity, with this data

TABLE 11.2   Mapping 25,000,000 64-bp-Long Simulated Reads to Human Chromosome 6 (166,880,988 bp)

| Program | Total Time | | Reads Aligned |
	Indexing	Mapping	
SOAP2	5 min 10 s	28 min 25 s	22,699,605
REAL -q 0	0 min 00 s	26 min 43 s	22,509,708
Bowtie	7 min 35 s	49 min 11 s	21,594,916
REAL -q 1	0 min 00 s	31 min 54 s	22,519,739

Note: All programs were run with 48-bp-long seed with at most two mismatches in the seed and reported best hits only.

TABLE 11.3   Mapping 24,543,488 70-bp-Long Simulated Reads to *Drosophila melanogaster* Chromosome 3L (24,543,557 bp)

| Program | Total Time | | Reads Aligned | Accuracy(%) |
	Indexing	Mapping		
SOAP2	0 min 45 s	16 min 02 s	21,126,303	99.98
REAL -q 0	0 min 00 s	10 min 44 s	21,134,692	99.98
Bowtie	0 min 59 s	40 min 28 s	18,920,716	96.09
REAL -q 1	0 min 00 s	15 min 42 s	21,134,699	99.98

Note: All programs were run with 48-bp-long seed with at most two mismatches in the seed and reported the best hits only.

set, SOAP2 and REAL were more sensitive than Bowtie, with SOAP2 being slightly more sensitive than REAL.

As a further experiment, we compared the performance of REAL to the respective performance of SOAP2 and Bowtie for mapping 24,543,488 70-bp-long simulated single-end reads to the *Drosophila melanogaster* chromosome 3L (24,543,557 bp), Release 5.30, obtained from the NCBI. As it is demonstrated by the results in Table 11.3, REAL was able to complete the assignment much faster than SOAP2 and Bowtie. REAL -q 0 finished in 10 min 44 s, SOAP2 in 16 min 47 s, REAL -q 1 in 15 min 42 s, and Bowtie in 41 min 27 s. In terms of sensitivity, with this data set, SOAP2 and REAL were more sensitive than Bowtie, with REAL being slightly more sensitive than SOAP2. Due to the fact that the reads were simulated, and thus we were able to know the exact locations they were derived from, we also measured the accuracy of each program by checking whether the reads were mapped back to the exact same locations. As it is demonstrated by the results in Table 11.4, with this data set, REAL and SOAP2 had an accuracy of 99,98%, while Bowtie had an accuracy of 96,09%.

As a further experiment, we compared the performance of REAL to the respective performance of SOAP2 and Bowtie for mapping 24,163,065 76-bp-long real single-end reads[*] to the human genome, *H. sapiens* (human), Build 37.2, obtained from the NCBI. As it is demonstrated by the results in Table 11.4, SOAP2 was able to complete the assignment slightly faster than REAL, while Bowtie was much slower. SOAP2 finished in 3 h 50 min

---

[*]Data produced by the Exome Sequencing Programme at the NIHR Biomedical Research Centre at Guy's and St. Thomas' NHS Foundation Trust in partnership with King's College London.

TABLE 11.4   Mapping 24,163,065 76-bp-long Real Reads to the Human Genome

| Program | Total Time | | Reads Aligned |
	Indexing	Mapping	
SOAP2	1 h 58 min 07 s	1 h 52 min 21 s	12,664,760
REAL -q 0	0 min 00 s	4 h 08 min 47 s	11,813,271
Bowtie	3 h 29 min 59 s	1 h 56 min 41 s	10,789,260
REAL -q 1	0 min 00 s	4 h 20 min 37 s	11,738,732

Note: All Programs were run with 48-bp-long seed with at most two mismatches in the seed and reported the best hits only.

TABLE 11.5   Mapping 31,116,663 25-bp-Long and 3,619,970 35-bp-Long Real Reads to Mouse Genome

Program	Reads Aligned (25-bp Long)	Reads Aligned (35 bp Long)
SOAP2	11,326,042	1,766,474
REAL -q 0	14,219,094	1,732,507

Note: Both programs were run with 25-bp-long seed for the 25-bp-long reads and 32-bp-long seed for the 35-bp-long reads with at most two mismatches in the seed and reported the best hits only.

28 s, REAL -q 0 in 4 h 08 min 47 s, REAL -q 1 in 4 h 20 min 37 s, and Bowtie in 5 h 26 min 40 s. In terms of sensitivity, with this data set, SOAP2 is more sensitive than REAL, while Bowtie is significantly less sensitive. However, in this case, we were not able to measure the accuracy of each program, due to the fact that we are not aware of the locations from which the reads were derived.

It is a known fact that SOAP2 has technical difficulties to handle reads of length less than 35 bp, resulting in poor accuracy [27] and poor sensitivity [13]. In order to verify this, we mapped 31,116,663 25-bp-long real single-end reads obtained from RNA-Seq experiments [36] and 3,619,970 35-bp-long real single-end reads obtained from RNA-Seq experiments [20] back to the mouse genome, *Mus musculus* (laboratory mouse), Build 37.2, obtained from NCBI. From the results demonstrated in Table 11.5, it becomes evident that SOAP2 does not perform well in terms of sensitivity with reads of length less than 35 bp. However, since the data processed is real, we believe that current short-read alignment programs should be able to handle it, regardless of the fact that the length of the reads, produced by the next-generation sequencers, tends to increase rather than decrease.

11.4   CREAL: MAPPING SHORT READS TO A GENOME WITH CIRCULAR STRUCTURE

Unlike the linear DNA of vertebrates, strain or species of bacteria with circular organization of their chromosomes or plasmids are the most common. Until the end of the 1980s, when the technology for examining chromosomes and plasmids improved, all bacteria were thought to have a single circular chromosome [6]. In fact, not all bacteria have a single circular chromosome; some bacteria have multiple circular chromosomes [53–56], and many bacteria have linear chromosomes and linear plasmids [58]. Bacterial genomes range in size from about 160,000 to 12,200,000 bp, depending on the type considered [37].

In this section, as most of the bacterial chromosomes contain a circular DNA macro-molecule, we present cREAL, a simple extension of REAL (see Section 11.3), specifically designed for mapping millions of short reads to a genome with circular structure. In particular, we define this problem as a *circular pattern-matching* (CPM) problem, reduce it to a classical pattern-matching problem, and make use of REAL to efficiently map the reads to the reference sequence.

We denote the produced short reads by the set $\{p_1, p_2, \ldots, p_r\}$, typically $r > 10^6$, and we call them *patterns*. The length m of each pattern, produced by Illumina's Solexa sequencer, is currently typically between 25 and 150 bp long. We denote the circular reference sequence of length n, typically $n > 10^6$, by $C(t)$, and we call it *circular text*.

We formally define the problem of mapping millions of short reads to a circular reference sequence, as follows.

Problem 11.2 *Circular Mapping* Find whether the pattern $p_i = p_i[0, \ldots, m-1]$ for all $1 \le i \le r$ with $p_i \in \Sigma^+$, $\Sigma = \{A,C,G,T\}$, occurs, with at most k mismatches in the circular text $C(t)$ of length n with $C(t) \in \Sigma^+$.

11.4.1 Algorithm

An outline of the proposed algorithm for solving Problem 11.2 follows.

(i) *Linearizing Circular Text* The idea is to first find a way to convert the circular text $C(t)$ to a text t' that is equivalent to the circular one, thereby reducing the problem to a classical pattern-matching problem, where we need to find all the occurrences of a given pattern p in text t' with at most k mismatches.

This is accomplished by first splitting $C(t)$ at an arbitrary point along the string. The outcome of this process is a string $t = t[0, \ldots, n-1]$ with two extremities: the leftmost position, which is the start of the string, and the rightmost position, which is the end of the string. The resulting string t is still not equivalent to the original string, since there is a possibility of some of the patterns occurring at the point where $C(t)$ was split. To make string t equivalent to the circular text $C(t)$, we append the prefix of length $m-1$ of t, that is, $t[0, \ldots, m-2]$, as a suffix, resulting in a new string $t' = t[0, \ldots, n]t[0, \ldots, m-2]$, which is equivalent to $C(t)$. We have now reduced the problem to finding whether pattern p_i for all $1 \le i \le r$ occurs in $t' = t'[0, \ldots, n+m-2]$ with at most k mismatches.

Example 11.7 The circular text $C(t)$, shown in Figure 11.3, illustrates this process; the string produced by splitting $C(t)$ at the point the arrow head touches the oval arrow is $t = \text{TGCACATGGTGCGTACCTTG}$. Suppose we have a pattern $p = \text{TGTGC}$. Then, we have an occurrence of p in $C(t)$, but we do not have an occurrence of p in linearized string t due to the pattern occurring across the split. A linearized string covering all possible factors across the split for patterns of length $m = 5$ can be obtained by copying the first $m-1$ letters, that is, $t[0, \ldots, 3] = \text{TGCA}$, and appending them to t. The outcome of this procedure is a string $t' = \text{TGCACATGGTGCGTACCTTGTGCA}$, which covers every possible match position around $C(t)$.

(ii) *Mapping* Make use of REAL (see Section 11.3) to search for the patterns in t'.

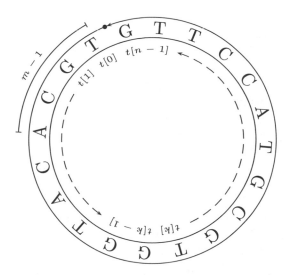

FIGURE 11.3 Circular text $C(t)$. The point where the arrow head touches the oval arrow is where the string is split. To search for a pattern p of length m in this circular text, the first $m - 1$ letters of the string are taken from the point of the split starting at $t[0]$ and added to the end $t[n - 1]$.

Complexities Step (i) can be done in time $\Theta(m)$. Step (ii) can be done in time $\mathcal{O}\big(\binom{q}{q-k}(n + r \log n)\big)$ (see Section 11.3).

Hence, overall, the proposed algorithm requires time $\mathcal{O}\big(\binom{q}{q-k}(n + r \log n)\big)$.

The space required is $\Theta\big(\binom{q}{q-k}n\big)$.

11.4.2 Experimental Results

cREAL, the simple extension of REAL, was implemented in the Perl programming language and was developed under the GNU/Linux operating system.

The experiments were conducted on a desktop PC using a single core of a 2.40-GHz Intel Xeon E7340 CPU and 8 GB of main memory running the GNU/Linux operating system. REAL is distributed under the GNU GPL. The implementation is available at a website [43], which is set up for maintaining the source code and the documentation.

To evaluate the performance of cREAL, we compared its performance to the respective performance of SOAP2 (v2.20) and Bowtie (v0.2.17), which are, to date, two of the most popular short-read alignment programs. In each case, effort was made to make the programs run in as similar a way as possible so that the efficiency, sensitivity, and accuracy comparisons are fair. Thus, SOAP2 and Bowtie were always given the modifier -l <INT>, to adjust the length of the seed to be equal to the one of REAL. The programs were set to report only best—nonrepetitive—hits; otherwise the reported hits of SOAP2 would be chosen at random between equal hits. In SOAP2, this was achieved with the use of -M 4 -r 0 modifiers and in Bowtie with the use of -best. Furthermore, since Bowtie makes use of the corresponding quality scores of the reads in FASTQ format, while SOAP2 does not, two versions of REAL were used: one with the modifier -q 0, to ignore the quality scores, and one with -q 1, to make use of the quality scores.

TABLE 11.6 Mapping 9,105,777 52-bp-Long Simulated Reads to
Bradyrhizobium japonicum **Genome**

| Program | Total Time | | Reads Aligned | Accuracy(%) |
	Indexing	Mapping		
SOAP2	0 min 22 s	3 min 51 s	8,746,116	99.99
cREAL -q 0	0 min 00 s	4 min 26 s	8,747,172	99.99
Bowtie	0 min 16 s	9 min 00 s	8,248,842	98.78
cREAL -q 1	0 min 00 s	5 min 16 s	8,747,233	99.99

Note: All programs were run with 32-bp-long seed with at most two mismatches in the seed and reported best hits only.

As a reference, we used the single circular chromosome of *Bradyrhizobium japonicum* (9,105,828 bp), obtained from [23]. The short reads were obtained by simulating 9,105,777 52-bp-long single-end reads from the same sequence. As it is demonstrated by the results in Table 11.6, cREAL and SOAP2 were able to complete the assignment much faster than Bowtie. SOAP2 finished in 4 min 13 s, cREAL -q 0 finished in 4 min 26 s, cREAL -q 0 finished in 5 min 16 s, while Bowtie finished in 9 min 16 s. In terms of sensitivity, with this data set, cREAL was slightly more sensitive than SOAP2 and Bowtie. Due to the fact that the reads are simulated, and thus we are able to know the exact locations they were derived from, we measured the accuracy of each program, by checking whether the reads were mapped back to the exact same locations. As it is demonstrated by the results in Table 11.6, with this data set, cREAL and SOAP2 had an accuracy of 99,99%, while Bowtie had an accuracy of 98,78%.

Similar results were obtained in Tables 11.7–11.9; in Table 11.7, for mapping 3,294,805 64-bp-long simulated single-end reads to the *Brucella melitensis 16M* genome, obtained from [19], which consists of two circular chromosomes (2,124,241 bp and 1,162,204 bp); in Table 11.8, for mapping 6,264,333 72-bp-long simulated single-end reads to the single circular chromosome of *Pseudomonas aeruginosa PAO1* (6,264,403 bp), obtained from [52]; and in Table 11.9, for mapping 2,475,055 6-bp-long simulated single-end reads to the single circular chromosome of *Xylella fastidiosa M12* (2,475,130 bp), obtained from [5].

As a last experiment, we compared the performance of cREAL to the respective performance of SOAP2 and Bowtie for mapping 5,288,154 36-bp-long real single-end reads obtained from the European Nucleotide Archive [10] to the single circular chromosome of *Escherichia coli* str. K-12 substr. MG1655 obtained from GenBank [14]. By the results in

TABLE 11.7 Mapping 3,294,805 64-bp-Long Simulated Reads to
Brucella melitensis **16M Genome**

| Program | Total Time | | Reads Aligned | Accuracy(%) |
	Indexing	Mapping		
SOAP2	0 min 17 s	1 min 26 s	3,214,557	99.99
cREAL -q 0	0 min 00 s	2 min 10 s	3,214,472	99.99
Bowtie	0 min 05 s	2 min 56 s	2,962,644	99.26
cREAL -q 1	0 min 00 s	2 min 31 s	3,214,485	99.99

Note: All programs were run with 32-bp-long seed with at most two mismatches in the seed and reported best hits only.

TABLE 11.8   Mapping 6,264,333 72-bp-Long Simulated Reads to
Pseudomonas aeruginosa **PAO1 Genome**

Program	Total Time		Reads Aligned	Accuracy(%)
	Indexing	Mapping		
SOAP2	0 min 19 s	3 min 36 s	6,035,526	99.99
cREAL -q 0	0 min 00 s	3 min 17 s	6,037,765	99.99
Bowtie	0 min 10 s	7 min 46 s	4,896,047	99.24
cREAL -q 1	0 min 00 s	4 min 17 s	6,037,765	99.99

Note: All programs were run with 32-bp-long seed with at most two mismatches in the seed and reported best hits only.

TABLE 11.9   Mapping 2,475,055 76-bp-Long Simulated Reads to
Xylella fastidiosa **M12 Genome**

Program	Total Time		Reads Aligned	Accuracy(%)
	Indexing	Mapping		
SOAP2	0 min 15 s	1 min 14 s	2,255,798	99.99
cREAL -q 0	0 min 00 s	1 min 13 s	2,257,124	99.99
Bowtie	0 min 04 s	2 min 45 s	1,918,988	96.53
cREAL -q 1	0 min 00 s	1 min 50 s	2,257,117	99.99

Note: All programs were run with 32-bp long seed with at most two mismatches in the seed and reported best hits only.

TABLE 11.10   Mapping 5,288,154 36-bp-Long Real Reads to
Escherichia coli **Chromosome**

Program	Total Time		Reads Aligned
	Indexing	Mapping	
SOAP2	0 min 18 s	2 min 14 s	3,532,761
cREAL -q 0	0 min 00 s	2 min 30 s	3,255,228
Bowtie	0 min 07 s	6 min 20 s	3,646,029
cREAL -q 1	0 min 00 s	2 min 48 s	3,255,266

Note: All programs were run with 32-bp-long seed with at most two mismatches in the seed and reported best hits only.

Table 11.10, no difference is observed regarding the efficiency, while, with this data set, Bowtie is slightly more sensitive than cREAL and SOAP2. However, in this case, we were not able to measure the accuracy of each program, due to the fact that we are not aware of the locations from which the reads were derived.

11.5 DYNMAP: MAPPING SHORT READS TO MULTIPLE CLOSELY RELATED GENOMES

Many algorithms and programs have been published recently to deal with the task of efficiently mapping millions of short reads to a reference sequence, namely Bowtie [26],

BWA [27], SOAP2 [30], and REAL [13]. However, none of these address the inherent genomic variability between individuals, opting instead to simply treat it as mismatches and punish the presence of differences accordingly. But, most importantly, since the reads are quite short, even few changes in the reference sequence, as part of the natural diversity, can cause a read to seemingly best match with a different location of the reference than the one it actually corresponds to, while other reads will fail to be mapped entirely. Misaligned reads, in turn, lead to false identification of novel variation.

For instance, the high level of individual differences in natural inbred strains of *Arabidopsis* creates a substantial challenge [47]. It has been observed that parts of the reference sequence are either missing or very divergent in other strains of this species. Hence the simple short-read alignment, especially by algorithms that do not accommodate many mismatches and gaps, will not cover the case of this inaccessible region.

In addition, incorporating known polymorphisms [59] increases the genome space against which the reads are aligned, further improving the mapping results. Moreover, the incorporation of missing or inserted bases in the reference would reduce sequencing costs as more reads would be placed on the genome [47]. Finally, the simple short-read alignment against a single reference biases the analysis toward a comparison within the sequence space, which is highly conserved with the reference. On the other hand, taking into consideration inherent genomic variability would reduce this bias.

Very few programs have been published to also take into account this natural variability. GenomeMapper [47] and GSNAP [59] address the issue by accepting a list of known variations and including them in their indexes. GenomeMapper uses an index with a graph structure which consists of the reference sequence of one of the genomes and a list of differences in the other genomes compared to the first one to do the mapping. GSNAP implements the ability to align reads not just against a single reference sequence but also to a reference "space" of all possible combinations of major and minor alleles from databases like dbSNP [8].

In this section, we introduce a new approach to this problem. Accepting that the mutation rate between two random individuals is limited, for example, 0.1%, on average, for humans [22], we present DynMap, an efficient, sensitive, and accurate short-read alignment program for mapping millions of short reads to multiple closely related genomes.

In particular, the proposed algorithm makes provision to accommodate dynamical changes that may occur in the reference sequence. With the increasing knowledge of variants, one could simply align against all known genomes for a species separately. This would come with the overhead of redundant alignments in conserved regions. Therefore, if a small number of differences occur within the reference sequence, it is more appropriate to alter the already mapped reads to the reference dynamically. In order to represent the new changes, instead of starting to align the reads against a new closely related sequence again from scratch, we propose a faster approach which encompasses a suitable data structure that will allow this flexibility and dynamic effects. Thus the proposed algorithm can take as input a single reference sequence and lists of differences in other sequences compared to the first one and produce a separate file with the hits, one for each related sequence, as output.

We denote the produced short reads by the set $\{p_1, p_2, \ldots, p_r\}$, typically $r > 10^6$, and we call them *patterns*. The length m of each pattern, produced by Illumina's Solexa sequencer, is currently typically between 25 and 150 bp long. We denote the reference sequence of length n, typically $n > 10^6$, by t, and we call it *text*.

We also denote the array of differences of size h by H, where $0 < h \ll n$, similarly as in [47]. Array H holds tuple (o, p, c) in $H[i]$ for all $0 \leq i < h$, where $H[i] \cdot o$ represents the

	0	1	2	3	4	5	6	7	8	9	10	11	$H{\cdot}o$	$H{\cdot}p$	$H{\cdot}c$	P
t	G	C	A	G	T	A	C	A	G	T	A		-1	4		-1
	G	C	A	G	A	C	A	G	T	A			1	7	T	0
	G	C	A	G	A	C	T	A	G	T	A		1	7	C	1
	G	C	A	G	A	C	C	T	A	G	T	A	-1	8		0
$\hat{t}$	G	C	A	G	A	C	C	T	A	T	A					

FIGURE 11.4 Array of differences H and array of prefix sums P.

edit operation (0 for substitution, -1 for deletion, 1 for insertion) applied at position $H[i] \cdot p$ in t. In the case of substitution or insertion, $H[i] \cdot c$ represents the new letter. The array is constructed in such a way that it is already sorted by $H[i] \cdot p$, that is, $H[i] \cdot p \leq H[i+1] \cdot p$ for all $0 \leq i < h - 1$. As an example of array H, see Figure 11.4. Notice that H describes how text t can evolve into a new text $\hat{t}$. In the case that $t = t[0, \ldots, n-1]$, $\hat{t}$, and threshold h are given instead, such that $\delta_E(t, \hat{t}) \leq h$, array H can be computed in $\Theta(hn)$ time and space [18].

We formally define the problem of mapping millions of short reads to a dynamically changing reference sequence, as follows.

Problem 11.3 *Dynamic Mapping*   Find whether the pattern $p_i = p_i[0, \ldots, m-1]$ for all $1 \leq i \leq r$ with $p_i \in \Sigma^+$, $\Sigma = \{A,C,G,T\}$, occurs, with at most k mismatches in text $t = t[1, \ldots, n]$ and/or in text $\hat{t}$ with $t, \hat{t} \in \Sigma^+$ given the array of differences $H[0, \ldots, h-1]$.

11.5.1 Algorithm

The focus of this section is to describe a suitable data structure that will allow us to dynamically alter the already mapped patterns of a text. Thus, if we have a text t and a non exact copy of t, say $\hat{t}$, then we want to change the already mapped patterns of t to reflect the ones that are present in $\hat{t}$. Therefore, if the patterns have already been mapped to t, we want to avoid the mapping to $\hat{t}$ from scratch, but rather alter the already mapped patterns of t.

We make use of word-level operations to preprocess the text t by transforming factors (k-mers) of t into *signatures*. We get the signature $\sigma(x)$, where $\sigma : \Sigma^+ \to \mathbb{Z}^+$, of a non empty string x by transforming x to a unique arithmetic value, using two-bits-per-base encoding of the DNA alphabet $\Sigma = \{A,C,G,T\}$ (see Table 11.1 in this regard). We consider approximate string-matching by the strategy of *partitioning into exact matches* (see Section 11.3 for details).

An outline of the proposed algorithm for solving Problem 11.3 follows.

(i) *Creating Lists* We partition t into a set $\{t_0, t_1, \ldots, t_{n-m}\}$ of factors by using the sliding-window mechanism such that $t_i = t[i, \ldots, i+m-1]$ for all $0 \leq i \leq n - m$, and, without loss of generality, we split each factor into $q > k$ equal fragments $t_i^j = t[i + jm/q, \ldots, i + (j+1)m/q - 1]$ of length m/q for all $0 \leq j < q$. We build an array X of singly linked lists $X[s]$ for all $0 \leq s < 2^{\log |\Sigma| m/q}$. We compute the signature $\sigma(t_i^j)$ of each fragment and insert the tuple $e = (u, s, \text{PF}, \text{NF}, P)$ in $X[s]$, where $e \cdot u$ represents the starting position of t_i^j in t, $e \cdot s$ represents the signature of t_i^j, $e \cdot \text{PF}$ and $e \cdot \text{NF}$ point to the previous and to the next nonoverlapping fragment of t_i^j, respectively, and $e \cdot P$ is the list of patterns

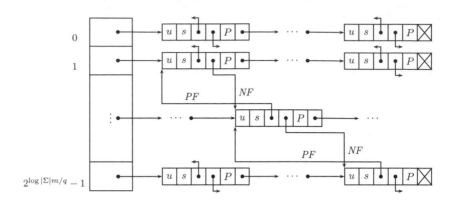

FIGURE 11.5 List $X[s]$ for all $0 \le s < 2^{\log |\Sigma| m/q}$ after step (i).

which are mapped to $t[u - (q-1)m/q, \dots, u - (q-1)m/q + m - 1]$ (see Figure 11.5). Thus it is not difficult to see that the tuples $(u, s, \text{PF}, \text{NF}, P)$ of $X[s]$ are sorted by u for all $0 \le s < 2^{\log |\Sigma| m/q}$ since we process the text from left to right.

(ii) *Mapping* Assume that we have a query pattern p of length m. We partition p into q equal fragments $p^j = t[jm/q, \dots, (j+1)m/q - 1]$ of length m/q for all $0 \le j < q$ and compute the signature $\sigma(p^j)$ of p^j. Let $\text{bitop}(\sigma(x), \sigma(y))$ be a word-level operation that, given two signatures $\sigma(x)$ and $\sigma(y)$ of two strings x and y, respectively, such that $|x| = |y|$ and $\lceil \log |\Sigma| \rceil |x| \le w$, returns $\delta_H(x, y)$ in constant time. For simplicity, consider the case when choosing $q = 3$ and $k = 2$. By Lemma 11.1, we can match at least one fragment exactly, and so the following hold:

- For each $e = (u, \sigma(p^0), \text{PF}, \text{NF}, P)$ in $X[\sigma(p^0)]$, if

$$\text{bitop}(e \cdot \text{NF} \cdot s, \sigma(p^1)) + \text{bitop}(e \cdot \text{NF} \cdot \text{NF} \cdot s, \sigma(p^2)) \le k$$

  then p occurs in t with at most k mismatches and it is added to $e \cdot \text{NF} \cdot \text{NF} \cdot P$.
- For each $e = (u, \sigma(p^1), \text{PF}, \text{NF}, P)$ in $X[\sigma(p^1)]$, if

$$\text{bitop}(e \cdot \text{PF} \cdot s, \sigma(p^0)) + \text{bitop}(e \cdot \text{NF} \cdot s, \sigma(p^2)) \le k$$

  then p occurs in t with at most k mismatches and it is added to $e \cdot \text{NF} \cdot P$.
- For each $e = (u, \sigma(p^2), \text{PF}, \text{NF}, P)$ in $X[\sigma(p^2)]$, if

$$\text{bitop}(e \cdot \text{PF} \cdot \text{PF} \cdot s, \sigma(p^0)) + \text{bitop}(e \cdot \text{PF} \cdot s, \sigma(p^1)) \le k$$

  then p occurs in t with at most k mismatches and it is added to $e \cdot P$.

If p does not occur in t, then it is added to a new list U.

(iii) *Dynamic Update* Assume that we have the array of differences H. We can easily construct $\hat{t}$ from t using H.

Assume that we have an edit operation $H[\lambda] \cdot o$ for some $0 \le \lambda < h$ applied at position $p = H[\lambda] \cdot p$ in t. We compute the signatures of all the m/q fragments of t affected by operation $H[\lambda] \cdot o$. Let s_j denote the signature of the jth affected fragment of t and $X[s_j][v]$

	0	1	2	3	4	5	6	7	8	9	10
t	G	C	A	G	T	A	C	A	G	T	A
$\hat{t}$	G	C	A	G	A	C	C	T	A	T	A

FIGURE 11.6 Affected fragments: $t[4 - 3 + 1 + i, \ldots, 4 + i]$ for all $0 \leq i < 3$, which are $t[2, \ldots, 4] = \text{AGT}$, $t[3, \ldots, 5] = \text{GTA}$, and $t[4, \ldots, 6] = \text{TAC}$; $t[7 - 3 + 1 + i, \ldots, 7 + i]$ for all $0 \leq i < 2$, which are $t[5, \ldots, 7] = \text{ACA}$ and $t[6, \ldots, 8] = \text{CAG}$; $t[7 - 3 + 1 + i, \ldots, 7 + i]$ for all $0 \leq i < 2$, which are $t[5, \ldots, 7] = \text{ACA}$ and $t[6, \ldots, 8] = \text{CAG}$; $t[8 - 3 + 1 + i, \ldots, 8 + i]$ for all $0 \leq i < 3$, which are $t[6, \ldots, 8] = \text{CAG}$, $t[7, \ldots, 9] = \text{AGT}$, and $t[8, \ldots, 10] = \text{GTA}$.

the vth tuple of the linked list $X[s_j]$. For each edit operation $H[\lambda] \cdot o$, for all $0 \leq \lambda < h$, the affected fragments are defined as follows:

- *Substitution*: $t[p - m/q + 1 + i, \ldots, p + i]$ for all $0 \leq i < m/q$
- *Insertion*: $t[p - m/q + 1 + i, \ldots, p + i]$ for all $0 \leq i < m/q - 1$
- *Deletion*: $t[p - m/q + 1 + i, \ldots, p + i]$ for all $0 \leq i < m/q$

We find and delete the tuple of the affected fragment from $X[s_j]$ such that $X[s_j][v] \cdot u = p - m/q + 1 + i$, to denote that it is no longer a fragment of $\hat{t}$. As an example of the affected fragments, see Figure 11.6 for $m = 6$ and $q = 2$, which uses the array H from Figure 11.4.

If $X[s_j][v] \cdot P$ is not empty, that is, there exist mapped patterns to the affected fragment of t, we need to unmap those patterns by adding them to list U, where we keep the unmapped patterns. In addition, we need to unmap the patterns which are mapped to other fragments of t affected by the deletion of the affected fragment. For each deleted fragment $t[p - m/q + 1 + i, \ldots, p + i]$, we also unmap the patterns from the tuples of the following fragments:

$$t[p + 1 + i + jm/q, \ldots, p + i + (j + 1)m/q] \quad \text{for all } 0 \leq j < q - 1$$

We compute the signatures of all the m/q new fragments of $\hat{t}$ affected by $H[\lambda] \cdot o$. Let s_j denote the signature of the jth new fragment of $\hat{t}$. We insert the new fragment as the vth tuple $X[s_j][v]$ of $X[s_j]$ to denote that it is a fragment of $\hat{t}$ by preserving the ascending order of the positions in the tuples.

We also compute a new array P, where $P[i] = \sum_{j=0}^{i-1} H[j] \cdot o$ represents the prefix sum of $H[i] \cdot o$, for all $0 \leq i < h$. As an example of array P, see Fig. 11.4. Let $\text{bsm}(H, \text{pos})$ be a binary search operation that, given a sorted array H of tuples and a position p as the key, returns the maximum index i such that $H[i] \cdot p \leq p$. We compute and store in place the new position of each fragment in our structure. The new positions can be computed as $P[\text{bsm}(p, H)] + p$. As an example, see Figure 11.7.

	0	1	2	3	4	5	6	7	$H \cdot p$	$H \cdot o$	P
t	C	A	T	G	G	A	C	A	1	0	0
	C	G	T	G	G	A	C	A	2	-1	-1
	C	G	G	G	A	C	A		7	1	0
$\hat{t}$	C	G	G	G	A	C	G	A			

FIGURE 11.7 New position of $t[4, \ldots, 6] = \text{GAC}$ is $P[\text{bsm}(p, H)] + p = P[1] + 4 = 3$.

	0	1	2	3	4	5	6	7	8	9	10
t	G	C	A	G	T	A	C	A	G	T	A
$\hat{t}$	G	C	A	G	A	C	C	T	A	T	A

FIGURE 11.8 New fragments: $\hat{t}[4 - 1 - i, \ldots, 4 - 1 + 3 - 1 - i]$ for all $0 \le i < 2$, which are $\hat{t}[3, \ldots, 5] = \text{GAC}$, $\hat{t}[2, \ldots, 4] = \text{AGA}$; $\hat{t}[7 + 0 - i - 1, \ldots, 7 + 0 + 3 - 2 - i]$ for all $0 \le i < 3$, which are $\hat{t}[6, \ldots, 8] = \text{CTA}$, $\hat{t}[5, \ldots, 7] = \text{CCT}$, $\hat{t}[4, \ldots, 6] = \text{ACC}$; $\hat{t}[7 + 1 - i - 1, \ldots, 7 + 1 + 3 - 2 - i]$ for all $0 \le i < 3$, which are $\hat{t}[7, \ldots, 9] = \text{TAT}$, $\hat{t}[6, \ldots, 8] = \text{CTA}$, $\hat{t}[5, \ldots, 7] = \text{CCT}$; $\hat{t}[8 + 0 - i, \ldots, 8 + 0 + 3 - 1 - i]$ for all $0 \le i < 2$, which are $\hat{t}[8, \ldots, 10] = \text{ATA}$, $\hat{t}[7, \ldots, 9] = \text{TAT}$.

For each edit operation $H[\lambda] \cdot o$, for all $0 \le \lambda < h$, the new fragments are defined as follows:

- *Substitution*: $\hat{t}[p + P[\lambda] - i, \ldots, p + P[\lambda] + m/q - 1 - i]$ for all $0 \le i < m/q$
- *Insertion*: $\hat{t}[p + P[\lambda] - 1 - i, \ldots, p + P[\lambda] + m/q - 2 - i]$ for all $0 \le i < m/q$
- *Deletion*: $\hat{t}[p + P[\lambda] - i, \ldots, p + P[\lambda] + m/q - 2 - i]$ for all $0 \le i < m/q - 1$

As an example of the new fragments, see Figure 11.8 for $m = 6$ and $q = 2$, which uses the array H from Figure 11.4.

In Figures 11.9 and 11.10, it is demonstrated how we maintain the pointers to the previous and to the next nonoverlapping fragments for each edit operation for the case that the length of the fragment is 3. The underlined fragments of t represent the affected fragments, which have to be found and removed from X. The vertical arrows represent the pointers to the previous (PF) and to the next (NF) nonoverlapping fragments. The horizontal arrows show how the affected fragments should be moved to represent the new changes in $\hat{t}$. The underlined fragments of $\hat{t}$ represent the new fragments which have to be inserted in X. In the case of an insertion or a deletion, the fragments underlined with the dashed line are neither removed nor inserted. However, they play an important role in the maintenance of the pointers. For example, in Figure 11.10, fragment GGT becomes the next nonoverlapping fragment of ACT and the previous of AAG.

(iv) *Remapping* The algorithm for remapping the patterns of list U to the new sequence $\hat{t}$ is identical to step (ii).

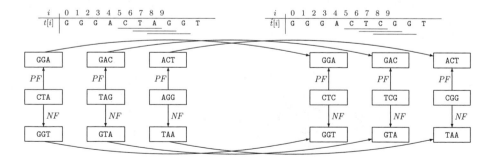

FIGURE 11.9 Substitution at position 6 in t.

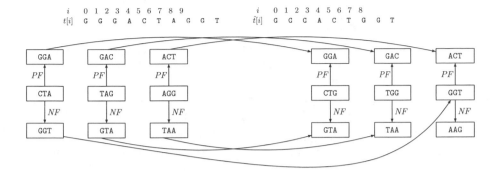

FIGURE 11.10   Deletion at position 6 in t.

In practice, for long patterns (e.g., $m \geq 40$), it is not possible to choose $q = 3$ since the memory complexity of storing X grows exponentially and becomes impractical for $m/q > 13$. Hence, the supported lengths of fragment range from 5 to 13, similarly as in [47] and [59]. We apply the strategy of *seed and extend*, that is, we apply step (i), with $q = 3$ and $k' = 2$, only for a prefix of length $m' < m$ such that $5 \leq m'/q \leq 13$, which we call *seed*. For example, if the length of fragment $m'/q = 12$ and $q = 3$, we only consider the seed of length $m' = 36$ to do the mapping. In step (ii), as soon as a match is located, with at most k' mismatches, it is extended to the right to complete the alignment. Hence, we allow at most k' mismatches in the seed of length m' and the rest in the suffix of the pattern of length $m - m'$.

Our method ensures that all alignments within a given number of mismatches are found provided they share at least one identical fragment, similarly as in [47]. No other constraints are imposed on the number of mismatches. Hence, this step can be easily configured to report either the best alignments or all hits within the specified range of mismatches. As expected, the latter will come with an increase in runtime, especially for highly repetitive genomes. In addition, it is not difficult to see that increasing the length of the fragment would result in a decrease in runtime and accuracy.

Complexities   By using the sliding-window mechanism, we read $t[0, \ldots, n - 1]$ from left to right, computing the signature $\sigma(t_i^j)$ of each factor of length m/q of t, $t_i^j = t[i + jm/q, \ldots, i + (j + 1)m/q - 1]$, for all $0 \leq i < n - m + 1, 0 \leq j < q$, and adding the tuple

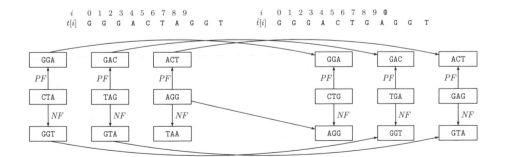

FIGURE 11.11   Insertion at position 6 in t.

$(i + jm/q, \sigma(t_i^j), \text{PF}, \text{NF}, P)$ as the last tuple of $X[\sigma(t_i^j)]$ in constant time. As soon as we compute $\sigma(t_0^0)$, then each of the rest signatures can be retrieved in constant time, using word-level operations, resulting in a total of $\Theta(n)$ for step (i). Maintaining the pointers to the previous and to the next nonoverlapping fragments is of no extra cost. According to Lemma 11.1, for each pattern, we have to try $\binom{q}{q-k}$ combinations, resulting in a total of $r|X_{\max}|\binom{q}{q-k}$ for step (ii), where $|X_{\max}|$ is the size of the largest linked list in X. The total amount of time is $\mathcal{O}(n + r|X_{\max}|\binom{q}{q-k})$ for steps (i) and (ii).

For each edit operation $H[i] \cdot o$, for all $0 \leq i < h$, we need to find and delete $\mathcal{O}(m/q)$ tuples from X, unmap the patterns of $\mathcal{O}(m)$ tuples of X, and add $\mathcal{O}(m/q)$ new tuples to X. The array P of the prefix sums can be computed in time $\Theta(h)$ from H. We compute the new position of each fragment of $\hat{t}$ in our structure by using a binary-search operation on array P in time $\mathcal{O}(n \log h)$. Maintaining the pointers to the previous and to the next nonoverlapping fragments is of no extra cost. Step (iv), which is identical to step (ii), requires time $\mathcal{O}(|U||X_{\max}|\binom{q}{q-k})$, where $|U|$ is the size of list U. The time required for steps (iii) and (iv) is $\mathcal{O}(hm|X_{\max}| + n \log h + |U||X_{\max}|\binom{q}{q-k})$.

Hence, overall, the proposed algorithm requires time $\mathcal{O}(r|X_{\max}|\binom{q}{q-k} + hm|X_{\max}| + n \log h)$ since $|U| \leq r$.

The array X consists of exactly $2^{\log|\Sigma|m/q}$ linked lists indexing the $2^{\log|\Sigma|m/q}$ possible signatures. A text of length n consists of exactly $n - m/q + 1$ factors of length m/q, and thus the total number of tuples contained in the linked lists of X is exactly $n - m/q + 1$. In addition, rm space is required for keeping the r patterns, each of length m, in memory. Hence, asymptotically, the overall space required is $\Theta(2^{\log|\Sigma|m/q} + n - m/q + rm)$.

11.5.2 Experimental Results

DynMap was implemented in the C programming language and was developed under GNU/Linux. The program takes as input arguments a file with a single reference sequence, in FASTA format, lists of differences of other sequences compared to the first one, and a file with the short reads in FASTA format. It then produces a separate tab-delimited text file with the hits, one for each sequence, as output. In addition, it produces a file in FASTA format with all the reads, which were not aligned to any of the sequences.

The fact that we are interested in reporting the best hits complicated the implementation of the algorithm. For instance, notice that a best hit on the first sequence is not necessarily a best hit on the second, since a potential difference in the second sequence may result in that read to be aligned more than once against the second sequence.

The experiments were conducted on a desktop PC using a single core of a 2.40-GHz Intel Xeon E7340 CPU and 8 GB of main memory running the GNU/Linux operating system. DynMap is distributed under the GNU GPL. The implementation is available at a website [9] that maintains the source code and the documentation.

To validate the correctness of DynMap, we used a 1-Mbp reference sequence and three list of differences, in the following manner, as input: The first list constructs the second sequence by simulating 1000 random mixed substitutions, deletions, and insertions to the reference sequence; the second list reconstructs the initial reference sequence; the third list reconstructs the second sequence. As a reference, we used a 1-Mbp *Escherichia coli* strain K-12 substrain MG1655 region obtained from GenBank. The short reads were obtained by simulating 999,949 52-bp-long single-end reads from the same sequence. In addition, to

TABLE 11.11   Mapping 999,949 52-bp-Long Simulated Reads to Four Sequences of *E. coli* Chromosome Region (1 Mbp) and 999,937 52-bp-Long Simulated Reads to Four Sequences of *D. melanogaster* Chromosome 3L Region (1 Mbp) using DynMap

Reference	First Alignment	Second Alignment	Third Alignment	Fourth Alignment
E. coli	94.17%	91.21%	94.17%	91.21%
D. melanogaster	95.82%	91.94%	95.82%	91.94%

Note: The program was run with 39-bp-long seed with at most two mismatches in the seed and reported best hits only.

further validate the correctness of DynMap, we conducted another experiment, in the same manner, to map 999,937 52-bp-long simulated single-end reads, produced from a 1 Mbp *Drosophila melanogaster* chromosome 3L region, obtained from the NCBI, back to the same sequence.

The results in Table 11.11 demonstrate the correctness of DynMap in practice: The percentage of aligned reads in the first and second alignments is exactly the same as the third and the fourth, respectively. After the first alignment, which is done in step (ii), the rest of the alignment is done in step (iv), which is based only on step (iii), thus avoiding mapping all the reads from scratch. The main advantage of the proposed approach becomes evident in Table 11.12: The number of reads to be aligned decreases significantly after the first alignment.

To evaluate the performance of DynMap, we compared its performance with a reference sequence and two lists of differences to the respective performance of three runs (one for each sequence) of SOAP2 (v2.20) [30] and REAL (v0.0.28) [13], which are, up to date, two of the most efficient known short-read alignment programs. In each case, effort was made to make the three programs run in as similar a way as possible so that the speed and sensitivity comparisons are fair. Thus, SOAP2 and REAL were always given the modifier -l <INT>, to adjust the length of the seed to be equal to the one of DynMap. The programs were set to report only the best, nonrepetitive, hits; otherwise the reported hits of SOAP2 would be chosen at random between equal hits. In SOAP2, this was achieved with the use of -M 4 -r 0 modifiers, and in REAL with the use of -u 1. As a reference sequence, we used the *D. melanogaster* chromosome 3L (24,543,557 bp) obtained from the NCBI. The second and third sequences were constructed by simulating 20,000 mixed substitutions, deletions, and insertions in the reference sequence. The short reads were obtained by simulating 24,543,488 70-bp-long single-end reads from the reference sequence.

As it is demonstrated by the results in Table 11.13, DynMap was able to complete the assignment much faster. DynMap finished in 583 s, while SOAP2 in 2975 s and REAL in 1217 s. In terms of sensitivity, with this data set, all programs report a similar amount of aligned reads for all three sequences, a fact that further demonstrates the correctness of

TABLE 11.12   Total Number of Reads to Be Aligned by DynMap in Each Alignment

Reads	First Alignment	Second Alignment	Third Alignment	Fourth Alignment
E. coli	999,949	132,592	133,807	132,592
D. melanogaster	999,937	133,197	134,325	133,197

Note: See Table 11.11.

TABLE 11.13 Mapping 24,543,488 70-bp-Long Simulated Reads to Three Sequences of *Drosophila melanogaster* Chromosome 3L (24,543,557 bp)

Program	Total Time	First Alignment	Second Alignment	Third Alignment
SOAP2	2975 s	89.85%	86.77%	83.85%
REAL	1217 s	89.51%	86.36%	83.37%
DynMap	583 s	89.95%	85.59%	83.91%

Note: SOAP2 and REAL were run with 40-bp-long seed and DynMap with 39-bp-long seed. All programs were run with at most two mismatches in the seed and reported best hits only.

DynMap in practice. In Table 11.14, the individual elapsed times for each step of DynMap for the same experiment are reported. It is demonstrated that after the first mapping the total time required for a dynamic update and a following remapping is much less than the time required for the first mapping.

To evaluate the accuracy of DynMap, we have simulated 2,000,000 52-bp-long simulated single-end reads from human chromosome 17 (76,037,631 bp), *H. sapiens* (human), Build 37.2, obtained from the NCBI and used DynMap, SOAP2, and REAL to map them back to the chromosome, from which they came. Due to the fact that the reads were simulated, and thus we were able to know the exact locations they were derived from, we measured the accuracy of each program by checking whether the reads were mapped back to the exact same locations. The results in Table 11.15 demonstrate the high accuracy of DynMap. In terms of sensitivity, with this data set, DynMap appears to have higher sensitivity than SOAP2 and REAL with almost the same accuracy.

As a further test, we compared the performance of DynMap with one reference sequence and a list of differences to the respective performance of GenomeMapper (v0.3) [47]. As mentioned in GenomeMapper's manual [15], the limiting factors of Genomapper are time and sensitivity of the resulting mappings. As a reference, we used the *E. coli* strain K-12 substrain MG1655 chromosome (4,639,675 bp), obtained from GenBank, and one list of differences with 5000 mixed substitutions, deletions, and insertions. We mapped 5,288,154 Illumina Solexa 36-bp-long real single-end reads obtained from the European Nucleotide Archive. As expected, the results in Table 11.16 demonstrate that DynMap was able to complete the assignment much faster, and with much higher sensitivity. Notice that in

TABLE 11.14 Individual Elapsed Times for Each Step of DynMap

Step	Elapsed Time
Creating lists	18 s
Mapping	287 s
Dynamic update	89 s
Remapping	53 s
Dynamic update	80 s
Remapping	56 s

Note: See Table 11.13.

TABLE 11.15   Mapping 2,000,000 52-bp-Long Simulated Reads to Human Chromosome 17 (76,037,631 bp)

Program	Aligned Reads	Correctly Aligned	Misaligned	Accuracy (%)
SOAP2	1,648,698	1,639,847	8851	99.46
REAL	1,648,904	1,641,500	7404	99.55
DynMap	1,650,697	1,642,902	7795	99.53

Note: SOAP2 and REAL were run with 40-bp-long seed and DynMap with 39-bp-long seed. All programs were run with at most two mismatches in the seed and reported best hits only.

TABLE 11.16   Mapping 5,288,154 36-bp-Long Real Reads to Two References of *Escherichia coli* Chromosome (4,639,675 bp) Using List of Differences of Second Sequence Compared to First

Program	Total Time	Alignment
GenomeMapper	95 s	47.73%
DynMap	66 s	66.84%

Note: Both programs were run with 12-bp-long fragment with at most two mismatches in the seed and reported best hits only.

TABLE 11.17   Mapping 4,639,624 52-bp-Long Simulated Reads to *Escherichia coli* Chromosome (4,639,675 bp) Using DynMap

Length of Fragment	Total Time	Accuracy (%)
11	51 s	95.89
12	35 s	95.25
13	31 s	94.40

Note: The program was run with at most two mismatches in the seed and reported best hits only.

Table 11.16 the percentage of aligned reads represents the total number of reads aligned to any of the two sequences.

As a last test, we mapped 4,639,624 52-bp-long simulated singe-end reads to the *E. coli* strain K-12 substrain MG1655 chromosome (4,639,675 bp) using DynMap with different lengths of fragment. The results in Table 11.17 show that DynMap is faster, but less accurate, as the length of the fragment increases, confirming our theoretical results.

11.6   CONCLUSION

In this chapter, we considered the well-known and challenging application of resequencing, which is useful for cataloging sequence variation and understanding its biological consequences.

We presented REAL, an efficient, sensitive, and accurate short-read alignment program for mapping millions of short reads to a genome. It is based on a new algorithm, different from what has been done so far. We demonstrated that it can match, or even outperform, current popular short-read alignment program such as Bowtie and SOAP2 in terms of efficiency, sensitivity, and accuracy. The two main advantages of REAL, over the most popular programs, are: Its performance, in terms of sensitivity and accuracy, is consistent and irrespective of the length of reads, while it can match, or even outperform, current popular programs, and in terms of efficiency, with large genomes, it is always more efficient with small ones. The main disadvantage of REAL is that it does not create a permanent index of the reference sequence, which could be reused across alignment runs, in particular for large genomes. Furthermore, we presented cREAL, a simple extension of REAL, specifically designed for mapping millions of short reads to a genome with circular structure, for example, strain or species of bacteria with circular organization of their chromosomes or plasmids.

Finally, we presented DynMap, an efficient, sensitive, and accurate short-read alignment program for mapping millions of short reads to multiple closely related genomes. We demonstrated that it can outperform current popular short-read alignment program such as GenomeMapper in terms of efficiency, sensitivity, and accuracy. It must be made clear that DynMap cannot compete, in terms of efficiency, with the most efficient short-read alignment programs, for example, REAL, SOAP2, and Bowtie, for mapping a set of reads to a single genome. Since it focuses on the alignment between a set of the reads and multiple closely related genomes, its advantage becomes much more drastic once many genomes are incorporated into the structure. In turn, this improves the work flow, as the separate handling of separate references, by the current existing programs becomes increasingly impractical.

REFERENCES

1. S. F. Altschul, W. Gish, W. Miller, E. W. Myers, and D. J. Lipman. Basic Local Alignment Search Tool. *J. Mol. Biol.*, 215(3):403–410, Oct. 1990.

2. P. Antoniou, J. W. Daykin, C. S. Iliopoulos, D. Kourie, L. Mouchard, and S. P. Pissis. Mapping uniquely occurring short sequences derived from high throughput technologies to a reference genome. In *Proceedings of Information Technology and Applications in Biomedicine (ITAB 09)*, 2009.

3. P. Antoniou, C. S. Iliopoulos, L. Mouchard, and S. P. Pissis. A fast and efficient algorithm for mapping short sequences to a reference genome. In H. R. Arabnia (Ed.), *Advances in Computational Biology*, Vol. 680 of *Advances in Experimental Medicine and Biology*. Springer New York, 2011, pp. 399–403.

4. M. Burrows and D. J. Wheeler. A block-sorting lossless data compression algorithm. Technical Report 124, 1994.

5. J. Chen, G. Xie, S. Han, O. Chertkov, D. Sims, and E. L. Civerolo. Whole genome sequences of two *Xylella fastidiosa* strains (M12 and M23) causing almond leaf scorch disease in California. *J. Bacteriol.*, 192(17):4534, 2010.

6. S. T. Colem and I. Saint-Girons. Bacterial genomes—All shapes and sizes. *Organization of the Prokaryotic Genome*, 291:35–62, 1999.

7. A. Cox. ELAND: Efficient local alignment of nucleotide data. Unpublished.

8. dbSNP: http://www.ncbi.nlm.nih.gov/projects/SNP/, Aug. 2011.

9. DynMap: http://www.inf.kcl.ac.uk/pg/dynmap/, Aug. 2011.

10. European Nucleotide Archive (ENA): http://www.ebi.ac.uk/ena/data/view/, Aug. 2011.

11. P. Ferragina and G. Manzini. Opportunistic data structures with applications. In *Proceedings of the 41st Annual Symposium on Foundations of Computer Science*. IEEE Computer Society, Washington, DC, 2000, pp. 390–398.

12. M. C. Frith, R. Wan, and P. Horton. Incorporating sequence quality data into alignment improves DNA read mapping. *Nucleic Acids Res.*, 38:1–9, 2010.

13. K. Frousios, C. S. Iliopoulos, L. Mouchard, S. P. Pissis, and G. Tischler. REAL: An efficient REad ALigner for next generation sequencing reads. In *Proceedings of the First ACM International Conference on Bioinformatics and Computational Biology (BCB '10)*. ACM, New York, 2010, pp. 154–159.

14. GenBank: http://www.ncbi.nlm.nih.gov/genbank/, Aug. 2011.

15. GenomeMapper: http://www.1001genomes.org/software/genomemapper.html, Aug. 2011.

16. L. P. Gilbert, et al. Whole-genome shotgun sequencing of mitochondria from ancient hair shafts. *Science*, 317(5846):1927–1930, Sept. 2007.

17. W. Gish and S. F. Altschul. Improved sensitivity of nucleic acid database searches using application-specific scoring matrices. *Methods*, 3:66–70, 1991.

18. D. Gusfield. *Algorithms on Strings, Trees, and Sequences: Computer Science and Computational Biology*. Cambridge University Press, New York, 1997.

19. S. M. Halling, B. D. Peterson-Burch, B. J. Bricker, R. L. Zuerner, Z. Qing, L.-L. Li, V. Kapur, D. P. Alt, and S. C. Olsen. Completion of the genome sequence of *Brucella abortus* and comparison to the highly similar genomes of *Brucella melitensis* and *Brucella suis*. *J. Bacteriol.*, 187(8):2715–2726, 2005.

20. X. Han, X. Wu, W.-Y. Chung, T. Li, A. Nekrutenko, N. S. Altman, G. Chen, and H. Ma. Transcriptome of embryonic and neonatal mouse cortex by high-throughput RNA sequencing. *Proc. Nat. Acad. Sci.*, 106(31):12741–12746, Aug. 2009.

21. H. Jiang and W. H. Wong. SeqMap: Mapping massive amount of oligonucleotides to the genome. *Bioinformatics*, 24(20):2395–2396, 2008.

22. L. B. Jorde and S. P. Wooding. Genetic variation, classification and race. *Nat. Genet. Suppl.*, 36(11):S28–S33, 2004.

23. T. Kaneko, Y. Nakamura, S. Sato, K. Minamisawa, T. Uchiumi, S. Sasamoto, A. Watanabe, K. Idesawa, M. Iriguchi, K. Kawashima, M. Kohara, M. Matsumoto, S. Shimpo, H. Tsuruoka, T. Wada, M. Yamada, and S. Tabata. Complete genomic sequence of nitrogen-fixing symbiotic bacterium *Bradyrhizobium japonicum* USDA110. *DNA Res.*, 9(6):189–197, 2002.

24. W. J. Kent. BLAT—The BLAST-Like Alignment Tool. *Genome Res.*, 12:656–664, 2002.

25. T. W. Lam, W. K. Sung, S. L. Tam, C. K. Wong, and S. M. Yiu. Compressed indexing and local alignment of DNA. *Bioinformatics*, 24(6):791–797, 2008.

26. B. Langmead, C. Trapnell, M. Pop, and S. L. Salzberg. Ultrafast and memory-efficient alignment of short DNA sequences to the human genome. *Genome Biol.*, 10(3):R25+, 2009.

27. H. Li and R. Durbin. Fast and accurate short read alignment with Burrows-Wheeler transform. *Bioinformatics*, 25(14):1754–1760, 2009.

28. H. Li, J. Ruan, and R. Durbin. Mapping short DNA sequencing reads and calling variants using mapping quality scores. *Genome Res.*, 18(11):1851–1858, Nov. 2008.

29. R. Li, Y. Li, K. Kristiansen, and J. Wang. SOAP: Short oligonucleotide alignment program. *Bioinformatics*, 24(5):713–714, Mar. 2008.

30. R. Li, C. Yu, Y. Li, T.-W. Lam, S.-M. Yiu, K. Kristiansen, and J. Wang. SOAP2: An improved ultrafast tool for short read alignment. *Bioinformatics*, 25(16):1966–1967, 2009.

31. R. Li, H. Zhu, J. Ruan, W. Qian, X. Fang, Z. Shi, Y. Li, S. Li, G. Shan, K. Kristiansen, S. Li, H. Yang, J. Wang, and J. Wang. De novo assembly of human genomes with massively parallel short read sequencing. *Genome Res.*, 20(2):265–272, Feb. 2010.

32. R. A. Lippert. Space-efficient whole genome comparisons with Burrows-Wheeler transforms. *J. Comput. Bio. J. Comput. Mol. Cell Bio.*, 12(4):407–415, May 2005.

33. M. Margulies, et al. Genome sequencing in microfabricated high-density picolitre reactors. *Nature*, 437(7057):376–380, July 2005.

34. A. M. Maxam and W. Gilbert. A new method for sequencing DNA. *Proc. Nat. Acad. Sci. USA*, 74(2):560–564, Feb. 1977.

35. J. R. Miller, S. Koren, and G. Sutton. Assembly algorithms for next-generation sequencing data. *Genomics*, 95(6):315–327, 2010.

36. A. Mortazavi, B. A. A. Williams, K. McCue, L. Schaeffer, and B. Wold. Mapping and quantifying mammalian transcriptomes by *RNA-Seq*. *Nat. Methods*, 5:621–628, May 2008.

37. A. Nakabachi, A. Yamashita, H. Toh, H. Ishikawa, H. E. Dunbar, N. A. Moran, and M. Hattori. The 160-kilobase genome of the bacterial endosymbiont carsonella. *Science*, 314(5797):267, 2006.

38. National Center for Biotechnology Information (NCBI): `http://www.ncbi.nlm.nih.gov/`, Aug. 2011.

39. G. Navarro. A guided tour to approximate string matching. *ACM Comput. Surv.*, 33:31–88, Mar. 2001.

40. S. B. Ng, K. J. Buckingham, C. Lee, A. W. Bigham, H. K. Tabor, K. M. Dent, C. D. Huff, P. T. Shannon, E. W. Jabs, D. A. Nickerson, J. Shendure, and M. J. Bamshad. Exome sequencing identifies the cause of a Mendelian disorder. *Nat. Genet.*, 42(1):30–35, Jan. 2010.

41. P. Ostergaard, M. A. Simpson, G. Brice, S. Mansour, F. C. Connell, A. Onoufriadis, A. H. Child, J. Hwang, K. Kalidas, P. S. Mortimer, R. Trembath, and S. Jeffery. Rapid identification of mutations in GJC2 in primary lymphoedema using whole exome sequencing combined with linkage analysis with delineation of the phenotype. *J. Med. Genet.*, 48(4):251–255, 2010.

42. W. R. Pearson and D. J. Lipman. Improved tools for biological sequence comparison. *Proc. Natl. Acad. Sci. USA*, 85:2444–2448, 1988.

43. REad ALigner (REAL): `http://www.inf.kcl.ac.uk/pg/real/`, Aug. 2011.

44. F. Sanger, G. M. Air, B. G. Barrell, N. L. Brown, A. R. Coulson, C. A. Fiddes, C. A. Hutchison, P. M. Slocombe, and M. Smith. Nucleotide sequence of bacteriophage phi X174 DNA. *Nature*, 265(5596):687–695, Feb. 1977.

45. F. Sanger and A. R. Coulson. A rapid method for determining sequences in DNA by primed synthesis with DNA polymerase. *J. Mol. Biol.*, 94:441–448, 1975.

46. F. Sanger, S. Nicklen, and A. R. Coulson. DNA sequencing with chain-terminating inhibitors. *Proc. Natl. Acad. Sci. USA*, 74:5463–5467, 1977.

47. K. Schneeberger, J. Hagmann, S. Ossowski, N. Warthmann, S. Gesing, O. Kohlbacher, and D. Weigel. Simultaneous alignment of short reads against multiple genomes. *Genome Bio.*, 10(9):R98+, Sept. 2009.

48. J. A. Schneider, M. S. Pungliya, J. Y. Choi, R. Jiang, X. J. Sun, B. A. Salisbury, and J. C. Stephens. DNA variability of human genes. *Mechanisms Ageing Develop.*, 124(1):17–25, 2003.

49. J. Shendure, Gr. J. Porreca, N. B. Reppas, X. Lin, J. P. McCutcheon, A. M. Rosenbaum, M. D. Wang, K. Zhang, R. D. Mitra, and G. M. Church. Accurate multiplex polony sequencing of an evolved bacterial genome. *Science*, 309(5741):1728–1732, Sept. 2005.

50. J. T. Simpson, K. Wong, S. D. Jackman, J. E. Schein, S. J. M. Jones, and İ. Birol. Abyss: A parallel assembler for short read sequence data. *Genome Res.*, 19(6):1117–1123, June 2009.

51. M. A. Simpson, M. D. Irving, E. Asilmaz, M. J. Gray, D. Dafou, F. V. Elmslie, S. Mansour, S. E. Holder, C. E. Brain, B. K. Burton, K. H. Kim, R. M. Pauli, S. Aftimos, H. Stewart, C. A. Kim, M. Holder-Espinasse, S. P. Robertson, W. M. Drake, and R. C. Trembath. Mutations in NOTCH2 cause Hajdu-Cheney syndrome, a disorder of severe and progressive bone loss. *Nat. Genet.*, 43:303–305, 2011.

52. C. K. Stover, X. Q. Pham, A. L. Erwin, S. D. Mizoguchi, P. Warrener, M. J. Hickey, F. S. Brinkman, W. O. Hufnagle, D. J. Kowalik, M. Lagrou, R. L. Garber, L. Goltry, E. Tolentino, S. Westbrock-Wadman, Y. Yuan, L. L. Brody, S. N. Coulter, K. R. Folger, A. Kas, K. Larbig, R. Lim, K. Smith, D. Spencer, G. K. Wong, Z. Wu, I. T. Paulsen, J. Reizer, M. H. Saier, R. E. Hancock, S. Lory, and M. V. Olson. Complete genome sequence of *Pseudomonas aeruginosa* PAO1, an opportunistic pathogen. *Nature*, 406(6799):959–964, Aug. 2000.

53. A. Suwanto and S. Kaplan. Physical and genetic mapping of the *Rhodobacter sphaeroides* 2.4.1 genome: Genome size, fragment identification, and gene localization. *J. Bacteriol.*, 171(11):5840–5849, 1989.

54. A. Suwanto and S. Kaplan. Physical and genetic mapping of the *Rhodobacter sphaeroides* 2.4.1 genome: Presence of two unique circular chromosomes. *J. Bacteriol.*, 171(11):5850–5859, 1989.

55. A. Suwanto and S. Kaplan. A self-transmissible, narrow-host-range endogenous plasmid of *Rhodobacter sphaeroides* 2.4.1: Physical structure, incompatibility determinants, origin of replication, and transfer functions. *J. Bacteriol.*, 174(4):1124–1134, 1992.

56. A. Suwanto and S. Kaplan. Chromosome transfer in *Rhodobacter sphaeroides*: Hfr formation and genetic evidence for two unique circular chromosomes. *J. Bacteriol.*, 174(4):1135–1145, 1992.

57. J. R. ten Bosch and W. W. Grody. Keeping up with the next generation: Massively parallel sequencing in clinical diagnostics. *J. Mol. Diagnost.*, 10(6):484–492, 2008.

58. J.-N. Volff and J. Altenbuchner. A new beginning with new ends: Linearisation of circular chromosomes during bacterial evolution. *FEMS Microbiol. Lett.*, 186(2):143–150, 2000.

59. T. D. Wu and S. Nacu. Fast and SNP-tolerant detection of complex variants and splicing in short reads. *Bioinformatics*, 26(7):873–881, Feb. 2010.

CHAPTER 12

GENE REGULATORY NETWORK IDENTIFICATION WITH QUALITATIVE PROBABILISTIC NETWORKS

ZINA M. IBRAHIM,[1] ALIOUNE NGOM,[2] and AHMED Y. TAWFIK[3]
[1]Social Genetic and Developmental Psychiatry Centre, King's College London, London, United Kingdom
[2]School of Computer Science, University of Windsor, Windsor, Ontario, Canada
[3]Information Systems Department, French University of Egypt, El-Shorouk, Egypt

In this chapter, we explore the use of qualitative probabilistic networks (QPNs) in constructing gene regulatory networks from microarray expression data. The chapter aims at demonstrating the usefulness of QPNs in aiding dynamic Bayesian networks (DBNs) in the process of learning the structure of gene regulatory networks from microarray gene expression data. We present a study which shows that QPNs define monotonic relations that are capable of identifying regulatory interactions in a manner that is less susceptible to the many sources of uncertainty that surround gene expression data. Moreover, we construct a model that maps the regulatory interactions of genetic networks to QPN constructs and show its capability in providing a set of candidate regulators for target genes, which is subsequently used to establish a prior structure that the DBN learning algorithm can use and which (1) distinguishes spurious correlations from true regulations; (2) enables the discovery of sets of coregulators of target genes; and (3) results in a more efficient construction of gene regulatory networks. The model is compared to existing literature using the known gene regulatory interactions of *Drosophila melanogaster*.

Before delving into the model presented here, the chapter begins by taking a detailed look at the process of gene expression followed by an examination of network-based methods for understanding the complexity of biological systems and defining the task of gene regulatory network construction.

12.1 CENTRAL DOGMA: GENE EXPRESSION IN A CELL

The success of whole-genome sequencing, exemplified by the completion of the first stages of the human genome project [7], has made available a plethora of and unprecedented volumes of biological data. The current challenges facing researchers today lie in analyzing the

Biological Knowledge Discovery Handbook: Preprocessing, Mining, and Postprocessing of Biological Data,
First Edition. Edited by Mourad Elloumi and Albert Y. Zomaya.
© 2014 John Wiley & Sons, Inc. Published 2014 by John Wiley & Sons, Inc.

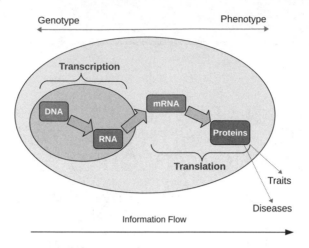

FIGURE 12.1   Gene expression process.

wealth of data available and developing a functional understanding of the system dictated by the genomic structure. This entails isolating functional components in the human genome sequence (i.e., genes) and uncovering their roles in forming the regulatory mechanisms that govern various cellular functionalities, which include reactions to internal and external signals (e.g., temperature variation) or protein synthesis. Understanding how these functionalities drastically vary across individuals despite having almost similar genomic data provides a critical foundation for understanding individual genomic variations, leading to advances in medicine, basic research, and clinical diagnostic technologies.

Each gene is a stretch of DNA whose sequence encodes the information needed for the production of one or more end products such as proteins. When a gene is active, it is transformed into the corresponding end product(s) via the process of *gene expression* [19]. The different proteins synthesized from different genes perform virtually every function within the cell, are responsible for the traits the organism shows (e.g., hair color), and are essential for its survival. Therefore, understanding this process is critical to obtaining insight about the working of the cell [43].

A simplified model of the expression process is shown in Figure 12.1 and consists of three stages, each ending with the formation of one or more end products. First, when a gene is active, it is processed by a specialized enzyme called RNA polymerase (RNAp) and is *transcribed* into messenger RNA (mRNA). mRNA is in turn receptive to other chemical products that *translate* it into a chain of amino acids. This chain serves as the base from which proteins, the main actors performing most cellular activities, are made. The process of expressing the information located on the DNA of a single gene to functional proteins is so important to modern biology that it is called the *central dogma* of molecular biology [8]. Therefore, gene expression serves as the base for studying the flow of information during the cellular life cycle in order to understand biological systems at the cellular level [19].

It is now established that genes and their end products do not work in isolation; they are connected via large and highly structured networks that dictate cellular activities. For example, the expression of one gene may produce one or more proteins which can serve as catalysts or inhibitors to the expression of several other genes. Moreover, the process of gene expression can be triggered by several cellular and external factors (e.g., change in pH level and temperature). The result is a complex web of interactions responsible for regulating cellular mechanisms and is responsible for its survival. The aim of network-based biology is to study the processes by which inheritable information located on the genes is made into protein and other functional end products and the generated network of the interacting components. This in turn enables the analysis of phenotypical traits by unearthing the relations between the end products responsible for their production and the corresponding genotype variants that encode these proteins.

Among the thousands of genes encoded by the genome, only a small fraction of the genes are *expressed* under a given set of conditions, and it is this subset that delivers the unique properties to each cell type and performs the functions required at the time. Gene expression is a highly complex and tightly regulated process that allows a cell to respond dynamically both to environmental stimuli and to its own changing needs. This mechanism acts an *activation/supression* switch to control which genes are expressed in a cell as well as a *volume control* that increases or decreases the level of expression of particular genes as necessary. As a result, in order to obtain insight into how the cell responds to the changing needs of itself and the environment, one must measure the expression level of the different genes during different time slots or under different cellular conditions [10].

Given the large size of genomes, identifying the genes that are expressed under any conditions entails the need for simultaneously measuring the expression levels of a large set of genes and a method for distinguishing those genes that are expressed form those that are not. This is where *microarray technology* comes into play and is discussed next.

12.2 MEASURING EXPRESSION LEVELS: MICROARRAY TECHNOLOGY

In the last decade, technical breakthroughs in spotting hybridization probes and advances in genome-sequencing efforts led to development of DNA microarrays, which simultaneously measure the expression level for thousands of genes and provide a snapshot of transcription levels within the cell. This parallel whole-genome expression detection [52] is achieved using a small slide made of glass, plastic, silicon, gold, gel, or membrane or even beads at the end of fiber-optic bundles commonly referred to as chips. The slides contain thousands of spots, each holding a single-stranded DNA sequence of one gene (also called cDNA, for complementary DNA) [10].

Hence, the thousands of spots of a microarray contain single DNA strands of a whole genome. The microarray works by hybridizing prelabeled mRNA samples contained in solutions which bind to the different spots on the surface, as shown in Figure 12.2.

The figure shows an example of an experiment aiming at discovering the expression profile (i.e., which genes are expressed) of a certain cell culture under a certain set of conditions (e.g., the absence of oxygen). The experiment starts by obtaining a cellular sample from the culture after allowing it to be in the condition being examined (and as a result, given the organism the chance to adapt to the conditions by launching the expression of the genes required for the set of conditions). mRNA molecules corresponding to the expressed genes are then extracted from the cellular culture* and is colored with a fluorescent dye for ease of detection. Then, the extracted mRNA is poured over the microarray containing the DNA of the respective cellular culture. If the DNA at a certain spot has a corresponding

---

*Details pertaining to the technical biologicals can be found in [10] for an elaborate discussion.

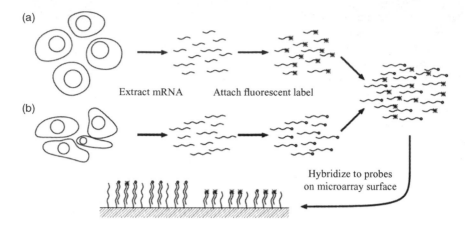

FIGURE 12.2 Experiment for measuring gene expression levels.

mRNA in the extracted cellular sample, it binds to it* and the corresponding spot on the microarray is illuminated with the fluorescent dye that colored the mRMA.

This slide containing the bound mRNA fragments is then viewed by a microarray scanner, which measures the amount of matching in the spots containing matched sequences. This is often reported as some amount of fluorescent intensity resulting from the colored sequences used. The scanner then detects the intensity for each spot in the slide, and from knowing where each gene marker is located on the slides (i.e., the spot where it is located), the activity level of the corresponding gene is inferred [13].

The idea of network-based expression studies is to infer the causal interactions between the genes and their end product from the expression levels obtained from microarrays. Despite the novelty and usefulness of microarrays, using the data they generate to use as input for computational models presents several challenges. The next section examines these challenges.

In what follows, the most important difficulties associated with using microarrays are presented. They can be classified as experimental difficulties and data-related difficulties as detailed next:

1. *Experimental Difficulties* Time-series experiments of gene expression data are per-formed by exploding the cell at different time points without changing the experi-mental condition the cell has undergone. Because the cells are exploded, what we are gathering are sparse momentary snapshots of the cell's activities at the instants the experiments are performed. This implies that all the activities that have taken place during the gaps which do not have corresponding snapshots will not be modeled. As a result, cellular activities taking place during these gaps are unknown. This becomes problematic if the gaps contain biologicals relevant to the biological insight sought after [3, 10].

2. *Data-Related Difficulties* Microarrays measure the expression levels of protein end products indirectly by measuring the amount of cRNA (or cDNA) hybridization to target mRNA transcripts [13]. The assumption made is that the level of cRNA

---

*The process is called hybridization [10].

measured (via the intensity of the florescent dye) provides an indication of the level of protein produced. This assumption, however, is not necessarily supported as current studies have shown varying levels of correlations between mRNA levels and protein levels and have given varying results depending on (1) the technology used and (2) biological factors that remain poorly understood [15, 34, 35]. As a result, mRNA-to-protein expression correlations vary from being poor [35] to moderately good [15]. This indirect measure has several implications that must be taken into account. First, the expression process is not one to one; when an mRNA transcript is translated to a polypeptide of amino acids, this polypeptide may correspond to a number of functionally different proteins. The reason behind this is that the type and functionality of the resulting protein does depends not only on the amino acids present in the polypeptide chain but also on the final three-dimensional (3D) structure that the chain assumes to produce the final protein molecule. The final 3D structure is in turn decided by a process known as *posttranslational modification*, in which the shape of the polypeptide is made depending on chemical and positional factors within the cell [36]. There, one linear chain of amino acids may result in differently shaped proteins that have different functionalities.

Because of the above, microarrays do not exactly capture if a gene's functional products (proteins) are currently present, but only whether the associated gene is currently being expressed. Because the resulting proteins may serve as activators or inhibitors to the expression of other genes, one can only assume their activities and infer it with uncertainty from the kind of data available.

Another issue is due to the fact that mRNA degrades much faster than the molecules it produces (e.g., proteins) [28]. As a result, a protein may be working in the cell and performing activating or inhibiting actions while the mRNA that produced it has degraded. Combined with the gaps induced by the nature of microarray experiments explained above, more regulatory relations may be missed from the experiments [41], making microarray extremely noisy and difficult to analyze [39, 43].

It is worth noting that large-scale protein expression measurements are currently present but tend to be much more noisy than microarray data and lack a great deal of sensitivity and specificity [10]. For an overview of other types of data, the reader may refer to [3].

12.3 UNDERSTANDING GENE REGULATORY NETWORKS: BASIC CONCEPTS

As the simplified picture of the central dogma given above shows, the cellular components do not work in isolation. Genes and the biological molecules produced during the transcription and translation processes (i.e., mRNA and proteins) exhibit complicated interactions that govern the diverse cellular functionalities. For instance, at the genome or DNA level, different proteins bind to DNA segments and cause the activation or inhibition of the gene located at the segment. Since these proteins are themselves products of genes, the ultimate effect is that genes regulate each others' expression as part of a large network. Similarly, at the protein level, proteins can participate in diverse posttranslational modifications of other proteins or form protein complexes and pathways together with other proteins that assume new roles, creating another level of interactions modeled by networks [5, 27].

In this chapter, we focus on one type of such networks, namely gene regulatory networks (GRNs). GRNs are high-level graphical visualizations of cellular biochemistry [5, 39] in which only genes and their (indirect) interactions are explicitly represented. In other words, a relationship defined in a GRN between two genes implies an indirect interaction between the two genes through their end products (e.g., the expression of the first gene produces a transcription factor protein which in turn activates the expression of the second gene). In such networks, the underlying biochemical processes leading to the gene–gene interactions are only implied and are not explicitly present [5].

GRNs are represented by graphs where each node represents one gene and each edge connecting two nodes describes an interaction between the two corresponding genes. The edges between the different GRN nodes are directed, implying a causal interaction in which the expression of the source gene influences that of the destination. This influence is quantified by a sign and a number, describing the type (i.e., activation or inhibition) and strength of the influence exerted. The process of inferring the existence of the edges among the genes modeled by the network and quantifying them with the type and strength of the interactions from microarray gene expression data uses *reverse engineering gene regulatory networks* and is discussed next.

12.3.1 Constructing GRNs from Microarray Data

The objective of reverse engineering is to infer the topology of the network describing the regulatory interactions among genetic variables from gene expression data automatically and in the absence of general theories [20]. The task aims at distinguishing true gene–gene interactions from spurious ones using the gene expression profiles.

Formally, we are given a data set D consisting of M measurements of the expression levels of N genes. For each gene represented by some variable X_i, $1 \leq i \leq N$, the data set D consists of the realization of the expression levels of X_i for the M measurements, that is, $x_1, x_2, \ldots, x_M$. The aim is to find a graph structure $G = (V(G), Q(G))$ having V as its set of nodes and Q as its set of edges that formalizes the dependencies embedded in the expression profiles given by D.

For the resulting network G, $X_1, \ldots, X_N$ will make up the nodes modeled by the network $V(G)$. The aim of reverse engineering is to find the components of $Q(G)$. The difficulties of the task stems not only from the challenges presented by the nature of gene expression data outlined in Section 12.2 but also because microarray data provide the expression levels of whole genomes (usually thousands of genes) at different but relatively few (usually a few dozens) temporal intervals or experimental conditions. From a computational point of view, the data available make the number of unknown variables (N) exponentially larger than the number of samples available (M) [13]. As a result, not enough observations are present for algorithms to produce a good estimate [27]. This is known as a the *curse-of-dimensionality problem*, which recognizes that the search space of the problem grows exponentially with the number of features (i.e., unknown variables) and for which many machine learning and data-mining methods have been proposed to tackle [27].

Another computational difficulty pertains to the nature of GRN structures. Gene regulatory networks adhere to a structural property termed free-scale topology. This structure is present in most natural networks [17, 44] and dictates that only a few nodes, termed hub nodes, are well connected (i.e., are connected to many other nodes), with the rest of the nodes having very few connections, as Figure 12.3 shows. For instance, [1, 31] suggest that in higher metazoa a gene or protein is estimated to interact with four to eight genes and is involved in 10 biological functions on average. The result is that GRNs are sparse, having

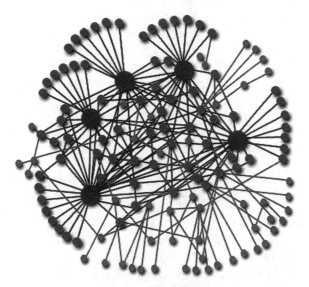

FIGURE 12.3   Free-scale network.

few connections given the number of nodes, which makes the task of inferring its structure
from the noisy and high-dimensional data computationally challenging [27].

12.3.2 Models for Reverse Engineering GRNs

The literature contains a variety of approaches to tackle the reverse engineering task differing
the level of details at which the gene–gene interactions are described [47]. At the most basic
level, clustering methods [12] offer a fast but coarse-grained approach which enables the
extraction of information about the coexpression profiles of the genes. However, clustering
is not useful if we want to uncover more refined interactions. On the other extreme, systems
of differential equations provide fine-grained details about the cellular biophysical processes
but they do not scale well to large systems and are therefore limited in usage [14].

Compromises between these two extremes are presented by Boolean networks [26],
neural networks [48], fuzzy systems [18], genetic programming [45], and Bayesian networks
[13, 32]. While each of these models has advantages and pitfalls, the Bayesian approach
has attracted special attention because of its ease of interpretation, natural way of capturing
the genetic interactions, and inherent capability to capture the stochastic nature and noise
of microarray data [10, 13]. More specifically, DBNs, which extend Bayesian networks to
capture temporal information and cyclic relations, have been successfully applied to extract
regulatory information from time-series microarray data [32, 50, 51] and learn large-scale
networks. The next section is concerned with introducing Bayesian networks and their use
in reconstructing GRN structures from microarray data.

12.4 BAYESIAN NETWORKS FOR LEARNING GRNs

The Bayesian method for reconstructing GRNs relies on modeling the data generated by
the microarray experiment, that is, D, by a joint probability distribution in which the genes
are represented by random variables and their expression levels are used as the probabilities

of the distribution. The hypothesis is that if knowing information about some gene A can provide information about another gene B, then, the two genes are said to be correlated and one can be a potential cause for the expression of the other gene. If this is the case, then, the conditional probabilities of the two variables (measured from their expression levels) can be used to construct the direction and quantify the parameters of the edge connecting the two. Before delving into the details of this approach, an introductory overview of Bayesian networks is given first.

12.4.1   Bayesian Networks

A Bayesian network (BN) is a compact graphical representation of a joint probability distribution Pr [25, 38] defined over a set of variables Ω. The network consists of a directed acyclic graph (DAG) in which the nodes correspond to random variables and the arcs represent direct dependencies between the linked variables [38].

If a directed edge in the graph exists from node X to node Y, then X is said to be a *parent Y* and Y conversely is termed X's child. The topology of the network implied by the directed edges can be used to model a causal influence between the connected nodes and constitute the qualitative aspect of the BN.

To fully specify a BN, the conditional probabilities of each node given its immediate predecessors are assigned, giving each node a local conditional probability distribution with respect to its predecessors [37]. Together, the qualitative and quantitative parts of a BN uniquely define a joint probability distribution on the set of variables under study. Formally:

Definition 12.1   *Bayesian Networks*   Given a probability distribution Pr, a BN representation of Pr is a directed acyclic graph $G = (V(G), Q(G))$, where $V(G)$ is the set of nodes capturing the variables of the domain and $Q(G)$ is the set of arcs capturing the conditional independence among the variables in the following way:

1. $\forall X, Y \in V(G)$, if $(X, Y) \in Q(G)$, then there exists a direct probabilistic dependence relationship between X and Y in which Y is directly dependent on X.
2. $\forall X, Y \in V(G)$, if $(X, Y) \in Q(G)$, then X is said to be an immediate predecessor or parent of Y, $X \in \pi(Y)$, where $\pi(Y)$ is the set of all parents of Y.
3. $\forall X_i \in V(G)$, X_i is described in terms of a conditional probability distribution $Pr(X_i|\pi(X_i))$ defined on X_i, where $Pr(X_i|\pi(X_i))$ reduces to an unconditional distribution if $\pi(X_i) = \phi$.

Hence, the independence relations of Pr are captured by the topology of the graph G in the following ways [38]:

1. A node is conditionally independent of its nondescendants given its parents.
2. A node is conditionally independent of all other nodes in the network given its parents, children, and children's parents (a node's parents, children, and children's parents are termed its Markov blanket).

Given these conditional independence properties, the only probabilities required to fully specify the joint distribution represented by the network are the conditional probability of the nodes given their parents and the prior probabilities of the root nodes. The result is a

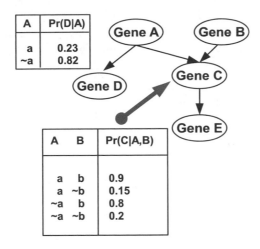

FIGURE 12.4 Bayesian network.

chain rule that can be used to recursively factorize the joint probability over all variables as given in Definition 12.2.

Definition 12.2 *Chain Rule*

$$\Pr(V(G)) = \Pr(X_1|X_2, \ldots, X_n) \Pr(X_2|X_3, \ldots, X_n) \cdots \Pr(X_n)$$
$$= \prod_{X_i \in V(G)} \Pr(X_i|\pi(X_i))$$

Figure 12.4 shows an example of a BN. In the figure, $V(G) = \{$gene A, gene B, gene C, gene D, gene $E\}$ and $Q(G) = \{$(gene A, gene D),(gene A, gene C),(gene B, gene C), (gene C, gene E)$\}$. According to Definition 12.1, the only probabilities required to fully specify the joint distribution are $\Pr(D|A)$, $\Pr(C|A, B)$, and $\Pr(E|C)$ and have the conditional probability table listed in the figure. Accordingly, the joint probability distribution defined by the five variables [i.e., $\Pr(A, B, C, D, E)$] can be found by applying the chain rule as

$$\Pr(A, B, C, D, E) = \Pr(A) \Pr(B) \Pr(C|A, B) \Pr(D|A) \Pr(E|C)$$

12.4.2 Dynamic Bayesian Networks

Despite the compact representation BNs provide, they are unable to handle the cyclic edges [33] due to their acyclic nature. However, the regulation relations we are after may contain cycles. To overcome this difficulty, DBNs [33] were employed to model cyclic relations by giving nodes a temporal dimension and regarding cycles as noncyclic connections between two nodes at different time slots, as shown in Figure 12.5.

In the figure, a BN cannot be used to model the cyclic network given in the left-hand side of the figure. However, the cycle (nodes: $A \rightarrow D \rightarrow E$) can be captured by a DBN by grouping the states of the nodes (genes A to D) into different time slots and dividing the edges making up the cycle among the time slots. More elaboration on DBNs and their use for modeling gene regulatory relations will be given in Section 12.6.1.3.

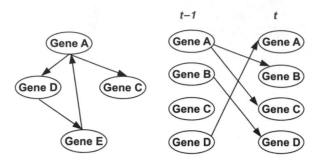

FIGURE 12.5 Constructing DBN from cyclic network.

12.4.3 Learning GRNs

Once the (dynamic) Bayesian network is constructed, its structure and parameters are used to model GRNs such that (1) its nodes represent the genes in the GRN; (2) its arcs represent the regulatory relations between the genes, where the existence of an arc between two nodes implies a regulation relation and lack thereof implies no regulation; and (3) the amount of regulation is captured by the local conditional probability distribution involving the connected nodes.

Nevertheless, the pressing problem is that of learning the unknown topology of the (dynamic) BN from microarray expression data D. Let M denote the structure of the BN representing the GRN underlying D; the learning task is to find a structure M that is most supported by the data, that is, one which has the most suitable posterior probability given D, $P(M|D)$.

There are essentially two schools of thought for Bayesian learning. The first proceeds by formulating hypotheses about possible conditional independences among triplets of variables and then verifying the hypotheses from the data accordingly [9]. Although this approach seems to be the natural way to learn the structure of the network from data, a large percentage of structure learning algorithms adhere to the second school of thought, mainly score and search methods [9]. These methods are based on the idea of a *scoring function*, which measures how well the candidate model M is described by the data D and ranks the possible models accordingly. Scoring metrics that have been used in the learning of Bayesian networks from data are penalized maximum-likelihood, Bayesian scores (like marginal likelihood) and scores based on information theory [9].

However, the number of possible graphs constructed using D grows exponentially to the size of the data D (for a data set D with N variables, there are N^2 possible interactions to be searched). Hence, it is nearly impossible to directly apply a score-based algorithm on large data [9, 27] as the problem is known to be NP hard [6].

In addition, because of the sparse nature of microarray data and the resulting curse-of-dimensionality problem mentioned in Section 12.3.1, the learned model will almost always suffer from overfitting [9], compromising the biological value of the network structures. Moreover, the sparseness of the data will cause any exact algorithm aiming to optimize for $P(M|D)$ to diffuse [20].

To tackle these issues, the next section describes how commonsense knowledge extracted from microarray data can be used to aid the structure-learning algorithm in DBNs.

12.5   TOWARD QUALITATIVE MODELING OF GRNs

Qualitative reasoning is now a well-established area in artificial intelligence [4, 36]. The field is concerned with explaining and predicting the behavior of physical phenomena without (or with the minimal use of) numerical information. It is motivated by the observation that people are capable of drawing subtle conclusions about many aspects of the physical world using less data than numerical and quantitative methods require. A subfield of qualitative reasoning is concerned with modeling probabilistic systems qualitatively and is based on the idea of building a reasoning system that makes full use of the principles underlying probabilistic reasoning without enumerating the exact probabilities required by BNs. Instead, what is captured is how probabilities change using categorial knowledge [46]. This is done by replacing conditional probabilities by relations describing how a variable's likelihood changes given the probability of the variables upon which it is conditionally dependent. The change is modeled by qualitative terms such as increase, decrease, no change, or an unknown change [46]. The idea has been extended to formulate qualitative equivalents of BNs, or QPNs.

When it comes to GRNs, we believe that QPNs can facilitate having a better-defined notion of regulation, one which exploits higher level commonsense information extracted from the gene expression profiles to complement the analysis of the data. The argument is is not only motivated by the many sources of uncertainty surrounding the data as the previous discussions have shown but also by several other merits specific to QPNs which can greatly help in the reverse engineering task. Therefore, in order to develop a good understanding of the purpose of this section we begin by listing the merits of using QPNs and qualitative reasoning in general.

12.5.1   Motivating Factors for Using Qualitative Models

In this section we justify the reasons for using QPNs in the reverse engineering of GRNs.

12.5.1.1   Abundance of Qualitative Information   The uncertainty surrounding microarray data does not prevent the extraction of useful qualitative information that can be used to uncover the underlying genetic interaction and effectively reason about it to obtain biological insight. In fact, microarray data contain information about the conditional independence among the genes in question, variable time delays, and the combined effects of complexes of end products over genes. Although this information can be modeled correctly using BNs (as done in [29]), there is other information of a strictly qualitative nature awaiting to be mined and which can be useful in uncovering the relations embedded in the data. More specifically, instead of using conditional probabilities to uncover the type of regulatory relation present between two (or more) genes (being of a stimulatory or an inhibiting nature), defining the conditions under which seemingly conditionally dependent genes do in fact exhibit regulatory ties is not directly derivable using the probabilistic model. Instead, the qualitative relations defined by QPNs can provide better clues to regulation as they have an explicitly defined notion of *influence* (to be discussed in Section 12.5.2), making one perfectly capable of formally defining the behavior of regulation relations and, if used properly, can be used to either uncover the network model or produce a candidate set of possible regulators that can reduce the search space for a DBN, which is the approach taken by the rest of the chapter.

12.5.1.2 Possibility for Extension   Biological pathways are intricate in nature, and their discovery remains an ongoing challenge. Moreover, it is now accepted that in order to obtain a biological insight, it is viable to examine data from different viewpoints with the aim of forming an integral examination of cellular interactions, for example, gene expression and protein–protein interactions [13]. Given this, discovering a biological pathway may require information for which there does not exist quantitative information (even noisy information). Having a model that can do away with this type of information makes it more portable and more capable of dealing with the surprises that may encounter the discovery process [24].

In order to perform such integral studies, we must first understand the biological principles that couple the measurements. In fact, it has been shown through stability analyses of gene expression models that describing models of gene networks requires information on both mRNA and protein levels [16]. Hence, while awaiting the development of acceptable large protein chip technology, a qualitative model can present a viable alternative.

12.5.1.3 Computational Efficiency   The dynamic nature of microarray time-series data requires the use of DBNs as regular BNs [32]. Despite the recent efforts to develop algorithms that are tailored to provide more efficient computations for uncovering genetic interactions [50, 51], inference in DBNs remains NP hard [6], as opposed to the polynomial–time arc-traversal algorithm for inference in QPNs [11].

Hence, qualitative probabilistic networks can be used to extract qualitative information from expression data which abstracts BNs while retaining their structural properties and use it to perform reasoning. Before introducing the framework that retrieves qualitative information from gene expression data, we first discuss the essentials of QPNs in the following section.

12.5.2 QPNs

QPNs are directed acyclic graphs that represent a qualitative abstraction of BNs [40, 46]. Formally, a QPN is given by a pair $G = (V(G), Q(G))$, where $V(G)$ is the set of nodes capturing random variables and $Q(G)$ is the set of arcs capturing the conditional dependence among the variables as in BNs. Instead of a known conditional probability distribution, the arcs of a QPN capture qualitative relations by finding monotonic characteristics in the local conditional probability distribution of each node [40]. The resulting relations are used to establish properties over the probabilities of events and are of two types, binary qualitative influences and tertiary qualitative synergies [46].

Influences describe how the change of the value of a single variable affects that of another, with the effect being categorized as positive, negative, constant, or unknown.

A positive influence exists between a parent node X and its child Y [X is said to positively influence Y, written as $I^+(X, Y)$] if observing higher values for X makes higher values of Y more probable, regardless of the value of any other node which may directly influence Y (i.e., any other parent of Y, denoted by W) as given in Definition 12.3. The definition assumes that the variables X and Y are binary and places a partial order on their values such that, for a variable X with two values x and $\neg x$, we have $x > \neg x$. Negative, constant, and unknown influences are analogously defined by replacing the $>$ sign by $<$, $=$, and ? respectively. While we use binary variables here to define influences for simplicity, the

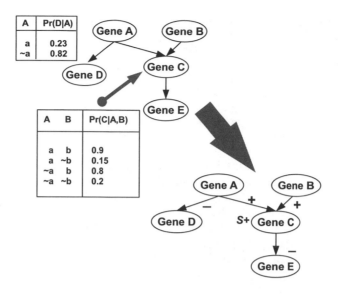

FIGURE 12.6 A BN with corresponding QPN.

definition can be easily extended for multivalued variables by placing the values in their appropriate locations in the inequality.

Definition 12.3 *Positive Influence* $I^+(X, Y)$ if and only if $\Pr(y|x, W) > \Pr(y|\neg x, W)$.

An example of a QPN illustrating influences is given in Figure 12.6, which shows the BN given as example in Figure 12.4 along with the QPN extracted from it. Instead of the conditional probabilities that are given in the BN, the only information encoded in the arcs is the signs of the influences from one node to another extracted from the conditional probability tables of each node. For instance, the negative influence exerted by gene A on gene D comes natural from gene D's conditional probability table given its parent gene A. A similar picture can be drawn to conclude $I^+(A, C)$ and $I^+(B, C)$. In the case of $I^+(A, C)$, W of Definition 12.3 is the set $\{B\}$ and the sign of the influence is obtained by comparing the probabilities $\Pr(c|a, B)$ (which is 1.05) and $\Pr(c|\neg a, B)$ (which is 1.0). With $I^+(B, C)$, W of Definition 12.3 is the set $\{A\}$ and the sign of the influence is the result of the comparison of probabilities $\Pr(c|b, A)$ (which is 1.7) and $\Pr(c|\neg b, A)$ (which is 0.35).

Although qualitative influences define the basic interactions among variables, they are not always sufficient to capture all the interactions that exist in the network. This is the case when it is necessary to identify the combined effect of a pair of parent nodes in union on another variable. For this, the concept of qualitative synergies is created in order to model the interaction among the influences between three nodes in a network's diagraph. Qualitative synergies are essentially of two classes depending on the type of interaction, mainly *additive* and *product* synergies, and can be positive, negative, constant, or unknown as in the case with influences. Since product synergies are not of direct relevance to this work, we will do away with a discussion about them.

Additive synergies describe the situations in which the combined influence of the parents on their common child is greater than the individual influence of each parent on the child [46]. For example, a positive additive synergy of two nodes X and Y on their common child

TABLE 12.1   **Sign Multiplication ($\otimes$) and Sign Addition ($\oplus$) Operators**

$\otimes$	+	−	0	?	$\oplus$	+	−	0	?
+	+	−	0	?	+	+	?	+	?
−	−	+	0	?	−	?	−	−	?
0	0	0	0	0	0	+	−	0	?
?	?	?	0	?	?	?	?	?	?

Z, written as $S^+(\{X, Y\}, Z)$, exists if the sum of their joint influence on Z is greater than the sum of their separate influences regardless of the value of any direct ancestor W of Z other than X and Y as given in Definition 12.4. As in the case of influences, the definition is stated for binary variables but can be similarly extended to multivalued ones.

Definition 12.4 *Positive Additive Synergy [46]* $S^+(\{X, Y\}, Z)$ if and only if, for any values x, y, z of X, Y, Z, respectively, and for any variable W such that $W \in \text{pa}(Z)/\{X, Y\}$, we have

$$\Pr(z|x, y, W) + \Pr(z|\neg x, \neg y, W) > \Pr(z|x, \neg y, W) + \Pr(z|\neg x, y, W)$$

where $\text{pa}(Z)$ denotes the set of Z's parents; therefore, $\text{pa}(Z)/\{X, Y\}$ is the set of all Z's parents except for X and Y.

In Figure 12.6, gene A and gene B exhibit a positive additive synergy on their common child gene C as the label $S+$ placed over the node C shows. This relation can be verified from gene C's conditional probability table given its parents; in this case, $W = \{\cdot\}$. Negative and constant additive synergies are analogously defined.

Observed evidence is propagated through the network via qualitative operators that combine influences and produce their net effects. There are two such operators serving different topologies of arcs. When evaluating the net effect of influences in a chain (such as the combined influence of gene A on gene E), the sign multiplication operator given in the left portion of Table 12.1 is used (resulting in a negative net influence). On the other hand, parallel connections (such as the individual influences of gene A on gene C and that of gene B on gene C) are evaluated using the sign addition operator given in the right portion of the table (resulting in a net positive influence). The signs propagate through the network until the net effect of the evidence is observed by the polynomial–time sign propagation algorithm [42].

It is worth noting that QPNs suffer from coarseness, which can result in many ambiguous signs, as Table 12.1 shows. However, because our aim is to use QPNs to only discover the topology of genetic networks, we will not discuss means for resolving the conflicts that can arise. The interested reader can refer to [40] for a general discussion and to [22] for a more biologically relevant application of conflict resolution.

12.6   QPNs FOR GENE REGULATION

Using the intuition that if some gene g_1 is said to regulate another gene g_2, then observing higher expression values for g_1 renders higher expression levels of g_2 more likely in the case of up regulation or less likely in the case of down regulation, one can map regulatory relations to qualitative QPN influences and use QPNs to model the topology of gene regulatory networks. Hence, the key to the approach presented here formally establishes a mapping between QPN constructs and gene regulation relations.

However, there are two crucial aspects in which QPNs and gene regulatory networks differ. First, because QPNs preserve the DAG structure of BNs, they are incapable of handling cyclic relations which are abundant in gene regulatory networks. Second, In contrast to binary influences and tertiary synergies, gene regulation relations may hold between an arbitrary number of parents and their children. To deal with these two limitations of QPNs, this section defines additional properties and constructs for QPNs to make them more usable for our purpose.

12.6.1 Dynamic QPNs

Here, we present dynamic QPNs (DQPNs) as a temporal extension of QPNs to enable them to handle time-series data and enable cyclic interactions based on the work presented in [21, 22, 30].

12.6.1.1 Terminology Let U be a set of n variables drawn from Pr, an unknown probability distribution on U, and let T be a totally ordered set of m temporal slices such that $T_1, \ldots, T_m \in T$. We denote the set of variables in each temporal slice by U^t ($1 \leq t \leq m$) and the set of n variables in U^t by X_i^t ($1 \leq i \leq n$).

Definition 12.5 *Temporal Snapshot* Let $G = (V(G), Q(G))$ be a DAG such that G is the qualitative probabilistic network representing U. An instance G_t of G represents a temporal snapshot of G in time slice T_t such that G_t retains the DAG structure of G.

Example 12.1 Consider Figure 12.7, representing a fictitious graph G capturing the I-map for Pr, the joint probability distribution on $U = \{A_1, A_2, A_3, A_4\}$. Each instance G_t of G ($1 \leq t \leq 3$ in the figure) represents a snapshot of G, where the variables in each temporal slice are given by $U_t = \{A_1^t, A_2^t, A_3^t, A_4^t\}$.

Definition 12.6 *Dynamic Instance* Let G_t be as given in Definition 12.5, where G_t defines a dynamic instance of the QPN whose structure is defined by G and is given by

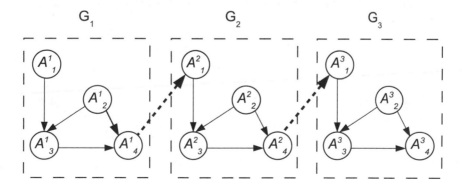

FIGURE 12.7 Example of G.

$G_t = (V(G_t), \{Q(G_t) \bigcup T(G_t)\}),^*$ where $V(G_t)$ and $Q(G_t)$ are instances of $V(G)$ and $Q(G)$, respectively, at time slot t and $T(G_t)$ describes the interslot conditional dependence between variables in $V(G_t)$ and its immediate neighbor $V(G_{t+1})$.

Example 12.2 In the graph given in Figure 12.7, for each G_t, $V(G_t) = U_t$, $Q(G_t) = \{(A_1^t, A_3^t), (A_2^t, A_3^t), (A_3^t, A_4^t), (A_2^t, A_4^t)\}$, and $T(G_t) = \{(A_4^t, A_1^{t+1})\}$.

Both $Q(G)$ and $T(G)$ encode a set of arcs for G to capture the set of qualitative relations representing how variables influence each other. For this, we redefine the concept of a qualitative influence to capture not only within-slot relations but also interslot ones. Before doing so, we first present the definition of a DQPN below.

Definition 12.7 *DQPN* Let $(G_1 = (V(G_1), \zeta(G_1)), \ldots, G_m = (V(G_m), \zeta(G_m)))$ be a total ordering of the m instances of G such that $T(G_t) \neq \emptyset$, $\forall 1 \leq t \leq m - 1$. Then the compound graph of $G_1, \ldots, G_m$ defines a DQPN over G and is given by

$$\bigcup_{t=1}^{m} G_t = \left(\bigcup_{t=1}^{m} V(G_t), \bigcup_{t=1}^{m} \zeta(G_t) \right)$$

12.6.1.2 *Qualitative Influences in a DQPN*

Definition 12.8 *Positive DQPN Influence* Let G_t and G_{t+1} be two adjacent subgraphs of the DQPN defined over G. Further, let X and Y be such that $X, Y \in V(G)$. A direct positive influence is exerted by node X over node Y, written as $I^+(X, Y)$, if and only if for all values x^i of X and $y^j, \neg y^j$ of Y and for all integer values i and j such that $1 \leq i, j \leq m$ and $i - j \in \{0, 1\}$ we have

$$\Pr(x^i | y^j, W) > \Pr(x^i | \neg y^j, W)$$

The superscripts i and j denote the temporal slot to which the instances x, y, and $\neg y$ belong. Moreover, the definition enforces a temporal order over its components by requiring that variables can only directly influence other variables that belong to the same temporal slot ($i = j$) or those that belong to the next immediate slot ($i = j = 1$). As in QPNs, W represents all other direct influences on Y other than X. Negative, zero, and unknown influences are analogously defined.

As the influences defined for DQPNs preserve the underlying principles of those defined for QPNs, they respect the combinatorial properties defined in Table 12.1 and can therefore be propagated according to their rules as in QPNs.

12.6.1.3 *Generalized Joint Influences* As stated earlier, because regulation is a many-to-many relationship, single influences and binary synergies are not sufficient for their description. There must be a way to establish the combined influence on many parent nodes over their common child in order to be able to define those relations. For this, we define the notion of a *generalized joint influence* of a set of k variables $X_1, \ldots, X_k$ over

---

*For readability purposes, we will refer to $\{Q(G_t) \bigcup T(G_t)\}$ as $\zeta(G_t)$ in this work.

a target variable Y which describes the monotonic relationship between the values of the variables $X_1, \ldots, X_k$ jointly and that of Y. Definition 12.9 illustrates a positive generalized joint influence $J^+(\{X_1, \ldots, X_k\}, Y)$. In the definition, the superscript i denotes the time slots at which the value of the child node y is observed while the superscripts $j_1, \ldots, j_k$ denote the time slots at which the influencing parents $X_1, \ldots, X_k$ are observed.

Definition 12.9 *Positive Generalized Joint Influence* $J^+(\{X_1, \ldots, X_k\}, Y)$ if and only if for value y of Y observed at time slot i and for any combination of values for variables $X_1, \ldots, X_k$ observed at time slots $j_1, \ldots, j_k$ such that $j_1, \ldots, j_k \leq i$:

$$\Pr(y^i|x_1{}^j, W) > \Pr(y^i|\neg x_1{}^j, W) \qquad k = 1$$
$$\Pr(y^i|x_1^{j_1}, \ldots, x_k^{j_k}, W) + \Pr(y^i|\neg x_1^{j_1}, \ldots, \neg x_k^{j_k}, W) > \wp \qquad k > 1$$

where $\wp$ is the sum of the conditional probability of Y given any combination of values for $X_1, \ldots, X_k$ other than $x_1^{j_1}, \ldots, x_k^{j_k}$ and $\neg x_1^{j_1}, \ldots, x_k^{j_k}$.

It can be seen that the case of binary synergies can be directly extracted from the definition by setting $k = 2$ and that negative and zero joint generalized influences can be analogously defined by replacing $>$ by $<$ and $=$, respectively.

In the next steps, we will use generalized joint influences of DQPNs to guide the process of identifying regulator genes for a given target. When referencing the influences defined above, we will use the notation $J^\wp(\{X_1, \ldots, X_k\}, Y)$ where $\wp \in \{+, -, 0\}$.

12.6.2 Approach

In this section, we describe the use of DQPNs and the generalized joint influences defined over them to aid in the construction of a DBN from microarray data. The approach is based on the following:

1. Using DQPN generalized joint influences to identify the set of regulators for each gene
2. Estimating time lags of regulations from the expression data
3. Infusing the qualitative knowledge in a DBN learning algorithm by using the candidate set of regulators to reduce the search space of possible models

The steps of the DQPN approach are detailed below.

12.6.2.1 *Constructing Qualitative Model* This step makes use of the monotonic relations corresponding to regulator–target interactions for the identification of the set of potential regulators of a specific gene. The step is twofold: First a quantitative analysis is performed based on comparing the times of significant initial change in expression levels of the genes to construct an initial set of candidate regulators for each gene; then another step follows to discover those candidates that exhibit a monotonic behavior with respect to the target gene and discard spurious interactions by building the subsets of regulators that jointly exhibit a generalized influence over the target gene, as described in Section 12.6.1.3.

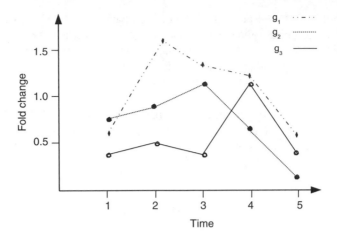

FIGURE 12.8 Hypothetical example illustrating possible regulators.

12.6.2.2 *Gathering Potential Regulators*

The quantitative step is not unique to DQPNs and is based on the hypothesis that more often than not regulators exhibit an earlier up or down change in their expression levels than that of the regulated genes [51]. This is of course not always the case, as will be clear in Section 12.6.3.2, but we think that it is a good estimator of regulation relations that can be improved in future models.

A gene is said to be up or down regulated if its expression level goes up (in the case of up regulation) or goes down (in the case of down regulation) by a certain fold change α. Since the aim of this step is to identify all potential regulators, we decided to use modest cutoffs of $\alpha = 1.1$ for up regulation or $\alpha = 0.9$ for down regulation in order not to overlook potential regulators.

Once the genes with significant fold changes have been identified, then for each gene g the genes with simultaneous or preceding fold changes are placed in the set of potential regulators of g. Establishing this set for every gene marks the completion of the quantitative part of this step.

A simple fictitious example illustrating this step is given in Figure 12.8. In the figure, gene g_3 has both g_1 and g_2 as potential regulators because its expression level had a significant increase at time step 4, which follows the time steps for which g_1 and g_2 had a significant increase in their expression levels.

12.6.2.3 *Extracting Most Likely Regulators*

A quick critical examination of the procedure described above reveals:

1. It can potentially incorporate many spurious relations because it assumes that change in expression levels entails a regulatory relation and does not consider a more well-defined notion of regulation (such as the one we provided in Section 12.6.1.3), which is the case for all stochastic approaches currently existing in the literature.
2. It does not distinguish between (i) coregulation, where several genes collectively activate or inhibit the expression of a target gene, and (ii) simple regulation, where a

ALGORITHM 12.1

Input: Gene g and set R of its potential regulators.
Output: Set O contains the most likely regulating sets of g.

```
 1:    for {k = |R| to 1 } do
 2:        ∀R_sub ⊆ R : |R_sub| = k
 3:            if ∀r₁^{i₁},...r_k^{i_k} ∈ R_sub, J^℘({r₁^{i₁},...,r_k^{i_k}}, g)  then
 4:                O ← R_sub
 5:            end if
 6:        end for
 7:    for { O_sub ⊂ O } do
 8:        if { ∃O_sub2 ⊆ O : O_sub2 ⊂ O_sub } then
 9:            O ← O - O_sub2
10:        end if
11:    end for
```

---

target gene has a set of regulators, each individually regulating the gene without the need for the other regulators to be present.

This is where the qualitative relations defined over DQPNs come into the picture in a procedure described in Algorithm 12.1. The idea is to find the maximum number of potential regulators that exhibit monotonic effects on the expression of the regulated gene and call the resulting set the most likely regulators of the gene. The algorithm receives as input a gene g along with the set R of its potential regulators identified using the quantitative method described above. The output is a collection O of subsets of R where each individual subset contains the genes that together coregulate g.

Lines 1–6 of the algorithm construct the subsets of R of decreasing size whose elements jointly exhibit a generalized influence over g. For each subset R_{sub} of R of size k (line 2), if the elements of R_{sub} satisfy some generalized influence $J^℘$ over g (condition in line 3), then R_{sub} is added to O, the set of most likely regulating sets of g (line 4).

The second phase of the algorithm (lines 7–11) removes redundant subsets by making sure that any proper subsets of O_{sub} (denoted by O_{sub2}) are not included in the set of all potential regulators given that its superset is included (line 8). This phase also establishes the distinction between joint and individual regulators by ensuring that for every subset of potential regulators O_{sub} of O one-element subsets made of its individual members are not included in the final output O as this corresponds to stating that each element of O_{sub} individually regulates g.

It is important to note that the time delays of the elements of the collection O for every regulated gene g are directly encoded in the construction of the set as the condition checks for the generalized joint influence given in line 3 shows.

Moreover, there are several points worth noting with respect to the use of generalized joint influences of Definition 12.9 and Algorithm 12.1 for discovering regulatory relationships. They are:

1. The temporal precedence properties of generalized joint influences are more relaxed than in Definition 12.8 of DQPN influences. This is to allow the discovery of regulation

relations between genes that may not belong to two consecutive time slots as fold changes of regulating genes may occur much earlier than those of target genes.

2. Generalized joint influences describe the combined influence of multiple parents such that all the influences yield the same sign, be it positive, negative, or constant. As a result, a target gene node may have two or more sets of generalized joint influences exerted on it by different subsets of its regulators according to how the elements of each subset satisfies the definition of the corresponding generalized joint influence.

3. Unknown influences generated by Definition 12.9 correspond to no regulation in the resulting gene regulatory network.

12.6.2.4 *Estimating Time Lag*   One issue with respect to the use of DBNs to model gene regulatory networks is that DBNs construct conditional distributions over fixed time intervals measured according to the time series. This has been found to be problematic [49] as it can miss potential regulation relations. However, DQPNs incorporate the time lag between each gene's expression and that of its potential regulators by marking the difference between their significant fold changes, and the resulting model will not suffer from this problem.

Hence, for each gene g the following were collected: (1) the sets of joint regulator genes O and (2) their corresponding time lags. The resulting adjacency list L of length N contains this information for all N genes such that for each gene in the list $L[j]$, $1 \leq j \leq N$, a linked list containing $L[j]$'s set of most likely regulators O is added where each node of the list represents one subset of joint regulators (O_{sub} in Algorithm 12.1) along with their times of significant fold changes, as the algorithm has shown.

12.6.2.5 *Aided Learning with Qualitative Joint Influences*   A score-maximizing learning algorithm that utilizes the additional aid of the list L was used to construct the target GRN. The corresponding criterion for maximizing the score is composed of two quantities. The first is the prior structure of the network established by L which contains the most likely regulators of every target gene constitutes a model that is used in this step as the base for a model search using DBN learning. The second is the marginal likelihood of the data, which measures how the model fits the microarray data. For each target gene, its conditional probability given its regulators is constructed from the expression data and was used to compute marginal likelihood scores.

12.6.3 Computational Experiments and Results

In this section we describe our computational experiments and discuss the results.

12.6.3.1 *Data and Preprocessing*   The data used are the gene expression time course data set the of *D. melanogaster* genetic network obtained from the *Drosophila* interaction database to compare the DQPN approach presented here with that of [51]. The data set contains 4028 genes whose expression levels were sampled at 74 time points covering the four life-cycle stages of embryonic, larval, pupal, and adulthood [2].

The original data set is quantized into a fold-change series by computing the ratio of expression of each gene g at two consecutive time points x_t and $x_{t+\Delta}$. The resulting set contains the fold changes enabling the establishment of times of significant change in expression for all the genes. Missing values are computed using a simple linear interpolation by obtaining the mean of the preceding and following neighbors in the expression time series for the specific gene. When the missing expression is a start or an end point in the time series, it is replaced by the nearest observed neighbor's value (resulting in no significant fold change).

12.6.3.2 *Accuracy Evaluation*

In order to obtain an initial visual image of the performance of the DQPN method, we first used it to construct the GRN of a selected set of 12 genes from our data set. The selected genes have been reported to describe the larval somatic muscle development stage of *D. melanogaster* and contains a total of 18 known interactions.

A comparison between the DQPNs and the approach presented in [51] for this set of genes is shown in Figure 12.9. While DQPNs successfully identified 15 interactions, using DBNs according to [51] only identified 11 of the total 18 interactions. Upon a close examination, we found that the missing interactions from the DQPN network are due to the assumption of regulators having an earlier or simultaneous expression time than regulated genes. For instance, examining CG9843, which regulates CG7447, it turns out that CG9843 has a much shorter half-life than CG7447. As a result, the regulator's mRNA will take much longer in reaching a steady-state level of up or down regulation compared to the regulated gene, resulting in an apparent later change of expression. Since this assumption is also made by [51], the method did not identify these interactions either. Moreover, using DQPNs identified coregulating genes using the synergetic definition of the initial model. These co-regulations along with feedforward loops, were largely missed by [51]'s method, resulting in a smaller number of identified relations. Apart from (G9843, G7447), the DQPN network is missing the interactions (CG6972, CG2046) and (CG13501, CG17440).

Comparison of larger subsets of the networks is given in Table 12.2. In the table, the experiments are labeled by $DBN_{qual}(N,I)$ or $DBN_{ZN}(N,I)$ denoting the approach used (DBN_{qual} refers to using DQPNs and DBN_{ZN} refers to using DBNs according to [51]) with N denoting the number of genes involved in the network while I refers to number of known interactions. The sizes of the networks were selected randomly and the subset of genes involved were based on the current interaction diagram of the *Drosophila* genetic network.

For each network size, 10 runs were performed and reported the average performance measures of the number of correctly identified edges or true positive edges (C); the number of misidentified edges or false positive edges (F), which have been identified by the learning algorithm but do not exist in the real network; and the number of missed edges (M), which are edges that exist in the real network but were either unidentified or given the wrong regulator-regulated gene direction in the inferred network. Precision is calculated as the ratio $C/(C + M)$ and recall as the ratio $C/(C + F)$ and are listed accordingly in Table 12.2.

The results given in the table show the clear improvement DQPNs present in terms of both precision and recall. The improved precision shown by DQPNs is due to the discovery of joint regulations and feedforward loop identifications as discussed earlier. Moreover, the increased recall is due to the better definition of regulation provided by the monotonic relations of the synergies and influences that QPNs provide. The numbers clearly show that this definition helps in eliminating many spurious correlations that do not correspond to regulatory relations.

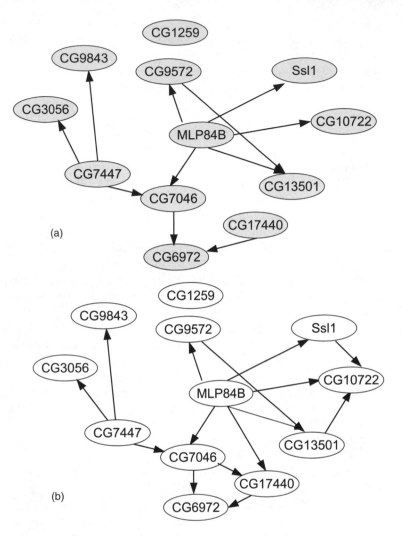

FIGURE 12.9 Muscle development network in *Drosophila* larval stage: (a) using DBN from [51]; (b) using DQPNs.

12.6.3.3 Efficiency Evaluation Table 12.2 shows the average running time of the algorithms at each experimental setup. The time taken by our algorithm does not include the step of generating the most likely regulators in our algorithm, so that the actual learning time of our algorithm can be compared with that of [51].

The improvement presented by DQPNs is contributed to the fact that Algorithm 12.1 provides a candidate set which minimizes the number of potential regulators so that the only possible regulators are those that exhibit the monotonicity of qualitative influences and synergies and excludes those exhibiting a correlation that does not correspond to a regulatory relation. This optimal candidate set is the main contributor to the better performance exhibited by our algorithm.

TABLE 12.2 Results of Comparing DBN$_{qual}$ and DBN$_{ZN}$ Using Differently Sized Sample Networks

	Correct Edges (C)			False Edges (F)			Missed Edges (M)			Precision	Recall	Average Time
	Min.	Max.	Avg.	Min.	Max.	Avg.	Min.	Max.	Avg.			
DBN$_{qual}$(12, 18)	13	17	15	0	4	2	1	3	2	0.88	0.88	12.9
DBN$_{ZN}$(12, 18)	9	12	10.5	2	9	5.5	5	5	5	0.66	0.66	19.5
DBN$_{qual}$(40, 80)	51	62	54.5	15	19	17	21	28	24.5	0.689	0.76	31.9
DBN$_{ZN}$(40, 80)	38	46	42	35	41	38	40	49	44.5	0.486	0.525	38.4
DBN$_{qual}$(50, 95)	61	69	65	29	42	35.5	28	34	31	0.677	0.647	23.1
DBN$_{ZN}$(50, 95)	45	51	48	48	57	52.5	51	68	54.5	0.468	0.478	34.3
DBN$_{qual}$(80, 100)	68	79	73.5	41	49	45	38	43	40.5	0.645	0.62	57.3
DBN$_{ZN}$(80, 100)	53	64	58.5	45	51	48	41	49	45	0.56	0.46	86.6

12.7 SUMMARY AND CONCLUSIONS

This chapter explored the use of qualitative reasoning to aid the process of reverse engineering gene regulatory networks from microarray data with DBNs. A model is presented where qualitative probability is used to discover monotonic relations among genes by comparing their expression profiles and using the discovered qualitative relations to aid the DBN learning algorithm in constructing better and more efficient models of the corresponding GRN. An experimental study was presented in which the results of the models given here are compared with an accepted benchmark for DBN learning [51]. The results show that the added qualitative knowledge highly improves the type of model inferred and the efficiency of the learning procedure. The results were compared using the *D. Melanogaster* gene regulation data set.

This research work is still ongoing, and we are planning to extend our DQPN approach in a number of ways:

1. Our definition of DQPN is a direct extension of the first-order DBN (FO-DBN) definition; that is, it also assumes that the expression value of a gene at time t depends only on the genes' expression values at time $t - r$ with $r = 1$. Thus, our first-order DQPN (FO-DQPN) cannot model time-delayed interactions in which most GRNs occur. We plan to propose high-order DQPNs (HO-DQPNs) to model time-delayed interaction; this is done by assuming an r-order Markov dependence of gene expression over time, with $r > 1$, and then extracting the qualitative information given a HO-DQPN structure and time-series gene expression data. This is essentially an extension of current HO-DBN approaches described in the literature.

2. currently, we do not *learn* a DQPN directly; given time-series expression data, we use DQPNs to extract the qualitative information from the data, then initialize a DBN structure using such information, and then subsequently learn the correct DBN (structure and parameters) identifying a best fit GRN (see Section 12.6.2.5). We plan to devise and approach for directly learning DQPNs (FO-DQPNs and HO-DQPNs) from time-series expression data. Different learning methods can be used, such as genetic algorithms (GAs) or Monte Carlo Markov chain (MCMC) optimization, to name a few.

3. Many of the (latest) techniques proposed in the identification of GRNs via DBN methods can also be studied for reverse engineering GRNs via DQPN methods.

4. Finally, we have only compared our DQPN approaches with the DBN methods of [51], and we plan to compare it with other methods and on different time-series expression data.

REFERENCES

1. M. Arnone and E. Davidson. The hardwiring of development: Organization and function of genomic regulatory systems. *Development*, 124:1851–1864, 1997.

2. M. Arbeitman et al. Gene expression during the life cycle of *Drosophila melanogaster. Science*, 297:2270–2275, 2002.

3. N. Barker. Learning genetic regulatory network connectivity from time series data. *IEEE Trans. Computat. Biol. Bioinformatics (TCBB)*, 8(1):152–165, 2011.

4. D. Berleant and B. Kuipers. Qualitative and quantitative simulation: Bridging the gap. *AI*, 95(2):215–255, 1997.

5. L. Chen, R. Wang, and X. Zhang. *Biomolecular Networks: Methods and Applications in Systems Biology, Wiley Series in Bioinformatics*, Wiley, Hoboken, NJ, 2009.

6. D. M. Chickering, D. Heckerman, and C. Meek. Large-sample learning of Bayesian networks is NP-hard. *J. Machine Learning Res.*, 5:1287–1330, 2004.

7. F. Collins, M. Morgan, and A. Patrinos. The Human Genome Project: Lessons from large-scale biology. *Science*, 300(5617):286–290, 2003.

8. F. Crick. Central dogma of molecular biology. *Nature*, 227:561–563, 1970.

9. A. Darwiche. *Modeling and Reasoning with Bayesian Networks*. Cambridge University Press, New York, NY, 2009.

10. P. D'haeseleer. Reconstructing gene networks from large scale gene expression data. Ph.D. Dissertation. University of New Mexico, 2000.

11. M. Druzdzel and M. Henrion. Efficient reasoning in qualitative probabilistic networks. In R. Fikes and W. G. Lehnert (Eds.), *Proceedings of the 11th National Conference on Artificial Intelligence*, AAAI Press/The MIT Press, Washington, DC, 1993, pp. 548–553.

12. Z. Fang et al. Comparisons of graph-structure clustering methods for gene expression data. *Acta Biochim. Biophys. Sinica*, 38(6):379–384, 2006.

13. N. Friedman. Inferring cellular networks using probabilistic graphical models. *Science*, 303:799–805, 2004.

14. J. Gebert, N. Radde, and G. Weber. Modeling gene regulatory networks with piecewise linear differential equations. *Eur. J. Oper. Res.*, 181(3):1148–1165, 2007.

15. Y. Guo et al. How is mRNA expression predictive for protein expression: A correlation study on human circulating monocytes. *Acta Biochim. Biophys. Sinica*, 40(5):426–436, 2008.

16. V. Hatzimanikatis and K. Lee. Dynamic analysis of gene networks requires both mRNA and protein expression information. *Metabol. Eng.*, 1:17, 1999.

17. A. Hernando et al. Unravelling the size distribution of social groups with information theory on complex networks. *Euro. Phys. J. B—Condens. Matter Complex Syst.* 76(1):87–97, 2011.

18. X. Hu et al. Mining, modeling and evaluation of sub-networks from large biomolecular networks and its comparison study. *IEEE Trans. Inform. Technol. Biomed.*, 13(2):184–194, 2009.

19. L. Hunter. Life and its molecules, a brief introduction. *AI Mag.*, 25(1):9–22, 2004.

20. D. Husmeier. Reverse engineering of genetic networks with Bayesian networks. *Biochem. Soc. Trans.*, 31(6):1516–1518, 2003.

21. Z. Ibrahim, A. Ngom, and A. Tawfik. Using qualitative probability in reverse-engineering gene regulatory networks. *IEEE/ACM Trans. Computat. Biol. Bioinformatics*, 8(2):326–334, 2011.

22. Z. Ibrahim, A. Tawfik, and A. Ngom. Qualitative motif detection in gene regulatory networks. In C. Wu and D. Xu (Eds.), Paper presented at the IEEE International Conference on Bioinformatics and Biomedicine (BIBM), Washington, DC, 2009, pp. 124–129.

23. Z. Ibrahim, A. Tawfik, and A. Ngom. A dynamic qualitative probabilistic network approach for extracting gene regulatory network motifs. In L. Chen, M. Ng, and L. Wong (Eds.), Paper presented at the IEEE International Conference on Bioinformatics and Biomedicine (BIBM), Hong Kong, 2010, pp. 380–385.

24. S. Iyenga and M. McGuire. Imprecise and qualitative probability in systems biology. Paper presented at the International Conference on Systems Biology, 2007.

25. F. Jensen. *Bayesian Networks and Decision Graphs*. Springer-Verlag, New York, 2001.

26. H. Lähdesmäki et al. On learning gene regulatory networks under the Boolean network model. *Machine Learning*, 52(1–2):147–167, 2003.

27. Pedro Larranaga et al. Machine learning in bioinformatics. *Brief. Bioinformatics*, 7(1):86–112, 2007.

28. B. Lehner and C. Sanderson. A protein interaction framework for human mRNA degradation. *Genomic Res.*, 14:1315–1323, 2004.

29. T. Liu and W. Sung. Learning gene network using conditional dependence. In C.-T. Lu and N. G. Bourbakis (Eds.), *18th IEEE International Conference on Tool with Artificial Intelligence*, Washington, DC, 2006, pp. 800–804.

30. W. Liu et al. Qualitative-probabilistic-network-based modeling of temporal causalities and its application to feedback loop identification. *Int. J. Inform. Sci.*, 178(7):1803–1824, 2008.

31. G. Miklos and G. Rubin. The role of the genome project in determining gene function: Insights from model organisms. *Cell*, 86(4):521–529, 1996.

32. K. Murphy and S. Mian. Modeling gene expression data using dynamic Bayesian networks. Technical report. University of California, Berkeley, CA, 1999.

33. K. Murphy. Dynamic Bayesian networks: Representation, inference and learning. Ph.D. Dissertation. University of California, Berkeley, 2002.

34. L. Nie, G. Wu, and W. Zhang. Correlation of mRNA expression and protein abundance affected by multiple sequence features related to translational efficiency in Desulfovibrio vulgaris, a quantitative analysis. *Genetics* 174:2229–2243, 2006.

35. L. Pascal et al. Correlation of mRNA and protein levels: Cell type-specific gene expression of cluster designation antigens in the prostate. *BMC Genomics*, 23(9):246–258, 2008.

36. S. Parsons. *Qualitative Methods for Reasoning under Uncertainty*. MIT Press, Cambridge, MA, 2001.

37. J. Pearl. Fusion, propagation, and structuring in belief networks. *AI Mag.*, 29(3):241–288, 1986.

38. J. Pearl. *Probabilistic Reasoning in Intelligent Systems: Networks of Plausible Inference*, Morgan Kaufmann, 1988.

39. A. Pisabarro et al. Genetic networks for the functional study of the genomes. *Brief. Funct. Genomics Proteomics*, 7(4):249–263, 2008.

40. S. Renooij and L. Van der Gaag. From qualitative to quantitative probabilistic networks. Paper presented at the International Conference on Uncertainty in Artificial Intelligence, 2002, pp. 422–429.

41. S. Torniuk and K. Hofmann. Microarray probe selection strategies. *Brief. Bioinformatics*, 2(4):329–340, 2001.

42. F. Van Kouwen, S. Renooij, and P. Schot. Inference in qualitative probabilistic networks revisited. *Int. J. Approximate Reasoning*, 50(5):708–720, 2009.

43. E. Van Someren et al. Genetic network modeling. *Pharmacogenomics*, 3(4):507–525, 2002.

44. M. Steyvers and J. Tenenbaum. The large-scale structure of semantic networks: Statistical analyses and a model of semantic growth. *Cognitive Sci.*, 29(1):41–78, 2005.

45. H. Wang and L. Qian. Inference of gene regulatory networks using genetic programming and Kalman filter. *IEEE Trans. Signal Process.* 56(7):3327–3339, 2008.

46. M. Wellman. Fundamental concepts of qualitative probabilistic networks. *AI*, 44:257–303, 1990.

47. L. Wessels, E. Someren, and M. Reinders. A comparison of genetic network models. Pacific Symposium on Biocomputing (PSB), 2001, pp. 508–519.

48. R. Xu, D. Wunsch II, and R. Frank. Inference of genetic regulatory networks with recurrent neural network models using particle swarm optimization. *IEEE/ACM Trans. Computat. Bio. Bioinformatics (TCBB)*, 4(4):681–692, 2007.

49. Z. Xiing and D. Wu. Modeling multiple time units delayed gene regulatory networks using dynamic Bayesian networks. IEEE International Conference on Data Minings, 2005, pp. 190–195.

50. Y. Zhang et al. Inferring gene regulatory networks from multiple data sources via a dyanamic Bayesian network with structural EM. Paper presented at the International Conference on Data Integration in the Life Sciences, 2007, pp. 204-214.

51. M. Zou and S. Conzen. A new dynamic Bayesian network (DBN) approach for identifying gene regulatory networks from time course microarray data. *Bioinformatics*, 2(1):70–71, 2005.

52. H. Zhu and M. Snyder. Protein arrays and microarrays. *Curr. Opin. Chem. Bio.*, 5:40-45, 2001.

PART D

BIOLOGICAL FEATURE SELECTION

CHAPTER 13

COMPARING, RANKING, AND FILTERING MOTIFS WITH CHARACTER CLASSES: APPLICATION TO BIOLOGICAL SEQUENCES ANALYSIS

MATTEO COMIN and DAVIDE VERZOTTO

Department of Information Engineering, University of Padova, Padova, Italy

13.1 INTRODUCTION

In biology the notion of motif plays a central role for describing various phenomena. For example, protein functional motifs, like the ones contained in the PROSITE database [20] (e.g. [FY]DPC[LIM][ASG]C[ASG]), are in general represented as motifs with character classes. These motifs are collected using semiautomatic procedures; nevertheless they are still manually verified.

The discovery of sequence motifs in proteins and genes is becoming increasingly important [2, 29]. Such motifs usually correspond to residues conserved during evolution due to some significant structural or functional role. Moreover, the increasing availability of biological sequences such as whole genomes from next-generation sequencing technologies to new protein discoveries has increased the need for automatic methods for their analysis and comparison.

In order to fill this gap, researchers have developed several approaches over the years. Typically these approaches follow in popular frameworks of motif discovery and matching [4, 6, 17, 23, 26, 30, 41, 44]. Although such methods have been exhaustively consolidated and successfully tested on small genomes and sets of proteins [12, 21, 25], the algorithm's outcome often exceeds the length of the original input [10, 36, 40], making it impossible to be handled and then interpreted for further analyses that require manual inspection. The main underlying difficulty of these frameworks is that, in order to model mutations and other evolutionary mechanisms, motifs have to account for some degree of variability. To this end, motifs are often modeled to include undetermined symbols, ?, called *don't care* (e.g., DPC?IM??C), or classes of symbols (e.g., [FY]DPC[LIM][ASG]C[ASG]). Unfortunately the discovery and matching of such motifs can be prohibitive. In fact, even in a simple string there might be an exponential number of motifs with don't care symbols.

The rest of the chapter is organized as follows. In Section 13.2, we give a characterization of motifs with character classes, following with the notion of *motif priority* for comparing and ranking different motifs together. In Section 13.3, we introduce the concept of *underlying motifs* for filtering any set of motifs with character classes into a new set that is linear in size with respect to a reference sequence. We then present an algorithm to compute this new set exploiting the notions of Section 13.2. Finally, in Section 13.4 we discuss some preliminary results on the identification of signals in protein sequences by means of underlying motifs.

13.1.1 Ranking and Clustering Motifs

To cope with the combinatorial explosion of motifs, motif discovery tools must first shrink the search space. In this regard, a number of different techniques have been proposed over the past two decades. In general, these techniques are based on the lexicographic composition of motifs [3, 5, 22, 28, 34] or on their statistical distribution [6, 33, 42]. Despite that, the number of motifs in output still remains in most cases intractable.

Moreover, all motif discovery tools must ultimately rank the output according to some measure of importance. For example, even if very sophisticated probabilistic scoring mechanisms are in place in a state-of-the-art tool such as Varun [4], there are cases where the direct interpretation of results is far from trivial. Let us consider, for instance, the worst case of [4] presented in Figure 13.1. The functionally relevant motif, shown in bold, appears at position 42, whereas almost all top motifs are somehow very similar. In order to filter out this output and enhance its readability, there are two main issues. On the one hand, most motifs are very similar in sequence and therefore they must be clustered together in some way. On the other hand, if we are interested in a specific region of the reference sequence, one would like to select the most important motif that appears in that region according to some rule. These two issues are in practice tightly related and they need to be addressed as one.

13.1.2 Ensemble Methods

In the last decade a number of ensemble methods have been developed [35, 43, 46]. The basic idea is that one can integrate the outcome of several motif discovery algorithms based on simple and efficient heuristics to improve the ability of finding functional motifs in specific contexts. The ensemble methods actually rank all predicted motifs according to some scoring functions and then report the top motifs. WebMotifs [35], ARCS-Motif [46], MotifMiner [11], and MotifVoter [43] assume that some of the motifs given by the consensus of several finders are likely to be functional motifs. They ultimately cluster all motifs and report only those from the best clusters. However, if none of the motifs from the individual finders can accurately capture the binding sites, the performance of the ensemble methods will suffer. Although these ensemble methods indeed help to improve the performance of motif finding, the improvement is usually not significant. For example, in Tompa's benchmark [39] and *Escherichia coli* data sets, the average sensitivity is only improved by 62%, but the average precision is reduced by 15%.

This relatively new topic deserves more attention, along with its mathematical and combinatorial foundations. In this chapter we will discuss the basic problems behind motif comparison and ranking. We will show how simple lexicographic properties can help to select a small subset of motifs, thus filtering the output of any finder to a more tractable size.

Rank	z-score	Motif
1	2,84E+09	Y???L???C??[FYW]A??[STAH]R??P??FNE[STAH]K?I?F[STAH]M
2	8,28E+07	V-(1,3,4)G???S??[STAH]????N???L????Q-(4)[STAH]????L?[DN]???[FYW]??F????P????Q??A???I
3	5,55E+07	L-(2,3)F???Q????[STAH][STAH]???L?[DN]???[FYW]??F?R??P?D??Q??A???I
4	4,27E+07	L-(2,3)F???Q?[STAH]??[STAH][STAH]????S????[FYW]??F?R??P?D??Q??A???I
5	4,23E+07	L????I???[STAH]??[STAH]????LS[DN]???[FYW]??F?R??P?D??Q??A???I
6	3,99E+07	LF-(3)Q????[STAH][STAH]????S[DN]???[FYW]??F?R??P?D??Q??A???I
7	3,38E+07	LF-(3)Q????[STAH]??L?[DN]???[FYW]??F?R??P?D??Q??A???I
8	3,38E+07	LF???Q????[STAH]-(4)L?[DN]???[FYW]??F?R??P?D??Q[STAH]?A???I
9	3,29E+07	I-(1)Q?[STAH]??[STAH]????LS[DN]???[FYW]??F?R??P?D??Q??A???I
10	3,29E+07	I?Q-(4)[STAH]????LS[DN]???[FYW]??F?R??P?D??Q[STAH]?A???I
11	3,29E+07	I?Q?[STAH]-(4)LS[DN]???[FYW]??F?R??P?D??Q??A???I
12	3,10E+07	L????Q-(1,4)[STAH]??[STAH]????LS[DN]???[FYW]??F?R??P?D??Q??A???I
13	2,77E+07	L[FYW]-(3)Q?[STAH]??[STAH]????LS????[FYW]??F?R??P?D??Q??A???I
14	2,58E+07	L-(4)Q?[STAH]??[STAH]????LS[DN]???[FYW]??F?R??P?D??Q??A???I
15	2,30E+07	S?[STAH]S-(2,4)LS[DN]???[FYW]??F?R??P?D??Q[STAH]?A???I
16	2,15E+07	L-(1,3,4)C??[FYW]A??[STAH]R??P??F?E?K?I?F?M
17	1,40E+07	F-(1)I?Q???[STAH][STAH]-(4)L[STAH]????[FYW]??F?R??P?D??Q??A???I
18	1,37E+07	L-(2,4)I???[STAH]?[STAH]-(3)LS????[FYW]??F?R??P?D??Q??A???I
19	1,02E+07	L??I-(1)Q????[STAH][STAH]????S????[FYW]??F?R??P?D??Q??A???I
20	8,65E+06	I-(1)Q????[STAH][STAH]??L?[DN]???[FYW]??F?R??P?D??Q??A???I
21	8,19E+06	S[STAH]-(1,2,3,4)LS[DN]???[FYW]??F?R??P?D??Q[STAH]?A???I
22	7,98E+06	Q-(3)[STAH][STAH]???LS[DN]???[FYW]??F?R??P?D??Q??A???I
23	6,82E+06	F-(3)Q????[STAH][STAH]???L[STAH]????[FYW]??F?R??P?D??Q??A???I
24	5,66E+06	A[STAH][STAH]-(2,3)LS[DN]???[FYW]??F?R??P?D??Q??A???I
25	5,57E+06	F?I-(3)[STAH]??[STAH]????L[STAH]????[FYW]??F?R??P?D??Q??A???I
26	5,18E+06	L?L-(4)Q????[STAH]????L-(1)[DN]???[FYW]??F?R??P?D??Q??A???I
27	3,61E+06	L?L-(2)I???[STAH]???[STAH]????[STAH]????[FYW]??F?R??P?D??Q??A???I
28	3,48E+06	[STAH]?[STAH]-(1,2,3)LS[DN]???[FYW]??F?R??P?D??Q??A???I
29	3,17E+06	[STAH]???[STAH]???LS[DN]???[FYW]??F?R??P?D??Q??A???I
30	2,47E+06	L????Q-(4)[STAH][STAH]????S????[FYW]??F?R??P?D??Q??A???I
31	2,43E+06	V-(1,3)N?L????I-(3)[STAH]???[STAH]????[STAH]????[FYW]??F????P?D??Q??A???I
32	2,22E+06	[STAH][STAH][STAH]-(1,2,3)LS????[FYW]??F?R??P?D??Q??A???I
33	2,06E+06	[STAH]?[STAH][STAH]????LS????[FYW]??F?R??P?D??Q??A???I
34	2,03E+06	Y???L???C??A???R??P??F?E?K?I-(1,4)[FYW][STAH]
35	1,99E+06	I?Q???[STAH]-(1)[STAH]????L?[DN]???[FYW]??F????P?D??Q??A???I
36	1,99E+06	I?Q-(1)[STAH]??[STAH]????L?[DN]???[FYW]??F????P?D??Q??A???I
38	1,97E+06	F?I???[STAH]-(3)[STAH]????L?[DN]???[FYW]??F????P?D??Q??A???I
40	1,97E+06	F?I-(3)[STAH]??[STAH]????L?[DN]???[FYW]??F????P?D??Q??A???I
41	1,91E+06	[STAH]??[STAH]?K-(1,4)P??FNE[STAH]K?I?F[STAH]M
42	**1,72E+06**	**CC[FYW]?C??C????[FYW]-(2,4)[DN]??[STAH]C??C**
43	1,57E+06	[STAH]-(1,3,4)[FYW]A??[STAH]R??P??F?E?K?I?F?M
44	1,49E+06	A-(1,3)[STAH]???L[STAH][DN]???[FYW]??F?R??P?D??Q??A???I
45	1,36E+06	Q???[STAH]?[STAH]-(3)L[STAH]????I[FYW]??F?R??P?D??Q??A???I
46	1,32E+06	I-(3)[STAH]??[STAH][STAH]????S????[FYW]??F?R??P?D??Q??A???I
47	1,31E+06	[STAH]I[STAH]-(1,2,3,4)L?[DN]???[FYW]??F?R??P?D??Q??A???I
48	1,24E+06	[STAH]??[STAH][STAH]-(1,3)LS????[FYW]??F?R??P?D??Q??A???I
49	1,19E+06	[FYW]-(1,3,4)[STAH]???P??FNE[STAH]K?I?F[STAH]M
50	1,12E+06	I???[STAH]-(3)[STAH]???L[STAH]????[FYW]??F?R??P?D??Q??A???I

FIGURE 13.1 One of the functionally relevant motifs is shown in bold for G-protein-coupled receptors family 3 (id PS00980). Output of Varun [4] for 25 sequences of about 25,000 amino acids each.

13.1.3 Motif Representation

In general, a motif is represented by an ordered sequence of symbols and a set of locations where it appears. Motifs, along with their lists of occurrences, are usually extracted from one or more reference sequences over a fixed-length alphabet Σ.

To model mutations and other evolutionary events, a number of formalisms have been introduced. For example, position-specific scoring matrices (PSSMs [7]) are widely used to model transcription factor binding sites, where each score represents the probability, or number of times, that a given symbol appears at a certain position. See Figure 13.2 for an example, including the multiple alignment of sequences that generates a PSSM.

Another popular model involves character classes, like the IUPAC alphabet.* For protein sequences a number of clustering approaches have been proposed [14, 19, 20, 24]. Similarly, other protocols exist for DNA [13] and for RNA. For example,

---

*IUPAC stands for International Union of Pure and Applied Chemistry. The alphabet main reference is: Nomenclature Committee of the International Union of Biochemistry (NC-IUB). Nomenclature for incompletely specified bases in nucleic acid sequences. Recommendations 1984. *J. Biol. Chem.*, 261, 13–17.

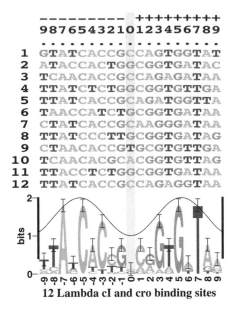

FIGURE 13.2 Example of sequence alignment logo taken from [37].

the PROSITE motif for the nickel-dependent hydrogenases large-subunit signature is
RG[LIVMF]E????????????????QESMP][RK]?C[GR][LIVM]C.

In this study we are interested in motifs with character classes. Most of the time, even if
the classification, say of amino acids, might lead to a partition of symbols, in practical cases
motifs show classes with nonempty intersections. For example, in the above motif there are
intersections between classes, like that of [RK] with [GR], and also subsets, like [LIVM]
with respect to [LIVMF]. If the motifs in input contain only partitions of the original alphabet
Σ, we can map the reference sequences into the new alphabet of symbols represented by the
partitions, thus considerably reducing the number of candidate motifs to be analyzed [40].
In all other cases this will result in the combinatorial explosion of candidate motifs that
consequently affects the efficiency of matching and discovering new motifs. In this chapter
we will set the basis to solve this fundamental problem.

13.1.4 Problem Statement

The main problem we want to address here is the following: Given a reference sequence s
that might be the concatenation of multiple biological sequences and a set of *motifs with
character classes* $\mathcal{M}$ that is the outcome of one or more motif finders, we aim to reduce the
set $\mathcal{M}$ to a small number of ordered representative motifs, say $\mathcal{U}$, such that the size of $\mathcal{U}$ is
linear with respect to the reference sequence s.

This reduction will allow us to manage the new set easier and will enhance its readability
and interpretation. The general idea behind this work is to identify interesting lexicographic
properties of motifs that are useful for the above problem. In particular, we will prove that
some properties, along with the notion of *minimality* that will be defined in the next section,
are capable of ranking all possible motifs with character classes and also of selecting a

representative subset of motifs, called the *underlying representative set U*. Inherently, with the notion of underlying motifs we want to discard those motifs that rank lower than others if located in the same occurrences on the reference sequence *s*.

In the following we first characterize motifs with character classes defining the notion of minimality, which makes the motifs more specific with respect to the reference sequence *s*. Then, we define the notion of *motif priority*, which permits to compare and rank different motifs together. The priority is defined using properties like the length of a motif, its composition (accounting also for character classes), and the list of its occurrences. This motif priority rule has proved to be useful for filtering a set of biological motifs $\mathcal{M}$. In particular, the mentioned lexicographic properties, combined with the list of occurrences of a motif, have been specifically designed for proteins by analyzing the results of [4, 12]. Nevertheless, we will prove that we are able to rank all minimal motifs using our motif priority rule, and we will show that it is possible to filter out a set of motifs $\mathcal{M}$ into a new set of linear size with respect to *s*.

In summary, using our simple motif priority rule, we can prove that any set $\mathcal{M}$ is *subordered*. Moreover, using the notion of minimality, we can map any set of motifs $\mathcal{M}$ into its *minimal representative set* $\mu(\mathcal{M})$ that is *totally ordered*. This lays the foundations for filtering any set of motifs into a set that is linear in size with respect to the reference sequence *s*. As a proof of concept we will present an algorithm that has time complexity $O(n|\mu(\mathcal{M})| \log|\mu(\mathcal{M})|)$, or $O(n \max\{|\mathcal{M}|, |\mu(\mathcal{M})| \log|\mu(\mathcal{M})|\})$, whenever the computation of minimal motifs is required, where *n* is the size of the sequence *s*.

We believe that such an approach can drastically reduce the number of candidate motifs to be analyzed in genomics and proteomics and can enhance their readability and interpretation. In this chapter we present a series of results on protein families that support the validity of the theoretical findings. Preliminary experiments on protein families show very good performance as a filter to reduce the number of motifs while keeping the most important ones.

13.2 MOTIFS WITH CHARACTER CLASSES: A CHARACTERIZATION

We define a *string* as a sequence of zero or more symbols from an alphabet Σ. The set of all strings over Σ is denoted by Σ^*. The length of a string *x* is defined as the number of its symbols, denoted by $|x|$, and the *i*th symbol of *x* is denoted by x_i, where $1 \leq i \leq |x|$.

For example, in genomics Σ corresponds to the set of nucleotides {A, C, G, T} or {A, C, G, U}, respectively, for DNA and RNA, while in proteomics Σ corresponds to the set of the 20 amino acids: {A, R, N, D, C, Q, E, G, H, I, L, K, M, F, P, S, T, W, Y, V}. Then, a symbol σ from Σ is called a *solid character*.

Throughout the chapter a string *s* composed of solid characters from Σ will be used as a reference sequence. Conversely, motifs will be represented by a more expressive alphabet, as explained in the following definitions.

Definition 13.1 *Character Class* Let R_Σ be a set of equivalence relations over Σ. A *character class* is a subset of Σ consisting of two or more equivalent solid characters with respect to some relation in R_Σ.

For instance, the hydrophobicity property can partition all 20 amino acids into disjoint classes. In this regard a number of different hydrophobicity scales have been developed over the years [8]. A hydrophobicity scale thus generates an equivalence relation $R \in R_\Sigma$ between solid characters such that each class of the resulting quotient set Σ / R can be defined as a character class. It is possible to define several character classes over Σ according to the equivalence relations in R_Σ. In particular, we consider the set of maximal character classes on R_Σ, that is, those classes that are not a proper subset of other classes. This argument will be further discussed in Section 13.2.1.

Given τ maximal character classes $\{C_i\}_1^\tau$ on Σ, $\bigcup_{i=1}^\tau 2^{C_i}$ represents all nonempty subsets of the classes.

Definition 13.2 *Pattern* A *pattern with character classes*, or simply a *pattern*, is a string defined on $\Sigma \cup (\bigcup_{i=1}^\tau 2^{C_i})$.

In the literature, a pattern with character classes is also called a *degenerate pattern* or an *indeterminate string* [1, 16, 27, 31, 32, 38, 45]. Given a pattern $p = p_1 p_2 \cdots p_k$ of length k, each symbol p_j, with $1 \leq j \leq k$, is either a solid character or a subset of a character class C. In the latter case, we write p_j by means of square brackets in the notation of PROSITE [20]: $p_j = [\sigma_1, \sigma_2, \ldots, \sigma_{r_j}]$.

Definition 13.3 *Pattern Occurrence* A pattern $p = p_1 p_2 \cdots p_k$ of length k is said to *occur* at a location l of a string s, with $1 \leq l \leq n$, if $s_{l+j-1} \in p_j$ for each $1 \leq j \leq k$.

Figure 13.3 shows an example of pattern and pattern occurrences, where $s = aabeadbace$, $\Sigma = \{a, b, c, d, e\}$, and the character classes are $C_1 = \{a, c, d\}$ and $C_2 = \{a, b, e\}$. In this case, $p = a[a, c, d][b, e]$ is a pattern of length $k = 3$ that occurs at locations 1, 5, 8 of s.

Hereafter we will assume that we are given a string s on Σ of length n, a set of character classes $\{C_i\}_1^\tau$, with $r = \max_{1 \leq i \leq \tau}\{|C_i|\}$, and a positive integer q, $2 \leq q \leq |s|$, called a *quorum*. A *motif* m is then defined as a pair $(p, \mathcal{L}_m)$, where p is a pattern of length k that occurs at the locations given by $\mathcal{L}_m$, and $\mathcal{L}_m$ is a set of at least q locations of s. For instance, as of Figure 13.3, $m = (p, \mathcal{L}_m)$ is a motif with pattern $p = a[a, c, d][b, e]$ of length $k = 3$ and location list $\mathcal{L}_m = \{1, 5, 8\}$ of cardinality $v = 3$. More formally:

FIGURE 13.3 Example of a pattern p with character classes along with its occurrences 1, 5, 8 in the string s.

Definition 13.4 *Motif and Location List* We say that $m = (p, \mathcal{L}_m)$ is a motif with pattern $p = p_1 p_2 \cdots p_k$ and location list $\mathcal{L}_m = (l_1, l_2, \ldots, l_v)$ if and only if all of the following hold:

(i) The length of m, denoted by $|m|$, is $|p| = k \geq 2$ symbols.

(ii) For each location $l \in \mathcal{L}_m$, p occurs at l in s and $|\mathcal{L}_m| = v \geq q$.

(iii) There does not exist a location $l' \notin \mathcal{L}_m$ such that p occurs at l' in s ($\mathcal{L}_m$ is complete).

We suppose now that an oracle has given us a set $\mathcal{M}$ of interesting motifs lying on the string s. Intuitively this set may be unusually large, with the number of elements that may reach up to $O(\sum_{k=2}^{n-q+1} (\min\{\tau 2^r + |\Sigma|, 2^{|\Sigma|}\})^k) = O((\min\{\tau 2^r, 2^{|\Sigma|}\})^n) = O(2^{|\Sigma|n})$ motifs. Thus, we want to characterize the whole set of motifs $\mathcal{M}$ with *representative motifs* that have to be $O(n)$ in number and dimensions in order to filter out the redundant information shared by some motifs and enhance their readability and interpretation.

Next sections lay the foundations for finding these particular representative motifs, which we will call *underlying*, which, in loose terms, are the most important for some regions of the string s according to the rules we will define in the following.

13.2.1 On Transitive Properties of Character Classes

Previously, we introduced the concept of a character class consisting of two or more solid characters obtained through some equivalence relation on Σ. In this case every character class is seen as an independent element wherewith building motifs. Then, since for patterns there is no distinction between a character class and its subsets, we consider maximal character classes as input for our problems.

Typical is the case where the considered relations of equivalence between solid characters, R_Σ, are not mutually transitive, since they might partition Σ in different ways [9, 41, 44]. For example, if σ_1, σ_2 are two solid characters belonging to a character class $C_1, \sigma_1, \sigma_3 \subset C_2$, and $\sigma_2, \sigma_3 \subseteq C_3$, then it could be the case that $\sigma_1, \sigma_2, \sigma_3$ do not belong to a common class C_4.

Consider, for simplicity, that R_Σ is mutually transitive on Σ. Then, the set of character classes partitions Σ, and we can map each solid character on Σ into either its maximal character class or itself. Call $R_\Sigma(\cdot)$ this function. Accordingly, we can map $s = s_1 s_2 \cdots s_n$ into $R_\Sigma(s)$, given by $R_\Sigma(s) = R_\Sigma(s_1) R_\Sigma(s_2) \cdots R_\Sigma(s_n)$. In this way every pattern becomes a pattern on the new restricted alphabet given by $R_\Sigma(\Sigma)$, that is, $\Sigma \cup \{C_i\}_1^\tau$. Moreover, the discovery of this type of pattern, called *exact pattern* in the literature, has been consolidated over the years [15, 18, 23, 25, 40]. In short, if R_Σ is mutually transitive, we can find a set of classes that is a partition of Σ. Then we can map the reference sequence on this new alphabet and use standard pattern techniques. As a consequence, every motif can be uniquely identified by its length and location list, and we can conclude that, for this particular case, there is no need of the notion of *minimality* that will be introduced in the next section.

More attention, however, deserves the general case where the transitivity does not hold. As stressed above, the main issue is that the character classes might not be a partition of Σ. Because of this, the motifs are not uniquely identified by their length and location list. In other words, there may exist two motifs m and m' lying on s that have equal length and location list, but different patterns p and p', because different character classes compose the corresponding symbols. Since classical motif discovery algorithms find motifs over the restricted alphabet $\Sigma \cup \{C_i\}_1^\tau$, because of its practicality and ease of computation, this may lead to a large number of motifs with the same location list. Thus, in the next section we study the notion of *minimality* specifically designed to address this issue.

13.2.2 Minimal Motifs and Motif Priority

Definition 13.5 *Minimal Representation* Given a motif m of length k, the *minimal representation* of its pattern p is a pattern $\mu(p)$ of length k with symbols $\mu(p)_j = \bigcup_{l \in \mathcal{L}_m} s_{l+j-1}$ for $1 \leq j \leq k$.

Fact 13.1 The minimal representation of a pattern is unique.

Remark 13.1 Since $\mu(p)$ is more specific than p, that is, $\mu(p)$ cannot have more occurrences than p in s, then the list of occurrences of $\mu(p)$ must be the same as for p.

Let $\mu(m) = (\mu(p), \mathcal{L}_m)$ be the minimal representation of a motif m with pattern p. Then Remark 13.1 suggests that $\mu(m)$ is consistent with the definition of motif, that is, the location list $\mathcal{L}_{\mu(m)}$ is complete:

Definition 13.6 *Minimal Motif* The minimal representation of m, given by $\mu(m) = (\mu(p), \mathcal{L}_m)$, is called a minimal motif.

Computing the minimal representation of a motif is useful when a motif is defined on $\Sigma \cup \{C_i\}_1^\tau$, rather than on specific characters. To have a more concrete idea about this concept, Figure 13.4 shows an example of the minimal representation $\mu(m)$ of a motif $m = ([a, c, d][a, c, d][a, b, e], \{1, 5, 8\})$, with pattern $\mu(p)$ and p, respectively, where the reference string is $s = aabeadbace$ and the character classes are $C_1 = \{a, c, d\}$ and $C_2 = \{a, b, e\}$. In this case we say that $m' = \mu(m) = (a[a, c, d][b, e], \{1, 5, 8\})$ is a minimal motif.

Let $\mathcal{M}$ be a set of motifs with character classes lying on the string s. From Fact 13.1, each motif $m \in \mathcal{M}$ has a unique minimal representation $\mu(m)$. Thus, one can easily check that the equivalence given by $\mu(m) = \mu(m')$ is an equivalence relation. The representatives of the induced partitions are the respective unique minimal motifs.

Fact 13.2 Let us map all the motifs in $\mathcal{M}$ into the set of their minimal representations $\mu(\mathcal{M})$, where each motif $m \in \mu(\mathcal{M})$ is the minimal representation $m = \mu(m')$ of some motif $m' \in \mathcal{M}$. Then, the set of motifs $\mathcal{M}$ is partitioned into equivalence classes by the binary relation of equality between minimal representations.

j	1	2	3
p	[a,c,d]	[a,c,d]	[a,b,e]
$\theta(p)$	a	[a,c,d]	[b,e]

FIGURE 13.4 Example of minimal representation $\mu(p)$ of a pattern p with reference string $s = aabeadbace$.

We call $\mu(\mathcal{M})$ the *minimal representative set* of $\mathcal{M}$. Since mapping $\mathcal{M}$ into $\mu(\mathcal{M})$ could mean a drastic reduction in the number of motifs, this is in practice a first step for filtering the original motifs in $\mathcal{M}$.

Remark 13.2 Two motifs in $\mathcal{M}$ or, equivalently, in $\mu(\mathcal{M})$ may have the same location list. However, two minimal motifs of equal length must have different location lists.

As a consequence of Remark 13.2, every minimal motifs in $\mu(\mathcal{M})$ can be uniquely identified by its length and location list within the minimal representative set. We can now define an important property of motifs with character classes, the *composition*, which is the sum of the number of characters within the symbols of a motif.

Definition 13.7 *Composition of Pattern and Composition of Motif* The *composition* of a pattern p of length k is defined as $c(p) = \sum_{j=1}^{k} |p_j|$. The composition of a motif $m = (p, \mathcal{L}_m)$, denoted by $c(m)$, is defined as the composition of its pattern $c(p)$.

For instance, given two patterns $p = a[a, c, d][b, e]$ and $p' = [a, d]b[a, b]$, their composition is $c(p) = 6$ and $c(p') = 5$, and we say that the latter is somehow more specific than p. Moreover, the composition of the motif $m = (a[a, c, d][b, e], \{1, 5, 8\})$ is equal to $c(p)$, that is, 6.

A fundamental point is the following definition of *priority* between motifs, a means for comparing different motifs. Here we give priority to motif length, then to motif composition, and finally to motifs that appear first in s.

Definition 13.8 *Motif Priority* A motif m of length k has *priority* over a motif m' of length k', denoted $m \rightarrow m'$, if and only if either $m = m'$ or

1. $k > k'$ or
2. $k = k'$ and $c(m) < c(m')$ or
3. $k = k', c(m) = c(m')$, and $\min\{l \mid l \in \mathcal{L}_m \setminus \mathcal{L}_{m'}\} < \min\{l \mid l \in \mathcal{L}_{m'} \setminus \mathcal{L}_m\}$ when both minima exist.

For instance, consider $s = aabeadbace$, $m = (a[a, c, d][b, e], \{1, 5, 8\})$, and $m' = ([a, d]b[a, b, e], \{2, 6\})$. Then, m has priority over m', written $m \rightarrow m'$, because of equal length and composition, but with different order of appearance in s: $\min\{l \mid l \in \mathcal{L}_m \setminus \mathcal{L}_{m'}\} = 1 < \min\{l \mid l \in \mathcal{L}_{m'} \setminus \mathcal{L}_m\} = 2$. If two distinct motifs m and m' have equal length and composition, but either $\mathcal{L}_m \subseteq \mathcal{L}_{m'}$ (that includes the equality case) or $\mathcal{L}_{m'} \subset \mathcal{L}_m$, then we consider m and m' *incomparable*; otherwise they are comparable. Nevertheless, we will solve this issue along with Theorem 13.2.

Given our binary relation, called *motif priority*, we want to prove that some intuitive properties hold:

Definition 13.9 *Acyclicity* A binary relation R over a set $\mathcal{M}$ is defined to be *acyclic* if there does not exist a chain of distinct elements of $\mathcal{M}$, $m_1, m_2, m_3, \ldots, m_t$, such that $m_1 R m_2, m_2 R m_3, \ldots, m_{t-1} R m_t$, and also $m_t R m_1$ (cycle).

Definition 13.10 *Subordered Set and Totally Ordered Set*   Let R be a binary relation over a set $\mathcal{M}$. Then, $\mathcal{M}$ is said to be *subordered* with respect to R if for all distinct elements $m_1, m_2, \ldots, m_t$ in $\mathcal{M}$:

   (i) $m_1 R m_1$ (reflexivity) and

   (ii) $\neg (m_1 R m_2 \text{ and } m_2 R m_1)$ (antisymmetry) and

   (iii) there does not exist a cycle between $m_1, m_2, \ldots, m_t$ (acyclicity).

If also (iv) $(m_1 R m_2 \text{ or } m_2 R m_1) \forall m_1, m_2 \in \mathcal{M}$ (totality), then m_1 and m_2 are said to be *comparable*, and $\mathcal{M}$ is *totally subordered*.

Furthermore, $\mathcal{M}$ is *totally ordered* if R is reflexive, antisymmetric, total, and transitive, that is, (v) $(m_1 R m_2 \text{ and } m_2 R m_3) \Rightarrow m_1 R m_3$.

One can prove that conditions (i) and (iii) of Definition 13.10 are sufficient to define a subordered set; nevertheless we have listed all three properties of subordered sets for clarity and completeness.

Lemma 13.1   A set $\mathcal{M}$ is totally ordered under a binary relation R if and only if it is totally subordered.

Proof   It is straightforward that transitivity and antisymmetry, together, imply acyclicity, that is, if $\mathcal{M}$ is totally ordered, then $\mathcal{M}$ is also totally subordered. Consider a chain of distinct elements in $\mathcal{M}$: $m_1 R m_2, m_2 R m_3, \ldots, m_{t-1} R m_t$. It follows that $m_1 R m_t$ for the transitivity and that $m_t R m_1$ cannot hold since R is antisymmetric.

We can also easily check that acyclicity and totality, together, imply transitivity. Consider the same chain of elements as above. Since for the acyclicity $m_t R m_1$ cannot hold, then, for the totality, $m_1 R m_t$. Therefore the transitivity holds, and the definitions of totally subordered and totally ordered coincide.   ∎

Now, before showing that some of these properties hold, we need to prove two preliminary results for the motif priority rule. At first, we observe:

Fact 13.3   The binary relation of motif priority is reflexive and antisymmetric since properties 1, 2, and 3 of Definition 13.8 are strictly defined.

Lemma 13.2 *Paired Occurrences*   Let m and m' be two distinct motifs with $\min\{l \mid l \in \mathcal{L}_m \setminus \mathcal{L}_{m'}\} < \min\{l \mid l \in \mathcal{L}_{m'} \setminus \mathcal{L}_m\}$ such that both minima exist, and define j to be $\min\{l \mid l \in \mathcal{L}_m \setminus \mathcal{L}_{m'}\}$. Then, the occurrences of m and m' at positions less than j must be the same. Furthermore, we call these occurrences *paired*.

Proof   We have to prove that, in case 3 of Definition 13.8, the occurrences of m and m' less than j are identical.

If m has an occurrence less than j that is not in $\mathcal{L}_{m'}$, then $\min\{l \mid l \in \mathcal{L}_m \setminus \mathcal{L}_{m'}\} < j$, that is, impossible by hypothesis. Conversely, if m' has occurrences less than j that are not in $\mathcal{L}_m$, then $\min\{l \mid l \in \mathcal{L}_{m'} \setminus \mathcal{L}_m\} < j = \min\{l \mid l \in \mathcal{L}_m \setminus \mathcal{L}_{m'}\}$ again contradicts our assumptions. Thus, the occurrences of the two motifs less than j must coincide, and we call them paired.

Finally, by assumptions, it trivially holds that $j \notin \mathcal{L}_{m'}$. ∎

Lemma 13.3 Let $m_1 \to m_2, m_2 \to m_3, \ldots, m_{t-1} \to m_t$ be a chain of distinct motifs of equal length and composition. Then, either $m_1 \to m_t$ or $\mathcal{L}_{m_t} \subset \mathcal{L}_{m_1}$ holds.

Proof We will prove the statement by induction on t. Let the basis be $t = 2$. In this case, the chain $m_1 \to m_2$ coincides with the result. We show now that, for $t > 2$, if it holds either $m_1 \to m_{t-1}$ or $\mathcal{L}_{m_{t-1}} \subset \mathcal{L}_{m_1}$, then either $m_1 \to m_t$ or $\mathcal{L}_{m_t} \subset \mathcal{L}_{m_1}$ holds.

Assume $\mathcal{L}_{m_{t-1}} \subset \mathcal{L}_{m_1}$. Define j to be $\min\{l \mid l \in \mathcal{L}_{m_{t-1}} \setminus \mathcal{L}_{m_t}\}$, and observe that it exists since $m_{t-2} \to m_{t-1}$, by property 3 of Definition 13.8. It follows that $j \in \mathcal{L}_{m_1}$ and, from Lemma 13.2, that the occurrences of m_{t-1} and m_t that are less than j are paired. Hence, these occurrences are also shared with m_1. Since $j \notin \mathcal{L}_{m_t}$, then either $m_1 \to m_t$, because j makes the difference between $\mathcal{L}_{m_1}$ and $\mathcal{L}_{m_t}$, or m_1 and m_t are incomparable. In the latter case, $\mathcal{L}_{m_{t-1}} \subset \mathcal{L}_{m_1}$ and $\mathcal{L}_{m_1} \subseteq \mathcal{L}_{m_t}$, together, imply that $\mathcal{L}_{m_{t-1}} \subset \mathcal{L}_{mt}$; that is impossible since m_{t-1} and m_t are comparable by hypothesis. This means that the latter case must be $\mathcal{L}_{m_t} \subset \mathcal{L}_{m_1}$.

Conversely, assume $m_1 \to m_{t-1}$. Define j as above, and $j' = \min\{l \mid l \in \mathcal{L}_{m_1} \setminus \mathcal{L}_{m_{t-1}}\}$. It holds that $j \notin \mathcal{L}_{m_t}$, as already observed, and that $j' \neq j$ because of $j' \notin \mathcal{L}_{m_{t-1}}$. Then, by Lemma 13.2, the occurrences of m_{t-1} and m_t that are less than j are paired and the same for occurrences of m_1 and m_{t-1} less than j'. In this way, if m_1 and m_t are comparable, then there exists an occurrence in $\mathcal{L}_{m_1}$ that appears first in s with respect to $\mathcal{L}_{m_t}$: If $j' < j$, the occurrences of m_1, m_{t-1}, and m_t less than j' are paired together, and thus j' makes the difference; otherwise $j' > j$, and the occurrences of m_1, m_{t-1}, and m_t less than j are paired together, and hence $j \in \mathcal{L}_1$ makes the difference. Alternatively, if m_1 and m_t are incomparable, then it must be the case of $\mathcal{L}_{m_t} \subset \mathcal{L}_{m_1}$. Otherwise, $\mathcal{L}_{m_1} \subseteq \mathcal{L}_{m_t}$ would imply that the occurrences of m_1 equal to or less than j' are also shared with m_t, which leads to $m_t \to m_{t-1}$; that is impossible. ∎

Theorem 13.1 Any set of motifs $\mathcal{M}$ is subordered with respect to the binary relation of motif priority.

Proof We have to prove that the relation of motif priority is reflexive, antisymmetric, and acyclic. The first two properties are stated in Fact 13.3. Now, following the work of Lemma 13.3, we can prove that the acyclicity holds too. First, observe that length and composition are intrinsic properties of the single motif and thus monotone functions. If all motifs $m, m' \in \mathcal{M}$ have different length or composition, then, by definition of motif priority, it is always true that either $m \to m'$ or $m' \to m$ holds, and a cycle can never exist because of different lengths and/or compositions.

Alternatively, consider a chain of distinct motifs $m_1 \to m_2, m_2 \to m_3, \ldots, m_{t-1} \to m_t$ of equal length and composition. In this case we must use property 3 of Definition 13.8 to compare the motifs together. From Lemma 13.3, it follows that a cycle of motif priority between any chain of distinct motifs is again impossible, and therefore the acyclicity holds. Furthermore, since there may exist a triad of motifs m_1, m_2, m_3 of equal length and composition such that $m_1 \to m_2$ and $m_2 \to m_3$ but $\mathcal{L}_{m_3} \subset \mathcal{L}_{m_1}$, then the motif priority rule is definitely not transitive on $\mathcal{M}$. ∎

Note that the nondecision on some binary comparisons finally discards the relations of totality and, as seen above, of transitivity. For instance, consider $s = aabeadbace$, $C_1 = \{a, c, d\}$, $C_2 = \{a, b, e\}$, and the motifs $m = ([a, d][a, b][a, e] \{2, 6\})$ and $m' = ([a, d][b, e][a, e], \{2, 6\})$ with the same list of occurrences: in short, $|m| = |m'| = 3$, $c(m) = c(m') = 6$, and $\mathcal{L}_m = \mathcal{L}_{m'}$. This means that we are not able to compare m and m' using the motif priority rule. Another example is given by $m_1 = (a[a, c, d][b, e], \{1, 5, 8\})$, $m_2 = ([b, e]a[a, c, d], \{4, 7\})$, and $m_3 = ([a, b][c, d][b, e], \{5, 8\})$. In this case, $m_1 \rightarrow m_2$ and $m_2 \rightarrow m_3$, but $m_1 \rightarrow m_3$ does not hold, since $\mathcal{L}_{m_3} \subset \mathcal{L}_{m_1}$. The issue is that m and m' may not be minimal motifs. In the following we set the basis to solve this problem.

Theorem 13.2 Given any set of motifs $\mathcal{M}$, its minimal representative set $\mu(\mathcal{M})$ is totally ordered under the binary relation of motif priority.

Proof According with Theorem 13.1, any set of motifs $\mathcal{M}$ is subordered under the motif priority rule; thus, also the set of minimal motifs $\mu(\mathcal{M})$ is subordered. Following the work of Lemma 13.1, we have to prove that the totality holds on this new set $\mu(\mathcal{M})$, that is, every pair of minimal motifs must be comparable under motif priority. In other words, if $m, m' \in \mu(\mathcal{M})$, either $m \rightarrow m'$ or $m' \rightarrow m$ must hold. To this end the proof of Lemma 13.1 tells us that length and composition are intrinsic properties of motifs, and thus every motif is comparable with another one in case of different length or composition.

From Remark 13.2 we have that $\mathcal{L}_m \neq \mathcal{L}_{m'}$ for two minimal motifs m and m' of equal length, and therefore we have, without loss of generality, two scenarios to consider: (1) $\mathcal{L}_m \nsubseteq \mathcal{L}_{m'}$ and $\mathcal{L}_{m'} \nsubseteq \mathcal{L}_m$ and (2) $\mathcal{L}_m \subset \mathcal{L}_{m'}$. In the former case, if we consider $\min\{l \mid l \in \mathcal{L}_m \setminus \mathcal{L}_{m'}\}$ and $\min\{l \mid l \in \mathcal{L}_{m'} \setminus \mathcal{L}_m\}$, then both minima exist and are different from each other. Hence either $m \rightarrow m'$ or $m' \rightarrow m$ holds if it is the case of equal length and composition of m and m', and the minimum between the two sets is either in $\mathcal{L}_m$ or in $\mathcal{L}_{m'}$, respectively. Conversely, in the latter case, since m and m' are minimal motifs and the respective location lists are complete, the respective patterns of m and m' must be different. Therefore $\mathcal{L}_m \subset \mathcal{L}_{m'} \Rightarrow c(m) < c(m')$, and hence $m \rightarrow m'$. Accordingly, for any set of minimal motifs under motif priority, the totality holds. From Lemma 13.1 we can conclude that any set of minimal motifs is totally ordered under the motif priority rule.   ∎

As a consequence of Theorem 13.2, all minimal motifs can be compared and ranked. We can further observe that, for property 2 of motif priority, every minimal motif has priority over all other motifs in $\mathcal{M}$ within its equivalence class, which is given by the paradigm of minimal representation.

Now it is clear that any set of motifs $\mathcal{M}$ can be mapped into its minimal representative set $\mu(\mathcal{M})$ and that we can build a measure of total order over this set, in particular using the motif priority rule, that otherwise would not be possible on the original set $\mathcal{M}$.

13.3 FILTERING BY MEANS OF UNDERLYING MOTIFS

In order to exploit the output of a motif discovery algorithm, our prior knowledge $\mathcal{M}$, and enhance its readability and interpretation, we aim to identify particular representative motifs of $\mathcal{M}$ that have to be $O(n)$ in number and dimensions, where n is the length of the reference string s.

Let R be a binary relation of priority between motifs. The objective is to select the most priority motifs in $\mathcal{M}$ for each location of s, according to R. If a motif m is selected, we discard all motifs with less priority that lie on the occurrences of m. The problem can be seen as a regional problem, in which we have to select some motifs for each considered region of the string s. These regions could be transcription factor binding sites or coding sequences if we consider genomes, otherwise functional regions if we consider a set of protein sequences. More formally:

Definition 13.11 *Region* A *region* $E_{j,x}$ of s is a set of x consecutive locations $\{j, j+1, \ldots, j+x-1\}$ corresponding to the symbols $s_j s_{j+1} \cdots s_{j+x-1}$, namely a substring of s, where $1 \leq j$ and $(j+x-1) \leq |s|$.

Definition 13.12 *Living in a Region* We say that a motif m of length k *lives* in the region $E_{j,x}$ if there exists a location $l \in \mathcal{L}_m$ such that $(E_{l,k} \cap E_{j,x}) \neq \emptyset$.

Furthermore, we say that every motif m *completely lives* in the regions defined by its occurrences.

Definition 13.13 *Tied Occurrence* Let m be a motif of length k. Then, we say that an occurrence l of m is *tied* to a motif m' if m' lives in $E_{l,k}$ and $m' R m$. Otherwise, we say that l is *untied* from m'.

Definition 13.14 *Underlying Representative Set and Underlying Motif* Let $\mathcal{M}$ be a set of motifs that lie on the string s, and let u be a positive integer called an *underlying quorum*. A set of motifs $\mathcal{U} \subseteq \mathcal{M}$ is said to be an *underlying representative set* of s if and only if

  (i) every motif m in $\mathcal{U}$, called an *underlying motif*, has at least u untied occurrences from any other motif in $\mathcal{U}$ and

  (ii) there does not exist a motif $m \in \mathcal{M} \setminus \mathcal{U}$ such that m has at least u untied occurrences from all motifs in $\mathcal{U}$.

In other words, given a string s and the information about all considered motifs $\mathcal{M}$, an underlying motif is a particular representative of some regions of s. Furthermore, considering the underlying quorum u as a fixed integer, it follows that Definition 13.14 of the underlying representative set converges to one and only one set of motifs $\mathcal{U}$ under certain conditions:

Theorem 13.3 Let $\mathcal{M}$ be a subordered set of motifs with respect to a binary relation R. Then there exists an underlying representative set $\mathcal{U} \subseteq \mathcal{M}$, and it is unique.

Proof We show first that a set $\mathcal{U}$, absolving the two conditions of Definition 13.14, exists. If $\mathcal{M}$ is subordered, then there does not exist a cycle of priority between some distinct motifs $m_1, m_2, \ldots, m_t$ in $\mathcal{M}$ (acyclicity). Consider, without loss of generality, $m_1 R m_t, m_2 R m_t, \ldots, m_{t-1} R m_t$ such that no other motif has priority over m_t. This means that, for each region $E_{l,k}$ of s where m_t completely lives, either m_t or some other motifs in $\{m_1, m_2, \ldots, m_{t-1}\}$ can have an untied occurrence in $E_{l,k}$; thus they must belong to some set of underlying motifs, say $\mathcal{U}$. Furthermore, any other motif m_{t+1} living in $E_{l,k}$ but with no priority relation with respect to m_t can also be an underlying motif in $\mathcal{U}$. Similarly, the occurrences of $\{m_1, m_2, \ldots, m_{t-1}\}$ living in $E_{l,k}$ must respect that rule. Since no cycle of priority is admitted, then, for all regions of s given by the occurrences of some motif m in $\mathcal{M}$, either m is in $\mathcal{U}$ or there are some other motifs in $\mathcal{U}$ that have untied occurrences from m and that cover those regions. In conclusion, there must be a set of underlying motifs $\mathcal{U}$.

In the opposite direction, we can prove that $\mathcal{U}$ is unique. Let us assume that there exists two distinct underlying representative sets $\mathcal{U}_1$ and $\mathcal{U}_2$. Then, for both sets, there exists at least one motif that is not in the other set; otherwise condition (ii) of Definition 13.14 does not hold. Suppose $m_1 \in \mathcal{U}_1 \setminus \mathcal{U}_2$. Since $m_1 \notin \mathcal{U}_2$, then, again for condition (ii), there must be an occurrence of m_1 in $\mathcal{U}_1$, say the region E_{l_1,k_1}, that in $\mathcal{U}_2$ is covered by some other motif m_2 with higher priority than m_1 such that $m_2 \notin \mathcal{U}_1$. For similar reasons, if m_2 is not in $\mathcal{U}_1$, then there must be another motif $m_3 \in \mathcal{U}_1$ with higher priority than m_2. Since $\mathcal{M}$ is subordered, then $m_3 \neq m_1$. Finally, as the number of motifs in $\mathcal{U}_1$ and $\mathcal{U}_2$ is finite, then the two sets must coincide. ∎

The following result is a consequence of the proof of Theorem 13.3:

Proposition 13.1 If $\mathcal{M}$ is totally ordered, then each underlying motif m has priority over all other underlying motifs in $\mathcal{U}$ in at least u regions of s.

From this proposition, we have that, if R is a total relation over $\mathcal{M}$, then the number of underlying motifs on a string s is $O(n)$.

Theorem 13.4 Let $\mathcal{M}$ be a totally ordered set under the binary relation R. Then, the number of underlying motifs in $\mathcal{U}$ is $\leq \lfloor n/2 \rfloor$, independently of the size of $\mathcal{M}$.

Proof From Proposition 13.1, every untied occurrence does not overlap with the untied occurrences of some other motifs in $\mathcal{U}$, and thus for every motif m in $\mathcal{U}$ its untied occurrences will not overlap with those of other motifs. Since every motif m has length $k \geq 2$, then m must cover at least $2 + u - 1$ characters of s, obtaining at most $n/(2 + u - 1) \leq n/2$ possible different motifs in $\mathcal{U}$, independently of the size of $\mathcal{M}$. Furthermore, $|\mathcal{U}| \leq \lfloor n/(2u) \rfloor$ in case of nonoverlapping occurrences for each of the motifs in $\mathcal{U}$. ∎

Let us now consider the *dimensions* of a set of motifs as the number of characters necessary to specify all its elements. This number coincides with the sum of compositions of all motifs. For instance, $m = (p, \mathcal{L}_m)$, with $p = a[a, c, d][b, e]$, is a motif with six characters and composition $c(m) = 6$. Let r be the maximum number of characters allowed in a motif symbol, that is, $r = \max_{1 \leq i \leq \tau}\{|C_i|\}$ as introduced in Section 13.2. Then:

Corollary 13.1 Given a string s of length n and a totally ordered set $\mathcal{M}$, any underlying representative set $\mathcal{U}$ over $\mathcal{M}$ has a total number of symbols, or total length, $\leq \lfloor n/2 \rfloor$ and dimensions no greater than $|\Sigma| n$.

Proof Following the proof of Theorem 13.4, all underlying motifs in $\mathcal{U}$ can be placed on their untied occurrences in s without overlaps with other motifs. Therefore, the total number of symbols for the whole set of motifs $\mathcal{U}$ is $\sum_{m \in \mathcal{U}} |m| \leq \lfloor n/2 \rfloor$. Hence $\mathcal{U}$ has dimensions $\leq r \lfloor n/2 \rfloor \leq |\Sigma| n$. ∎

For example, consider a scheme that encodes every solid character on Σ plus the two square brackets [and] in a simple injective way. Then, the dimension of each encoding would be at most $\lceil \log(|\Sigma| + 2) \rceil$. Therefore we can represent the symbols of a motif using at most $r\lceil \log(|\Sigma| + 2) \rceil$ bits per symbol. If we encode every underlying motif with this scheme, then the overall space needed to store all motifs in $\mathcal{U}$ would be at most $r\lceil \log(|\Sigma| + 2) \rceil \lfloor n/(2 + u - 1) \rfloor$ bits, or $r\lceil \log(|\Sigma| + 2) \rceil \lfloor n/(2u) \rfloor$ bits in case of nonoverlapping occurrences for each of the motifs in $\mathcal{U}$. This corresponds, in loose terms, to the result presented in Corollary 13.1. In conclusion, considering r as a constant, since it is bounded by $|\Sigma|$, any underlying representative set $\mathcal{U}$ has linear dimensions with respect to the size of the string s.

To summarize the results of the previous sections, we have that every set of motifs $\mathcal{M}$ that could be the output of some motif discovery algorithm can be transformed into its minimal representative set $\mu(\mathcal{M})$. This is the basis to enable the comparison of all motifs in $\mu(\mathcal{M})$ by means of the notion of motif priority that captures the lexicographic power of a motif. One can prove the validity of a series of properties that are fundamental for the global comparison of motifs. On this setting we can define the subset of underlying motifs that are, for some locations of the reference string s, the most important. In the next section we discuss an algorithm to find the set of underlying motifs, while in Section 13.4 we will describe a series of experiments to prove the validity of the latter.

13.3.1 Algorithm for Filtering Set of Motifs into Its Underlying Representative Set

Here we describe an application of motif priority and underlying motifs. We present an algorithm that filters a set of motifs $\mathcal{M}$ lying on a string s into its underlying representative set $\mathcal{U}$.

Let R be a binary relation of priority. In the following we show how to build an underlying representative set $\mathcal{U}$ in case of a totally ordered set $\mathcal{M}$ under R. The purpose is to select the most representative motifs with character classes in $\mathcal{M}$ according to R and to the definition of underlying motif. In practice, we filter out those motifs in $\mathcal{M}$ that rank lower than others if located in the same regions of s. From Corollary 13.1, since $\mathcal{M}$ is totally ordered, it follows that $\mathcal{U}$ has linear dimensions.

Consider Algorithm 13.1 for filtering the motifs in $\mathcal{M}$ into the underlying representative set $\mathcal{U} \subseteq \mathcal{M}$. This algorithm is presented as a proof of concept. It is unclear if a more efficient implementation exists or whether it is optimal. In this context we just analyze the

ALGORITHM 13.1

```
1. Rank all motifs in M using the binary relation R.
2. Initialize U to an empty set and iteratively select a motif m
   from M following the rank given by the priority.
3. At each step, if m has at least u untied occurrences from all
   motifs already in U:

   4. Add m to U and store the regions of s in which m completely
      lives.
   5. Otherwise, discard m.
```

---

correctness and the computational complexity of Algorithm 13.1. At first, we observe that the overall correctness follows from the proof of Theorem 13.3. Let n be the size of the string s, and let r be the maximum allowed size of a character class. If R corresponds to the motif priority rule, as of Section 13.2.2, in step 1 we may first preprocess the motifs in input, computing their lengths and compositions, in $O(rn|\mathcal{M}|)$ time. Then we sort all the motifs in $\mathcal{M}$ that are totally ordered in descending order. Considering the worst case, when we compare two motifs, we must also compare their lists of occurrences. Since for some motif m, $|\mathcal{L}_m|$ is $O(n)$, then the comparison of two ordered lists of occurrences costs $O(n)$ (see the pseudocode presented in the function CompareMotif). Thus, overall the first step costs $O(n|\mathcal{M}| \log |\mathcal{M}| + rn|\mathcal{M}|)$.

The main cycle, line 2, selects the top motifs from $\mathcal{M}$ and checks if they could be inserted in the set of underlying motifs $\mathcal{U}$. This loop can be stopped when no other motif can be added to the set $\mathcal{U}$.

After adding the first motif in the rank to $\mathcal{U}$, we check for untied occurrences of the next motif m' having length k'. For each motif m that has been selected by our algorithm in $\mathcal{U}$, we store the occurrences of m in a vector of Boolean $\Gamma[1, n]$ that represents all the locations of the string s. The value $\Gamma[i]$ is set to True if the location i is tied to some motif m in $\mathcal{U}$. This means that, if m is in $\mathcal{U}$, then $\forall l \in \mathcal{L}_m$ we store the value True at the locations of Γ that correspond to $E_{l,k}$, that is, $\Gamma[l, l + k - 1]$. Using the vector Γ, in the third instruction we have to check, for all $l' \in \mathcal{L}_{m'}$, whether some of the locations of $\Gamma[l', l' + k' - 1]$ corresponding to the region $E_{l',k'}$ are set to True. If it is the case, we say that l' is tied to some other motif with higher priority with respect to m'; otherwise, l' is untied. Accordingly, if m' has at least u untied occurrences, we add m' to the set $\mathcal{U}$; otherwise we discard m'. This step is detailed in the function CheckForUntiedOccurrences. The checking for untied occurrences of a motif m using the additional vector Γ thus costs $O(n)$.

In the fourth instruction we have to update the vector Γ with all locations of the newly added underlying motif m. This can be done by scanning all the occurrences of m and, $\forall l \in \mathcal{L}_m$, updating the values $\Gamma[l, l + k - 1]$ with no backtracking. To this end, we use a variable δ that takes the maximum between $l + k - 1$ and the next occurrence l' of m. This procedure is described in the function StoreCoverage. Again this step takes $O(n)$ in time. In conclusion, the whole cycle of instructions 2–5 has a total cost of $O(n|\mathcal{M}|)$.

Since a motif m added to $\mathcal{U}$ has higher priority than the motifs considered at the iterations that follow m, as of the second instruction, the following invariant holds: At each stage, condition (i) of Definition 13.14 is satisfied. Hence, from Theorem 13.3, $\mathcal{U}$ is the unique underlying representative set over $\mathcal{M}$.

In summary, the total complexity of Algorithm 13.1 is dominated by the first term $O(n|\mathcal{M}| \log |\mathcal{M}| + rn|\mathcal{M}|)$. Moreover, if we consider r to be a constant as above, then the total complexity of the algorithm becomes $O(n|\mathcal{M}| \log |\mathcal{M}|)$. For completeness, below you can find the pseudocode of the described implementation of Algorithm 13.1, which we called MotifFiltering.

Finally, in most cases we need first to compute the minimal representative set $\mu(\mathcal{M})$ before ranking the motifs by means of the priority rule. This further process costs $O(n^2|\mathcal{M}| + rn|\mathcal{M}|)$. Nevertheless, since we consider r as a constant, and typically the location lists of motifs have nonoverlapping occurrences, which is a realistic assumption for most applications in genomics and proteomics, then in practice the complexity of computing $\mu(\mathcal{M})$ becomes $O(n|\mathcal{M}|)$. In this regard, filtering the minimal motifs in $\mu(\mathcal{M})$ ultimately takes $O(n|\mu(\mathcal{M})| \log |\mu(\mathcal{M})|)$ time.

MotifFiltering

    Input: a sequence s, a list of motifs $\mathcal{M}$, an underlying quorum u, a binary relation R
    Output: the underlying representative set $\mathcal{U}$

```
1   n ← length(s)
2   Γ ← a vector of n booleans set to FALSE, representing E_{1,n}
3   sort(M, R)
4   for each motif m = (p, L_m) in M
5       do test ← CHECKFORUNTIEDOCCURRENCES(m, u, Γ)
6           if test is TRUE
7               then Γ ← STORECOVERAGE(m, Γ)
8                    U ← U ∪ {m}
9   return U
```

StoreCoverage

    Input: a motif m, a vector of booleans Γ
    Output: the new vector of booleans Γ

```
1   k ← length(m),  delta ← 0
2   for each location l in L_m
3       do delta ← max{delta, l}
4           store TRUE in the locations E_{delta,l+k-1} of Γ
5           delta ← l + k
6   return Γ
```

CheckForUntiedOccurrences

    Input: a motif m, an underlying quorum u, a vector of booleans Γ
    Output: the value TRUE, if the number of untied occurrences of m is at least u; the value FALSE, otherwise

```
1    k ← length(m),  delta ← 0
2    for each occurrence l in L_m
3        do count ← 0, untied ← TRUE
4            delta ← max{delta, l}
5            for each location i in E_{delta,l+k-1} such that
                (l + k - 1) ≤ |Γ|
6                do if Γ_i is TRUE
7                    then untied ← FALSE
8                         break for
9            if untied is TRUE
10               then count + +, i + +
11                   if count ≥ u
12                       then return TRUE
13           delta ← i
14   return FALSE
```

CompareMotifs

Input: two minimal motifs m, m'
Output: BEFORE, if $m \rightarrow m'$; AFTER, if $m' \rightarrow m$;
EQUAL, otherwise
1 **if** $m = m'$
2   **then return** EQUAL
3 **if** $length(m) > length(m')$
4   **then return** BEFORE
5 **if** $length(m) < length(m')$
6   **then return** AFTER
7 **if** $c(m) < c(m')$
8   **then return** BEFORE
9 **if** $c(m) > c(m')$
10   **then return** AFTER
11 ▷ At this stage, using the paired property described in
    Lemma 13.2, we can simply compare the two ordered
    lists of occurrences without any further check:
12 $i \leftarrow 0$
13 **while** TRUE
14   **do if** $\mathcal{L}_m.get(i) < \mathcal{L}_{m'}.get(i)$
15   **then return** BEFORE
16   **if** $\mathcal{L}_m.get(i) > \mathcal{L}_{m'}.get(i)$
17   **then return** AFTER
18        $i++$
19 **return** EQUAL

13.4 EXPERIMENTAL RESULTS AND DISCUSSION

In this section we discuss the ability of underlying motifs to efficiently capture meaningful information. A general problem in genome and proteome research is the identification of signals represented by means of motifs. Some motif discovery tools proved to be useful to analyze biological sequences in different contexts. Here we first collect the motifs in output from one of these tools, say a set of motifs $\mathcal{M}$. Then we present some preliminary results in order to support the theoretical properties shown in the above sections of the chapter.

More generally there are two types of scenarios where the notion of underlying motifs might be useful. The first case is when a region of interest has already been identified, so that it is possible to analyze and select only those motifs that are underlying with respect to that particular region without considering the whole set of motifs. Another possible application is the case where we just want to filter all motifs in $\mathcal{M}$ looking at the whole sequence.

In this context we present some results for the latter scenario. We take as input $\mathcal{M}$ the set of motifs extracted using the tool Varun [4]. The benchmark consists of two protein families for which Varun successfully extracts the functional motifs, as reported in the PROSITE database [20]. In particular, we consider the following protein families:

1. *Nickel-Dependent Hydrogenases (id PS00508)* These are enzymes that catalyze the reversible activation of hydrogen, and are further involved in the binding of nickel.

The family is composed by 22 sequences of about 23,000 amino acids. One of the most functionally significant motifs is detected by Varun in the top three out of 4150 extensible motifs.

2. *Coagulation Factors 5/8 Type C Domain (FA58C) (id PS01286)* This family is composed of 40 sequences of about 46,432 amino acids. Varun places one of the most important structural and functional motifs in this family in the top two motifs out of 80,290 extensible motifs.

To prove that the information captured by the underlying motifs is relevant with respect to the protein family under examination, we devised two kinds of tests. In the first test we compare the original set of motifs in input $\mathcal{M}$ with the set of underlying motifs in output $\mathcal{U}$ using global measures. In the second set of experiments we test the ability to filter meaningful motifs and retain the functional ones.

In the first set of experiments we use Varun to extract motifs from the above families of protein sequences for different quorums q. In all these experiments the quorum refers to the number of occurrences in the concatenation of all sequences of a certain family. Then, we use the extracted motifs as input $\mathcal{M}$ to our algorithm, presented in Section 13.3.1, in order to compute the underlying motifs $\mathcal{U}$. Three observations must be made at this point:

- The motifs extracted by Varun, $m \in \mathcal{M}$, are with character classes and no gaps.
- Before using Algorithm 13.1, we compute the set of minimal motifs $\mu(\mathcal{M})$.
- In our experiments we set the quorum for underlying motifs u to be the same as the original motifs in input; thus $u = q$.

For both sets of motifs $\mathcal{M}$ and $\mathcal{U}$ we compute some statistics. Figure 13.5 shows the number of motifs, the sum of lengths of all motifs, and their mean Z-score. The Z-score is computed employing the same formula reported in [4]. As expected, the number of underlying motifs is always much smaller than the number of original motifs. A similar conclusion can be drawn for the sum of lengths. More important, for small quorums the total length of original motifs exceeds the length of sequences in both families, indicating that the original motifs are even larger than the set of sequences under examination. Moreover, as seen above, the sum of lengths of underlying motifs is always bounded by the length of sequences. These first two measures indicate that, not only the number, but also the total length of underlying motifs, are much smaller than the original motifs. Thus the filtering process is space efficient.

Another important measure is the mean Z-score of $\mathcal{M}$ and $\mathcal{U}$. The mean Z-score is a global measure that captures the average quality of motifs in a set. In Figure 13.5 we can see that, for all quorums, the average Z-score of underlying motifs is always greater than those of original motifs, and in most cases the difference is one or two orders of magnitude. To summarize, this first test confirms that the number and span of underlying motifs is much more manageable than the original set and also that their average quality is improved.

Once we have verified that the notion of underlying is a suitable filter, in a second series of experiments we test the ability to retain meaningful motifs. To this end, we employ the motifs obtained from the previous experiments to test the presence of functional motifs, as reported in the PROSITE database. In particular, the first family, the nickel-dependent hydrogenases (id PS00508), contains two functional motifs: $Ni_1 = $ RG[FILMV]E???????????????[EMPQS][KR]?C[GR][ILMV]C and $Ni_2 = $ [FY]D[IP][CU][AILMV][AGS]C. Similarly,

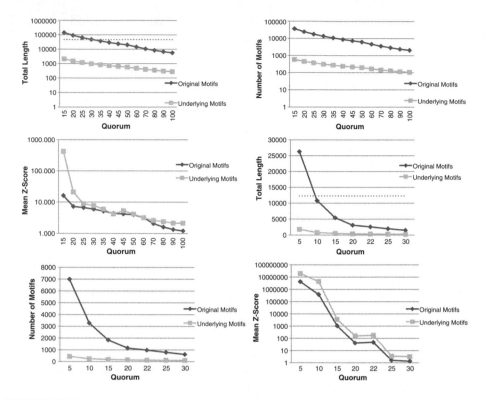

FIGURE 13.5 Total number, sum of lengths, and mean Z-score of the motifs extracted using Varun and their corresponding underlying motifs for two protein families: (*a*) nickel-dependent hydrogenases (id PS00508); (*b*) coagulation factors 5/8 type C domain (id PS01286). The dashed line in Total Length diagrams indicates the total size of each family. Note that in (*a*)–Mean Z-Score and (*b*)–all diagrams the ordinates are plotted on a logarithmic scale.

the second family, the coagulation factors 5/8 type C domain (FA58C) (id PS01286), shares the functional motifs $Fa_1 = $ [FWY][ILV]?[AFILV][DEGNST]??????[FILV]??[IV]? [ILTV][KMQT]G and $Fa_2 = $ [LM]R?[EG][ILPV]?GC. For each set of motifs $\mathcal{M}$ and $\mathcal{U}$, we compute the maximum similarity between each motif in the set and the two functional motifs. The similarity between two motifs m and m' is the number of shared characters, including character classes, in the best alignment of m versus m' without considering indels. Tables 13.1 and 13.2 summarize the maximum similarity for different quorums of $\mathcal{M}$ and

TABLE 13.1 Performance of Underlying Motifs on Family Nickel-Dependent Hydrogenases

Quorum	Max Sim Ni_1 (underlying/original)	Max Sim Ni_2 (underlying/original)
5	26/26	9/12
10	18/18	12/12
15	11/11	9/12
20	9/9	12/12
22	9/9	12/12
25	6/6	6/6
30	6/6	6/6

TABLE 13.2   Performance of Underlying Motifs on Family Coagulation Factors 5/8 Type C Domain

Quorum	Max Sim Fa_1 (underlying/original)	Max Sim Fa_2 (underlying/original)
15	11/12	11/12
20	11/12	12/12
25	12/12	8/10
30	10/12	8/10
35	10/12	9/10
40	10/12	8/8
45	12/12	8/8
50	12/12	8/8
60	10/10	8/8
70	10/10	8/8
80	9/10	8/8
90	9/10	8/8
100	9/10	8/8

$\mathcal{U}$ with each functional motif of the two protein families. The second and third columns report the maximum similarity for the set of underlying motifs divided by the similarity of the original set. For example, in the first row of Table 13.1 the quorum is 5. In this case, the maximum similarity of $\mathcal{M}$ with the functional motif Ni_1 is 26. The same value is obtained also for the corresponding set of underlying motifs $\mathcal{U}$, thus indicating that the motif Ni_1 is retained with the same degree of accuracy.

The values presented in Tables 13.1 and 13.2 confirm that, in most cases, the functional motifs that were present in $\mathcal{M}$ are also selected in the set of underlying motifs with a similar accuracy. Ultimately, although a more comprehensive experimental setting is desirable, this set of preliminary experiments supports the validity of the theoretical results presented in the previous sections and also proves their effectiveness.

13.5 CONCLUSION

In this chapter we have studied motifs with character classes, introducing basic properties for the comparison and ranking of motifs. We have proved several theoretical results that support the validity of these fundamental properties. Most important, our motif priority rule along with the notion of underlying motifs has proved to be valuable for the analysis of biological sequences. Preliminary experiments on protein families have shown very good performance as a filter to reduce the number of motifs in output while keeping the most important ones.

ACKNOWLEDGMENTS

Matteo Comin was partially supported by the Ateneo Project of the University of Padova and by the CaRiPaRo Project. Davide Verzotto was partially supported by Fondazione Ing. Aldo Gini while visiting the University of California, Riverside.

REFERENCES

1. K. Abrahamson. Generalized string matching. *SIAM J. Comput.*, 16:1039–1051, 1987.

2. A. Apostolico. Pattern discovery and the algorithmics of surprise. In *Proceedings of the NATO Advanced Study Institute on Artificial Intelligence and Heuristic Methods for Bioinformatics*, IOS Press, 2003, pp. 111–127.

3. A. Apostolico, M. Comin, and L. Parida. Conservative extraction of over-represented extensible motifs. *Bioinformatics*, 21(Suppl. 1):i9–i18, 2005. Proceedings of the Thirteenth International Conference on Intelligent Systems for Molecular Biology (ISMB 2005).

4. A. Apostolico, M. Comin, and L. Parida. VARUN: Discovering extensible motifs under saturation constraints. *IEEE/ACM Trans. Computat. Biol. Bioinformatics*, 7(4):752–762, Oct.–Dec. 2010.

5. A. Apostolico and L. Parida. Incremental paradigms of motif discovery. *J. Computat. Biol.*, 11:15–25, 2004.

6. T. L. Bailey, N. Williams, C. Misleh, and W. W. Li. MEME: Discovering and analyzing DNA and protein sequence motifs. *Nucleic Acids Res.*, 34(Web-Server-Issue):369–373, 2006.

7. I. E. Ben-Gal, A. Shani, A. Gohr, J. Grau, S. Arviv, A. Shmilovici, S. Posch, and I. Grosse. Identification of transcription factor binding sites with variable-order Bayesian networks. *Bioinformatics*, 21(11):2657–2666, 2005.

8. K. M. Biswas, D. R. DeVido, and J. G. Dorsey. Evaluation of methods for measuring amino acid hydrophobicities and interactions. *J. Chromatogr. A.*, 1000(1–2):637–655, 2003.

9. A. Chakravarty, J. M. Carlson, R. S. Khetani, C. E. DeZiel, and R. H. Gross. SPACER: Identification of cis-regulatory elements with non-contiguous critical residues. *Bioinformatics*, 23(8): 1029–1031, 2007.

10. A. Chattaraj and L. Parida. An inexact-suffix-tree-based algorithm for detecting extensible patterns. *Theor. Comput. Sci.*, 335(1):3–14, 2005.

11. M. Coatney and S. Parthasarathy. MotifMiner: A general toolkit for efficiently identifying common substructures in molecules. In *Proceedings of the Third IEEE Symposium on BioInformatics and BioEngineering (BIBE 2003)*. IEEE Computer Society, Washington, DC, 2003.

12. M. Comin and D. Verzotto. Classification of protein sequences by means of irredundant patterns. *BMC Bioinformatics*, 11(Suppl.1):S16, 2010. Selected articles from the Eighth Asia-Pacific Bioinformatics Conference (APBC 2010).

13. A. Cornish-Bowden. Nomenclature for incompletely specified bases in nucleic acid sequences: Recommendations 1984. *Nucleic Acids Res.*, 13(9):3021–3030, May 1985.

14. C. H. Q. Ding and I. Dubchak. Multi-class protein fold recognition using support vector machines and neural networks. *Bioinformatics*, 17(4):349–358, 2001.

15. M. Federico and N. Pisanti. Suffix tree characterization of maximal motifs in biological sequences. *Theor. Comput. Sci.*, 410(43):4391–4401, 2009.

16. K. Fredriksson and S. Grabowski. Efficient algorithms for pattern matching with general gaps, character classes, and transposition invariance. *Inform. Retrieval*, 11:335–357, 2008.

17. M. C. Frith, N. F. W. Saunders, B. Kobe, and T. L. Bailey. Discovering sequence motifs with arbitrary insertions and deletions. *PLoS Computat. Biol.*, 4(5):e1000071, 2008.

18. D. Gusfield. *Algorithms on Strings, Trees, and Sequences: Computer Science and Computational Biology*. Cambridge University Press, New York, 1997.

19. S. Henikoff and J. G. Henikoff. Amino acid substitution matrices from protein blocks. *Proc. Nat. Acad. Sci. USA*, 89(22):10915–10919, 1992.

20. N. Hulo, A. Bairoch, V. Bulliard, L. Cerutti, B. Cuche, E. de Castro, C. Lachaize, P. Langendijk-Genevaux, and C. Sigrist. The 20 years of PROSITE. *Nucleic Acids Res.*, 36 (database issue): D245–D249, 2008.

21. K. L. Jensen, M. P. Styczynski, I. Rigoutsos, and G. N. Stephanopoulos. A generic motif discovery algorithm for sequential data. *Bioinformatics*, 22(1):21–28, 2006.

22. H. Jiang, Y. Zhao, W. Chen, and W. Zheng. Searching maximal degenerate motifs guided by a compact suffix tree. In N. Back, I. R. Cohen, A. Lajtha, J. D. Lambris, R. Paoletti, and H. R. Arabnia, (Eds.), *Advances in Computational Biology*, Vol. 680 of *Advances in Experimental Medicine and Biology*, Springer New York, 2010, pp. 19–26.

23. R. M. Karp, R. E. Miller, and A. L. Rosenberg. Rapid identification of repeated patterns in strings, trees and arrays. In *Proceedings of the Fourth Annual ACM Symposium on Theory of Computing (STOC 1972)*, 1972, pp. 125–136.

24. I. Ladunga and R. F. Smith. Amino acid substitutions preserve protein folding by conserving steric and hydrophobicity properties. *Prot. Eng.*, 10(3):187–196, 1997.

25. C. S. Leslie, E. Eskin, A. Cohen, J. Weston, and W. S. Noble. Mismatch string kernels for discriminative protein classification. *Bioinformatics*, 20(4):467–476, 2004.

26. N. D. Mendes, A. C. Casimiro, P. M. Santos, I. Sá-Correia, A. L. Oliveira, and A. T. Freitas. MUSA: A parameter free algorithm for the identification of biologically significant motifs. *Bioinformatics*, 22(24):2996–3002, 2006.

27. G. Navarro and M. Raffinot. Fast and simple character classes and bounded gaps pattern matching, with applications to protein searching. *J. Computat. Biol.*, 10(6):903–923, 2003.

28. L. Parida. *Algorithmic Techniques in Computational Genomics*. Courant Institute of Mathematical Sciences, New York University, New York, 1998.

29. L. Parida. *Pattern Discovery in Bioinformatics: Theory and Algorithms*. Chapman and Hall/CRC Mathematical and Computational Biology, 2007.

30. N. Pisanti, A. M. Carvalho, L. Marsan, and M.-F. Sagot. RISOTTO: Fast extraction of motifs with mismatches. In J. R. Correa, A. Hevia, and M. A. Kiwi (Eds.), *Proceeding of Seventh Latin American Symposium on Theoretical Informatics (LATIN 2006)*, Vol. 3887 of *Lecture Notes in Computer Science*, Springer, 2006, pp. 757–768.

31. N. Pisanti, H. Soldano, M. Capentier, and J. Pothier. Implicit and explicit representation of approximated motifs. In C. Iliopoulos, K. Park, and K. Steinhofel (Eds.), *Algorithms for Bioinformatics*. King's College London Press, 2006.

32. N. Pisanti, H. Soldano, and M. Carpentier. Incremental inference of relational motifs with a degenerate alphabet. In *Proceedings of the 16th Annual Symposium on Combinatorial Pattern Matching (CPM 2005)*, 2005, pp. 229–240.

33. E. Redhead and T. L. Bailey. Discriminative motif discovery in DNA and protein sequences using the DEME algorithm. *BMC Bioinformatics*, 8(1), 2007.

34. I. Rigoutsos, A. Floratos, L. Parida, Y. Gao, and D. Platt. The emergence of pattern discovery techniques in computational biology. *Metabolic Eng.*, 2:159–177, 2000.

35. K. Romer, G. R. Kayombya, and E. Fraenkel. WebMOTIFS: Automated discovery, filtering and scoring of DNA sequence motifs using multiple programs and Bayesian approaches. *Nucleic Acids Res.*, 35(Web Server Issue):W217–W220, 2007.

36. M.-F. Sagot. Spelling approximate repeated or common motifs using a suffix tree. In *Proceedings of the Third Latin American Symposium: Theoretical Informatics (LATIN 1998)*, 1998, pp. 374–390.

37. M. C. Shaner, I. M. Blair, and T. D. Schneider. Sequence logos: A powerful, yet simple, tool. In T. N. Mudge, V. Milutinovic, and L. Hunter (Eds.), *Proceedings of the Twenty-Sixth Annual Hawaii International Conference on System Sciences (HICSS 1993)*, Vol. 1: *Architecture and Biotechnology Computing*. IEEE Computer Society, Los Alamitos, CA, 1993, pp. 813–821.

38. H. Soldano, A. Viari, and M. Champesme. Searching for flexible repeated patterns using a nontransitive similarity relation. *Pattern Recognition Lett.*, 16(3):233–246, 1995.

39. M. Tompa, N. Li, T. L. Bailey, G. M. Church, B. De Moor, E. Eskin, A. V. Favorov, M. C. Frith, Y. Fu, W. J. Kent, V. J. Makeev, A. A. Mironov, W. S. Noble, G. Pavesi, G. Pesole, M. Regnier, N. Simonis, S. Sinha, G. Thijs, J. van Helden, M. Vandenbogaert, Z. Weng, C. Workman, C. Ye, and Z. Zhu. Assessing computational tools for the discovery of transcription factor binding sites. *Nat. Biotechnol.*, 23(1):137–144, 2005.

40. E. Ukkonen. Maximal and minimal representations of gapped and non-gapped motifs of a string. *Theor. Comput. Sci.*, 410(43):4341–4349, 2009.

41. O. V. Vishnevsky and N. A. Kolchanov. ARGO: A web system for the detection of degenerate motifs and large-scale recognition of eukaryotic promoters. *Nucleic Acids Res.*, 33(Suppl. 2): W417–W422, 2005.

42. G. Wang, T. Yu, and W. Zhang. WordSpy: Identifying transcription factor binding motifs by building a dictionary and learning a grammar. *Nucleic Acids Res.*, 33(Suppl. 2):W412–W416, 2005.

43. E. Wijaya, S.-M. Yiu, N. T. Son, R. Kanagasabai, and W.-K. Sung. MotifVoter: A novel ensemble method for fine-grained integration of generic motif finders. *Bioinformatics*, 24:2288–2295, Oct. 2008.

44. R. Wu, C. Chaivorapol, J. Zheng, H. Li, and S. Liang. fREDUCE: Detection of degenerate regulatory elements using correlation with expression. *BMC Bioinformatics*, 8(1):399, 2007.

45. S. Wu and U. Manber. Fast text searching: Allowing errors. *Commun. ACM*, 35:83–91, 1992.

46. S. Zhang, W. Su, and J. Yang. ARCS-Motif: Discovering correlated motifs from unaligned biological sequences. *Bioinformatics*, 25:183–189, Jan. 2009.

CHAPTER 14

STABILITY OF FEATURE SELECTION ALGORITHMS AND ENSEMBLE FEATURE SELECTION METHODS IN BIOINFORMATICS

PENGYI YANG,[1] BING B. ZHOU,[1] JEAN YEE-HWA YANG,[2] and ALBERT Y. ZOMAYA[1]

[1]School of Information Technologies, University of Sydney, Sydney, Australia
[2]School of Mathematics and Statistics, University of Sydney, Sydney, Australia

14.1 INTRODUCTION

Feature selection is a key technique originated from the fields of artificial intelligence and machine learning [3, 10] in which the main motivation has been to improve sample classification accuracy [5]. Since the purpose is mainly on improving classification outcome, the design of feature selection algorithms seldom considers specifically which features are selected. Due to the exponential growth of biological data in recent years, many feature selection algorithms have been found to be readily applicable or with minor modification [32], for example, to identify potential disease-associated genes from microarray studies [35], proteins from *mass spectrometry* (MS)–based proteomics studies [23], or *single-nucleotide polymorphism* (SNP) from *genomewide association* (GWA) studies [37]. While sample classification accuracy is an important aspect in many of those biological studies such as discriminating cancer and normal tissues, the emphasis is also on the selected features as they represent interesting genes, proteins, or SNPs. Those biological features are often referred to as biomarkers and they often determine how the further validation studies should be designed and conducted.

One special issue arises from the application of feature selection algorithms in identifying potential disease-associated biomarkers is that those algorithms may give unstable selection results [19]. That is, a minor perturbation on the data such as a different partition of data samples, removal of a few samples, or even reordering of the data samples may cause a feature selection algorithm to select a different set of features. For those algorithms with stochastic components, to simply rerun the algorithm with a different random seed may result in a different feature selection result.

Biological Knowledge Discovery Handbook: Preprocessing, Mining, and Postprocessing of Biological Data, First Edition. Edited by Mourad Elloumi and Albert Y. Zomaya.
© 2014 John Wiley & Sons, Inc. Published 2014 by John Wiley & Sons, Inc.

The term *stability* and its counterpart *instability* are used to describe whether a feature selection algorithm is sensitive/insensitive to the small changes in the data and the settings of algorithmic parameters. The stability of a feature selection algorithm becomes an important property in many biological studies because biologists may be more confident on the feature selection results that do not change much on a minor perturbation on the data or a rerun of the algorithm. While this subject has been relatively neglected before, we saw fast-growing interests in recent years in finding different approaches for improving the stability of feature selection algorithms and different metrics for measuring them.

In this chapter, we provide a general introduction on the stability of feature selection algorithms and review some popular ensemble strategies and evaluation metrics for improving and measuring feature selection stability. In Section 14.2, we categorize feature selection algorithms and illustrate some common causes of feature selection instability. In Section 14.3, we describe some popular methods for building ensemble feature selection algorithms and show the improvement of ensemble feature selection algorithms in terms of feature selection stability. Section 14.4 reviews some typical metrics that are used for evaluating the stability of a given feature selection algorithm. Section 14.5 concludes the chapter.

14.2   FEATURE SELECTION ALGORITHMS AND INSTABILITY

Feature selection stability has been a minor issue in many conventional machine learning tasks. However, from the application of feature selection algorithms to bioinformatics problems, especially in disease-associated biomarker identification, has arisen the specific interests in selection stability as evidenced by several recent publications [4, 17]. In this section, we first categorize feature selection algorithms according to the way they select features. Then we demonstrate the instability of different feature selection algorithms using three case studies.

14.2.1   Categorization of Feature Selection Algorithm

From a computational perspective, feature selection algorithms can be broadly divided into three categories, namely *filter*, *wrapper*, and *embedded*, according to their selection manners [10]. Figure 14.1 shows a schematic view of these categories.

Filter algorithms commonly rank/select features by evaluating certain types of association or correlation with class labels. They do not optimize the classification accuracy of a given inductive algorithm directly. For this reason, filter algorithms are often computationally more efficient compared to wrapper algorithms. For numeric data analysis such as *differentially expressed* (DE) gene selection from microarray data or DE protein selection from mass spectrometry data, the most popular methods are probably the t-test and its variants [33]. As for categorical data types such as disease-associated SNP selection from GWA studies, the commonly used methods are χ^2-statistics, odds ratio, and increasingly the ReliefF algorithm and its variants [27].

Although filter algorithms often show good generalization on unseen data, they suffer from several problems. First, filter algorithms commonly ignore the effects of the selected features on sample classification with respect to the specified inductive algorithm. Yet the performance of the inductive algorithm can be useful for accurate phenotype classification [21]. Second, many filter algorithms are univariate and greedy based. They assume that each feature contributes to the phenotype independently and thus evaluate each feature

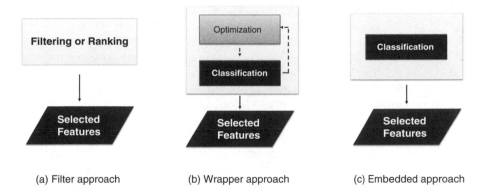

FIGURE 14.1 Categorization of feature selection algorithms: (a) filter approach, where feature selection is independent from the classification; (b) wrapper approach, where feature selection relies on an inductive algorithm for sample classification in an iterative manner; (c) embedded approach, where feature selection is performed implicitly by an inductive algorithm during sample classification.

separately. A feature set is often determined by first ranking the features according to certain scores calculated by filter algorithms and then selecting the top-k candidates. However, the assumption of independence is invalid in biological systems and the selection results produced in this way are often suboptimal.

Compared to filter algorithms, wrapper algorithms have several advantages. First, wrapper algorithms incorporate the performance of an inductive algorithm in feature evaluation and therefore are likely to perform well in sample classification. Second, most wrapper algorithms are multivariate and treat multiple features as unit for evaluation. This property preserves the biological interpretation of genes and proteins since they are linked by pathways and function in groups. A large number of wrapper algorithms have been applied to gene selection of microarray and protein selection of mass spectrometry. Those include evolution approaches such as *genetic algorithm* (GA)–based selection [15, 24, 25] and greedy approaches such as incremental forward selection [30] and incremental backward elimination [28].

Despite their common advantages, the wrapper approach often suffers from problems such as overfitting since the feature selection procedure is guided by an inductive algorithm that is fitted on training data. Therefore, the features selected by the wrapper approach may generalize poorly on new data sets if overfitting is not prevented. In addition, wrapper algorithms are often much slower compared to filter algorithms (by several orders of magnitude) due to their iterative training and evaluation procedures.

The embedded approach is somewhere between the filter approach and the wrapper approach where an inductive algorithm implicitly selects features during sample classification. Different from filter and wrapper approaches, the embedded approach relies on certain types of inductive algorithms and is therefore less generic. The most popular ones that apply to gene and protein selection are support vector machine recursive feature elimination (SVM-RFE) [11] and random forest–based feature evaluation [7].

14.2.2 Potential Causes of Feature Selection Instability

The instability of feature selection algorithms is typically amplified by the small sample sizes common in bioinformatics applications. This is often demonstrated by applying bootstrap sampling on the original data set and comparing the feature selection results from sampled data sets [1]. Beside the common cause of small sample size, the stability is also highly dependent on the types of feature selection algorithm in use. For example, wrapper-based approaches rely on partitioning data into training and testing sets where the training set is used to build the classification model and the testing set is used for feature evaluation [9]. Therefore, a different partition of the training and testing sets may cause different feature selection results and thus instability. Feature selection algorithms using stochastic search such as GA-based feature selection may give different selection results with a different random seed, initialization, and parameter setting. Some algorithms such as ReliefF-based algorithms are sensitive to the sample order in feature selection from a categorical data set [36].

In this section, we demonstrate several common cases where the instability of feature selection is observed. We select typical filter, wrapper, and embedded feature selection algorithms for this demonstration. The case studies are classified according to the causes of feature selection instability.

14.2.2.1 *Case Study I: Small Sample Size*
Small sample size is the common cause of feature selection instability. To demonstrate this effect, we applied bootstrap sampling on the colon cancer microarray data set [2]. The colon cancer microarray data set represents a typical microarray experiment where the normal samples and the tumor samples are compared. The data set has 40 tumor samples and 22 normal ones obtained from colon tissue. Giving the number of genes measured (i.e., 2000) and the total number of samples (i.e., 62), it is a typical small-sample-size data set with very high feature dimensionality.

Figure 14.2a shows the scatter plot of two runs of a filter algorithm known as the moderated *t*-test [33]. Each run of the moderated *t*-test is conducted on a bootstrap sampling from the original data set with a different seeding. The x and the y axes are the rankings of genes (in logarithm of base 2) in the first and the second runs, respectively, plotted against each other. The most informative gene is ranked as 1, the second most informative one as 2, and so on. If the rankings of all genes remain the same in these two runs, they should form a diagonal line with a Spearman correlation of 1. However, it is clear that the moderated

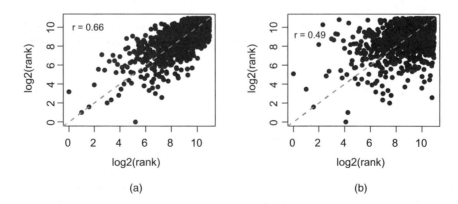

(a)   (b)

FIGURE 14.2 Instability demonstration for filter algorithm (moderated *t*-test) and embedded algorithm (SVM-RFE) in feature selection on colon cancer microarray data set [2]: (a) scatter plot of two runs of moderated *t*-test each calculated on bootstrap sampling of original data set; (b) scatter plot of two runs of SVM-RFE each calculated on bootstrap sampling of original data set. In each case, a Spearman correlation denoted as *r* is calculated.

t-test is highly unstable in ranking genes from a small-sample-size data set. A Spearman correlation (denoted as r) of 0.66 is observed from the two runs.

Figure 14.2b shows the result from using an embedded feature selection algorithm known as SVM-RFE. A SVM is built to evaluate features, and we eliminate 10% of total features in each iteration. The scatter plot of two runs of SVM-RFE each conducted on a separate bootstrap sampling indicates a low stability of a Spearman correlation of only 0.49. Therefore, similar to the moderated t-test, SVM-RFE is also highly unstable in ranking genes from the small-sample-size data set.

14.2.2.2 Case Study II: Sample Order Dependency

Feature selection results may be different even by changing the order of samples in the data set. This may occur if the feature selection algorithm scores each feature by evaluating partial as opposed to all samples in the data set, and the selection of the partial samples is dependent on the order of samples. This is best exemplified by using ReliefF-based feature selection algorithms [29] for categorical feature selection.

Consider a GWA study consisting of N SNPs and M samples. Define each SNP in the study as g_j and each sample as s_i where $j = 1, \ldots, N$ and $i = 1, \ldots, M$. The ReliefF algorithm ranks each SNP by updating a weight function for each SNP at each iteration as follows:

$$W(g_j) = W(g_j) - \frac{D(g_j, s_i, h_k)}{M} + \frac{D(g_j, s_i, m_k)}{M} \tag{14.1}$$

where s_i is the ith sample from the data set and h_k is the kth nearest neighbor of s with same the class label (called a *hit*) while m_k is the kth nearest neighbor to s_i with a different class label (called a *miss*). This weight -updating process is repeated for M samples selected randomly or exhaustively. Therefore, dividing by M keeps the value of $W(g_j)$ in the interval [-1,1]. Assume $D(\cdot)$ is a difference function that calculates the difference between any two samples s_a and s_b for a given gene g:

$$D(g, s_a, s_b) = \begin{cases} 0 & \text{if } G(g, s_a) = G(g, s_b) \\ 1 & \text{otherwise} \end{cases} \tag{14.2}$$

where $G(\cdot)$ denotes the genotype of the SNP g for sample s. The nearest neighbors to a sample are determined by the distance function, $MD(\cdot)$, between the pairs of samples (denoted as s_a and s_b), which is also based on the difference function [Eq. (14.2)]:

$$MD(s_a, s_b) = \sum_{j=1}^{N} D(g_j, s_a, s_b) \tag{14.3}$$

Turned ReliefF (TuRF) proposed by Moore and White [27] aims to improve the performance of the ReliefF algorithm in SNP filtering by adding an iterative component. The signal-to-noise ratio is enhanced significantly by recursively removing the low-ranked SNPs in each iteration. Specifically, if the number of iterations of this algorithm is set to R, it removes the N/R lowest ranking (i.e., least discriminative) SNPs in each iteration, where N is the total number of SNPs.

However, both ReliefF and TuRF are sensitive to the order of samples in the data set due to the assignment of hit and miss nearest neighbors of each sample. Since K nearest neighbors are calculated by comparing the distance between each sample in the data set

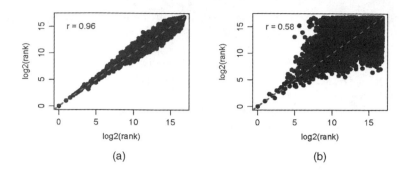

(a)   (b)

FIGURE 14.3 Instability demonstration for ReliefF and TuRF algorithms: (a) scatter plot of two runs of ReliefF on original AMD data set [20] and on sample order perturbed data set; (b) scatter plot of two runs of TuRF on original AMD data set and on sample order perturbed data set. In each case, a Spearman correlation denoted as r is calculated.

and the target sample s_i, a tie occurs when more than K samples have a distance equal or less than the Kth nearest neighbor of s_i. It is easy to show that a dependency on the sample order can be caused by using any tie-breaking procedure which forces exactly K samples out of all possible candidates to be the nearest neighbors of s_i, which causes a different assignment of hits and misses of nearest neighbors when the sample order is permuted.

We demonstrate the sample order dependency effect by using ReliefF and TuRF algorithms, respectively, on a GWA study of *an age-related macular degeneration* (AMD) data set [20]. In this experiment, we permuted the sample order in the original data set and applied ReliefF and TuRF to the original data set and the perturbed data set for SNP ranking. The ranking of each SNP in the two runs are log transferred and plotted against each other (Figures 14.3a,b). While such an inconsistency is relatively small for the ReliefF algorithm, it is enhanced through the iterative ranking procedure of TuRF. A Spearman correlation of only 0.58 is obtained from the original and the sample order perturbed data set.

14.2.2.3 *Case Study III: Data Partitioning*

Typical wrapper algorithms generally build classification models and evaluate features using the models for data classification. For the purpose of building models and evaluating features, the data set is partitioned into training and testing subsets where the training set is used with an inductive algorithm for creating classification models and the testing set is used for evaluating features using the models obtained from the training set. Note that partition of the data set is often necessary since using the entire data set for both model building and feature evaluation would overfit the model easily and produce ungeneralizable feature selection results. The feature selection result from wrapper algorithms could be unstable due to different splittings of data partition. Moreover, wrapper algorithms often rely on certain stochastic or heuristic algorithms (known as search algorithms) to evaluate features in combination so as to reduce the large search space. Therefore, a different seeding or initialization of the search algorithm or a different parameter setting in heuristic search could also produce different feature selection results.

Here we demonstrate the instability in wrapper-based feature selection algorithms using a wrapper of the GA with a k-nearest neighbor (kNN) as the induction algorithm for feature selection (GA/kNN). Since the initial work by Li et al. [25], this configuration and its variants have become very popular in biomarker selection from high-dimensional data. We fix the neighbor size as $k = 3$ in all experiments and the partition of the data set as

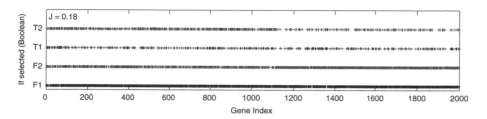

FIGURE 14.4 Instability demonstration for GA/kNN wrapper algorithm with colon cancer microarray data set. The x axis is the index of the 2000 genes in the colon cancer microarray data set [2]. The y axis is a boolean value indicating whether a gene is selected. Two separate runs of GA/kNN each with a different five-fold cross-validation partitioning of the data set. For example, a cross is added to the x axis of 200 and y axis of T2 if the gene with index of 200 in the data set is selected in the second run. A Jaccard set-based index denoted as J is calculated (see Section 14.4.2 for details).

five-fold cross validation. The parameter setting of the GA is also fixed to the default values as specified in the Weka package [12]. Figure 14.4 shows two separate runs of the GA/kNN wrapper algorithm each with a different five-fold cross-validation partitioning of a colon microarray data set [2] for model training and feature evaluation. After running GA/kNN, a gene is either selected or unselected. If the algorithm is not sensitive to a different partitioning of the data set, the genes selected in the first run should also be selected in the second run.

To quantify the concordance of the two runs in terms of the selected genes, we use a metric known as the Jaccard set-based index (see Section 14.4.2 for details) to compute the similarity of the two runs. A Jaccard set-based index of 0.18 indicates a low reproducibility of the GA/kNN wrapper algorithm on feature selection. Therefore, the algorithm is highly unstable when the data set is partitioned differently.

14.2.3 Remark on Feature Selection Instability

Although we have demonstrated some common causes of feature selection instability separately, they should not be considered independently. For example, a wrapper algorithm could suffer from a combination effect of small sample size and partition of the data set. A ReliefF-based algorithm could suffer from the sample order perturbation and a different size of k used to determine nearest neighbors. The SVM-RFE algorithm could suffer from a small sample size and a different step size of recursive feature elimination.

There are several possible ways to improve stability of feature selection algorithms such as using prior information and knowledge, feature grouping, and ensemble feature selection. We will focus specifically on ensemble feature selection, which is introduced in Section 14.3. A review for several other approaches can be found in [13].

The stability of feature selection algorithms is generally assessed by using certain metric. We have used the Spearman correlation and the Jaccard set-based index in our case studies. The details of those metrics and many others are described in Section 14.4.

14.3 ENSEMBLE FEATURE SELECTION ALGORITHMS

The purpose of composing ensemble feature selection algorithms is manyfold. Generally, the goals are to improve feature selection stability or sample classification accuracy or both at the same time as demonstrated in numerous studies [1, 16, 26]. In many cases, other aspects such as to identify important features or to extract feature interaction relationships could also be achieved in a higher accuracy using ensemble feature selection algorithms as compared to their single versions.

Depending on the type of feature selection algorithm, there may be many different ways to compose an ensemble feature selection algorithm. Here we describe two of the most commonly used approaches.

14.3.1 Ensemble Based on Data Perturbation

The first approach is based on data perturbation. This approach has been extensively studied and utilized [1, 4, 36]. The idea is built on the successful experience in ensemble classi-fication [8] and it has been found to stabilize the feature selection result. For example, a bootstrap sampling procedure can be used to create an ensemble of filter algorithms each giving a slightly different ranking of genes. The consensus is then obtained through com-bining those ranking lists. It is natural to understand that beside bootstrap sampling many other data perturbation methods (such as random spacing) can also be used to create multi-ple versions of the original data set in the same framework. A schematic illustration of this class of methods is shown in Figure 14.5.

14.3.2 Ensemble Based on Different Data Partitioning

The second approach is based on partitioning the training and testing data differently and is specific for wrapper-based feature selection algorithms. That is, data that are used for building the classification model and the data that are used for feature evaluation are parti-tioned using multiple cross validations (or any other random partitioning procedures). The

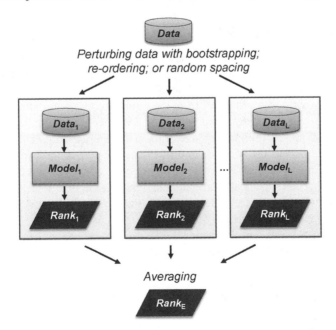

FIGURE 14.5   Schematic of ensemble of filters using data perturbation approach.

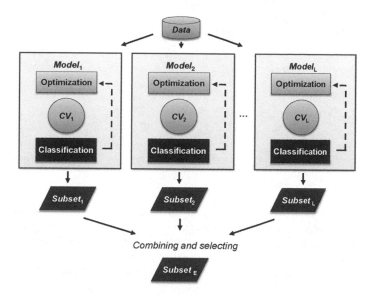

FIGURE 14.6   Schematic illustration of ensemble of wrappers using different partitions of internal cross validation for feature evaluation.

final feature subset is determined by calculating the frequency of each feature selected from each partitioning. If a feature is selected more than a given threshold, it is then included into the final feature set.

A schematic illustration of this method is shown in Figure 14.6. This method is first described in [9] where a *forward-feature selection* (FFS) wrapper and a *backward-feature elimination* (BFE) wrapper are shown to benefit from this ensemble approach.

Beside using different data partitioning, for stochastic optimization algorithms such as GA or *particle swarm optimization* (PSO), the ensemble can also be achieved by using different initializations or different parameter settings. For wrappers such as FFS or BFE, a different starting point in the feature space can result in a different selection result. Generally, bootstrap sampling or other random spacing approaches can also be applied to wrapper algorithms for creating ensembles.

14.3.3   Performance on Feature Selection Stability

We continue the examples in Section 14.2.2 and evaluate the performance of ensemble feature selection algorithms in terms of feature selection stability.

14.3.3.1   Small-Sample-Size Problem   For the small-sample-size problem, we evaluated the ensemble version of the moderated *t*-test and the ensemble version of SVM-RFE (Figures 14.7a,b). Each ensemble run of the moderated *t*-test was generated by aggregating (using averaging) 50 individual runs of bootstrap sampling from the original colon cancer data set [2]. An ensemble of 50 individual runs were combined and plotted against another ensemble of 50 individual runs, with each individual run conducted with a different bootstrap seeding. The same procedure was also used to create the ensemble of SVM-RFE.

It appears that the ensemble of the moderated *t*-test is much better in terms of feature selection stability, with most gene rankings clustering close to the diagonal line.

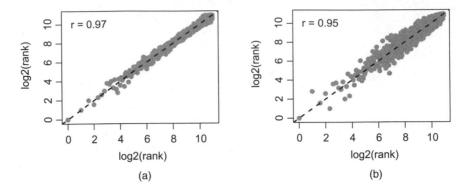

FIGURE 14.7 Ensemble feature selection algorithms for small sample size: (a) scatter plot of two runs of ensemble of moderated *t*-test each calculated on and combined from 50 bootstrap sampling of original colon cancer data set [2]; (b) scatter plot of two runs of ensemble of SVM-RFE each calculated on and combined from 50 bootstrap sampling of original colon cancer data set. Multiple ranking lists are combined by averaging. In each case, a Spearman correlation denoted as *r* is calculated.

A Spearman correlation of 0.97 is obtained compared to 0.66 from the single runs (Figure 14.2a). Similarly, the ensemble of SVM-RFE is able to increase the Spearman correlation from 0.49 to 0.95.

14.3.3.2 Sample Order Dependency Problem The ensembles of ReliefF and TuRF were created by using random sample reordering for generating multiple SNP ranking lists and the consensus is obtained by simple averaging. Figure 14.8 shows the ensemble versions of ReliefF and TuRF algorithms where an ensemble size of 50 is used.

It is clear that the ensemble approach for both ReliefF and TuRF algorithms can improve their consistency on feature selection when the sample order is perturbed. The improvement is especially encouraging for TuRF since two runs of a single TuRF only give a Spearman

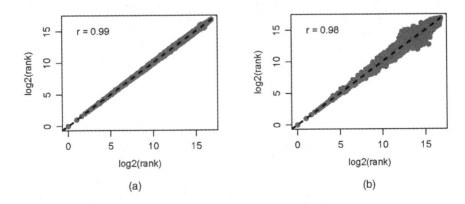

FIGURE 14.8 Ensemble feature selection algorithms for sample order dependency: (a) scatter plot of two runs of ensemble of ReliefF each calculated and combined from 50 sample order perturbed data sets from original AMD data set [20]; (b) scatter plot of two runs of ensemble of TuRF each calculated and combined from 50 sample order perturbed data sets from original AMD data set. In each case, a Spearman correlation denoted as *r* is calculated.

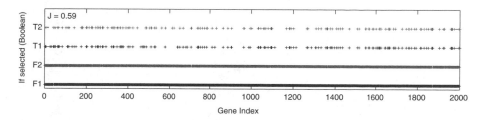

FIGURE 14.9 Ensemble feature selection algorithms for data partitioning. The x axis is the index of the 2000 genes in the colon cancer microarray data set [2]. The y axis is a Boolean value indicating whether a gene is selected. Two separate runs of ensemble of GA/kNN (an ensemble of 50) each with a different five-fold cross-validation partitioning of the data set. For example, a cross is added to the x axis of 200 and y axis of T2 if the gene with index of 200 in the data set is selected in the second run of the ensemble of GA/kNN. A Jaccard set-based index denoted as J is calculated (see Section 14.4.2 for details).

correlation of 0.58 (Figure 14.3b) whereas the ensembles of TuRF improve the Spearman correlation to 0.98 (Figure 14.8b).

14.3.3.3 Data-Partitioning Problem We conducted two separate runs of an ensemble of the GA/kNN wrapper algorithm (an ensemble size of 50 is used) each with a different five-fold cross-validation partitioning of the colon cancer data set [2]. Figure 14.9 shows the concordance of two ensembles of GA/kNN. The Jaccard set-based index increases from 0.18 (Figure 14.4) to 0.59, indicating that the ensemble version of GA/kNN can generate much more consistent feature selection results compared to the original GA/kNN algorithm.

14.3.4 Performance of Sample Classification

Besides improving stability, another goal is to achieve higher classification accuracy by using the ensemble feature selection approach [1]. Here we tested the classification accuracy using the genes selected by a moderated t-test from the colon cancer microarray data set [2] and compared those results with its ensemble version. The classification accuracy was calculated using a 10-fold cross validation with a k-nearest-neighbor classifier ($k = 3$).

From Figure 14.10, we observe that genes selected using the ensemble approach produce a minor improvement on sample classification as compared to the single approach. Since the sample size of the data set is small, we anticipate that a greater improvement on sample classification may be achieved by using a data set with larger sample size.

14.3.5 Ensemble Size

For ensemble feature selection, the choice of ensemble size may affect the performance of feature selection and stability. In this section, we evaluate the effect of different ensemble sizes on feature selection stability. All the evaluations are done on a colon cancer microarray data set [2]. Several different evaluation metrics are used to assess the stability. Those metrics are described in detail in Section 14.4.

From Figures 14.11a,b, we can see that the larger ensemble size of the moderate t-test corresponds to higher feature selection stability in terms of both the Spearman correlation

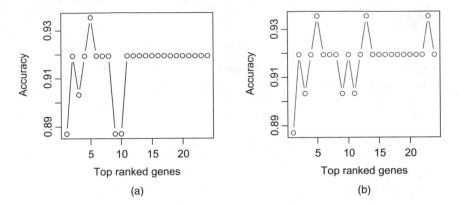

FIGURE 14.10 Sample classification accuracy using genes selected from colon cancer microarray data set [2] by (a) moderated t-test and (b) ensemble of moderated t-test.

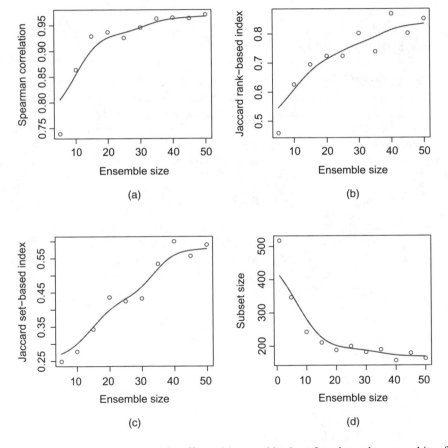

FIGURE 14.11 Ensemble size and its effects: (a) ensemble size of moderated t-test and its effect on feature selection stability measured by Spearman correlation; (b) ensemble size of moderated t-test and its effect on feature selection stability measured by Jaccard rank-based index; (c) ensemble size of GA/kNN and its effect on feature selection stability measured by Jaccard set-based index; (d) ensemble size of GA/kNN and its effect on selected feature subset size.

and the Jaccard rank-based index. A similar effect is also observed for the ensemble of GA/kNN where increasing ensemble size results in higher feature selection stability as indicated by the Jaccard set-based index (Figure 14.11c).

The size of the selected gene subsets has been used by many studies as an evaluation standard for wrapper algorithms [30]. Specifically, without sacrificing the performance (e.g., classification accuracy), small gene subsets are preferred. We observe that the larger the ensemble size of GA/kNN, the smaller the identified gene subset, as shown in Figure 14.11d.

14.3.6 Some Key Aspects in Ensemble Feature Selection Algorithms

Several key aspects may be of interest in designing ensemble feature selection algorithms. First, how to create multiple models is important and determines the quality of the final feature selection results. An ensemble of a certain feature selection algorithm may be created by using bootstrap sampling, random data partitioning, parameter randomization, or a combination of several. However, some ensemble approaches are specific to certain types of feature selection algorithms. For example, we can use sample order perturbation for creating an ensemble of ReliefF algorithm, but this approach will not help on a t-test filter. Similarly, we cannot use the data-partitioning approach for the filter-based feature selection algorithms as the classification is independent of the feature selection procedure.

The ensemble approach attempts to improve feature selection by increasing model complexity. Why the added complexity may improve the feature selection result leads to the second key aspect, known as diversity, which is intensively studied in designing ensembles of classification algorithms [34]. However, to our knowledge this aspect has not been systematically studied in ensembles feature selection. Therefore, it is interesting to evaluate the relationship between the performance of sample classification, the feature selection stability, and the diversity of ensemble models in ensemble feature selection algorithms.

The third key aspect of ensemble feature selection algorithms is the design of appropriate methods for combining multiple ranking lists or feature subsets. Some initial work has been done in this area [6], but the main approach still remains to be simple averaging. A more sophisticated approach is clearly needed for improving the finial feature selection result.

Several other aspects, such as model selection and model averaging, that have been studied in ensemble classification can also be applied to study ensemble feature selection algorithms.

14.4 METRICS FOR STABILITY ASSESSMENT

Stability metrics are used to assess the stability of multiple feature selection results. A feature selection algorithm is often considered as stable in terms of feature selection if the selected features are consistent over multiple runs of the algorithm with variants of the original data set. Depending on the type of feature selection algorithm, multiple variants of the original data set can be obtained by perturbing the original data set in a certain way, for example, bootstrapping, random partitioning, or reordering. We denote each feature selection result as $\mathcal{F}_i$, $i = 1, \ldots, L$, where L is the number of times the selections are repeated. To assess the stability, it is common to perform a pairwise comparison of each selection result with others and average the assessment with respect to the number of comparisons [9]. Formally, this procedure can be expressed as follows:

$$\overline{S}_p = \frac{2}{L(L-1)} \sum_{i=1}^{L} \sum_{j=i+1}^{L} S(\mathcal{F}_i, \mathcal{F}_j) \qquad (14.4)$$

where $\overline{S}_p$ is the assessment score of stability from averaged pairwise comparisons; $\mathcal{F}_i$ and $\mathcal{F}_j$ are the ith feature selection result and the jth feature selection result generated from different runs of a feature selection algorithm; and $S(\cdot)$ is a stability assessment metric which can be defined differently according to the type of feature selection algorithm and ones interest or emphasis in the assessment.

14.4.1 Rank-Based Stability Metrics

Rank-based metrics are used to assess the stability of multiple ranking lists in which the features are ranked based on certain evaluation criteria of a feature selection algorithm. Filter algorithms that produce a "goodness" score for each feature can be assessed using rank-based metrics whereas wrapper algorithms that generate a subset of features instead of ranking the features may not be assessed properly using rank-based metrics but require set-based stability metrics which will be introduced in Section 14.4.2.

Within the rank-based metrics, there are mainly two subcategories depending on whether a full- or partial-ranking list is considered. For the full-ranking list, one assesses stability based on the rank of all features, whereas for the partial list, a threshold is specified and only those that pass the threshold are used for stability assessment.

14.4.1.1 *Full-Ranking Metrics* The most widely used metric for the full-ranking list is the *Spearman correlation* [18, 19, 31]. For stability assessment, it is applied as

$$S_S(\mathcal{R}_i, \mathcal{R}_j) = 1 - \sum_{\tau=1}^{N} \frac{6(r_i^\tau - r_j^\tau)^2}{N(N^2-1)} \qquad (14.5)$$

where $S_S(\mathcal{R}_i, \mathcal{R}_j)$ denotes the stability score on ranking lists $\mathcal{R}_i$ and $\mathcal{R}_j$ using the Spearman correlation; N is the total number of features and τ is an index that goes through the first feature to the last one in the data set; and r_i^τ denotes the rank of the τth feature in the ith ranking list.

The spearman correlation ranges between -1 and 1 with 0 indicating no correlation and 1 or -1 indicating a perfect positive or negative correlation, respectively. For feature selection stability assessment, the higher (in positive value) the Spearman correlation, the more consistent the two ranking lists, and therefore the more stable the feature selection algorithm.

14.4.1.2 *Partial-Ranking Metrics* In contrast to the full-ranking metrics, partial-ranking metrics require us to prespecify a threshold and consider only features that pass the threshold [14]. For example, the *Jaccard rank-based index* is a typical partial-ranking metric used for assessing the stability of the feature selection algorithm in several studies [19, 31]. Here, one needs to make a decision on the percentage of top-ranked features that should be used or simply how many top-ranked features should be used for stability assessment. Let us use top k features in each list. The Jaccard rank-based index can be computed as

$$S_J^k(\mathcal{R}_i, \mathcal{R}_j) = \sum_{\tau=1}^{N} \frac{I(r_i^\tau \leqslant k \wedge r_j^\tau \leqslant k)}{2k - I(r_i^\tau \leqslant k \wedge r_j^\tau \leqslant k)} \qquad (14.6)$$

where $S_J^k(\mathcal{R}_i, \mathcal{R}_j)$ is the computing stability score on ranking lists $\mathcal{R}_i$ and $\mathcal{R}_j$ using the Jaccard rank-based index with top k ranked features and $I(\cdot)$ is an indicator function which gives 1 if an evaluation is true or 0 otherwise. As defined before, r_i^τ denotes the rank of the τth feature in the ith ranking list; $\wedge$ is the logic and.

The above function gives the intersection and union of the top k features from ranking list i and ranking list j and then computes the ratio of the intersection over the union. Clearly, if the top k features in both ranking lists are exactly the same, their intersection and the union will be the same and therefore the ratio is 1 (perfect stability). Otherwise the ratio will be smaller than 1 and reach 0 when none of the top k features in the two ranking lists are the same (no stability). Note that the Jaccard rank-based metric is undefined when $k = 0$ and it is always 1 if all features are considered ($k = N$). Both cases are meaningless in the context of feature selection. In other words, we need to specify a meaningful threshold k that fulfills the inequality $0 < k < N$.

Another partial-ranking metric is the *Kuncheva index* [22]:

$$S_I^k(\mathcal{R}_i, \mathcal{R}_j) = \sum_{\tau=1}^{N} I(r_i^\tau \leqslant k \wedge r_j^\tau \leqslant k) \frac{1 - k^2/N}{k - k^2/N} \qquad (14.7)$$

where N is the total number of features, $I(r_i^\tau \leqslant k \wedge r_j^\tau \leqslant k)$ as defined before computes the number of features in common in the top k features of the ranking lists of i and j, and N is the total number of features.

Similar to the Jaccard rank-based index, the Kuncheva index looks at the intersection of the top k features in the two ranking lists i and j. However, instead of normalizing the intersection using the union of the two partial lists as in the Jaccard rank-based index, the Kuncheva index normalizes the intersection using the length of the list (that is, k) and corrects for the chance of selecting common features at random among two partial lists with the term k^2/N. This is done by incorporating the total number of features N in the ranking list to the metric which takes into account the ratio of the number of features considered (k) and the total number of feature (N) in computing the index. The Kuncheva index is in the range of -1 to 1 with a greater value suggesting a more consistent feature selection result in the two runs. Similar to the Jaccard rank-based index, the Kuncheva index is undefined at both $k = 0$ and $k = N$, which is meaningless in practice and is often ignored.

14.4.2 Set-Based Stability Metrics

For algorithms that directly select features instead of ranking them, a Boolean value is produced indicating whether a feature is included or excluded in the feature selection result. In such a scenario, a set-based metric is more appropriate to evaluate the stability of the feature selection result.

The most common metric in this category is the *Hamming index*, which is adopted by Dunne et al. [9] for evaluating the stability of a few wrapper algorithms in the feature selection. Assume the feature selection results of two independent runs of a feature selection algorithm produces two Boolean lists $\mathcal{M}_i$ and $\mathcal{M}_j$ in which a 1 indicates that a feature is selected and a 0 that it is excluded. The stability of the algorithm can be quantified as

$$S_H(\mathcal{M}_i, \mathcal{M}_j) = 1 - \sum_{\tau=1}^{N} \frac{|m_i^\tau - m_j^\tau|}{N} \qquad (14.8)$$

where m_i^τ and m_j^τ denote the values of the τth position in the Boolean list of i and Boolean list of j, respectively. Those values could either be 0 or 1. As before N is the total number of features in the data set.

If the same features are included or excluded in the two Boolean lists, the term $\sum_{\tau=1}^{N} |m_i^\tau - m_j^\tau|/N$ will be 0, which will give a Hamming index of 1. On the contrary, if the feature selection results are exactly opposite to each other, the term $\sum_{\tau=1}^{N} |m_i^\tau - m_j^\tau|/N$ will be 1 and the Hamming index will be 0.

Besides the Hamming index, the Jaccard index can also be applied for evaluating the stability of the set-based feature selection results. We refer to it as the *Jaccard set-based index* so as to differentiate it from the Jaccard rank-based index. The Jaccard set-based index is defined as

$$S_J(\mathcal{M}_i, \mathcal{M}_j) = \sum_{\tau=1}^{N} \frac{m_i^\tau \wedge m_j^\tau}{m_i^\tau \vee m_j^\tau} \qquad (14.9)$$

where m_i^τ and m_j^τ as before denote the values of the τth position in the Boolean list of i and Boolean list of j. The term $m_i^\tau \wedge m_j^\tau$ over the sum of total number of features N gives the intersection of selected features in the two Boolean lists, whereas the term $m_i^\tau \vee m_j^\tau$ over the sum of total number of features gives the union of selected features.

14.4.3 Threshold in Stability Metrics

Depending on the feature selection algorithm and the biological questions, it may be more interesting to look at only the top-ranked genes from a ranking list instead of considering all genes. This is generally true in cancer studies where only a subset of top-ranked genes will be selected for followup validation. In such a case, metrics that rely on a predefined threshold for calculation are often applied to study the stability of the feature selection results. The question here is on what threshold to use (say, the top 100 or top 500 genes). Note that a different threshold may lead to a different conclusion on stability.

Figure 14.12 shows the stability evaluation across multiple thresholds of Jaccard rank-based index. In particular, Figure 14.12a is the result using SVM-RFE and Figure 14.12b is the result using ensemble of SVM-RFE all with colon cancer microarray dataset [2]. Genes are ranked by the score from SVM-RFE or ensemble of SVM-RFE, respectively. We applied the thresholds of top 10, 20, . . . , 2000 genes with a step of 10 genes for calculating the Jaccard rank-based index using bootstrap sampling datasets.

It is clear that the ensemble of SVM-RFE demonstrates much higher stability, especially at the very top of the ranking lists. The stability according to the Jaccard rank-based index is around 0.7 for the ensemble approach whereas for the single version of SVM-RFE it is less than 0.2. One important observation is that as more genes are included for calculation, the differences of the Jaccard rank-based index between the ensemble and the single approaches become smaller and eventually become 0 when all genes are included in the calculation. Therefore, it may be most informative to compare the very top of the ranking lists when

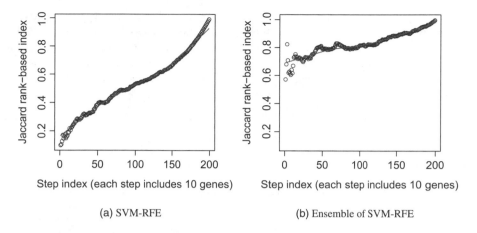

(a) SVM-RFE   (b) Ensemble of SVM-RFE

FIGURE 14.12 Evaluation of using different thresholds for computing stability. (a) SVM-RFE and (b) its ensemble are run on bootstraps on colon cancer microarray data set [2], respectively, and the stability values in terms of the Jaccard rank-based index are calculated using thresholds from the top 10 to top 2000 genes (that is, all genes) with a step of 10 (thus, 200 steps).

using the Jaccard rank-based index, whereas the comparison of a long list using the Jaccard rank-based index could be meaningless as both of them will have a value close to 1.

14.4.4 Remark on Metrics for Stability Evaluation

It is generally unnecessary or even impossible to determine which metric is the best one for evaluating stability across all scenarios [14, 19]. In practice, depending on the type of feature selection algorithm, a certain metric may appear to be more appropriate. Sometimes, different metrics can be applied to the same selection results, and they may help to determine different properties of a feature selection algorithm in terms of stability.

Since different metrics may score a feature selection algorithm differently, an algorithm that is more stable than another algorithm across multiple metrics is desirable for designing a method to improve feature selection.

14.5 CONCLUSIONS

The stability of feature selection algorithms has become an important research topic in bioinformatics where the selected features have important biological interpretations. The ensemble feature selection approach has been a general and promising solution in many scenarios where the performance of a single feature selection algorithm is highly unstable. In this chapter, we categorized feature selection algorithms into three types and demonstrated their instability in different scenarios. We focused on ensemble feature selection algorithms and compared their performance with their corresponding single versions. Several metrics that are commonly used for assessing feature selection stability are introduced and used in our comparison.

Ensemble feature selection algorithms appear to be much more stable in terms of generating a feature subset or feature ranking list. However, factors such as the size of the ensemble, the metric used for assessment, and the threshold used by some metrics should be taken into consideration when designing and comparing ensemble feature selection algorithms. We believe that ensemble feature selection algorithms are useful tools in bioinformatics applications where the goal is both accurate sample classification and biomarker identification.

ACKNOWLEDGMENT

Pengyi Yang is supported by the NICTA International Postgraduate Award (NIPA) and the NICTA Research Project Award (NRPA).

REFERENCES

1. T. Abeel, T. Helleputte, Y. Van de Peer, P. Dupont, and Y. Saeys. Robust biomarker identification for cancer diagnosis with ensemble feature selection methods. *Bioinformatics*, 26(3):392–398, 2010.

2. U. Alon, N. Barkai, D. A. Notterman, K. Gish, S. Ybarra, D. Mack, and A. J. Levine. Broad patterns of gene expression revealed by clustering analysis of tumor and normal colon tissues probed by oligonucleotide arrays. *Proc. Nat. Acad. Sci. USA*, 96:6745–6750, 1999.

3. A. L. Blum and P. Langley. Selection of relevant features and examples in machine learning. *AI*, 97(1–2):245–271, 1997.

4. A. L. Boulesteix and M. Slawski. Stability and aggregation of ranked gene lists. *Brief. Bioinformatics*, 10(5):556–568, 2009.

5. M. Dash and H. Liu. Feature selection for classification. *Intelligent Data Analysis*, 1(3):131–156, 1997.

6. R. P. DeConde, S. Hawley, S. Falcon, N. Clegg, B. Knudsen, and R. Etzioni. Combining results of microarray experiments: A rank aggregation approach. *Statist. Appl. Genetics Mol. Biol.*, 5:Article15, 2006.

7. R. Díaz-Uriarte and S. A. De Andres. Gene selection and classification of microarray data using random forest. *BMC Bioinformatics*, 7(1):3, 2006.

8. T. G. Dietterich. Ensemble methods in machine learning. In *Proceedings of the First International Workshop on Multiple Classifier Systems.* Springer-Verlag, London, UK, 2000, pp. 1–15.

9. K. Dunne, P. Cunningham, and F. Azuaje. Solutions to instability problems with sequential wrapper-based approaches to feature selection. Technical Report TCD-CS-2002-28. Department of Computer Science, Trinity College, Dublin, Ireland, 2002.

10. I. Guyon and A. Elisseeff. An introduction to variable and feature selection. *J. Machine Learning Res.*, 3:1157–1182, 2003.

11. I. Guyon, J. Weston, S. Barnhill, and V. Vapnik. Gene selection for cancer classification using support vector machines. *Machine Learning*, 46(1):389–422, 2002.

12. M. Hall, E. Frank, G. Holmes, B. Pfahringer, P. Reutemann, and I. H. Witten. The WEKA data mining software: An update. *ACM SIGKDD Explorations Newsletter*, 11(1):10–18, 2009.

13. Z. He and W. Yu. Stable feature selection for biomarker discovery. *Computat. Biol. Chem.*, 34(4):215–225, 2010.

14. I. B. Jeffery, D. G. Higgins, and A. C. Culhane. Comparison and evaluation of methods for generating differentially expressed gene lists from microarray data. *BMC Bioinformatics*, 7(1):359, 2006.

15. T. Jirapech-Umpai and S. Aitken. Feature selection and classification for microarray data analysis: Evolutionary methods for identifying predictive genes. *BMC Bioinformatics*, 6(1):148, 2005.

16. K. Jong, J. Mary, A. Cornuéjols, E. Marchiori, and M. Sebag. Ensemble feature ranking. In *Proceedings of the 8th European Conference on Principles and Practice of Knowledge Discovery in Databases*. Springer-Verlag, New York, 2004, pp. 267–278.

17. G. Jurman, S. Merler, A. Barla, S. Paoli, A. Galea, and C. Furlanello. Algebraic stability indicators for ranked lists in molecular profiling. *Bioinformatics*, 24(2):258, 2008.

18. A. Kalousis, J. Prados, and M. Hilario. Stability of feature selection algorithms. In *Proceedings of the Fifth IEEE International Conference on Data Mining*. IEEE, New York, 2005, pp. 218–225.

19. A. Kalousis, J. Prados, and M. Hilario. Stability of feature selection algorithms: A study on high-dimensional spaces. *Knowledge Inform. Syst.*, 12(1):95–116, 2007.

20. R. J. Klein, et al. Complement factor h polymorphism in age-related macular degeneration. *Science*, 308(5720):385–389, 2005.

21. R. Kohavi and G. H. John. Wrappers for feature subset selection. *Artif. Intell.*, 97(1–2):273–324, 1997.

22. L. I. Kuncheva. A stability index for feature selection. In *Proceedings of the 25th IASTED International Multi-Conference: Artificial Intelligence and Applications*. ACTA Press, Anaheim, CA, 2007, pp. 390–395.

23. I. Levner. Feature selection and nearest centroid classification for protein mass spectrometry. *BMC Bioinformatics*, 6(1):68, 2005.

24. L. Li, D. M. Umbach, P. Terry, and J. A. Taylor. Application of the GA/KNN method to SELDI proteomics data. *Bioinformatics*, 20(10):1638, 2004.

25. L. Li, C. R. Weinberg, T. A. Darden, and L. G. Pedersen. Gene selection for sample classification based on gene expression data: Study of sensitivity to choice of parameters of the ga/knn method. *Bioinformatics*, 17(12):1131–1142, 2001.

26. B. Liu, Q. Cui, T. Jiang, and S. Ma. A combinational feature selection and ensemble neural network method for classification of gene expression data. *BMC Bioinformatics*, 5(1):136, 2004.

27. J. Moore and B. White. Tuning relief for genome-wide genetic analysis. *Evolutionary Computation, Machine Learning and Data Mining in Bioinformatics*, 4447:166–175, 2007.

28. G. Potamias, L. Koumakis, and V. Moustakis. Gene selection via discretized gene-expression profiles and greedy feature-elimination. *Methods Appl. AI*, 3025:256–266, 2004.

29. M. Robnik-Šikonja and I. Kononenko. Theoretical and empirical analysis of ReliefF and RReliefF. *Machine Learning*, 53(1):23–69, 2003.

30. R. Ruiz, J. C. Riquelme, and J. S. Aguilar-Ruiz. Incremental wrapper-based gene selection from microarray data for cancer classification. *Pattern Recognition*, 39(12):2383–2392, 2006.

31. Y. Saeys, T. Abeel, and Y. Peer. Robust feature selection using ensemble feature selection techniques. In *Proceedings of the European Conference on Machine Learning and Knowledge Discovery in Databases—Part II*. Springer-Verlag, Antwerp, Belgium, 2008, pp. 313–325.

32. Y. Saeys, I. Inza, and P. Larrañaga. A review of feature selection techniques in bioinformatics. *Bioinformatics*, 23(19):2507–2517, 2007.

33. G. K. Smyth. Linear models and empirical Bayes methods for assessing differential expression in microarray experiments. *Statist. Appl. Genet. Mol. Biol.*, 3:Article3, 2004.

34. A. Tsymbal, M. Pechenizkiy, and P. Cunningham. Diversity in search strategies for ensemble feature selection. *Inform. Fusion*, 6(1):83–98, 2005.

35. E. P. Xing, M. I. Jordan, and R. M. Karp. Feature selection for high-dimensional genomic microarray data. In *Proceedings of the Eighteenth International Conference on Machine Learning*. Morgan Kaufmann Publishers, Williamstown, MA, 2001, pp. 601–608.

36. P. Yang, J. Ho, Y. Yang, and B. Zhou. Gene-gene interaction filtering with ensemble of filters. *BMC Bioinformatics*, 12(Suppl. 1):S10, 2011.

37. K. Zhang, Z. S. Qin, J. S. Liu, T. Chen, M. S. Waterman, and F. Sun. Haplotype block partitioning and tag snp selection using genotype data and their applications to association studies. *Genome Res.*, 14(5):908, 2004.

CHAPTER 15

STATISTICAL SIGNIFICANCE ASSESSMENT FOR BIOLOGICAL FEATURE SELECTION: METHODS AND ISSUES

JUNTAO LI,[1,2] KWOK PUI CHOI,[2] YUDI PAWITAN,[3] and RADHA KRISHNA MURTHY KARUTURI[1]

[1]Computational and Mathematical Biology, Genome Institute of Singapore, Singapore
[2]Department of Statistics and Applied Probability, National University of Singapore, Singapore
[3]Department of Medical Epidemiology and Biostatistics, Karolinska Institute, Stockholm, Sweden

15.1 INTRODUCTION

Biological knowledge discovery is aimed at quantifying the treatment effects and establishing functional and mechanistic characterization of drug, treatment, or disease [1, 2]. It involves eliciting information at multiple layers of granularity and generalization. It may be identifying gene(s) or proteins, gene–gene interactions, regulatory networks, and biological processes involved in a disease and other biological phenomena.

The different levels of granularity are achieved through both supervised and unsupervised analysis frameworks. Sample attributes [3] may be used to identify the genes contributing most and thereby establishing gene–disease associations. The unsupervised framework [4] is used for class discovery involving a multitude of clustering methodologies such as hierarchical/partitional clustering [5–7], biclustering [8], and consensus clustering. Alternatively, it may even be a combination of both supervised and unsupervised methodologies [9].

However, irrespective of the granularity of the hypothesis and the knowledge discovery framework, the necessary requirement is to identify feature sets consisting of genes, proteins, single-nucleotide polymorphisms (SNPs), linkage disequilibrium (LD) blocks, pathways, and interactions involved in the process under study from a huge number of possibilities present in the data. Furthermore, it may be required to analyze the biological implications of the identified genes or interactions based on the multitude of the knowledge available in the literature which too needs selection of a few from a huge number of interactions and pathways, described in the literature.

Biological Knowledge Discovery Handbook: Preprocessing, Mining, and Postprocessing of Biological Data, First Edition. Edited by Mourad Elloumi and Albert Y. Zomaya.
© 2014 John Wiley & Sons, Inc. Published 2014 by John Wiley & Sons, Inc.

Biological knowledge discovery is greatly facilitated by high-throughput technologies. The microarray [10] and sequencing [11] technologies facilitated, for example, high-throughput genome-scale profiling of gene expression, protein–DNA binding, epigenetic markers, SNPs, and structural variants in multiple samples to identify the markers and regulation mechanisms associated with the disease of interest. The number of profiled markers may range from tens of thousands to a few million. For example, a human sample profiling may involve the study of ~20,000 genes using ~60,000 probes [12], ~1 million SNPs [13], identifying 1000-40,000 binding sites of transcription factors from 3 billion base-pair genomes [14] and hundreds of millions of gene–gene interactions [15–17] and many-fold more SNP–SNP interactions [18]. Furthermore, knowledge of thousands of interactions between genes and loci and hundreds of pathways and processes is also available in the literature and databases [19–21]. As an interaction or pathway may play a role in multiple diseases, it may be necessary to identify which of the known interactions and pathways may be associated with the disease or process of interest.

A major concern in such a discovery process is the huge number of irrelevant features, potentially leading to a very large number of false positives even at the extremely low false positive rate. The presence of relatively more false positives in a feature set can hinder the true biological meaning. For example, a SNP discovery from a 1-million chip with a false positive rate of 0.1% can give rise to 1000 false positives. If the number of identified SNPs is not many-fold more than 1000, the identified SNP set may not represent real biology or association and the downstream knowledge discovery process may be hindered.

In practice, the false-positive rates are controlled using a suitable hypothesis-testing procedure to provide a statistical significance assessment to each feature under consideration (the multiple hypothesis-testing situation) and researchers may choose those with statistically acceptable false-positive rate. Hence, in this chapter, we introduce the hypothesis-testing framework and provide an overview of false-positive rate controlling procedures in multiple hypotheses-testing, estimation of the parameters, and other relevant issues.

15.2 STATISTICAL SIGNIFICANCE ASSESSMENT

Statistical hypothesis testing is a confirmatory data analysis technique whose roots are in the frequentist approach to statistical inference. Statistical inference was developed to assess whether an observed value of a quantity of interest is different from that expected due to chance, which could arise due to sampling variability. The hypothesis testing contrasts between expected value of a quantity of interest (called *null hypothesis H_0*) and its alternative (called *alternative hypothesis H_1*) using its estimate from a given data. For example, the expected expression of a gene is 0 and the observed expression (X) is 5. The question is whether the difference between the observed expression and the expected expressions can be due to chance given that the variation of the estimator of the observed expression is 2 (standard deviation σ). We write:

$H_0 : \mu = 0$ (null hypothesis)

$H_1 : \mu \neq 0$ (alternative hypothesis)

To test whether the data support H_0 or H_1, a statistic T is defined whose assumed distribution under the null hypothesis forms the basis for the testing. From the above example,

TABLE 15.1 Four Possible Hypothesis-Testing Outcomes

Statistical Inference	Fail to Reject Null Hypothesis	Reject Null Hypothesis	Total
True null hypotheses	U (true negative)	V (false positive)	m_0
False null hypotheses	F (false negative)	S (true positive)	m_1
Total	W	R	m

a possible definition of the statistic could be

$$T = \frac{X}{\sigma}$$

Assuming a normal distribution, $T \sim N(0, 1)$ under the null hypothesis. The observed statistic $T = 2.5$ and the p-value, the probability of the observed or more extreme T under the null hypothesis, is computed as

$$p = \Pr(|T| > 2.5) = \int_{-\infty}^{-2.5} N(0, 1)\,dx + \int_{2.5}^{\infty} N(0, 1)\,dx = 2 \int_{2.5}^{\infty} N(0, 1)\,dx$$

If the p-value is less than a predefined α, then H_0 is rejected and H_1 is confirmed.

Each test results in one of four possible outcomes, depending on whether the null hypothesis is true and the statistical testing rejects the null hypothesis (Table 15.1): The true null hypothesis is rejected (i.e., a false-positive or type I error); the true null hypothesis is not rejected (i.e., a true negative); the false null hypothesis is rejected (i.e., a true positive); or the false null hypothesis is incorrectly rejected (i.e., a false-negative or type II error).

Therefore there is a positive probability that the testing will produce an incorrect inference (V and F). When only one hypothesis is to be tested, the probability of each type of erroneous inference can be limited to a tolerable level by carefully planning the experiment and the statistical analysis. The probability of a false positive can be limited by preselecting the p-value threshold used to determine whether to reject the null hypothesis. For a given α, the probability of a false negative can be limited by performing an experiment with adequate replications. Statistical power calculations can determine how many replications are required to achieve a desired level of control of the probability of a false-negative result [22]. When multiple tests are performed, it is even more critical to carefully plan the experiment and statistical analysis to reduce the occurrence of erroneous inferences.

Every multiple testing procedure uses one or more error rates to measure the occurrence of incorrect inferences. Most error rates focus on the occurrence of false positives. Some error rates that have been used in the multiple testing are described next. For a detailed review of the procedures and their statistical properties, the reader may refer to [23].

15.2.1 Familywise Error Rates

Classical multiple testing procedures use the familywise error rate (FWER) control. The FWER is the probability of at least one type I error,

$$\text{FWER} = \Pr(V > 0) = 1 - \Pr(V = 0)$$

TABLE 15.2   FWER Procedures

FWER-Controlling Procedure	Single-Step Procedure	Step-Down Procedure
Bonferroni	$\tilde{p}_i = \min(mp_i, 1)$	
Sidak	$\tilde{p}_i = 1 - (1 - p_i)^m$	$\tilde{p}_{r_i} = \max_{k=1,\dots,i} \left\{ 1 - (1 - p_{r_k})^{(m-k+1)} \right\}$
Westfall and Young (minP)	$\tilde{p}_i = \Pr\left(\min_{1 \le l \le m} p_l \le p_i \vert H_{\mathcal{M}} \right)$	$\tilde{p}_{r_i} = \max_{k=1,\dots,i} \left\{ \Pr\left(\min_{1 \le l \le m} p_{r_l} \le p_{r_k} \vert H_{\mathcal{M}} \right) \right\}$
Westfall and Young (maxT)	$\tilde{p}_i = \Pr\left(\max_{1 \le l \le m} \vert T_l \vert \ge t_i \vert H_{\mathcal{M}} \right)$	$\tilde{p}_{s_i} = \max_{k=1,\dots,i} \left\{ \Pr\left(\min_{1 \le l \le m} \vert T_{s_l} \vert \ge t_{s_k} \vert H_{\mathcal{M}} \right) \right\}$
Holm	–	$\tilde{p}_{r_i} = \max_{k=1,\dots,i} \left\{ \min\left((m-k+1)p_{r_k}, 1 \right) \right\}$

The familywise error rates may be controlled using the simple but too conservative single-step procedures of Bonferroni, Sidak [24], and Westfall and Young [25]. Alternatively, slightly complex but less conservative compared with single-step procedures, the step-down procedures of Holm [26], Sidak, or Westfall and Young may be used. They are listed in Table 15.2.

The FWER was quickly recognized as being too conservative for the analysis of genome scale data, because in many applications, the only way to limit the probability that any of thousands of statistical tests yield a false-positive inference is to not allow any result to be deemed significant. A similar but less stringent error rate is the generalized familywise error rate (gFWER). The gFWER is the probability that more than k of the significant findings are actually false positives.

$$gFWER(k) = \Pr(V > k)$$

When $k = 0$, the gFWER reduces to the usual familywise error rate, FWER (see Table 15.3). Recently, some procedures have been proposed to use the gFWER to measure the occurrence of false positives [27].

15.2.2   False Discovery Rate

The false discovery rate [28] (FDR) control is now recognized as a very useful measure of the relative occurrence of false positives in omics studies [29]. The FDR is the expected

TABLE 15.3   gFWER Procedures [27]

gFWER-Controlling Procedure	Adjusted p-Values
Common quantile	$\tilde{p}_{r_i} = \Pr_{f_0}\left(p_{r_{k+1}} \le p_{r_i} \right)$
Common cut-off	$\tilde{p}_{r_i} = \Pr_{f_0}\left(Z_{r_{k+1}} > T_i \right)$

TABLE 15.4   FDR-Controlling Procedures: BH FDR, BY FDR

FDR-Controlling Procedure	Step-Up Procedure
Benjamini–Hocheberg (BH)	$\tilde{p}_{r_i} = \max\limits_{k=1,\ldots,m} \left\{ \min\left(\dfrac{m}{k} p_{r_k}, 1 \right) \right\}$
Benjamini–Yekuteili (BY) (dependence is considered)	$\tilde{p}_{r_i} = \max\limits_{k=1,\ldots,m} \left\{ \min\left(\dfrac{m \sum_{l=1}^{m} 1/l}{k} p_{r_k}, 1 \right) \right\}$

value of the proportion of type I errors among the rejected hypotheses,

$$\text{FDR} = E\left[\frac{V}{R} 1_{\{R>0\}} \right]$$

If all null hypotheses are true, all R rejected hypotheses are false positives, and hence $V/R = 1$ and FDR = FWER = $\Pr(V > 0)$. FDR-controlling procedures therefore also control the FWER in the weak sense. In general, because $V/R \leq 1$, the FDR is less than or equal to the FWER for any given multiple testing procedure.

The assumption FDR = 0 for $R = 0$ leads to the Benjamini–Hochebcrg (BH) procedure and the Benjamini–Yekuteili (BY) procedure under dependence [30]: see Table 15.4.

15.2.3 Positive FDR

If we are only interested in estimating an error rate when positive findings have occurred, then the positive FDR (pFDR) [31] is appropriate. It is defined as the conditional expectation of the proportion of type I errors among the rejected hypotheses given that at least one hypothesis is rejected,

$$\text{pFDR} = E\left[\frac{V}{R} | R > 0 \right]$$

This dcfinition is intuitively pleasing and has a nice Bayesian interpretation. Suppose that identical hypothesis tests are performcd with the independent statistics T and rejection region Γ. Also suppose that a null hypothesis is true with a priori probability π_0. Then

$$\text{pFDR}(\Gamma) = \frac{\pi_0 \Pr(T \in \Gamma | H = 0)}{\Pr(T \in \Gamma)} = \Pr(H = 0 | T \in \Gamma)$$

where $\Pr(T \in \Gamma) = \pi_0 \Pr(T \in \Gamma | H = 0) + (1 - \pi_0) \Pr(T \in \Gamma | H = 1)$. Here H is the random variable such that $H = 0$ if the null hypothesis and $H = 1$ if the alternative hypothesis and $\pi_0 = \Pr(H = 0)$.

15.2.4 Conditional FDR

The conditional false discovery rate (cFDR) [32] is the FDR conditional on the observed number of rejections $R = r$ and is defined as

$$\text{cFDR} = E\left(\frac{V}{R} | R = r \right) = \frac{E(V | R = r)}{r}$$

provided that $r > 0$ and cFDR = 0 for $r = 0$.

The cFDR is a natural measure of proportion of false positives among the r most signif-icant tests. Further, under Storey's mixture model [31], Tsai et al. [32] have shown that

$$\text{cFDR}(\alpha) = \text{pFDR}(\alpha) = \frac{\pi_0 \alpha m}{r}$$

15.2.5 Local FDR

A major criticism of FDR is its cumulative measure and a measure for a set of r most significant tests. An rth significance test may have an acceptable FDR only due to it being part of the r most significant tests. To address this anomaly, in 2001, Efron et al. [33] introduced the local false discovery rate (lFDR), which is a variant of Benjamini–Hochberg's FDR. It gives each tested null hypothesis its own FDR. While the FDR is defined for a whole rejection region, the lFDR is defined for a particular value of the test statistic:

$$\text{lFDR}(t) = \Pr(H = 0 | T = t)$$

The local nature of the lFDR is an advantage for interpreting results from individual test statistic. Moreover, lFDR is the average of global FDR given $T \in \Gamma$, that is,

$$\text{FDR}(\Gamma) = \text{E}(\text{lFDR}(T) | T \in \Gamma)$$

From the two-component mixture model of the test statistics $f(p) = \pi_0 f_0(p) + (1 - \pi_0) f_1(p)$, $\text{lFDR}(t) = \pi_0 f_0(t)/f(t)$. Several procedures have been proposed in the literature to estimate lFDR. Efron et al. [33] proposed a distribution-free procedure, that is, f_0 does not have to be uniform under the null hypothesis; instead it is estimated from the data. But the assumptions of the procedure are (1) the transformation of p-values into z-values leading to standard normal distribution and (2) $\pi_0 > 0.9$. Efron's procedure [34] estimates densities of z-values by modeling $\log(f(z))$ by a seven-degree natural spline function and computes π_0 by the ratio of the means $\overline{f(z)}/\overline{f_0(z)}$ and $\text{lFDR}(z) = \pi_0 f(z)/f_0(z)$.

On the other hand, Aubert et al. [35], Scheid and Spang [36], and Broberg [37] assume uniform distribution of f_0 and separate estimation of π_0 and $f(p)$. Aubert et al. rank p-values from most significant to least significant ($p_{r_1} \le p_{r_2} \le \cdots \le p_{r_i} \le p_{r_{i+1}} \le \cdots \le p_{r_m}$) and compute

$$\text{lFDR}(p_{r_i}) = \tfrac{1}{2} m \pi_0 (p_{r_{i+1}} - p_{r_i})$$

the π_0 estimated using procedures available in the literature. Scheid and Spang [36] proposed a smoothing spline estimator of $f(p)$ over equidistant 100 bins of p-values, and π_0 is estimated by iteratively eliminating genes that minimize the Kolmogoroff-Smirnoff score [36] leading to a maximal set that follows a uniform distribution and computes

$$\text{lFDR}(p) = \frac{\pi_0}{f(p)}$$

Note that $f_0 = 1$ for the uniformity assumption under the null hypothesis. Broberg proposed to estimate f by Poisson regression and the pooling adjacent violators algorithm [37] that guarantees monotonocity. Assume $\pi_0 = \min[f(p)]$ and

$$\text{lFDR}(p) = \frac{\pi_0}{f(p)}$$

for $0 \le p \le 1$.

Dalmasso et al. [38] argued that the above procedures only estimate the upper bound of lFDR. Aubert et al. yield an estimator with higher variance, Scheid and Spang require extensive computational resources, and Broberg's procedure may substantially underestimate lFDR. Based on these observations, Dalmasso et al. proposed a polynomial regression under monotony and convexity constraints of the empirical $F(p)$, which can achieve an estimated upper bound of lFDR with small variability.

Liao et al. [39] proposed a mixture model-based estimator for lFDR based on the observation that the stochastic order can be imposed on f_1 and f_0, $F_1(p) \geq F_0(p)$. They used a proportional hazards model, which can impose the stochastic order, leading to $f_1 = \text{beta}(1, \theta(p))$. The function $\theta(p)$ is p dependent hazards, chosen to be a piecewise constant function with a smoothing model imposed. The parameters and the model are estimated using Bayesian inference.

15.2.6 2D-lFDR

Ploner et al. [40] generalized the local FDR as a function of multiple statistics, combining a common test statistic with its standard error information, and proposed 2D-lFDR. If two different statistics Z_1 and Z_2 capture different aspects of the information contained in the data, the 2D-lFDR can be defined as

$$2\text{D-lFDR}(z_1, z_2) = \pi_0 \frac{f_0(z_1, z_2)}{f(z_1, z_2)}$$

where $f(z)$ is the density function of the statistics z and $f_0(z) = f(z | z \in H_0)$. 2D-lFDR is very useful to deal with small standard error problems. The procedure is described in [40].

The FDR, cFDR, pFDR, lFDR and 2D-lFDR are reasonable error rates because they can naturally be translated into the costs of attempting to validate false-positive results. In practice the first three concepts lead to similar values, and most statistical software will usually report only one of the three.

15.3 *p*-VALUE DISTRIBUTION AND π_0 ESTIMATION

The appropriate FDR estimation depends on the precise p-values from each test and the validity of the underlying assumptions of the distribution. Therefore, p-value distribution and π_0 estimation are crucial in statistical significance assessment.

15.3.1 *p*-Value Distribution

A density plot (or histogram) of p-values is a useful tool for determining when problems are present in the analysis. This simple graphic assessment can indicate when crucial assumptions such as the tests are independent and the distribution of the test statistic under the null hypothesis is accurate have been grossly violated [41].

Additionally, it can be helpful to add a horizontal reference line to the p-value density plot at the value of the estimated π_0 null proportion [31]. A line falling far below the height of the shortest bar suggests that the estimate of the null proportion may be downward biased. Conversely, a line high above the top of the shortest bar may suggest that the method is overly conservative.

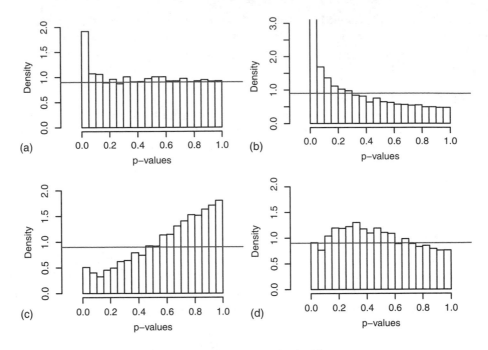

FIGURE 15.1 Four p-value density histograms.

Furthermore, adding the estimated density curves to the p-value histogram can aid in assessing the model fit [42]. Large discrepancies between the density of the fitted model and the histogram indicate a lack of fit. This diagnostic can identify when some methods produce unreliable results. This is a good graphic diagnostic for any of the smoothing based and model-based methods that operate on p-values.

If the test statistics from multiple testing can be well modeled using a certain distribution and p-values are well defined, the p-value distribution can be used to validate whether the statistical significance is appropriately estimated or not. In Figure 15.1, there are four different p-value density plot examples. The most desirable shape of the p-value density plot is the one in which the p-values are most dense near zero, become less dense as the p-values increase, and have a stable tail toward 1 (Figure 15.1a).

This shape does not indicate any violation of the assumptions of methods operating on p-values and suggests that several features are differentially expressed, though they may not be statistically significant after adjusting for multiple testing. A very sharp p-value density plot without constant tail close to 1 (Figure 15.1b) and $f(1) < 0.5$ may indicate overassessment of significance, that is, undermeasure p-values. It suggests that fewer features are significant than observed. A right triangle p-value density plot with $f(0) < f(1)$ and $f(1) > 1$ (Figure 15.1c) may also indicate overmeasure p-values, suggesting that more features are differentially expressed than observed. A p-value density plot with one or more humps in the middle (Figure 15.1d) can indicate that an inappropriate statistical test was used to compute the p-values, some heterogeneity data were included in the analysis, or a strong and extensive correlation structure is present in the data set.

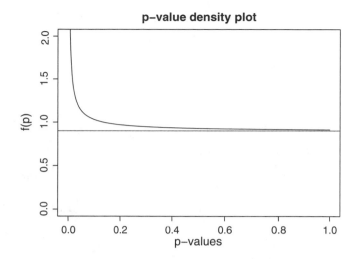

FIGURE 15.2   The π_0 estimation as density of $f(p)$ at $p = 1$.

15.3.2   Mixture Model as Basis for π_0 Estimation

An important quantity to be estimated in the assessment significance is π_0, the fraction of true null hypotheses. The *p*-values from multiple hypothesis testing, for m hypotheses, can be described by a mixture model $f(p)$ with two components: one component $f_0(p)$ originates from true null hypotheses and follows uniform distribution $U(0, 1)$ [43], and the other component $f_1(p)$ results from true alternative hypotheses and follows a distribution confined to the *p*-values close to 0 [44]. The mixing parameter π_0 is the proportion of true null hypotheses in the data. More precisely,

$$f(p) = \pi_0 f_0(p) + (1 - \pi_0) f_1(p)$$
$$= \pi_0 + (1 - \pi_0) f_1(p) \quad \text{as} \quad f_0(p) = 1 \quad \text{since} \quad f_0(p) \sim U(0, 1)$$

where $f_0(p) = 1$ denotes the probability density function of a uniform distribution over [0, 1] and $f_1(p) \approx 0$ for p close to 1. Therefore, $f(p)$ will be close to a constant (i.e., π_0) for p close to 1.

The basis of all π_0 estimation procedures is the mixture model and the assumption that $f_1(p) \approx 0$ for sufficiently large values of p. The extreme case is when $p = 1$, $f(p) \approx \pi_0$, which means the density of *p*-values at $p = 1$ is π_0; see Figure 15.2.

15.3.3 π_0 Estimation

To better estimate π_0, the following estimator was proposed by Storey [31]:

$$\hat{\pi}_0 = \frac{\{\#p > \beta\}}{[(1 - \beta)m]}$$

The rationale for the estimator is, for $f_1(p) \approx 0$ for $p > \beta$, the expected number of *p*-values above β will be $m(1 - \beta)$. The choice of β is usually taken as 0.25, 0.5 or 0.75.

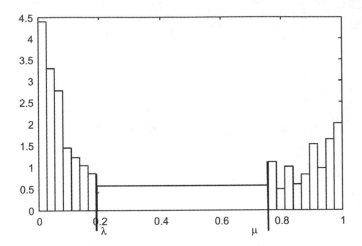

FIGURE 15.3 Two-parameter estimation of π_0 [45].

ALGORITHM 15.1 Two-Parameter Estimation of π_0 [45]

```
1: For each partition I ∈ I, define p̂(I) = Argmin_p MSE̅(I; p).
2: Find the best partition Î = Argmin_{I∈I} R̂_{p̂(I)}(I).
3: From Î, get (λ̂, μ̂).
4: Compute the estimator π̂_0 = Card{i : P_i ∈ [λ̂, μ̂]}/m(μ̂ − λ̂).
```

Here I is defined as $[\lambda, \mu]$ and the objective function $\text{MSE}(I, x)$ is the sum of squares of bias and variance of the estimator.

As certain p-value distributions might exhibit a valley for medium to large values of $p < 1$, Celisse and Robin [45] proposed a two-parameter extension of Storey's estimator (Figure 15.3).

The fraction $\hat{\pi}_0$ is estimated by the procedure outlined in Algorithm 15.1.

To circumvent the difficulty of the choice of parameters in the above estimators, Dalmasso et al. [46] proposed a simple parameter-free estimator. Their procedure is based on the observation that the area under $(1 - \pi_0)f_1(p)$ is sufficiently smaller than π_0. Under such an assumption π_0 is estimated as an integral of $f(p)$:

$$\hat{\pi}_0 = \frac{2}{m} \sum_{i=1}^{m} p_i$$

To reduce the bias of the above π_0 estimator, they proposed a transformation of p-values by a function $g(p)$. It was shown that if $g(p)$ satisfies the properties (i) $\lim_{p \to 1} g(p) = +\infty$, (ii) $\lim_{p \to 0} g(p) < +\infty$, (iii) $g(\cdot)$ is convex, and (iv) $g(E_0(P)) \geq E_0(P)$, then the bias will be less than the original estimator. Under such a transformation, π_0 is estimated using $g(p) = -\log(1 - p)$ as

$$\hat{\pi}_{0_{(n)}} = \frac{(1/m) \sum_{i=1}^{m} [-\log(1 - p_i)]^n}{n!}$$

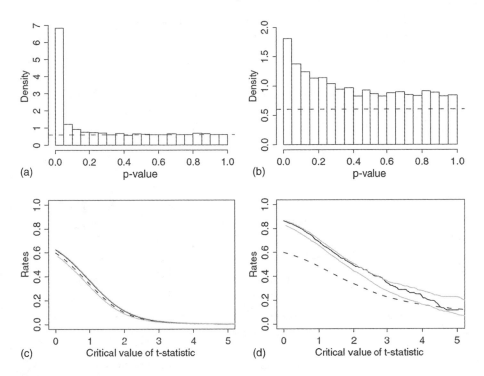

FIGURE 15.4 Bias in π_0 estimation and its influence on FDR calculation. (a) Histogram of 10000 *p*-values of the *t*-statistics for two-group comparisons of data simulated for $\pi_0 = 0.6$ and log-fold change $D = 1.33$. The horizontal line is at $\pi_0 = 0.6$. (b) The same as (a), except for a smaller log-fold change of $D = 0.45$. (c) Estimated FDR (solid) and true FDR (dashed) for the data simulated with a large log-fold change of $D = 1.33$. The gray lines indicate a pointwise 90% confidence band for the estimated FDR, based on 100 additional simulated data sets. The curves are very close to each other. (d) The same as (c), except for the smaller log-fold change of $D = 0.45$ [22].

where *n* is a suitably chosen positive integer. Here *n* balances the bias and the variance of the estimator: Larger *n* results in smaller bias but larger variance.

All of the above procedures may still lead to bias in the estimator of π_0 as demonstrated by Pawitan et al. [22]; see Figure 15.4. The bias was estimated to be increasing with $(1 - \pi_0)$ and $f_1(1)$:

$$\text{Bias} = (1 - \pi_0)f_1(1)$$

They proposed a direct Gaussian mixture modeling of the test statistics and π_0 as the mixing proportion. For such a modeling, the distribution of the statistic under the null and alternative hypotheses needs to be approximately Gaussian. Their simulations demonstrated a remarkable improvement in the π_0 estimation, especially for smaller π_0, where the bias could be large; see Figure 15.5.

On the other hand, Pounds and Morris [44] proposed the beta uniform-mixture (BUM) model for the distribution of observed *p*-values where the beta distribution models $f_1(p)$ and uniform distribution models $f_0(p)$.

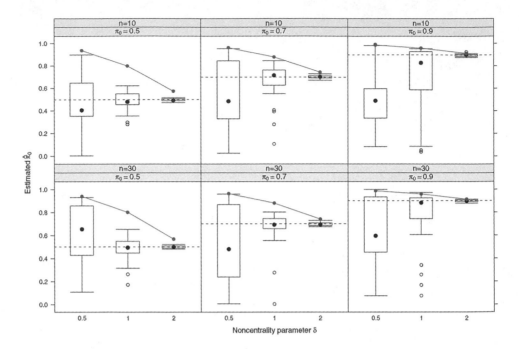

FIGURE 15.5 Reduced bias using mixture modeling of statistics compared to estimator $f(1)$. Simulation results of the estimation of π_0 in the mixture model. Each boxplot summarizes 25 independent replications. The target parameter π_0 is drawn as a dashed line, and the biased values $f(1)$ for π_0 are shown as connected dots at the top of each panel [22].

Broberg [37] carried out an extensive study of comparing different π_0 estimation procedures. Though the study did not include the methods of Dalmasso et al. [46] and Pawitan et al. [22], it sheds good light on the performance of different methods. All methods demonstrate larger bias for smaller values of π_0, as demonstrated by Pawitan et al., which implies even larger relative error for smaller values of π_0. The BUM estimator is least biased for $\pi_0 < 0.8$ and its bias increases faster for $\pi_0 > 0.8$. The bias is significantly higher for dependent data compared to the independent data. The readers are referred to [37] for detailed results and description of other methods of π_0 estimation. In the light of many more methods proposed and many more technologies in place, a comprehensive comparative study is due in the literature.

15.4 OBTAINING CONTROL AND BACKGROUND ESTIMATION

To conduct proper statistical testing, a good estimate of the distribution of the test statistic under the null hypothesis (also called *background distribution*) is as important as the choice of the testing model. To obtain appropriate background distribution, a control group/population needs to be well defined. It can be obtained directly from an explicitly well-designed control group. For example, in clinical studies a treatment group is directly compared with the placebo or untreated group [47]. In human genetics studies a disease population is compared with that of the normal population [48]. In binding site analysis, a

ChIP-chip library is directly compared with a mock ChIP-chip library. On the other hand, to conduct GO analysis for functional enrichment discovery of a gene set, the remaining genes are taken as the control group [49, 50]. However, direct control data may not always be available or insufficient. For example, analysis of ChIP-seq data without mock ChIP-seq data or cohorts of the disease group with little useful clinical labels needs to be analyzed by properly building up the control population from the data. A correlation network analysis involves assessment of the significance of its quantifiable properties, which have to be done through generation of appropriate null or randomized graphs as control group.

The second problem is obtaining the background distribution of the test statistic under the null hypothesis. It may be directly obtained by appropriate parametric assumptions of the data as in the t-test [51] or by permuting the data for more complex statistics. Both approaches have their own advantages and disadvantages.

15.4.1 Testing with Explicit Control Data

In some experimental settings, it is common to have internal controls such as housekeeping genes for gene expression studies or nonbinding regions for DNA–protein interaction studies of transcription factors. While the chosen controls may provide information of the quality of the experiment, they may not be directly useful to estimate the significance of the differential signal, as shown in Johnson et al. [14]. They have designed a chip to identify novel REST binding sites, with probes (RE1 probes) selected to be close to the candidates sites containing REST motif RE1. Multiple control probes were also provided and a large fraction of binding sites were expected to be positive, that is, $\pi_0 < 0.5$. However, many control probes had poorer signal than that of the RE1 probes with no the RE1 binding and some control probes appeared to be closer to the RE1 binding sites. This resulted in poor background distribution if the signals from the control probes are directly used. To circumvent this problem, Johnson et al. performed Gaussian mixture modeling (GMM) [52] with a Bayesian information criterion (BIC) [53] for model selection on RE1 probes as well as on control probes separately. In each model, the Gaussian with lowest mean is treated as the one representing the null distribution, that is, the null Gaussian. The null Gaussians in both models were used to equalize the signal distributions of the RE1 probes and control probes. The ratio of the mixing proportions of the null Gaussians of the RE1 probes and control probes was used as the estimate of π_0. FDR was computed using the equalized distributions and this π_0 estimation.

Similarly, Gibbons et al. [54] use the slope of the left-side ChIP-chip signal distribution to estimate the null distribution under the assumption of normality and derive the statistical significance of the ChIP enrichment.

15.4.1.1 ConReg-R Similar to the above, in many applied testing problems, the p-values could be undermeasured or overmeasured for many known or unknown reasons. The violation of p-value distribution assumptions may lead to inaccurate FDR estimation as almost all significance assessment procedures are based on the assumption $f_0 = 1$ for $0 \leq p \leq 1$. Dependence among the test statistics is one of the major factors [56, 57].

Moreover, many applied testing methods modified the standard testing methods (e.g., modifying the t-statistic to the moderated t-statistic [58] to increase their power. As the modified test statistics only approximately follow some known distribution, the approximate p-value estimation may influence the significance assessment. Resampling strategies may better estimate the underlying distributions of the test statistics. However, due to small sample size and data correlation, the limited number of permutations and resampling bias [59] may limit their use. To address the above problems, Li et al. [55] proposed an extrapolative recalibration procedure called *Constrained Regression Recalibration* (ConReg-R), which models the empirical distribution of p-values in multiple hypothesis tests and recalibrates the imprecise p-value calculation to better approximated p-values to improve the significance estimation. See Figure 15.6.

ConReg-R focuses on p-values as the p-values from true null hypotheses are expected to follow the uniform distribution and the interference from the distribution of p-values from alternative hypotheses is expected to be minimal toward $p = 1$.

ConReg-R first maps the observed p-values to predefined uniformly distributed p-values preserving their rank order and estimates the recalibration mapping function by performing constrained polynomial regression to the k highest p-values. The constrained polynomial regression is implemented by quadratic programming solvers. Finally, the p-values are recalibrated using the normalized recalibration function. FDR is estimated using the recalibrated p-values and π_0 can be determined during ConReg-R procedure.

15.4.2 Testing Using Permutation

A permutation procedure may be adopted if the accurate analytical form of the null distribution of the test statistic is not readily known. However, to get an accurate null distribution, the permutation procedure has to be carefully designed and the distribution obtained needs to be interpreted appropriately. The issues are explained with a variety of examples.

15.4.2.1 Distribution Standardization
Gene set enrichment analysis for functional discovery is carried out using predefined sets of functional categories such as Gene Ontology categories. GSEA [60] uses random resampling of array labels and a form of restandardization of the observed statistics by carrying out zero-mean, one-variance standardization. On the other hand, GSA [59] uses permutation of sample labels to generate the null distribution. The issue with this approach is that the location and scale parameters of the computed null distribution may be completely different from those of the actual null, as shown in Figure 15.7. Due to this discrepancy, one may observe unexpectedly large number of enriched categories.

To address the discrepancy, GSA restandardizes the computed null distribution by equating its median and variance to those of the observed distribution of the statistic. The re standardized score S^{**} is defined as

$$S^{**} = \mu + \frac{\sigma}{\sigma^*}(S^* - \mu^*)$$

where S^{**} is the re standardized permutation value and (μ, σ) and (μ^*, σ^*) are the mean and standard deviation of the observed statistic S and permuted statistic S^*, respectively.

15.4.2.2 Bias in Binding Site Functional Analysis
Another example of incorrect null distribution is the functional analysis of DNA binding proteins. It is carried out by identifying their binding sites, mapping the binding sites to nearby genes, and analyzing the functional enrichment of the mapped genes using typical gene set enrichment analysis methods. It has been recently pointed out (GREAT [61] and reFABS [62]) that such a procedure is flawed. It is true especially for large-range assignment of binding sites to

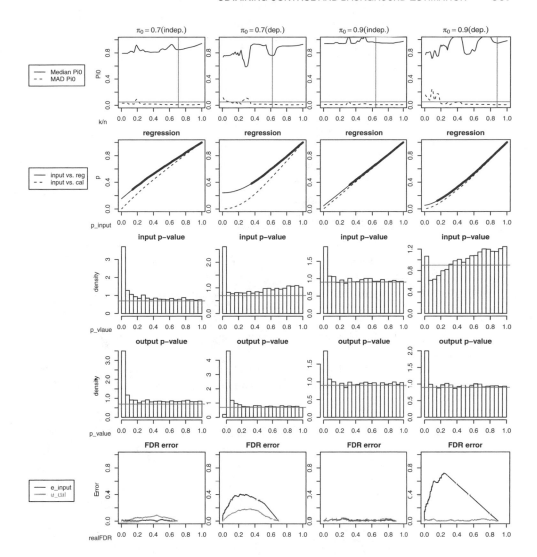

FIGURE 15.6 ConReg-R: Plots demonstrating the procedure and improvement obtained using ConReg-R procedures. The plots in the first row show $\hat{\pi}_0$ and $e_{\hat{\pi}_0}$ at different k/n, where $e_{\hat{\pi}_0}$ is the error of $\hat{\pi}_0$, n is the total number of p-values, and k is the number of p-values for recalibration. The black solid curve indicates $\hat{\pi}_0$ and the black dashed curve indicates $e_{\hat{\pi}_0}$, the grey horizontal line indicates the cutoff of $e_{\hat{\pi}_0}$ (here we used 0.05), the grey vertical line indicates the choice of k/n at which locally minimized $\hat{\pi}_0$ under $e_{\hat{\pi}_0} < 0.05$ is obtained. The plots in the second row show the regression procedure. The black thick curve indicates the (p_i, p_i'), $i = 1, \ldots, k$, the solid curve is the regression line $h_k(\cdot)$, and the dashed curve is the regression line $f(\cdot)$ after transformation. The plots in the third and fourth rows show the p-value histograms before and after applying ConReg-R and the gray horizontal line indicates the π_0. The plots in the last row show the FDR estimation errors between real FDR and the FDR estimated by p-values before (black) and after (grey) applying ConReg-R [55].

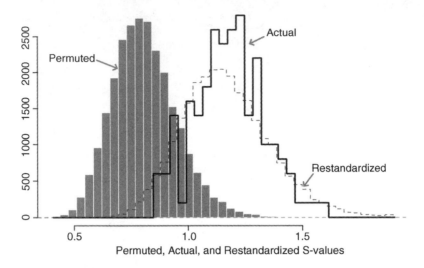

FIGURE 15.7 Discrepancy between actual and computed (perms) null distributions [59].

genes due to varying lengths of genes and intergenic regions, as demonstrated by Jair et al. [62]; see Figure 15.8.

GREAT used a genomic footprint-based testing model, whereas reFABS used randomization-based estimation of the null distribution. Using such a procedure, both GREAT and reFABS have shown that the bias in the functional analysis of transcription factors could be reduced; see Figure 15.9. The major difference between GREAT and re-FABS is that in GREAT each binding site assigned to a gene carries a weight of 1 whereas in reFABS all binding sites assigned to a gene carry a weight of 1 together; that is, all binding sites assigned to a gene are merged and counted as one binding site.

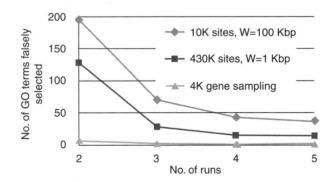

FIGURE 15.8 Bias in GO enrichment analysis of transcription factors. Cumulative distribution of the number of GO terms repeatedly selected for each random selection of genes over all five runs. The direct random sampling of genes results in very few GO categories enriched, indicating absence of bias. Analysis of the genes obtained by mapping 10K random sites using window of 100 kbp resulted in 40 GO categories repeatedly selected in all five runs and 200 were commonly selected in at least two runs, which demonstrates large bias in the functional analysis. However, it reduced substantially for the mapping using a reduced window size of 1 kbp [62].

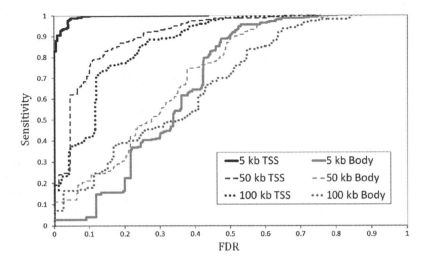

FIGURE 15.9 Bias for varying window sizes on estrogen receptor (ER) binding site data [63]. The plot shows sensitivity–FDR curves. In the absence of bias, the curve should trace the points (0,0)–(0,1)–(1,1). Solid curves are for TSS (transcription start site) reference and broken curves are for gene body reference for the assignment of binding sites to genes. Gene body reference shows larger bias irrespective of range of assignment and higher the range of assignment indicates higher bias [62].

15.4.2.3 *Bias in RNA-seq Functional Analysis*   Similar to the binding site analysis, the functional analysis of the RNA-seq enriched genes also may be biased to longer genes; see Young et al. [64]. They developed a procedure called GOseq to solve the problem by generating a probability weighting function between gene length and bias and used a generalized hypergeometric distribution to find the enrichment. The GOseq method is a three-step methodology to correct for bias in testing. First, the genes that are significantly differentially expressed (DE) genes between conditions are identified. The GOseq method works with any procedure for identifying DE genes. Second, the likelihood of DE as a function of transcript length is quantified. This is obtained by fitting a monotonic function to DE versus transcript length data. Finally, the DE-versus-length function is incorporated into the statistical test of each category's significance. This final step takes into account the lengths of the genes that make up each category. The GOseq method is able to account for such biases when performing GO analysis. The new method makes a substantial difference to the categories identified as the most significant. The paper shows that the GOseq method is better able to recover well-established microarray results than existing methods of GO analysis of RNA-seq data.

15.4.2.4 *Permutation in Differential Expression Studies*   In the generation of the null distribution of the t-statistic or its modifications for differential expression analyses, one may encounter problems especially if there is a reasonably large fraction of differentially expressed gene; that is, π_0 is significantly less than 1. In such a case the variance of the computed null distribution could be different from the actual [65]. It is contributed by the fact that the null estimated by permuting the expression of differentially expressed (DE) genes will have different variance compared with that of the nondifferentially expressed genes (nonDE) whose variance remains the same before and after permutation. As the

Sample number	1	2	3	4	5	6	7	8	
Sample class	1	1	1	1	2	2	2	2	
Sample batch	1	1	1	1	2	2	2	2	Batch Confounding
Ideal Sample Batch	1	1	2	2	1	1	2	2	

FIGURE 15.10 Batch-confounded experiment. The first row indicates the sample numbers. The second row indicates two classes, first four samples belong to class 1 and last four belong to class 2. The third row indicates the batch-confounded case, where two batch assignments are the same as class. The last row indicates the ideal batch assignment, which assigns two batches mixed with two classes.

fraction of DE genes increases, it might lead to discrepancies between actual and estimated null distributions. As shown by Xie et al. [65], large DE genes may contribute to inflation of the variance of the t-statistic and small DE genes may lead to deflation. To circumvent this problem, Xie et al. have proposed to use only the nonDE genes in the first step to generate the null distribution.

The extreme case is batch-confounded or batch-biased data. The batch-confounded data is illustrated in Figure 15.10. Batch-confounded data may be practically unavoidable in many situations. For example, one wants to compare the data from one experiment or laboratory to data from another experiment or laboratory, which essentially means batch-confounded biological groups. Time course experiments spread over long time horizons may also inevitably result in batch confounding when samples from different time points are compared for change of expression. Similarly, batch confounding is unavoidable in huge experiments even though all groups are generated in the same laboratory. The problem of global batch effects may be solved using SVD (singular-value decomposition) / PCA (principal-component analysis) [66, 67], DWD (distance-weighted discrimination) [68], or empirical Bayes methods [69]. The methods treat the batch as a factor and work well provided the experimental batches are not confounded with the biological groups of interest; that is, each batch contains arrays of samples from different biological groups.

The use of non-permutation- or permutation-based approaches may lead to over- or underestimation of significance of a large number of genes, as shown in the QQ plots of expected and observed statistics in Figure 15.11.

In Figure 15.11a, the expected score (expected test statistics) and observed score (test statistics) are aligned with the diagonal. This indicates the statistical significance is appropriately measured. If the expected test statistics deviate much from test statistics (Figures 15.11b,c), the statistical significance will be over-/undermeasured. Figure 15.11d shows that the location and scale parameters of the estimated null are completely different from the actual.

Furthermore, the problem may be aggravated by particular biases arising from the design of experiment and data filtering leading to computation of the null distribution whose variance as well as mean are different from the actual null distribution.

The solution for such problems is using permutation in conjunction with null distribution renormalization. A procedure similar to GSA may be used. However, it is not desirable as π_0

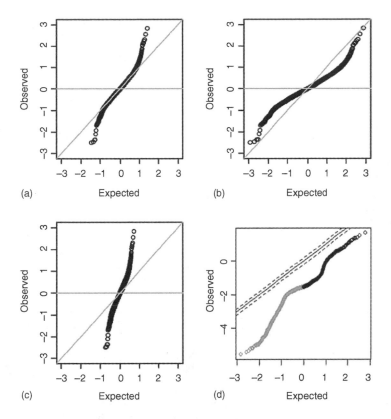

FIGURE 15.11   QQ plots for expected score (permutation statistics) versus observed score (test statistics) of over- or underestimation of significance of large fraction of genes: (a) QQ plot with statistical significance appropriately estimated; (b) The QQ plot with overestimation of significance; (c) The QQ plot with underestimation of significance; (d) QQ plot deviated from origin.

is much smaller than 1, which means the variance of the actual null may be overestimated from the observed distribution of the statistic. Furthermore, the GSA-like restandardization procedure may not be appropriate for one-sided test statistics as in ANOVA or if the differential expression is biased toward overexpression or repression. The iPLR (iterative piecewise linear regression) [71] procedure offers a solution for such problems.

iPLR reestimates the expected statistics under the assumption that the expression difference due to batch variation is smaller than that of the biological variation. FDR is estimated using the reestimated expected statistics; iPLR was demonstrated to be more accurate in assessing statistical significance; see Figure 15.12.

15.5   STATISTICAL SIGNIFICANCE IN INTEGRATIVE ANALYSIS

Integrative analysis of heterogeneous genome-scale data sets is a common practice to discover relevant biological knowledge. Gene expression data sets from multiple cohorts of patients may have to be analyzed together to improve power, and GO category enrichment results from different analyses (from binding site or expression or both) may have to be combined and reliable categories found for further analysis. Different strategies need to be

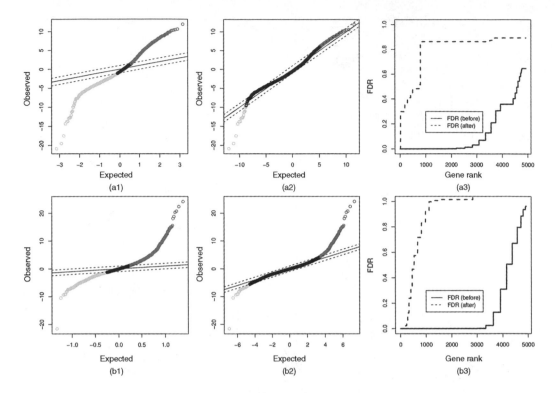

FIGURE 15.12   iPLR: SAM plot and FDR comparison (before and after iPLR reestimation) for Schizosaccharomyces. pombe data set [70]. (a1) The SAM plot before iPLR reestimation for wt1/wt1 versus wt2/wt2 dataset. (a2) The SAM plot after reestimation for wt1/wt1 versus wt2/wt2 data set. (a3) FDR comparison for wt1/wt1 versus wt2/wt2 dataset. Solid line indicates estimated FDR before iPLR reestimation and dashed line indicates estimated FDR after iPLR reestimation. (b1) The SAM plot before reestimation for wt/wt versus Δmip1/wt dataset. (b2) The SAM plot after reestimation for wt/wt versus Δmip1/wt dataset. (b3) FDR comparison for wt/wt versus Δmip1/wt dataset. Solid line indicate estimated FDR before iPLR re-estimation and the dashed line indicates estimated FDR after iPLR reestimation. The results are encouraging and iPLR is a practically useful technique [71].

employed for the best use of the data and elicit the best possible knowledge. Meta-analysis procedures are commonly used for integrative analysis. Nonparametric analysis is most useful for integrating data of different types, such as expression and binding site data.

15.5.1   *p*-Value-Controlling Meta-Analysis (Nonparametric Meta-Analysis)

Traditionally, *p*-values of a hypothesis from different sources is combined using nonparametric methods under the assumption of uniform distribution of *p*-values over the interval [0,1] under the null hypothesis. The meta-analysis could range from most conservative to most liberal. After having performed a meta-analysis for all hypotheses, type I error rate control can be carried using the methods described before.

Min Analysis   Here, an intermediate *p*-value of a hypothesis p' is defined as the minimum of *p*-values from all k available sources, that is, $p' = \min(p_1, p_2, \ldots, p_k)$.

Then the meta p-value, p_0, of the hypothesis is $1 - (1 - p')^k$. Min analysis provides the most liberal analysis.

Max Analysis An intermediate p-value of a hypothesis p' is defined as maximum p-values from all k available sources, that is, $p' = \max(p_1, p_2, \ldots, p_k)$. Then the meta p-value, p_0, of the hypothesis is p'^k. The Max analysis provides the most conservative analysis.

Inv Chi-Square Analysis An intermediate statistic X is defined using the p-values from all k available sources, that is, $p' = \Pi_{i=1}^{k} p_i$. Then the meta p-value, p_0, of the hypothesis is computed using the chi-square distribution of $-2 \log p'$ with $2k$ degrees of freedom.

Though weighted meta-analysis methods are available in the literature, they are rarely used in genomics studies as the weights have to be carefully chosen and their implications may not be clear to the researcher. The reader may refer to [72] for more details on meta-analysis methods.

15.5.2 FDR-Controlling Meta-Analysis

Instead of using all p-values in the *Inv chi-square method*, Zaykin et al. [73] proposed the truncated product method (TPM) in which only those p-values less than a threshold τ are considered for the meta-analysis to reduce false negatives. TPM computes the statistic $W = \Pi_{i=1}^{k} p_i^{I(p_i \leq \tau)}$ and the null distribution of W is computed. The method may be seen as a special case of the weighted Inv chi-square method. TPM requires at least one p-value to be better than the predefined type I error rate of α.

Pyne et al. [74] suggested the use of FDR as a determining criterion to choose τ for the study. That is, they modified W to $\Pi_{i=1}^{k} p_i^{I(p_i \leq \tau_{i,\alpha'})}$, where $\tau_{i,\alpha'}$ is the p-value threshold for the ith study at the FDR cutoff of α'. It helps in the choice of different τ for different studies depending on their quality and extensiveness.

15.6 CONCLUSIONS

Statistical significance assessment plays a major role in the selection of biological features essential for downstream analysis and interpretation of the high-throughput data. A hypothesis-testing framework is predominantly used and the statistical significance is assessed using a p-value, a measure of false-positive rate. Adjusted p-values need to be used in assessing multiple features simultaneously, a multiple hypothesis testing, to control false positives effectively. We have presented an overview of the error rates for multiple hypothesis testing and procedures to obtain adjusted p-values to control them. Of the broad range of error rates, FDR and lFDR are most commonly used lFDR is the average of global FDR. Since selection of the control group is as important as the selection of the test, we discussed the issues posed by the choice of control group. Though permutation or "good" biological controls appear to be natural choices, they may result in grossly overestimated or underestimated error rates. These typically result in extremely low or high FDR estimation and can be figured out by examining the density plots of the test statistics of the actual data and control data for discrepancy in their location and scale parameters. We have presented a few typical instances and discussed procedures to appropriately reestimate the significance.

Furthermore, all error control procedures are based on the assumption that the distribution of p-values under the null hypothesis is uniform on [0, 1]. It could be violated in many practical testing situations and the error rates estimated could be grossly wrong. To ensure this assumption is met, we can examine the density plot of p-values for its near uniformity for p-values close to 1 and the estimated π_0, which is not expected to be either too low (i.e., < 0.5) or more than 1. A few procedures to estimate the error rates in such cases are presented. Finally, we presented procedures to assess statistical significance in integrative analysis, which is inevitable in the biological knowledge discovery based on a multitude of data. On the whole, the chapter may serve as a good starting point for researchers in the biological knowledge discovery community to understand the error control, the caveats in using the standard procedures for feature selection and interpretation.

SYMBOLS

α	Significance level of a test
$E(\cdot)$	Expectation function
Γ	Region of rejection
$f(\cdot)$	Probability density function
$f_0(\cdot)$	Probability density function under null hypothesis
$f_1(\cdot)$	Probability density function under alternative hypothesis
H_0	Null hypothesis
H_1	Alternative hypothesis
$N(\mu, \sigma^2)$	Normal distribution with mean μ and variance σ^2
m	Total number of tests
p_i	ith p-value
$\tilde{p}_i$	ith adjusted p-value
p_{r_i}	ith rank ascending ordered p-value
π_0	Probability that null hypothesis is correct
$\hat{\pi}_0$	Estimate of π_0
$\mathbf{Pr}(\cdot)$	Probability function
T	Test statistic
$U(0, 1)$	Uniform distribution on [0,1]
$N(\mu, \sigma^2)$	Normal distribution with mean μ and variance σ^2

ACKNOWLEDGMENTS

The authors thank Edison T. Liu for his constant encouragement and support during this work. We appreciate Philippe Broet and Cyril Dalmasso for their valuable comments. This work was supported by the Genome Institute of Singapore, Biomedical Research Council, Agency for Science, Technology and Research (A*STAR), Singapore.

REFERENCES

1. J. Tan, X. Yang, L. Zhuang, X. Jiang, W. Chen, P. L. Lee, R. K. Murthy Karuturi, P. Boon Ooi Tan, E. T. Liu, and Q. Yu. Pharmacologic disruption of polycomb-repressive complex 2-mediated gene repression selectively induces apoptosis in cancer cells. *Genes Devel.*, 21(9):1050–1063, 2007.

2. P. Broët, C. Dalmasso, E. Huat Tan, M. Alifano, S. Zhang, J. Wu, M. H. Lee, J.-F. Régnard, D. Lim, H. N. Koong, T. Agasthian, L. D. Miller, E. Lim, S. Camilleri-Broët, and P. Tan. Genomic profiles specific to patient ethnicity in lung adenocarcinoma. *Clin. Cancer Res. Offic. Am. Assoc. Cancer Res.*, 17(11):3542–3550, 2011.

3. G. C. Cawley and N. L. C. Talbot. Gene selection in cancer classification using sparse logistic regression with Bayesian regularization. *Bioinformatics*, 22(19):2348 –2355, 2006.

4. M. B. Eisen, P. T. Spellman, P. O. Brown, and D. Botstein. Cluster analysis and display of genome-wide expression patterns. *Proc. Nat. Acad. Sci. USA,*, 95(25):14863–14868, 1998.

5. I. S. Dhillon, E. M. Marcotte, and U. Roshan. Diametrical clustering for identifying anti-correlated gene clusters. *Bioinformatics*, 19(13):1612–1619, 2003.

6. T. R. Golub, D. K. Slonim, P. Tamayo, C. Huard, M. Gaasenbeek, J. P. Mesirov, H. Coller, M. L. Loh, J. R. Downing, M. A. Caligiuri, C. D. Bloomfield, and E. S. Lander. Molecular classification of cancer: Class discovery and class prediction by gene expression monitoring. *Science*, 286(5439):531–537, 1999.

7. B. Mirkin. *Mathematical Classification and Clustering*. Springer, The Netherlands, 1996.

8. B. Kuan Hui Chia and R. Krishna Murthy Karuturi. Differential co-expression framework to quantify goodness of biclusters and compare biclustering algorithms. *Algorithms Mol. Biol.*, 5:23, 2010.

9. E.-J. Yeoh, M. E. Ross, S. A. Shurtleff, W. K. Williams, D. Patel, R. Mahfouz, F. G. Behm, S. C. Raimondi, M. V. Relling, A. Patel, C. Cheng, D. Campana, D. Wilkins, X. Zhou, J. Li, H. Liu, C.-H. Pui, W. E. Evans, C. Naeve, L. Wong, and J. R. Downing. Classification, subtype discovery, and prediction of outcome in pediatric acute lymphoblastic leukemia by gene expression profiling. *Cancer Cell*, 1(2):133–143, 2002.

10. E. S. Lander. Array of hope. *Nat. Genet.*, 21(Suppl.1):3–4, 1999.

11. S. C. Schuster. Next-generation sequencing transforms today's biology. *Nat. Methods*, 5(1): 16–18, 2008.

12. A. Watson, A. Mazumder, M. Stewart, and S. Balasubramanian. Technology for microarray analysis of gene expression. *Cur. Opini. Biotechnol.*, 9(6):609–614, 1998.

13. J. G. Hacia, J. B. Fan, O. Ryder, L. Jin, K. Edgemon, G. Ghandour, R. A. Mayer, B. Sun, L. Hsie, C. M. Robbins, L. C. Brody, D. Wang, E. S. Lander, R. Lipshutz, S. P. Fodor, and F. S. Collins. Determination of ancestral alleles for human single-nucleotide polymorphisms using high density oligonucleotide arrays. *Nat. Genet.*, 22(2):164–167, 1999.

14. D. S. Johnson, A. Mortazavi, R. M. Myers, and B. Wold. Genome-wide mapping of in vivo protein-DNA interactions. *Science*, 316(5830):1497–1502, 2007.

15. D. Kostka and R. Spang. Finding disease specific alterations in the co-expression of genes. *Bioinformatics*, 20 (Suppl 1):i194–199, 2004.

16. H. Li and R. Krishna Murthy Karuturi. Significance analysis and improved discovery of disease-specific differentially co-expressed gene sets in microarray data. *Int. J. Data Mining Bioinformatics*, 4(6):617–638, 2010.

17. A. Choon Tan, D. Q. Naiman, L. Xu, R. L. Winslow, and D. Geman. Simple decision rules for classifying human cancers from gene expression profiles. *Bioinformatics*, 21(20):3896–3904, 2005.

18. V. Ummiye Onay, L. Briollais, J. A. Knight, E. Shi, Y. Wang, S. Wells, H. Li, I. Rajendram, I. L Andrulis, and H. Ozcelik. SNP-SNP interactions in breast cancer susceptibility. *BMC Cancer*, 6:114, 2006.

19. M. Ashburner, C. A. Ball, J. A. Blake, D. Botstein, H. Butler, J. M. Cherry, A. P. Davis, K. Dolinski, S. S. Dwight, J. T. Eppig, M. A. Harris, D. P. Hill, L. Issel-Tarver, A. Kasarskis, S. Lewis, J. C. Matese, J. E. Richardson, M. Ringwald, G. M. Rubin, and G. Sherlock. Gene ontology: Tool for the unification of biology. The gene ontology consortium. *Nat. Genet.*, 25(1):25–29, 2000.

20. M. Kanehisa, S. Goto, S. Kawashima, Y. Okuno, and M. Hattori. The KEGG resource for deciphering the genome. *Nucleic Acids Res.*, 32(database issue):D277–280, 2004.

21. M. P. Platt, Z. Soler, R. Metson, and K. M. Stankovic. Pathways analysis of molecular markers in chronic sinusitis with polyps. *Otolaryngology—Head Neck Surg. Official J. Am. Acad. Otolaryngol—Head Neck Surg.*, 144(5):802–808, 2011.

22. Y. Pawitan, R. Krishna Murthy Karuturi, S. Michiels, and A. Ploner. Bias in the estimation of false discovery rate in microarray studies. *Bioinformatics*, 21(20):3865–3872, 2005.

23. Y. Ge, S. Dudoit, and T. P. Speed. Resampling-based multiple testing for microarray data analysis. *Test*, 12(1):1–77, 2003.

24. Z. Sidak. Rectangular confidence regions for the means of multivariate normal distributions. *J. Am. Statist. Assoc.*, 62(318):626–633, 1967.

25. P. H. Westfall and S. S. Young. *Resampling-Based Multiple Testing: Examples and Methods for P-Value Adjustment.* Wiley, New York, 1993.

26. S. Holm. A simple sequentially rejective multiple test procedure. *Scand. J. Statist.*, 6(2):65–70, 1979.

27. S. Dudoit, M. J. van der Laan, and K. S. Pollard. Multiple testing. Part i. Single-step procedures for control of general type i error rates. *Statist. Appl. Genet. Mol. Biol.*, 3:Article13, 2004.

28. Y. Benjamini and Y. Hochberg. Controlling the false discovery rate: A practical and powerful approach to multiple testing. *J. R. Statist. Soc. Ser. B (Methodol.)*, 57:289–300, 1995.

29. J. D. Storey and R. Tibshirani. Statistical significance for genomewide studies. *Proc. Natl. Acad. Sci. USA*, 100:9440–9445, 2003.

30. Y. Benjamini and D. Yekutieli. The control of the false discovery rate in multiple testing under dependency. *Ann. Statist.*, 29(4):1165–1188, 2001.

31. J. D. Storey. A direct approach to false discovery rates. *J. R. Statist. Soc. Ser. B*, 64:479–498, 2002.

32. C.-A. Tsai, H. Hsueh, and J. J Chen. Estimation of false discovery rates in multiple testing: Application to gene microarray data. *Biometrics*, 59:1071–1081, 2003.

33. B. Efron, R. Tibshirani, J. D. Storey, and V. Tusher. Empirical Bayes analysis of a microarray experiment. *J. Am. Statist. Assoc.*, 96(456):1151–1160, 2001.

34. B. Efron. Large-Scale simultaneous hypothesis testing. *J. Am. Statist. Assoc.*, 99:96–104, 2004.

35. J. Aubert, A. Bar-Hen, J.-J. Daudin, and S. Robin. Determination of the differentially expressed genes in microarray experiments using local FDR. *BMC Bioinformatics*, 5(1):125, 2004.

36. S. Scheid and R. Spang. A stochastic downhill search algorithm for estimating the local false discovery rate. *IEEE/ACM Trans. Computat. Biol. Bioinformatics*, 1(3):98–108, 2004.

37. P. Broberg. A comparative rcview of estimates of the proportion unchanged genes and the false discovery rate. *BMC Bioinformatics*, 6:199, 2005.

38. C. Dalmasso, A. Bar-Hen, and P. Broët. A constrained polynomial regression procedure for estimating the local false discovery rate. *BMC Bioinformatics*, 8:229, 2007.

39. J. G. Liao, Y. Lin, Z. E. Selvanayagam, and W. J. Shih. A mixture model for estimating the local false discovery rate in DNA microarray analysis. *Bioinformatics*, 20(16):2694–2701, 2004.

40. A. Ploner, S. Calza, A. Gusnanto, and Y. Pawitan. Multidimensional local false discovery rate for microarray studies. *Bioinformatics*, 22(5):556–565, 2006.

41. S. B. Pounds. Estimation and control of multiple testing error rates for microarray studies. *Brief. Bioinformatics*, 7:25–36, 2006.

42. S. Pounds and C. Cheng. Improving false discovery rate estimation. *Bioinformatics*, 20: 1737–1745, 2004.

43. E. L. Lehmann and J. P. Romano. *p*-Values. In *Testing Statistical Hypotheses*, Third ed., Springer, New York, 2005. pp. 63–65.

44. S. Pounds and S. W. Morris. Estimating the occurrence of false positives and false negatives in microarray studies by approximating and partitioning the empirical distribution of *p*-values. *Bioinformatics*, 19:1236–1242, 2003.

45. A. Celisse and S. Robin. A cross-validation based estimation of the proportion of true null hypotheses. *J. Statist. Planning Inference*, 140(11):3132–3147, 2010.

46. C. Dalmasso, P. Broët, and T. Moreau. A simple procedure for estimating the false discovery rate. *Bioinformatics*, 21(5):660–668, 2005.

47. M. Eshaghi, L. Zhu, Z. Chu, J. Li, C. Seng Chan, A. Shahab, R. Krishna Murthy Karuturi, and J. Liu. Deconvolution of chromatin immunoprecipitation-microarray (ChIP-chip) analysis of MBF occupancies reveals the temporal recruitment of rep2 at the MBF target genes. *Eukaryotic Cell*, 10(1):130–141, 2011.

48. J.-X. Bei, Y Li, W.-H. Jia, B.-J. Feng, G. Zhou, L.-Z. Chen, Q.-S. Feng, H.-Q. Low, H. Zhang, F. He, E. Shyong Tai, T. Kang, E. T. Liu, Jianjun Liu, and Y.-X. Zeng. A genome-wide association study of nasopharyngeal carcinoma identifies three new susceptibility loci. *Nat. Genet.*, 42(7):599–603, 2010.

49. Q. Zheng and X.-J. Wang. GOEAST: a web-based software toolkit for gene ontology enrichment analysis. *Nucleic Acids Res.*, 36(Web Server issue):W358–363, 2008.

50. D. Wei Huang, B. T. Sherman, and R. A. Lempicki. Systematic and integrative analysis of large gene lists using DAVID bioinformatics resources. *Nat. Protocols*, 4(1):44–57, 2009.

51. K. A. Baggerly, K. R. Coombes, K. R. Hess, D. N. Stivers, L. V. Abruzzo, and W. Zhang. Identifying differentially expressed genes in cDNA microarray experiments. *J. Computat. Biol.*, 8(6):639–659, 2001.

52. D. M. Titterington, A. F. M. Smith, and U. E. Makov. *Statistical Analysis of Finite Mixture Distributions*. Wiley, New York, 1985.

53. G. Schwarz. Estimating the dimension of a model. *Ann. Statist.*, 6(2):461–464, Mar. 1978.

54. F. D. Gibbons, M. Proft, K. Struhl, and F. P. Roth. Chipper: Discovering transcription-factor targets from chromatin immunoprecipitation microarrays using variance stabilization. *Genome Biol.*, 6(11):R96, 2005.

55. J. Li, P. Paramita, K. Choi, and R. Krishna Karuturi. ConReg-R: Extrapolative recalibration of the empirical distribution of *p*-values to improve false discovery rate estimates. *Biol. Direct*, 6:27, 2011.

56. B. Efron. Correlation and large-scale simultaneous significance testing. *J. Am. Statist. Assoc.*, 102(477):93–103, 2007.

57. X. Qiu, L. Klebanov, and A. Yakovlev. Correlation between gene expression levels and limitations of the empirical Bayes methodology for finding differentially expressed genes. *Statist. Appl. Genet. Mol. Bio.*, 4(1):34, 2005.

58. G. K. Smyth. Linear models and empirical Bayes methods for assessing differential expression in microarray experiments. *Statist. Appl. Genet. Mol. Bio.*, 3(1):3, 2004.

59. B. Efron and R. Tibshirani. On testing the significance of sets of genes. *Ann. Appl. Statist.*, 1(1):107–129, 2007.

60. A. Subramanian, P. Tamayo, V. K. Mootha, S. Mukherjee, B. L Ebert, M. A. Gillette, A. Paulovich, S. L. Pomeroy, T. R. Golub, E. S. Lander, and J. P. Mesirov. Gene set enrichment analysis: A knowledge-based approach for interpreting genome-wide expression profiles. *Proc. Natl. Acad. Sci. USA*, 102(43):15545–15550, 2005.

61. C. Y. McLean, D. Bristor, M. Hiller, S. L. Clarke, B. T. Schaar, C. B. Lowe, A. M. Wenger, and G. Bejerano. GREAT improves functional interpretation of cis-regulatory regions. *Nat. Biotechnol.*, 28(5):495–501, 2010.

62. J. Z, H. Li, and R. Krishna Murthy Karuturi. Bias in genome scale functional analysis of transcription factors via binding sites data. In preparation.

63. C.-Y. Lin, V. B. Vega, J. S. Thomsen, T. Zhang, S. Li Kong, M. Xie, K. Ping Chiu, L. Lipovich, D. H. Barnett, F. Stossi, A. Yeo, J. George, V. A. Kuznetsov, Y. Kok Lee, T. Howe Charn, N. Palanisamy, L. D. Miller, E. Cheung, B. S. Katzenellenbogen, Y. Ruan, G. Bourque, C.-L. Wei, and E. T. Liu. Whole-genome cartography of estrogen receptor alpha binding sites. *PLoS Genet.*, 3(6):e87, 2007.

64. M. D. Young, M. J. Wakefield, G. K. Smyth, and A. Oshlack. Gene ontology analysis for RNA-seq: Accounting for selection bias. *Genome Bio.*, 11:R14, 2010.

65. Y. Xie, W. Pan, and A. B. Khodursky. A note on using permutation-based false discovery rate estimates to compare different analysis methods for microarray data. *Bioinformatics*, 21(23): 4280–4288, 2005.

66. O. Alter, P. O. Brown, and D. Botstein. Singular value decomposition for genome-wide expression data processing and modeling. *Proc. Natl. Acad. Sci. USA*, 97(18):10101–10106, 2000.

67. T. O. Nielsen, R. B. West, S. C. Linn, O. Alter, M. A. Knowling, J. X. O'Connell, S. Zhu, M. Fero, G. Sherlock, J. R. Pollack, P. O. Brown, D. Botstein, and M. va de Rijn. Molecular characterisation of soft tissue tumours: A gene expression study. *Lancet*, 359(9314):1301–1307, 2002.

68. M. Benito, J. Parker, Q. Du, J. Wu, D. Xiang, C. M. Perou, and J. S. Marron. Adjustment of systematic microarray data biases. *Bioinformatics*, 20(1):105–114, 2004.

69. W. E. Johnson, C. Li, and A. Rabinovic. Adjusting batch effects in microarray expression data using empirical Bayes methods. *Biostatistics*, 8(1):118–127, 2007.

70. Z. Chu, J. Li, M. Eshaghi, R. Krishna Murthy Karuturi, K. Lin, and J. Liu. Adaptive expression responses in the pol-gamma null strain of *S. pombe* depleted of mitochondrial genome. *BMC Genomics*, 8:323, 2007.

71. J. Li, C. Kwok Pui, and R. Krishna Karuturi. Iterative piecewise linear regression to accurately assess statistical significance in batch confounded differential expression analysis. In *Bioinformatics Research and Applications (ISBRA)*, Vol. 7292. Springer, 2012, pp. 153–164.

72. L. V. Hedges and I. Olkin. *Statistical Methods for Meta-Analysis*. Academic, 1985.

73. D. V. Zaykin, L. A. Zhivotovsky, P. H. Westfall, and B. S. Weir. Truncated product method for combining *p*-values. *Genet. Epidemiol.*, 22(2):170–185, 2002.

74. S. Pyne, B. Futcher, and S. Skiena. Meta-analysis based on control of false discovery rate: Combining yeast ChIP-chip datasets. *Bioinformatics*, 22(20):2516–2522, 2006.

CHAPTER 16

SURVEY OF NOVEL FEATURE SELECTION METHODS FOR CANCER CLASSIFICATION

OLEG OKUN

SMARTTECCO, Stockholm, Sweden

16.1 BIOLOGICAL BACKGROUND

This chapter concentrates on gene selection for microarray gene expression–based cancer classification. Before going to the machine learning aspects of this task, let us briefly consider its biological aspects.

Let us first recall the "central dogma" of biology as it is described in [6]: Deoxyribonucleic acid, or DNA, is a nucleic acid that stores genetic information needed for the development and functioning of all living beings; DNA is used to construct proteins in the following way: A section of DNA called a gene is transcribed to a molecule called a messenger RNA (ribonucleic acid), or mRNA, and then translated into a protein by a ribosome; proteins carry out most functions of cells such as regulation of translation and transcription and DNA replication. DNA and mRNA molecules are sequences of 4 different nucleotides. Proteins are sequences of 20 different amino acids.

After the protein is constructed, the gene is said to be expressed. Transcription and translation can be considered as a kind of transformation, one of which is applied to DNA while the other one is applied to mRNA. The entire process can be expressed as follows: DNA→mRNA→protein. As you can see, genes, being the essential parts of DNA, play the important role in this process. Gene expression is often viewed as the process of protein synthesis (though proteins are not the only possible products of gene expression). By monitoring gene expression, one can get an indirect estimate of protein abundance, which is important for determining biological function.

The expressed genes within mammalian cells can be divided into housekeeping and tissue-specific ones [40]. Housekeeping genes are responsible for maintaining viability of all cell types in the body; they carry out biological functions common to all cell types. On the other hand, the tissue-specific genes produce proteins that are specifically associated with a given tissue.

Biological Knowledge Discovery Handbook: Preprocessing, Mining, and Postprocessing of Biological Data,
First Edition. Edited by Mourad Elloumi and Albert Y. Zomaya.
© 2014 John Wiley & Sons, Inc. Published 2014 by John Wiley & Sons, Inc.

Microarray technology helps to get the expression levels of many genes at once. It is thanks to this technology that we are flooded nowadays with plenty of such measurements, however, done for a few samples.

A DNA microarray is an array of thousands of locations, each containing DNA for a different gene [6, 24]. This array or (glass, plastic) slide contains a large library of thousands of single-stranded cDNA (complementary DNA, i.e., DNA complementary to mRNA) clones (probes), corresponding to different genes; that is, each spot on the slide corresponds to a specific gene. A typical use of microarrays is to extract two mRNA samples from two cell cultures or tissues (e.g., normal and cancerous), separately reverse transcribe them into cDNA, and using fluorescence labeling, dye the cDNA in these samples red (for the sample extracted from cancerous tissue) and green (for the sample extracted from healthy tissue), respectively [6]. Both samples are then spread across the microarray and left to hybridize to their corresponding complementary cDNA (labeled cDNA try to bind to their complementary cDNA on the microarray in order to form a double-stranded molecule in the process called hybridization). Hybridization thus acts like a detector of the presence of a certain gene. The slide is then scanned to obtain numerical intensities of each dye. The result of scanning is an image. Finally, image processing is used to find out the color at each location of the array. The four variants are possible: If genes are expressed in both samples, the color will be yellow; if genes are expressed in neither sample, the color will be black; if genes are only expressed in one sample, the color will be either red or green. The intensity of a color indicates the level of expression, that is, the number of mRNA transcribed. Given two differently dyed cDNA, the goal is to compare the intensity values I_R and I_G of the red and green channels at each spot of the microarray. The most popular statistic is the intensity log ratio: $\log_2(I_R/I_G)$ [7, 19, 33].

DNA microarrays are described in detail in several good books (see, e.g., [7, 19, 23, 26, 27, 30, 33, 42]). In addition, the following books include a description of the most commonly applied bioinformatics algorithms: [2, 19, 23, 26, 27, 30, 33, 42].

Cancer or a malignant (invasive, metastatic) tumor can be seen as a disease of DNA due to gene alterations and mutations, which results in uncontrolled growth of cells (cell proliferation). That is, tumor does not appear from nowhere (it is not a foreign body): It arises from mutated normal cells [29, 40]. Once a cancerous cell has been created, it undergoes clonal expansion via cell division. In other words, "parents" of the first-generation cancerous cells are mutated and altered normal cells while "parents" of the next-generation cancerous cells are the first-generation cancerous cells, and so on.

Detailed biology of cancer is described in [29, 40]. The book [29] includes chapters on biology of different cancer types such as colon, bladder, prostate, and breast.

As genes undergo changes during progression of cancer, so do gene expressions. That is, for a given gene or a set of genes, the expression level or levels in the normal (healthy) state can be different from those in the cancerous state. Based on this fact, the idea of cancer classification sprang. In other words, it is assumed that comparing microarray gene expression levels of healthy and cancerous cells, it is possible to distinguish between these two states and to diagnose cancer. However, in some cancers and for some tumor progression states, this difference is more profound than for others. Besides, as cancerous cells originate from mutated normal cells, these two types of cells may share many genes for which expression levels are almost identical. In addition, during cancer development tumor may rapidly mutate, which affects tissue-specific gene expression values. Some cancers change their phenotype to resemble cells from a different tissue in a process called metaplasia [29]. One also needs to take into account the fact that different cancer types generally have different sets of tissue-specific expressed genes. Therefore, the task of assigning a patient to one of the two classes (healthy or diseased) is not as straightforward as it may seem. The sheer number of genes makes this task even more challenging. This is where machine learning is typically called for help.

16.2 INTRODUCTION

A typical gene expression data set contains a matrix X of real numbers. Let D and N be the number of its rows and columns, respectively. As there are thousands of gene expressions and only a few dozens of samples, D (the number of genes) is of order 1000–10,000 while N (the number of biological samples) is somewhere between 10 and 100. Such a condition makes the application of many traditional statistical methods impossible as those techniques were developed under the assumption that $N \gg D$. You may ask: What's a problem?

The problem is in an underdetermined system where there are only a few equations versus many more unknown variables [19]. Hence, the solution of such a system is not unique. In other words, multiple solutions exist. By translating this into the biological language of the applied problem treated in this book, this means that multiple subsets of genes may be equally relevant to cancer classification [8, 9]. However, in order to reduce a chance for noisy and/or irrelevant genes to be included into one of such subsets, one needs to eliminate irrelevant genes before the actual classification.

You may also wonder why it is impossible to increase N. The answer is that this is difficult as the measurement of gene expression requires a functionally relevant tissue taken under the right conditions, which is sadly rare due to the impossibility to meet all requirements at once in practice (read more about these problems in [19]). So, we are left with the necessity to live and to deal with high-dimensional data.

From the machine learning point of view, gene selection removes meaningless (i.e., not related to a studied disease) genes, thus mitigating overfitting of a classifier on high-dimensional microarray data. Overfitting is plague when there are a lot of features and only few samples or instances characterized by these features. Overfitting leads to very good and often perfect classification performance (zero or close to zero error rate) on the training data, but this seemingly wonderful result does automatically translate to new, out-of-sample data. Put differently, a researcher neglecting the harmful effect of overfitting in the case of microarray data would find a small set of genes which he or she claims to predict a certain type of cancer. However, when biologists and/or doctors try to pay attention to expression levels of these genes when observing test volunteers and/or real patients, they see no value of those genes, because during the machine learning stage healthy and diseased patients were separated purely based on the noise present in microarray measurements rather than on the disease presence or absence. This happened because without prior removal of irrelevant genes, the classification problem is known as the small-sample-size problem (the number of features far exceeds the number of samples in a data set) in statistics and machine learning. For such problems, the lack of classifier generalization to new data is a norm rather than an exception unless a data dimensionality is dramatically reduced.

Gene selection methods can be divided into filters and wrappers. Wrappers rely on an external classifier to find important genes while filters extract the information on gene importance from the data without employing a classifier. Thus, filters are independent of any classifier and hence seem to be less biased than wrappers. As unbiasedness in gene selection is of paramount importance when a data set is small, this chapter concentrates exclusively on filter models. Those who are interested in comparing filters versus wrappers are advised to read [15].

The purpose of this chapter is to provide a short tutorial on three gene selection filters by explaining all details of their implementation in pseudocode, which could readily be used to write a computer code. I tried to choose as diverse algorithms as possible in order to demonstrate different approaches to gene selection. It was not my purpose to compare algorithms as the no-free-lunch theorem says that there is no algorithm that would be significantly better than other algorithms on all data sets.

16.3 KERNEL-BASED FEATURE SELECTION WITH HILBERT–SCHMIDT INDEPENDENCE CRITERION

Kernel methods are a class of pattern analysis algorithms that project the data into a high-dimensional feature space Φ, where relations hidden in the data can better be revealed than when doing pattern analysis in the original space of features. One does not need to know the explicit form of this projection, since it can be done via the inner products between images of all pairs of data in Φ. The inner products are embedded into the definition of a kernel. The complete set of all inner products forms an $N \times N$ kernel matrix. As N is small for typical gene expression data sets, the computation of this matrix is fast.

In a series of works [31, 32] a feature/gene filtering algorithm was proposed that is based on measuring dependence between features (gene expressions) and class labels in the kernel-induced space Φ. The key assumption is that good, that is, relevant for classification, features will maximize this dependence that is formulated through a mutual-information-like quantity called the Hilbert–Schmidt independence criterion (HSIC) (see [11] for explanation of this name and mathematical derivation). The HSIC is defined as

$$\text{HSIC} = \frac{1}{N(N-3)} \left[\text{tr}(KL) + \frac{I'KII'LI}{(N-1)(N-2)} - \frac{2}{N-2} I'KLI \right] \quad (16.1)$$

where I is an $N \times 1$ vector of 1's, I' is the transposed I, $\text{tr}(\cdot)$ is the trace of a square matrix, and

$$K_{ij} = (1 - \delta_{ij})k(x_i, x_j)$$
$$L_{ij} = (1 - \delta_{ij})l(y_i, y_j)$$
$$\delta_{ij} = \begin{cases} 1 & \text{if } i = j \\ 0 & \text{if } i \neq j \end{cases}$$
$$k(x_i, x_j) = \langle x_i, x_j \rangle \qquad l(x_i, x_j) = \langle y_i, y_j \rangle$$

In these formulas, $\langle \cdot, \cdot \rangle$ is the inner product, $x_i(x_j)$ is a vector, $y_i(y_j)$ is a scalar, and K and L are $N \times N$ kernel matrices: K is the data kernel matrix while L is the class label kernel matrix.

It is easy to see that the HSIC is a number. As a number, it can take negative, zero, and positive values. The positive values indicate that there is a strong dependence between data and class labels. Thus, the HSIC sign and magnitude serve as criteria for gene selection.

As for the mechanism of gene selection, in [11, 31, 32] it was backward elimination belonging to the class of greedy feature selection approaches. Backward elimination iteratively removes features according to a certain criterion until the desired number of features is collected or a termination condition is satisfied [12]. In contrast to its cousin—forward selection that iteratively adds features according to a certain criterion until the desired number of features is collected or a termination condition is satisfied—backward elimination is more time consuming because in order to select 10 features out of 100 it is much faster to add 10 features than to remove 90 features. However, backward elimination provides better features, in general, since candidate features are assessed within the context of many others. In terms of backward elimination, the minimum value of the HSIC points to a feature or a subset of features to be eliminated.

Pseudocode of the algorithm called backward-elimination HSIC (BAHSIC) is shown in Algorithm 16.1. In the beginning, each feature is normalized (independently of other features) to zero mean and unit variance. This operation makes all features to have the same domain and neutralizes a scale difference between features. As the part of initialization, the kernel matrix of labels is computed, too, since it does not change in later stages.

Algorithm 16.1 appends the features deleted from S to another list $S^\dagger$. In the beginning, S includes the full set of features (expression levels of genes). Because the most relevant features will join $S^\dagger$ last, the feature selection problem can be simply solved by taking the

ALGORITHM 16.1

```
BAHSIC algorithm {
        add indices of all features to the list S;
        set to empty the list of selected features; S† ← ∅;
        set the number of feature subsets, ℓ, to check for removal;
        set the number of features, t, to be selected;
        normalize each feature to zero mean and unit variance;
        compute the kernel matrix L for class labels;
        while S is not empty
        {
            adjust σ if a Gaussian (RBF) kernel is chosen:
            σ = 1/(2d), d =| S | −1;
            for each i, i ∈ {1,...,ℓ}
            {
                randomly sample the ith feature subset Tᵢ
                of size 0.1| S | from S;
                initialize accumulator; sᵢ = 0
                for each j, j ∈ Tᵢ
                {
                    temporarily remove the jth feature from S;
                    compute HSIC(σ, L, S \ {j}) using Eq. (16.1);
                    add the obtained HSIC to accumulator sᵢ;
                }
            }
            find a subset Tₖ such that k = arg min₁≤ᵢ≤ℓ sᵢ;
            delete Tₖ from S; S ← S \ Tₖ;
            add Tₖ to S†; S† ← S† ∪ Tₖ;
        }
        pick t last elements of S† as indices of selected features.
}
```

last t elements from $S^\dagger$. BAHSIC fills $S^\dagger$ recursively while eliminating the least relevant features from the current S. Since removing one feature at a time would be inefficient when there are a lot of irrelevant features, Song et al. advocate to delete a feature subset at a time (its size is 10% of the current features, i.e., $0.1 \,|\, S\,|$, which is a good trade-off between speed and the risk to lose relevant features).

The important question not explicitly discussed by Song et al. is how to choose subsets for elimination. Pseudocode in [32] nevertheless implicitly assumes that there are several subsets—candidates for elimination. However, only one of them is eventually removed from S. Complemented BAHSIC with such an option is complemented by providing an extra parameter ℓ to set up. This parameter defines the number of subsets, each of size $0.1 \,|\, S\,|$, to be randomly sampled from the current S.

The contribution of the ith subset $T_i, i = 1, \ldots, \ell$, is composed of contributions of the individual features, belonging to it. In particular, the jth feature $(j = 1, \ldots, 0.1 \,|\, S\,|)$ is temporarily removed from the current S and HSIC is computed for the remaining features. This operation is repeated for each feature in T_i, and all HSIC values thus obtained are summed up together to produce a single composite value of HSIC for the whole subset T_i. The minimum of the composite HSIC values is then found, pointing to the subset to be removed from S and be added to $S^\dagger$.

The algorithm iterates until S is empty. After that, the last t features appended to $S^\dagger$ are considered as the most relevant features and they are selected.

The other important question is the kernel choice. Microarray data are likely linearly separable in the original feature space due to their high dimensionality. Thus, a linear kernel for the data and class labels would likely work well. Besides the linear kernel, a Gaussian or radial basis function (RBF) kernel could be used as well, as Song et al. demonstrated in [32]. The parameter σ of the RBF kernel can be adjusted as shown in Algorithm 16.1, where it increases as the size of S decreases. This adjustment is an adaptation to the potential scale of the nonlinearity present in the data. In order to emphasize this adaptation of the RBF kernel parameter σ, it was explicitly included into the definition of the HSIC in the pseudocode. At each round of the BAHSIC, only the data kernel matrix K is recomputed while the label kernel matrix L remains the same all the time.

Following extensive experiments, Song et al. [31] concluded that the linear kernel outperforms many comparative methods (see their article for details) both for binary and multiclass problems. Only if nonlinearities are known to exist in data (e.g., when one class contains two or more overlapping subclasses), then the RBF kernel can provide superior classification results to those achieved by employing the linear kernel. It could also be said that if gene interactions are important for cancer prediction, then the RBF kernel may be a better choice than its linear counterpart. However, RBF success, of course, depends on the correct choice of the kernel parameter. Determining such an optimal value can be a nontrivial task.

In [31], it was also demonstrated that several well-known feature selectors commonly used in bioinformatics research are, in fact, the instances of BAHSIC. Among them are the Pearson's correlation [10, 37], centroid [3, 14], shrunken centroid [35, 36], and t-score [14].

16.4 REDUNDANCY-BASED GENE SELECTION

Yu [41] proposed a filter model based on the first- and second-order relationships between features and the class membership. In this model, not only is the dependence of a single feature and the class used, but also is the dependence of a pair of features and the class. Computing higher order interactions (e.g., involving three or more features) not only would be computationally expensive but also would be imprecise due to the small size of typical gene expression data sets.

Before describing Yu's main idea, let us introduce a number of useful definitions.

16.4.1 Feature Relevance and Redundancy

Let $P(C \mid F)$ be the probability distribution of the class C given the features F. In other words, P is the conditional distribution, because the probability of the class C depends on conditions on F. Let F be a full set of features, F_i a feature i, and $S_i = F \setminus F_i$, which means the set F with the feature F_i removed from F. Kohavi and John [20] classified features into three nonoverlapping groups: strongly relevant, weakly relevant, and irrelevant. These notions can be defined as follows.

Definition 16.1 *Strong Relevance* A feature F_i is strongly relevant if and only if

$$P(C \mid F_i, S_i) \neq P(C \mid S_i)$$

Definition 16.2 *Weak Relevance* A feature F_i is weakly relevant if and only if

$$P(C \mid F_i, S_i) = P(C \mid S_i)$$

and $\exists S_i' \subset S_i$ such that $P(C \mid F_i, S_i') \neq P(C \mid S_i')$.

Definition 16.3 *Irrelevance* A feature F_i is irrelevant if and only if

$$\forall S_i' \subseteq S_i, P(C \mid F_i, S_i') = P(C \mid S_i')$$

If a feature is strongly relevant, this feature is always necessary for the optimal subset of features because its deletion from the optimal subset results in loss of discriminative power. This is reflected by the symbol $\neq$ between the probability of the class C when F_i is given in addition to S_i and the probability of the class C when just S_i is given with no knowledge about F_i. That is, the sign that a feature is strongly relevant is the change (typically decrease) in probability if a strongly relevant feature is excluded from a subset of features.

Weak relevance implies that the feature is not always necessary to have among selected features in the optimal subset. However, under certain circumstances such a feature may become relevant, for example, in combination with another feature. Compared to strong relevance, the weak-relevance definition looks totally different. In other words, the fact that a weakly relevant feature is included or not into a given subset of already selected features (it is useful to think of S_i as the optimal subset) does not affect the probability value. However, among features in S_i there are probably certain features that change the status of weak relevance to strong relevance when combined together with a weakly relevant feature. This state transition can be seen in the second line of the weak-relevance definition.

Finally, an irrelevant feature is the feature that can be safely omitted from the optimal subset, since it does not influence classification performance in any way. Hence, adding an irrelevant feature to other previously selected features does not change the probability value.

The important implication of all three definitions above is that features are not considered in isolation from each other anymore! This allows taking into account interactions among features; hence, more complex relations between features can be discovered.

The optimal subset of features must include all strongly relevant and some weakly relevant features. However, the definition of weak relevance is rather vague; it does not indicate how one can distinguish between important weakly relevant and unimportant weakly relevant features. Hence, the concept of feature redundancy is necessary.

Redundancy can be defined in terms of correlation. Indeed, two features are redundant if their values are completely correlated. However, such an ideal case is quite rare in practice. In order to efficiently utilize feature redundancy, the following definition of a feature's Markov blanket is used [28].

Definition 16.4 *Markov Blanket* Given a feature F_i, let $M_i \subset F(F_i \notin M_i)$, where M_i is a Markov blanket for F_i if and only if

$$P(F \setminus \{M_i, F_i\}, C \mid F_i, M_i) = P(F \setminus \{M_i, F_i\}, C \mid M_i)$$

A Markov blanket is a feature associated with F_i. However, it is still useful to think of it as a kind of "blanket" that "covers" or "does not cover" a certain feature. Notice that a Markov blanket does not exist per se; it is only useful if linked to the feature of interest. Intuitively, you might already determine when a given feature is redundant or not: if a Markov blanket exists for it, it is redundant; otherwise, it is not.

It is easy to see that if M_i is a Markov blanket of F_i (pay attention that both M_i and F_i are excluded from the original feature set F when calculating probabilities), the class C is conditionally independent of F_i given M_i, that is, knowing F_i does not bring extra information about C.

Moreover, the Markov blanket condition is stronger than conditional independence, because it requires that M_i subsumes the information F_i has not only about C but also about all of the other features. In [21] it was pointed out that an optimal subset can be obtained by using Markov blankets as the basis for feature elimination. Let G be the current set of features ($G = F$ in the beginning). At any step, if there exists a Markov blanket for F_i within G, F_i is deemed to be unnecessary for the optimal subset and thus it can be removed from G. It is proved that this process guarantees that a feature eliminated at an earlier stage will still have a Markov blanket at any later stages [21]. As a result, this means that if a feature has been removed at an earlier stage, one does not have to worry that this feature might be needed to check at a later stage.

Based on the feature relevance definitions, it is clear that a strongly relevant feature does not have the corresponding Markov blanket. On the other hand, a Markov blanket always exists for an irrelevant feature; therefore, such a feature will always be detected and removed from further analysis. This implies that we are left with ambiguous weakly relevant features, which may include both useful and useless features.

Definition 16.5 *Redundant Feature* Let G be the current set of features. Then a feature is redundant and should be removed from G if and only if it is weakly relevant and has a Markov blanket within G.

After removal of irrelevant and weakly relevant but redundant genes, only strongly relevant and weakly relevant but nonredundant features form an optimal subset of the features of interest. However, the number of genes in microarray data is so huge that the task of finding the exact Markov blanket seems to be impractical due to its combinatorial complexity. Hence, Yu [41] suggested searching for a suboptimal subset of genes by resorting to an approximate solution for a Markov blanket.

16.4.2 Main Idea

There are two types of correlation between genes and the class on which Yu's algorithm is based: individual C-correlation and combined C-correlation.

Definition 16.6 *Individual C-Correlation* The correlation between gene F_i and the class C is called individual C-correlation.

Definition 16.7 *Combined C-Correlation* The correlation between the pair of genes F_i and F_j $(i \neq j)$ and the class C is called combined C-correlation.

In the combined C-correlation, two genes are treated as a single gene. For simplicity it is assumed that gene expression levels are represented by nominal values instead of continuous values. This would, of course, require discretization of the whole range $] - \infty, +\infty[$ into the small number of discrete values, each associated with its own subinterval. In order to avoid any ambiguity, there is no overlap between adjacent subintervals. Under such conditions, if both genes take nominal values -1, 0, and $+1$, there will be nine pairs of values covering all possible states: $(-1,-1)$, $(-1,0)$, $(-1,+1)$, $(0,-1)$, $(0,0)$, $(0,+1)$, $(+1,-1)$, $(+1,0)$, $(+1,+1)$. In this case, the combined correlation measures the correlation between each of the nine states and the class C. Of course, individual C-correlations are also calculated for nominal data.

The method proposed by Yu determines if a single gene F_i can be an approximate Markov blanket for another gene F_j based on both individual C-correlations and the combined C-correlation. It assumes that a gene with a larger individual C-correlation possesses more information about the class than a gene with a smaller individual C-correlation. For two genes F_i and F_j, if the individual C-correlation for F_i is larger than or equal to the individual C-correlation for F_j, then the next check is to evaluate whether gene F_j is approximately redundant to gene F_i. In addition, if combining two genes F_i and F_j does not give more information about the class than F_i alone, it is heuristically decided that F_i forms an approximate Markov blanket for F_j. Therefore, an approximate Markov blanket is defined as follows.

Definition 16.8 *Approximate Markov Blanket* For two genes F_i and F_j, F_i forms an approximate Markov blanket for F_j if and only if (1) the individual C-correlation for F_i is larger than or equal to the individual C-correlation for F_j and (2) the individual C-correlation for F_i is larger than or equal to the combined C-correlation for F_i and F_j.

Consequences of gene removal based on an approximate Markov blanket are not the same as those with the exact Markov blanket. In particular, if F_j is the only gene forming an approximate Markov blanket for F_k and F_i forms an approximate Markov blanket for F_j, then after removing F_k based on F_j, further removal of F_j based on F_i will result in no approximate Markov blanket for F_k (this implies that one is not certain that there is no need to check F_k for relevance again; hence, the whole backward-elimination scheme may collapse). Fortunately, it is possible to circumvent this problem by removing a gene only if an approximate Markov blanket exists for it that formed by a predominant gene defined below.

Definition 16.9 *Predominant Gene* A gene is predominant if and only if it does not have any approximate Markov blanket in the current set.

Predominant genes (there can be several of them) will not be removed at any stage. This is what distinguishes them from other genes. If a certain gene is removed based on a predominant gene, it is guaranteed that a Markov blanket for it will still exist at any later stage when another gene is removed. To find predominant genes, all genes are sorted in decreasing order of their individual C-correlation. The gene with the highest value of C-correlation does not have an approximate Markov blanket, and hence, it is one of the predominant genes that will be used to filter out unimportant genes. In other words, the goal of Yu's method is to discover all predominant genes while eliminating all other genes. Compared to the approaches treating each gene separately from the others, this method offers the following advantages:

- Redundancy among relevant genes is efficiently handled.
- Gene-to-gene interactions (though only pairwise, but not higher order) are taken into account.
- Irrelevant and weakly relevant but redundant genes are removed.

The last characteristic makes it unnecessary to determine a threshold value for partitioning all genes into important and unimportant for classification, since all predominant genes will be among the ones selected and iterations will stop when the list of gene ends. It is possible, of course, to extend the method so that it can handle higher order gene interactions, but there are two reasons why it might not be a good idea: (1) dramatic increase in computational time and (2) oversearching problem [17] due to the combination of small-sample-size and high-dimensional data.

16.4.3 Algorithm

I first show how to compute certain measures employed in the algorithm as well as how discretization of continuous values has been done followed by the algorithm itself in detail.

Discretization of continuous values into a number of nominal states is usually intended to reduce noise. Various techniques for doing so can be employed (see, e.g., [25]), but in [41] the following approach was exercised.

The number of different nominal values was set to three: -1, 0, and $+1$, representing underexpression, baseline, and overexpression, respectively. These nominal values correspond to $]-\infty, \mu - \sigma/2[$, $[\mu - \sigma/2, \mu + \sigma/2]$, and $]\mu + \sigma/2, +\infty[$, respectively, where μ and σ are the mean and standard deviation of expression levels for a given gene across all samples. The algorithm of discretization is thus straightforward: If a continuous expression level comes into $]-\infty, \mu - \sigma/2[$, it is replaced with -1; if it lies within $[\mu - \sigma/2, \mu + \sigma/2]$, it is assigned to 0; and if it falls into $]\mu + \sigma/2, +\infty[$, it is set to +1.

Once deciding upon discretization, the individual and combined C-correlations are defined in terms of information-theoretic measures based on entropy.

For nominal variables, entropy and conditional entropy are defined by

$$H(X) = -\sum_{i=1}^{m} P(x_i) \log_2 P(x_i) \tag{16.2}$$

$$H(X \mid C) = -\sum_{k=1}^{m} P(c_k) \sum_{i=1}^{m} P(x_i \mid c_k) \log_2 P(x_i \mid c_k) \tag{16.3}$$

where $m = 3$ because of three possible nominal values (-1, 0, +1), $P(x_i)$ is the probability that the nominal variable X takes the value x_i, $P(c_k)$ is the class c_k probability, and $P(x_i \mid c_k)$ is the probability that the nominal variable X takes the value x_i given that the class is c_k.

For combined C-correlation, the formulas above are changed into

$$H(X) = -\sum_{i,j-1}^{m} P(x_i, x_j) \log_2 P(x_i, x_j) \tag{16.4}$$

$$H(X \mid C) = -\sum_{k=1}^{m} P(c_k) \sum_{i,j=1}^{m} P(x_i, x_j \mid c_k) \log_2 P(x_i, x_j \mid c_k) \tag{16.5}$$

Interpretation of conditional probabilities in these formulas is essentially the same as in those for the individual C-correlation; the only difference is that x_i is now replaced with the pair (x_i, x_j). Since the nominal variable in our case can take only three distinct values, there are nine pairs for which probabilities and hence entropies need to be calculated. These pairs are $(-1,-1), (-1,0), (-1,+1), (0,-1), (0,0), (0,+1), (+1,-1), (+1,0), (+1,+1)$.

Having defined entropies, both types of correlation are finally expressed through symmetrical uncertainty SU as

$$\text{SU}(X, C) = 2\left[\frac{\text{IG}(X \mid C)}{H(X) + H(C)}\right] = 2\left[\frac{H(X) - H(X \mid C)}{H(C) + H(X)}\right] \tag{16.6}$$

where X stands for the nominal values of a single gene (individual C-correlation) or the nominal values of a pair of genes (combined C-correlation) and $\text{IG}(X \mid C) = H(X) - H(X \mid C)$ is information gain from knowing the class information, meaning that the more information we know about the relation between X and C, the larger the entropy decrease is, that is, the less uncertain we are about X.

SU defines both kinds of correlations. It is a normalized characteristic whose values lie between 0 and 1, where 0 indicates that X and C are independent, that is, knowing C does not affect our knowledge about X. It should be noted that instead of symmetrical uncertainty, other definitions for correlation can also be applied.

The algorithm abbreviated as RBF is shown as Algorithm 16.2, where the list S includes genes that have been selected by the algorithm; the end of this list is marked with NULL, which is borrowed from programming languages, where it usually means the end of a file or other structure storing data.

ALGORITHM 16.2

```
redundancy-based gene selection algorithm {
        compute the individual C-correlation for each gene
        by using Eqs. (16.2),(16.3),(16.6);
        sort correlations in descending order;
        put genes into the list S in the sorting order;
        get the first element Fᵢ from S;
        while Fᵢ ≠ NULL
        {
            get the next element Fⱼ from S;
            while Fⱼ ≠ NULL
            {
                compute the combined C-correlation of Fᵢ and Fⱼ
                by using Eqs. (16.4),(16.5),(16.6);
                if (the individual correlation for Fᵢ is larger than
                or equal to the combined correlation for Fᵢ and Fⱼ)
                    S = S \ Fⱼ;
                get the next element Fⱼ from S;
            }
            get the next element Fᵢ from S.
        }
}
```

The algorithm starts from computing an individual C-correlation for each gene and sorting all correlations in descending order of magnitude. The gene with the largest correlation is considered as predominant (no approximate Markov blanket exists for it) and hence it is put to the list S of the selected genes.

After that, the iteration begins with picking the first gene F_i from S in order to filter out other genes which are not in S. For all remaining genes, if F_i forms an approximate Markov blanket for any gene F_j, the latter is removed from further analysis. The following conditions must be satisfied for this to happen:

- The individual C-correlation for F_i must be larger than or equal to the individual C-correlation for F_j, which implies that a gene with a larger individual correlation provides more information about the class than a gene with a smaller individual correlation. This condition is automatically fulfilled after gene sorting based on the individual C-correlation.

- The individual C-correlation for F_i must be larger than or equal to the combined C-correlation for genes F_i and F_j, which means that if combining genes F_i and F_j does not provide more discriminating power than F_i alone, F_j is decided to be useless.

After one iteration of filtering based on F_i, the algorithm takes the next, still unfiltered gene (according to the magnitude of the individual C-correlation), and the filtering process is repeated over and over again. The algorithm halts if there are no more predominant genes to be selected.

Since a lot of genes are typically removed in each round (recall that gene expression data contain a lot of redundancy) and removed genes do not appear in the next iterations, RBF is much faster than the typical hill climbing (greedy forward selection or backward elimination where one gene at a time is either added or removed). Only in the worst case when no gene can be redundant or irrelevant, which is extremely rare or even impossible in case of microarray data, the computational complexity of RBF is comparable to the ones of the greedy search algorithms.

16.5 UNSUPERVISED FEATURE SELECTION

Varshavsky et al. [38] proposed several variants of an unsupervised feature selection algorithm which is based on singular-value decomposition (SVD), where features are selected according to their contribution to the SVD entropy, which is the entropy defined for the distribution of eigenvalues of a square data matrix. Because SVD looks for eigenvalues of a matrix, it is akin to principal-component analysis.

Unsupervised feature selection algorithms are rare because class labels are typically used one way or another to judge on feature usefulness or relevance. Such algorithms are naturally associated with filter models. In bioinformatics, a typical example of the unsupervised feature filtering is gene shaving [13].

In [38] authors introduced three variants of unsupervised feature selection: simple feature ranking, forward feature selection, and backward feature elimination. Due to time-consuming computations in the backward feature elimination variant, I do not describe it here. Readers are advised to consult the original article for details.

16.5.1 Singular-Value Decomposition

Let A be a $D \times N$ data matrix containing as its rows the expression levels of D genes measured in N samples. The A can be written as $A = USV'$, where U is a $D \times D$ orthogonal matrix, V is an $N \times N$ orthogonal matrix, and S is a $D \times N$ diagonal matrix with nonnegative values. Such a decomposition of the matrix A into the product of three other matrices is called singular-value decomposition [22].

An algorithm to find the SVD is given in [34] as follows:

1. Find the eigenvalues λ_i, $i = 1, \ldots, N$, of the $N \times N$ matrix $A'A$ and arrange the eigenvalues in descending order.
2. Find the number of nonzero eigenvalues of the matrix $A'A$ and denote this number by r.
3. Find the orthogonal eigenvectors v_i of the matrix $A'A$ corresponding to the obtained eigenvalues and arrange them in the same order to form column vectors of the $N \times N$ matrix V.
4. Form a $D \times N$ matrix S by placing on the leading diagonal of it quantities $\sigma_i = \sqrt{\lambda_i}$, $i = 1, \ldots, \min(N, D)$. These quantities are called singular values.
5. Find the first r column vectors of the $D \times D$ matrix U:

$$u_i = \frac{1}{\sigma_i} A v_i \qquad i = 1, \ldots, r$$

These column vectors are the left-singular (u_i) and right-singular (v_i) vectors, respectively.

6. Add to the matrix U the rest of the $D - r$ vectors using the Gram-Schmidt orthogonalization process.

16.5.2 Feature Ranking by SVD Entropy

An SVD entropy of a data set was first introduced in [1]. It is defined by

$$E = -\frac{1}{\log N} \sum_{i=1}^{N} S_i \log S_i$$

where $S_i = \sigma_i^2 / (\sum_{j=1}^{N} \sigma_j^2)$ is the normalized relative value.

This entropy varies between 0 and 1: $E = 0$ (low entropy, high order) corresponds to a data set that can be explained by a single eigenvector associated with the only nonzero eigenvalue and $E = 1$ (high entropy, low order) corresponds to the data set for which eigenvalues are uniformly distributed, that is, all eigenvalues are equal in magnitude. As one can notice, there is a certain similarity between the Shannon entropy and its SDV analog. However, instead of probability, SVD entropy is based on the distribution of eigenvalues or singular values.

Having defined SVD entropy, the next step is to define the contribution of the ith feature:

$$CE_i = E(A_{m \times N}) - E(A_{(m-1) \times N})$$

where $E(A_{m \times N})$ means the SVD entropy computed for the data contained in matrix $A_{m \times N}$ and $E(A_{(m-1) \times N})$ means the SVD entropy computed for the data contained in matrix $A_{(m-1) \times N}$ with the ith row (feature) removed. That is, features are temporarily removed from the data set one by one and the difference before and after each feature removal is calculated. Intuitively, if a feature is not important, there would be no effect on the SVD entropy after this feature has been removed. In other words, CE for this feature will be zero. On the contrary, if a feature is significant for data characterization, its contribution will be positive.

After computing the contribution of each feature, the obtained contribution values are sorted in decreasing order of magnitude. Let c and d be the average of all feature contributions and their standard deviation, respectively. Then three groups of features can be distinguished:

- $CE_i > c + d$ (features with high contribution)
- $c + d > CE_i > c - d$ (features with average contribution)
- $CE_i < c - d$ (features with low contribution)

Features of the first category are only considered relevant since removal of such features leads to decrease in the entropy for the whole data set. Features of other two categories are deemed to be unimportant and therefore they can be filtered out, because the second category includes neutral features (entropy does not change much if one deletes them), while the third category is comprised of redundant features.

Let the number of features in the first category be m_c. This is the upper limit and the target for three feature selection algorithms described in the next section. In other words, features are selected until the number of selected features reaches m_c.

16.5.3 Algorithms

Let *selected* and *remaining* denote lists storing indices of already selected features and features that were not yet analyzed, respectively. In the following sections, three algorithms utilizing CE are given. The simplest of them is feature ranking.

16.5.3.1 *Simple Ranking (SR)*

In this algorithm, CE for each individual feature is calculated, all CE values are ranked, and the top m_c features with the highest contribution are selected. It is the fastest algorithm among all the three, but its speed results from the fact that joint contributions of several features are not considered. To remedy this, Varshavsky et al. [38] also proposed two variants of the forward feature selection.

16.5.3.2 *Forward Selection 1 (FS1)*

FS1 chooses the first feature according to the highest CE. Next, another feature—candidate for selection—is sought, which, together with the first feature, produces a two-feature subset with highest entropy ($D - 1$ features are candidates for inclusion into the list of selected features). After that, the third, fourth, ..., features are iteratively selected so that in combination with already selected features they comprise a 3-, 4-, ..., m_c-feature subsets with highest SVD entropy (see Algorithm 16.3).

ALGORITHM 16.3

```
forward selection 1 algorithm {
        selected = ∅;  remaining = {1,...,D};
        let A_full be the original D × N data matrix
        whose rows are genes
        for each i, i ∈ {1,...,D}
        {
            compute the contribution of the i gene:
            CE_i = E(A_full)   E(A_full\remaining_i);
        }
        let j = arg max_{i=1,...,D} CE_i;
        selected = selected ∪j;
        remaining = remaining \j;
        while | selected |< m_c
        {
            for each i, i ∈ {1,...,| remaining |}
            {
                compute the joint contribution to SVD-entropy
                of genes that have been selected and
                the ith remaining gene:
                CE_i = E(A_{selected∪remaining_i}) − E(A_{selected});
            }
            let j = arg max_{i=1,...,|remaining|} CE_i
            selected = selected ∪j;
            remaining = remaining \j.
        }
}
```

ALGORITHM 16.4

```
forward selection 2 algorithm {
        selected = ∅;  remaining = {1, ..., D};
        let A_full be the original D × N data matrix
        whose rows are genes
        for each i,  i ∈ {1, ..., D}
        {
                compute the contribution of the i gene:
                CE_i = E(A_full) − E(A_full\remaining_i);
        }
        let  j = arg max_{i=1,...,D} CE_i;
        selected = shape selected ∪ j;
        remaining = remaining \ j;
        while | selected | < m_c
        {
                for each i,  i ∈ {1, ..., | remaining |}
                {
                        compute the contribution to SVD-entropy of
                        the ith remaining gene:
                        CE_i = E(A_remaining) − E(A_remaining\remaining_i);
                }
                let  j = arg max_{i=1,...,|remaining|} CE_i
                selected = selected ∪ j;
                remaining = remaining \ j.
        }
}
```

16.5.3.3 Forward Selection 2 (FS2) In this variant of forward feature selection, the first feature is selected in the same manner as in FS1. This feature is then deleted from the set of features, the contributions of the remaining $D - 1$ features to the SVD entropy are recalculated, and the feature with the highest contribution is added to the set of selected features. The second selected feature is afterward removed from the set of available features and the contributions of the remaining $D - 2$ features are again recalculated in order to find the third feature to be selected, and so on. Such operations continue until m_c features are found. Algorithm 16.4 shows the details of FS2.

16.5.3.4 Brief Comments on Algorithms In all three algorithms, the optimal number of features to find is automatically determined. Although the criterion based on which this number is determined is rather heuristic, this is nevertheless a step forward compared to the manually set number of features, which may often be far from being optimal. Thus, the algorithms in [38] offer a certain advantage for a researcher since it is unnecessary to guess the optimal number of features.

However, as experimental results in [38] showed, both simple ranking and forward-selection algorithms find too many features (100–250). Therefore they can serve as prefilters filling a pool of candidate features, some of which might be irrelevant or weakly relevant. From this pool of features more aggressive (and often time-consuming) filters or wrappers (e.g., those based on the Markov blanket [18, 21]) can further select strongly relevant features. But because these feature selection methods are applied to a smaller subset of the

TABLE 16.1   Summary of Algorithms

	Algorithm 16.1	Algorithm 16.2	Algorithms 16.3 and 16.4
Principle	Kernel-based hill climbing	Markov blanket–based hill climbing	SVD-based hill climbing
Automatic cutoff	No	Yes	Yes

original set of features, this results in faster feature selection, compared to the case of the full feature set.

Given three different algorithms, one may ask which of them could be better than the others. Experiments in [38] leave this question open, since though one could expect that FS1, taking into account feature interactions, would perform better than SR, one experiment showed almost no difference between FS1 and SR. This fact indicates that there could be problems where the simplest solution is as good as a much more computationally intensive one. However, such exceptions should not mislead one into thinking that FS1 or conceptually similar algorithms cannot offer significant advantages over simple ranking.

16.6   SUMMARY OF ALGORITHMS

Three considered algorithms are summarized in Table 16.1. All algorithms were implemented in MATLAB and can be obtained from the author by writing to olegokun@yahoo.com.

All algorithms operate in the hill climbing matter when genes are incrementally added or removed to a set of previously selected genes. In other words, the solutions they deliver might not be globally optimal.

Algorithm 16.2 needs gene expression value discretization before its application whereas other algorithms do not require it.

"Automatic cutoff" in Table 16.1 refers to the need to preset the number of genes to be selected; "yes" means that no cutoff threshold is necessary because an algorithm automatically halts, while "no" implies that a user has to set up this number before running an algorithm. Automatic determination of relevant genes might be desired, especially if one does not know how many of them exist in advance. On the other hand, it does not allow exploring other possibilities that are possible if a user can vary the number of selected genes.

16.7   CONCLUSION

Given the fact that no algorithm can be overwhelminly better than other algorithms on all kinds of data sets, it is natural to ask when filter models of gene selection described in this chapter might be useful in practice. I recommend to apply them together with classifier ensembles, especially those which include nontrainable ensemble members/combiners. Inclusion of different gene selection algorithms would inject diversity of predictions among individual classifiers and, hence, improve the overall ensemble performance.

In my opinion, faced with scarcity of data samples in many biological data sets, it is important to avoid any training in both gene selection and data classification stages because the training process would likely lead to overfitting and therefore poor generalization of a classifier system. Despite their widespead use, traditional k-fold cross validation and bootstraping are inadequate in solving the overfitting issue [16].

When one cannot avoid using a trainable classifier, I advise the artificial sample generation introduced in [4]. With this approach, the original data set is intact and it serves as training data, while samples, artificially produced from the training data based on random-number generation, function as test data. Low-bias, low-variance classification error associated with such an approach is called bolstered error [4].

REFERENCES

1. O. Alter, P. O. Brown, and D. Botstein. Singular value decomposition for genome-wide expression data processing and modeling. *Proc. Nat. Acad. Sci. USA*, 97(18):10101–10106, 2000.

2. P. Baldi and S. Brunak. *Bioinformatics: The Machine Learning Approach*. MIT Press, Cambridge, MA, 2001.

3. J. Bedo, K. Sanderson, and A. Kowalczyk. An efficient alternative to SVM based recursive feature elimination with applications in natural language processing and bioinformatics. In A. Sattar and B. H. Kang, (Eds.), *Lecture Notes in Computer Science 4304. Proceedings of the 19th Australian Joint Conference on Artificial Intelligence*, 2006, Hobart, TAS. Springer-Verlag, Berlin/Heidelberg, 2006, pp. 170–180.

4. U. M. Braga-Neto and E. R. Dougherty. Bolstered error estimation. *Pattern Recognition*, 36(7):1267–1281, 2004.

5. P. O. Brown and D. Botstein. Exploring the new world of the genome with DNA microarrays. *Nat. Genet.*, 21(Suppl. 1):33–37, 1999.

6. W. W. Cohen. *A Computer Scientist's Guide to Cell Biology*. Springer Science+Business Media, New York, 2007.

7. S. Drăghici. *Data Analysis Tools for DNA Microarrays*. Chapman & Hall/CRC Press, Boca Raton, FL, 2003.

8. R. Díaz-Uriarte and S. Alvarez de Andrés. Gene selection and classification of microarray data using random forest. *BMC Bioinformatics*, 7(3), 2006. doi:10.1186/1471-2105-7-3.

9. L. Ein-Dor, I. Kela, G. Getz, D. Givol, and E. Domany. Outcome signature genes in breast cancer: Is there a unique set? *Bioinformatics*, 21(2):171–178, 2005.

10. L. Ein-Dor, O. Zuk, and E. Domany. Thousands of samples are needed to generate a robust gene list for predicting outcome in cancer. *Proc. Nat. Acad. Sci. USA* 103(15):5923–5928, 2006.

11. A. Gretton, O. Bousquet, A. Smola, and B. Schölkopf. Measuring statistical dependence with Hilbert-Schmidt norms. In S. Jain, H.-U. Simon , and E. Tomita, (Eds.), *Lecture Notes in Artificial Intelligence 3734. Proceedings of the 16th International Conference on Algorithmic Learning Theory*, 2005, Singapore. Springer-Verlag, Berlin/Heidelberg, 2005, pp. 63–77.

12. I. Guyon and A. Elisseeff. An introduction to variable and feature selection. *J. Machine Learning Res.*, 3:1157–1182, 2003.

13. T. Hastie, et al. "Gene shaving" as a method for identifying distinct sets of genes with similar expression patterns. *Genome Biol.* 1(2):research0003.1–0003.21, 2000.

14. T. Hastie, R. Tibshirani, and J. Friedman. *The Elements of Statistical Learning*. Springer-Verlag, New York, 2001.

15. I. Inza, P. Larrañaga, R. Blanco, and A. J. Cerrolaza. Filter versus wrapper gene selection approaches in DNA microarray domains. *Artif. Intell. Med.* 31(2):91–103, 2004.

16. A. Isaksson, M. Wallman, H. Göransson, and M. Gustafsson. Cross-validation and bootstrapping are unreliable in small sample classification. *Pattern Recognition Lett.* 29(14):1960–1965, 2008.

17. D. D. Jensen and P. R. Cohen. Multiple comparisons in induction algorithms. *Machine Learning*, 38(3):309–338, 2000.

18. T. A. Knijnenburg, M. J. Reinders, and L. F. Wessels. Artifacts of Markov blanket filtering based on discretized features in small sample size applications. *Pattern Recognition Lett.* 27(7):709–714, 2006.

19. I. S. Kohane, A. T. Kho, and A. J. Butte. *Microarrays for an Integrative Genomics*. MIT Press, Cambridge, MA, 2003.

20. R. Kohavi and G. H. John. Wrappers for feature subset selection. *Artif. Intell.*, 97(1–2):273–324, 1997.

21. D. Koller and M. Sahami. Toward optimal feature selection. In L. Saitta, (Ed.), *Proceedings of the 13th International Conference on Machine Learning*, 1996, Bari, Italy. Morgan Kaufmann, San Francisco, CA, 1996, pp. 284–292.

22. D. C. Lay. *Linear Algebra and Its Applications*. Pearson Education, Upper Saddle River, NJ, 2003.

23. M.-LT. Lee. *Analysis of Microarray Gene Expression Data*. Kluwer Academic, Boston, MA, 2004.

24. C. Li, G. C. Tseng, and W. H. Wong. Model-based analysis of oligonucleotide arrays and issues in cDNA microarray analysis. In T. Speed, (Ed.), *Statistical Analysis of Gene Expression Microarray Data*. Chapman & Hall/CRC Press, Boca Raton, FL, 2003, pp. 1–34.

25. H. Liu, F. Hussain, C. L. Tan, and M. Dash. Discretization: An enabling technique. *Data Mining Knowledge Discov.* 6(4):393–423, 2002.

26. O. Lund, M. Nielsen, C. Lundegaard, C. Keşmir, and S. Brunak. *Immunological Bioinformatics*. MIT Press, Cambridge, MA, 2005.

27. B. K. Mallick, D. Gold, and V. Baladandayuthepani. *Bayesian Analysis of Gene Expression Data*. Wiley, Hoboken, NJ, 2009.

28. J. Pearl, (Ed.). *Probabilistic Reasoning in Intelligent Systems: Networks of Plausible Inference*. Morgan Kaufmann, San Francisco, 1988.

29. W. A. Schulz. *Molecular Biology of Human Cancers: An Advanced Student's Textbook*. Springer, Dordrecht, The Netherlands, 2007.

30. R. M. Simon, E. L. Korn, L. M. McShane, M. D. Radmacher, G. W. Wright, and Y. Zhao. *Design and Analysis of DNA Microarray Investigations*, Springer-Verlag, New York, 2003.

31. L. Song, J. Bedo, K. M. Borgwardt, A. Gretton, and A. J. Smola. Gene selection via the BAHSIC family of algorithms. *Bioinformatics*, 23(13):i490–i498, 2007.

32. L. Song, A. Smola, A. Gretton, K. Borgwardt, and J. Bedo. Supervised feature selection via dependence estimation. In Z. Ghahramani, (Ed.), *Proceedings of the 24th International Conference on Machine Learning*, 2007, Corvallis, OR, ACM, New York, NY, pp. 823–830.

33. T. Speed, (Ed.). *Statistical Analysis of Gene Expression Microarray Data*. Chapman & Hall/CRC Press, Boca Raton, FL, 2003.

34. W.-H. Steeb. *Problems and Solutions in Introductory and Advanced Matrix Calculus*. World Scientific, Singapore, 2006.

35. R. Tibshirani, T. Hastie, B. Narasimhan, and G. Chu. Diagnosis of multiple cancer types by shrunken centroids of gene expression. *Proc. Nat. Acad. Sci. USA*, 99(10):6567–6572, 2002.

36. R. Tibshirani, T. Hastie, B. Narasimhan, and G. Chu. Class prediction by nearest shrunken centroids, with applications to DNA microarrays. *Statist. Sci.* 18(1):104–117, 2003.

37. L. J. van 't Veer, et al. Gene expression profiling predicts clinical outcome of breast cancer. *Nature* 415:530–536, 2002.

38. R. Varshavsky, A. Gottlieb, M. Linial, and D. Horn. Novel unsupervised feature filtering of biological data. *Bioinformatics* 22(14):e507–e513, 2006.

39. V. E. Velculescu, L. Zhang, B. Vogelstein, and K. W. Kinzler. Serial analysis of gene expression. *Science*, 270(5235):484–487, 1995.

40. R. A. Weinberg. *The Biology of Cancer*. Garland Science, New York, 2007.

41. L. Yu. Feature selection for genomic data analysis. In H. Liu and H. Motoda, (Eds.), *Computational Methods of Feature Selection*. Chapman & Hall/CRC, Boca Raton, FL, 2008, pp. 337–354.

42. A. Zhang. *Advanced Analysis of Gene Expression Microarray Data*. World Scientific, Singapore, 2006.

CHAPTER 17

INFORMATION-THEORETIC GENE SELECTION IN EXPRESSION DATA

PATRICK E. MEYER and GIANLUCA BONTEMPI

Machine Learning Group, Computer Science Department, Université Libre de Bruxelles, Brussels, Belgium

17.1 INTRODUCTION

Genomewide patterns of gene expression represent a snapshot of the state of a cell in a given condition. Using different snapshots taken under different conditions, it becomes possible to build statistical models that can efficiently classify and predict new snapshots. A typical application of such techniques consists in discovering new molecular signatures of tumor cells for diagnostic and prognostic purposes [52, 53]. However, the detection of functional relationships between genes as well as the design of effective models from expression data is a major statistical challenge, mainly because of the data dimensionality. Expression data sets are typically characterized by a low number of noisy samples together with a high number of variables. As a result, even a simple predictive model such as a linear regression cannot be used without eliminating irrelevant and redundant variables as a first step [30]. A number of experimental studies [6, 28, 46] have shown that the elimination of irrelevant and redundant variables as well as the selection of synergetic variables [24, 35] can dramatically increase the predictive accuracy of models built from data. Moreover, variable selection can decrease future measurements and storage requirements [20] while increasing the intelligibility of a model.

In order to derive efficient methods of variable selection, formal definitions of *relevance, redundancy*, and *synergy* of variables have been defined. *Information theory*, a theory introduced for data transmission and signal compression [48] and widely used in areas such as statistics, physics, economics or biology, provides a particularly adapted framework for measuring, quantifying, and defining variable interactions [38].

The outline of this chapter is the following. Section 17.2 introduces the curse of dimensionality. Section 17.3 focuses on widely used variable exploration strategies. Section 17.4 intoduces the information-theoretic framework. Section 17.5 recalls variable selection techniques which have been proposed in the literature. Section 17.6 introduces

Biological Knowledge Discovery Handbook: Preprocessing, Mining, and Postprocessing of Biological Data, First Edition. Edited by Mourad Elloumi and Albert Y. Zomaya.
© 2014 John Wiley & Sons, Inc. Published 2014 by John Wiley & Sons, Inc.

estimation techniques that can be used for implementing the selection strategies on the basis of observed data.

17.2 CURSE OF DIMENSIONALITY

A natural question arises when it comes to make experiments or measurements: "how many experiments do I need in order to obtain a clear signal in my data?" or even "how many genes can I select when I have made 100 experiments"?

Although the question cannot be answered directly, it is easy to give an intuition behind "the curse of dimensionality." Most expression data sets provide continuous measurements of gene activities. However, in order to illustrate the problem, we will consider discretized variables, such as binary variables, that is, genes that can be either "on" or "off." Binary variables have been studied extensively in statistics and the question that was raised at the time was "how many tosses of a coin should I make in order to assess if the coin is fair?" Although genes and coins are very different entities of a physical world, statisticians view them both as *random variables*. The more experiments you have, the more confident you are in your estimate of the probability distribution of a random variable. Let us assume that you need an average of 5 samples per possible event (on or off) in order to have a good estimate of the distribution of a random variable, that is, you require 10 samples in order to assess if a coin is fair. Now if you consider a joint distribution of 2 binary variables, you are estimating a distribution that has four distinct possibilities (gene 1 on–gene 2 on, gene 1 on–gene 2 off, gene 1 off–gene 2 on, gene 1 off–gene 2 off). You then require 20 samples. As you are estimating a joint distribution of 4 ternary variables (on, off, or in between), you have $3 \times 3 \times 3 \times 3 = 81$ possibilities. Hence with the requirement of 5 samples by possibilities, you now need 405 samples to have an estimate of a joint distribution of only 4 ternary variables. In general, if you consider estimating a d-variate probability distribution of variables, each one discretized in p bins and you need an average of 5 samples per bin, then you need $5p^d$ samples. You can, however, reduce the number of samples required by decreasing your estimation accuracy requirements (less than an average of 5 samples by possibilities) or by making more constraining assumptions on the joint distribution of these variables (such as assuming that some events are unlikely).

17.3 VARIABLE SELECTION EXPLORATION STRATEGIES

Let us consider the following problem: Given d number of variables to select, is there an algorithm that can select the optimal subset of variables of a given size?

Unfortunately, various results, like the theorem by Cover and Van Campenhout [14], show that finding the optimal subset of size d among n variables requires to test all $\binom{n}{d}$ combinations of subsets. However, this is impossible in practice, since it would take too much time to compute all of them. Hence, search heuristics have been used to reach a good predictive subset of variables.

Let us denote A the search space of $\binom{n}{d}$ subsets of random variables of X having size d. Variable selection can be seen as a combinatorial optimization problem [28] which depends on:

1. A method of exploring the space A (including the starting point and the stop criterion)
2. An evaluation function returning a measure of accuracy

More formally the problem is: Given n input variables X and a performance measure $F : A \rightarrow \mathbb{R}$, find the subset $X_S \subset X$ which maximizes the performance,

$$X_S^{\max} = \arg \max_{X_S \in A} F(X_S) \qquad (17.1)$$

Exploration strategies can be classified into three main categories of combinatorial optimization algorithms, namely, *optimal search*, *stochastic search*, and *sequential search* (see [21], Chapter 4):

1. Optimal search strategies include exhaustive search and branch-and-bound methods [21]. Their high computational complexity makes them impracticable with a high number of inputs and, for this reason, they are not discussed in this work.

2. Stochastic search strategies are also called *randomized* or *nondeterministic* [45] because two runs of these methods (with the same inputs) will not necessarily lead to the same result [16]. These methods explore a smaller portion of the search space A by using rules often inspired by nature. Some examples are simulated annealing [16], tabu search [16], and genetic algorithms [16, 55].

3. Sequential search strategies are also called *deterministic heuristics* [45]. These methods are widely used for variable selection [9, 17, 18, 43]. Most of them use a neighbor search (two subsets are said neighbors if they differ from one variable) to discover a local optimum. Some examples are forward selection (see Section 17.3.1), backward elimination (see Section 17.3.2), and bidirectional search (see Section 17.3.3).

Because of their simplicity and their wide adoption in the variable selection community, we focus here on the three main sequential strategies, namely, the forward selection, the backward one, and the bidirectional one.

In the following, we denote by X the complete initial set of variables and by $X_i^{\text{METH}} \in X$, $i \in A = \{1, 2, \ldots, n\}$, the variable selected at each step by the method METH; X_S and X_R are the sets of selected variables and remaining variables, respectively. Hence, at each step $X = \{X_S, X_R\}$; X_i or X_j usually denotes a variable in X_R or in X_S, respectively.

17.3.1 Forward Selection Search

Forward selection [9, 28] is a sequential search method that starts with an empty set of variables $X_S = \emptyset$. At each step, it selects the variable X_t that brings the best improvement [in terms of a given evaluation criterion $F(\cdot)$]. A pseudo code of the method is given in Algorithm 17.1. As a consequence of the sequential process, each selected variable influences the evaluations of the following steps.

This search has been widely used in variable selection, (see [6, 9, 28]). The forward-selection algorithm selects a subset of $d < n$ variables in d steps and explores only $\sum_{i=0}^{d-1} (n - i)$ subsets.

However, this search has some weaknesses:

1. Two variables that are synergetic (i.e., highly relevant only once taken together; see Section 17.4.3) appear as not relevant if taken individually and are as a consequence ignored by this procedure,

ALGORITHM 17.1

```
Inputs:  input variables X, the output variable Y, a maximal subset
size d > 0, a performance measure F(·) to maximize
```

$X_S := \phi$
$X_R := X$
while $(|X_S| < d)$
      $maxscore := -\infty$
      for all the inputs X_i in the search space X_R
            Evaluate $F(X_{S,i})$ for the variable X_i with X_S the subset
of selected variables.
            if $(F(X_{S,i}) > maxscore)$
                $X_t := X_i$
                $maxscore := F(X_{S,i})$
            end-if
      end-for
      $X_S := X_{S,t}$
      $X_R := X_{R-t}$
end-while
```
```
Output: the subset X_S
```

2. Selecting the best variable at each step does not mean selecting the best subset. Indeed, suppose that we have the following situation:

$$Y = f(X_5, X_4, X_3) + N(0, \sigma_1) = f(X_1, X_2) + N(0, \sigma_2) \qquad (17.2)$$

where $N(\mu, \sigma)$ denotes a normally distributed noise with mean $\mu$ and variance $\sigma$. If we have the order of univariate relevance

$$\text{rel}(X_5) > \text{rel}(X_1) > \text{rel}(X_2) > \text{rel}(X_4) \geq \text{rel}(X_3) \qquad (17.3)$$

and

$$\sigma_1 > \sigma_2 \qquad (17.4)$$

the best subset should be $X_{1,2} = \{X_1, X_2\}$ because the variance of the noise is smaller. Also, there are less variables in the latter combination, which usually leads to a lower number of parameters to estimate in a model. However, the forward-selection algorithm will, in many cases, select the subset $X_{3,4,5} = \{X_5, X_4, X_3\}$. Indeed, it first selects $X_5$ because $X_5$ is the most relevant variable. Given $X_5$, the best improvement can be brought by $X_4$, and given $\{X_5, X_4\}$, $X_3$ can be the best variable to select.

### 17.3.2 Backward-Elimination Search

Backward elimination [9, 28, 39] is a search method that starts by evaluating a subset containing all the variables $X_S = X$ and progressively discards the least relevant variables. For instance, at the second step, the method compares $n$ subsets of $n - 1$ inputs. The variable $X_t$ associated with the least favorable improvement of accuracy is eliminated. The process
```

ALGORITHM 17.2

```
Inputs: input variables X (the input space), the output variable
Y, a minimal subset size d > 0, and a performance measure F(·)
to maximize
```

$X_S := X$
while $(|X_S| > d)$
      $worstscore := \infty$
      for all inputs X_j in the subset X_S
            Evaluate $F(X_{S-j})$, with all inputs of the subset X_S
without X_j
                if ($F(X_{S-j}) < worstscore$)
                    $X_t := X_i$
                    $worstscore := F(X_{S-j})$
                end-if
        end-for
        $X_S := X_{S-t}$
end-while
```
Output: the subset $X_S$
```

---

is repeated until it yields the chosen number of inputs d (see Algorithm 17.2). This method does not suffer from the risk of ignoring a pair of complementary variables as it is the case for forward selection.

17.3.3 Bidirectional Search

The strengths of forward selection and of backward elimination can be combined in different manners.

As an example, let 26 random variables constitute the search space and be denoted by letters of the alphabet. Let the best subset of four variables be denoted by the letters $\{B, E, S, T\}$. The forward and the backward approaches can be combined in different ways:

- *Using Backward Elimination on Subset Selected with Forward Search* [9] If a forward selection has selected the subset $\{C, B, E, S, T, D, F, G\}$, then we can use backward elimination to keep the most important variables of the subset and reach the subset $\{B, E, S, T\}$.
- *Performing Stepwise Approach* [9, 39] At each step, choose the best action between eliminating a variable or selecting one. In our example, we may at some stage have selected the subset $\{E, A, S, T\}$. The stepwise algorithm chooses between adding a variable that brings the best improvement $\{B, E, A, S, T\}$ or eliminating the less important variable $\{E, S, T\}$.
- *Using Sequential Replacement* [9, 39] This procedure consists in replacing $k \geq 1$ variables at each step. In our example, we can imagine at some stage having the subset $\{P, E, S, T\}$ that becomes the subset $\{B, E, S, T\}$ after an iteration. The pseudo code of the algorithm for $k = 1$ is described in Algorithm 17.3.

ALGORITHM 17.3

Inputs: a selected subset of inputs X_S, the set of remaining
variables X_R, the output variable Y, and a performance measure
$F(\cdot)$ to maximize

do

   for all inputs X_i in the remaining variables X_R
        Evaluate $F(X_{S,i})$
   end-for
   $X_{t1} := \arg\max_{X_i} F(X_{S,i})$
   for all for all inputs X_j in the subset X_S
        Evaluate the $F(X_{S-j})$
   end-for
   $X_{t2} := \arg\max_{X_j} F(X_{S-j})$
   $X_S := X_{(S,t1)-t2}$
   $X_R := X_{(R,t2)-t1}$
end-do while $X_{t1} \neq X_{t2}$
Output: the subset X_S

17.4 RELEVANCE, REDUNDANCY, AND SYNERGY

In order to improve the resolution of the two variable selection problems stated above, that is, subset estimation and search of good combination, many variable selection criteria have been developed in the past decade. These criteria focus on (1) selecting relevant variables without having to estimate accurately the full joint distribution of a subset and (2) guiding the heuristic search in the space of combinations.

These variable selection criteria have been built around three main notions: relevance, redundancy, and synergy. These three notions can be efficiently formulated in an information-theoretic framework that is introduced in the following sections. For simplicity, we consider here discrete variables though the theory can be extended to the continuous-variable case.

17.4.1 Relevance

In this section entropy, conditional entropy, and mutual information are defined. These notions will be intensively used in the following in order to define relevance, redundancy, and synergy.

The *entropy* [10] of a discrete random variable Y with probability mass function $p(Y)$ is defined by

$$H(Y) = H(p(Y)) = -\sum_{y \in \mathcal{Y}} p(y) \log p(y) = E_Y \left[\log \frac{1}{p(y)} \right] \qquad (17.5)$$

Note that this definition remains valid for a discrete random vector (i.e., a subset of random variables).

The usual unit of the entropy is the *bit*. However, other units are sometimes chosen for this measure. The unit depends on the base taken for the logarithm of Equation (17.5), base

2 for bit, base 10 for *ban*. The *deciban* (one-tenth of a ban) is also known as a useful measure of belief since 10 decibans correspond to an odds ratio of 10 : 1; 20 decibans to 100 : 1 odds, 30 decibans to 1000 : 1, and so on [25]. The natural logarithm (base e) is increasingly used for computational reasons and in this case the unit is the *nat*.

The *conditional entropy* of Y given X is

$$H(Y|X) = H(Y, X) - H(X) \tag{17.6}$$

This quantity measures the uncertainty of a variable once another one is known.

The reduction of entropy due to conditioning can be quantified by a symmetric measure called *mutual information* [10]:

$$H(Y) - H(Y|X) = I(Y; X) = I(X; Y) = H(X) - H(X|Y) \tag{17.7}$$

The *mutual information* between X and Y is

$$I(Y; X) = \sum_{x \in \mathcal{X}} \sum_{y \in \mathcal{Y}} p(x, y) \log\left(\frac{p(x, y)}{p(x)p(y)}\right) \tag{17.8}$$

Mutual information can be also viewed as a divergence between the joint distribution $p(X, Y)$ and the product distribution $p(X)p(Y)$ [10] or between the marginal distribution $p(X)$ and a conditional distribution $p(X|Y)$. As a consequence, when two variables are independent, their mutual information is null and the higher the dependency between the variables, the higher the value of the mutual information. When the two variables are identical, this measure reaches its maximum and is equal to the entropy of the variable, that is, $I(X; X) = H(X)$.

The mutual information is a natural measure of relevance since it quantifies the dependency level between random variables. The use of mutual information as relevance measure traces back to [11]. Later, [50] introduced a selection criterion called the *information bottleneck*, which also uses mutual information as a a relevance measure. Kojadinovic [29] defines the *relevance* of a set X_S to an output variable Y as the mutual information $I(X_S; Y)$.

As a result, the relevance of an input variable X_i knowing a set X_S to an output variable Y is the gain of relevance resulting from using X_i additionally to X_S:

$$I(X_i; Y|X_S) = I(\{X_S, X_i\}; Y) - I(X_S; Y) \tag{17.9}$$

This quantity is precisely the conditional mutual information [10]. Its normalized version (i.e., constrained to range between zero and one) has been introduced by [5] in a variable selection procedure.

Note that it is possible to increase the information of a variable with another by appropriate conditioning, as shown in the following example.

Let Y and X be two independent random variables and Z be a random variable defined as a deterministic function of Y and X [see Equation (17.10)].

$$X \rightarrow Z \leftarrow Y \tag{17.10}$$

As X and Y are independent, we have $I(X; Y) = 0$, and since $Z = f(X, Y)$, we obtain $I(X; Y|Z) > 0$. As a result, the conditional mutual information is higher than the mutual information, that is, $I(X; Y|Z) > I(X; Y)$, which means that conditioning can increase relevance.

17.4.2 Redundancy

According to [54], a redundancy measure should be symmetric, nonnegative, and nondecreasing with the number of variables. The monotonicity is justified by the fact that, unlike relevance, the amount of redundancy of a variable can never decrease when more variables are added. As a result, [54] proposed to use multi-information [34]. This measure used in [49] is called *total correlation* in [23]. The multi-information between n sets of random variables $X_1, X_2, \ldots, X_n$ is

$$R(X_i; \ldots; X_n) = \sum_{i=1}^{n} H(X_i) - H(X_1, X_2, \ldots, X_n) \tag{17.11}$$

Note that in the two-variables case

$$R(X_i; X_j) = H(X_i) + H(X_j) - H(X_i, X_j) = I(X_i; X_j) \tag{17.12}$$

While the relevance measure concerns the relation between inputs and outputs, the bivariate redundancy measure applies exclusively to input variables.

17.4.3 Synergy

Synergy and redundancy are two sides of a coin that has been called *variable interaction*. The definition of variable interaction in information-theoretic terms can be found in the seminal paper of [34] and, more recently, in [23].

The interaction among n sets of random variables $X_1, X_2, \ldots, X_n$ is defined as

$$C(X_1; X_2; \ldots; X_n) = \sum_{k=1}^{n} \sum_{S \subseteq \{1, \ldots, n\}: |S| = k} (-1)^{k+1} H(X_S) \tag{17.13}$$

Given a random vector X and a random variable Y the link between mutual information $I(X; Y)$ and interaction information is made explicit by the following formula from [29]:

$$I(X; Y) = \sum_{i \in A} C(X_i; Y) - \sum_{i, j \in A} C(X_i; X_j; Y) \\ + \cdots + (-1)^{n+1} C(X_1; X_2; \ldots; X_n; Y) \tag{17.14}$$

with $C(X_i; Y) = I(X_i; Y)$.

In plain words, mutual information can be seen as a series where higher order terms are corrective terms that represent the effect of the multivariate interaction. In most cases, the measure of interaction is positive and it indicates that the n sets of variables share a common information (redundancy). However, interaction can be negative. In the latter case, the variables are said to be complementary [35] or synergetic [2].

The synergy effect was mentioned in several variable selection papers [20, 23, 24, 28] and has been explicitly used in variable selection algorithms only recently [29, 35, 59].

In particular, the synergy between two random features X_i and X_j and the output Y

$$-C(X_i; X_j; Y) = -H(X_i) - H(X_j) - H(Y) \\ + H(X_i, X_j) + H(X_i, Y) + H(X_j, Y) - H(X_i, X_j, Y) \tag{17.15} \\ = I(X_{i,j}; Y) - (I(X_i; Y) + I(X_j; Y))$$

measures the gain resulting from using the joint mutual information of two variables X_i and X_j instead of the sum of the univariate informations. It is well known, indeed, that the joint information of two random variables, that is, $I(X_{i,j}; Y)$ can be higher than the sum of their individual information $I(X_i; Y)$ and $I(X_j; Y)$.

An example of synergy is Equation (17.10), where conditioning increases relevance. Another known illustration of this phenomenon is the XOR problem as pointed out by [28]:

X_1	X_2	$Y = X_1 \oplus X_2$
1	1	0
1	0	1
0	1	1
0	0	0

One can see that X_1 and X_2 have a null relevance individually, that is, $I(X_1; Y) = 0$, $I(X_2; Y) = 0$, whereas together $X_{1,2}$ has a maximal relevance, that is, $I(X_{1,2}; Y) = H(Y) > 0$. Synergy explains why a combination of apparently irrelevant variables can perform efficiently in a learning task. It also gives an intuition behind the Cover and Van Campenhout theorem [14] mentionned earlier, which requires that all combinations of the subset be tested to find the optimal one.

17.5 INFORMATION-THEORETIC FILTERS

Variable selection methods based on mutual information are also called *information-theoretic filters*.

Let us start by stating the objective of an *information-theoretic filter*: *Given a training data set D_m of m samples, an output variable Y, n input variables X, and an integer $d \le n$, find the subset $X_S \subseteq X$ of size d that maximizes the mutual information $I(X_S; Y)$.*

In other words, the objective of *filter variable selection* (for a given d) is to find the subset X_S, with $|X_S| = d$, such that

$$X_S^{\max} = \arg \max_{X_S \subseteq X : |X_S| = d} I(X_S; Y) \tag{17.16}$$

This is a particular case of (17.1), where the evaluation function $F(X_S)$ is the mutual information $I(X_S; Y)$. We assume that the number of variables d has been determined by some a priori knowledge or by some cross-validation techniques. As filters often rank the variables according to their relevance measure, variables can be added one by one in a predictive model until the cross-validated performances decrease. This procedure allows to reach an adequate number of variables for a given predictive model. Other strategies can be adopted such as the information bottleneck [50], Bayesian confidence on parametric estimations [27], or resampling techniques [19].

In the following, we review the most important filter selection methods found in the literature which are based on information theory. We present the algorithms by stressing when and where the notions of relevance, redundancy, and synergy are used.

17.5.1 Variable Ranking

The *variable-ranking* (RANK) method returns a ranking of variables on the basis of their individual mutual informations with the output. This means that, given n input variables, the method first computes n times the quantity $I(X_i, Y)$, $i = 1, \ldots, n$, then ranks the variables according to this quantity, and eventually discards the least relevant ones [3, 17].

The main advantage of this method is its low computational cost. Indeed, it requires only n computations of bivariate mutual information. The main drawback derives from the fact that possible redundancies between variables are not taken into account. Indeed, two redundant variables, yet highly relevant taken individually, will be both well ranked. On the contrary, two variables could be synergetic to the output (i.e., highly relevant together) while being poorly relevant once each is taken individually. As a consequence, these variables could be badly ranked, or even eliminated, by a ranking filter.

17.5.2 Fast Correlation–Based Filter

Fast correlation–based filtering (FCBF) is a ranking method combined with a redundancy analysis which has been proposed in [58]. The FCBF starts by selecting the variable (in the remaining variables X_R) with the highest mutual information, denoted by X_i^{FCBF}. Then, all the variables which are less relevant to Y than redundant to X_i^{FCBF} are eliminated from the list. For example, X_i is removed from the remaining variable set X_R if

$$I\left(X_i; X_i^{\text{FCBF}}\right) > I(X_i; Y) \tag{17.17}$$

At the next step, the algorithm repeats the selection and the elimination steps. The procedure stops when no more variables remain to be taken into consideration.

In other words, at each step, the set of selected variables X_S is updated with the variable

$$X_i^{\text{FCBF}} = \arg \max_{X_i \in X_R} I(X_i; Y) \tag{17.18}$$

and the set of remaining variables X_R is updated by removing the set

$$\left\{ X_i \in X_{R-i} : \ I(X_i; Y) < I\left(X_i; X_i^{\text{FCBF}}\right) \right\} \tag{17.19}$$

This method is affordable because a few (less than n^2) evaluations of bivariate mutual information are computed. However, although the method addresses redundancy, it presents the risk of eliminating relevant and synergetic variables. Another drawback of this method is that it does not return a complete ranking of the variables of the data set. In [58], this approach is shown competitive with two filters [1, 31]. Note that in [58] a normalized measure of mutual information called *symmetrical uncertainty* is used, that is,

$$\text{SU}(X, Y) = \frac{2I(X; Y)}{H(X) + H(Y)} \tag{17.20}$$

This measure helps to improve the performances of the selection by penalizing inputs with large entropies.

17.5.3 Backward Elimination and Relevance Criterion

Let $X_S^{\max} \subset X$ be the target subset, that is, the subset X_S of size d, that achieves the maximal mutual information with the output (17.16). By the chain rule for mutual information [10],

$$I(X; Y) = I\left(X_S^{\max}; Y\right) + I\left(X_R^{\max}; Y | X_S^{\max}\right) \tag{17.21}$$

where $X_R = X_{-S}$ is the set difference between the original set of inputs X and the set of variables X_S selected so far.

The backward elimination (using mutual information) [47] starts with $X_S = X$ and, at each step, eliminates from the set of selected variable X_S, the variable X_j^{back} having the lowest relevance on Y,

$$X_j^{\text{back}} = \arg \min_{X_j \in X_S} I(X_j; Y | X_{S-j}) \tag{17.22}$$

In other words, X_j^{back} is an approximation of $X_R^{\max}$ in (17.21). The approximation is exact for a subset size $d = n - 1$ of one variable less than the complete set. The elimination process is then repeated until the desired size is reached. However, this approach is intractable for large variable sets since the beginning of the procedure requires the estimation of a multivariate density that includes the whole set of variables X.

17.5.4 Markov Blanket Elimination

The Markov blanket elimination [30] consists in approximating $I(X_j; Y | X_{S-j})$ in (17.22) by $I(X_j; Y | X_{M_j})$ with $X_{M_j} \subset X_{S-j}$ a subset of variables, that is, the Markov blanket, having limited fixed size k. The algorithm proceeds in two phases. First, for every variable X_j in the selected set X_S, k variables X_{M_j} are selected among the variables X_{S-j}. Second, the least relevant variable X_j^{MB} (conditioned on the selected subset $X_{M_j} \subseteq X_{S-j}$) is eliminated, that is, $X_S = X_S \setminus X_j^{\text{MB}}$:

$$X_j^{\text{MB}} = \arg \min_{X_j \in X_S} I(X_j; Y | X_{M_j}) \tag{17.23}$$

The process is repeated until the selected variable set X_S contains no more irrelevant and redundant variables or when the desired subset size is reached. The method is named from the fact that X_{M_j} is an approximate Markov blanket. In [30], the Pearson correlation coefficient [26] is used in order to find the k variables most correlated to the candidate X_j. These k variables are considered as the Markov blanket X_{M_j} of the candidate X_j. In this way, only linear dependencies between variables are considered. However, more complex functions can make the algorithm very slow. In fact, finding a Markov blanket is itself a variable selection task. As a result, this method is adapted to large dimensionality problems only with very strong assumptions on the structure of X_M.

17.5.5 Forward Selection and Relevance Criterion

A way to sequentially maximize the *relevance* (REL) quantity $I(X_S; Y)$ in (17.16) is provided by the chain rule for mutual information [10]:

$$I(X_{S'}; Y) = I(X_S; Y) + I(X_i; Y | X_S) \tag{17.24}$$

where $X_{S'} = X_{S,i}$ is the updated set of variables. Rather than maximizing the left-hand-side term directly, the idea of the forward selection combined with the relevance criterion consists in maximizing sequentially the second term of the right-hand term, $I(X_i; Y | X_S)$. In other words, the approach consists in updating a set of selected variables X_S with the variable X_i^{REL} featuring the maximum relevance.

In analytical terms, the variable X_i^{REL} returned by the relevance criterion at each step is

$$X_i^{\mathrm{REL}} = \arg \max_{X_i \in X_R} \{I(X_i; Y | X_S)\} \tag{17.25}$$

where $X_R = X_{-S}$ is the difference between the original set of inputs X and the set of variables X_S selected so far. This strategy prevents from selecting a variable which, though relevant to Y, is redundant with respect to a previously selected one. This algorithm has been used in [3, 5, 7, 47]. In [5], a normalized version of relevance is used.

Although this method is appealing, it presents some major drawbacks. The estimation of the relevance requires the estimation of large multivariate densities. For instance, at the dth step of the forward search, the search algorithm requires $n - d$ evaluations, where each evaluation requires in turn the computation of a $(d + 1)$-variate density. It is known that for a large d the estimations are poorly accurate and/or computationally expensive [44]. In particular, in the small-sample settings (around 100), having an accurate estimation of large $(d > 3)$ multivariate densities is difficult (see Section 17.2). For these reasons, the recent filter literature adopt selection criteria based on bi- and trivariate densities at most.

17.5.6 Forward Selection and Conditional Mutual Information Maximization Criterion

The *conditional mutual information maximization* (CMIM) *criterion* approach [18] proposes to select the variable $X_i \in X_R$ whose minimal relevance $I(X_i; Y | X_j)$ conditioned to each selected variable taken separately, $X_j \in X_S$, is maximal. This requires the computation of the mutual information of X_i and the output Y conditioned on each variable $X_j \in X_S$ previously selected.

Formally, the variable returned according to the CMIM is

$$X_i^{\mathrm{CMIM}} = \arg \max_{X_i \in X_R} \{ \min_{X_j \in X_S} I(X_i; Y | X_j) \} \tag{17.26}$$

A variable X_i can be selected only if its information to the output Y has not been caught by an already selected variable X_j.

The CMIM criterion is an approximation of the relevance criterion,

$$X_i^{\mathrm{REL}} = \arg \max_{X_i \in X_R} \{I(X_i; Y | X_S)\} \tag{17.27}$$

where $I(X_i; Y | X_S)$ is replaced by $\min_{X_j \in X_S}(I(X_i; Y | X_j))$.

Fleuret [18] shows experiments where CMIM is competitive with FCBF [58] in selecting binary variables for a pattern recognition task. This criterion selects relevant variables, avoids redundancy, avoids estimating high-dimensional multivariate densities, and does not ignore complementarity two-by-two. However, it does not necessarily select a variable complementary to the already selected variables. Indeed, a variable that has a high negative interaction to the already selected variable will be characterized by a large conditional mutual information with that variable but not necessarily by a large minimal conditional information. In the XOR problem, for instance, the synergetic variables have a null relevance taken alone. In that case, $\min_{X_j \in X_S} I(X_i; Y | X_j) = 0$ and CMIM would not select those variable.

17.5.7 Forward Selection and Minimum Redundancy–Maximum Relevance Criterion

The *minimum redundancy–maximum relevance* (MRMR) criterion has been proposed in [43, 44, 51] in combination with a forward-selection search strategy. Given a set X_S of selected variables, the method updates X_S with the variable $X_i \in X_R$ that maximizes $v_i - z_i$, where v_i is a relevance term and z_i is a redundancy term. More precisely, v_i is the relevance of X_i to the output Y alone, and z_i is the average redundancy of X_i to each selected variables $X_j \in X_S$:

$$v_i = I(X_i; Y) \tag{17.28}$$

$$z_i = \frac{1}{|X_S|} \sum_{X_j \in X_S} I(X_i; X_j) \tag{17.29}$$

$$X_i^{\text{MRMR}} = \arg \max_{X_i \in X_R} \{v_i - z_i\} \tag{17.30}$$

At each step, this method selects the variable which has the best trade-off between relevance and redundancy. This selection criterion is fast and efficient. At step d of the forward search, the search algorithm computes $n - d$ evaluations where each evaluation requires the estimation of $d + 1$ bivariate densities (one for each already selected variable plus one with the output). As a result, MRMR avoids the estimation of multivariate densities by using multiple bivariate densities.

A justification of MRMR given by the authors [44] is that

$$I(X; Y) = H(X) + H(Y) - H(X, Y) \tag{17.31}$$

with

$$R(X_1; X_2; \ldots; X_n) = \sum_{i=1}^{n} H(X_i) - H(X) \tag{17.32}$$

and

$$R(X_1; X_2; \ldots; X_n; Y) = \sum_{i=1}^{n} H(X_i) + H(Y) - H(X, Y) \tag{17.33}$$

Hence

$$I(X; Y) = R(X_1; X_2; \ldots; X_n; Y) - R(X_1; X_2; \ldots; X_n) \tag{17.34}$$

where:

- The minimum of the second term $R(X_1; X_2; \ldots; X_n)$ is reached for independent variables since, in that case, $H(X) = \sum_i H(X_i)$ and $R(X_1; X_2; \ldots; X_n) = \sum_i H(X_i) - H(X) = 0$. Hence, if a subset of variables X_S is already selected, a variable X_i should have a minimal redundancy $I(X_i; X_S)$ with the subset. Pairwise independency does not guarantee independency. However, the authors approximate $I(X_i; X_S)$ with $\frac{1}{|S|} \sum_{j \in S} I(X_i; X_j)$.
- The maximum of the first term $R(X_1; X_2; \ldots; X_n; Y)$ is attained for maximally dependent variables.

Qualitatively, in a sequential setting where a selected subset X_S is given, independence between the variables in X is reached by minimizing $(1/|X_S|) \sum_{X_j \in X_S} I(X_i; X_j) \simeq I(X_i; X_S)$ and maximizing dependency between the variables of X and of Y, that is, by maximizing $I(X_i; Y)$.

Although the method addresses the issue of bivariate redundancy through the term z_i, it does not capture synergy between variables. This can be ineffective in situations like see Equation (17.10), where, although the set $\{X, Z\}$ is very relevant for predicting Y, once X has been selected Z will not since:

1. The redundancy term z_i is large due to the redundancy of X and Z.
2. The relevance term v_i is small since Z alone is not relevant to Y.

Nonetheless, MRMR has been sucessfully used for network inference tasks when coupled with forward, backward, and bidirectional searches [36, 37].

17.5.8 Forward Selection and Minimum Interaction–Maximum Relevance Criterion

The *minimum interaction–maximum relevance* (MIMR) criterion, also called *double-input symmetrical relevance* (DISR) in a previous version, has been proposed in [8, 35] in combination with a forward-selection search strategy. Given a set X_S of selected variables, the method updates X_S with the variable $X_i \in X_R$ that maximizes $v_i - w_i$, where v_i is a relevance term and w_i is an interaction term. As in MRMR, v_i is the relevance of X_i to the output Y alone; however, in MIMR the second term w_i is an average interaction of X_i to each selected variable $X_j \in X_S$:

$$v_i = I(X_i; Y) \tag{17.35}$$

$$w_i = \frac{1}{|X_S|} \sum_{X_j \in X_S} C(X_i; X_j; Y) \tag{17.36}$$

$$X_i^{\text{MIMR}} = \arg \max_{X_i \in X_R} \{v_i - w_i\} \tag{17.37}$$

At each step, this method selects the variable which has the best trade-off between relevance and interaction. At step d of the forward search, the search algorithm computes $n - d$ evaluations where each evaluation requires the estimation of a bivariate density plus d trivariate ones. Assuming normally distributed variables, trivariate densities can even be computed with bivariate terms, leading to much faster selection of variables. This criterion eliminates redundant variables (because they are penalized by a positive w_i) but also tends to select synergetic variables (because of their negative w_i) while avoiding the estimation of multivariate densities.

A theoretical justification of MIMR given by the authors is that

$$I(X_S; Y) \geq \frac{1}{\binom{d}{2}} \sum_{X_i \in X_S} \sum_{X_j \in X_S} I(X_{i,j}; Y) \tag{17.38}$$

TABLE 17.1   Comparison of Relevance, Redundancy and Synergy, Ability to Avoid Estimation of Large Multivariate Densities and Ability to Rank Variables Selection Criterion

Methods	RANK	FCBF	REL	CMIM	MRMR	MIMR
Select relevance	Yes	Yes	Yes	Yes	Yes	Yes
Eliminate redundancy	No	Yes	Yes	Yes	Yes	Yes
Two-variable synergy	No	No	Yes	No	No	Yes
Avoid multivariate density	Yes	Yes	No	Yes	Yes	Yes
Return ranking	Yes	No	Yes	Yes	Yes	Yes

TABLE 17.2   Computational Cost of Variable Evaluation Using Rel, CMIN, MRMR, and MIMR

Variable Evaluation	RANK	REL	CMIM	MRMR	MIMR
Calls of mutual information	1	1	d	$d+1$	$d+1$
k-Variate density	2	$d+1$	3	2	3
Computational cost	$O(C)$	$O(d \times C)$	$O(d \times C)$	$O(d \times C)$	$O(d \times C)$

Note: C the cost of a mutual information estimation.

with

$$\arg \max_{X_i \in X_S} \sum_{X_j \in X_S} I(X_{i,j}; Y) = \arg \max_{X_i \in X_S} \left\{ I(X_i; Y) - \frac{1}{|X_S|} \sum_{X_j \in X_S} C(X_i; X_j; Y) \right\} \quad (17.39)$$

17.5.9 Theoretical Comparison of Filters

The presented criteria can be analyzed under different perspectives. In Table 17.1 we stress:

1. Which issues, among relevance, redundancy, and synergy, are taken into account
2. The ability of a criterion to avoid the estimation of large multivariate densities
3. Whether it returns a ranking of variables

Table 17.2 reports a comparative analysis of the different techniques in terms of computational complexity of the evaluation step.

We observe from Tables 17.1 and 17.2 that the MIMR criterion avoids redundant variables and multivariate density estimation but selects synergetic variables (up to the second order) at the same computational cost as CMIM and MRMR. Numerous experimental studies have shown the performances of MRMR and MIMR on expression data sets [8, 38].

17.6 FAST MUTUAL INFORMATION ESTIMATION

Table 17.2 shows that the computational complexity of most filters strongly depends on the cost of estimation of bi - and trivariate mutual information. We present here two very simple estimators that have shown good trade-off between computational load and accuracy in variable selection [38, 41]. However, it should be noted that most filters exposed above could be used with other estimators or even with other evaluation functions/similarity measures than mutual information.

Mutual information computation requires the determination of three entropy terms (see Section 17.4.1):

$$I(X; Y) = H(X) + H(Y) - H(X, Y) \qquad (17.40)$$

An effective entropy estimation is then essential for computing mutual information. Entropy estimation has gained much interest over the last decade [13] and most approaches focus on reducing the bias inherent in entropy estimation.

For microarray data sets, bias reduction should not be the only criterion to choose an estimator. Bias reduction should be traded with speed/computational complexity of the estimator. Indeed, in variable selection and network inference, mutual information estimation routines are expected to be called a huge number of times and used for estimating tasks with the same number of variables and the same amount of samples. Since filters consist mainly in comparing information-theoretic quantities, the correct ranking of the estimated quantities is much more important than the correct estimation of the quantities. A similar conclusion has been reached in [33, 41]. We refer the reader to [4, 12, 13, 40, 42] for alternative approaches of entropy and mutual information estimation.

17.6.1 Discretizing Variables and Empirical Estimation

We describe here the equal-frequency discretization since it has been reported in [57] as one of the most efficient discretization method.

The equal-frequency discretization scheme consists in partitioning the interval $[a, b]$ into $|\mathcal{X}_i|$ intervals, each having the same number $m/|\mathcal{X}_i|$ of data points [15, 32, 56]. As a result, the intervals can have different sizes. If the $|\mathcal{X}_i|$ intervals have equal frequency, then the computation of entropy is straightforward: $\log(1/|\mathcal{X}_i|)$.

The value of the number of bins $|\mathcal{X}_i|$ controls a trade-off. With a too high $|\mathcal{X}_i|$, each bin will contain a few number of points, and hence the variance is increased, whereas a too low $|\mathcal{X}_i|$ will introduce a too high loss of information [10]. A classical choice of $|\mathcal{X}_i|$ is given by the sample square root $\sqrt{m}$ [56]. One justification given for that choice is that the ratio $m/|\mathcal{X}_i|$ becomes $m/\sqrt{m} = \sqrt{m}$, and hence there are as many bins as the average number of points per bin. Note also that when estimating the entropy of a bivariate distribution where each variable has $\sqrt{m}$ bins, the number of bins of the joint distribution is upper bounded by $|\mathcal{X}_i| \leq \sqrt{m} \times \sqrt{m} = m$. As a result, the empirical entropy estimator should not be too biased when combined with this choice of $|\mathcal{X}_i|$.

In order to compute the joint entropy of two discrete variables, the empirical estimator can be used. The empirical entropy estimator (also called "plug-in" "maximum likelihood," or "naive" [42]) is simply the entropy of the empirical distribution:

$$\hat{H}^{\text{emp}}(X) = -\sum_{x \in \mathcal{X}} \frac{\#(x)}{m} \log \frac{\#(x)}{m} \qquad (17.41)$$

where $\#(x)$ is the number of data points having value x. Because of the convexity of the logarithmic function, underestimates of $p(x)$ cause errors on $E\{1/[\log p(x)]\}$ that are larger than errors due to overestimations. As a result, entropy estimators are biased downward, that is,

$$E[\hat{H}^{\text{emp}}(X)] \leq H(X). \tag{17.42}$$

It has been shown in [42] that:

1. The variance of the empirical estimator is upper bounded by a term $((\log m)^2/m)$ which depends only on the number of samples.
2. The asymptotic bias is $-(|\mathcal{X}| - 1)/(2m)$ and depends on the number of bins $|\mathcal{X}|$ [42]. As $|\mathcal{X}| \gg m$, this estimator can still have a low variance but the bias can become very large [42].

The computation of $\hat{H}^{\text{emp}}(X)$ has an $O(m)$ complexity cost.

The Miller–Madow correction is given by the following formula, which is the empirical entropy corrected for the asymptotic bias:

$$\hat{H}^{\text{mm}}(X) = \hat{H}^{\text{emp}}(X) + \frac{|\mathcal{X}| - 1}{2m} \tag{17.43}$$

where $|\mathcal{X}|$ is the number of bins with nonzero probability. This correction, while adding no computational cost, reduces the bias without changing variance. As a result, the Miller–Madow estimator is often preferred to the naive empirical entropy estimator.

17.6.2 Assuming Normally Distributed Variables

Another way to deal with continuous variables without discretizing variables and decreasing the computational cost is to assume that variables follow a well-known probability distribution such as the Gaussian.

Let X be a multivariate Gaussian, having a density function

$$f(X) = \frac{1}{\sqrt{(2\pi)^n |V|}} \exp^{[-1/2(x-\mu)^T V^{-1}(x-\mu)]} \tag{17.44}$$

with mean μ and covariance matrix V.

The (differential) entropy of this distribution is [10]

$$H(X) = \tfrac{1}{2} \ln[(2\pi e)^n |V|] \tag{17.45}$$

where $|V|$ is the determinant of the covariance matrix [10].

As a result, the mutual information between two normal distributions is given by [22]

$$I(X_i, X_j) = \tfrac{1}{2} \log\left(\frac{\sigma_{ii}\sigma_{jj}}{|V|}\right) \tag{17.46}$$

where σ_{ii} and σ_{jj} are the standard deviations of X_i and X_j, respectively. Hence

$$I(X_i, X_j) = -\tfrac{1}{2} \log(1 - \rho^2) \tag{17.47}$$

with ρ being the Pearson correlation [26] between X_i and X_j. Note that the complexity of estimating $\hat{\rho}^2$ is $O(m)$, where m is the number of samples.

17.7 CONCLUSIONS

Variable selection algorithms are mostly composed of two parts: a search strategy and an evaluation function. In the case of information-theoretic filters a third component is given by the mutual information estimator. In this chapter we have introduced eight different information-theoretic evaluation functions together with three heuristics searches and two mutual information estimators. The three sequential heuristic searches introduced, namely forward, backward, and bidirectional selection, share with the two mutual information estimators, the empirical and the Gaussian, a low computational cost coupled with a growing literature of good empirical results. Having a low computational cost is critical in large data sets such as microarray data where the number of subset combinations is very high. An additional requirement brought by typical expression data sets is the ability to deal with a low number of samples. Most of the selection criteria presented here use combinations of only bi- and trivariate probability distributions in order to reduce the effect of the curse of dimensionality. Indeed, the latter require exponentially more samples for estimating larger joint distribution. Finally, we have introduced the notions of relevance, redundancy, and synergy out of an information-theoretic framework in order to understand and compare each method's ability to combine those bi- and trivariate distributions in an efficient setting.

REFERENCES

1. H. Almuallim and T. G. Dietterich. Learning with many irrelevant features. In *Proceedings of the Ninth National Conference on Artificial Intelligence (AAAI91)*. AAAI Press, Washington, DC, 1991, pp. 547–552.

2. D. Anastassiou. Computational analysis of the synergy among multiple interacting genes. *Mol. Sys, Biol.*, 3(83), 2007.

3. R. Battiti. Using mutual information for selecting features in supervised neural net learning. *IEEE Trans. Neural Networks*, 5:537–550, 1994.

4. J. Beirlant, E. J. Dudewica, L. Gyofi, and E. van der Meulen. Nonparametric entropy estimation: An overview. *J. Statist.*, 6:17–39, 1997.

5. D. A. Bell and H. Wang. A formalism for relevance and its application in feature subset selection. *Machine Learning*, 41(2):175–195, 2000.

6. A. Blum and P. Langley. Selection of relevant features and examples in machine learning. *Artif. Intell.*, 97:245–271, 1997.

7. B. V. Bonnlander and A. S. Weigend. Selecting input variables using mutual information and non-parametric density estimation. In *Proceedings of the 1994 International Symposium on Artificial Neural Networks (ISANN94)*, 1994.

8. G. Bontempi and P. E. Meyer. Causal filter selection in microarray data. In *International Conference on Machine Learning (ICML)*, 2010.

9. R. Caruana and D. Freitag. Greedy attribute selection. In *International Conference on Machine Learning*, 1994, pp. 28–36.

10. T. M. Cover and J. A. Thomas. *Elements of Information Theory*. Wiley, New York, 1990.

11. R. T. Cox. *Algebra of Probable Inference*. John Hopkins Press, Baltimore, 1961.

12. G. Darbellay and I. Vajda. Estimation of the information by an adaptive partitioning of the observation space. *IEEE Trans. Inform. Theory*, 45:1315–1321, 1999.

13. C. O. Daub, R. Steuer, J. Selbig, and S. Kloska. Estimating mutual information using b-spline functions—An improved similarity measure for analysing gene expression data. *BMC Bioinformatics*, 5, 2004.

14. L. Devroye, L. Györfi, and G. Lugosi. *A Probabilistic Theory of Pattern Recognition*. Springer-Verlag, 1996.

15. J. Dougherty, R. Kohavi, and M. Sahami. Supervised and unsupervised discretization of continuous features. In *International Conference on Machine Learning*. 1995, pp. 194–202.

16. J. Dreo, A. Petrowski, P. Siarry, and E. Taillard. *Métaheuristiques pour l'Optimisation Difficile*. Eyrolles, 2003.

17. W. Duch, T. Winiarski, J. Biesiada, and A. Kachel. Feature selection and ranking filters. In *International Conference on Artificial Neural Networks (ICANN) and International Conference on Neural Information Processing (ICONIP)*. June 2003, pp. 251–254.

18. F. Fleuret. Fast binary feature selection with conditional mutual information. *J. Machine Learning Res.*, 5:1531–1555, 2004.

19. D. François, F. Rossi, V. Wertz, and M. Verleysen. Resampling methods for parameter-free and robust feature selection with mutual information. *Neurocomputing*, 70(7–9):1276–1288, 2007.

20. I. Guyon and A. Elisseeff. An introduction to variable and feature selection. *J. Machine Learning Res.*, 3:1157–1182, 2003.

21. I. Guyon, S. Gunn, M. Nikravesh, and L. A. Zadeh. *Feature Extraction: Foundations and Applications*. Springer-Verlag, New York, 2006.

22. S. Haykin. *Neural Networks: A Comprehensive Foundation*. Prentice-Hall International, 1999.

23. A. Jakulin and I. Bratko. Quantifying and visualizing attribute interactions, report: Arxiv 0308002, 2003.

24. A. Jakulin and I. Bratko. Testing the significance of attribute interactions. In *Proceedings of 21st International Conference on Machine Learning (ICML)*. 2004, pp. 409–416.

25. E. T. Jaynes. *Probability Theory: The Logic of Science*. Cambridge University Press, 2003.

26. M. G. Kendall, A. Stuart, and J. K. Ord. *Kendall's Advanced Theory of Statistics*. Oxford University Press, 1987.

27. M. B. Kennel, J. B. Shlens, H. D. I. Abarbanel, and E. J. Chichilnisky. Estimating entropy rates with Bayesian confidence intervals. *Neural Comput.*, 17(7):1531–1576, 2005.

28. R. Kohavi and G. H. John. Wrappers for feature subset selection. *Artif. Intell.*, 97(1–2):273–324, 1997.

29. I. Kojadinovic. Relevance measures for subset variable selection in regression problems based on *k*-additive mutual information. *Computat. Statist. Data Anal.*, 49:1205–1227, 2005.

30. D. Koller and M. Sahami. Toward optimal feature selection. In *International Conference on Machine Learning*. 1996, pp. 284–292.

31. I. Kononenko. Estimating attributes: Analysis and extensions of RELIEF. In *European Conference on Machine Learning*. 1994, pp. 171–182.

32. H. Liu, F. Hussain, C. Lim Tan, and M. Dash. Discretization: An enabling technique. *J. Data Mining Knowledge Discov.*, 6(4):393–423, 2002.

33. A. A. Margolin, I. Nemenman, K. Basso, C. Wiggins, G. Stolovitzky, R. Dalla Favera, and A. Califano. ARACNE: An algorithm for the reconstruction of gene regulatory networks in a mammalian cellular context. *BMC Bioinformatics*, 7, 2006.

34. W. J. McGill. Multivariate information transmission. *Psychometrika*, 19(2):97–116, 1954.

35. P. E. Meyer and G. Bontempi. On the use of variable complementarity for feature selection in cancer classification. In F. Rothlauf et al. (Eds.), *Applications of Evolutionary Computing:*

EvoWorkshops, Vol. 3907 of *Lecture Notes in Computer Science*, Springer, Budapest, 2006, pp. 91–102.

36. P. E. Meyer, K. Kontos, F. Lafitte, and G. Bontempi. Information-theoretic inference of large transcriptional regulatory networks. *EURASIP J. Bioinformatics Syst. Biol.*, Special Issue on Information-Theoretic Methods for Bioinformatics, 2007.

37. P. E. Meyer, D. Marbach, S. Roy, and M. Kellis. Information-theoretic inference of gene networks using backward elimination. In *International Conference on Bioinformatics and Computational Biology (BioComp)*, Las Vegas, 2010.

38. P. E. Meyer, C. Schretter, and G. Bontempi. Information-theoretic feature selection using variable complementarity. *IEEE J. Spec. Topics Signal Process.*, 2(3):261–274, 2008.

39. A. J. Miller. *Subset Selection in Regression*, 2nd ed. Chapman and Hall, 2002.

40. I. Nemenman, W. Bialek, and R. de Ruyter van Steveninck. Entropy and information in neural spike trains: Progress on the sampling problem. *Phys. Rev. Lett.*, 69(5):056111, 2004.

41. C. Olsen, P. E. Meyer, and G. Bontempi. On the impact of entropy estimation on transcriptional regulatory network inference based on mutual information. *EURASIP J. Bioinformatics Syst. Biol.*, 2009(1):308959, 2009.

42. L. Paninski. Estimation of entropy and mutual information. *Neural Computat.*, 15(6):1191–1253, 2003.

43. H. Peng and F. Long. An efficient max-dependency algorithm for gene selection. In *36th Symposium on the Interface: Computational Biology and Bioinformatics*, 57:65, May 2004.

44. H. Peng, F. Long, and C. Ding. Feature selection based on mutual information: Criteria of max-dependency, max-relevance, and min-redundancy. *IEEE Trans. Pattern Anal. Machine Intell.*, 27(8):1226–1238, 2005.

45. L. Portinale and L. Saitta. Feature selection. *Appl. Intell.*, 9(3):217–230, 1998.

46. G. Provan and M. Singh. Learning Bayesian networks using feature selection. In *Fifth International Workshop on Artificial Intelligence and Statistics*. 1995, pp. 450–456,

47. F. Rossi, A. Lendasse, D. François, V. Wertz, and M. Verleysen. Mutual information for the selection of relevant variables in spectrometric nonlinear modelling. *Chemometr. Intell. Lab. Syst.*, 2:215–226, 2006.

48. C. E. Shannon. A mathematical theory of communication. *Bell Syst. Tech. J.*, 28(4):656–715, 1949.

49. M. Studený and J. Vejnarová. The multiinformation function as a tool for measuring stochastic dependence. In *Proceedings of the NATO Advanced Study Institute on Learning in Graphical Models*. 1998, pp. 261–297.

50. N. Tishby, F. Pereira, and W. Bialek. The information bottleneck method. In *Proceedings of the 37th Annual Allerton Conference on Communication, Control and Computing*. 1999.

51. G. D. Tourassi, E. D. Frederick, M. K. Markey, and C. E. Floyd, Jr. Application of the mutual information criterion for feature selection in computer-aided diagnosis. *Med. Phys.*, 28(12):2394–2402, 2001.

52. M. J. van de Vijver, Y. D. He, L. J. van't Veer, H. Dai, A. A. Hart, D. W. Voskuil, G. J. Schreiber, J. L. Peterse, C. Roberts, M. J. Marton, M. Parrish, D. Atsma, A. Witteveen, A. Glas, L. Delahaye, T. van der Velde T, H. Bartelink H, S. Rodenhuis, E. T. Rutgers, S. H. Friend, and R. Bernards. A gene-expression signature as a predictor of survival in breast cancer. *New Engl. J. Med.*, 347(25):1999–2009, 2002.

53. L. J. van 't Veer, H. Dai, M. J. van de Vijver, Y. D. He, A. A. Hart, M. Mao, H. L. Peterse, K. van der Kooy, M. J. Marton, A. T. Witteveen, G. J. Schreiber, R. M. Kerkhoven, C. Roberts, P. S. Linsley, R. Bernards, and S. H. Friend. Gene expression profiling predicts clinical outcome of breast cancer. *Nature*, 415(6871):530–536, 2002.

54. W. Wienholt and B. Sendhoff. How to determine the redundancy of noisy chaotic time series. *Int. J. Bifurcation Chaos*, 6(1):101–117, 1996.

55. J. Yang and V. Honavar. Feature subset selection using A genetic algorithm. In *Genetic Programming 1997: Proceedings of the Second Annual Conference*. Morgan Kaufmann, 1997, p. 380.

56. Y. Yang and G. I. Webb. Discretization for naive-Bayes learning: managing discretization bias and variance. *Machine Learning*, 74(1):39–74, 2009.

57. Y. Yang and G. I. Webb. On why discretization works for naive-bayes classifiers. *AI 2003: Advances in Artificial Intelligence*. Springer, Berlin, 2003, pp. 440–452.

58. L. Yu and H. Liu. Efficient feature selection via analysis of relevance and redundancy. *J. Machine Learning Res.*, 5:1205–1224, 2004.

59. Z. Zhao and H. Liu. Searching for interacting features. In *Proceedings of the 20th International Joint Conference on Artificial Intelligence (IJCAI-07)*. 2007.

CHAPTER 18

FEATURE SELECTION AND CLASSIFICATION FOR GENE EXPRESSION DATA USING EVOLUTIONARY COMPUTATION

HAIDER BANKA,[1] SURESH DARA,[1] and MOURAD ELLOUMI[2,3]

[1]Department of Computer Science and Engineering, Indian School of Mines, Dhanbad, India

[2]Laboratory of Technologies of Information and Communication and Electrical Engineering (LaTICE)

[3]University of Tunis-El Manar, Tunisia

18.1 INTRODUCTION

Computational molecular biology is an interdisciplinary subject involving fields as diverse as biology, computer science, information technology, mathematics, physics, statistics, and chemistry. One needs to analyze and interpret the vast amount of data that are available, involving the decoding of around 24,000–30,000 human genes. Specifically, high-dimensional feature selection is important for characterizing gene expression data involving many attributes, indicating that data-mining methods hold promise in this direction.

Unlike a genome, which provides only static sequence information, microarray experiments produce gene expression patterns that provide dynamic information about cell function. This information is useful while investigating complex interactions within the cell. For example, data-mining methods can ascertain and summarize the set of genes responding to a certain level of stress in an organism [1]. Microarray technologies have been utilized to evaluate the level of expression of thousands of genes in colon, breast, and blood cancer classification [2, 5, 9, 20] as well as clustering [16, 19].

In addition to the combinatorial approach for solutions, there also exists scope for soft computing, especially for generating low-cost, low-precision, good solutions. *Soft computing* is a consortium of methodologies that works synergistically and provides flexible information processing capability for handling real-life ambiguous situations [24]. Its aim is to exploit the tolerance for imprecision, uncertainty, approximate reasoning, and partial truth in order to achieve tractability, robustness, and low-cost solutions. Various soft computing methodologies (like fuzzy logic, neural networks, genetic algorithms, and rough sets)

Biological Knowledge Discovery Handbook: Preprocessing, Mining, and Postprocessing of Biological Data,
First Edition. Edited by Mourad Elloumi and Albert Y. Zomaya.
© 2014 John Wiley & Sons, Inc. Published 2014 by John Wiley & Sons, Inc.

have been applied to handle the different challenges posed by data mining [13], involving large heterogeneous data sets.

One of the important problems in extracting and analyzing information from large databases is the associated high complexity. Feature selection is helpful as a preprocessing step for reducing dimensionality, removing irrelevant data, improving learning accuracy, and enhancing output comprehensibility. There are two basic categories of feature selection algorithms, namely *filter* and *wrapper* models [15]. The filter model selects feature subsets independently of any learning algorithm and relies on various measures of the general characteristics of the training data. The wrapper model uses the predictive accuracy of a predetermined learning algorithm to determine the goodness of the selected subsets and is computationally expensive. Use of fast filter models for efficient selection of features, based on correlation for relevance and redundancy analysis, has been reported in the literature [22, 23] for high-dimensional data.

Microarray data are a typical example presenting an overwhelmingly large number of features (genes), the majority of which are not relevant to the description of the problem and could potentially degrade the classification performance by masking the contribution of the relevant features. The key informative features represent a base of reduced cardinality for subsequent analysis aimed at determining their possible role in the analyzed phenotype. This highlights the importance of feature selection, with particular emphasis on microarray data. Recent approaches in this direction include *probabilistic neural networks* [11], *support vector machines* [4], *neuro-fuzzy computing* [6], and *neuro-genetic hybridization* [12].

Rough-set theory [14] provides an important and mathematically established tool for this sort of dimensionality reduction in large data. A basic issue addressed, in relation to many practical applications of knowledge databases, is the following. An information system consisting of a domain U of objects/observations and a set A of attributes/features induces a partitioning (classification) of U by A. A block of the partition would contain those objects of U that share identical feature values, that is, are *indiscernible* with respect to the given set A of features. But the whole set A may not always be necessary to define the classification/partition of U. Many of the attributes may be superfluous, and we may find *minimal* subsets of attributes which give the same classification as the whole set A. These subsets are called *reducts* in rough-set theory. In terms of feature selection, therefore, reducts correspond to the *minimal feature sets* that are *necessary* and *sufficient* to represent a *correct* decision about classification of the domain. One is thus provided with another angle of addressing the problem of dimensionality based on the premise that the initial set of features may render objects of the domain indiscernible due to lack of complete information.

The task of finding reducts is reported to be NP hard [17]. The high complexity of this problem has motivated investigators to apply various approximation techniques to find near-optimal solutions. There are some studies reported in the literature, for example, [3, 21], where *genetic algorithms* (GAs) [10] have been applied to find reducts.

GAs provide an efficient search technique in a large solution space based on the theory of evolution. It involves a set of evolutionary operators, like *selection*, *crossover*, and *mutation*. A population of chromosomes is made to evolve over generations by optimizing a fitness function, which provides a quantitative measure of the fitness of individuals in the pool. When there are two or more conflicting characteristics to be optimized, often the single-objective GA requires an appropriate formulation of the single fitness function in terms of an additive combination of the different criteria involved. In such cases *multiobjective*

GAs (MOGAs) [7] provide an alternative more efficient approach to searching for optimal solutions.

Each of the studies in [3, 21] employs a single objective function to obtain reducts. The essential properties of a reduct are (i) to classify among all elements of the universe with the same accuracy as the starting attribute set and (ii) at the same time to be of small cardinality. A close observation reveals that these two characteristics are of a conflicting nature. Hence the determination of reducts is better represented as a two-objective optimization problem.

In the present work, we consider microarray data consisting of three sets of two-class cancer samples. Since such data typically contain a large number of features, most of which are not relevant, an initial redundancy reduction is done on the (attribute) expression values. The idea is to retain only *those* genes that play a major role in arriving at a decision about the output classes. This preprocessing aids faster convergence, mainly because the initial population is now located nearer the optimal solution in the huge search space. Reducts or minimal features are then generated from these reduced sets using MOGA. Among the different multi-objective algorithms, it is observed that the *nondominated sorting genetic algorithm* (NSGA-II) [8] has the features required for a good MOGA. NSGA-II is adapted here to handle large data sets more effectively.

Section 18.2 describes the relevant preliminaries on rough-set theory, MOGAs, and microarray gene expression data. We assume that the readers are sufficiently familiar with the basics of classical GAs [10] and hence do not go into its details here. The redundancy reduction to better handle the high-dimensional data, the basic notions used in the evolutionary-rough feature selection algorithm, and the algorithm itself are described in Section 18.3. The performance of the algorithm is demonstrated, in Section 18.4, on microarray gene expression data involving very high-dimensional attributes. Comparative study and analysis of the results are also included. Finally, Section 18.5 concludes the chapter.

18.2 PRELIMINARIES

In this section we briefly discuss the basic concepts of rough-set theory, MOGAs, and microarray gene expression data.

18.2.1 Rough-Set Theory

Rough sets [14] constitute a major mathematical tool for managing uncertainty that arises from granularity in the domain of discourse—due to incomplete information about the objects of the domain. The granularity is represented formally in terms of an *indiscernibility* relation that partitions the domain. If there is a given set of *attributes* ascribed to the objects of the domain, objects having the same attribute values would be indiscernible and would belong to the same block of the partition. The intention is to approximate a *rough* (imprecise) concept in the domain by a pair of *exact* concepts. These exact concepts are called *lower* and *upper approximations* and are determined by the indiscernibility relation. The *lower approximation* is the set of objects definitely belonging to the rough concept, whereas the *upper approximation* is the set of objects possibly belonging to the same. Figure 18.1 provides an illustration of a rough set with its approximations. The formal definitions of the above notions and others required for the present work are given below.

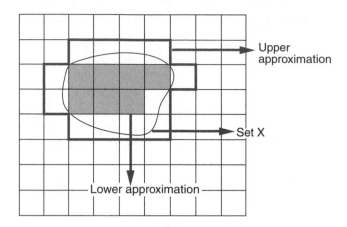

FIGURE 18.1   Lower and upper approximations of rough set.

Definition 18.1   An *information system* $\mathcal{A} = (U, A)$ consists of a nonempty, finite set U of objects (cases, observations, etc.) and a nonempty, finite set A of attributes a (features, variables) such that $a : U \rightarrow V_a$, where V_a is a value set. We shall deal with information systems called *decision tables* in which the attribute set has two parts ($A = C \cup D$) consisting of the condition and decision attributes (in the subsets C, D of A respectively). In particular, the decision tables we take will have a single decision attribute d and will be *consistent, that is*, whenever objects x, y are such that for each condition attribute a, $a(x) = a(y)$, then $d(x) = d(y)$.

Definition 18.2   Let $B \subset A$. Then a *B-indiscernibility relation* IND(B) is defined as

$$\text{IND}(B) = \{(x, y) \in U : a(x) = a(y) \; \forall a \in B\} \tag{18.1}$$

It is clear that IND(B) partitions the universe U into equivalence classes

$$[x_i]_B = \{x_j \in U : (x_i, x_j) \in \text{IND}(B)\} \qquad x_i \in U \tag{18.2}$$

Definition 18.3   The *B-lower* and *B-upper approximations* of a given set $X(\subseteq U)$ are defined, respectively, as follows:

$$\underline{B}X = \{x \in U : [x]_B \subseteq X\} \qquad \overline{B}X = \{x \in U : [x]_B \cap X \neq \phi\}$$

The *B*-boundary region is given by $BN_B(X) = \overline{B}X \setminus \underline{B}X$.

18.2.1.1 Reducts   In a decision table $\mathcal{A} = (U, C \cup D)$, one is interested in eliminating redundant condition attributes, and actually relative *D*-reducts are computed.

Let $B \subseteq C$, and consider the *B-positive region* of D, namely, $\text{POS}_B(D) = \bigcup_{[x]_D} \underline{B}[x]_D$. An attribute $b \in B(\subseteq C)$ is D dispensable in B if $\text{POS}_B(D) = \text{POS}_{B \setminus \{b\}}(D)$; otherwise b is D indispensable in B. Here B is said to be D independent in $\mathcal{A}$ if every attribute from B is D indispensable in B.

Definition 18.4 $B(\subseteq C)$ is called a *D-reduct* in $\mathcal{A}$ if B is D independent in $\mathcal{A}$ and $\text{POS}_C(D) = \text{POS}_B(D)$.

Notice that, as decision tables with a single decision attribute d are taken to be consistent, $U = \text{POS}_C(d) = \text{POS}_B(D)$ for any d-reduct B.

18.2.1.2 Discernibility Matrix D-reducts can be computed with the help of D-discernibility matrices [17]. Let $U = \{x_1, \ldots, x_m\}$. A D-discernibility matrix $M_D(\mathcal{A})$ is defined as an $m \times m$ matrix of the information system $\mathcal{A}$ with the (i, j)th entry c_{ij} given by

$$c_{ij} = \{a \in C : a(x_i) \neq a(x_j) \qquad (x_i, x_j) \notin \text{IND}(D)\} \qquad i, j \in \{1, \ldots, m\} \qquad (18.3)$$

A variant of the discernibility matrix, that is, a *distinction table* [21], is used in our work to enable faster computation.

Definition 18.5 A *distinction table* is a binary matrix with dimensions $(m^2 - m)/2 \times N$, where N is the number of attributes in A. An entry $b((k, j), i)$ of the matrix corresponds to the attribute a_i and pair of objects (x_k, x_j) and is given by

$$b((k, j), i) = \begin{cases} 1 & \text{if } a_i(x_k) \neq a_i(x_j) \\ 0 & \text{if } a_i(x_k) = a_i(x_j) \end{cases} \qquad (18.4)$$

The presence of a 1 signifies the ability of the attribute a_i to discern (or distinguish) between the pair of objects (x_k, x_j).

18.2.2 Genetic Algorithms

Genetic algorithms [10] are heuristic techniques applied to solve complex search and optimization problems. They are motivated by the principles of natural genetics and natural selection. Unlike classical optimization methods, GAs deal with a population of solutions/individuals. With the basic genetic/evolutionary operators, like *selection*, *crossover*, and *mutation*, new solutions are generated. A population of chromosomes, representing solutions, is made to evolve over generations by optimizing a fitness function which provides a quantitative measure of the fitness of individuals in the pool. The selection operator selects better solutions to participate into crossover. The crossover operator is responsible for creating new solutions from the old ones. Mutation also creates new solutions, but only in the vicinity of old solutions. The mutation operator plays a major role in multimodal problems.

When there are two or more conflicting objectives to be optimized, often the weighted sum of objectives is taken to convert them to a single-objective problem. In such cases multiobjective GAs provide an alternative, more efficient approach to searching for optimal solutions.

18.2.3 Multiobjective Genetic Algorithms

Most real-world search and optimization problems typically involve multiple objectives. A solution that is better with respect to one objective requires a compromise in other objectives. Let us consider the decision-making problem regarding the purchase of a car. It is expected that an inexpensive car is likely to be less comfortable. If a buyer is willing to sacrifice the cost to some extent, he or she can find another car with a better comfort level than the cheapest one. Thus in problems with more than one conflicting objective there exists no single optimum solution. Rather, there exists a set of solutions which are all optimal involving trade-offs between conflicting objectives. For example, the various factors to be optimized in the problem of buying a car include the total finance available, distance to be driven each day, number of passengers riding in the car, fuel consumption and cost, depreciation value, road conditions where the car will be mostly driven, physical health of the passengers, and social status.

Unlike single-objective optimization problems, the MOGA tries to optimize two or more conflicting characteristics represented by fitness functions. Modeling this situation with single-objective GA would amount to heuristic determination of a number of parameters involved in expressing such a scalar-combination-type fitness function. Multiobjective genetic algorithms, on the other hand, generate a set of *Pareto-optimal* solutions [7] which simultaneously optimize the conflicting requirements of the multiple fitness functions.

Among the different multiobjective algorithms, it is observed that NSGA-II [8] possesses all the features required for a good MOGA. It has been shown that this can converge to the global Pareto front while simultaneously maintaining the diversity of the population. We describe here the characteristics of NSGA-II, like nondomination, crowding distance, and crowding selection operator. This is followed by the actual algorithm.

18.2.3.1 Nondomination

The concept of optimality, behind the multiobjective optimization, deals with a set of solutions. The conditions for a solution to be *dominated* with respect to the other solutions are given below.

Definition 18.6 If there are M objective functions, a solution $x^{(1)}$ is said to dominate another solution $x^{(2)}$ if both conditions (a) and (b) are true:

(a) The solution $x^{(1)}$ is no worse than $x^{(2)}$ in all the M objective functions.

(b) The solution $x^{(1)}$ is strictly better than $x^{(2)}$ in at least one of the M objective functions.

Otherwise the two solutions are *nondominating* to each other. When a solution i dominates solution j, then rank $r_i < r_j$.

The major steps for finding the nondominated set in a population P of size $|P|$ are outlined below.

1. Set solution counter $i = 1$ and create an empty nondominated set P'.
2. For a solution $j \in P$ ($j \neq i$), check if solution j dominates solution i. If yes, then go to step 4.
3. If more solutions are left in P, increment j by one and go to step 2. Else set $P' = P' \cup \{i\}$.
4. Increment i by one. If $i \leq |P|$, then go to step 2; else declare P' as the nondominated set.

After all the solutions of P are checked, the members of P' constitute the nondominated set at the first level (front with rank 1). In order to generate solutions for the next higher level (dominated by the first level), the above procedure is repeated on the reduced population $P = P - P'$. This is iteratively continued until $P = \emptyset$.

18.2.3.2 Crowding Distance

In order to maintain diversity in the population, a measure called *crowding distance* is used. This assigns the highest value to the boundary solutions and the average distance of two solutions [$(i+1)$th and $(i-1)$th] on either side of solution i along each of the objectives. The following algorithm computes the crowding distance d_i of each point in the front $\mathcal{F}$:

1. Let the number of solutions in $\mathcal{F}$ be $l = |\mathcal{F}|$ and assign $d_i = 0$ for $i = 1, 2, \ldots, l$.
2. For each objective function $f_k, k = 1, 2, \ldots, M$, sort the set in its worse order.
3. Set $d_1 = d_l = \infty$.
4. For $j = 2$ to $l - 1$, increment d_j by $f_{k_{j+1}} - f_{k_{j-1}}$.

18.2.3.3 Crowding Selection Operator A *crowded tournament selection* operator is defined as follows. A solution i wins a tournament with another solution j if any one of the following is true:

- Solution i has better rank, that is, $r_i < r_j$.
- Both the solutions are in the same front, that is, $r_i = r_j$, but solution i is less densely located in the search space, that is, $d_i > d_j$.

18.2.3.4 NSGA-II The multiobjective algorithm NSGA-II is characterized by the use of the above-mentioned three characteristics while generating the optimal solution. Let us now outline the main steps of NSGA-II [8]:

1. Initialize the population randomly.
2. Calculate the multiobjective fitness function.
3. Rank the population using the dominance criteria of Section 18.2.3.1.
4. Calculate the crowding distance based on Section 18.2.3.2.
5. Do selection using the crowding selection operator of Section 18.2.3.3.
6. Do crossover and mutation (as in conventional GA) to generate the children population.
7. Combine parent and children populations.
8. Replace the parent population by the best members of the combined population. Initially, members of lower fronts replace the parent population. When it is not possible to accommodate all the members of a particular front, then that front is sorted according to the crowding distance. Selection of individuals is done on the basis of higher crowding distance. The number selected is that required to make the new parent population size the same as the size of the old one.

18.2.4 Microarray and Gene Expression Data

Microarrays are used in the medical domain to produce molecular profiles of diseased and normal tissues of patients. Such profiles are useful for understanding various diseases and aid in more accurate diagnosis, prognosis, treatment planning, and drug discovery.

DNA microarrays (gene arrays or gene chips) [1] usually consist of thin glass or nylon substrates containing specific DNA gene samples spotted in an array by a robotic printing device. Researchers spread fluorescently labeled messenger RNA (mRNA) from an experimental condition onto the DNA gene samples in the array. This mRNA binds (hybridizes) strongly with some DNA gene samples and weakly with others, depending on the inherent double-helical characteristics. A laser scans the array and sensors to detect the fluorescence levels (using red and green dyes), indicating the strength with which the sample expresses each gene.

The logarithmic ratio between the two intensities of each dye is used as the gene expression data. The relative abundance of the spotted DNA sequences in a pair of DNA or RNA samples is assessed by evaluating the differential hybridization of the two samples to the sequences on the array. Gene expression levels can be determined for samples taken (i) at multiple time instants of a biological process (different phases of cell division) or (ii) under various conditions (tumor samples with different histopathological diagnosis). Each sample corresponds to a high-dimensional row vector of its gene expression profile.

18.3 EVOLUTIONARY REDUCT GENERATION

Over the past few years, there has been a good amount of study in effectively applying GAs to find reducts. We describe here the reduct generation procedure, incorporating initial redundancy reduction, in a multiobjective framework. NSGA-II is adapted to handle large data sets more effectively. We focus our analysis on two-class problems.

18.3.1 Redundancy Reduction for Microarray Data

Gene expression data typically consist of a small number of samples with very large number of features, of which many are redundant. We consider here two-class problems, particularly diseased and normal samples, or two varieties of diseased samples. In other words, there is a single decision attribute d having only two members in its value set V_d. We first do a redundancy reduction on the (attribute) expression values to retain only those genes that play a highly decisive role in choosing in favor of either output class. Note that this preprocessing phase is a simple, fast, heuristic thresholding with the objective of generating an initial crude redundancy reduction among features. Subsequent reduct generation with MOGA determines the actual, refined minimal feature sets that are necessary and sufficient to represent a correct classification decision.

Normalization leads to scaling of intensities, thereby enabling comparison of expression values between different microarrays within an experiment. *Preprocessing* aims at eliminating the ambiguously expressed genes (neither too high nor too low) as well as the constantly expressed genes across the tissue classes. During reduct generation we select an appropriate minimal set of differentially expressed genes, across the classes, for subsequent efficient classification:

1. Attributewise normalization by

$$a'_j(x_i) = \frac{a_j(x_i) - \min_j}{\max_j - \min_j} \ \forall i \qquad (18.5)$$

where $\max_j$ and $\min_j$ correspond to the maximum and minimum gene expression values for attribute a_j over all samples. This constitutes the normalized gene data set, that is, a (continuous) attribute value table.

2. Choose thresholds Th_i and Th_f, based on the idea of quantiles [13]. Let the N patterns be sorted in the ascending order of their values along the jth axis. In order to determine the partitions, we divide the measurements into a number of small class intervals of equal width d and count the corresponding class frequencies fr_c. The position of the kth partition value ($k = 1, 2, 3$ for four partitions) is calculated as

$$Th_k = l_c + \frac{R_k - c\,fr_{c-1}}{fr_c}\delta \tag{18.6}$$

where l_c is the lower limit of the cth class interval, $R_k = Nk/4$ is the rank of the kth partition value, and $c\,fr_{c-1}$ is the cumulative frequency of the immediately preceding class interval such that $c\,fr_{c-1} \le R_k \le cfr_c$. Here we use $Th_i = Th_1$ and $Th_f = Th_3$.

3. Convert the attribute value table to binary (0/1) form as follows:

```
If a'(x) ≤ Th_i, then put 0.
Else, if a'(x) ≥ Th_f, then put 1.
Else, put * (don't care).
```

4. Find the average occurrences of ∗ over the entire attribute value table. Choose this as threshold Th_a.

5. Remove from the table those attributes for which the number of ∗'s are $\ge Th_a$. This is the *modified* (reduced) *attribute value table* A_r.

18.3.2 *d*-Distinction Table

For a decision table A with N condition attributes and a single decision attribute d, the problem of finding a d-reduct is equivalent to finding a minimal subset of columns $R(\subseteq \{1, 2, \ldots, N\})$ in the distinction table [cf. Section 18.2, Definition 18.5, Equation (18.4)] satisfying $\forall(k, j)\exists i \in R : b((k, j), i) = 1$ whenever $d(x_k) \ne d(x_j)$. So, in effect, we may consider the distinction table to consist of N columns and rows corresponding to only those object pairs (x_k, x_j) such that $d(x_k) \ne d(x_j)$. Let us call this shortened distinction table a *d-distinction table*. Note that, as A is taken to be consistent, there is no row with all zero entries in a d distinction table.

Accordingly, to find d-reducts in the present case, the reduced attribute value table A_r (as obtained in Section 18.3.1) is used for generating the d-distinction table. As mentioned earlier, d has the two output classes as the only members in its value set V_d.

- As object pairs corresponding to the same class do not constitute a row of the d-distinction table, there is a considerable reduction in its size, thereby leading to a decrease in computational cost.

- Additionally,

  If either of the objects in a pair, has '∗' as an entry under an attribute in table A_r

  Then in the distinction table, put '0' at the entry for that attribute and pair.

- The entries 1 in the matrix correspond to the attributes of interest for arriving at a classification decision. Let the number of objects initially in the two classes be m_1 and m_2, respectively. Then the number of rows in the d-distinction table becomes $m_1 m_2 < m(m-1)/2$, where $m_1 + m_2 = m$. This reduces the time complexity of fitness computation to $O(Nm_1 m_2)$.

18.3.3 Using MOGA

Algorithms reported in the literature (e.g., [3, 21]) vary more or less in defining the fitness function and typically use combined single-objective functions. Upon closely observing the nature of the reduct, we find that one needs to concentrate on generating a minimal set of attributes that are necessary and sufficient in order to arrive at an acceptable (classification) decision. These two characteristics of reducts, being conflicting to each other, are well suited for multiobjective modeling. In order to optimize the pair of conflicting requirements, the fitness function of [21] was split in a two-objective GA setting. We use these two objective functions in the present work in a modified form.

The reduct candidates are represented by binary strings of length N, where N is the number of condition attributes. In the bit representation, a 1 implies that the corresponding attribute is present while 0 means that it is not. So, if there are three attributes a_1, a_2, a_3 (i.e., $N = 3$), $v = (1, 0, 1)$ in the search space of the GA would actually indicate the reduct candidate $\{a_1, a_3\}$. As we are looking for *minimal* nonredundant attribute sets, an objective then is to obtain a minimal number of 1's in a solution. We note that a reduct is a minimal set of attributes that *discerns between all objects* [cf. Equation (18.4)]. Now v would discern between an object pair (k, j) (say) provided at least one of the attributes present in v assigns a 1 to the pair, that is, in the d-distinction table, $b((k, j), i) = 1$ for some a_i in v. Thus the second objective is to maximize the number of such object pairs for a solution.

Accordingly, two fitness functions f_1 and f_2 are considered for each individual. We have

$$f_1(v) = \frac{N - L_v}{N} \tag{18.7}$$

$$f_2(v) = \frac{C_v}{(m^2 - m)/2} \tag{18.8}$$

where v is the reduct candidate, L_v represents the number of 1's in v, m is the number of objects, and C_v indicates the number of object combinations v can discern between. The fitness function f_1 gives the candidate credit for containing less attributes (fewer 1's), while the function f_2 determines the extent to which the candidate can discern among objects.

Thus, by generating a reduct we are focusing on that minimal set of attributes which can essentially distinguish between all patterns in the given set. In this manner, a reduct is mathematically more meaningful as the most appropriate set of nonredundant features selected from high-dimensional data.

The crowding binary tournament selection of Section 18.2.3.3 is used. One-point crossover is employed with probability $p_c = 0.7$. Probability p_m of mutation on a single position of an individual was taken as 0.05. Mutation of one position means replacement of 1 by 0 or 0 by 1. The probability values were chosen after several experiments.

18.3.4 The Algorithm

In this chapter NSGA-II is modified to effectively handle large data sets. Since we are interested in interclass distinction, the fitness function of Equation (18.8) is modified as

$$f_2(v) = \frac{C_v}{m_1 m_2} \tag{18.9}$$

where m_1 and m_2 are the number of objects in the two classes. The basic steps of the proposed algorithm are summarized as follows:

1. Redundancy reduction is made for the high-dimensional microarray data, as described in Section 18.3.1, to get the reduced attribute value table $\mathcal{A}_r$.
2. The d-distinction table is generated from $\mathcal{A}_r$ for the two classes being discerned.
3. A random population of size n is generated.
4. The two fitness values f_1, f_2 for each individual are calculated using Equations (18.7) and (18.9).
5. Nondomination sorting is done as discussed in Section 18.2.3.1 to identify different fronts.
6. Crowding sort based on crowding distance is performed to get a wide spread of the solution.
7. Offspring solution of size n is created using *fitness* tournament selection, crossover, and mutation operators. This is a modification of the crowded tournament selection of Section 18.2.3.3, with f_1 being accorded a higher priority over f_2 during solution selection from the same front. This implies precedence to the classification efficiency of a solution over its cardinality. Specifically, for $r_i = r_j$ we favor solution i if $f_{1_i} > f_{1_j}$ (instead of $d_i > d_j$).
8. Select the best populations of size $n/2$ each from both the parent and offspring solutions based on nondominated sorting to generate a combined population of size n. This modification enables effective handling of larger population sizes in case of large data sets along with computational gain.
9. Steps 4–8 are repeated for a prespecified number of generations.

18.4 EXPERIMENTAL RESULTS

We have implemented the proposed minimal feature selection algorithm on microarray data consisting of three different cancer samples. The availability of literature about the performance of other related algorithms on these data sets, summarized in Table 18.1, prompted us to select them for our study. All results are averaged over several (3–5) runs involving different random seeds. No significant change was observed in the performance using different seeds.

The colon cancer data set (http://microarray.princeton.edu/oncology) is a collection of 62 gene expression measurements from colon biopsy samples. There are 22 normal (class C_2) and 40 colon cancer (class C_1) samples, having 2000 genes (features).

TABLE 18.1   Usage Details of Two-Class Microarray Data

Data Used	Number of Attributes	Number of Attributes after Preprosessing	Classes	Number of Samples
Colon	2000	1102	Colon cancer	40
			Normal	22
Lymphoma	4026	1867	Other type	54
			B-cell lymphoma	42
Leukemia	7129	3783	ALL	47
			AML	25

Fifty percent of the samples $(20 + 11 = 31)$ was considered the training set, while the remaining 50% $(20 + 11 = 31)$ constituted the test set.

The lymphoma data set (`http://llmpp.nih.gov/lymphoma/data/figure1/figure1.cdt`) provides expression measurements from 96 normal and malignant lymphocyte samples containing 42 cases of diffused large B-cell lymphomas (DLBCLs) (class C_2) and 54 cases of other types (class C_1). There are 4026 genes present. Here also, 50% of the samples $(27 + 21 = 48)$ was considered the training set, while the remaining 50% $(27 + 21 = 48)$ constituted the test set.

The leukemia dataset (`http://www.genome.wi.mit.edu/MPR`) is a collection of gene expression measurements from 38 leukemia samples. There are 27 cases of acute lymphoblastic leukemia (ALL) and 11 cases of acute myeloblastic leukemia (AML). An independent test set, composed of 20 ALL and 14 AML samples, was used for evaluating the performance of the classifier. The gene expression measurements were taken from high-density oligonucleotide microarrays containing 7129 genes (attributes).

After the initial redundancy reduction, by the procedure outlined in Section 18.3.1, the feature sets were reduced that are shown in Table 18.2.

The MOGA of Section 18.3.4 is run on the d-distinction table by using the fitness functions of Equations (18.7) and (18.8), with different population sizes, to generate reducts upon convergence. Results are provided in Table 18.2 for the minimal reduct, on the three sets colon, lymphoma, and leukemia of two-class microarray gene expression data after 15,000 generations. Note that a reduct implies 100% discrimination over the training set, consisting of object pairs from the d-distinction table. The corresponding recognition scores (%) (on the test set) by the powerful k-nearest-neighbor (k-NN) classifier [18] for different values of k are also presented in the table. We do not use other classifiers like ID-tree which typically deal with symbolic (nonnumeric) data. Neural networks were not explored since our objective was to focus on the classification ability of the reducts generated and not to further improve upon the recognition at the expense of increased computational complexity.

It is observed that the number of features get reduced considerably with the evolutionary progression of reduct generation. A larger initial population size leads to a smaller size of reducts faster and hence a correspondingly higher fitness value. This is depicted in Figure 18.2. However, the associated computational complexity also increases, with a larger size of population, thereby resulting in a limitation in terms of available space and time.

The Pareto-optimal front, with a population size of 100 chromosomes, is illustrated in Figure 18.3 for the three data sets. Here we plot the reduct size versus the number of misclassifications over the training set (as obtained from the object pairs in the d-distinction table) at the end of 15,000 generations.

We found that with the increase in number of generations the $f_1(\nu)$ component of Equation (18.7) gains precedence over the $f_2(\nu)$ component of Equation (18.8) in the fitness function. Thereby the number of minimal reducts (having 100% discrimination between training samples) decreases, as compared to those having less number of attributes but incapable of perfect discrimination.

Figure 18.4 depicts sample normalized gene expression values of a set of three genes for leukemia data. The partitions Th_i and Th_f of Equation (18.6) are marked parallel to the abscissa. The samples are listed classwise and sequentially, such that one can observe the marked change in gene expression values of these attributes corresponding to the two output classes. This also serves to highlight the importance of these selected features (in reduct) in arriving at a good discriminatory decision.

TABLE 18.2 Reduct Generation and Classification of Gene Expression Data Using MOGA

Data Set	Population Size	Minimal Reduct Size	$k=1$ C_1	C_2	Net	$k=3$ C_1	C_2	Net	$k=5$ C_1	C_2	Net	$k=7$ C_1	C_2	Net
Colon:	50	10	80.0	90.9	83.9	75.0	90.9	80.6	75.0	81.8	77.4	75.0	72.7	74.2
number of genes 2000,	100	9	90.0	90.9	90.3	90.0	90.9	90.3	90.0	81.8	87.1	90.0	63.6	80.6
reduce to 1102	200	8	85.0	90.9	87.1	90.0	81.8	87.1	90.0	90.9	90.3	95.0	81.8	90.3
	300	8	75.0	72.7	74.2	80.0	72.7	77.4	80.0	63.6	74.2	80.0	63.6	74.2
Lymphoma:	50	2	92.6	90.5	91.7	96.3	95.2	95.8	96.3	95.2	95.8	96.3	95.2	95.8
number of genes 4026,	100	3	92.6	90.5	91.7	96.3	95.2	95.8	96.3	95.2	95.8	96.3	95.2	95.8
reduce to 1867	200	3	96.3	90.5	93.8	96.3	95.2	95.8	96.3	95.2	95.8	96.3	95.2	95.8
	300	2	92.6	90.5	91.7	96.3	95.2	95.8	96.3	95.2	95.8	96.3	95.2	95.8
Leukemia:	50	3	100.0	85.7	94.1	100.0	78.6	91.2	100.0	78.6	91.2	100.0	71.4	88.2
number of genes 7129,	100	3	100.0	78.6	91.2	95.0	85.7	91.2	100.0	78.6	91.2	100.0	78.6	91.2
reduce to 3783	150	2	90.0	71.4	82.4	90.0	100.0	94.1	90.0	85.7	88.2	90.0	85.7	88.2
	180	2	95.0	71.4	85.3	100.0	71.4	88.2	100.0	71.4	88.2	100.0	71.4	88.2

k-Nearest-Neighbors Classification (%) on Test Set

Note: C_1 and C_2 are two classes and Net is the average classification score of both classes.

433

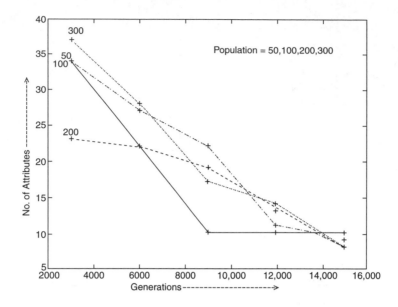

FIGURE 18.2   Plot of minimal reduct size versus generations with different population sizes for multiobjective optimization on colon data.

18.4.1 Comparison

Feature selection has been reported in the literature [4, 6, 11]. Huang [11] used a probabilistic neural network for feature selection based on correlation with class distinction. In the case of leukemia data, there is 100% correct classification with a 10-gene set. For colon data, a 10-gene set produces a classification score of 79.0%. From Table 18.2 we obtain a correct classification of 90.3% with a 9-gene set, whereas the reduced attribute size comes down to two or three for leukemia data.

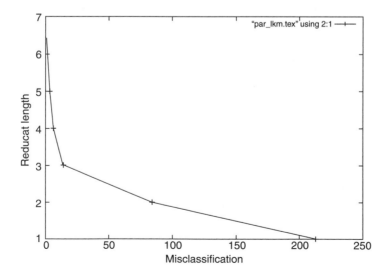

FIGURE 18.3   Pareto-optimal front for colon data set.

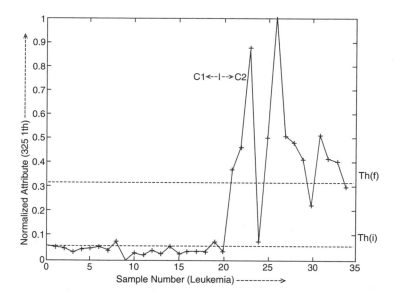

FIGURE 18.4 Plot of normalized gene expression value of attributes U46499 leukemia data set.

Chu et al. [6] employ a *t*-test-based feature selection with a fuzzy neural network. A five-gene set provides 100% correct classification for lymphoma data. From Table 18.2, we determine a misclassification on just two samples from the test data using a two-gene set for lymphoma.

Cao et al. [4] apply saliency analysis to support vector machines for gene selection in tissue classification. The importance of genes is ranked by evaluating the sensitivity of the output to the inputs in terms of the partial derivative. The *recursive saliency analysis* (RSA) algorithm is developed to remove irrelevant genes in leukemia and colon data. Table 18.3 lists a comparative study of RSA with the proposed evolutionary-rough method in terms of the number of misclassifications on the test data.

We also made a comparative study with some other logically similar fitness functions [3, 21] involving combinations of

$$f_1(v) = \frac{1}{L_v} \tag{18.10}$$

$$f_2(v) = \begin{cases} \dfrac{C_v}{(m^2-m)/2} & \text{if } C_v < \dfrac{m^2-m}{2} \\ \left(\dfrac{C_v}{(m^2-m)/2} + \dfrac{1}{2}\right)\dfrac{1}{2} & \text{if } C_v = \dfrac{m^2-m}{2} \end{cases} \tag{18.11}$$

TABLE 18.3 Comparative Performance as Number of Misclassification

Data Set	Leukemia			Colon	
Number of genes	2	3	8	9	10
Number of misclassifications for evolutionary-rough	2	2	3	3	5
Number of genes	2	4	2	4	8
Number of misclassifications for RSA	4	2	8.5 ± 0.58	6.5 ± 1.73	5.0 ± 1.41

as adapted in the multiobjective framework. There was no observable improvement in performance here while using the multiobjective algorithm, as compared to that employing the functions of Equations (18.7) and (18.8).

Reduct generation with single-objective (classical) GA [21] was also investigated for different population sizes. The fitness function $F_t = \alpha_1 f_1(\mathbf{v}) + \alpha_2 f_2(\mathbf{v})$ was used in terms of Equations (18.7) and (18.8) with the parameters $\alpha_1 = \alpha_2 = 1$. Additionally, we investigated with $0 < \alpha_1, \alpha_2 < 1$ for $\alpha_1 = 1 - \alpha_2$. Sample results are provided in Table 18.4 for a population size of 100 with optimal values being generated for $\alpha_1 = 0.9$. It is observed that for different choices of α_1 and α_2 the sizes of the minimal reduct were 15, 18, and 19 for colon, lymphoma, and leukemia data, respectively. This is more than the reduct size generated by the proposed multiobjective approach illustrated in Table 18.2. Moreover, the classification performance in Table 18.4 is also observed to be poorer. Comparison is provided for the same set of parameter initializations with runs over the same number of generations using similar objective functions. It is observed that the plots stabilize at a larger reduct size in single-objective as compared to multiobjective optimization. Moreover, there is a convergence to noticeably homogeneous solutions in the population in single-objective GA resulting in stagnation of performance.

A data reduction technique based on *principal-component analysis* (PCA) [18] has been very popular in data mining [13]. Eigenvectors of the covariance matrix of a data set identify a linear projection that produces uncorrelated features. PCA allows extraction of the most relevant eigenvalues and eigenvectors, which provides a good approximation for the discrimination. We employed PCA to generate an optimal set of n_o transformed features (eigenvalues) subject to a threshold of 99% approximation for the decision function. These features were subsequently evaluated using a k-NN classifier (for $k = 1, 3, 5, 7$) on the test set. The best performance (% recognition scores) for the three cancer data sets were as follows:

Colon: $k = 1$ with $n_o = 7$ eigenvalues, $C_1 = 90.0$, $C_2 = 66.7$, Net $= 80.7$.

Lymphoma: $k = 3$ with $n_o = 8$ eigenvalues, $C_1 = 95.5$, $C_2 = 96.3$, Net $= 95.8$.

Leukemia: $k = 1$ with $n_o = 8$ eigenvalues, $C_1 = 100.0$, $C_2 = 64.3$, Net $= 85.3$. Our evolutionary-rough strategy is found to work better in all cases.

18.5 CONCLUSION

We have described an evolutionary-rough feature selection algorithm using redundancy reduction for effective handling of high-dimensional microarray gene expression data. The NSGA-II has been modified to more effectively handle large data.

Since microarray data typically consist of a large number of redundant attributes, we have done an initial preprocessing for redundancy reduction. The objective was to retain only those genes that play a major role in discerning between objects. This preprocessing aids faster convergence along the search space. Moreover, a reduction in the rows (object pairs) of the distinction table was made by restricting comparisons only between objects belonging to different classes, giving the d-distinction table. This is intuitively meaningful, since our objective here is to determine the reducts that can discern between objects belonging to different classes. A further reduction in computational complexity is thereby achieved.

TABLE 18.4 Comparative Performance on Gene Expression Data Using Single-Objective GA

Data Set	Minimal Reduct Size	k = 1			k = 3			k = 5			k = 7		
		C_1	C_2	Net	C_1	C_2	Net	C_1	C_2	Net	C_1	C_2	Net
Colon	15	75.0	63.6	71.0	70.0	36.4	58.1	75.0	0.0	48.4	90.0	9.1	61.3
Lymphoma	18	85.2	71.4	79.2	81.5	90.5	85.4	92.6	81.0	87.5	92.6	85.7	89.6
Leukemia	19	90.0	50.0	75.5	90.0	57.1	76.5	95.0	14.3	61.7	100.0	14.3	64.7

k-Nearest-Neighbor Classification (%) on Test Set

437

Selection of the most frequently occurring attributes among the reducts may prove significant for biologists. This is because the attributes in the core [14] (the intersection of the reducts) could be the relevant genes responsible for a certain medical condition. For example, let us consider the results presented in Table 18.2 to illustrate selection of important attributes (or genes) in the reducts. It is found that generally genes $Hsa.8147$ and $Hsa.1039$ occurred most frequently among the reducts in colon data. Similar analysis on lymphoma data led to a focus on genes $1559X$ and $1637X$. In leukemia data, the genes $U46499$, $M28130$, and $Y00787$ are found to be in the core. In the next phase, we plan to collaborate with biological experts to validate these findings.

REFERENCES

1. Special Issue on Bioinformatics. *IEEE Computer*, 35(7), July 2002.

2. S. Ando and H. Iba. Artificial immune system for classification of cancer: Applications of evolutionary computing. *Lecture Notes in Computer Science*, 2611:1–10, 2003.

3. A. T. Bjorvand. "Rough Enough": A system supporting the rough sets approach. In *Proceedings of the Sixth Scandinavian Conference on Artificial Intelligence (SCAI '97)*, Helsinki, Finland, IOS Press, Amsterdam, The Netherlands, 1997, pp. 290–291.

4. L. Cao, H. P. Lee, C. K. Seng, and Q. Gu. Saliency analysis of support vector machines for gene selection in tissue classification. *Neural Comput. Appl.*, 11:244–249, 2003.

5. S. -B. Cho and H. -H. Won. Data mining for gene expression profiles from DNA microarray. *Int. J. Software Eng. Knowledge Eng.*, 13:593–608, 2003.

6. F. Chu, W. Xie, and L. Wang. Gene selection and cancer classification using a fuzzy neural network. In *Fuzzy Information, 2004. IEEE Annual Meeting of the North American Fuzzy Information Processing Society (NAFIPS '04)*, Vol. 2, 2004, pp. 555–559.

7. K. Deb. *Multi-Objective Optimization Using Evolutionary Algorithms*. Wiley, London, 2001.

8. K. Deb, S. Agarwal, A. Pratap, and T. Meyarivan. A fast and elitist multiobjective genetic algorithm: NSGA-II. *IEEE Trans. Evolutionary Computat.*, 6:182–197, 2002.

9. M. E. Futschik, A. Reeve, and N. Kasabov. Evolving connectionist systems for knowledge discovery from gene expression data of cancer tissue. *Artif. Intell. Med.*, 28:165–189, 2003.

10. D. E. Goldberg. *Genetic Algorithms in Search, Optimization and Machine Learning*, 1st ed. Addison-Wesley Longman, Boston, MA, 1989.

11. C. -J. Huang. Class prediction of cancer using probabilistic neural networks and relative correlation metric. *Appl. Artif. Intell.*, 18:117–128, 2004.

12. M. Karzynski, A. Mateos, J. Herrero, and J. Dopazo. Using a genetic algorithm and a perceptron for feature selection and supervised class learning in DNA microarray data. *Artif. Intell. Rev.*, 20:39–51, 2003.

13. S. Mitra and T. Acharya. *Data Mining: Multimedia, Soft Computing, and Bioinformatics*. Wiley, New York, 2003.

14. Z. Pawlak. *Rough Sets, Theoretical Aspects of Reasoning about Data*. Kluwer Academic, Dordrecht, 1991.

15. P. E. Hart and R. O. Duda. *Pattern Classification*, 2nd ed. Wiley InterScience, Canada, 2001.

16. V. Roth and T. Lange. Bayesian class discovery in microarray datasets. *IEEE Trans. Biomed. Eng.*, 51:707–718, 2004.

17. A. Skowron and C. Rauszer. The discernibility matrices and functions in information systems. In R. Slowiński (Ed.), *Intelligent Decision Support, Handbook of Applications and Advances of the Rough Sets Theory*. Kluwer Academic, Dordrecht, 1992, pp. 331–362.

18. J. T. Tou and R. C. Gonzalez. *Pattern Recognition Principles*. Addison-Wesley, London, 1974.

19. Y. Turkeli, A. Ercil, and O. U. Sezerman. Effect of feature extraction and feature selection on expression data from epithelial ovarian cancer. In *Engineering in Medicine and Biology Society, 2003. Proceedings of the 25th Annual International Conference of the IEEE*, Vol. 4, 2003, pp. 3559–3562.

20. H. -H. Won and S. -B. Cho. Ensemble classifier with negatively correlated features for cancer classification. *J. KISS: Software Appl.*, 30:1124–1134, 2003.

21. J. Wroblewski. Finding minimal reducts using genetic algorithms. Technical Report 16/95. Warsaw Institute of Technology—Institute of Computer Science, Poland, 1995.

22. L. Yu and H. Liu. Feature selection for high-dimensional data: A fast correlation-based filter solution. In *Proceedings of the Twentieth International Conference on Machine Learning (ICML '03)*, Vol. 20, AAAI Press, Washington DC, 2003, pp. 856–863.

23. L. Yu and H. Liu. Efficient feature selection via analysis of relevance and redundancy. *J. Machine Learning Res.*, 5:1205–1224, 2004.

24. L. A. Zadeh. Fuzzy logic, neural networks, and soft computing. *Commun. ACM*, 37:77–84, 1994.

BIOLOGICAL DATA MINING

PART E

REGRESSION ANALYSIS
OF BIOLOGICAL DATA

CHAPTER 19

BUILDING VALID REGRESSION MODELS FOR BIOLOGICAL DATA USING STATA AND R

CHARLES LINDSEY[1] and SIMON J. SHEATHER[2]
[1]StataCorp, College Station, Texas
[2]Department of Statistics, Texas A&M University, College Station, Texas

19.1 INTRODUCTION

Regression analysis explores the nature of a response conditioned on a control. Knowledge of the control or predictor variables provides insight into the response. Linear regression is a technique which is widely used to model the relationship between a response and its predictor variables.

In these models, at fixed values of the predictors the mean of the response is a linear combination of the predictor values. So for predictors $x_1, \ldots, x_k$ and response y, we have

$$E[y|\mathbf{x}] = \mathbf{x}'\boldsymbol{\beta} = \beta_0 + \beta_1 x_1 + \cdots + \beta_k x_k \qquad (19.1)$$

We can also describe this setting by

$$y = \beta_0 + \beta_1 x_1 + \cdots + \beta_k x_k + e \qquad (19.2)$$

where e is a zero-mean error term. We assume that this has constant variance.

In this chapter we will show how linear regression can be applied to model relationships in biological data. The example response variables include brain weight, size of fish populations, HDL (high-density lipoprotein) cholesterol level, and diabetes progression. Our approach emphasizes multiple diagnostics and graphics. In this way, those who practice the methods we describe will be careful and thorough, and the technique will be correctly applied. The statistical software R [23] and Stata [29] are used to perform our analyses. The program code used can be downloaded at www.stat.tamu.edu/~sheather/. We boldface which commands we use in the text.

When fitting a regression model to data, we argue that it is important to determine whether the proposed regression model is a valid model (i.e., determine whether it provides an adequate fit to the data). The main tools we will use to validate regression assumptions are plots involving standardized residuals and/or fitted values. We shall see that these plots

Biological Knowledge Discovery Handbook: Preprocessing, Mining, and Postprocessing of Biological Data,
First Edition. Edited by Mourad Elloumi and Albert Y. Zomaya.
© 2014 John Wiley & Sons, Inc. Published 2014 by John Wiley & Sons, Inc.

enable us to assess visually whether the assumptions are being violated and, under certain conditions, point to what should be done to overcome these violations. We shall also consider a tool, called *marginal model plots*, which have wider application than residual plots.

Examination of the residual plots can demonstrate whether the assumption of constant error variance is reasonable. If this assumption is violated, it may invalidate inference on the model. If the variance is not constant, we will show how transforming the variables can lead to a valid model.

We will also show how to assess the extent of collinearity among the predictor variables. High collinearity among the predictors bloats the variance of estimation and prediction using the fitted model. We will use variance inflation factors to check collinearity.

It is also advsiable to determine which (if any) of the data points are outliers, that is, points which do not follow the pattern set by the bulk of the data, when one takes into account the given model. We will briefly discuss outlier analysis here. In addition to checking for outliers, one should determine which (if any) of the data points have predictor values that have an unusually large effect on the estimated regression model (such points are called *leverage points*).

An alternative to examination of the variance inflation factors and the fitted model coefficient estimates is the examination of added variable plots. These can be used to assess the effect of each predictor variable on the response variable, having adjusted for the effect of other predictor variables.

Further details on outlier analysis, leverage points, and added variable plots are found in [26].

19.2 FITTING THE MODEL

On observing a sample on the response y and predictor variables $\mathbf{x}$, we will demonstate how the regression function $E[y|\mathbf{x}]$ can be estimated. The regression of y on $\mathbf{x}$ can be modeled in Stata with the **regress** command. In R, the **lm** function can be used. Use of these commands, or an analogous command in another software package, is the first step in modeling a linear regression. This is called *fitting the model* and provides an estimate of β.

Our first example is taken from [32]. Its contents were recorded in 1996 by the Minnesota Department of Natural Resources. Their goal was to study the abundance of black crappies (a fish species) in Swan Lake, Minnesota. The response variable is *lcpue*, the logarithm of the catch of 200 mm or longer black crappies per unit of fishing effort.

The lone predictor variable is *day*, the day of sampling, measured as the number of days after June 19, 1996. No samples were taken when the lake was frozen in winter, and some were taken in spring of the following year. All samples were taken before the next population of fish was born in late June of 1997.

We fit the linear regression of *lcpue* on *day*:

$$E[lcpue|day] = \beta_0 + \beta_1 day \tag{19.3}$$

Fitting the model using the **regress** command discussed earlier, we obtain the results in Table 19.1.

The top right column of the output in Table 19.1 displays summary information on the model. We have 27 observations in the data. A test of the F-statistic [calculated as $F(1, 25)$] shows that the model is statistically significant at the .01 level (**Prob > F**). The R^2 value

TABLE 19.1   Model (19.3)

```
. regress lcpue day

      Source |       SS       df       MS              Number of obs =      27
- - - - - - -+- - - - - - - - - - - - - - -           F( 1,    25) =   16.83
       Model | 17.9303408        1  17.9303408         Prob > F      =  0.0004
    Residual | 26.627575        25   1.065103          R-squared     =  0.4024
- - - - - - -+- - - - - - - - - - - - - - -           Adj R-squared =  0.3785
       Total | 44.5579158       26  1.71376599         Root MSE      =   1.032


- - - - - - - - - - - - - - - - - - - - - - - - - - - - - - - - - - - - - - - -
       lcpue |     Coef.   Std. Err.        t    P>|t|     [95% Conf. Interval]
- - - - - - -+- - - - - - - - - - - - - - - - - - - - - - - - - - - - - - - - -
         day |  .0080404   .0019596      4.10    0.000     .0040044    .0120763
       _cons |  1.641772    .321429      5.11    0.000     .9797768    2.303768
- - - - - - - - - - - - - - - - - - - - - - - - - - - - - - - - - - - - - - - -
```

is 0.4024, so we estimate that the model explains 40% of the variation in lcpue. So our estimation of *lcpue* should be substantially better when we condition on day. The **root MSE** is an estimate of the variance of *lcpue* at fixed values of *day*. The **source** section contains information used in calculating the F and R^2 statistics.

The *lcpue* section of the output shows the individual estimates for $\boldsymbol{\beta}$. These are in the **Coef** column. Their standard errors and confidence intervals are also listed. The *p*-values for the Wald test of the coefficient being zero is given in the $P > |t|$ column. We find both coefficients have a statistically significant difference from zero.

Based on this output, the model seems fine. We can predict the mean of *lcpue* linearly with the value of *day*. This course of action would be naive. We will show how to assess the validity of a linear regression model in the next section. After evaluating the numeric output produced by the methods described in this section and using the graphical methods detailed in the next section, the model estimates can be used with confidence.

19.3 VALIDITY OF THE MODEL

After an estimate of $\boldsymbol{\beta}$, $\hat{\boldsymbol{\beta}}$, is made, we can estimate fitted or predictive values of the response y at certain predictor values. We predict y with its conditional mean $E[y|\mathbf{x}] = \mathbf{x}'\boldsymbol{\beta}$.

For the *i*th observation in the sample, define the fitted value as

$$\hat{y}_i = \mathbf{x}_i'\hat{\boldsymbol{\beta}} \tag{19.4}$$

This is our estimate of the mean of y at the predictor values of observation i. The residuals are defined as the response minus the fitted values:

$$\hat{e}_i = y_i - \hat{y}_i \tag{19.5}$$

If the regression function $E[y|\mathbf{x}]$ captures all of the information about y that $\mathbf{x}$ provides, then our model is valid. Formally, the regression model is valid if $y - E[y|\mathbf{x}]$ is statistically independent of the $\mathbf{x}$ variables.

The residuals are estimates of $y - E[y|\mathbf{x}]$ in the sample. So we can assess the validity of the model by examining whether the residuals depend on $\mathbf{x}$. We should see random scatters when plotting the residuals versus each predictor or any linear combination of them.

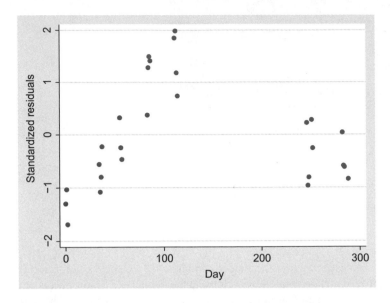

FIGURE 19.1   Model (19.3) standardized residuals.

The residuals can be standardized such that they have constant variance. This will ensure that patterns in the residual plots are not distorted. Each unit of the standardized residuals will correspond with a standard deviation as well. So identification of the **outliers**, points which fall far from the main group of residuals, which the model does not explain well can be more easily classified and investigated. Details on outlier analysis can be found in [26].

Now we plot the standardized residuals for model (19.3) versus days in Figure 19.1. The **predict** command with the **rstandard** option is used to produce the standardized residuals.

Figure 19.1 does not show a random scatter. We see two clusters. The leftmost appears to be sloping upward, while the right slopes downward. This suggests a quadratic pattern. In Figure 19.2, we fit a quadratic function to the points with the Stata command **qfit** and redraw the graph.

The presence of this quadratic pattern suggests that we are not explaining all of the effect of *day* on *lcpue* with the linear term for *day* in (19.3).

We can account for this quadratic pattern by adding a quadratic term for *day* to model (19.3). We treat this new term as a separate predictor. The linear regression, while no longer linear in *day*, is linear in the coefficients of *day* and day^2.

We make a note of caution here. The variable *day* is positive, and so it may be highly correlated with day^2. This correlation, called multicollinearity since it happens between predictors, will affect the estimates of variance of the individual predictor coefficients. So it will be hard to discern what individual effect a predictor has on the response.

We now fit the full quadratic model:

$$E[lcpue|day] = \beta_0 + \beta_1 day + \beta_2 day^2 \tag{19.6}$$

Use of the **regress** command in Stata provides the estimates in Table 19.2.

The quadratic term is very significant, while the intercept _cons is no longer significant. We estimate the model explained over 80% of the variance of *lcpue*. We can assess whether there are problems with multicollinearity by calculating the *variance inflation factors*. These

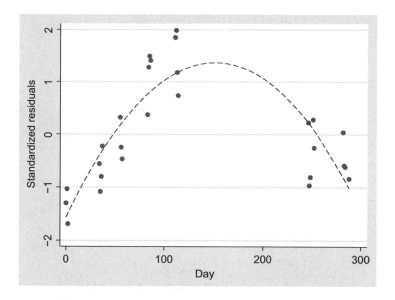

FIGURE 19.2 Model (19.3) standardized residuals with quadratic line.

are created by regressing the predictors on each other, measuring their linear relation. Variance inflation factors above 5 are cause for concern. Stata performs this calculation with the **vif** command. We show the results in Table 19.3.

This is a disturbingly high variance inflation factor. So we should be cautious about using model (19.6).

We can fix model (19.6) so that multicollinearity is no longer a problem. By centering *day*, we reduce the correlation between the linear and quadratic forms. Rather than having day zero at June 19, 1996, day zero becomes October 25, 1996. And we measure days before and after this date. The direction of association between *day* and *lcpue* will remain the same. The new day variable is called *dayc*:

$$E[lcpue|dayc] = \beta_0 + \beta_1 dayc + \beta_2 dayc^2 \tag{19.7}$$

TABLE 19.2 Model (19.6)

Source	SS	df	MS		
Model	36.7168453	2	18.3584226		
Residual	7.84107055	24	.326711273		
Total	44.5579158	26	1.71376599		

Number of obs = 27
F(2, 24) = 56.19
Prob > F = 0.0000
R-squared = 0.8240
Adj R-squared = 0.8094
Root MSE = .57159

lcpue	Coef.	Std. Err.	t	P>|t|	[95% Conf. Interval]
day	.0466052	.0052002	8.96	0.000	.0358725 .057338
day2	-.0001273	.0000168	-7.58	0.000	-.0001619 -.0000926
_cons	.0921151	.2710245	0.34	0.737	-.4672519 .6514821

TABLE 19.3   Model (19.6) Variance Inflation Factors

```
. vif

    Variable |       VIF       1/VIF
-------------+----------------------
         day |     22.96    0.043560
        day2 |     22.96    0.043560
-------------+----------------------
    Mean VIF |     22.96
```

TABLE 19.4   Model (19.7)

```
. reg lcpue dayc dayc2

      Source |       SS       df       MS              Number of obs =      27
-------------+------------------------------           F(  2,    24) =   56.19
       Model | 36.7168452        2  18.3584226         Prob > F      =  0.0000
    Residual | 7.84107058       24  .326711274         R-squared     =  0.8240
-------------+------------------------------           Adj R-squared =  0.8094
       Total | 44.5579158       26  1.71376599         Root MSE      =  .57159

-----------------------------------------------------------------------------
       lcpue |      Coef.   Std. Err.      t    P>|t|     [95% Conf. Interval]
-------------+---------------------------------------------------------------
        dayc |   .0137816   .0013233    10.41   0.000     .0110504    .0165128
       dayc2 |  -.0001273   .0000168    -7.58   0.000    -.0001619   -.0000926
       _cons |   3.985949   .2044999    19.49   0.000     3.563882    4.408016
-----------------------------------------------------------------------------
```

While the coefficient for the quadratic term remains the same in Table 19.4, the coefficient for day has been reduced, and its standard error estimate is smaller. The constant is now significant again. The very high R^2 value is still present.

We show the variance inflation factors in Table 19.5. The variance inflation factors are much lower now, and well below 5, so we should not worry about multicollinearity.

Finally, to check that (19.7) is a valid model, we look at a plot of the standardized residuals versus centered days in Figure 19.3.

This is a random scatter, showing no quadratic pattern. We conlude that model (19.7) is a valid and powerful model. So we can confidently predict *lcpue* using the centered day of measurement.

TABLE 19.5   Model (19.7) Variance Inflation Factors

```
. vif

    Variable |       VIF       1/VIF
-------------+----------------------
        dayc |      1.49    0.672662
       dayc2 |      1.49    0.672662
-------------+----------------------
    Mean VIF |      1.49
```

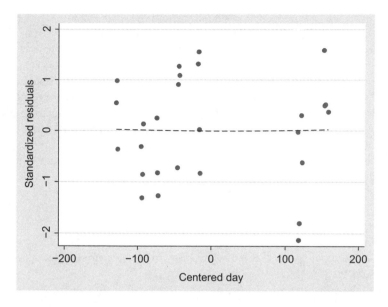

FIGURE 19.3   Model (19.7) standardized residuals with quadratic line.

19.4   NONCONSTANT VARIANCE AND VARIABLE TRANSFORMATION

Patterns in the standardized residual plots can indicate nonconstant variance of the response variable as the predictors vary. This can be problematic for prediction.

At large values of one predictor, you may obtain a very precise prediction of the response, while at low values of another predictor, your prediction of the response is much wider. We should have only a single estimate for the variance of the prediction of the response on the predictors. The specific values of the predictors should only affect the mean of the response. The variance of the response, when conditioned on the predictors, should be constant. In the Swan lake example, the square root of this variance was estimated in the **root MSE** part of the regression table.

One way to deal with nonconstant variance is to use robust estimation for fitting the regression. Stata supports this option through using the **vce()** option in **regress**. Sometimes the model is misspecified such that the response and predictors do not have a direct linear relationship but have a linear relationship under monotone transformations. Nonconstant variance can suggest this scenario. In this case, even a robust adjustment of the standard errors will not be adequate to fit the model.

Basically, we observe the data in the wrong scale and must transform it to the correct scaling to see the proper linear regression relationship between the response and predictors. This involves exponentiating the variables to be transformed or taking their logarithms. Transformations that move the variables to the correct scale for regression can also stabilize the conditional variance of the response. There are a variety of methods to perform these transformations.

An inverse response plot estimates a transformation for the response variable such that the tranformed response and predictors have a linear relationship. This actually uses the fitted values from the regression of the untransformed response on the predictors, $\hat{y}_i$. A plot of $\hat{y}_i$ and the response y is created, and a curve is fit to the scatter points. The power of this curve is the optimal power that should be used to transform the response y. The user-written Stata command **irp** [20] peforms inverse-response plots in Stata. The inverse-response plot was developed by [6], based on results from [10].

Box–Cox transformations may also be used [3]. Here predictors are held constant and the response transformed or predictors transformed based on the constant response. There are also univariate and multivariate forms of these transformations, which do not use the predictor/response regression settting [30]. The Stata command **boxcox** performs the conditional transformations that use the relationship between the predictors and response. The user-written Stata command **mboxcox** [19] performs the full multivariate transformation and univariate transformation.

The Box–Cox transformation transforms its input variables to multivariate normality. As a result, they become approximately linearly related, constant in conditional variance, and each becomes marginally normal.

We examine a data set from [32] (originally studied in [2]) containing body and brain weights of 62 mammal species. Brain weight (*brain*) is measured in grams, while body weight (*body*) is measured in kilograms.

We regress the variable *brain* on *body*:

$$E[brain|body] = \beta_0 + \beta_1 body \qquad (19.8)$$

We obtain a powerful model. The results are shown in Table 19.6. We estimate that body weight explains 87% of the variability in brain weight. Both the constant and coefficient for *body* are significant as well. The standardized residual plot in Figure 19.4 puts the model in a more negative light.

The labeled points, corresponding to Asian and African elephant species and humans, are severe outliers. Recall that each unit of the standardized outlier scale is a standard deviation. Further, the points are very densely clustered above zero. We will examine a plot without the three outliers in Figure 19.5 to more thoroughly investigate the clustering.

When we examine the points that are not outliers, we still see heavy clustering close to zero. This suggests that the variance of the brain weight of small-body-weight mammals is lesser than the variance of the brain weight of larger body weight mammals. So our prediction of brain weight on body weight cannot use a single standard error estimate. A power transformation may solve this problem.

TABLE 19.6 Model (19.8)

```
. regress brain body

      Source |       SS       df       MS              Number of obs =      62
-------------+------------------------------           F(  1,    60) =  411.12
       Model |  46067328.8        1  46067328.8         Prob > F      =  0.0000
    Residual |  6723217.22       60  112053.62          R-squared     =  0.8726
-------------+------------------------------           Adj R-squared =  0.8705
       Total |  52790546.1       61  865418.788         Root MSE      =  334.74


       brain |      Coef.   Std. Err.       t    P>|t|     [95% Conf. Interval]
-------------+----------------------------------------------------------------
        body |   .9664599   .0476651    20.28   0.000     .8711156    1.061804
       _cons |   91.00864   43.55574     2.09   0.041     3.884194    178.1331
```

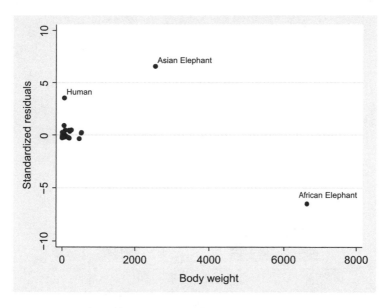

FIGURE 19.4   Model (19.8) standardized residuals.

A look at the univariate box plots for brain and body weight in Figure 19.6 shows that both are severely skewed.

The outlying human and elephant species are omitted from the plots in Figure 19.6. Their inclusion makes the variables even more skewed. Linear regression works better on symmetric variables than skewed. So we may try transforming both brain and body

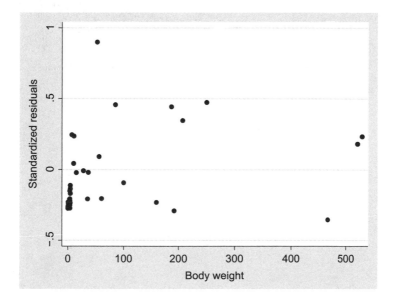

FIGURE 19.5   Model (19.8) standardized residuals without severe outliers.

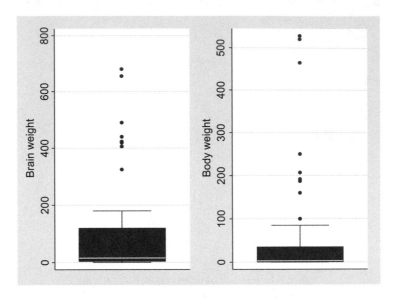

FIGURE 19.6   Box plots of brain and body weight.

weight. Two approaches using the Box–Cox and inverse-response plot techniques will be demonstrated. These two approaches are advocated in [7] and later again in [26].

In the first, we will transform the variable body to normality using a univariate Box–Cox transformation. This will make it symmetric. Then the response variable brain will be transformed using an inverse-response plot. The **mboxcox** command is used to estimate the Box–Cox tranformation.

The Box–Cox transformation estimates are shown in Table 19.7. Our estimate of the power transformation for *body* is −0.0195531. The confidence interval for our estimate includes zero, and the likelihood ratio test cannot reject that the power transformation

TABLE 19.7   Box–Cox Transformation for Body Weight

```
. mboxcox body
Multivariate boxcox transformations
                                             Number of obs   =       62


Likelihood Ratio Tests
- - - - - - - - - - - - - - - - - - - - - - - - - - - - - - - - - - - -
Test          | Log Likelihood     Chi2         df           Prob > Chi2
- - - - - - - + - - - - - - - - - - - - - - - - - - - - - - - - - - - -
All powers -1 | -374.4313          442.0717     1            0
All powers  0 | -153.5353          .2795279     1            .59701081
All powers  1 | -421.6921          536.5932     1            0
- - - - - - - - - - - - - - - - - - - - - - - - - - - - - - - - - - - -


- - - - - - - - - - - - - - - - - - - - - - - - - - - - - - - - - - - -
              |    Coef.    Std. Err.      z    P>|z|    [95% Conf. Interval]
- - - - - - - + - - - - - - - - - - - - - - - - - - - - - - - - - - - -
lambda        |
        body  |  -.0195531   .0370105   -0.53   0.597   -.0920924    .0529861
- - - - - - - - - - - - - - - - - - - - - - - - - - - - - - - - - - - -
```

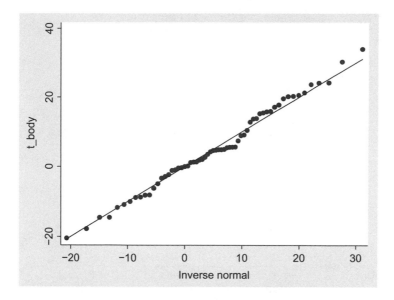

FIGURE 19.7 Normal quantile plot of ln(body).

parameter is zero. This implies that our power transformation should be the natural logarithm of body weight.

Rather than simply raising a variable to a power, a simple power transformation, we use a modified-scaled power transformation. This transformation uses the geometric mean of the original variable and the scale of the transforming power. The variable is transformed such that it maintains its original unit of measurement and correlation direction with other variables. The variable also still gains the benefits of the normalizing transformation. The modified-scaled power transformation is implemented in the user-written command **mbctrans**. The transformed version of *body* is saved as *t_body*.

Note that the additional scaling of the variables does not affect how well the transformation linearizes the relationship between them or forces them to have constant conditional variance. It only eases their interpretation once they are examined in the new scale.

In Figure 19.7, We graph the quantiles of the transformed version of *t_body* versus the quantiles of a normal random variable with the same mean and variance. The plot suggests that the log-transformed body variable is consistent with a normal distribution.

Now we use the **irp** command to produce an inverse-response plot for transforming brain based on the transformed body weight variable *t_body*.

The fitted values in Table 19.8 are from the regression of *brain* on the transformed *body*. The optimal power 0.0117948 is calculated by minimizing the residual sum of squares of the fitted values on the transformed response. This means that we choose the transformation power such that the best model of the fitted values on the transformed response is chosen. Figure 19.8 contains the inverse-response plot.

We see in the graph that the zero power and optimal power of 0.0117948 yield very similar fits to the scatter points. So we will transform *brain* using the zero power by taking its natural logarithm. Again, we use a modified-scaled transformation. So **mbctrans** is used on *brain* to create *t_brain*.

TABLE 19.8   Inverse-Response Plot Optimal Power

```
. irp brain t_body, opt try(0)

+ - - - - - - - - - - - - - - - - - - - - - - - - - - - - - - - - - - - +
| Response  | brain                                                     |
| - - - - - + - - - - - - - - - - - - - - - - - - - - - - - - - - - - - |
|  Fitted   | 41.71*t_body + 67.8                                       |
+ - - - - - - - - - - - - - - - - - - - - - - - - - - - - - - - - - - - +


+ - - - - - - - - - - - - - +
| Optimal Power |  .0117948 |
+ - - - - - - - - - - - - - +


+ - - - - - - - - - - - - - +
|     Power | RSS( F | R ) |
| - - - - - + - - - - - - - +
|  .0117948 |    1217531    |
|         0 |    1221686    |
+ - - - - - - - - - - - - - +
```

As an alternative, our second method of transformation estimates a multivariate Box–Cox transformation for *brain* and *body* together. The results of this estimation are shown in Table 19.9.

The estimated parameters differ slightly from those of the first method. However, the conclusion that 0 is an appropriate power of transformation is still supported. The **Prob > Chi2** *p*-value in the **All powers 0** row shows that we cannot reject that zero is the appropriate transformation power for both *brain* and *body*. So a logarithmic transformation to both variables is suggested by this second method as well as the first.

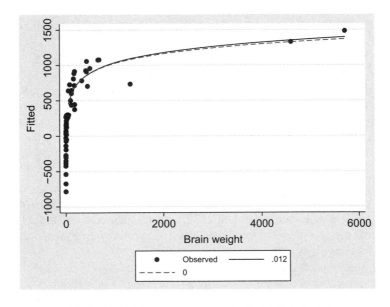

FIGURE 19.8   Inverse-response plot for brain‖ln(body).

TABLE 19.9   Multivariate Box–Cox for Brain and Body Weight

```
. mboxcox brain body
Multivariate boxcox transformations
                                              Number of obs   =        62

Likelihood Ratio Tests
- - - - - - - - - - - - - - - - - - - - - - - - - - - - - - - - - - - - -
Test          | Log Likelihood    Chi2         df           Prob > Chi2
- - - - - - - + - - - - - - - - - - - - - - - - - - - - - - - - - - - - -
All powers -1 | -704.1436         759.9946     2            0
All powers  0 | -325.0938         1.895042     2            .38770092
All powers  1 | -781.6084         914.9243     2            0
- - - - - - - - - - - - - - - - - - - - - - - - - - - - - - - - - - - - -


              |      Coef.    Std. Err.      z     P>|z|    [95% Conf. Interval]
- - - - - - - + - - - - - - - - - - - - - - - - - - - - - - - - - - - - - -
lambda        |
        brain | -.028513     .0352485    -0.81    0.419    -.0975987    .0405727
         body | -.0355785    .0265709    -1.34    0.181    -.0876564    .0164994
- - - - - - - - - - - - - - - - - - - - - - - - - - - - - - - - - - - - -
```

Now we will refit our original regression using the transformed versions of *brain* and *body*:

$$E[t\_brain|t\_body] = \beta_0 + \beta_1 t\_body \tag{19.9}$$

We see similar directions for the coefficients in model (19.9) as in model (19.8). Both the coefficient for *t_body* and the constant intercept are significant as well. Based on R^2, the model is slightly more powerful than (19.9). Figure 19.9 contains the standardized residual plot.

The standardized residual plot shows no clear pattern. The elephant species are no longer outliers, though humanity is. The residual plot supports that we have found a valid regression model between ln(*brain*) and ln(*body*).

TABLE 19.10   Model (19.9)

```
. regress t_brain t_body

      Source |      SS          df      MS            Number of obs =      62
- - - - - - - + - - - - - - - - - - - - - - -        F( 1,    60) =  697.42
       Model | 179524.833        1   179524.833       Prob > F      =  0.0000
    Residual | 15444.6826       60   257.411377       R-squared     =  0.9208
- - - - - - - + - - - - - - - - - - - - - - -        Adj R-squared =  0.9195
       Total | 194969.515       61   3196.22156       Root MSE      =  16.044


     t_brain |      Coef.    Std. Err.      t     P>|t|    [95% Conf. Interval]
- - - - - - - + - - - - - - - - - - - - - - - - - - - - - - - - - - - - - -
      t_body |  4.499638    .1703841    26.41    0.000    4.158819    4.840457
       _cons |  49.33164    2.21941     22.23    0.000    44.89216    53.77112
- - - - - - - - - - - - - - - - - - - - - - - - - - - - - - - - - - - - -
```

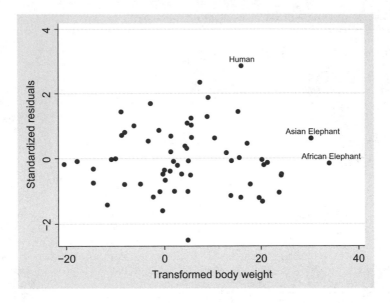

FIGURE 19.9   Model (19.9) standardized residuals.

19.5   MARGINAL MODEL PLOTS

We have discussed how to fit a linear regression model and determine the validity of a model's fit with standardized residual plots. We also described how patterns in the residual plots can suggest improvements to the model. The improvements may be the addition of functions of the predictors (e.g., adding a quadratic term) or transforming both the predictor and response.

In this section we will describe another graphical fit assessment technique, marginal model plots. These can be used in addition to standardized residual plots and can be extended to other regression models beside the linear regression models that we investigate here.

The software R will be used in this section, with the CAR package [9].

Consider the situation when we have two predictors x_1 and x_2. We wish to visually assess whether

$$y = \beta_0 + \beta_1 x_1 + \beta_2 x_2 + e \tag{19.10}$$

is an adequate model for $E[y|\mathbf{x}]$. The variable e is a zero-mean random-error term. We wish to compare the fit from (19.10) with a fit from the nonparametric regression model

$$y = f(x_1, x_2) + e \tag{19.11}$$

Under model (19.11), we can estimate $E_{19.11}[y|x_1]$ by adding a nonparametric fit to the plot of y against x_1. We want to check that the estimate of $E_{19.11}[y|x_1]$ is close to the estimate of $E_{19.10}[y|x_1]$.

Under model (19.10)

$$E_{19.10}[y|x_1] = E[\beta_0 + \beta_1 x_1 + \beta_2 x_2 + e|x_1] = \beta_0 + \beta_1 x_1 + \beta_2 E[x_2|x_1] \qquad (19.12)$$

Notice that this includes the unknown $E_{19.10}[x_2|x_1]$ and that in general there would be $p - 1$ unknowns, where p is the number of unknowns in model (19.10). Cook and Weisberg [5] overcome this problem by utilizing the following result:

$$E_{19.10}[y|x_1] = E[E_{19.10}(y|\mathbf{x})|x_1] \qquad (19.13)$$

The result follows from the well-known general result regarding conditional expectations. However, it is easy and informative to demonstrate the result in this special case. First note that

$$E_{19.10}[y|\mathbf{x}] = E_{19.10}[\beta_0 + \beta_1 x_1 + \beta_2 x_2 + e|\mathbf{x}] = \beta_0 + \beta_1 x_1 + \beta_2 x_2 \qquad (19.14)$$

so that

$$E[E_{19.10}(y|\mathbf{x})|x_1] = E[\beta_0 + \beta_1 x_1 + \beta_2 x_2|x_1) = \beta_0 + \beta_1 x_1 + \beta_2 E[x_2|x_1] \qquad (19.15)$$

matching what we found above for $E_{19.10}[y|\mathbf{x}]$.

Under model (19.10), we can estimate $E_{19.10}[y|\mathbf{x}] = \beta_0 + \beta_1 x_1 + \beta_2 x_2$ by the fitted values $\hat{y} = \hat{\beta}_0 + \hat{\beta}_1 x_1 + \hat{\beta}_2 x_2$. Utilizing (19.13), we can therefore estimate $E_{19.10}[y|x_1] = E[E_{19.10}(y|\mathbf{x})|x_1]$ by estimating $E[E_{19.10}(y|\mathbf{x})|x_1]$ with an estimate of $E[\hat{y}|x_1]$.

In summary, we wish to compare estimates under models (19.11) and (19.10) by comparing nonparametric estimates of $E(y|x_1)$ and $E(\hat{y}|x_1)$. If the two nonparametric estimates agree, then we conclude that x_1 is modeled correctly by model (19.10). If not, then we conclude that x_1 is not modeled correctly by model (19.10). We will demonstrate with an example.

Vittinghoff et al. [31] provide many examples using data from the Heart and Estrogen/Progestin Study, a clinical trial of hormone therapy for prevention of reccurrent heart attacks and death among 2763 postmenopausal women with existing coronary heart disease [15]. For example, on page 110 of [31], a regression model for HDL level based on predictors including age and body mass index (*BMI*) is considered.

We first considered the model

$$\log(HDL) = \beta_0 + \beta_1 BMI + \beta_2 age + e \qquad (19.16)$$

A log transformation of *HDL* was taken to remove skewness and model (19.16) was fit to the 2747 cases for which data were available for *HDL*, *age*, and *BMI*.

We obtain the results of the regression of model (19.16) by using the **lm** function in R. The results are shown in Table 19.11.

We find all coefficients are highly significant. An individual's age has a positive effect on their $\log(HDL)$ levels, while their body mass index has a negative effect.

Now we will assess the validity of the model. In Figure 19.10, we will render marginal model plots based on model (19.16) for $\log(HDL)$ and *BMI*, $\log(HDL)$ and *age*, and $\log(HDL)$ and $\hat{y}$, respectively.

TABLE 19.11   Model (19.16)

```
> m1 <- lm(log(HDL)~age+BMI,data=hers)
> summary(m1)

Call:
lm(formula = log(HDL) ~ age + BMI, data = hers)

Residuals:
      Min       1Q    Median       3Q      Max
-1.26626 -0.16873  0.00089  0.15643  0.96525

Coefficients:
              Estimate Std. Error t value Pr(>|t|)
(Intercept)  3.8810147  0.0578999  67.030  < 2e-16 ***
age          0.0034343  0.0007239   4.744 2.2e-06 ***
BMI         -0.0078797  0.0008707  -9.049  < 2e-16 ***
- - -
Signif. codes:  0 .***. 0.001 .**. 0.01 .*. 0.05 ... 0.1 . . 1

Residual standard error: 0.2489 on 2744 degrees of freedom
Multiple R-squared: 0.0423,     Adjusted R-squared: 0.0416
F-statistic:  60.6 on 2 and 2744 DF,  p-value: < 2.2e-16
```

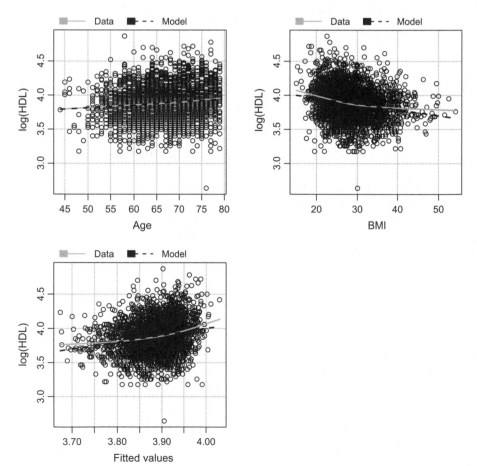

FIGURE 19.10   Model (19.16) marginal model plots.

TABLE 19.12   Model (19.17)

```
> hers$BMIc <- hers$BMI-mean(hers$BMI)
> hers$BMIc2 <- hers$BMIc^2
> m2 <- lm(log(HDL)~age+BMIc+BMIc2,data=hers)
> summary(m2)

Call:
lm(formula = log(HDL) ~ age + BMIc + BMIc2, data = hers)

Residuals:
     Min       1Q   Median       3Q      Max
-1.25180 -0.16930  0.00402  0.15574  0.95224

Coefficients:
              Estimate Std. Error t value Pr(>|t|)
(Intercept)  3.6417749  0.0484669  75.139  < 2e-16 ***
age          0.0034526  0.0007219   4.783 1.82e-06 ***
BMIc        -0.0096966  0.0009772  -9.923  < 2e-16 ***
BMIc2        0.0004219  0.0001041   4.053 5.21e-05 ***
- - -
Signif. codes:  0 .***. 0.001 .**. 0.01 .*. 0.05 ... 0.1 . . 1

Residual standard error: 0.2482 on 2743 degrees of freedom
Multiple R-squared: 0.048,      Adjusted R-squared: 0.04696
F-statistic:  46.1 on 3 and 2743 DF,  p-value: < 2.2e-16
```

Consider the top left-hand plot. The solid curve is the loess estimate of $E[\log HDL|age]$ while the dashed curve is the loess estimate of $E[\hat{y}|age]$. Loess estimation is a nonparametric estimation technique [4]. It is clear that these two curves agree quite well, suggesting that the effect of age is correctly modeled by (19.16). Consider the top right-hand plot in Figure 19.10. The solid curve is the loess estimate of $E[\log(HDL)|BMI]$, while the dashed curve is the loess estimate of $E[\hat{y}|BMI]$. It is clear that these two curves do not agree well, suggesting that the effect of *BMI* is not correctly modeled by (19.16). Thus we conclude that (19.16) is not a valid model for the data and that *BMI* is misspecified in the model.

In view of the curvature present in the loess estimate of $E[\hat{y}|BMI]$, we expand model (19.16) by including a quadratic term in *BMI*. As in the Swan Lake example, we center *BMI* so that it is not strongly correlated with its square. Given this, we consider the model

$$\log(HDL) = \beta_0 + \beta_1\, BMIc + \beta_2\, BMIc^2 + \beta_3\, age + e \qquad (19.17)$$

All coefficients are higly significant in Table 19.12. The coefficient for *age* remains close to what it was in (19.16). The coefficient of the centered *BMI* in (19.17) is negative, like the sign of *BMI* in (19.16). We see a positive coefficient for the square of the centered *BMI*.

The variance inflation factors for model (19.17) are all within acceptable levels as well. We show them in Table 19.13.

TABLE 19.13   Model (19.17)
Variance Inflation Factors

```
> vif(m2)
      age      BMIc     BMIc2
1.026206 1.299746 1.274676
```

TABLE 19.14   Model (19.18)

```
> m3 <- lm(log(HDL)~age+BMI+I(BMI^2),data=hers)
> summary(m3)

Call:
lm(formula = log(HDL) ~ age + BMI + I(BMI^2), data = hers)

Residuals:
     Min       1Q   Median       3Q      Max
-1.25180 -0.16930  0.00402  0.15574  0.95224

Coefficients:
              Estimate Std. Error t value Pr(>|t|)
(Intercept)  4.2633199  0.1106025  38.546  < 2e-16 ***
age          0.0034526  0.0007219   4.783 1.82e-06 ***
BMI         -0.0338091  0.0064569  -5.236 1.76e-07 ***
I(BMI^2)     0.0004219  0.0001041   4.053 5.21e-05 ***
- - -
Signif. codes:  0 .***. 0.001 .**. 0.01 .*. 0.05 ... 0.1 . . 1

Residual standard error: 0.2482 on 2743 degrees of freedom
Multiple R-squared: 0.048,      Adjusted R-squared: 0.04696
F-statistic:  46.1 on 3 and 2743 DF,  p-value: < 2.2e-16
```

Suppose we fit the model without centering:

$$\log(HDL) = \beta_0 + \beta_1\, BMI + \beta_2\, BMI^2 + \beta_3\, age + e \tag{19.18}$$

In Table 19.14, we find that the coefficient for *BMI* is larger in magnitude, while the standard error of the intercept has more than doubled.

The variance inflation factors in Table 19.15 are incredibly large, far beyond acceptable levels. This reinforces our advice to center before adding a quadratic term.

Returning to model (19.17), we draw the marginal model plots for $\log(HDL)$ and the centered *BMI*, $\log(HDL)$ and age, and $\log(HDL)$ and $\hat{y}$, respectively. Figure 19.11 contains these plots.

Consider the top right-hand plot in Figure 19.11. The solid curve is the loess estimate of $E[\log(HDL)|BMIc]$ while the dashed curve is the loess estimate of $E[\hat{y}|BMIc]$. It is clear that these two curves agree well, suggesting that the effect of *BMI* is correctly modeled by (19.17).

TABLE 19.15   Model (19.18)
Variance Inflation Factors

```
> vif(m3)
      age       BMI   I(BMI^2)
 1.026206 56.744598 56.733543
```

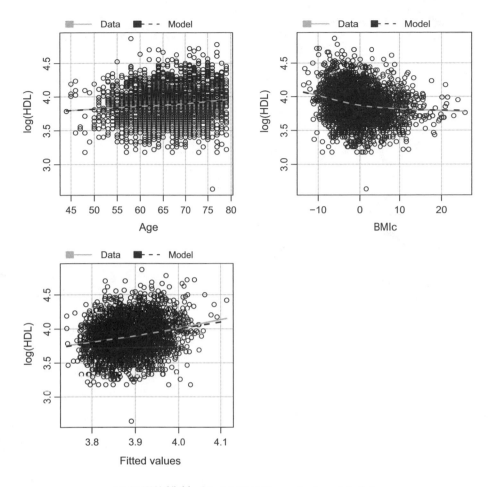

FIGURE 19.11 Model (19.16) marginal model plots.

19.6 PATTERNS IN RESIDUAL PLOTS

A pattern in the standardized residual plots will always indicate that the model is not valid, but it will not always directly indicate how the model is misspecified.

Two conditions must be met for the standardized residual plots to provide this direct information:

$$E[y|\mathbf{x}] = g(\beta_0 + \beta_1 x_1 + \cdots + \beta_k x_k) \tag{19.19}$$

$$E[x_i|x_j] \sim \alpha_0 + \alpha_1 x_j \tag{19.20}$$

It is hard to verify (19.19), but (19.20) is simple to verify. Now we will provide a generated example in which (19.20) does not hold. The data consist of $n = 601$ points generated from the model

$$y = x_1 + 3\,\sin(x_2) + e \tag{19.21}$$

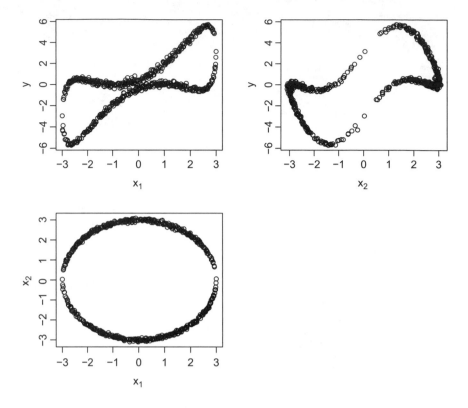

FIGURE 19.12   Model (19.21) scatter plots of response and predictors.

where

$$E(x_2^2|x_1) = 9 - x_1^2 \qquad (19.22)$$

The variable x_1 is equally spaced from -3 to 3 and the errors are normally distributed with standard deviation equal to 0.1. Now we examine scatter plots of the data in Figure 19.12. These are generated using R. The nonlinear relationship between x_1 and x_2 is clearly evident.

We consider the following model for y, x_1, and x_2:

$$y = \beta_0 + \beta_1 x_1 + \beta_2 x_2 + e \qquad (19.23)$$

We fit (19.23) using the R fuction **lm**. The results are given in Table 19.16.

Our estimation shows positive and significant coefficients for x_1 and x_2. The R^2 value is also large.

We use the **Rstandard** function to generate the standardized residuals. Then we examine the standardized residual plots in Figure 19.13.

The nonrandom nature of the plots in Figure 19.13 is indicative that model (19.23) is not a valid model for the data. The usual interpretation of the plot of standardized residuals against x_1 is that a complicated periodic function of x_1 is missing from the model. However, this is not true in this case. The highly nonlinear relationship between the two predictors has produced the nonrandom pattern in the plot of standardized residuals against x_1. Since

TABLE 19.16   Model (19.23)

```
> m1 <- lm(y~x1+x2)
> summary(m1)

Call:
lm(formula = y ~ x1 + x2)

Residuals:
     Min      1Q   Median      3Q      Max
-2.51336 -1.11048  0.01572  1.04648  2.41664

Coefficients:
            Estimate Std. Error t value Pr(>|t|)
(Intercept)  0.05786    0.05115   1.131    0.258
x1           0.94086    0.02951  31.879   <2e-16 ***
x2           0.55357    0.02095  26.426   <2e-16 ***
- - -
Signif. codes:  0 .***. 0.001 .**. 0.01 .*. 0.05 ... 0.1 . . 1

Residual standard error: 1.254 on 598 degrees of freedom
Multiple R-squared: 0.7319,    Adjusted R-squared: 0.731
F-statistic: 816.2 on 2 and 598 DF,  p-value: < 2.2e-16
```

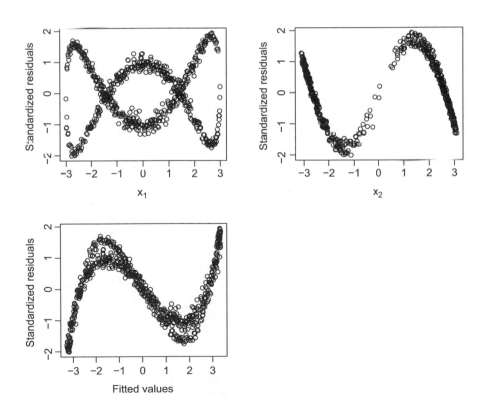

FIGURE 19.13   Model (19.23) standardized residuals.

the linearity condition between the predictors does not hold, all we can say in this case is that the model fit to the data is invalid. Based on residual plots, we cannot say anything about what part of the model is misspecified.

19.7 VARIABLE SELECTION

In previous sections, we mentioned the variance inflation factor measure. High values of this measure can indicate highly correlated predictors in a linear regression. In earlier examples, we were able to center one of the predictors and the high correlation disappeared. We will not be able to correct our models in this way generally. Variable selection techniques can be used to determine which are the most important variables in the model.

The more predictors a regression uses, the more accurate it is, and the lower a residual sum of squares (RSS) it has. The RSS is the sum of squared residuals. This is also an estimate of the conditional variance of the response that is scaled by the sample size. So lowering the RSS lowers the conditional variance of the response and makes the model more powerful. This means that predictions made using the model are less biased and more accurate. But the addition of extra predictors increases the variance of prediction.

When there are a small number of predictors, the partial F-test can be used to determine whether to include certain groups of predictors in the model. The predictors are divided into two groups. The base group is included in the model. The other group, suspected, may or may not be included in the model. The regression model containing all predictors in both the base and suspected is the FULL model. The regression model containing only the base predictors is the RED (reduced) model.

The partial F-test has the following test statistic:

$$F = \frac{(\text{RSS}_{\text{RED}} - \text{RSS}_{\text{FULL}})/(df_{\text{RED}} - df_{\text{FULL}})}{\text{RSS}_{\text{FULL}}/df_{\text{FULL}}} \tag{19.24}$$

Under the null hypothesis that the reduced model RED is true (all the predictor coefficients for suspected are zero), F has an $F(df_{\text{RED}} - df_{\text{FULL}}, df_{\text{FULL}})$ distribution. When we accept the null hypothesis, we have support to use the RED (reduced) model. Rejecting the null hypothesis indicates that we should not ignore the predictors in suspected (at least one of the predictor coefficients are not zero). We can then reperform the test using subsets of suspected to determine which predictors to include in the model. The partial F-test may be easily performed in Stata via the command **nestreg**.

When the suspected predictor list grows large, it is no longer feasible to use the partial F-test method to determine the final regression model. There are a variety of variable selection algorithms that can deal with this situation. They take the specification of the FULL model and output an optimal RED model. In this section, we demonstrate the best-subset Leaps-and-Bounds algorithm [11]. This is implemented by the Stata command **vselect** [21].

Note that inference on the models produced by variable selection algorithms is not equivalent to the inference on the same models that the users find independently without the algorithms. Each step of a variable selection algorithm will fit one or more models and then make an inference on the next step using information from these models. Many inferences are made before the final model is produced.

So the significance levels of the final model are not as they appear. The situation is similar to performing multiple comparisons on the factor means after an ANOVA tells you there is a significant effect. Each of these comparisons should be evaluated at a different significance level than that of the original factor effect.

Cross-validation methods handle this multiple-inference difficulty. These methods generally perform variable selection on subsets of the data and then use an average measure of the results on the subsets to find the final model. They may also split the data into two parts, performing variable selection on one part (*train*) and using the other for evaluating the resulting model (*test*). Details of this method and a general discussion of the multiple-inference problem in variable selection are given in [26].

The definition of optimal is not uniformly agreed upon. The optimal model is one that optimizes one or more information criteria. There are multiple information criteria. There are also a variety of guidelines for the quantity and type of information criteria that should be satisfied.

An information criterion is a function of a model's explanatory power and complexity. Explanatory power increases the criterion in the desirable direction, while the complexity of the model (number of predictors) moves the criterion in the undesirable direction. We detail five information criteria relevant to linear regression: C, R^2_{ADJ}, AIC, AIC_C, and BIC. We use the definitions of these criteria in [26] and [18].

The R^2 adjusted information criterion, R^2_{ADJ}, is an improvement to the R^2 measure of a model's explanatory power. We abbreviate the RSS_{RED} notation to simply RSS. The SST notation refers to the total sum of squares. With this notation, we defined R^2 as

$$R^2 = 1 - \frac{RSS}{SST}$$

A penalty for unnecessary predictors is introduced by a multiplication by $(n-1)/(n-p-1)$, where n is the sample size and p the number of predictors:

$$R^2_{ADJ} = 1 - \frac{n-1}{n-p-1}\frac{RSS}{SST}$$

As R^2_{ADJ} increases, the model becomes more desirable. Akaike's information criterion [1] works in the opposite way: As the criterion decreases, the model becomes more desirable.

The explanatory power of the model is measured by the maximized log-likelihood of the predictor coefficients (assuming a normal model) and error variance. The complexity penalization comes from an addition of the number of predictors:

$$AIC = 2[-\log L(\hat{\beta}_0, \hat{\beta}_1, \ldots, \hat{\beta}_p, \hat{\sigma}^2 | Y) + p + 2]$$

After we formulate the regression model in terms of a normal distribution likelihood, we have

$$AIC = n \log \frac{RSS}{n} + 2p + n + n \log(2\pi)$$

Hurvich and Tsai [16] developed a bias corrected version of AIC, AIC_C. AIC_C is preferred for small sample sizes or when the number of predictors is large relative to sample size. Using our simplified version of AIC,

$$AIC_C = AIC + \frac{2(p+2)(p+3)}{n-(p+2)-1}$$

Let $b = p + 1$. As in the previous section, we use RSS_{FULL} to refer to the residual sum of squares under the model that contains all predictors. Suppose we have k possible predictors, including the intercept. In [18], the information criterion C, or Mallows' C, is defined by

$$C_b = (n-k)\frac{RSS}{RSS_{FULL}} - (n-2b)$$

According to the C_b criterion, good models have $C_b \approx b$. The full model will always satisfy this criterion. Further, as noted in [14], models with small values of Mallows' C may be preferred as well. The Mallows' C criterion was originally developed in [17].

Our final information criterion BIC was proposed by [25]. Raftery [24] provides another development and motivation for the criterion. BIC is similar to AIC but adjusts the penalty term for complexity based on the sample size:

$$BIC = -2 \log L(\hat{\beta}_0, \hat{\beta}_1, \ldots, \hat{\beta}_p, \hat{\sigma}^2|Y) + (p+2) \log n$$

This reduces to

$$BIC = n \log \frac{RSS}{n} + p \log n + n + n \log(2\pi)$$

There is controversy over what should be called the *best information criterion*. According to [26], choosing a model based solely on R^2_{ADJ} generally leads to overfitting (having too many predictors). There is debate over whether AIC or AIC_C should be used in preference to BIC as well. This is demonstrated by comparing page 46 of [27] and page 208 of [12]. Mallows' C suffers from similar controversies. Inference using C is asymptotically equivalent to AIC, but both will share different properties than BIC [18].

Note that for each predictor size p the best model under each of the information criteria for that predictor size p is the model that minimizes RSS. All other terms are constant for the same predictor size. Therefore, at each predictor size we can find the best model of that size by minimizing the residual sum of squares. This remarkable result can greatly simplify the variable selection process.

The Leaps-and-Bounds algorithm actually gives p different models. Each model contains a different number of predictors and is the most optimal model among models of that predictor size. The **vselect** command produces the five information criteria for each of the models produced by Leaps-and-Bounds. The optimal model is the one model with the smallest value of AIC, AIC_C, and BIC and largest value of R^2_{ADJ}, and a value of Mallows' C that is close to the number of predictors in the models + 1 or smallest among other Mallows' C-values. This avoids the controversy about which information criterion is the best.

Sometimes there is no single model that optimizes all the criteria. There are not fixed guidelines for this situation. We narrow the choices down to a few models that are close in optimization and then make an arbitrary choice among them. Each model in our final group is close together in fit, so we do not lose or gain much explanatory power by choosing one over another.

As explained in [11], the Leaps-and-Bounds algorithm organizes all possible models in a tree structure and scans through them, skipping (or *leaping*) over those that are definitely not optimal. The original description of the algorithm is done with large amounts of Fortran code. Ni and Huo [22] provide a description of the original algorithm that is easier to understand.

We demonstrate variable selection using the five mentioned criteria and the Leaps-and-Bounds algorithm with data from a diabetes study.

Efron et al. [8] examined a study with 442 diabetes patients. They are measured on 10 baseline predictor variables and one measure of disease progression. The predictors include *age*, *sex*, body mass index (*bmi*), blood pressure (*bp*), and six serum measurements ($s_1 - s_6$). The progression variable *prog* is our models' response and was recorded a year after the 10 baseline predictors:

$$prog = \beta_0 + \beta_1\, age + \beta_2\, sex + \beta_3\, bmi + \beta_4\, bp + \beta_5 s_1 + \beta_6 s_2 + \beta_7 s_3$$
$$+ \beta_8 s_4 + \beta_9 s_5 + \beta_{10} s_6 + e \tag{19.25}$$

First we fit the model with **regress**. The results are shown in Table 19.17.

Some of the variance inflation factors are incredibly high. We obtain these using the **vif** command. They are shown in Table 19.18.

TABLE 19.17   Model (19.25)

```
. regress prog age sex bmi bp s1 s2 s3 s4 s5 s6

      Source |       SS          df       MS              Number of obs =      442
-------------+------------------------------            F( 10,    431) =    46.27
       Model |  1357023.32       10   135702.332         Prob > F       =   0.0000
    Residual |  1263985.8       431   2932.68168         R-squared      =   0.5177
-------------+------------------------------            Adj R-squared  =   0.5066
       Total |  2621009.12      441   5943.33135         Root MSE       =   54.154


        prog |      Coef.   Std. Err.       t     P>|t|    [95% Conf. Interval]
-------------+----------------------------------------------------------------
         age |  -.0363613   .2170414     -0.17   0.867    -.4629526    .3902301
         sex |  -22.85965   5.835821     -3.92   0.000    -34.32986   -11.38944
         bmi |   5.602962   .7171055      7.81   0.000     4.193503    7.012421
          bp |   1.116808   .2252382      4.96   0.000     .6741061    1.55951
          s1 |  -1.089996   .5733318     -1.90   0.058     -2.21687    .0368782
          s2 |   .7464501   .5308344      1.41   0.160     -.296896    1.789796
          s3 |   .3720042   .7824638      0.48   0.635    -1.165915    1.909924
          s4 |   6.533831   5.958638      1.10   0.273    -5.177772    18.24543
          s5 |   68.48312   15.66972      4.37   0.000     37.68454    99.28169
          s6 |   .2801171    .273314      1.02   0.306     -.257077    .8173111
       _cons |  -334.5671   67.45462     -4.96   0.000     -467.148   -201.9862
```

TABLE 19.18 Model (19.25) Variance Inflation Factors

```
. vif

        Variable |       VIF        1/VIF
- - - - - - - -+- - - - - - - - - - - -
              s1 |     59.20     0.016891
              s2 |     39.19     0.025515
              s3 |     15.40     0.064926
              s5 |     10.08     0.099246
              s4 |      8.89     0.112473
             bmi |      1.51     0.662499
              s6 |      1.48     0.673572
              bp |      1.46     0.685200
             sex |      1.28     0.782429
             age |      1.22     0.821486
- - - - - - - -+- - - - - - - - - - - -
        Mean VIF |     13.97
```

Now we will draw the standardized residual plots in Figure 19.14. We generate the standardized residuals using **predict** with the **sr** option. We will also want to draw a plot of the fitted values versus the standardized residuals. We use the **predict** with the **xb** option to produce these.

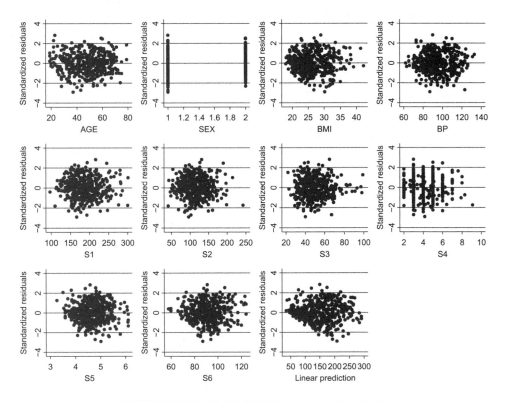

FIGURE 19.14 Model (19.25) standardized residuals.

TABLE 19.19   Model (19.25) Best Subset Selection

```
. vselect prog age sex bmi bp s1 s2 s3 s4 s5 s6, best
Response :              prog
Fixed Predictors :
Selected Predictors:   bmi bp s5 sex s1 s2 s4 s6 s3 age

Actual Regressions   29
Possible Regressions 1024

 Optimal Models Highlighted:

   # Preds     R2ADJ          C        AIC       AICC        BIC
         1  .3424327  148.3513  4912.038   6166.435   4920.221
         2  .4570228  47.07119  4828.398   6082.832   4840.672
         3  .4765213  30.66302  4813.226   6067.705   4829.591
         4   .487366  21.99793  4804.963   6059.498   4825.419
         5  .5029966  9.147958  4792.264   6046.863   4816.811
         6  .5081925  5.560187  4788.603   6043.278   4817.243
         7  .5084884  6.303253   4789.32   6044.079   4822.051
         8  .5085553  7.248507  4790.241   6045.093   4827.062
         9  .5076694  9.028067  4792.015    6046.97   4832.928
        10  .5065593        11  4793.986   6049.055     4838.99


 Selected Predictors

 1  :  bmi
 2  :  bmi s5
 3  :  bmi bp s5
 4  :  bmi bp s5 s1
 5  :  bmi bp s5 sex s3
 6  :  bmi bp s5 sex s1 s2
 7  :  bmi bp s5 sex s1 s2 s4
 8  :  bmi bp s5 sex s1 s2 s4 s6
 9  :  bmi bp s5 sex s1 s2 s4 s6 s3
10  :  bmi bp s5 sex s1 s2 s4 s6 s3 age
```

TABLE 19.20   Model (19.25) Optimal Six-Predictor Model

```
. regress prog bmi bp s5 sex s1 s2

      Source |       SS        df        MS          Number of obs =      442
- - - - - - -+- - - - - - - - - - - - - -          F(  6,   435) =    76.95
       Model | 1349515.11    6   224919.184          Prob > F      =   0.0000
    Residual | 1271494.02  435   2922.97476          R-squared     =   0.5149
- - - - - - -+- - - - - - - - - - - - - -          Adj R-squared =   0.5082
       Total | 2621009.12  441   5943.33135          Root MSE      =   54.065


- - - - - - - - - - - - - - - - - - - - - - - - - - - - - - - - - - - - - -
        prog |      Coef.   Std. Err.       t    P>|t|    [95% Conf. Interval]
- - - - - - -+- - - - - - - - - - - - - - - - - - - - - - - - - - - - - - - -
         bmi |   5.711107   .7072624     8.07    0.000     4.32103    7.101183
          bp |   1.126553   .2158433     5.22    0.000    .7023271    1.550778
          s5 |   73.30653   7.308257    10.03    0.000    58.94264    87.67041
         sex |  -21.59101   5.705638    -3.78    0.000   -32.80506   -10.37697
          s1 |  -1.042876   .2207508    -4.72    0.000   -1.476747   -.6090056
          s2 |   .8432769   .2297536     3.67    0.000    .3917118    1.294842
       _cons |  -313.7666   25.38477   -12.36    0.000   -363.6587   -263.8746
- - - - - - - - - - - - - - - - - - - - - - - - - - - - - - - - - - - - - -
```

**TABLE 19.21   Model (19.25) Optimal
Six-Predictor Model Variance Inflation
Factors**

```
. vif

        Variable |       VIF        1/VIF
- - - - - - - +- - - - - - - - - - -
              s1 |      8.81     0.113561
              s2 |      7.37     0.135750
              s5 |      2.20     0.454745
             bmi |      1.47     0.678813
              bp |      1.34     0.743677
             sex |      1.23     0.815832
- - - - - - - +- - - - - - - - - - -
        Mean VIF |      3.74
```

Each plot in Figure 19.14 shows a random pattern. Thus, model (19.25) appears to be a valid model for the data.

Now we use **vselect** to perform the Leaps-and-Bounds algorithm on model (19.25). The **best** option tells **vselect** to use the Leaps-and-Bounds algorithm. The results are shown in Table 19.19.

Only the full model has an optimal Mallows C criterion value, while the six-predictor model had the smallest value. The choices of best model predictor sizes were five for BIC, six for AIC and AIC_C, and eight for R^2_{ADJ}. Given all of this and the closeness of the optimal BIC and R^2_{ADJ} values to their values under six predictors, the six-predictor model seems like a prudent choice. The six-predictor model is fit in Table 19.20.

Using the six-predictor model, we still find some high variance inflation factors between the first and second serum variables. They are far lower in magnitude than they were under the full model. The variance inflation factors are shown in Table 19.21.

We are concerned about this multicollinearity, so we try the five-predictor model that BIC chose. This is fit in Table 19.22. The variance inflation factors are given in Table 19.23:

$$prog = \beta_0 + \beta_1\,sex + \beta_2\,bmi + \beta_3\,bp + \beta_4 s_3 + \beta_5 s_5 + e \qquad (19.26)$$

TABLE 19.22   Model (19.26)

```
. regress prog bmi bp s5 sex s3

      Source |       SS        df        MS            Number of obs =      442
- - - - - - -+- - - - - - - - - - - - - -            F( 5,    436) =    90.26
       Model | 1333127.95       5   266625.591        Prob > F      =   0.0000
    Residual | 1287881.17     436   2953.8559         R-squared     =   0.5086
- - - - - - -+- - - - - - - - - - - - - -            Adj R-squared =   0.5030
       Total | 2621009.12     441   5943.33135        Root MSE      =   54.349


        prog |     Coef.   Std. Err.       t    P>|t|    [95% Conf. Interval]
- - - - - - -+- - - - - - - - - - - - - - - - - - - - - - - - - - - - - - - -
         bmi |   5.643077   .7037408     8.02   0.000    4.259931    7.026223
          bp |   1.123165   .2171875     5.17   0.000    .6963002    1.55003
          s5 |   43.23441   5.987446     7.22   0.000    31.46657    55.00226
         sex | -22.47424    5.764026    -3.90   0.000   -33.80297  -11.14551
          s3 | -1.064416    .241683     -4.40   0.000   -1.539425   -.5894075
       _cons | -217.6849   35.76377     -6.09   0.000   -287.9757   -147.394
```

**TABLE 19.23   Model (19.26) Variance
Inflation Factors**

```
. vif

        Variable |       VIF       1/VIF
- - - - - - - + - - - - - - - - - - - -
            s5 |      1.46    0.684663
            s3 |      1.46    0.685455
           bmi |      1.44    0.692867
            bp |      1.35    0.742260
           sex |      1.24    0.807833
- - - - - - - + - - - - - - - - - - - -
      Mean VIF |      1.39
```

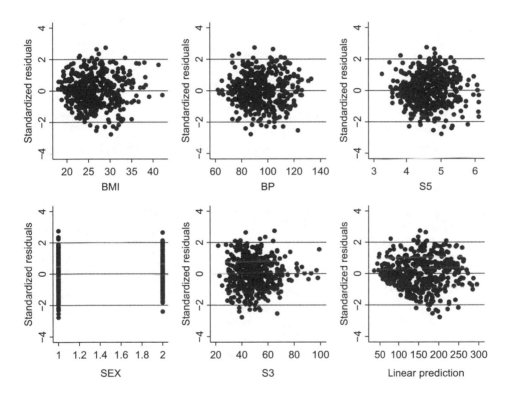

FIGURE 19.15   Model (19.26) standardized residuals.

These variance inflation factors are all within tolerance. Examination of the standardized residual plots in Figure 19.15 shows that the model is accurate as well.

REFERENCES

1. H. Akaike. A new look at the statistical model identification. *IEEE Trans. Automatic Control*, 19:716–723, 1974.

2. T. Allison and D. V. Cicchetti. Sleep in mammals: Ecological and constitutional correllates. *Science*, 194:732–734, 1976.

3. G. E. P. Box and D. R. Cox. An analysis of transformations. *J. Roy. Statis. Soc. Ser. B*, 26:211–252, 1962.

4. W. Cleveland. Robust locally weighted regression and smoothing scatterplots. *J. Am. Statist. Assoc.*, 74:829–836, 1979.

5. R. D. Cook and S. Weisberg. Graphics for assessing the adequacy of regression models. *J. Am. Statist. Assoc.*, 92:490–499, 1997.

6. R. D. Cook and S. Weisberg. Transforming a response variable for linearity. *Biometrika*, 81:731–737, 1994.

7. R. D. Cook and S. Weisberg. *Applied Regression Including Computing and Graphics*. Wiley, New York, 1999.

8. B. Efron, T. Hastie, I. Johnstone, and R. Tibshirani. Least angle regression. *Ann. Statist.*, 32:407–499, 2004.

9. J. Fox and S. Weisberg. *An R Companion to Applied Regression*, 2nd ed. Sage, Thousand Oaks, CA, 2011.

10. K. C. Li and N. Duan. Regression analysis under link violation. *Ann. Statist.*, 17:1009–1052, 1989.

11. G. M. Furnival and R. W. Wilson, Jr. Regressions by leaps and bounds. *Technometrics*, 16:499–511, 1974.

12. T. Hastie, R. Tibshirani, and J. Friedman. *The Elements of Statistical Learning*. Springer, New York, 2001.

13. T. Hastie, R. Tibshirani, and J. Friedman. *The Elements of Statistical Learning*, 2nd ed. Springer, New York, 2009

14. R. R. Hocking. The analysis and selection of variables in linear regression. *Biometrics*, 32:1–50, 1976.

15. S. Hulley, D. Grady, T. Bush, C. Furberg, D. Herrington, B. Riggs, and E. Vittinghoff. Randomized trial of estrogen plus progestin for secondary prevention of heart disease in postmenopausal women. The Heart and Estrogen/Progestin Replacement Study. *J. Am. Med. Assoc.*, 280(7):605–613, 1998.

16. C. M. Hurvich and C. H. Tsai. Regression and time series model selection in small samples. *Biometrika*, 76:297–307, 1989.

17. C. L. Mallows. Some comments on Cp. *Technometrics*, 15:661–675, 1973.

18. A. J. Izenman. *Modern Multivariate Statistical Techniques: Regression, Classification, and Manifold Learning*. Springer, New York, 2009.

19. C. D. Lindsey and S. J. Sheather. Power transformation via multivariate Box-Cox. *Stata J.*, 10:69–81, Stata Press, College Station, TX, 2010.

20. C. D. Lindsey and S. J. Sheather. Optimal power transformation via inverse response plots. *Stata J.*, 10:200–214, Stata Press, College Station, TX, 2010.

21. C. D. Lindsey and S. J. Sheather. Variable selection in linear regression. *Stata J.*, 10:650–669, 2010.

22. X. Ni and X. Huo. Enhanced leaps-and-bounds method in subset selections with additional optimality tests. *INFORMS QSR Best Student Paper Competition*. Available: `http://qsr.section.informs.org/qsr activities.htm`, 2005.

23. R Development Core Team. *R: A Language and Environment for Statistical Computing*. R Foundation for Statistical Computing, Vienna, Austria. Available: `http://www.R-project.org/`, 2011.

24. A. E. Raftery. Bayesian model selection in social research. *Sociol. Methodol.*, 25:111–163, 1995.

25. G. Schwarz. Estimating the dimension of a model. *Ann. Statist.*, 6:461–464, 1978.

26. S. J. Sheather. *A Modern Approach to Regression with R*. Springer, New York, 2009.

27. J. S. Simonoff, *Analyzing Categorical Data*. Springer, New York, 2003.

28. T. Stamey, J. Kabalin, J. McNeal, I. Johnstone, F. Freiha, E. Redwine, and N. Yang. Prostate specific antigen in the diagnosis and treatment of adenocarcinoma of the prostate II, radical prostatectomy treated patients. *J. Urol.*, 16:1076–1983, 1989.

29. StataCorp. *Stata Statistical Software: Release 12*. StataCorp, College Station, TX, 2011.

30. S. Velilla. A note on the multivariate Box-Cox transformation to normaility. *Statist. Probabil. Lett.*, 17:259–263, 1993.

31. E. Vittinghoff, D. V. Glidden, S. C. Shiboski, and C. E. McCulloch. *Regression Methods in Biostatistics*. Springer, New York, 2005.

32. S. Weisberg. *Applied Linear Regression*, 3rd ed., Wiley, New York, 2005.

CHAPTER 20

LOGISTIC REGRESSION IN GENOMEWIDE ASSOCIATION ANALYSIS

WENTIAN LI[1] and YANING YANG[2]
[1]Robert S. Boas Center for Genomics and Human Genetics, Feinstein Institute for Medical Research, North Shore LIJ Health System, Manhasset, New York
[2]Department of Statistics and Finance, University of Science and Technology of China, Hefei, China

20.1 INTRODUCTION

Regression analysis is a branch of statistics that examines the relationship between a dependent variable (y) and a set of independent variables ($x_1, x_2, \ldots, x_p$). The directionness from independent to dependent variables makes regression analysis different from correlation analysis, in which there is no direction between the two sets of variables.

In principle, the functional form describing the relationship between y and $(x_1, x_2, \ldots, x_p)$ can be arbitrarily complicated, such as those in neural networks or polynomial functions. Nevertheless, the most popular regression is still the simple linear regression

$$E[y] = a_0 + a_1 x_1 + a_2 x_2 + \cdots + a_p x_p \tag{20.1}$$

where $E[y]$ means the "average" of y, and its extensions are called the generalized linear model [71]:

$$h(E[y]) = a_0 + a_1 x_1 + a_2 x_2 + \cdots + a_p x_p \tag{20.2}$$

where h is a *link function*. Note that the contributions from independent variables are weighted (by $\{a_i\}$) and summed.

To illustrate the motivation for the generalized linear model, we consider the situation where the probability P of a tossing coin outcome is the dependent variable. The independent variables can be any factors that may affect this outcome, such as wind direction, wind speed, and roughness of the surface on which the coin would drop. It can be seen that one serious problem with linear regression in this situation is the possibility that the sum of the linear combination of multiple variables could be negative or larger than 1, which is not appropriate for a probability $P \in (0, 1)$.

Biological Knowledge Discovery Handbook: Preprocessing, Mining, and Postprocessing of Biological Data, First Edition. Edited by Mourad Elloumi and Albert Y. Zomaya.
© 2014 John Wiley & Sons, Inc. Published 2014 by John Wiley & Sons, Inc.

A solution to this problem is to transform P by a function so that $h(P)$ ranges from $-\infty$ to ∞. Logit$h(P) = \log[P/(1 - P)]$ is such a function, which was first used by Bartlett [6] and given its name by Berkson [8]. This is the logistic regression:

$$\log \left(\frac{P}{1 - P} \right) = a_0 + a_1 x_1 + a_2 x_2 + \cdots + a_p x_p$$

or equivalently,

$$P = \frac{1}{1 + e^{-(a_0 + a_1 x_1 + a_2 x_2 + \cdots + a_p x_p)}} \tag{20.3}$$

More on the history of logistic regression can be found in the Appendix of [1]. Because of the logit function, the relationship between P and $\{x_j\}$ is nonlinear.

A genetic association study is a method to associate genetic polymorphisms with a phenotype or disease status. Genetic polymorphisms can be any measurable differences in DNA sequence between individuals. Genetic polymorphisms have been used as genetic markers [60] in examining the potential relation between one or several genomic DNA changes and a phenotype.

Genetic markers might be classified according to the number of base pairs on a DNA sequence where the polymorphism occurs. A *single-nucleotide polymorphism* (SNP) [23] is a single base change, insertion–deletion variant (indel) [94] refers a plus or minus of $\sim$10 bases, and *copy number variants* (CNVs) [91] are deletions or duplications/multiplications of DNA segments of from 10^3 bases (kb) to 10^6 bases (Mb).

Phenotype can be continuous and may be distributed as a normal distribution in the population (e.g., height, blood pressure) or binary and follow a binomial distribution (e.g., sick with a certain disease versus healthy). The former phenotype is called a quantitative trait and the latter a qualitative trait. Logistic regression is well suited for genetic association analysis of qualitative traits because:

1. A genotype–phenotype relationship has a causal direction from genotype to phenotype, and not the other way around [63], and it is well suited to the directionness in regression analysis.

2. Disease risk is defined as the probability of having the disease (a binary trait), so it is in the range of $(0, 1)$, the same as the P discussed above, and logit(P) is simply the log-odds (to be defined in the next section).

3. Although there is no theoretical reason that the genetic polymorphisms from different chromosome regions have to additively contribute to the disease risk, it is one of the simplest assumptions. Same additiveness of the effects of independent variables is also assumed in (logistic) regression.

Compared to other approaches in genetic association studies, logistic regression has an advantage of being able to easily incorporate other nongenetic (environmental) [15, 66] risk factors in modeling. This again assumes that the contributions from genetic and nongenetic terms are additive. When the additive assumption becomes a limitation, nonadditive "interaction" terms can be introduced (to be discussed in later sections).

Note that logit is not the only function to transform the range $(0,1)$ to $(-\infty, \infty)$. The inverse of the cumulative distribution, in particular, that of normal distributions, called the probit *function*, also achieves this goal. There are other S-shaped sigmoid functions, such as the arctangent function. In this sense, the logit function is not the unique choice, only a convenient one.

20.2 SINGLE GENETIC MARKER: BASIC CONCEPTS

Consider a SNP with two alleles (triallelic SNPs do exist [43, 46] are but less common) a and A (in real DNA sequences, these two alleles can represent, e.g., nucleotides guanine and adenine on the reference strand) and the diploid genotype of that SNP can be $a/a, a/A, A/A$ (see Figure 20.1a). We may assume A to be the lower frequency (minor) allele, which is either potentially a disease-causing mutation or in linkage disequilibrium (to be discussed later) with one. Usually a point mutation that led to the minor allele is evolutionarily deleterious, if not neutral. Then, the minor allele would not spread in the population to become the major allele.

How to create a numerical independent variable x from the categorical genotype is an issue of coding. One strategy of coding is to use the indicator variable, 1 for presence and 0 for absence. If we treat the three genotypes $a/a, a/A, A/A$ as three categories and use three indicator variables to represent them (only two are independent), then the logistic regression is

$$\text{Genotype indicator:} \quad P = \frac{1}{1 + e^{-a_0 - \sum_{k(-1)} a_k x_k}} \tag{20.4}$$

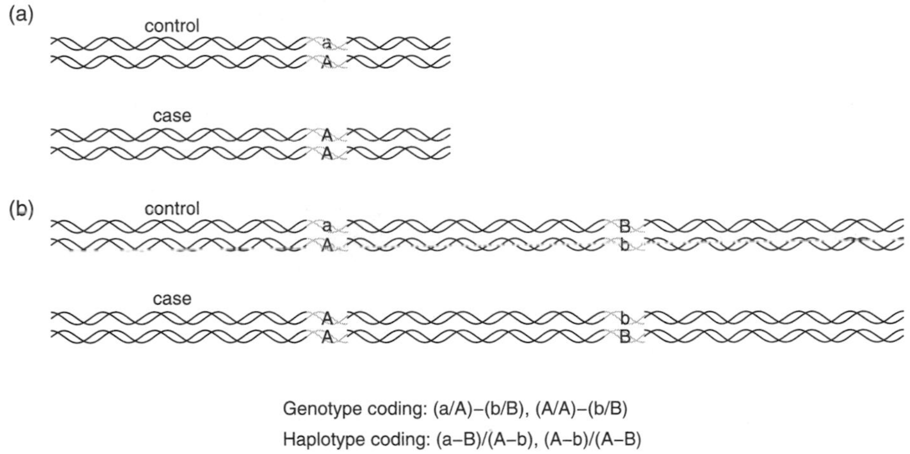

Genotype coding: (a/A)–(b/B), (A/A)–(b/B)

Haplotype coding: (a–B)/(A–b), (A–b)/(A–B)

FIGURE 20.1 (a) Single SNP marker of control (unaffected) and case (affected with disease) samples. Since human is a diploid species, there are two copies of a chromosome (each copy contains a double-helix DNA molecule). The control sample has the a/A genotype and the case sample has A/A genotype. The molecular detail of an allele is important in molecular biology but is usually ignored in genetics (e.g., allele a can be the 5′-guanine-3′ and 3′-cytosine-5′ base pair, allele A can be the 5′-adenine-3′ and 3′-thymine-5′ base pair). (b) Two SNP markers of control and case samples. For the control sample, a at SNP1 and B at SNP2 are on the same haplotype (derived from a same parent); similarly, A and b are on the same haplotype. The two-SNP genotype configuration can either be represented by joining the two genotypes at the two SNPs (e.g., a/A and b/B genotypes) or, if the haplotype is known, by joining the two haplotypes (e.g., $a–B$ and $A–b$ haplotypes).

We use the notation -1 to indicate that less than one of the full rank $(3 - 1 = 2)$ is ranged in summation.

If we do not consider a genotype as a category, but its component allele is, then the indicator variable is used to show the presence or absence of an allele. There are at least two versions of this approach. For example, two indicator variables can be used for maternally and paternally derived alleles, if that information is known. Note that out of the two allele values, only $2 - 1 = 1$ is independent, so the the summation $\sum_{k(-1)}$ becomes a single term:

$$\text{Allele indicator by parental origin:} \quad P = \frac{1}{1 + e^{-a_0 - a_p x_p - a_m x_m}} \quad (20.5)$$

where $x_p, x_m = 1, 0$ indicates that the paternally or maternally derived allele is A or a. An alternative version is to indicate whether the genotype contains allele a or A:

$$\text{Allele indicator by presence in genotype:} \quad P = \frac{1}{1 + e^{-a_0 - a_1 x_a - a_2 x_A}} \quad (20.6)$$

Table 20.1 compares these three types of indicator variables: All use two independent variables to represent the genotype.

In Equations (20.4)–(20.6), the number of fitting parameters is 3. A strategy to reduce the number of parameters, and thus to improve statistical power, is to convert the genotype to a scaled numerical variable, from low for the aa genotype to high for the A/A genotype. For example, the mapping $x : (a/a, a/A, A/A) \rightarrow (0, s, 1)$, where $0 \leq s \leq 1$. The corresponding logistic regression is

$$\text{Scaled numerical coding:} \quad P = \frac{1}{1 + e^{-a_0 - a_1 x}} \quad (20.7)$$

The classical additive, recessive, dominant genetic models correspond to $s = 0.5, 0, 1$ (here we do not consider disease model information as part of the genetic association signal, but there are works on detecting them as an independent signal, often related to violation of Hardy–Weinberg equilibrium [30, 51, 62, 79, 101, 121]). The overdominant model with $s > 1$ is rarely discussed in the literature. The last column of Table 20.1 (allele counting) is equivalent to the additive model. Despite the similarity of the last two columns in Table 18.1,

TABLE 20.1   Three Indicator Variables and One Scaled Variable

Genotype	Genotype Indicator[a]			Parental Origin		Allele Containing		Allele Counting[b]	
	x_{aa}	x_{aA}	x_{AA}	$x_F = A$	$x_M = A$	x_a	x_A	x_{na}	x_{nA}
a/a	1	0	0	0	0	1	0	2	0
a/A	0	1	0	1	0	1	1	1	1
				0	1				
A/A	0	0	1	1	1	0	1	0	2

Note: *Genotype indicator variable* (column 2): presence (1) or absence (0) of the three genotypes (only two are independent). *Allele with parental origin indicator* (column 3): presence or absence of A allele in the paternally (maternally) derived allele. *Allele-containing indicator* (column 4): indication of whether the genotype contains a ($x_a = 1$) or A ($x_A = 1$). *Allele-counting variable* (column 5, a scaled numerical variable): number of copies of a or A (only one variable is independent).
[a] $x_{aa} + x_{aA} + x_{AA} = 1$.
[b] $x_{na} + x_{nA} = 2$.

TABLE 20.2   Common Quantities Defined by Single-SNP Logistic Regression Using Numerical Coding of Genotypes [Equation (20.7)]

Name	Definition	Expression
Genotype frequencies	$P(x)\,(x=0,s,1)$	$(1-p_A)^2, 2(1-p_A)p_A, p_A^2$
Prevalence	$P(D=1)=\langle P(D=1|x)\rangle_x$	$\dfrac{(1-p_A)^2}{1+e^{-a_0}}+\dfrac{2p_A(1-p_A)}{1+e^{-a_0-sa_1}}+\dfrac{p_A^2}{1+e^{-a_0-a_1}}$
Odds	$\dfrac{P(D=1|x)}{P(D=0|x)}$	$e^{a_0+a_1 x}$
Log-odds	$\log(\text{odds})$	$a_0+a_1 x$
Baseline log-odds	$\log(\text{odds})(x=0)$	a_0
Odds ratio (OR)	$\dfrac{\text{odds}(x=1)}{\text{odds}(x=0)}$	e^{a_1}
	$\dfrac{\text{odds}(x=s)}{\text{odds}(x=0)}$	$e^{a_1 s}$
Log-OR	$\log(\text{OR})$	a_1 or $a_1 s$
Relative risk (RR)	$\dfrac{P(D=1|x=1)}{P(D=1|x=0)}$	$\dfrac{e^{a_0}+1}{e^{a_0}+1/e^{a_1}}\sim\dfrac{\text{odds}+1}{\text{odds}+1/\text{OR}}$
	$\dfrac{P(D=1|x=s)}{P(D=1|x=0)}$	$\dfrac{e^{a_0}+1}{e^{a_0}+1/e^{a_1 s}}\sim\dfrac{\text{odds}+1}{\text{odds}+1/\text{OR}}$
Disease group genotype frequency	$P(x|D=1)\,(x=0,s,1)$	$\propto (1-p_A)^2, 2(1-p_A)p_A e^{sa_1}, p_A^2 e^{a_1}$
		$\propto \dfrac{(1-p_A)^1}{1+e^{-a_0}}, \dfrac{2p_A(1-p_A)}{1+e^{-a_0-a_1 s}}, \dfrac{p_A^2}{1+e^{a_0 a_1}}$

the additive model in Equation (20.7) fundamentally differs from the presence/absence model in Equation (20.6) because it assumes an extra copy of the same allele doubles the allelic effect.

Several useful quantities can be obtained using Equation (20.7), such as disease prevalence $P(D=1)$ [note that P in Equation (20.7) is simply the conditional probability $P(D=1|x)$], odds [defined as $P(D=1|x)/P(D=0|x)$], odds ratio [defined as $\text{odds}(x=1)/\text{odds}(x=0)$], and relative risk [defined as $P(D=1|x=1)/P(D=1|x=0)$]. The formula for these are listed in Table 20.2. The symbol p_A denotes the population allele frequency for A, and the Hardy–Weinberg equilibrium is usually assumed in the population.

In general, the two coefficients in logistic regression Equation (20.7) have very different meanings: a_0 is the log-odds for baseline genotype $x=0$, a_1 is the log-OR between two genotypes ($x=1$ and $x=0$). The relationship between RR and OR is only approximately true: If the population odds is small and if OR is high, then

$$\text{RR}\sim\frac{\text{odds}(x=0)+1}{\text{odds}(x=0)+1/\text{OR}}\approx\text{OR}$$

Sometimes, one may need to simulate the genotype frequencies in the diseased group [124], whereas those in the healthy group are more or less the same as those in the whole population $(1 - p_A)^2, 2p_A(1 - p_A), p_A^2$. Using Bayes's theorem, we have

$$\frac{P(x|D = 1)}{P(x|D = 0)} = \frac{P(D = 1|x)P(x)P(D = 1)^{-1}}{P(D = 0|x)P(x)P(D = 0)^{-1}}$$

$$= \text{Odds}(x) \times \frac{1 - P(D = 1)}{P(D = 1)} \propto \text{Odds}(x) \qquad (20.8)$$

Another approach is to compare $P(x|D = 1)$ with $P(x)$:

$$\frac{P(x|D = 1)}{P(x)} = \frac{P(D = 1|x)}{P(D = 1)} \propto \frac{1}{1 + e^{-a_0 - a_1 x}} \qquad (20.9)$$

Since $P(x|D = 0) \approx P(x)$, the last two lines in Table 20.2 are roughly the same (after normalization).

To summarize this section, there are several coding schemes to represent a two-allele SNP by either the indicator variable or the scaled numerical variable. The optimal coding scheme is related to the underlying disease model (e.g., dominant or recessive model). Coefficients in a logistic regression model are related to some population measures of the disease (e.g., a_0 is the baseline log-odds, a_1 is the log-OR).

20.3 SINGLE GENETIC MARKER: STATISTICAL TESTS

Given a genetic data set, that is, the number of diseased or healthy samples with certain genotypes, parameters a_0, a_1 in Equation (20.7) in a logistic regression can be estimated. There are three ways to collect samples: random selection samples from a population, selecting roughly equal number of diseased and healthy samples ("cases" and "controls"), and selecting equal number of samples with or without certain risk factors (e.g., smokers and nonsmokers, carriers and noncarriers of a certain genetic defect marker). For a rare disease, random sampling is unlikely to pick up any diseased person, so it is impractical. The third option (prospective cohort study) is ideally suited by logistic regression [51], but the cost for waiting for a disease to develop can be high. The second option (retrospective case–control study) is more practical, and fortunately, its conditioning on outcome first will not affect the logistic regression result as shown below [13].

We introduce a new variable S for being sampled ($S = 1$) or not ($S = 0$). We would like to show that $P(y = 1|x)$ and $P(y = 1|S = 1, x)$ have mostly the same form of logistic regression except one parameter. Suppose the probability of a patient being sampled is $\pi_1 = P(S = 1|y = 1)$ and that of an unaffected patient being sampled is $\pi_0 = P(S = 1|y = 0)$. Under case–control design for rare diseases, $\pi_1 \gg \pi_0$. Within the sampled data ($S = 1$), the probability of being affected ($y = 1$) using logistic regression, by Bayes's theorem, is [13]

$$P(y = 1|S = 1, x)$$

$$= \frac{P(S = 1|y = 1, x)P(y = 1|x)}{P(S = 1|y = 0, x)P(y = 0|x) + P(S = 1|y = 1, x)P(y = 1|x)}$$

$$= \frac{\pi_1 e^{a_0 + a_1 x}}{\pi_0 + \pi_1 e^{a_0 + a_1 x}} = \frac{1}{1 + e^{-(a_0 + \log(\pi_1/\pi_0)) - a_1 x}} = \frac{1}{1 + e^{-a_0' - a_1 x}} \qquad (20.10)$$

In other words, it is still a logistic regression with the same log-OR, only that the baseline log-odds is incorrectly estimated, as $a_0' = a + 0 + \log(\pi_1/\pi_0)$.

Because logistic regression is insensitive to whether equal number of cases and controls or equal number of exposed and unexposed is collected [13], its use is quite flexible. In genetic studies, case–control is the main sample collection design [59]. Fortunately, only the parameter a_1 is informative for genetic association analysis. The null hypothesis that the SNP is not associated with the disease is $a_1 = 0$. There are several ways to test the null hypothesis: Wilks's likelihood-ratio test, Wald's test, and Rao's score test (pp. 11–12 of [1]). In Wilks's likelihood-ratio test [118, 119], data are fitted twice, once with both a_0 and a_1 and another with a_0 only. If our data are $\{x_i, y_i\}(i = 1, 2, \ldots, n)$ where $\{x_i\}$ is the coded values for SNP genotypes, $\{y_i\}$ is the disease status of n samples, the two maximized likelihoods are

$$
\begin{aligned}
\hat{L}_1 &= \prod_{i=1}^{n} \left(\frac{1}{1 + e^{-\hat{a}_0 - \hat{a}_1 x_i}} \right)^{y_i} \left(1 - \frac{1}{1 + e^{-\hat{a}_0 - \hat{a}_1 x_i}} \right)^{1-y_i} \\
&= \prod_{i=1}^{n} \left(\frac{1}{1 + e^{-\hat{a}_0 - \hat{a}_1 x_i}} \right)^{y_i} \left(\frac{1}{1 + e^{\hat{a}_0 + \hat{a}_1 x_i}} \right)^{1-y_i} = \prod_{i=1}^{n} \frac{1}{1 + e^{(1-2y_i)(\hat{a}_0 + \hat{a}_1 x_i)}} \\
\hat{L}_0 &= \prod_{i=1}^{n} \frac{1}{1 + e^{(1-2y_i)\hat{a}_0}}
\end{aligned}
\tag{20.11}
$$

where the hat denotes the fitted value after a maximum-likelihood procedure. If $\Lambda = \hat{L}_1/\hat{L}_0$ is the ratio of the two maximized likelihoods, $-2 \log \Lambda$ follows a χ^2 distribution (with one degree of freedom) under the null hypothesis in the large-sample limit [119]. Given the observed Λ, one can calculate the p-value from the $\chi^2_{df=1}$ distribution.

The Wald test [112] follows the similar idea as the z transformation, that is, any variable or parameter can be converted to a standard normal variable/parameter after subtracting the mean and divided by the standard deviation (or standard error for parameters). The square of z is simply a chi-square variable (with one degree of freedom). For testing $a_1 = 0$, Wald's test statistic is defined as

$$
W = \frac{(\hat{a}_1 - 0)^2}{\mathrm{Var}(\hat{a}_1)} = \hat{a}_1^2 I(\hat{a}_1)
\tag{20.12}
$$

where $I(\hat{a}_1)$ is the Fisher information $I(a_1)$,

$$
I(a_1) = \left\langle -\frac{\partial^2 \log L_1(a_1, \{x_i, y_i\}, n)}{\partial a_1^2} \right\rangle_{x,y}
\tag{20.13}
$$

evaluated at $a_1 = \hat{a}_1$. This test is not recommended when $\hat{a}_1$ is large (p. 172 of [1]).

Rao's score test [93] relies on the fact that if the maximum-likelihood estimate $\hat{a}_1$ is close to the null hypothesis of $a_1 = 0$, then the slope at $a_1 = 0$ should be close to zero. One only needs to normalize the slope at $a_1 = 0$ appropriately so that it is a standard normal variable. Rao's choice was the score function

$$
S(a_1) = \left(\left\langle \frac{\partial \log L_1(a_1, \{x_i, y_i\}, n)}{\partial a_1} \right\rangle_{x,y} \right)^2 \Big/ I(a_1)
\tag{20.14}
$$

TABLE 20.3 Genotype Counts of SNP in *FTO* Gene

	TT	*AT*	*AA*	*T*	*A*	*TT + AT*	*AA*
Normal-weight T2D	220	349	71	789	491	569	71
	34.4%	54.5%	11.1%	61.6%	38.4%	88.9%	11.1%
Overweight T2D	1495	2414	934	5404	4282	3909	934
	30.9%	49.8%	19.3%	55.8%	44.2%	80.7%	19.3%

Source: Data taken from first three lines of Table S2(a) in [32], UK cases (WTCCC), UK T2D cases, and UKT2D GCC cases are combined.

evaluated at $a_1 = 0$. Although $-2 \log \Lambda$, W, and S all have the same null distribution ($\chi^2_{df=1}$), Rao's test uses the information at $a_1 = 0$, Wald's test uses that at $a_1 = \hat{a}_1$, and Wilks's likelihood-ratio test uses both. In the large-sample limit, all three are equivalent.

To compare the logistic regression analysis and the more standard Pearson chi-square test (see, e.g., [59]), we use the data for SNP (rs9939609) in gene *FTO* (on chromosome 16) comparing the overweight type II diabetes patients with normal-weight type II diabetes (T2D) [32]. The *A* allele in rs9939609 is a risk for overweight (allele frequency 44.2% in overweight T2D patients versus 38.4% in normal-weight T2D patients) (Table 20.3). In a standard procedure, ORs can be calculated: $\text{OR}_A = 1.27$, $\text{OR}_{AA} = 1.94$, $\text{OR}_{TA} = 1.02$, and p-values from Pearson's chi-square test: 7.3×10^{-5} (allelic test), 4.8×10^{-7} (recessive model), 0.072 (dominant model), 3.1×10^{-6} (two-degree-of-freedom genotype test). Because there is strong evidence for the recessive model, we can combine the *TT* and *TA* genotype counts (Table 20.3), and the OR for this new table is $\text{OR}_{AA/(TT+AT)} = 1.91$.

Using the glm function in R (http://www.r-project.org) [111], testing $a_1 = 0$ in Equation (20.7) leads to p-values of 6.1×10^{-5} (additive model), 0.072 (dominant model), 7.1×10^{-7} (recessive model), and for the general model, p-values for testing $a_1 = 0$ and $a_2 = 0$ in Equation (20.15) are 0.85 and 3.7×10^{-6}. All these test results by logistic regression are very close to the corresponding test results from Pearson's chi-square test. In the current implementation of glm, the Wald test (under the z-value and $\Pr(> |z|)$) is used for testing nonzero regression coefficients, while Rao's score test is not used, and the likehood ratio is used to calculate the "deviance difference" (2 times the log-likelihood ratio) though the corresponding p-value is not given.

To summarize this section, even if patients are biased sampled in the data set, logistic regression still provides a correct estimation of the log-OR. It is one reason logistic regression is a popular choice in case–control study designs. The relevance of an independent (x) variable to the dependent variable (y) can be cast in a statistical test: testing the coefficient in the logistic regression to be zero. Several test statistics can be used, and all are equivalent in the large-sample limit.

20.4 TWO GENETIC MARKERS AND FISHER'S NONADDITIVITY INTERACTION

An illustration of the situation with two SNP markers is shown in Figure 20.1b, where the possible genotypes at the second SNP are b/b, b/B, and B/B. We follow the similar strategy in coding the single-SNP genotype to represent marker genotypes at both markers, which is much more complicated.

The two-locus (two-SNP) genotype indicator strategy is to use nine indicator variables for nine two-locus genotypes (eight are independent) $\{x_{\alpha\beta}\}(\alpha, \beta = 1, 2, 3)$:

$$\text{2L genotype indicator:} \qquad P = \frac{1}{1 + e^{-a_0 - \sum_{\alpha\beta(-1)} a_{\alpha\beta} x_{\alpha\beta}}} \qquad (20.15)$$

To compare with single-SNP logistic regression using the one-locus genotype indicator, one can write this one-locus "main-effect" plus "interaction" form:

$$\text{1L + interaction:} \qquad P = \frac{1}{1 + e^{-a_0 - \sum_{\alpha(-1)} a_\alpha x_\alpha - \sum_{\beta(-1)} b_\beta y_\beta - \sum_{\alpha(-1)\beta(-1)} c_{\alpha\beta} x_\alpha y_\beta}} \qquad (20.16)$$

It can be checked that there are eight variable terms in Equation (20.16): two terms for the single-locus effect from SNP1, two from SNP2, and four from interaction.

A claim of interaction is by rejecting the null hypothesis of $\{c_{\alpha\beta}\} = 0$ for all α, β's. The definition of interaction by deviation from additivity can be traced back to Fisher in his study of gene–gene interaction or epistasis [31]. However, this statistical definition of interaction is not unique as one also has to specify toward what quantity this additivity is used. In Equation (20.16), the additivity is toward the log-odds $\log(P/(1 - P))$, instead of toward the disease risk itself (i.e., $P = a_0 + a_1 x_1 + a_2 x_2$), or toward the log-risk [i.e., $\log(P) = a_0 + a_1 x_1 + a_2 x_2$, which is equivalent to the multiplicative model $P = kx'_1 x'_2$, where $k = e^{a_0}$, $x'_1 = e^{a_1 x_1}$, $x'_2 = e^{a_2 x_2}$], among others. These equations are all different, and additivity or lack of interaction toward one quantity is typically nonadditive or interactive toward another [21].

The genetic epistasis concept introduced by Bateson [7] distinguishes two types of factors in an interaction. The main-effect factor is a major contributor of the disease risk and a modifier either modifies or masks the effect of the first factor. The modifier itself usually does not contribute significantly to the disease risk. The two variables in Equation (20.16), representing two SNPs, are symmetric, and thus it is hard to imagine that the equation can be used to describe Bateson's interaction where the symmetry between the two factors is lacking. Since there are many ways to be asymmetric whereas only one way to be symmetric, the difficulty in modeling a Bateson interaction is partly due to the large number of two-locus models to choose from [57] and the fact that the true model is unknown [81]. Work has been done to reduce the number of model types for two-locus disease models [39, 57].

Beyond statistical/genetic interaction [110], there are also concepts of epistasis motivated by other branches of biology, such as protein–protein contact in a molecular complex, protein–protein interaction in an enzymatic activity, and multiple proteins on the same biochemical pathway [90]. There are numerous examples when protein–protein contact is known, whereas their corresponding genes do not exhibit statistical interaction as defined in Equation (20.16) in a genetic association analysis. This should not come as a total surprise as the definitions of interaction used are different.

Besides the representation of a two-locus genotype by grouping two alleles at a SNP first [e.g., $(a/A)–(B/b)$ in Figure 20.1], another representation is by grouping alleles from the same haplotype first [113] [e.g., $(a–B)/(A–b)$]. The distinct number of 2-SNP haplotype pairs (ignoring parental origin) is 10, as compared to the number of 9 for a two-locus genotype by combing the SNP genotype first. The correspondence between the haplotype pairs and the two-locus genotype combination is illustrated in Figure 20.2. We notice, first, for the SNP-first representation, $(a/A) - (b/B)$ can be either $(a–b)/(A–B)$ or $(a–B)/(A–b)$, increasing the number of two-locus genotypes from 9 to 10; second, for the haplotype-first

	b/b	b/B	B/B
a/a	1	2	3
a/A	4	5 / 6	7
A/A	8	9	10

	a–b	a–B	A–b	A–B
a–b	1	2	4	5
a–B		3	6	7
A–b			8	9
A–B				10

FIGURE 20.2 Left: Single-SNP genotype-first representation of two-locus genotypes. The three genotypes of the first (second) SNP are written as $a/a, a/A, A/A$ ($b/b, b/B, B/B$). The (a/A)–(b/B) may correspond to two-haplotype-first representations: $(a-b)/(A-B)$ or $(a-B)/(A-b)$. Right: haplotype-first representation of two-locus genotypes. The four two-locus haplotypes are written as $a-b, a-B, A-b, A-B$. By ignoring the parental origin of haplotypes, the number of haplotype pairs is reduced from 16 to 10. The numbers 1–10 are used to map one representation to another.

representation, ignoring the parental origin of haplotypes reduces the number from 16 to 10.

The logistic regression using the haplotype pair indicator variables can be written as $\{H_\alpha\}(\alpha = 1, 2, \cdots 10)$:

$$\text{Haplotype pair indicator:} \quad P = \frac{1}{1 + e^{-a_0 - \sum_{\alpha(-1)} a_\alpha H_\alpha}} \tag{20.17}$$

Of the 10 haplotype pairs, 4 are homozygous [e.g., $(a-b)/(a-b)$] and 6 are heterozygous [e.g., $(a-b)/(A-b)$]. Besides the haplotype pair indicator variable, the single haplotype indicator variable can also be used [116]. The ambiguity in constructing the haplotype pair [5 and 6 in Figure 20.1 (left)] creates a missing value problem. This problem has been addressed in [98] by a mixture model.

To summarize this section, the coding scheme for genotypes at two chromosome locations (loci) is more complicated. The common choices include 9 two-locus genotypes and 10 haplotype pairs. Fisher's statistical interaction in the logistic regression context is defined as a cross-product term. But a claim of statistical interaction in logistic regression may not imply a statistical interaction in linear or log-linear regression. Besides Fisher's statistical interaction, there are also Bateson's epistasis and biochemical interactions.

20.5 MANY GENETIC MARKERS IN GENOMEWIDE ASSOCIATION ANALYSIS: VARIABLE REDUCTION AND PENALIZED REGRESSION

Genomewide association studies (GWASs) are simply an extension of genetic association analysis from one or two genetic markers to all markers typed in a genome. The number of SNPs available genomewide depends on the biotechnology used. Genotyping microarrays, those that use unique flanking sequences for locating and array technology for genotyping genome wide SNPs, typically contain 0.3 to 1 million SNPs (p_{gwas}). Next-generation sequencing-based detection of polymorphisms [80] can produce several million SNPs.

Logistic regression using the numerically coded variable in Equation (20.7) can be extended to all SNPs in the genome (or at least to multiple-candidate gene regions) easily without or with pairwise (second-order) interaction terms:

Numerically coded without interaction terms:

$$P = \frac{1}{1 + \exp(-a_0 - \sum_j a_j x_j)}$$

Numerically coded with interaction terms:

$$P = \frac{1}{1 + \exp(-a_0 - \sum_j a_j x_j - \sum_j \sum_{j' > j} a_{jj'} x_j x_{j'})} \tag{20.18}$$

The ease with which the equation can be written, however, does not translate to ease with which to solve the equation. The large number of fitting parameters often leads to many local minima for mean-square error (or local maxima for likelihood) that can trap an iterative procedure for optimization.

A quick estimation shows that we will never have enough number of samples for an appropriate regression with all interaction terms included. To fill the p_{gwas}-dimensional grid ($p_{\text{gwas}} \sim 500,000 - 1,000,000$) with three allele values in each dimension, $3^{p_{\text{gwas}}} \sim 10^{238,000} - 10^{477,000}$ samples are needed. Even with the minimum requirement that the sample size has to be more than the number of parameters leads to the sample size of $\sim 10^5 - 10^6$. The only solution to this problem is variable selection (subset selection, variable reduction) [58, 74].

SNPs close to each other may be statistically correlated with each other. These SNPs are said to be in *linkage disequilibrium* (LD). These correlations are gradually destroyed by recombinations during meiosis. Since recombinations tend to occur in certain chromosomal locations (hot spots), SNPs can be clustered into LD blocks. There are more than 25,000 recombination hot spots claimed [75], leading to roughly 25,000 LD blocks (p_{ld}). Replacing p_{gwas} by p_{ld} greatly reduces the required sample sizes, but the number is still astronomical. Further reduction of variables is needed.

The textbook technique for variable selection is the stepwise regression (either forward from zero number of variable, adding one extra variable at the time, or backward from the full set of variables, removing one variable at the time) using one of the decision criteria (e.g. [22, 37, 61, 109]). For example, the *step* function in R [111] uses the *Akaike information criterion* (AIC) [2, 61] to decide whether to continue or stop the stepwise operation.

Stepwise regression involves a large number of decisions or tests, and each time the least-squares or maximum-likelihood results are compared with and without a given variable. The more elegant approach is to carry out least-squares or maximum-likelihood estimation only once, but the quantity to be minimized or maximized is a "penalized" square error or likelihood [41, 69].

The standard maximum-(log)-likelihood estimation of regression coefficients for Equation (20.18) is [see Equation (20.11)] (arg max means to choose the parameter value which maximized the expression)

$$\{\hat{a}_j\} = \arg\max_{\{a_j\}} \log L(\{a_j\})$$

$$= \arg\max_{\{a_j\}} \left\{ -\sum_{i=1}^{n} \log \left[1 + \exp \left((1 - 2y_i)(a_0 + \sum_{j=1}^{p} a_j x_{ij}) \right) \right] \right\} \tag{20.19}$$

In other words, given the data $\{\{x_{ij}\}, y_i\}$ [$i = 1, 2, \ldots, n$ for sample index, $j = 1, 2, \ldots, p$ for SNP marker or LD block index, $y \in (0, 1)$ for disease affection status, $x = 0, 1, 2$ for three genotypes], the estimated regression coefficients $\{\hat{a}_j\}$ are those that maximize the log-likelihood function.

Subtracting an extra term (penalty) to the log-likelihood that involves a sum of regression coefficients will force these coefficients to be relatively small. Other names for penalized regression are regularized regression, shrinkage, and so on [41]. At least four types of penalty terms can be used in estimating the regression coefficients:

1. Ridge regression [44]:

$$\{\hat{a}_j\}_{\text{RR}} = \arg\max_{\{a_j\}} \left\{ \log L(\{a_j\}) - \lambda \sum_{j=1}^{p} a_j^2 \right\} \tag{20.20}$$

2. *Least absolute shrinkage and selection operator* (LASSO) [86, 105]:

$$\{\hat{a}_j\}_{\text{LASSO}} = \arg\max_{\{a_j\}} \left\{ \log L(\{a_j\}) - \lambda \sum_{j=1}^{p} |a_j| \right\} \tag{20.21}$$

3. Elastic net [127]:

$$\{\hat{a}_j\}_{\text{EN}} = \arg\max_{\{a_j\}} \left\{ \log L(\{a_j\}) - \lambda_1 \sum_{j=1}^{p} |a_j| - \lambda_2 \sum_{j=1}^{p} a_j^2 \right\} \tag{20.22}$$

4. *Octagonal shrinkage and clustering algorithm for regression* (OSCAR) [10, 89]:

$$\{\hat{a}_j\}_{\text{OSCAR}} = \arg\max_{\{a_j\}} \left\{ \log L(\{a_j\}) - \lambda_1 \sum_{j=1}^{p} |a_j| - \lambda_2 \sum_{j<j'} \max(|a_j|, |a_{j'}|) \right\} \tag{20.23}$$

Typically, independent variables $\{x_j\}$ are standardized with zero mean and unit variance, so that their coefficients $\{a_j\}$ can be treated equally. Since $E[x_j] = 2p_{Aj}$ (where p_{Aj} is the minor allele frequency of the jth SNP), $\text{Var}[x_j] = 2p_{Aj}(1 - p_{Aj})$, the $x_j \to x_j' = (x_j - 2p_{Aj})/[2p_{Aj}(1 - p_{Aj})]$ transformation might be needed before a variable selection.

These equations are derived from the optimization with inequality constraints (Kuhn–Tucker multiplier [54]): To maximize function $f(a)$ with the $g(a) < c$ constraint, we can maximize the new function $f(a) - \lambda[g(a) - c]$ instead. Since λc is not a function of a, we can maximize $f(a) - \lambda g(a)$. The constraints used in these penalized regressions are (1) $\sum_{j=1}^{p} a_j^2 \leq c$ (also called L_2 constraint) for ridge, (2) $\sum_{j=1}^{p} |a_j| \leq c$ (an L_1 constraint) for LASSO, and (3) $\sum_{j=1}^{p} a_j^2 \leq c_1$ and $\sum_{j=1}^{p} |a_j| \leq c_2$ ($L_1 + L_2$ constraint) for elastic net. Note that stepwise variable selection is to limit $\sum_{j=1}^{p} 0/1 \leq c < p$, which is a L_0 constraint. Also note that the intercept term a_0 is determined by an overall statistic of the data set and is not restricted by the constraints. The R package glmnet [34] can be used for all these penalized regressions, lasso2 [82] and lars [29] packages for LASSO.

Ridge regression has been used to remove SNPs that are in LD with each other [70] to enhance the multilocus signal [52, 65], reduce the number of interaction terms [87], and others [25]. LASSO has been applied to GWAS for reducing both the number of SNPs included and the number of interaction terms [14, 38, 42, 99, 109, 120, 122, 123] as well as for collapsing rare alleles in a gene [103, 126]. Bayesian LASSO [88] (which is not discussed here) has also been applied to GWAS [9, 56]. An L_1 regularized regression (which makes them to be LASSO) has been used to remove the large number of haplotypes within a sliding window [64]. The elastic net has been applied to GWAS as well [17, 18]. There are other penalized regressions that are not standard [16, 102, 104]. For a review of these applications, see [3].

The constraint in penalized regressions forces many regression coefficients to be small, effectively removing them from the regression. However, LASSO (L_1) is more effective than ridge regression (L_2) in variable reduction [105]; for example, LASSO may shrink a coefficient a_j to 0 whereas ridge regression may only shrink it to half of the original size. The reason for this is because, for small a_j values, $|a_j|$ is much larger than a_j^2 and the constraint $\sum_j |a_j| \leq c$ is stronger than $\sum_j a_j^2 \leq c$ [122].

To summarize this section, variable reduction is a very important part of the application of logistic regression in GWAS. Either the number of SNPs or the number of LD blocks are too large for a regression with only a few hundred samples. Textbook methods for variable selection employ stepwise adding or removing of variables. However, modern approaches impose a constraint on all regression coefficients, in effect forcing many of them to zero (penalized or regularized regression). Among the penalized regression, LASSO (L_1 constraint) is currently the most popular choice.

20.6 LATENT VARIABLES AND DIMENSION REDUCTION: PARTIAL LEAST-SQUARES REGRESSION

So far, we have discussed the modeling of the dependent variable y by independent variables $\{x_j\}$ through logit link function and the need to reduce the number of independent variables if they do not contribute to the fitting performance. On the other hand, if some independent variables are highly correlated or naturally joined together as a group based on biological information or based on high-order modeling, artificially constructed variables can be used. These variables are not by themselves observable, and thus their existence cannot be verified. However, these variables can aid in the mathematical description of the data. We use the term *latent variable* here, but other names may provide a similar meaning, such as hidden variables, constructs, composites, dimensions, and so on [24].

The well-known latent variables outside the field of regression analysis include *hidden variable* in hidden Markov models [92], *factors* in factor analysis [100], *component scores* or *principal components* in principal-component analysis [49], and *canonical variables* in canonical correlation analysis [45]. Approaches that involve latent variables $\{t_j\}$ ($j = 1, 2, \ldots, K \leq p$) for an explanation of the dependent variable y include path analysis [55] and structural equation modeling [50]. Here we cover two latent-variable-based regressions: partial least-squares regression and logic regression.

Latent variable construction can be considered as a separate step before carrying out the logistic regression. Suppose K latent variables are constructed: $\{t_j\}$ which are linear combinations of the original variable $\{x_j\}$. For example, the first latent variable t_1 is defined as

$$t_1 = \sum_{k=1}^{p} x_k w_{k1} \qquad (20.24)$$

(there is no constant term as we assum x_k's are centralized (zero mean). The *partial least-square* (PLS) constructs the weights by maximizing the covariance between the latent variable and the output y. Again, for the first latent variable (t_{i1} is the t_1-value for sample i),

$$\{w_{k1}\} = \arg\max \left(\sum_{i=1}^{n} \frac{y_i t_{i1}}{n} - \sum_i \frac{y_i}{n} \cdot \sum_i \frac{t_{i1}}{n} \right)$$

$$= \arg\max_{w_{k1}} \sum_{i=1}^{n} y_i \sum_{k=1}^{p} x_{ik} w_{k1} \tag{20.25}$$

with the condition of

$$\sum_{k=1}^{p} w_{k1}^2 = 1 \tag{20.26}$$

Such maximization (or least squares) can be iteratively continued to the second, the third, and so on, latent variables ($j = 2, 3, \ldots, K$):

$$\{w_{kj}\} = \arg\max_{w_{kj}} \sum_{i=1}^{n} y_i \sum_{k=1}^{p} x_{ik} w_{kj} \tag{20.27}$$

with two conditions

$$\sum_{k=1}^{p} w_{kj}^2 = 1 \qquad \sum_{k=1}^{p} w_{kj} \left(\sum_{i=1}^{n} x_{ij} x_{ij'} \right) w_{kj'} = 0 \qquad (j \neq j') \tag{20.28}$$

so that the latent variables are

$$t_j = \sum_{k=1}^{p} x_k w_{kj} \tag{20.29}$$

A more compact derivation can be written by using the matrix representation (see Appendix). PLS is often compared to the *principal-component analysis* (PCA) in which the weights are determined by maximizing the variance of the latent variables, also under the unitary and orthogonal conditions.

Once the latent variables are constructed, we can use the logistic regression

$$\log\left(\frac{P}{1 - P} \right) = a_0 + a_1 t_1 + a_2 t_2 + \cdots + a_K t_K \tag{20.30}$$

If the latent variables are constructed by PCA, the corresponding regression is called *principal-component regression* [114]. Since the latent variables $\{t_j\}$ are ordered—t_1 is mostly correlated with the dependent variable, t_2 is the second mostly correlated, and so on—the forward latent variable selection can be applied, and the appropriate number of latent variables to be used in Equation (20.30) can be decided by leave-one-out cross-validation. The variable selection on latent variable $\{t_j\}$ is different from that on the original variable $\{x_j\}$ in the sense that even if only one latent variable is selected, it may still include contribution from all genes. We call the first selection *dimension reduction* and the second one *variable reduction*.

In [115], PLS is used for dimension reduction for latent variables constructed from the gene–gene or gene–environment interaction, while the number of SNPs is limited to only a few candidate gene regions. In [19, 20], the distinction between dimension reduction and variable (gene) reduction is made. PLS has also been applied to the genetic association of quantitative traits, in which y is a continuous variable instead of a binary trait [125]: Even though that work is outside the scope of logistic regression, its application of PLS to genetic association is very similar to the theme of this section.

In the penalized regression discussed in the last section, variable reduction is achieved by imposing a constraint on the magnitudes of parameters. The sparse partial least square [19], similar to the sparse principal-component analysis [117], is to apply a similar constraint on weights in the maximization of Equation (20.27). The goal of sparse PLS is to carry out variable reduction and dimension reduction at the same time. For GWAS with $\sim 10^5$–10^6 SNPs, some sort of variable reduction is clearly needed even before PLS. On the other hand, for SNPs in a candidate gene, the number of SNPs is much smaller, ~ 10–10^2, and then PLS could be applied directly [125].

To summarize this section, PLS is a method to construct a linear combination of the independent variables (these are called *latent variables*) so that the covariance between the latent variables and the dependent variable is maximized. PLS can be useful in combining effects from all SNPs in a gene region (a locus). PLS should outperform latent variable construction by PCA in classification tasks because PCA does not take the dependent variable into account.

20.7 LATENT VARIABLES: LOGIC REGRESSION

Logic regression (not to be confused with logistic regression) is an attempt to construct latent variables that are Boolean combinations of the (binary) independent variables [95]. If the dependent variable is also binary, the logic function construction of binary independent variables can be combined to the logistic regression to be *logic logistic regression*.

There are three basic logic functions, AND, OR, NOT (see Table 20.4), plus many derived logic functions, such as exclusive-OR (XOR) or inequality and equality [XOR is the same as $(x \wedge y^C) \vee (x^C \wedge y)$]. Multiple logic expressions can represent the same functional relationship. We will illustrate this by the two-locus disease model in Table 20.5. An interpretation of this model is that the second gene has a modifying effect on the first recessive gene [57, 77]. A person is affected if he or she carries two copies of the first gene's mutant allele A or one copy of A as well as one copy of the second gene's mutant allele B.

A logic function to represent the two-locus disease model in Table 20.5 is

$$y = x_{AA} \vee (x_{aA} \wedge x_{BB}) \tag{20.31}$$

TABLE 20.4   Basic Logic Functions

Name	Symbols	In Programs (C, R, Perl)
AND, conjunction	$x \wedge y, x \cap y, x \times y, x \cdot y$	$x \& y$
OR, disjunction	$x \vee y, x \cup y, x + y$	$x \vert y$
NOT, negation, complement	$\neg x, x^C, x', \overline{x}$	$!x$

Note: Three basic logic functions (AND, OR, NOT) and their commonly used symbols.

TABLE 20.5 Two-Locus Disease Model Representing Modifying Effect by Second Locus

	bb	bB	BB
aa	0	0	0
aA	0	0	1
AA	1	1	1

Note: Rows are the genotypes of the first locus (aa, aA, AA), columns are those of the second locus (bb, bB, BB). In binary value (0, 1) is the probability that a person with the two-locus genotype will be affected by the disease. In this model, a person is affected with either the AA genotype at the first locus by itself or the combination of aA and bB genotypes.

where x_{AA}, x_{aA}, x_{BB} are indicator variables of genotype AA, aA, BB, and so on, and y is the disease affection status. If we use the NOT function to model the unaffected status, an alternative logic expression can be written as

$$y = [x_{aa} \vee (x_{aA} \wedge x_{BB}^C)]^C. \tag{20.32}$$

In fact, any two-input logic function is guaranteed to have an alternative expression due to de Morgan's law: $x \wedge y = (x^C \vee y^C)^C$ or $x \vee y = (x^C \wedge y^C)^C$. This duality leads to two canonical forms of logic functions: *sum of products* (using OR to join subfunctions) and *product of sums* (using AND to join subfunctions).

With a large number of independent variables, finding latent variables constructed by the logic function is not easy. The proposal in the original logic regression paper is to use simulated annealing and other stochastic and greedy search algorithms such as the *Markov chain Monte Carlo* (MCMC) [95]. Once K latent variables $\{L_j\}$ ($j = 1, 2, \ldots, K$, with $K \ll p$) are constructed, logistic regression is applied as before:

$$\log\left(\frac{P}{1-P}\right) = a_0 + a_1 L_1 + a_2 L_2 + \cdots + a_K L_K \tag{20.33}$$

In [95], K is limited to less than 8. Other applications use a very small number of latent variables as well [35, 53, 96].

To summarize this section, logic regression is a method to combine effect from multiple genes by three logic functions (AND, OR, NOT). Since logic functions are highly nonlinear, they have the potential to model complicated gene–gene interactions more efficiently than linear combinations.

20.8 DISCUSSION

Like any other statistical classifiers, logistic regression can be used for two purposes. One is for prediction/classification and another is for measuring the importance of variables. Two major outputs of random forest analysis, for example, are out-of-bag classification errors and a measure of variable importance [12]. Unlike random forest, which can keep a reasonably large number of independent variables [26, 58], whether to include some variables or not in a logistic regression requires the extra step of variable/dimension reduction. For GWAS, even for random forest, the number of SNPs included needs to be filtered down from 10^5–10^6 to 10^2–10^3, especially if interaction terms are included [48, 68].

Besides the biostatician's familiarity with logistic regression and its flexiblity in modeling [40, 76, 83–85], which makes it easily acceptable, another reason it is applied to genetic analysis is due to its protection against population substructures [5, 97]. To account for population stratifications, one may include a set of phenotypically neutral whereas ethnic-group sensitive SNPs in a multiple logistic regression. These SNPs will account for the population stratifications. Any test of significance of other SNPs will be conditional upon these noncausal effects and thus unlikely to be false positives. (Note added after proof: using mixed models within the regression framework to account for population structure and family relatedness is an active research topic.)

As SNPs themselves are often not causal factors for diseases, it is important to move from the SNP level to the gene level. Introducing latent variables is a crucial step toward this goal. It was shown in [15] that if the interaction is specified at the latent variable level instead of the SNP level, the number of parameters in the model is greatly reduced. This formulation of a parsimonious modeling of the interaction parallels Tukey's modeling of nonadditivity in a two-way *analysis of variance* (ANOVA) [106]. In fact, moving up in levels always leads to a simpler description of a complex system.

Because logistic regression is a standard statistical method, computer programs are readily available. Table 20.6 lists some R packages (http://www.r-project.org) [111] relevant to the discussion in this chapter.

To conclude, *logistic regression* (LR) complements standard statistical tests such as the chi-square test and the Cochran–Armitage trend test [5, 59] in analyzing data for GWAS. LR is more flexible in handling population stratification, in considering gene–gene and gene–environment interaction, and in assessing classification performance. There are still many topics not covered in this chapter, such as the random-effect LR [4], clustering of haplotypes for variable reduction [28, 47, 107, 108], and nonparametric kernel machine LR [36, 85], showing how diverse this topic is.

TABLE 20.6 Selected R Packages

Function/Package Name	Full Name	Details	First Author
glm/-	Generalized linear model	family=binomial	Davies
step/-	Stepwise selection		Ripley
haplo.ccs	Haplotype case–control		French [33]
gl1ce/lasso2	L_1 LASSO	family=binomial	Lokhorst [67]
grplasso/grplasso	Group LASSO	model=LogReg()	Meier [72]
glmnet/glmnet	Penalized GLM	family=binomial	Hastie
penalized/penalized	Penalized GLM	model="logistic"	Goeman
pcr/pls	PLS regression		Wehrens [73]
glplsia/gpls	Generalized PLS		Ding [27]
spls/spls	Sparse PLS		Chung
spca/elasticnet	Sparse PCA		Zou
logreg/logreg	Logic regression		Kooperberg

APPENDIX: MATRIX REPRESENTATION OF PARTIAL LEAST-SQUARES REGRESSION

We use bold uppercase symbols for matrices and bold lowercase symbols for column vectors. Matrix $\mathbf{X}(n \times p)$ contains the observed data of p independent variables in n samples (each independent variable is standardized, i.e., zero mean and unit variance); column vector $\mathbf{y}(n \times 1)$ is the n observations of the dependent variable. Denote K latent variables as $t_1, t_2, \ldots, t_K$ and their n values form the matrix $\mathbf{T}(n \times K)$.

The latent variables are a linear combination of the original independent variable, and this linear relationship can be represented by a matrix product:

$$\mathbf{T}_{n \times K} = \mathbf{X}_{n \times p} \mathbf{W}_{p \times K} \tag{20.34}$$

If we pick the jth column from both sides,

$$\mathbf{t}_j = \mathbf{X} \mathbf{w}_j \qquad j = 1, 2, \ldots, K \tag{20.35}$$

which are the jth latent variable values in n samples.

We choose the latent variables (i.e., the weights in $\mathbf{W}$) so that

$$
\begin{aligned}
\mathbf{t}_j^T \mathbf{t}_j &= 1 & (j = 1, 2, \ldots, K) \\
\mathbf{t}_j^T \mathbf{t}_{j'} = \mathbf{w}_j^T (\mathbf{X}^T \mathbf{X}) \mathbf{w}_{j'} &= 0 & (j = 1, 2, \ldots, K-1, j' = j+1, \ldots, K) \\
\mathbf{y}^T \mathbf{t}_j \text{ is maximized} & & (j = 1, 2, \ldots, K)
\end{aligned}
\tag{20.36}
$$

These are equivalent to

$$\mathbf{w}_j = \arg\max_{\mathbf{w}_j} \left(\mathbf{y}^T \mathbf{X} \mathbf{w}_j \right) \qquad (j = 1, 2, \ldots, K)$$

$$\text{where} \qquad \mathbf{W}^T \mathbf{X}^T \mathbf{X} \, \mathbf{W} = \mathbf{I} \tag{20.37}$$

and $\mathbf{I}$ $(K \times K)$ is the identity matrix and $\mathbf{X}^T \mathbf{X}$ $(p \times p)$ is the variance–covariance matrix.

ACKNOWLEDGMENTS

We thank David Ballard and Hyonho Chun for discussions. YY is supported by a China NSF grant.

REFERENCES

1. A. Agresti. *Categorical Data Analysis*, 2nd ed. Wiley-Interscience, Hoboken, NJ, 2002.

2. H. Akaike. A new look at the statistical model identification. *IEEE Trans. Automatic Control*, 19:716–723, 1974.

3. K. L. Ayers and H. J. Cordell. SNP selection in genome-wide and candidate gene studies via penalized logistic regression. *Genet. Epid.*, 34:879–891, 2010.

4. P. G. Bagos and G. K. Nikolopoulos. A method for meta-analysis of case-control genetic association studies using logistic regression. *Stat. Appl. Genet. Mol. Biol.*, 6:17, 2007.

5. D. J. Balding. A tutorial on statistical methods for population association studies. *Brief. Bioinformatics*, 7:781–791, 2006.

6. M. S. Bartlett. Some examples of statistical methods of research in agriculture and applied biology. *J. Roy. Stat. Soc. Suppl.*, 4:137–183, 1937.

7. W. Bateson. *Mendel's Principles of Heredity*. Cambridge University Press, Cambridge, UK, 1909.

8. J. Berkson. Application of the logistic function to bio-assay. *J. Am. Stat. Assoc.*, 39:357–365, 1944.

9. S. Biswas and S. Lin. Logistic Bayesian LASSO for identifying association with rare haplotypes and application to age-related macular degeneration. *Biometrics*, 68:587–597, 2012.

10. H. D. Bondell and B. J. Reich. Simultaneous regression shrinkage, variable selection and clustering of predictors with OSCAR. *Biometrics*, 64:115–123, 2008.

11. A. L. Boulesteix and K. Strimmer. Partial least squares: A versatile tool for the analysis of high-dimensional genomic data. *Brief. Bioinformatics*, 8:32–44, 2006.

12. L. Breiman. Random forests. *Machine Learning*, 45:5–32, 2001.

13. N. E. Breslow and N. E. Day. *Statistical Methods in Cancer Research*, Vol 1: *The Analysis of Case-Control Studies*. International Agency for Research on Cancer, Lyon, 1980.

14. R. M. Cantor, K. Lange, and J. S. Sinsheimer. Prioritizing GWAS results: A review of statistical methods and recommendations for their application *Am. J. Hum. Genet.*, 86:6–22, 2010.

15. N. Chatterjee, Z. Kalaylioglu, R. Moslehi, U. Peters, and S. Wacholder. Powerful multilocus tests of genetic association in the presence of gene-gene and gene-environment interactions. *Am. J. Hum. Genet.*, 79:1002–1016, 2006.

16. L. S. Chen, C. M. Hutter, J. D. Potter, Y. Liu, R. L. Prentice, U. Peters, and L. Hsu. Insights into colon cancer etiology via a regularized approach to gene set analysis of GWAS data. *Am. J. Hum. Genet.*, 86:860–871, 2010.

17. S. Cho, H. Kim, S. Oh, K. Kim, and T. Park. Elastic-net regularization approaches for genome-wide association studies of rheumatoid arthritis. *BMC Proc.*, 3(Suppl. 7):S25, 2009.

18. S. Cho, K. Kim, Y. J. Kim, J. K. Lee, Y. S. Cho, J. Y. Lee, B. G. Han, H. Kim, J. Ott, and T. Park. Joint identification of multiple genetic variants via elastic-net variable selection in a genome-wide association analysis. *Ann. Hum. Genet.*, 74:416–428, 2010.

19. H. Chun and S. Keleş. Sparse partial least square regression for simultaneous dimension reduction and variable selection. *J. R. Stat. Soc. B*, 72:3–25, 2010.

20. H. Chun, D. H. Ballard, J. Cho, and H. Zhao. Identification of association between disease and multiple markers via sparse partial least-square regression. *Genet. Epid.*, 35:479–486, 2011.

21. H. J. Cordell. Epistasis: What it means, what it doesn't mean, and statistical methods to detect it in humans *Hum. Mol. Genet.*, 11:2463–2468, 2002.

22. H. J. Cordell and D. G. Clayton. A unified stepwise regression procedure for evaluating the relative effects of polymorphisms within a gene using case/control or family data: Application to HLA in type 1 diabetes. *Am. J. Hum. Genet.*, 70:124–141, 2001.

23. R. G. H. Cotton. Detection of single base changes in nucleic acids. *Biochem. J.*, 263:1–10, 1989.

24. D. R. Cox and N. Wermuth. *Multivariate Dependencies*. Chapman & Hall, London, UK, 1996.

25. E. Cule, P. Vineis, and M. De Iorio. Significance testing in ridge regression for genetic data. *BMC Bioinformatics*, 12:372, 2011.

26. R. Díaz-Uriarte and S. Alvarez de Andrés. Gene selection and classification of microarray data using random forest. *BMC Bioinformatics*, 7:3, 2006.

27. B. Ding and R. Gentleman. Classification using generalized partial least squareas. *J. Comp. Graph. Stat.*, 14:280–298, 2005.

28. C. Durrant, K. T. Zondervan, L. R. Cardon, S. Hunt, P. Deloukas, and A. P. Morris. Linkage disequilibrium mapping via cladistic analysis of single-nucleotide polymorphism haplotypes. *Am. J. Hum. Genet.*, 75:35–43, 2004.

29. B. Efron, T. Hastie, I. Johnstone, and R. Tibshirani. Least angle regression. *Ann. Stat.*, 32:407–499, 2004.

30. J. N. Feder et al. A novel MHC class I-like gene is mutated in patients with hereditary haemochromatosis. *Nat. Genet.*, 13:399–408, 1996.

31. R. A. Fisher. The correlation between relatives on the supposition of Mendelian inheritance. *Trans. Roy. Soc. Edin.*, 52:399–433, 1918.

32. T. M. Frayling et al. A common variant in the FTO gene is associated with body mass index and predisposes to childhood and adult obesity. *Science*, 316:889–894, 2007.

33. B. French, T. Lumley, S. A. Monks, K. M. Rice, L. A. Hindorff, A. P. Reiner, and B. M. Psaty. Simple estimates of haplotype relative risks in case-control data. *Genet. Epid.*, 30:485–494, 2006.

34. J. H. Friedman, T. Hastie, and R. Tibshirani. Regularization paths for generalized linear models via coordinate descent. *J. Stat. Soft.*, 33:1–22, 2010.

35. A. Fritsch and K. Ickstadt. Comparing logic regression based methods for identifying SNP interactions. *Lecture Notes Comp. Sci.*, 4414:90–103, 2007.

36. Q. Gao, Y. He, Z. Yuan, J. Zhao, B. Zhang, and F. Xue. Gene- or region-based association study via kernel principal component analysis. *BMC Genet.*, 12:75, 2011.

37. X. Gu, R. F. Frankowski, G. L. Rosner, M. Relling, B. Peng, and C. I. Amos. A modified forward multiple regression in high-density genome-wide association studies for complex traits. *Genet. Epid.*, 33:518–525, 2008.

38. W. Guo, R. C. Elston, and X. Zhu. Evaluation of a LASSO regression approach on the unrelated samples of Genetic Analysis Workshop 17. *BMC Proc.*, 5(Suppl. 9):S12, 2011.

39. I. B. Hallgrímsdóttir and D. S. Yuster. A complete classification of epistatic two-locus models. *BMC Genet.*, 9:17, 2008.

40. F. Han and W. Pan. Powerful multi-marker association tests: Unifying genomic distance-based regression and logistic regression. *Genet. Epid.*, 34:680–688, 2010.

41. T. Hastie, R. Tibshirani, and J. Friedman. *The Elements of Statistical Learning*, 2nd ed. Springer, New York, 2009.

42. A. G. Heidema, J. M. A. Boer, N. Nagelkerke, E. C. M. Mariman, D. L. van der A, and E. J. M. Feskens. The challenge for genetic epidemiologists: How to analyze large numbers of SNPs in relation to complex diseases. *BMC Genet.*, 7:23, 2006.

43. A. Hodgkinson and A. Eyre-Walker. Human triallelic sites: Evidence for a new mutational mechanism? *Genetics*, 184:233–241, 2010.

44. A. E. Hoerl and R. Kennard. Ridge regression: Biased estimation for nonorthogonal problems. *Technometrics*, 12:55–67, 1970.

45. H. Hotelling. Relations between two sets of variates. *Biometrika*, 28:321–377, 1936.

46. C. Hüebner, I. Petermann, B. L. Browning, A. N. Shelling, and L. R. Ferguson. Triallelic single nucleotide polymorphisms and genotyping error in genetic epidemiology studies: MDR1 (ABCB1) G2677/T/A as an example. *Cancer Epid. Biomarkers Prevention*, 16:1185–1192, 2007.

47. R. P. Igo, Jr., J. Li, and K. A. B. Goddard. Association mapping by generalized linear regression with density-based haplotype clustering. *Genet. Epid.*, 33:16–26, 2009.

48. R. Jiang, W. Tang, X. Wu, and W. Fu. A random forest approach to the detection of epistatic interactions in case-control studies. *BMC Bioinf.*, 10(Suppl. 1):S65, 2009.

49. I. T. Jolliffe. *Principal Component Analysis*, 2nd ed. Springer, New York, 2002.

50. K. G. Jöreskog. A general method for analysis of covariance structures. *Biometrika*, 57:239–251, 1970.

51. S. Kim, N. J. Morris, S. Won, and R. C. Elston. Single-marker and two-marker association tests for unphased case-control genotype data, with a power comparison. *Genet. Epid.*, 34:67–77, 2010.

52. O. Kohannim, D. P. Hibar, J. L. Stein, N. Jahanshad, C. R. Jack, M. W. Weiner, A. W. Toga, and P. M. Thompson. Boosting power to detect genetic associations in imaging using multi-locus, genome-wide scans and ridge regression. In *2011 IEEE International Symposium on Biomedical Imaging: From Nano to Macro*. IEEE, 2011, pp. 1855–1859.

53. C. Kooperberg and I. Ruczinski. Identifying interacting SNPs using Monte Carlo logic regression. *Genet. Epid.*, 28:157–170, 2005.

54. H. W. Kuhn and A. W. Tucker. Nonlinear programming. In J. Neyma (Ed.), *Proceedings of the Second Berkeley Symposium on Mathematical Statistics and Probability*. University of California Press, 1950, pp. 481–492.

55. C. C. Li. *Path Analysis: A Primer*. Boxwood Press, Pacific Grove, CA, 1975.

56. J. Li, K. Das, G. Fu, R. Li, and R. Wu. The Bayesian lasso for genome-wide association studies. *Bioinformatics*, 27:516–523, 2011.

57. W. Li. A complete enumeration and classification of two-locus disease models. *Hum. Hered.*, 50:334–349, 2000.

58. W. Li. The-more-the-better and the-less-the-better. *Bioinformatics*, 22:2187–2188, 2006.

59. W. Li. Three lectures on case-control genetic association analysis. *Brief. Bioinformatics*, 9:1–13, 2008.

60. W. Li. Genetic marker. In W. Dubitzky, O. Wolkenhauer, K. H. Cho, and H. Yokota, (Eds.), *Encyclopedia of Systems Biology*. Springer Science+Business Media, New York, 2013.

61. W. Li and D. R. Nyholt. Marker selection by Akaike information criterion and Bayesian information criterion. *Genet. Epid.*, 21(Suppl. 1):S272–S277, 2001.

62. W. Li, Y. J. Suh, and Y. Yang. Exploring case-control genetic association tests using phase diagrams. *Comp. Biol. Chem.*, 32:391–399, 2008.

63. W. Li, M. Wang, P. Irigoyen, and P. K. Gregersen. Inferring causal relationships among intermediate phenotypes and biomarkers. A case study of rheumatoid arthritis. *Bioinformatics*, 22:1503–1507, 2006.

64. Y. Li, W. K. Sung, and J. J. Liu. Association mapping via regularized regression analysis of single-nucleotide-polymorphism haplotypes in variable-sized sliding windows. *Am. J. Hum. Genet.*, 80:705–715, 2007.

65. Z. Liu, Y. Shen, and J. Ott. Multilocus association mapping using generalized ridge logistic regression. *BMC Bioinformatics*, 12:384, 2011.

66. I. Lobach, R. J. Carroll, C. Spinka, M. H. Gail, and N. Chatterjee. Haplotype-based regression analysis and inference of case-control studies with unphased genotypes and measurement errors in environmental exposures. *Biometrics*, 64:673–684, 2008.

67. J. Lokhorst, B. A. Turlach, and W. N. Venables. Lasso2: An S-PLUS library to solve regression problems while imposing an L^1 constraint on the parameters. Preprint. Department of Statistics, University of Adelaide, Australia, 1999.

68. K. L. Lunetta, L. B. Hayward, J. Segal, and P. Van Eerdewegh. Screening large-scale association study data: Exploiting interactions using random forests. *BMC Genet.*, 5:32, 2004.

69. E. Makalic and D. F. Schmidt. Review of modern logistic regression methods with application to small and medium sample size problems. *Lecture Notes in Computer Science*, 6464/2011:213–222, 2011.

70. N. Malo, O. Libiger, and N. J. Schork. Accommodating linkage disequilibrium in genetic-association analyses via ridge regression. *Am. J. Hum. Genet.*, 82:375–385, 2008.

71. P. McCullagh and J. A. Nelder. *Generalized Linear Models*, 2nd ed. Chapman & Hall/CRC, Boca Raton, FL, 1989.

72. L. Meier, S. Van De Geer, and P. Bühlmann. The group lasso for logistic regression. *J. Roy. Stat. Soc.*, 70:53–71, 2008.

73. B. H. Mevik and R. Wehrens. The pls package: Principal component and partial least squares regression in R. *J. Stat. Soft.*, 18:1–24, 2007.

74. A. Miller. *Subset Selection in Regression*, 2nd ed. Chapman and Hall/CRC, Boca Raton, FL, 2002.

75. S. Myers, L. Bottolo, C. Freeman, G. McVean, and P. Donnelly. A fine-scale map of recombination rates and hotspots across the human genome. *Science*, 310:321–324, 2005.

76. N. J. Nagelkerke, B. Hoebee, P. Teunis, and T. G. Kimman. Combining the transmission disequilibrium test and case-control methodology using generalized logistic regression. *Eur. J. Hum. Genet.*, 12:964–970, 2004.

77. R. J. Newman and J. P. Rice. Two-locus models of diseases. *Genet. Epid.*, 9:347–365, 1992.

78. D. V. Nguyen and D. N. Rocke. Tumor classification by partial least squares using microarray gene expression data. *Bioinformatics*, 18:39–50, 2002.

79. D. M. Nielsen, M. G. Ehm, and B. S. Weir. Detecting marker-disease association by testing for Hardy-Weinberg disequilibrium at a marker locus. *Am. J. Hum. Genet.*, 63:1531–1540, 1998.

80. R. Nielsen, J. S. Paul, A. Albrechtsen, and Y. S. Song. Genotype and SNP calling from next-generation sequencing data. *Nat. Rev. Genet.*, 12:443–451, 2011.

81. B. V. North, D. Curtis, and P. C. Sham. Application of logistic regression to case-control association studies involving two causative loci. *Hum. Hered.*, 59:79–87, 2005.

82. M. R. Osborne, B. Presnell, and B. A. Turlach. On the LASSO and its dual. *J. Comp. Graph. Stat.*, 9:319–337, 2000.

83. W. Pan. A unified framework for detecting genetic association with multiple SNPs in a candidate gene or region: Contrasting genotype scores and LD patterns between cases and controls. *Hum. Hered.*, 69:1–13, 2010.

84. W. Pan. Statistical tests of genetic association in the presence of gene-gene and gene-environment interactions. *Hum. Hered.*, 69:131–142, 2010.

85. W. Pan. Relationship between genomic distance-based regression and kernel machine regression for multi-marker association testing. *Genet. Epid.*, 35:211–216, 2011.

86. M. Y. Park and T. Hastie. L1 regularization-path algorithm for generalized linear models. *J. Roy. Stat. Soc. B*, 69:659–677, 2007.

87. M. Y. Park and T. Hastie. Penalized logistic regression for detecting gene interactions. *Biostatistics*, 9:30–50, 2008.

88. T. Park and G. Casella. The Bayesian LASSO. *J. Am. Stat. Assoc.*, 103:681–686, 2008.

89. S. Petry and G. Tutz. The OSCAR for generalized linear models. Preprint. Institute of Statistics, Ludwig-Maximilians-Universität, München, Germany, 2011.

90. P. C. Phillips. Epistasis—The essential role of gene interactions in the structure and evolution of genetic systems. *Nat. Rev. Genet.*, 9:855–867, 2008.

91. D. Pinkel et al. High resolution analysis of DNA copy number variation using comparative genomic hybridization to microarrays. *Nat. Genet.*, 20:207–211, 1998.

92. L. R. Rabiner. A tutorial on hidden Markov models and selected applications in speech recognition. *Proc. IEEE*, 77:257–286, 1989.

93. C. R. Rao. Score test: Historical review and recent developments. In N. Balakrishnan, N. Kannan, H. N. Nagaraja (Eds.) *Advances in Ranking and Selection, Multiple Comparisons, and Reliability.* Birkhauser, Boston, 2005, pp. 3–20.

94. B. Rigat et al. An insertion/deletion polymorphism in the angiotensin I-converting enzyme gene accounting for half the variance of serum enzyme levels. *J. Clin. Invest.*, 86:1343–1346, 1990.

95. I. Ruczinski, C. Kooperberg, and M. L. LeBlanc. Logic regression. *J. Comp. Graph. Stat.*, 12:475–511, 2003.

96. H. Schwender and K. Ickstadt. Identification of SNP interactions using logic regression. *Biostatistics*, 9:187–198, 2008.

97. E. Setakis, H. Stirnadel, and D. J. Balding. Logistic regression protects against population structure in genetic association studies. *Genome Res.*, 16:290–296, 2006.

98. P. C. Sham, F. V. Rijsdijk, J. Knight, A. Makoff, B. North, and D. Curtis. Haplotype association analysis of discrete and continuous traits using mixture of regression models. *Behav. Genet.*, 34:207–214, 2004.

99. W. Shi, K. Lee, and G. Wahba. Detecting disease causing genes by LASSO-patternsearch algorithm. *BMC Proc.*, 1(Suppl. 1):S60, 2007.

100. C. Spearman. General intelligence: Objectively determined and measured. *Am. J. Psych.*, 15:201–292, 1904.

101. K. Song and R. C. Elston. A powerful method of combining measures of association and Hardy-Weinberg disequilibrium for fine-mapping in case-control studies. *Stat. Med.*, 25:105–126, 2006.

102. S. Srivastava and L. Chen. Model selection methods for genome wide association studies. *Commun. Infom. Syst.*, 10:39–52, 2010.

103. Y. V. Sun, Y. J. Sung, N. Tintle, and A. Ziegler. Identification of genetic association of multiple rare variants using collapsing methods. *Genet. Epid.*, 35:S101–S106, 2011.

104. S. Szymczak, J. M. Biernacka, H. J. Cordell, O. González-Recio, I. R. König, H. Zhang, and Y. V. Sun. Machine learning in genome-wide association studies. *Genet. Epid.*, 33(Suppl. 1):S51–S57, 2009.

105. R. Tibshirani. Regression shrinkage and selection via the lasso. *J. Roy. Stat. Soc. B*, 58:267–288, 1996.

106. J. W. Tukey. One degree of freedom for non additivity. *Biometrics*, 5:232–242, 1949.

107. J. Y. Tzeng, C. H. Wang, J. T. Kao, and C. K. Hsiao. Regression-based association analysis with clustered haplotypes through use of genotypes. *Am. J. Hum. Genet.*, 78:231–242, 2006.

108. J. Y. Tzeng, D. Zhang, S. M. Chang, D. C. Thomas, and M. Davidian. Gene-trait similarity regression for multimarker-based association analysis. *Biometrics*, 65:822–832, 2009.

109. H. W. Uh, B. J. A. Mertens, H. J. van der Wijk, H. Putter, H. C. van Houwelinge, and J. J. Houwing-Duistermaat. Model selection based on logistic regression in a highly correlated candidate gene region. *BMC Proc.*, 1(Suppl. 1):S114, 2007.

110. K. Van Steen. Travelling the world of gene-gene interaction. *Brief. Bioinformatics*, in press.

111. W. N. Venables and B. D. Ripley. *Modern Applied Statistics with S*, 4th ed. Springer, New York, 2010.

112. A. Wald. Tests of statistical hypotheses concerning several parameters when the number of observations is large. *Thans. Am. Math. Soc.*, 54:426–482, 1943.

113. S. Wallenstein, S. E. Hodge, and A. Weston. Logistic regression model for analyzing extended haplotype data. *Genet. Epid.*, 15:173–181, 1998.

114. K. Wang and D. Abbott. A principal components regression approach to multilocus genetic association studies. *Genet. Epid.*, 32:108–118, 2008.

115. T. Wang, G. Ho, K. Ye, H. Strickler, and R. C. Elston. A partial least-square approach for modelling gene-gene and gene-environment interactions when multiple markers are genotyped. *Genet. Epid.*, 33:6–15, 2009.

116. J. M. S. Wason and F. Dudbridge. Comparison of multimarker logistic regression models, with application to a genomewide scan of schizophrenia. *BMC Genet.*, 11:80, 2010.

117. D. M. Witten, R. Tibshirani, and T. Hastie. A penalized matrix decomposition, with applications to sparse principal components and canonical correlation analysis. *Biostatistics*, 10:515–534, 2009.

118. S. S. Wilks. The likelihood test of independence in contingency tables. *Ann. Math. Stat.*, 6:190–196, 1935.

119. S. S. Wilks. The large-sample distribution of the likelihood ratio for testing composite hypotheses. *Ann. Math. Stat.*, 9:60–62, 1938.

120. S. Winham, C. Wang, and A. A. Motsinger-Reif. A comparison of multifactor dimensionality reduction and L1-penalized regression to identify gene-gene interactions in genetic association studies. *Stat. Appl. Genet. Mol. Biol.*, 10:4, 2011.

121. S. Won and R. C. Elston. The power of independent types of genetic information to detect association in a case-control study design. *Genet. Epid.*, 32:731–756, 2008.

122. T. T. Wu, Y. F. Chen, T. Hastie, E. Sobel, and K. Lange. Genome-wide association analysis by lasso penalized logistic regression. *Bioinformatics*, 25:714–721, 2009.

123. Z. Wu, C. Aporntewan, D. H. Ballard, J. Y. Lee, J. S. Lee, and H. Zhao. Two-stage joint selection method to identify candidate markers from genome-wide association studies. *BMC Proc.*, 3(Suppl. 7):S29, 2009.

124. Y. Yang, E. F. Remmers, C. B. Ogunwole, D. L. Kastner, P. K. Gregersen, and W. Li. Effective sample size: Quick estimation of the effect of related samples in genetic case-control association analyses. *Comp. Biol. Chem.*, 35:40–49, 2011.

125. F. Zhang, X. Guo, and H. W. Deng. Multilocus association testing of quantitative traits based on partial least-squares analysis. *PLoS ONE*, 6:e16739, 2011.

126. H. Zhou, M. E. Sehl, J. S. Sinsheimer, and K. Lange. Association screening of common and rare genetic variants by penalized regression. *Bioinformatics*, 26:2375–2382, 2010.

127. H. Zou and T. Hastie. Regularization and variable selection via the elastic net. *J. Roy. Stat. Soc. B*, 67:301–320, 2005.

CHAPTER 21

SEMIPARAMETRIC REGRESSION METHODS IN LONGITUDINAL DATA: APPLICATIONS TO AIDS CLINICAL TRIAL DATA

YEHUA LI

Department of Statistics and Statistical Laboratory, Iowa State University, Ames, Iowa

21.1 INTRODUCTION

In many clinical trials, the variables of interest are repeatedly measured during the follow-up period of the study. This type of data is commonly referred to as *longitudinal data* [2]. In this chapter, we illustrate the statistical methodology to analyze such data using an example from the CD4 count data from the AIDS Clinical Trial Group 193A Study [12]. CD4 (cluster of differentiation 4) is a glycoprotein considered as an indicator for HIV progression.

The clinical trial is a randomized, double-blind study of AIDS patients with initial CD4 counts of less than or equal to 50 cells/mm^3. The patients were randomized to one of four treatments; each consisted of a daily regimen of 600 mg of zidovudine. Treatment 1 is zidovudine alternating monthly with 400 mg didanosine; treatment 2 is zidovudine plus 2.25 mg of zalcitabine; treatment 3 is zidovudine plus 400 mg of didanosine; and treatment 4 is a triple therapy with zidovudine plus 400 mg of didanosine and 400 mg of nevirapine.

Measurements of CD4 counts were scheduled to be collected at baseline (i.e., before the start of the treatment) and at 8-week intervals during the 40 weeks of follow-up. However, the real observation times were unbalanced due to mistimed measurements, skipped visits, and dropouts. The number of measurements of CD4 counts during the 40 weeks of follow-up varied from 1 to 9, with a median of 4. The response variable was the log-transformed CD4 counts, $Y = \log(\text{CD4 counts} + 1)$. Covariates, such as gender and baseline age, were also collected for each patient.

A total of 1309 subjects were enrolled in the study. We eliminated the 122 subjects who dropped out immediately after the baseline measurement. For the remaining patients, there are 1044 males and 143 females. There are roughly the same number of subjects (about 297) for each of the four treatment groups.

Figure 21.1 shows 10 randomly sampled CD4 count trajectories from each of the four treatment groups. The little squares in the graphs indicate the visit times. As we can see,

Biological Knowledge Discovery Handbook: Preprocessing, Mining, and Postprocessing of Biological Data,
First Edition. Edited by Mourad Elloumi and Albert Y. Zomaya.
© 2014 John Wiley & Sons, Inc. Published 2014 by John Wiley & Sons, Inc.

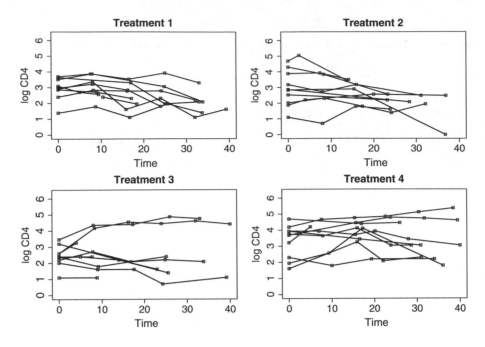

FIGURE 21.1   Ten randomly sampled CD4 count trajectories from each of four treatment groups.

every subject has a measurement at the baseline, but the rest of the visiting times are quite irregular. It is commonly assumed that the subjects are independent of each other, but, as we can also see from the graphs, the CD4 counts within the same subject tend to take similar values. For example, if a patient has relatively low CD4 count at the baseline, he or she tends to have low counts for the rest of the measurements during the follow-up. In statistics, this phenomenon is described by within-subject correlation.

In this application, we are interested in modeling how the CD4 count changes over time and how is it related to other covariates, for example, gender and baseline age. The covariate effects are modeled parametrically. In other words, we assume that the relationship between CD4 count and the covariates has a certain structure, for example, a linear relationship. The time effect, on the other hand, is modeled nonparametrically. We assume that the mean CD4 count level changes continuously over time and do not assume any structure for this temporal trend. The semiparametric model described below combines the efficiency of parametric modeling and the flexibility of nonparametric modeling. We are also interested in comparing the four treatments. After eliminating the effects of gender and age, we want to see whether the mean CD4 levels have different functional forms under different treatments.

21.2   MODELING A SINGLE TREATMENT GROUP USING A SEMIPARAMETRIC PARTIALLY LINEAR MODEL

Before comparing different treatments, we start with modeling data within the same treatment group using a partially linear model. Such semiparametric models have been considered by Zeger and Diggle [28], Lin and Carroll [17], and Wang et al. [25].

21.2.1 Model Assumptions

Suppose all longitudinal observations from different subjects or clusters are made on a fixed time interval $\mathcal{T} = [a, b]$. The data consist of n independent clusters, with the ith cluster having m_i observations. Let $T_i = (T_{i1}, \ldots, T_{im_i})^T$ be the vector of random observation times in the ith cluster. Within the ith cluster, at time T_{ij}, we observe a response variable Y_{ij} and a p-dimensional covariate vector X_{ij}. Let $Y_i = (Y_{i1}, \ldots, Y_{im_i})^T$ and $X_i = (X_{i1}, \ldots, X_{im_i})^T$. The number m_i may vary for different subjects, and let $N = \sum_{i=1}^{n} m_i$.

We consider a more general setting than the application mentioned before and allow the covariate vector X to be time dependent. We view both $Y_i(t)$ and $X_i(t)$ as random processes defined on continuous time $t \in \mathcal{T}$, with $X_i(t)$ being a multivariate process. Then Y_i and X_i are observations on these processes at discrete times. We model the relationship between Y and X by a semiparametric partially linear model [17, 25]:

$$E\{Y_i(t)|X_i(s), s \in \mathcal{T}\} = E\{Y_i(t)|X_i(t)\} = X_i^T(t)\beta + \theta(t) \qquad t \in \mathcal{T} \qquad (21.1)$$

where β is an unknown coefficient vector and $\theta(\cdot)$ is an unknown smooth function that represents the time effect. In model (21.1), the effect of X is assumed to be linear and therefore is parametric. The time effect $\theta(t)$, on the other hand, does not have any specific functional structure and is modeled nonparametrically.

We model the covariance of the longitudinal response Y conditional on X as

$$\mathcal{R}(t_1, t_2) = \text{cov}\{Y_i(t_1), Y_i(t_2)|X_i(s), s \in \mathcal{T}\} \qquad t_1, t_2 \in \mathcal{T} \qquad (21.2)$$

To be a valid covariance function, $\mathcal{R}(\cdot, \cdot)$ needs to be a positive semidefinite function with $\sum_{j_1=1}^{k} \sum_{j_2=1}^{k} a_{j_1} a_{j_2} \mathcal{R}(t_{j_1}, t_{j_2}) \geq 0$ for any $\{t_1, \ldots, t_k\}$ and any constants $\{a_1, \ldots, a_k\}$.

Moreover, we assume that the observation times are random but not informative, that is, $E(Y_{ij}|X_i, T_i) = X_{ij}^T\beta + \theta(T_{ij})$ and $\text{cov}(Y_{ij}, Y_{ij'}|X_i, T_i) = \mathcal{R}(T_{ij}, T_{ij'})$; these assumptions are very common (see, e.g., [17, 25]).

21.2.2 Semiparametric Profile Estimator Assuming Working Independence

Lin and Carroll [17] proposed a class of profile-kernel estimators for model (21.1), where various working covariance models can be used. Their asymptotic theory shows that the most efficient estimator within this class is the one assuming working independence. In other words, we should treat the data as if there is no within-cluster correlation. This method is described below.

The nonparametric function $\theta(t)$ is estimated by a local linear estimator [4]. For T_{ij} within a radius h of a fixed time point t, $\theta(T_{ij})$ is approximated by a linear function $\theta(T_{ij}) \approx \alpha_0 + \alpha_1(T_{ij} - t)$, where $\alpha_0 = \theta(t)$ and $\alpha_1 = \theta^{(1)}(t)$. For a given value β, let $\widehat{\alpha} = \widehat{\alpha}(t, \beta) = \{\widehat{\alpha}_0(t, \beta), \widehat{\alpha}_1(t, \beta)\}^T$ be the solution of the local estimating equation

$$N^{-1} \sum_{i=1}^{n} \sum_{j=1}^{m_i} T_{ij}(t) K_h(T_{ij} - t)\{Y_{ij} - \mu(X_{ij}, t)\} = 0 \qquad (21.3)$$

where $T_{ij}(t) = \{1, (T_{ij} - t)\}^T$, $\mu(X_{ij}, t) = X_{ij}^T\beta + T_{ij}^T(t)\alpha$, $K(\cdot)$ is a symmetric probability density function, $K_h(t) = h^{-1}K(t/h)$, and h is the bandwidth. Then the kernel estimator for $\theta(t)$ is given by $\widehat{\theta}(t, \beta) = \widehat{\alpha}_0(t, \beta)$. Examples of kernel functions include the uniform kernel

$K(t) = 0.5I(t \in [-1, 1])$, Gaussian kernel $K(t) = (2\pi)^{-1/2} \exp(-t^2/2)$, and the Epanechnikov kernel $K(t) = 0.75(1 - t^2)I(t \in [-1, 1])$.

Denote $\widetilde{T}(t) = (\mathbf{1}, T - t)$, where $\mathbf{1}$ is N-dimensional vector of 1's and $T^T = (T_1^T, \ldots, T_n^T)$. It can be easily seen that the solution of (21.3) is

$$\widehat{\theta}(t, \beta) = \mathcal{S}_{\mathrm{WI}}^T(t)(Y - X\beta) \tag{21.4}$$

where $Y = (Y_1^T, \ldots, Y_n^T)^T$, $X = (X_1^T, \ldots, X_n^T)^T$, $\mathcal{S}_{\mathrm{WI}}^T(t) = e^T\{\widetilde{T}^T(t)K_{dh}(t)\widetilde{T}(t)\}^{-1}\widetilde{T}^T(t)$ $K_{dh}(t)$, $K_{dh}(t) = \mathrm{diag}\{K_h(T_{11} - t), \ldots, K_h(T_{nm_n} - t)\}$, and $e = (1, 0)^T$.

We then proceed to estimate β by solving the profile estimating equation

$$\frac{1}{N} \sum_{i=1}^n \sum_{j=1}^{m_i} \left\{ X_{ij} + \frac{\partial\widehat{\theta}(T_{ij}, \beta)}{\partial\beta} \right\} [Y_{ij} - \{X_{ij}^T\beta + \widehat{\theta}(T_{ij}, \beta)\}] = 0 \tag{21.5}$$

Given the expression (21.4), we have $\partial\widehat{\theta}/\partial\beta(T_{ij}, \beta) = -X^T\mathcal{S}_{\mathrm{WI}}(T_{ij})$. Putting $\widetilde{X}_{ij} = X_{ij} - X^T\mathcal{S}_{\mathrm{WI}}(T_{ij})$, $\widetilde{Y}_{ij} = Y_{ij} - Y^T\mathcal{S}_{\mathrm{WI}}(T_{ij})$, $\widetilde{X}_i = (\widetilde{X}_{i1}, \ldots, \widetilde{X}_{im_i})^T$, and $\widetilde{Y}_i = (\widetilde{Y}_{i1}, \ldots, \widetilde{Y}_{im_i})^T$, the solution of (21.5) is given by

$$\widehat{\beta} = \left(\sum_{i=1}^n \widetilde{X}_i^T \widetilde{X}_i \right)^{-1} \left(\sum_{i=1}^n \widetilde{X}_i^T \widetilde{Y}_i \right) \tag{21.6}$$

The final estimator for the nonparametric component is then given by

$$\widehat{\theta}(t) = \mathcal{S}_{\mathrm{WI}}^T(t)(Y - X\widehat{\beta}) \tag{21.7}$$

Lin and Carroll [17] studied the asymptotic properties of the working independence estimators in (21.6) and (21.7) and proved the following results.

Theorem 21.1 [17] Let Σ be the true within-subject covariance matrix, Σ_d be a diagonal matrix with the diagonal elements of Σ, $\widetilde{X}_j = X_j - E(X_j|T_j)$, and $\widetilde{X} = (\widetilde{X}_1, \ldots, \widetilde{X}_m)^T$. Then

$$n^{1/2}(\widehat{\beta} - \beta) \to \mathrm{Normal}(\mathbf{0}, V_\beta) \quad \text{in distribution}$$

where $V_\beta = \{E(\widetilde{X}^T\Sigma_d^{-1}\widetilde{X})\}^{-1}\{E(\widetilde{X}^T\Sigma_d^{-1}\Sigma\Sigma_d^{-1}\widetilde{X})\}\{E(\widetilde{X}^T\Sigma_d^{-1}\widetilde{X})\}^{-1}$. Suppose the visit time T is randomly distributed on $\mathcal{T}$ with a density $f(t)$ and $\theta(t)$ is twice continuously differentiable. Let $\sigma^2(t) = \mathrm{var}\{Y(t)|X(t)\}$, $\sigma_K^2 = \int t^2 K(t)\,dt$, and $v_K = \int K^2(t)\,dt$. Under some mild conditions,

$$(nh)^{1/2}\{\widehat{\theta}(t) - \theta(t) - B(t)\} \to \mathrm{Normal}\{0, V_\theta(t)\} \quad \text{in distribution}$$

where the bias term is $B(t) = h^2\sigma_K^2\theta^{(2)}(t)/2 + o_p(h^2)$ and the asymptotic variance is $V_\theta(t) = v_K\sigma^2(t)/f(t)$.

The working independence estimator is not as efficient as the one described in the following section, yet it provides good initial estimates for β and $\theta(t)$ which enable us to estimate the covariance function using the residuals. Such an approach will be further discussed in Section 21.3.

We now apply the working independence estimator to each treatment group in the CD4 count data. Li [14] analyzed the same data set but only focused on the male patients.

TABLE 21.1   Estimated Regression Coefficients for CD4 Count Data

	Treatment 1	Treatment 2	Treatment 3	Treatment 4
Age	0.0027 (0.0065)	0.0235 (0.0063)	0.0079 (0.0068)	0.0132 (0.0072)
Gender	0.1987 (0.1521)	−0.2178 (0.1399)	−0.1201 (0.1880)	−0.3643 (0.1857)

Note: Each treatment group is analyzed separately using the working independence estimators. The numbers in parentheses are the standard errors estimated by the sandwich formula in Section 21.2.4.

We include both gender groups in our analysis, and X includes baseline age and gender. The estimated regression coefficients and standard error for the covariates are provided in Table 21.1.

Let β_j, $j = 1, \ldots, 4$, be the regression coefficients in the four treatment groups respectively and denote $\mathcal{B} = (\beta_1, \ldots, \beta_4)$. The first hypothesis that we want to test is whether there is any interaction between the treatments and the covariates. In other words, the null hypothesis of interest is $H_0 : \beta_1 = \cdots = \beta_4$. Let

$$
\mathcal{C} = \begin{pmatrix} 1 & 1 & 1 \\ 1 & -1 & -1 \\ -1 & 1 & -1 \\ -1 & -1 & 1 \end{pmatrix}
$$

be a matrix of linear contrasts. The null hypothesis can be rewritten as $\mathcal{BC} = \mathbf{0}$, where $\mathbf{0}$ is a 2×3 matrix of 0's.

Let A^{vec} be the vector by stacking all columns of a matrix A, and $\otimes$ denotes the Kronecker product of matrices [20]. By the asymptotic theory, $\widehat{\beta}_j$ is approximately distributed with Normal$(\beta_j, V_{\beta, j})$, $j = 1, \ldots, 4$. Because the four treatment groups are analyzed separately, the $\widehat{\beta}_j$'s are independent with each other, and hence $\widehat{\mathcal{B}}^{\text{vec}} \sim$ Normal$(\mathcal{B}^{\text{vec}}, \widetilde{V}_\beta)$, where $\widetilde{V}_\beta =$ diag$(V_{\beta, 1}, \ldots, V_{\beta, 4})$. Then a test statistic for H_0 can be constructed as

$$
T_\beta = (\widehat{\mathcal{B}}^{\text{vec}})^T \widetilde{\mathcal{C}} (\widetilde{\mathcal{C}}^T \widetilde{V}_\beta \widetilde{\mathcal{C}})^{-1} \widetilde{\mathcal{C}}^T \widehat{\mathcal{B}}^{\text{vec}}
$$

where $\widetilde{\mathcal{C}} = \mathcal{C} \otimes I$ and I is a two-dimensional identity matrix. Under the null hypothesis, T_β follows an asymptotic χ^2-distribution with six degrees of freedom. The asymptotic variances $V_{\beta, j}$'s are unknown but can be substituted with the sandwich estimators in Section 21.2.4. We apply this test to the data and obtain a p-value of 0.066. Judging with a commonly used level of 0.05, the interaction between treatments and X is small.

The estimated time effects $\widehat{\theta}(t)$ for the four treatment groups are presented in Figure 21.2. In each panel, a pointwise confidence interval for $\theta(t)$ is provided by $\widehat{\theta}(t) \pm \text{SE}_\theta(t)$, where the standard errors are calculated using the sandwich formula in Section 21.2.4. It seems that different treatments have very different effects on the mean CD4 level, but a rigorous test on this claim will be deferred to Section 21.4, where all treatment groups are modeled simultaneously by one model.

21.2.3   Efficient Semiparametric Regression Method

The working independence profile-kernel method in Section 21.2.2 ignores the longitudinal correlation and hence is not fully efficient. Wang et al. [25] proposed another class of estimators based on the seemingly unrelated kernel estimator of Wang [24], which makes

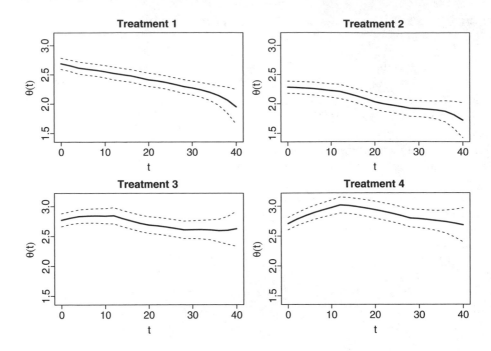

FIGURE 21.2   Estimated time effects for CD4 count data, where each treatment group is analyzed separately using the working independence estimators. In each panel, the dotted curves are $\widehat{\theta}(t) \pm 2\,SE_\theta(t)$.

use of within-cluster correlation information and is semiparametrically efficient. When the true covariance model is used, the method of Wang et al. [25] has smaller asymptotic variance than that of the working independence estimator.

The seemingly unrelated kernel estimator of Wang [24] is equipped with an iterative algorithm which is applicable to various types of response variables, including binary and Poisson responses. For Gaussian-type responses, which is the case we are primarily interested in, Lin et al. [18] proposed a noniterative algorithm in their Proposition 1. We now describe this algorithm based on a local linear smoother.

Let V_i be the working covariance matrix within the ith subject, V_i^d be a diagonal matrix containing the diagonal entries of V_i^{-1}, $\widetilde{V} = \text{diag}(V_1, \ldots, V_n)$, and $\widetilde{V}^d = \text{diag}(V_1^d, \ldots, V_n^d)$. Let $K(\cdot)$ be a kernel function as described above, h be the bandwidth, and $\widetilde{T}(t)$ and $K_{dh}(t)$ defined as in Section 21.2.2. Put $K_{dh}(t) = \text{diag}\{K_h(T_{11} - t), \ldots, K_h(T_{nm_n} - t)\}$ and $e = (1, 0)^T$.

For a given value β, the seemly unrelated kernel estimator for $\theta(t)$ is

$$\widehat{\theta}(t, \beta) = \mathcal{S}_{\text{SU}}^T(t)(Y - X\beta) \tag{21.8}$$

where

$$\mathcal{S}_{\text{SU}}^T(t) = K_{wh}^T(t)\{I + (\widetilde{V}^{-1} - \widetilde{V}^d)K_w\}^{-1}\widetilde{V}^{-1}$$
$$K_{wh}^T(t) = e^T\{\widetilde{T}^T(t)K_{dh}(t)\widetilde{V}^d\widetilde{T}(t)\}^{-1}\widetilde{T}^T(t)K_{dh}(t)$$
$$K_w = \{K_{wh}(T_{11}), \ldots, K_{wh}(T_{nm_n})\}^T$$

The estimator $\widehat{\beta}$ is then obtained by solving the profile estimating equation

$$\sum_{i=1}^{n} \left\{ X_i + \frac{\partial \widehat{\theta}(T_i, \beta)}{\partial \beta} \right\}^T V_i^{-1}[Y_i - \{X_i\beta + \widehat{\theta}(T_i, \beta)\}] = 0 \tag{21.9}$$

where $\widehat{\theta}(T_i, \beta) = \{\widehat{\theta}(T_{i1}, \beta), \ldots, \widehat{\theta}(T_{im_i}, \beta)\}^T$. Given the expression for the seemingly un-related kernel estimator (21.8), it is easy to derive that the solution of (21.9) has a close form

$$\widehat{\beta} = \left(\sum_{i=1}^{n} \widetilde{X}_i^T V_i^{-1} \widetilde{X}_i \right)^{-1} \left(\sum_{i=1}^{n} \widetilde{X}_i^T V_i^{-1} \widetilde{Y}_i \right) \tag{21.10}$$

where $\widetilde{X}_{ij} = X_{ij} - X^T S_{SU}(T_{ij})$, $\widetilde{Y}_{ij} = Y_{ij} - Y^T S_{SU}(T_{ij})$, $\widetilde{X}_i = (\widetilde{X}_{i1}, \ldots, \widetilde{X}_{im_i})^T$, and $\widetilde{Y}_i = (\widetilde{Y}_{i1}, \ldots, \widetilde{Y}_{im_i})^T$. Finally, the nonparametric component is updated as

$$\widehat{\theta}(t) = S_{SU}^T(t)(Y - X\widehat{\beta}) \tag{21.11}$$

Wang et al. [25] provided the asymptotic properties for the estimators defined in (21.10) and (21.11). Some notation and assumptions are required before introducing these results. Suppose T_{ij} are randomly distributed on interval $\mathcal{T}$ with density $f(t)$. For ease of exposition, assume $m_i = m$ for all subjects. Let Σ_i be the true covariance matrix within the ith subject, $\widetilde{X}_i = X_i - \varphi(T_i, \beta)$, and $\varphi(t)$ be the solution of a Fredholm integral equation of the second kind,

$$\sum_{j=1}^{m} \sum_{\ell=1}^{m} E[v^{j\ell}\{X_\ell - \varphi(T_\ell)\} \mid T_j = t]f(t) = 0$$

where $v^{j\ell}$ denotes the (j, ℓ)th entry of V^{-1}. For a complete list of the conditions, the readers are referred to Wang et al. [25].

Theorem 21.2 [24, 25] Under some mild conditions, we have the following convergence in distribution:

$$n^{-1/2}(\widehat{\beta} - \beta) \to \text{Normal}\{0, \Omega(V, \Sigma)\}$$

where $\Omega(V, \Sigma) = \widetilde{A}^{-1}(V)\widetilde{B}(V, \Sigma)\widetilde{A}^{-1}(V)$, $\widetilde{A}(V) = E(\widetilde{X}_i V_i^{-1} \widetilde{X}_i)$, and $\widetilde{B}(V, \Sigma) = E(\widetilde{X}_i V_i^{-1} \Sigma_i V_i^{-1} \widetilde{X}_i)$. The nonparametric estimator has the following pointwise asymptotic distribution:

$$(nh)^{1/2}\{\widehat{\theta}(t) - \theta(t) - h^2 B_*(t)\} \to \text{Normal}\{0, V_\theta(t)\}$$

The asymptotic bias is $B_*(t) = b_*(t) \times \{1 + o(1)\}$ with $b_*(t)$ satisfying the integral equation $b_*(t) = \theta^{(2)}(t) - W_2^{-1}(t) \sum_j \sum_{\ell \neq j} E\{v^{j\ell}b_*(T_\ell) \mid T_j = t\}f(t)$, where $W_2(t) = \sum_{j=1}^{m} E\{v^{jj} \mid T_j = t\}f(t)$. The asymptotic variance is

$$V_\theta(t) = v_K W_2^{-2}(t) \left[\sum_{j=1}^{m} E\{\eta_{jj} \mid T_j = t\}f(t) \right]$$

where η_{jj} is the (j, j)th element of $V^{-1}\Sigma V^{-1}$.

As shown in Wang et al. [25], when the correct covariance model is used, that is, $V_i = \Sigma_i$ for $i = 1, \ldots, n$, the estimators defined in (21.10) and (21.11) have the smallest possible asymptotic variance among all estimators. In other words, these estimators are semiparametrically efficient when the true covariance matrices are used. In real life, these covariance matrices need to be estimated. Li [14] showed that when the working covariance matrices V_i's are substituted with uniformly consistent covariance estimators $\widehat{\Sigma}_i$, the estimators in (21.10) and (21.11) are still semiparametrically efficient. Modeling and estimating the covariance will be further discussed in Section 21.3.

21.2.4 Bandwidth Selection and Inference

Both methods described in Sections 21.2.2 and 21.2.3 depend on the choice of the bandwidth. Bandwidth selection is an important step for all nonparametric and semiparametric regressions. One widely used approach is cross-validation (CV). The idea is to leave one subject out at a time, use the rest of the data to fit the model under the current bandwidth, and then use data that have been left out to validate the fitted model. The CV criterion provides essentially an estimate of the mean-squared prediction error under a given bandwidth, and the optimal bandwidth is chosen as the one that minimizes the prediction error, that is, $h^* = \arg\min_h \text{CV}(h)$. The CV criterion is defined as

$$\text{CV}(h) = \frac{1}{n} \sum_{i=1}^{n} \| Y_i - X_i \widehat{\beta}_h^{(i)} - \widehat{\theta}_h^{(i)}(T_i) \|^2$$

where $\widehat{\beta}_h^{(i)}$ and $\widehat{\theta}_h^{(i)}$ are the estimators by deleting the ith subject from the data and using bandwidth h.

The variance of both $\widehat{\beta}$ and $\widehat{\theta}(t)$ can be estimated by some sandwich formulas. For both methods described in Sections 21.2.2 and 21.2.3, the profile nonparametric estimator can be written as

$$\widehat{\theta}(t, \beta) = \mathcal{S}^T(t)(Y - X\beta) \tag{21.12}$$

where the smoothing matrix $\mathcal{S}(t)$ is either the working independence smoother (21.4) or the seemingly unrelated kernel smoother (21.8). As a result,

$$\frac{\partial}{\partial \beta} \widehat{\theta}(t, \beta) = -X^T \mathcal{S}(t)$$

A sandwich formula for estimating the covariance of $\widehat{\beta}$ is

$$\widehat{\text{var}}(\widehat{\beta}) = \left(\sum_{i=1}^{n} \widetilde{X}_i^T V_i^{-1} \widetilde{X}_i \right)^{-1} \left\{ \sum_{i=1}^{n} \widetilde{X}_i^T V_i^{-1} (Y_i - \widehat{\mu}_i)(Y_i - \widehat{\mu}_i)^T V_i^{-1} \widetilde{X}_i \right\}$$
$$\times \left(\sum_{i=1}^{n} \widetilde{X}_i^T V_i^{-1} \widetilde{X}_i \right)^{-1} \tag{21.13}$$

where $\widetilde{X}_i = X_i + \partial \widehat{\theta}(T_i, \beta)/\partial \beta$, $\widehat{\mu}_i = X_i \widehat{\beta} + \widehat{\theta}(T_i)$, and V_i is an identity matrix for the working independence estimator and is the working covariance matrix for the efficient profile estimators in Section 21.2.3.

Since $\widehat{\theta}$ is a linear smoother, and by (21.12), we have

$$\mathrm{var}\{\widehat{\theta}(t, \beta_0)\} = \mathcal{S}^T(t)\,\mathrm{cov}(Y)\mathcal{S}(t)$$

Notice that $\mathrm{cov}(Y)$ is a block diagonal matrix, with the ith block on the diagonal being the covariance matrix within the ith cluster. Therefore a sandwich-type variance estimator is

$$\widehat{\mathrm{var}}\{\widehat{\theta}(t)\} = \mathcal{S}^T(t)\widehat{\Sigma}_{\mathrm{Sand}}\mathcal{S}(t) \tag{21.14}$$

where $\widehat{\Sigma}_{\mathrm{Sand}} = \mathrm{diag}(\widehat{\Sigma}_{i,\mathrm{Sand}})_{i=1}^n$, with $\widehat{\Sigma}_{i,\mathrm{Sand}} = (Y_i - \widehat{\mu}_i)(Y_i - \widehat{\mu}_i)^T$.

21.3 MODELING WITHIN-SUBJECT COVARIANCE

As discussed in Section 21.2.3, in order to gain efficiency in longitudinal data analysis, it is crucial to model the within-subject covariance. There has been a vast volume of work on modeling covariance matrices in longitudinal data. Some recent work includes Wu and Pourahmadi [26] and Huang et al. [13]. However, most of these methods assume that the observations are made on a regular time grid and therefore are not suitable for longitudinal data collected at irregular and subject-specific times. In this section, we will be mainly focused on two types of covariance models: (a) the semiparametric covariance models proposed by Fan et al. [5] and Fan and Wu [7] and (b) the nonparametric covariance models advocated by Yao et al. [27] and Hall et al. [10].

21.3.1 Semiparametric Covariance Estimation

Fan et al. [5] modeled the variance function and correlation function separately. Specifically, in their setting the covariance function can be written as

$$\mathcal{R}(t_1, t_2) = \sigma(t_1)\sigma(t_2)\rho(t_1, t_2; \vartheta)$$

where $\sigma^2(t)$ is the conditional variance of Y at time t modeled completely nonparametrically and $\rho(t_1, t_2; \vartheta)$ is a correlation function from a known family with only a few unspecified parameters. Examples of correlation models include:

(a) The AR(1) correlation: $\rho(t_1, t_2; \varphi) = \exp(-|t_1 - t_2|/\varphi)$ for $\varphi > 0$
(b) The ARMA(1,1) correlation: $\rho(t_1, t_2; \gamma, \varphi) = \gamma \exp(-|t_1 - t_2|/\varphi)$ for $0 \le \gamma \le 1$ and $\varphi > 0$
(c) The CARMA(p,q) correlation with $q < p$: $\rho(t_1, t_2; \gamma_1, \ldots, \gamma_p, \varphi_1, \ldots, \varphi_p) = \sum_{i=1}^p \gamma_i \exp(-|t_1 - t_2|/\varphi_i)$, where $0 \le \gamma_i \le 1$, $\varphi_i > 0$, for $i = 1, \ldots, p$ and $\sum_{i=1}^p \gamma_i = 1$

The variance function is estimated applying a smoother to the squares of residuals. Let $\widehat{\beta}$ and $\widehat{\theta}(t)$ be the initial estimators, for example, the working independence estimators described in Section 21.2.2, and define the residuals as $\widehat{\epsilon}_{ij} = Y_{ij} - X_{ij}^T\widehat{\beta} - \widehat{\theta}(T_{ij})$. Then $\sigma^2(t)$ can be estimated by a local linear estimator $\widehat{\sigma}^2(t) = \widehat{\alpha}_0$, where $(\widehat{\alpha}_0, \widehat{\alpha}_1)$ minimizes

$$\frac{1}{N}\sum_{i=1}^n\sum_{j=1}^{m_i}\{\widehat{\epsilon}_{ij}^2 - \alpha_0 - \alpha_1(T_{ij} - t)\}^2 K_h(T_{ij} - t) \tag{21.15}$$

and $K(\cdot)$ and h are the kernel function and bandwidth as described before.

Fan et al. [5] also proposed a quasi-maximum-likelihood estimator (QMLE) for the correlation parameters. Letting $\widehat{\epsilon}_i = (\widehat{\epsilon}_{i1}, \ldots, \widehat{\epsilon}_{im_i})^T$, $\widehat{D}_i = \text{diag}\{\widehat{\sigma}(T_{i1}), \ldots, \widehat{\sigma}(T_{im_i})\}$, and $C_i(\vartheta) = \{\rho(T_{ij}, T_{ij'}; \vartheta)\}_{j,j'=1}^{m_i}$ be the correlation matrix for the ith cluster, we have

$$\widehat{\vartheta} = \text{argmax}_\vartheta \sum_{i=1}^{n} \left\{ -\frac{1}{2} \log |C_i(\vartheta)| - \frac{1}{2}\widehat{\epsilon}_i^T \widehat{D}_i^{-1} C_i^{-1}(\vartheta)\widehat{D}_i^{-1}\widehat{\epsilon}_i \right\} \qquad (21.16)$$

Fan and Wu [7] showed the consistency and asymptotic normality for the QMLE estimator in (21.16)

We now apply the semiparametric covariance estimation to the CD4 count data. We assume that the covariance structures are the same for all treatment groups, which is a common assumption in analysis-of-variance (ANOVA) models. We pool residuals from all treatment groups and apply the QMLE estimator, assuming ARMA(1,1) correlation structure. The estimated variance function is shown in Figure 21.3a, and it seems that the variance is increasing with time. The estimated parameters for the ARMA(1,1) correlation structure are $\widehat{\gamma} = 0.7653$ and $\widehat{\varphi} = 109.4323$. The semiparametric covariance $\mathcal{R}$ as a two-dimensional function is shown in Figure 21.3b. As we can see, there is a ridge on the diagonal of the covariance surface. The discontinuity can be explained by the existence of measurement errors or the nugget effect, which will be explained with more details in the next section.

21.3.2 Nonparametric Covariance Estimation

The semiparametric covariance estimation in Section 21.3.1 provides valid yet flexible models for the covariance structure, but it depends on correctly specifying the correlation model. To extend this idea further, one can model the covariance function completely non-parametrically. Such models have become increasingly popular in functional data analysis [22]. A incomplete list of work on nonparametric covariance function estimation includes Rice and Silverman [23], Diggle and Verbyla [3], Yao et al. [27], Hall et al. [10], and Li and Hsing [15].

We model $\mathcal{R}(t_1, t_2)$ as a bivariate nonparametric function, which is smooth except for the points on the diagonal line, $\{t_1 = t_2\}$, to allow possible nugget effects. To see this point, let $\epsilon_i(t) = Y_i(t) - \{X_i(t)^T\beta + \theta(t)\}$ be the error process, and by definition $\text{cov}\{\epsilon_i(t_1), \epsilon_i(t_2)\} = \mathcal{R}(t_1, t_2)$. We assume that $\epsilon_i(t)$ can be decomposed into two independent components, $\epsilon_i(t) = \epsilon_{i0}(t) + \epsilon_{i1}(t)$, where $\epsilon_{i0}(\cdot)$ is a longitudinal process with smooth covariance function $\mathcal{R}_0(t_1, t_2)$, $\epsilon_{i1}(\cdot)$ is a white noise process usually caused by measurement errors. Let $\sigma_1^2(t) = \text{var}\{\epsilon_{i1}(t)\}$. Then

$$\mathcal{R}(t_1, t_2) = \mathcal{R}_0(t_1, t_2) + \sigma_1^2(t_1)I(t_1 = t_2) \qquad (21.17)$$

where $I(\cdot)$ is an indicator function. In Equation (21.17), $\sigma_1^2(\cdot)$ is the nugget effect causing discontinuity in $\mathcal{R}(\cdot, \cdot)$. We assume that both $\mathcal{R}_0(\cdot, \cdot)$ and $\sigma_1^2(\cdot)$ are smooth functions. As a result, $\mathcal{R}(t_1, t_2)$ is a smooth surface except on the diagonal points where $t_1 = t_2$, and it is also smooth along the diagonal direction. For time-series data, without additional assumptions, some confounding will occur if both the mean and covariance functions are modeled nonparametrically. However, as illustrated by Yao et al. [27] and Hall et al. [10],

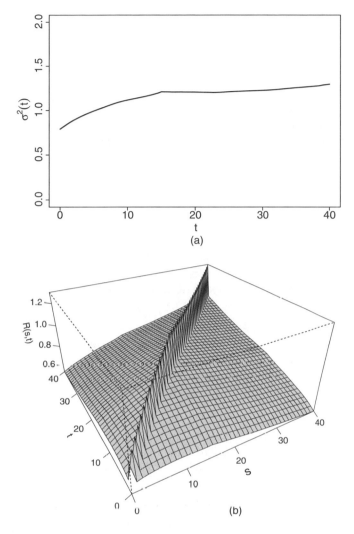

FIGURE 21.3 Estimated semiparametric covariance function for CD4 count data by pooling residuals from all treatment groups: (a) variance function $\widehat{\sigma}^2(t)$; (b) estimated covariance function by QMLE method assuming ARMA(1,1) correlation structure.

this identifiability issue will not occur for longitudinal data because of the independence structure between subjects.

Let $\widehat{\epsilon}_{ij} = Y_{ij} - \{X_{ij}^T\widehat{\beta} + \widehat{\theta}(T_{ij}, \widehat{\beta})\}$ be the residual based on some initial estimators $\widehat{\beta}$ and $\widehat{\theta}(t)$. Suppose $\mathcal{R}$ has a decomposition as in (21.17); we first estimate the smooth part $\mathcal{R}_0$ using a bivariate local linear smoother. Let $\widehat{\mathcal{R}}_0(t_1, t_2) = \widehat{\alpha}_0$, where $(\widehat{\alpha}_0, \widehat{\alpha}_1, \widehat{\alpha}_2)$ minimizes

$$\frac{1}{n}\sum_{i=1}^{n}\sum_{j=1}^{m_i}\sum_{j' \neq j}\left\{\widehat{\epsilon}_{ij}\widehat{\epsilon}_{ij'} - \alpha_0 - \alpha_1(T_{ij} - t_1) - a_2(T_{ij'} - t_2)\right\}^2$$
$$\times K_h(T_{ij} - t_1)K_h(T_{ij'} - t_2) \tag{21.18}$$

Define $N_R = \sum_{i=1}^{n} m_i(m_i - 1)$,

$$S_{pq} = \frac{1}{N_R} \sum_{i=1}^{n} \sum_{j=1}^{m_i} \sum_{j' \neq j} \left(\frac{T_{ij} - t_1}{h}\right)^p \left(\frac{T_{ij'} - t_2}{h}\right)^q K_h(T_{ij} - t_1) K_h(T_{ij'} - t_2)$$

$$R_{pq} = \frac{1}{N_R} \sum_{i=1}^{n} \sum_{j=1}^{m_i} \sum_{j' \neq j} \widehat{\epsilon}_{ij} \widehat{\epsilon}_{ik} \left(\frac{T_{ij} - t_1}{h}\right)^p \left(\frac{T_{ij'} - t_2}{h}\right)^q$$

$$\times K_h(T_{ij} - t_1) K_h(T_{ij'} - t_2)$$

Then the following solution for (21.18) is given in Hall et al. [10]:

$$\widehat{\mathcal{R}}_0(s, t) = (\mathcal{A}_1 R_{00} - \mathcal{A}_2 R_{10} - \mathcal{A}_3 R_{01}) \mathcal{B}^{-1} \tag{21.19}$$

where $\mathcal{A}_1 = S_{20}S_{02} - S_{11}^2$, $\mathcal{A}_2 = S_{10}S_{02} - S_{01}S_{11}$, $\mathcal{A}_3 = S_{01}S_{20} - S_{10}S_{11}$, and $\mathcal{B} = \mathcal{A}_1 S_{00} - \mathcal{A}_2 S_{10} - \mathcal{A}_3 S_{01}$.

As described above, the diagonal values on $\mathcal{R}(\cdot, \cdot)$ require a special treatment. The variance function can be written as $\sigma^2(t) = \mathcal{R}_0(t, t) + \sigma_1^2(t)$ and be estimated by the local linear smoother in (21.15). The covariance function is estimated by

$$\widehat{\mathcal{R}}(s, t) = \widehat{\mathcal{R}}_0(s, t) I(s \neq t) + \widehat{\sigma}^2(t) I(s = t) \tag{21.20}$$

Li and Hsing [15] and Li [14] proved that the nonparametric covariance function estimator in (21.20) is uniformly consistent to the true covariance function

$$\sup_{s, t \in T} |\widehat{\mathcal{R}}(s, t) - \mathcal{R}(s, t)| = o_p(1)$$

The detailed convergence rate for the nonparametric covariance estimator can be found in Li [14]. However, as noted in previous literature [9, 16], the kernel covariance estimator in (21.20) is not guaranteed to be positive semidefinite, and therefore some adjustment is needed to enforce the condition. One possible adjustment is through a spectral decomposition of the covariance estimator.

A commonly used spectral decomposition of the covariance functions for longitudinal data is [10, 27]

$$\mathcal{R}_0(s, t) = \sum_{k=1}^{\infty} \omega_k \psi_k(s) \psi_k(t)$$

where $\omega_1 \geq \omega_2 \geq \cdots \geq 0$ are the eigenvalues of the covariance function and $\psi_k(t)$ are the corresponding eigenfunctions with $\int_T \psi_k(t) \psi_{k'}(t) \, dt = I(k = k')$.

An adjustment procedure has been proposed and theoretically justified by Hall et al. [11] to transform $\widehat{\mathcal{R}}_0$ into a valid covariance function. We take a spectral decomposition of $\widehat{\mathcal{R}}_0$ and truncate the negative components. Letting $\widehat{\omega}_k$ and $\widehat{\psi}_k(\cdot)$, $k = 1, 2, \ldots$, be the eigenvalues and eigenfunctions of $\widehat{\mathcal{R}}_0$, and $K_n = \max\{k; \widehat{\omega}_k > 0\}$, the adjusted estimator for $\mathcal{R}$ is

$$\widetilde{\mathcal{R}}_0(s, t) = \sum_{k=1}^{K_n} \widehat{\omega}_k \widehat{\psi}_k(s) \widehat{\psi}_k(t)$$

$$\widetilde{\mathcal{R}}(s, t) = \widetilde{\mathcal{R}}_0(s, t) I(s \neq t) + \widehat{\sigma}^2(t) I(s = t) \tag{21.21}$$

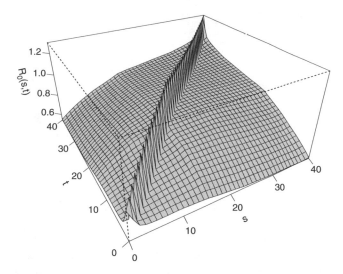

FIGURE 21.4 Nonparametric covariance estimator $\widehat{\mathcal{R}}(s, t)$ for CD4 count data by pooling residuals from all treatment groups.

We now apply the kernel nonparametric covariance estimator to the CD4 count data. As discussed before, we will assume the covariance structures are the same for all treatment groups, and the estimation is carried out by pooling the residuals from all groups. The estimated covariance function is presented in Figure 21.4, where the ridge on the diagonal of the covariance surface is the nugget effect. By comparing Figure 21.4 with Figure 21.3, the semiparametric ARMA (1,1) covariance in Section 21.3.1 seems to provide a reasonable fit to the data.

21.4 MODELING MULTIPLE TREATMENT GROUPS

21.4.1 Functional Analysis of Covariance Model

Li [14] proposed the following semiparametric model for longitudinal data from multiple treatment groups:

$$Y_{k,ij} = X_{k,ij}^T \beta + \theta_k(T_{k,ij}) + \epsilon_{k,ij}$$
$$i = 1, \ldots, n_k \qquad j = 1, \ldots, m_i \qquad k = 1, \ldots, q \qquad (21.22)$$

where $Y_{k,ij}$ is the response (log CD4 count) for the jth visit of the ith subject within the kth treatment group, q is the number of treatment groups, and $X_{k,ij}$ include the covariates and possibly their interactions with the treatment. The time effects, $\theta_k(T)$, are modeled nonparametrically and are allowed to be different among different treatment groups.

In model (21.22), the data within each treatment are modeled with a partially linear model as in (21.1). Since the main effect of the kth treatment is given by the function θ_k, this model can be considered as a functional ANOVA model, as in Brumback and Rice [1]. Since the model also accommodates the effects of covariates (e.g., baseline age, gender), it is named as a functional analysis-of-covariance (fANCOVA) model by Li [14]. We assume each treatment group has the same within-subject covariance function, which is a common assumption in ANOVA. In other words, we assume $\mathrm{cov}(\epsilon_{k,ij}, \epsilon_{k,ij'}) = \mathcal{R}(T_{k,ij}, T_{k,ij'})$ for all k.

The profile method described in both Sections 21.2.2 and 21.2.3 can be easily extended to this new model. Given β, $\theta_k(\cdot)$ can be estimated by $\widehat{\theta}_k(t, \beta) = \mathcal{S}_k^T(t)(Y_k - X_k\beta)$, where Y_k and X_k are the response vector and design matrix within the kth treatment group. For the working independence estimator, $\mathcal{S}_k$'s are the local linear kernel smoothers defined as in (21.4); for the semiparametric efficient profile estimator of Wang et al. [25], $\mathcal{S}_k$'s are the seemingly unrelated kernel smoothers in (21.8).

To estimate β, we need to solve an estimating equation that pools all treatment groups together:

$$\sum_{k=1}^{q}\sum_{i=1}^{n_k}\left\{X_{k,i} + \frac{\partial}{\partial\beta}\widehat{\theta}_k(T_{k,i}, \beta)\right\}^T V_{k,i}^{-1}\{Y_{k,i} - X_{k,i}\beta - \widehat{\theta}_k(T_{k,i}, \beta)\} = 0 \qquad (21.23)$$

where $V_{k,i}$'s are identity matrices for the working independence estimator and are the working covariance matrices for the semiparametric efficient profile estimator.

Given the expression of $\widehat{\theta}_k(t, \beta)$, we can easily show that $(\partial\widehat{\theta}_k/\partial\beta)(t, \beta) = -X_k^T\mathcal{S}_k(t)$, and solution for Equation (21.23) is given by

$$\widehat{\beta} = \left(\sum_{k=1}^{q}\sum_{i=1}^{n_k}\widetilde{X}_{k,i}^T V_{k,i}^{-1}\widetilde{X}_{k,i}\right)^{-1}\left(\sum_{k=1}^{q}\sum_{i=1}^{n_k}\widetilde{X}_{k,i}^T V_{k,i}^{-1}\widetilde{Y}_{k,i}\right)$$

where $\widetilde{X}_{k,ij} = X_{k,ij} - X_k^T\mathcal{S}_k(T_{k,ij})$, $\widetilde{Y}_{k,ij} = Y_{k,ij} - Y_k^T\mathcal{S}_k(T_{k,ij})$, $\widetilde{X}_{k,i} = (\widetilde{X}_{k,i1}, \ldots, \widetilde{X}_{k,im_i})^T$ and $\widetilde{Y}_{k,i} = (\widetilde{Y}_{k,i1}, \ldots, \widetilde{Y}_{k,im_i})^T$. Then the nonparametric estimators are updated as $\widehat{\theta}_k(t) = \widehat{\theta}_k(t, \widehat{\beta})$, $k = 1, \ldots, q$.

The variances of $\widehat{\beta}$ and $\widehat{\theta}_k(t)$ can be estimated by sandwich formulas similar to those given before,

$$\widehat{\mathrm{var}}(\widehat{\beta}) = \left(\sum_{k=1}^{q}\sum_{i=1}^{n_k}\widetilde{X}_{k,i}^T V_{k,i}^{-1}\widetilde{X}_{k,i}\right)^{-1}\left\{\sum_{k=1}^{q}\sum_{i=1}^{n_k}\widetilde{X}_{k,i}^T V_{k,i}^{-1}\widehat{\Sigma}_{k,i,\mathrm{Sand}} V_{k,i}^{-1}\widetilde{X}_{k,i}\right\}$$

$$\times\left(\sum_{k=1}^{q}\sum_{i=1}^{n_k}\widetilde{X}_{k,i}^T V_{k,i}^{-1}\widetilde{X}_{k,i}\right)^{-1}$$

$$\widehat{\mathrm{var}}\{\widehat{\theta}_k(t)\} = \mathcal{S}_k^T(t)\widehat{\Sigma}_{k,\mathrm{Sand}}\mathcal{S}_k(t)$$

where $\widehat{\Sigma}_{k,i,\mathrm{Sand}} = (Y_{k,i} - \widehat{\mu}_{k,i})(Y_{k,i} - \widehat{\mu}_{k,i})^T$, $\widehat{\mu}_{k,i} = X_{k,i}\widehat{\beta} + \widehat{\theta}_k(T_{k,i})$, and $\widehat{\Sigma}_{k,\mathrm{Sand}} = \mathrm{diag}(\widehat{\Sigma}_{k,i,\mathrm{Sand}})_{i=1}^{n_k}$.

We now apply the fANCOVA model (21.22) to the CD4 count data. As the analysis in Section 21.2.2 suggested, the interactions between the covariates and the treatments are insignificant, and therefore such interactions are not considered in the subsequent analysis and X only includes baseline age and gender. We first apply the working independence estimator to the data and then use the residuals to estimate the covariance function using both the semiparametric QMLE estimator assuming ARMA(1,1) correlation structure and the nonparametric kernel covariance estimator. The results are already shown in Figures 21.3 and 21.4. We then apply the semiparametric efficient profile estimator in Section 21.2.3 using the covariance functions in Figures 21.3 and 21.4 as the working covariance structure. The estimated regression coefficients for age and gender are reported in Table 21.2 by three estimation methods: the working independence estimator (WI), the efficient semiparametric

**TABLE 21.2   Estimated Regression Coefficients (COEF), Standard Error (SE), and
p-Value for fANOVA Model in CD4 Count Data**

	Age			Gender		
	Coef	SE	*p*-Value	Coef	SE	*p*-Value
WI	0.01167	0.00345	0.00071	−0.13150	0.08584	0.12555
ESPR-ARMA	0.01171	0.00096	0.00000	−0.11592	0.02610	0.00001
ESPR-NPC	0.01168	0.00094	0.00000	−0.12158	0.02551	0.00000

Note: The three estimation methods are the working independence estimator (WI), the efficient semiparametric profile estimator with a semiparametric ARMA (1,1) covariance structure (ESPR-ARMA), and the efficient semiparametric profile estimator with a nonparametric covariance function (ESPR-NPC).

profile estimator with a semiparametric ARMA (1,1) covariance structure (ESPR-ARMA), and the efficient semiparametric profile estimator with a nonparametric covariance function (ESPR-NPC). We also report the standard errors and *p*-values of these parameters. As we can see, the three methods essentially give the same estimates for β, but the ESPR-ARMA method and the ESPR-NPC method have much smaller standard errors, indicating great efficiency gain by considering within-subject correlations. This efficiency gain is translated into improved power when testing the significance of the these regression coefficients. For example, the WI method reports the effect of gender as insignificant, with a *p*-value of 0.126, but both of the two ESPR methods report gender as strongly significant. The effect of baseline age is reported as significant by all three methods.

The estimated time effects $\widehat{\theta}_k(t)$ and their pointwise confidence intervals using the ESPR-NPC method are shown in Figure 21.5. The WI and ESPR-ARMA methods give similar estimates for these functions but slightly wider pointwise confidence intervals. As discussed above, under model (21.22), these functions represent the treatment effects. From the figure, it seems the four treatments yield very different response curves. Especially treatment 4 seems to be most effective, since the patients in this groups seem to have higher mean CD4 count during the follow-up. A rigorous statistical test on these treatment effects will be provided in Section 21.4.2.

21.4.2 Test for Treatment Effects

Under model (21.22), the treatment effects are represented by the functions $\theta_k(t)$, $k = 1, \ldots, q$. To test the hypothesis $H_0 : \theta_1(t) = \cdots = \theta_q(t)$, Li [14] proposed using a generalized likelihood ratio (GLR) test. The GLR test was first proposed by Fan et al. [8] and Fan and Jiang [6], and they studied the theoretical properties of the GLR test under many important nonparametric models, including the varying coefficient models and the additive models. Adapting to our setting, the GLR test works as follows. Assuming $\epsilon_{k,ij}$ are Gaussian errors, the estimated likelihood under the full model (i.e., the alternative hypothesis) is

$$\widehat{\ell}_{\text{full}} = -\frac{1}{2} \sum_{k=1}^{q} \sum_{i=1}^{n_k} \log(|V_{k,i}|) + (Y_{k,i} - \widehat{\mu}_{k,i})^T V_{k,i}^{-1} (Y_{k,i} - \widehat{\mu}_{k,i})$$

where $\widehat{\mu}_{k,i} = X_{k,i}\widehat{\beta} + \widehat{\theta}_k(T_{k,i})$ and $V_{k,i}$ is the working covariance matrix. The estimated likelihood under the reduced model (or under the null hypothesis), denoted as $\widehat{\ell}_{\text{red}}$, is defined similarly under the assumption that the θ_k's are the same. The generalized likelihood ratio test statistic is defined as $\lambda_n(H_0) = \widehat{\ell}_{\text{full}} - \widehat{\ell}_{\text{red}}$.

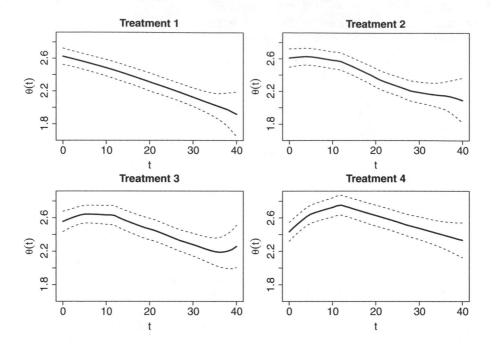

FIGURE 21.5 Estimated time effects for CD4 count data using fANCOVA model (21.22) and assuming a nonparametric covariance structure. In each panel, the solid curve is $\widehat{\theta}_k(t)$ and the two dotted curves are $\widehat{\theta}(t) \pm 2 \times SE_\theta(t)$.

Under different models and for independent data, Fan et al. [8] showed that the GLR test statistic converges in distribution to a χ^2 random variable with the degree of freedom diverging to infinity. One important property of the GLR test is the so-called *Wilks phenomenon* [8], which means the asymptotic distribution of the GLR statistic under the null hypothesis does not depend on the true functions in the model. This property enables us to approximate the null distribution of the test statistic by a bootstrap method [6].

To assess the null distribution of $\lambda_n(H_0)$ in our problem, Li [14] proposed the following stratified conditional bootstrap procedure:

1. To generate data satisfying the null hypothesis, take the residuals within each treatment group, $Y_{k,ij}^* = Y_{k,ij} - \widehat{\theta}_k(T_{k,ij})$ for all k, i, and j.
2. Sample with replacement n_k subjects within the kth treatment group and include the residuals Y^* within the resampled subjects into the bootstrap sample.
3. Calculate the generalized likelihood ratio test statistic $\lambda_n^*(H_0)$ in the bootstrap sample.
4. Repeat steps 2 and 3 a large number of times and use the empirical distribution of $\lambda_n^*(H_0)$ to approximate the null distribution of $\lambda_n(H_0)$.

The p-value of the test is estimated by the empirical frequencies of λ_n^*, which are greater than the observed test statistic λ_n.

We now apply this test procedure to the CD4 data. With a bootstrap sample size of 1000, we find the p-value for the null hypothesis to be 0.018. Therefore, we conclude that the four treatments have different effects.

21.5 SUMMARY

Semiparametric models, such as those considered in this chapter, combine the efficiency of a parametric model and the flexibility of a nonparametric model. The fANCOVA model (21.22) discussed in Section 21.4 provides flexible estimation of the treatment effects while controlling the effects of other covariates.

In longitudinal data analysis, it is particularly important to incorporate covariance information in order to construct fully efficient estimators for the parameters in the model. Such improved efficiency is then translated into the increased power of detecting significant factors. As shown in our analysis of the CD4 count data, the gender effect, which is declared to be insignificant by an inefficient working independence method, is eventually proven to be significant by the efficient semiparametric profile methods that take into account the covariance information. There are a number of methods to model the covariance structure in longitudinal data, and we review two flexible methods which received a lot of attention in recent literature: the semiparametric covariance modeling of Fan et al. [5] and the nonparametric covariance modeling from functional data analysis.

In many longitudinal studies, the response variable may not be Gaussian as in our CD4 count example. For example, Y_{ij} may be binary or Poisson counts. Such response variables are usually modeled by generalized (non)linear mixed models. Efficient semiparametric regression methods for such general longitudinal data were studied in Wang et al. [25] and Lin and Carroll [19].

ACKNOWLEDGMENT

The author's research is partially supported by the U.S. National Science Foundation, grants DMS-1105634 and DMS-1317118.

REFERENCES

1. B. A. Brumback and J. A. Rice. Smoothing spline models for the analysis of nested and crossed samples of curves. *J. Am. Stat. Assoc.*, 93:961–976, 1998.

2. P. J. Diggle, P. Heagerty, K.-Y. Liang, and S. L. Zeger. *Analysis of Longitudinal Data*, 2nd ed. Oxford University Press, New York, 2002.

3. P. J. Diggle and A. P. Verbyla. Nonparametric estimation of covariance structure in longitudinal data. *Biometrics*, 54:401–415, 1998.

4. J. Fan and I. Gijbels. *Local Polynomial Modeling and Its Applications*. Chapman & Hall, London, 1996.

5. J. Fan, T. Huang, and R. Li. Analysis of longitudinal data with semiparametric estimation of covariance function. *J. Am. Stat. Assoc.*, 102:632–641, 2007.

6. J. Fan and J. Jiang. Nonparametric inferences for additive models. *J. Am. Stat. Assoc.*, 100:890–907, 2005.

7. J. Fan and Y. Wu. Semiparametric estimation of covariance matrixes for longitudinal data. *J. Am. Stat. Assoc.*, 103:1520–1533, 2008.

8. J. Fan, C. Zhang, and J. Zhang. Generalized likelihood ratio statistics and Wilks phenomenon. *Ann. Stat.*, 29:153–193, 2001.

9. P. Hall, N. I. Fisher, and B. Hoffman. On the nonparametric estimation of covariance functions. *Ann. Stat.*, 22:2115–2134, 1994.

10. P. Hall, H. G. Müller, and J. L. Wang. Properties of principal component methods for functional and longitudinal data analysis. *Ann. Stat.*, 34:1493–1517, 2006.

11. P. Hall, H. G. Müller, and F. Yao. Modelling sparse generalized longitudinal observations with latent Gaussian processes. *J. R. Stat. Soc. B.*, 70:703–723, 2008.

12. K. Henry, A. Erice, C. Tierney, H. H. Balfour Jr., M. A. Fischl, A. Kmack, S. H. Liou, A. Kenton, M. S. Hirsch, J. Phair, A. Martinez, and J. O. Kahn. A randomized, controlled, double-blind study comparing the survival benefit of four different reverse transcriptase inhibitor therapies (three-drug, two-drug, and alternating drug) for the treatment of advanced AIDS. *J. Acquir. Immune Defic. Syndrome Hum. Retrovirol.*, 19:339–349, 1998.

13. J. Z. Huang, L. Liu, and N. Liu. Estimation of large covariance matrices of longitudinal data with basis function approximations. *J. Comp. Graph. Stat.*, 16:189–209, 2007.

14. Y. Li. Efficient semiparametric regression in longitudinal data with nonparametric covariance estimation. *Biometrika*, 98:355–370, 2011.

15. Y. Li and T. Hsing. Uniform convergence rates for nonparametric regression and principal component analysis in functional/longitudinal data. *Ann. Stat.*, 38:3321–3351, 2010.

16. Y. Li, N. Wang, M. Hong, N. Turner, J. Lupton, and R. J. Carroll. Nonparametric estimation of correlation functions in spatial and longitudinal data, with application to colon carcinogenesis experiments. *Ann. Stat.*, 35:1608–1643, 2007.

17. X. Lin and R. J. Carroll. Semiparametric regression for clustered data using generalized estimating equations. *J. Am. Stat. Assoc.*, 96:1045–1056, 2001.

18. X. Lin, N. Wang, A. H. Welsh, and R. J. Carroll. Equivalent kernels of smoothing splines in nonparametric regression for clustered/longitudinal data. *Biometrika*, 91:177–193, 2004.

19. X. Lin and R. J. Carroll. Semiparametric estimation in general repeated measures problems. *J. R. Stat. Soc. B*, 68:69–88, 2006.

20. K. V. Mardia, J. T. Kent, and J. M. Bibby. *Multivariate Analysis*. Academic, New York, 1979.

21. E. Masry. Multivariate local polynomial regression for time series: Uniform strong consistency and rates. *J. Time Ser. Anal.*, 17:571–599, 1995.

22. J. O. Ramsay and B. W. Silverman. *Functional Data Analysis*, 2nd ed. Springer-Verlag, New York, 2005.

23. J. A. Rice and B. W. Silverman. Estimating the mean and covariance structure nonparametrically when the data are curves. *J. R. Stat. Soc. B*, 53:233–243, 1991.

24. N. Wang. Marginal nonparametric kernel regression accounting for within-subject correlation. *Biometrika*, 90:43–52, 2003.

25. N. Wang, R. J. Carroll, and X. Lin. Efficient semiparametric marginal estimation for longitudinal/clustered data. *J. Am. Stat. Assoc.*, 100(469):147–157, 2005.

26. W. B. Wu and M. Pourahmadi. Nonparametric estimation of large covariance matrices of longitudinal data. *Biometrika*, 90:831–844, 2003.

27. F. Yao, H. G. Müller, and J. L. Wang. Functional data analysis for sparse longitudinal data. *J. Am. Stat. Assoc.*, 100:577–590, 2005.

28. S. L. Zeger and P. J. Diggle. Semiparametric models for longitudinal data with application to CD4 cell numbers in HIV seroconverters. *Biometrics*, 50:689–699, 1994.

BIOLOGICAL DATA CLUSTERING

CHAPTER 22

THE THREE STEPS OF CLUSTERING IN THE POST-GENOMIC ERA

RAFFAELE GIANCARLO,[1] GIOSUÉ LO BOSCO,[1,4] LUCA PINELLO,[2,3,4] and FILIPPO UTRO[5]

[1]Department of Mathematics and Informatics, University of Palermo, Palermo, Italy
[2]Department of Biostatistics, Harvard School of Public Health, Boston, Massachusetts
[3]Department of Biostatistics and Computational Biology, Dana-Farber Cancer Institute, Boston, Massachusetts
[4]I.E.ME.S.T., Istituto Euro Mediterraneo di Scienza e Tecnologia, Palermo, Italy
[5]Computational Genomics Group, IBM T.J. Watson Research Center, Yorktown Heights, New York

22.1 INTRODUCTION

In recent years, the advent of high-density arrays of oligonucleotides and cDNAs has had a deep impact on biological and medical research. Indeed, the new technology enables the acquisition of data that are proving to be fundamental in many areas of the biological sciences, ranging from the understanding of complex biological systems to diagnosis (e.g., [3]).

Although clustering microarray expression data is by now a fundamental aspect of microarray data analysis [22, 73], the application of such a powerful and well-established methodology to postgenomic data seems to be rather ad hoc. Motivated by such an observation, Handl et al. [41] have produced a key paper with the intent of bringing to the attention of both bioinformatics researchers and end users some of the fundamental aspects of the methodology. In order to place this chapter in the proper context, it is useful to recall from Handl et al. that clustering can be seen as a three-step process: (1) choice of a distance function, (2) choice of a clustering algorithm, and (3) choice of a methodology to assess the statistical significance of clustering solutions. Although computational methods for the analysis of microarray data have witnessed an exponential growth, very little has been done in trying to assess their merits [56]. Consequently, the need for a through evaluation of the entire analysis process for microarray data is being recognized and a few benchmarking studies are starting to appear (i.e., [30, 35]). Following that novel research trend, all three

Biological Knowledge Discovery Handbook: Preprocessing, Mining, and Postprocessing of Biological Data, First Edition. Edited by Mourad Elloumi and Albert Y. Zomaya.
© 2014 John Wiley & Sons, Inc. Published 2014 by John Wiley & Sons, Inc.

of the clustering steps are considered here with a separate section devoted to each of them. In particular, this chapter is organized as follows.

The experimental set-up used for the results reported here is presented in Section 22.2. Those results are simply highlighted here, referring the interested reader to the studies from which they have been extracted.

Section 22.3 is dedicated to distance functions; in particular, new approaches [33, 34] to assess the intrinsic separation ability of many standard distance functions and their use in conjunction with clustering algorithms are both presented.

Section 22.4 is devoted to clustering algorithms, in particular to nonnegative matrix factorization (NMF) [54]. Indeed, following the work by Brunet et al. [14] on molecular pattern discovery, NMF has become a reference pattern discovery method in bioinformatics [20]. Although it is well known that it is quite demanding in terms of computer time, its worthiness compared to other clustering algorithms has been studied only recently [81]. It involves the assessment of the method with respect to both its ability to cluster data and the time it takes for that task as well as comparison with other clustering algorithms.

Section 22.5 discusses the assessment of the statistical significance of a clustering solution. Attention is given to a particular aspect of this rather general question [47]: the identification of the correct number of clusters in a given data set. This class of statistical methods is usually referred to as internal validation measures. Moreover, the focus is on data-driven ones, particularly on those designed for and tested on microarray data. Measures in this class assume nothing about the structure of the data set, which is inferred directly from the data. Attention is given to consensus clustering (`Consensus`) [60] because of its paradigmatic nature for stability-based validation measures and its excellent discriminative power [35, 81]. Due to those two properties and to its high computational demand, it is a natural candidate for a speed-up [37], which is also reported here.

22.2 EXPERIMENTAL SET-UP

The entire area of clustering has a strong experimental flavor. Therefore, in order to obtain a fair evaluation of the various methods, a sound experimental methodology is required. In what follows, the one used for the results presented in this chapter is detailed. As will be evident, it is a de facto standard in this area.

22.2.1 Data Sets

A generic data set is denoted by $\mathbf{X}$ and is assumed to be a set of n m-dimensional observations $\mathbf{x}_1, \mathbf{x}_2, \ldots, \mathbf{x}_n$. Practically, a data set can be represented by a real matrix X in which each row corresponds to an element to be clustered and each column to an experimental condition. Technically speaking, a *gold solution* for a data set is a partition C of the data in a number of classes known a priori. Membership of a class is established by assigning the appropriate class label to each element. In less formal terms, the partition of the data set into classes is based on external knowledge that leaves no ambiguity as to the actual number of classes and the membership of elements within classes. Although there exist real microarray data sets for which such an a priori division is known, as in a few previous studies of relevance here, a more relaxed criterion has been adopted to also allow data sets with high-quality partitions that have been inferred by analyzing the data, that is, by the use of internal knowledge via data analysis tools such as clustering algorithms. In strict technical terms, there is a difference between the two types of gold solutions. For their data sets, Dudoit and Fridlyand [25] elegantly make clear that the difference in a related study and their approach is closely followed here.

The six data sets that are used here for the experiments together with the acronyms used in this chapter are reported next. For conciseness, only some relevant facts about them are mentioned. The interested reader can find additional information in Dudoit and Fridlyand [25] for the lymphoma and NCI60 data sets, Handl et al. for the leukemia data set [41], and Di Gesù et al. [23] for the remaining ones. In all of the referenced papers, the data sets were used mainly for validation studies and can be considered a reference for benchmarking studies in the clustering literature. Indeed, they are referred to as `benchmark 1` data sets in [37, 81]. That notation is also kept here.

CNS Rat   The data set gives the expression levels of 112 genes during rat central nervous system development. It is a 112×17 data matrix studied by Wen et al. [84]. There are no a priori known classes for this data set, but the analysis by Wen et al. [84] suggests a partition of the genes into six classes, four of which are composed of biologically, functionally related, genes. That partition is taken as the gold solution, which is the same one used for the validation of figure of merit (FOM) [87].

Leukemia   The data set is the one used by Handl et al. [41] in their survey of computational cluster validation to illustrate the use of some measures. It is a 38×100 data matrix, where each row corresponds to a patient with acute leukemia and each column to a gene. For this data set, there is an a priori partition into three classes, which is taken as the gold solution.

Lymphoma   The data set comes from the study of Alizadeh et al. [4] on the three most common adult lymphoma tumors. It is an 80×100 matrix, where each row corresponds to a tissue sample and each column to a gene. There is an a priori partition into three classes, which is taken as the gold solution. The data set has been obtained from the original microarray experiments as described by Dudoit and Fridlyand [25].

NCI60   This data set originates from a microarray study in gene expression variation among the 60 cell lines of the National Cancer Institute anticancer drug screen [2]. It is a 57×200 data matrix, where each row corresponds to a cell line and each column to a gene. There is an a priori partition of the data set into eight classes, which is taken as the gold solution. The data set has been obtained from the original microarray experiments as described by Dudoit and Fridlyand [25].

PBM   The data set contains 2329 cDNAs with a fingerprint of 139 oligos. This gives a 2329×139 data matrix. According to Hartuv et al. [45], the cDNAs in the data set originated from 18 distinct genes; that is, the a priori classes are known. The partition of the data set into 18 groups was obtained by laboratory experiments at Novartis in Vienna. Following that study, those classes and the class labels assigned to the elements are taken as the gold solution. It was used by Hartuv et al. to test their clustering algorithm.

Yeast   The data set is part of that studied by Spellman et al. [74] and is a 698×72 data matrix. There are no a priori known classes for this data set, but the analysis by Spellman et al. suggests a partition of the genes into five functionally related classes.

That partition is taken as the gold solution, which has been used by Shamir and Sharan for a case study on the performance of clustering algorithms [70].

22.2.2 Algorithms and Hardware

For the experiments reported here, our own C/C++ implementation of nonnegative matrix factorization (NMF) is based on the Matlab script available at the Broad Institute [1]. Indeed, it has been converted to a C/C++ version, then validated by ensuring it produces the same results, in a number of simulations, as for the Matlab version. In addition to NMF, a suite of algorithms has been chosen, that is, K-means among *partitional methods* and average, complete, and single link (Hier-A, Hier-C, and Hier-S, respectively) among the *hierarchical methods*. Moreover, the minimum spanning tree (MST) [16] has also been used as a partitional algorithm. With the exception of NMF, all of the mentioned algorithms are standard and well known and therefore they are not described here. The interested reader, however, will find a detailed description of them in a classic book on the subject by Jain and Dubes [48]. It goes without saying that each of the above algorithms has already been used for data analysis of microarrays (e.g., [23, 36, 85]). Moreover, both K-means and NMF, rather than starting from a random partition of the data, can take as input the partition produced by another algorithm, for instance, Hier-A. In what follows, in order to make clear how each of those algorithms is initialized, the suffix R is used to indicate random initialization; for example, K-means-R indicates that the algorithm has been used with a random initial partition of the data. In the case of hierarchical initialization, the letter corresponding to the linkage policy is used as a suffix; for example, K-means-A indicates that the algorithm has been used with an initial partition of the data produced by Hier-A.

All experiments were performed, in part, on several state-of-the-art PCs and, in part, on a 64-bit AMD Athlon 2.2-GHz biprocessor with 1 GB of main memory running Windows Server 2003. All the timing experiments reported were performed on the biprocessor using one processor per run. All of the operating systems supervising the computations have 32-bit precision.

22.2.3 External Indices

Once a gold solution is known for a given data set, it is possible to benchmark the performance of, say, a clustering algorithm by comparing the partition produced by the algorithm with the gold solution. That comparison is usually done via external indices: They measure the level of agreement between two partitions. Moreover, those indices can also be used to evaluate the intrinsic discriminative ability of distance functions, as discussed in Section 22.3. Since they are essential for the benchmarking of several procedures of relevance for this chapter, they will be defined next.

Formally, let $C = \{c_1, \ldots, c_r\}$ be the partition of the items in data set $\mathbf{X}$ into r clusters, corresponding to the gold solution for that data set. Let $P = \{p_1, \ldots, p_t\}$ be an analogous partition, possibly produced by a clustering algorithm.

External indices are usually defined via an $r \times t$ contingency table T, where T_{ij} represents the number of items in both c_i and p_j, $T_{i.} = |c_i|$, $T_{.j} = |p_j|$, for $1 \le i \le r$, $1 \le j \le t$.

Among the many external indices that have been introduced [48] for the experiments reported in this chapter, the adjusted Rand (R_A) index, the Fowlkes and Mallows (FM) index, and the F index have been used because of their "popularity" in computational biology applications. Their formulas are reported next, although it is worth pointing out that additional details about them can be found in [36]:

$$R_A = \frac{\sum_{i,j} \binom{T_{ij}}{2} - [\sum_i \binom{T_{i\cdot}}{2} \sum_j \binom{T_{\cdot j}}{2}]/\binom{n}{2}}{\frac{1}{2}[\sum_i \binom{T_{i\cdot}}{2} + \sum_j \binom{T_{\cdot j}}{2}] - [\sum_i \binom{T_{i\cdot}}{2} \sum_j \binom{T_{\cdot j}}{2}]/\binom{n}{2}} \tag{22.1}$$

$$\text{FM} = \frac{\sum_{i,j} T_{ij}^2 - n}{\sqrt{(\sum_i T_{i\cdot}^2 - n)(\sum_j T_{\cdot j}^2 - n)}} \tag{22.2}$$

$$F = \sum_{c_i \in C} \frac{T_{i\cdot}}{n} \max_{p_k \in P} \frac{2(T_{ij}/T_{\cdot j})(T_{ij}/T_{i\cdot})}{(T_{ij}/T_{\cdot j}) + (T_{ij}/T_{i\cdot})} \tag{22.3}$$

The FM and F indices assume a value in $[0, 1]$; while R_A has an expected value of zero, its maximum is unity and it can assume negative values [27, 86]. The larger the value of each of those indices, the better agreement there is between the two partitions.

22.3 DISTANCES

Although points 2 and 3 mentioned in the introduction lead into two well-established and rich research areas in data analysis, point 1 has only been marginally investigated regarding this microarray. Among the plethora of distance and similarity functions available in the mathematical literature [21], the most common ones used for microarray data analysis are the *Euclidean distance* and the *Pearson correlation* coefficient or those closely related ones. The choice of those two functions is due, primarily, to their widespread and well-justified use in other application areas, rather than to an appraisal of their merits within microarray applications. Indeed, there are very few results shedding light on which distance function is most appropriate for which task in microarray data analysis (see [22, 33, 65] and references therein). This section outlines the current research status on such a choice.

In what follows, distance, similarity, and dissimilarity functions are referred to with the generic term *distance functions*. However, the proper term is used when those functions are formalized via mathematical formulas.

22.3.1 State of the Art

Gentleman et al. [32] provide an overview of the distance function for microarray data analysis available within the R statistical computing environment, giving also valuable guidelines for their practical use. The remaining part of the literature on this topic can be broadly divided into three main categories. The first is devoted to the use of distance functions in relation to technological issues in microarrays, the second deals with the relation between distance functions and clustering algorithms, and the more recent third one tries to assess the intrinsic discriminative abilities of distance functions for microarray data analysis as well as to identify biases in their use in conjunction with clustering algorithms. Next, the main results for the first two types of contribution are outlined, while a somewhat more detailed review is given for the third type.

Gibbons et al. [38] provide useful information about the appropriate distance when dealing with different kinds of microarray measurements. That experimental study applies the clustering algorithms K-means, Hier-A, Hier-S, and SOM [76] in conjunction with Euclidean, 3-norm, Manhattan, Hausdorff, and Pearson correlation distances (see Section 22.3.4 for definitions) over two ratio-based (i.e., two-color cDNA) and two non ratio-based (Affymetrics) yeast data sets, showing that Euclidean distance performs at least as well as other distances when used on ratio-style data, while Pearson correlation has the same behavior on non-ratio-style ones. That is due to the fact that it captures linear relations among data, a property that is very useful in analyzing time course data for gene expression profiles.

The study by Costa et al. [17] summarizes very well the relation between distance functions and clustering algorithms. Indeed, the algorithms K-means, Click [71], dynamical clustering [24], SOM, and Hier-A have been used in conjunction with cosine, Pearson correlation, and Euclidean distances (see Section 22.3.4 for definitions). The performance of a clustering algorithm in combination with a specific distance function has been evaluated via external criteria, that is, R_A, on four time course versions of the yeast cell cycle data set [26]. The main finding of that paper is a suggestion of the best algorithm–distance combination: The Pearson correlation is more appropriate for SOM, Hier-A, and Click, while cosine and Euclidean distances fit best with the rest of the algorithms.

It is also well known that one can measure the correlation between "items" via information measures, mainly normalized mutual information (MI). Indeed, a recent study by Priness et al. [65] investigates how its theoretic ability to capture any kind of statistical dependency among data translates in the real world of microarrays. In particular, those authors have shown the superiority of MI in conjunction with the sIB clustering algorithm [78] versus K-means, Click, and SOM, all using both the Euclidean distance and Pearson correlation. In that study, the evaluation methodology is based on internal criteria, such as cluster homogeneity and separation, rather than the more stringent external criteria that are based on the indices introduced in Section 22.2.3.

The third category of investigations has recently been initiated by Giancarlo et al. [33, 34] and resulted in extensions, in several directions, of the results by Costa et al. [17] and Priness et al. [65] by using:

- A wider collection of data sets that consist of time course, cancer studies, and cDNAs microarrays, that is, the ones in Section 22.2.1.
- A wider collection of distances, including also MI, defined in Section 22.3.3.
- An external validation methodology, described in Section 22.3.4, that uses both the three external indices defined in Section 22.2.3 and *receiver operating characteristic* (ROC) analysis [57].

Among the clustering algorithms mentioned in Section 22.2.2, K-means-R, Hier-A, Hier-C, and MST have been used. The techniques and findings by Giancarlo et al. [33, 34] are presented next.

22.3.2 Problem Statement

In order to gain deeper insights into the use of distance functions for microarray data analysis, one needs to address the following three related problems:

(a) Assessment of the intrinsic separation ability of a distance, that is, how well a distance discriminates independently of its use within a clustering algorithm

(b) Assessment of the predictive clustering algorithm ability of a distance, that is, which distance function grants the best performance when used within a clustering algorithm

(c) The interplay between (a) and (b)

22.3.3 Basic Definitions

Let $\mathbb{X}$ be a set. A function $\delta : \mathbb{X} \times \mathbb{X} \to \mathbb{R}$ is a *distance* (or *dissimilarity*) on $\mathbb{X}$ if, $\forall \mathbf{x}, \mathbf{y} \in \mathbb{X}$, it satisfies the following three conditions:

1. $\delta(\mathbf{x}, \mathbf{y}) \geq 0$ (*nonnegativity*)
2. $\delta(\mathbf{x}, \mathbf{y}) = \delta(\mathbf{y}, \mathbf{x})$ (*symmetry*)
3. $\delta(\mathbf{x}, \mathbf{x}) = 0$

Conversely, a *similarity* (or *proximity*) function $\sigma : \mathbb{X} \times \mathbb{X} \to \mathbb{R}$ on $\mathbb{X}$ must satisfy the following three conditions $\forall \mathbf{x}, \mathbf{y} \in \mathbb{X}$:

1. $\sigma(\mathbf{x}, \mathbf{y}) \geq 0$ (*nonnegativity*)
2. $\sigma(\mathbf{x}, \mathbf{y}) = \delta(\mathbf{y}, \mathbf{x})$ (*symmetry*)
3. $\sigma(\mathbf{x}, \mathbf{y}) \leq \sigma(\mathbf{x}, \mathbf{x})$ and $\sigma(\mathbf{x}, \mathbf{y}) = \sigma(\mathbf{x}, \mathbf{x}) \Leftrightarrow \mathbf{x} = \mathbf{y}$

There are some simple and well-known relations between distance and similarity functions defined on the same set $\mathbb{X}$ that are recalled next for the convenience of the reader. A similarity function σ naturally defines a distance $\delta_o(\mathbf{x}, \mathbf{y}) = \sigma(\mathbf{x}, \mathbf{x}) - o(\mathbf{x}, \mathbf{y})$. The converse does not hold. However, when $\mathbb{X}$ is bounded, a distance δ always defines a similarity function $\sigma_\delta(\mathbf{x}, \mathbf{y}) = r - \delta(\mathbf{x}, \mathbf{y})$, where r is the diameter of $\mathbb{X}$ with respect to δ.

In the case of microarray data, $\mathbb{X} = \mathbb{R}^m$; that is, each data point is a vector in m-dimensional space. Note that the available data set $\mathbf{X}$ is a finite subset of $\mathbb{X}$. One can categorize distance functions according to three broad classes: *geometric*, *correlation based*, and *information based*. Functions in the first class capture the concept of *physical* distance between two objects. They are strongly influenced by the magnitude of changes in the measured components of vectors $\mathbf{x}$ and $\mathbf{y}$, making them sensitive to noise and outliers. Functions in the second class capture dependencies between the coordinates of two vectors. In particular, they usually have the benefit of capturing positive, negative, and linear relationships between two vectors. Functions in the third class are defined via well-known quantities in information theory such as entropy and mutual information [18]. They have the advantage of capturing statistical dependencies between two discrete data points, even if they are not linear. Unfortunately, when one tries to apply them to points in $\mathbb{R}^m$, a suitable discretization process must be carried out, known as *binning*, which usually poses some nontrivial challenges [19, 72].

The functions of interest for this chapter are now formally defined, starting with the geometric ones.

The *Minkowski distance* is a parametric distance defined as

$$d_\ell(\mathbf{x}, \mathbf{y}) = \sqrt[\ell]{\sum_{i=1}^{m} |x_i - y_i|^\ell} \tag{22.4}$$

where $\mathbf{x} = (x_1, \ldots, x_m)$, $\mathbf{y} = (y_1, \ldots, y_m)$.

The functions d_1 and d_2 are important special cases, the first being the well-known *Manhattan* or *city block distance*, and the second being the *Euclidean* or *2-norm distance*.

The *cosine distance* (also known as either *Orchini distance* or *angular distance*) is defined as

$$d_{\cos}(\mathbf{x}, \mathbf{y}) = 1 - \frac{\mathbf{x} \cdot \mathbf{y}}{\sqrt{\mathbf{x} \cdot \mathbf{x}} \sqrt{\mathbf{y} \cdot \mathbf{y}}} \tag{22.5}$$

which corresponds to $1 - \cos \phi$, where ϕ is the angle between the two vectors $\mathbf{x}$ and $\mathbf{y}$.

Let $\mathbf{S}$ denote the *covariance matrix of* $\mathbf{X}$, that is, a matrix of size $m \times m$ with entries defined as

$$\mathbf{S} = \frac{1}{n-1} \sum_{j=1}^{n} (\mathbf{x}_j - \bar{\mathbf{x}}) \otimes (\mathbf{x}_j - \bar{\mathbf{x}})$$

where $\bar{\mathbf{x}} = (1/n) \sum_j \mathbf{x}_j$ and $\otimes$ denotes the *outer product* of vectors.

The *Mahalanobis distance* is defined as

$$d_M(\mathbf{x}, \mathbf{y}) = \sqrt{(\mathbf{x} - \mathbf{y}) \mathbf{S}^{-1} (\mathbf{x} - \mathbf{y})^T} \tag{22.6}$$

It is related to *principal-component analysis* (PCA) [46] since it measures the Euclidean distance between vectors in a new reference system where the data become uncorrelated.

In order to define and compute d_M, $\mathbf{S}$ must be invertible, which is granted if and only if its eigenvalues are positive.

Among the correlation-based distances, the most well known are the *Pearson distance* d_r, the *Spearman distance* d_ρ, and the *Kendall distance* d_τ, defined as

$$d_r(\mathbf{x}, \mathbf{y}) = 1 - r = 1 - \frac{\sum_{i=1}^{m} (x_i - \bar{x})(y_i - \bar{y})}{\sum_{i=1}^{m} (x_j - \bar{x})^2 \sum_{j=1}^{m} (y_j - \bar{y})^2} \tag{22.7}$$

$$d_\rho(\mathbf{x}, \mathbf{y}) = 1 - \rho = 1 - \frac{6 \sum_{i=1}^{m} \Delta_i^2}{n(n^2 - 1)} \tag{22.8}$$

$$d_\tau(\mathbf{x}, \mathbf{y}) = 1 - \tau = \frac{n_c - n_d}{\frac{1}{2} n(n-1)} \tag{22.9}$$

where $\bar{x} = (1/m) \sum_i x_i$, $\bar{y} = (1/m) \sum_i y_i$, Δ_i is the difference between the ranks of x_i and y_i, and n_c and n_d are their number of concording and discording pairs, respectively.

It is worth pointing out that, in the formulas above, r, ρ and τ are the Pearson, Spearman, and Kendall correlation coefficients, respectively.

Formally, the *mutual information* of two discrete random variables Y and Z assuming values $\{y_1, \ldots, y_m\}$ and $\{z_1, \ldots, z_m\}$ respectively is

$$I(Y; Z) = \sum_{i=1}^{m} \sum_{j=1}^{m} p_{ij} \log \frac{p_{ij}}{p_i p_j} \tag{22.10}$$

where $p_i = P(Y = y_i)$ and $p_j = P(Z = z_j)$ are the marginal probability mass functions of Y and Z and $p_{ij} = P(Y = y_i, Z = z_j)$ is their joint probability mass function. Several normalized variants of the mutual information have been defined in the literature [58, 75], but among all of them there exists a particular normalization [75] which induces a distance referred to as the *mutual information distance*:

$$d_{MI}(\mathbf{x}, \mathbf{y}) = 1 - \frac{I(X; Y)}{\max(H(X), H(Y))} \tag{22.11}$$

where $H(Y)$ and $H(Z)$ are the marginal entropies of Y and Z, respectively, defined for a generic variable Y as

$$H(Y) = \sum_{i=1}^{m} -p_i \log p_i \tag{22.12}$$

When dealing with such a distance, the key problem is the estimation of the marginal and joint probability mass functions. The method outlined in Priness et al. [65] is based on the computation of a histogram using a specific binning methodology [72]. Here we follow a different approach to perform the same task, one based on kernel density estimation methodologies.

22.3.4 Criteria to Evaluate Performance of Distance Function

The techniques supporting a quantification of points (a)–(c) stated in Section 22.3.2 are now outlined.

Criteria for point (a)   The intrinsic separation ability is a measure of how well a distance is able (by itself) to separate the objects in a data set. Such an evaluation is now reduced to the classic problem of quantifying the quality of a binary classifier via ROC analysis [57].

It is worth recalling that the data set $\mathbf{X}$ is composed of m-dimensional observations $\mathbf{x}_1, \mathbf{x}_2, \ldots, \mathbf{x}_n$. Let D be the $n \times n$ distance matrix for a given distance d, that is, $D(i, j) = d(\mathbf{x}_i, \mathbf{x}_j)$. Moreover, D is assumed to be normalized, that is, $D(i, j) \in [0, 1]$ (distance matrices obtained from the functions defined in Section 22.3.3 can always be normalized and, for the experiments reported here, such a normalization process has in fact been done).

Given a threshold value $\phi \in [0, 1]$ and the distance matrix D, let I_ϕ be a vector such that

$$I_\phi(k) = \begin{cases} 1 & \text{if } D(i, j) \le \phi \\ 0 & \text{otherwise} \end{cases} \tag{22.13}$$

where $i = [(k-1)\text{div } n)] + 1$ and $j = [(k-1)\text{mod } n] + 1$.

Since, in this chapter, it is assumed that the gold solution $C = \{c_1, \ldots, c_r\}$ is known for $\mathbf{X}$, one can define the *learning set* J as follows:

$$J(k) = \begin{cases} 1 & \text{if } \mathbf{x}_i \text{ and } \mathbf{x}_j \text{ belong to the same cluster} \\ 0 & \text{otherwise} \end{cases} \tag{22.14}$$

Now, the measurement of the separation abilities of a distance is formally reduced to the evaluation of the performance of a binary classifier: The outcomes of such a classifier are stored in I_ϕ, while the real class labels are stored in J. This latter is a classic problem in data analysis that can be addressed via ROC analysis. For the convenience of the reader, an outline of the method is briefly given next, pointing out that additional details can be found in [57].

A useful visualization tool for the performance of a classifier, not necessarily binary, is the *confusion matrix* or *matching matrix*, which is a matrix where each row represents the instances in a predicted class, while each column represents the instances in an actual class. In the case of a binary classification, the 2×2 confusion matrix stores the number of elements of class 0 classified as 0, denoted T_0, and the number of elements of class 0 classified as 1, denoted F_1. One defines T_1 and F_0 analogously. In this context, the *sensitivity* S_e and *specificity* S_p are defined as follows:

$$S_e = \frac{T_0}{T_0 + F_1} \qquad S_p = \frac{T_1}{T_1 + F_0}$$

A ROC plane [42] is a plane where $y = S_e$ and $x = S_p = 1 - S_e$, and it is useful to measure a classification in terms of S_e and S_p rates, once it has been established to represent with 0 the positive class. It is worth noting that, since a classifier assigns data items to classes, S_e is the percentage of item pairs correctly assigned to different classes, while S_p is the percentage of item pairs incorrectly assigned to different classes. It is then useful to define a curve in the ROC plane, which is referred to as ROC curve, providing a two-dimensional visualization of S_e versus $1 - S_p$, for different values of the threshold ϕ. The area under the curve (AUC) can be used to quantify the performance of a classifier. Indeed, it takes values in the range [0, 1], where a value of 0.5 corresponds to the performance of a classifier with a random assignment rule, while the closer AUC is to unity, the better is the performance of the classifier. A value below 0.5 suggests an incorrect label assignment by the classifier, which is solvable by simply flipping its outcomes.

As discussed in [42], the AUC also represents the probability that a random pair of elements belonging to different classes will be correctly ranked. By analogy, in the case being considered here, the AUC represents the probability of the following event: two couples $(\mathbf{x}, \mathbf{x}')$ and $(\mathbf{y}, \mathbf{z})$ such that $\mathbf{x}, \mathbf{x}'$ belong to the same cluster while $\mathbf{y}, \mathbf{z}$ belong to different clusters and satisfy the relation $d(\mathbf{y}, \mathbf{z}) > d(\mathbf{x}, \mathbf{x}')$. Figure 22.1 illustrates the evaluation process just described for one data set.

Criteria for point (b)   First, each distance function is used in conjunction with a clustering algorithm to produce a partition of a given data set in a number of clusters equal to the number of classes in the gold solution of the data set. Then, all three indices defined in Section 22.2.3 are used to evaluate the agreement between the generated partition and the gold solution.

Criteria for point (c)   Giancarlo et al. [34] address point (c) by:

(c1) Showing how to map a clustering solution into the ROC plane
(c2) Introducing a distance between a clustering solution and the gold solution in the ROC plane
(c3) Showing how (c1) and (c2) can be used to gain deeper insights into the interplay between the intrinsic ability of the distance function and a clustering algorithm, such as the introduction of biases

The interested reader will find an outline of the details in [34].

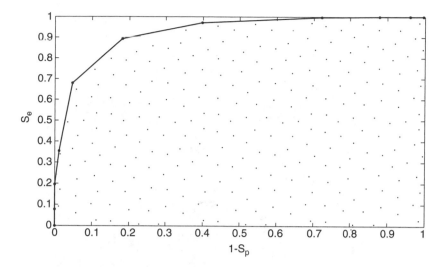

FIGURE 22.1   ROC curve for Euclidean distance d_2 on leukemia data set. In this case, the AUC value is 0.9258.

22.3.5 Some Benchmarking Results

The presentation in this chapter is limited to giving the results of Giancarlo et al. [33] regarding points (a) and (b). The interested reader can find a preliminary account of the results for point (c) in [34].

The results of the intrinsic separation ability can naturally be organized in a table, where each row corresponds to a distance and each column to a data set. The value stored in an entry of that table is the AUC of the corresponding experiment. The table has a total of 54 elements, each corresponding to an experiment (data not shown and available upon request).

In order to get a synoptic description of the performance of each distance across data sets, a distance that is at most 5% away from the maximum value in the corresponding column is labeled as a *winner*. Indeed, it is not to be expected that one distance would consistently perform best. Rather, it is reasonable to expect a division of the set of distances considered here in classes, according to their ability, to consistently perform well across data sets. Figure 22.2 displays a histogram of the winning percentage, that is, the number of times it won divided by the number of times it was evaluated.

One has the following indications from those results: d_1, d_2, d_3, $d_{\cos}$, d_r have the best intrinsic separation ability since they have a performance within 5% of the best over all the considered data sets. The distances d_ρ, d_τ have a reasonable intrinsic separation ability because they have performed as well as the distances just mentioned, except for the PBM data set. The worst performers are the normalized mutual information d_{MI} and the Mahalanobis distance d_M. The former seems to be suitable only for the CNS Rat and PBM data sets, while the latter has shown to be definitely not suitable for any of the data sets. One reason for such a poor performance may be that the Mahalanobis distance suffers from a sample size problem on small- and medium-sized data sets, such as the ones that have been used in this study. Indeed, that type of data gives rise to biases in the estimation of the covariance matrix. The same problem seems to affect d_{MI}: Data sets of small or moderate size can lead to significant numerical errors when using a binning procedure [19].

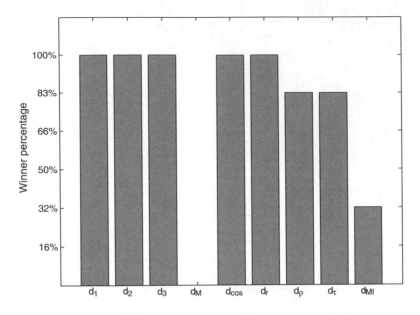

FIGURE 22.2 Summary of results of intrinsic separation ability for each considered distance.

In analogy with results reported for point (a) above, those for the assessment of the predictive clustering algorithm ability can naturally be organized in three tables, that is, one table for each of the three external indices. The total number of entries in those tables is 648, each corresponding to an experiment: 9 distances × 4 algorithms × 6 data sets × 3 indices (data not shown and available upon request).

In each table, a row corresponds to a combination algorithms–distance and each column to a data set. In analogy with the histogram for point (a), a distance is labeled as a winner according to a given index and on a given data set if the entry algorithm–distance on that column is again within 5% of the maximum in the column. Again, the goal is to divide the distances in classes, testing their level of reliability across algorithms and data sets. The histogram in Figure 22.3 summarizes the winner percentage, which is the percentage of times a distance has been a winner, irrespective of the index used, over the relative set of experiments.

It is evident that the best results are for the cosine distance d_{cos}, 3-norm distance d_3, Pearson distance d_r, Euclidean distance d_2, and Manhattan distance d_1, since they have shown themselves to be robust across algorithms and data sets.

22.3.6 Some Recommendations

The results presented so far extend the ones reported in Costa et al. in several ways. First, and most important, they show that the recommendations in that paper obtained for time course microarray data extend to other types of microarray experiments. Indeed, the study outlined here shows that the choice of Pearson, cosine, and Euclidean distances is the most appropriate for microarray data analysis. In addition, by using an analysis of both the intrinsic qualities of a distance and the same distance within a clustering algorithm,

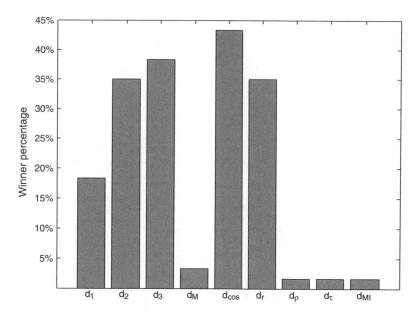

FIGURE 22.3 Summary of results of the predictive clustering algorithm ability for each combination of distance, algorithm, data set, and external index.

one receives an indication that the three mentioned distances are the most versatile and flexible among the ones considered here. Moreover, further light is also shed on the use of MI for microarray data analysis. Indeed, results show it be a poor performer here. Taking into account such a fact, together with the results by Priness et al. [65], one receives an indication that MI may be superior to other distances only in conjunction with clustering algorithms specifically designed for its use. That is, although theoretically superior to other distances in terms of its ability to capture statistical dependency, it does not seem to offer the same flexibility and versatility as other well-known distances. The reason for such a poor performance seems to be due to difficulties in its estimation on relatively small sample spaces such as a single data set.

It is also worthy of mention that preliminary conclusions which can be drawn from the study of point (c) by Giancarlo et al. [34] show that the comparative methodology introduced there is able to establish that K-means and Hier-A improve upon the intrinsic separation ability of a distance with respect to clustering. That is, those two algorithms amplify the discriminative ability of a distance function.

22.4 CLUSTERING ALGORITHMS

The second step of the clustering process is to compute a partition of $\mathbf{X}$ via a clustering algorithm. Recall from the Introduction that a choice of a distance function may be required. Due to the importance, in many areas of science, of dividing data into groups, there is a great proliferation of research on clustering algorithms within and across many disciplines, for example, statistics, mathematical optimization, and computer science [43, 44, 47, 48, 50,

59, 66]. The advent of high-thoughput technologies, such as microarrays, and the pioneering work by Eisen et al. [26] in the application of clustering to the analysis of those new types of data have resulted in a *revival* of this entire area [22, 25, 70]. However, difficulties persist in identifying the *ultimate* clustering algorithm for genomic applications, and many of the new methods do not even seem to be justified [56].

From the above introductory remarks, it is clear that a comprehensive review and comparison of all available clustering algorithms are virtually impossible. Therefore, in what follows, the focus is on some major points that are either essential for clustering or particularly novel. Accordingly, this section is organized as follows. In Section 22.4.1, an outline is given of the various ways of dividing clustering algorithms into classes and, based on the few reliable benchmarking studies available for clustering of genomic data, an attempt is made to extract their common denominator indicating the best performing algorithms. Due to its methodological importance, in Section 22.4.2, a very basic technique that can be used to evaluate the performance of a clustering algorithm is presented. Due to its leading role in biological data mining [20], the first benchmarking of NMF as a clustering algorithm is provided in Section 22.4.3: It brings to light several of its limitations in comparison with other classic clustering algorithms [37, 81]. Finally, a few recommendations are offered in Section 22.4.4.

22.4.1 State of the Art

A widely accepted division of clustering algorithms into classes is *partitional*, *hierarchical*, and *density based* (see [41, 47, 48] and references therein), with obvious meaning. A more refined, and somewhat less justified, division into classes is provided in [5]. Indeed, the merit of that paper is in providing a list of desirable properties that a clustering algorithm should have and then in providing, for each of the algorithms reviewed in that paper, a synopsis on how well each algorithm satisfies those properties. Unfortunately, such an assessment seems to come from theoretic analysis available in the literature rather than from experimental performance evaluations conducted on biological data. In addition, the paper provides a list of the biological domains where each algorithm has been applied together with information on where to find implementations of the algorithm.

Handl et al. [41], viewing clustering as an optimization process, propose a very formal and elegant division of algorithms into classes, based on the objective function they try to optimize. The following three classes are reported.

Compactness   Algorithms in this class try to keep interclass variation small (e.g., K-means).

Connectedness   Algorithms in this class try to group items so that "neighboring" data items should share the same cluster (e.g., Hier-S).

Spatial Separation   Algorithms in this class try to optimize spatial separation and make essential use of sophisticated optimization heuristics [41].

Once a new clustering algorithm is proposed, its performance is usually evaluated versus well-known algorithms, usually K-means. Unfortunately, there are very few comparative studies with a substantial amount of experimental benchmarking on genomic data. To date, the only one that has explicitly attempted such a task is [49], where several algorithms have been compared, most of them being based on graph-theoretic strategies. The study indicates that such a latter class of algorithms outperforms classic methods, including SOM [76]. In particular, CAST [7] is among the top performers. Unfortunately, the conclusions of that study are based on experiments conducted on one gene expression data set only. Fortunately, earlier related work by Di Gesú et al. [23] for the validation of their algorithm Genclust can be used to provide a more robust estimation about the quality of CAST. Indeed, they use five microarray data sets for their experimentation, three of which are part of the benchmark 1 data sets. Experiments by Di Gesú et al. [23] show that Genclust and CAST have analogous discriminative performances, certainly superior to K-means and hierarchical algorithms. Another point in favor of CAST is given by a study in [70], although only the YCC data set is used for the experiments.

On the other hand, results in [22, 30] report that hierarchical algorithms, with the exception of Hier-S and K-means, seem to be the most appropriate for microarray data clustering. However, the review by D'Haeseleer [22] is very basic and accounts only for the initial use of clustering in gene expression data analysis. The more recent study by Freyhult et al. [30] tries to analyze the entire microarray data processing pipeline. Therefore, it is certainly extensive in that respect but somewhat limited in regard to the comparison of clustering algorithms. Indeed, apart from hierarchical and K-means, they include only Mclust, SOM, and PAM in their study (see [30] and references therein for details and definitions). Nevertheless, given the amount of experimentation carried out, the indications from that study are quite reliable. In particular, hierarchical clustering with Ward's method [83] seems to be among the best performers.

None of the mentioned studies are concerned with the time performance of clustering algorithms, which is a serious limitation. Indeed, as genomic data sets are growing larger and larger, the need for fast algorithms is now acute [28]. In the computer science literature, hierarchical clustering and K-means algorithms have been the object of several speed-ups (see [11, 29, 69] and references therein). However, those efficient implementations do not seem to be used in computational biology. Rather, the need for computational performance in the area of clustering for microarray data is addressed by developing implementations of well-known algorithms, such as K-means, specific for multicore architectures [51] as opposed to being addressed by designing efficient algorithms.

22.4.2 Criteria to Evaluate Performance of Clustering Algorithms

It is worth recalling, from Section 22.2.1, that all of the data sets used in this chapter for experimentation have a gold solution and, from Section 22.2.3, that an external index measures how well a clustering solution computed by an algorithm agrees with the gold solution of a given data set. In particular, for the benchmarking of NMF detailed in Section 22.4.3.2, all three indexes presented in Section 22.2.3 are used. In order to evaluate the precision of a clustering algorithm, that is, its ability to identify a good partition of the data, a very simple and rather demanding methodology, used here for the reported experiments, is as follows. With the use of a given clustering algorithm, a partition of X into i clusters is generated for $i \in [k_{min}, k_{max}]$ where the endpoints of the interval are determined based on the number of classes in the true solution. Indeed, the interval should be such that its maximum is well away from the number of classes in the data set. For our experiments, the interval [2, 30] is used. For each partition so generated, its agreement with the gold solution is measured via an external index. Then, all those values are plotted to obtain a curve. For a good algorithm, one expects the curve to have a maximum in the proximity of the number of clusters in the gold solution and to decrease sharply after that point. For a comparison among algorithms in terms of time, the total time, in milliseconds, that the algorithm takes in order to generate all of those solutions should also be reported.

It goes without saying that many other criteria can be used to evaluate the performance of clustering algorithms, in particular for genomic data. The interested reader can find details about them in the benchmarking studies mentioned in Section 22.4.1.

22.4.3 Important Special Case: NMF

In this section, a general outline of matrix factorization (MF) is given and then two restricted versions of it are presented: positive matrix factorization (PMF) and the already mentioned NMF.

MF Let X be the matrix of size $n \times m$, where m denotes the number of features and n denotes the number of items in **X**. Given X and an integer $r < \min\{n, m\}$, one wants to find two matrix factors V and W of size $n \times r$ and $r \times m$, respectively, such that

$$X \approx V \times W \qquad (22.15)$$

One has that $x \approx vW$, where x and v are homologous rows in X and V, respectively. That is, each row x is approximated by a linear combination of the columns of W weighted by the components of v. Therefore, W can be regarded as containing a basis.

PMF It is a variant of MF, by Paatero and Tapper [64], since X is constrained to be a positive matrix. One possible solution can be obtained by computing a positive low-rank approximation of $V \times W$ via an optimization of the function

$$\min_{V, W \geq 0} \| A \circ (X - V \times W) \|_F$$

where A is a weighted matrix whose elements are associated with the elements of X, $\circ$ is the Hadamard product, and $\| \cdot \|_F$ denotes the Frobenius norm [39]. Paatero and Tapper also proposed an alternative least-squares algorithm in which one of the two matrices is fixed and the optimization is solved with respect to the other one and vice versa. Later, Paatero developed a series of algorithms [61–63] using a longer product of matrices to replace the approximate $V \times W$.

NMF A variant of PMF, NMF allows X to be nonnegative, this latter being a constraint much more suitable for data analysis tasks. It also offers several advantages [31, 54]:

1. The constraint that the matrix factors are nonnegative allows for their intuitive interpretation as real underlying components within the context defined by the original data. The basis components can be directly interpreted as parts or basis samples, present in different proportions in each observed sample.
2. NMF generally produces sparse results, implying that the basis and/or the mixture coefficients have only a few nonzero entries.

3. Unlike other decomposition methods such as singular-value decomposition [79] or independent component analysis [6, 15], the aim of NMF is not to find components that are orthogonal or independent, therefore allowing overlap among the components.

22.4.3.1 General NMF Scheme

In order to compute an NMF, all the methods proposed in the literature use the same simple paradigm, that is, Algorithm 22.1 below, where the following "ingredients" must be specified:

(i) An initialization for matrices V and W
(ii) An update rule
(iii) A stopping criterion

Procedure NMF (X) // Algorithm 22.1
```
initialize V and W;
while condition is true do
 update V and W;
```

The scheme is iterative: It starts from the two initial matrices V and W, which are repeatedly updated via a fixed rule until the stopping criterion is satisfied.

For point (i), the matrices V and W are initialized at random. In that case, different runs of NMF, with the same input, are likely to produce different results. However, it is worth pointing out that sophisticated deterministic initialization methods have been proposed to choose appropriate initial values referred to as *seed NMF algorithms*. When one uses the same initial seed, the procedure is deterministic, that is, it always produces the same output on a given input. Relevant references can be found in [81].

With respect to points (ii) and (iii), many numerical algorithms have been developed for NMF.

For (ii), the most popular use at least one of the following principles and techniques: *alternating direction iterations, projected Newton, reduced quadratic approximation*, and *descent search*. Correspondingly, specific implementations can be categorized into *alternating least-squares algorithms, multiplicative update algorithms* combined with *gradient descent search*, and *hybrid algorithms*. For the interested reader, it is worth pointing out that a general assessment of these methods can be found in [53, 80].

As for (iii), the most "popular" stopping criteria are a fixed number of iterations, the stabilization of a suitably defined matrix, referred to as *consensus* (see [14] for formal definitions), and stationarity of the objective function value.

22.4.3.2 Some Benchmarking Results

In what follows, the results of the experiments performed according to the methodology described in Section 22.4.2 are presented. They are limited to the `benchmark 1` data sets, with the use of the algorithms mentioned in Section 22.2.2 . However, the interested reader will find in [37, 81] a more extensive evaluation, from which the one reported here has been extracted.

The execution time (in milliseconds) of each algorithm on each data set is reported in Table 22.1. A dash indicates that the experiment was stopped because of its high computational demand. Indeed, given the dimension of the PBM data sets, NMF was stopped after four days. From the results in Table 22.1, it is possible to see that NMF is very slow, at

TABLE 22.1 Timing Results (ms) for All Algorithms on `benchmark` 1 Data Sets

	CNS Rat	Leukemia	NCI60	Lymphoma	Yeast	PBM
Hier-A	875	219	500	921	594	4.4×10^5
Hier-C	865	250	469	750	625	4.6×10^5
Hier-S	860	296	516	641	609	4.3×10^5
K-means-R	3.2×10^3	2.1×10^3	3.2×10^3	7.2×10^3	1.1×10^5	1.1×10^6
K-means-A	3.2×10^3	1.1×10^3	4.2×10^3	4.4×10^3	1.1×10^5	1.7×10^6
K-means-C	2.9×10^3	1.1×10^3	4.0×10^3	4.2×10^3	1.0×10^5	1.3×10^6
K-means-S	3.3×10^3	1.3×10^3	5.2×10^3	5.4×10^3	1.2×10^5	1.4×10^6
NMF-R	9.0×10^6	8.6×10^4	3.9×10^5	5.2×10^5	2.9×10^8	—
NMF-A	3.0×10^6	2.4×10^4	7.9×10^4	1.1×10^5	5.5×10^7	—
NMF-C	2.4×10^6	2.5×10^4	7.4×10^4	1.1×10^5	5.9×10^7	—
NMF-S	5.7×10^6	2.3×10^4	6.9×10^4	1.1×10^5	4.5×10^7	—

Note: For PBM, the experiments were terminated due to their high computational demand (weeks to complete).

least four orders of magnitude of difference with the other clustering algorithms. Moreover, NMF is not able to complete the experiment on the PBM data set.

The experiments assessing the discriminative ability of NMF, compared with the other algorithms, is reported next. The PBM data set is excluded from the evaluation, since NMF did not complete execution on it.

Adjusted Rand Index   For this index, the relevant plot is in Figures 22.4 and 22.5. It is worth pointing out that the experiments for PBM on NMF were terminated due to their high computational demand and the corresponding plots have been removed from the figure. Based on that, it is possible to see that all the algorithms perform very well on the leukemia and NCI60 data sets. For the remaining three data sets, their performance is somewhat mixed, and sometimes they are not precise, in particular the Hier-S, NMF-R, and NMF-S algorithms.

FM Index   For this index, the relevant plot is in Figures 22.6 and 22.7. It is worth pointing out that the experiments for PBM on NMF were terminated due to their high computational demand and the corresponding plots have been removed from the figure. Based on that, it is possible to see that Hier-S and NMF-S are still the worst among the algorithms. However, now there is no consistent indication given by the other algorithms.

F Index   For this index, the relevant plot is in Figures 22.8 and 22.9. It is worth pointing out that the experiments for PBM on NMF were terminated due to their high computational demand and the corresponding plots have been removed from the figure. Based on that, it is possible to see that Hier-S and NMF-S are still the worst among the algorithms and the indications in this case about the other algorithms are essentially the same as in the case of R_A.

22.4.4 Some Recommendations

From the brief description of the state of the art given in Sections 22.4.1 and 22.4.3.2, one has the indication that, although hierarchical, and K-means, seem to be the algorithms

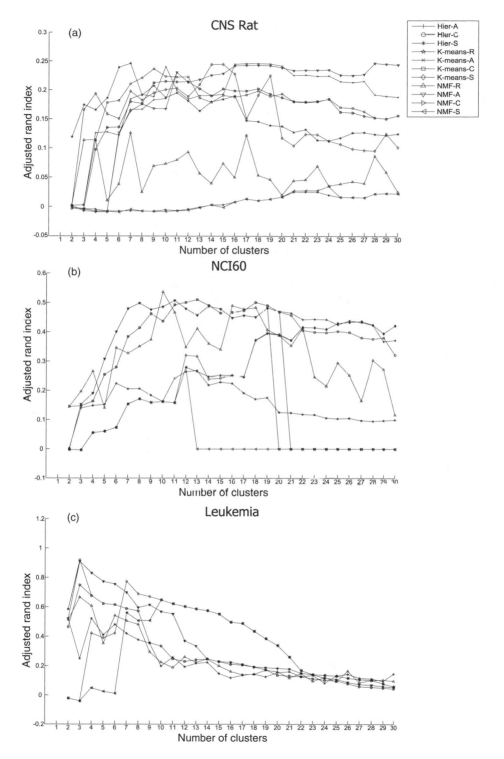

FIGURE 22.4 `Adjusted Rand` index curves for (a) CNS Rat, (b) NCI60, and (c) Leukemia data sets: plots of index as function of number of clusters.

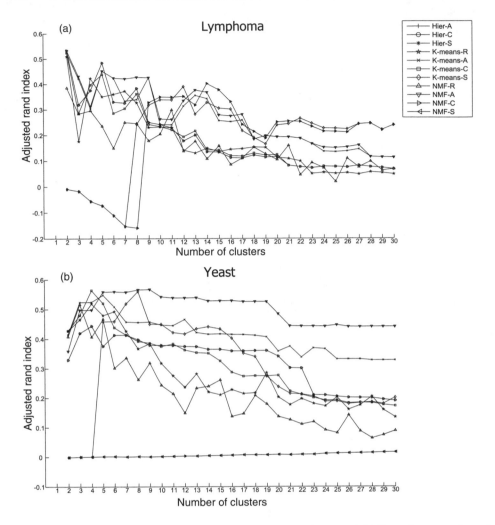

FIGURE 22.5   Adjusted Rand index curves for (a) Lymphoma and (b) Yeast data sets: plots of index as function of number of clusters.

of choice, it is also evident that their performance can be quite disappointing on some data sets (see Figures 22.4 and 22.5 again). Therefore, for genomic studies where clustering is required, it is advisable to use K-means and at least one of Hier-A and Ward's hierarchical [83]. Indeed, one important aspect well quantified by the study of Di Gesú et al. [23] is that there is no significantly large difference in the performance of classic algorithms and the novel ones that have been specifically designed for genomic analysis.

Regarding NMF, it is evident that, although it has been used as a clustering algorithm (e.g., [14]), its ability to identify a good partition of the data is not substantially better than the ability of classic algorithms. However, it can be orders of magnitude slower in time. Although such a limitation was intuitively known in the literature [20], it is well quantified in

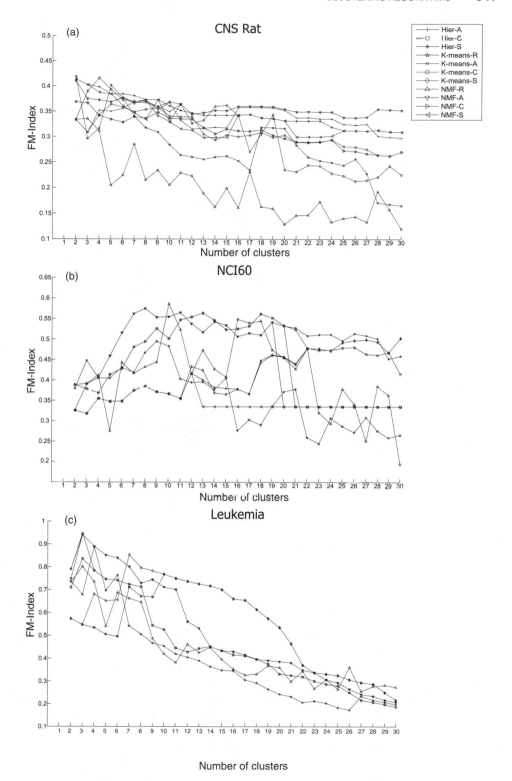

FIGURE 22.6 `FM-index` curves for (a) CNS Rat, (b) NCI60, and (c) Leukemia data sets: plots of index as function of number of clusters.

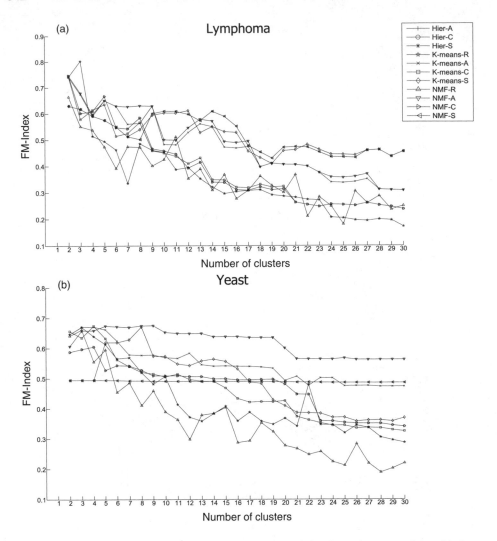

FIGURE 22.7 FM-index curves for (a) Lymphoma and (b) Yeast data sets: plots of index as function of number of clusters.

[37, 81] (see Section 22.4.3.2 again). Therefore, the use of such a powerful pattern discovery technique as a clustering algorithm seems to be rather artificial and unjustified.

One last word about the design of new clustering algorithms is appropriate. In his review of clustering algorithms for gene expression data analysis, D'Haeseleer on the second page of the paper [22] states that it is easy and tempting to design a new clustering algorithm. However, "it is much harder to do a fair evaluation of how well a new algorithm will perform on typical gene expression data sets, how it compares with those dozens of other published algorithms and under which circumstances one algorithm should be preferred over another." Therefore, the proposal of a new algorithm should really be made having a strong case of superiority in performance with respect to at least a few leading algorithms in this area.

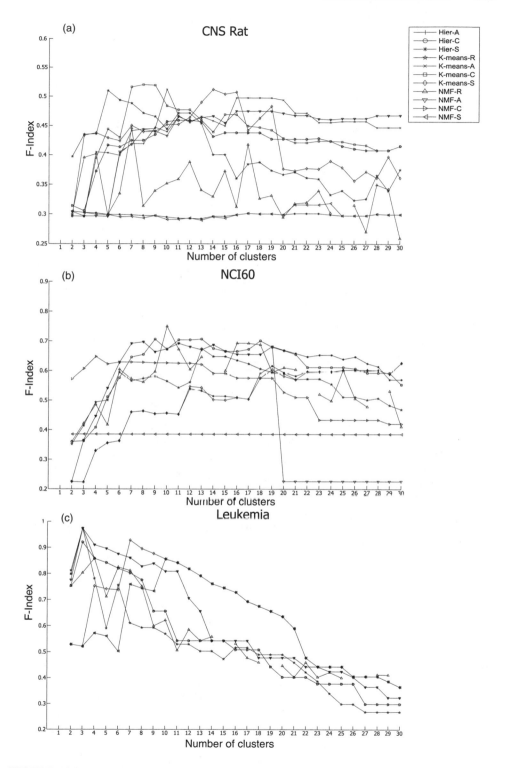

FIGURE 22.8 F-index curves for (a) CNS Rat, (b) NCI60, and (c) Leukemia data sets: plots of index as function of number of clusters.

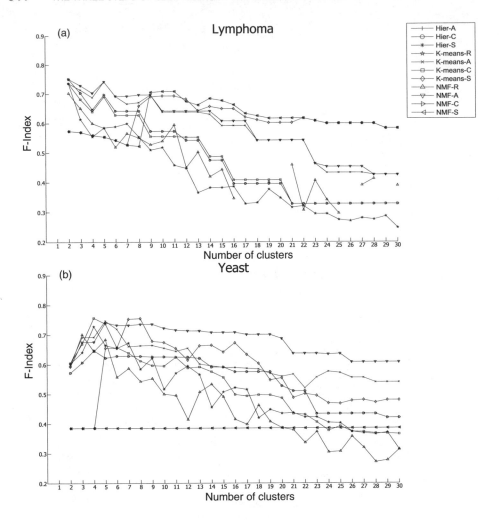

FIGURE 22.9 F-index curves for (a) Lymphoma and (b) Yeast data sets: plots of index as function of number of clusters.

22.5   INTERNAL VALIDATION MEASURES

The last step of the clustering process is to assess the statistical significance of a clustering solution via a validation measure. There are at least three meaningful ways to perform such a task [47]: (a) quantify the agreement of a clustering solution with external knowledge via one of the indices mentioned in Section 22.2.3; (b) quantify how statistically meaningful is a single clustering solution by comparing it with a clustering solution on a data set generated via a null model, this latter formalizing the intuition of "random clustering structure in the data" [35, 40, 81]; and (c) quantify which, among many clustering solutions, is the "best one."

Measures in class (b) are referred to as *internal*, while those in class (c) are referred to as *relative*. However, since measures in the latter class are based on those in the former, in most cases both classes assume the same name, that is, internal. That notation is also followed here, although this chapter concentrates on relative indices, in particular the data-driven ones.

22.5.1 State of the Art

Handl et al. [41], in their fundamental review on clustering in the postgenomic era, point out the need for a more extensive use of cluster validation measures for the analysis of biological data. Following up on that contribution, Giancarlo et al. [35] have recently proposed an extensive comparative analysis of measures taken from the most relevant paradigms in the area: (a) *assessment of cluster compactness* (e.g., [52]); (b) *hypothesis testing in statistics* (e.g., [77]); (c) *stability-based techniques* (e.g., [8, 25, 60]); and (d) *jackknife techniques* (e.g., [87]). Those benchmarks consider both the ability of a measure to predict the correct number of clusters in a data set and, departing from the current state of the art in that area, the computer time it takes for a measure to complete its task. Moreover, in that study, the idea of designing fast approximation algorithms for the computation of those measures is also introduced and investagated, with preliminary results indicating its great potential. Some facts that have emerged from the mentioned study summarizing quite well the state of the art are outlined next:

1. There is a very natural hierarchy of internal validation measures, with the fastest and less precise at the top. In terms of time, there is a gap of at least two orders of magnitude between the fastest, within-cluster sum of squares (WCSS) [77], and the slowest ones.

2. All measures considered in that study have severe limitations on large data sets with a large number of clusters, either in their ability to predict the correct number of clusters or to finish their execution in a reasonable amount of time, for example, a few days.

3. Although among the slowest, Consensus [60] displays some quite remarkable properties that, accounting for 1 and 2, make it the measure of choice, among the measures benchmarked in [35], for small- and medium-sized data sets. Indeed, it is very reliable in terms of its ability to predict the correct number of clusters in a data set, in particular when used in conjunction with hierarchical clustering algorithms. Moreover, such a performance is stable across the choice of basic clustering algorithms, that is, various versions of hierarchical clustering and K-means, used to produce clustering solutions.

4. The fast approximation algorithms proposed for the computation of a few measures, in particular the gap statistics [77] (Gap), are at least one order of magnitude faster than the exact procedures, yet grant nearly the same predictive ability.

Since a stability-based measure such as Consensus appears to be the best among a wide collection of measures and in light of the encouraging results regarding the use of approximation algorithms, it is a natural candidate for further studies in this area. Indeed, Utro [81] has added a few relevant results that have Consensus as a special case. Namely:

5. All of the stability-based measures are instances of a single algorithmic paradigm that generalizes, in several aspects, previous work by Breckenridge [12], Breiman [13],

and Valentini [82]. To the best of our knowledge, the following methods are all the ones that fall into that class [8–10, 25, 55, 67].

6. The idea of fast approximation algorithms can be successfully applied to Consensus and therefore, because of point 5, to all of the stability-based measures. In particular, FC, the proposed speed-up of Consensus [37, 81], is two orders of magnitude faster than Consensus while granting the same precision.

In what follows, the techniques leading to point 6 are outlined, referring the interested reader to [37, 81] for a full account. Moreover, the interested reader can find a detailed description of most of the validation measures that have been proposed in the literature and used for genomic analysis in [35, 41, 81].

22.5.2 Consensus

Consensus is a stability-based technique best presented as a procedure taking as input Sub, H, X, $\mathcal{A}$, $k_{\max}$. The resampling scheme Sub is a means of sampling from one data set in order to build a new one. For the experiments reported here, the resampling scheme extracts, uniformly and at random, a given percentage p of the rows of the data set matrix X. Finally, H is the number of resampling steps, $\mathcal{A}$ is the clustering algorithm, and $k_{\max}$ is the maximum number that is considered as candidates for the "correct" number k^* of clusters in $\mathbf{X}$.

Procedure Consensus (Sub, H, X, $\mathcal{A}$, $k_{\max}$)

1. For $2 \leq k \leq k_{\max}$, initialize to empty the set M of connectivity matrices and perform steps (a) and (b):
   (a) For $1 \leq h \leq H$, compute a perturbed data matrix $X^{(h)}$ using resampling scheme Sub; cluster the elements in k clusters using algorithm $\mathcal{A}$ and $X^{(h)}$. Compute a connectivity matrix $M^{(h)}$ and insert it into M.
   (b) Based on the connectivity matrices in M, compute a consensus matrix $\mathcal{M}^{(k)}$.
2. Based on the $k_{\max} - 1$ consensus matrices, return a prediction for k^*.

As for the connectivity matrix $M^{(h)}$, one has $M^{(h)}(i, j) = 1$ if items i and j are in the same cluster and zero otherwise. Moreover, it is useful to define an indicator matrix $I^{(h)}$ such that $I^{(h)}(i, j) = 1$ if items i and j are both in $X^{(h)}$ and zero otherwise. Then, the consensus matrix $\mathcal{M}^{(k)}$ is defined as a properly normalized sum of all connectivity matrices in all perturbed data sets:

$$\mathcal{M}^{(k)} = \frac{\sum_h M^{(h)}}{\sum_h I^{(h)}} \tag{22.16}$$

Based on experimental observations and sound arguments, Monti et al. [60] derive a "rule of thumb" in order to estimate the real number k^* of clusters present in X. The presentation here is limited to the key points, since the interested reader can find a full discussion in Monti et al. [60]. Let n be the number of items to cluster, $\gamma = n(n-1)/2$, and $\{x_1, x_2, \ldots, x_\gamma\}$ be the list obtained by sorting the entries of the consensus matrix. Moreover, let the empirical cumulative distribution CDF, defined over the range $[0, 1]$, be

$$\text{CDF}(c) = \frac{\sum_{i<j} l\{\mathcal{M}(i, j) \le c\}}{\gamma}$$

where c is a chosen constant in $[0, 1]$ and l equals unity if the condition is true and zero otherwise.

For a given value of k, that is, number of clusters, consider the CDF curve obtained by plotting the values of $\text{CDF}(x_i)$, $1 \le i \le \gamma$, with the use of the corresponding consensus matrix. In an ideal situation in which there are k clusters and the clustering algorithm is more than adequate to provide a perfect classification, such a curve is bimodal, with peaks at zero and unity. Monti et al. [60] observe and validate experimentally that the area under the CDF curves is an increasing function of k. That result has also been confirmed by the experiments in Giancarlo et al. [35]. In particular, for values of $k \le k^*$, that area has a significant increase, while its growth flattens out for $k > k^*$. For instance, with reference to Figure 22.10a, one sees an increase in the area under the CDFs for $k = 2, \dots, 13$. The growth rate of the area is decreasing as a function of k and it flattens out for $k \ge k^* = 3$. The point in which such a growth flattens out can be taken as an indication of k^*. However, operationally, Monti et al. [60] propose a closely associated method, described next. For a given k, the area of the corresponding CDF curve is estimated as follows:

$$A(k) = \sum_{i=2}^{m}[x_i - x_{i-1}]\text{CDF}(x_i)$$

Again, $A(k)$ is observed to be an increasing function of k, with the same growth rate as the CDF curves. Now, let

$$\Delta(k) = \begin{cases} A(k) & k = 2 \\ \dfrac{A(k+1) - A(k)}{A(k)} & k > 2 \end{cases}$$

be the proportion increase of the CDF area as a function of k and as estimated by $A(k)$. Again, Monti et al. [60] observe experimentally that:

(i) For each $k \le k^*$, there is a pronounced decrease of the Δ curve. That is, the incremental growth of $A(k)$ decreases sharply.

(ii) For $k > k^*$, there is a stable plot of the Δ curve. That is, for $k > k^*$, the growth of $A(k)$ flattens out.

From this behavior, the "rule of thumb" to identify k^* with the use of the Δ curve is: Take as k^* the abscissa corresponding to the smallest nonnegative value where the curve starts to stabilize; that is, no big variation in the curve takes place from that point on. An example is given in Figure 22.10b.

A few remarks are in order. From the observations outlined above, one has that the value of the area under the CDF is not very important. Rather, its growth as a function of k is key.

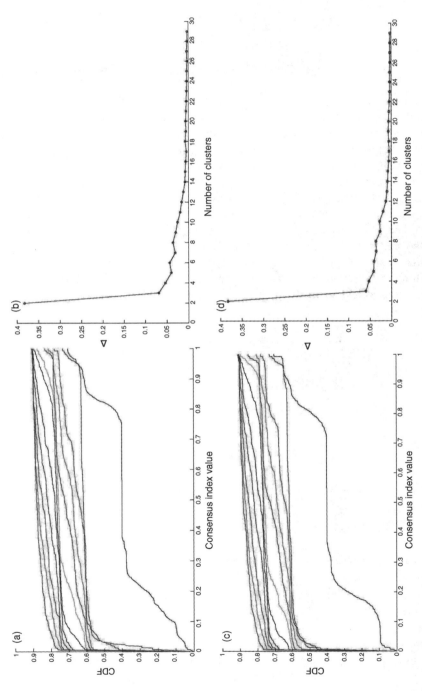

FIGURE 22.10 Example of number of cluster predictions using CONSENSUS and FC. The experiment is derived with the Leukemia data set as input, with the use of the K-means-A clustering algorithm. (a) Plot of CDF curves as function of k obtained by CONSENSUS with $H = 250$ and $p = 80\%$. For clarity, only the curves for k in [2, 13] are shown. From bottom to top, the rank of each curve corresponds to the number of clusters in the solution used to compute it, starting with two clusters. It is evident that there are increasing values of the area under the CDF for increasing values of k. The flattening effect in the growth rate of the area is evident for $k \geq k^* = 3$. (b) Plot of corresponding Δ curve for k in [2, 30], where flattening effect indicating k^* is evident for $k \geq k^* = 3$. (c) Plot of CDF curves obtained by FC with $H = 250$ and $p = 80\%$ in analogy with (a). (d) Plot of Δ curve obtained by FC with $H = 250$ and $p = 80\%$ in analogy with (b).

Moreover, experimentally, the Δ curve is nonnegative. Such an observation has been confirmed by Giancarlo et al. [35]. However, there is no theoretic justification for such a fact. Even more importantly, the growth of the CDF curves also gives an indication of the number of clusters present in X. Such a fact, together with the use of the Δ curve, contributes to the quality of the prediction since $A(k)$ is only an approximation of the real area under the CDF curve and it may give spurious indications that can be "disambiguated" with the use of the CDF curves. It is quite remarkable that there is usually excellent agreement in the prediction between the Δ curve and the CDF curves. For the convenience of the reader, it is worth pointing out that many internal validation methods are based on the identification of a "knee" in a suitably defined curve, for example, WCSS and FOM [87], in most cases via a visual inspection of the curve. For specific measures, there exist automatic methods that identify such a point, some of them being theoretically sound [77], while others are based on heuristic geometric observations [35, 68]. For Consensus, the identification of a theoretically sound automatic method for the prediction of k^* is open and it is not clear that heuristic approaches will yield appreciable results.

Consensus is quite representative of the area of internal validation measures [37]. Indeed, the main, and rather simple, idea sustaining that procedure is the following. For each value of k in the range $[2, k_{\max}]$, the procedure extracts H new data matrices from the original one and, for each of them, a partition into k clusters is generated. The better the agreement among those solutions, the higher the "evidence" that the value of k under scrutiny is a good estimate of k^*. That level of agreement is measured via the consensus matrices. As discussed in [81], such a scheme is characteristic of stability-based internal validation measures (see point 5 above). It is also worth noting that each of the $k_{\max} \times H$ clustering solutions needed is computed from a distinct data set. As is shown in the next section, this leads to inefficiencies, in particular in regard to agglomerative clustering algorithms, such as the hierarchical ones. Indeed, their ability to quickly compute a clustering solution with k clusters from one with $k + 1$, typical of these methods, cannot be used within Consensus because, for each k, the data set changes. The same holds true for divisive methods.

22.5.3   FC

Intuitively, a large number of clustering solutions, each obtained via a sample of the original data set, seem to be required in order to identify the correct number of clusters. However, there is no theoretic reason indicating that those clustering solutions must each be generated from a *different* sample of the input data set, as Consensus does. Based on this observation, Giancarlo and Utro [37, 81] propose to perform, first, a sampling step to generate a data matrix $X^{(h)}$, which is then used to generate all clustering solutions for k in the range $[2, k_{\max}]$. In terms of code, that implies a simple switch of the two iteration cycles in steps 1 and 1a of the Consensus procedure. In turn, and with reference to the discussion at the end of Section 22.5.2, that switch allows us to obtain a speed-up since costly computational duplications are avoided when the clustering algorithm $\mathcal{A}$ is hierarchical. Indeed, once the switch is done, it becomes possible to interleave the computation of the measure with the level bottom-up construction of the hierarchical tree underlying the clustering algorithms. Specifically, only one dendrogram construction is required rather than the repeated and partial construction of dendrograms as in the Consensus procedure. Therefore, the main characteristics of agglomerative algorithms are used in full, as briefly discussed in Section 22.5.2.

Procedure FC(Sub, H, X, $\mathcal{A}$, k_{max})

1. For $1 \leq h \leq H$, compute a perturbed data matrix $X^{(h)}$ using the resampling scheme Sub:
    (1a) For $2 \leq k \leq k_{max}$, initialize to empty the set $M^{(k)}$ of connectivity matrices and cluster the elements in k clusters using algorithm $\mathcal{A}$ and $X^{(h)}$. Compute a connectivity matrix $M^{(h,k)}$.
2. For $2 \leq k \leq k_{max}$, based on the connectivity matrices in M, compute a consensus matrix $\mathcal{M}^{(k)}$.
3. Based on the $k_{max} - 1$ consensus matrices, return a prediction for k^*.

The "rule of thumb" one uses to predict k^*, via FC, is the same as for Consensus. An example is reported in Figures 22.10c,d. It is worth pointing out that both the CDFs and Δ curve shapes for FC closely track those of the respective curves for Consensus.

Finally, although the idea behind FC is simple, it has a general applicability that goes beyond the speed-up of Consensus. Indeed, as discussed earlier, all other stability-based methods available in the literature follow the same strategy for the construction of a large number of clustering solutions. Therefore, the FC speed-up applies also to them, although experiments have been conducted only with Consensus since it seems to be the best, in terms of precision, in this category of measures.

22.5.4 Some Benchmarking Results

Using the benchmark 1 data sets, Giancarlo et al. [35] show that there is a natural hierarchy, in terms of time, among the most established internal validation measures used for postgenomic data analysis. Moreover, the faster the measure, the less accurate it is. Based on those findings, FC has been compared in [37, 81] with the fastest and best performing measures from [35], in addition to Consensus. Parts of the results of those experiments are reported in Tables 22.2 and 22.3: They are limited to the benchmark 1 data sets and to the fastest measures. The full set of results is available in [37, 81]. It is worth pointing out, referring the interested reader to [35, 37], that (a) WCSS-R-R5 and FOM-R-R5 are two approximations of WCSS and FOM based on a combination of K-means and hierarchical clustering; (b) G-Gap is a geometric approximation of Gap, where the suffix refers to the clustering algorithm used together with the measure; (c) the suffix succeeding FOM has the same meaning as the one for G-Gap; DIFF-FOM, proposed in [35], is an extension of the Krzanowski and Lai index [52] to FOM—the suffix has the same meaning as the one for G-Gap. For all experiments, the range of values in which k^* has been searched is [2, 30].

22.5.5 Some Recommendations

Based on the above results, FC seems to be the measure of choice for small- and medium-sized data sets. Indeed, when used in conjunction with hierarchical clustering algorithms, it has the same outstanding precision of Consensus while being within only one order of magnitude away from the fastest measures. WCSS is still the fastest and, due to its simplicity, it is very unlikely that a stability-based measure will match its time performance. Therefore,

TABLE 22.2 Summary of Precision for Fastest Measures on Benchmark 1 Data Sets [37]

	CNS Rat	Leukemia	NCI60	Lymphoma	Yeast
WCSS-K-means-C	5	3	8	8	4
WCSS-R-R0	5	4	8	3	4
G-Gap-K-means-R	7	3	4	4	6
G-Gap-R-R5	5	4	2	1	4
FOM-K-means-C	7	8	8	4	4
FOM-K-means-S	5	3	8	8	4
FOM-R-R5	5	3	7	5	4
FOM-Hier-A	7	3	7	6	6
DIFF-FOM-K-means-C	7	3	7	4	3
FC-Hier-A	7	3	8	3	4
FC-Hier-C	5	4	8	5	6
Gold solution	**6**	**3**	**8**	**3**	**5**

Note: FC has been used with $H = 250$ and $p = 80\%$. Each cell in the table displays the prediction of the number of clusters in a data set given by a measure. A number in a circle with a black background indicates a prediction in agreement with the number of classes in the data set; a number in a circle with a white background indicates a prediction that differs, in absolute value, by 1 from the number of classes in the data set; a number in a square indicates a prediction that differs, in absolute value, by 2 from the number of classes in the data set; a number not in a circle/square indicates the remaining predictions.

the one-order-of-magnitude gap in speed between WCSS and FC seems to be a small price to pay for the robustness of the latter measure with respect to the former. As for large data sets, that is, thousands of elements to cluster, none of the most popular measures available in the literature seem to be of any use, due to either lack of precision or to excessive computational demand (week to complete on a state-of-the-art PC) or both.

TABLE 22.3 Summary of Timing for Fastest Measures on Benchmark 1 Data Sets [37]

	CNS Rat	Leukemia	NCI60	Lymphoma
WCSS-K-means-C	1.7×10^3	1.3×10^3	5.0×10^3	4.0×10^3
WCSS-R-R0	1.2×10^3	8.0×10^2	4.1×10^3	3.0×10^3
G-Gap-K-means-R	2.4×10^3	2.0×10^3	8.3×10^4	8.4×10^3
G-Gap-R-R5	1.2×10^3	8.0×10^2	4.5×10^4	3.2×10^3
FOM-K-means-C	1.9×10^4	9.4×10^4	5.5×10^5	2.6×10^5
FOM-K-means-S	2.9×10^4	1.0×10^5	7.1×10^5	3.6×10^5
FOM-R-R5	3.9×10^3	3.7×10^4	2.1×10^5	7.6×10^4
FOM-Hier-A	1.6×10^3	7.5×10^3	5.1×10^4	1.8×10^4
DIFF-FOM-K-means-C	1.9×10^4	9.4×10^4	5.5×10^5	2.6×10^5
FC-Hier-A	5.9×10^4	2.7×10^4	7.0×10^4	6.8×10^4
FC-Hier-C	5.9×10^4	2.7×10^4	6.5×10^4	6.7×10^4

Note: FC has been used with $H = 250$ and $p = 80\%$. Each cell in the table displays timing results reported in milliseconds. Consistent with the studies in [35, 37], only the timing results for CNS Rat, Leukemia, NCI60, and Lymphoma are reported, since for the Yeast and PBM data sets the experiments have been performed on a computer other than the AMD Athlon.

22.6 CONCLUSIONS

This chapter shows a broad study concerning the three steps that mainly distinguish the clustering process: (1) choice of a distance function, (2) choice of a clustering algorithm, and (3) choice of a methodology to assess the statistical significance of clustering solutions. Regarding point 1, we focus on new methodologies to evaluate the performance of a distance function. The results shown in this chapter implicitly strengthen the state of the art and point out the bias between a distance and a clustering algorithm. Point 2 gives an indication that the benchmarking of a new clustering algorithm and a justification of it, in view of what is already available in the Literature, are far more difficult than designing the new algorithm itself. Moreover, a concrete benchmarking example is also provided: the NMF. The results quantify what was intuitively known in the literature: It is a computationally expensive procedure, even on data sets of moderate size, quite manageable by other algorithms, and its use as a clustering algorithm is discouraged. Point 3 gives attention to the so-called *internal validation measures*. Measures in this class assume nothing about the structure of the data set, which is inferred directly from the data. Attention is given to Consensus, and because of its high computational demand, a speed-up of this measure, FC, is proposed. FC is perceived as a nontrivial step forward in the identification of a validation measure for microarray data analysis that is both fast in execution time and accurate in its prediction of the number of clusters in a data set.

ACKNOWLEDGMENT

The authors are grateful to Margaret Gagie for proofreading and comments on earlier versions of this chapter.

REFERENCES

1. Broad institute. Available: `http://www.broadinstitute.org/cgi-bin/cancer/publications/pub_paper.cgi?mode=view&paper_id=89`.
2. NCI 60 Cancer Microarray Project. Available: `http://genome-www.stanford.edu/NCI60`.
3. Stanford microarray database. Available: `http://genome-www5.stanford.edu/`.
4. A. A. Alizadeh, M. B. Eisen, R. E. Davis, C. Ma, I. S. Lossos, A. Rosenwald, J. C. Boldrick, H. Sabet, T. Tran, X. Yu, J. I. Powell, L. Yang, G. E. Marti, T. Moore, J. Jr Hudson, L. Lu, D. B. Lewis, R. Tibshirani, G. Sherlock, W. C. Chan, T. C. Greiner, D. D. Weisenburger, J. O. Armitage, R. Warnke, R. Levy, W. Wilson, M. R. Grever, J. C. Byrd, D. Botstein, P. O. Brown, and L. M. Staudt. Distinct types of diffuse large b-cell lymphoma identified by gene expression profiling. *Nature*, 403:503–511, 2000.
5. B. Andreopoulos, A. An, X. Wang, and M. Schroeder. A roadmap of clustering algorithms: Finding a match for a biomedical application. *Brief. Bioinformatics*, 10:297–314, 2009.
6. A. J. Bell and T. J. Sejnowski. The "independent components" of natural scenes are edge filters. *Vis. Res.*, 37:3327–3338, 1997.
7. A. Ben-Dor, R. Shamir, and Z. Yakhini. Clustering of gene expression patterns. *J. Computat. Biol.*, 6:281–297, 1999.
8. A. Ben-Hur, A. Elisseeff, and I. Guyon. A stability based method for discovering structure in clustering data. In *Seventh Pacific Symposium on Biocomputing.*, 2002, pp. 6–17.

9. A. Bertoni and G. Valentini. Randomized maps for assessing the reliability of patients clusters in DNA microarray data analyses. *Artif. Intell. Med.*, 37:85–109, 2006.

10. P. Bertrand and G. Bel Mufti. Loevinger's measures of rule quality for assessing cluster stability. *Computat. Stat. Data Anal.*, 50:992–1015, 2006.

11. A. Borodin, R. Ostrovsky, and Y. Rabani. Subquadratic approximation algorithms for clustering problems in high dimensional space. *Machine Learning*, 56:153–167, 2004.

12. J. N. Breckenridge. Replicating cluster analysis: Method, consistency, and validity. *Multivariate Behav. Res.*, 24:147–161, 1989.

13. L. Breiman. Bagging predictors. *Machine Learning*, 24:123–140, 1996.

14. J. P. Brunet, P. Tamayo, T. R. Golub, and J. P. Mesirov. Metagenes and molecular pattern discovery using matrix factorization. *Proc. Nat. Acad. Sci. USA*, 101:4164–4169, 2004.

15. A. Cichocki and S. Amari. *Adaptive Blind Signal and Image Processing: Learning Algorithms and Applications.* Wiley, West Sussex, United Kingdom, 2002.

16. T. H. Cormen, C. Stein, R. L. Rivest, and C. E. Leiserson. *Introduction to Algorithms.* McGraw-Hill Higher Education, Boston, MA, 2001.

17. I. G. Costa, F. A. de Carvalho, and M. C. de Souto. Comparative analysis of clustering methods for gene expression time course data. *Genet. Mol. Biol.*, 27:623–631, 2004.

18. T. M. Cover and J. A. Thomas. *Elements of Information Theory.* Wiley-Interscience, New York, 1991.

19. C. Daub, R. Steuer, J. Selbig, and S. Kloska. Estimating mutual information using b-spline functions—An improved similarity measure for analysing gene expression data. *BMC Bioinformatics*, 5:118, 2004.

20. K. Devarajan. Non-negative matrix factorization: An analytical and interpretive tool in computational biology. *PLoS Computat. Biol.*, 4:e1000029, 2008.

21. E. Deza and M. M. Deza. *Dictionary of Distances.* Elsevier, Amsterdam, The Netherlands, 2006.

22. P. D'Haeseleer. How does gene expression cluster work? *Nat. Biothechnol.*, 23:1499–1501, 2006.

23. V. Di Gesú, R. Giancarlo, G. Lo Bosco, A. Raimondi, and D. Scaturro. Genclust: A genetic algorithm for clustering gene expression data. *BMC Bioinformatics*, 6:289, 2005.

24. E. Diday and J. C. Simons. Clustering analysis. In K. S. Fu (Ed.), *Digital Pattern Recognition.* Springer, Heidelberg, Germany, 1976, pp. 47–92.

25. S. Dudoit and J. Fridlyand. A prediction-based resampling method for estimating the number of clusters in a data set. *Genome Biol.*, 3(7):research0036.21, 2002.

26. M. B. Eisen, P. T. Spellman, P. O. Brown, and D. Botstein. Cluster analysis and display of genome-wide expression patterns. *Proc. Nat. Acad. Sci. USA*, 95:14863–14868, 1998.

27. D. Fisher and P. Hoffman. The adjusted Rand statistic: A SAS macro. *Psychometrika*, 53:417–423, 1988.

28. P. Flicek. The need for speed. *Genome Biol.*, 10:212, 2009.

29. G. Frahling and C. Sohler. A fast K-means implementation using coresets. In N. Amenta and O. Cheong (Eds.), *Proceedings of the Twenty-Second Annual Symposium on Computational Geometry 2006*, Sedona, Arizona, USA, June 5–7, 2006, ACM, pp. 135–143.

30. E. Freyhult, M. Landfors, J. Önskog, T. R. Hvidsten, and P. Rydén. Challenges in microarray class discovery: A comprehensive examination of normalization, gene selection and clustering. *BMC Bioinformatics*, 11:503, 2010.

31. R. Gaujoux and C. Seoighe. A flexible R package for non-negative matrix factorization. *BMC Bioinformatics*, 11:367, 2010.

32. R. Gentleman, B. Ding, S. Dudoit, and J. Ibrahim. Distance measures in DNA microarray data analysis. In W. Wong, M. Gail, K. Krickeberg, A. Tsiatis, and J. Samet (Eds.), *Bioinformatics and*

Computational Biology Solutions Using R and Bioconductor, Statistics for Biology and Health. Springer, New York, 2005, pp. 189–208.

33. R. Giancarlo, G. Lo Bosco, and L. Pinello. Distance functions, clustering algorithms and microarray data analysis. In C. Blum and R. Battiti, (Eds.), *Learning and Intelligent Optimization*, Vol. 6073 of *Lecture Notes in Computer Science*. Springer, Heidelberg, Germany, 2010, pp. 125–138.

34. R. Giancarlo, G. Lo Bosco, L. Pinello, and F. Utro. The three steps of clustering in the postgenomic era: A synopsis. In R. Rizzo and P. Lisboa (Eds.), *Computational Intelligence Methods for Bioinformatics and Biostatistics*, Vol. 6685 of *Lecture Notes in Computer Science*. Springer, Heidelberg, Germany, 2011, pp. 13–30.

35. R. Giancarlo, D. Scaturro, and F. Utro. Computational cluster validation for microarray data analysis: Experimental assessment of Clest, Consensus Clustering, Figure of Merit, Gap Statistics and Model Explorer. *BMC Bioinformatics*, 9:462, 2008.

36. R. Giancarlo, D. Scaturro, and F. Utro. Statistical indices for computational and data driven class discovery in microarray data. In *Biological Data Mining*, Chapman & Hall/CRC Data Mining and Knowledge Discovery. CRC Press, Boca Raton, FL, 2009, pp. 295–335.

37. R. Giancarlo and F. Utro. Speeding up the consensus clustering methodology for microarray data analysis. *Algorithms Mol. Biol.*, 6:1, 2011.

38. F. D. Gibbons and F. P. Roth. Judging the quality of gene expression-based clustering methods using gene annotation. *Genome Res.*, 12:1574–1581, 2002.

39. G. H. Golub and C. F. Van Loan. *Matrix Computations*, 3rd ed. Johns Hopkins University Press, Baltimore, MD, 1996.

40. A. D. Gordon. Null models in cluster validation. In W. Gaul and D. Pfeifer (Eds.), *From Data to Knowledge: Theoretical and Practical Aspects of Classification, Data Analysis, and Knowledge Organization*, Springer, Heidelberg, 1996, pp. 32–44.

41. J. Handl, J. Knowles, and D. B. Kell. Computational cluster validation in post-genomic data analysis. *Bioinformatics*, 21:3201–3212, 2005.

42. J. A. Hanley and B. J. McNeil. The meaning and use of the area under a receiver operating characteristic (ROC) curve. *Radiology*, 143:29–36, 1982.

43. P. Hansen and P. Jaumard. Cluster analysis and mathematical programming. *Math. Prog.*, 79: 191–215, 1997.

44. J. A. Hartigan. *Clustering Algorithms*. Wiley, New York, 1975.

45. E. Hartuv, A. Schmitt, J. Lange, S. Meier-Ewert, H. Lehrach, and R. Shamir. An algorithm for clustering of cDNAs for gene expression analysis using short oligonucleotide fingerprints. *Genomics*, 66:249–256, 2000.

46. T. Hastie, R. Tibshirani, and J. Friedman. *The Elements of Statistical Learning*. Springer, New York, 2003.

47. A. K. Jain and R. C. Dubes. *Algorithms for Clustering Data*. Prentice-Hall, Englewood Cliffs, NJ, 1988.

48. A. K. Jain, M. N. Murty, and P. J. Flynn. Data clustering: A review. *ACM Comput. Surv.*, 31:264–323, 1999.

49. J. J. Jay, J. D. Eblen, Y. Zhang, M. Benson, A. D. Perkins, A. M. Saxton, B. H. Voy, E. J. Chesler, and M. A. Langston. A systematic comparison of genome scale clustering algorithms. In J. Chen, J. Wang, and A. Zelikovsky (Eds.), *International Symposium on Bioinformatics Research and Applications*, Vol. 6674 of *Lecture Notes in Computer Science*. Springer, Heidelberg, Germany, 2011, pp. 416–427.

50. L. Kaufman and P. J. Rousseeuw. *Finding Groups in Data: An Introduction to Cluster Analysis*. Wiley, New York, 1990.

51. J. Kraus and H. Kestler. A highly efficient multi-core algorithm for clustering extremely large data sets. *BMC Bioinformatics*, 11:169, 2010.

52. W. Krzanowski and Y. Lai. A criterion for determining the number of groups in a data set using sum of squares clustering. *Biometrics*, 44:23–34, 1985.

53. A. Langville, C. Meyer, R. Albright, J. Cox, and D. Duling. Algorithms, initializations, and convergence for the non-negative matrix factorization. In *Twelfth Annual SIGKDD International Conference on Knowledge Discovery and Data Mining*. 2006.

54. D. D. Lee and H. S. Seung. Learning the parts of objects by non-negative matrix factorization. *Nature*, 401:788–791, 1999.

55. E. Levine and E. Domany. Resampling method for unsupervised estimation of cluster validity. *Neural Computat.*, 13:2573–2593, 2001.

56. T. Mehta, M. Tanik, and D. B. Allison. Towards sound epistemological foundations of statistical methods for high-dimensional biology. *Nat. Gen.*, 36:943–947, 2004.

57. C. E. Metz. Basic principles of ROC analysis. *Semin. Nucl. Med.*, 8:283–298, 1978.

58. G. S. Michaels, D. B. Carr, M. Askenazi, S. Fuhrman, X. Wen, and R. Somogyi. Cluster analysis and data visualization of large-scale gene expression data. *Pac. Symp. Biocomput.*, 3:42–53, 1998.

59. B. Mirkin. *Mathematical Classification and Clustering*. Kluwer Academic, London, 1996.

60. S. Monti, P. Tamayo, J. Mesirov, and T. Golub. Consensus clustering: A resampling-based method for class discovery and visualization of gene expression microarray data. *Machine Learning*, 52:91–118, 2003.

61. P. Paatero. Least squares formulation of robust non-negative factor analysis. *Chemomet. Intell. Lab. Syst.*, 37:23–25, 1997.

62. P. Paatero. A weighted non-negative least squares algorithm for three-way 'PARAFAC' factor analysis. *Chemomet. Intell. Lab. Syst.*, 38:223–242, 1997.

63. P. Paatero. The multilinear engine: A table-driven, least squares program for solving multilinear problems, including the n-way parallel factor analysis model. *J. Computat. Graph. Stat.*, 8:854–888, 1999.

64. P. Paatero and U. Tapper. Positive matrix factorization: A non-negative factor model with optimal utilization of error estimates of data values. *Environmetrics*, 5:111–126, 1994.

65. I. Priness, O. Maimon, and I. Ben-Gal. Evaluation of gene-expression clustering via mutual information distance measure. *BMC Bioinformatics*, 8:1–12, 2007.

66. J. A. Rice. *Mathematical Statistics and Data Analysis*. Wadsworth, Pacific Grove, CA, 1996.

67. V. Roth, T. Lange, M. Braun, and J. Buhmann. A resampling approach to cluster validation. In *Proc. 15th Symposium in Computational Statistics*. 2002, pp. 123–128.

68. S. Salvador and P. Chan. Determining the number of clusters/segments in hierarchical clustering/segmentation algorithms. In *Proc. 16th IEEE International Conference on Tools with Artificial Intelligence (ICTAI)*. 2004, pp. 576–584.

69. S. Seal, S. Comarina, and S. Aluru. An optimal hierarchical clustering algorithm for gene expression data. *Inform. Process. Lett.*, 93:143–147, 2004.

70. R. Shamir and R. Sharan. Algorithmic approaches to clustering gene expression data. In T. Jiang, T. Smith, Y. Xu, and M. Q. Zhang (Eds.), *Current Topics in Computational Biology*, Computational Molecular Biology. MIT Press, Cambridge, MA, 2003, pp. 120–161.

71. R. Sharan, A. Maron-Katz, and R. Shamir. CLICK and EXPANDER: A system for clustering and visualizing gene expression data. *Bioinformatics*, 19:1787–1799, 2003.

72. B. W. Silverman. *Density Estimation for Statistics and Data Analysis*, Chapman & Hall/CRC Monographs on Statistics & Applied Probability. Chapman and Hall/CRC, London, 1986.

73. T. P. Speed. *Statistical Analysis of Gene Expression Microarray Data*. Chapman & Hall/CRC, Boca Raton, FL, 2003.

74. P. T. Spellman, G. Sherlock, M. Q. Zhang, V. R. Iyer, K. Anders, M. B. Eisen, P. O. Brown, D. Botstein, and B. Futcher. Comprehensive identification of cell cycle regulated genes of the yeast *Saccharomyces cerevisiae* by microarray hybridization. *Mol. Biol. Cell*, 9:3273–3297, 1998.

75. R. Steuer, J. Kurths, C. O. Daub, J. Weise, and J. Selbig. The mutual information: Detecting and evaluating dependencies between variables. *Bioinformatics*, 18:S231–S240, 2002.

76. P. Tamayo, D. Slonim, J. Mesirov, S. Zhu, S. Kitareewan, E. Dmitrovsky, E. S. Lander, and T. R. Golub. Interpreting patterns of gene expression with self-organizing maps: Methods and application to hematopoietic differentiation. *Proc. Nat. Acad. Sci. USA*, 96:2907–2912, 1999.

77. R. Tibshirani, G. Walther, and T. Hastie. Estimating the number of clusters in a data set via the gap statistics. *J. R. Stat. Soc. B.*, 2:411–423, 2001.

78. N. Tishby and N. Slonim. Data clustering by Markovian relaxation and the Information Bottleneck Method. *Adv. Neural Inform. Proc. Syst.*, Papers from Neural Information Processing Systems, 13:640–646, 2001.

79. L. N. Trefethen and D. Bau. *Numerical Linear Algebra*. Society for Industrial and Applied Mathematics, Philadelphia, NJ, 1997.

80. J. A. Tropp. Literature survey: Non-negative matrix factorization. Available: `http://citeseerx.ist.psu.edu/viewdoc/summary?doi=10.1.1.84.9645`.

81. F. Utro. Algorithms for internal validation clustering measures in the Post Genomic Era. Ph.D. Dissertation. University of Palermo. Available: `http://arxiv.org/abs/1102.2915v1`, 2011.

82. G. Valentini. Mosclust: A software library for discovering significant structures in biomolecular data. *Bioinformatics*, 23:387–389, 2007.

83. J. H. Ward. Hierarchical grouping to optimize an objective function. *J. Am. Stat. Assoc.*, 58:236–244, 1963.

84. X. Wen, S. Fuhrman, G. S. Michaels, G. S. Carr, D. B. Smith, J. L. Barker, and R. Somogyi. Large scale temporal gene expression mapping of central nervous system development. *Proc. Nat. Acad. Sci. USA*, 95:334–339, 1998.

85. Y. Xu, V. Olman, and D. Xu. Clustering gene expression data using a graph-theoretic approach: An application of minimum spanning tree. *Bioinformatics*, 18:526–535, 2002.

86. K. Y. Yeung. Cluster analysis of gene expression data. Ph.D. Dissertation. University of Washington, 2001.

87. K. Y. Yeung, D. R. Haynor, and W. L. Ruzzo. Validating clustering for gene expression data. *Bioinformatics*, 17:309–318, 2001.

CHAPTER 23

CLUSTERING ALGORITHMS OF MICROARRAY DATA

HAIFA BEN SABER,[1,2] MOURAD ELLOUMI,[1,3] and MOHAMED NADIF[4]

[1]Laboratory of Technologies of Information and Communication and Electrical Engineering (LaTICE)
[2]University of Tunis, Tunisia
[3]University of Tunis-El Manar, Tunisia
[4]LIPADE, University of Paris-Descartes, Paris, France

23.1 INTRODUCTION

Microarray data can be represented by a data matrix M, where the ith row corresponds to the ith gene, the jth column corresponds to the jth condition, and the cell m_{ij} represents the expression level of the ith gene under the jth condition [18, 25]. In this chapter, we make a brief survey on clustering algorithms of microarray data. There are three main types of clustering algorithms: *geometric* [4], *model based* [5, 6, 14, 19], and *formal concepts based* [24, 28]. So, the rest of the chapter is organized as follows: In Section 23.2, we briefly review *geometric* clustering algorithms. In Section 23.3, we present *model-based* clustering algorithms. Section 23.4 is devoted to *formal concepts–based clustering* algorithms. In Section 23.5, we review some clustering webtools. In Section 23.6, we present microarray data sets commonly used. Finally, in the last section, we conclude our chapter.

23.2 GEOMETRIC CLUSTERING ALGORITHMS

In geometric clustering algorithms, we distinguish between *hierarchical* and *partitioning* clustering algorithms [4, 8, 9, 17].

23.2.1 Hierarchical Clustering Algorithms

The aim of *hierachical* algorithms is to create a hierachical decomposition of a set of objects E. On E we have a dissimilarity measure such that the closest objects are grouped in the clusters with the smallest index. The *index* on a hierarchy H is a mapping denoted by i from H to $\mathbf{R}^+$ verifying the following properties: $h \subset h'$ and $h \neq h' \Rightarrow i(h) < i(h')$ (i is a

Biological Knowledge Discovery Handbook: Preprocessing, Mining, and Postprocessing of Biological Data,
First Edition. Edited by Mourad Elloumi and Albert Y. Zomaya.
© 2014 John Wiley & Sons, Inc. Published 2014 by John Wiley & Sons, Inc.

strictly increasing function) and $\forall x \in E \; i(\{x\}) = 0$. There exists two principal approaches, *divisive* and *agglomerative*, which we describe below; for details see, for instance, [21].

- *Divisive Approach*   this approach is also called a *top-down* approach. We start with just one cluster containing all objects. In each successive iteration, we split up clusters into two or more clusters until generally each object is in one cluster. Note that other stop conditions can be used, and the division into clusters is defined by the verification or not of a property.
- *Agglomerative Approach*   Opposed to the divisive approach, we start by assuming n clusters, where each object forms a singleton cluster. In each successive iteration, we merge the closest clusters until we obtain one cluster which is the set E. In the following, we focus on this approach, which is the most frequently used.

While in the process of grouping the clusters in the agglomerative approach, it is necessary to define a distance between the clusters in order to merge the closest ones. Generally, from the dissimilarity measure on E, we define a *distance D* between the clusters. In fact, D is just a dissimilarity measure. The measures commonly used are *single* linkage, *complete* linkage, *average* linkage, and the *Ward* criterion. Now, we briefly present the different steps of the algorithm:

Initialization   Each object is a singleton partition. Compute the dissimilarity measure between these objects.
Repeat

- Merge two closest clusters according to D.
- Compute the distance between the obtained new cluster and the old clusters not merged.

Until   the number of clusters is equal to 1.

The advantages of agglomerative hierarchical clustering algorithms are as follows:

- They can produce an ordering of the objects (genes/conditions) which may be informative for data display.
- They generate smaller clusters which can be helpful for analysis.

The drawbacks of agglomerative hierarchical clustering algorithms are as follows:

- They cannot relocate objects (genes/conditions) that may have been badly clustered at an earlier stage.
- The use of different metrics for measuring distances between clusters may generate different results.

23.2.2 Partitioning Clustering Algorithms

Partitioning clustering consists in splitting the objects (genes/conditions) into K homogeneous clusters. The most popular partitionning algorithms are K-means and *self-organizing maps* (SOMs):

1. The K-means algorithm is one of the simplest clustering algorithm. The K-means version commonly used is due to Forgy [12]. It follows a simple and easy way to cluster given objects (genes or conditions) in a number K of clusters (K is fixed a priori). K-means operates as follows:

   (a) Randomly select K objects of E which form the K first cluster means.

   (b) While not converging:

      (i) Assign each object of E to the cluster with the nearest cluster mean. If this one is not unique, the object is assigned to the cluster with the smallest subscript.

      (ii) The cluster means computed become the new cluster means.

   The advantages of K-means are:

   - If K is small, then with a large number of variables K-means may be faster than hierarchical clustering algorithms. In fact, it is scalable.
   - K-means may produce tighter clusters than hierarchical clustering algorithms.

   The drawbacks of K-means are:

   - Different initial partitions may affect the final result clustering.
   - It is difficult to predict the best value of K that will produce the best clustering.
   - It tends to give spherical clusters. Note that model-based clustering allows us to overcome this drawback.

2. The SOM algorithm, introduced by Kohonen [7, 15], can be viewed as a spatially smoothed version of K-means algorithm clustering. SOM operates as follows: First, it randomly choose nodes, that is, centers of clusters of genes. Then, at each iteration, it chooses an object (gene) and finds a node that is the closest to the object according to the Euclidean distance. If the object is not closest to the node of its own cluster, then SOM moves it into the cluster of the closest node and defines the new nodes of both clusters. SOM repeats this process until no object moves from one cluster to another. By its simplicity SOM has had much success for decades even if, until now, there is not any criterion whose optimization implies the formula of the updates of the cluster means. Actually, the proof of the convergence in the general context does not exist. The convergence has been proved only on special cases and in particular for one-dimensional data.

23.3 MODEL-BASED CLUSTERING ALGORITHMS

Model-based clustering algorithms can be used for different types of data by using appropriated *mixtures* such as *Gaussian, von Mises–Fisher, multinomial*, and *Bernoulli*. Model-based clustering considers two approaches: *maximum likelihood* (ML) and *classification maximum likelihood* (CML). The former is based on the maximization of the observed likelihood of data, and the latter is based on the maximization of the classification (or complete data) likelihood. These maximizations can be performed respectively by the *expectation–maximization* (EM) [1] and *classification* EM (CEM) algorithms [6]. Note that this approach offers considerable flexibility and provides solutions to the problem of the number of clusters. Its associated estimators of posterior probabilities give rise to fuzzy or hard clustering using the *maximum a posteriori principle* (MAP). Hereafter we review the definition of the *mixture model* and classical clustering algorithms used.

23.3.1   Finite-Mixture Model

Finite-mixture models underpin a variety of techniques in major areas of statistics, including cluster analysis [19]. With mixture model–based clustering, it is assumed that the data to be clustered are generated by a *mixture* of underlying probability distributions in which each component represents a different cluster. Given observations $x = (x_1, \ldots, x_m)$, $\varphi_k(x_i; \alpha_k)$ is the density of an observation x_i from the kth component, where the α_k's are the corresponding parameters of the K components in the mixture. The *probability density function* is

$$f(x_i; \theta) = \sum_{k=1}^{K} \pi_k \varphi_k(x_i; \alpha_k)$$

where π_k is the probability that an observation belongs to the kth component and θ is the vector of the unknown parameters $(\pi_1, \ldots, \pi_K; \alpha_1, \ldots, \alpha_K)$.

23.3.2   EM Algorithm

The EM algorithm is a method for maximizing the log-likelihood $L(\theta)$ iteratively using the maximization of the conditional expectation of the complete-data log-likelihood given a previous current estimate $\theta^{(c)}$ and the observed data x. In mixture modeling, we take the complete data to be the vector (x, z) where the unobservable $m \times K$ binary matrix $z = (z_{ik})$ indicates the label data: $z_{ik} = 1$ if x_i belongs to the kth component and $z_{ik} = 0$ otherwise. The optimized conditional expectation can then be written as

$$Q(\theta, \theta^{(c)}) = \sum_{i,k} s_{ik}^{(c)} \log[\pi_k \varphi_k(x_i; \alpha_k)]$$

where

$$s_{ik}^{(c)} = P(z_{ik} = 1 | x, \theta^{(c)}) = \frac{\pi_k^{(c)} \varphi_k(x_i; \alpha_k^{(c)})}{\sum_{k'=1}^{g} \pi_{k'}^{(c)} \varphi_{k'}(x_i; \alpha_{k'}^{(c)})}$$

denotes the conditional probability, given x and $\theta^{(c)}$ that x_i arises from the mixture component with density $\varphi_k(x_i; \alpha_k)$. Each iteration of EM has two steps, an E-step and an M-step, defined as follows:

- The estimation step computes the current posterior probabilities $s_{ik}^{(c)}$.
- The maximization step computes the ML estimates $\theta^{(c+1)} = (\pi_k^{(c)}, \alpha_k^{(c)})$.

Note that in the M-step this leads to $\pi_k^{(c+1)} = \sum_{i,k} s_{ik}^{(c)} / m$ and the exact formulas for $\alpha_k^{(c+1)}$ will depend on the involved parametric family of distribution probabilities.

At convergence the clusters are deduced by using the MAP.

23.3.3 Classification EM Algorithm

The *classification* EM (CEM) algorithm is seen as a hard version of EM [6]; it is performed in each iteration (c) by substituting $Q(\theta, \theta^{(c)})$ by $L_C(\theta)$, a hard expectation where the s_{ik}'s are converted to z_{ik}'s:

$$L_C(\theta) = \sum_{i=1}^{m} \sum_{k=1}^{K} z_{ik}^{(c)} \log[\pi_k \varphi_k(x_i; \alpha_k)]$$

The main modifications imported to EM therefore concern the conditional maximization of complete data log-likelihoods with respect to z given θ, and the missing component indicator vectors (z_{ik}) of each sample point are included in the data set. Although the estimates of the CML don't converge to the ML estimates [19].

Starting from an initial θ^0, a classification step is introduced between the two steps E and M. The classifcation step consists in assigning each point x_i to the component which maximizes the conditional probability s_{ik}. Hence, the CEM estimators are

$$\pi_k^{(c+1)} = \frac{\sum_{i=1}^{m} z_{ik}^{(c)}}{m}$$

and $\alpha_k^{(c+1)}$ depends on the parameter of the chosen distribution $\varphi_k(.; \alpha_k)$. In particular, note that when we consider the Gaussian mixture model under certain constraints, CEM is an extension of the K-means algorithm.

23.3.4 Stochastic EM Algorithm

The *stochastic* EM (SEM) algorithm [5] is a stochastic version of EM. It incorporates between the E- and the M-steps a restoration of the unknown component labels $(z_{ik}, i = 1, \ldots, m; k = 1, \ldots, K)$ by drawing them at random from their current conditional distribution, starting from an initial parameter. It is a stochastic step S in which the algorithm assigns each point at random to one of the mixture components according to the multinomial distribution e_{ik} with parameters the values of the posterior probabilities s_{ik}. The algorithm is as follows:

- *E-step:* Compute the conditional probabilities $s_{ik}^{(c)}$ $(i = 1, \ldots, m, k = 1, \ldots, K)$.
- *The stochastic S-step:* Assign each point x_i at random to a component according to the multinomial distribution with parameters to produce a partition $z^{(c)}$.
- *M-step:* Compute the ML estimator $\theta^{(c+1)}$ using the partition result of the S-step.

Note that this stochastic version does not converge pointwise, and SEM generates a Markov chain in which the distribution is more or less concentrated around the ML estimates.

23.4 FORMAL CONCEPT–BASED CLUSTERING ALGORITHMS

The *analysis of formal concepts* (AFC) [21] is a domain of applied mathematics which restructures the theory of the lattices to facilitate its use in applications of the real world and to also allow the interpretation of its concepts from the theoretical framework by mathematicians as well as nonmathematicians. The basic notions of lattice theory are *binary relation*, *formal context*, and *formal concept*.

The construction of the Galois lattice of a binary relation can be broken up into three steps: enumeration of the maximum rectangles (closed), search for a partial order relation between these rectangles, and construction of the lattice chart [15, 20]. We distinguish three types of formal concepts–based clustering algorithms [11, 20]: *batch*, *incremental*, and *assembly*, by considering the distribution of the algorithms, according to their strategies of data acquisition starting from a formal context.

23.4.1 Batch Algorithms

Batch algorithms are the first generation of the algorithms of extraction of the Galois lattices. By taking in the entire formal context, these algorithms calculate the formal concepts and the order between these concepts simultaneously or sequentially. Among the most known of these algorithms is the one by Chein [2, 20, 23] generating the concepts by levels: The algorithm is iterative. Its starting point is the set L_1 of couples (X_i, Y_i) representing the lines of the formal context. To each step i, the algorithm starts from a set L_i and builds the elements of L_{i+1}. An element (X_3, Y_3) of L_{i+1} is obtained by combining two elements (X_1, Y_1) and (X_2, Y_2) from L_i as follows: $X_3 = X_1 \cup X_2$ and $Y_3 = Y_1 \cap Y_2$. The elements of L_i included in at least an element of L_{i-1} are not maximum and are thus removed. The algorithm stops when L_{i+1} contain less than two elements. The elements not removed after the stop of the algorithm are the concepts of the formal context considered. The time complexity of Chein's algorithm is $O(|E|^3|F||L|)$, where $|E|$ is the number of objects in the context, $|F|$ the number of attributes, and $|L|$ the number of formal concepts in the obtained lattice.

The sets of maximum rectangles calculated by Chein's algorithm [20] starting from the formal context is given in Table 23.1. The barred rectangles (Table 23.1) correspond to nonmaximum rectangles. The rectangles which contain them are indicated in parentheses and the iteration during which they were calculated is given by the number of asterisks. For example, 1 X adg **(12 X adg) is interpreted as follows: The rectangle 1 X adg is not maximum; it is replaced by 12 X adg found with the second iteration of the algorithm.

23.4.2 Incremental Algorithms

The incremental algorithms [16, 20] consider the formal context line by line (or column by column) and build the Galois lattice by successive additions of lines or columns while preserving its structure. With a step K, the concepts corresponding to K first lines of the formal context are calculated. The addition of the $(K + 1)$th line involves modification of part of the concepts calculated at step K and the addition of possible new concepts. The incremental algorithms manage the dynamic contexts, where the number of objects and/or attributes can evolve, without having to compute again the lattice from zero following a modification of the context. The first incremental algorithm published in 1978 by Norris [21] remains among the most powerful algorithms. The time complexity of Norris's algorithm is $O(|E|^3|F||L|)$.

TABLE 23.1 Sets of Maximum Rectangles Calculated by Algorithm of Chein

L_1		L_2		L_3	L_4
~~1 × adg~~	**(12 × adg)	12 × adg		12349 × a	∅
~~2 × adg~~	**(12 × adg)	~~13 × ad~~	**(134 × ad)	3456789 × f	
~~3 × adf~~	**(34 × adf)	~~134 × ad~~	**(1234 × ad)		
~~4 × adf~~	**(34 × adf)	~~19 × a~~	**(129 × a)		
~~5 × cef~~	**(56 × cef)	1234 × ad			
~~6 × cef~~	**(56 × cef)	~~129 × a~~	***(12349 × a)		
~~7 × bef~~	**(78 × bef)	34 × adf			
~~8 × bef~~	**(78 × bef)	~~35 × f~~	**(356 × f)		
9 × aef		356 × f	**(3567 × f)		
		~~3567 × f~~	**(35678 × f)		
		~~35678 × f~~	**(345678 × f)		
		~~39 × af~~	**(349 × af)		
		~~345678 × f~~	***(3456789 × f)		
		349 × af			
		56 × cef			
		~~57 × ef~~	**(578 × ef)		
		~~578 × ef~~	**(5789 × ef)		
		~~5789 × ef~~	**(56789 × ef)		
		56789 × ef			
		78 × bef			

23.4.3 Assembly Algorithms

These algorithms constitute an evolution of the incremental algorithms which generalize the incremental character to set (groups) objects/attributes [20]. They divide a formal context into two parts, vertically or horizontally, and then calculate the lattice of concepts corresponding to each part and finally assemble the lattices obtained in only one (Figure 23.1).

The steps of the incremental construction of the lattice of concepts correspond to the formal context. The addition of a new line to the lattice built is symbolized by $(\overrightarrow{+n})$, where n indicates the number of the line considered. The modifications generated by such an addition are indicated in red on the lattice. To illustrate the principle of this approach, we again consider the formal context given in Figure 23.2, where one context will divide into two ($\mathbb{C}1$ on the left and $\mathbb{C}2$ on the right). The lattices $P(\mathbb{C}1)$ and $P(\mathbb{C}2)$ correspond to the two contexts $\mathbb{C}1$ and $\mathbb{C}2$, and it is the same for the bond between the Galois lattices $P(\mathbb{C}1)$ and $P(\mathbb{C}2)$ and those of the lattice $P(\mathbb{C})$.

23.5 CLUSTERING WEBTOOLS

In this section, we introduce some clustering webtools.

WLPT@DNA-Array WLPT@DNA-Array is a webtool for the management and analysis of DNA microarrays by using *weighted trees* [8, 26]. It computes the *appearance probability* of a DNA microarray, to compare the informational distances in the expression of

(a)

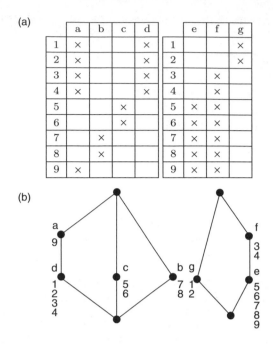

(b)

FIGURE 23.1   Concepts lattice corresponding to the formal contexts.

genes between DNA microarrays, and determines the group of candidate genes related to a pathology.

WLPT@DNA-Array is available at `http://www.genopole-lille.fr/spip`.

Lattice Miner   *Lattice Miner* (LM) is a formal concept analysis webtool for the construction, visualization, and manipulation of concept lattices. It allows the generation of formal concepts and association rules as well as the transformation of formal contexts via apposition, subposition, reduction, and object/attribute generalization and the manipulation of concept lattices via approximation, projection, and selection. LM also allows the drawing of nested line diagrams.

LM is available at `http://sourceforge.net/projects/lattice-miner/`.

FAM   *Formal concept Analysis–based association rule Miner* (FAM) was designed and implemented considering a user's facility of information retrieval such as context editing, concept and lattice exploring, query submitting, and showing the association rules in response to the query.

FAM is available at `http://bike.snu.ac.kr/`.

BicAT   *Biclustering Analysis Toolbox* (BicAT) is a webtool to help biologists with the analysis and exploration of gene expression data, for example, microarrays. It provides a number of algorithms to find biclusters (or clusters) within expression data as well as a number of postprocessing utilities useful for further analysis of the results.

BicAT is available at `http://www.tik.ee.ethz.ch/sop/bicat/`.

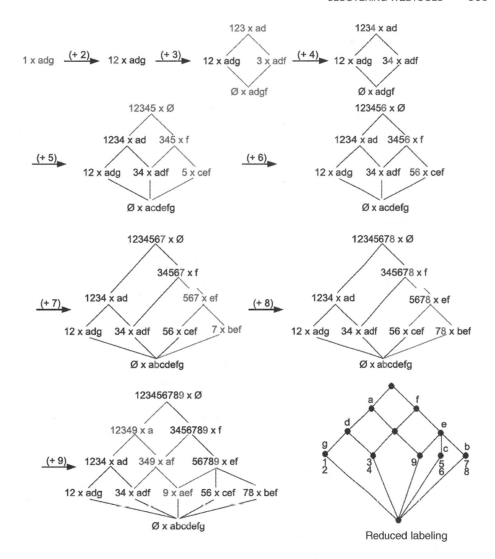

FIGURE 23.2   Steps of incremental concept lattice construction corresponding to formal context.

SPECLUST   SPECLUST is a webtool for hierarchical clustering of peptide mass spectra obtained from protease-digested proteins. Mass spectra are clustered according to the peptide masses they contain such that mass spectra containing similar masses are clustered together. Hierarchical clustering of *mass spectra* (MS) with SPECLUST can in particular be useful for MS screening of large proteomic data sets derived from 2D gels. SPECLUST can also be used to identify masses shared by mass spectra. Masses present in the majority of the mass spectra in a data set are likely to be contaminants. With SPECLUST, MS/MS can be focused on noncontaminant shared masses in a cluster, facilitating investigations of protein isoforms. Within a cluster, shared and unique masses represent peptides from regions that are similar and different, respectively, between protein isoforms. Taken together, SPECLUST is a versatile tool for analysis of mass spectrometry data.

SPECLUST is available at `http://bioinfo.thep.lu.se/speclust.html`.

Mixmod The *Mixture Modelling* (Mixmod) webtool fits mixture models to a given data set with a density estimation, a clustering, or a discriminant analysis. A large variety of algorithms to estimate the mixture parameters are proposed (EM, CEM, SEM) and it is possible to combine them to lead to different strategies in order to get a sensible maximum of the likelihood (or complete-data likelihood) function. Mixmod is currently focused on multivariate Gaussian mixtures and 14 different Gaussian models. It can be considered according to different assumptions on the component presented by the variance matrix eigenvalue decomposition. Moreover, different information criteria for choosing a parsimonious model (the number of mixture components, for instance), some of them favoring either a cluster analysis or a discriminant analysis view point, are included. Written in *C*++, Mixmod is interfaced with Scilab and Matlab.

Mixmod, the statistical documentation, and the user guide are available at `http://www-math.univ-fco mte.fr/mixmod/index.php`.

23.6 MICROARRAY DATA SETS

Real data are also used because artificial data can only be used to test the effect of certain aspects such as noise level and overlap degree of the bicluster problems on different models/algorithms. We introduce the AML/ALL, *central nervous system* (CNS), lung cancer, and colon cancer data sets. All these data sets can be obtained directly from `http://sdmc.lit.org.sg/GEDatasets/`:

AML-ALL Data Set This data set, as a golden standard in the cancer classification community, includes two types of human tumor–acute myelogenous leukemia (AML, 11 samples) and acute lymphoblastic leukemia (ALL, 27 samples). Also ALL can be divided into two subtypes–ALL-T (8 samples) and ALL-B (19 samples).

CNS Data Set This data set consists of 34 samples: 10 classic medulloblastomas, 10 malignant, 10 rhabdoids, and 4 normals.

Lung Cancer Data Set This data set is composed of 32 samples which are about *malignant pleural mesothelioma* (MPM, 16 samples) and *adenocarcinoma* (ADCA, 16 samples) of the lung.

Colon Cancer Data Set Murali and Kasif [27] used a colon cancer data set originated in [22] to test XMOTIF. The matrix contains 40 colon tumor samples and 22 normal colon samples over about 6500 genes. This data set is available at `http://www.weizmann.ac.il/physics`.

We can investigate whether a set of genes discovered by a biclustering algorithms shows significant enrichment with respect to a specific *Gene Ontology* (GO) annotation provided by the GO Consortium. The GO Consortium is available at `http://www.geneontology.org`.

We can also use the webtool *FuncAssociate* [13] to evaluate the discovered biclusters. FuncAssociate first uses *Fisher's exact test* [10] to compute the *hypergeometric functional score* [3] of a gene set, then uses the Westfall and Young procedure [7] to compute the *adjusted significant score* of the gene set. The analysis is performed on the gene expression data of *Saccharomyces cerevisiae*.

23.7 CONCLUSION

In this chapter, we have briefly reviewed clustering algorithms of microarray data. We have reported advantages and drawbacks of certain algorithms. Although clustering of microarray data has been the subject of much research, none of the existing clustering algorithms are perfect and the construction of biologically significant groups of clusters for large microarray data is still a problem. Biological validation of clustering algorithms of microarray data is one of the most important open issues.

REFERENCES

1. N. M. Laird, A. P. Dempster, and D. B. Rubin. Maximum likelihood from incomplete data via the EM algorithm. *J. Roy. Stat. Soc.*, 51:1–38, 1977.

2. Y. Bastide, R. Taouil, N. Pasquier, G. Stumme, and L. Lakhal. Pascal: Un algorithme d'extraction des motifs fréquents. *Tech. Sci. Inform.*, 21(1):65–95, 2002.

3. F. Bravo-Marquez, G. L'Huillier, S. A. Rios, and J. D. Velasquez. Hypergeometric language model and zipf-like scoring function for web document similarity retrieval. In E. Chavez and S. Lonardi (Eds.), *Proceedings of the 17th International Symposium (SPIRE 2010)*, Vol. 6393 of *Lecture Notes in Computer Science*. Springer, Los Cabos, Mexico, October 11–13, 2010, pp. 303–308.

4. G. Carlsson. Topology and data. *Bull. Am. Math. Soc.*, 46(2):255–308, 2009.

5. G. Celeux and J. Diebolt. L'algorithme SEM: Un algorithme d'apprentissage probabiliste pour la reconnaissance de mélange de densités. *Road Safety Authority*, 34(2):35–52, 1986.

6. G. Celeux and G. Govaert. A classification EM algorithm for clustering and two stochastic versions. *Comput. Stat. Data Anal.*, 14:315–332, 1992.

7. D. D. Cox and J. S. Lee. Pointwise testing with functional data using the westfall–young randomization method. *Biometrika*, 95(3):621–634, 2008.

8. S. Draghici. *Data Analysis Tools for DNA Microarrays*. CRC Press, Boca Raton, FL, 2003.

9. M. Elati, F. Radvanyi, and C. Rouveirol. Fouille de données pour l'extraction de grands réseaux de régulation génétique. *Technique et Science Informatiques*, 26:1–2, 2007.

10. M. P. Fay. Confidence intervals that match fisher's exact or blaker's exact tests. *Biostatistics*, 11(2):373–374, 2010.

11. R. D. Fleischmann et al. Whole-genome random sequencing and assembly of *Haemophilus influenzae* Rd. *Science*, 269(5223):496, 1995.

12. E. Forgy. Cluster analysis of multivariate data: Efficiency versus interpretability of classifications. *Biometrics*, 21:768–780, 1965.

13. F. B. Gabriel, D. K. Oliver, B. Barbara, C. Sander, and F. P. Roth. Characterizing gene sets with FuncAssociate. *Bioinformatics*, 19(18):2502–2504, 2003.

14. G. Govaert and M. Nadif. Comparison of the mixture and the classification maximum likelihood in cluster analysis when data are binary. *Computat. Stat. Data Anal.*, 23:65–81, 1996.

15. D. Ignatov and S. Kuznetsov. Frequent Itemset mining for clustering near duplicate Web documents. *Conceptual Structures: Leveraging Semantic Technologies*, Vol. 5662 of *Lecture Notes in Computer Science*. Springer, 2009, pp. 185–200.

16. H. Katzan, Jr. Batch, conversational, and incremental compilers. In *Proceedings of the May 14–16, 1969, Spring Joint Computer Conference*. ACM, 1969, pp. 47–56.

17. L. Kaufman and P. J. Rousseeuw. *Finding Groups in Data: An Introduction to Cluster Analysis*, Wiley Series in Probability and Statistics. Wiley, New York, 2005.

18. Y. Kluger, R. Basri, J. T. Chang, and M. Gerstein. Spectral biclustering of microarray data: Coclustering genes and conditions. *Genome Res.*, 13(4):703, 2003.

19. G. Mclachlan and D. Peel. *Finite Mixture Models*, Wiley Series in Probability and Statistics. Wiley-Interscience, New York, 2000.

20. N. Messai. Analyse de concepts formels guidée par des connaissances de domaine: Application à la découverte de ressources génomiques sur le Web. Thesis. Thèse, Henri Poincaré, University, Nancy 2009.

21. M. Nadif and G. Govaert. Cluster analysis. In G. Govaert (Ed.), *Data Analysis*, ISTE-Wiley, New York, 2009, pp. 215–256.

22. A. Noga, H. S. Joel, and P. Erdős. *The Probabilistic Method*. Wiley-Interscience Series in Discrete Mathematics and Optimization, Wiley, 1992.

23. N. Pasquier, Y. Bastide, R. Taouil, and L. Lakhal. Discovering frequent closed itemsets for association rules. *Database Theory ICDT 99*. 1999, pp. 398–416.

24. N. Pasquier, Y. Bastide, R. Taouil, and L. Lakhal. Efficient mining of association rules using closed itemset lattices* 1. *Inform. Syst.*, 24(1):25–46, 1999.

25. M. Steenman, G. Lamirault, N. Le Meur, M. Le Cunff, D. Escande, and J. J. Léger. Distinct molecular portraits of human failing hearts identified by dedicated cDNA microarrays. *Eur. J. Heart Failure*, 7(2):157, 2005.

26. T. Tran, C. C. Nguyen, and N. M. Hoang. Management and analysis of DNA microarray data by using weighted trees. *J. Global Optimiz.*, 39(4):623–645, 2007.

27. C. J. Wu, Y. Fu, and T. Y. Murali. Gene expression module discovery using gibbs sampling. *Genome Inform.*, 15:2004, 2004.

28. M. J. Zaki and C. J. Hsiao. CHARM: An efficient algorithm for closed itemset mining. In *2nd SIAM International Conference on Data Mining*, Vol. 15. Citeseer, 2002.

CHAPTER 24

SPREAD OF EVALUATION MEASURES FOR MICROARRAY CLUSTERING

GIULIA BRUNO[1] and ALESSANDRO FIORI[2]

[1]Dipartimento di Ingegneria Gestionale e della Produzione, Politecnico di Torino, Torino, Italy

[2]Dipartimento di Automatica e Informatica, Politecnico di Torino, Torino, Italy

24.1 INTRODUCTION

During the last decade, with the development of new technologies and revolutionary changes in biomedicine and biotechnologies, there was an explosive growth of biological data. Particularly, gene expression data generated by DNA microarray technology has become a fundamental tool in genomic research [31, 49, 65, 75]. As a consequence, scientists started to develop informatics tools for the analysis and the information extracted from these data, which led to an explosive growth of publications addressing microarray analysis. Among data-mining techniques, clustering plays a crucial role in the analysis of microarray data [40]. Clustering aims at finding groups of genes that share a similar behavior under different experimental conditions. Many conventional clustering algorithms have been applied or adapted to gene expression data, and new algorithms have been proposed specifically aimed at gene expression data (see particularly [15, 53] for surveys on microarray clustering and biclustering).

The critical issue of applying clustering algorithms to microarray data is the validation of results. Differently from other data-mining tasks, for example, classification, in which the evaluation of the resulting models is an integral part of the process and there are well-accepted evaluation measures and procedures, clustering evaluation is not a well-developed or frequently used part of analysis [73]. Furthermore, since background knowledge on groups of genes is not always available, it is difficult to compare the clustering results obtained by different approaches.

Classical data-mining indexes can be applied to evaluate clustering results. Such measures are usually divided into internal and external measures. The internal measures are based on the concept of distance among cluster objects and evaluate cluster results in terms of intracluster cohesion and intercluster separation. On the contrary, the external measures assume that the true partition of objects is known and compare the obtained clusters with the actual class labels. Since in the biological context the "ground truth" is not always available,

Biological Knowledge Discovery Handbook: Preprocessing, Mining, and Postprocessing of Biological Data, First Edition. Edited by Mourad Elloumi and Albert Y. Zomaya.

there is the need of measures able to incorporate biological information from other sources (e.g., ontologies). For this reason, a number of biological measures have been proposed to evaluate how much the genes in a cluster represent a particular biological function.

When a new clustering algorithm for microarray data is proposed, it is compared by exploiting one or more quality indexes to assess its superiority with respect to previous ones. Some papers have already presented a review of validation indexes exploited in the microarray context [6–8, 10, 33, 57, 78], but they analyze only some aspects of validation or present only a subset of measures. For example, in [6] only some internal indexes are analyzed, while in [7, 10, 57] some internal and biological measures are described and compared. In [78] and [8] a comparison of internal and external indexes is presented, and [33] gives the most complete overview of internal and external measures.

Differently from other surveys, our aim is to present a snapshot of the spread of validation measures belonging to the three categories. Since an exhaustive review is infeasible due to the large amount of literature on this topic, we planned a search procedure to select the most relevant papers in this context, which is detailed in the next section. Then, a section for each measure category (i.e., internal, external, and biological) is presented. In the discussion section the spread of different validation measures and their applicability to different problems are discussed. A section on data sets frequently used for clustering analysis is also provided.

24.2 SEARCH PROCEDURE AND CLASSIFICATION OF EVALUATION MEASURES

The search procedure to identify the state of art of evaluation measures for microarray clustering is summarized in Figure 24.1. All the papers published from 2000 to 2009 which contain the words *microarray* and *clustering* were selected by using Google Scholar and the Harzing Publish or Perish (POP) tool [34]. POP is a software program that retrieves and analyzes academic citations. It uses Google Scholar to obtain the raw citations, then analyzes them and presents a wide range of citation metrics in a user-friendly format.

We based our work on the assumption that the most cited papers have to be included in our review, because they represent the consolidate state-of-art of research. Thus, we sorted the papers by citation count. However, this criterion penalizes recent works, which are also important to determine the direction of new research. For this reason, we also considered all the 2009 papers in a separate list.

Then we restricted the analysis to articles published by four publishers: (i) ACM Portal, (ii) IEEE Xplore, (iii) *Bioinformatics Journal*, and (iv) *BMC Bioinformatics Journal*. They are named respectively ACM, IEEE, BIO, and BMC in the following. We considered these four publishers as representative of the microarray clustering context because ACM and IEEE are among the most known and wide computer science communities, and BIO and BMC are among the international bioinformatics journals with the highest impact factor. We maintained different lists depending on the publisher to select information from different sources and we considered the top 100 papers for each list.

Finally, since few overview works are included in the lists, we performed manual queries on Google Scholar with additional keywords to complete our set of papers which deal with validation approaches for microarray data clustering.

Among this large set of articles, we performed a manual inspection to prune the papers which do not address the topic of microarray gene clustering. We considered only papers

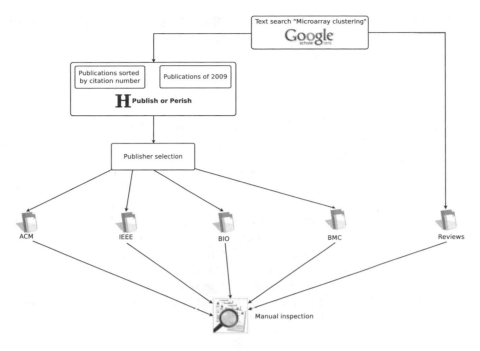

FIGURE 24.1   Search procedure to choose most relevant papers in microarray clustering context.

which address the gene clustering problem and not sample clustering problem for two reasons: (i) sample clustering is less challenging because sample labels are always known and (ii) sample clustering validation can be performed by exploiting a subset of gene clustering validation techniques (i.e., both internal and external measures).

At the end of the searching process, a set of about 50 articles have been selected for the analysis (see Table 24.2 in Section 24.6 for the complete list of analyzed papers).

By following previous classifications in both the general [73] and microarray [15, 33, 57] context, we classified cluster evaluation methods into the following categories:

Internal Measures   Indexes which evaluate the cluster cohesion or separation without knowing the real class of objects.

External Measures   Indexes which evaluate the agreement between the obtained clusters and the "ground truth," that is, the actual class division.

Biological Measures   Indexes which involve the comparison with biological databases (e.g., Gene Ontology [14]) to measure the biological homogeneity of clusters.

24.3 INTERNAL MEASURES

The basic idea behind internal measures stems from the definition of clustering as a solution which groups objects so that objects within each cluster are more similar to each other than objects from different clusters. All measures that evaluate clusters without knowing the true partition of objects are grouped in this category. These measures can be further categorized among measures defined on a single gene, on a single cluster, or on the whole clustering. In this category we also include measures of stability against data perturbation and measures of predictive power.

24.3.1 Preliminaries

Let N be the number of genes and M the number of samples in the microarray experiments. After the clustering process, k clusters are generated, $C_1, C_2, \ldots, C_k$, and each gene x belongs to a cluster. Let n_i be the number of genes in cluster C_i. The notation $d(x, y)$ represents the distance measure between genes x and y, computed according to the distance measure exploited in the clustering process (e.g., Euclidean, Manhattan). Analogously, the notation $d(C_i, C_j)$ represents the distance measure between clusters C_i and C_j, computed according to the cluster distance measure exploited in the clustering process (e.g., single linkage, average linkage, complete linkage). Sometimes, instead of a distance measure there is a similarity measure among elements (e.g., Pearson correlation). We refer to similarity between objects with the notation $s(x, y)$ and also this measure depends on the exploited clustering algorithm. If there is the need to switch from distance to similarity or vice versa, if both are normalized in the range [0,1], the following relation holds: $d(x, y) = 1 - s(x, y)$ [73].

24.3.2 Evaluation of Single Gene

A first analysis on clustering results can be focused on the contribution of each single gene to a cluster. The "silhouette" measure [63] is used to evaluate the appropriateness of a gene being in a cluster rather than in another. For each gene x, let $a(x)$ be the average distance between x and all other data within the same cluster C_i. For any other cluster $C_j \neq C_i$, let $d(x, C_j)$ be the average distance between gene x and all genes of C_j. The scalar $b(x)$ is the smallest of that average distances (i.e., it represents the distance between x and its "neighbor" cluster). The silhouette of gene x is computed by

$$\text{Silhouette}_x = \frac{b(x) - a(x)}{\max\{a(x), b(x)\}} \tag{24.1}$$

The silhouette value lies between -1 and 1. When it is close to 1, it means that the gene is appropriately clustered, while if it is close to -1, it means it would be more appropriate if gene x was clustered in its neighboring cluster. When the value is near zero, it means that the gene is on the border of two clusters.

Even if the silhouette is defined for a single gene, it can be computed also for a single cluster or the whole clustering simply by summing the silhouettes of genes in a cluster or in all clusters, respectively. The average silhouette of genes in a cluster is a measure of how tightly grouped the data are in the cluster and the average silhouette of the entire data set is a measure of how appropriately the data have been clustered.

The silhouette measure is among the most frequently used internal measures to evaluate clustering results [4, 6, 10, 12, 21, 42, 54].

24.3.3 Evaluation of Single Cluster

By considering a single cluster, two measures are used to quantify the similarity of elements in the same cluster, that is, homogeneity [69] and heterogeneity [35]:

$$\text{Homogeneity } i = \frac{2}{n_i(n_i - 1)} \sum_{x,y \in C_i, x<y} s(x, y) \tag{24.2}$$

$$\text{Heterogeneity } i = \frac{\sum_{x \in C_i} d(x, z_i)}{n_i} \tag{24.3}$$

where z_i is the cluster representative (e.g., centroid). Homogeneity increases if the solution improves, while heterogeneity increases if the solution gets worse. Both homogeneity and heterogeneity can be defined for the whole clustering as the average value of all clusters.

Homogeneity is widely used as a validation technique [10, 12, 15, 67–69], while heterogeneity is less frequent [35].

24.3.4 Evaluation of Whole Clustering

Since usually more than one cluster is produced, most measures are defined to evaluate clustering in terms of intercluster separation and trade-off between inter-cluster separation and intracluster homogeneity.

The separation measure [69] evaluates if the distance between members of the same cluster is lower than the distance between members of different clusters. It is defined as

$$\text{Separation} = \frac{2}{N(N-1) - Q} \sum_{x \in C_i, j \in C_j, i \neq j, x<y} s(x, y) \tag{24.4}$$

where Q is the total number of gene pairs that are in the same cluster [i.e., $Q = \sum_{i=1}^{k} n_i(n_i - 1)$]. The separation decreases if the solution improves. This measure is conflictual with homogeneity (24.2), as an improvement in one will usually worsen the other. In fact, separation is often used in the literature and is evaluated together with homogeneity [10, 15, 67–69].

Some indexes have been defined to combine the intracluster and intercluster distances in a unique function to evaluate homogeneity and separation simultaneously.

One of them is the Davies–Bouldin validity index (DBI) [19], which measures the average similarity between a cluster and its most similar one. It is defined as

$$\text{DBI} = \frac{1}{k} \sum_{i=1}^{k} \max_{j, j \neq i} \left\{ \frac{d_{\text{intra}}(C_i) + d_{\text{intra}}(C_j)}{d(C_i, C_j)} \right\} \tag{24.5}$$

where $d_{\text{intra}}(C_i)$ is the average distance between values and the centroid of the cluster i, that is, $d_{\text{intra}}(C_i) = (1/n_i) \sum_{x \in C_i} d(x, z_i)$. Low values of DBI correspond to good cluster quality. In [42, 52, 85] authors exploit it to compare different clustering algorithms and different numbers of clusters.

Another index to evaluate homogeneity and separation is the Dunn index [23]. It is defined as the ratio of the smallest distance between observations not in the same cluster to the largest intracluster distance and is computed as

$$
\text{Dunn} = \min_{1 \leq i \leq k} \left\{ \min_{1 \leq j \leq k, j \neq i} \left\{ \frac{d(C_i, C_j)}{\max_{C_m \in C} \text{diam}(C_m)} \right\} \right\}
\tag{24.6}
$$

where $\text{diam}(C_m)$ is the maximum distance between genes in cluster C_m (intracluster distance). The main goal of the Dunn index is to maximize the intercluster distances while minimizing intracluster distances. Since the index assumes values from 0 to ∞, high values correspond to good clusters. This index can be used to determine the optimal number of clusters on a data set. In [6, 42] authors exploit the silhouette, DBI, and Dunn indexes to assess cluster quality.

To measure the compactness of clusters, another index, the dynamic validity index (DVI), is proposed in [70]. It takes care of both the intra- and the intercluster distances and is defined as follows (apart from a normalization factor):

$$
\text{DVI} = \text{Intra} + \gamma \, \text{Inter}
\tag{24.7}
$$

where γ is the penalty factor that is equal to 1 if there is no noise or is less than 1 if the data are noisy. The other terms are defined by

$$
\text{Intra} = \frac{1}{N} \sum_{i=1}^{k} \sum_{x \in C_i} ||x - z_i||^2
\tag{24.8}
$$

$$
\text{Inter} = \frac{\max_{i,j} \left(||z_i - z_j||^2 \right)}{\min_{i \neq j} \left(||z_i - z_j||^2 \right)} \sum_{i=1}^{k} \left(\frac{1}{\sum_{j=1}^{k} \left(||z_i - z_j||^2 \right)} \right)
\tag{24.9}
$$

where z_i denotes the center of cluster C_i.

The Intra term represents the overall compactness of clusters while Inter represents the overall separateness of clusters. The Intra term computes the average sum of squares of the distance from the data points to the cluster centers. It generally decreases with cluster number since the clusters become more and more compact. On the other hand, the Inter term tends to increase with the number of clusters since it is influenced by the geometry of the cluster centers. This index is used in [28] to determine the optimal number of clusters.

24.3.5 Evaluation of Cluster Stability

Another property that assesses clustering quality is its stability (or consistency) against data perturbation (e.g., data removal, addition of noise).

The basic idea of evaluating consistency against data removal is to repeat the clustering M times by deleting the observation i at each iteration for each $i = 1, 2, \ldots, M$. For each gene x, let $C_{x,i}$ be the cluster containing gene x in the clustering obtained on the data set without the observation i. Let $C_{x,0}$ be the cluster containing gene x in the clustering obtained on the original data set. The three proposed measures are the average proportion of genes that are not put in the same cluster (V_1), the average distance between the mean expression ratios of all genes that are put in the same cluster (V_2), and the average distance between the expression levels of all genes that are put in the same cluster (V_3). They are computed as follows:

$$V_1 = \frac{1}{NM} \sum_{x=1}^{N} \sum_{j=1}^{M} \left(1 - \frac{\#(C_{x,j} \cap C_{x,0})}{\#C_{x,0}} \right) \tag{24.10}$$

$$V_2 = \frac{1}{NM} \sum_{x=1}^{N} \sum_{j=1}^{M} \left[d(\bar{e}_{x,j}, \bar{e}_{x,0}) \right] \tag{24.11}$$

$$V_3 = \frac{1}{NM} \sum_{x=1}^{N} \sum_{j=1}^{M} \frac{1}{\#C_{x,0}\#C_{x,j}} \sum_{x \in C_{x,0}, k \in C_{x,j}} d(e_x, e_k) \tag{24.12}$$

where e_x is the expression profile of gene x and $\bar{e}_{x,j}$ is the average expression profiles for genes across cluster $C_{x,j}$. In [18] the authors exploit these three validation criteria to evaluate the consistency of several clustering algorithms. According to such measures, there is not a clear winner among the algorithms. For example, the hierarchical clustering with correlation similarity is the best according to V_1 and V_2, while it is the worst according to V_3.

Cluster stability can be evaluated also against missing values (i.e., single gene expression values instead of entire observations). In [20] the authors used the conserved pairs proportion (CPP) index to compute the percentage of genes found associated with the original clusters and again found an association with the cluster generated from the data with missing values. To this aim, they first compute the clustering on a real data set without missing values, and then they generate missing values in the data and reapply the clustering. The two clustering results are compared by using the formula

$$\text{CPP} = \frac{1}{N} \sum_{i=1}^{k} \max_{1 \leq j \leq k} \left\{ \sum_{x \in C_{i,0}} \sum_{y \in C_{j,mv}} \delta_{xy} \right\} \tag{24.13}$$

where δ_{xy} is the Kronecker delta, which is equal to 1 when the genes x and y are identical and 0 otherwise. The CPP index is used to measure the influence of missing values on the clustering algorithms. It decreases when the percentage of missing values increases.

The evaluation against noise can be performed by measuring the ability of the algorithms to identify standard patterns of genes (i.e., patterns of true clusters) by adding fold noises (i.e., permutation of real gene expression data) to a data set. In [41] the similarity between standard patterns and average expression profiles for each cluster is computed for different clustering algorithms. The authors showed that their algorithm, even at increasing noise rate, discover gene patterns more similar to the original ones than do other methods.

Finally, clustering stability can also be evaluated by applying a perturbation of original expression values. In [10] the clustering stability against perturbation is evaluated by the weighted average discrepant pairs (WADP). This index is computed as the ratio of pairs of genes in an original cluster and the number of gene pairs that are not grouped together on the perturbed data. It assumes that values are between 0 and 1, where 0 means that two clustering results match perfectly.

24.3.6   Evaluation of Predictive Power of Clustering

Another idea to evaluate a cluster is to measure its predictive power, that is, its ability to predict the value of an element (an expression value or a sample label) by using the information of gene clusters.

One of these measure is the figure of merit (FOM) [83], which estimates the predictive power of a clustering algorithm by doing the following steps: (i) the experiment j is removed from the data set, (ii) the genes are clustered based on the remaining data, and (iii) the within-cluster similarity of expression values in experiment j is measured. Particularly, when the experiment j is removed from the data, the FOM is defined as

$$\text{FOM}(j) = \sqrt{\frac{1}{N} \sum_{i=1}^{k} \sum_{x \in C_i} \left(e_{xj} - \bar{e}_{j,i}\right)^2} \qquad (24.14)$$

where e_{xj} is the expression value of gene x in experiment j in the raw data and $\bar{e}_{j,i}$ is the average expression value in condition j of genes in cluster C_i. This estimation is repeated M times to compute the aggregate FOM which evaluates the total predictive power of the clustering algorithm over all the conditions. The FOM measure is frequently used as an internal validation technique [12, 27, 29, 83].

Another definition of predictive power is proposed in [52], and it is based on the idea that if the discovered clusters are valid and of good quality, they should contain meaningful patterns. If these patterns are used to classify some testing data, the classification accuracy can reflect how valid and how good the qualities of the discovered clusters are. Thus, the authors select a set of training genes from each cluster to construct a classifier. Then, based on the classifier, the cluster memberships of those genes that were not selected for training are predicted. The percentage of accurate predictions can be defined as being the classification accuracy. If a clustering algorithm is effective, the clusters that are discovered should contain hidden patterns that can be used to accurately predict the cluster membership of the testing data. Otherwise, the clusters do not contain patterns and the grouping is more or less random. In this second case, the predictive power is expected to be low.

The predictive power can also be measured by the accuracy to classify sample labels reached by a classification model built on representative genes of clusters. For example, in [3] the authors select a subset of genes from each cluster to make up a gene pool, and then they run classification experiments to see whether or not the representative genes are able to correctly classify samples. The good accuracy reached by selecting a few representative genes from the obtained clusters reveals that the clustering effectively groups genes based on their sample classification capability. This work represents an interesting integration of clustering, feature selection, and classification. Furthermore, it evaluates clustering by exploiting also the sample class information, which usually is not considered in the previously described measures. Due to its particularity, this method can be applied only if the sample class labels are available (e.g., it is not suitable for time series). However, it can be successfully exploited in tumor microarray data sets, where the true partition of genes is usually not known.

24.4   EXTERNAL MEASURES

The indexes that are used to measure the agreement between cluster labels and externally supplied class labels (i.e., the true partition) are usually named external indexes. If the cluster number and the object labels are a priori known, the clustering result can be compared with the true partition. To this aim, a number of measures that compare the results of two partitions can be exploited.

These indexes can be divided in the following three categories, which are described in the next sections:

- *Classification-Oriented Measures* Evaluate the accuracy of clustering approaches in identifying the true partition.
- *Similarity-Oriented Measures* Compute the similarity of two clusters obtained by different methods (e.g., clustering algorithm and true class labels).
- *Naïve Statistics* Measure only some characteristics of obtained clusters (e.g., number of genes in each cluster) disregarding the distribution of clustered items.

In the following, we refer to $T_1, T_2, \ldots, T_h$ as the true class partition, while the obtained clustering is referred as previously described by $C_1, C_2, \ldots, C_k$. The number of objects of class j in cluster i is referred by n_{ij}.

24.4.1 Classification-Oriented Measures

Some external measures are based on the effectiveness of a classification model in predicting true class labels [73]. Such measures can also be exploited to evaluate a clustering result and are named classification-oriented measures.

Two famous measures mostly used for classification problems are precision and recall. The precision of a cluster i with respect to a class j is the fraction of objects of class j in cluster i, while the recall of a cluster i with respect to a class j is the extent to which cluster i contains all objects of class j. They are computed as

$$\text{Precision}(i, j) = \frac{n_{ij}}{n_i} \qquad (24.15)$$

$$\text{Recall}(i, j) = \frac{n_{ij}}{n_j} \qquad (24.16)$$

where n_j is the number of object in class j.

The precision and recall values can be combined to measure the extent to which a cluster contains only objects of a particular class and all objects of that class. Such a measure is called the F-measure [43] and is calculated as

$$F(i, j) = \frac{2\,\text{Precision}(i, j)\,\text{Recall}(i, j)}{\text{Precision}(i, j) + \text{Recall}(i, j)} \qquad (24.17)$$

The F-measure values are in the interval [0, 1], and the larger its values, the better the clustering quality. Among the analyzed papers, the F-measure is used only in [52] to demonstrate the superiority of the proposed clustering algorithm.

Another classification-oriented measure is the error rate (ER) [48], computed as

$$\text{ER} = 1 - \sum_{i=1}^{k} \frac{n_{ii}}{N} \qquad (24.18)$$

where n_{ii} is the number of genes correctly put in the right cluster (i.e., $C_i = T_i$). The same quantity is also used under different names, such as the misclassification index or the overall error rate [48, 80, 85].

The classification-oriented measures are not widely used in the microarray clustering evaluation, mainly because the true class partition is not often available. Thus, they are usually computed on simulated data where the true partition is a priori known [48, 52, 80] or on a subset of data sets for which the class labels are provided [85].

24.4.2 Similarity-Oriented Measures

Some measures have been defined with the aim of comparing results of two partitions. Thus they are named similarity-oriented measures. They can be used to compare the obtained clusters both to the true class partition and to a partition obtained by a different clustering algorithm.

The most used similarity-oriented measure are the Rand index [58] and the Jaccard coefficient [32]. The Rand index is defined as the fraction of agreement between two partitions, that is, the number of object pairs that are either in the same groups in both partitions or in different groups in both partitions divided by the total number of objects. It lies between 0 and 1, and it is 1 if the two partitions agree perfectly. Sometimes, it also called simple matching [77]. The Jaccard coefficient also measures the similarity between two partitions by using a little different formula. If there is the need of presenting the proportion of disagreement instead of agreement between two partitions, the Minkowski measure [72] can be exploited.

Considering two partitions C and B of N objects, for each pair of objects (i, j) there are four possible cases: (1) i and j are in the same cluster in both C and B, (2) i and j are in the same cluster in C but in different clusters in B, (3) i and j are in the same cluster in C but in different clusters in B, and (4) i and j are in different clusters in both C and B.

Assuming that a, b, c, and d are the number of object pairs in cases 1, 2, 3, and 4, respectively, the formulas of the previously described measures are as follows:

$$\text{Rand} = \frac{a + d}{a + b + c + d} \tag{24.19}$$

$$\text{Jaccard} = \frac{a}{a + b + c} \tag{24.20}$$

$$\text{Minkowski} = \sqrt{\frac{b + c}{a + c}} \tag{24.21}$$

A lot of works exploit the Rand index [15, 30, 48, 64, 77, 82, 83] and the Jaccard coefficient [15, 42, 67–69, 77] to evaluate clustering results, while the Minkowski index is less used [15, 68].

A problem with the Rand index is that its expected value of two random partitions does not take a constant value (i.e., zero). Thus, the adjusted Rand index (ARI) [36] has been proposed to adjust the score so that its expected value in the case of random partitions is zero. As for the Rand index, a high ARI value indicates a high level of agreement between two partitions. The ARI is used in [82].

Another similarity-oriented measure is Hubert's Γ-statistics [77], which represents the correlation between two $N \times N$ matrices X and Y. Elements of X and Y are 1 or 0, depending on if the corresponding genes are grouped in the same cluster or not, respectively, in C and

B. For example, an element of the X matrix is defined as 1 if i and j are grouped in the same cluster in C and 0 otherwise. Hubert's Γ-statistics is defined as

$$\text{Hubert's } \Gamma = \frac{1}{Q} \sum_{i=1}^{N-1} \sum_{j=i+1}^{N} X(i,j)Y(i,j) \tag{24.22}$$

It is exploited in [77] together with the Rand index and the Jaccard coefficient to compare clustering results on both synthetic and real data.

Finally, another measure to assess clustering results is the Bayesian information criterion (BIC) or Schwarz criterion [66]. The BIC is an increasing function of the residual sum of squares from the estimated model and an increasing function of the number of parameters. Thus, unexplained variations in the dependent variable and the number of explanatory variables increase the value of BIC. Hence, a lower BIC implies either fewer explanatory variables or a better fit. It is computed as

$$\text{BIC} = -2 \ln(L) + v \ln(M) \tag{24.23}$$

where L is the maximum value of the likelihood function for the estimated model, v is the number of free parameters, and M is the number of observations (i.e., samples). Given any two estimated models, the model with the lower value of BIC is the one to be preferred. Few works exploit the BIC as clustering evaluation technique [56, 82] .

24.4.3 Naïve Statistics

A number of other measures have been exploited to compare the obtained clusters with the true partition. However, they give only a qualitative measure of the goodness of clustering results, and thus we classify them as naïve statistics.

A simple evaluation method is to compile a list of differences between the correct clusters and the obtained ones. For example, in [51], for each real cluster the list of correct clustered, added, and missed genes is reported. This approach contains detailed information for the analyzed clusters, but it is not appropriate when the number of clusters is high. Moreover, this validation approach does not give a quantity measure about the quality of obtained clusters.

Sometimes the clustering is validated by considering only the number of obtained clusters without evaluating the genes in each cluster [81] or by visually comparing the expression profiles of genes in the obtained clusters with respect to the ones in the true clusters [41, 54]. Other simple measures were introduced to evaluate the clustering results. For example, in [86] the average variance across a given dimension across all clusters is exploited. In [10] the cluster size distribution is evaluated to estimate the structural quality of clusters.

All these measures give only an approximate idea of the quality of obtained clusters and introduce critical issues for the comparison among different algorithms in order to select the best one.

24.5 BIOLOGICAL MEASURES

The application of external measures is rarely possible on real data sets because, differently from other contexts, the true partition is not a priori known and there are few benchmarks to evaluate and compare algorithms. Since genes with similar expression profiles may imply similarity among their functions in the biological activities, gene clusters may represent specific biological functions. The idea of biological measures is to analyze biological annotations of genes in the same cluster and verify if they are coherent.

The most used biological measure is the functional enrichment. A cluster of genes is said to be functionally enriched for a category if the proportion of genes within the cluster known to be in that category exceeds the number that could reasonably be expected from random chance [62]. This score sometimes is also called correspondence plot [84]. The degree of functional enrichment for a given cluster and category can be quantitatively assessed by the hypergeometric data distribution (P). For each category, the probability of observing such an overlap by chance is calculated by

$$P = 1 - \sum_{i=0}^{k-1} \frac{\binom{C}{i}\binom{G-C}{n-1}}{\binom{G}{n}} \qquad (24.24)$$

where G is the size of the genome, C is the number of genes of the genome in the considered category, n is the cluster size, and k is the number of genes in the cluster which are in the same category. If this probability is sufficiently low (e.g., lower than 0.01), then the cluster is said to be enriched for that category. Some other statistical tests can be used to compute the functional enrichment of clusters such as the binomial test, the chi-square test, or Fisher's test [10]. A comparison and clarification of relationships between these tests are presented in [61]. In particular, the authors conclude that the hypergeometric test and Fisher's test are equivalent and all the other tests are valid only if a large set of samples is available.

Many works exploit the functional enrichment to evaluate clustering results [9, 12, 15, 16, 21, 22, 25, 28, 39, 44–47, 50, 54, 59, 60, 62, 67, 69, 71, 74, 76, 84, 86].

Usually the biological enrichment is evaluated according to the Gene Ontology categories (e.g., [45–47]). However, other databases can be used to evaluate the enrichment of clusters, such as the MIPS [1] functional catalog database [21].

Some tools have been developed to compute the biological enrichment based on the previous formula (24.24). For example, in [62] the FunSpec tool (available at `http://funspec.med.utoronto.ca/`), which finds the category for which a set of genes is enriched, is presented. Another tool which implements the estimation of the enrichment is Onto-Express (available at `http://vortex.cs.wayne.edu/projects.htm`) and is presented in [39]. This tool automatically translates lists of differentially regulated genes into functional profiles characterizing the impact of the condition studied. Moreover, it constructs functional profiles using GO terms and the statistical significance values are calculated for each category. A comparison of tools for identifying significantly enriched GO categories is presented in [5].

Other measures consider statistics of cluster enrichment, such as sensitivity, specificity, and coverage [59]. Sensitivity is the fraction of clusters that are significantly enriched with genes that have the same annotation. Specificity measures the fraction of genes in each significantly annotated cluster that have the same significantly enriched annotation found for that cluster. Coverage describes both the fraction of all observed genes and experimental conditions in the data which are included in at least one cluster and the fraction of all groups in a given class that are significantly enriched in at least one cluster. In [59] authors evaluate the clustering performance by considering the trade-off among these three measures.

In [17] two more complex biological measures are defined: the biological homogeneity index (BHI) and the biological stability index (BSI). The BHI measures how biologically homogeneous the clusters are, while the BSI measures the clustering algorithm ability to produce biologically meaningful clusters when applied repeatedly to similar data sets. Let x and y be two annotated genes belonging to the same cluster and $F(x)$ and $F(y)$ be their functional categories. The indicator function $I(F(x) = F(y))$ is 1 if and only if $F(x)$ and $F(y)$ are equal. The BHI is an average proportion of gene pairs of the same functional category that are in the same cluster and is computed as

$$\text{BHI} = \frac{1}{k} \sum_{i=1}^{k} \frac{1}{n_i(n_i - 1)} \sum_{x \neq y \in C_i} I(F(x) = F(y)) \tag{24.25}$$

By following a procedure similar to formulas (24.10)–(24.12), the BSI aims at capturing the stability of a clustering by analyzing results when an observation in turn is deleted. Suppose we have M samples. Then the clustering is repeated M times by deleting the observation i at each iteration for each $i = 1, 2, \ldots, M$. For each gene x, let $C_{x,i}$ be the cluster containing gene x in the clustering obtained on the data set without the observation i. Let $C_{x,0}$ be the cluster containing gene x in the clustering obtained on the original data set. The cardinality of a set C is denoted by $n(C)$. The BSI is computed as

$$\text{BSI} = \frac{1}{k} \sum_{i=1}^{k} \frac{1}{n(C_i)(n(C_i) - 1)M} \sum_{j=1}^{M} \sum_{x \neq y \in C_i} \frac{n(C_{x,0} \cap C_{y,j})}{n(C_{x,0})} \tag{24.26}$$

A successful clustering should be characterized by high values of both BSI and BHI. The authors suggest using the most suitable database to retrieve the functional information for each gene. Since these validation indexes are quite new, they are only exploited in [17].

24.6 DISCUSSION

Tables 24.1 and 24.2 present a summary of results. Table 24.1 shows, for each measure, the list of papers which exploit it, while Table 24.2 shows, for each paper, the list of measures it exploits. The majority of works consider only one kind of measure in the experimental evaluation, while only four studies [15, 54, 67, 69] analyze all three aspects (i.e., internal, external and biological) of clustering results.

Both tables highlight that most of the works consider the functional enrichment as the preferred evaluation method. Often this measure is considered alone as representative of clustering quality and the other two types of measures are not considered.

This behavior is explicable by the fact that in many cases the application of external measures is unfeasible due to the lack of class labels. Instead, if the information about gene annotations or biological functions are available, a biological measure should be exploited to evaluate the algorithm efficacy. Gene Ontology is the most-used resource for computing cluster enrichment and demonstrates that an algorithm succeeds in finding meaningful groups of genes. The requirement for applying biological measures is that the biological database must reflect the cluster division that is found. In fact, a cluster can have different enrichment values depending on the exploited annotation (e.g., molecular function, biological process, cellular component) because each gene can contain multiple annotations. Thus, the right biological database must be chosen. Another critical aspect is the fact that some genes do not have any annotation. For these genes, the biological measures have no way of assessing similarity with other genes.

TABLE 24.1 Spread of Clustering Evaluation Measures for Microarray Data

Category	Measure	References
Internal	Silhouette	[4, 6, 10, 12, 21, 42, 54]
	Homogeneity	[10, 12, 15, 67–69]
	Separation	[10, 15, 67–69]
	DBI	[6, 42, 52, 85]
	FOM	[12, 27, 29, 83]
	Dunn	[6, 42]
	Heterogeneity	[35]
	DVI	[28]
	V_1, V_2, V_3	[18]
	CPP	[20]
	Pattern similarity	[41]
	WADP	[10]
	Pattern classification accuracy	[52]
	Sample classification accuracy	[3]
External	Rand	[15, 30, 48, 64, 77, 82, 83]
	Jaccard	[15, 42, 67–69, 77]
	Naïve	[10, 41, 51, 54, 81, 86]
	ER	[41, 48, 80, 85]
	Minkowski	[15, 68]
	BIC	[56, 82]
	F measure	[52]
	Hubert's Γ	[77]
Biological	Enrichment	[9, 12, 15, 16, 21, 22, 25, 28, 39, 44–47, 50, 54, 59, 60, 62, 67, 69, 71, 74, 76, 84, 86]
	BHI	[17]
	BSI	[17]

Among the internal measures, silhouette (24.1), homogeneity (24.2), and separation (24.4) are the most used. They are usually exploited together with an external measure if comparisons among more algorithms are presented. All the internal measures are based on the concept of distance (or similarity) among intra- or intercluster elements. For clustering algorithms, the distance is usually a parameter, and several distance measures can be exploited (e.g., Euclidean, Manhattan) as well as similarity measures (e.g., Pearson, cosine correlation) to create a distance matrix among elements. In fact, the formulas of internal measures do not indicate the distance in explicit form because it should be consistent with the distance used in the clustering process. If two clustering algorithms exploit two different distance measures, they cannot be compared by using an internal measure because they could produce different results also depending on the different distance and not only on the different algorithm. Instead, to compare two clustering algorithms (e.g., a partition and a hierarchical one) which exploit the same distance metric, the internal measures can be used to determine the superiority of one of them. Furthermore, if any threshold is a priori known, the internal measures can be used to support the validity of a single clustering or to decide the optimal number of clusters. For example, silhouette (24.1) is typically computed for a clustering algorithm repetitively for different cluster number to select the best parameter setting.

TABLE 24.2   List of Evaluation Measures Exploited by Each Analyzed Paper

Internal Measures	External Measures	Biological Measures	Reference
Homogeneity, separation	Rand, Jaccard, Minkowski	Enrichment	[15]
Silhouette, DBI, Dunn			[6]
Homogeneity, silhouette, separation, WADP	Naïve		[10]
Silhouette		Enrichment	[21]
Silhouette	Naïve	Enrichment	[54]
Silhouette, DBI, Dunn	Jaccard		[42]
Homogeneity, silhouette, FOM		Enrichment	[12]
Silhouette			[4]
Homogeneity, separation	Jaccard	Enrichment	[69]
Heterogeneity			[35]
Homogeneity, separation	Jaccard	Enrichment	[67]
Homogeneity, separation	Jaccard, Minkowski		[68]
DBI, pattern classification accuracy	F-measure		[52]
DVI		Enrichment	[28]
V_1, V_2, V_3			[18]
CPP			[20]
Pattern similarity	ER, Naïve		[41]
FOM	Rand		[83]
FOM			[29]
FOM			[27]
Sample classification accuracy			[3]
	Rand, ER		[48]
DBI	ER		[85]
	ER		[80]
	Hubert's Γ, Rand, Jaccard		[77]
	Rand, BIC		[82]
	Rand		[30]
	Rand		[64]
	BIC		[56]
	Naïve		[51]
	Naïve		[81]
	Naïve	Enrichment	[86]
		Enrichment	[62]
		Enrichment	[84]
		Enrichment	[74]
		Enrichment	[71]
		Enrichment	[25]
		Enrichment	[9]
		Enrichment	[76]
		Enrichment	[50]
		Enrichment	[47]
		Enrichment	[46]
		Enrichment	[39]

(continued)

TABLE 24.2   (*Continued*)

Internal Measures	External Measures	Biological Measures	Reference
		Enrichment	[45]
		Enrichment	[16]
		Enrichment	[22]
		Enrichment	[44]
		Enrichment	[60]
		Enrichment	[59]
		BHI, BSI	[17]

The external measures can be used to compare different clustering algorithms which also exploit different distance measures. In fact, if the actual class labels are known, one of the external measures can be computed to assess the superiority of one algorithm with respect to another. Such measures can also be exploited to evaluate a new distance metric among genes. By applying the same clustering algorithm, the external measures can enable to determine which distance measure permits good performance. The most used measures for this purpose are the Rand (24.19) and the Jaccard (24.20) indexes, which can be applied also to compare results of two clustering algorithms. If the true class label are a priori known, also the error rate (24.18) and the F-measure (24.17) can be used. The naïve statistics can be exploited to describe the macroscopic characteristics of obtained clusters and to give a qualitative measure of the partitioning approach. However, even if widely used, they are not the best method to determine the superiority of a clustering algorithm or a new distance measure.

As explained, each kind of measure has some merits and some drawbacks, and different measures can be used depending on the aim and, above all, the considered data set. However, all three aspects should be considered for good evaluation of clustering results.

Some tools were proposed to build and evaluate clustering results. Among the analyzed papers, the Expander tool [67, 69] seems to be the more complete with respect to the clustering validation and visualization topics. It is a Java-based tool which integrates several microarray analysis steps, including data preprocessing, normalization, identification of differential genes, clustering, biclustering, and network-based analysis of gene expression data. For microarray clustering validation, it implements the two internal measures of homogeneity and separation and the biological measure of enrichment (in particular, analyses of Gene Ontology functional categories, TF binding sites in promoter regions, microRNA sites in 3′-UTRs, and chromosomal locations can be performed). It also offers the possibility of visualizing the mean patterns of each cluster and the dendrogram trees (for the hierarchical clustering).

24.7   DATA SETS

The main problem in clustering microarray data is to have a data set on which one can evaluate results. Several works applied their proposed clustering algorithms to simulated gene expression data for which the correct distribution of genes over clusters is known a priori. Several other works also perform some experiments on real data sets, for which some kind of cluster information is known.

TABLE 24.3 Most Frequently Used Microarray Data Sets for Gene Clustering

Name	Website	References
Alizadeh	`http://llmpp.nih.gov/lymphoma/`	[20, 74, 84]
Cho	`http://genomics.stanford.edu/yeast_cell_` `cycle/cellcycle.htm`	[15, 30, 41, 50–52, 68, 71, 82, 83]
Chu	`http://cmgm.stanford.edu/pbrown/sporulation/`	[17, 18]
Eisen	`http://genome-www.stanford.edu/clustering/`	[4, 81]
Huges	`http://www.rii.com/publications/2000/cell_` `hughes.html`	[15, 35, 46, 47, 52, 69, 74, 77]
Iyer	`http://genome-www.stanford.edu/serum/`	[15, 21, 41, 69, 81]
Spellman	`http://genome-www.stanford.edu/cellcycle/`	[15, 20, 41, 45, 51, 52, 69, 77, 80–82, 86]
Whitfield	`http://genome-www.stanford.edu/Human-` `CellCycle/HeLa/`	[67, 69]

The most frequently used microarray data sets for clustering validation are reported in Table 24.3 and their main characteristics are described in the following:

Alizadeh [2] The data set contains the expression profiles of 4026 genes for 96 samples to characterize gene expression in B-cell lymphoma (DLBCL), the most common subtype of non-Hodgkin's lymphoma.

Cho [11] The data set contains time course expression profiles of 6220 genes with 17 time points for each gene taken at 10-min intervals covering nearly two yeast cell cycles (160 min).

Chu [13] The data set contains 97% of the known and predicted genes involved in sporulation in budding yeast over 6118 genes in total, measured at seven time points during the biological process. The sporulation process consists of meiosis and spore morphogenesis.

Eisen [24] The data set is an aggregation of data from experiments on the budding yeast *Saccharomices cerevisiae*, including time courses of the mitotic cell division cycle, sporulation, the diauxic shift, and shock responses. For all the 2467 genes, the authors collected 79 data points.

Huges [37] The data set contains the expression profiles of 6000 genes corresponding to 300 diverse mutations and chemical treatments in *S. cerevisiae*.

Iyer [38] The data set contains a study on the response of several human fibroblasts to serum. The expressions levels of 8613 human genes after the stimulation by the addition of serum to human fibroblasts were monitored for 48 h. Expression levels were measured at 12 time points after the stimulation. Additional data points were obtained from a separate asynchronized sample by obtaining a final data set of 18 data points.

Spellman [26] The original data set contains samples from yeast cultures synchronized by four independent methods as well as separated experiments in which some cyclings were induced. The raw data contain the expression levels of 6178 genes for 206 total conditions, but the authors identified 800 genes among them that are cell cycle regulated.

Whitfield [79] The purpose of the work was to identify the genes periodically expressed in the human cell cycles and study the correlation of them with the proliferative state of tumors. The data set contains the expression profiles of synchronized HeLa cells in five independent experiments using three synchronization methods. Three experiments contain 76 conditions and represent about 29,600 genes.

Since these sets of microarray experiments are not considered as a benchmark, in some works the raw data are preprocessed in different ways or integrated with other data sets. For example, in [67], the authors use the data set published by Murray [55] which integrates the Withfield data set with another study on human cell lines exposed to various stressful conditions. Otherwise, all these data sets store the information about the Gene Ontology annotations which can be used for biological evaluation.

24.8 CONCLUSIONS

Microarray clustering gave rise to a lot of attention in recent years in the scientific community. Many tools and algorithms were proposed to address microarray clustering, while less attention has been devoted to the definition of an evaluation procedure of clustering results. In this overview we analyzed the evaluation indexes most frequently used in the microarray clustering domain.

The indexes exploited to evaluate clustering results on microarray data can be categorized in three categories: internal, external, and biological measures. Each of them evaluates the capability of clustering algorithms to identify well-formed clusters according to some criteria. The internal indexes evaluate the capability of clustering algorithms to identify groups of similar genes without knowing the true gene labels. The external measures compare the partitions obtained by the clustering approaches to the true class partitions, while the biological indexes are addressed to measure to what extent the genes in the same partition share biological functions according to information stored in biological resources (e.g., Gene Ontology). A good evaluation procedure should deal with all these aspects in order to measure the quality of clustering results to demonstrate the superiority of the proposed approach.

In our review we have also analyzed the most used microarray data exploited with clustering algorithms in order to identify possible benchmarks for further works.

REFERENCES

1. Mips functional categories. Available: `http://mips.helmholtz-muenchen.de/genre/proj/yeast/`.

2. A. A. Alizadeh et al. Distinct types of diffuse large B-cell lymphoma identified by gene expression profiling. *Nature*, 403(6769):503–511, 2000.

3. W.-H. Au, K. C. C. Chan, A. K. C. Wong, and Y. Wang. Attribute clustering for grouping, selection, and classification of gene expression data. *IEEE/ACM Trans. Computat. Biol. Bioinformatics*, 2(2):83–101, Apr.–June 2005.

4. A. Ben-Hur, A. Elisseeff, and I. Guyon. A stability based method for discovering structure in clustered data. In *Pacific Symposium on Biocomputing 2002: Kauai, Hawaii, 3-7 January 2002.* World Scientific Publishing Company, 2002, p. 6.

5. B. Berg, C. Thanthiriwatte, P. Manda, and S. Bridges. Comparing gene annotation enrichment tools for functional modeling of agricultural microarray data. *BMC Bioinformatics*, 10(Suppl 11):S9, 2009.

6. N. Bolshakova and F. Azuaje. Cluster validation techniques for genome expression data. *Signal Process.*, 83(4):825–833, 2003.

7. G. Brock, V. Pihur, S. Datta, and S. Datta. clvalid: An r package for clustering validation. *J. Stat. Software*, 25(4):3201–3212, 2008.

8. M. Brun, C. Sima, J. Hua, J. Lowey, B. Carroll, E. Suh, and E. R. Dougherty. Model-based evaluation of clustering validation measures. *Pattern Recognition*, 40(3):807–824, 2007.

9. P. Carmona-Saez, R. Pascual-Marqui, F. Tirado, J. Carazo, and A. Pascual-Montano. Biclustering of gene expression data by non-smooth non-negative matrix factorization. *BMC Bioinformatics*, 7(1):78, 2006.

10. G. Chen, S. A. Jaradat, N. Banerjee, T. S. Tanaka, M. S. H. Ko, and M. Q. Zhang. Evaluation and comparison of clustering algorithms in analyzing ES cell gene expression data. *Stat. Sinica*, 12(1):241–262, 2002.

11. R. J. Cho, et al. A genome-wide transcriptional analysis of the mitotic cell cycle. *Mol. Cell*, 2(1):65–73, 1998.

12. J. W. Chou, T. Zhou, W. K. Kaufmann, R. S. Paules, and P.R. Bushel. Extracting gene expression patterns and identifying co-expressed genes from microarray data reveals biologically responsive processes. *BMC Bioinformatics*, 8(1):427, 2007.

13. S. Chu, J. DeRisi, M. Eisen, J. Mulholland, D. Botstein, PO Brown, and I. Herskowitz. The transcriptional program of sporulation in budding yeast. *Science*, 282(5389):699, 1998.

14. Gene Ontology. Gene Ontology Consortium, www.genntology.org.

15. C. Tang, D. Jiang, and A. Zhang. Cluster analysis for gene-expression data: A survey. *IEEE Trans. Knowledge Data Eng.*, 16(11):1370–1386, 2004.

16. X. Dai, T. Erkkila, O. Yli-Harja, and H. Lahdesmaki. A joint finite mixture model for clustering genes from independent Gaussian and beta distributed data. *BMC Bioinformatics*, 10(1):165, 2009.

17. S. Datta and S. Datta. Methods for evaluating clustering algorithms for gene expression data using a reference set of functional classes. *BMC Bioinformatics*, 7(1):397, 2006.

18. S. Datta and S. Datta. Comparisons and validation of statistical clustering techniques for microarray gene expression data. *Bioinformatics*, 19(4):459–466, 2003.

19. D. L. Davies and D. W. Bouldin. A cluster separation measure. *IEEE Trans. Pattern Anal. Machine Intell.*, 1(2):224–227, 1979.

20. A. de Brevern, S. Hazout, and A. Malpertuy. Influence of microarrays experiments missing values on the stability of gene groups by hierarchical clustering. *BMC Bioinformatics*, 5(1):114, 2004.

21. D. Dembele and P. Kastner. Fuzzy C-means method for clustering microarray data. *Bioinformatics*, 19(8):973–980, 2003.

22. S. Dharan and A. Nair. Biclustering of gene expression data using reactive greedy randomized adaptive search procedure. *BMC Bioinformatics*, 10(Suppl. 1):S27, 2009.

23. J. C. Dunn. Well-separated clusters and optimal fuzzy partitions. *Cybernet. Syst.*, 4(1):95–104, 1974.

24. M. B. Eisen, P. T. Spellman, P. O. Brown, and D. Botstein. Cluster analysis and display of genome-wide expression patterns. *Proc. Nat. Acad. Sci.*, 95(25):14863, 1998.

25. J. Ernst, G. J. Nau, and Z. Bar-Joseph. Clustering short time series gene expression data. *Bioinformatics*, 21:159–168, 2005.

26. G. R. Fink, P. T. Spellman, G. Sherlock, M. Q. Zhang, V. R. Iyer, K. Anders, M. B. Eisen, P. O. Brown, D. Botstein, and B. Futcher. Comprehensive identification of cell cycle-regulated genes

of the yeast *Saccharomyces cerevisiae* by microarray hybridization. *Mol. Biol. Cell*, 9(12):3273–3297, 1998.

27. L. Fu and E. Medico. FLAME, a novel fuzzy clustering method for the analysis of DNA microarray data. *BMC Bioinformatics*, 8(1):3, 2007.

28. A. Ghouila, S. B. Yahia, D. Malouche, H. Jmel, D. Laouini, F. Z. Guerfali, and S. Abdelhak. Application of multi-SOM clustering approach to macrophage gene expression analysis. *Infect., Genet. Evol.*, 9(3):328–336, 2009.

29. R. Giancarlo, D. Scaturro, and F. Utro. Computational cluster validation for microarray data analysis: Experimental assessment of Clest, Consensus Clustering, Figure of Merit, Gap Statistics and Model Explorer. *BMC Bioinformatics*, 9(1):462, 2008.

30. P. Glenisson, J. Mathys, and B. De Moor. Meta-clustering of gene expression data and literature-based information. *ACM SIGKDD Explor. Newsl.*, 5(2):101–112, 2003.

31. T. R. Golub et al. Molecular classification of cancer: Class discovery and class prediction by gene expression monitoring. *Science*, 286(5439):531, 1999.

32. M. Halkidi, Y. Batistakis, and M. Vazirgiannis. On clustering validation techniques. *J. Intell. Inform. Syst.*, 17(2):107–145, 2001.

33. J. Handl, J. Knowles, and D. B. Kell. Computational cluster validation in post-genomic data analysis. *Bioinformatics*, 21(15):3201, 2005.

34. A. W. Harzing. Harzing's Publish or Perish, 2008. Available: `http://www.harzing.com/pop.htm`.

35. J. Herrero, A. Valencia, and J. Dopazo. A hierarchical unsupervised growing neural network for clustering gene expression patterns. *Bioinformatics*, 17(2):126–136, 2001.

36. L. Hubert and P. Arabie. Comparing partitions. *J. Classification*, 2(1):193–218, 1985.

37. T. R. Hughes et al. Functional discovery via a compendium of expression profiles. *Cell*, 102(1):109–126, 2000.

38. V. R. Iyer et al. The transcriptional program in the response of human fibroblasts to serum. *Science*, 283(5398):83, 1999.

39. D. Jiang, J. Pei, M. Ramanathan, C. Tang, and A. Zhang. Mining coherent gene clusters from gene-sample-time microarray data. In *Proceedings of the Tenth ACM SIGKDD International Conference on Knowledge Discovery and Data Mining*. ACM New York, 2004. pp. 430–439.

40. D. Jiang, C. Tang, and A. Zhang. Cluster analysis for gene expression data: A survey. *IEEE Trans. Knowledge Data Eng.*, 16(11):1370–1386, 2004.

41. D. Jiang, J. Pei, and A. Zhang. Dhc: A density-based hierarchical clustering method for time series gene expression data. In *Proceedings of the Third IEEE Symposium on Bioinformatics and Bioengineering*. 2003, pp. 393–400.

42. S. Jonnalagadda and R. Srinivasan. Nifti: An evolutionary approach for finding number of clusters in microarray data. *BMC Bioinformatics*, 10(1):40, 2009.

43. B. Larsen and C. Aone. Fast and effective text mining using linear-time document clustering. In *Proceedings of the Fifth ACM SIGKDD International Conference on Knowledge Discovery and Data Mining*. ACM, New York, 1999, pp. 16–22.

44. J. Liu, Z. Li, X. Hu, and Y. Chen. Biclustering of microarray data with MOSPO based on crowding distance. *BMC Bioinformatics*, 10(Suppl. 4):S9, 2009.

45. J. Liu, W. Wang, and J. Yang. A framework for ontology-driven subspace clustering. In *Proceedings of the Tenth ACM SIGKDD International Conference on Knowledge Discovery and Data Mining*. ACM, New York, 2004, pp. 623–628.

46. J. Liu, W. Wang, and J. Yang. Gene ontology friendly biclustering of expression profiles. In *Proceedings of the CSB 2004 Computational Systems Bioinformatics Conference*. IEEE, New York, 2004, pp. 436–447.

47. J. Liu, J. Yang, and W. Wang. Biclustering in gene expression data by tendency. In *Proceedings of the CSB 2004 Computational Systems Bioinformatics Conference*. IEEE, New York, 2004, pp. 182–193.

48. T. Liu, N. Lin, N. Shi, and B. Zhang. Information criterion-based clustering with order-restricted candidate profiles in short time-course microarray experiments. *BMC Bioinformatics*, 10(1):146, 2009.

49. D. J. Lockhart, E. L. Brown, G. G. Wong, M. Chee, and T. R. Gingeras. Expression monitoring by hybridization to high density oligonucleotide arrays. U.S. Patent Application 10/998,518, November 23, 2004.

50. Y. Lu, S. Lu, F. Fotouhi, Y. Deng, and S. Brown. Incremental genetic k-means algorithm and its application in gene expression data analysis. *BMC Bioinformatics*, 5(1):172, 2004.

51. A. V. Lukashin and R. Fuchs. Analysis of temporal gene expression profiles: Clustering by simulated annealing and determining the optimal number of clusters. *Bioinformatics*, 17(5):405–414, 2001.

52. P. C. H. Ma, K. C. C. Chan, X. Yao, and D. K. Y. Chiu. An evolutionary clustering algorithm for gene expression microarray data analysis. *IEEE Trans. Evol. Comput.*, 10(3):296–314, 2006.

53. S. C. Madeira and A. L. Oliveira. Biclustering algorithms for biological data analysis: A survey. *IEEE/ACM Trans. Comput. Biol. Bioinformatics*, 1(1):24–45, 2004.

54. U. Maulik, A. Mukhopadhyay, and S. Bandyopadhyay. Combining Pareto-optimal clusters using supervised learning for identifying co-expressed genes. *BMC Bioinformatics*, 10(1):27, 2009.

55. J. I. Murray, M. L. Whitfield, N. D. Trinklein, R. M. Myers, P. O. Brown, and D. Botstein. Diverse and specific gene expression responses to stresses in cultured human cells. *Mol. Biol. Cell*, 15(5):2361, 2004.

56. W. Pan. Incorporating gene functions as priors in model-based clustering of microarray Gene expression data. *Bioinformatics*, 22(7):795, 2006.

57. V. Pihur, G. N. Brock, S. Datta, and S. Datta. Cluster validation for microarray data: An appraisal. *Multivariate Statistical Methods*, Vol. 5, World Scientific Press, 2009, pp. 79–94.

58. W. M. Rand. Objective criteria for the evaluation of clustering methods. *J. Am. Stat. Assoc.*, 66(336):846–850, 1971.

59. D. Reiss, N. Baliga, and R. Bonneau. Integrated biclustering of heterogeneous genome-wide data sets for the inference of global regulatory networks. *BMC Bioinformatics*, 7(1):280, 2006.

60. A. L. Richards, P. Holmans, M. C. O'Donovan, M. J. Owen, and L. Jones. A comparison of four clustering methods for brain expression microarray data. *BMC Bioinformatics*, 9(1):490, 2008.

61. I. Rivals, L. Personnaz, L. Taing, and M. C. Potier. Enrichment or depletion of a go category within a class of genes: Which test? *Bioinformatics*, 23(4):401–407, 2007.

62. M. Robinson, J. Grigull, N. Mohammad, and T. Hughes. Funspec: A web-based cluster interpreter for yeast. *BMC Bioinformatics*, 3(1):35, 2002.

63. P. J. Rousseeuw. Silhouettes: A graphical aid to the interpretation and validation of cluster analysis. *Computat. Appl. Math.*, 20:53–65, 1987.

64. R. Savage, K. Heller, Y. Xu, Z. Ghahramani, W. Truman, M. Grant, K. Denby, and D. Wild. R/bhc: Fast Bayesian hierarchical clustering for microarray data. *BMC Bioinformatics*, 10(1):242, 2009.

65. M. Schena, D. Shalon, R. W. Davis, and P. O. Brown. Quantitative monitoring of gene expression patterns with a complementary DNA microarray. *Science*, 270(5235):467, 1995.

66. G. E. Schwarz. Estimating the dimension of a model. *Ann. Stat.*, 6(2):461–464, 1978.

67. R. Shamir, A. Maron-Katz, A. Tanay, C. Linhart, I. Steinfeld, R. Sharan, Y. Shiloh, and R. Elkon. Expander—An integrative program suite for microarray data analysis. *BMC Bioinformatics*, 6(1):232, 2005.

68. R. Sharan and R. Shamir. CLICK: A clustering algorithm with applications to gene expression analysis. *Proc. Int. Conf. Intell. Syst. Mol. Biol*, 8:307–316, 2000.

69. R. Sharan, A. Maron-Katz, and R. Shamir. CLICK and EXPANDER: A system for clustering and visualizing gene expression data. *Bioinformatics*, 19(14):1787–1799, 2003.

70. J. Shen, S. I. Chang, E. S. Lee, Y. Deng, and S. J. Brown. Determination of cluster number in clustering microarray data. *Appl. Math. Comput.*, 169(2):1172–1185, 2005.

71. F. De Smet, J. Mathys, K. Marchal, G. Thijs, B. De Moor, and Y. Moreau. Adaptive quality-based clustering of gene expression profiles. *Bioinformatics*, 18(5):735–746, 2002.

72. R. R. Sokal. Clustering and classification: Background and current directions. *Classification and Clustering*, 3, 1977.

73. P. N. Tan, M. Steinbach, and V. Kumar. *Introduction to Data Mining*. Pearson Addison Wesley, Boston, 2005.

74. A. Tanay, R. Sharan, and R. Shamir. Discovering statistically significant biclusters in gene expression data. *Bioinformatics*, 18:S136–144, 2002.

75. R. C. Thompson, M. Deo, and D. L. Turner. Analysis of microRNA expression by in situ hybridization with RNA oligonucleotide probes. *Methods*, 43(2):153–161, 2007.

76. P. Toronen. Selection of informative clusters from hierarchical cluster tree with gene classes. *BMC Bioinformatics*, 5(1):32, 2004.

77. V. S. Tseng and C.-P. Kao. Efficiently mining gene expression data via a novel parameterless clustering method. *IEEE/ACM Trans. Computat. Biol. Bioinformatics*, 2(4):355–365, 2005.

78. K. Wang, B. Wang, and L. Peng. Cvap: Validation for clustering analyses. *Data Sci. J.*, 8:88–93, 2009.

79. M. L. Whitfield et al. Identification of genes periodically expressed in the human cell cycle and their expression in tumors. *Mol. Biol. Cell*, 13(6):1977, 2002.

80. S. Wu, A. W.-C. Liew, H. Yan, and M. Yang. Cluster analysis of gene expression data based on self-splitting and merging competitive learning. *IEEE Trans. Inform. Technol. Biomed.*, 8(1):5–15, 2004.

81. Y. Xu, V. Olman, and D. Xu. Clustering gene expression data using a graph-theoretic approach: An application of minimum spanning trees . *Bioinformatics*, 18(4):536–545, 2002.

82. K. Y. Yeung, C. Fraley, A. Murua, A. E. Raftery, and W. L. Ruzzo. Model-based clustering and data transformations for gene expression data. *Bioinformatics*, 17(10):977–987, 2001.

83. K. Y. Yeung, D. R. Haynor, and W. L. Ruzzo. Validating clustering for gene expression data. *Bioinformatics*, 17(4):309, 2001.

84. S. Yoon, C. Nardini, L. Benini, and G. De Micheli. Discovering coherent biclusters from gene expression data using zero-suppressed binary decision diagrams. *IEEE/ACM Trans. Computat. Biol. Bioinformatics*, 2(4):339–354, 2005.

85. Y. Zeng, J. Tang, J. Garcia-Frias, and G. R. Gao. An adaptive meta-clustering approach: Combining the information from different clustering results. In *CSB '02: Proceedings of the IEEE Computer Society Conference on Bioinformatics*, 2002, pp. 276–288.

86. L. Zhao and M. J. Zaki. Tricluster: An effective algorithm for mining coherent clusters in 3d microarray data. In *Proceedings of the 2005 ACM SIGMOD International Conference on Management of Data*, ACM New York, 2005, pp. 694–705.

CHAPTER 25

SURVEY ON BICLUSTERING OF GENE EXPRESSION DATA

ADELAIDE VALENTE FREITAS,[1] WASSIM AYADI,[2,3] MOURAD ELLOUMI,[2,4]
JOSÉ LUIS OLIVEIRA,[5] and JIN-KAO HAO[3]

[1]DMat/CIDMA, University of Aveiro, Portugal
[2]Laboratory of Technologies of Information and Communication and Electrical
Engineering (LaTICE)
[3]LERIA, University of Angers, Angers, France
[4]University of Tunis-El Manar, Tunisia
[5]DETI/IEETA, University of Aveiro, Portugal

25.1 INTRODUCTION

Microarrays allow measuring the expression level of a large number of genes under different experimental samples or environmental conditions. The data generated from them are called *gene expression data*. The extraction of biological relevant knowledge from these data is not a trivial task. Gene expression data are usually represented by a matrix M (see Table 25.1), where the ith row represents the ith gene, the jth column represents the jth condition, and the cell m_{ij} represents the expression level of the ith gene under the jth condition.

There are several objectives when analyzing gene expression data, such as grouping subsets of genes that are coexpressed under subsets of conditions or classifying new genes, given the expression of other genes with known classification. Discovering such coexpressions can be helpful to uncover genomic knowledge such as gene networks or gene interactions. That is why it is of utmost importance to make a simultaneous clustering of rows (genes) and columns (conditions) of the data matrix to identify clusters of genes that are coexpressed under clusters of conditions. This type of clustering is called *biclustering* [14]. The resulting clusters are called *biclusters*. A bicluster is a subset of genes showing similar behavior under a subset of conditions of the original expression data matrix. Let us note that a gene/condition can belong to more than one bicluster.

Formally, a bicluster can be defined as follows: Let $I = \{1, 2, \ldots, n\}$ be a set of indices of n genes, $J = \{1, 2, \ldots, m\}$ be a set of indices of m conditions, and $M(I, J)$ be a data matrix associated with I and J. A bicluster associated with the data matrix $M(I, J)$ is a couple (I', J') such that $I' \subseteq I$ and $J' \subseteq J$.

Biological Knowledge Discovery Handbook: Preprocessing, Mining, and Postprocessing of Biological Data,
First Edition. Edited by Mourad Elloumi and Albert Y. Zomaya.

TABLE 25.1 Gene Expression Data Matrix

	Condition 1	$\ldots$	Condition j	$\ldots$	Condition m
Gene 1	m_{11}	$\ldots$	m_{1j}	$\ldots$	m_{1m}
$\ldots$	$\ldots$	$\ldots$	$\ldots$	$\ldots$	$\ldots$
Gene i	m_{i1}	$\ldots$	m_{ij}	$\ldots$	m_{im}
$\ldots$	$\ldots$	$\ldots$	$\ldots$	$\ldots$	$\ldots$
Gene n	m_{n1}	$\ldots$	m_{nj}	$\ldots$	m_{nm}

The *biclustering problem* can be formulated as follows: Given a data matrix M, construct a group of biclusters B_{opt} associated with M such that

$$f(B_{\text{opt}}) = \max_{B \in \text{BC}(M)} f(B) \tag{25.1}$$

where f is an objective function measuring the *quality*, that is, degree of coherence, of a group of biclusters and $\text{BC}(M)$ is the set of all the possible groups of biclusters associated with M.

Clearly, biclustering is a highly combinatorial problem with a search space size $O(2^{|I|+|J|})$. In its general case, biclustering is NP hard [14, 31].

In this chapter, we make a survey on biclustering of gene expression data. The rest of the chapter is organized as follows: First, we present the different types of biclusters and groups of biclusters. Then, we present *evaluation functions* and *systematic* and *stochastic* biclustering algorithms. Next, we discuss bicluster validation. Finally, we present our conclusion.

25.2 TYPES OF BICLUSTERS

A bicluster can be in one of the following forms:

1. *Bicluster with Constant Values* It is a bicluster where all the values are equal to a constant c:

$$m_{ij} = c \tag{25.2}$$

2. *Bicluster with Constant Values on Rows or Columns*
   - *Bicluster with Constant Values on Rows* It is a bicluster where all the values can be obtained by using one of the following equations:

$$m_{ij} = c + a_i \tag{25.3}$$

$$m_{ij} = c * a_i \tag{25.4}$$

   where c is a constant and a_i is the adjustment for the row i, $1 \le i \le n$.
   - *Bicluster with Constant Values on Columns* It is a bicluster where all the values can be obtained by using one of the following equations:

$$m_{ij} = c + b_j \tag{25.5}$$

$$m_{ij} = c * b_j \tag{25.6}$$

   where c is a constant and b_j is the adjustment for the column j, $1 \le j \le m$.

3. *Bicluster with Coherent Values* This bicluster can be obtained by using one of the following equations:

$$m_{ij} = c + a_i + b_j \tag{25.7}$$

$$m_{ij} = c * a_i * b_j \tag{25.8}$$

4. *Bicluster with Linear Coherent Values* It is a bicluster where all the values can be obtained by using the following equation:

$$m_{ij} = c * a_i + b_j \tag{25.9}$$

5. *Bicluster with Coherent Evolution* It is a bicluster where all the rows (respectively columns) induce a linear order across a subset of columns (respectively rows).

25.3 GROUPS OF BICLUSTERS

A group of biclusters can be in one of the following forms [31]:

1. Single bicluster (Figure 25.1a)
2. Exclusive rows and columns group of biclusters (Figure 25.1b)
3. Nonoverlapping group of biclusters with checkerboard structure (Figure 25.1c)
4. Exclusive rows group of biclusters (Figure 25.1d)

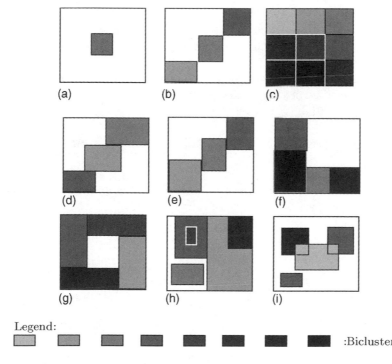

FIGURE 25.1 Possible structures of group of biclusters in data matrix.

5. Exclusive columns group of biclusters (Figure 25.1e)
6. Nonoverlapping group of biclusters with tree structure (Figure 25.1f)
7. Nonoverlapping nonexclusive group of biclusters (Figure 25.1g)
8. Overlapping group of biclusters with hierarchical structure (Figure 25.1h)
9. Arbitrarily positioned overlapping group of biclusters (Figure 25.1i)

A natural way to visualize a group of biclusters consists in assigning a different color to each bicluster and in reordering the rows and the columns of the data matrix so that we obtain a data matrix with colored blocks, where each block represents a bicluster.

25.4 EVALUATION FUNCTIONS

An evaluation function is an indicator of the performance of a biclustering algorithm. We distinguish two main classes of evaluation functions: *intra-bicluster* evaluation functions and *inter-bicluster* ones. While the former are used to quantify the coherence degree within each bicluster, the last are measures of match scores between two groups of biclusters provided by different biclustering strategies and are used to assess the ability of an algorithm to recover biclusters detected by another one.

There are several intra-bicluster evaluation functions [3, 4, 13, 14, 21, 26, 44]. Most of these functions are particular cases of the *average similarity score* (AVSS) introduced in [30]. Given a bicluster (I', J'), the AVSS $E_{\text{AVSS}}(I', J')$ is defined as

$$E_{\text{AVSS}}(I', J') = \frac{\sum_{i \in I'} \sum_{j \in J'} s_{ij}}{|I'||J'|} \tag{25.10}$$

for some similarity measure s_{ij} among elements of the row i and the column j with other elements belonging to I' and J'.

The most popular intra-bicluster evaluation function is the *mean-squared residue* (MSR) function, E_{MSR}, proposed in [14] [Equation (25.11)]. It is used by several algorithms like [3, 11, 13, 19, 34, 46, 49]. It is given by

$$E_{\text{MSR}}(I', J') = \frac{\sum_{i \in I'} \sum_{j \in J'} (m_{ij} - m_{iJ'} - m_{I'j} + m_{I'J'})^2}{|I'||J'|} \tag{25.11}$$

where $m_{I'J'}$ is the average over the whole bicluster, $m_{I'j}$ is the average over the column j, and $m_{iJ'}$ is the average over the row i. Since

$$\sum_{i \in I'} \sum_{j \in J'} (m_{ij} - m_{iJ'} - m_{I'j} + m_{I'J'})^2$$

$$= \sum_{i \in I'} \sum_{j \in J'} (m_{ij} - m_{I'J'})^2 - \sum_{i \in I'} \sum_{j \in J'} (m_{iJ'} - m_{I'J'})^2 - \sum_{i \in I'} \sum_{j \in J'} (m_{I'j} - m_{I'J'})^2$$

E_{MSR} represents the variation associated with the interaction between the rows and the columns in the bicluster.

A low (respectively high) E_{MSR} value, that is, *close* to zero (respectively higher than a fixed threshold), indicates that the bicluster is strongly (respectively weakly) coherent. If a bicluster has a value of E_{MSR} lower than a given threshold δ, then it is called a δ-bicluster. However, the E_{MSR} function is inadequate to assess certain types of biclusters [1, 37, 44].

Angiulli et al. [3] and Divina and Aguilar-Ruiz [21] propose to use E_{MSR}, the *average row variance*, E_{ARV}, and the *volume* (or *size*), E_V, of a bicluster. The average row variance (E_{ARV}) is defined as

$$E_{\text{ARV}}(I', J') = \frac{\sum_{i \in I'} \sum_{j \in J'} (m_{ij} - m_{iJ'})^2}{|I'||J'|} \tag{25.12}$$

Note that

$$E_{\text{ARV}}(I', J') = \frac{\sum_{i \in I'} \text{Variance of row } i}{|I'|} \tag{25.13}$$

Biclusters that contain individuals (rows) with large changes in their values for different attributes (columns) are characterized by high values of variance per individual (row). It follows that average row variance can be used to guarantee that a bicluster captures individuals exhibiting coherent trends under some subset of attributes. Note that both E_{MSR} and E_{ARV} are E_{AVSS}: Equation (25.10) coincides with Equation (25.11) when $s_{ij} = (m_{ij} - m_{iJ'} - m_{I'j} + m_{I'J'})^2$, and Equation (25.10) coincides with Equation (25.12) when $s_{ij} = (m_{ij} - m_{iJ'})^2$.

The volume $E_V(I', J')$ of a bicluster (I', J') is used to maximize the size of this bicluster. It is defined by

$$E_V(I', J') = |I'||J'| \tag{25.14}$$

Das et al. [17] propose to find the maximum-sized bicluster that does not exceed a certain *coherence* value. Coherence is expressed as a MSR score. Hence, Das et al. try to maximize the volume $E_V(I', J')$ [Equation (25.14)] and find biclusters with a value of E_{MSR} lower than a given threshold δ for some $\delta \geq 0$ [Equation (25.11)].

Teng and Chan [44] propose the *average correlation value* (ACV) function, E_{ACV}, to evaluate the homogeneity of a bicluster. It is defined by

$$E_{\text{ACV}}(I', J') = \max \left\{ \frac{\sum_{i \in I'} \sum_{j \in I'} |r_{ij}| - |I'|}{|I'|(|I'| - 1)}, \quad \frac{\sum_{k \in J'} \sum_{l \in J'} |r_{kl}| - |J'|}{|J'|(|J'| - 1)} \right\} \tag{25.15}$$

where r_{ij} $(i \neq j)$ is Pearson's correlation coefficient associated with the row indices i and j in the bicluster (I', J') [36] and r_{kl} $(k \neq l)$ is Pearson's correlation coefficient associated with the column indices k and l in the bicluster (I', J').

Let us note that the values of E_{ACV} belong to [0, 1]. A high (respectively low) E_{ACV} value, that is, close to 1 (respectively close to 0), indicates that the bicluster is strongly (respectively weakly) coherent. However, the performance of the E_{ACV} function decreases when noise exists in the data matrix [13]. Some examples are illustrated to assess the E_{ACV} evaluation function [44].

Cheng et al. [13] propose to use the E_{ACV} and E_{MSR} functions. A bicluster with a high coherence has a low E_{MSR} value and a high E_{ACV} value.

Ayadi et al. propose three evaluation functions:

(i) The first one is the *average Spearman's rho* function [4], E_{ASR}. It is defined as

$$E_{\text{ASR}}(I', J') = 2 \max \left\{ \frac{\sum_{i \in I'} \sum_{j \in I', j \geq i+1} \rho_{ij}}{|I'|(|I'| - 1)}, \quad \frac{\sum_{k \in J'} \sum_{l \in J', l \geq k+1} \rho_{kl}}{|J'|(|J'| - 1)} \right\}$$

(25.16)

where ρ_{ij} ($i \neq j$) is Spearman's rank correlation associated with the row indices i and j in the bicluster (I', J') [28] and ρ_{kl} ($k \neq l$) is Spearman's rank correlation associated with the column indices k and l in the bicluster (I', J').

Let us note that the values of Spearman's rank correlation belong to $[-1, \ldots, 1]$. A high (respectively low) Spearman's rank correlation value, that is, close to 1 (respectively close to -1), indicates that the two vectors are strongly (respectively weakly) coherent [28]. So, the values of the E_{ASR} function belong also to $[-1, \ldots, 1]$. Hence, a high (respectively low) E_{ASR} value, that is, close to 1 (respectively close to -1), indicates that the bicluster is strongly (respectively weakly) coherent. Furthermore, it has been shown that Spearman's rank correlation is less sensitive to the presence of noise in data. Since the E_{ASR} function is based on Spearman's rank correlation, E_{ASR} is also less sensitive to the presence of noise in data.

(ii) The second one is the *average correspondence similarity index* [6], E_{ACSI}. In order to calculate E_{ACSI}, we first discretize the initial data matrix $M(I, J) = [m_{i,j}]$, $I = \{1, 2, \ldots, n\}$ and $J = \{1, 2, \ldots, m\}$, into a matrix $M' = [m'_{i,l}]$ defined as

$$m'_{i,l} = \begin{cases} 1 & \text{if } m_{i,l} < m_{i,l+1} \\ -1 & \text{if } m_{i,l} > m_{i,l+1} \\ 0 & \text{if } m_{i,l} = m_{i,l+1} \end{cases}$$

(25.17)

with $i \in \{1, 2, \ldots, n\}$ and $l \in \{1, 2, \ldots, m - 1\}$.

Let the *correspondence similarity list* (CSL) between *gene i* and *gene j* ($i < j$), denoted by $\text{CSL}_{i,j}$, be the list where each element is represented by $T(m'_{i,l} = m'_{j,l})$ where $T(\exp) = 1$ when exp is true, and $T(\exp) = 0$ otherwise. Let $\text{NumCSL}_{i,j}$ be the number of times where we have a true value in $\text{CSL}_{i,j}$ and $\text{MaxCSL}_i = \max\{\text{NumCSL}_{i,i+1}, \text{NumCSL}_{i,i+2}, \ldots, \text{NumCSL}_{i,n}\}$. We define the *correspondence similarity index* (E_{CSI}) as follows:

$$E_{\text{CSI}}(i, j, k) = \frac{\sum_{l=1}^{m-1} T(m'_{i,l} = m'_{j,l} = m'_{k,l})}{\text{MaxCSL}_i}$$

(25.18)

with $i \in \{1, 2, \ldots, n - 2\}$, $j \in \{2, \ldots, n - 1\}$, $k \in \{3, \ldots, n\}$, $i < j < k$.

The function $E_{\text{CSI}}(i, j, k)$ indicates the proportion of trues, that is, the change in the same direction that exists between rows i, j, and k in the same set of columns. This enables us to see how *gene i*, *gene j* and *gene k* behave over a subset of conditions.

Finally, for the whole bicluster, we define the *average correspondence similarity index* (E_{ACSI}) for the row $i(i \in I'$ and $i < j < k)$:

$$E_{\text{ACSI}_i}(I', J') = 2\frac{\sum_{j \in I'; j \geq i+1} \sum_{k \in I'; k \geq j+1} E_{\text{CSI}}(i, j, k)}{(|I'| - 1)(|I'| - 2)} \qquad (25.19)$$

(iii) The last one is the E_S evaluation function [5]. In order to calculate E_S, we first discretize the initial data matrix $M(I, J) = [m_{i,j}]$, $I = \{1, 2, \ldots, n\}$ and $J = \{1, 2, \ldots, m\}$, into a matrix $M' = [m'_{i,l}]$ defined as

$$m'_{i,l} = \begin{cases} 1 & \text{if } m_{i,k} < m_{i,q} \\ -1 & \text{if } m_{i,k} > m_{i,q} \\ 0 & \text{if } m_{i,k} = m_{i,q} \end{cases} \qquad (25.20)$$

with $i \in \{1, 2, \ldots, n\}$, $l \in \{1, 2, \ldots, m(m-1)/2\}$, $k \in \{1, 2, \ldots, m-1\}$, $q \in \{2, 3, \ldots, m\}, q \geq k + 1$.

The matrix M' is constructed progressively by merging pairs of columns (conditions) from the input data matrix M. Since M has n rows and m columns, there are $m(m-1)/2$ distinct combinations.

Given a bicluster $b = (I', J')$, the quality of b is assessed via the following evaluation function $E_S(b)$:

$$E_S(b) = \frac{\sum_{i \in I'} \sum_{j \in I', j \geq i+1} F_{ij}}{|I'|(|I'| - 1)/2} \qquad (25.21)$$

with F_{ij} defined as

$$F_{ij} = \frac{\sum_{l \in J'} T(m'_{i,l} = m'_{j,l})}{|J'|} \qquad (25.22)$$

where $i \in I', j \in I', j \geq i + 1$.

Let us note that $0 \leq F_{ij} \leq 1$. A high (respectively low) F_{ij} value, close to 1 (respectively close to 0), indicates that *gene i* and *gene j* (under the given conditions) are strongly (respectively weakly) correlated [5]. Likewise for E_S, a high (respectively low) $E_S(b)$ value, close to 1 (respectively close to 0), indicates that the bicluster b is strongly (respectively weakly) correlated.

Regarding inter-bicluster evaluation functions, [38] introduced the so-called *gene match score* (GMS) given by

$$E_{\text{GMS}}(B_1, B_2) = \frac{1}{|B_1|} \sum_{(I_1, J_1) \in B_1} \max_{(I_2, J_2) \in B_2} \frac{|I_1 \cap I_2|}{|I_1 \cup I_2|} \qquad (25.23)$$

where B_1, B_2 are two groups of biclusters. Thereafter, more similar measures of match scores have been introduced [2, 13, 23, 30]. For instance, the evaluation functions, herein called *row and column match scores*, E_{RCMS_1} and E_{RCMS_2}, are proposed in [30] and [23], respectively. E_{RCMS_1} is given by

$$E_{\text{RCMS}_1}(B_1, B_2) = \frac{1}{|B_1|} \sum_{(I_1, J_1) \in B_1} \max_{(I_2, J_2) \in B_2} \frac{|I_1 \cap I_2| + |J_1 \cap J_2|}{|I_1 \cup I_2| + |J_1 \cup J_2|} \qquad (25.24)$$

and E_{RCMS_2} by

$$E_{\mathrm{RCMS}_2}(B_1, B_2) = \frac{1}{|B_1|} \sum_{(I_1, J_1) \in B_1} \max_{(I_2, J_2) \in B_2} \frac{|I_1 \cap I_2| + |J_1 \cap J_2|}{|I_1| + |J_1|} \qquad (25.25)$$

All these measures of match score are used to assess the accuracy of an algorithm to recover known biclusters and reveal true ones. Both E_{RCMS_1} and E_{RCMS_2} have the advantage of reflecting, simultaneously, the match of the row and column dimensions between biclusters, as opposed to E_{GMS} which does not take into account column match. They vary between 0 and 1 (the higher the better the accuracy). Let B_{opt} denote the set of true implanted biclusters in the data matrix M and B the set of the output biclusters of a biclustering algorithm. Thus, $E_{\mathrm{GMS}}(B_{\mathrm{opt}}, B)$ and $E_{\mathrm{RCMS}_1}(B_{\mathrm{opt}}, B)$ express how well each of the true biclusters are detected by the algorithm under consideration.

The function $E_{\mathrm{RCMS}_2}(B_X, B_Y)$, where B_X (respectively B_Y) denotes the set of biclusters detected by the algorithm X (respectively algorithm Y), has the particularity to allow the quantification of how well each bicluster identified by the algorithm X is contained into some bicluster detected by the algorithm Y.

All the evaluation functions above are deterministic in the sense that no statistical significance is provided for the degree of coherence of any bicluster detected by a biclustering algorithm. When a biclustering algorithm is applied on microarray data sets, enrichment analysis with respect to *Gene Ontology* (GO) annotations or other specific biological networks like metabolic and protein–protein interaction networks has usually been applied to check the biological significance of each found bicluster [30, 38, 42]. On a general data matrix M (not necessarily microarray data), Freitas et al. [23] recently presented a useful proposal to assign the statistical significance of biclusters. It is given in terms of how "unusually dense" a bicluster is, comparatively, with M. Concretely, the initial data matrix M is transformed into a binary matrix $M_b = \left[b_{ij} \right]$ through a discretization defined by

$$b_{ij} = \begin{cases} 1 & m_{ij} \in \mathcal{C} \\ 0 & \text{otherwise} \end{cases} \qquad (25.26)$$

where $\mathcal{C}$ is a set of real numbers satisfying the criterion that depends on the strategy defined by the biclustering algorithm. An example of $\mathcal{C}$ applied for the *iterative signature algorithm* (ISA) can be found in [23]. Assuming that the binary matrix M_b contains k 1's, a bicluster B will be considered as *potentially significant*, if its observed number of 1's is significantly greater than the real proportion $p = k/(|I| * |J|)$ of 1's in M. For this statistical testing, the p-value is calculated as

$$p\text{-value}(B) = 1 - \phi\left(\frac{|1_B|/|B| - p}{\sqrt{p(1-p)/|B|}} \right) \qquad (25.27)$$

where ϕ is the standard normal distribution function and $|1_B|$ represents the number of 1's in the bicluster B. Thus, when $p\text{-value}(B) < \alpha$, B will be classified as a bicluster *potentially significant* at a level of significance α.

Some biclustering methods identify no more than one bicluster for each application. With this evaluation strategy one can execute several times the biclustering algorithm upon M and assign for each time a statistical significance for the identified bicluster.

25.5   SYSTEMATIC AND STOCHASTIC BICLUSTERING ALGORITHMS

As we mentioned in the introduction of this chapter, the biclustering problem is NP hard [14, 31]. Consequently, heuristic search algorithms are typically used to approximate the problem by finding suboptimal solutions.

We distinguish two main classes of biclustering algorithms: *systematic search* algorithms and *stochastic search* algorithms, also called *metaheuristic* algorithms.

25.5.1   Systematic Biclustering Algorithms

Systematic search algorithms are based on one of the following general approaches:

1. *Divide-and-Conquer* (DAC) *Approach*   Generally, this approach divides repeatedly the problem into smaller subproblems with similar structures to the original problem until these subproblems become small enough to be solved directly. The solutions to the subproblems are then combined to create a solution to the original problem. With this approach, we start with a bicluster representing the whole data matrix; then we partition this matrix in two submatrices to obtain two biclusters. We reiterate recursively this process until we obtain a certain number of biclusters verifying a specific set of properties. For instance, Prelic et al. [38] partition the data matrix M' (M' is a discretization of a data matrix M which contains only binary values where a cell m_{ij} contains 1 if *gene i* is expressed under condition j and 0 otherwise) into three submatrices, one of which contains only 0 cells. The algorithm is then recursively applied to the remaining two submatrices and ends if the current matrix represents a bicluster which contains only 1's. The advantage of this approach is that it is fast; however, its biggest disadvantage is that it may ignore good biclusters by partitioning them before identifying them. Representative examples of algorithms adopting this approach are given by Dufiy and Quiroz [22], Hartigan [26], and Prelic et al. [38].

2. *Greedy Iterative Search* (GIS) *Approach*   This approach constructs a solution in a step-by-step way using a given quality criterion. Decisions made at each step are based on information at hand without worrying about the effect these decisions may have in the future. Moreover, once a decision is taken, it becomes irreversible and is never reconsidered. By applying this approach to the biclustering problem, at each iteration, we construct submatrices of the data matrix by adding/removing a row/column to/from the current submatrix that maximizes/minimizes a certain function. We reiterate this process until no other row/column can be added/removed to/from any submatrix. For instance, the *maximum similarity biclusters* [30] algorithm starts by constructing a similarity matrix based on a reference gene. A greedy strategy of removing rows/columns iteratively is employed to provide the maximum similarity bicluster in polynomial time. Shabalin et al. [40] extract large average submatrices according to a *Bonferroni-based* significance score. Several graph-theoretic approaches have also been proposed. Another recent work was reported by Ayadi et al. [6] which constructs a *directed acyclic graph* (DAG) to combine a subset of genes under a subset of conditions iteratively by adopting the evaluation functions E_{ACSI} and E_{ASR}.

   This approach presents the similar advantage and disadvantage of the DAC one. Representative examples of algorithms based on this approach are given by Ben-Dor et al. [10], Cheng et al. [13], Ihmels et al. [27], Liu and Wang [30], Shabalin et al. [40], Teng and Chan [44], Yang et al. [46, 48], and Ayadi et al. [6].

3. *Bicluster Enumeration* (BE) *Approach*   This approach tries to enumerate (explicitly or implicitly) all the solutions for an original problem. The enumeration process is generally represented by a search tree.

By applying this approach to the biclustering problem, we identify all the possible groups of biclusters in order to keep the *best* one. Ayadi et al. [4] use a *bicluster enumeration tree* (BET) to find all the biclusters (nodes) of interest reachable from the root of the BET by adopting to the E_{ASR} evaluation function. To reduce the size of the BET, a quality threshold is employed to cut branches that cannot lead to biclusters of desired quality.

This approach has the advantage of being able to obtain the best solutions. Its disadvantage is that it is costly in computing time and in memory space. Representative examples of algorithms adopting this approach are given by Liu and Wang [29], Tanay et al. [42], and Ayadi et al. [4, 7].

25.5.2 Stochastic Biclustering Algorithms

Stochastic search algorithms are based on one of the following general approaches:

1. *Neighborhood Search* (NS) *Approach*   Neighborhood search, also called *local search*, is based on the notion of neighborhood and a strategy exploiting this neighborhood. A neighborhood search algorithm starts with an initial solution s and then moves iteratively to a neighboring solution thanks to the neighborhood exploitation strategy. A neighboring solution is generally generated by applying a transformation operator, also called a *move operator*, to the current solution. At each iteration, the neighborhood exploitation strategy decides the neighboring solution to be selected to become the new current solution. For instance, the basic *hill-climbing* strategy replaces the current solution by a neighboring solution of better quality while other strategies based on *simulated annealing* and *tabu search* may substitute the current solution with a worse neighboring solution.

By applying this approach to the biclustering problem, we start by an initial solution which can be a cluster, a bicluster, or the whole matrix. Then, at each iteration, we try to improve this solution by adding and/or removing some genes/conditions to minimize/maximize a certain function. The difference with the greedy search algorithms is that if we delete, for example, one gene/condition, we can later add this gene/condition to the solution.

Cheng and Church [14] are probably the first to apply this concept to the biclustering problem. Their goal is to find biclusters with a E_{MSR} value lower than a fixed threshold. Hence, they proposed a local search procedure which deletes/adds genes/conditions to the biclusters. The multiple-node deletion method removes all genes and conditions with a E_{MSR} score lower than a fixed threshold. The single-node deletion method iteratively removes the gene or column that has low quality according to E_{MSR}. Finally, the node addition method adds genes and conditions that do not decrease the quality of the actual bicluster. In order to find a given number of biclusters, this approach is iteratively executed on the remaining genes and conditions that are not present in the previous obtained biclusters.

The move operator used by Ayadi et al. [5] is based on the drop/add operation which removes a *gene i* where $i \in I'$ from the bicluster $b = (I', J')$ and adds one *gene v*, where $v \notin I'$, or various *gene v, ..., gene w*, where $v \notin I', ..., w \notin I'$, to b. The move operator can be defined as follows: We first choose a pair of genes {*gene i*, *gene j*} from b which have a bad quality according to an evaluation function. Such a pair of genes contribute negatively to the quality of the bicluster b. Then we look for other pairs of genes {*gene j*, *gene* r_1}, {*gene j*, *gene* r_2}, ..., {*gene j*, *gene* r_n}, where $r_1 \notin I'$, ..., $r_n \notin I'$ which have a good quality according to the evaluation function. Hence, *gene j* contributes positively to the quality of the bicluster when it is associated with *gene* r_1 ... *gene* r_n. Finally, we replace *gene i* in b by *gene* r_1, *gene* r_2, ..., *gene* r_n. In Das and Idicula [18], the authors generate initial solutions using a K-means clustering algorithm. These solutions are then extended by adding more rows and columns using a *cardinality-based greedy randomized adaptive search* procedure. Their greedy strategy makes a choice that optimizes a local gain in the hope that this choice will lead to a globally good solution.

The advantage of this approach lies in the ability to explore large search spaces. This approach also offers the possibility of trade-off between solution quality and running time. Indeed, when the quality of a solution tends to improve gradually over time, the user can stop the execution at a chosen time. The disadvantage of this approach is that the search lead to suboptimal solutions (local maxima). Representative examples of algorithms adopting this approach are given by Bryan et al. [12], Cheng and Church [14], Dharan and Nair [19], Das and Idicula [18], and Ayadi et al. [5, 8].

2. *Evolutionary Computation* (EC) *Approach*   The evolutionary computation approach is based on the natural evolutionary process such as population, reproduction, mutation, recombination, and selection. Candidate solutions of the given problem are sampled by a set of individuals in a population. An evaluation mechanism (fitness evaluation) is established to assess the quality of each individual. Evolution operators eliminate some (less fit) individuals and produce new individuals from selected individuals.

By applying this approach to the biclustering problem, we start from an initial population of solutions, that is, clusters, biclusters, or the whole matrix. Then, we measure the quality of each solution of the population by the fitness function. We select a number of solutions to produce new solutions by recombination and mutation operators. This process ends when a prefixed stop condition is verified. For instance, Divina and Aguilar-Ruiz [20] generate a population representing biclusters of dimension 1 because these biclusters have a high E_{MSR} score. From this population, selection, crossover, and mutation are repeatedly applied to the population. A number of biclusters are selected for reproduction with a tournament selection operator. In other words, a certain number of biclusters are first selected randomly, and the best one according to E_{MSR} is chosen. Each selected pair of parents is recombined by a crossover operator. For this, three crossover (one point, two points and uniform) operators are applied with equal probability. The resulting offspring is mutated by using three mutation operators: the standard mutation operator and two mutation operators where one adds a row and the other a column to the bicluster. Since mutation is a highly random operation, it is applied with a low probability. The process is repeated with the new generation of offspring until a maximum number of generations is reached.

This approach shares the similar advantages and disadvantages with the neighborhood search approach. Few evolutionary algorithms are reported in the literature for the biclustering problem. Two examples are given by Divina and Aguilar-Ruiz [20, 21].

3. *Hybrid* (H) *Approach*   The hybrid approach, also called the *memetic approach*, tries to combine both the neighborhood search and the evolutionary approaches. This hybrid approach is known to be quite successful in solving many hard combinatorial search problems. The purpose of such an approach is to take advantage of the complementary nature of the evolutionary and neighborhood search methods. Indeed, it is generally believed that the evolutionary framework offers more facilities for exploration, while neighborhood search has more capability for exploitation. Combining them may offer a better balance between exploitation and exploration, which is highly desirable for an effective search.

Mitra and Banka [34] present a *multiobjective evolutionary algorithm* (MOEA) based on Pareto dominance. The authors try to find biclusters with maximum size and homogeneity by using a multiobjetive *nondominated sorting genetic algorithm* (NSGA-II) [15] in combination with the local search procedure. Gallo et al. [24] present another hybrid algorithm based on MOEA combined with a local search strategy. They extract biclusters with multiple criteria like maximum rows, columns, homogeneity, and row variance. A mechanism for reorienting the search in terms of row variance and size is provided. The mutation operator is performed when the individual needs to be mutated by means of the probability assigned to the operator. Hence, the gene/condition of the bicluster is mutated at a random position. The crossover operator is applied over both the genes and the conditions. Hence, when both children are obtained by combining at the end and at the center each of the two parents, the individual to select as the only descendant is the nondominated one. If both are nondominated, one of them is chosen at random. The authors apply the local search procedure based on Cheng and Church [14] on all the individuals in the resulting population of each generation.

Representative examples of algorithms adopting this approach are given by Bleuler et al. [11], Gallo et al. [24], and Mitra and Banka [34].

Table 25.2 shows microarray data sets used to evaluate biclustering algorithms. Let us note that some data sets contain missing values. To deal with this problem, Cheng and Church [14] propose to replace the missing values by random ones. Unfortunately, these random values can affect the discovery of coherent biclusters [47]. Another method to deal with missing values consists in removing the genes/conditions that contain such values [33]. Unfortunately, the removed genes/conditions can affect the discovery of coherent biclusters.

Now, we briefly present some biclustering tools that are publicly available for microarray data analysis:

1. GEMS [45] is a Web server for biclustering of microarray data. It is based on a Gibbs sampling paradigm [41]. GEMS is available at: `http://genomics10.bu.edu/terrence/gems/`.
2. BicAT [9] is a biclustering analysis toolbox that is mostly used by the community and contains several implementations of biclustering algorithms like the *order-preserving submatrix* (OPSM) algorithm [10], Cheng and Church's algorithm [14], the *iterative signature algorithm* (ISA) [27], the xMotif algorithm [35] and the Bimax algorithm [38]. BicAT is available at `http://www.tik.ee.ethz.ch/sop/bicat`.
3. BiVisu [13] is a biclustering algorithm based on *parallel coordinate* (PC) formulation. It can visualize the detected biclusters in a 2D setting by using PC plots. BiVisu is available at `http://www.eie.polyu.edu.hk/nflaw/Biclustering/index.html`.

TABLE 25.2 Microarray Data Sets Used to Evaluate Biclustering Algorithms

Data Set	Number of Genes	Number of Conditions	Website
Arabidopsis thaliana	734	69	`http://www.tik.ethz.ch/sop/bimax/`
Colon rectal cancer	2,000	62	`http://microarray.princeton.edu/oncology/affydata/index.html`
Human B-cell lymphoma	4,026	96	`http://arep.med.harvard.edu/biclustering/`
Leukemia	7,129	72	`http://sdmc.lit.org.sg/GEDatasets/Datasets.html`
Lung cancer	12,533	181	`http://sdmc.lit.org.sg/GEDatasets/Datasets.html`
Ovarian cancer tumor	15,154	253	`http://sdmc.lit.org.sg/GEDatasets/Datasets.html`
Prostate cancer	12,600	136	`http://sdmc.lit.org.sg/GEDatasets/Datasets.html`
Saccharomyces cerevisiae	2,993	173	`http://www.tik.ethz.ch/sop/bimax/`
Yeast cell cycle	2,884	17	`http://arep.med.harvard.edu/biclustering/`

4. Bayesian biclustering (BBC) [25] is a biclustering algorithm based on the Monte Carlo procedure. BBC is available at `http://www.people.fas.harvard.edu/junliu/BBC/`.

5. BicOverlapper [39] is a visual framework that supports:
   - Simultaneous visualization of one or more sets of biclusters
   - Visualization of microarray data matrices as heatmaps and PC
   - Visualization of *transcription regulatory networks*
   - Linkage of different visualizations and data to achieve a broader analysis of experiment results

   BicOverlapper is available at `http://vis.usal.es/bicoverlapper/`.

6. e-CCC-Biclustering [32] is a biclustering algorithm that can find and report all maximal contiguous column-coherent biclusters with approximate expression patterns. e-CCC-Biclustering is available at `http://kdbio.inesc-id.pt/software/e-ccc-biclustering`.

25.6 BICLUSTER VALIDATION

Biological validation can qualitatively evaluate the capacity of an algorithm to extract meaningful biclusters from a biological point of view. Assessing the biological meaning of the results of a biclustering algorithm is not a trivial task because there do not exist general guidelines in the literature on how to achieve this task. Several authors use artificial data sets to validate their approaches. However, an artificial scenario is inevitably biased regarding the underlying model and only reflects certain aspects of biological reality.

One possible validation concerns the *coverage* of biclusters. In fact, in the biclustering domain, it is interesting to have a good compromise between the size and the coherence of a bicluster. However, this is not enough to have a good group of biclusters. It is very important that the final group of biclusters provide good coverage of the data set. A large coverage of the data set is very important in several applications that employ biclusters. Indeed, the higher the number of highlighted correlations, the greater the amount of extracted information.

To assess the biclusters biologically, we can use GO annotation [16]. In GO, genes are assigned to three structured, controlled vocabularies, that is, *ontologies*, which describe gene products in terms of associated *biological processes, cellular components*, and *molecular functions* in a species-independent manner. Users measure the degree of enrichment, that is, p-value, by using a cumulative *hypergeometric* distribution that involves the probability of observing the number of genes from a particular GO category, that is, biological processes, cellular components, and molecular functions, within each bicluster. Statistical significance is evaluated for the genes in each bicluster by computing p-values which indicate how well they match with the different GO categories. Let us note that a smaller p-value, close to zero, is indicative of a better match [43].

The *Gene Ontology Consortium* (GOC) [16] (http://www.geneontology.org) is involved in the development and application of the GO. In the following, we present examples of Web tools related to the GOC:

1. GO Term Finder (http://db.yeastgenome.org/cgi-bin/GO/goTermFinder) searches for significant shared GO terms or parents of GO terms used to annotate gene products in a given list.

2. FuncAssociate (http://llama.med.harvard.edu/cgi/func/funcassociate) is a Web-based tool that accepts as input a list of genes and returns a list of GO attributes that are over-/underrepresented among the genes of the input list. Only those over-/underrepresented genes are reported.

3. GENECODIS (http://genecodis.dacya.ucm.es/) is a Web-based tool for the functional analysis of a list of genes. It integrates different sources of information to search for annotations that frequently co-occur in a list of genes and ranks them according to their statistical significance.

4. GeneBrowser (http://bioinformatics.ua.pt/genebrowser2/) is a Web-based tool that, for a given list of genes, combines data from several public databases with visualisation and analysis methods to help identify the most relevant and common biological characteristics. The functionalities provided include the following: a central point with the most relevant biological information for each inserted gene; a list of the most related papers in PubMed (http://www.ncbi.nlm.nih.gov/pubmed) and gene expression studies in ArrayExpress; and an extended approach to functional analysis applied to GO, homologies, gene chromosomal localization, and pathways.

The microarray data sets presented in Table 25.2 are such that each experimental condition corresponds to a patient presenting a kind of pathology. For example, the leukemia data set discriminates patients affected by either *lymphoblastic* or *myeloid leukemia*. Thus, we do not know the biological coherence between genes, while we know the medical classification of conditions. In this case, we can evaluate the ability of an algorithm to separate the samples according to their known classification. To this end, we can compute the number of columns labeled with the same class and belonging to the same bicluster. Obviously, the higher the number of columns in a bicluster labeled with the same class label, the higher its biological quality. In fact, this means that many patients with the same diagnosis are grouped together with respect to a subset of genes. Thus we could induce that those genes probably have similar functional category and characterize the majority class of patients.

25.7 CONCLUSION

The biclustering of microarray data has been the subject of much research. None of the existing biclustering algorithms are perfect and the construction of biologically significant groups of biclusters for large microarray data is still a problem that requires a continuous work.

Biological validation of biclusters of microarray data is one of the most important open issues. So far, there are no general guidelines in the literature on how to biologically validate such biclusters.

ACKNOWLEDGMENTS

Research partially supported by FEDER funds through COMPETE—Operational Programme Factors of Competitiveness and by Portuguese funds through the CIDMA and the Portuguese Foundation for Science and Technology (FCT—Fundação para a Ciência e a Tecnologia), under project PEst-C/MAT/UI4106/2011 with COMPETE No. FCOMP-01-0124-FEDER-022690.

REFERENCES

1. J. S. Aguilar-Ruiz. Shifting and scaling patterns from gene expression data. *Bioinformatics*, 21:3840–3845, 2005.

2. W. Ahmad and A. Khokhar. chawk: An efficient biclustering algorithm based on bipartite graph crossing minimization. In *Proceedings of the 2007 VLDB Workshop on Data Mining in Bioinformatics*. ACM, New York, 2007, pp. 1–12.

3. F. Angiulli, E. Cesario, and C. Pizzuti. Random walk biclustering for microarray data. *J. Inform. Sci.*, 178(6):1479–1497, 2008.

4. W. Ayadi, M. Elloumi, and J. K. Hao. A biclustering algorithm based on a bicluster enumeration tree: Application to DNA microarray data. *BioData Mining*, 2(1):9, 2009.

5. W. Ayadi, M. Elloumi, and J. K. Hao. Iterated local search for biclustering of microarray data. In Dijkstra et al. (Eds.) *Proceedings of 5th IAPR International Conference on Pattern Recognition in Bioinformatics (PRIB 2010)*, Vol. 6282 of *Lecture Notes in Computer Science*. Springer-Verlag, Berlin Heidelberg, 2010, pp. 219–229.

6. W. Ayadi, M. Elloumi, and J. K. Hao. Bicfinder: A biclustering algorithm for microarray data analysis. *Knowledge Inform. Syst. Int. J.*, 30(2):341–358, 2012.

7. W. Ayadi, M. Elloumi, and J. K. Hao. Bimine+: An efficient algorithm for discovering relevant biclusters of DNA microarray data. *Knowl.-Based Syst.*, 35:224–234, 2012.

8. W. Ayadi, M. Elloumi, and J. K. Hao. Pattern-driven neighborhood search for biclustering of microarray data. *BMC Bioinformatics*, 13(Suppl 7):S11, 2012.

9. S. Barkow, S. Bleuler, A. Prelic, P. Zimmermann, and E. Zitzler. Bicat: A biclustering analysis toolbox. *Bioinformatics*, 22(10):1282–1283, 2006.

10. A. Ben-Dor, B. Chor, R. Karp, and Z. Yakhini. Discovering local structure in gene expression data: The order-preserving submatrix problem. In G. Myers et al. (Eds.) *Recomb'02: Proceedings of the Sixth Annual International Conference on Computational Biology*. ACM, New York, 2002, pp. 49–57.

11. S. Bleuler, A. Prelic, and E. Zitzler. An EA framework for biclustering of gene expression data. In *Proceedings of Congress on Evolutionary Computation*, IEEE, Vol. 1, 2004, pp. 166–173.

12. K. Bryan, P. Cunningham, and N. Bolshakova. Application of simulated annealing to the biclustering of gene expression data. *IEEE Trans. Inform. Technol. Biomed.*, 10(3):519–525, 2006.

13. K. O. Cheng, N. F. Law, W. C. Siu, and A. W. Liew. Identification of coherent patterns in gene expression data using an efficient biclustering algorithm and parallel coordinate visualization. *BMC Bioinformatics*, 9(210):1282–1283, 2008.

14. Y. Cheng and G. M. Church. Biclustering of expression data. In R. Altman et al. (Eds.) *Proceedings of the Eighth International Conference on Intelligent Systems for Molecular Biology.*, AAAI Press, Washington, DC, 2000, pp. 93–103.

15. C. A. Coello Coello, G. B. Lamont, and D. A. Van Veldhuizen. *Evolutionary Algorithms for Solving Multi-Objective Problems (Genetic and Evolutionary Computation)*, 2nd ed., Springer Science + Business Media, New York, 2007.

16. Gene Ontology Consortium. Gene Ontology: Tool for the unification of biology. *Nat. Genet.*, 25:25–29, 2000.

17. R. Das, S. Mitra, H. Banka, and S. Mukhopadhyay. Evolutionary biclustering with correlation for gene interaction networks. In A. Ghosh et al. (Eds.), *Pattern Recognition and Machine Intelligence*, Vol. 4815 of *Lecture Notes in Computer Science*, Springer, Heidelberg, 2007, pp. 416–424.

18. S. Das and S. M. Idicula. Application of cardinality based grasp to the bi clustering of gene expression data. *Int. J. Comput. Appl.*, 1(18):44–53, 2010.

19. A. Dharan and A. S. Nair. Biclustering of gene expression data using reactive greedy randomized adaptive search procedure. *BMC Bioinformatics*, 10(Suppl. 1):S27, 2009.

20. F. Divina and J. S. Aguilar-Ruiz. Biclustering of expression data with evolutionary computation. *IEEE Trans. Knowledge Data Eng.*, 18(5):590–602, 2006.

21. F. Divina and J. S. Aguilar-Ruiz. A multi-objective approach to discover biclusters in microarray data. In *gecco'07: Proceedings of the 9th Annual Conference on Genetic and Evolutionary Computation*. ACM, New York, 2007, pp. 385–392.

22. D. Dufiy and A. Quiroz. A permutation based algorithm for block clustering. *J. Classification*, (8):65–91, 1991.

23. A. Freitas, V. Afreixo, M. Pinheiro, J. L. Oliveira, G. Moura, and M. Santos. Improving the performance of the iterative signature algorithm for the identification of relevant patterns. *Stat. Anal. Data Mining*, 4(1):71–83, 2011.

24. C. A. Gallo, J. A. Carballido, and I. Ponzoni. Microarray biclustering: A novel memetic approach based on the pisa platform. In *EvoBIO '09: Proceedings of the 7th European Conference on Evolutionary Computation, Machine Learning and Data Mining in Bioinformatics*, Springer-Verlag, Berlin and Heidelberg, 2009, pp. 44–55.

25. J. Gu and J. S. Liu. Bayesian biclustering of gene expression data. *BMC Genomics*, 9(Suppl. 1):S4, 2008.

26. J. A. Hartigan. Direct clustering of a data matrix. *J. Am. Stat. Assoc.*, 67(337):123–129, 1972.

27. J. Ihmels, S. Bergmann, and N. Barkai. Defining transcription modules using large-scale gene expression data. *Bioinformatics*, 13:1993–2003, 2004.

28. E. L. Lehmann and H. J. M. D'Abrera. *Nonparametrics: Statistical Methods based on Ranks*, rev. ed. Prentice-Hall, Englewood Cliffs, NJ, 1998, pp. 292–323.

29. J. Liu and W. Wang. Op-cluster: Clustering by tendency in high dimensional space. *IEEE International Conference on Data Mining*, 2003, pp. 187–194.

30. X. Liu and L. Wang. Computing the maximum similarity bi-clusters of gene expression data. *Bioinformatics*, 23(1):50–56, 2007.

31. S. C. Madeira and A. L. Oliveira. Biclustering algorithms for biological data analysis: A survey. *IEEE/ACM Trans. Computat. Biol. Bioinformatics (TCBB)*, 1(1):24–45, 2004.

32. S. C. Madeira and A. L. Oliveira. A polynomial time biclustering algorithm for finding approximate expression patterns in gene expression time series. *Algorithms Mol. Biol.*, 4:8, 2009.

33. S. C. Madeira and A. L. Oliveira. An efficient biclustering algorithm for finding genes with similar patterns in time-series expression data. In D. Sankoff et al. (Eds.) *Proceedings of the 5th Asia Pacific Bioinformatics Conference*, Vol. 5 of *Series on Advances in Bioinformatics and Computational Biology*, Imperial College Press, London, 2007, pp. 67–80.

34. S. Mitra and H. Banka. Multi-objective evolutionary biclustering of gene expression data. *Pattern Recognition*, 39(12):2464–2477, 2006.

35. T. M. Murali and S. Kasif. Extracting conserved gene expression motifs from gene expression data. *Pacific Symp. Biocomput.*, 8:77–88, 2003.

36. J. L. Myers and D. W. Arnold. *Research Design and Statistical Analysis*, 2nd ed., Lawrence Erlbaum Associates, New Jersey, 2003.

37. B. Pontes, F. Divina, R. Giráldez, and J. S. Aguilar-Ruiz. Virtual error: A new measure for evolutionary biclustering. In E. Marchiori, J. H. Moore, and J. C. Rajapakse (Eds.), *Evolutionary Computation, Machine Learning and Data Mining in Bioinformatics*, Vol. 4447 of *Lecture Notes in Computer Science*. Springer, Berlin Heidelberg, 2007, pp. 217–226.

38. A. Prelic, S. Bleuler, P. Zimmermann, P. Buhlmann, W. Gruissem, L. Hennig, L. Thiele, and E. Zitzler. A systematic comparison and evaluation of biclustering methods for gene expression data. *Bioinformatics*, 22(9):1122–1129, 2006.

39. R. Santamaria, R. Therón, and L. Quintales. A visual analytics approach for understanding biclustering results from microarray data. *BMC Bioinformatics*, 9:247, 2008.

40. A. A. Shabalin, V. J. Weigman, C. M. Perou, and A. B. Nobel. Finding large average submatrices in high dimensional data. *Ann. Appl. Stat.*, 3(985):985–1012, 2009.

41. Q. Sheng, Y. Moreau, and B. De Moor. Biclustering microarray data by Gibbs sampling. *Bioinformatics*, 19:II196–II205, 2003.

42. A. Tanay, R. Sharan, and R. Shamir. Discovering statistically significant biclusters in gene expression data. *Bioinformatics*, 18:S136–S144, 2002.

43. S. Tavazoie, J. D. Hughes, M. J. Campbell, R. J. Cho, and G. M. Church. Systematic determination of genetic network architecture. *Nat. Genet.*, 22:281–285, 1999.

44. L. Teng and L. Chan. Discovering biclusters by iteratively sorting with weighted correlation coefficient in gene expression data. *J. Signal Process. Syst.*, 50(3):267–280, 2008.

45. C. J. Wu and S. Kasif. Gems: A web server for biclustering analysis of expression data. *Nucleic Acids Res.*, 33:W596–W599, 2005.

46. J. Yang, H. Wang, W. Wang, and P. Yu. Enhanced biclustering on expression data. In *bibe'03: Proceedings of the 3rd IEEE Symposium on BioInformatics and BioEngineering*. IEEE Computer Society, Washington, DC, 2003, p. 321.

47. J. Yang, W. Wang, H. Wang, and P. S. Yu. delta-clusters: Capturing subspace correlation in a large data set. In D. Agrawal et al. (Eds.) *Proceedings of the 18th IEEE Conference on Data Engineering*, IEEE Computer Society. Los Alamitos, CA, 2002, pp. 517–528.

48. Y. H. Yang, S. Dudoit, P. Luu, D. M. Lin, V. Peng, J. Ngai, and T. P. Speed. Normalization for cdna microarray data: A robust composite method addressing single and multiple slide systematic variation. *Nucleic Acids Res.*, 30:1–12, 2002.

49. Z. Zhang, A. Teo, B. C. Ooi, and K. L. Tan. Mining deterministic biclusters in gene expression data. *IEEE Int. Symp. Bioinformatic Bioeng.*, 283–292, 2004.

CHAPTER 26

MULTIOBJECTIVE BICLUSTERING OF GENE EXPRESSION DATA WITH BIOINSPIRED ALGORITHMS

KHEDIDJA SERIDI, LAETITIA JOURDAN, and EL-GHAZALI TALBI

INRIA Lille Nord Europe, Villeneuve d'Ascq, France

26.1 INTRODUCTION

Studying thousands of gene activities under several experimental conditions (environmental, individual, tissue, etc.) simultaneously is now possible using microarray technologies.

Microarrays use results of a large amount of data usually presented in 2D matrices, where rows represent genes and columns represent experimental conditions. The analysis of the resulting data consists in extracting genes that have similar behavior (coexpress) under a subset of conditions. This analysis is usually done by using data-mining methods such as *biclustering*. Biclustering performs simultaneously the selection of rows and columns of a data matrix leading to the discovery of biclusters. A *bicluster* is essentialy a submatrix revealing a certain homogeneity. Two main approaches for biclustering can be found in the literature: *systematic search approach* and *stochastic search or metaheuristic approach*. The systematic search approaches can be divided into five groups: *iterative row and column clustering combination* [12, 21], *divide and conquer, greedy iterative search* [5], *exhaustive bicluster enumeration*, and *distribution parameter identification* [15] (for a review see [19]). The second group is based on metaheuristics. Among the metaheuristic methods, we can mention *neighborhood-based algorithms* like *simulated annealing* [4], GRASP [10], and *evolutionary and hybrid algorithms* [11, 20].

In this work, we propose *a multiobjective model* for the biclustering problem, and we present two *hybrid multiobjective algorithms* called $MOBI_{nsga}$ and $MOBI_{ibea}$ which are based on the well-known metaheuristics NSGA-II [9] and IBEA [24]. A comparative study between them is proposed. This chapter is organized as follows: in Section 26.2, the definitions related to biclustering are presented. *Multiobjective concepts* and *biclustering multiobjective modeling* are explained in Section 26.3. In Section 26.4, we give a description of our multiobjective framework for solving the model. Experimental results and a comparative analysis are discussed in Section 26.5. The last section concludes the chapter.

Biological Knowledge Discovery Handbook: Preprocessing, Mining, and Postprocessing of Biological Data,
First Edition. Edited by Mourad Elloumi and Albert Y. Zomaya.
© 2014 John Wiley & Sons, Inc. Published 2014 by John Wiley & Sons, Inc.

TABLE 26.1 Gene Expression Data Matrix

	Con. 1	...	Con. j	...	Con. M
Gene 1	a_{11}	...	a_{1j}	...	a_{1M}
...	...	...	...	...	...
Gene i	a_{i1}	...	a_{ij}	...	a_{iM}
...	...	...	...	...	...
Gene N	a_{N1}	...	a_{Nj}	...	a_{NM}

Note: Conditions (Con.) are in columns and genes are in rows

26.2 BICLUSTERING PROBLEM IN MICROARRAY DATA

Microarray data can be presented in a matrix form $A = (X, Y)$ (see Table 26.1), where $X = \{i_1, i_2, \ldots, i_N\}$ is a set of N genes and $Y = \{j_1, \ldots, j_M\}$ a set of M conditions. Assume $a_{ij} \in A$ ($i \in X, i \in Y$) corresponds to the expression level of gene i under condition j. A bicluster $B = (I, J)$ ($I \subseteq X, J \subseteq Y$) is a submatrix of A that satisfies some specific characteristic of homogeneity. A bicluster with constant values in the genes (rows) is called a *flat bicluster*. The biclustering problem consists of extracting biclusters with maximal size and respecting a certain homogeneity constraint. The homogeneity of a bicluster can be defined using the *mean-squared residue*.

26.2.1 Mean-Squared Residue

The mean-squared residue (MSR) is a measure defined by Cheng and Church [5] in order to assess the overall quality of a bicluster.

Given a bicluster $B = (I, J)$. The residue $r(a_{ij})$ of an element $a_{ij} \in B$ is given by the equation

$$r(a_{ij}) = a_{ij} - a_{iJ} - a_{Ij} + a_{IJ} \tag{26.1}$$

where

$$a_{Ij} = \frac{\sum_{i \in I} a_{ij}}{|I|} \tag{26.2}$$

$$a_{iJ} = \frac{\sum_{j \in J} a_{ij}}{|J|} \tag{26.3}$$

$$a_{IJ} = \frac{\sum_{i \in I, j \in J} a_{ij}}{|I||J|} \tag{26.4}$$

The MSR of the bicluster is

$$\mathrm{MSR}(I, J) = \frac{1}{|I||J|} \sum_{i \in I, j \in J} r(a_{ij})^2 \tag{26.5}$$

The lower the MSR value of the bicluster, the better its quality. A bicluster with MSR value less than δ is called a *δ-bicluster*.

26.2.2 Mean Row Variance

A bicluster with a low MSR value, indicates that the expression levels fluctuate in unison [5]. This includes flat biclusters (the same expression value for each gene under all the conditions). For gene expression data, we are interested in biclusters with genes that exhibit significant fluctuations in the different conditions, that is, biclusters with significant row variances. To evaluate the variance in the bicluster's rows, we define the mean row variance Rvar:

$$\text{Rvar}(I, J) = \frac{1}{|I||J|} \sum_{i \in I, j \in J} (a_{ij} - a_{iJ})^2 \qquad (26.6)$$

26.3 MULTIOBJECTIVE MODEL FOR BICLUSTERING IN GENE EXPRESSION DATA

In this section, we give some multiobjective optimization concepts. Then, we present our multiobjective biclustering model.

26.3.1 Multiobjective Optimization

26.3.1.1 *Multiobjective Optimization Problem*   A *multiobjective optimization problem* (MOP) may be defined as

$$\text{MOP} = \begin{cases} \min F(x) = (f_1(x), f_2(x), \dots, f_n(x)) \\ x \in S \end{cases}$$

where n ($n \geq 2$) is the number of objectives, $x = (x_1, \dots, x_k)$ is the vector representing the decision variables, and S represents the set of feasible solutions associated with equality and inequality constraints and explicit bounds, $F(x) = (f_1(x), f_2(x), \dots, f_n(x))$ is the vector of objectives to be optimized.

The search space S represents the decision space of the MOP. The space in which the objective vector belongs to is called the *objective space*. The vector F can be defined as a cost function from the decision space in the objective space that evaluates the quality of each solution $(x_1, \dots, x_k)$ by assigning an objective vector $(y_1, \dots, y_n)$ which represents the quality of the solution (fitness).

As the criteria are usually in conflict, it is not usual to have a solution x^* associated with a decision variable vector where x^* is optimal for all the objectives. Other concepts were established to consider optimality. A partial order relation could be defined, known as the dominance relation (see Figure 26.1).

26.3.1.2 *Pareto Dominance*   For a minimization MOP, an objective vector $u = (u_1, \dots, u_n)$ is said to *dominate* $v = (v_1, \dots, v_n)$ (denoted by $u \prec v$) if and only if no component of v is smaller than the corresponding component of u and at least one component of u is strictly smaller, that is,

$$\forall i \in [1, \dots, n] : u_i \leq v_i \land \exists i \in [1, \dots, n] : u_i < v_i$$

26.3.1.3 *Pareto Optimality*   A solution $x^* \in S$ is *Pareto optimal* if, for every $x \in S$, $F(x)$ does not dominate $F(x^*)$, that is, $\forall F(x) \nprec F(x^*)$.

26.3.1.4 *Pareto Optimal Set*   For a given MOP(F, S), the *Pareto-optimal set* is defined as $P^* = \{x \in S / \nexists x' \in S, F(x') \prec F(x)\}$.

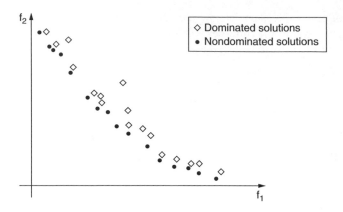

FIGURE 26.1   Dominated and nondominated solutions in objective space (minimization problem).

Figure 26.1 illustrates the dominance concept in the objective space.

26.3.1.5   Pareto Front   For a given MOP(F, S) and its Pareto-optimal set P^*, the *Pareto front* is defined as $PF^* = \{F(x), x \in P^*\}$.

The Pareto front is the image of the Pareto-optimal set in the objective space. Obtaining the Pareto front of a MOP is the main goal of the multiobjective optimization. However, given that the Pareto front can contain a large number of points, a good approximation of the Pareto-optimal set may contain a limited number of Pareto solutions that satisfy two properties [8]:

- The closeness to Pareto-optimal set
- Diversification of solutions.

Multiobjective evolutionary algorithms (MOEAs) and other metaheuristics have been successfully applied to both theoretical and practical MOPs [8].

MOEAs are population-based metaheuristics where a set of solutions (population) is iteratively handled in order to get a final set of solutions.

For a given solution, a fitness assignment procedure maps a fitness vector to a single value. The fitness scalar value measures the quality of the solution. According to the fitness assignment strategy, multiobjective metaheuristics can be classified into four main categories:

1. *Scalar Approaches*   They are based on the MOP transformation into a mono-objective problem.
2. *Criterion-Based Approaches*   The search is performed by treating the various non-commensurable objectives separately.
3. *Dominance-Based Approaches*   Dominance-based approaches use the concept of dominance and Pareto optimality to guide the search process. The objective vectors are scalarized using the dominance relation. Most dominance-based approaches are evolutionary multiobjective algorithms. The commonly used ones are NSGA-II [9] and SPEA2 [23].

4. *Indicator-Based Approaches* In indicator-based approaches, the metaheuristics use performance quality indicators to drive the search toward the Pareto front. Example: IBEA [24].

26.3.1.6 *Quality Indicators* To evaluate the quality of the different multiobjective metaheuristics, various metrics have been suggested, but there exist no generally accepted standard for performance evaluation. Quality indicators may be classified using different properties, such as arity (unary, binary) and complementary performance goals (convergence to the optimal Pareto front and diversity of solutions along the front). In the following we present two well-known quality indicators: *hypervolume* and *epsilon* indicators.

1. *Hypervolume Indicator* The *hypervolume indicator* (I_H) was proposed by Zitzler et al. [22]. In its unary form, the hypervolume indicator I_H associated with an approximation A is given by the volume of the objective space portion that is weakly dominated by the set A. This intuitive quality indicator needs the specification of a reference point Z_{ref} that denotes an upper bound over all the objectives (Figure 26.2). In its binary form, computing the *hypervolume metric* needs a reference set Z_N^*. It represents the hypervolume dominated by Z_N^* and not by A (Figure 26.2). The choice of the reference point affects the ordering of nondominated sets. The reference point Z_{ref} may be fixed as $(1.05\, z_1^{\max}, \ldots, 1.05\, z_n^{\max})$, where $z_i^{\max}$ represents the upper bound of the objectives obtained from the reference set. The more this measure is close to zero, the better is the approximation A.

2. *Additive Epsilon Indicator* The ϵ-*indicator* family was introduced by Knowles et al. [13]. The unary additive ϵ-indicator $I_{\epsilon+}^1$, which is a distance-based indicator, gives the minimum factor by which an approximation A has to be translated in the objective space to weakly dominate the reference set Z_N^*. Define $I_{\epsilon+}^1$ as

$$I_{\epsilon+}^1(A) = I_{\epsilon+}(A, Z_N^*)$$

where

$$I_{\epsilon+}^1(A, B) = \min_{\epsilon \in R}\{\forall z \in B, \exists z' \in A : z_i' - \epsilon \le z_i, \forall A \le i \le n\}$$

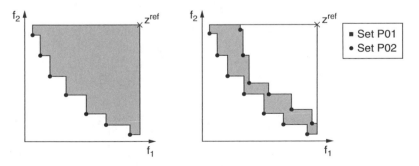

FIGURE 26.2 Unary versus binary hypervolume indicator for nondominated approximation set of solutions. The binary hypervolume indicator is computed for two Pareto sets of solutions.

26.3.2 Multiobjective Biclustering

Extracting biclusters from a data matrix can be seen as a combinatorial optimization problem, where two objectives are to be maximized: the similarity (homogeneity) between the bicluster's elements and its size. When optimizing the similarity criterion using MSR, the trivial solutions S (bicluster with only one row and one column) are optimal solutions, since $\text{MSR}(a_{ij}) = 0$ and increasing the size of the bicluster increases its MSR value. We can therefore deduce that the problem of biclustering is a multiobjective optimization problem.

In this way, some multiobjective models have been proposed to formulate the biclustering problem [14, 16–18, 20]. Some of the existing methods to solve the multiobjective models are based on *hybrid evolutionary algorithms* [20], and others are based on *swarm intelligence optimization* [14, 16–18].

26.3.2.1 *Proposed Model*   Given a data matrix $A = (X, Y)$, the size of a bicluster $B = (I, J) (I \subseteq X, J \subseteq Y)$ is defined by its number of elements: $|I||J|$. Using this definition as an objective, we give more chance to the number of rows to be maximized since the total number of rows is higher than the total number of columns. Lashkarghir et al. [14] proposed to separate rows and columns and to consider two objective functions (one for rows and the other for columns).

In our model we use only one objective function to evaluate the size of the bicluster, which gives the same chance to the number of rows and the number of columns to be maximized:

$$f_1(I, J) = \frac{1}{2}\frac{|I|}{|X|} + \frac{1}{2}\frac{|J|}{|Y|}$$

To model the biclustering problem, we use the following functions:

$$f_1(I, J) = \frac{1}{2}\frac{|I|}{|X|} + \frac{1}{2}\frac{|J|}{|Y|}$$

$$f_2(I, J) = \begin{cases} \dfrac{\text{MSR}(I, J)}{\delta} & \text{if } \text{MSR}(I, J) \leqslant \delta \\ 0 & \text{else} \end{cases}$$

$$f_3(I, J) = \frac{1}{\text{Rvar}(I, J) + 1}$$

Such that

$$\text{MSR}(I, J) \leqslant \delta$$

Note that f_1 and f_2 are to be maximized, while f_3 is to be minimized. The user threshold δ represents the maximum dissimilarity allowed within the bicluster. As the size and similarity criteria are conflicting, we allow the function f_2 to be maximized as long as the residue does not exceed the threshold δ, while f_1 (size) is always maximized and f_3 is always minimized.

26.4   BIOINSPIRED ALGORITHMS FOR BICLUSTERING

To solve this model, we propose two hybrid multiobjective evolutionary algorithms called $\text{MOBI}_{\text{nsga}}$ and $\text{MOBI}_{\text{ibea}}$, based on NSGA-II[9] and IBEA[24], respectively.

We start by giving the main components of the MOBI algorithm, which can be instantiated using any MOEA. Then we give the definitions of NSGA-II and IBEA.

26.4.1 General Presentation of MOBI Algorithms

(a) *Encoding* In the existing metaheuristics for solving the biclustering problem [14, 20], a solution (bicluster) is usually represented by a fixed-size binary string, with a bit string for genes appended by another bit string for conditions. A bit is set to unity if the corresponding gene/condition is present in the bicluster and to zero otherwise. When using the local search (Cheng and Church's algorithm), we need to explore all the rows and all the columns of each bicluster, which is very time consuming if the classical binary representation is considered, since the microarray data have high numbers of rows and columns. In our algorithm, we choose to represent a bicluster as a list of four parts: The first part is an ordered-row index the second an ordered-column index, the third the row number, and the fourth the column number. By this representation we aim to reduce time and memory space, especially for the local search. A similar representation was used in [7].

Example: Given the data matrix presented in Table 26.2, the list {1 3 2 3 2 2} represents the following bicluster compound of two rows (1 and 3) and two columns (2 and 3):

TABLE 26.2 Example Data Matrix

6	3	11
5	17	2
1	0	4

$$\{1\ 3\ 2\ 3\ 2\ 2\} \Longrightarrow \begin{bmatrix} 3 & 11 \\ 0 & 4 \end{bmatrix}$$

(b) *Initial Population* The initial population is generated randomly.

(c) *Operators* For the proposed encoding, we define the following crossover and mutation operators which are used to generate a new offspring in each generation:

1. *Crossover Operator* Single-point crossover is used in each part of the solution (row part and column part). Each part undergoes crossover separately.

   Let parents be chromosomes $P_1 = \{r_1, \ldots, r_n, c_1, \ldots, c_m, r_{nb}, c_{nb}\}$ and $P_2 = \{r'_1, \ldots, r'_l, c'_1, \ldots, c'_k, r'_{nb}, c'_{nb}\}$, where $r_n \leqslant r'_l$.

   The crossover in the row part is performed as follows: The crossover point in P_1, and λ_1 is generated as a random integer in the range $2 \leqslant \lambda_1 \leqslant r_n$. the crossover point in P_2, $\lambda_2 = r'_j$, where $r'_j \geqslant \lambda_1$ and $r'_{j-1} \leqslant \lambda_1$. In the same way, the crossover in the columns part is performed.

   For example, consider the following parents:

   P_1 : 1 4 15 18 22 28 | 2 5 7 | 6 | 3
   P_2 : 3 5 8 13 16 27 35 | 1 2 4 6 8 | 7 | 5

   Suppose the third gene index and the second condition index of P_1 are selected, so $\lambda_1 = 15$ and $\lambda'_1 = 5$; then $\lambda_2 = 16$ and $\lambda'_2 = 6$.
   Hence, after crossover the resultant children are

   C_1 : 1 4 15 16 27 35 | 2 5 6 8 | 6 | 4
   C_2 : 3 5 8 13 18 22 28 | 1 2 4 7 | 7 | 4

2. *Mutation Operator* In our algorithms, we replace the mutation operation by Cheng and Church's (CC) algorithm [5]. The CC algorithm was the first biclustering algorithm applied to gene expression problems, and it is based on the concept of δ-biclusters. The goal of CC is to obtain K δ-biclusters for a given data set. The CC algorithm starts with a single bicluster, representing the whole data set, and iteratively removes rows and columns of this bicluster until the residue is equal to or less than δ. After that, it starts to insert rows and columns (that are not in the bicluster yet) sequentially until the insertion of any other row or column increases the residue to a value above δ. After the first bicluster is constructed, the rows and columns already present in this bicluster are replaced by random values in the original data set, and the whole process is restarted until a predefined number K of biclusters is created.

The algorithm starts from a solution of this set. The irrelevant genes or conditions having mean-squared residue above (or below) a certain threshold are eliminated (or added) using the following conditions (Algorithm 26.1). A "node" refers to a gene or a condition.

ALGORITHM 26.1

```
/* CC Algorithm[5] */
/*Multiple node deletion*/
```

1 Compute a_{iJ}, a_{Ij}, a_{IJ} and $MSR(I, J)$
2   **if** ($\frac{1}{|J|} \sum_{j \in J}(a_{ij} - a_{iJ} - a_{Ij} + a_{IJ})^2 > \alpha MSR(I, J)$)
        Remove the rows $i \in I$
    endif
3 Recompute a_{iJ}, a_{Ij}, a_{IJ} and $MSR(I, J)$.
4   **if** ($\frac{1}{|I|} \sum_{i \in I}(a_{ij} - a_{iJ} - a_{Ij} + a_{IJ})^2 > \alpha MSR(I, J)$)
        Remove the columns $j \in J$
endif

```
/*Single node deletion*/
```

1   **while** ($MSR(I, J) > \delta$)
        Recompute a_{iJ}, a_{Ij}, a_{IJ} and $MSR(I, J)$.
        Find the node d (row or column) with the largest squared residue.
        Delete d.
    endwhile

```
/*Multiple node addition*/
```

1 Recompute a_{iJ}, a_{Ij}, a_{IJ} and $MSR(I, J)$.
2   **if** ($\frac{1}{|I|} \sum_{i \in I}(a_{ij} - a_{iJ} - a_{Ij} + a_{IJ})^2 \leqslant MSR(I, J)$)
        Add the columns $j \notin J$
    endif
3 Recompute a_{iJ}, a_{Ij}, a_{IJ} and $MSR(I, J)$.
4   **if** ($\frac{1}{|J|} \sum_{j \in J}(a_{ij} - a_{iJ} - a_{Ij} + a_{IJ})^2 \leqslant MSR(I, J)$)
        Add the rows $i \notin I$
    endif

26.4.2 Nondominated Sorting Genetic Algorithm II (NSGA-II)

NSGA-II is probably the most widely used multiobjective resolution method [9]. At each NSGA-II generation, solutions from the current population are ranked into several classes. Individuals mapping to vectors from the first nondominated set all belong to the best efficient set; individuals mapping to vectors from the second nondominated set all belong to the second best efficient set; and so on. Two values are then assigned to each population member. The first one corresponds to the rank to which the corresponding solution belongs and represents the quality of the solution in terms of convergence.

The second one, the crowding distance, consists in estimating the density of solutions surrounding a particular point of the objective space and represents the quality of the solution in terms of diversity. A solution is said to be better than another one if it has a best rank value or, in case of equality, if it has the best crowding distance. The selection strategy is a deterministic tournament between two random solutions. At the replacement step, only the best individuals are kept with respect to a predefined population size. Furthermore, it has to be noted that, in addition to the original NSGA-II, an external population is added, the so-called *archive*, in order to store the whole set of potentially efficient solutions found during the search.

The main steps of NSGA-II are illustrated in Algorithm 26.2.

26.4.3 Indicator-Based Multiobjective Evolutionary Algorithm (IBEA)

IBEA is an evolutionary multiobjective algorithm proposed by Zitzler and Kunzli in 2004 [24]. The optimization goal is established in terms of a binary indicator defining the selection operator. The fitness assignment scheme is based on a pairwise comparison of solutions contained in a population by using a binary quality indicator. No diversity preservation technique is required, according to the indicator being used. The selection scheme for reproduction is a binary tournament between randomly chosen individuals. The replacement strategy is an environmental one that consists of deleting, one by one, the worst individuals and in updating the fitness values of the remaining solutions each time there is a deletion; this is continued until the required population size is reached. Moreover, an archive stores solutions mapping to potentially nondominated points in order to prevent their loss during the stochastic search process.

ALGORITHM 26.2

```
/*NSGA-II[9]*/
1 Initialize the population randomly.
2 Calculate the multiobjective fitness function.
3 Rank the population using the dominance criteria.
4 Calculate the crowding distance.
5 Do selection using crowding distance operator.
6 Do crossover and mutation to generate offspring population.
7 Replace the parent population by the best members of the
combined using crowded.
8 Termination test.
```

ALGORITHM 26.3

```
/* IBEA[24]*/
1 Initialize the population randomly.
2 Calculate the multi-objective fitness function.
3 Perform environmental selection.
4 Termination test.
5 Perform binary tournament selection with replacement.
6 Add the generated offspring to the population.
7 Do crossover and mutation to generate offspring population.
```

The main steps of the IBEA are given in Algorithm 26.3.

26.5 RESULTS AND DISCUSSIONS

In this section, we present the results obtained using the proposed algorithms $MOBI_{nsga}$ and $MOBI_{ibea}$ over well-known data sets. The results are compared to results obtained from the literature using the multiobjective biclustering algorithms NSGA2B [20] and MOP-SOB [18] and CC algorithm [5]. NSGA2B is a hybrid algorithm which combines NSGA-II and the CC algorithm. In NSGA2B, the CC algorithm is applied both after the generation of the initial population and after the application of the operators (crossover and mutation). The aim of NSGA2B is to extract biclusters with large size and mean-squared residue value under an upper bound δ, for which NSGA2B maximizes the mean-squared residue as long as it is smaller than δ. While MOPSOB is a multiobjective particle swarm algorithm that aims to extract biclusters of large size, low-mean-squared residue, and high row variances.

26.5.1 Data

In our experiments we used the well-known *yeast cell cycle* [6], *human B-cell expression* [6], and *colon cancer* [1] data sets to allow comparison of our results with the literature:

> *Yeast Cell Cycle*   [6] contains 2884 genes and 17 conditions. Two of the 2884 rows contain missing values. The missing values are replaced by random numbers between 0 and 800 as in [20].
>
> *Human B-Cell Expression*   contains 4026 genes and 96 conditions, with 12.3% missing values. We replaced the missing values by random numbers between −800 and 800 as in [20].
>
> *Colon Cancer*   contains 2000 genes and 62 samples.

26.5.2 Parameters

For all the data sets (yeast cell cycle [6], human B-cell expression [6], and colon cancer [1]), we ran 20 times each algorithm for 400 generations with a population of size 200. The crossover and mutation probabilities are set to 0.5 and 0.4, respectively. For the local search we set α to 1.8. These parameters have been set experimentally. The value of δ (maximum allowable mean-squared residue) is set to 300 for the yeast cell cycle data set [6], 1200 for the Human B-cell expression data set [6], and 500 for the colon cancer data set [1], as recommended in [2].

26.5.3 Comparative Results

In this section, we perform a comparative study of the performance for the two proposed algorithms. Furthermore, we compare the quality of the extracted biclusters with NSGA2B [20], MOPSOB [18], and CC [5] algorithms.

1. *Performance Assessment* In order to evaluate the quality of the nondominated front approximations obtained for a specific test instance, we follow the protocol given by Knowles et al. [13]. For a specific instance, we first compute a reference set $Z_N^\star$ of nondominated points extracted from the union of all these fronts. Second, we define $z^{\max} = (z_1^{\max}, z_2^{\max}, z_3^{\max})$, where $z_1^{\max}$, $z_2^{\max}$, $z_3^{\max}$ denote the upper bounds of the first, second, and third objectives in the whole nondominated front approximations. Then, to measure the quality of an output set A in comparison to $Z_N^\star$, we compute the difference between these two sets by using the unary hypervolume metric [22], $(1.05z_1^{\max}, 1.05z_2^{\max}, 1.05z_3^{\max})$ being the reference point. As illustrated in Figure 26.2, the hypervolume difference indicator (I_H^-) computes the portion of the objective space that is weakly dominated by $Z_N^\star$ and not by A.

   Furthermore, we also consider the additive ϵ-indicator $(I_{\epsilon+}^-)$. This indicator is used to compare nondominated set approximations, and not solutions. The *unary additive ϵ-indicator* $(I_{\epsilon+}^1)$ gives the minimum factor by which an approximation A has to be translated in the criterion space to weakly dominate the reference set $Z_N^\star$. Define $I_{\epsilon+}^1$ as

   $$I_{\epsilon+}^1(A) = I_{\epsilon+}(A, Z_N^\star) \tag{26.7}$$

   where

   $$I_{\epsilon+}(A, B) = \min_{\epsilon}\{\forall z \in B, \exists z' \in A \text{ such that } z_i' - \epsilon \le z_i, \forall 1 \le i \le n\} \tag{26.8}$$

   As a consequence, for each test instance, we obtained 20 hypervolume differences and 20 epsilon measures, corresponding to the 20 runs, per algorithm. As suggested by Knowles et al. [13], once all these values are computed, we perform a statistical analysis on pairs of optimization methods for a comparison on a specific test instance. To this end, we use the Mann-Whitney statistical test as described in [13].

   Note that all the performance assessment procedures have been achieved using the performance assessment tool suite provided in PISA [3].

   Table 26.3 gives a comparison of $MOBI_{ibea}$ and $MOBI_{nsga}$ with regard to the hypervolume indicator (I_H^-) and the epsilon indicator $(I_{\epsilon+})$, respectively.

   The obtained results show that the two algorithms are almost equivalent. In fact, $MOBI_{nsga}$ outperforms $MOBI_{ibea}$ and thus with regard to the hypervolume (I_H^-) and epsilon indicator $(I_{\epsilon+})$ in the case of the yeast cell cycle data set [6], while $MOBI_{ibea}$ outperforms $MOBI_{nsga}$ with regard to the hypervolume indicator in the case of the human B-cell expression data set [6], and they are equivalent for the same instance with regard to the epsilon indicator. The performance of $MOBI_{nsga}$ and $MOBI_{ibea}$ is

TABLE 26.3 Comparison of Different Metaheuristics for I_H^- and $I_{\epsilon+}$ Metrics Using Mann-Whitney Statistical Test with p-Value of 5%

Instance	Algorithm	I_H^-		$I_{\epsilon+}$	
		MOBI$_{ibea}$	MOBI$_{nsga}$	MOBI$_{ibea}$	MOBI$_{nsga}$
Yeast	MOBI$_{ibea}$	—	$\prec$	—	$\prec$
	MOBI$_{nsga}$	$\succ$	—	$\succ$	—
Human	MOBI$_{ibea}$	—	$\succ$	—	$\equiv$
	MOBI$_{nsga}$	$\prec$	—	$\equiv$	—
Colon	MOBI$_{ibea}$	—	$\equiv$	—	$\equiv$
	MOBI$_{nsga}$	$\equiv$	—	$\equiv$	—

Note: According to the metric under consideration, the results of the algorithm located at a specific row are significantly better than those of the algorithm located at a specific column ($\succ$) or they are worse ($\prec$) or there is no significant difference between them ($\equiv$).

TABLE 26.4 Comparative Results of Two Multiobjective Biclustering Algorithms with Proposed Algorithms Using Yeast Cell Cycle Data Set [6]

Algorithm	Average Size	Average MSR Value	Maximum Size
NSGA2B [20]	10,176.5	234.87	14,828
MOPSOB [18]	10,267.4	218.54	**15,613**
CC [5]	2,004	**204.29**	—
MOBI$_{nsga}$	11,250.81	296.96	14,400
MOBI$_{ibea}$	**11,262.95**	297.54	12,168

also the same in the case of the colon cancer [1] data set, with regard to hypervolume and epsilon indicators.

2. *Solution Quality* In this section, the proposed algorithms (MOBI$_{nsga}$ and MOBI$_{ibea}$) are compared with the classical multiobjective biclustering algorithms NSGA2B [20] and MOPSOB [18] and the CC algorithm [5].

Tables 26.4 and 26.5 display information about extracted biclusters from the yeast cell cycle [6] and human B-cell expression [6] data sets using the different methods, namely the average size of the found biclusters, the average mean-squared residue, and the maximum bicluster size found.

Concerning the yeast cell cycle [6] data set, Table 26.4 shows that, on average, the biclusters found by our algorithms (MOBI$_{nsga}$ and MOBI$_{ibea}$) are characterized by a higher size (11,250.81) than those found by NSGA2B (10,176.5), MOPSOB (10,267.4), and CC

TABLE 26.5 Comparative Results of Two Multiobjective Biclustering Algorithms with Proposed Algorithms Using Human B-Cell Expression Data Set [6]

Algorithm	Average Size	Average MSR Value	Maximum Size
NSGA2B [20]	33,463.69	915.81	37,560
MOPSOB [18]	**36,204.68**	**902.41**	37,666
MOBI$_{nsga}$	15,077.2	1,104.81	**43,486**
MOBI$_{ibea}$	18,379.23	1,191.6	22,448

TABLE 26.6 Number of Genes and Conditions, Mean-Squared Residue and Row Variance of Four Biclusters in Yeast Cell Cycle [6] Data Set for $\delta = 300$ Using MOBI$_{nsga}$

Bicluster	Conditions	Genes	Residue	Row Variance
a	12	1191	299.9	421.19
b	10	1273	299.72	445.9
c	17	648	299.6	402.55
d	7	1521	299.9	486.03

(2004), while the maximum bicluster size is more important in the case of NSGA2B and MOPSOB (15,613) compared to MOBI$_{nsga}$ (14,400). From these results we can deduce that our algorithms find several biclusters of interesting sizes, while NSGA2B and MOPSOB find some biclusters of large sizes and others of small sizes. On the other hand, we can see that biclusters found by MOBI$_{ibea}$ are, on average, larger than those found using MOBI$_{nsga}$. In fact, the biclusters extracted using MOBI$_{ibea}$ are, on average, characterized by the highest size (11,262.95). The mean-square residue of biclusters found by our algorithms are slightly higher than those found by NSGA2B, MOPSOB, and CC. In fact, since the values of the mean-square residues do not exceed the threshold value (300 in this case), these biclusters are considered to be of a good quality.

For the human B-cell expression [6] data set, Table 26.5 shows that, on average, the biclusters found by our algorithms are smaller (15,077.2) than those found by NSGA2B and MOPSOB (36,204.68), while the maximum bicluster size found by MOBI$_{nsga}$ (43,486) is more important than all the other algorithms.

26.5.4 Some Extracted Biclusters

Tables 26.6 and 26.7 display some interesting biclusters extracted from the yeast cell cycle [6] data set using MOBI$_{nsga}$ and MOBI$_{ibea}$, respectively. These biclusters are characterized by high sizes (number of genes and number of conditions) and acceptable values of the means of the row variances and a mean-square residue always below the used threshold ($\delta = 300$ for the yeast cell cycle [6] data set). As mentioned before, the aim is to extract biclusters with maximal size and mean-square residue under the threshold value δ.

Figure 26.3 shows a Pareto front projection on two objectives for the colon cancer data set [1] using MOBI$_{nsga}$. We can observe that the front contains a large number of solutions (295 solutions). The solutions are characterized by a good diversification mainly for f_1 (size).

TABLE 26.7 Number of Genes and Conditions, Mean-Squared Residue and Row Variance of Four Biclusters in Yeast Cell Cycle [6] Data Set for $\delta = 300$ Using MOBI$_{ibea}$

Bicluster	Conditions	Genes	Residue	Row Variance
a	12	1014	299.89	429.06
b	17	618	297.9	393.46
c	6	1497	298.2	523.1
d	10	1128	299.4	447.55

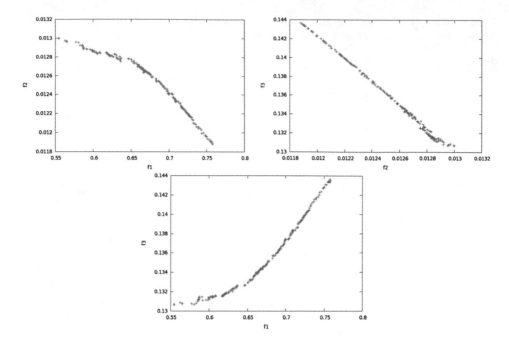

FIGURE 26.3 Resulting Pareto front projections onto two objectives for colon data using NSGA-II: size (f_1) and MSR (f_2) (top left); size (f_1) and variance (f_3) (top right); MSR (f_2) and variance (f_3) (bottom).

26.6 CONCLUSION

In this study, we presented a multiobjective model for the biclustering problem applied to microarray data. This model aims to extract biclusters with large size (large number of rows and columns), low mean-square residue, and high row variances. To solve for this model, we have proposed two algorithms called $MOBI_{nsga}$ and $MOBI_{ibea}$ based on the well-known bioinspired algorithms, NSGA-II [9] and IBEA [24], in addition the CC algorithm [5]. In our algorithms we chose to use a string of integers as a solution representation instead of the classical representation (bits string) in order to reduce time and memory consummation. For this representation, we proposed an adapted crossover operator.

The performance comparison between the two proposed algorithms showed that they are practically equivalent and behave similarly. In terms of solution quality, $MOBI_{nsga}$ extracts biclusters of high (and low) sizes while $MOBI_{ibea}$ extracts biclusters of average sizes. The results in the yeast cell cycle data set [6] confirm the good quality of the extracted biclusters. A comparative study shows that our algorithms are able to extract good-quality biclusters with larger sizes than biclusters extracted using NSGA2B, MOPSOB, and CC algorithms.

The results in the human B-cell expression data set [6] show that the algorithm based on $MOBI_{nsga}$ can extract biclusters with maximal size. According to the presented results, MOBI algorithms seem to be interesting. More experiments over other data sets may be effected to affirm their quality.

REFERENCES

1. U. Alon, N. Barkai, D. A. Notterman, K. Gish, S. Ybarra, D. Mack, and A. J. Levine. Broad patterns of gene expression revealed by clustering analysis of tumor and normal colon tissues probed by oligonucleotide arrays. *Proc. Nat. Acad. Sci. USA*, 96(12):6745–6750, 1999.

2. F. Divina, R. Giraldez, J. Aguilar-Ruiz, and B. Pontes. Improved biclustering on expression data through overlapping control. *Int. J. Intell. Comput. Cybernet.*, 2:477–493, 2009.

3. S. Bleuler, M. Laumanns, L. Thiele, and E. Zitzler. PISA—a platform and programming language independent interface for search algorithms. In C. M. Fonseca, P. J. Fleming, E. Zitzler, K. Deb, and L. Thiele (Eds.), *Conference on Evolutionary Multi-Criterion Optimization (EMO 2003)*, Vol. 2632 of *Lecture Notes in Computer Science (LNCS)*, Springer-Verlag, Faro, Portugal, 2003, pp. 494–508.

4. K. Bryan, P. Cunningham, and N. Bolshakova. Application of simulated annealing to the biclustering of gene expression data. *IEEE Trans. Inform. Technol. Biomed.*, 10(3):519–525, 2006.

5. Y. Cheng and G. M. Church. Biclustering of expression data. In P. E. Bourne, M. Gribskov, R. B. Altman, N. Jensen, D. A. Hope, T. Lengauer, J. C. Mitchell, E. D. Scheeff, C. Smith, S. Strande, and H. Weissig (Eds.), *Proceedings of the Eighth International Conference on Intelligent Systems for Molecular Biology*, August 19–23, 2000, La Jolla, San Diego, CA, AAAI Press, Washington, DC, 2000, pp. 93–103.

6. Y. Cheng and G. M. Church. Biclustering of expression data. (supplementary information). Technical Report, 2006. Available: http://arep.med.harvard.edu/biclustering/.

7. P. A. D. de Castro, F. O. de França, H. M. Ferreira, and F. J. Von Zuben. Applying biclustering to text mining: An immune-inspired approach. In L. N. de Castro, F. J. Von Zuben, and H. Knidel (Eds.) *Proceedings of the 6th International Conference on Artificial Immune Systems (ICARIS'07)*, Springer, Heidelberg, 2007, pp. 83–94.

8. K. Deb. *Multi-Objective Optimization Using Evolutionary Algorithms*. Wiley-Interscience Series in Systems and Optimization. Wiley, Chichester, 2001.

9. K. Deb, S. Agrawal, A. Pratap, and T. Meyarivan. A fast elitist non-dominated sorting genetic algorithm for multi-objective optimization: NSGA-II. *IEEE Trans. Evol. Comput.*, 6:182–197, 2000.

10. A. Dharan and A. S. Nair. Biclustering of gene expression data using reactive greedy randomized adaptive search procedure. *BMC Bioinformatics*, 10(Suppl. 1):S27, 2009.

11. F. Divina and J. S. Aguilar-Ruiz. Biclustering of expression data with evolutionary computation. *IEEE Trans. Knowledge Data Eng.*, 18, 2006, pp. 590–602.

12. G. Getz, E. Levine, and E. Domany. Coupled two-way clustering analysis of gene microarray data. *Proc. Natl. Acad. Sci. USA*, 97:12079–12084, 2000.

13. J. Knowles, L. Thiele, and E. Zitzler. A tutorial on the performance assessment of stochastic multiobjective optimizers. Technical Report. Computer Engineering and Networks Laboratory (TIK), ETH Zurich, Switzerland, 2006 (revised version).

14. M. Lashkargir, S. A. Monadjemi, and A. B. Dastjerdi. A new biclustering method for gene expersion data based on adaptive multi objective particle swarm optimization. In K. Jusoff, S. S. Mahmoud, and R. Sivakumar (Eds.) *Proceedings of the 2009 Second International Conference on Computer and Electrical Engineering*, Vol. 01 *(ICCEE '09)*. IEEE Computer Society, Washington, DC, 2009, pp. 559–563.

15. L. Lazzeroni and A. Owen. Plaid models for gene expression data. *Stat. Sinica*, 12:61–86, 2000.

16. J. Liu, Z. Li, X. Hu, and Y. Chen. Biclustering of microarray data with mospo based on crowding distance. *BMC Bioinformatics*, 10(Suppl. 4):S9, 2009.

17. J. Liu, Z. Li, X. Hu, and Y. Chen. Multi-objective ant colony optimization biclustering of microarray data. In *IEEE International Conference on Granular Computing (GrC'09)*. 2009, pp. 424–429.

18. J. Liu, Z. Li, F. Liu, and Y. Chen. Multi-objective particle swarm optimization biclustering of microarray data. *IEEE International Conference on Bioinformatics and Biomedicine (BIBM '08)*, 2008, pp. 363–366.

19. S. C. Madeira and A. L. Oliveira. Biclustering algorithms for biological data analysis: A survey. *IEEE/ACM Trans. Computat. Biol. Bioinformatics*, 1:24–45, 2004.

20. S. Mitra and H. Banka. Multi-objective evolutionary biclustering of gene expression data. *Pattern Recognition*, 39(12):2464–2477, 2006.

21. C. Tang, L. Zhang, M. Ramanathan, and A. Zhang. Interrelated two-way clustering: An unsupervised approach for gene expression data analysis. In *Proceedings of the 2nd IEEE International Symposium on Bioinformatics and Bioengineering (BIBE '01)*. IEEE Computer Society, Washington, DC, 2001, pp. 41–48.

22. E. Zitzler and L. Thiele. Multiobjective evolutionary algorithms: A comparative case study and the strength pareto approach. *IEEE Trans. Evol. Computat.*, 3(4):257–271, 1999.

23. E. Zitzler, M. Laumanns, and L. Thiele. SPEA2: Improving the strength Pareto evolutionary algorithm for multiobjective optimization. In K. C. Giannakoglou et al. (Eds.), *Evolutionary Methods for Design, Optimisation and Control with Application to Industrial Problems (EUROGEN 2001)*, International Center for Numerical Methods in Engineering (CIMNE), 2002, pp. 95–100.

24. S. E. Zitzler. Indicator-based selection in multiobjective search. *Parallel Problem Solving from Nature, PPSN*, 3242:832–842, 2004.

CHAPTER 27

COCLUSTERING UNDER GENE ONTOLOGY DERIVED CONSTRAINTS FOR PATHWAY IDENTIFICATION

ALESSIA VISCONTI,[1] FRANCESCA CORDERO,[1] DINO IENCO,[2] and RUGGERO G. PENSA[1]
[1]Department of Computer Science, University of Torino, Turin, Italy
[2]Institut de Recherche en Sciences et Technologies pour l'Environnement, Montpellier, France

27.1 INTRODUCTION

Understanding complex functional mechanisms at the basis of cells requires a global analysis of different cellular processes. Several high-throughput techniques have become mandatory in this kind of study. Among the others, microarrays are still the most-used technology to monitor the expression of tens of thousands of genes in parallel [30]. Microarray technologies are usually fruitful to analyze the gene expression in several samples captured at different time points or in different experimental conditions. Hence, microarrays become crucial in molecular biology research; this technology is also used for pharmacogenomic research, studying infectious and genetic disease, cancer diagnostics, and forensic identification. Additionally, microarray technologies are now used for many protcomic and cell based applications. The amounts of data produced by microarray techniques are huge. This leads to the need for the development of new computational techniques to manage and evaluate the data and even to formulate new biological hypotheses.

To this purpose, clustering techniques are widely used in microarray data analysis that enable to discover homogeneous experimental clusters or genes clusters based on a distance measure quantifying the degree of correlation of expression profiles [25]. Clustering allows to partition data into groups such that each data object is similar to all objects within the same group (cluster) and is dissimilar from any other object belonging to any other group. Genes that are clustered together are supposed to share similar expression profiles. Similar techniques could be applied to experimental conditions, thus producing a grid of coclusters (clusters of genes associated to clusters of conditions). Coclusters provide a first insight on gene expression data, and allow to identify potential transcription modules (genes regulated by the same transcription factors), that are more likely to concern genes that are coexpressed in the same group of conditions. A limitation of traditional clustering techniques is that they are applied on gene sets or sample sets independently. To exceed this view, coclustering algorithms [37] have been proposed: These identify groups of genes that show similar activity patterns under a specific subset of the experimental conditions. From an algorithmic point of view, clustering genes and conditions simultaneously is different than clustering them separately, since the metric to be optimized takes into account the correlation between the partition of genes and the partition of conditions.

As we anticipated, the goal of coclustering algorithms emphasizes one of the major targets in computational biology: the discovery of regulatory modules that control gene transcription in biological model systems. Approaches based on coclustering process genes and conditions simultaneously and enable the discovery of more coherent and meaningful groups. The main practical reasons are that biological systems are inherently modular and that grouping genes into modules reduces the effective complexity of a given data set. For instance, the association of these modules with a specific histological cancer class may be exploited within an effective diagnostic tool.

In many applications, distance metrics based only on expression levels fail in capturing biologically meaningful clusters. Moreover, approaches based on clustering that identify gene signatures in specific conditions tend to base the analysis on their signal in the conditions under study. But a simple list of genes associated with a certain tumor type is far from identifying the regulatory modules in which genes are involved. Indeed, several works proposed to define distance metrics based on different sources of information. As an advantage, additional information could help in resolving ambiguities or in avoiding erroneous linking based on spurious similarities. Different sources of information have been employed to complete gene expression data metrics: biological networks [28], operon annotation, intergenic distance, and transcriptional coresponse [50]. Another preferred source of information which is widely used in gene expression data analysis validation is Gene Ontology (GO) [4], which provides annotation for gene and gene product attributes across all species and has been used in combination with standard clustering measures [14]. All these approaches derive some metrics from the complementary sources of information and combine them with standard metrics on gene expression values in standard clustering frameworks. These works, in fact, do not perform coclustering on both genes and samples at the same time.

Designing new measures to combine different sources of information is not an easy task. However, when we consider applications where knowledge coming from external sources is injected in the analysis process, we must recall that, in data mining, a typical solution consists in pushing some user-defined constraint during the mining process [24]. Constraint-based data mining has been widely employed as a means to reduce the search space in local pattern-mining algorithms. Approaches such as frequent itemset mining and close pattern mining often produce untractable collections of patterns. In many cases, the mining process is simply unfeasible, due to the explosion of the search space. Constraints are a simple but efficient means to (1) reduce the output of pattern-mining algorithms to those patterns that really interest the user and (2) prune the search space and reduce the computational time required to complete the mining process. Mining local patterns under constraints has been extensively studied, also in the case of gene expression data analysis [11, 12]. In recent years, the data-mining and machine learning communities started to also study constraints for global patterns such as clustering and coclustering [10]; however, only few works addressed the problem of finding partitions of gene expression data under constraints [39, 40].

Instead of combining ontology-based metrics and expression-based metrics within the same distance measure, we propose a methodology in which a standard expression-based coclustering algorithm is enhanced by sets of constraints which take into account the similarity/dissimilarity (inferred by some background knowledge) between pairs of genes. Using constraints has been proven to be very effective in many applications, including gene expression analysis [40] and sequence analysis [18], since the user can decide which type of biological knowledge leads to the association among gene clusters and condition clusters. In this way the list of genes associated with a set of conditions may assume a specific meaning. Moreover, constraints can be generated by mixing different semantics, while combining different semantics in a single measure is not straightforward. Defining these constraints by hand is not that simple either. Since the advantage of modularity is crucial in learning biologically meaningful clusters from data, we decided to use the expressive power provided by GO to construct a set of similarity (*must-link*) and dissimilarity (*cannot-link*) constraints automatically.

Furthermore, for a correct usage of the technique presented in [40], similar to all coclustering techniques, the user has to specify the desired number of clusters on rows and columns. Deciding an adequate number of clusters is not trivial, and a bad choice may influence negatively the quality of coclustering results. Thus, we adopt a preprocessing method that automatically determines a congruent number of clusters per rows and columns.

In a nutshell, we propose a new methodology that minimizes the intervention of the analyst within the coclustering process and that provides meaningful coclusters whose discovery and interpretation are enhanced by embedding GO annotations. To show the effectiveness of our approach, we apply our methodology on a gene expression data set consisting on different stress conditions for *Saccharomyces cerevisiae* (baker's yeast).

The remainder of this chapter is organized as follows: Section 27.2 explores the related bibliography in details. Section 27.3 briefly introduces the constrained coclustering algorithm (presented in [40]) that we use in our framework. Section 27.4 describes the core of this chapter, that is, our methodology for coclustering using GO-derived constraints. Section 27.5 presents a case study on a real gene expression data set. Finally, Section 27.6 concludes.

27.2 RELATED WORK

Many coclustering methods have been developed, possibly dedicated to gene expression data analysis. Kluger et al. [35] propose a spectral coclustering method. First, they perform an adequate normalization of the data set to emphasize coclusters if they exist. Then, they consider that the correlation between two columns is better estimated by the expression level mean of each column with respect to a partition of the rows. The bipartition is computed by the algebraic eigenvalue decomposition of the normalized matrix. Their algorithm critically depends on the normalization procedure. Dhillon et al. [23] and Robardet et al. [43] have considered the two searched partitions as discrete random variables whose association must be maximized. Different measures can be used. Whereas Cocluster [23] uses the loss in mutual information, Bi-Clust [43] uses Goodman-Kruskal's τ coefficient to evaluate the link strength between the two variables. In both algorithms, a local optimization method is used to optimize the measure by alternatively changing a partition when the other one is fixed. The main difference between these two approaches is that the τ measure is independent of the number of coclusters and thus Bi-Clust can automatically determine the number of coclusters. Lazzeroni et al. [36] propose to consider each matrix value as a sum of variables. Each variable represents a particular phenomenon in the data and corresponds to a cocluster. In each cocluster, column or row values are linearly correlated. Then, the method consists in determining the model minimizing the Euclidean distance between the matrix and the modeled values. This method is similar to the eigenvalue decomposition used in [35] without the orthogonal constraint on the computed variables. Notice also that the problem of matrix partitioning has been investigated in other contexts, such as for parallel processing purposes [29], where the goal is to provide a block diagonal structure of sparse matrices in order to parallelize some common and frequent operations like matrix–vector products. A new and significant result has been presented in [3]. The authors show that the coclustering problem is NP hard, and they propose a constant-factor approximation algorithm for any norm-based objective functions. Concerning recent contributions to coclustering, they have focused on hierarchical [31], overlapping [22], and Bayesian [46] models. Recently, Banerjee et al. have proposed in [5] a coclustering setting based on matrix approximation. The approximation error is measured using a large class of loss functions called Bregman divergences. They introduce a meta-algorithm whose special cases include the algorithms from [23] and [17].

In the context of gene expression data analysis, several authors have considered the computation of potentially overlapping local patterns that they call *biclusters* (see [37] for a survey). Ihmels et al. [32] propose a simple algorithm which builds in two steps a single association called a bicluster starting from a column set. First, they consider that the rows having a high score (greater than a threshold on the normalized matrix) on these columns belong to the bicluster. Then, they use the same principle to increase the original column set. In [16], Cheng et al. propose a so-called *biclustering* approach for gene expression data. They define a bicluster as a subset of rows and a subset of columns with a low mean-squared residue. When the measure is equal to zero, the bicluster contains rows having the same value on the bicluster columns. When the measure is greater than zero, one can remove rows or columns to decrease the value. Thus the method consists in finding maximal-size biclusters such that the measure is less than a threshold. Various heuristics can be used for this purpose. The same definition of residue is used in [17] to define the objective function which is also used in this work. Authors propose two different residue measures and show that the one proposed by Cheng et al. fits better to gene expression data analysis. Then, they introduce their coclustering algorithm which optimizes the sum-squared residue functions.

Constrained clustering is a recent and active research domain (see, e.g., [10] for a state-of-the-art survey). It has been mainly studied in the context of semisupervised learning for which an alternative approach is the so-called *metric-based method* (i.e., learning a metric considering labeled data before applying standard clustering). Semisupervised clustering can support classification tasks when labeled data are limited and/or expensive to collect. A solution is to use the knowledge given by available labeled instances within a clustering algorithm. In [52], a simple adaptation of k-means which enforces must-link and cannot-link constraints during the clustering process is described. Basu et al. [8] propose a constrained clustering approach which uses labeled data during the initialization and clustering steps. An example of metric-based approach is given in [34]. Notice that [13] integrates both constraint-based and metric-based approaches in a k-means-like algorithm. In [9], the authors propose a probabilistic model for semisupervised clustering which also combines the two approaches. Other related work focuses on constraint feasibility on a k-means-like scheme [21] and on an agglomerative hierarchical clustering scheme [20]. Other applications of constrained clustering are the so-called *sensor network* and *k-anonymity* problems. In both applications, a possible solution is to find compact clusters containing a balanced number of objects. For instance, the discovery of balanced clusters is considered in [6, 7]. Ge et al. describe an algorithm which finds an unspecified number of compact clusters under the combination of minimum-significance constraints and minimum-variance constraints [27].

Constrained coclustering is a new approach to gene expression data analysis. The first work that addressed the problem of coclustering under user-defined constraints is [41], extended in [42]. In this work, the authors employ local pattern collections to build bipartitions under constraints. They propose to transform the cluster-level constraints into local pattern constraints. Then a k-means-like approach is used to cluster local patterns and build the bipartitions on data. Direct coclustering of data matrices under constraints was first presented in [39]. In this work the authors extend the approach of [17] by allowing the satisfaction of must-link, cannot-link, and interval constraints. In [40], the authors propose a constrained coclustering formulation that generalizes the approach proposed in [39] by exploiting Bregman divergences. This is also the approach that we use in this work for building bipartitions. Other more recent approaches of coclustering under constraints have been applied to textual data [47, 49].

Designing new measures to combine different source of information is not an easy task in bioinformatics. The pioneers of this stream of works is Hanisch et al. [28], who proposed a novel approach that allows for an entirely exploratory joint analysis of gene expression data and biological networks. The authors proposed a combined measure derived from gene expression data and metrics on biological networks into a single distance function that they use as a distance measure in a hierarchical average linkage clustering algorithm. Starting from Hanish's work, Steinhauser et al. [50] proposed a new measure that involves operon annotations, intergenic distance, and transcriptional coresponse data into a distance metric used in hierarchical clustering algorithms. More recently, Brameier et al. [14] presented a coclustering approach based on self-organizing maps (SOMs), where center-based clustering of standard SOMs have been combined with a representative-based clustering. The authors developed a two-level cluster selection where the nearest cluster according to the GO distance is selected among the best matching clusters according to gene expression distance. In this work, coclustering means that GO-based clustering and expression-based clustering are performed in parallel. None of these methods perform coclustering on both genes and samples at the same time.

Finally, this chapter is a significant extension of the preliminary work presented in [19].

27.3 CONSTRAINED COCLUSTERING

In this section we briefly describe the constrained coclustering algorithm presented in [40] and which is central to our methodology.

Let $X \in \mathbb{R}^{m \times n}$ denote a data matrix. Let x_{ij} be the element corresponding to row i and column j. For instance, x_{ij} might contain the expression level of gene i in the experimental condition j. Let x_i and y_j denote the vectors associated to, respectively, row i and column j.

A coclustering $C^{k \times l}$ over X produces simultaneously a set of $k \times l$ coclusters (a partition C^r into k groups of rows associated to a partition C^c into l groups of columns). To obtain a first-quality criterion, we first try to optimize a certain objective function. Let I be the set of indices of the rows belonging to a row cluster and J the set of indices of the columns belonging to a column cluster. The submatrix of X defined by I and J is called a *cocluster*.

Given an element x_{ij} of X, the residue of x_{ij} in the cocluster defined by the sets of indices I and J and whose respective cardinalities are $|I|$ and $|J|$ is given by

$$h_{ij} = x_{ij} - x_{Ij} - x_{iJ} + x_{IJ} \tag{27.1}$$

where

$$x_{IJ} = \frac{\sum_{i \in I, j \in J} x_{ij}}{|I| \cdot |J|} \qquad x_{Ij} = \frac{\sum_{i \in I} x_{ij}}{|I|} \qquad x_{iJ} = \frac{\sum_{j \in J} x_{ij}}{|J|}$$

This formulation [Equation (27.1)] is the measure designed by Cheng and Church [16] for local pattern discovery in gene expression data.

Let $H = [h_{ij}] \in \mathbb{R}^{m \times n}$ denote the matrix of residues computed using the previous definition. The objective function to be minimized is the sum of squared residues [17] computed as

$$||H||^2 = \sum_{I,J} ||h_{IJ}||^2 = \sum_{I,J} \sum_{i \in I, j \in J} h_{ij}^2 \tag{27.2}$$

We can rewrite the residue matrix in a more compact form [17]. Let us introduce the matrices $R \in \mathbb{R}^{m \times k}$ and $C \in \mathbb{R}^{n \times l}$ which are defined as follows: Each element (i, r) $(1 \leq r \leq k)$ of R is equal to $m_r^{-1/2}$ if i is in cocluster r (m_r is the number of rows in r) and zero otherwise. Each element (j, c) $(1 \leq c \leq l)$ of the matrix C is equal to $n_c^{-1/2}$ if j is in c (n_c being the number of columns in c), and zero otherwise. The residue matrix becomes

$$H = (I - RR^T)X(I - CC^T) \tag{27.3}$$

Our goal is to inject external knowledge into the coclustering process. To this purpose, we consider the two well-known must-link (similarity) and cannot-link (dissimilarity) constraints, also referred as pairwise constraints, since they involve pairs of objects. They are defined as follows: If rows i_a and i_b (respectively columns j_a and j_b) are involved in a must-link constraint, denoted $c_=(i_a, i_b)$ [respectively $c_=(j_a, j_b)$], they must be in the same cluster of $C^r = r_1, \ldots, r_k$ (respectively $C^c = c_1, \ldots, c_l$); if rows i_a, i_b (respectively columns j_a and j_b) are involved in a cannot-link constraint, denoted $c \neq (i_a, i_b)$ [respectively $c \neq (j_a, j_b)$], they cannot be in the same cluster of $C^r = r_1, \ldots, r_k$ (respectively $C^c = c_1, \ldots, c_l$).

Such types of constraints have been studied in the context of semisupervised clustering [13]. It is here generalized in order to apply them on both row and column sets. In a gene expression matrix, it is then possible to exploit the knowledge about genes and/or experimental conditions. For example, if we know that gene i_a and gene i_b have the same function (say F) in the biological process, we can enforce a must-link constraint between these two genes to focus the search for coclusters associating genes having such a function F. We could also add some cannot-link constraints to avoid associations between experimental conditions which we want to separate, for example, avoiding to mix conditions that are related to different stages of a disease.

Transitivity of must-link constraints is a well-known property. We can transform a set of must-link constraints over rows into a collection $\mathcal{M}_r = M_1, \ldots, M_N$, where each M_i is a set of rows involved by the same transitive closure of must-link constraints. Let us denote $\mathcal{M}_c$ as the same set built for columns and let $\mathcal{C}_r$ and $\mathcal{C}_c$ be the sets of cannot-link constraints for rows and columns, respectively.

The coclustering algorithm builds a $k \times l$ coclustering over X, trying to minimize the objective function (27.2), and satisfying constraints $\mathcal{M}_r$, $\mathcal{M}_c$, $\mathcal{C}_r$, and $\mathcal{C}_c$. The approach uses the introduced "ping-pong" technique that processes columns and rows alternately by means of a k-means method. It means that matrix C is updated only after determining the nearest column cluster for each column (and similarly for rows). Therefore, the algorithm decomposes the objective function captured by Equation (27.3) in terms of columns. Given $X^P = (I - RR^T)X$, $X^C = (I - RR^T)XC$, and $\hat{X}^P = (I - RR^T)XCC^T = X^C C^T$, the specified objective function can be rewritten as

$$||X^P - \hat{X}^P||^2 = \sum_{c=1}^{l} \sum_{j \in J_c} ||X^P_{.j} - \hat{X}^P_{.j}||^2$$

$$= \sum_{c=1}^{l} \sum_{j \in J_c} ||X^P_{.j} - (X^C C^T)_{.j}||^2$$

$$= \sum_{c=1}^{l} \sum_{j \in J_c} ||X^P_{.j} - n_c^{1/2} X^C_{.c}||^2$$

In the same way, setting $X^P = X(I - CC^T)$, $X^R = R^T X(I - CC^T)$, and $\hat{X}^P = RR^T X(I - CC^T) = RX^R$, the following decomposition in terms of rows holds:

$$||X^P - \hat{X}^P||^2 = \sum_{r=1}^{k} \sum_{j \in I_r} ||X^P_{i.} - m_r^{1/2} X^R_{r.}||^2$$

Then, matrices X^C and X^R correspond to the cluster centroids for columns and rows, respectively.

We can now provide the whole constrained coclustering algorithm presented in [40].

Algorithm 27.1 solves the coclustering problem with conjunctions of must-link and cannot-link constraints. First, the algorithm initializes matrices C and R. Then, during each iteration, the algorithm associates each column (respectively row) to the nearest column (respectively row) cluster which does not introduce any cannot-link violation. If a column j (respectively row i) is involved in a must-link constraint (see Algorithms 27.2 and 27.3), the algorithm associates the whole set of columns M_v (respectively set of rows M_u) involved in the transitive closure of this constraint to the column (respectively row) cluster such that the average distance is minimum, and controlling that there is no cannot-link constraint which is violated by this operation. Since the assignment step is order dependent, rows and columns are randomly ordered at each iteration. Then the algorithm updates the matrix C (respectively R) following the assignment schema resulting from the previously described operations. This process is iterated until the diminution of the objective function value turns to be smaller than a user-defined threshold τ.

ALGORITHM 27.1 CoClust($X, k, l, \mathcal{M}_r, \mathcal{M}_c, \mathcal{C}_r, \mathcal{C}_c$)

Input: Data matrix X, k, l, *cannot-link* sets $\mathcal{C}_r$ and $\mathcal{C}_c$, collections $\mathcal{M}_r$ and $\mathcal{M}_c$

Output: Matrices R and C

Initialize R and C;

$\Delta = ||X||^2$; $\quad \tau = 10^{-5}||X||^2$;

$t = 0$;

$obj^t = ||(I - RR^T)X(I - CC^T)||^2$;

while $\Delta > \tau$ **do**

    $t = t + 1$;

    $X^C = (I - RR^T)XC$; $\quad X^P = (I - RR^T)X$;

    foreach $1 \leq j \leq n$ **do**

        $L = \emptyset$;

        if $\exists M_v \in \mathcal{M}_c$ s.t. $j \in M_v$ **then**

            | MLColumnAssign($X, l, L, M_v, \mathcal{C}_c$);

        else

            $L = \{1 \leq c \leq l \mid \nexists j_c \mid \gamma^t[j_c] = c \wedge c \neq (j, j_c) \in \mathcal{C}_c\}$;

            $\gamma^t[j] = \mathrm{argmin}_{c \in L}||X^P_{.j} - n_c^{-1/2}X^C_{.c}||^2$;

        end

    end

    Update C using γ;

    $X^R = R^T X(I - CC^T)$; $\quad X^P = X(I - CC^T)$;

    foreach $1 \leq i \leq m$ **do**

        $L = \emptyset$;

        if $\exists M_u \in \mathcal{M}_r$ s.t. $i \in M_u$ **then**

            | MLRowAssign($X, k, L, M_u, \mathcal{C}_r$);

        else

            $L = \{1 \leq r \leq k \mid \nexists i_r \mid \rho^t[i_r] = r \wedge c \neq (i, i_r) \in \mathcal{C}_r\}$;

            $\rho^t[i] = \mathrm{argmin}_{r \in L}||X^P_{i.} - m_r^{-1/2}X^R_{r.}||^2$;

        end

    end

    $obj^t = ||(I - RR^T)X(I - CC^T)||^2$;

    $\Delta = |obj^t - obj^{t-1}|$;

end

ALGORITHM 27.2 MLColumnAssign($X, l, L, M_v, \mathcal{C}_c$)

---

foreach $j_v \in M_v$ **do**

    | $L = L \cup \{1 \leq c \leq l \mid \nexists j_c \mid \gamma^t[j_c] = c \wedge c \neq (j_v, j_c) \in \mathcal{C}_c\}$;

end

$\gamma^t[M_v] = \mathrm{argmin}_{c \in L} \dfrac{\sum_{j_v \in M_v}||X^P_{.j} - n_c^{-1/2}X^C_{.c}||^2}{|M_v|}$;

ALGORITHM 27.3 MLRowAssign($X, k, L, M_u, \mathcal{C}_r$)

---

foreach $i_u \in M_u$ **do**

    | $L = L \cup \{1 \leq r \leq k \mid \nexists i_r \mid \rho^t[i_r] = c \wedge c \neq (i_u, i_r) \in \mathcal{C}_r\}$;

end

$\rho^t[M_u] = \mathrm{argmin}_{r \in L} \dfrac{\sum_{r_u \in M_u}||X^P_{i.} - m_r^{-1/2}X^C_{r.}||^2}{|M_u|}$;

27.4 PARAMETERLESS METHODOLOGY FOR GO-DRIVEN COCLUSTERING

Our framework is motivated by the necessity of using the previously described coclustering algorithm on gene expression data by limiting the number of parameters a user has to specify. So far, the user has to provide the following parameters: (i) number of row clusters; (ii) number of column clusters; (iii) a set of pairwise constraints (optional); and (iv) convergence criterion (optional).

Providing a correct number of clusters is crucial for every clustering algorithm, since a wrong number might considerably alter the quality of the results. Unfortunately, this is not an easy task, and some heuristics should be used to determine a correct number of clusters.

Providing a coherent and useful set of constraints is also a hard task. In classic semisupervised applications, constraints are automatically selected from labeled samples by selecting random pairs of labeled objects and setting a must-link or a cannot-link constraint depending on their class label. We will show how to extend this setting to gene expression data analysis.

Figure 27.1 shows an overview of the crucial steps of our methodology. The first two steps are performed independently. From one side, microarray experiments (a) are preprocessed to build a gene expression matrix consisting of normalized expression values. Other preprocessing techniques, such as missing-value replacement and gene or sample filtering, are possibly performed (c). The resulting matrix is then processed using the method described in [45] in order to determine a congruent number of row/column clusters (e). From the other side, the GO graph (b) is processed in order to obtain nodes consisting of multiple regulated GO terms linked by similarity relationships (d). The retained set of genes is mapped into the obtained GO graph to identify groups of similar and dissimilar genes, that contributes to the

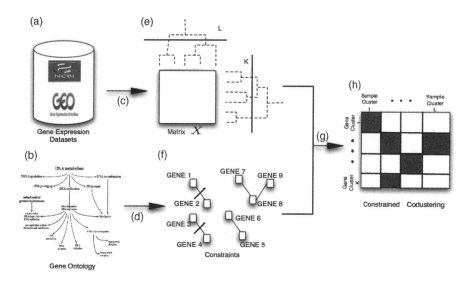

FIGURE 27.1 Methodology overview: microarray data (a) are preprocessed (c) in order to determine a congruent number of row/column clusters (e); multiple regulated GO terms are extracted (d) from the Gene Ontology graph (b); must-link and cannot-link constraints are defined (f); finally, coclustering is performed (g) in order to identify a set of row clusters described by GO annotations and a set of columns clusters described by experiment information (h).

definition of must-link and cannot-link constraints (f). The central step is the constrained coclustering algorithm (g) performed over the gene expression matrix obtained at step (c) using the number of row/column clusters discovered at step (e) and embedding the set of constraints built during step (f). The result (h) is a set of row clusters described by GO annotations and a set of columns clusters described by experiment information.

In the following, we describe in full detail steps (e) and (f) of the methodology described beforehand.

27.4.1 Determining Suitable Number of Coclusters

To estimate parameters k and l (i.e., the number of row and column clusters), we adopt the method described in [45], namely the *L-method*, which aims at selecting the number of clusters that provides the best result in a hierarchical clustering setting. It consists of the following steps:

Step 1. Hierarchical Clustering To build a cluster hierarchy over rows, we must first construct a distance matrix. The chosen distance metric is given by Equation (27.1) and has been modified to enable the comparison between two rows. In particular, we consider Equation (27.2) for the submatrices of X consisting in each pair of rows (considered as singleton clusters) and n singleton column clusters. The resulting distance matrix is then processed using a standard hierarchical clustering algorithm.

For columns, we do not process the transposed matrix directly, but we first reduce its dimensions using principal-component analysis (PCA) [33]. This choice is motivated by the fact that in gene expression data analysis usually $n \ll m$. On the resulting matrix we apply a standard hierarchical clustering algorithm using the Euclidean distance.

Step 2. Analysis of Dendrograms Once the dendrogram has been constructed, we analyze its levels. This analysis is performed in three steps:

1. Starting from the bottom of the hierarchy, for each level we identify the two clusters that are joined at the next level.
2. We compute a representative for each of the two clusters by averaging the features of the members belonging to each of them.
3. We compute a distance between the two representatives using the above-mentioned metrics (Cheng and Church for rows and Euclidean distance for columns).

This process results in pairs of values (number of clusters and distance) which identify a series of points.

Step 3. Determination of Number of Clusters The crucial phase of the L-method presented in [45] consists in determining a suitable number of clusters. It is performed in four steps:

1. We consider the $n - 1$ points (where n is the number of rows or columns) generated at the previous step. We choose a point c (which, in the first iteration, is equal to 2). This point divides the whole set of points in two subsets that graphically represent two intervals: the left interval L_c, containing points $[1, c]$, and the right interval R_c, containing points $[c + 1, n - 1]$.

2. For each of these subsets, we construct the line approximating them using linear regression.

3. For each line, we compute the root mean-square error (RMSE). We obtain a value for the line built on the left subset [RMSE(L_c)] and another one for the line built on the right subset [RMSE(R_c)].

4. Those values are then combined using the following formula [45]:

$$\text{RMSE}_c = \frac{c-1}{n-1}\text{RMSE}(L_c) + \frac{n-c}{n-1}\text{RMSE}(R_c)$$

We iterate these steps until $c = n - 1$. The estimated number of clusters is then given by $\hat{c} = \min_c \text{RMSE}_c$.

27.4.2 Definition of Constraints

To create sets of must-link and cannot-link constraints, we decided to use the information stored in GO [4].

The GO is a controlled vocabulary for the consistent description of attributes of gene and gene products maintained by the Gene Ontology Consortium. The ontologies are in the form of hierarchically direct acyclic graphs whose nodes represent GO terms and edges represent the relationships between GO terms. The nodes can be associated by five types of relationships: is_a, part_of, regulates, positively_regulates, and negatively_regulates. This ontology is organized in three key domains that are shared by all organisms: *molecular function*, *biological process*, and *cellular component*. These are represented by separate disconnected subgraphs of the root node.

The is_a relationship is a class–subclass relationship, where A is_a B means that A is a subclass of B. Instead, it is defined C part_of D if, whenever C is present, it is always a part of D, but C does not always have to be present. In other words, a child class is either a part_of the parent class or is_a more specific variant. The regulates, positively_regulates, and negatively_regulates relationships describe interactions between biological processes and other biological processes, molecular functions, or biological qualities. When a biological process E regulates a function or a process F, it modulates the occurrence of F. If F is a biological quality, then E modulates the value of F. In this work, we do not consider the cellular component domain.

We reformat the regulative information contained in GO in order to obtain a more concise representation of regulative relationships between the GO classes.

We built a weighted graph, where each node is a set of GO terms linked together by *regulative* relationships. If there is at least one is_a relationship among GO terms in two different nodes, we put an edge among these two vertices. The resulting graph contains 1537 GO macronodes. The weight associated to each edge is given by the number of is_a relationships existing among two nodes. By extracting the cliques in that graph, we obtain 202 cliques that represent strongly connected regulative *modules*.

Then, each gene of X is mapped into GO cliques following its GO annotation. Clearly, genes that are involved in multiple biological process/molecular functions are likely to belong to more than one clique. To construct the set of must-link constraints, we perform the following steps: First, since we perform hard (nonoverlapping) coclustering, we do not consider genes that belong to more than one clique; then those genes (among the remaining ones) belonging to one clique are associated to a unique transitive closure of must-link constraints.

Finally, to provide a set of cannot-link constraints, we consider all pairs of cliques associated to the transitive closures of must-link constraints generated before. If they do not share any gene, then we set a cannot-link constraint between an arbitrary pair of genes belonging to the associated transitive closures.

27.5 CASE STUDY

To evaluate the reliability of the proposed methodology, we download from the Gene Expression Omnibus (GEO) [1] database five microarray experiments performed over *S. cerevisiae*. The GEO data set IDs are GDS777, GDS1299, GDS2196, GDS2508, and GDS2713. From each microarray experiment we randomly single out a subset of 29 stress condition samples. We consider the fold changes of the gene expression levels, that is, the ratio of gene expression level in the stress condition on its expression level in the reference (control) condition. The GO annotations have also been extracted from the GEO website.

27.5.1 Methodology Instantiation

Following the steps described in the workflow reported in Figure 27.1, we introduce in detail the instantiation of our approach:

- *Construction of Matrix X* We built a gene expression matrix X composed of 9335 rows and 29 columns joining the subset conditions extracted from the selected GEO data sets.
- *Selection of Suitable Number of Row/Column Clusters* We process the matrix X using the method described in Section 27.4.1, obtaining a suggested number of 1677 row clusters ($k = 1677$) and of 9 column clusters ($l = 9$).
- *Generation of Collection of Constraints* We generate a collection of must-link constraints $\mathcal{M}$ and a set of cannot-link constraints $\mathcal{C}$ as described in Section 27.4.2. A total of 2151 genes (23%) were constrained in 52 transitive closures of must-link constraints and in 39 cannot-link constraints.
- *Constrained Coclustering* Using the previously discovered k and l parameters and the constraints belonging to $\mathcal{M}$ and $\mathcal{C}$, we perform 40 trials of the coclustering algorithm. The coclustering process stops when $||H||_{t-1}^2 - ||H||_t^2 < 10^{-5}$, where $||H||_t^2$ and $||H||_{t-1}^2$ are values of the objective function at the iteration t and $t - 1$, respectively.

27.5.2 Validation of Results

To assess the quality and the biological meaning of our results, we performed several analyses. We start by showing the accuracy of column clusters. Then, we evaluate the homogeneity of the row clusters. Finally, we associate row and column clusters and we discuss such associations from a biological point of view.

Accuracy of Column Clusters We evaluated the accuracy of the columns clusters with respect to the reference partition given by the GEO accession ID. To measure the accuracy we used the normalized mutual information (NMI) [51]. It provides a value impartial with respect to the number of clusters. NMI measures the information shared between clustering results and true class assignment. We denote by $\mathbf{C} = \{C_1, \ldots, C_J\}$ the partition built by the clustering algorithm on objects and by $\mathbf{P} = \{P_1, \ldots, P_I\}$ the partition inferred by the original classification. The symbols J and I represent respectively the number of clusters $|\mathbf{C}|$ and the number of classes $|\mathbf{P}|$. We denote by n the total number of objects. NMI is computed as the average mutual information between every pair of clusters and classes:

$$\mathbf{NMI} = \frac{\sum_{i=1}^{I} \sum_{j=1}^{J} p_{ij} \log(np_{ij}/p_i p_j)}{\sqrt{\sum_{i=1}^{I} p_i \log(p_i/n) \sum_{j=1}^{J} p_j \log(p_j/n)}}$$

where p_{ij} is the cardinality of the set of objects that occurs both in cluster C_j and in class P_i; p_j is the number of objects in cluster C_j; and p_i is the number of objects in class P_i. Its values ranges from 0 to 1. The column partitioning was quite stable over the 40 trials: We achieved an average NMI of 0.8514 (with a standard deviation of 0.0661). The best trial corresponds to an NMI value of 0.9199. The corresponding coclustering shows 4 column clusters and 1310 row clusters. This is the trial we retain for the in-depth analysis. In particular, we check whether the samples belonging to the same clusters are related to similar experimental conditions. We discover that three column clusters correspond exactly to three of the microarray experiments, confirming the meaningfulness of our clusters. In detail, column cluster 1 (CC_1) contains all the experiments related to cultures grown in either aerobic or anaerob conditions (GDS777). Column cluster 2 (CC_2) contains gene expression levels of yeast subjected to controlled air drying and subsequent rehydration (GDS2713). The experiments that belong to column cluster 3 (CC_3) are all related to stresses caused by drug and radiation administration (GDS2508). The fourth column cluster (CC_4) contains experimental conditions belonging to two different GEO data sets. They are related to stresses induced by cytotoxic compounds (GDS1299) and to treatments with sterol biosynthesis inhibitors (GDS2196).

Homogeneity of Row Clusters   To assess the homogeneity of the row clusters, we used a *homogeneity* score, defined as the ratio of each involved GO term (for both biological process and molecular function subontologies) in each cluster. It takes values between 0 and 1, where a value of 1 means that all genes are involved in at least one common GO term. We obtained an average score of 0.6105 (with a standard deviation of 0.3966), and in 70% of the cases it is greater than 0.50. We suppose that low homogeneity values arose because most genes are annotated on different GO terms, even though they are strictly connected to each other. To test our hypothesis we employed the FuncSpec Web application [44]. It takes as input a list of gene names and it gives as output a summary of functional classes that are functionally enriched in that list. A cluster of genes can be said to be *functionally enriched* for an attribute if the proportion of genes within the cluster known to have that attribute exceeds the number that could reasonably be expected from random chance [44]. FuncSpec provides a *p*-value that represents the probability that the intersection of a given list with any given functional category occurs by chance. For each row cluster we analyzed all the MIPS functional classifications with a *p*-value lower than 0.01. The functional classes are downloaded from the MIPS database [38]. We analyzed 229 clusters containing a number of genes ranging between 5 and 50. For sake of brevity, we report only two examples, but we experienced similar results for the other analyzed clusters. We discovered that genes *UTP*14, *ERB*1, *RNT*1, *DBP*6, *RIX*1, *URB*2, *RPA*12, and *UTP*13, which belong to a cluster showing a low homogeneity value, are all related to *ribosomal processing*. Also the set of genes $ALD6$, $DLD1$, $SNA2$, $MPM1$, $OPI3$, $MCR1$, $SDH2$, $COQ10$, $SDH4$, $SDH3$, and $SDH1$ show a low homogeneity value, but all of them participate in *cellular respiration*. More specifically, they are involved in Fe/S binding, electron transport and membrane-associated energy conservation, aerobic respiration, and electron transport. All these functional categories occur with a p-value lower than 10^{-7}.

The second aspect that we assess is the presence of putative transcription modules. As reported in the Section 27.1, coclustering algorithms are able to identify potential transcription modules, that is, genes whose expression level is enhanced/repressed by the same set of transcription factors (TFs). This ability is enhanced by using constraints chosen to highlight the regulation relationships codified in the GO. In fact, 101 gene clusters out of the 229 analyzed contain at least one TF. To assess the correlation among the TFs and the other genes in the cluster, we checked the enriched biological process. For example, the cluster containing $PRP45$, $MDV1$, $TAM41$, $GLN3$, $ATG9$, $VPS4$, $GYP5$, and $SEC2$ is enriched (among others) for the *nitrogen catabolite activation of transcription from the RNA polymerase II promoter* pathway. Interestingly, $GLN3$ (the only TF belonging to that cluster) is involved in the nitrogen metabolism as reported by the *YTF* website [2]. We derived similar results also for other clusters. $RAP1$, a TF involved in the regulation of telomere turnover in yeast, is clustered with $RPC37$, $TPA1$, $MSI1$, and $YNG1$, which are enriched for *nuclear telomere cap complex* and for *protection from nonhomologous end joining at telomere*. $BEM1$, a TF related to cell–cell signal, belongs to a row cluster composed of 18 genes enriched for the *cell communication* process.

Cluster Association   To provide also a clinical interpretation to the extracted gene clusters, we tried to associate functional modules (described by the row clusters) to specific experimental conditions (characterized by each column cluster) by means of an associative measure. For each column cluster defined by the set of indices J, we evaluated for all row clusters (defined by indices I_r with $r \in 1, \ldots, k$) using the following measure:

$$\mathrm{assoc}(I_r, J) = \frac{\sum_{j \in J} \sum_{i \in I_r} |x_{ij}|}{\sum_{j \in J} \sum_i^m |x_{ij}|}$$

Then, we associated to columns J all the genes that belong to the first 10 row clusters that maximize such a measure.

Finally, we analyzed the obtained four gene sets to verify that the enriched pathways are correctly related to the experimental conditions described in the respective four column clusters. To carry out this analysis we used Eu.Gene Analyzer [15], a stand-alone application that implements the Fisher exact test to identify enriched pathways. Eu.Gene Analyzer offers to the user the possibility of using a nonredundant set of pathways derived from multiple databases, such as Reactome and KEGG.

Here we discuss the obtained results only for column clusters CC_2 and CC_3. We recall that they contain samples belonging respectively to GDS2713 and to GDS2508.

The GDS2713 experimental setting is described in the paper by Singh et al. [48]. In detail, they analyze the response of a yeast to controlled air drying and subsequent rehydration under minimal glucose conditions. Singh et al. observed that the expression levels of genes involved in both fatty acid oxidation and the glyoxylate cycle increased during drying and remained in this state during the rehydration phase. The top-10 row clusters associated to this column cluster contain 169 genes. According to Eu.Gene Analyzer, they are all related to *gluconeogenesis* and *fatty acid biosynthesis*.

The GDS2508 data set is described in the work by Fry et al. [26]. They exposed the yeast to three antibiotics that are known to damage DNA. Moreover, such antibiotics perform a widespread reprogramming of gene expression because they affect also proteins, RNA, and lipids. The 52 genes contained in the top-10 associated row clusters are related to several pathways coherent with the antibiotics effects: *APC/C-mediated degradation of cell cycle proteins*, *gluconeogenesis*, *glycolysis*, *glucose metabolism*, *purine biosynthesis*, and *metabolism of carbohydrates*.

The strength of these results is twofold. On the one hand, they prove that the associated genes are meaningful from a biological point of view. On the other hand, they highlight the ability of our approach to group genes that are differentially expressed under a given stress condition.

27.6 CONCLUSION

In this chapter we presented an ontology-driven coclustering approach for the identification of gene clusters characterized by similar expression profiles under a set of conditions. The proposed methodology, based on a constrained coclustering algorithm, provides a method for selecting the number of column/row clusters automatically as well as a congruent set of constraints. The possibility of imposing some biological constraints enabled us to discover more biologically coherent and meaningful gene groups in an application to baker's yeast. In particular, deriving constraints from the regulative relationships stored in GO led to a more accurate identification of transcription modules. Indeed, we showed that the 44% of row clusters contain at least one transcription factor and the genes in the same cluster are strongly related among them in a regulative function. In addition, we also assessed the biological meaning of the association between clusters of genes and clusters of experimental conditions.

REFERENCES

1. http://www.ncbi.nlm.nih.gov/geo/.

2. http://biochemie.web.med.uni-muenchen.de/YTFD/index.htm.

3. A. Anagnostopoulos, A. Dasgupta, and R. Kumar. A constant-factor approximation algorithm for co-clustering. *Theory Comput.*, 8(1):597–622, 2012.

4. M. Ashburner, C. A. Ball, J. A. Blake, D. Botstein, H. Butler, J. M. Cherry, A. P. Davis, K. Dolinski, S. S. Dwight, J. T. Eppig, M. A. Harris, D. P. Hill, L. Issel-Tarver, A. Kasarskis, S. Lewis, J. C. Matese, J. E. Richardson, M. Ringwald, G. M. Rubin, and G. Sherlock. Gene ontology: Tool for the unification of biology. The Gene Ontology Consortium. *Nat. Genet.*, 25:25–29, 2000.

5. A. Banerjee, I. Dhillon, J. Ghosh, S. Merugu, and D. S. Modha. A generalized maximum entropy approach to bregman co-clustering and matrix approximation. *J. Machine Learning Res.*, 8:1919–1986, 2007.

6. A. Banerjee and J. Ghosh. On scaling up balanced clustering algorithms. In R. L. Grossman, J. Han, V. Kumar, H. Mannila, and R. Motwani (Eds.), *Proceedings of the Second SIAM International Conference on Data Mining*, SIAM, Arlington, VA, April 11–13, 2002, pp. 333–349.

7. A. Banerjee and J. Ghosh. Scalable clustering algorithms with balancing constraints. *Data Mining Knowledge Discov.*, 13(3):365–395, 2006.

8. S. Basu, A. Banerjee, and R. J. Mooney. Semi-supervised clustering by seeding. In C. Sammut and A. G. Hoffmann (Eds.), *Proceedings of the Nineteenth International Conference (ICML 2002)*, University of New South Wales, Sydney, Australia, July 8–12, 2002, pp. 27–34.

9. S. Basu, M. Bilenko, and R. J. Mooney. A probabilistic framework for semi-supervised clustering, In W. Kim, R. Kohavi, J. Gehrke, and W. DuMouchel (Eds.), *Proceedings of the Tenth ACM SIGKDD International Conference on Knowledge Discovery and Data Mining*, ACM, Seattle, WA, August 22–25, 2004, pp. 59–68.

10. S. Basu, I. Davidson, and K. Wagstaff (Eds.). *Constrained Clustering: Advances in Algorithms, Theory and Applications*, Data Mining and Knowledge Discovery Series, Chapman & Hall/CRC Press, New York, 2008.

11. C. Becquet, S. Blachon, B. Jeudy, J.-F. Boulicaut, and O. Gandrillon. Strong-association-rule mining for large-scale gene-expression data analysis: A case study on human sage data. *Genome Biol.*, 3(12):0067.1–0067.16, 2002.

12. J. Besson, C. Robardet, J.-F. Boulicaut, and S. Rome. Constraint-based concept mining and its application to microarray data analysis. *Intell. Data Analysis*, 9(1):59–82, 2005.

13. M. Bilenko, S. Basu, and R. J. Mooney. Integrating constraints and metric learning in semi-supervised clustering. In C. E. Brodley (Ed.), *Proceedings of the Twenty-first International Conference (ICML 2004)*, Banff, Alberta, Canada, July 4–8, 2004, pp. 81–88.

14. M. Brameier and C. Wiuf. Co-clustering and visualization of gene expression data and gene ontology terms for *Saccharomyces cerevisiae* using self-organizing maps. *J. Biomed. Inform.*, 40:160–173, 2007.

15. D. Cavalieri, C. Castagnini, S. Toti, K. Maciag, T. Kelder, L. Gambineri, S. Angioli, and P. Dolara. Eu.gene analyzer a tool for integrating gene expression data with pathway databases. *Bioinformatics*, 1:2631–2632, 2007.

16. Y. Cheng and G. M. Church. Biclustering of expression data. In P. E. Bourne, M. Gribskov, R. B. Altman, N. Jensen, D. A. Hope, T. Lengauer, J. C. Mitchell, E. D. Scheeff, C. Smith, S. Strande, and H. Weissig (Eds.), *Proceedings of the Eighth International Conference on Intelligent Systems for Molecular Biology*, August 19–23, 2000, La Jolla, San Diego, CA, pp. 93–103.

17. H. Cho, I. S. Dhillon, Y. Guan, and S. Sra. Minimum sum-squared residue co-clustering of gene expression data. In M. W. Berry, U. Dayal, C. Kamath, and D. B. Skillicorn (Eds.), *Proceedings of the Fourth SIAM International Conference on Data Mining*, Lake Buena Vista, FL, April 22–24, 2004, pp. 114–125.

18. F. Cordero, A. Visconti, and M. Botta. A new protein motif extraction framework based on constrained co-clustering. In S. Y. Shin and S. Ossowski (Eds.), *Proceedings of the 2009 ACM Symposium on Applied Computing (SAC)*, Honolulu, HI, March 9–12, 2009, pp. 776–781.

19. F. Cordero, R. G. Pensa, A. Visconti, D. Ienco, and M. Botta. Ontology-driven co-clustering of gene expression data. In *Proceedings of AI*IA 2009*, Reggio Emilia, Italy, Vol. 5883 of *Lecture Notes in Computer Science*. Springer, 2009, pp. 426–435.

20. I. Davidson and S. S. Ravi. Agglomerative hierarchical clustering with constraints: Theoretical and empirical results. In *Proceedings PKDD 2005*, Porto, Portugal, Vol. 3721 of *Lecture Notes in Computer Science*. Springer, 2005, pp. 59–70.

21. I. Davidson and S. S. Ravi. Clustering with constraints: Feasibility issues and the k-means algorithm. In *Proceedings SIAM SDM 2005*, Newport Beach, CA, 2005.

22. M. Deodhar, G. Gupta, J. Ghosh, H. Cho, and I. S. Dhillon. A scalable framework for discovering coherent co-clusters in noisy data. In *Proceedings ICML 2009*, Montreal, Quebec, Canada, 2009, pp. 241–248.

23. I. S. Dhillon, S. Mallela, and D. S. Modha. Information-theoretic co-clustering. In *Proceedings ACM SIGKDD 2003*, Washington, DC, 2003, pp. 89–98.

24. S. Dzeroski, B. Goethals, and P. Panov (Eds.). *Inductive Databases and Constraint-Based Data Mining*, Springer, New York, 2010.

25. M. B. Eisen, P. T. Spellman, P. O. Brownand, and D. Botstein. Cluster analysis and display of genome-wide expression patterns. *Proc. Natl. Acad. Sci. USA*, 95:14863–14868, 1998.

26. R. C. Fry, M. S. DeMott, J. P. Cosgrove, T. J. Begley, L. D. Samson, and P. C. Dedon. The dna-damage signature in *Saccharomyces cerevisiae* is associated with single-strand breaks in dna. *BMC Genomics*, 12:300–313, 2006.

27. R. Ge, M. Ester, W. Jin, and I. Davidson. Constraint-driven clustering. In *Proceedings of ACM SIGKDD 2007*, San Jose, CA, 2007, pp. 320–329.

28. D. Hanisch, A. Zien, R. Zimmer, and T. Lengauer. Co-clustering of biological networks and gene expression data. *Bioinformatics*, 18:S145–S154, 2002.

29. B. Hendrickson and T. G. Kolda. Partitioning rectangular and structurally unsymmetric sparse matrices for parallel processing. *SIAM J. Sci. Comput.*, 21:2048–2072, 1999.

30. J. D. Hoheisel. Microarray technology: Beyond transcript profiling and genotype analysis. *Nat. Rev. Genet.*, 7:200–210, 2006.

31. D. Ienco, R. G. Pensa, and R. Meo. Parameter-free hierarchical co-clustering by n-ary splits. In *Proceedings ECML PKDD 2009*, Bled, Slovenia, Vol. 5781 of *Lecture Notes in Computer Science*. Springer, 2009, pp. 580–595.

32. J. Ihmels, G. Friedlander, S. Bergmann, O. Sarig, Y. Ziv, and N. Barkai. Revealing modular organization in the yeast transcriptional network. *Nat. Genet.*, 31:370–377, Aug. 2002.

33. I. Jolliffe. *Principal Component Analysis*, Springer, New York, 1986.

34. D. Klein, S. D. Kamvar, and C. D. Manning. From instance-level constraints to space-level constraints: Making the most of prior knowledge in data clustering. In *Proceedings ICML 2002*, Sydney, Australia, 2002, pp. 307–314.

35. Y. Kluger, R. Basri, J. T. Chang, and M. Gerstein. Spectral biclustering of microarray data: Coclustering genes and conditions. *Genome Res.*, 13:703–716, 2003.

36. L. Lazzeroni and A. Owen. Plaid models for gene expression data. Technical Report. Stanford University, Stanford, CA, 2000.

37. S. C. Madeira and A. L. Oliveira. Biclustering algorithms for biological data analysis: A survey. *IEEE/ACM Trans. Computat. Biol. Bioinformatics*, 1(1):24–45, 2004.

38. H. W. Mewes, D. Frishman, U. Güldener, G. Mannhaupt, K. Mayer, M. Mokrejs, B. Morgenstern, M. Münsterkötter, S. Rudd, and B. Weil. Mips: A database for genomes and protein sequences. *Nucleic Acids Res.*, 30(1):31–34, 2002.

39. R. G. Pensa and J-F. Boulicaut. Constrained co-clustering of gene expression data. In *Proceedings SIAM SDM 2008*, Atlanta, GA, 2008, pp. 25–36.

40. R. G. Pensa, J.-F. Boulicaut, F. Cordero, and M. Atzori. Co-clustering numerical data under user-defined constraints. *Stat. Anal. Data Mining*, 3(1):38–55, 2010.

41. R. G. Pensa, C. Robardet, and J.-F. Boulicaut. Towards constrained co-clustering in ordered 0/1 data sets. In *Proceedings ISMIS 2006*, Bari, Italy, Vol. 4203 of *Lecture Notes in Computer Science*. Springer, 2006, pp. 425–434.

42. R. G. Pensa, C. Robardet, and J.-F. Boulicaut. Constraint-driven co-clustering of 0/1 data. In *Constrained Clustering: Advances in Algorithms, Theory and Applications*, Data Mining and Knowledge Discovery Series, Chapman & Hall/CRC Press, Boca Raton, FL, 2008, pp. 123–148.

43. C. Robardet and F. Feschet. Efficient local search in conceptual clustering. In *Proceedings DS 2001*, Washington, DC, Vol. 2226 of *Lecture Notes in Computer Science*. Springer, 2001, pp. 323–335.

44. M. D. Robinson, J. Grigull, N. Mohammad, and T. R. Hughes. Funspec: A web-based cluster interpreter for yeast. *BMC Bioinformatics*, 3(1):35, 2002.

45. S. Salvador and P. Chan. Determining the number of clusters/segments in hierarchical clustering/segmentation algorithms. In *Proceedings of the 16th IEEE International Conference on Tools with AI*, 2004, pp. 576–584.

46. H. Shan and A. Banerjee. Bayesian co-clustering. In *Proceedings ICDM 2008*, Pisa, Italy. IEEE Computer Society, 2008, pp. 530–539.

47. X. Shi, W. Fan, and P. S. Yu. Efficient semi-supervised spectral co-clustering with constraints. In *Proceedings of ICDM 2010*, Sydney, Australia, 2010, pp. 1043–1048.

48. J. Singh, D. Kumar, N. Ramakrishnan, V. Singhal, J. Jervis, J. F. Garst, S. M. Slaughter, A. M. DeSantis, M. Potts, and R. F. Helm. Transcriptional response of *Saccharomyces cerevisiae* to desiccation and rehydration. *Appl. Environ. Microbiol.*, 71:8752–8763, 2005.

49. Y. Song, S. Pan, S. Liu, F. Wei, M. X. Zhou, and W. Qian. Constrained coclustering for textual documents. In *Proceedings of AAAI 2010*, AAAI Press, Atlanta, GA, 2010.

50. D. Steinhauser, B. H. Junker, A. Luedemann, J. Selbig, and J. Kopka. Hypothesis-driven approach to predict transcriptional units from gene expression data. *Bioinformatics*, 20:1928–1939, 2004.

51. A. Strehl and J. Ghosh. Cluster ensembles—A knowledge reuse framework for combining multiple partitions. *J. Machine Learning Res.*, 3:583–617, 2002.

52. K. Wagstaff, C. Cardie, S. Rogers, and S. Schrödl. Constrained k-means clustering with background knowledge. In *Proceedings ICML 2001*, Williamstown, MA, 2001, pp. 577–584.

PART G

BIOLOGICAL DATA CLASSIFICATION

CHAPTER 28

SURVEY ON FINGERPRINT CLASSIFICATION METHODS FOR BIOLOGICAL SEQUENCES

BHASKAR DASGUPTA and LAKSHMI KALIGOUNDER

Department of Computer Science, University of Illinois at Chicago, Chicago, Illinois

28.1 INTRODUCTION

Since the discovery of the double-helical structure of DNA, the molecular biology field has undergone a significant transformation via nucleic acids sequencing to determine genetic information at the most fundamental level. This revolution in biology has created a huge volume of data, estimated by many to grow at an exponential rate, by directly reading DNA sequences. One important reason for this exceptional growth rate of biological data lies in the medical use of such information in the design of therapeutics. Naturally, such a large amount of data poses a serious challenge in storing, retrieving, and analyzing biological information.

In this chapter, we provide a survey of a classification problem involving genetic sequences, namely the problem of classifying fingerprint vectors with missing values. Oligonucleotide fingerprinting is a powerful DNA array-based method to characterize complementary DNA (cDNA) and ribosomal DNA (rDNA) gene libraries and has many applications such as gene expression profiling and DNA clone classification. For example, Herwig et al. [18] used oligonucleotide fingerprinting as an efficient and fast approach to extract parallel gene expression information about all genes that are represented in a cDNA library from a specific tissue under analysis. The information obtained by monitoring gene expression levels in different development stages, tissue types, clinical conditions, and organisms can fuel an understanding of gene function and gene networks and may assist in diagnostics of disease conditions and effects of medical treatments.

The main focus of this chapter is motivated by the recent development of a *discrete* classification approach by Figueroa, Borneman, and Jiang in 2004 [11], called the binary clustering with missing-values (BCMV) problem, for analyzing oligonucleotide fingerprints, especially in applications such as DNA clone classifications. In this approach, fingerprint data were first normalized and binarized using control DNA clones. Because there may exist unresolved ("missing") values in the binarization process, they formulated the

Biological Knowledge Discovery Handbook: Preprocessing, Mining, and Postprocessing of Biological Data,
First Edition. Edited by Mourad Elloumi and Albert Y. Zomaya.

classification of (binary) oligonucleotide fingerprints as a combinatorial optimization problem that attempted to identify clusters and resolve the missing values in the fingerprints *simultaneously*.

The rest of the chapter is organized as follows. In Section 28.2 we state some basic mathematical definitions that will be useful in understanding the underlying computational problems more effectively. In Section 28.3 we provide a brief survey of various other classification approaches to provide the reader with a global perspective, and in Section 28.4 we provide a brief overview of several approaches for estimating missing values in the genomic data. In Section 28.5 we survey in more detail the BCMV problem and its variations. We assume that the reader is familiar with standard textbook concepts of algorithmic complexity theory such as found in [8, 23].

28.2 BASIC DEFINITIONS AND PROBLEM STATEMENTS

Fingerprint   Formally, we define a fingerprint vector (in short, fingerprint) as a vector with each component (element) from $\Sigma \cup \{N\}$ for some finite alphabet Σ not containing the symbol N that consists of the hybridization intensity values between the clone and each probe. The value N in a component of the vector corresponds to a component with missing values. The number of elements of a fingerprint is its *length*.

Oligonucleotide Probe   A short DNA sequence (usually 8–50 bases) which is applied to hybridize with the clones.

Compatible Fingerprints   Two fingerprint vectors $f_1 = \langle f_1[1], f_1[2], \ldots, f_1[\ell] \rangle$ and $f_2 = \langle f_2[1], f_2[2], \ldots, f_2[\ell] \rangle$ are *compatible* if for any position i where they differ at least one of $f_1[i]$ and $f_2[i]$ is equal to N. See Figure 28.1 for an illustration.

Resolved Vector   A vector r is called a *resolved vector* of a fingerprint vector f if it is identical with f on all positions having an alphabet from Σ in f and has a symbol from Σ in each position of f that had the symbol N.

28.3 OVERVIEW OF VARIOUS CLASSIFICATION APPROACHES

Classification approaches are not very new to biologists; hierarchical classification has been used for a long time to create taxonomic ranks (kingdom, phylum, class, order, family,

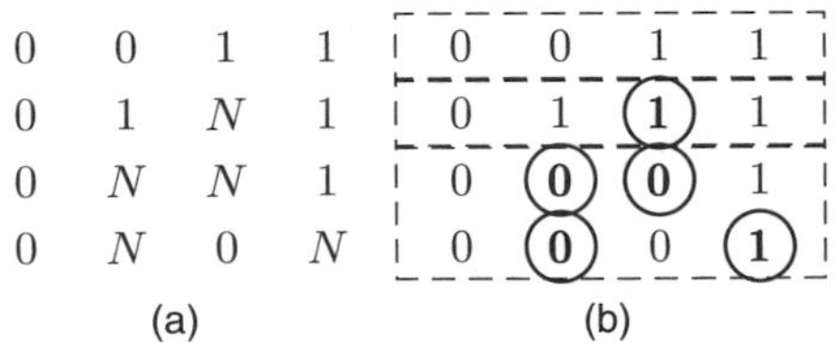

FIGURE 28.1   (a) Four fingerprint vectors $\Sigma = \{0, 1\}$. (b) A possible resolution of them. Each compatible fingerprint group is enclosed by a dashed rectangle.

genus, and species) of all living things. However, with the arrival of fast computational tools and large amounts of genetic information, classification and clustering approaches have increased their applicability considerably to efficiently analyze the genomic data. Classification and clustering remains, in general to a certain extent, an art since there are no universally agreed-upon criteria for evaluating solutions, and there is no ultimate algorithm. In this section, we briefly review a few classification approaches that have been used in the past in bioinformatics; for a more comprehensive treatment, see, for example, [24].

Shamir and Sharan in [26] discuss some algorithmic approaches for clustering *gene expression data*. A key step in the analysis of gene expression data is the identification of groups of genes that manifest similar expression patterns. The goal is to partition the elements into subsets, which are called *clusters*, so that two criteria are satisfied: *homogeneity* (elements in the same cluster are highly similar to each other) and *separation* (elements from different clusters have low similarity to each other).

In the *hierarchical* classification approach, the solutions are typically represented by a dendrogram. Algorithms for generating such solutions often work either in top-down manner, by repeatedly partitioning the set of elements, or in a bottom-up fashion.

Another classical classification approach is k-means [2, 21]. It assumes that the number of clusters K is known and aims to minimize the distance between elements and the centroids of their assigned clusters. The HCS [16, 17] and CLICK [25] algorithms use a similar graph-theoretic approach for classification. The input data are represented as a similarity graph. The algorithm recursively partitions the current set of elements into two subsets. Before a partition, the algorithm considers the subgraph induced by the current subset of elements. If the subgraph satisfies a stopping criterion, then it is declared a kernel. Otherwise, a minimum-weight cut is computed in that subgraph, and the set is split into the two subsets separated by that cut. The output is a list of kernels that serve as a basis for the eventual clusters. HCS and CLICK differ in the similarity graph they construct, their stopping criteria, and the postprocessing of the kernels. In another graph-theoretic approach, Ben-Dor et al. [4] developed a polynomial algorithm called CAST (clustering affinity search technique) for finding true clustering with high probability. The correct cluster structure is represented by a graph that is a disjoint union of cliques, and errors are subsequently introduced in the graph by independently removing and adding edges between pairs of vertices with some probability. If all clusters are of size at least $\Omega(n)$, the algorithm solves the problem to a desired accuracy with high probability.

Self-organizing maps (SOMs) [20] were developed as a method for fitting a number of ordered discrete reference vectors to the distribution of vectorial input samples. A SOM assumes that the number of clusters is known.

To summarize, the hierarchical method gives an overall view of the structure without an attempt to force a hard classification, whereas the other methods aim to split the universe of elements into clusters, either by geometric approaches that move cluster centers (SOM, k-means) or by the graph-theoretic approach. The last approach may take a global view (CLICK) or single out one affinity-stable cluster at a time (CAST).

28.4 MISSING-VALUE ESTIMATION METHODS

The value of N in the sequence for fingerprint classification corresponds to some unknown (missing) spots on the sequence during the laboratory process due to various factors (e.g., machine error, gene expression microarray experiments, generating data sets with multiple expression values, insufficient resolution in microarray experiments, etc.). There are many options for dealing with missing values, each of which reaches drastically different results.

Ignoring missing values is obviously the simplest method and is frequently applied. This approach however has its flaws. Because it is often very costly or time consuming to repeat the experiment, molecular biologists, statisticians, and computer scientists have investigated the possibility of recovering the missing gene expression values by ad hoc or systematic methods. Methods like hierarchical clustering and *k-means* clustering are not robust against missing data and may lose effectiveness even with a few missing values. Other standard supervised statistical microarray analysis techniques such as support vector machine classification, principal-component analysis, or singular-value component analysis often may not be applicable to a data set with missing values. Thus methods for imputing missing data are needed.

One solution to deal with the missing values is to do the same experiment and replicate the data. This extra labor work strategy has been used in many experimental scientists and wet laboratories so far. If the cost of the experiment is not expensive, it may be a practical solution, but certain type of experiments such as patient-specific time course experiments are very expensive or may even be impossible to be reproduced. Less labor work and a simple tentative solution is to fill the missing values by zeros, average of the gene expressions, or average of overall expression values.

Two recent popular methods of inputting missing values are the KNNimpute method [28] and the LLSimpute method [3, 19], which uses the *k*-nearest-neighbor clustering, least-square, and Bayesian optimization. The basic strategy of this type is to find similar expression patterns having missing values by clustering methods and then to predict the missing value from the corresponding values in the same cluster. In these two methods, the recovery of missing data is done independently; that is, the estimation of each missing entry does not influence the estimation of other missing entries. Another approach is to use high-rank Eigengenes in a hidden concept space to predict the missing value. Representative methods of this type are the SVDimpute method [1], which uses singular-value decomposition, and the BPCAimpute method [22], which uses principal-component analysis and Bayesian optimizations. The basic strategy of this type of approach is to find bases of expression space and then to reconstruct a matrix with the dominant bases. During the reconstruction process, the missing values are filled. The basis is called Eigengene, and Eigengene shows a gene expression fluctuation which is orthogonal to each other in an expression pattern space. Another approach similar to SVDimpute- and BPCAimpute-type prediction is the fixed rank approximation algorithm (FRAA) of Friedland, Niknejad, and Chihara [13] to predict missing entries by using Eigengenes. In this approach the estimation of missing entries is done simultaneously; that is, the estimation of one missing entry influences the estimation of the other missing entries. They showed that FRAA is more accurate than replacing missing values with zeros or with row means. FRAA by itself is a very useful tool for gene data analysis without using clustering methods. The number of high-rank Eigengenes should be close to the rank of the perfect matrix, but it is hard to guess the correct number of high-rank Eigengenes from a data with missing entries. To find the optimal number, BPCAimpute uses Bayesian statistics while SVDimpute uses a given fixed number. FRAA also requires the fixed number of major Eigengenes, but the uniqueness of FRAA is that it has an iteration process which can increase the importance of these high-rank Eigengenes in a reconstructed matrix on each step. However, it is still difficult to guess the correct number of Eigengenes or rank of a perfect matrix and therefore even FRAA itself is powerful but not useful in a practical case. The other drawback of FRAA is that the result heavily deepens on initial tentative values for missing entries. Friedland et al. [14] suggested a hybrid method IFRAA (improved FRAA), which is a combination of FRAA and a good clustering algorithm.

There is no general consensus about which type of algorithms is better. Past experiments in [19, 22] suggest that BPCAimpute and LLSimpute predict generally better than the others, and the performances of these two methods are almost comparable depending on the data sets. Troyanskaya et al. [28] observed that KNNimpute is a more robust and sensitive method for missing-value estimation than SVDimpute and both SVDimpute and KNNimpute surpass the commonly used row average method. Gan, Liew, and Yan [15] proposed a hybrid approach called POCS (projection onto convex set), which is the best combination of SVDimpute and KNNimpute. They experimentally showed that POCS achieves a reduction of 16–20% error than KNNimpute and SVDimpute. The FRAA method has been used by several computational biologists and experimental results on various data sets show its robustness. To further improve upon the FRAA approach, one needs to combine it with an algorithm for gene clustering. A possible implementation is as follows. First, apply FRAA to the corrupted data set. Next, using this estimated data set, partition the genes into clusters of genes with similar traits. Now apply FRAA again to the missing entries of genes in each cluster.

In the next section, we survey in more detail a combinatorial approach to determining missing values originally proposed by Figueroa, Borneman, and Jiang [11], the main focus of this chapter.

28.5 FINGERPRINT CLASSIFICATION: COMBINATORIAL APPROACH FOR ESTIMATING MISSING VALUES

In this approach, called binary clustering with missing values (BCMV), fingerprint data are first normalized and binarized using control DNA clones. To resolve the missing values in the binarization process, Figueroa et al. formulated the classification of (binary) oligonucleotide fingerprints as several combinatorial optimization problems as described below that attempt to identify clusters and resolve the missing values in the fingerprints *simultaneously*. They studied the computational complexity of these problems and their parameterized versions where the maximum number of N's in a fingerprint vector is bounded by an integer parameter p.

In the following problem formulations, we assume that $\Sigma = \{0, 1\}$:

- *Binary Clustering with Missing Values* (BCMV) The problem of clustering with p missing values [CMV(p) for short] is to partition a set F of n fingerprint vectors, each of of length ℓ with at most p symbols that are N, into *disjoint* subsets $F_1, F_2, \ldots, F_k$ such that, for each $1 \leq i \leq k$, any two fingerprints in F_i are compatible. The objective is to *minimize* the number of partitions. Intuitively, the CMV problem aims to resolve the fingerprints using the minimum number of resolved vectors.

- *Inside Edge Binary Clustering with Missing Values* (IEBCMV) The problem of inside compatible clustering with p missing values [IEBCMV(p) for short] is defined analogously except that the number of compatible pairs of vectors within the same partition is maximized instead of the minimization of the cardinality of the partition. That is, the objective now is to *maximize* the number of coclustered pairs of fingerprints.

- *Outside Edge Binary Clustering with Missing Values* (OEBCMV) The problem of outside compatible clustering with p missing values [OEBCMV(p) for short] is again defined analogously except that now the number of compatible pairs of vectors belonging to different clusters is minimized. That is, the new objective is to *minimize* the number of pairs of compatible fingerprints assigned to different clusters.

28.5.1 Algorithmic Complexity Results

BCMV(p)   BCMV(p) was first considered and motivated in [11]. For arbitrary p, the following strong inapproximability result can be shown.

Theorem 28.1 [9] For any constant $0 < \varepsilon < 1$ and unrestricted p, BCMV(p) cannot be approximated to within a ratio of $n^{1-\varepsilon}$ unless NP $\subseteq$ ZPP.

Sketch of Proof   In the standard graph coloring problem, the goal is to produce an assignment of colors to vertices of a given graph $G = (V, E)$ such that no two adjacent vertices have the same color and the number of colors is *minimized*. Let $\chi^*(G)$ denote the minimum number of colors in a coloring of G. The following inapproximability result is known [10]: For any constant $0 < \varepsilon < 1$, $\chi^*(G)$ cannot be approximated to within a factor of $|V|^{1-\varepsilon}$ unless NP $\subseteq$ ZPP.

Given an instance $G = (V, E)$ with n vertices and m edges, one can construct an instance of BCMV(p) in the following manner. There is a sequence f_v of length m for every node v of G. Consider any arbitrary ordering of the m edges of G. For the ith edge in the order, say $\{u, v\}$, we have $f_u[i] = 0$, $f_v[i] = 1$, and $f_x[i] = N$ for every $x \in V \setminus \{u, v\}$. See Figure 28.2 for an illustration. The proof can then be completed by showing that G can be colored with y colors if and only if BCMV(p) outputs a solution with y partitions.

However, in practice, the number of N's in a binarized fingerprint vector is often upper bounded by a small constant, depending on the quality of hybridization intensity values and choice of control clones. Thus, it behooves to look at the problem with restricted values of p. Figueroa, Borneman, and Jiang [11] showed the problem to be NP hard even when $p = 3$ and polynomial-time solvable when $p = 1$. The polynomial-time solvability for BCMV(1) was shown by reducing it to a vertex cover problem on *bipartite graphs* and observing that the later problem is well known to be solvable in polynomial time by matching techniques. Figueroa et al. in 2005 [12] further showed that BCMV(2) is NP hard by giving a reduction from the minimum vertex cover problem on planar, cubic, 3-connected, and triangle-free graphs, which is known to be NP hard [29], to the BCMV(2) problem.

In a subsequent paper, Bonizzoni, Della Vedova, Dondi, and Mauri [7] showed some improvements in closing the gaps between the known lower bounds and upper bounds on

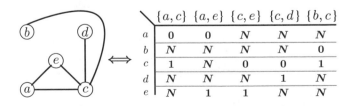

FIGURE 28.2   An illustration of the reduction in Theorem 28.1.

the approximability of variants of the original problem proposed in [12]. They showed that, even when each fingerprint contains only two unknown positions, BCMV(2) is APX hard[†] by giving an L-reduction from minimum vertex cover on cubic graphs which is known to be APX hard. In particular, to prove that BCMV(2) is APX hard, they combined two L-reductions: the first one from the minimum vertex cover problem on a graph G to the minimum vertex cover on a graph gadget G' and the second one from the minimum vertex cover problem on a graph gadget G' to BCMV(2).

As the proof of Theorem 28.1 suggests, BCMV(p) can be easily formulated as one of finding a *minimum clique partition* of a graph in the following manner:

> Given a set of fingerprint vectors F, define a graph $G_F = (F, E_F)$, where two nodes (fingerprints) are adjacent if and only if they are compatible.

The graph G_F is known as the *compatibility graph* of F. Hence BCMV of F is equivalent to the problem of finding a minimum clique partition (MCP) on G_F. However, it is also well known that finding MCP of a graph is in general an NP-hard problem. Nonetheless, based on such a reformulation, The authors in [11, 12] presented efficient algorithmic approaches for BCMV(p) by taking advantage of some unique properties of the graph G_F, resulting in several results such as the following:

- There exists a greedy algorithm with an approximation ratio of $\min\{1 + \ln n, 2 + p \ln \ell\}$ that can be implemented to run in $O(n\ell 2^p)$ time. For $p = O(\log n)$ this approximation algorithm runs in polynomial time.
- There exists a polynomial-time heuristics that achieves an approximation ratio of 2^p.
- They provide a practical greedy heuristics based on iterating on building the largest possible cluster that has a worst-case running time of $O(p^{2^p} n^2)$. Since p is usually small compared to n in practice, the running time of the algorithm is practically efficient. To find a small clique partition of G_F, one keeps on finding unique *maximal* cliques and removing it from the graph (and updates the graph accordingly) until no unique maximal cliques can be found. Then, a greedy action takes place by removing a maximum clique from the graph and the same process is repeated until all vertices of G_F have been included in some clique.

IEBCMV(p) and OEBCMV(p) These two variants of the original optimization problems in [12], introduced in [7], aim to solve the fingerprint classification problem based on slightly different optimization criteria. The first variant, termed as the problem of inside compatible clustering with at most p missing values [IECBMV(p) for short] is defined analogously to BCMV(p) with the exception that the number of compatible pairs of vectors within the same clusters is maximized instead of the minimization of the cardinality of the partition. The second variant, termed as the problem of outside compatible clustering with at most p missing values [OECBMV(p) for short], is again defined analogously to BCMV(p) with the exception that now the number of compatible pairs of vectors belonging to different

---

[†]A problem that is APX hard cannot be approximated within a factor of $1 + \varepsilon$ for some positive constant $\varepsilon > 0$ in polynomial time unless $P = NP$.

clusters is minimized. Various results on these problems that were reported in the papers [7, 12] include the following:

- It was shown in [12] that, when $p = O(\log n)$, IECMV(p) can be approximated in polynomial time within a factor of 2^{2p-1}, whereas, in the special case when no two compatible vectors have N at the same position, OECMV(p) can be approximated in polynomial time within a ratio of $2\left(1 - 2^{-2p}\right)$. To obtain these results, they reduced IECBMV(p) and the restricted version of OECBMV(p) to special variants of maximum and minimum satisfiability problems which yielded polynomial-time constant-factor approximations for both problems.

  They showed that IECBMV(p) can be expressed as a variant of the maximum satisfiability problem where the Boolean formula is in disjunctive normal form (DNF). By a result of Trevisan [27], the maximum satisfiability problem for DNF formulas with conjunctive clauses of length at most k admits a polynomial-time approximation algorithm with an approximation ratio of 2^{k-1}, which leads to an approximation ratio of 2^{2p-1} for the IECBMV(p) problem.

  By taking the negation of the above DNF formula and applying De Morgan's laws, they obtained a formula Φ in conjunctive normal form (CNF) with clauses of length at most $2p$. Now, the problem of finding the minimum number of clauses in Φ that can be simultaneously satisfied is easily seen to be equivalent to the OECBMV(p) problem. Furthermore, if no two compatible vectors contain N at the same position, then there is a one-to-one correspondence between satisfied clauses and compatible pairs of fingerprints that are in different clusters. Using the fact that the problem of minimum k-satisfiability admits a polynomial-time approximation algorithm with an approximation ratio of $2\left(1 - 2^{-k}\right)$ [6], they obtained an approximation ratio of $2\left(1 - 2^{-2p}\right)$ for the so-restricted version of the OECBMV(p) problem.

- Further improvements of the results of [12] are reported in a subsequent paper [7]. Here, they proved that both of these problems are APX hard. The APX hardness of IECBMV(2) is obtained via an L-reduction from a maximum independent set on 3-regular graphs which is known to be APX hard [5], and their results show that it is NP hard to approximate IECBMV(2) with a ratio better than $1 + \frac{1}{3479}$.

  On the positive side, these authors presented a fixed-parameter tractable approximation algorithm whose running time is $O(2^p n^3 \ell)$ and achieved an approximation ratio of 2. Despite the hardness of these restricted versions of the problem, they also showed that the general clustering problem on an unbounded number of missing values such that these missing values occur for every fixed position of at most one input fingerprint vector can be solved in polynomial time. Finally, they gave a polynomial-time algorithm for solving the BCMV(p) problem for the special case where, for each position of a fingerprint vector, there is at most one fingerprint with an N symbol in such a position. They denoted such a restriction by 1-BCMV and showed that their proposed algorithm run in $O(n^2 \ell)$ time.

28.5.2 Experimental Results

The experimental results on simulation and real data demonstrated that the greedy heuristics in [11] run faster and perform better (in the context of DNA clone classification) than popular clustering methods such as UPGMA, CLUSTER, and CLICK. If the ratio between the largest and the smallest intensity values is above some prespecified threshold, the intensity of the clone was considered as a missing value, and the reliability of hybridization intensities were evaluated using clones spotted twice. The results on real data from the classification of microbial rDNA clones suggested that this discrete approach is more accurate than clustering methods based on real intensity values in terms of separating clones that have different characteristics with respect to the given oligonucleotide probes. An important advantage of the discrete approach was that binarized fingerprints were essentially reproducible whereas (normalized) real intensity values were generally not.

28.5.3 Open Problems for Future Research

As observed in [7, 12], several open problems remain for the future on the algorithmic complexity side. For example:

- Is there a constant-factor approximation algorithm for OECBMV(p) in the general case and a nontrivial approximation ratio for greedy heuristics for IECMV(p)? Can we discover any nontrivial relationship between the various problem BCMV(p), IECBMV(p), and OECBMV(p) in terms of their hardness of approximation? Some experimental work could be helpful for this purpose to develop intuitions about the special structure of the input data.
- Naturally, one could relate resolving the fingerprint vectors with construction of the phylogenetic trees of the corresponding resolved sequences. For instance, a natural objective could be to find an assignment to the N positions which will yields phylogenetic trees optimizing a specific evolutionary objective (e.g., perfect phylogeny, phylogenetic tree of minimum size or a minimum number of mutations, etc.). After the rDNA clone libraries are constructed, the clones can classified by individual hybridization experiments on DNA microarrays with a series of short DNA oligonucleotides into clone types or operational taxonomic units (OTUs), where an OTU is a set of DNA clones sharing the same set of oligonucleotides that have successfully hybridized. Once classified, the nucleotide sequence of representative clones from each OTU can then be obtained by DNA sequencing to provide phylogenetic descriptions of the microorganisms.

ACKNOWLEDGMENTS

We thank Paola Bonizzoni and Riccardo Dondi for useful discussions. This work was partially supported by National Science Foundation Grant No. DBI-1062328.

REFERENCES

1. O. Alter, P. O. Brown, and D. Botstein. Singular value decomposition for genome-wide expression data processing and modeling. *Proc. Natl. Acad. Sci. USA*, 97:10101–10106, 2000.
2. C. H. Ball and D. J. Hall. A clustering technique for summarizing multivariate data. *Behav. Sci.*, 12:153–155, 1967.

3. T. H. Be, B. Dysvik, and I. Jonassen. LSimpute: Accurate estimation of missing values in microarray data with least squares methods. *Nucl. Acids Res.*, 32(3):e34, 2004.

4. A. Ben-Dor, R. Shamir, and Z. Yakhini. Clustering gene expression patterns. *J. Computat. Biol.*, 6(3–4):281–297, 1999.

5. P. Berman and M. Karpinski. On some tighter inapproximability results (extended abstract). In J. Wiedermann, P. Boas Emde, and M. Nielsen (Eds.) *Automata, Languages and Programming*, Vol. 1644 of *Lecture Notes in Computer Science*, Springer, Heidelberg, 1999, pp. 200–209.

6. D. Bertsimas, C-P. Teo, and R. Vohra. On dependent randomized rounding algorithms. In W. Cunningham, S. T. McCormick, and M. Queyranne (Eds.) *Integer Programming and Combinatorial Optimization*, Vol. 1084 of *Lecture Notes in Computer Science*, Springer, Heidelberg, 1996, pp. 330–344.

7. P. Bonizzoni, G. Della Vedova, R. Dondi, and G. Mauri. Fingerprint clustering with bounded number of missing values. *Algorithmica*, 58(2):282–303, 2010.

8. T. H. Cormen, C. E. Leiserson, R. L. Rivest, and C. Stein. *Introduction to Algorithms*. MIT Press, Cambridge, MA, 2001.

9. B. DasGupta and R. Dondi. Some improved inapproximability results for fingerprint classification, unpublished manuscript, 2011.

10. U. Feige and J. Kilian. Zero knowledge and the chromatic number. *J. Comput. Syst. Sci.*, 57(2):187–199, 1998.

11. A. Figueroa, J. Borneman, and T. Jiang. Clustering binary fingerprint vectors with missing values for DNA array data analysis. *J. Computat. Biol.*, 11(5):887–901, 2004.

12. A. Figueroa, A. Goldstein, T. Jiang, M. Kurowski, A. Lingas and M. Paterson. Approximate clustering of fingerprint vectors with missing values. *Proc. 2005 Australasian Symp. Theory Comput.*, 41:57–60, 2005.

13. S. Friedland, A. Niknejad, and L. Chihara. A simultaneous reconstruction of missing data in DNA microarrays. *Lin. Alg. Appl.*, 416(1):8–28, 2006.

14. S. Friedland, A. Niknejad, M. Kaveh, and H. Zare. An algorithm for missing value estimation for DNA microarray data. In *Proceedings of IEEE International Conference on Acoustics, Speech and Signal Processing*, Vol. 2, IEEE Press, 2006, pp. 1092–1095.

15. X. Gan, A. W.-C. Liew, and H. Yan. Missing microarray data estimation based on projection onto convex set method. *Proc. 17th Int. Conf. Pattern Recognition*, 3:782–785, 2004.

16. E. Hartuv and R. Shamir. A clustering algorithm based on graph connectivity. *Inform. Process. Lett.*, 76(4–6):175–181, 2000.

17. E. Hartuv, A. O. Schmitt, J. Lange, S. Meier-Ewert, H. Lehrach, and R. Shamir. An algorithm for clustering cDNAs for gene expression analysis. *Genomics*, 66(3):249–256, 2000.

18. R. Herwig, A. J. Poustka, C. Miller, C. Bull, H. Lehrach, and J. O'Brien. Large-scale clustering of cDNA fingerprint data. *Genome Res.*, 9(11):1093–1105, 1999.

19. H. Kim, G. H. Golub, and H. Park. Missing value estimation for DNA microarray gene expression data: Local least squares imputation. *Bioinformatics*, 21(2):187–198, 2005.

20. T. Kohonen. *Self-Organizing Maps*, 3rd extended ed., Springer, Heidelberg, 2001.

21. J. MacQueen. Some methods for classification and analysis of multivariate observations. In L. M. Le Cam and J. Neyman (Eds.), *Proceedings of the Fifth Berkeley Symposium on Mathematical Statistics and Probability*, Vol. 1. University of California Press, 1967, pp. 281–297.

22. S. Oba, M. Sato, I. Takemasa, M. Monden, K. Matsubara, and S. Ishii. A Bayesian missing value estimation method for gene expression profile data. *Bioinformatics*, 19(16):2088–2096, 2003.

23. C. H. Papadimitriou. *Computational Complexity*. Addison-Wesley, Reading, MA, 1994.

24. C. Romesburg. *Cluster Analysis for Researchers*. Lulu Press, 2004.

25. R. Sharan and R. Shamir. CLICK: A clustering algorithm with applications to gene expression analysis. *Proc. Int. Conf. Intell. Syst. Mol. Biol.*, 8:307–316, 2000.

26. R. Shamir and R. Sharan. Algorithmic approaches to clustering gene expression data. In T. Jiang, T. Smith, Y. Xu, and M. Zhang (Eds.) *Current Topics in Computational Biology*, MIT Press, Cambridge, MA, 2003, pp. 269–300.

27. L. Trevisan. Positive linear programming, parallel approximation and PCP's. In J. Diaz and M. Serna (Eds.) *Algorithms: ESA '96*, Vol. 1136 of *Lecture Notes in Computer Science*, Springer, Heidelberg, 1996, pp. 62–75.

28. O. Troyanskaya, M. Cantor, G. Sherlock, P. Brown, T. Hastie, R. Tibshirani, D. Botstein, and R. B. Alman. Missing value estimation methods for DNA microarray. *Bioinformatics*, 17(6):520–525, 2001.

29. R. Uehara. NP-complete problems on a 3-connected cubic planar graph and their applications. Technical Report TWCU-M-0004. Tokyo Woman's Christian University, 1996.

CHAPTER 29

MICROARRAY DATA ANALYSIS: FROM PREPARATION TO CLASSIFICATION

LUCIANO CASCIONE,[1] ALFREDO FERRO,[1] ROSALBA GIUGNO,[1]
GIUSEPPE PIGOLA,[2] and ALFREDO PULVIRENTI[1]
[1]Department of Clinical and Molecular Biomedicine, University of Catania, Italy
[2]IGA Technology Services, Udine, Italy

29.1 INTRODUCTION

Microarray is a well-established technology to analyze the expression of many genes in a single reaction whose applications range from cancer diagnosis to drug response. Their functionality relies on the biological fact that DNA is formed by pairs of matching bases which always bind in the same way and DNA fixes on solid support. Thus, they are matrices, built on microscope glass slides (alternatively may be silicon chips or nylon membranes), where known samples of DNA, cDNA, or oligonucleotides, called *probes*, combine with mRNA sequences. The combination process is called *hybridization* and each entry of the matrix contains an immobilized probe hybridized with a mRNA target. The expression level of genes is given by the amount of mRNA binding to each entry. All expressions in the matrix form a gene profile (see Figure 29.1 for an experiment outline).

In cancer classification and prediction, microarrays help by analyzing the expression of genes in tumor cells taken from different tissues [50]. The problem is that cancers, when known, are divided into classes. A given cancer A may have subtypes $A_1, \ldots, A_n$. Each A_i represents a specific tumor which must be properly treated. Subtypes may have different clinical histories, survival probabilities, and chemotherapy responses. The process of finding a new subtype of a cancer is called *class discovery*. Unfortunately, for many tumors the specification in subclasses is not known. (Figure 29.2 reports a subtype classification of breast cancer.) Moreover, recognizing the subtype of a cancer is also crucial. The difficulty lies in the fact that cells may appear different even though they are of the same subtype.

Data analysis algorithms and methods play a central role in exploiting the wealth of such data [14]. A typical analysis work flow consists of the following steps. First, the researchers (biologists, epidemiologists, etc.) formulate the *biological question*. Then they establish, with the help of statisticians, the experimental design. This consists of deciding what kind of microarray platform (cDNA, GeneChip, etc.) must be used, which mRNAs have to be hybridized, how many slides must be generated, and so on [19, 64]. By making

Biological Knowledge Discovery Handbook: Preprocessing, Mining, and Postprocessing of Biological Data,
First Edition. Edited by Mourad Elloumi and Albert Y. Zomaya.

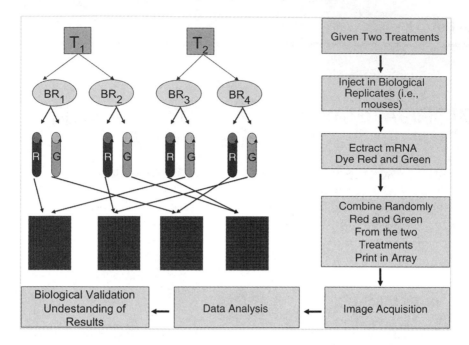

FIGURE 29.1 Work flow of microarray experimental design. Setting a microarray experiment is a process that goes into the following phases: define a specific and well-thought biological question, design the experiments, prepare the data, and set the microarray, acquisition of image, data analysis, and biological validation. Randomization applied to treatments assignments and sampling is very important to guarantee statistical significance of the experiments.

proper decisions, researchers save time and money and achieve more significant results. The next step consists of extracting numerical data from microarray images and normalizing them [57]. Such a phase includes background correction and data standardization. Once the data are normalized, these are ready for a high-level analysis. Such a phase is the core of the whole analytical process. It formulates the basic knowledge relevant to the biological phenomenon under study [29]. In this phase, statistical models are fit to estimate the magnitude and the significance of differentially expressed genes. Statistical significance is established on the basis of its corresponding p-values and adjusted p-values [22, 27, 28]. Afterward, specific supervised and unsupervised learning methods to investigate the predictive power of the candidate gene sets are applied [6, 44, 69]. High-level analyses allow the formulation of significant biological conclusions (see [23] for a review).

The rest of the chapter is organized as follows. In Sections 29.2 and 29.3 we sketch the experimental design and the normalization of microarrays. In Section 29.4 we survey the most used statistical tests for the gene ranking. Next, in Section 29.5, we focus on the commonly used classification methods for profiling data. We review state-of-the art approaches and then, in Section 29.6, we present a new classification method, called *Microarray Interval Discriminant CLASSifier* (MIDClass). MIDClass is based on association rules built on top of gene expression intervals. In Section 29.7 we present a comparative analysis on a case study of statistical tests. Then we give a wide experimental evaluation on the classification techniques showing the effectiveness of MIDClass compared to the most prominent classification approaches. Finally, in Section 29.8, we give our conclusions.

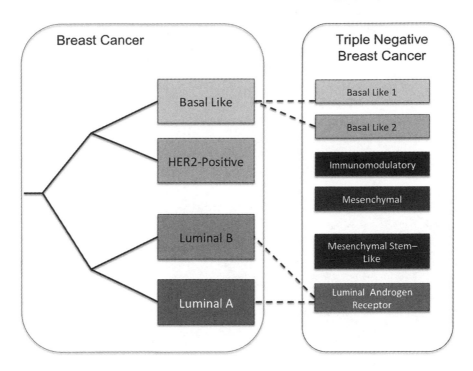

FIGURE 29.2 Subtype classification of Sotiriou et al. [68] concerning breast cancer in general and triple-negative breast cancer subtyping proposed by Lehmann et al. [52]. Here we can identify four groups of breast cancer (hierarchically organized according to their molecular properties) and six triple-negative subtypes: two *basal-Like* (BL1 and BL2), *immunomodulatory* (IM), *mesenchymal* (M), *mesenchymal stemlike* (MSL), and *luminal androgen receptor* (LAR).

29.2 EXPERIMENT DESIGN

Designing an experiment involves the choice of the mRNAs to be hybridized, those that should go in the same slide, how many slides must be used, and so on [19, 76]. Appropriate decisions may lead to better technical and economic results. Figure 29.3 illustrates the hybridization of samples. Nodes are samples and edges represent hybridization. Edge labels indicate how many times each hybridization will be replicated. The samples are directly compared among them. Depending on the biological question to answer, mRNA samples may be treated as reference, control, treatment, and so on. Let us consider as an example the cancer subtype discovery problem. A microarray experiment design fitting this biological problem could be the one depicted in Figure 29.3b; where T_i are the mRNAs taken from several tumor tissues. They are hybridized with the same RNA reference. Comparisons may be either direct or indirect. For example, in Figure 29.3d hybridizations are realized among all possible pairs. The comparison between A and B is direct and may be indirect through C. A cycle may be seen as a loop [46] (Figure 29.3e). The loop may be as long as the designer wants. However, the imprecision of comparisons among nodes increases along with their distances in the loop.

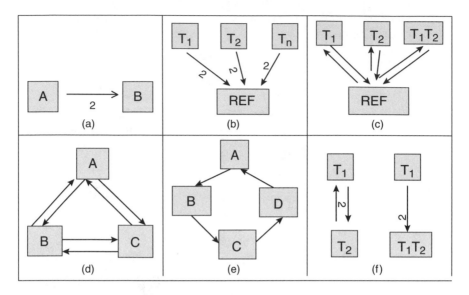

FIGURE 29.3 Different kinds of experimental design.

The designs in Figure 29.3e,f are called *multifactorial*. They are used to evaluate the effect of each treatment rather than their composition. Here, T_1 and T_2 are two treatments, C is a control, and $T_1 T_2$ are the two treatments jointly applied.

Finally, in the case that n treatments are analyzed and the corresponding samples are taken in n different times, the biological problem may require to compare variations on $n - 1$ treatments all compared to the same reference (called time course experiments).

For each design, researchers should evaluate the number of slides needed and the variation obtained through comparisons. Moreover, a large number of experiment replications should be executed. The lack of replications restricts the ability to understand if the measured intensity is statistically significant.

29.3 NORMALIZATION

Each element of a microarray is a comparison between two gene expression values, the reference (probe) named G_i and the query named R_i. In order to evaluate the change in the expression values, one could take the ratios $T = R_i/G_i$, which has the disadvantage to treat up- and down-regulated genes differently. This is avoided by transforming all values by $\log_2$ scaling. Thus, $M = \log_2(R_i/G_i)$ is the log ratio of the expression. Assume $M = 0$ means equal expression, $M = 2$ means two-fold change between the RNA samples, and negative values of M mean missing values. The significant values are the log ratios which are different from zero (see [57, 60, 67] for reviews).

Before analyzing the data, their quality must be checked out by computing the *normalized unscaled standard error* (NUSE) and the *relative logarithmic expression* (RLE). NUSE tends to identify any array which has high standard errors relative to other arrays in the data set. Arrays showing a consistently increased standard error are probably of lower quality.

RLE is computed by comparing the log-scale expression values of each probeset on each slide to the median expression of this probeset across all slides. The median RLE value should be zero for the assumption that most of the genes are not deregulated under a given treatment. Each array, which shows a deviation of the median from the zero line or increased spread on a box plot of the RLE values, is presumably of low-quality. Microarrays with low-quality data are discarded whereas the remaining ones are normalized.

The simplest normalization method sets the median of differences to zero. This can be applied under the assumption that genes are randomly sampled in the array and there is an equal quantity of mRNA into each sample. A more drastic normalization method (called *quantile*) adjusts all variances without taking the median. This may be done by sorting the expressions values.

Other methods are based on using reference values to adjust the desired expressions. For example, one can use a set of invariant genes such that either their expression values are constant on all arrays or they cover the ranges of observed values.

The above methods are also used to evaluate sensitivity and specificity of the microarray experiments, the accuracy and reproducibility of the measurements, and the assessment of technical variability introduced by labeling procedure, hybridization, and image scanning, together with visualization tools which show scatter plots or MA plots [the log ratio of the expression M by the average, A, intensity $\frac{1}{2} \times \log_2(R_i \times G_i)$].

29.4 RANKING

The problem of identifying differentially expressed genes across specified conditions in designed microarray experiments is a massive multiple testing problem where tests are executed for each of tens of thousands of genes. The simplest method for identifying differentially expressed genes is to evaluate the fold change. This is defined as a logarithmic ratio between two expressions where we consider as differentially expressed all genes that differ by more than one arbitrary *cutoff* value [24, 63].

Such an approach reveals many critical drawbacks. First of all, it is not a statistical test and consequently there is no associated value controlling the level of confidence in the designation of genes as differentially expressed [17]. On the other hand, by using this method the small number of biological replicates together with the large heterogeneous variation of samples could make the discovery of differentially expressed genes unfeasible. For this reason several authors have proposed sophisticated testing methods to deal with this kind of biological data. Different methods produce dissimilar gene lists, yielding dramatically different discrimination performance when trained as gene classifiers. In what follows we survey various parametric and nonparametric statistical tests that are commonly used.

The simplest statistical method is the *t*-test [2, 15]. It can be used to compare two conditions when there is replication of samples. The *t*-test calculates the observed *t*-statistic [2, 15] for each gene. The idea is to compare the between-group difference (the numerator) and the within-group difference (the denominator) and then compute the *p*-value [45] of the *t*-statistic for each gene by using the *t*-distribution [2]. The test statistic is obtained by dividing the difference of the means by its standard error. When the difference of the measured expression is very large with respect to the noise, it is claimed significant. The analysis yields a *p*-value for each gene which represents the chance of getting the *t*-statistic as large as or larger than the observed one under the hypothesis of no differential expression. When the variances of the conditions are different, the *Welch t-test* can be performed [58].

In the case that samples are paired, the *paired t-test* is used [3]. Other variations include the regularized *t*-test [3] and the *B*-statistics [53].

Limma [66] fits a linear model to the data and uses an empirical Bayes method for assessing differential expression. The empirical Bayes method is a moderated *t*-statistic providing a more complex model of the gene variance. The Bayesian statistic also provides *p*-values and has the advantage that it can be adapted to deal with data sets having more than two classes.

The *t*-statistic methods performed relatively poorly when there are high levels of noise in microarray data together with low sample size. In this case, the estimated variance (denominator of the *t*-statistic) can be skewed by genes having a low variance. These genes will have a large *t*-statistic and will be falsely predicted to be differentially expressed. Several ad hoc modified *t*-statistics have been proposed to address this problem. *Significance analysis of microarrays* (SAM)* [73] performs moderately well except when applied to data with low sample size and to noisy data sets. SAM adds a constant factor to the variance of the *t*-statistic.

When there are more than two conditions in an experiment, we cannot simply compute ratios; a more general concept of relative expression is needed. One approach uses the *analysis-of-variance* (ANOVA) model to estimate the relative expression *Variety×Gene* (VG) for each gene in each sample [20].

When it cannot be assumed that the data are drawn from a normal distribution, a non-parametric test can be performed. The *Wilcoxon rank-sum test* [49] establishes whether the measurements of two samples come from the same distribution. The test is alternative to the two-sample *t*-test and is commonly applied to find differentially expressed gene candidates under the two conditions. The extension of the test to deal with arbitrary sample size is called the *Mann-Whitney test* [49].

The *rank product* [10, 40] method allows the identification of differentially expressed genes by computing the ranks of fold changes. The success of this method relies on the ability to analyze data sets from different sources (e.g., to perform microarray meta-analysis) or variable environments. A rank product can also be applied to paired samples. Comprehensive surveys on statistical tests can be found in [22, 28].

A key step in the discriminant gene identification is the strict control of the error rates. This can be done by using multiple-testing adjusted *p*-values [27] instead of simple *p*-values [22]. The numbers of false positives and false negatives obtained after a statistical test belong to the following two classes: In the type I error we reject the null hypothesis even though it holds, whereas in the type II error the null hypothesis is false but we do not reject it. The goal is therefore to identify as many significant genes as possible while incurring a relatively low proportion of false positives [71]. To solve the multiple-testing problem, many procedures to control the error rates have been proposed. The *Bonferroni correction* [27] allows to control the *familywise error rate* (FWER) [38] in which we want to keep low the probability of having one or more false positives. In this case any hypothesis with unadjusted *p*-value less than or equal than a threshold is rejected. Less conservative corrections can be found in [12, 38, 39]. For example, the *false discovery rate* (FDR) [7] procedure has been proposed to control the expected proportion of incorrectly rejected null hypotheses (type I errors). An extended presentation of the adjusted *p*-value methodology can be found in Doduit et al. [27].

---

*Although SAM is an extension of the *t*-test, following [43] it can be classified as a nonparametric statistical test.

29.5 BRIEF REVIEW OF APPROACHES OF MICROARRAY DATA CLASSIFICATION

The next step in the analysis pipeline of expression data consists of the application of unsupervised or supervised machine learning methods. Supervised learning can be used to establish whether the interested classes can be predicted from expression profiles or to provide what genes underlie the differences between classes [6, 77].

Microarray data are very large; each column may contain thousands of genes. This implies to deal with a highly dimensional space. More precisely, let us assume that in a microarray of gene expression there are N training samples $\{x_i, y_i\}_{i=1}^{N}$, where x_i is an M-dimensional vector in the feature space and $y_i \in \{0, \ldots, K - 1\}$ is the class label.

Several classification methods may be used for high-dimensional classification: *support vector machines* (SVMs) [74], *diagonal linear discriminant analysis* [34], *artificial neural networks* (ANNs) [55], *naïve Bayes* [25], *k-nearest neighbors* [21], *nearest centroids* [72], *decision trees* [61], and *random forests* [9]. However, most of these methods produce a so-called *black-box model*, in which prediction is based on mathematical formulas which are difficult to be interpreted by experts.

In what follows, we briefly review common classification approaches of gene expression data.

Support Vector Machine   SVMs [74] are powerful binary classification methods which take as input a training set of data, each belonging to one of the two classes. It builds a separating hyperplane which will be used to classify new uncategorized samples. The construction of a model based on SVMs have the following problems:

- *Overfitting* Generally, in microarray data, M is much larger than N. This can lead to the problem known as the "curse of dimensionality." The resulting model will accurately fit only sample members of the training set. SVMs avoid overfitting by choosing the hyperplane that maximizes the minimum distance from the hyperplane to the closest training point.
- *Nonseparable Data* This is the case in which data are nonlinearly separable and therefore a hyperplane that successfully separates the two classes in the training set does not exist. SVMs solve this problem in two main ways: (i) by finding the hyperplane that splits samples as cleanly as possible (soft-margin method) or (ii) by mapping the M-dimension points in a higher-dimensional space by means of a *kernel function* in which the separating hyperplane can be found. By appropriately choosing the kernel functions, any set of data can be made separable.

SVMs can be successfully applied also to multicategorial classification by using the "one-against-all" methodology. That is, a data point would be classified under a certain class if and only if SVM accepted that class and all other classes are rejected.

Classification Trees and Random Forests   *Classification trees* [8, 61] are popular data-mining methods which have several applications in bioinformatics such as sequence annotation [16], protein structure and function prediction [16], and protein–protein interactions [16]. The tree-building procedure is usually a top-down heuristic. Starting from a training set (the root node), a set of features is evaluated in order to decide how well they classify the training set. Then, the best feature is chosen to split the root node into descendant nodes. The procedure recursively continues until a certain stopping criterion is reached. Because the procedure never backtracks and does not reconsider the previous choices, it can be considered as a greedy algorithm. The tree construction may generate too many nodes, and this may produce overfitting. For this reason, the procedure is generally followed by a pruning step which removes unimportant nodes or subtrees. The key point in the tree construction is the selection of the best feature. Generally, two measures establishing the *degree of impurity* in the residual data set with respect to the class label are considered. Given a node n in the tree, the *information gain* and its variant, the *gain ratio* [61], use the *entropy*

$$H(p_1, p_2, \ldots, p_K) = -\sum_{i=1}^{K} p_i \log_2 p_i$$

whereas the *Gini index* [8] is defined as

$$\text{Gini}(p_1, p_2, \ldots, p_K) = 1 - \sum_{i=1}^{K} p_i^2$$

and is used in connection to binary partitions.

Here, $1, \ldots, K$ are the classes and $p_1, p_2, \ldots, p_K$ are the proportions of samples in each class in the residual subset rooted at the node n. Both information gain and the Gini index can be used to determine how well a feature condition performs. The degree of impurity of the parent node before splitting is compared with the degree of impurity of the child nodes after splitting. The larger their distance is, the better the feature condition is. The size or the homogeneity of a node are commonly used [8, 61] as stopping criteria.

Classification based on single trees may have a low accuracy in the prediction. A single tree may be unstable because the number of samples in the training set is much smaller than the number of features. Classification can be improved by using forests of trees. *Random forests* [9] build hundreds of trees. Each tree refers to a random variant of the same data. A single tree in the forest is built by using a bootstrap sample obtained from the training set. The splitting procedure of a node is performed considering a small subset of randomly chosen features. *Deterministic forests* [78] and *smallest forests* [70] are variants of random forests which try to build forests of similar trees and reduce the number of trees in the forest, respectively.

Bayesian Classification   *Bayesian classifier* assigns the most probable a posteriori class to a given instance. The naïve Bayes [25] classifier is the simplest among the Bayesian classifiers. It is based on the assumption of conditional independence of the predictive variables. Although this assumption is commonly not true, this basic paradigm yields good results. On the other hand, the Bayesian network classifier approach [33] takes into account the relationships among the variables. The extensions include the *seminaive Bayes* [59] classifier, the *tree augmented naive Bayes* [33], and the *k-dependence Bayesian* (kDB) classifier [18].

Artificial Neural Networks   The ANNs are based on the idea of mathematically modeling human intellectual abilities [55]. The elementary processing units (also called *nodes* or *neurons*) are organized in layers. Commonly, only those units belonging to two consecutive layers are connected. In a feed-forward neural network, a unit receives information from several units belonging to the previous layer. The simplest network is the *perceptron* (a one-neuron classifier) that, by making use of a threshold activation function, separates two classes by a linear discrimination function. Then, the more complex multilayer perceptron network structures can be obtained by connecting perceptrons. In ANNs, there is no limitation in the number of hidden layers and perceptrons. Furthermore, a multilayer perceptron with two hidden layers of threshold nodes can approximate any classification region guaranteeing a given precision. Once the structure of the multilayer perceptron is chosen and fixed, the problem of determining the values of the weights for all nodes is solved through backpropagation [62].

Nearest-Neighbor Classifier   The *nearest-neighbor* (NN) classifier [32] assigns to an unknown phenotype the label associated to the nearest sample tuple. The natural extension of the nearest-neighbor rule is the *k*-NN classifier. In this case, the new tuple label will be the most represented in the *k*-NN tuples. The distance from the new tuple is also used as weight in the classification. This method has the drawback that tends to be slow for large training sets. Common indexing approaches are used to avoid such a bottleneck (see [37] for a survey).

29.6 MIDCLASS: A NOVEL APPROACH TO EFFECTIVE MICROARRAY DATA CLASSIFICATION

In what follows we introduce a new simple and accurate method for gene expression data classification, called Microarray Interval Discriminant CLASSifier. The method relies on associative classification [54] and it is supported by the idea that the expression range of genes may efficiently identify subtypes in the same class. Other approaches have been proposed for the gene expression analysis in connection to association rule mining [5, 35, 56].

MIDClass operates as follows. First, a statistical test is applied to filter the genes whose expression does not present any significant change across the classes. Next, a discretization algorithm allows to partition the gene expression range into subranges presenting strong discriminant power in each class. In the last phase, the gene expression ranges are treated as *items*. Each phenotype of a class is considered as a record containing a set of items. Therefore, phenotypes of each class are given as input to an algorithm to extract *maximal frequent itemsets* which will characterize subclasses. Those *frequent itemsets* are then used as rules in which the antecedent part is the conjunction of gene expression interval conditions, and the consequence is the class label. In what follows, we give the details of MIDClass.

Discriminant Gene Filtering   Generally, only a small fraction of gene expression values are truly discriminant and useful for classification purposes. Moreover, the presence of not-informative genes might negatively affect the classification. Therefore, by applying standard parametric or nonparametric statistical tests [3, 73], MIDClass filters out the genes that are not statistically significant.

Discretization   Let $\phi_m(x)$ be the expression value of sample x on the mth gene, with $m = 1, \ldots, M$. Let k be a class label and ω_k represent the set of phenotypes x_i belonging to class k. MIDClass discretizes gene expression values ϕ_m by partitioning its range into subintervals called items. Each gene expression value $\phi_m(x)$ is represented by the unique item (interval) containing it. We refer to this new set of items as $\overline{\Phi} = \left\{\overline{\phi_m}\right\}_{m=1}^{M}$. The set of items falling into the kth class is denoted by $\overline{\omega_k}$. MIDClass uses those gene expression intervals to build the classification rules.

Model Construction and Classification   Once the data have been discretized, MIDClass extracts the maximal frequent itemsets. This is based on one of the most classical problems in data mining, that is, the *association rule discovery* [1]. More precisely, let I be a set of items. We call $X \subseteq I$ an *itemset*. Let T be a multiset of itemsets and let support(X) be the percentage of itemsets Y in T such that $X \subseteq Y$. The support measures how often X occurs in T. If support(X) $\geq$ minSup, then X is a frequent itemset. Let FI be the set of frequent itemsets. If X is frequent and no superset of X is frequent, then X is a maximal. Let MFI be the set of maximal frequent itemsets. Although useful, raw FI could be difficult to analyze since a combinatorial explosion in the number of subsets could be present. For this reason we use MFI in our classification system since they can be viewed as a compress representation of the FI knowledge (MFI consists in a lossy representation of the FI knowledge since the exact support of each subset of a MFI is not available). MIDClass extracts MFI by using the MAFIA algorithm [13].

Once FI is constructed, association rules can be extracted from them. An association rule is an implication of the form $X \Longrightarrow Y$, where $X \subset I$, $Y \subset I$, and $X \cap Y = \emptyset$. The rule $X \Longrightarrow Y$ holds in the set T with support($X \cup Y$) $= s$, where s is the percentage of subsets in T that contain $X \cup Y$. The rule $X \Longrightarrow Y$ has confidence c in T, where c is the percentage of subsets of T containing X that also contain Y. Rules satisfying both a minimum-support threshold and a minimum-confidence threshold are called *strong* [36].

Frequent patterns and their corresponding association rules characterize interesting relationships between attribute conditions and class labels. For this reason they have been recently used for effective classification.

We can easily model the problem of gene expression data classification with an associative classification method as follows. For each class we compute the MFI. In this way, $\text{MFI}(i) \cap \text{MFI}(j) = \emptyset$ for each $i, j = 0, \ldots, K - 1$ with $i < j$ (i.e., all the MFIs are distinct).

The set of values $\overline{\Phi}$ represents the set of all possible items and each M-dimensional vector $[\overline{\phi_1(x_i)}, \overline{\phi_2(x_i)}, \ldots, \overline{\phi_M(x_i)}]$ for $i = 1, \ldots, N$ represents the set of gene intervals in the phenotypes $1, \ldots, N$, respectively.

The identification of MFIs for each class $k \in \{0, \ldots, K - 1\}$ automatically induces a set of association rules $R^k = \left\{r_1^k, \ldots, r_{h_k}^k\right\}$.

Without loss of generality, fixed a class k (e.g., disease phenotype), the correspondent MFI(k) has h_k elements. The vth itemset can be written as $mfi_v(k) = \{I_i, \ldots, I_j\}$.

Each item I_l stores a range of values which are relative to a gene in $\overline{\omega_k}$. The association rule induced by $mfi_v(k)$ can be viewed as a quantitative association rule having quantitative attributes on the antecedence of the rule (i.e., discretized values) and one categorical attribute on the right-hand side of the rule (i.e., the class $k \in \{0, \ldots, K - 1\}$): $r_v^k : I_i \wedge I_{i+1} \wedge \cdots \wedge I_{j-1} \wedge I_j \Longrightarrow k$. Let $R^k = \left\{r_1^k, \ldots, r_{h_k}^k\right\}$ be the association rules for $k = 0, \ldots, K - 1$ and $\overline{x} = \{I_1, \ldots, I_M\}$ be an unknown discretized sample (phenotype). We evaluate how many rules are satisfied, even partially, in each R^k. The sample is assigned to the class whose rules are maximally satisfied by the following criterion. Fixed a class k, we evaluate $\overline{x}$ under a generic rule $r_v^k = \{I_i, \ldots, I_j\}$ assigning a score in the following way:

$$\text{EVAL}(r_v^k, \bar{x}) = \frac{(|r_v^k \cap \bar{x}|/|r_v^k|) \log |r_v^k|}{|R^k|}$$

Notice that $\text{EVAL}(r_v^k, \bar{x})$ takes into account the number of items in the sample contained in the rule together with the cardinality of the rule $|r_v^k|$. The value is normalized by the number of rules $|R^k|$ in the class k. Finally, the score assigned to the sample $\bar{x}$ with respect to the class k is then given by $\sum_{v=1}^{h_k} \text{EVAL}(r_v^k, \bar{x})$ (i.e. the sum of the scores of each satisfied rule). In order to consider really discriminant rules, we considered only r_i^k such that $|r_i^k| > 1$.

29.7 EXPERIMENTAL STUDY

Statistical Tests   Farmer et al. [31] present a study of tumor samples taken from 49 patients affected by large operable or locally advanced breast cancers. Their study originally identified three groups of breast tumors: *luminal*, *basal*, and *molecular apocrine*. The data have been normalized using *robust multichip average* (RMA) [41]. We selected genes differentially expressed between luminal and basal samples (a total of 43 samples, 27 luminal and 16 basal) by making use of seven diffcrent statistical tests: four nonparametric tests—SAM, *Wilcoxon's test* [49], *local-pooled-error* (LPE) [42], and *rank product*—and three parametric tests—*t*-test, *Welch's t-test*, and *limma*. Then we selected the top 100 genes claimed to be discriminant by each statistical test. The aim of this test is to establish the concordance of the statistical tests and their capability of recovering those genes that have been proved discriminant by [4, 30]. From the experiments (see Figure 29.4a) we highlight that nonparametric statistical tests commonly yield very different putative gene lists and a very low consensus can be observed. On the other hand parametric tests (Figure 29.4b) show that limma and the *t*-test recover almost the same top 100 genes. Results obtained by all statistical tests have been compared with the known biomarkers for luminal and basal breast cancer [30]. Figures 29.4c,d show that, although statistical tests find subsets of common biomarkers, each method identifies subsets of markers that are not recovered by the others. We can conclude that a consensus among several statistical tests could result in a more robust candidate identification. However, a statistical test with no common candidate markers could result in a new lead of investigation.

Classification   Comparisons among different classification paradigms (NN classifiers, linear discriminant analysis, decision trees, bagging and boosting, SVMs, ANNs, and different ensemble classifiers) can be found in several papers [6, 11, 26, 47, 51, 69, 70, 77]. From these works it can be concluded that no method outperforms the others in all the cases. We compared MIDClass with the other systems on the same 11 data sets used in [75] through a *leave-one-out cross-validation* (LOOCV) [48]. Wang and Simon in [75] [hereafter *single-gene classifier* (SGC)] claim that in most cases a single gene is enough to obtain a reliable classification compared to the state of the art. However, we show that MIDClass, by using MFIs [13] together with the discretizer ID3 [61], outperforms the SGC in almost all cases and in particular on those data sets in which SGC had poor performance (see Table 29.1). From these results we can conclude that in some cases MIDClass rules are able to capture clusters of phenotypes defining possible cancer subtypes.

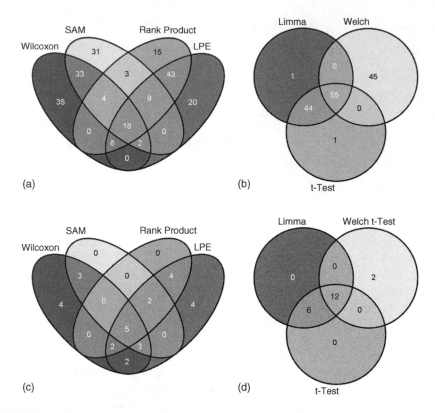

FIGURE 29.4   Concordance on significant gene sets obtained with (a) nonparametric and (b) parametric statistical tests. We extract the top 100 genes showing the best p-value/FDR. (c, d) Behavior of each statistical test crossed with known biomarkers for luminal and basal breast cancer described in [30].

Our approach depends on a parameter that is the support threshold of the MFI. We experimentally established that the best performance of MIDClass are obtained when this parameter is ≤ 0.2. All the data sets we used are publicly available and data were downloaded from the *BRB-ArrayTools Data Archive* for *Human Cancer Gene Expression* repository [65].

TABLE 29.1   LOOCV Classification Accuracy (%)

Data Set	MIDClass	SGC	DLDA	k-NN	SVM	RF
Melanoma	**98,5**	97	97	97	97	97
Breast cancer 1	**71**	69	61	53	52	43
Brain cancer	**83**	80	65	73	60	70
Breast cancer 2	**88**	58	73	67	73	67
Gastric tumor	94	89	81	96	**97**	95
Lung cancer 1	**98**	**98**	95	**98**	**98**	**98**
Lung cancer 2	**99**	93	**99**	**99**	**99**	**99**
Lymphoma	69	**74**	66	52	59	57
Myeloma	**84**	68	75	78	74	79
Pancreatic cancer	78	**90**	63	61	65	55
Prostate cancer	92	89	78	**93**	**93**	**93**

TABLE 29.2   Description of Data Sets Used for Classifiers Analysis

Data Set	Description
Melanoma	70 samples, 45 cases of malignant melanoma patients and 25 of nonmalignant patients
Breast cancer 1	99 samples, patients that did ($n = 45$) and did not ($n = 54$) relapse
Brain cancer	60 samples, 46 patients with classic and 14 patients with desmoplastic brain cancer
Breast cancer 2	60 samples, disease free ($n = 32$) or cancer recurred ($n = 38$)
Gastric tumor	132 samples, 103 tumor samples and 20 normal controls
Lung cancer 1	41 samples, squamous cell lung carcinoma (21) or pulmonary carcinoid (20)
Lung cancer 2	181 samples, 31 mesothelioma samples and 150 adenocarcinoma
Lymphoma	58 samples, patients that did ($n = 32$) and did not ($n = 26$) cured
Myeloma	173 samples, 137 patients with bone lytic lesions, 36 patients without
Pancreatic cancer	49 samples, 24 ductal carcinoma samples and 24 normal controls
Prostate cancer	102 samples, 50 non–tumor prostate and 52 prostate tumors

TABLE 29.3   Number of Genes Used by Each Classifier

Data Set	MIDClass	SGC	DLDA	k-NN	SVM	RF
Melanoma	55	1	7200	7200	7200	7200
Breast cancer 1	14	1	17	17	17	15
Brain cancer	239	1	14	14	14	14
Breast cancer 2	16	1	176	176	176	176
Gastric tumor	23	1	848	848	848	848
Lung cancer 1	101	1	7472	7472	7472	7472
Lung cancer 2	55	1	3207	3207	3207	3207
Lymphoma	3	1	2	2	2	2
Myeloma	27	1	169	169	169	169
Pancreatic cancer	22	1	56	56	56	44
Prostate cancer	45	1	798	798	798	798

In Table 29.2 we give the details of each data set. In Table 29.3 we report the number of genes used by all the tested classifiers.

29.8   CONCLUSION

In this chapter we reviewed the protocol used in the analysis of profile expression data. In particular, we focused in the phase of normalization end high-level analysis. The high-level analysis consists of extracting those genes exhibiting a statistical significant different behavior in each class supported by a p-value and a proper FDR. The list of genes can then be used in connection to learning methods such as clustering or classification. In particular, we focused on classification reviewing the most prominent approaches. Finally we introduced a new classification method, called MIDClass, based on a synergistic combination of discretization of gene expression intervals and MFI construction used as classification rules. Our classifier exhibited very good performances compared to state-of-the-art approaches.

REFERENCES

1. R. Agrawal and R. Srikant. Fast algorithms for mining association rules. *Proc. 20th Int. Conf. Very Large Data Bases VLDB*, 1215:487–499, 1994.

2. S. M. Arfin, A. D. Long, E. T. Ito, L. Tolleri, M. M. Riehle, E. S. Paegle, and G. Hatfield. Global gene expression profiling in Escherichia colik12. *J. Biol. Chem.*, 275(38):29672, 2000.

3. P. Baldi and A. D. Long. A Bayesian framework for the analysis of microarray expression data: Regularized *t*-test and statistical inferences of gene changes. *Bioinformatics*, 17(6):509, 2001.

4. T. Barrett, D. B. Troup, S. E. Wilhite, P. Ledoux, D. Rudnev, C. Evangelista, I. F. Kim, A. Soboleva, M. Tomashevsky, and R. Edgar. Ncbi geo: Mining tens of millions of expression profiles database and tools update. *Nucleic Acids Res.*, 35(Suppl. 1):D760–D765, 2007.

5. C. Becquet, S. Blachon, B. Jeudy, J. F. Boulicaut, and O. Gandrillon. Strong-association-rule mining for large-scale gene-expression data analysis: A case study on human sage data. *Genome Biol.*, 3(12):research0067, 2002.

6. A. Ben-Dor, L. Bruhn, N. Friedman, I. Nachman, M. Schummer, and Z. Yakhini. Tissue classification with gene expression profiles. *J. Computat. Biol.*, 7(3–4):559–583, 2000.

7. Y. Benjamini and Y. Hochberg. Controlling the false discovery rate: A practical and powerful approach to multiple testing. *J. R. Stat. Soc. Series B Stat. Methodol.*, 57(1):289–300, 1995.

8. L. Breiman, J. H. Friedman, R. A. Olshen, and C. J. Stone. *Classification and Regression Trees.* Chapman & Hall/CRC, Boca Raton, FL, 1984.

9. L. Breiman. Random forests. *Machine Learning*, 45(1):5–32, 2001.

10. R. Breitling, P. Armengaud, A. Amtmann, and P. Herzyk. Rank products: A simple, yet powerful, new method to detect differentially regulated genes in replicated microarray experiments. *FEBS Lett.*, 573(1):83–92, 2004.

11. M. P. S. Brown, W. N. Grundy, D. Lin, N. Cristianini, C. W. Sugnet, T. S. Furey, M. Ares, and D. Haussler. Knowledge-based analysis of microarray gene expression data by using support vector machines. *Proc. Nat. Acad. Sci.*, 97(1):262, 2000.

12. A. S. Bryk and S. W. Raudenbush. *Hierarchical Linear Models: Applications and Data Analysis Methods.* Sage, 1992.

13. D. Burdick, M. Calimlim, J. Flannick, J. Gehrke, and T. Yiu. Mafia: A maximal frequent itemset algorithm. *IEEE Trans. Knowledge Data Eng.*, 17(11):1490–1504, 2005.

14. A. Butte. The use and analysis of microarray data. *Nat. Rev. Drug Discov.*, 1(12):951–960, 2002.

15. M. J. Callow, S. Dudoit, E. L. Gong, T. P. Speed, and E. M. Rubin. Microarray expression profiling identifies genes with altered expression in hdl-deficient mice. *Genome Res.*, 10(12):2022–2029, 2000.

16. X. Chen, M. Wang, and H. Zhang. The use of classification trees for bioinformatics. *Wiley Interdisciplinary Rev. Data Mining Knowledge Discov.*, 1(1):55–63, 2011.

17. Y. Chen, E. R. Dougherty, and M. L. Bittner. Ratio-based decisions and the quantitative analysis of cdna microarray images. *J. Biomed. opt.*, 2(4):364–374, 1997.

18. C. Chow and C. Liu. Approximating discrete probability distributions with dependence trees. *IEEE Trans. Inform. Theory*, 14(3):462–467, 1968.

19. G. A. Churchill. Fundamentals of experimental design for cdna microarrays. *Nature Genet. Suppl.*, 32:490–495, 2002.

20. G. A. Churchill. Using anova to analyze microarray data. *Biotechniques.*, 37:173–175, 2004.

21. T. Cover and P. Hart. Nearest neighbor pattern classification. *IEEE Trans. Inform. Theory*, 13(1):21–27, 1967.

22. X. Cui and G. A. Churchill. Statistical tests for differential expression in cdna microarray experiments. *Genome Biol.*, 4(4):210, 2003.

23. H. De Jong. Modeling and simulation of genetic regulatory systems: A literature review. *J. Computat. Biol.*, 9(1):67–103, 2002.

24. S. Draghici et al. Statistical intelligence: Effective analysis of high-density microarray data. *Drug Discov. Today*, 7(11):55, 2002.

25. R. O. Duda, P. E. Hart, and D. G. Stork. *Pattern Classification*, 2nd ed. John Wiley & Sons, Inc., 2012.

26. S. Dudoit, J. Fridlyand, and T. P. Speed. Comparison of discrimination methods for the classification of tumors using gene expression data. *J. Am. Stat. Assoc.*, 97(457):77–87, 2002.

27. S. Dudoit, J. P. Shaffer, and J. C. Boldrick. Multiple hypothesis testing in microarray experiments. *Statist. Sci.*, 71–103, 2003.

28. S. Dudoit, Y. H. Yang, M. J. Callow, and T. P. Speed. Statistical methods for identifying differentially expressed genes in replicated cdna microarray experiments. *Statist. Sinica*, 12(1):111–140, 2002.

29. A. Dupuy and R. M. Simon. Critical review of published microarray studies for cancer outcome and guidelines on statistical analysis and reporting. *J. Natl. Cancer Inst.*, 99(2):147–157, 2007.

30. J. Eeckhoute, J. S. Carroll, T. R. Geistlinger, M. I. Torres-Arzayus, and M. Brown. A cell-type-specific transcriptional network required for estrogen regulation of cyclin d1 and cell cycle progression in breast cancer. *Genes Devel.*, 20(18):2513–2526, 2006.

31. P. Farmer et al. Identification of molecular apocrine breast tumours by microarray analysis. *Breast Cancer Res.*, 7:1–1, 2005.

32. E. Fix and J. L. Hodges. Discriminatory analysis. Nonparametric discrimination: Consistency properties. *Int. Stat. Rev.*, 57(3):238–247, 1989.

33. N. Friedman, D. Geiger, and M. Goldszmidt. Bayesian network classifiers. *Machine learning*, 29(2):131–163, 1997.

34. K. Fukunaga. *Introduction to Statistical Pattern Recognition*. Access Online via Elsevier, 1990.

35. E. Georgii, L. Richter, U. Rückert, and S. Kramer. Analyzing microarray data using quantitative association rules. *Bioinformatics*, 21(Suppl. 2):ii123–ii129, 2005.

36. J. Han, M. Kamber, and J. Pei. *Data Mining: Concepts and Techniques*. Morgan Kaufmann, 2006.

37. M. L. Hetland. The basic principles of metric indexing. *Swarm Intelligence for Multi-Objective Problems in Data Mining*. Springer, Heidelberg, 2009, pp. 199–232.

38. Y. Hochberg. A sharper Bonferroni procedure for multiple tests of significance. *Biometrika*, 75(4):800–802, 1988.

39. G. Hommel. A stagewise rejective multiple test procedure based on a modified Bonferroni test. *Biometrika*, 75(2):383–386, 1988.

40. F. Hong, R. Breitling, C. W. McEntee, B. S. Wittner, J. L. Nemhauser, and J. Chory. Rankprod: A bioconductor package for detecting differentially expressed genes in meta-analysis. *Bioinformatics*, 22(22):2825, 2006.

41. R. A. Irizarry, B. Hobbs, F. Collin, Y. D. Beazer-Barclay, K. J. Antonellis, U. Scherf, and T. P. Speed. Exploration, normalization, and summaries of high density oligonucleotide array probe level data. *Biostatistics*, 4(2):249, 2003.

42. N. Jain, J. Thatte, T. Braciale, K. Ley, M. O'Connell, and J. K. Lee. Local-pooled-error test for identifying differentially expressed genes with a small number of replicated microarrays. *Bioinformatics*, 19(15):1945–1951, 2003.

43. M. Jeanmougin, A. De Reynies, L. Marisa, C. Paccard, G. Nuel, and M. Guedj. Should we abandon the *t*-test in the analysis of gene expression microarray data: A comparison of variance modeling strategies. *PloS One*, 5(9):e12336, 2010.

44. D. Jiang, C. Tang, and A. Zhang. Cluster analysis for gene expression data: A survey. *IEEE Trans. Knowledge Data Eng.*, 16(11):1370–1386, 2004.

45. D. H. Johnson. The insignificance of statistical significance testing. *J. Wildlife Manag.*, 63(3):763–772, 1999.

46. M. K. Kerr and G. A. Churchill. Statistical design and the analysis of gene expression microarray data. *Genet. Res.*, 89(5–6):509–514, 2007.

47. K. J. Kim and S. B. Cho. Prediction of colon cancer using an evolutionary neural network. *Neurocomputing*, 61:361–379, 2004.

48. R. Kohavi. A study of cross-validation and bootstrap for accuracy estimation and model selection. In *International Joint Conference on Artificial Intelligence*, Vol. 14. Morgan Kaufmann Publishers Inc., Montreal, Quebec, Canada, 1995, pp. 1137–1145.

49. W. H. Kruskal. Historical notes on the wilcoxon unpaired two-sample test. *J. Am. Statist. Assoc.*, 52(279):356–360, 1957.

50. R. Kumar, A. Sharma, and R. K. Tiwari. Application of microarray in breast cancer: An overview. *J. Pharm. Bioallied Sci.*, 4(1):21–26, 2012.

51. J. W. Lee, J. B. Lee, M. Park, and S. H. Song. An extensive comparison of recent classification tools applied to microarray data. *Computat. Statist. Data Anal.*, 48(4):869–885, 2005.

52. B. D. Lehmann, J. A. Bauer, X. Chen, M. E. Sanders, A. B. Chakravarthy, Y. Shyr, and J. A. Pietenpol. Identification of human triple-negative breast cancer subtypes and preclinical models for selection of targeted therapies. *J. Clin. Investig.*, 121(7):2750, 2011.

53. I. Lönnstedt and T. P. Speed. Replicated microarray data. *Statist. Sinica*, 12(1):31–46, 2002.

54. B. Liu, W. Hsu, and Y. Ma. Integrating classification and association rule mining. In *Proceedings of the Fourth International Conference on Knowledge Discovery and Data Mining (KDD-98)*. AAAI, New York City, NY, 1998, pp. 80–86.

55. W. S. McCulloch and W. Pitts. A logical calculus of the ideas immanent in nervous activity. *Bull. Math. Biol.*, 5(4):115–133, 1943.

56. T. McIntosh and S. Chawla. High confidence rule mining for microarray analysis. *IEEE/ACM Trans. Computat. Biol. Bioinformatics*, 4(4):611–623, 2007.

57. J. Onskog, E. Freyhult, M. Landfors, P. Ryden, and T. R. Hvidsten. Classification of microarrays; synergistic effects between normalization, gene selection and machine learning. *BMC Bioinformatics*, 12(390), 2011.

58. W. Pan. A comparative review of statistical methods for discovering differentially expressed genes in replicated microarray experiments. *Bioinformatics*, 18(4):546, 2002.

59. M. J. Pazzani. Searching for dependencies in Bayesian classifiers. In *Lecture Notes in Statistics*. Springer Verlag, New York, 1996, pp. 239–248.

60. J. Quackenbush. Microarray data normalization and transformation. *Nature Genet. Suppl.*, 32:496–501, 2002.

61. J. R. Quinlan. *C4. 5: Programs for Machine Learning*. Morgan Kaufmann, San Francisco, CA, 1993.

62. D. E. Rumelhart, G. E. Hintont, and R. J. Williams. Learning representations by back-propagating errors. *Nature*, 323(6088):533–536, 1986.

63. M. Schena, D. Shalon, R. Heller, A. Chai, P. O. Brown, and R. W. Davis. Parallel human genome analysis: Microarray-based expression monitoring of 1000 genes. *Proc. Nat. Acad. Sci.*, 93(20):10614, 1996.

64. W. Shi, C. A. De Graaf, S. A. Kinkel, A. H. Achtman, T. Baldwin, L. Schofield, H. S. Scott, D. J. Hilton, and G. H. Smyth. Estimating the proportion of microarray probes expressed in an rna sample. *Nucleic Acids Res.*, 38(7):2168–2176, 2010.

65. R. Simon, A. Lam, M. C. Li, M. Ngan, S. Menenzes, and Y. Zhao. Analysis of gene expression data using brb-array tools. *Cancer Informatics*, 3:11, 2007.

66. G. Smyth. Limma: Linear models for microarray data. In R. Gentleman (Ed.) *Bioinformatics and Computational Biology Solutions Using R and Bioconductor*, Vol. XIX. Springer, New York, 2005, pp. 397–420.

67. G. K. Smyth and T. P. Speed. Normalization of cdna microarray data. *Methods*, 31:265–273, 2003.

68. C. Sotiriou, S. Y. Neo, L. M. McShane, E. L. Korn, P. M. Long, A. Jazaeri, P. Martiat, S. B. Fox, A. L. Harris, and E. T. Liu. Breast cancer classification and prognosis based on gene expression profiles from a population-based study. *Proc. Nat. Acad. Sci. USA*, 100(18):10393, 2003.

69. A. Statnikov, C. F. Aliferis, I. Tsamardinos, D. Hardin, and S. Levy. A comprehensive evaluation of multicategory classification methods for microarray gene expression cancer diagnosis. *Bioinformatics*, 21(5):631–643, 2005.

70. A. Statnikov, L. Wang, and C. Aliferis. A comprehensive comparison of random forests and support vector machines for microarray-based cancer classification. *BMC Bioinformatics*, 9(1):319, 2008.

71. J. D. Storey and R. Tibshirani. Statistical significance for genomewide studies. *Proc. Nat. Acad. Sci. USA*, 100(16):9440, 2003.

72. R. Tibshirani, T. Hastie, B. Narasimhan, and G. Chu. Class prediction by nearest shrunken centroids, with applications to dna microarrays. *Statist. Sci.*, 18(1):104–117, 2003.

73. V. G. Tusher, R. Tibshirani, and G. Chu. Significance analysis of microarrays applied to the ionizing radiation response. *Proc. Nat. Acad. Sci.*, 98(9):5116, 2001.

74. V. N. Vapnik. *The Nature of Statistical Learning Theory*. Springer, New York, NY, 2000.

75. X. Wang and R. Simon. Microarray-based cancer prediction using single genes. *BMC Bioinformatics*, 12(1):391, 2011.

76. Y. H. Yang and T. Speed. Desig issues for cdna microarray experiments. *Nature Rev. Genet.*, 3:579–588, 2002.

77. C. H. Yeang, S. Ramaswamy, P. Tamayo, S. Mukherjee, R. M. Rifkin, M. Angelo, M. Reich, E. Lander, J. Mesirov, and T. Golub. Molecular classification of multiple tumor types. *Bioinformatics*, 17(Suppl. 1):S316, 2001.

78. H. Zhang, C. Y. Yu, and B. Singer. Cell and tumor classification using gene expression data: Construction of forests. *Proc. Nat. Acad. Sci.*, 100(7):4168, 2003.

CHAPTER 30

DIVERSIFIED CLASSIFIER FUSION TECHNIQUE FOR GENE EXPRESSION DATA

SASHIKALA MISHRA,[1] KAILASH SHAW,[2] and DEBAHUTI MISHRA[1]
[1]Institute of Technical Education and Research, Siksha O Anusandhan University, Bhubaneswar, Odisha, India
[2]Department of CSE, Gandhi Engineering College, Bhubaneswar, Odisha, India

30.1 INTRODUCTION

Classification is a technique where we discover the hidden class level of the unknown data. Different classification methods produce different accuracy according to the class level; classifier fusion is the solution to achieve more accuracy in every level of the input data. Selection of a suitable classifier in classifier fusion is a tedious task. In the proposed model, the output of the three classifiers is fed to the dynamic classifier fusion technique. This model will use each classifier for every individual data. We have used principal-component analysis (PCA) to deal with issues of high dimensionality in biomedical classification. It is observed that data size, number of classes, and dimension of feature space and interclass separability affect the performance of any classifier. For a long time, efforts are made in improving efficiency, accuracy, and reliability of classifiers for a wide range of applications. Different optimization algorithms such as particle swarm optimization (PSO) and simulated annealing (SA) have been used to enhance the accuracy of classifiers. *Bat algorithm* is also a metaheuristic search algorithm which is use to solve the multiobjective engineering problem. In this chapter, a model has been proposed for classification using the bat algorithm to update the weights of a functional link artificial neural network (FLANN) classifier. The bat algorithm is based on the echolocation behavior of bats. The proposed model has been compared with the multilayer perceptron (MLP) and particle swarm optimization functional link artificial neural network (PSO-FLANN). Three types of classification techniques on microarray data like MLP, BAT-FLANN (bat functional link artificial neural network), and PSO-FLANN have been implemented and compared; it has been observed that BAT-FLANN is showing better results. We have also proposed a model for classifier fusion, where the model will choose the relevant classifiers according to the different regions of

Biological Knowledge Discovery Handbook: Preprocessing, Mining, and Postprocessing of Biological Data, First Edition. Edited by Mourad Elloumi and Albert Y. Zomaya.
© 2014 John Wiley & Sons, Inc. Published 2014 by John Wiley & Sons, Inc.

data sets. Simulation shows that the proposed classification technique with the bat algorithm is superior and faster than others.

High dimensionality of microarray data sets is a crucial issue to be considered while designing classifiers [1–4]. To handle the curse of high dimensionality, the data sets need to be preprocessed by reducing the redundant and irrelevant features. By removing such features or attributes, we can also reduce the computational complexity. PCA is used to deal with the curse of dimensionality for microarray data sets. The ultimate goal of any pattern recognition system is to achieve the best possible classification performance for a given problem domain. *Classification* is the process of assigning unknown input patterns of data to some known classes based on their properties [1–5]. For a long time many research areas in designing classifiers have focused on improving efficiency, accuracy, and reliability of the classifier for a wide range of applications. Fusing output of more classifiers is an alternative method to build more reliable classifiers [6, 7]. It is well known that in many situations combining [7–10] output of several classifiers leads to improved classification results. This occurs because each classifier produces an error on different areas of the input space. In other words, a subset of the input space that each classifier labels correctly will differ from one classification to another. This implies that by using information from more than one classifier, it is probable that the better overall accuracy can be obtained for a given problem. On the other hand, instead of picking up just one classifier, a better approach would be to use [11–18] more than one classifier while averaging the output. The new classifier might not be better than the single best classifier, but it will distinguish or eliminate the risk of picking an inadequate single classifier. For any pattern classification [19–23], while designing a fused classifier, increase in the performance of the fusion technique can be achieved by considering four parameters: accuracy, speed of performance, solution correctness, and solution quality.

Metaheuristic algorithms like PSO and SA are the powerful methods for solving many optimization problems. The fine adjustment of the parameters of the above techniques enhances the accuracy of the classifiers. In this chapter, the *bat algorithm* is used to update the weights of a FLANN classifier. Bats emit sounds of various wavelength and frequency in the search for prey and direction [27]. Bats fly with velocity v at position x with different sound frequency f. Bats adjust their velocity, direction, and frequency on hearing an echo signal. In this paper, a new metaheuristic, the bat algorithm, has been formulated and also the whole working principle of the algorithm is explained.

Section 30.2 describes the background study, Section 30.3 gives information about preliminaries, Section 30.4 deals with the proposed model, Section 30.5 describes the experimental evaluation, and Section 30.6 deals with conclusions and future work.

30.2 BACKGROUND STUDY

Chen et al. [11] proposed a multiple-kernel support vector machine (SVM) data-mining system. Multiple tasks, including feature selection, data fusion, class prediction, decision rule extraction, associated rule extraction, and subclass discovery, are incorporated in an integrated framework. The all-AML leukemia data set is used to demonstrate the performance of the system.

Kilic et al. [12] investigate two kinds of classifier systems which are capable of estimating how much to weight each base classifier dynamically during the calculation of overall output for a given test data instance:

1. In a referee-based system, a referee is associated with each classifier which learns the area of expertise of its associated classifier and weights it accordingly.
2. When number of classifiers are present, the referee will decide which classifier will be selected for the input space.

The study shows that, by using a well-trained selection unit, we can get accuracy as high as using all the base classifiers with a drastic decrease in the number of base classifiers used, thus improving accuracy.

Garcia-Pedrajas et al. [13] suggest that there are two different tasks: (1) training and construction of an ensemble of classifiers, with each one being able to solve a multiclass problem, and (2) the fusion of binary classifiers, with each one solving a different two-class problem to construct a multiclass classifier. The paper presents a study of the different class binarization methods for the various multiclass classification problems.

Feng et al. [14] introduced a fused model, which comprehensively compares four fuzzy integrals in multiple-classifier fusions to give the foundation for selecting a Choquet integral. According to the theoretical and experimental analysis, the paper gives the conclusion that the choquet integral is the best for classifier fusion.

Huang et al. [15] proposed a new multiple-classifier fusion method that integrates classifier selection and classifier combination. This paper is based on interval-valued fuzzy permutation. First, all classifier posterior probabilities are normalized using a priori knowledge of the corresponding classifier recognition rate. Second, a decision matrix for the multiple-classifier system is converted into an interval-valued fuzzy decision matrix. Third, the grade of possibility of each input sample class is determined for the multiple-classifier system. Finally, the best classifier in the current pattern recognition task is selected using interval-valued fuzzy permutation. The experiments have shown that the new multiple-classifier fusion approach using interval-valued fuzzy permutation can provide much better accuracy compared to the independent classifier and some other fusion methods.

Ei-Bakry [16] proposed an efficient algorithm for pattern detection using the combine classifier and data fusion. In this paper, efficient neural networks for face detection are presented. Such classifiers are designed based on cross-correlation in the frequency domain between the input matrix and the input weight of the neural network. This approach is developed to reduce the computation steps required by ENNs for the search process.

Mangai et al. [17] have done a survey of decision fusion and feature training strategies for pattern classification. The technique uses databases from the University of California (UCI) Repository, vistexture, speech, and medical image for exhibiting the performance. The authors also proposed a framework which uses decision and feature fusion for a better classification result. The result is presented using three benchmark data sets from the UCI Repository.

Likuncheva et al. [18] proposed a simple rule for adapting the class combiner to the application. The decision templates are estimated with the same training set that is used for the classifier set. These templates are then matched to the decision profile of new incoming objects by some similarity measure. The authors compared 11 versions of the proposed model with 14 other techniques for classifier fusion on the Sitimage Phoneme data set from the database ELENA.

Matteore et al. [24] evaluated the performance of three basic ensembles to integrate six different sources of high-dimensional biomolecular data. They also studied the performances resulting from the simple greedy classifier selection scheme.

Albert et al. [19] proposed a pairwise fusion matrix transformation which produces reliable probabilities for the classifier combination and can be amalgamaped with most existing fusion function for the combining classifier. The PFM pairwise fusion requires crisp class label outputs from classifiers and is suitable for high-class problems or problems with training samples. The experimental results suggest that the performance of a PFM can be a notch above that of a simple majority voting rule, and a PFM can work on a problem where a behavior–knowledge space might not be applicable.

Yang [25] proposed a bat algorithm and uses wavelengths for ease of implementation. Bats automatically adjust the wavelength of their emitted pulses and the rate of pulse emission. Hermann et al. [26] developed an alternative solution in the area of parametric and nonparametric modeling of short-time signals. The work presents the possibility of using the suggested parameterization methods in automatic species identification. Altringham [27] describes the behavior of bats.

30.3   PRELIMINARIES

PCA is a mathematical procedure that uses an orthogonal transformation to convert a set of observations [20] of possibly corelated variables into a set of uncorrelated variables called *principal components*.

FLANN is a mathematical model or computational model that is inspired by structural and/or functional aspects of biological neural networks [21]. It consists of an interconnected group of artificial neurons and it processes information using a model.

PSO is a stochastic-based search algorithm widely used to find the optimum solution introduced by Kennedy and Eberthart [28] in 1995. PSO is used in this paper to update the weight of a FLANN model. PSO as an optimization tool provides a population-based search procedure in which individuals called *particles* change their position (state) with time. The velocity V_{id} and X_{id} position of the ith particle are updated as follows:

$$V_{id} = V_{id} + c_1 \, \text{rand1}_{id} \, (\text{pbest}_{id} - X_{id}) + c_2 \, \text{rand2}_{id} \, (\text{gbest}_{id} - X_{id}) \quad (30.1)$$

$$X_{id} = X_{id} + V_{id} \quad (30.2)$$

where X_i is the position and V_i is the velocity of the particle; pbest is the best previous position yielding the best fitness value for the ith particle and gbest is the best position discovered by the whole population; c_1 and c_2 and are the acceleration constants reflecting the weighting of stochastic acceleration terms that pull each particle toward pbest and gbest positions, respectively; and rand1_{id} and rand2_{id} are two random numbers in the range (0,1).

In our work the FLANN model is trained with biologically inspired soft computing [13] technique, that is, PSO. The weight of the model has been updated by PSO. Each input vector passed through the model, the error is calculated, and the parameters are updated by PSO.

MLP is a network of simple neurons called *perceptrons* [15]. The basic concept of a single perceptron was introduced by Rosenblatt in 1958. The perceptron computes a single output from multiple real-valued inputs by forming a linear combination according to its input weights and then possibly puts the output through some nonlinear activation function. Mathematically this can be written as

$$y = \psi \left(\sum w_i x_i + b \right) = \psi(w^T x + b) \quad (30.3)$$

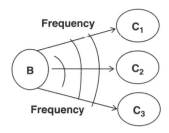

FIGURE 30.1 Bat sends sound signal with frequency c.

where w denotes the vector of weights, x is the vector of inputs, b is the bias, and ψ is the activation function.

30.3.1 Working Procedure of BAT

A bat sends a signal with loudness of frequency 20–200 kHz, as shown in Figure 30.1. After striking an object this signal deflects back to the bat as an echo, as given in Figure 30.2, which is used to calculate the distance S. The minimum distance from the bat to any object is the destination of the bat [25]. The bat flies toward the minimum-distance object. The bat reduces its pulse rate as it approaches the object and continues to do so until distance becomes zero [26, 27]. To calculate the distance, the new position, and the frequency of a bat, the following methods have been used.

30.3.2 Calculation of Frequency

Consider the data set D is represented as an $n \times m$ matrix. Let the number of bats be $B_1, B_2, \ldots, B_k, \ldots, B_n$. For each row one bat is considered. Every bat emits different sound signals with different wavelengths and pulse rates. Let us denote the frequency of sound as f for a bat B. To find the frequency f_k of bat B_k we use Equation (30.4), where c_1 is the pulse rate used to control the frequency f_k of bat B_k and, when it reaches near or far from the object, the value of c_1 is autoadjusted in each iteration by (30.8):

$$f_k = \frac{c_1 \sum (d_k)}{m} \tag{30.4}$$

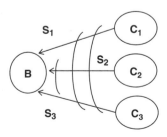

FIGURE 30.2 Echo signal used to calculate the distance S.

30.3.3 Calculation of Distance

The distance S of the object z from bat B_k is calculated by multiplying D_k with some random weight value multiplied by f_k for each object z, where, $z \in T$, T being the number of class labels. For example, in Figures 30.1 and 30.2 the value of $T = 3$:

$$S_{\text{object}z} = f_k D_k wt \tag{30.5}$$

In (30.2) wt is a weight matrix of value between -0.5 and 0.5 of size mT.

30.3.4 Updated Position of BAT

Each object denotes a class. After calculating the error by (30.3), the bat position can be changed by (30.7):

$$E_k = S_{\text{object}z} - 1 \tag{30.6}$$
$$P_k = P_k + E_k \tag{30.7}$$

When the bat starts flying, it assumes that the position is initialized to zero. Its position keeps on changing when it reaches nearer to the object. As it gets closer to the pray, error E_k and position P_k are reduced to zero.

30.3.5 Increased Frequency (*f*) and Weight (*wt*) After Bat Changes Position

When bat comes nearer to the object, the frequency starts reducing. That can be done by controlling the value of c_1 in (30.1) by using (30.5). Assume c_2 is a constant treated as the bat learning parameter. We have taken it nearer to 0.0011:

$$c_1 = f_k + c_2 E_k^2 P_k \tag{30.8}$$
$$wt = wt + 2\mu E_k \tag{30.9}$$

30.4 PROPOSED MODEL

Feature extraction aims to reduce the computational cost of feature measurement, increase classifier efficiency, and allow greater classification accuracy based on the process of deriving new features from the original features. In feature extraction the whole feature space is projected onto another dimensional space for a better analysis of the features. The dimension of a data set can be reduced by, for example, principal-component analysis, linear discriminant analysis, factor analysis, and independent-component analysis.

In the model (Figure 30.3) the dimension of microarray data (MAD) has been reduced using PCA, the data were classified using three classifiers (Bat-FLANN, MLP, and PSO-FLANN), and the result of the three classification techniques is fused together using dynamic classifier fusion (DCF) for better accuracy.

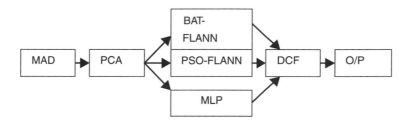

FIGURE 30.3 Proposed DCF model.

30.5 EXPERIMENTAL EVALUATION

The breast cancer data set [29] has been used for experimental evaluation. The dimension of this data set is 98×1213. After implementing PCA, the original data set is reduced to 98×97. The breast cancer data set contains three class levels: 1–11 features for class level 1, 12–62 for class level 2, and the rest belong to class level 3. The input vector for the classification contains 98 genes with 97 conditions using PCA and also the classification is observed on the original data set (without PCA). The weight of each classifier is initially chosen using a random function. The mean-square error (MSE) graph is used as the cost function of the classification techniques. PSO is used in PSO-FLANN and the back-propagation algorithm is used in MLP. The result of three classifiers is fused together using DCF. DCF chooses the classifier according to the best class regions. The MLP classifier with hidden layer 4, $\eta = 0.4$, $\alpha = 0.7$ (both are the learning parameters in MLP), and 1000 iterations gives the confusion matrix in Table 30.1. PSO-FLANN with $p_{\text{num}} = 10$, $\mu = 0.001$, $c_1 = 0.4$, and $c_2 = 0.3$ with 1000 iterations gives the confusion matrix shown in Table 30.1. DCF as shown in Table 30.2 is achieved by fusing Table 30.1. From Table 30.1, it is noted that BAT-FLANN gives better results as compared to MLP and PSO-FLANN. The input vector for our BAT-FLANN classifier has 98 genes with 97 conditions. Each row is assumed to be a bat; therefore, for the breast cancer data set we have $B_1, B_2, \ldots, B_{98}$, or 98 bats. Also we used a different microarray data set, for example, lung cancer Reference [30] having dimension 197×581 and St. Judel leukemia having dimension 248×985 [29]. Table 30.2 presents a comparison of classification results of all the above data sets. We have implemented the BAT-FLANN algorithm in MATLAB. We have successfully achieved more than 90% accuracy, as shown in Table 30.1 for the breast cancer data set. We have also compared our result with PSO-FLANN [11] and normal MLP with other cancer data sets [4, 10]. The comparison is shown in Table 30.2.

TABLE 30.1   Comparison of Classification Result

	Actual Size	After PCA	MLP	PSO-FLANN	BAT-FLANN
Breast cancer	98×1213	98×97	70	69.6	91.61
Lung cancer	197×581	197×81	78.8	76.7	96.3
St. Judel leukemia	248×985	248×91	76.6	74.9	94.7

TABLE 30.2   Result Obtained Using DCF

	MLP	PSO-FLANN	BAT-FLANN	DCF
Breast cancer	70	69.696	91.61	91.61
Lung cancer	78.8	76.7	96.3	96.3
St. Judel leukemia	76.6	74.9	94.7	94.7

30.6   CONCLUSION

In this chapter, the bat algorithm was successfully formulated and is used to update the weight of the FLANN classifier. Wide knowledge of bat echolocation signals and their specific features results in good accuracy in the FLANN model. Implementation of BAT-FLANN has been compared and it has been observed to be a very promising algorithm. It is more powerful than PSO. The primary reason is that the bat algorithm incorporates the major advantages of PSO. In the future, a natural extension to the current bat algorithm can be used in other engineering application areas. Ensemble learning or classifier fusion is an ever-growing field, with a wide scope of interdisciplinary research in the fields of computer science, mathematics, statistics, and machine learning. In the future, one can expect rich concepts from widely varying areas such as information theory, optimization theory, rough fuzzy sets, soft computing, and evolutionary computation to contribute and enrich this problem domain in the field of pattern recognition.

REFERENCES

1. H. Yu, G. Gu, H. Liu, J. Shen, and C. Zhu. A novel discrete particle swarm optimization algorithm for microarray databased tumor marker gene selection. In *IEEE International Conference on Computer Science and Software Engineering (CSSE)*, Wuhan, China, 2008, pp. 1057–1060.

2. Y. Leung and Y. Hung. A multi-filter-multi-wrapper approach to gene selection and microarray date classification. *IEEE/ACM Trans. Computat. Biol. Bioinformatics*, 7(1):108–117, 2010.

3. C.-J. Huang and W.-C. Liao. A comparative study of feature selection methods for probabilistic neural networks in cancer classification. *Proc. 15th IEEE Int. Conf. Tools Artif. Intell. (ICTAI'03)*, 3:1082–3409, 2003.

4. J. Shim, I. Sohn, S. Kim, J. W. Lee, P. E. Green, and C. Hwang. Selecting marker genes for cancer classification using supervised weighted kernel clustering and the support vector machine. *Computat. Stat. Data Anal.*, 53:1736–1742, 2009.

5. D. Lin, M. Jinwen, and P. Jian. Rank sum method for related gene selection and its application to tumor diagnosis. *Chinese Sci. Bull.*, 49(15):1652–1657, 2004.

6. P. A. Mundra and J. C. Rajapakse. Gene and sample selection for cancer classification with support vectors based *t*-statistic. *Neurocomputing*, 73:2353–2362, 2010.

7. S. Hengpraprohm and P. Chongstitvatana. Selecting informative genes from microarray data for cancer classification with genetic programming classifier using *k*-means clustering and SNR ranking. In *Frontiers in the Convergence of Bioscience and Information Technologies (FBIT)*, 2007, pp. 211–218.

8. S. Huda, J. Yearwood, and A. Stranieri. Hybrid wrapper-filter approach for input feature selection using maximum relevance and artificial neural network input gain measurement approximation. In *IEEE Fourth International Conference On Network and System Security*, 2010, pp. 442–449.

9. M. Rangasamy and S. Venketraman. An efficient statistical model based classification algorithm for classifying cancer gene expression data with minimal gene subsets, *Int. J. Cyber Soc. Educ.*, 2(2):51–66, 2009.

10. N. Revathy and R. Amalraj. Accurate cancer classification using expressions of very few genes. *Int. J. Comput. Appl.*, 14(4):0975–8887, 2011.

11. Z. Chen, J. Li, L. W. Wei, W. Xu, and Y. Shi. Multiple kernel SVM based multiple-task oriented data mining system for gene expression data analysis. *Expert Syst. Appl.*, 38:12151–12159, 2011.

12. E. Kilic and E. Alpaydin. Learning the areas of expertise of classifiers in an ensemble. *Proc. Comput. Sci.*, 3:74–82, 2011.

13. N. Garcia, B. Pedrajas, and B. Ortiz. An empirical study of binary classifier fusion methods for multi class classification. *Inform. Fusion*, 12:111–130, 2011.

14. H. M. Feng, X. F. Li, and J. F. Chen. A comparative study of four fuzzy integrals for classifier fusion. *Proc. Int. Conf. Machine Learning Cybernet.*, 1:332–338, 2010.

15. J. Huange, M. Wang, B. Gu, and Z. Chen. Multiple classifier combination based on interval-valued fuzzy permutation. *J. Computat. Inform. Syst.*, 6:1759–1768, 2010.

16. M. Hazem and E. Bakry. An efficient algorithm for pattern detection using combined classifiers and data fusion. *Inform. Fusion*, 11:133–148, 2010.

17. U. G. Mangai, S. Samanta, S. Das, and P. R. Chowdhury. A survey of decision fusion and feature training strategies for pattern classification. *IETE Tech. Rev.*, 27:293–307, 2010.

18. L. I. Kuncheva, J. C. Bezbek, and R. P. W Duin. Decision template for multiple classifier fusion: An experimental comparison. *Pattern Recognition*, 34:299–314, 2010.

19. H. R. Albert, R. Ko, R. Sabourin, A. S. Britto, and L. Oliveira. Pair wise fusion matrix for combining classifiers. *Pattern Recognition*, 40:2198–2210, 2007.

20. E. Peterson. Partitioning large-sample microarray-based gene expression profile using principal component analysis. *Comput. Methods Program. Biomed.*, 107–119, 2003.

21. A. M. Sarhan. Cancer classification based on micro array gene expression data using DCT and ANN. *Proc. Int. Conf. Gen. Theor. Appl. Inform. Technol.*, 70(2):208–216, 2009.

22. R. Kumar, M. S. B. Saithij, S. Vaddadi, and S. V. K. K. Anoop. An intelligent functional link artificial neural network for channel equalization. *Proc. Int. Conf. Signal Proc. Robot. Automation*, 240–245, 2009.

23. W. Chen, S. Chen, and C. Lin, A speech recognition method based on the sequential multi-layer perceptrons. *Neural Networks*, 9:655–699, 1996.

24. M. Re and G. Valentini. An ensemble based data fusion for gene function prediction. In *Multiple Classifier Systems*. Springer, 2009, pp. 448–457.

25. X. S. Yang. Anewmetaheuristic bat-inspired algorithm. In J. R. Gonzalez, D. A. Pelta, C. Cruz, G. Terrazas, and N. Krasnogor (Eds.), *Nature Inspired Cooperative Strategies for Optimization*, Springer, Heidelberg, 2010, pp. 65–74.

26. H. Herman and T. Gudra. New approach in bats' sonar parameterization and modelling. *Physics Procedia*, 3:217–224, 2010.

27. J. D. Altringham. *Bats: Biology and Behaviour*. Oxford University Press, UK, 2000.

28. J. Kennedy and R. Eberhart. Particle swarm optimization. *Proc. IEEE Int. Conf. Neural Networks*, 1942–1948, 1995.

29. UCI Machine Learning Repository, archive.ics.uci.edu.

30. Machine Learning Data Set Repository, mldata.org.

CHAPTER 31

RNA CLASSIFICATION AND STRUCTURE PREDICTION: ALGORITHMS AND CASE STUDIES

LING ZHONG, JUNILDA SPIROLLARI, JASON T. L. WANG, and DONGRONG WEN

Department of Computer Science, New Jersey Institute of Technology, Newark, NJ

31.1 INTRODUCTION

RNA is a remarkable biomolecule with an ample diversity in size, shape, and function, as observed from the small microRNAs involved in posttranscriptional regulation of genes [6] to the large ribosomal macromolecules responsible for making proteins [3, 39, 44]. In this chapter, we present two case studies related to RNA data analysis. The first case study is focused on classification of microRNA precursors (also known as pre-miRNAs). We develop new algorithms to classify given RNA sequences as pre-miRNAs or not. The second case study is focused on prediction of RNA secondary structures, including pseudoknots. Pseudoknots are important RNA tertiary motifs. We develop a probabilistic method for predicting these tertiary motifs. Experimental results demonstrate the superiority of our algorithms over competing methods. In the following sections we describe in detail the problems we study and solutions we propose, first being pre-miRNA classification, then RNA pseudoknot prediction.

31.2 CLASSIFICATION OF RNA SEQUENCES

MicroRNAs are noncoding RNAs of approximately 22 nucleotides that are known to regulate posttranscriptional expression of protein-coding genes [4, 6]. Lee et al. [28] first reported that in *Caenorhabditis elegans*, lin-4 regulates the translation of lin-14 mRNA via an antisense RNA–RNA interaction. Since then, many roles for miRNAs have been discovered, including, for example, the control of left/right neuronal asymmetry in *C. elegans* [21] and cell proliferation in *Drosophila* [8] as well as the regulation of flowering time in plants [2]. Their role in cancer development has also been reported [31]. However, these roles are only

Biological Knowledge Discovery Handbook: Preprocessing, Mining, and Postprocessing of Biological Data, First Edition. Edited by Mourad Elloumi and Albert Y. Zomaya.
© 2014 John Wiley & Sons, Inc. Published 2014 by John Wiley & Sons, Inc.

a small portion of total miRNA functions [9]. So, exploring miRNAs and their functions continues to be a highly active area of research.

miRNAs are derived from pre-miRNAs that often fold into stem–loop hairpin structures. These characteristic stem–loop structures are highly conserved in different species [27]. One challenging research problem is to distinguish pre-miRNAs from other sequences with similar stem–loop structures (referred to as pseudo pre-miRNAs). Many computational methods have been developed to tackle this challenge. A common approach is to transform the classification of real and pseudo pre-miRNAs to a feature selection problem.

Lim et al. [29] reported some characteristic features in phylogenetically conserved stem–loop pre-miRNAs that derive known miRNAs. Lai et al. [27] considered hairpin structures predicted by mfold [48] as well as the nucleotide divergence of pre-miRNAs. Xue et al. [45] decomposed stem–loop hairpin structures into local structure–sequence features and used these features in combination with a support vector machine to classify pre-miRNAs. Bentwich et al. [5] proposed a scoring function for pre-miRNAs with thermodynamic stability and certain structural features, which capture the global properties of the hairpin structures in the pre-miRNAs. Ng and Mishra [34] employed a Gaussian radial basis function kernel as a similarity measure for 29 global and intrinsic hairpin folding attributes, and characterized a pre-miRNA based on its dinucleotide subsequences, hairpin folding, nonlinear statistical thermodynamics, and topology. Huang et al. [19] evaluated features valuable for pre-miRNA classification, such as the local secondary-structure differences of the stem regions of real pre-miRNA and pseudo pre-miRNA hairpins, and established correlations between different types of mutations and the secondary structures of real pre-miRNAs. More recently, Zhao et al. [46] considered structure–sequence features and minimum free energy of RNA secondary structure, along with the double-helix structure with free nucleotides and base-pairing features. In general, the quality of selected features directly affects the classification accuracy achieved by a method.

In this section we present a combinatorial feature mining method for pre-miRNA classification. Our method, named MirID, identifies and classifies an input RNA sequence as pre-miRNA or not. MirID considers different combinations of features extracted from pre-miRNA. For each combination or set of features, we create a *support vector machine* (SVM) [13, 15] model based on that feature set. SVM models whose accuracy is above a user-determined threshold are then used to build a classifier ensemble. This classifier ensemble will be refined through several iterations until its accuracy cannot be enhanced further. We next construct new feature sets based on existing feature sets by performing pairwise union and split operations on the feature sets. We then repeat the above procedure by building a SVM model based on each new feature set, constructing a classifier ensemble from the SVM models, refining the ensemble until it cannot be improved further. Finally we output the best ensemble obtained through this iterative procedure, which is used for pre-miRNA classification.

31.2.1 Materials and Methods

In this section we present the data used in our study and the algorithm employed by MirID.

31.2.1.1 Data Sets   We collected real pre-miRNAs and pseudo pre-miRNAs from 20 species (Table 31.1). The real pre-miRNAs were downloaded from miRBase available at `http://www.mirbase.org/` [26]. We used RNAfold [18] to predict the secondary structures of all the RNA sequences. Some real pre-miRNAs downloaded from miRBase cannot

TABLE 31.1   Number of Training and Test Sequences Used in pre-miRNA Classification

Species	Real pre-miRNAs Training/Test	Pseudo pre-miRNAs Training/Test
Arabidopsis thaliana	66/67	114/114
Caenorhabditis briggsae	66/67	400/400
Caenorhabditis elegans	84/85	288/289
Canis familiaris	161/161	400/400
Ciona intestinalis	160/160	400/400
Danio rerio	170/170	468/468
Drosophila melanogaster	81/82	370/370
Drosophila pseudoobscura	98/99	115/116
Epstein–Barr virus	12/13	30/31
Gallus gallus	241/241	336/336
Macaca mulatta	222/223	387/387
Medicago truncatula	111/111	117/118
Mus musculus	315/315	780/781
Oryza sativa	172/172	358/359
Physcomitrella patens	73/74	186/186
Populus trichocarpa	94/95	558/558
Pristionchus pacificus	60/61	47/48
Rattus norvegicus	193/193	250/250
Schmidtea mediterranea	72/73	102/102
Taeniopygia guttata	94/95	269/270

be folded into a stem–loop structure using RNAfold. These pre-miRNAs were excluded from our data set. The lengths of the real pre-miRNAs in the final data set ranged from 60 to 120 nucleotides (nt).

The pseudo pre-miRNAs used in this study were collected from GenBank (http://www.ncbi.nlm.nih.gov/genbank/). We searched for the protein-coding regions of the genome sequences of the 20 species in Table 31.1 and divided them into shorter sequences, each of them having 100 nucleotides. The pseudo pre-miRNAs were chosen from those 100-nucleotide sequences. The criteria used in choosing the pseudo pre-miRNAs are: (i) they must contain at least 18 base pairs, including Watson–Crick and GU wobble base pairs, on the stem region of the stem–loop structure and (ii) their secondary structures have a maximum of -15 kcal/mol free energy without multiple hairpin loops [26]. These criteria guarantee that the stem–loop structures of the pseudo pre-miRNAs are similar to those of the real pre-miRNAs. Finally we divided the sets of real pre-miRNAs and pseudo pre-miRNAs into two parts respectively, one for the training set and the other for the test set. Table 31.1 presents the number of real pre-miRNAs and pseudo pre-miRNAs used for training and test, respectively.

31.2.1.2 *Feature Pool*

In designing our pre-miRNA classification method, we examined multiple features extracted from a pre-miRNA sequence and its secondary structure. Some of these features were taken from our previous studies on noncoding RNA (ncRNA) prediction [16, 43] while others were suggested in the literature [40, 45, 47]. These features included the sequence length, the number of base pairs, GC content, the ratio between the number of base pairs and the sequence length, the number of nucleotides contained in the hairpin loop (the loop size), the free energy of the sequence secondary structure obtained from RNAfold [18], the number of bulge loops, and the size of the largest bulge loop in the secondary structure.

In addition, we considered the features described in [47]. These features included the difference of the lengths of the two tails in the secondary structure where a tail represented the strand of unpaired bases in the 5′ or 3′ end of the structure, the number of tails, and the length of the larger tail. In addition, several combined features were considered. They included the length difference of two tails plus the larger tail length, the size of the hairpin loop plus the larger tail length, the size of the hairpin loop plus the largest bulge size, the ratio between the larger tail length and the sequence length, the ratio between the size of the hairpin loop and the sequence length, the ratio between the largest bulge size and the sequence length, the ratio between the largest bulge size and the number of base pairs, the normalized free energy [41], which is the minimum free energy divided by the sequence length, and the ratio between the normalized free energy and the GC content.

The next set of features included the triplet structure–sequence elements described in [45]. Here we used the dot-bracket notation [18] to represent an RNA secondary structure. A triplet is composed of the 3 continuous sub structures and the nucleotide at the middle. For example, the structure–sequence elements "A(((" and "A((." are two triplets. There are 32 triplets, and hence 32 such features in total.

Finally we considered the symmetric and asymmetric loops defined in [40]. We refer to the portion of the sequence from the 5′ end to the hairpin loop as the left arm and the portion of the sequence from the hairpin loop to the 3′ end as the right arm. In a symmetric (internal) loop, the number of nucleotides in the left arm equals the number of nucleotides in the right arm. In an asymmetric (internal) loop, the number of nucleotides in the left arm is different from the number of nucleotides in the right arm. Features related to these loops included the size of each loop, the average size of the loops, the average distance between the loops, the length of the longest symmetric region, and the length of the arm in the region. Other features included the proportion of A/C/G/U in the stem, the proportion of A–U/C–G/G–U base pairs in the stem, and the proportion of A/C/G/U and A–U/C–G/G–U base pairs in the symmetric region. Totally, there are 74 features in the feature pool.

31.2.1.3 *Algorithm for Classification of Pre-miRNAs*   MirID adopts a novel feature-mining algorithm for pre-miRNA classification. Initially the algorithm randomly creates N feature sets (in the study presented here, N is set to 100). Each feature set contains between 1 and 150 features randomly chosen with replacement from the feature pool. Some features may be repeated in a feature set (thus a bagging approach is used here [7]). We build a support vector machine model based on each feature set. The SVM used in this study is the LIBSVM downloaded from http://www.csie.ntu.edu.tw/~cjlin/libsvm/ [15]. We use the polynomial kernel provided in the LIBSVM package. The polynomial kernel achieves the highest accuracy among all kernel functions included in the package.

We then remove the SVM models whose accuracy is less than a user-determined threshold. (In the study presented here, the threshold is set to 0.8.) The feature sets used to build those removed SVM models are also eliminated from further consideration. We construct a classifier ensemble from the remaining SVM models. The ensemble works by taking the majority vote from the individual SVM models used to build the classifier ensemble. This ensemble will be refined through several iterations until its accuracy cannot be enhanced further.

Since different combinations of remaining features may still yield a better classifier, our algorithm next performs pairwise union and split operations on the feature sets used to build the best classifier ensemble obtained so far. In doing so, MirID takes four steps: (1) pick every pair of feature sets S_1 and S_2; (2) merge them into a single feature set S with, say, n features; (3) randomly generate a number k; and (4) randomly assign k features into a set S_1' and assign the remaining $n - k$ features into another set S_2'. Thus, these four steps take two feature sets S_1 and S_2 as input and produce two new feature sets S_1' and S_2' as output. These pairwise union and split operations yield new feature sets. The new feature sets are used to build new SVM models. The above procedure is then repeated to obtain a best possible classifier ensemble using the new feature sets. Figure 31.1 summarizes our feature mining algorithm, which produces a classifier ensemble.

31.2.1.4 Web Server   We have implemented the pre-miRNA classification method presented here into a Web server which is freely available at `http://bioinformatics.njit.edu/MirID`. The Web server takes an RNA sequence in FASTA format as input and classifies the input sequence as pre-miRNA or not. Figure 31.2 shows a sample input sequence, and Figure 31.3 shows the output generated by the Web server based on the sample input in Figure 31.2.

31.2.2 Results

We carried out a series of experiments to evaluate the proposed MirID method and compare it with two closely related methods, PMirP [46] and Triplet-SVM [45]. Like MirID, both PMirP and Triplet-SVM were implemented using SVMs. PMirP adopted a hybrid coding scheme, combining features such as free bases, base pairs, and minimum free energy of secondary structure, among others. Triplet-SVM used triplet structure–sequence elements, which are also included in our feature pool. Table 31.2 shows the accuracy rates of MirID on 12 species taken from Table 31.1. These 12 species were previously tested by PMirP and Triplet-SVM too [45, 46]. A method is said to classify a test sequence in Table 31.1 correctly if the sequence is a pre-miRNA (pseudo pre-miRNA, respectively) and the method indicates that the sequence is indeed a pre-miRNA (pseudo pre-miRNA, respectively). A method is said to classify a test sequence in Table 31.1 incorrectly if the sequence is a pre-miRNA (pseudo pre-miRNA, respectively) but the method mistakenly indicates that the sequence is a pseudo pre-miRNA (pre-miRNA, respectively). For each species in Table 31.2, the accuracy rate of a method is defined as the number of correctly classified test sequences of that species divided by the total number of test sequences of that species. For each species, the highest accuracy rate yielded by a method is in bold. It can be seen that MirID outperforms the two competing methods, yielding the highest overall accuracy rate among the three methods. Table 31.3 shows the accuracy rates of MirID on nine species in Table 31.1 that were not tested by PMirP and Triplet-SVM previously. MirID achieves high accuracy on all the nine species.

31.2.3 Summary

In this section we present a novel feature-mining algorithm for pre-miRNA classification. Our method, named MirID, achieves high accuracy on the 20 species tested in the study. When compared with two closely related methods, PMirP and Triplet-SVM, our method

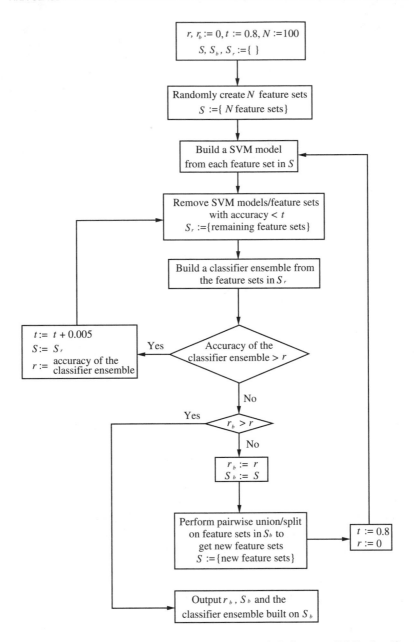

FIGURE 31.1   Feature-mining algorithm employed by MirID for pre-miRNA classification.

yields a higher accuracy rate than the two competing methods. Since all the three methods were implemented using SVMs with similar features, we conclude that the superiority of our method is due to the new feature-mining algorithm proposed in the section. We are currently exploring other data-mining techniques to further improve the performance of our tool on pre-miRNA classification as well as the prediction of other RNA motifs.

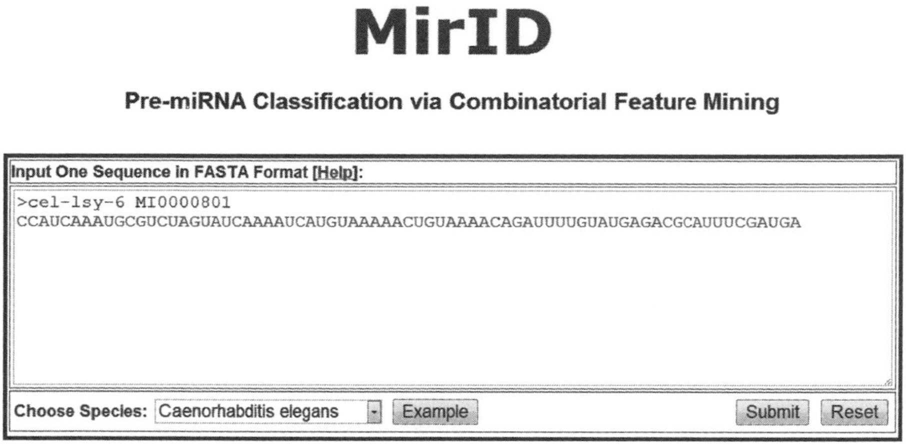

MirID

Pre-miRNA Classification via Combinatorial Feature Mining

Input One Sequence in FASTA Format [Help]:

```
>cel-lsy-6 MI0000801
CCAUCAAAUGCGUCUAGUAUCAAAAUCAUGUAAAAACUGUAAAACAGAUUUUGUAUGAGACGCAUUUCGAUGA
```

Choose Species: Caenorhabditis elegans   Example   Submit   Reset

FIGURE 31.2 Screenshot showing input of MirID.

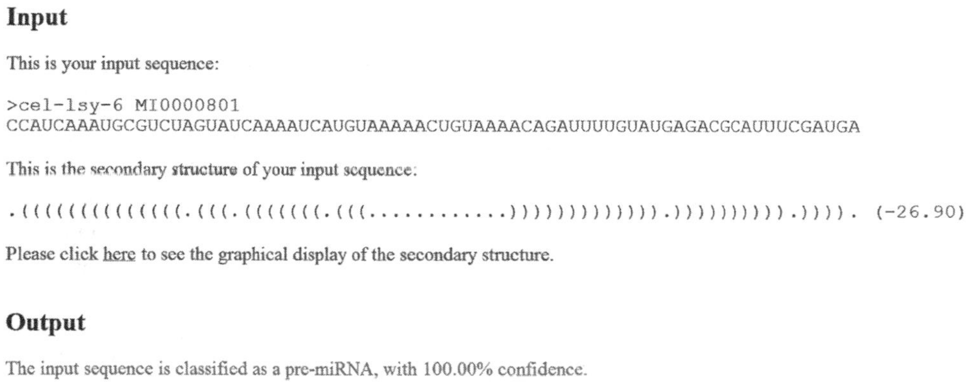

Input

This is your input sequence:

```
>cel-lsy-6 MI0000801
CCAUCAAAUGCGUCUAGUAUCAAAAUCAUGUAAAAACUGUAAAACAGAUUUUGUAUGAGACGCAUUUCGAUGA
```

This is the secondary structure of your input sequence:

```
.((((((((((((((.(((.(((((((.(((............)))))))))))))))).))))))))))).)))). (-26.90)
```

Please click here to see the graphical display of the secondary structure.

Output

The input sequence is classified as a pre-miRNA, with 100.00% confidence.

FIGURE 31.3 Screenshot showing output of MirID.

TABLE 31.2 Comparison of Three Studied pre-miRNA Classification Methods (%)

Species	MirID	PMirP	Triplet-SVM
Mus musculus	91.9	**94.4**	**94.4**
Rattus novegicus	**94.6**	92	80
Gallus gallus	95	**100**	84.6
Dnio rerio	**90.9**	83.3	66.7
Caenorhabditis briggsae	94.2	**97.3**	95.9
Caenorhabditis elegans	**93**	86.4	86.4
Drosophila pseudoobscura	**96.3**	91.5	90.1
Drosophila melanogaster	**97.3**	95.8	91.5
Oryza sativa	94.9	**100**	94.8
Arabidopsis thaliana	95	**96**	92
Estein–Barr virus	**100**	80	**100**
Overall/average	**94.83**	92.42	88.76

692 RNA CLASSIFICATION AND STRUCTURE PREDICTION: ALGORITHMS AND CASE STUDIES

TABLE 31.3 Accuracy Rates of MirID on Nine Species

Species	Accuracy Rate (%)
Canis familiaris	98.0
Ciona intestinalis	99.6
Macaca mulatta	93.1
Medicago truncatula	95.6
Physcomitrella patens	96.2
Populus trichocarpa	97.1
Pristionchus pacificus	94.5
Schmidtea mediterranea	94.3
Taeniopygia guttata	92.3

31.3 IN SILICO PREDICTION OF RNA PSEUDOKNOTS

After describing our method for pre-miRNA classification, we now turn to the problem of pseudoknot prediction. Heuristic methods have been developed to predict RNA secondary structures with pseudoknots. Some of these methods require a prior analysis of training data [20]; others are ab initio methods capable of performing pseudoknot prediction without prior knowledge of the characteristics and peculiarity of data. Well-known ab initio methods include HotKnots [1], FlexStem [11], and PknotsRG [36].

HotKnots uses a heuristic approach to explore alternative pseudoknot-included secondary structures for a given sequence. The tool provides multiple possible structures, but the choices are not exhaustive and it might miss some pseudoknot structures. FlexStem takes stems as the elements of RNA secondary structures and predicts a secondary structure by adding stems in a stepwise manner and adopting a comprehensive energy model that allows complex pseudoknots. PknotsRG is based on the minimum free-energy model using Turner's parameters [33] and offers three methods for predicting secondary structures: (i) with minimum free energy, containing a pseudoknot or not, (ii) with at least one pseudoknot, and (iii) with the best energy-to-length ratio.

In this section we present a new method, named KnotFold, for RNA pseudoknot prediction. KnotFold is an ab initio method that regards a secondary structure as a set of stems and combines an ensemble of RNA folding tools and a search technique for finding appropriate stems to be included in a predicted structure. The input to the KnotFold tool is a single RNA sequence in FASTA format. The output of the tool is a set of possible secondary structures given as lists of stems along with their score, ranked in descending order of the score. The software package, available from `http://bioinformatics.njit.edu/KnotFold`, contains binary executables of the other state-of-the-art RNA folding programs employed by our method.

31.3.1 Methods

In this section we describe the heuristics and algorithm used by KnotFold.

31.3.1.1 Ensemble Approach KnotFold computes and generates results through a two-phase process. During the first phase, three state-of-the-art RNA folding programs are combined to produce a list of common pseudoknot-free stems shared by the predicted secondary structures of a given RNA sequence. A majority rule is used to build the common stem list. Specifically, if a stem is predicted by at least two of the three RNA folding programs, then that stem is added to the common stem list. During the second phase, a search technique based on stem probabilities is employed to select remaining stems with probabilities that maximize an objective function, which are part of possible secondary structures. These possible secondary structures constitute the output of our tool.

We adopt three widely used programs, including two pseudoknot-free RNA folding tools, RNAfold [17, 18] and CentroidFold [38], and one pseudoknot prediction tool, HotKnots [1, 37]. The expectation is that the stems in the common stem list, produced by the combination of the three state-of-the-art tools, are very likely to occur in the real structure. We use this list as our initial stem list and remove all nucleotides involved in the list from the original sequence. The new shorter sequence is then used as the input to our second phase described in the following section.

Notice that HotKnots [1] produces multiple possible structures where some may contain pseudoknots and some may not. As a consequence, there are also many possible common stem lists generated in the first phase and, hence, many possible secondary structures predicted by our KnotFold method.

31.3.1.2 Stem-Based Estimator for Secondary-Structure Prediction
We propose an estimator, called the α-estimator, reminiscent of the γ-estimator used by CentroidFold [38], to predict high-sensitivity secondary structures. A high-sensitivity secondary structure is one with a large number of true base pairs. Unlike the γ-estimator, our approach is to examine stems instead of base pairs. More precisely, we maximize the expected number of true-positive and true-negative stems in a predicted structure. Before giving the derivation for the expected value, we first define some terms.

Representation of RNA Secondary Structure   A *stem s* is a secondary-structure component that contains two or more consecutive base pairs. A secondary structure r of a sequence A is represented as a list of stems, $r = s_1; s_2; \ldots; s_n$. A valid secondary structure should satisfy the constraint that there exist no two stems s_i and s_j with common bases [41]. We denote by $R(A)$ the set of all secondary structures of sequence A.

Figure 31.4 shows an RNA secondary structure with a pseudoknot. There are three stems in this structure. The first stem contains two subsequences; the first subsequence begins at position 0 and ends at position 3 while the second subsequence begins at position 12 and ends at position 15. The first stem is represented as 0–3, 12–15. The secondary structure is represented as a list of three stems separated by semicolons, namely 0–3,12–15; 7–9,16–18; 21–26,33–38. In general, a pseudoknot results from the formation of base pairs between a hairpin loop and a single-stranded region outside the loop. In this example, the stem 7–9,16–18 contains the base pairs that give rise to the pseudoknot.

Proposed Stem-Based Estimator   The γ-estimator employed in the CentroidFold algorithm [38] maximizes the expectation of the linear function $\gamma \times TP_{bp} + TN_{bp}$, where TP_{bp} (TN_{bp}, respectively) is the number of true-positive (true negative, respectively) base pairs in a predicted structure. The motivation for introducing the γ-estimator is that the structures predicted by the minimum free-energy (MFE) approach are not accurate. They generally have a very small probability of being in the real structure and sometimes are not even optimal structures with respect to the number of true-positive base pairs [10]. In other cases, many near-optimal structures based on the MFE approach have high probabilities of being in the real structure [38]. This indicates that the MFE solution does not represent

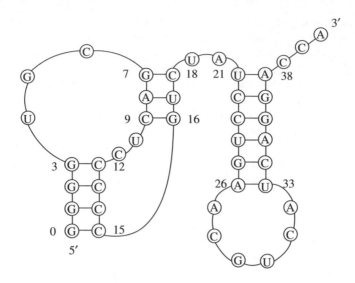

FIGURE 31.4   Illustration of RNA secondary structure with pseudoknot.

the most accurate secondary structure over the entire probability distribution $p(r/A)$ [10]. Therefore, alternative approaches, instead of finding the solution with the minimum free energy, would improve the accuracy [38]. A good alternative would be to produce estimators that maximize the expectation of an objective function related to the accuracy of the prediction. An example is the γ-estimator used in CentroidFold [38]. In our work, we propose the α-estimator to maximize a linear function $\alpha \times \mathrm{TP}_{\mathrm{stem}} + \mathrm{TN}_{\mathrm{stem}}$, where $\mathrm{TP}_{\mathrm{stem}}$ and $\mathrm{TN}_{\mathrm{stem}}$ are numbers of the true-positive and true-negative stems in a predicted structure. A true-positive stem is a correctly predicted stem, whereas a true-negative stem is a stem that is correctly predicted as nonmatching. Our goal is to maximize the expected number of true-positive and true-negative stems in a predicted structure.

Let pr be a predicted structure with a probability distribution $p(\mathrm{pr}/A)$ and let rr be the reference secondary structure of sequence A, with $S(A)$ being the set of all possible stems over A. We define $\mathrm{TP}_{\mathrm{stem}}$, $\mathrm{FP}_{\mathrm{stem}}$, $\mathrm{FN}_{\mathrm{stem}}$, and $\mathrm{TN}_{\mathrm{stem}}$ in the context of a stem as follows:

$$\mathrm{TP}_{\mathrm{stem}} = \sum_{s_i \in S(A)} f(s_i \in \mathrm{pr}) \times f(s_i \in \mathrm{rr}) \tag{31.1}$$

$$\mathrm{FP}_{\mathrm{stem}} = \sum_{s_i \in S(A)} f(s_i \in \mathrm{pr}) \times f(s_i \notin \mathrm{rr}) \tag{31.2}$$

$$\mathrm{FN}_{\mathrm{stem}} = \sum_{s_i \in S(A)} f(s_i \notin \mathrm{pr}) \times f(s_i \in \mathrm{rr}) \tag{31.3}$$

$$\mathrm{TN}_{\mathrm{stem}} = \sum_{s_i \in S(A)} f(s_i \notin \mathrm{pr}) \times f(s_i \notin \mathrm{rr}) \tag{31.4}$$

where $f(\cdot)$ is an indicator function with a value of 1 or 0 depending on whether $(\cdot)$ is true or false. Using these two structures pr and rr we denote by $g_\alpha(\mathrm{pr}, \mathrm{rr})$ the linear function whose maximization expectation will determine the predicted structure and which is defined as

$$g_\alpha(\text{pr}, \text{rr}) = \alpha \times \text{TP}_{\text{stem}} + \text{TN}_{\text{stem}} \tag{31.5}$$

Thus, we propose the estimator that predicts the structure pr that maximizes the expectation value of $g_\alpha(\text{pr}, \text{rr})$ with respect to $p(\text{pr}/A)$,

$$E_{\text{pr}/A}(g_\alpha) = \sum_{\text{pr} \in R(A)} g_\alpha(\text{pr}, \text{rr}) p(\text{pr}/A) \tag{31.6}$$

Equation (31.6) can be rewritten as

$$
\begin{aligned}
E_{\text{pr}/A}(g_\alpha) &= \sum_{\text{pr} \in R(A)} g_\alpha(\text{pr}, \text{rr}) p(\text{pr}/A) \\
&= \sum_{\text{pr} \in R(A)} \sum_{s \in S(A)} \{\alpha f(s \in \text{pr}) f(s \in \text{rr}) + f(s \notin \text{pr}) f(s \notin \text{rr})\} p(\text{pr}/A) \\
&= \sum_{s \in S(A)} \left\{ (\alpha+1) \sum_{\text{pr} \in R(A)} f(s \in \text{pr}) p(\text{pr}/A) - 1 \right\} f(s \in \text{rr}) \\
&\quad + \sum_{s \in S(A)} \left\{ 1 - \sum_{\text{pr} \in R(A)} f(s \in \text{pr}) p(\text{pr}/A) \right\} \\
&= \sum_{s \in S(A)} \{(\alpha+1) p_s - 1\} f(s \in \text{rr}) + \sum_{s \in S(A)} (1 - p_s) \\
&= \sum_{s \in S(A)} \{(\alpha+1) p_s - 1\} f(s \in \text{rr}) + C \tag{31.7}
\end{aligned}
$$

Here $C = \sum_{s \in S(A)} (1 - p_s)$ and p_s is the stem pseudo probability, which is computed as the sum of probabilities of all base pairs (i, j) in the stem [12, 14, 25, 41], that is,

$$p_s = \sum_{i,j} p_{i,j} \tag{31.8}$$

We use Rfold [25] to compute the base-pair probabilities $p_{i,j}$. Notice that the value of p_s may be greater than 1, in which case $1 - p_s$ in Equation (31.7) is set to zero.

Equation (31.7) indicates that, in order to maximize $E_{\text{pr}/A}(g_\alpha)$, the sum of stem probabilities larger than $1/(\alpha+1)$ must be maximized, which equivalently will maximize $\alpha \times \text{TP}_{\text{stem}} + \text{TN}_{\text{stem}}$. In this study the value of α was set to 2^{10}. Finally, we define the pseudoprobability score, or simply the score, of stem s (the score of a structure S, respectively) as follows:

$$\text{score}(s) = (\alpha+1) p_s - 1 \tag{31.9}$$
$$\text{score}(S) = \sum_{s \in S} \text{score}(s) \tag{31.10}$$

31.3.1.3 *Algorithm for Prediction of RNA Pseudoknots* As mentioned above, given an RNA sequence A_o, we use Rfold [25] to compute the probability matrix of all

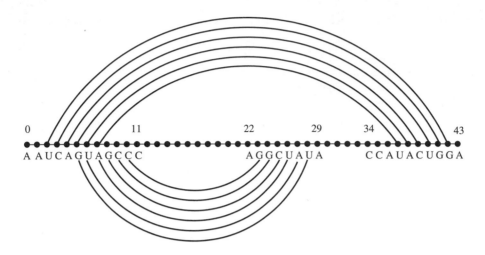

FIGURE 31.5   Conflicting stems, contiguous maximal stems, and contiguous difference stems in sequence A_o.

possible base pairs in sequence A_o. We consider in this study the Watson–Crick base pairs A–U, U–A, C–G, G–C and wobble base pairs G–U, U–G. During the first phase of the KnotFold algorithm, we apply the ensemble approach described in Section 31.3.1.1 to compute a common stem list, treated as an initial stem list. Since HotKnots predicts multiple possible secondary structures, there are several possible initial stem lists. Consider each initial stem list I. Our approach predicts that all stems in I should be in the secondary structure of A_o. Next, we remove from the original sequence A_o all nucleotides in I. The remaining shorter sequence, called A, is processed during the second phase of the KnotFold algorithm. We introduce some definitions below to facilitate the description of the second phase of our algorithm.

Definition 31.1   A *contiguous stem* is a stem made up of contiguous nucleotides from the original sequence A_o.

Definition 31.2   A *maximal stem* is a stem that is not a substem of another stem.

Definition 31.3   A *contiguous maximal stem* is a maximal stem made up of contiguous nucleotides in the original sequence A_o. Referring to Figure 31.5, the stem 2–7,37–42 is a contiguous maximal stem.

Definition 31.4   *Conflicting stems* are stems that share nucleotides. For example, the stem 2–7,37–42 and the stem 5–10,23–28 in Figure 31.5 are conflicting.

Definition 31.5   A *contiguous difference stem* s' of stem s_1 with respect to stem s_2 is a substem of s_1 that is nonconflicting with s_2. Furthermore, s' is contiguous and has at least three base pairs. For example, in Figure 31.5, the stem 8–10,23–25 is a contiguous difference stem of the stem 5–10,23–28 with respect to the stem 2–7,37–42.

We maintain a candidate stem list CL which is composed of all possible contiguous maximal stems from the original sequence A_o, sorted by their score calculated by

```
Procedure: KnotFold
Input: Single RNA sequence A_o
Output: A set of predicted secondary structures of A_o represented as lists of stems
        /* RS is the set of all predicted secondary structures. */
1.    RS := Ø;
2.    PM := probability matrix (all base-pair probabilities);
3.    I := initial stem list (constructed by using the ensemble approach);
4.    A := new shorter sequence constructed by removing from A_o all nucleotides in I;
5.    CL := candidate stem list made up from original sequence A_o composed of
      contiguous maximal stems sorted by their score calculated using Equation (31.9);
6.    while the total number of nucleotides in CL is greater than δ do
7.      begin
8.          RL := CL;
            /* PR is a predicted structure. */
9.          PR := I;
10.         while RL ≠ Ø and the total number of nucleotides in PR is less than θ do
11.           begin
12.             add to PR the stem with the highest score, s, in RL;
13.             remove s from RL;
14.             remove from RL all conflicting stems of s;
15.             add to RL all stems s', where s' is a contiguous difference stem of
                a removed stem with respect to s;
16.           end;
17.         add PR to RS;
18.         remove from CL the stem with the highest score;
19.       end;
20.     display all secondary structures in RS;
```

FIGURE 31.6 KnotFold algorithm for pseudoknot prediction.

Equation (31.9). The KnotFold algorithm is summarized in Figure 31.6. Notice that this algorithm is a greedy heuristic; that is, the optimality of the algorithm with respect to the scoring function in Equation (31.10) is not guaranteed. Nevertheless, as our experimental results show later, the proposed algorithm achieves good performance when compared with existing methods.

On average, 54% of the nucleotides in an RNA sequence are involved in the base pairs of its secondary structure [32]. In step 10 of the KnotFold algorithm, the value of θ is set to 60% of the nucleotides in the original sequence A_o. (A pseudoknotted RNA secondary structure has slightly more base pairs than a pseudoknot-free secondary structure and hence we use 60% for the threshold θ here.) The value of δ in step 6 is set to $|A_o| \times (1 - \theta) - |I|$, where $|\cdot|$ is the number of nucleotides in the indicated sequence. Notice that since HotKnots predicts many possible structures, there are many initial stem lists I in step 3 and, as a consequence, many structures predicted by KnotFold.

31.3.2 Experiments and Results

In this section we present the data used in our study and some experimental results.

31.3.2.1 Data We tested and compared KnotFold against three other methods: HotKnots, FlexStem, and PknotsRG. They are all ab initio methods, capable of performing RNA pseudoknot prediction without prior knowledge of the characteristics and peculiarity of data. The experiments were done on PseudoBase entries [42] as well as sequences from other sources. We used four different data sets. The first one, referred to as pk168 and used in [11, 20], included 168 entries taken from PseudoBase, with sequence lengths less than 140 nucleotides. The second set, referred to as pkLL2 and used in [20], included 9 sequences taken from PseudoBase with lengths less than 121 nucleotides. The third and fourth sets, referred to as ShPK and LoPK, respectively, were acquired from the HotKnots website [1]. ShPK consisted of 78 short pseudoknotted sequences with lengths less than 40 nucleotides, while LoPK contained 20 long pseudoknotted sequences with lengths more than 140 nucleotides [1]. Every sequence used in our experimental study had a reference structure.

31.3.2.2 *Experimental Results* We use two performance measures to assess the accuracy of the four studied tools. These measures include sensitivity (SN), which is defined as the ratio of number of correctly predicted base pairs to the number of base pairs in the reference structure, that is,

$$SN = \frac{TP_{bp}}{TP_{bp} + FN_{bp}} \tag{31.11}$$

and positive predictive value (PPV), which is defined as the ratio of number of correctly predicted base pairs to the number of base pairs in the predicted structure, that is,

$$PPV = \frac{TP_{bp}}{TP_{bp} + FP_{bp}} \tag{31.12}$$

Here, TP_{bp} is equal to the number of correctly predicted base pairs, FP_{bp} is equal to the number of incorrectly predicted base pairs, and FN_{bp} is equal to the number of base pairs in the reference structure that were not predicted.

Table 31.4 shows the average accuracy of the four studied tools over the four data sets used in the experiments. The highest accuracy achieved for each data set is shown in bold. Notably, KnotFold has higher sensitivity in all data sets, while HotKnots has higher PPV.

31.3.3 Example

We present here an example of the execution of KnotFold, showing a sample input and output of the tool. Note that HotKnots predicts multiple secondary structures. As a consequence, KnotFold also produces several possible secondary structures as the output. Refer to the example in Table 31.5. The input sequence begins at position 0. Each predicted structure is displayed as a list of stems. For example, in structure 1, there are three predicted stems separated by semicolons. The first stem contains two subsequences; the first subsequence

TABLE 31.4 Comparison of Accuracy of Four Studied Pseudoknot Prediction Methods (%)

	pk168		pkLL2		ShPK		LoPK	
	SN	PPV	SN	PPV	SN	PPV	SN	PPV
FlexStem	75.9	71.3	64.6	59.3	78.1	75.7	48.5	41.6
PknotsRG	77.2	75.3	67.4	71.1	79.8	80.9	50.6	46.8
HotKnots	79.0	**81.2**	78.8	**80.1**	85.5	**88.6**	58.4	**59.6**
KnotFold	**83.7**	77.2	**85.3**	78.3	**88.1**	80.6	**60.5**	48.7

TABLE 31.5   Example of Execution of KnotFold

Sequence name is: pkb13
Sequence: GGGGUGCGACUCCCCCGUCUAUCCUGAACGUCAUCAGGACCA

Predicted structure 1:
Score: 9080172.0
0–3,12–15; 7–9,16–18; 21–26,33–38

Predicted structure 2:
Score: 6979616.0
0–3,11–14; 7–9,16–18; 21–26,33–38

Predicted structure 3:
Score: 6053400.0
7–9,16–18; 0–3,10–13; 21–26,33–38

Predicted structure 4:
Score: 6008610.5
0–4,8–12; 5–7,15–17; 21–26,33–38

Predicted structure 5:
Score: 5995131.5
0–3,10–13; 5–7,15–17; 21–26,33–38

begins at position 0 and ends at position 3 while the second subsequence begins at position 12 and ends at position 15. A graphical representation of this secondary structure is given in Figure 31.4.

31.3.4   Summary

In this section we propose a new approach, called KnotFold, for predicting RNA secondary structures with pseudoknots. KnotFold is an ab initio method that regards a secondary structure as a set of stems and combines an ensemble of RNA folding tools and a search technique for finding appropriate stems to be included in a predicted structure. Our experimental results show that the new method achieves higher sensitivity than three existing methods. In the future, we plan to explore more heuristics to further enhance the performance of KnotFold and to integrate it into our RNA data-mining toolkit (RADAR) [22–24, 30].

31.4   CONCLUSION

We present in this chapter two case studies concerning RNA classification and structure prediction. Specifically we propose a combinatorial feature-mining algorithm for pre-miRNA classification, and a probabilistic method for predicting RNA secondary structures including pseudoknots. These case studies demonstrate new ways for applying data-mining techniques to solving RNA bioinformatics problems. We hope the work will make contributions to the field of computational bioinformatics, in particular data mining in bioinformatics.

REFERENCES

1. M. S. Andronescu, C. Pop, and A. E. Condon. Improved free energy parameters for RNA pseudoknotted secondary structure prediction. *RNA*, 16:26–42, 2010.

2. M. J. Aukerman and H. Sakai. Regulation of flowering time and floral organ identity by a microRNA and its APETALA2-like target genes. *Plant Cell*, 15(11):2730–2741, 2003.

3. N. Ban, P. Nissen, J. Hansen, P. B. Moore, and T. A. Steitz. The complete atomic structure of the large ribosomal subunit at 2.4 A resolution. *Science*, 289:905–920, 2000.

4. D. P. Bartel. MicroRNAs: Genomics, biogenesis, mechanism, and function. *Cell*, 116(2):281–297, 2004.

5. I. Bentwich, A. Avniel, Y. Karov, R. Aharonov, S. Gilad, O. Barad, A. Barzilai, P. Einat, U. Einav, E. Meiri, E. Sharon, Y. Spector, and Z. Bentwich. Identification of hundreds of conserved and nonconserved human microRNAs. *Nat. Genet.*, 37(7):766–770, 2005.

6. R. S. Bindra, J. T. L. Wang, and P. S. Bagga. Bioinformatics methods for studying microRNA and ARE-mediated regulation of post-transcriptional gene expression. *Int. J. Knowledge Discov. Bioinformatics*, 1(3):97–112, 2010.

7. L. Breiman. Bagging predictors. *Machine Learning*, 24(2):123–140, 1996.

8. J. Brennecke, D. R. Hipfner, A. Stark, R. B. Russell, and S. M. Cohen. *bantam* encodes a developmentally regulated microRNA that controls cell proliferation and regulates the proapoptotic gene *hid* in *Drosophila*. *Cell*, 113(1):25–36, 2003.

9. N. Bushati and S. M. Cohen. microRNA functions. *Annu. Rev. Cell. Devel. Biol.*, 23:175–205, 2007.

10. L. Carvalho and C. Lawrence. Centroid estimation in discrete high-dimensional spaces with applications in biology. *Proc. Natl. Acad. Sci. USA*, 105:3209–3214, 2008.

11. X. Chen, S. M. He, D. Bu, F. Zhang, R. Chen, and W. Gao. FlexStem: Improving predictions of RNA secondary structures with pseudoknots by reducing the search space. *Bioinformatics*, 24:1994–2001, 2008.

12. P. Clote and J. Straubhaar. Symmetric time warping, Boltzmann pair probabilities and functional genomics. *J. Math. Biol.*, 53:135–161, 2006.

13. C. Cortes and V. Vapnik. Support-vector networks. *Machine Learning*, 20(3):273–297, 1995.

14. Y. Ding, C. Y. Chan, and C. E. Lawrence. RNA secondary structure prediction by centroids in a Boltzmann weighted ensemble. *RNA*, 11:1157–1166, 2005.

15. R. Fan, P. Chen, and C. Lin. Working set selection using the second order information for training SVM. *J. Machine Learning Res.*, 6:1889–1918, 2005.

16. S. J. Griesmer, M. Cervantes-Cervantes, Y. Song, and J. T. L. Wang. In silico prediction of noncoding RNAs using supervised learning and feature ranking methods. *Int. J. Bioinformatics Res. Appl.*, 7(4):355–375, 2011.

17. A. R. Gruber, R. Lorenz, S. H. Bernhart, R. Neubock, and I. L. Hofacker. The Vienna RNA websuite. *Nucleic Acids Res.*, 36:W70–W74, 2008.

18. I. L. Hofacker. Vienna RNA secondary structure server. *Nucleic Acids Res.*, 31:3429–3431, 2003.

19. T. H. Huang, B. Fan, M. F. Rothschild, Z. L. Hu, K. Li, and S. H. Zhao. MiRFinder: An improved approach and software implementation for genome-wide fast microRNA precursor scans. *BMC Bioinformatics*, 8:341, 2007.

20. X. Huang and H. Ali. High sensitivity RNA pseudoknot prediction. *Nucleic Acids Res.*, 35:656–663, 2007.

21. R. J. Johnston and O. Hobert. A microRNA controlling left/right neuronal asymmetry in *Caenorhabditis elegans*. *Nature*, 426(6968):845–849, 2003.

22. M. Khaladkar, V. Bellofatto, J. T. L. Wang, B. Tian, and B. A. Shapiro. RADAR: A web server for RNA data analysis and research. *Nucleic Acids Res.*, 35:W300–W304, 2007.

23. M. Khaladkar, J. Liu, D. Wen, J. T. L. Wang, and B. Tian. Mining small RNA structure elements in untranslated regions of human and mouse mRNAs using structure-based alignment. *BMC Genomics*, 9:189, 2008.

24. M. Khaladkar, V. Patel, V. Bellofatto, J. Wilusz, and J. T. L. Wang. Detecting conserved secondary structures in RNA molecules using constrained structural alignment. *Computat. Biol. Chem.*, 32:264–272, 2008.

25. H. Kiryu, T. Kin, and K. Asai. Rfold: An exact algorithm for computing local base pairing probabilities. *Bioinformatics*, 24:367–373, 2008.

26. A. Kozomara and S. Griffiths-Jones. miRBase: Integrating microRNA annotation and deep-sequencing data. *Nucleic Acids Res.*, 39:D152–D157, 2011.

27. E. C. Lai, P. Tomancak, R. W. Williams, and G. M. Rubin. Computational identification of *Drosophila* microRNA genes. *Genome Biol.*, 4(7):R42, 2003.

28. R. C. Lee, R. L. Feinbaum, and V. Ambros. The *C. elegans* heterochronic gene lin-4 encodes small RNAs with antisense complementarity to lin-14. *Cell*, 75(5):843–854, 1993.

29. L. P. Lim, M. E. Glasner, S. Yekta, C. B. Burge, and D. P. Bartel. Vertebrate microRNA genes. *Science*, 299(5612):1540, 2003.

30. J. Liu, J. T. L. Wang, J. Hu, and B. Tian. A method for aligning RNA secondary structures and its application to RNA motif detection. *BMC Bioinformatics*, 6:89, 2005.

31. G. S. Mack. MicroRNA gets down to business. *Nat. Biotechnol.*, 25:631–638, 2007.

32. D. H. Mathews, A. R. Banerjee, D. D. Luan, T. H. Eickbush, and D. H. Turner. Secondary structure model of the RNA recognized by the reverse transcriptase from the R2 retrotransposable element. *RNA*, 3:1–16, 1997.

33. D. H. Mathews, J. Sabina, M. Zuker, and D. H. Turner. Expanded sequence dependence of thermodynamic parameters improves prediction of RNA secondary structure. *J. Mol. Biol.*, 288:911–940, 1999.

34. K. L. Ng and S. K. Mishra. De novo SVM classification of precursor microRNAs from genomic pseudo hairpins using global and intrinsic folding measures. *Bioinformatics*, 23(11):1321–1330, 2007.

35. D. W. Opitz. Feature selection for ensembles. *Proc. 16th Nat. Conf. Artif. Intell.*, 379–384, 1999.

36. J. Reeder and R. Giegerich. Design, implementation and evaluation of a practical pseudoknot folding algorithm based on thermodynamics. *BMC Bioinformatics*, 5:104, 2004.

37. J. Ren, B. Rastegari, A. Condon, and H. H. Hoos. HotKnots: Heuristic prediction of RNA secondary structures including pseudoknots. *RNA*, 11:1494–1504, 2005.

38. K. Sato, M. Hamada, K. Asai, and T. Mituyama. CentroidFold: A web server for RNA secondary structure prediction. *Nucleic Acids Res.*, 37:W277–W280, 2009.

39. F. Schluenzen, A. Tocilj, R. Zarivach, J. Harms, M. Gluehmann, D. Janell, A. Bashan, H. Bartels, I. Agmon, F. Franceschi, and A. Yonath. Structure of functionally activated small ribosomal subunit at 3.3 angstroms resolution. *Cell*, 102(5):615–623, 2000.

40. A. Sewer, N. Paul, P. Landgraf, A. Aravin, S. Pfeffer, M. J. Brownstein, T. Tuschl, E. van Nimwegen, and M. Zavolan. Identification of clustered microRNAs using an *ab initio* prediction method. *BMC Bioinformatics*, 6:267, 2005.

41. J. Spirollari, J. T. L. Wang, K. Zhang, V. Bellofatto, Y. Park, and B. A. Shapiro. Predicting consensus structures for RNA alignments via pseudo-energy minimization. *Bioinformatics Biol. Insights*, 3:51–69, 2009.

42. F. H. van Batenburg, A. P. Gultyaev, and C. W. Pleij. PseudoBase: Structural information on RNA pseudoknots. *Nucleic Acids Res.*, 29:194–195, 2001.

43. J. T. L. Wang and X. Wu. Kernel design for RNA classification using support vector machines. *Int. J. Data Mining Bioinformatics*, 1(1):57–76, 2006.

44. B. T. Wimberly, D. E. Brodersen, W. M. Clemons, R. J. Morgan-Warren, Jr., A. P. Carter, C. Vonrhein, T. Hartsch, and V. Ramakrishnan. Structure of the 30S ribosomal subunit. *Nature*, 407:327–339, 2000.

45. C. Xue, F. Li, T. He, G. P. Liu, Y. Li, and X. Zhang. Classification of real and pseudo microRNA precursors using local structure-sequence features and support vector machine. *BMC Bioinformatics*, 6:310, 2005.

46. D. Zhao, Y. Wang, D. Luo, X. Shi, L. Wang, D. Xu, J. Yu, and Y. Liang. PMirP: A pre-microRNA prediction method based on structure-sequence hybrid features. *Arti. Intell. Med.*, 49:127–132, 2010.

47. Y. Zheng, W. Hsu, M. L. Lee, and L. Wong. Exploring essential attributes for detecting microRNA precursors from background sequences. *Lecture Notes Comput. Sci.*, 4316:131–145, 2006.

48. M. Zuker. Mfold web server for nucleic acid folding and hybridization prediction. *Nucleic Acids Res.*, 31:3406–3415, 2003.

AB INITIO PROTEIN STRUCTURE PREDICTION: METHODS AND CHALLENGES

JAD ABBASS,[1,2] JEAN-CHRISTOPHE NEBEL,[1] and NASHAT MANSOUR[2]

[1]Faculty of Science, Engineering and Computing, Kingston University, London, United Kingdom

[2]Department of Computer Science and Mathematics, Lebanese American University, Beirut, Lebanon

32.1 INTRODUCTION

Proteins represent approximately 20% of a eukaryotic cell's weight, that is, the largest percentage after water [1]. They are involved in the most critical functions: Structural proteins are an organism's basic building blocks; enzymes, the largest class, are known to be involved in 4000 biochemical reactions [2]; and transmembrane proteins are essential in the cellular environment's maintenance.

A protein is a linear sequence of *amino acids* (AAs) which generally folds in a high-speed spontaneous process into a unique three-dimensional conformation; this conformation typically represents a global energy minimum [3]. A protein's lack of structure, or misfold, may be harmful since a protein's biological function is highly related to its three-dimensional structure. Indeed, it has been shown that many serious diseases like Alzheimer's, Parkinson's, Creutzfeldt–Jakob disease, cystic fibrosis, and many cancers are linked to protein misfolding [4]; see Figure 32.1. Thus, predicting the native structure of some proteins may not only contribute to a better understanding of the biochemistry of diseases but also have an invaluable contribution in drug design. Consequently, predicting a final structure from a sequence of AAs has been qualified as deciphering "the second half of the genetic code" and referred to the "holy grail of molecular biology" [5]. This quest has attracted researchers from many disciplines, including biology, biochemistry, biophysics, and computer science.

It is estimated that about 100,000 different structures of proteins can be found in the human body [6]. However, fewer than 10% of them have been discovered so far [7]. Since experimental techniques for protein structure determination [i.e., X-ray crystallography and *nuclear magnetic resonance* (NMR) spectroscopy] are very expensive and time consuming, there is a great incentive in generating such knowledge via computational means. *Protein structure prediction* (PSP) aims at predicting computationally the three-dimensional (3D)

Biological Knowledge Discovery Handbook: Preprocessing, Mining, and Postprocessing of Biological Data, First Edition. Edited by Mourad Elloumi and Albert Y. Zomaya.
© 2014 John Wiley & Sons, Inc. Published 2014 by John Wiley & Sons, Inc.

FIGURE 32.1   Structures of normal prion protein (PrP^c) and disease-causing prion (PrP^{Sc}). Misfolded molecule believed to be responsible for Creutzfeldt–Jakob (mad cow) disease. (Retrieved from: `http://www.cmpharm.ucsf.edu/cohen/media/pages/gallery.html`.)

structure of proteins from their sequences of AAs. Nevertheless, even for short sequences, the search space is enormous and is computationally intractable [8]. This NP-hard problem has been a target for computer scientists who have tackled it using a variety of techniques including heuristic algorithms and parallel programming.

The approaches used to predict the final 3D structure of a protein are usually classified in three categories: *comparative*, *threading*, and *ab initio* modeling. Whereas ab initio modeling is based solely on amino acid sequences, the first two classes rely on the worldwide repository of protein 3D structures—the *Protein Data Bank* (PDB, `http://www.pdb.org`) [7]—where they infer new structures from previous known structures. Consequently, these two approaches are also referred to as *template-based* modeling [9]. The main difference between comparative modeling and threading is that the former requires the existence of the structure of a homologous sequence in the PDB. In other words, comparative modeling relies on sequence–sequence alignment, while threading is based on a sequence–structure alignment.

In principle, ab initio approaches do not rely on previous known structures. They are usually based on thermodynamic rules expressing interactions among atoms and energy functions, and thus, the most stable structure is found by determining the energy minimization through one of the *force field* (FF) energy models. For this reason, ab initio approaches can also be referred as *physics-based* methods [10], free modeling (FM) [11], or de novo [12]. An FF model aims at evaluating structures using an energy-scoring function. This function usually quantifies chemical reactions and physical forces that occur within the conformation. Initially, when the PDB was relatively small and thus the chance to find the sought structure was low, ab initio methods were seen as "fallback position" where both modeling and threading failed [13]. However, this view is changing in light of the progress achieved by ab initio methods.

This chapter presents the state of the art of the PSP problem from a computational science perspective. It reports major and latest findings concerning protein folding and focuses on ab initio computational approaches. Although they are the most challenging methods, they are also the most promising ones since they are applicable, in principle, to any protein whose sequence is known. Moreover, this survey evaluates ab initio methods in the latest competition and discusses both the computational and biological complexities that still hinder improvements.

32.2   PROTEIN-FOLDING PROBLEM MILESTONES AT A GLANCE

Emil Fischer is considered the first to conduct investigations on protein structures and functions. In 1894, he proposed the "lock-and-key model" regarding enzyme interaction: An enzyme can perform its catalysis function only if its corresponding substrate has a specific geometric shape that allows it to fit into the enzyme [14]. Consequently, he was the first to suggest that a unique rigid 3D structure determines a protein's function. Hsien Wu introduced the concept of protein denaturation in 1931 [15]. He showed that denaturation was purely due to an unfolding process and not to some chemical alteration of the protein. He also predicted that misfolding would lead to a loss of protein function. In the early 1950s, Frederick Sanger proposed an experimental method which led him to sequence a protein, that is, insulin [16, 17]. In 1958, John Kendrew et al. resolved the first 3D structure of a protein called *myoglobin* using X-ray crystallography [18]. In 1961, Christian Anfinsen et al. proposed a theory concerning the native structure of proteins [3]. They stated that the correct conformation has the lowest potential energy among all possible structures. Although this theory has not been proved and seems to be contradicted by a few experimental structures, it has been widely accepted. This is the basis of ab initio PSP, which searches for the optimal solution using heuristics. Another milestone is the Ramachandran plot that was first established in 1963 [19] and further elaborated in 1968 [20]. It reveals the possible local conformations in protein structures which lead to their secondary structure, that is, the presence of α helices and β-sheets. This is illustrated in Figure 32.2.

In 1969, Cyrus Levinthal raised the question of why and how a sequence of AAs can fold into its native structure provided that the number of geometrically possible structures is humongous [21]. In his three-page article, which led to what is now known as Levinthal's

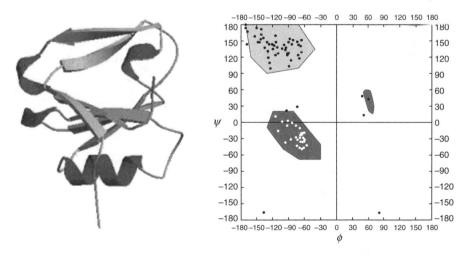

FIGURE 32.2   Structure of fragment of human hepatocyte growth factor (pdb:3hms) and positions of each AA on Ramachandran plot according to their main rotation angles φ and ψ. Light gray and dark gray represent β-sheet and α-helix configurations, respectively.

paradox [8], he compares the astronomical number of possible conformations with the folding time in nature which is measured using millisecond or even microsecond time scales. Even if a protein had the ability to fold into 100 billion different structures per second, hundreds of billion years would be required by a small protein to evaluate all possible conformations. In 1973, Anfinsen demonstrated that the conformation of a protein can be inferred only from its sequence of AAs [22]. He introduced his thermodynamics hypothesis, later known as *Anfinsen's dogma*, which states that protein folding is a pure physical process, that is, it is not biological, that depends only on the specific AA sequence and the surrounding solvent. This theory has been considered the main support and motive for advocates of ab initio protein structure prediction.

In order to evaluate and stimulate the development of computational methods that attempt to predict the native structure of a protein, a biannual community-wide experiment called *critical assessment of structure prediction* (CASP) was created in 1994 by John Moult [23]. This event is now the benchmark for research groups that work in the field of PSP: Prediction methods are evaluated through blind tests of proteins structures. In the latest edition—CASP9 (2010)—more than 60,000 3D models were submitted. The results of the competition are publicly available on the website of the community (predictioncenter.org) and published as a special issue of a journal [24].

32.3 AB INITIO PROTEIN STRUCTURE PREDICTION

The classification of PSP approaches in three categories, that is, comparative modeling, threading, and ab initio, is becoming more and more blurred. More and more methods that are classified in the ab initio category, for example, fragment based and hybrid, use knowledge extracted from known secondary and supersecondary structures to build final native structures. This arose for historical reasons because, when a fragment-based method was first introduced in 1996, it was assessed to be ab initio since it was applied in the discovery of new folds [13]. Consequently, the ab initio category has now been subdivided into subclasses to differentiate between *fragment-based* and *biophysics-based* methods. They have been called *first-principles methods that employ database information* and *first-principles methods without database information* [25], physics-based and knowledge-based or simply de novo and ab initio [26]. In this chapter, we call them simply ab initio *with database information* and *pure* ab initio methods.

Despite the variety of the proposed ab initio methods, they all rely on minimization of an energy function over the conformation parameters. A general approach for ab initio methods is based on a four-step procedure aiming at finding the conformation which has the lowest energy: (1) Start with an unfolded/arbitrary folded conformation; (2) generate alternative conformations using some heuristics; (3) estimate their corresponding energy; and (4) go to step 2 and repeat until the ending criterion is reached. In general, three parameters play critical roles in any ab initio method: energy function accuracy, search algorithm efficiency, and selection of the best models among several structures.

32.4 PURE AB INITIO PREDICTION

Pure ab initio approaches are motivated by three important points. First, they are a direct implementation of Anfinsen's thermodynamics hypothesis since they consider the protein sequence the sole source and they search for the minimum free energy of the protein in its environment. Accordingly, it is the closest method to mimic and simulate the folding process. Second, since new protein structures are continually discovered, only a pure ab initio method can, in principle, derive the native structure of any new protein. Third, these methods give researchers some insights into the folding mechanisms and pathways that are essential to biochemists.

Since pure ab initio methods attempt to replicate in silico the folding process, quantum mechanics should be used to model and estimate the interactions that take place among atoms. Currently, despite the availability of high-performance computing facilities, the computational complexity is such that no system is based on quantum mechanics. Instead, ab initio methods rely on FF or energy functions which attempt to express a variety of atomic interactions such as van der Waals, torsion angles, electrostatics, and bond length. Energy functions are usually associated with a search procedure in order to locate the conformation with the minimum-energy function value. The most popular optimization methods are molecular dynamics [27, 28] and Monte Carlo simulations [29].

In spite of the usage of FF, pure ab initio techniques remain computationally expensive, which has limited their scope to the prediction of the structure of small protein chains [30]. In order to address this limitation, researchers have proposed ways of simplifying the PSP task. First, they suggested simplifying the atomic representation of a protein by considering only some atoms [31, 32] or using lattice models [33, 34]. Second, they investigated the narrowing of FF terms by taking into account few dominant forces [35]. Finally, protein conformational space was reduced using dihedral angle restrictions to limit their motions [36, 37].

After presenting the key components of an ab initio system, that is, FF, search strategies, some popular approaches are detailed.

32.4.1 Force Fields

The FF models are empirical and attempt to provide an atomic description of quantum mechanics. They quantify bonded and nonbonded interactions between atoms so that the inner energy of a whole molecular system can be estimated by adding the values associated to each interaction between pairs of atoms. Whereas bonded interactions are expressed by terms related to bonds, angles, and torsion angles, nonbonded ones deal with van der Waals and electrostatic interactions. Since van der Waals interactions, which can be either repulsive or attractive, vanish quickly, they can be estimated accurately by considering only atom pairs whose distance is under a certain threshold value. On the other hand, electrostatic interactions have long-range properties which make them computationally expensive to calculate.

Energy functions can be classified into two major groups; see [30] for a recent survey: physics based and knowledge based. While the latter is based on previous knowledge and statistics extracted from the known protein structures by observing folded protein properties, the former relies on basic physical theories. CHARMM [38], AMBER [39], UNRES [40], and the one used in ASTRO-FOLD [41] are physics based. On the other hand, the energy functions used in TASSER [42], Chunk-TASSER [43], and I-TASSER [44] are knowledge based. ROSETTA [36] is a popular example of PSP where the function is a combination of terms of both types.

32.4.2 Molecular Dynamics Simulations

Molecular dynamics (MD) simulation is a computational method that calculates the time-based behavior of a molecular system. It attempts to mimic a protein's motion based on

Newton's equation of motion, $F = ma$, where F is the force applied on the particle and m and a are respectively the particle's mass and acceleration. Although other equations of motion could describe a protein's motion, that is, the time-dependent Schrodinger equation for quantum-mechanical systems [45] and Langevin's equation for stochastic systems [46], properties such as conservation of energy, linear and angular momentum, and time reversibility make the use of the laws of classical mechanics and Newton's equation more attractive.

Motions occurring in a protein can be classified into four categories according to scale and time: *Local motions* involve atomic fluctuation and side-chain motions, *medium-scale motions* include loop and helices motion, *large-scale motions* describe motions between domains, and finally *global motions* include helix–coil transition and the folding/unfolding process.

Originally, MD was introduced to study hard-sphere interactions [27, 28], simulation of liquid argon [47], and liquid water [48]. Protein MD simulation was conducted for the first time in 1977 on the *bovine pancreatic trypsin inhibitor* (BPTI) [49]. Since then, MD has given valuable information regarding protein fluctuations, stability, conformational changes, and especially folding pathways [50].

The main limitation of MD is its computational time. Typically, a single CPU requires around a day to simulate a nanosecond, whereas a protein folds generally on the tens of microsecond time scale [51]. Consequently, MD is often used in structure refinement rather than simulating the whole folding process starting from a random coil. Besides their essential use in computational methods, especially ab initio, MD simulation techniques have made a valuable contribution in experimental methods like X-ray crystallography and NMR.

32.4.3 Monte Carlo Simulations

The *Monte Carlo* (MC) method was established in the 1940s to approximately solve intractable problems [29]. It is based on generating several random samples of the problem and aggregating their results to constitute the final one. In general, Monte Carlo methods can be summarized in four steps: (1) definition of the domain of the problem, (2) generation of several random samples that cover the domain, (3) calculation of the result for each sample, and (4) estimation of the final solution based on the sample results.

Monte Carlo simulations are very popular to discover the conformational space of proteins. However, since they may converge toward local minima due to the jagged surface of the energy landscape, many extensions of MC have been proposed. They include multicanonical ensemble [52], entropic ensemble [53], *replica exchange MC* method (REM) [54], *parallel hyperbolic sampling* (PHS) [55], and *Monte Carlo with minimization* (MCM) [56] that has been used in Rosetta. Although historically *simulated annealing* (SA) [57] has been the most popular optimization algorithm due to its simplicity, it is usually outperformed by the most recent MC-based approaches [30].

32.4.4 LINUS

In 1995, Rose and Srinivasan introduced an ab initio Monte Carlo–based method called LINUS which stands for *local independently nucleated units of structure* [35, 58]. LINUS relies on a hierarchical procedure that simulates the folding process as discrete hierarchical phases. The rationale behind this approach comes from the decomposition of globular protein structures into secondary structures, supersecondary structures, domains, and so on [59, 60]. The term "folding by hierarchic condensation" was first introduced by Rose himself in 1979. He had proposed that close chain sites interacted to form small structures, which in turn interacted iteratively to form larger structures.

The essence of the hierarchical approach lies in constraining some favorable conformations found in previous stages, so that good structures are accumulated. The algorithm works as follows: It starts from an initial extended conformation where both the φ and ψ angles are set to $120°$ with a small interval of allowed interactions. After each iteration, this interval increases and a new conformation is chosen based on the Metropolis criterion [61]. Each iteration involves the random selection of three residues whose torsion angle values are amended, whereas bond angles and length are kept constant to "ideal" values [62]. At each stage a simplified energy function is used to assess the most favorable conformation among a set of candidates. The function only considers three main types of interactions: steric overlap, hydrogen bonds, and polarity, that is, hydrophobic burial. A protein's geometric representation in LINUS can be seen as medium grain where all nonhydrogen atoms are taken into account.

In 2000, LINUS contributed in CASP4 when new fold approaches were considered to be in their infancy [63]. Although their overall RMSDs ranged from 8.7 to 16.2 Å, some fragments of around 50 AAs displayed RMSDs of around 4 Å, which highlighted the strength of the method. Furthermore, from a secondary-structure prediction perspective, α-helix predictions were evaluated as one of the best among all competitors. LINUS is available to download at no cost at `http://roselab.jhu.edu/dist/index.html`. Unfortunately LINUS's latest contribution to the competition was in 2002.

32.4.5 ASTRO-FOLD

ASTRO-FOLD is considered one of the successful first-principle methods in PSP competition. It was created by Floudas and co-workers in 2003 [41] and has been in permanent development since then.

ASTRO-FOLD is a framework that combines several approaches [64]. Its main structure can be summarized in four main points.

1. α-Helices are predicted since they are observed as the first stage of hierarchical folding [65]. This phase uses an all-atom physics-based energy function called ECEPP/3, which takes into account electrostatic, bonded, nonbonded, and torsion angles [66].
2. Then, β-sheets are predicted based on a process called *hydrophobic collapse*. This occurs when hydrophobic side chains interact and assemble. This dramatic event has many consequences, including rejecting water molecules outside the protein, forming the hydrophobic core, and forming β-sheets. The integer linear programming approach [67] is used to formulate an objective function that evaluates hydrophobic interaction energy.
3. The third phase deals with the development of restraints as well as side-chain modeling.
4. Finally, the overall tertiary structure prediction involves a combination of several approaches: αBB global optimization, an algorithm based on branch-and-bound strategy [68]; the stochastic method of *conformational space annealing* (CSA) [69]; and an MD algorithm which is applied to the torsion angle space.

ASTRO-FOLD 2.0 ("FLOUDAS" was used as the group name) contributed to the latest CASP event, that is, CASP9, through the prediction of 47 models [70]. The majority of the structures showed a RMSD range between 2.0 and 8.0 Å. Four models were predicted with an RMSD below 1.80 Å. However, taking into account the average of all models submitted as "first models" for all targets, ASTRO-FOLD did not achieve good results.

32.5 AB INITIO PREDICTION WITH DATABASE INFORMATION

Instead of aiming at simulating the folding mechanism as physics-based ab initio approaches do, this category of methods focuses only on predicting as accurately as possible a protein's final configuration. As a consequence, it is reasonable to take advantage of the known 3D structures which are held in the PDB to extract peptide fragments, secondary structures, and statistical information.

The most successful methods in this category are called fragment based. The rationale behind these methods is that, at the local level, there is a strong correlation between an amino acid sequence and its structure [71]. Besides, it has been shown that incorporating information from independent secondary-structure predictions has improved scoring functions [72]. These methods, first, search in the PDB for known structure fragments which match subsequences of the protein of interest. Once candidate fragments have been selected, compact structures can be formed by randomly assembling fragments using, for example, the SA technique [73]. Then, with the aid of scoring functions the fitness of each conformation is evaluated and the most promising ones are optimized. Since scoring functions are loosely related to energy functions and fragment assembly along with optimization algorithms are conceptually similar to free-energy optimization, these approaches somehow abide by the law of physics that governs the protein-folding process. Consequently, they were originally categorized as ab initio. Nevertheless, they cannot be considered as a direct application of Anfinsen's hypothesis and do not have a protein sequence as sole input. However, as illustrated in CASP9, pure ab initio approaches remain less accurate than fragment-based techniques; see the Appendix.

32.5.1 FRAGFOLD

Although some researchers refer to Bowie and Eisenberg as being the small-fragment assembly pioneers [74], FRAGFOLD is considered the first fragment-based method developed by Jones in 1996 [13]. Its results in CASP2 (1996) seemed promising for a totally new approach and paved the way for the development of similar methods. Beside pairwise and solvation potentials, Jones took into consideration compactness of low-energy folds, hydrogen bonds, and steric overlaps to constitute a weight-based energy function. Its minimization was carried out using an SA-based approach. FRAGFOLD relies on four types of supersecondary structural fragments, that is, α-hairpin, α-corner, β-hairpin, and β-α-β unit, which are defined as motifs containing two or three sequential secondary structures extracted from a library of protein structures. The length of each supersecondary structure is between 9 and 31 residues.

Since then FRAGFOLD has been continuously improved, including an extended library of supersecondary structures [75], several enhancements of secondary-structure prediction algorithms, and the removal of the compactness-related term in their energy function [76]. Jones achieved excellent results in CASP9, where his system was ranked on average in the 24th place overall and 7th in the ab initio category (see Appendix). FRAGFOLD's main components, including THREADER [77] and PSIPRED [78], can be downloaded at `http://bioinf.cs.ucl.ac.uk`.

32.5.2 TASSER

TASSER is another successful fragment-based method and was initially created in 2004 by Zhang and Skolnick [42]. Later, it led to the development of two remarkably improved versions: Chunk-TASSER [43] and I-TASSER [44]. TASSER is a hierarchical approach that encompasses three phases which gave it its name: threading/assembly/refinement. The first step is based on a threading program called PROSPECTOR_3 [79]. It is based on an iterative sequence–structure alignment algorithm that results in three category targets— easy, medium, and hard—that depend on score value and alignment consistency. Then, the assembly step uses parallel hydrophobic Monte Carlo sampling by rearranging the template fragments [80]. In order to decrease computation, a preliminary model is built using only $C\alpha$ and side-chain coordinates. Finally, a refinement stage is performed using a clustering program called SPICKER [81]. The full-atom optimization is conducted using the CHARMM22 force field.

TASSER achieved an average RMSD of 5.4 Å on all CASP6's 90 targets. Further improvements were achieved at CASP7 with an average RMSD of 4.9 Å on 124 models [82] by using better templates from 3D-jury and applying two additional threading software, that is, SP^3 [83] and SPARKS [9]. In the latest CASP, TASSER participated using different versions. The group called Zhang, which represents I-TASSER, was the best ab initio server among all competitors. Moreover, it achieved second place overall (see the Appendix). TASSER is available online at `http://cssb.biology.gatech.edu/`.

32.5.3 ROSETTA

ROSETTA's principle is based on simulating the mutual effect of both local and global interactions in order to reach the final native conformation. Accordingly, after selecting fragments from libraries to construct secondary structures, nonlocal interactions are taken into consideration using scoring functions to evaluate the fitness of the conformations. The assembly phase is conducted by merging selected fragments using a MC SA heuristic search. The length of the fragments, which are extracted from the PDB via PSI-BLAST, is between three and nine residues. They are evaluated according to (1) minimum steric overlap, (2) appropriate torsion angles, and (3) secondary-structure prediction results using respectively PSIPRED [78], SAM-T99 [84], and JUFO [85]. An important particularity of ROSETTA is the exploitation of Bayes statistical theorem as a scoring function using a large database where sequences have known structures [86]:

$$P(\text{Structure}|\text{Sequence}) = P(\text{Structure})\frac{P(\text{Sequence}|\text{Structure})}{p(\text{Sequence})}$$

Two different energy functions are used in ROSETTA: a coarse-grained one that is faster but less accurate and a fine-grained one, or what is called *all-atoms* scoring functions to be used when high resolution is required. The main difference is that the former relies on the dihedral angles and the side chains are represented as one centroid. Details about all terms in each function are described in [87].

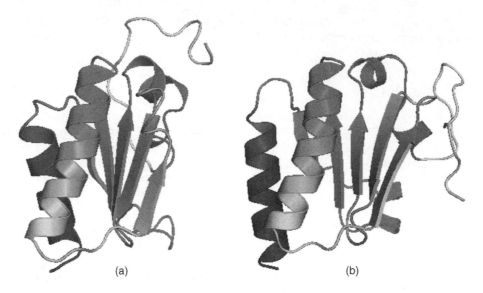

(a)　　　　　　　　　　　　　　　(b)

FIGURE 32.3 (a) Native structure of CASP7 target T0354 and (b) predicted structure by ROSETTA (right) with an RMSD of 3.3 Å over 90 residues. (Reprinted from R. Das et al. Structure prediction for CASP7 targets using extensive all-atom refinement with Rosetta@home. *Proteins: Structure, Function and Bioinformatics*, 69:118–128. Copyright 2007 with permission from Wiley.)

ROSETTA is arguably the most popular fragment assembly approach, and it was assessed as the most accurate de novo PSP by CASP7 when it contributed for the second time; see Figure 32.3 [88]. Besides, its results in FM targets in CASP were truly remarkable. In CASP9, Rosetta server achieved the eighth place in the ab initio category. All services related to ROSETTA, including downloads, can be found at `http://www.rosettacommons.org/`.

32.6 DISCUSSION AND CHALLENGES

Although more and more protein 3D structures have been resolved experimentally—on December 14, 2011, the PDB contained 77,878 entries—and this number increases at an exponential pace, the gap between the number of available sequences and known structures continues to widen dramatically; see Table 32.1. Consequently, computational techniques remain essential to protein structure prediction.

The state of the field of PSP has been monitored and quantitatively evaluated since 1994 by the biennial CASP event. This community-wide experiment has grown significantly from a set of 33 targets which attracted around 100 models (CASP1, 1994) to a set of 129 targets which led to the submission of more than 60,000 models (CASP9, 2010). Despite the fact that progress in CASP9 was a little bit disappointing compared with the previous ones, enormous advances have taken place in the three types of computational approaches since CASP started [24, 89]. However, they all suffer from inconsistency: Although they may be successful at predicting some targets, they fail for others. In particular, predictions for large- and medium-size proteins (i.e., 300+ residues) tend to be below acceptable levels. An attractive compromise would be to, at least, be able to assess a priori the quality of generated models. As a consequence, the development of *quality assessment* (QA) programs has become an important field of research. Although they are quite accurate at ranking a set of alternative models according to accuracy, their ability to evaluate the quality of a

TABLE 32.1   Comparison of Growth of PDB^a and UniProtKB/TrEMBL^b

Date	Number of Nonredundant Sequence Entries in UniProtKB/TrEMBL	Number of Known Structures Found in PDB
2011^c	18,510,272	77,878
2010	12,347,303	70,120
2009	8,926,016	59,790
2008	6,964,485	54,798
2007	5,072,048	47,829

^{a}http://www.pdb.org/pdb/statistics/contentGrowthChart.
do?content=total&seqid=100.
^{b}http://www.ebi.ac.uk/uniprot/TrEMBLstats/.
^{c}December 14, 2011: date of UniProtKB/TrEMBL latest release.

single model is still limited [90]. Moreover, models whose accuracy can be considered as equivalent as experimental techniques are still limited to *template-based Modeling* (TBM) associated with very high sequence identity [24]. Therefore, it can be concluded that, despite a lot of progress, there is still a lot of scope of improvement for protein structure prediction.

Analysis of the outcome of the latest CASP shows that ab initio methods are still considered for many successful groups as a backup plan when template-based techniques fail (see the Appendix). Consequently, the majority of algorithms/servers whose category is "hybrid" use ab initio as the last approach to be applied. This is mainly due to the facts that, first, relevant homology modeling is very accurate, and, second, ab initio methods have a very high computational cost even when parallel processing is available. In the ab initio category, it is clear that fragment-based techniques like TASSER, FRAGFOLD, and ROSETTA perform much better than pure ab initio ones like ASTRO-FOLD, which are rarely practical due to their additional computational complexities. It should also be mentioned that due to the small number of (FM) targets in CASP (e.g. only 4 out of 129 in CASP9), the experiment tends to favor model-based methods. This has led the CASP community to launch, in November 2011, a new competition called CASP ROLL dedicated to FM targets, which should allow a fairer assessment of ab initio methods.

Besides the computational issues stated above, it is important to realize that even if they were solved, PSP would remain a challenge for many classes of proteins. Indeed, nature has evolved proteins whose folding includes additional biological complexities which are rarely considered by any existing method. Here we will review four of these classes: membrane proteins, proteins whose folding is chaperone assisted, proteins with more than one stable structure, and intrinsically unstructured proteins.

While PSP methodologies generally target proteins located within the cell, membrane proteins are located in the membrane of a cell, which presents a very different chemical environment. As a consequence, membrane proteins, except for some peripheral enzymes, are not water soluble and their environment is heterogeneous and complicated; see Figure 32.4b [91]. These proteins are particularly important because not only do they represent around 30% of proteins found in eukaryotic cells [92] but also they are the target of more than 50% of current drugs [93]. Consequently, a deep understanding of their structure and function has been assessed as "invaluable" in the world of drug design [94]. However, the fact they are not water soluble represents a serious obstacle to predict their structures experimentally [91]. As a consequence, up to November 11, 2011, only 304 structures have been determined (http://blanco.biomol.uci.edu/mpstruc/listAll/list), which represents only 0.4% of the total number of proteins found in the PDB. The small number of high-resolution templates available so far has limited advances in computational approaches, especially comparative modeling techniques which rely on the availability of templates [95]. As a consequence, prediction of membrane proteins is currently excluded from CASP. Attempts have been made to predict these proteins using ab initio methods. However, this means that, besides the AA sequence, a detailed structural and thermodynamic knowledge of the membrane environment is also required [96]. Ab initio methods with membrane database information, such as ROSETTA [97], have been proposed but with limited success. Recent research on helix–turn–helix supersecondary structures, also known

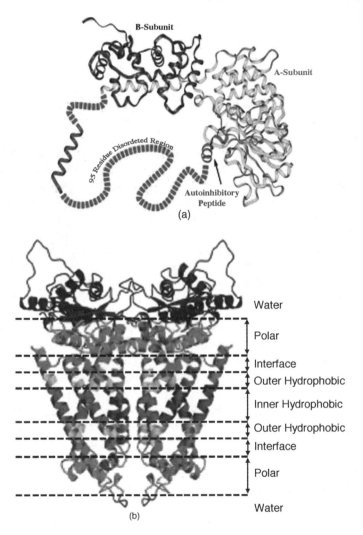

(a)

(b)

FIGURE 32.4 (a) The 3D structure of a protein called *calcineurin*. The discete part shows a 95-residue disordered region. (b) The bilayer and surrounding solvent region of membrane proteins is divided into five layers: Water-exposed, interface, outer hydrophobic, and inner hydrophobic. [(a) Reprinted from A. K. Dunker et al. Intrinsically disordered protein. *Journal of Molecular Graphics and Modelling*, 19:26–59. Copyright 2001 with permission from Elsevier. (b) Reprinted from V. Yarov-Yarovoy et al. Multipass membrane protein structure prediction using Rosetta. *Proteins: Structure, Function and Bioinformatics*, 62:1010–1025. Copyright 2005 with permission from Wiley.)

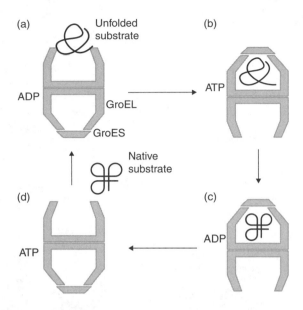

FIGURE 32.5   Model of chaperone-assisted folding. (Reprinted with permission from J. C. Young et al. Pathways of chaperone-mediated protein folding in the cytosol. *Nature Reviews Molecular Cell Biology*, 5:781–791, 2004.)

as *helix packing*, appears promising to predict structures of α helical *transmembrane* (TM) protein by narrowing the search space of the possible conformations due to their prevalence and similarities [98].

In addition to membrane proteins which fold in a nonaqueous environment, some proteins are not able to fold correctly on their own. They require the assistance of a specific type of protein, called *chaperones*, to conform to their proper 3D structures [99] or to prevent them from aggregating [100]. Those molecular chaperones can distinguish between folded and unfolded proteins by their ability to recognize hydrophobic AAs in the unfolded ones [101]. Since the role of chaperones has not been well understood biologically and they create folding environments which are several orders of magnitude more complex than those currently modeled (see Figure 32.5), existing PSP methods do not consider chaperone-assisted folding and are unlikely to do it for the foreseeable future.

Whereas PSP methods attempt to find the structure of a protein, it has been shown that some proteins can have more than one partially folded intermediate state that may play a critical biological role [102, 103]. The *molten globule* (MG) is a distinct intermediate conformational state, but not very thermodynamically stable, that takes place between the unfolded state (U) and the native one (N) for most proteins; see Figure 32.6 [104]. MG is characterized by its compact size with the presence of significant amounts of most secondary structures, however with the absence of a specific tertiary structure due to the tight packing of side chains and high mobility of the loops [105]. A popular study suggests that MG can be seen as a third phase [102] where the N/U/MG diagram of protein phases is similar to the solid/vapor/liquid diagram of fluid phases. In other words, each state has its own thermodynamic phase which corresponds to a local free energy. MG along with the jagged surface of the energy landscape represents a real obstacle, especially for heuristic algorithms in ab initio methods. MGs are currently not addressed by PSP.

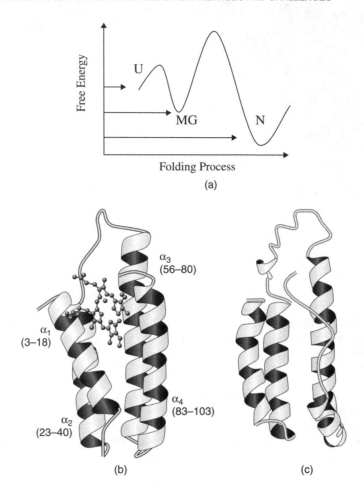

FIGURE 32.6 (a) Free energy of MG state is lower than unfolded state but higher than native one. (b, c) Native and molten globule structures of cytochrome b_{562}. (Reprinted from K. E. Laidig and V. Daggett. Molecular dynamics simulations of apocytochrome b562—The highly ordered limit of molten globules. In *Folding and Design*, Vol. 1, pp. 335–346. Copyright 1996 with permission from Elsevier.)

Finally, the *intrinsically unstructured proteins* (IUPs), also known as *natively unfolded* or *intrinsically disordered proteins* (IDPs), may be the most interesting type of proteins by breaching the standard wisdom about proteins. They simply lack, partially or completely, stable tertiary structure but are able to perform their functions in the cell (see Figure 32.4a). Such a finding was first seen in 1996 [106] and has been considered so far the first experimental proof that the lack of structure does not necessarily make some kind of protein harmful or even useless and thus an exception to the conventional rule of proteins [6]. It has been suggested that 32% of all human proteins could have some unstructured regions in which the lock-and-key concept cannot be applied [107]. To date, around 600 partially or totally unstructured proteins have been recorded in the Database of Protein Disorder (http://www.disprot.org) [108]. Unstructured parts of proteins are indeed a problem in predicting the structure of such molecules; however, they play a critical role in many biological functions. For this reason, the CASP community has created a category since

CASP5 to predict the disordered regions in proteins [109]. Since then, this category has been gaining importance; more than 5000 models were submitted in CASP9 [110].

32.7 APPENDIX: CASP9

Besides the main category of CASP9, which is *tertiary structure* (TS) prediction (the heart of this survey), four additional categories exist in CASP9: *residue–residue* (RR) contact pre-

TABLE 32.2   Subset of CASP9 Results

Rank	Ab Initio Rank	Group Name	Category	URL
1		Mufold	Hybrid	
2	1	Zhang	Fragment based	http://zhanglab.ccmb.med.umich.edu/I-TASSER
3		elofsson	Hybrid	http://www.pcons.net/
4		Seok-meta	Hybrid	
5	2	Chicken_George	Fragment based	
6	3	RecombineIt	Fragment based	
7	4	McGuffin	Fragment based	
8		prmls	Hybrid	
9	5	QUARK	Fragment based	http://zhanglab.ccmb.med.umich.edu/QUARK
10		fams-multi	Comparative modeling	
11	6	Sternberg	Fragment based	
12		TASSER	Hybrid	http://cssb.biology.gatech.edu/
13		RaptorX-MSA	Hybrid	http://velociraptor.ttic.edu
14		TMD3D	Comparative modeling	http://www.proteinhub.net
15		RaptorX	Hybrid	http://velociraptor.ttic.edu.
16	7	Jones-UCL	Fragment based	http://bioinf.cs.ucl.ac.uk
17		bujnicki-kolinski	Fragment based	
18		GeneSilico	Hybrid	
19	8	BAKER	Fragment based	http://www.rosettacommons.org
20		BIO_ICM	Comparative modeling + fold recognition	
21		KnowMIN	Comparative modeling	http://csb.stanford.edu/koba_stable/
22		LEE	Hybrid	
23		HHpredA	Comparative modeling	
24		Bilab-solo	Hybrid	
25		MULTICOM-NOVEL	Comparative modeling	http://casp.rnet.missouri.edu/multicom_3d.html.

diction, *disordered regions* (DR) prediction, function (binding sites) (FN) prediction, and QA. The main criterion CASP uses to assess prediction accuracy is the GDT_TS (GlobalDistanceTest_TotalScore), where GDT_TS = (GDT_P1 + GDT_P2 + GDT_P4 + GDT_P8)/4. GDT_Pn is the percent of predicted residues whose RMSD is less than or equal nÅ, where $n \in \{1, 2, 4, 8\}$.

Table 32.2 shows a subset of CASP9's official results found at (`http://predictioncenter.org/casp9/groups_analysis.cgi`). This subset shows the best 25 groups were related to the TS category only. Groups are ordered based on the models submitted as "first models." Besides the overall rank and the group name, we have added the corresponding ab initio rank, category, and URL (if any). Some groups that used the same server were summarized by mentioning the best group.

REFERENCES

1. A. Brazma, H. Parkinson, T. Schlitt, and M. Shojatalab. A quick introduction to elements of biology—cells, molecules, genes, functional genomics, microarrays. European Bioinformatics Institute, 2001. Available: `http://www.ebi.ac.uk/microarray/biology_intro.html`.

2. A. Bairoch. The ENZYME database in 2000. *Nucleic Acids Res*, 28(1):304–305, 2000.

3. C. B. Anfinsen, E. Haber, M. Sela, and F. H. White. The kinetics of formation of native ribonuclease during oxidation of the reduced polypeptide chain. *Proc. Natl. Acad. Sci. USA*, 47:1309–1314, 1961.

4. C. M. Dobson. The structural basis of protein folding and its links with human disease. *Phil. Trans. R. Soc. Lond. B*, 356:133–145, 2001.

5. G. Kolata. Trying to crack the second half of the genetic code. *Science*, 233:1037–1039, 1986.

6. A. K. Dunker and R. W. Kriwacki. The orderly chaos of proteins. *Sci. Am.*, 304:68–73, 2011.

7. H. M. Berman, J. Westbrook, Z. Feng, G. Gilliland, T. N. Bhat, H. Weissig, I. N. Shindyalov, and P. E. Bourne. The Protein Data Bank. *Nucleic Acids Res.*, 28:235–242, 2000.

8. R. Zwanzig, A. Szabo, and B. Bagchi. Levinthal's paradox. *Proc. Natl. Acad. Sci. USA*, 89:20–22, 1992.

9. H. Zhou and Y. Zhou. Fold recognition by combining sequence profiles derived from evolution and from depth-dependent structural alignment of fragments. *Proteins*, 58:321–328, 2005.

10. K. A. Dill, S. B. Ozkan, M. S. Shell, and T. R. Weikl. The protein folding problem. *Annu. Rev. Biophys.*, 37:289–316, 2008.

11. A. Hagler, E. Euler, and S. Lifson. Energy functions for peptides and proteins I. Derivation of a consistent force field including the hydrogen bond from amide crystals. *J. Am. Chem. Soc.*, 96:5319–5327, 1974.

12. P. Bradley, K. M. Misura, and D. Baker. Toward high-resolution de novo structure prediction for small proteins. *Science*, 309(5742):1868–1871, 2005.

13. D. T. Jones. Successful ab initio prediction of the tertiary structure of NK-Lysin using multiple sequences and recognized supersecondary structural motifs. *Proteins*, 1:185–191, 1997.

14. F. Cramer. Emil Fischer's lock-and-key hypothesis after 100 years—Towards a supracellular chemistry. In J.-P. Behr (Ed.), *Perspectives in Supramolecular Chemistry: The Lock-and-Key Principle*, Vol. 1. Wiley, Chichester, 2007.

15. H. Wu. Studies on denaturation of proteins. XIII. A theory of denaturation. *Chinese J. Physiol.*, 5:321–344, 1931.

16. F. Sanger, and E. O. P. Thompson. The amino-acid sequence in the glycyl chain of insulin. 1. The investigation of lower peptides from partial hydrolysates. *Biochem. J.*, 53:353–366, 1953.

17. F. Sanger and E. O. P. Thompson. The amino-acid sequence in the glycyl chain of insulin. 2. The investigation of peptides from enzymic hydrolysates. *Biochem. J.*, 53:366–374, 1953.

18. T. Takano. Structure of myoglobin refined at 2.0 Å resolution. II. Structure of deoxymyoglobin from sperm whale. *J. Mol. Biol.,* 110:569–584, 1977.

19. G. N. Ramachandran, C. Ramakrishnan, and V. Sasisekharan. Stereochemistry of polypeptide chain configurations.*J. Mol. Biol.*, 7:95–99, 1963.

20. G. N. Ramachandran and V. Sasisekharan. Conformations of polypeptides and proteins. *Adv. Protein Chem.*, 23:283–437, 1968.

21. C. Levinthal. Are the pathways for protein folding? *J. Chem. Phys.*, 65:44–45, 1968.

22. C. B. Anfinsen. Principles that govern the folding of protein chains. *Science*, 181(4096):223–230, 1973.

23. J. Moult, J. T. Pedersen, R. Judson, and K. Fidelis. A large-scale experiment to assess protein structure prediction methods. *Proteins*, 23:2–5, 1995.

24. J. Moult, K. Fidelis, A. Kryshtafovych, and A. Tramontano. Critical assessment of methods of protein structure prediction (CASP)—Round IX. *Proteins: Struct., Funct. Bioinformatics*, 79:1–5, 2011.

25. C. A. Floudas. Computational methods in protein structure prediction. *Biotechnol. Bioeng.*, 97:207–213, 2007.

26. M. Punta, L. R. Forrest, H. Bigelow, A. Kernytsky, J. Liu, and B. Rost. Membrane protein prediction methods. *Methods*, 41:460–474, 2007.

27. B. J. Alder and T. E. J. Wainwright. Phase transition for a hard sphere system. *J. Chem. Phys.*, 27:1208 1209, 1957.

28. B. J. Alder and T. E. Wainwright. Studies in molecular dynamics. I. General method. *J. Chem. Phys.*, 31:459, 1959.

29. N. Metropolis. The beginning of the Monte Carlo method. *Los Alamos Sci.* (1987 Special Issue dedicated to Stanisław Ulam):125–130, 1987.

30. J. Lee, S. Wu, and Y. Zhang. Ab initio protein structure prediction. In D. J. Rigden (Ed.), *From Protein Structure to Function with Bioinformatics.* Springer, London, 2009, pp. 1–26.

31. S. Sun. Reduced representation model of protein structure prediction: Statistical potential and genetic algorithms. *Protein Sci.*, 2:762–85, 1993.

32. J. Pilardy, C. Czaplewski, A. Liwo, W. J. Wedemeyer, J. Lee, D. R. Ripoll, P. Arlukowicz, S. Oldziej, Y. A. Arnautova, and H. A. Scheraga. Development of physics-based energy functions that predict medium-resolution structures for proteins of the a,b, and a/b structural classes. *J. Phys. Chem.*, 105:7299–7311, 2001.

33. R. Agarwala, S. Batzogloa, V. Dančík, S. E. Decatur, S. Hannenhalli, M. Farach, S. Muthukrishnan, and S. Skiena. Local rules for protein folding on a triangular lattice and generalized hydrophobicity in the HP model. *J. Comp. Biol.*, 4(3):276–296, 1997.

34. W. E. Hart and A. Newman. Protein structure prediction with lattice models. In S. Aluru (Ed.), *Handbook of Computational Molecular Biology*, CRC Computer and Information Science Series. Chapman & Hall, Boca Raton, FL, 2005.

35. R. Srinivasan, P. J. Fleming, and G. D. Rose. Ab initio protein folding using LINUS. *Methods Enzymol.*, 383:48–66, 2004.

36. C. A. Rohl, C. E. M. Strauss, D. Chivian, and D. Baker. Modeling structurally variable regions in homologous proteins with Rosetta. *Proteins: Struct. Funct. Bioinformatics*, 55:656–677, 2004.

37. J. L. Klepeis, M. T. Pieja, and C. A. Floudas. Hybrid global optimization algorithms for protein structure prediction: Alternating hybrids. *Biophys. J.*, 84:869–882, 2003.

38. B. R. Brooks, R. E. Bruccoleri, B. D. Olafson, D. J. States, S. Swaminathan, and M. Karplus. CHARMM: A program for macromolecular energy minimization, and dynamics calculations. *J. Comp. Chem.*, 4:187, 1983.

39. D. A. Pearlman, D. A. Case, J. W. Caldwell, W. R. Ross, T. E. Cheatham III, S. DeBolt, D. Ferguson, G. Seibel, and P. Kollman. AMBER, a computer program for applying molecular mechanics, normal mode analysis, molecular dynamics and free energy calculations to elucidate the structures and energies of molecules. *Comp. Phys. Commun.*, 91:1–41, 1995.

40. S. Oldziej, C. Czaplewski, A. Liwo, M. Chinchio, M. Nanias, J. A. Vila, M. Khalili, Y. A. Arnautova, A. Jagielska, M. Makowski, H. D. Schafroth, R. Kazmierkiewicz, D. R. Ripoll, J. Pillardy, J. A. Saunders, Y. K. Kang, K. D. Gibson, and H. A. Scheraga. Physics-based protein-structure prediction using a hierarchical protocol based on the UNRES force field: Assessment in two blind tests. *Proc. Natl. Acad. Sci. USA*, 102(21):7547–7552, 2005.

41. J. L. Klepeis and C. A. Floudas. ASTRO-FOLD: A combinatorial and global optimization framework for ab initio prediction of three dimensional structures of proteins from the amino acid sequence. *Biophys. J.*, 85:2119–2146, 2003.

42. Y. Zhang and J. Skolnick. Automated structure prediction of weakly homologous proteins on a genomic scale. *Proc. Natl. Acad. Sci. USA*, 101:7594–7599, 2004.

43. H. Zhou and J. Skolnick. Ab initio protein structure prediction using chunk-TASSER. *Biophys. J.*, 93(5):1510–1518, 2007.

44. S. Wu, J. Skolnick, and Y. Zhang. Ab initio modeling of small proteins by iterative TASSER simulations. *BMC Biol.*, 5:17, 2007.

45. E. Schrödinger. An undulatory theory of the mechanics of atoms and molecules. *Phys. Rev.*, 28(6):1049–1070, 1926.

46. W. T. Coffey, Y. P. Kalmykov, and J. T. Waldron. *The Langevin Equation: With Applications to Stochastic Problems in Physics, Chemistry and Electrical Engineering.* World Scientific, Singapore, 1996.

47. A. Rahman. Correlations in the motion of atoms in liquid argon. *Phys. Rev.*, 136:405–411, 1964.

48. F. H. Stillinger and A. J. Rahman. Improved simulation of liquid water by molecular dynamics. *J. Chem. Phys.*, 60:1545–1557, 1974.

49. J. A. McCammon, B. R. Gelin, and M. Karplus. Dynamics of folded proteins. *Nature*, 267:585–590, 1977.

50. Y. Duan and P. A. Kollman. Pathways to a protein folding intermediate observed in a 1-microsecond simulation in aqueous solution. *Science*, 282(5389):740–744, 1998.

51. V. A. Voelz, G. R. Bowman, K. Beauchamp, and V. S. Pande. Molecular simulation of ab initio protein folding for a millisecond folder NTL9(1–39). *J. Am. Chem. Soc.*, 132:1526–1528, 2010.

52. B. A. Berg and T. Neuhaus. Multicanonical ensemble: A new approach to simulate first-order phase transitions. *Phys. Rev. Lett.*, 68(1):9–12, 1992.

53. J. Lee. New Monte Carlo algorithm: Entropic sampling. *Phys. Rev. Lett.*, 71(2):211–214, 1993.

54. D. Kihara, H. Lu, A. Kolinski, and J. Skolnick. TOUCHSTONE: An ab initio protein structure prediction method that uses threading-based tertiary restraints. *Proc. Natl. Acad. Sci. USA*, 98(18):10125–10130, 2001.

55. Y. Zhang, A. Kolinski, and J. Skolnick. TOUCHSTONE II: A new approach to ab initio protein structure prediction. *Biophys. J.*, 85(2):1145–1164, 2003.

56. Z. Li and H. A. Scheraga. Monte Carlo-minimization approach to the multiple-minima problem in protein folding. *Proc. Natl. Acad. Sci. USA*, 84(19):6611–6615, 1987.

57. S. Kirkpatrick, C. D. Gelatt, and M. P. Vecchi. Optimization by simulated annealing. *Science*, 220(4598):671–680, 1983.

58. R. Srinivasan and G. D. Rose. LINUS: A hierarchic procedure to predict the fold of a protein. *Proteins: Struct. Funct. Bioinformatics*, 22:81–99, 1995.

59. G. M. Crippen. The tree structural organization of proteins. *J. Mol. Biol.*, 126:315–332, 1978.

60. G. D. Rose. Hierarchic organization of domains in globular proteins. *J. Mol. Biol.*, 134:447–470, 1979.

61. N. Metropolis, A. W. Rosenbluth, M. N. Rosenbluth, A. H. Teller, and E. Teller. Equation of calculations by fast computing machines. *J. Chem. Phys.*, 21:1087–1092, 1953.

62. R. A. Engh and R. Huber. Accurate bond and angle parameters for X-ray protein structure refinement. *Acta Cryst.*, A47:392–400, 1991.

63. R. Srinivasan and G. D. Rose. Ab initio prediction of protein structure using LINUS. *Proteins: Struct. Funct. Bioinformatics*, 47:489–495, 2002.

64. C. A. Floudas, H. K. Fung, S. R. McAllister, M. Mönnigmann, and R. Rajgaria. Advances in protein structure prediction and de novo protein design: A review. *Chem. Eng. Sci.*, 61:966–988, 2006.

65. J. L. Klepeis and C. A. Floudas. Ab initio prediction of helical segments of polypeptides. *J. Comput. Chem.*, 23:246–266, 2002.

66. G. Nemethy, K. D. Gibson, K. A. Palmer, C. N. Yoon, G. Paterlini, A. Zagari, S. Rumsey, and H. A. Scheraga. Energy parameters in polypeptides. X. Improved geometrical parameters and nonbonded interactions for use in the ECEPP/3 algorithm, with application to proline-containing peptides. *J. Phys. Chem.*, 96:6472–6484, 1992.

67. C. A. Floudas. *Nonlinear and Mixed-Integer Optimization: Fundamentals and Applications.* Oxford University Press, New York, 1995.

68. C. S. Adjiman, I. P. Androulakis, C. D. Maranas, and C. A. Floudas. A global optimization method, aBB, for process design. *Comput. Chem. Eng.*, 20:S419–S424, 1996.

69. J. Lee, H. A. Scheraga, and S. Rackovsky. New optimization method for conformational energy calculations on polypeptides: Conformational space annealing. *J. Computat. Chem.*, 18:1222–1232, 1997.

70. A. Subramani, Y. Wei, and C. A. Floudas. ASTRO-FOLD 2.0: An enhanced framework for protein structure prediction. *AIChE J.*, 58:1619–1637, 2011.

71. W. Lu and H. Liu. Correlations between amino acids at different sites in local sequences of protein fragments with given structural patterns. *Chin. J. Chem. Phys.,* 20:71, 2007

72. K. T. Simons, I. Ruczinski, C. Kooperberg, B. A. Fox, C. Bystroff, and D. Baker. Improved recognition of native-like protein structures using a combination of sequence-dependent and sequence-independent features of proteins. *Proteins*, 34:82–95, 1999.

73. S. Kirkpatrick, C. D. Gelatt, and M. P. Vecchi. Optimization by simulated annealing. *Science,* 220(4598):671–680, 1983.

74. J. U. Bowie and D. Eisenberg. An evolutionary approach to folding small alpha-helical proteins that uses sequence information and an empirical guiding fitness function. *Proc. Natl. Acad. Sci. USA*, 91(10):4436–4440, 1994.

75. D. T. Jones. (2001), Predicting novel protein folds by using FRAGFOLD. *Proteins: Struct., Funct. Bioinformatics*, 45:127–132, 2001.

76. D. T. Jones and L. J. McGuffin. Assembling novel protein folds from supersecondary structural fragments. *Proteins: Struct., Funct. Genet.*, 53:480–485, 2003.

77. D. T. Jones. THREADER: Protein sequence threading by double dynamic programming. In S. Salzberg, D. Searls, and S. Kasif (Eds.), *Computational Methods in Molecular Biology.* Elsevier Science, Amsterdam, 1998, Chapter 13.

78. D. T. Jones. Protein secondary structure prediction based on position-specific scoring matrices. *J. Mol. Biol.*, 292:195–202, 1999.

79. J. Skolnick, D. Kihara, and Y. Zhang. Development and large scale benchmark testing of the PROSPECTOR_3 threading algorithm. *Proteins*, 56:502–518, 2004.

80. Y. Zhang, A. Arakaki, and J. Skolnick. TASSER: An automated method for the prediction of protein tertiary structures in CASP6. *Proteins*, 61:91–98, 2005.

81. Y. Zhang and J. Skolnick. SPICKER: A clustering approach to identify near-native protein folds. *J. Comput. Chem.*, 25(6):865–871, 2004.

82. H. Zhou, S. B. Pandit, S. Y. Lee, J. Borreguero, H. Chen, L. Wroblewska, and J. Skolnick. Analysis of TASSER-based CASP7 protein structure prediction results. *Proteins: Struct. Funct. Bioinformatics*, 69:90–97, 2007.

83. H. Zhou and Y. Zhou. Single-body residue-level knowledge-based energy score combined with sequence-profile and secondary structure information for fold recognition. *Proteins*, 55:1005–1013, 2004.

84. K. Karplus, C. Barrett, and R. Hughey. Hidden Markov models for detecting remote protein homologies. *Bioinformatics*, 14:846–856, 1998.

85. J. Meiler, M. Müller, A. Zeidler, and F. Schmäschke. Generation and evaluation of dimension-reduced amino acid parameter representations by artificial neural networks. *J. Mol. Model*, 7:360–369, 2001.

86. K. T. Simons, C. Kooperberg, E. Huang, and D. Baker. Assembly of protein tertiary structures from fragments with similar local sequences using simulated annealing and Bayesian scoring functions. *J. Mol. Biol.*, 268:209–225, 1997.

87. C. A. Rohl, C. E. Strauss, K. M. Misura, and D. Baker. Protein structure prediction using Rosetta. *Methods Enzymol.*, 383:66–93, 2004.

88. R. Jauch, H. C. Yeo, P. R. Kolatkar, and N. D. Clarke. Assessment of CASP7 structure predictions for template free targets. *Proteins,* 69(Suppl. 8):57–67, 2007.

89. A. Kryshtafovych, K. Fidelis, and J. Moult. CASP9 results compared to those of previous CASP experiments. *Proteins*, 79(10):196–207, 2011.

90. A. Kryshtafovych, K. Fidelis, and A. Tramontano. Evaluation of model quality predictions in CASP9. *Proteins: Struct. Funct. Bioinformatics*, 79:91–106, 2011.

91. T. Cross, S. Mukesh, Y. Myunggi, and Z. Huan-Xiang. Influence of solubilizing environments on membrane protein structures. *Trends Biochem. Sci.*, 36:117–125, 2011.

92. A. L. Hopkins and C. R. Groom. The druggable genome. *Nat. Rev. Drug. BMC Bioinformatics*, 11:533, 2002.

93. S. H. White. Biophysical dissection of membrane proteins. *Nature*, 459:344–346, 2009.

94. S. Ahamd, Y. H. Singh, Y. Paudel, T. Mori, Y. Sugita, and K. Mizuguchi. Integrated prediction of one-dimensional structural features and their relationships with conformational flexibility in helical membrane proteins. *BMC Bioinformatics*, 11:533, 2010.

95. L. R. Forrest, C. L. Tang, and B. Honig. On the accuracy of homology modeling and sequence alignment methods applied to membrane proteins. *Biophys. J.*, 91:508–517, 2006.

96. V. Goder, T. Junne, and M. Spiess. Sec61p contributes to signal sequence orientation according to the positive-inside rule. *Mol. Biol. Cell*, 15:1470–1478, 2004.

97. V. Yarov-Yarovoy, J. Schonbrun, and D. Baker. Multipass membrane protein structure prediction using Rosetta. *Proteins*, 62:1010–1025, 2006.

98. R. F. S. Walters and W. F. De Grado. Helix-packing motifs in membrane proteins. *Proc. Natl. Acad. Sci.*, 103:13658–13663, 2006.

99. S. Lee and F. T. Tsai. Molecular chaperones in protein quality control. *J. Biochem. Mol. Biol.*, 38:259–265, 2005.

100. F. U. Hartl and M. Hayer-Hartl. Molecular chaperones in the cytosol: From nascent chain to folded protein. *Science*, 295:1852–1858, 2002.

101. F. Engin and G. S. Hotamisligil. Restoring endoplasmic reticulum function by chemical chaperones: An emerging therapeutic approach for metabolic diseases. *Diabet. Obesity Metab.*, 12:108–115, 2010.

102. V. S. Pande and D. S. Rokhsar. Is the molten globule a third phase of proteins? *Proc. Natl. Acad. Sci. USA*, 95:1490–1494, 1998.

103. K. E. Laidig and V. Daggett. Molecular dynamics simulations of apocytochrome b562—The highly ordered limit of molten globules. *Folding and Design*, 1(5):335–346, 1996.

104. O. B. Ptitsyn. Molten globule and protein folding. *Adv. Prot. Chem.*, 47:83–229, 1995.

105. L. Regan. Molten globules move into action. *Proc. Natl. Acad. Sci. USA*, 100:3553–3554, 2003.

106. R. W. Kriwacki, L. Hengst, L. Tennant, S. I. Reed, and P. E. Wright. Structural Studies of p21$^{\text{Waf1/Cip1/Sdi1}}$ in the free and Cdk2-bound state: Conformational disorder mediates binding diversity. *Proc. Nat. Acad. Sci. USA*, 93:11504–11509, 1996.

107. Y. Cheng, T. LeGall, C. J. Oldfield, A. K. Dunker, and V. N. Uversky. Abundance of intrinsic disorder in protein associated with cardiovascular disease. *Biochemistry*, 45:10448–10460, 2006.

108. M. Sickmeier, J. A. Hamilton, T. LeGall, V. Vacic, M. S. Cortese, A. Tantos, B. Szabo, P. Tompa, J. Chen, V. N. Uversky, Z. Obradovic, and A. K. Dunker. DisProt: The database of disordered proteins. *Nucleic Acids Res.*, 35:D786–793, 2007.

109. E. Melamud and J. Moult. Evaluation of disorder predictions in CASP5. *Proteins: Struct. Funct. Bioinformatics*, 53:561–565, 2003.

110. B. Monastyrskyy, K. Fidelis, J. Moult, A. Tramontano, and A. Kryshtafovych. Evaluation of disorder predictions in CASP9. *Proteins: Struct. Funct. Bioinformatics*, 79:107–118, 2011.

CHAPTER 33

OVERVIEW OF CLASSIFICATION METHODS TO SUPPORT HIV/AIDS CLINICAL DECISION MAKING

KHAIRUL A. KASMIRAN,[1] ALI AL MAZARI,[1] ALBERT Y. ZOMAYA,[1] and ROGER J. GARSIA[2]

[1]School of Information Technologies, The University of Sydney, Sydney, Australia
[2]Department of Clinical Immunology, Royal Prince Alfred Hospital, Sydney, Australia

Acquired immunodeficiency syndrome (AIDS) is a disease which still has no cure. Despite dramatic advances in medical science, the latest UNAIDS report in 2012 estimated that 34 million people live infected with human immunodeficiency virus (HIV), the virus that causes AIDS [1]. The treatments available do dramatically slow down or even reverse the progression to AIDS, prolonging life and allowing a better quality of life for the HIV/AIDS patient. However, optimal application of these treatments depends on a number of factors which relate to the patient, the HIV virus, and their complex interaction. The development of sophisticated bioinformatics-assisted classification methods suitable for use in understanding host–virus interactions and in guiding therapeutic decisions remains an area of intense interest and research activity for laboratory-based clinical teams.

Previous research has introduced many bioinformatics classification methods for reporting HIV parameters based on genotype correlated with phenotype. Assessing their true contribution to clinical decision making is problematic, as in many cases the data have only become available in retrospect. From many studies it has emerged that population viral gene sequencing can contribute toward identifying and evaluating HIV drug resistance, coreceptor usage, mutation evolution, subtype, and the antiretroviral treatment applied—factors that can have some bearing on the future progression of HIV/AIDS in an individual patient and in communities at large. This chapter seeks to provide a brief description of these methods, potentially highlighting the significant relationships between HIV genotype and phenotype.

33.1 PREDICTING RESISTANCE TO DRUGS

The current resistance of an HIV infection to a particular antiretroviral drug determines the effectiveness of the drug in keeping viral loads low and has a direct impact on the well-being of a patient. Resistance can occur when HIV proteins such as its protease and reverse

Biological Knowledge Discovery Handbook: Preprocessing, Mining, and Postprocessing of Biological Data, First Edition. Edited by Mourad Elloumi and Albert Y. Zomaya.
© 2014 John Wiley & Sons, Inc. Published 2014 by John Wiley & Sons, Inc.

transcriptase enzymes gather mutations, preventing antiretroviral drugs from interacting effectively with them. A measure of intrinsic sensitivity to antiviral drugs is the virus IC_{50} or the drug concentration needed to inhibit viral replication by half. In vitro culture-based or molecular assays can be used to directly estimate the resistance of a specific HIV sample [2]. However, they are expensive to use routinely and the estimate does not take patient factors into account [3]. A more practical option is to indirectly determine the resistance through genetic analysis. Explicit expert-derived rules [4–6] have been derived from the literature for this purpose. However, their current role depends on the speed of which new knowledge is published and assessed, and they may not reflect the latest developments in the evolution of the HIV virus [7]. Therefore, there is interest in using computational methods to extract these rules from the patient data itself, and a number of methods using various techniques have been developed.

One tool used to infer from a patient's HIV genotype the level of resistance to specific drugs is the *decision tree*. It [8, 9] has the advantages of being simple and easy to understand, and it is clear how the decision tree arrives at a particular conclusion. Example decision trees specific to HIV can be found in Beerenwinkel et al. [10] depicting the rules that classify dichotomously whether a HIV-1 genotype is resistant or susceptible to various drugs, including zidovudine, nevirapine, and amprenavir. The method used was C4.5 [8] with partitions determined by the discriminative information provided by a particular codon.

Apart from decision trees, *support vector machines* (SVMs) have also been employed by Beerenwinkel et al. [11, 12]. The initial investigation used linear SVMs as a binary classifier, treating protein sequences as points in a coordinate space and establishing a linear boundary that divides the coordinate space into two areas, the resistant sequence area and the susceptible sequence area [11]. SVM performance was comparable to decision trees. A follow-up investigation used linear SVMs to build a *linear regression model* that stated how resistance varies with different protein sequences with the resistance then classified as either resistant or susceptible based on a two-component *Gaussian mixture model* [12].

Resistance classification via *regression* has also been investigated using *linear models* and cutoff thresholds. In [13], the linear model developed was used to predict the IC_{50} fold change from protease and reverse transcriptase mutations, and the research showed that a linear model can have high performance in predicting resistance. The research also suggested that interactions between mutations may not be of significant importance, but follow-up research dispelled that notion and showed that interactions need to be taken into account [14]. In [15], the variable predicted was the IC_{50} category (resistant or sensitive), and the model was used to determine which mutations best predict resistance to drugs.

Resistance classification can also be done via *clustering*, where genotypes that are similar according to some measure are grouped together. Further interpretation of the clusters is needed to determine their general level of resistance, but once that is done, the resistance of new genotypes can be estimated based on their cluster membership. A clustering technique that has been used in the HIV literature is *Kohonen networks* with *metaclassing* [16]. In this study, the authors performed clustering on both structural and sequence features derived from HIV genotypes and found that drug resistance can be predicted from either type of feature.

For comparison between methods, Rhee et al. [17] evaluated five statistical learning methods (*decision trees, neural networks, support vector regression, least-squares regression, and least-angle regression*) in classifying genetic sequences as susceptible, low/intermediate resistant, or highly resistant to a particular drug. Least-angle regression was found to perform significantly better than the other methods.

33.2   PREDICTING CORECEPTOR USAGE

The HIV-1 virus enters target cells through two entry points: one is the CD4 receptor and the other is either the coreceptor CCR5 or CXCR4 [18]. CCR5-using viruses dominate the early stage of infection, and then in around 50% of infected patients, CXCR4-using viruses start to appear. This switch is of interest to clinicians for it has been associated with quicker CD4 cell depletion and could therefore be an important indicator of HIV progression [19]. The V3 loop of the envelope protein gp120 has been identified as a major determinant for coreceptor usage [20]. It consists of 35 amino acids. A simple rule to predict whether CXCR4 will be used is the existence of a positively charged residue at positions 11 and 25 [21], but several bioinformatics classification methods have been developed that appear to have more predictive power [21–27].

Working mainly from V3 sequence data, several techniques were applied by early researchers to predict coreceptor usage. Resch et al. [21] applied *neural networks* to the task and demonstrated that they have better performance than the 11/25 rule. Through SVM and decision trees, Pillai et al. [22] showed that other sequence positions besides 11 and 25 can be used for prediction. Jensen et al. [23] developed a method based on the position-specific scoring matrix (PSSM) that assigned scores to V3 sequences indicating their tendency to use CXCR4 as a co-receptor with defined cutoff values for categorization.

Recent approaches have concentrated more on combining V3 sequence data with other kinds of data, such as clinical and structural data. Sing et al. [24] demonstrates through an SVM-based approach that taking into account clinical and host data such as viral load and CD4 count as well results in improved performance over just using sequence data. Inclusion of structural data was found to increase performance of methods by Sander et al. [25], who developed SVM and random forest-based approaches, and by Lamers et al. [26], who used evolutionary computation to evolve neural networks. Prosperi et al. [27] showed that including the whole *env* region (of which the V3 loop is part), several physicochemical properties and clinical markers as input increased performance over just having the V3 loop as input, for several machine learning approaches including logistic regression and SVM.

33.3   IDENTIFYING SUBTYPE

There are two major types of HIV, HIV-1 and HIV-2. The HIV-1 type can be further subdivided into four subtype groups: M (main), O (outlier), N and P. Under the M group, there is recognition of 9 pure HIV-1 subtypes (A–D, F–H, J, and K). HIV viruses from multiple pure subtypes can infect the same person and possibly recombine with each other. Recombinant HIV viruses that have their structure show up in at least 3 independent viral strains are known as *circulating recombinant forms* (CRFs) and 43 CRFs are currently known [28]. The subtype properties have been shown to not affect current HIV treatment efficiency [29], however these properties can be significant for HIV transmission and pathogenic potential [30]. A number of Web resources are available for subtyping that employ sequence alignment: the National Center for Biotechnology Information (NCBI) Genotyping Program [31], the Los Alamos Recombinant Identification Program [32], and the Stanford HIVseq Program [33]. In the literature, several bioinformatics classification methods that use other techniques have been developed that demonstrate excellent subtyping performance with only portions of the HIV genome as input [34–38].

One portion that has been used is the HIV *env* gene which codes for the envelope protein on the virus surface. The *env* gene shows considerable genotypic variability within HIV subtypes [39, 40]. Aires-de-Sousa and Aires-de-Sousa [34] have clustered *env* sequences using a type of neural network called the *Kohonen map*, representing sequences with a concept they call virtual potentials. They report excellent results despite the lack of data. The *pol* gene has also been the focus of bioinformatics methods despite being highly conserved compared to the *env* gene since it codes for the protease and reverse transcriptase enzymes. Since mutations of these enzymes are important for determining resistance, there is therefore an abundance of data from which to do subtyping. This abundance has been utilized by Gale et al. [35] to develop a subtyping algorithm—the *SubType AnalyzeR* (STAR)—using PSSMs. These scoring matrices represent the results of a frequency analysis of the amino acids of each subtype, which are then used to assign subtype similarity scores to a query sequence based on its amino acids. STAR was reported to have a mean accuracy of 99% in assigning subtypes. For better detection of recombinant sequences, an improvement to the STAR scoring mechanism was developed using odds ratios [36]. Another subtyping approach is phylogenetic analysis, which determines a query sequence's subtype based on its estimated position within an evolutionary tree. The REGA subtyping tool [37] achieves excellent results using this approach with *pol*, *env*, and *gag* sequences as well as full-genome sequences. Another investigation using the same general approach developed an HIV-1 subtyping method based on a second-order Markov model that selected the most informative nucleotide composition strings and used only their composition values to represent whole genomes [38]. The method had 100% accuracy on their test data set.

33.4   IDENTIFYING MUTATION SELECTION PRESSURE

Genotype mutations undergo selection pressure which depends on the contribution of that mutation on genotype fitness. Knowing the type of pressure mutations are under in a particular time is important because such pressure can determine the future evolution of the genotype [41, 42]. In the specific case of HIV, the high error rate of the HIV reverse transcriptase enzyme allows mutations to emerge at a considerable rate [43–45]. Mutations can change the structure of HIV proteins and thus may cause them to resist interaction with antiretroviral drugs reducing their efficiency [46, 47]. However, each possible mutation is not equally likely to emerge and become predominant in the HIV population of a patient. The likelihood depends on a multitude of factors, including how beneficial the mutation would be to the replication rate of the virus, drug pressure, immune system pressure, and the presence of previous mutations. There are three types of selection pressure: neutral, positive, or negative. Under neutral selection, there is no selection pressure on that mutation and thus it will appear and disappear randomly. Under positive selection the mutation will become more prevalent in the genotype population as time goes on, while under negative selection the opposite will occur and the mutation will be substituted with other mutations. Several bioinformatics classification methods have been developed to analyze and classify this phenomenon and also have a focus on HIV [48–52].

One method used is to model substitution rates at codon sites using continuous-time Markov processes and classify sites according to the selection pressure on them (mainly neutral/positive/negative). One study compared two evolution models of protein-coding DNA sequences: "neutral model" and "positive-selection model." From analysis of sequence data from HIV-1 envelope genes, the positive-selection model was favored over the neutral model [48]. Models that accounted for different selective pressures among amino acid sites were also developed. Analysis of HIV-1 *env*, *vif*, and *pol* genes showed that selective pressure is highly heterogeneous among sites [49]. In [50], Bayes's theorem was used to develop an algorithm for the classification of the evolutionary behavior of mutational patterns or combinations of mutations.

Another method developed was the *sitewise likelihood ratio* (SLR) method for detecting nonneutral evolution. The authors showed that the SLR method was more powerful than previously published methods for identifying positive-selection sites, especially if strength of selection is low [51]. Maximum-likelihood techniques were used in an inference method of positive selection that is robust to the presence of recombination. It was shown that where recombination causes standard methods to have high false-positive rates, the proposed method has an acceptable false-positive rate while retaining high power [52].

33.5 MAKING TREATMENT-RELATED DECISIONS

After obtaining all information on the patient and virus, a clinician will then need to integrate and consider all the information and ultimately render a decision on the treatment for the patient. This is a complicated process, involving many factors, treatment options, and drug interactions with high rates of cross-drug resistance. Of particular concern is the ability of the virus to quickly acquire mutations to a single drug [46]. Therefore, current treatment guidelines recommend a combination of drugs that attack different components of the virus [53, 54]. Given the various patient and virus factors, the problem of determining the optimal treatment is still unresolved, but various researchers have taken steps toward obtaining a solution [55–57].

Some researchers have developed statistical classifiers that attempt to predict whether a drug combination will be successful given various other factors. Altmann et al. [55] have employed *linear discriminant analysis*, *least-squares regression*, and *linear* SVM, C4.5, *logistic regression*, and *logistic model trees* for this purpose and tested them with different encodings of the viral genotype and drug combination. Their results showed that the input encoding used affects performance more than the classification technique used. Larder et al. [56] have built neural networks that combine the genotype with a variety of clinical variables such as baseline $CD4^+$ and baseline viral load, with results suggesting that additional clinical variables can provide additional predictive power. Rosen-Zvi et al. [57] have developed three prediction engines on different inputs, that is, an *evolutionary engine*, a *generative discriminative engine*, and a *mixture-of-effects engine*, and demonstrated that combining the engines can improve prediction performance over the individual engines alone.

33.6 FUTURE DIRECTIONS

33.6.1 Clinical Research Directions

This survey has shown that many computational methods have been developed that can aid in HIV clinical decision making. However, there are various aspects to the clinical decision-making process and not all of them have been adequately addressed in the literature. Here, we identified throughout the literature the following aspects as major areas of interest to clinicians due to their potential as prognostic factors:

1. Choosing the optimal intervention point (optimal timing of therapy commencement)
2. Choosing an optimal regimen having due regard to patient-specific factors
3. Choosing an appropriate target in terms of degree of viral suppression or immuno-logical recovery to be deemed adequate to justify continuation of a regimen
4. Identifying the components of second-line regimens that are likely to result in viral suppression when first-line regimens have failed (salvage therapy)
5. Identifying the reasons for regimen failure, such as drug interactions interfering with maintenance of adequate drug levels, so that the causes can be addressed in future treatment approaches for that individual
6. Characterizing and profiling drug-resistant viruses
7. Recognizing novel treatment approaches which hold particular promise for certain individuals (individualized therapy approaches)

33.6.2 Computational Research Directions

For optimum decision making, it would be best if there was a fully tested and validated com-putational model that accurately represents all the relevant interactions between HIV/AIDS variables and allows prognosis of the future state of the patient, preferably in a manner that can be easily interpreted. Working toward this goal, we suggest current research to be extended further according to the following guidelines:

- *Additional Features*   There should a focus toward extracting features from the data that provide significant new information that is not easily derived from currently available features. In particular, these new features should not be derived just from simple algebraic manipulation of currently available features.
- *Feature Integration*   Both the patient and the virus are complex systems and any features of these systems may be due to multiple disparate factors. Therefore, there should be further efforts to integrate the features available into one predictive system since the combination may have better performance than if the features are considered in isolation.
- *Low-Quality Patient Data*   Population selection is a significant part of developing a predictive algorithm, ensuring that the input to the algorithm fits within certain constraints and has a certain quality level. However, a practical situation may see these constraints violated and patients excluded, and therefore further efforts are needed toward graceful algorithm performance degradation in the face of low-quality data and greater patient inclusion in the input.

There should also be greater focus on the following technical issues when developing bioinformatics methods for the analysis of HIV/AIDS data sets:

- *Data Set Noise and Inconsistency*   Measurements performed separately may be af-fected by unknown factors, despite proper control for all known factors. Information about HIV patients may be incomplete, and there will be need to represent the missing information in some way. Some data may have been entered manually, and there could be input errors.

- *Data Set Accuracy Uncertainty* Patients may not adhere to treatment as well as reported. Assays used may be incorrectly calibrated or may produce measurements that have a large standard deviation or high ambiguity.

- *Integration Issues with Data Sets from Multiple Institutions* Same type of data from different data sets might be in different formats, have slightly different interpretations, or be classified into different categories. Some data may be available in one source but missing from another source.

- *Method Expansion and Futureproofing* Methods should be flexible enough to allow integration of information regarding new mutations, new classes of drugs, or even new knowledge about HIV/AIDS. Implementation source code should be open for inspection and extension.

33.7 CONCLUSION

There have been numerous bioinformatics classification methods in the literature that have the potential to support HIV/AIDS decision making; analysis shows that they use disparate approaches. They cover various aspects of HIV: its resistance to drugs, coreceptor usage, subtype, mutation selection pressure, and suitability of treatment. Integrating these aspects is an area that is currently under active research. Complementing these classification methods with other computational techniques such as *regression* and *optimization* is another active research area that could also be beneficial for treatment decision making.

REFERENCES

1. UNAIDS. Global report: UNAIDS report on the global AIDS epidemic, UNAIDS/JC2417E, 2012.

2. L. Demeter and R. Haubrich. International perspectives on antiretroviral resistance. Phenotypic and genotypic resistance assays: Methodology, reliability, and interpretations. *J. Acquir. Immune Defic. Syndr.*, 26(1):S3–9, 2001.

3. T. Lengauer and T. Sing. Bioinformatics-assisted anti-HIV therapy. *Nat. Rev. Microbiol.*, 4:790–797, 2006.

4. Stanford HIVdb. Available: `http://hivdb.stanford.edu`, last accessed Aug. 14, 2011.

5. K. Van Laethem, A. De Luca, A. Antinori, A. Cingolani, C. F. Perna, and A. M. Vandamme. A genotypic drug resistance interpretation algorithm that significantly predicts therapy response in HIV-1-infected patients. *Antivir. Ther.*, 7:123–129, 2002.

6. J. L. Meynard, M. Vray, L. Morand-Joubert, E. Race, D. Descamps, G. Peytavin, S. Matheron, C. Lamotte, S. Guiramand, D. Costagliola, F. Brun-Vezinet, F. Clavel, and P. M. Girard. Phenotypic or genotypic resistance testing for choosing antiretroviral therapy after treatment failure: A randomized trial. *AIDS*, 16:727–736, 2002.

7. A. De Luca, A. Antinori, S. D. Giambenedetto, A. Cingolani, M. Colafigli, C. F. Perno, and R. Cauda. Interpretation systems for genotypic drug resistance of HIV-1. *Scand. J. Infect. Dis.*, 35:29–34, 2003.

8. J. R. Quinlan. *C4.5: Programs for Machine Learning*. Morgan Kaufmann, San Francisco, CA, 1993.

9. L. Breiman, J. Friedman, C. J. Stone, and R. A. Olshen. *Classification and Regression Trees.* Chapman & Hall/CRC, Boca Raton, FL, 1984.

10. N. Beerenwinkel, B. Schmidt, H. Walter, R. Kaiser, T. Lengauer, D. Hoffmann, K. Korn, and J. Selbig. Diversity and complexity of HIV-1 drug resistance: A bioinformatics approach to predicting phenotype from genotype. *Proc. Natl. Acad. Sci. USA*, 99:8271–8276, 2002.

11. N. Beerenwinkel, T. Lengauer, J. Selbig, B. Schmidt, H. Walter, K. Korn, R. Kaiser, and D. Hoffmann. Geno2pheno: Interpreting genotypic HIV drug resistance tests. *IEEE Intell. Syst.*, 16:35–41, 2001.

12. N. Beerenwinkel, M. Daumer, M. Oette, K. Korn, D. Hoffmann, R. Kaiser, T. Lengauer, J. Selbig, and H. Walter. Geno2pheno: Estimating phenotypic drug resistance from HIV-1 genotypes. *Nucl. Acids Res.*, 31:3850–3855, 2003.

13. K. Wang, E. Jenwitheesuk, R. Samudrala, and J. E. Mittler. Simple linear model provides highly accurate genotypic predictions of HIV-1 drug resistance. *Antivir. Ther.*, 9:343–352, 2004.

14. H. Vermeiren, E. Van Craenenbroeck, P. Alen, L. Bacheler, G. Picchio, and P. Lecocq. Prediction of HIV-1 drug susceptibility phenotype from the viral genotype using linear regression modeling. *J. Virol. Methods*, 145:47–55, 2007.

15. A. D. Sevin, V. DeGruttola, M. Nijhuis, J. M. Schapiro, A. S. Foulkes, M. F. Para, and C. A. B. Boucher. Methods for investigation of the relationship between drug-susceptibility phenotype and human immunodeficiency virus type 1 genotype with applications to AIDS clinical trials group 333. *J. Infect. Dis.*, 182:59–67, 2000.

16. S. Draghici and R. B. Potter. Predicting HIV drug resistance with neural networks. *Bioinformatics*, 19:98–107, 2003.

17. S.-Y. Rhee, J. Taylor, G. Wadhera, A. Ben-Hur, D. L. Brutlag, and R. W. Shafer. Genotypic predictors of human immunodeficiency virus type 1 drug resistance. *Proc. Natl. Acad. Sci. USA*, 103:17355–17360, 2006.

18. E. A. Berger, P. M. Murphy, and J. M. Farber. Chemokine Receptors as HIV-1 Coreceptors: Roles in viral entry, tropism, and disease. *Annu. Rev. Immunol.*, 17:657–700, 1999.

19. R. R. Regoes and S. Bonhoeffer. The HIV coreceptor switch: A population dynamical perspective. *Trends Microbiol.*, 13:269–277, 2005.

20. R. A. Fouchier, M. Groenink, N. A. Kootstra, M. Tersmette, H. G. Huisman, F. Miedema, and H. Schuitemaker. Phenotype-associated sequence variation in the third variable domain of the human immunodeficiency virus type 1 gp120 molecule. *J. Virol.*, 66:3183–3187, 1992.

21. W. Resch, N. Hoffman, and R. Swanstrom. Improved success of phenotype prediction of the human immunodeficiency virus type 1 from envelope variable loop 3 sequence using neural networks. *Virology*, 288:51–62, 2001.

22. S. Pillai, B. Good, D. Richman, and J. Corbeil. A new perspective on V3 phenotype prediction. *AIDS Res. Hum. Retrovir.*, 19:145–149, 2003.

23. M. A. Jensen, F.-S. Li, A. B. van 't Wout, D. C. Nickle, D. Shriner, H.-X. He, S. McLaughlin, R. Shankarappa, J. B. Margolick, and J. I. Mullins. Improved coreceptor usage prediction and genotypic monitoring of R5-to-X4 transition by motif analysis of human immunodeficiency virus type 1 env V3 loop sequences. *J. Virol.*, 77:13376–13388, 2003.

24. T. Sing, A. J. Low, N. Beerenwinkel, O. Sander, P. K. Cheung, F. S. Domingues, J. Buch, M. Daumer, R. Kaiser, T. Lengauer, and P. R. Harrigan. Predicting HIV coreceptor usage on the basis of genetic and clinical covariates. *Antivir. Ther.*, 12:1097–1106, 2007.

25. O. Sander, T. Sing, I. Sommer, A. J. Low, P. K. Cheung, P. R. Harrigan, T. Lengauer, and F. S. Domingues. Structural descriptors of gp120 V3 loop for the prediction of HIV-1 coreceptor usage. *PLoS Comput. Biol.*, 3:e58, 2007.

26. S. L. Lamers, M. Salemi, M. S. McGrath, and G. B. Fogel. Prediction of R5, X4, and R5X4 HIV-1 coreceptor usage with evolved neural networks. *IEEE/ACM Trans. Comput. Biol. Bioinform.*, 5:291–300, 2008.

27. M. C. F. Prosperi, I. Fanti, G. Ulivi, A. Micarelli, A. De Luca, and M. Zazzi. Robust supervised and unsupervised statistical learning for HIV type 1 coreceptor usage analysis. *AIDS Res. Hum. Retrovir.*, 25:305–314, 2009.

28. S. L. Kosakovsky Pond and D. M. Smith. Editorial commentary: Are all subtypes created equal? The effectiveness of antiretroviral therapy against non–subtype B HIV-1. *Clin. Infect. Dis.*, 48:1306–1309, 2009.

29. A. M. Geretti, L. Harrison, H. Green, C. Sabin, T. Hill, E. Fearnhill, D. Pillay, and D. Dunn. Effect of HIV-1 subtype on virologic and immunologic response to starting highly active antiretroviral therapy. *Clin. Infect. Dis.*, 48:1296–1305, 2009.

30. A. M. Geretti. HIV-1 subtypes: Epidemiology and significance for HIV management. *Curr. Opin. Infect. Dis.*, 19:1–7, 2006.

31. NCBI Genotyping Program. Available: `http://www.ncbi.nlm.nih.gov/projects/genotyping/`, last accessed Aug. 14, 2011.

32. Los Alamos Recombinant Identification Program. Available: `http://www.hiv.lanl.gov/content/sequence/RIP/RIP.html`, last accessed Aug. 14, 2011.

33. Stanford HIVseq Program. Available: `http://hivdb.stanford.edu/pages/algs/HIVseq.html`, last accessed Aug. 14, 2011.

34. J. Aires-de-Sousa and L. Aires-de-Sousa. Representation of DNA sequences with virtual potentials and their processing by (SEQREP) Kohonen self-organizing maps. *Bioinformatics*, 19:30–36, 2003.

35. C. V. Gale, R. Myers, R. S. Tedder, I. G. Williams, and P. Kellam. Development of a novel human immunodeficiency virus type 1 subtyping tool, subtype analyzer (STAR): Analysis of subtype distribution in London. *AIDS Res. Hum. Retrovir.*, 20:457–464, 2004.

36. R. E. Myers, C. V. Gale, A. Harrison, Y. Takeuchi, and P. Kellam. A statistical model for HIV-1 sequence classification using the subtype analyser (STAR). *Bioinformatics*, 21:3535–3540, 2005.

37. T. de Oliveira, K. Deforche, S. Cassol, M. Salminen, D. Paraskevis, C. Seebregts, J. Snoeck, E. J. van Rensburg, A. M. J. Wensing, D. A. van de Vijver, C. A. Boucher, R. Camacho, and A.-M. Vandamme. An automated genotyping system for analysis of HIV-1 and other microbial sequences. *Bioinformatics*, 21:3797–3800, 2005.

38. X. Wu, Z. Cai, X.-F. Wan, T. Hoang, R. Goebel, and G. Lin. Nucleotide composition string selection in HIV-1 subtyping using whole genomes. *Bioinformatics*, 23:1744–1752, 2007.

39. L. Buonaguro, M. L. Tornesello, and F. M. Buonaguro. Human immunodeficiency virus type 1 subtype distribution in the worldwide epidemic: Pathogenetic and therapeutic implications. *J. Virol.*, 81:10209–10219, 2007.

40. B. Korber, B. Gaschen, K. Yusim, R. Thakallapally, C. Kesmir, and V. Detours. Evolutionary and immunological implications of contemporary HIV-1 variation. *Br. Med. Bull.*, 58:19–42, 2001.

41. A. J. L. Brown and E. C. Holmes. Evolutionary biology of human immunodeficiency virus. *Annu. Rev. Ecol. Syst.*, 25:127–165, 1994.

42. F. Seillier-Moiseiwitsch, B. H. Margolin, and R. Swanstrom. Genetic variability of the human immunodeficiency virus: Statistical and biological issues. *Annu. Rev. Genet.*, 28:559–596, 1994.

43. J. M. Coffin. HIV population dynamics in vivo: Implications for genetic variation, pathogenesis, and therapy. *Science*, 267:483–489, 1995.

44. J. D. Roberts, K. Bebenek, and T. A. Kunkel. The accuracy of reverse transcriptase from HIV-1. *Science*, 242:1171–1173, 1988.

45. B. D. Preston, B. J. Poiesz, and L. A. Loeb. Fidelity of HIV-1 reverse transcriptase. *Science*, 242:1168–1171, 1988.

46. F. Clavel and A. J. Hance. HIV drug resistance. *N. Engl. J. Med.*, 350:1023–1035, 2004.

47. R. W. Shafer and J. M. Schapiro. HIV-1 drug resistance mutations: An updated framework for the second decade of HAART. *AIDS Rev.*, 10:67–84, 2008.

48. R. Nielsen and Z. Yang. Likelihood models for detecting positively selected amino acid sites and applications to the HIV-1 envelope gene. *Genetics*, 148:929–936, 1998.

49. Z. Yang, R. Nielsen, N. Goldman, and A. M. Pedersen. Codon-substitution models for heterogeneous selection pressure at amino acid sites. *Genetics*, 155:431–449, 2000.

50. A. Al Mazari, A. Y. Zomaya, M. Charleston, and R. J. Garsia. A novel algorithm for adaptive and neutral evolutionary patterns associated with HIV drug resistance. Paper presented at the Fifth ACS/IEEE International Conference on Computer Systems and Applications (AICCSA-07), Amman, Jordan, 2007.

51. T. Massingham and N. Goldman. Detecting amino acid sites under positive selection and purifying selection. *Genetics*, 169:1753–1762, 2005.

52. K. Scheffler, D. P. Martin, and C. Seoighe. Robust inference of positive selection from recombining coding sequences. *Bioinformatics*, 22:2493–2499, 2006.

53. S. M. Hammer, J. J. Eron, Jr., P. Reiss, R. T. Schooley, M. A. Thompson, S. Walmsley, P. Cahn, M. A. Fischl, J. M. Gatell, M. S. Hirsch, D. M. Jacobsen, J. S. G. Montaner, D. D. Richman, P. G. Yeni, and P. A. Volberding. Antiretroviral treatment of adult HIV infection: 2008 recommendations of the International AIDS Society—USA Panel. *JAMA*, 300:555–570, 2008.

54. Panel on Antiretroviral Guidelines for Adults and Adolescents. Guidelines for the use of antiretroviral agents in HIV-1-infected adults and adolescents. Department of Health and Human Services, Washington, DC, 2008.

55. A. Altmann, N. Beerenwinkel, T. Sing, I. Savenkov, M. Doumer, R. Kaiser, S. Y. Rhee, W. J. Fessel, R. W. Shafer, and T. Lengauer. Improved prediction of response to antiretroviral combination therapy using the genetic barrier to drug resistance. *Antivir. Ther.*, 12:169–178, 2007.

56. B. Larder, D. Wang, A. Revell, J. Montaner, R. Harrigan, F. De Wolf, J. Lange, S. Wegner, L. Ruiz, M. J. Perez-Elias, S. Emery, J. Gatell, A. D. Monforte, C. Torti, M. Zazzi, and C. Lane. The development of artificial neural networks to predict virological response to combination HIV therapy. *Antivir. Ther.*, 12:15–24, 2007.

57. M. Rosen-Zvi, A. Altmann, M. Prosperi, E. Aharoni, H. Neuvirth, A. Sonnerborg, E. Schulter, D. Struck, Y. Peres, F. Incardona, R. Kaiser, M. Zazzi, and T. Lengauer. Selecting anti-HIV therapies based on a variety of genomic and clinical factors. *Bioinformatics*, 24:i399–406, 2008.

PART H

ASSOCIATION RULES LEARNING FROM BIOLOGICAL DATA

CHAPTER 34

MINING FREQUENT PATTERNS AND ASSOCIATION RULES FROM BIOLOGICAL DATA

IOANNIS KAVAKIOTIS, GEORGE TZANIS, and IOANNIS VLAHAVAS

Department of Informatics, Aristotle University of Thessaloniki, Thessaloniki, Greece

34.1 INTRODUCTION

During the last years biology and computer science have been characterized by major advances that have attracted a lot of interest. Nowadays the collaboration between biologists and computer scientists is deemed a vital necessity for the further progress of biological research. Bioinformatics is a novel research area that has emerged as a solution to the aforementioned need for collaboration. Two relative subfields of computer science, data mining and machine learning, have provided biologists, as well as experts from other areas, a powerful set of tools to analyze new data types in order to extract various types of knowledge efficiently and effectively. These tools combine powerful techniques of artificial intelligence, statistics, mathematics, and database technology. This fusion of technologies aims to overcome the obstacles and constraints posed by the traditional statistical methods.

Association rule (AR) mining has attracted the attention of the data-mining research community since the early 1990s as a means of unsupervised, exploratory data analysis. ARs were first introduced by Agrawal et al. [1] as a market basket analysis tool. However, since then, they have been effectively applied to many other application domains, including biology and bioinformatics. An AR implies the coexistence of a number of items in a portion of a transaction database. The goal of this exploratory data analysis is to provide the decision maker with valuable knowledge about a certain domain modeled by a transaction database. The frequent existence of two or more items in the same transaction implies a relationship among them. For example, the existence of bread and butter in the same baskets implies a possible buying behavior pattern that can be further investigated in order to improve the sales of both products. Similarly, the coexistence of high-expression values of a number of genes in the same transactions–experiments indicates a possible coexpression pattern of these genes. Conversely, the rare or the absolutely non-coexistence of two products could also imply a negative association (e.g., a mutual exclusion) among them.

Biological Knowledge Discovery Handbook: Preprocessing, Mining, and Postprocessing of Biological Data,
First Edition. Edited by Mourad Elloumi and Albert Y. Zomaya.
© 2014 John Wiley & Sons, Inc. Published 2014 by John Wiley & Sons, Inc.

Many algorithms for mining ARs and others that extend the concept of AR mining have been proposed so far. Agrawal and Srikant [2] proposed APRIORI, the first algorithm for mining ARs. APRIORI is a levelwise algorithm which works by generating candidate sets of items and testing if they are frequent by scanning the database. It is one of the most popular data-mining algorithms and will be described in more detail later in the chapter. About the same time Mannila et al. [3] independently discovered a variation of APRIORI, the OCD algorithm. The large number of algorithms that have been proposed since then either improve efficiency, such as FP-GROWTH [4] and ECLAT [5], or address different problems from various application domains, such as spatial [6], temporal [7], and intertransactional ARs [8].

One of the major problems in AR mining is the large number of often uninteresting rules extracted. Some approaches that are based on concept hierarchies try to deal with this problem. Srikant and Agrawal [9] presented the problem of mining for generalized ARs. These rules utilize item taxonomies (concept hierarchies) in order to discover more interesting rules. Thomas and Sarawagi [10] proposed a technique for mining generalized ARs based on Structured Query Language (SQL) queries. Han and Fu [11] also describe the problem of mining "multiple-level" ARs based on taxonomies and propose a set of top-down progressive deepening algorithms.

Another kind of approach deals with negative associations between items. Savasere et al. [12] introduced this kind of problem. Negative associations relate to the problem of finding rules that imply what items are not likely to appear in a transaction when a certain set of items appears in the transaction. The approach of Savasere et al. demands the existence of a taxonomy and is based on the assumption that items belonging to the same parent of taxonomy are expected to have similar types of associations with other items. In another work Wu et al. [13] presented an efficient method for mining positive and negative associations and proposed a pruning strategy and an interestingness measure. Finally, another kind of negative association that has been studied concerns the mining of mutually exclusive items [14, 15].

The process of *knowledge discovery from databases* (KDD) consists of a number of steps that can be grouped in three categories: preprocessing, data mining, and postprocessing (Figure 34.1). Although the core of the process is the data-mining step, where a data-mining algorithm (e.g., APRIORI for mining of ARs) is applied, the preprocessing and postprocessing phases are particularly important and contribute sensibly to the extraction of valuable knowledge. The preprocessing phase usually includes the selection of an

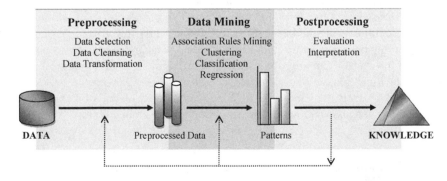

FIGURE 34.1   The KDD process.

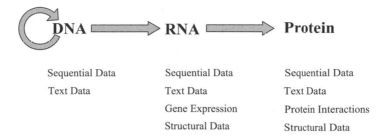

FIGURE 34.2 Central dogma of molecular biology and main kinds of biological data.

appropriate portion of the data, the cleaning of the selected data, and the transformation of the data. The postprocessing phase deals with the management of the produced patterns and focuses on the evaluation and interpretation of data-mining results.

The central dogma of molecular biology, as coined by Francis Crick [16], describes the flow of biological information (Figure 34.2). In most organisms DNA is transcribed into RNA and then RNA is translated into protein. The circular arrow around DNA denotes its ability to replicate itself. The figure also describes the basic kinds of data that can be produced by various biological experiments in relation to the three basic molecules of life.

It is important to mention that AR mining is a very prominent tool in application domains that include a large number of binary attributes and the associations among these attributes could be meaningful. A convenient application domain in biology is gene expression data, which include a large number of attributes (genes), and the associations among different genes are often particularly important. Although the expression values of genes are not binary, an appropriate discretization algorithm can convert these values to a suitable format for applying an AR mining algorithm successfully. Even though gene expression data are quite convenient for association analysis, AR mining is also applied to other kinds of biological data. These applications will be presented in the following sections.

In the next section, the problem of mining ARs will be defined. Then, some important mining algorithms, preprocessing and postprocessing methods, will be described. In the rest sections, the application of AR mining algorithms to various kinds of biological data will be presented. Finally, the chapter will be concluded and summarized.

34.2 DEFINITION OF AR MINING PROBLEM

The original definition of the AR mining problem has been given by Agrawal et al. in 1993 [1]. Let $I = \{i_1, i_2, \ldots, i_N\}$ be a finite set of binary attributes called *items* and $D = \{t_1, t_2, \ldots, t_N\}$ be a finite multiset of transactions called the *database*. Each *transaction* t_i contains a subset of items chosen from I and has a unique transaction ID. A set of items is referred to as an *itemset*. If an itemset contains k items, it is called a k-itemset. The number k is called the *size* or *length* of the itemset. The itemset that does not contain any items is called an empty itemset. A transaction $T \in D$ is said to contain an itemset $X \subseteq I$, if $X \subseteq T$.

An AR is an implication of the form $X \Rightarrow Y$ where $X \subset I$, $Y \subset I$, and $X \cap Y = \emptyset$. The itemset X is called the *antecedent* or *left-hand-side* (LHS) of the rule and the itemset Y is called the *consequent* or *right-hand-side* (RHS) of the rule.

TABLE 34.1 Example of Binary Gene Expression Matrix

Transaction ID	Gene 1	Gene 2	Gene 3	Gene 4
T1	0	1	0	0
T2	0	0	0	1
T3	1	1	0	0
T4	0	0	1	0
T5	1	1	1	0

There are many measures that have been proposed in order to evaluate a rule's interestingness. The most popular are *support* and *confidence*. They respectively reflect the usefulness and certainty of discovered rules. More specifically, support determines how often a rule is applicable to a given data set, whereas confidence determines how frequently items in Y appear in transactions that contain X. The support of a rule $X \Rightarrow Y$ is equal to the support of the itemset $X \cup Y$ and is defined as the fraction of transactions in the database which contain the itemset. The support of an itemset X is calculated as presented in the following equation:

$$\text{support}_D(X) = \frac{|\{T \in D | X \subseteq T\}|}{|D|}$$

The confidence of the rule $X \Rightarrow Y$ is defined as the fraction of transactions in the database that contain $X \cup Y$ over the number of transactions that contain only X. In other words, confidence is equal to the fraction of the support of $X \cup Y$ in D over the support of X in D. The equation that defines confidence is presented below:

$$\text{confidence}_D(X \Rightarrow Y) = \frac{\text{supp}_D(X \cup Y)}{\text{supp}_D(X)}$$

In order to make the concepts presented above more clear, a detailed example is presented. Table 34.1 presents a binary data matrix (database) concerning the expressions of four genes. Every transaction represents a separate measurement of gene expression levels. All measurements have been discretized so that only two levels of gene expression are possible. A value of zero represents a gene that is underexpressed, whereas a value of unity represents a gene that is overexpressed.

In this example the set of items is $I = \{\text{gene 1, gene 2, gene 3, gene 4}\}$. In the database there are five transactions, for example, $t_3 = \{\text{gene 1, gene 2}\}$. An example of a rule for this database could be $\{\text{gene 1, gene 2}\} \Rightarrow \{\text{gene 3}\}$. The support for this rule is $\frac{1}{5}$ (20%), because only one transaction (t_5) out of five contains gene 1, gene 2 and gene 3. The confidence of the rule is $\frac{1}{2}$ (50%), because the support of itemset $\{\text{gene 1, gene 2}\}$ (the antescedent of the rule) is $\frac{2}{5}$ and the support of itemset $\{\text{gene 1, gene 2, gene 3}\}$ is $\frac{1}{5}$.

The AR mining problem can be decomposed in two major subtasks:

1. *Frequent-Itemset Generation* Its purpose is to find all itemsets that satisfy a user-specified minimum-support threshold (min_sup). These itemsets are called *frequent itemsets*.

2. *Rule Generation* Its purpose is to extract from the frequent itemsets all the rules that satisfy a user-specified minimum-confidence threshold (min_conf).

The first subtask is the more computationally complex and has concentrated all the focus of the research community. The second subtask is a straightforward task and does not attract the interest of researchers.

34.3 ALGORITHMS FOR MINING ARs

In this section three popular algorithms that are based on three main methodologies for mining all frequent itemsets and consequently ARs will be presented.

34.3.1 APRIORI

Most of the algorithms for mining frequent itemsets are based on the principle of downward closure. This principle imposes that all nonempty subsets of a frequent itemset are also frequent. For example, if itemset {gene 1, gene 2, gene 5} is frequent according to a minimum-support threshold, then itemsets {gene 1, gene 2}, {gene 1, gene 5}, {gene 2, gene 5}, {gene 1}, {gene 2}, and {gene 5} must also be frequent according to the same minimum-support threshold. The most popular algorithm that employs this principle is APRIORI [2].

APRIORI works by constructing candidate frequent itemsets and then checks which of them are indeed frequent (Table 34.2). For the generation of candidate k-frequent itemsets, the set of $(k-1)$-frequent itemsets is exploited according to the principle of downward closure. Thus, the process of frequent-itemset mining in APRIORI is a two-step process:

1. The set of candidate frequent itemsets C_i is constructed.
2. Then the set of frequent itemsets L_i is constructed by scanning the database and checking which candidates in C_i using the minimum-support threshold.

To clarify the process, the algorithm initially constructs all the candidate frequent 1-itemsets (C_1), which actually include all the items. Then it is checked by scanning the database whether the minimum-support threshold is satisfied for these candidates and so the set of frequent 1-itemsets (L_1) is generated. Next, L_1 is used in order to generate the set of

TABLE 34.2 Pseudocode of APRIORI Algorithm

Input: Database D, minimum support threshold (min_sup)
Output: All the frequent itemsets

```
L₁ ← {frequent items}
for (k ← 2; Lₖ₋₁!=∅; k++) do
    Cₖ ← {candidates from Lₖ₋₁} (Lₖ₋₁× Lₖ₋₁ and downward closure)
        for each t ∈ D  do
            for  each c ∈ Cₖ  do
                if (c ⊆ t)
                    c.count++
    Lₖ ← {c ∈ Cₖ | c.count = min_sup}
return ⋃ Lₖ
       k
```

candidate frequent 2-itemsets (C_2), exploiting the downward closure principle. Following the same process the 2-frequent dataset (L_2) is generated. The process ends in a specific number of iterations or when there are no more candidate frequent itemsets. The number of APRIORI's database scans is equal to the length of the longest candidate frequent.

34.3.2 FP-GROWTH

The main drawbacks of the APRIORI algorithm is that it not only generates a huge number of candidate itemsets but also scans the database several times. Both drawbacks are very costly. Han et al. [4] proposed an algorithm, called FP-GROWTH, that is not based on the generation of candidate frequent itemsets. In general, the algorithm uses a tree structure, the *frequent-pattern tree* (FP-Tree), which stores all the database. This structure can compress the data up to 200 times, and it is stored to the computer's memory, which leads to a more effective rule extraction. Moreover, this algorithm uses a divide-and-conquer approach in order to decompose the rule extraction process in simpler parts.

More specifically, in the first step, the algorithm compresses the database into an FP-Tree structure that is highly condensed but is complete for the purposes of frequent pattern mining. The beneficial consequent is that it avoids costly database scans during candidate generation. Then, in the second step, it extracts frequent itemsets directly from the FP-Tree using the divide-and-conquer methodology. Generally FP-GROWTH is faster than APRIORI.

34.3.3 ECLAT

Zaki [5] proposed a new algorithm for mining frequent patterns, called *equivalence class transformation* (ECLAT). The main difference between the two algorithms presented previously and ECLAT is that the first two mine frequent itemsets from a set of transactions in horizontal data format while ECLAT mines frequent itemsets in a vertical data format.

First, the algorithm builds the TID_set of all items in the transaction database. As in APRIORI, in ECLAT the frequent k-itemsets are generated from the frequent $(k - 1)$-itemsets. In order to clarify the process, an example is presented below. In this example the minimum-support threshold is set to 20%. Table 34.3 presents the transaction database in which the first column represents the transaction ID (TID) and the second the items included in each transaction.

TABLE 34.3   Example Transaction Database

TID	Item IDs
T1	I4, I5
T2	I1, I3, I4, I5
T3	I1, I3, I5
T4	I3, I4
T5	I3, I4
T6	I4, I5
T7	I2, I3, I5
T8	I2, I5
T9	I3, I4, I5

TABLE 34.4 Transactional Database of Table 34.3 in Vertical Data Format

Itemset	TID_set
{I1}	T2, T3
{I2}	T7, T8
{I3}	T2, T3, T4, T5, T7, T9
{I4}	T1, T2, T4, T5, T6, T9
{I5}	T1, T2, T3, T6, T7, T8, T9

TABLE 34.5 Frequent 2-Itemsets (highlighted)

Itemset	TID_set	Support (%)
{I1, I3}	T2, T3	22
{I1, I4}	T2	11
{I1, I5}	T2, T3	22
{I2, I3}	T7	11
{I2, I5}	T7, T8	22
{I3, I4}	T2, T4, T5, T9	44
{I3, I5}	T2, T3, T7, T9	44
{I4, I5}	T1, T2, T6, T9	44

TABLE 34.6 Frequent 3-Itemsets

Itemset	TID_set	Support (%)
{I1, I3, I5}	T2, T3	22
{I3, I4, I5}	T2, T9	22

Table 34.4 presents the transactional database of Table 34.3 in vertical-data format. The first column represents the itemset and the second column the transactions which contain the particular itemset.

By intersecting the TID_set, the frequent 2-itemsets (highlighted) in vertical data format are generated. These itemsets are presented in Table 34.5.

Again, by intersecting the TID_sets, the frequent 3-itemsets (Table 34.6) in vertical-data format are generated. An optimization based on the principle of downward closure is that there is no need to intersect {I1, I5} and {I4, I5} because {I1, I4} is not frequent and as a concequence {I1, I4, I5} cannot be frequent.

The process ends when there are no more candidate frequent itemsets or frequent itemsets.

34.4 PREPROCESSING AND POSTPROCESSING

As previously discussed, data preprocessing is an essential step before applying a data-mining algorithm. The preprocessing phase usually includes the selection of an appropriate portion of the data and the cleaning and transformation of the data. In AR mining problems the most necessary and most frequently used preprocessing procedure is discretization, which involves the transformation of the continuous range of an attribute's values to discrete intervals.

34.4.1 Discretization

Many algorithms in data mining and the vast majority of AR discovery algorithms and their derivations work only with categorical attributes. So it is essential to use data discretization techniques in order to reduce the number of values for a given continuous attribute by dividing the range of the attribute into intervals. In other words the aim of discretization techniques is to convert the numeric attributes into nominal ones. There are three axes by which discretization methods can be classified: *global/local, supervised/unsupervised*, and *static/dynamic* [17].

Local discretization algorithms produce partitions that are applied to localized regions of the instance space. Instead, global algorithms group values of each feature into intervals by considering other features. Supervised discretization algorithms are applicable only when the data are divided into classes. On the other hand, unsupervised algorithms do not consider the class value. Lastly, static algorithms discretize each feature in one iteration independent of the other features, whereas dynamic algorithms search for all possible intervals for all features simultaneously. In the rest of this section some of the most popular discretization strategies will be presented according to the second categorization (supervised/usupervised).

Supervised discretization is used when dealing with classification problems or a dataset in which a label attribute is assigned to each instance. This label indicates the class to which the instance belongs. This information is used to guide the discretization process. The most well known approach for supervised discretization is the one proposed by Fayyad and Irani [18]. This method uses the information gain in order to recursively define the best bins. The entropy of each bin should be minimal. The method works by recursively splitting the intervals until a stopping criterion is reached.

Let S be a training set. All instances in the training set should belong to one of c different classes. Each class is denoted by a number from 1 to c. Considering the above, entropy E of the set S is defined by the equation

$$E(S) = - \sum_{i=1}^{c} p_i \, \log_2(p_i)$$

In the above equation, p_i is the fraction of instances in S that belong to class c_i. The entropy of S decreases when the homogeneity of S with respect to the class where each instance belongs increases. For example, entropy is zero when all instances belong to the same class. On the contrary, entropy increases when the homogeneity of the instances decreases. By definition, if p_i is zero, then the term $p_i \, \log_2(p_i)$ is also equal to zero.

Let $T = \{t_1, \ldots, t_N\}$ be an arranged set of N split points for the values of an attribute A which splits the training set S into $N + 1$ subsets $\{S_1, \ldots, S_{N+1}\}$. Then, information gain G is defined as

$$G(S; A, T) = E(S) - \sum_{i=1}^{N+1} \frac{|S_i|}{|S|} E(S_i)$$

Information gain measures the reduction of the entropy which is caused if the values of attribute A are divided in the $N + 1$ intervals which are generated from the N split points included in T. The main purpose is the minimization of the heterogeneity among the instances that belong to the same interval of the attribute values. In other words, from the candidate splits of the data set, the one which minimizes the entropy and maximizes the information gain should be chosen.

On the contrary, unsupervised discretization is used in the absence of any knowledge of the class memberships of the instances. Thus, unsupervised discretization methods are generally based on the distribution of attribute values. The basic and simplest unsupervised strategy is the *equal-interval-width* discretization, which divides the values of the attribute into k equal bins, where k is a user-specified parameter. This method is vulnerable to outliers, namely observations that are numerically distant from the data, which may skew the range.

Another basic and simple unsupervised strategy is the *equal-frequency-interval* discretization, which divides a continuous attribute into k intervals which include the same number of values. Each interval contains n/k bins where n is the number of values.

These methods are rather simple but have some drawbacks which are very important in AR mining [19]. First of all, discretization must reflect the original distribution of the attribute. Second, discretization intervals should not hide the association and the patterns which exist in the values and, last, intervals should be semantically meaningful and must make sense to human experts.

Some interesting approaches which take under consideration the drawbacks mentioned before have been proposed. Three methods that can be grouped under the term *threshold methods* because they calculate a threshold which helps the discretization process are presented below. These methods [20] were used for discretizing gene expression data that were produced using the *serial analysis of gene expression* (SAGE) method [21].

The first discretization method is called max minus x% and includes the identification of the highest expression value (max) initially and then the replacement of each value that is greater than max-$x/100$ with the value of unity and the replacement of all other values with the value of zero.

The second approach is the *midrange-based cutoff*. This consists of identifying the highest and lowest expression values for each gene and then the calculation of their arithmetic mean. All expression values below or equal to the arithmetic mean are set to zero and all the expression values exceeding the arithmetic mean are set to unity.

The last method is *x% of highest value*. This consists of finding the $x\%$ of the highest values and replacing them with the value of unity. The rest are assigned the value of zero.

Vanucci and Colla [19] proposed an unsupervised discretization method for dicretizing data for the purposes of AR mining. The main thought is to preserve the original sample distribution. One idea was to use the K-means algorithm in order to generate K number of partitions which reflect the original distribution of the partitioned attribute. The main drawback of using the K-means algorithm was that the result obtained was very sensitive to the value of K because the value must be given by the user before the execution of the algorithm. So a false estimation of the K value could lead to unsatisfactory results. To overcome this disadvantage, a *self-organizing map* (SOM) [22] can be used. The SOM also preserves the initial distribution. The basic advantage of SOMs is that the number of clusters that will be generated is not required to be known in advance, as in the case with K-means. The only parameter that should be given before the execution of the algorithm is the maximum number of clusters (intervals).

An interesting approach in discretizing continuous attributes for AR mining was proposed by Ludl and Widmer [23]. The *relative unsupervised discretization* (RUDE) algorithm combines aspects of both supervised and unsupervised discretization. The method does not require a class attribute and hence belongs to unsupervised methods. Furthermore, the split points for an attribute are constructed in dependence of the other attributes and hence it is called relative. The basic idea when discretizing a particular attribute (the target attribute) is to consider information about the distribution of the values of the other attributes (source attributes).

34.4.2 Postprocessing of ARs

As already mentioned in the introduction, the large number of ARs that are discovered poses a great challenge in the data-mining research community. The vast amount of generated rules makes interpretation much more complex and often guides to misleading conclusions and consequently to wrong decisions. The assessment of the usefulness of the generated rules becomes an essential necessity and introduces the need to effectively deal with various kinds of redundant and uninteresting data.

Postprocessing usually consists of four phases: pruning, summarizing, grouping, and visualization [24]. In the pruning phase, rules are deleted because they are uninteresting or redundant. The summarizing phase tries to summarize the rules into more general concepts (usually using taxonomies). Then, the remaining rules are grouped into rule packets in the grouping phase. Finally, the extracted useful knowledge is illustrated in a visualization phase. Often the distinction among these phases is not very strict, and there are major interactions among each other. However, they comprise different steps that could be integrated in any postprocessing procedure.

34.5 GENE EXPRESSION DATA MINING

Gene expression is the process by which the genetic information encoded in DNA is converted into a functional product that can be either a protein or an RNA molecule in the case of non-protein-coding genes such as rRNA or tRNA genes.

Each organism contains a number of genes that code the synthesis of an mRNA or protein molecule. Every cell in an organism—with only few exceptions—has the same set of chromosomes and genes. However, two cells may have very different properties and functions. This is due to the differences in abundance of proteins. The abundance of a protein is partly determined by the levels of mRNA, which in turn are determined by the expression levels of the corresponding gene.

A popular tool for the measurement of gene expression is the *microarray* [25]. A microarray experiment measures the relative mRNA levels of thousands of genes, providing the ability to compare the expression levels of different biological samples. These samples may correlate with different time points taken during a biological process or with different tissue types such as normal cells and cancer cells [26]. Another method for measuring gene expression is SAGE, which allows the quantitative profiling of a large number of mRNA transcripts [21]. Although this method is more expensive than microarrays, it has the advantage that the experimenter does not have to preselect the mRNA sequences that will be studied.

The gene expression data are represented by an $M \times N$ matrix (Table 34.7). Biologists conduct a number of experiments measuring gene expression levels of a cell or group of cells under various conditions affecting these expression levels [27]. The M columns of the matrix represent the samples (e.g., microarray experiments or SAGE libraries), which can be related to the type of tissue, the age of the organism, or the environmental conditions. The N columns represent all the genes. The values included in the cells of the matrix are either counts of mRNA molecules (SAGE) or ratios that indicate the variance between the

TABLE 34.7   **Typical Gene Expression Matrix**

	Gene 1	Gene 2	$\cdots$	Gene N
Sample 1	a_{11}	a_{12}	$\cdots$	a_{1N}
Sample 2	a_{21}	a_{22}	$\cdots$	a_{2N}
$\vdots$	$\vdots$	$\vdots$	$\ddots$	$\vdots$
Sample M	a_{M1}	a_{M2}	$\cdots$	a_{MN}

TABLE 34.8   **Horizontal- and Vertical-Data Format**

Horizontal Format		Vertical Format	
TID	Items	Items	TID_set
1	G1, G3	G1	1, 4
2	G2, G4, G5	G2	2, 4
3	G4, G5	G3	1
4	G1, G2, G5	G4	2, 3
		G5	2, 3, 4

expression of the respective gene in the particular sample and the expression of the same gene in a control sample (microarrays).

Although the results of the experiments are expressed as real numbers, biologists are usually not interested in those values. These values are used in comparison to normal expression levels in an organism. For that reason, the absolute values are normalized under certain normalization criteria and discretized according to certain predetermined thresholds. After this process the values are grouped under three different levels: unchanged, upregulated (or overexpressed), and downregulated (or underexpressed).

The most common way to mine frequent patterns from a set of transactions is when these transactions are in horizontal-data format, that is, {TID: Itemset}, where TID is the transaction ID and Itemset is the set of items found in that transaction. Another way to mine frequent items (see ECLAT algorithm above) is when the data are in the vertical format, that is, {item: TID_set}. Table 34.8 presents an example database in both horizontal and vertical format. The vertical-data format is popular in application domains, where the data consist of many features (items) and a few samples, as is the case with gene expression data.

34.5.1 Mining in Horizontal-Data Format

As mentioned before, the most popular AR mining algorithm is APRIORI. A detailed example of the application of APRIORI on gene expression data is presented below.

In this example the minimum-support threshold (min_sup) is set to 40% and the minimum-confidence threshold (min_conf) is set to 80%. The matrix presented in Table 34.9 is a discretized gene expression matrix. A value of zero represents a gene that is underexpressed, whereas a value of unity represents a gene that is overexpressed. The samples that represent various experimental conditions C_i are in rows, whereas the genes G_j are in columns. Moreover, the data are transformed in transactional format.

TABLE 34.9 Discretized Gene Expression Matrix Converted in Transactional Format

	G1	G2	G3	G4		TID	Items
C1	1	0	0	0		C1	G1
C2	1	1	0	0		C2	G1, G2
C3	1	0	1	1		C3	G1, G3, G4
C4	1	1	1	1		C4	G1, G2, G3, G4
C5	1	1	1	0	$\Longrightarrow$	C5	G1, G2, G3
C6	0	0	1	1		C6	G3, G4
C7	0	1	1	1		C7	G2, G3, G4
C8	0	1	0	1		C8	G2, G4
C9	0	1	1	0		C9	G2, G3
C10	0	1	1	1		C10	G2, G3, G4

In the first step of the APRIORI algorithm, the support of every single gene (item) is calculated, and the genes that satisfy the minimum-support threshold constitute the set of frequent 1-itemsets. The support for every gene in Table 34.9 is presented below:

- support($\{G1\}$) = 5/10 = 50% $\geq$ min_sup
- support($\{G2\}$) = 7/10 = 70% $\geq$ min_sup
- support($\{G3\}$) = 7/10 = 70% $\geq$ min_sup
- support($\{G4\}$) = 6/10 = 60% $\geq$ min_sup

Consequently the set of frequent 1-itemsets contains all the genes: $L_1 = \{G1, G2, G3, G4\}$.

In the next step, APRIORI generates all the pairs of genes using L_1. The set of candidate frequent 2-itemsets is $C_2 = \{\{G1, G2\}, \{G1, G3\}, \{G1, G4\}, \{G2, G3\}, \{G2, G4\}, \{G3, G4\}\}$. After the construction of C_2, the support of each pair is calculated by scanning the database and counting the appearance of the pairs in each transaction. The support for every candidate frequent 2-itemset is presented below:

- support($\{G1, G2\}$) = 30% < min_sup
- support($\{G1, G3\}$) = 30% < min_sup
- support($\{G1, G4\}$) = 20% < min_sup
- support($\{G2, G3\}$) = 50% $\geq$ min_sup
- support($\{G2, G4\}$) = 40% $\geq$ min_sup
- support($\{G3, G4\}$) = 50% $\geq$ min_sup

Only three out of the six pairs of genes have support greater than or equal to the threshold (40%). Consequently the set of frequent 2-itemsets is $L_2 = \{\{G2, G3\}, \{G2, G4\}, \{G3, G4\}\}$.

In the next step, from the L_2 will arise the C_3, the set which contains all the candidate frequent 3-itemsets. Since the items included in each itemset are ordered according to their ID, then only the itemsets that have the first item in common are merged in order to provide the candidate frequent 3-itemsets. So by merging $\{G2, G3\}$ and $\{G2, G4\}$, the 3-itemset $\{G2, G3, G4\}$ arises that is the only candidate. Moreover, all the subsets of this itemset are frequent, since they are included in L_1 and in L_2, so this itemset is not pruned due to violation of the downward-closure principle. So $C_3 = \{\{G2, G3, G4\}\}$. Next, the support of this itemset is calculated by scanning the database. Its support is equal to 30%, which is below the minimum-support threshold. As a result, L_3 is an empty set (L3=$\{\}$), thus the frequent itemset mining procedure terminates.

The next step of the APRIORI algorithm includes the generation of the rules which occur from L_2 and then the calculation of the confidence for every rule in order to determine which ones satisfy the minimum-confidence threshold:

- $\{G2, G3\}$
    - $G2 \Rightarrow G3 = 5/7 = 71\% < \text{min\_conf}$ (discarded)
    - $G3 \Rightarrow G2 = 5/7 = 71\% < \text{min\_conf}$ (discarded)
- $\{G3, G4\}$
    - $G3 \Rightarrow G4 = 5/7 = 71\% < \text{min\_conf}$ (discarded)
    - $G4 \Rightarrow G3 = 5/6 = 83\% \geq \text{min\_conf}$ (accepted)
- $\{G2, G4\}$
    - $G2 \Rightarrow G4 = 4/7 = 57\% < \text{min\_conf}$ (discarded)
    - $G4 \Rightarrow G2 = 4/6 = 66\% < \text{min\_conf}$ (discarded).

Finally, only one rule is generated ($G4 \Rightarrow G3$). It is very clear that if the minimum-confidence threshold had been set to 70%, then four rules would have been generated. This indicates that it is very important to make a careful choice of the interestingness measures (e.g., support and confidence) thresholds before mining the ARs. The AR that was generated could mean that when gene 4 (G4) is overexpressed, then it is also likely, with a high possibility (83%), that gene 3 (G3) is also overexpressed.

The majority of frequent pattern-mining algorithms are based on the APRIORI candidate generation procedure. The main drawback of these methods is the high computational cost of the evaluation of all candidates. For this reason a lot of algorithms that are inspired by the FP-GROWTH algorithm and exploit the use of a tree structure have been proposed. Kotala et al. [28] proposed a method for mining microarray data using *Peano count trees* (P-Trees). This method treats the microarray data as spartial data.

Two interesting approaches which are based on the frequent closed-pattern idea are [29] and [30]. The definition of a closed pattern as is given by Han et al. [31], states that a is a closed frequent pattern in a database D if a is frequent in D and there exists no proper superpattern b such that b has the same support as a in D. Mining closed itemsets provides an interesting alternative to mining frequent itemsets because it generates a much smaller set of results and so it achieved better scalability and interpretability.

34.5.2 Mining in Vertical-Data Format

As already mentioned before, gene expression data usually contain a very large number of columns, which represent the genes, in comparison to rows, which are the experiments. For example, a gene expression matrix may contain 10,000–100,000 columns but only 100–1000 rows. As a result, it became obvious that the methods which use the horizontal-data format for these data sets are not very suitable. Thus, many new algorithms were proposed in order to handle high-dimensional data, such as gene expression data, in vertical-data format.

The first algorithm designed to handle a microarray data set in vertical-data format was CARPENTER [32]. CARPENTER discovers frequent closed patterns by performing depth-first rowwise enumeration instead of the conventional feature (column) enumeration. Furthermore, pruning techniques are used in order to optimize the algorithm's efficiency.

Another approach, called FARMER, has been proposed by Cong et al. [33]. FARMER finds interesting rule groups and builds classifiers based on them. The concept of rule groups implies that rules supported by exactly the same set of rows are grouped together. FARMER is designed specifically to generate rules of the form $X \Rightarrow C$, where X is a set of genes and C is a class label. For that reason, each experiment in microarray data should be related to a class label, such as cancer or noncancer.

Pan et al. extended the CARPENTER algorithm in order to handle data sets with large numbers of both columns and rows. The algorithm, which is called COBBLER [34], switches dynamically between column and row enumeration based on the estimated cost of processing. Moreover, COBBLER is more efficient than the previously mentioned algorithms: CHARM, CLOSET+, and CARPENTER.

Finally, another interesting approach was proposed in 2006 by Liu et al. [35]. They developed an algorithm, TD-CLOSE, to find the complete set of frequent closed itemsets. The main difference with the existing approaches is that TD-CLOSE adapts a top-down row enumeration search strategy which enables the use of the minimum-support threshold to dramatically prune the search space.

34.6 SEQUENTIAL DATA MINING

Technological advances of the last decades have driven the collection of vast amounts of biological sequences. After the completion of genome-sequencing projects, the sequenced genomes have to be analyzed and annotated. The observed paradigm shift from static structural genomics to dynamic functional genomics [36] and the assignment of functional information to known sequences are considered particularly important. Gene prediction is the step that usually follows sequencing and is concerned with the identification of stretches of DNA that are biologically functional. As it is not a straightforward task, especially for the more complex eukaryotic genomes, the use of advanced techniques, including data mining, is required.

For example, eukaryotic genes consist of coding parts, called *exons*, that are separated by intervening noncoding sequences, called *introns*. Introns are removed from the transcribed RNA sequence by the process of splicing. The recognition of the splice sites, namely the boundaries between adjacent exons and introns, is a difficult problem that exploits data-mining methods. The problem becomes even more challenging if one considers the possibility of alternative splicing, that is, the production of different mature mRNA molecules, depending on the number of the exons that are finally concatenated.

Other important sequence analysis tasks are the prediction of regulatory regions, that is, promoters and enhancers, which are segments of DNA where regulatory proteins bind preferentially and thus control gene expression and consequently protein abundance. The prediction of the transcription start site, where transcription of DNA to RNA starts, the prediction of translation initiation site, where translation of mRNA to protein initiates, and the prediction of polyadenylation sites where a polyA (multiple adenines) tail is added at the 3' end of an mRNA sequence are also some important sequence analysis tasks.

Quite often, around these important sites there are found some signals or patterns that appear with variable frequency in each case. These patterns could be exported using frequent itemset mining algorithms. Moreover, various patterns or sequence parts that are found near specific sequence signals could be associated to each other using ARs. In most cases the representation of a particular biological sequence is accomplished by a number of features that should be extracted from this sequence. These features usually record the frequencies of some variable-length nucleotide patterns. In such a case, if a frequent-itemset mining algorithm should be used, it is essential to apply a discretization method first in order to transform the continuous-valued features to categorical ones.

An approach which used association analysis and combined gene expression and biological sequences was proposed by Icev et al. [37]. In their approach they focused on characterization of the expression patterns of genes based on their promoter regions. The promoter region contains short sequences called motifs to which may bind gene regulatory proteins which possibly control the gene expression mechanisms. The *distance-based AR mining* (DARM) algorithm is based on the APRIORI algorithm. DARM has the ability to involve multiple motifs and to predict expression in multiple cell types. Moreover, ARs in DARM are enhanced with information about the distances among the motifs that are present in the rules in order to investigate whether the order and spacing of the motifs can affect expression.

Another category of frequent pattern that can be used for discriminating two classes is the emerging patterns. In a recent study [38], a method called PolyA-iEP, which exploits the advantages of emerging patterns as well as a distance-based scoring method, has been proposed. This method aims to effectively predict polyadenylation sites in biological sequences and can be used for both descriptive and predictive analysis.

Emerging patterns [39] are itemsets whose supports increase significantly from one data set to another. Given two data sets D_1 and D_2, the *growth rate* of an itemset X from D_1 to D_2 is defined as follows (indices 1 and 2 are used instead of D_1 and D_2):

$$gr_{1 \to 2}(X) = \begin{cases} 0 & \text{if } supp_1(X) = 0 \text{ and } supp_2(X) = 0 \\ \infty & \text{if } supp_1(X) = 0 \text{ and } supp_2(X) > 0 \\ \dfrac{supp_2(X)}{supp_1(X)} & \text{otherwise} \end{cases}$$

Given a minimum growth rate threshold $\rho > 1$, an itemset X is said to be ρ-*emerging pattern*, or simply an *emerging pattern*, from D_1 to D_2 if $gr_{1 \to 2}(X) \geq \rho$, where D_1 is called the *background data set* and D_2 the *target data set*.

The *strength* of an emerging pattern X from D_1 to D_2 is defined as

$$strength_{1 \to 2}(X) = \begin{cases} supp_2(X) & \text{if } gr_{1 \to 2}(X) = \infty \\ supp_2(X)\dfrac{gr_{1 \to 2}(X)}{gr_{1 \to 2}(X) + 1} & \text{otherwise} \end{cases}$$

In contrast to other patterns or models, emerging patterns are easily interpretable and understood. Moreover, emerging patterns, especially those with a large growth rate and strength, provide a great potential for discriminating examples of different classes. This twofold benefit of emerging patterns makes them a useful tool for exploring domains that are not well understood, providing the means for descriptive and predictive analysis as well.

A disadvantage of emerging pattern mining is that the number of emerging patterns may be huge, especially when minimum-support and minimum-growth-rate thresholds are set very low. Increasing the thresholds is not an ideal solution, since valuable emerging patterns may not be discovered. For example, if the minimum-support threshold is set high, then those emerging patterns with a low support but with a high growth rate will be lost. Conversely, if the minimum-growth-rate threshold is set high, then those emerging patterns with a low growth rate but with a high support will be lost. Some interestingness measures have been proposed to reduce the number of mined emerging patterns without sacrificing valuable emerging patterns, or at least sacrificing as less as possible. Such an interestingness measure includes a special kind of emerging pattern, called a *chi emerging pattern* [40], defined as follows: Given a background dataset D_1 and a target dataset D_2, an itemset X is called a *chi emerging pattern* if all the following conditions are true:

1. $\text{supp}_2(X) \geq \sigma$, where σ is a minimum support threshold.
2. $\text{gr}_{1 \rightarrow 2}(X) \geq \rho$, where ρ is a minimum growth rate threshold.
3. $\forall Y \subset X, \text{gr}_{1 \rightarrow 2}(Y) < \text{gr}_{1 \rightarrow 2}(X)$
4. $|X| = 1 \vee |X| > 1 \wedge (\forall Y \subset X \wedge |Y| = |X| - 1 \wedge \text{chi}(X, Y) \geq \eta)$, where $\eta = 3.84$ is a minimum chi value threshold and $\text{chi}(X, Y)$ is computed using the chi-squared test.

The first condition ensures that the mined emerging patterns will have at least a minimum coverage over the training data set in order to generalize well on new instances. The second condition ensures that the mined emerging patterns will have an adequate discriminating power. The third condition is used to filter out those emerging patterns that have a subset with higher or equal growth rate and higher or equal support (any itemset has equal or greater support than any of its supersets). Since the subset has fewer items, there is no reason to keep this emerging pattern. Finally, the fourth condition ensures that an emerging pattern has a significantly (95%) different support distribution in target and background data sets than the distributions of its immediate subsets.

34.7 STRUCTURAL DATA MINING

Structural bioinformatics is the subfield of bioinformatics which is related to the analysis and prediction of the three-dimensional structure of biological macromolecules, especially for proteins. The application of machine learning and data mining in structural bioinformatics is quite challenging, since structural data are not linear. Moreover, the search space for most structural problems is continuous and infinite and demands highly efficient and heuristic algorithms.

Important problems of structural bioinformatics that utilize machine learning and data-mining methods are the RNA secondary-structure prediction, the inference of a protein's function from its structure, the identification of protein–protein interactions, and the efficient design of drugs based on structural knowledge of their target.

Machine learning and data-mining methods are also applied for protein secondary-structure prediction. This problem has been studied for over 35 years and many techniques have been developed. Initially, statistical approaches were adopted to deal with this problem. Later, more accurate techniques based on information theory, Bayes theory, nearest neighbors, and neural networks were developed. Combined methods such as integrated multiple-sequence alignments with neural network or nearest-neighbor approaches improve prediction accuracy.

Secondary-structure prediction methods can be divided in four generations [41]: First-generation methods were based on single amino acid propensities. Second-generation methods used prospensities of 3–51 adjacent residues. The prediction accuracy was at 60% [42]. The accuracy is defined as the percentage of residues predicted correctly in one of the tree states: helix, strand, and other. Third-generation methods used information from homologue sequences and machine learning methods. Lastly, in fourth-generation methods, a matching between secondary and tertiary protein structure was used. Using the fourth-generation approaches, the accuracy reached around 77%. Nowadays a great amount of research has been focused on better representations of secondary-structure features which is believed will improve significantly the prediction accuracy of the algorithms. The better representation is achieved by discovering frequent patterns in protein databases.

An approach to the representation of secondary structure has been proposed by Birzele and Kramer [43]. In their approach they used the levelwise search strategy [44], which is a string-mining algorithm, in order to find frequent patterns in protein databases. From those frequent patterns were extracted features to be used in the prediction of the secondary structure using *support vector machines* (SVMs).

Finally, Beccerra et al. [45] proposed an algorithm for biological sequence feature classification. The approach includes two main features. First, the use of association analysis in order to extract interesting relationships hidden in biological data sets and, second, the use of machine learning classifiers trained with the data obtained from the association analysis. More specifically, the first feature consists of three main phases. First, the sequences are scanned as subsequences of *N* symbols (*N*-grams). The *N*-grams represent patterns of variable size in the biological sequence and are represented as binary vectors which allow the application of association analysis. The second step consists of finding frequent patterns in the sequences. The third step consist of finding ARs. In this approach the APRIORI algorithm was used for the AR extraction process.

34.8 PROTEIN INTERACTIONS: GRAPH DATA MINING

Proteins are the most versatile macromolecules in living systems. They are the building blocks from which the cells are assembled, and they constitute most of the cell's dry mass. Proteins not only provide the cell with shape and structure but also execute nearly all its numerous functions [46, 47]. Following are some of their numerous and versatile functions:

- *Function as catalyst in chemical reactions.* Enzymes are proteins that increase the rates of chemical reactions.
- *Transport and store other molecules such as oxygen.* For example, hemoglobin carries oxygen to the erythrocytes (red blood cells).
- *Provide mechanical support.* For example, collagen is the main component of connective tissue and is the most abundant protein in mammals.
- *Immune protection.* Antibodies are proteins used by the immune system to identify and neutralize foreign objects like bacteria and viruses.
- *Generate movement.* For instance, myosin in skeletal muscle cells provides the motive force for humans to move.
- *Detects and transmits nerve impulses to the cells' response machinery.* For instance, rhodopsin in the retina detects light.
- *Control growth and differentiation.*

It is obvious that proteins have a wide range of functions. In fact, a protein almost never performs its function in isolation. It should interact with other proteins in order to accomplish a certain function. It has been discovered that the vast majority of proteins interact with multiple partners (on average six to eight other proteins) and thousands of different proteins form intricate interaction networks or highly regulated pathways [48]. The most common way for the representation of these networks are as undirected graphs. In these graphs the proteins are represented as nodes and the interactions are represented as edges between two nodes (proteins).

The last years many interactions have been discovered by researchers. This has been achieved through new high-throughput methods which have been recently proposed. The huge number of interactions discovered have been stored in many databases. Xenarios and Eisenberg [49] have reviewed and presented many of them, including DIP, BIND, MIPS, PROTEOME, PROTONET, CURAGEN, and PIM.

Although a huge amount of information is contained in these databases, there are several issues associated with them and the most important is the large amount of noise that is present in high-throughput interaction data [50]. The noise can affect the efficacy of the algorithms at the task of function prediction between different data sets [51].

Recently, some data-mining techniques have been proposed to determine the reliability of a given interaction. One of them [52] uses the *h-confidence* measure [53] from the field of association analysis which can be used to estimate the similarity between two proteins based on the number of their shared neighbors. The importance of using the *h*-confidence measure for all pairs of proteins in this network is twofold. First, it can address the problem of noise in the data mentioned before. For instance, when an interaction is already known, the *h*-confidence measure between the two particular proteins is low. Second, it can also address another important problem of the interaction data, which is the problem of incompleteness. For example, if an interaction between two proteins is not known and the *h*-confidence measure for these proteins is high, then it is probable that an interaction between those two proteins exists.

Association analysis can be used to predict protein functions from a protein interaction network. In the context of graphs the frequent patterns stand for the frequent subgraphs in a set of graphs [54]. In the context of protein interaction networks a set of graphs may be a set of protein interaction networks and frequent patterns (subgraphs) may be functional modules. The discovered network modules can be used in many biological applications such as the prediction of the function of unknown genes or the construction of the transcription modules.

Hu et al. [55] developed an algorithm, called CODENCE, to efficiently mine frequent coherent dense subgraphs across a large number of massive graphs. The two main steps of the algorithm include the construction of a summary graph across multiple relation graphs $G_1, \ldots, G_n$ and then the mining of dense summary graphs using the MODES algorithm [56]. It is worth mentioning that this method can integrate heterogeneous network data, such as protein interaction networks, genetic interaction networks, and coexpression networks to reveal consistent biological signals.

Also, Xiong et al. [57] proposed a hyperclique pattern discovery approach in order to extract functional modules from protein complexes. A *hyperclique pattern* is a type of association pattern that contains highly affiliated proteins, that is, every pair of proteins in the same hyperclique pattern is guaranteed to have the cosine similarity above a certain level. For that reason, if a protein is found to belong in a protein complex, then it is very probable that the other proteins in the same hyperclique pattern also belong to the same protein complex. The h-confidence measure mentioned before is designed to capture the strength of this association. The definitions of h-confidence and hyperclique pattern are given below according to [57]:

- The h-confidence of a pattern $X = \{p_1, p_2, \ldots, p_m\}$, denoted as hconf($X$), is a measure that reflects the overall affinity among proteins within the pattern. This measure is defined as $\min(\text{conf}(\{p_1\} \Rightarrow \{p_2, p_3, \ldots, p_m\}), \text{conf}(\{p_2\} \Rightarrow \{p_1, p_3, \ldots, p_m\}), \text{conf}(\{p_3\} \Rightarrow \{p_1, p_2, \ldots, p_m\}), \ldots \text{conf}(\{p_m\} \Rightarrow \{p_1, p_2, \ldots, p_{m-1}\})$, where conf is the confidence of AR.
- A pattern X is a hyperclique pattern if hconf(X) $\geq h_c$, where h_c is a user-specified minimum h-confidence threshold. A hyperclique pattern is a maximal hyperclique pattern if no superset of this pattern is also a hyperclique pattern.

Another approach to the field of protein interaction networks was proposed by Besemann et al. [58], who introduced the concept of differential AR mining to study the annotations of proteins in the context of one or more interaction networks. The goal of this technique was to highlight the differences among items belonging to different interacting nodes or different networks, something that could not be achieved with the standard relational AR mining techniques.

Another perspective to the field of protein interaction networks is to find frequent subnetworks in a given network in a different manner than in the previously described approaches which focused on mining frequent subgraphs in a set of networks. Such an algorithm is NeMoFINDER, which was proposed by Chen et al. [59] and was inspired by the APRIORI algorithm.

34.9 TEXT MINING

Text mining in molecular biology, defined as the automatic extraction of information about genes, proteins, and their functional relationships from text documents [60], has emerged as a hybrid discipline on the edges of the fields of information science, bioinformatics, and computational linguistics.

It is critically important for biologists to have access to the most up-to-date information on their field of research. Current research practice involves online search for gene-related information utilizing the latest technologies in information retrieval, semantic Web, and text mining. A new term lately used by bioinformaticians to describe the text body where they can extract information such as ontology, interaction, and function between biological entities is the *textome*. Generally, it can include all parseable and computable scientific text body.

The rapid progress in biomedical research has led to a dramatic increase in the amount of available information in terms of published articles, journals, books, and conference proceedings. Pubmed is a free database accessing primarily the MEDLINE database of references and abstracts on life sciences and biomedical topics. As of July 1, 2011, PubMed has over 21 million records, 11.0 milion articles are listed with their abstracts, and 3.3 milion articles are available full text for free. Every year about 500,000 new records are added. In total, more than 5000 journals are currently indexed by PubMed. Although PubMed is by far the richest database of abstracts, citations, and full text articles, there is a plethora of such sources of scientific publications on biology such as NCBI BookShelf for e-books and a large number of online resources. The researchers' need to exploit this enormous volume of available information, along with the availability of high-performance and efficient data mining, natural language processing, and information retrieval tools, has given birth to a new field of research and application called *bioinformatics text mining* (BTM). Other terms for BTM are bio(logical) text mining and biomedical text mining.

From a data miner's point of view, biomedical literature has certain characteristics that require special attention, such as heavy use of domain-specific terminology, polysemic words (word sense disambiguation), low-frequency words (data sparseness), creation of new names, and terms and different writing styles [61].

Several studies have categorized the tasks of BTM from different points of view. Cohen and Hersh [62] provide a high-level categorization identifying the main tasks to be the following:

- *Named Entity Recognition* (NER)   The goal is to find and classify atomic elements in text into predefined categories.
- *Text Classification*   The goal is to determine whether a document has particular characteristics, usually based on whether the document includes certain types of information.
- *Synonym and Abbreviation Extraction*   This task deals with the problem that many biological entities have multiple names, so in the biomedical literature there are many synonyms and abbreviations.
- *Relationship Extraction*   The goal of relationship extraction is to find a specific type of relationship between a pair of entities of given types.
- *Hypothesis Generation*   The goal is to find relationships that are not present in text but are inferred by other explicit relationships.

An early work which used ARs for text mining was proposed by Hristovski et al. [63]. The goal of the system they presented was to discover new, potentially meaningful relations of a given concept of interest with other concepts that have not been published in the medical literature before. All the known relations among the concepts came from MEDLINE. Each citation in MEDLINE is associated with a set of *medical subject heading* (MeSH) terms that describe the content of the item in the database. The main idea was the use of ARs to find all concepts Y that are related to the starting concept X and then to find all the concepts Z that are related to the concept Y. The next step included examination of whether the concepts X and Z are found together in the medical literature. If they do not appear, it is possible that a new relation has been discovered. Evaluation of the discovered associations was done by human experts, laboratory methods, or clinical investigations, depending of the nature of X and Z.

Another interesting approach that used ARs for biomedical text mining was proposed by Berardi et al. [64]. The purpose of their method was to detect associations between concepts as an indication of the existence of the biomedical relation. This method also used the MEDLINE abstract and MeSH taxonomy. The hierarchical nature of the MeSH taxonomy made it possible to mine multilevel ARs (generalized ARs) [9]. Generalized ARs include ARs of the form $X \Rightarrow Y$, where no item in Y is an ancestor of any item in X in a given taxonomy.

34.10 CONCLUSION

Frequent patterns and ARs are useful data-mining tools that have attracted research interest since 1993 as a means of unsupervised, exploratory data analysis. Although they were initially proposed as a market basket analysis tool, they were almost immediately applied to other application domains and nowadays include a large number of applications. The community of biologists and bioinformaticians have used ARs for analyzing a quite variable set of biological data. Gene expression data, biological sequences, biological structural data, protein interaction networks, and biological texts are the most popular kinds of biological data that have been effectively analyzed using these data-mining tools.

As already done in the past, it is deemed that several new algorithms for mining ARs more efficiently as well as for mining new kinds of patterns and extending the concept of ARs will be proposed in the future. All these novel AR mining tools will provide the means for more efficient and effective analyses of biological data. As a result, the research efforts of biologists will be enhanced by the gain of new biological insights and the rise of new biological questions that will guide unexplored research directions.

REFERENCES

1. R. Agrawal, T. Imielinski, and A. Swami. Mining association rules between sets of items in large databases. In P. Buneman and S. Jajodia (Eds.), *Proceedings of the 1993 ACM SIGMOD International Conference on Management of Data*, Washington, DC, May 26–28, 1993, ACM Press, 1993.

2. R. Agrawal and R. Srikant. Fast algorithms for mining association rules in large databases. J. B. Bocca, M. Jarke, and C. Zaniolo (Eds.). *Proceedings of the 20th International Conference on Very Large Data Bases (VLDB'94)*, Santiago de Chile, Chile, September 12–15, 1994, Morgan Kaufmann, 1994.

3. H. Mannila, H. Toivonen, and A. I. Verkamo. Efficient algorithms for discovering association rules. In U. M. Fayyad and R. Uthurusamy (Eds.), *Knowledge Discovery in Databases: Papers from the 1994 AAAI Workshop*, Technical Report WS-94-03, AAAI Press, Seattle, WA, July 1994, pp. 181–192.

4. J. Han, J. Pei, and Y. Yin. Mining frequent patterns without candidate generation. In W. Chen, J. F. Naughton, and P. A. Bernstein (Eds.), *Proceedings of the 2000 ACM SIGMOD International Conference on Management of Data*, Dallas, TX, May 16–18, 2000, ACM, 2000, pp. 1–12.

5. M. J. Zaki. Scalable algorithms for association mining. *IEEE Trans. Knowledge Data Eng.*, 12:372–390, 2000.

6. K. Koperski and J. Han. Discovery of spatial association rules in geographic information databases. In M. J. Egenhofer and J. R. Herring (Eds.), *Advances in Spatial Databases: Proceedings of the 4th International Symposium (SSD'95)*, Portland, ME, August 6–9, 1995, *Lecture Notes in Computer Science*, Springer, 1995, pp. 47–66.

7. X. Chen and I. Petrounias. Discovering temporal association rules: Algorithms, language and system. In *Proceedings of the 16th International Conference on Data Engineering*, 2000.

8. A. K. H. Tung, H. Lu, J. Han, and L. Feng. Efficient mining of intertransaction association rules. *IEEE Trans. Knowledge Data Eng.*, 15(1):43–56, 2003.

9. R. Srikant and R. Agrawal. Mining generalized association rules. In U. Dayal, P. M. D. Gray, and S. Nishio, *Proceedings of 21st International Conference on Very Large Data Bases (VLDB'95)*, Zurich, Switzerland, September 11–15, 1995, Morgan Kaufmann, 1995, pp. 407–419.

10. S. Thomas and S. Sarawagi. Mining generalized association rules and sequential patterns using SQL queries. In R. Agrawal, P. E. Stolorz, and G. Piatetsky-Shapiro (Eds.), *Proceedings of the Fourth International Conference on Knowledge Discovery and Data Mining (KDD'98)*, New York City, NY, August 27–31, 1998, AAAI Press 1998, pp. 344–348.

11. J. Han and Y. Fu. Discovery of multiple-level association rules from large databases. In U. Dayal, P. M. D. Gray, S. Nishio, *Proceedings of 21st International Conference on Very Large Data Bases (VLDB'95)*, Zurich, Switzerland, September 11–15, 1995, Morgan Kaufmann, 1995, pp. 420–431.

12. A. Savasere, E. Omiecinski, and S. B. Navathe. Mining for strong negative associations in a large database of customer transactions. In *Proceedings of 14th International Conference on Data Engineering*, Orlando, FL, February 23–27, 1998, pp. 494–502.

13. X. Wu, C. Zhang, and S. Zhang. Efficient mining of both positive and negative association rules. *ACM Trans. Inform. Syst.*, 22(3):381–405, 2004.

14. G. Tzanis and C. Berberidis. Mining for mutually exclusive items in transaction databases. *Int. J. Data Warehousing Mining*, 3(3):45–59, 2007.

15. G. Tzanis, C. Berberidis, and I. Vlahavas. On the discovery of mutually exclusive items in a market basket database. In *Proceedings of the 2nd ADBIS Workshop on Data Mining and Knowledge Discovery*, Thessaloniki, Greece, 2006.

16. F. H. C. Crick. On protein synthesis. *Sympo. Soc. Exp. Biol.*, 12:139–163, 1958.

17. J. Dougherty, R. Kohavi, and M. Sahami. Supervised and unsupervised discretization of continuous features. In A. Prieditis and S. J. Russell (Eds.), *Machine Learning: Proceedings of the Twelfth International Conference on Machine Learning*, Tahoe City, CA, July 9–12, 1995, Morgan Kaufmann, 1995.

18. U. Fayyad and K. Irani. On the handling of continuous-valued attributes in decision tree generation. *Machine Learning*, 8:87–102, 1992.

19. M. Vannucci and V. Colla. Meaningful discretization of continuous features for association rules mining by means of a SOM. In *Proceedings of the ESANN2004 European Symposium on Artificial Neural Networks*, Belgium, 2004, pp. 489–494.

20. C. Becquet, S. Blachon, B. Jeudy, J.-F. Boulicaut, and O. Gandrillon. Strong-association-rule mining for large-scale gene-expression data analysis: A case study on human SAGE data. *Genome Biol.*, 3(12): 2002.

21. V. E. Velculescu, L. Zhang, B. Vogelstein, and K. W. Kinzler. Serial analysis of gene expression. *Science*, 270(5235):484–487, 1995.

22. T. Kohonen. The self-organizing map. *Proc. IEEE*, 78(9):1464–1480, 1990.

23. M.-C. Ludl and G. Widmer. Relative unsupervised discretization for association rule mining. In *Proceedings of the Fourth European Conference on Principles and Practice of Knowledge Discovery in Databases*, 2000.

24. B. Baesens, S. Viaene, and J. Vanthienen. Postprocessing of association rules. In *Proceedings of the Workshop Post Processing in Machine Learning and Data Mining: Interpretation, Visualization, Integration, and Related Topics, Sixth ACM SIGKDD International Conference on Knowledge Discovery and Data Mining*, Boston, MA, 2000.

25. M. Schena, D. Shalon, R. W. Davis, and P. O. Brown. Quantitative monitoring of gene expression patterns with a complementary DNA microarray. *Science* 270(5235):467–470, 1995.

26. K. Aas. Microarray data mining: A survey. NR Note. SAMBA, Norwegian Computing Center, Oslo, 2001.

27. A. Tuzhilin and G. Adomavicius. Handling very large numbers of association rules in the analysis of microarray data. In *Proceedings of the Eighth ACM SIGKDD International Conference on Data Mining and Knowledge Discovery*, Edmonton, Canada, July 23–26, 2002, pp. 396–404.

28. P. Kotala, A. Perera, and J. K. Zhou. Gene expression profiling of DNA microarray data using peano count tree (p-trees). In *Proceedings of the First Virtual Conference on Genomics and Bioinformatics*, North Dakota State University, 2001, pp. 15–16.

29. J. Wang, J. Han, and J. Pei. Closet+: Searching for the best strategies for mining frequent closed itemsets. In L. Getoor, T. E. Senator, P. Domingos, and C. Faloutsos (Eds.), *Proceedings of the Ninth ACM SIGKDD International Conference on Knowledge Discovery and Data Mining*, Washington, DC, August 24–27, 2003, ACM, 2003.

30. M. J. Zaki and C. J. Hsiao. CHARM: An efficient algorithm for closed itemset mining. In *Proc. 2002 SIAM Int. Conf. Data Mining*, Arlington, VA, 2002, pp. 457–473.

31. J. Han, H. Cheng, D. Xin, and X. Yan. Frequent pattern mining: Current status and future directions. *Data Mining Knowledge Discov.*, 15(1):55–86, 2007.

32. F. Pan et al. Carpenter: Finding closed patterns in long biological datasets. In L. Getoor, T. E. Senator, P. Domingos, and C. Faloutsos (Eds.), *Proceedings of the Ninth ACM SIGKDD International Conference on Knowledge Discovery and Data Mining*, Washington, DC, August 24–27, 2003, pp. 637–642.

33. G. Cong, A. K. H. Tung, X. Xu, F. Pan, and J. Yang. Farmer: Finding interesting rule groups in microarray datasets. *Proceedings of the 2004 ACM SIGMOD International Conference on Management of Data*, Paris, France, June 13–18, 2004.

34. F. Pan, A. Tung, G. Cong, and X. Xu. COBBLER: Combining column and row enumeration for closed pattern discovery. In *Proceedings of the 16th International Conference on Scientific and Statistical Database Management*, 2004, pp. 21–30.

35. H. Liu, J. Han, D. Xin, and Z. Shao. Mining frequent patterns from very high dimensional data: A top-down row enumeration approach. In *Proceeding of the 2006 SIAM International Conference on Data Mining (SDM 06)*, Bethesda, MD, Citeseer, 2006, pp. 280–291.

36. J. L. Houle, W. Cadigan, S. Henry, A. Pinnamaneni, and S. Lundahl. Database mining in the Human Genome Initiative. Whitepaper, Bio-databases.com, Amita Corporation. Available: http://www.biodatabases.com/whitepaper01.html, last Accessed July 15, 2011.

37. A. Icev, C. Ruiz, and E. F. Ryder. Distance-based association rules mining. M. J. Zaki, J. T.-L. Wang, and H. Toivonen (Eds.), *Proceedings of the 3rd ACM SIGKDD Workshop on Data Mining in Bioinformatics (BIOKDD'03)*, August 27, 2003, Washington, DC, 2003, pp. 34–40.

38. G. Tzanis, I. Kavakiotis, and I. Vlahavas. PolyA-iEP: A data mining method for the effective prediction of polyadenylation sites. *Expert Syst. Appl.*, 38(10):12398–12408, 2011.

39. G. Dong and J. Li. Efficient mining of emerging patterns: Discovering trends and differences. In U. M. Fayyad, S. Chaudhuri, and D. Madigan (Eds.), *Proceedings of the Fifth ACM SIGKDD International Conference on Knowledge Discovery and Data Mining*, San Diego, CA, August 15–18, 1999, ACM 1999, pp. 43–52.

40. H. Fan. Efficient mining of interesting emerging patterns and their effective use in classification. Ph.D. Thesis. University of Melbourne, Australia, 2004.

41. F. Birzele. Data mining for protein secondary structure prediction. Master's thesis. Technische Universität München, Jan. 2005.

42. B. Rost. Review: Protein secondary structure prediction continue torise. *J. Struct. Biol.*, 134:204–218, 2001.

43. F. Birzele and S. Kramer. A new representation for protein secondary structure prediction based on frequent patterns. *Bioinformatics*, 22:2628–2634, Nov. 2006.

44. H. Mannila and H. Toivonen. Levelwise search and borders of theories in knowledge discovery. *Data Mining Knowledge Discov.*, 3:241–258, 1997.

45. D. Becerra, D. Vanegas, G. Cantor, and L. Niño. An association rule based approach for biological sequence feature classification. In *Proceedings of the Eleventh CEC*, IEEE, 2009, pp. 3111–3118.

46. B. Alberts, D. Bray, K. Hopkin, A. Johnson, J. Lewis, M. Raff, K. Roberts, and P. Walter. *Essential Cell Biology*, 2nd ed. Garland Publishing, 2004.

47. L. Stryer. *Biochemistry*, 3rd ed. W. H. Freeman, 1988.

48. A. Panchenko and T. Przytycka. *Protein–Protein Interactions and Networks. Identification, Computer Analysis and Prediction*. Springer, 2008.

49. I. Xenarios and D. Eisenberg. Protein interaction databases. *Curr. Opin. Biotechnol.*, 12:334–339, 2001.

50. G. Pandey, V. Kumar, and M. Steinbach. Computational approaches for protein function prediction: A survey. Technical Report 06-028. Department of Computer Science and Engineering, University of Minnesota, Twin Cities, MN, 2006.

51. M. Deng, F. Sun, and T. Chen. Assessment of the reliability of protein–protein interactions and protein function prediction. *Pac. Symp. Biocomput.*, 140–151, 2003.

52. G. Pandey, M. Steinbach, R. Gupta, T. Garg, and V. Kumar. Association analysis-based transformations for protein interaction networks: A function prediction case study. In P. Berkhin, R. Caruana, and X. Wu (Eds.), *Proceedings of the 13th ACM SIGKDD International Conference on Knowledge Discovery and Data Mining*, San Jose, CA, August 12–15, 2007, pp. 540–549.

53. H. Xiong, P.-N. Tan, and V. Kumar. Hyperclique pattern discovery. *Data Mining Knowledge Discov.*, 13(2):219–242, 2006.

54. M. Kuramochi and G. Karypis. An efficient algorithm for discovering frequent subgraphs. *IEEE Trans. Knowledge Data Eng.*, 16(9):1038–1051, 2004.

55. H. Hu, X. Yan, Y. Huang, et al. Mining coherent dense subgraphs across massive biological networks for functional discovery. *Bioinformatics*, 21, 2005.

56. E. Hartuv and R. Shamir. A clustering algorithm based on graph connectivity. *Inform. Process. Lett.*, 76:4–6, 175–181, 2000.

57. H. Xiong, X. He, C. Ding, Y. Zhang, V. Kumar, S. R. Holbrook. Identification of functional modules in protein complexes via hyperclique pattern discovery. In *Proc. Pacific Symposium on Biocomputing (PSB)*, 2005, pp. 221–232.

58. C. Besemann, A. Denton, and A. Yekkirala. Differential association rule mining for the study of protein-protein interaction networks. Paper presented at BIOKDD04: 4th Workshop on Data Mining in Bioinformatics (with SIGKDD Conference), Seattle, WA, 2004, pp. 72–80.

59. J. Chen, W. Hsu, M. L. Lee, and S.-K. Ng. NeMoFinder: Dissecting genome-wide protein–protein interactions with meso-scale network motifs. In T. Eliassi-Rad, L. H. Ungar, M. Craven, and D. Gunopulos (Eds.), *Proceedings of the Twelfth ACM SIGKDD International Conference on Knowledge Discovery and Data Mining*, Philadelphia, PA, August 20–23, 2006. ACM, 2006, pp. 106–115.

60. M. Krallinger and A. Valencia. Text-mining and information-retrieval services for molecular biology. *Genome Biol.*, 6:224, 2005.

61. G. Tzanis, C. Berberidis, and I. Vlahavas. Machine learning and data mining in bioinformatics. In L. C. Rivero, J. H. Doorn, and V. E. Ferraggine (Eds.), *Handbook of Research on Innovations in Database Technologies and Applications: Current and Future Trends*. IGI Global, 2009.

62. A. M. Cohen and W. R. Hersh. A survey of current work in biomedical text mining. *Brief. Bioinformatics*, 6(1):57–71, 2005.

63. D. Hristovski, J. Stare, B. Peterlin, and S. Dzeroski. Supporting discovery in medicine by association rule mining in Medline and UMLS. *Stud. Health Technol. Inform.*, 84(Part 2):1344–1348, 2001.

64. M. Berardi, M. Lapi, P. Leo, and C. Loglisci. Mining generalized association rules on biomedical literature. *Lecture Notes Comput. Sci.*, 3533:500–509, 2005.

CHAPTER 35

GALOIS CLOSURE BASED ASSOCIATION RULE MINING FROM BIOLOGICAL DATA

KARTICK CHANDRA MONDAL and NICOLAS PASQUIER
Laboratory I3S, University of Nice Sophia-Antipolis, Sophia-Antipolis, France

35.1 INTRODUCTION

The association rule mining task was introduced in pattern mining and knowledge discovery no more than two decades ago. Many intensive and extensive researches have been conducted to improve this task since then. As a result, several scalable and efficient methods and techniques are now available to ascertain association rules from very large data repositories. The greater extent of these researches have concentrated on the different concepts, methods, and data structures to efficiently identify the most relevant association rules. First applications have pointed out that mining association rules using frequent-itemset-based approaches, such as the state-of-the-art a priori algorithm, can be computationally expensive and generate a large quantity of rules. Several theoretical frameworks were proposed to minimize the search space and improve the efficiency of the association rule extraction from the data set. To reduce the number of rules generated, two main approaches have been studied: condensed representations and interestingness measures of association rules. Condensed representations minimize the number of association rules with minimal information loss. Interestingness measures are used to filter uninteresting and useless rules or group of rules with identical coverage in the data set. They are usually classified into three categories: objective (data-driven), subjective (user-driven), and semantic (context-driven) measures. Results of these works have been adapted and applied for mining association rules from biological data. These applications have been successful to contribute to the understanding of biological processes and diseases. This chapter presents the different theoretical frameworks, condensed representations, interestingness measures, and biological applications of association rule mining.

Association rule mining was introduced in the early 1990s by Agrawal et al. [3]. Since then, intensive research works produced many efficient association rule mining techniques some of which are specific to peculiar application domains. The term *association rules* came from the idea of showing the associations, companionship, and juxtaposition between two groups of variable values, called *items*, in a data set. Each group of items in the data set is called an *itemset* and a directed conditional relationship, or association rule, between two

Biological Knowledge Discovery Handbook: Preprocessing, Mining, and Postprocessing of Biological Data, First Edition. Edited by Mourad Elloumi and Albert Y. Zomaya.

itemsets is represented using the arrow implication symbol. The distribution of an itemset, that is, the number of instances the items appear together in the data set, is the *support* of the itemset. For each itemset containing more than one item, several association rules can be generated by dividing the items into different antecedents and consequents. For instance, for an itemset $\{X, Y, Z\}$ possible association rules are $\{X\} \rightarrow \{Y, Z\}$, $\{Y\} \rightarrow \{X, Z\}$, $\{Z\} \rightarrow \{X, Y\}$, $\{X, Y\} \rightarrow \{Z\}$, $\{X, Z\} \rightarrow \{Y\}$, and $\{Y, Z\} \rightarrow \{X\}$. The itemset on the left side of an association rule is called the *antecedent* of the rule and the itemset on the right side is called the *consequent*. For example, $\{X, Y\}$ is the antecedent and $\{Z\}$ is the consequent for rule $\{X, Y\} \rightarrow \{Z\}$. All association rules derived from an itemset have the same support that is equal to the support of the itemset itself. The *confidence* of an association rule is the conditional probability of appearance of the consequent of the rule among rows of the data set containing the antecedent. Association rules generated from the same itemset can thus have different confidence values as probabilities of the association relationship between their antecedent and their consequent can be dissimilar. The statistical measures of support and confidence associated to each association rule have as an objective to state respectively the coverage and the precision of the rule in the data set.

The number of possible itemsets in a data set is exponential in the number of items of the data set: For n items there are 2^n possible itemsets. For large data sets, where the number of itemsets is high, the resulting association rules can be of the order of hundreds of thousands, or even millions. To counter this problem and since, in general, neither rare combinations of items nor association rules with low conditional probabilities are relevant, using user-defined minimum-support and minimum-confidence threshold values is a common conception. If the frequency of an itemset is greater than or equal to the minimum-support threshold value minsup, this itemset is said to be a *frequent itemset*. Then, for a particular application, only frequent itemsets will generate association rules. Similarly, if the confidence of an association rule is greater than or equal to the minimum-confidence threshold value minconf, this rule is said to be a *valid* or *strong association rule*. For a particular application, only valid association rules will be generated.

Even if minsup and minconf values limit the number of association rules generated, their number can still be too large for visualizing and interpreting them. Moreover, several applications have pointed out that an important proportion of redundant association rules can be generated, lessening the informative property of the set of extracted rules. Informally, redundant association rules are rules that convey the same information to the end user. These problems are particularly important in the case of dense sets of highly correlated data where the number of frequent itemsets and valid association rules are huge, even for high values of minsup and minconf. Finding the most interesting rules in a compact set, containing maximal information, is one of the major challenges in association rule mining. Several ideas have been proposed for solving this particular problem. These proposals can be divided into two categories: *interestingness measures* and *condensed representations* of association rules. Condensed representations use the structural properties of association rules, such as inclusion relationships between antecedents and consequents or identical or close coverage and statistical precision values, to construct a small set of rules with the highest predictive power and coverage in the dataset. The *frequent-closed-itemset* framework introduced in the late 1990s has been used to define and characterize several condensed representations in this category. This comes from the fact that this framework is particularly well adapted to this problem as frequent closed itemsets identify groups of itemsets, or *equivalence classes*, that have the same coverage in the data set and *generators* that are the minimal common properties of these groups. Frequent closed itemsets, defined using the *Galois closure*, are the maximal common properties of these groups. A detailed discussion on this topic is given in Section 35.3. Interestingness measures are statistical values associated to each rule and used, in combination with minimum-support and minimum-confidence threshold, to discard a posteriori rules with a low predictive power. An interesting short summary of association rule interestingness measures can be found in [29]. A detailed discussion on this topic is given in Section 35.4. Interestingness measures and condensed representations are complementary approaches that can be used together to enhance as much as possible the predictive power of extracted association rule collections.

Association rule mining was applied in a wide range of application domains from business to health through telecommunications and the Internet. These applications have shown the efficiency and the adequacy of this methodology to support decision making, to optimize processes, and to get profit from individuals. One of the most active actual field of research is biological data analysis, or bioinformatics. Biological data mining presents several specificities and challenges for association rule mining. These are related to the nature of biological data, which are heterogeneous, noisy and uncertain, the need to integrate existing biological knowledge, represented in bio-ontologies, research reports, knowledge bases, graphs, and so on, in the process and the specific requirements of biological applications and tools. In Section 35.5, we discuss applications in biology in terms of genomics and proteomics. We concentrate on this particular domain of association rule mining, from higher level to genome and proteome analyses, as it is the most prolific domain of association rule application in bioinformatics. Even if a large number of works have been conducted in this intensive field of research, a lot of research issues are still open.

This chapter presents concepts and frameworks for association rule mining and their applications in biology, especially in genomics and proteomics. First, we give a short introduction to association rule mining background. The different theoretical frameworks proposed for itemset representation and frequent-itemset extraction are described in Section 35.2. The two following sections describe the proposed solutions for reducing sets of extracted association rules to the most relevant and useful rules. This is an important topic in association rule mining as several thousands, and sometimes millions, of association rules can be generated for large databases, with most often numerous redundant information. The different condensed representations of association rules, such as minimal covers, bases, and inference systems, along with their properties are presented in Section 35.3. Section 35.4 presents subjective and objective interestingness measures that can be used for selecting the most relevant association rules. In Section 35.5, we concentrate on biological applications of association rule mining, particularly in the genomic and proteomic fields of study. Section 35.6 concludes the chapter.

35.2 ASSOCIATION RULE MINING FRAMEWORKS

Research works in the association rule mining domain can be divided into two main segments: selecting the most relevant sets of items and generating the most pertinent association rules, either directly or indirectly, from these selected sets of items. Works in the first segment focus on the generation of different categories of sets of items, such as frequent itemsets, closed itemsets, free itemsets, and regular itemsets, with different structural properties in regard to the data set. In the second segment, works focus on association rule generation either indirectly, by using the itemsets previously extracted from the data set, or directly from the data set when they are based on evolutionary approaches. According to the notions

TABLE 35.1 Binary Matrix Representation of Data Set Đ

O-id	A	B	C	D	E	F
1	1	1	1	1	0	0
2	0	1	0	1	0	0
3	1	0	1	0	1	0
4	0	1	1	1	0	0
5	1	1	1	1	0	1

mentioned above, the frameworks for association rule mining can be classified into five categories:

- Based on the theoretical framework of the algorithms
- Based on the search space traversals of the algorithms
- Based on the data structure used by the algorithms
- Based on the databases dealing with the algorithms
- Based on the applications used for the algorithms.

In this section, we describe the most prominent of these frameworks: frequent-itemset (or classical) framework, closed-itemset framework, free-set framework, regular-set framework, and evolutionary computation framework.

Data representation has an important impact on the efficiency of any algorithm for extracting association rules. When data are coming from several sources, all approaches require to combine them into a unique matrix for processing. Transactional and binary matrices are the most widely used data representations used. Tables 35.1 and 35.2 give the representation in binary matrix and transactional format, respectively, of an example data set Đ. This data set will be used as a supporting example throughout the chapter for describing the different concepts. It contains five objects or rows, identified by their O-id or transaction number ranging from 1 to 5, and each of these objects contains a list of at most six items, namely A, B, C, D, E, and F. Throughout this chapter, we also use 0.4 (40%) for minimum-support and minimum-confidence threshold values unless explicitly stated otherwise.

35.2.1 Frequent-Itemset Framework

The first theoretical framework, defined in [3] together with the association rule mining problem, is the *frequent-itemset framework*. In this work, the frequent, or large, itemsets

TABLE 35.2 Transactional Representation of Data Set Đ

Transaction	Items
1	A, B, C, D
2	B, D
3	A, C, E
4	B, C, D
5	A, B, C, D, F

were defined as itemsets with support greater than or equal to the user-defined minsup threshold value in the data set. It was shown that all supersets of an *infrequent itemset*, that is, an itemset with support lower than *minsup*, are infrequent. The valid, or strong, association rules were also defined along with their support, which is the support of the itemset resulting from the union of the antecedent and the consequent of the rule, and their confidence, which is the ratio between the support of the consequent and the support of the union of the antecedent and the consequent of the rule. It was also shown that all valid association rules, that is, association rules with support and confidence greater than or equal to the user-defined minsup and minconf threshold values, respectively, can be generated from the frequent itemsets and their support. Considering the properties mentioned above, the association rule mining problem can be divided into two successive phases:

- Mining frequent itemsets, with their support, in the data set
- Generating valid association rules, with their support and confidence, from frequent itemsets and their support

Once frequent itemsets and their support are extracted, all valid association rules can be generated from them in a straightforward manner. Generating these rules is a much less computationally expensive task compared to the frequent-itemset mining process that requires accessing the data set. Optimizing the frequent-itemset mining process has thus been the subject of intensive research works for nearly two decades and many algorithms and theories have been proposed for this in the literature.

The difficulties of the frequent-itemset extraction lies in two points: First, it requires several costly scans of the data set that are usually stored in secondary memory. Second, the size of the search space is exponential in the number of items in the data set. If the data set contains n items, then the size of the search space is 2^n and the frequent itemset mining problem was shown to be NP complete [11]. This search space constitutes the subset lattice, or *itemset lattice*. The itemset lattice for database Đ that contains six items is given in Figure 35.1. We can see that, for a minimum-support threshold of 40%, there are 15 frequent itemsets and one maximal frequent itemset, all other itemsets being infrequent. Since all supersets of infrequent itemsets are infrequent, the maximal frequent itemsets, defined according to the inclusion relation, form a border above which all itemsets are infrequent and below which all itemsets are frequent.

Several algorithms for traversing the itemset lattice have been proposed in the literature to optimize this computationally expensive task. The state-of-the-art Apriori algorithm [4] introduced the principle of *levelwise traversal* to improve the efficiency of frequent-itemset extraction. Many algorithms derived from Apriori have then been proposed since. However, frequent-itemset-based approaches suffer from the problem of the huge number of frequent itemsets and association rules generated in the case of dense data sets [32]. Overviews of algorithms and descriptions of trends in frequent-itemset and association rule mining can be found in [40, 146, 200].

35.2.2 Closed-Itemset Framework

The *closed-itemset framework* was introduced to address the problem of association rule mining in dense data sets [141]. Closed itemsets are defined according to the closure operator γ of the Galois connection used in formal concept analysis and concept lattice theories

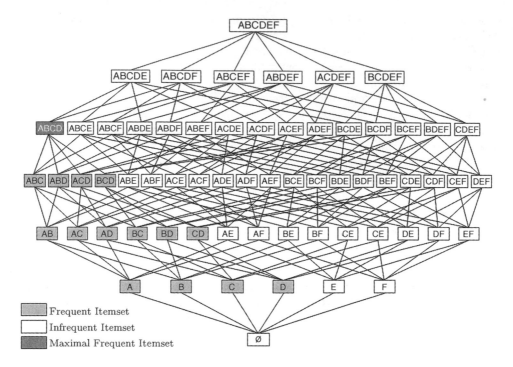

FIGURE 35.1 Itemset lattice with infrequent, frequent, and maximal frequent itemsets (minsup = 40%).

[21, 60]. The Galois closure of an itemset is equal to the intersection of all objects containing it and an itemset I is closed if it is equal to its closure, that is, if $I = \gamma(I)$. Each closed itemset defines a membership class, or *equivalence class*, that includes all itemsets contained in the same data set objects and consequently have the same support value as the closed itemset [16]. By definition, the unique maximal itemset of an equivalence class is a closed itemset. An itemset that is both frequent, according to the minsup threshold, and closed is called a *frequent closed itemset*. The frequent closed itemsets and their equivalence class in the itemset, lattice for data set Ð and for a minimum-support threshold of 40% are shown in Figure 35.2.

Since all frequent itemsets and their support can be deduced from the set of frequent closed itemsets and their support, this set constitutes a lossless condensed representation of all frequent itemsets. Using this property, the search space of frequent-itemset mining can be reduced to the frequent closed itemsets and the association rule mining problem can be divided into the two following successive phases:

- Mining frequent closed itemsets, with their support, in the data set
- Generating valid association rules, with their support and confidence, from frequent closed itemsets and their support

The search space of frequent-closed-itemset algorithms is a suborder of the itemset lattice. The reduction of this search space depends on the proportion of frequent itemsets that are closed since once a frequent closed itemset is identified, all frequent itemsets in its equivalence class can be deduced. In the case of dense data sets, equivalence classes are

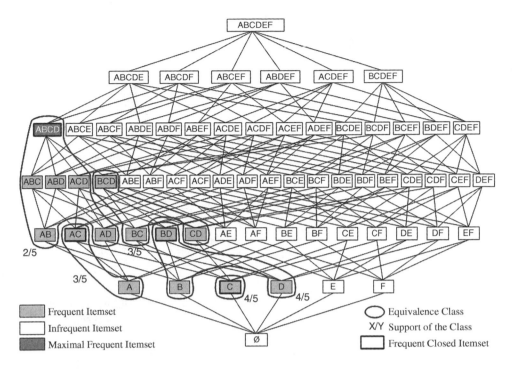

FIGURE 35.2 Itemset lattice with frequent closed itemsets and equivalence classes (minsup — 40%).

large as few frequent itemsets are closed and the first phase execution times are notably improved compared to frequent-itemset mining. However, this approach does not improve association rule mining for sparse data sets, such as market basket data sets. For such data sets, equivalence classes are small, as most frequent itemsets are closed, and closure computations increase execution times compared to frequent-itemset mining.

To improve the efficiency of this approach, the minimal itemsets of an equivalence class, called *generators*, can be identified in a levelwise manner and used to generate the frequent closed itemsets [143]. This subsequently reduces the computational cost as they are the smallest itemsets in an equivalence class. The lattice structure of the suborder defined by the frequent closed itemsets, for example, database Đ and minsup = 40%, is depicted in Figure 35.3.

This lattice contains five equivalence classes corresponding to the five frequent closed itemsets and their seven generators. For the second phase, condensed representations for association rules can be generated from frequent closed itemsets and generators, which further reduces the processing time of association rule generation. The use of generators in the definition of condensed representations for association rules is described in Section 35.3. Recent surveys on frequent-closed-itemset mining of associating rules can be found in [157, 184].

35.2.3 Free-Set Framework

Frequent-itemset and closed-itemset frameworks are sensitive to noise in the data that is common in some applications. The *free-set framework* was proposed to overcome this

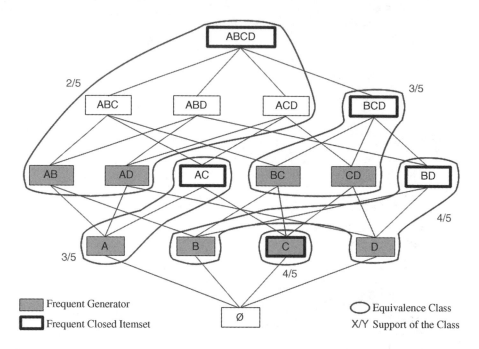

FIGURE 35.3 Suborder of itemset lattice with frequent closed itemsets and their generators (minsup = 40%).

problem [24, 25]. This framework is based on the ϵ-adequate condensed representation presented in [119]. Free sets are also referred to as δ-free sets defined according to δ-strong rules. An itemset I is a δ-free set if and only if there is no δ-strong rule $I_1 \rightarrow I_2$ with I_1 and $I_2 \subset I$ and $I_1 \notin I_2$. An association rule of the form $I_1 \rightarrow I_2$ with $I_1, I_2 \in I$ is a δ-strong if support(I_1) - support(I) $\leq \delta$. The value of δ is proportional to the confidence of the rule, that is, minimizing δ is equivalent to maximizing the confidence of rules. The δ-strong rules for $\delta = 0$ are exact association rules, that is, rules with confidence equals to 1, and mining δ-free sets for $\delta = 0$ is equivalent to mining generators. The minimal elements of an equivalence class, that is, the generators of the class, are free sets [34, 149].

An important property of free sets is anti-monotonicity: All subsets of a free set are also free. A levelwise frequent-free-set mining algorithm was proposed in [25] with an additional search space reduction for the case where $\delta \neq 0$. Free sets constitute an approximate representation of the frequent-itemsets as an approximation of the frequent-itemset supports can be deduced from their supports [25]. A constraint-based frequent-free-set mining algorithm was proposed in [26]. A recent review on free-set-based condensed representations can be found in [34].

35.2.4 Regular Framework

Condensed representations aim at optimizing memory usage and execution time of the extraction phase of association rule mining while allowing to get the correct complete information during a postprocessing operation. In the *regular framework*, regular itemsets allow to specify which items or itemsets may or may not be present in the itemsets of

TABLE 35.3   Frequent Regular Itemsets for Data Set Đ (minsup = 40%)

Closed Itemsets	0-Free Sets	Regular Itemsets	Support	Cover
$ABCD$	AB, AD	$AC?\{BD\}^+$	2	1, 5
BCD	BC, BD	$B\{CD\}^*$	3	1, 4, 5
AC	A	$AC?$	3	1, 3, 5
BD	B, D	$\{BD\}^+$	4	1, 2, 4, 5
C	C	C	4	1, 3, 4, 5

the condensed representation. A regular itemset E can be represented by *regular grammar* and is called *extended representation of the itemset*, or *extended itemset* for short: $E ::= X|X?|\{X_1, \ldots, X_i\}^*|\{X_1, \ldots, X_j\}^+$, where X is an itemset and X_n are items with $i \geq 0$ and $j > 0$. In this regular itemset:

- First argument X represents an itemset.
- Second argument $X?$ indicates that the itemset X may or may not be present in the regular itemsets.
- Third argument $\{X_1, \ldots, X_i\}^*$ means that any subset of the itemset $\{X_1, \ldots, X_i\}^*$, including the null, or empty, set, participates in the formation of the regular itemsets.
- Last argument $\{X_1, \ldots, X_j\}^+$ represents the participation of the nonempty subset of the itemset $\{X_1, \ldots, X_j\}$ to the formation of regular itemsets.

For example, the extended itemset $AB\{CE\}+$ represents itemsets containing both A and B and possibly C and E. This itemset thus designates the set of itemsets $\{AB, ABC, ABE, ABCE\}$. The semantic of an extended itemset E is represented as $S(E)$ and E is called regular when $\text{cover}(I_1) = \text{cover}(I_2)$, where $\text{cover}(I)$ is the list of data set objects containing I, which implies $\text{support}(I_1) = \text{support}(I_2)$, for all itemsets $I_1, I_2 \in S(E)$. This representation, is a lossless representation unlike free sets. The set of regular itemsets for dataset Đ is presented in Table 35.3.

The "cover" column of the table represents the list of data set objects containing the corresponding itemset. The RegularMine algorithm for generating a set of regular itemsets as a concise representation of frequent itemsets and a detailed discussion on semantics and procedural descriptions can be found in [149].

35.2.5 Evolutionary Framework

Evolutionary approaches have been used for association rule mining to overcome some problems encountered with preceding frameworks in some applications:

- The number of attribute and value pairs (i.e., items) can be huge in some databases, rendering it difficult to handle these data.
- In the case of continuous-valued attributes, making a binary discretization of those attributes to transform them into discrete values can be difficult. Hence, choosing the proper discretization method for making the process lossless can be nontrivial.
- Supplying appropriate values for the minimum-support and minimum-confidence threshold parameters is most often application specific and can be difficult.

The *evolutionary framework* was introduced to address applications where the above-mentioned problems appear. This framework regroups several strategies such as genetic algorithms, genetic programming, genetic network programming, and differential evolution, among others. Some approaches perform the rule mining task as a combination of several of these strategies, such as, for example, combining genetic algorithms and genetic network programming as in [68]. In this framework, the association rule mining process is divided into the two following phases:

Rule Generation   During the rule generation process, the rules are encoded in the chromosome according to one of the following approaches:

- In the *Pittsburg approach*, a set of rules are encoded in a single chromosome and the length of the chromosome restricts the number of generated association rules [51].
- In the *Michigan approach*, each rule is encoded in a single chromosome divided into the antecedent and the consequent parts of the rule [65].

Rule Selection   After rule set generation, several evolutionary criteria, such as support, confidence, or one of the measures presented in Section 35.4, are used to select the most pertinent rules. The rule sets generated by this selection process are also known as *Pareto-optimal rule sets*.

An interesting feature of evolutionary approaches is that, instead of using only support and confidence measures, they can extend the problem to the optimization of multiple-objective measures such as those presented in Table 35.10 later in the chapter. This principle, called *multiobjective optimization*, for generating Pareto-optimal rule sets can notably improve the results. Multiobjective optimization has been successfully applied to classification association rules and associative rule mining using support and confidence. For example, the Pareto-optimal associative rules based on combined support and confidence measure optimization remarkably improved results in some cases, as was demonstrated in [18]. The most prominent evolutionary strategies used for association rule mining are described below.

Genetic Algorithms   These algorithms represent rules as individual chromosomes with a fixed population size, that is, number of chromosomes, which is a user-defined parameter. This can be a problem in some applications as interesting rules can be missed if an inadequate population size was defined. Increasing the population size is not a viable solution to this problem as too high values will lead to important execution times. An interesting review of single-objective and multiobjective optimizations for association rule mining based on genetic algorithms can be found in [50]. Genetic algorithms were used for Pareto-optimal association rule mining [65], Pareto-optimal fuzzy association rule mining [90], Pareto-optimal classification rule mining [84], and multiobjective fuzzy-rule-based classifiers [83, 85]. Recent surveys on genetic-algorithm-based association rule mining are available in [58, 65, 82, 200].

Genetic Programming   This theory is a biologically inspired evolutionary theory for solving multiobjective optimization problems. However, this approach suffers from the drawback of a possible generation of invalid itemsets or association rules due to crossover and mutation operations used [122]. Genetic programming was used for mining association rules in temporal data [79] and an extension called *Grammar Guided Genetic Programming* (G3P) for solving the problem of generating invalid individuals was proposed [47, 179]. The generation of valid association rules from continuous-valued numerical attributes using the G3P method was also the subject of research works [57, 114].

Genetic Network Programming   This extension of genetic programming is a graph-based evolutionary approach for optimizing multiobjective searches. It uses directed graph data structures for solving the problem of continuous-valued attributes in association rule mining. This approach was introduced in the association rule mining domain in [159] and implemented using genetic algorithms in [68]. Recent developments in association rule mining using genetic network programming are described in [158, 167, 186]. Few research works have done in this field and some interesting perspectives on this topic require more attention by researchers.

Differential Evolution   This evolutionary approach is an adaptation of natural evolution to solve optimization problems. Algorithms based on this theory were the first adapted to association rule mining as they are well fitted to solve the problem of association rule mining from continuous-valued numerical attributes [7]. Although differential evolution was introduced as a single-objective optimization approach, it was shown to be an effective solution to the multiobjective association rule mining problem [7]. The use of differential evolution to solve multiobjective optimization problems is studied in [1, 152, 165].

The use of evolutionary approaches for association rule mining presents interesting perspectives for several practical problems encountered in some applications. Their combination with deterministic symbolic approaches, to benefit from their respective capabilities and strengths, is a promising field of research.

35.3   CONDENSED REPRESENTATIONS OF ASSOCIATION RULES

Many application reports pointed out that frequent-itemset-based association rule mining generates huge sets of rules, with an important proportion of redundant rules, for large or dense data sets. Redundant association rules are rules resulting from different combinations of items in the antecedent and the consequent covering the same sets of objects in the data set. Two different types of solutions have been proposed to eliminate these uninformative rules: interestingness measures and condensed representations of association rules.

35.3.1   Representation Systems

Different representation systems have been proposed to summarize association rule sets in a minimal collection called *condensed representation* of association rules. These condensed representations are minimal sets of strong rules satisfying the user's requirements and containing the same information as the set of all valid rules. They follow some properties to restrict as much as possible their size [119]. A condensed representation is said to be *lossless* if all valid association rules can be deduced, with support and confidence, from it. From such condensed representations, all valid association rules are deduced using an inference system for particular application requirements. A recent study on condensed representations of association rule sets and inference systems for association rule mining can be found in [140]. The definition of condensed representations relies in the notion of redundant association rules that are considered as noninformative from the end user's viewpoint.

35.3.1.1 Redundant Association Rules

Redundancies among association rules is a fundamental concept for improving the relevance of association rule sets. A redundancy is present whenever a relationship represented in a rule that holds in the data set is also represented in another rule of the set. An association rule is redundant if its structure, that is, its antecedent and consequent, and statistical measures, such as support and confidence, can be deduced from another rule. Such redundant association rules are considered uninformative as they do not add information from the end user's viewpoint [17, 197]. They must be discarded from the output rule set to improve its relevance and to minimize the difficulties and time required for domain experts to process information from the outputs. Works on this topic include definitions, characterizations, and relationship studies among redundant rules and several approaches have been proposed to avoid redundancies in association rule sets [93]. Most of these works use the equivalence class framework to characterize properties and reduction constraints of association rules as this framework defines two classes of association rules with distinct structural and semantical properties: exact and approximate association rules. A lossless condensed representation containing no redundant association rule is called a *basis of association rules*. A recent study on the reduction of redundancy in rule bases can be found in [14].

35.3.1.2 Exact and Approximate Association Rules

Exact association rules are rules with a confidence equal to 1, that is, rules that are verified for all data set objects and thus have no counterexample in the data set. Approximate, or partial, association rules are rules with a confidence less than 1, that is, rules that are not verified for all data set objects and an approximate association rule R has a proportion of counterexamples in the data set equal to $1 - \text{confidence}(R)$. Equivalence classes, defined using the closed-itemset framework, provide a theoretical framework to characterize these two categories of association rules:

Exact Association Rules   By definition, two itemsets I_1 and I_2 within the same equivalence class have the same support value. Since the confidence of a rule $R : I_1 \rightarrow I_2 \setminus I_1$ is defined by the ratio between the supports of I_2 and I_1, respectively, the confidence of rules between two itemsets of the same equivalence class is equal to 1. All rules between two itemsets in an equivalence class are thus exact association rules and cover identical sets of data set objects. All valid exact association rules in data set D for minsup $= 40\%$ are represented as directed links in the equivalence classes in Figure 35.4.

Approximate Association Rules   By definition, two itemsets I_1 and I_2 related by inclusion and belonging to different equivalence classes have different support values. Each pair of such itemsets $I_1 \subset I_2$ form an approximate association rule $R : I_1 \rightarrow I_2 \setminus I_1$ which confidence is less than 1 since support$(I_2) >$ support(I_1). All rules are between two itemsets of different equivalence classes and are thus approximate association rules covering identical sets of data set objects. All valid approximate association rules between three equivalent classes in data set Đ for minsup $= 40\%$ and minconf

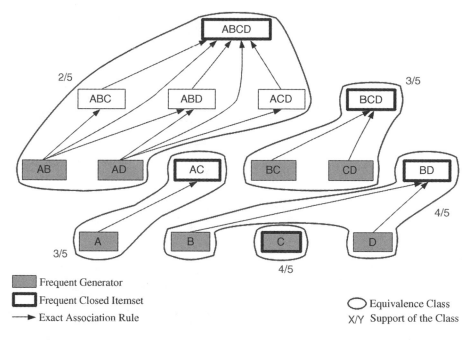

FIGURE 35.4 Exact association rules and frequent equivalence classes (minsup = 40%).

= 40% are represented in Figure 35.5. These rules correspond to all possible combinations of two itemsets of the equivalence classes defined by the frequent closed itemsets $\{C\}$, $\{BD\}$, and $\{BCD\}$ related by inclusion.

35.3.1.3 *Inference Systems*

The deduction of the complete set of valid association rules using an inference system relies on a set of rules called *inference rules.* Association rules are basically implications between two sets of variable values and can be related to functional dependencies in database theory [118, 178]. The inference system of the Armstrong axioms [12] is a method for generating the closure of a set of functional dependencies between attribute values. The inference rules of the Armstrong axioms are:

Reflexivity $X \supseteq Y \vdash X \rightarrow Y$

Transitivity $X \rightarrow Y \wedge Y \rightarrow Z \vdash X \rightarrow Z$

Union $X \rightarrow Y \wedge X \rightarrow Z \vdash X \rightarrow YZ$

Augmentation $X \rightarrow Y \vdash XZ \rightarrow YZ$

Decomposition $X \rightarrow YZ \vdash X \rightarrow Y \wedge X \rightarrow Z$

Pseudotransitivity $X \rightarrow Y \wedge WY \rightarrow Z \vdash XW \rightarrow Y$

Armstrong's axioms are used in database design to generate the closure of a set of functional dependencies by repeated application of these inference rules. Adapating this inference system to the framework of association rule mining requires to consider statistical measures, such as support and confidence, of the rules [144]. This led to the definition of new inference systems to generate minimum-size covers, or bases, for approximate association rules [144].

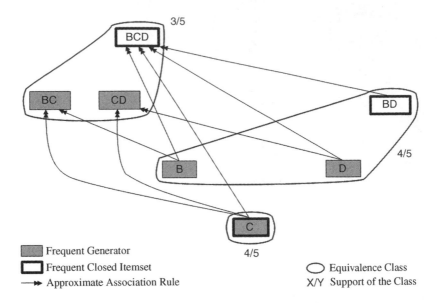

FIGURE 35.5 Approximate association rules and frequent equivalence classes (minsup = 40%, minconf = 40%).

35.3.1.4 *Informative Bases* Getting the maximum information in a minimal set of rules is crucial for the understandability and usefulness of extracted association rules. Most data-mining applications depend on the interpretation by the end user of extracted knowledge patterns. The set of rules presented to the end user must contain all information about co-occurrences of the itemsets. To guarantee that information is contained in suppressed association rules, the deduction must be natural and intuitive [67]. This is achieved by eliminating redundancies and defining natural inference rules, defined for human reasoning on information in a collection of rules, derived from Armstrong's axioms [49]. To verify the preceding characteristics, the rule set must have the following properties:

Itemset Covering   All combinations of items in the set of valid association rules must be covered in the condensed representation.

Object Covering   All objects in the data set covered by valid association rules must be covered in the condensed representation.

Condensed representations with these two properties are called *informative bases* [75, 144].

35.3.2 Bases of Association Rules

A basis of association rules is a lossless condensed representation of a set of valid association rules. Different bases can be defined depending on the inference system considered as the inference rules determine which association rules are considered redundant and are thus suppressed. In this section, we present several widely used bases of association rules. Other bases, with variations and adaptations to specific application contexts of the notions presented here, were proposed in the literature. This is, for example, the case for the reliable approximate basis for eliminating redundancies in approximate association rule sets [183].

TABLE 35.4   Duquenne–Guigues Basis of Exact Association Rules (minsup = 40%)

Pseudoclosed Itemset	Closure	Association Rule	Support
A	AC	$A \rightarrow C$	3/5
B	BD	$B \rightarrow D$	4/5
D	BD	$D \rightarrow B$	4/5

35.3.2.1 Duquenne–Guigues Basis

The Duquenne–Guigues basis was defined to reduce to a set as small as possible a set of global implication rules [54]. It was adapted to the association rule mining framework for generating a basis of nonredundant exact association rules in [142]. This basis is a set of rules generated from the *frequent pseudoclosed itemset* that is minimal with respect to the number of rules [16, 60, 142]. The definition of this basis relies on the following inference rules:

(i) $X \rightarrow Y \bigwedge Z \rightarrow W \vdash XZ \rightarrow YW$

(ii) $X \rightarrow Y \bigwedge Y \rightarrow Z \vdash X \rightarrow Z$

However, for this basis, supports of frequent closed itemsets are necessary for computing the statistical measures of inferred association rules [49, 96]. The Duquenne–Guigues basis extracted from dataset Đ for minsup = 40% is presented in Table 35.4.

35.3.2.2 Luxenburger Basis

The Luxenburger basis was defined to reduce a set of partial implication rules in the context of formal concept analysis [117]. Partial implication rules are rules between two sets of variables with an associated precision measure equivalent to confidence but no coverage measure like support. This basis is also known as the proper basis and was adapted to the association rule mining framework in [142]. It contains the nonredundant approximate association rules generated from pairs of frequent closed itemsets that belong to two different equivalence classes and are related by the inclusion relation. The definition of this basis relies on the transitivity Armstrong axiom for transitive reduction, that is, to suppress deducible transitive association rules. For example, the transitive rule $R : I_1 \rightarrow I_3$ is inferred from $R_1 : I_1 \rightarrow I_2$ and $R_2 : I_2 \rightarrow I_3$ and we have confidence$(R) = $ confidence$(R_1) \times$ confidence(R_2). The Luxenburger basis of approximate association rules for dataset Đ and minsup = 40% and minconf = 40% is given in Table 35.5.

TABLE 35.5   Luxenburger Basis of Approximate Association Rules (minsup = 40%, minconf = 40%)

Generator	⊂	Closed Set	Association Rule	Support	Confidence
A		ABCD	$A \rightarrow BCD$	2/5	2/3
B		BCD	$B \rightarrow CD$	3/5	3/4
B		ABCD	$B \rightarrow ACD$	2/5	2/4
C		AC	$C \rightarrow A$	3/5	3/4
C		BCD	$C \rightarrow BD$	3/5	3/4
C		ABCD	$C \rightarrow ABD$	2/5	2/4
D		BCD	$D \rightarrow BC$	3/5	3/4
D		ABCD	$D \rightarrow ABC$	2/5	2/4

The union of the Duquenne–Guigues basis and the proper basis is a losless basis of exact and approximate association rules as it solves the problem of deriving support values of inferred rules [96, 142]. Nevertheless, these bases are defined for an automated treatment, such as the computation of a normalized conceptual database schema, and do not consider the problem of the end-user interpretation of the rules. They are very small sets of rules that can be more easilly managed and treated and from which all rules that hold can be inferred on demand.

35.3.2.3 Generic Basis   The quantity of information brought by association rules and their interpretability are related to the size of their antecedent and consequent. Smaller antecedents make rules easier to interpret and comprehend as revealed in several studies based on diverse subjective interestingness measures and techniques [95, 121, 174]. The generic basis of association rules was defined using the frequent equivalence class framework to maximize information in each rule and facilitate their usage [16]. Rules in the generic basis have minimal antecedent and maximal consequent. This basis is also known as the min–max basis of association rules.

An association rule $R_1 : I_1 \rightarrow I_2$ is a generic association rule if and only if there is no other rule with identical support and confidence which antecedent is a subset of I_1 and which consequent is a superset of I_2. As generators are the minimal itemsets and frequent closed itemsets are the maximal itemsets in equivalence classes, rules between two of these itemsets constitute the generic basis of association rules. The generic basis can be divided into two distinct complete sets for respectively exact and approximate association rules.

Generic exact association rules are composed of a frequent generator in the antecedent and its closure, that is, the frequent closed itemset of its equivalence class, in the consequent. The number of generic exact association rules is therefore proportional to the number of generators in frequent equivalence classes. The generic basis of exact association rules extracted from data set Ð for minsup $= 40\%$ is presented in Table 35.6.

Generic approximate association rules are composed of a frequent generator in the antecedent and a frequent closed superset of its closure, that is, a frequent closed itemset of another equivalence class, in the consequent. The generic basis of approximate association rules in data set Ð for minsup $= 40\%$ and minconf $= 40\%$ is given in Table 35.7.

Transitive reduction can also be applied to the generic basis for approximate association rules. This discards rules with the lowest confidence among all rules covering the same set of items. Hence, since the confidence of a transitive rule $R : I_1 \rightarrow I_3$ inferred from $R_1 : I_1 \rightarrow I_2$ and $R_2 : I_2 \rightarrow I_3$ is equal to the product of R_1 and R_2 confidences, we have

TABLE 35.6   Generic Basis of Exact Association Rules (minsup $= 40\%$)

Generators	Closure	Association Rule	Support
A	AC	$A \rightarrow C$	3/5
B	BD	$B \rightarrow D$	4/5
D	BD	$D \rightarrow B$	4/5
BC	BCD	$BC \rightarrow D$	3/5
CD	BCD	$CD \rightarrow B$	3/5
AB	$ABCD$	$AB \rightarrow CD$	2/5
AD	$ABCD$	$AD \rightarrow BC$	2/5

TABLE 35.7 Generic Basis of Approximate Association Rules (minsup = 40%, minconf = 40%)

Generator	⊂	Closed Set	Association Rule	Support	Confidence
A		ABCD	A → BCD	2/5	2/3
B		ABCD	B → ACD	2/5	2/4
C		ABCD	C → ABD	2/5	2/4
D		ABCD	D → ABC	2/5	2/4
B		BCD	B → CD	3/5	3/4
C		BCD	C → BD	3/5	3/4
D		BCD	D → BC	3/5	3/4
BC		ABCD	BC → AD	2/5	2/3
CD		ABCD	CD → AB	2/5	2/3

confidence(R) < confidence(R_1) and confidence(R) < confidence(R_2). The generic basis for exact and approximate association rules gives a lossless compact set of rules that are informative for the end user. The total number of rules in this basis depends linearly on the number of frequent equivalence classes extracted.

35.3.2.4 Min–Min Basis

Association rules with minimal antecedent and minimal consequent is another informative basis that can be characterized by frequent equivalence classes defined in [197]. This basis is also defined according to the principle that small antecedents make the rules easier to interpret [95, 121, 174]. Generators, which are the minimal elements of equivalence classes, are used as antecedents of these rules.

Min–min exact association rules consist of a generator as antecedent and one of its minimal supersets in the equivalence class as consequent. The min–min basis of exact association rules for dataset Đ and minsup = 40% is given in Table 35.8.

Min–min approximate association rules consist of a generator as antecedent and one of its minimal supersets within another equivalence class as consequent. The min–min basis of approximate association rules extracted from data set Đ for minsup = 40% and minconf = 40% is given in Table 35.9.

As the generic basis, the min–min basis is lossless, since all valid rules can be inferred with their statistical measures, and its number of rules is also linear in the number of frequent equivalence classes [198]. An extension of the concept of min–min bases for condensed representation of association rules is given in [67].

TABLE 35.8 Exact Association Rules of Min–Min Basis (minsup = 40%)

Generators	Closure	Association Rule	Support
A	AC	A → C	3/5
AB	ABCD	AB → C	2/5
AB	ABCD	AB → D	2/5
AD	ABCD	AD → C	2/5
AD	ABCD	AD → B	2/5
BC	BCD	BC → D	3/5
CD	BCD	CD → B	3/5
B	BD	B → D	4/5
D	BD	D → B	4/5

TABLE 35.9   Approximate Association Rules of Min–Min Basis
(minsup = 40%, minconf = 40%)

Generator	Equivalence Class	Association Rule	Support	Confidence
A	$ABCD$	$A \to BC$	2/5	2/3
A	$ABCD$	$A \to BD$	2/5	2/3
A	$ABCD$	$A \to CD$	2/5	2/3
B	$ABCD$	$B \to AC$	2/5	2/4
B	$ABCD$	$B \to AD$	2/5	2/4
B	BCD	$B \to C$	3/5	3/4
B	BCD	$B \to D$	3/5	3/4
C	AC	$C \to A$	3/5	3/4
C	BCD	$C \to B$	3/5	3/4
C	BCD	$C \to D$	3/5	3/4
C	$ABCD$	$C \to AB$	2/5	2/4
C	$ABCD$	$C \to AD$	2/5	2/4
D	$ABCD$	$D \to AB$	2/5	2/4
D	$ABCD$	$D \to AC$	2/5	2/4
D	BCD	$D \to C$	3/5	3/4

35.4   INTERESTINGNESS MEASURES

Several interestingness measures were proposed to assess the usefulness of an association rule or a group association rule. These measures aim at filtering extracted association rules to minimize the size of the rule set and help the end user in the deduction of information for decision making. In Section 35.4.1, different types of interestingness measures for single association rules and their properties, along with the criteria used to define them, are studied. In Section 35.4.2, an overview of interestingness measures for assessing interestingness of groups of association rules is given.

A hierarchical representation of the different categories of interestingness measures is shown in Figure 35.6. In this figure, the diagram shows the classification of the different interestingness measures of association rules according to their domain of application (individual or group of rules), the type of measures (objective, subjective, or semantic), and their structural properties (symmetric or asymmetric).

These measures follow several criteria for deciding whether a pattern, that is, a rule or a group of rules, is really interesting. In [63], the following nine such criteria, which are used in most works on this topic, are studied in detail:

Conciseness   Describes how compact one pattern is.

Generality   Is defined in terms of maximal coverage of the items in the data set.

Reliability   Characterizes whether a pattern is reliable in terms of occurrences is the application areas.

Peculiarity   Depicts how a pattern is different from the others in the generated output.

Diversity   Defined in terms of differences of the item characteristics in an itemset and between the itemsets in the extracted patterns.

Surprisingness   A pattern is said to be surprising if it is out of the end user's expectedness.

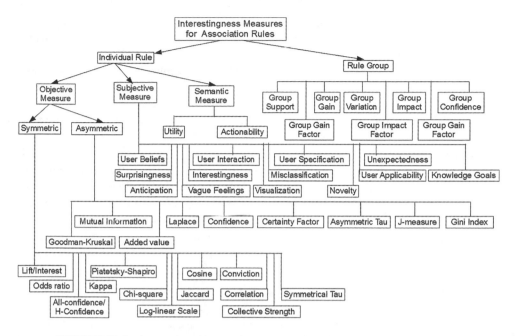

FIGURE 35.6 Categories of interestingness measures for association rule mining.

Novelty   Defines to what extent the patterns mined are novel to the end user's knowledge.

Utility   Defines the usefulness of a pattern.

Applicability   Characterizes whether extracted patterns are appropriated to the application or not.

35.4.1 Interestingness Measures for Individual Association Rules

These interestingness measures are used for evaluating the importance of association rules, on their own, in the data set. These measures help to reduce the size of the list of extracted rules by selecting the most interesting ones. A recent overview of such interestingness measures can be found in [121]. These measures can be divided into three categories: *objectives, subjectives*, and *semantic*.

35.4.1.1 *Objective Measures*   Measures in this category evaluate the statistical significance of the rule in the data set. Several properties were defined to assess the relevance of these interestingness measures. Detailed reviews of these properties can be found in [63, 169]. Values of objective measures are calculated under the contingency table, and they can be evaluated according to different properties:

- *Symmetry Property*   This property refers to the symmetry of measure values under variable permutation. A measure of association rule interestingness which value is not modified when the antecedent and the consequent are interchanged is called a *symmetric measure*. Other measures, which value change when interchanging antecedent and consequent, are called *asymmetric*. A recent review on symmetric interestingness measures is presented in [123].

- *Null-Addition Property*   This property refers to whether the value of the measure remains constant when the number of objects not covering the rule is increased in the data set. A measure with this property is called *null invariant*. Cosine and Jaccard measures are null invariant but odds ratio, correlation coefficient, and interest factor are not for instance.

- *Row/Column Scaling Property*   This property refers to the constancy of the measure value after rescaling the contingency table with some positive constant. Odds ratio is one example of this property.

- *Inversion Property*   This property, which is a special case of the row/column scaling property, refers to whether the measure value remains constant after exchanging the frequency counts in the contingency table. Inversion property includes the correlation coefficient, odds ratio, collective strength, and kappa symmetric measures and interest, cosine, Piatetsky–Shapiro, and Jaccard asymmetric measures.

- *Piatetsky–Shapiro's Properties*   Piatetsky and Shapiro proposed three properties for qualifying relevant measures [145]:

  (i) The value of the measure is zero when antecedent and consequent parts are statistically independent.

  (ii) The value of the measure monotonically increases with the support of the rule when the individual support of both antecedent and consequent are unchanged.

  (iii) The value of the measure monotonically decreases with the support of the antecedent (respectively the consequent) when the supports of the rule and of the consequent (respectively the antecedent) remain constant.

Added value, two-way support, and Piatetsky–Shapiro measures are examples of measures following these three properties. An extended version of these properties is described in [88].

- *Lenca et al.'s Properties*   Eight properties for classifying interestingness measures were proposed in [100]. Among these eight properties, five are normative properties and three are subjective properties. The five normative properties are:

  (i) Easiness to define the threshold values

  (ii) Ability of the measures to identify asymmetricity of the rule

  (iii) Constancy of the measure values in the absence of counterexamples

  (iv) Uniformity of measure values in the case of independent attributes

  (v) Decrease of the measure values with increase in the number of records covering only the consequent of the rule

The three subjective properties are based on the multicriteria decision analysis performed by the analyst. They assess measure interestingness according to the end user's viewpoint and depend on the following criteria:

  (vi) Increase of the measure values when the size of the database is increased

  (vii) Semantics of the measures that are easily expressed and are thus relevant

(viii) Without significant loss of measure values to tolerate some counterexamples that do not notably lessen rule interestingness

These properties were applied to classify a list of 20 measures in [100].

* *Gang and Hamilton's Properties* Gang and Hamilton [63] proposed some properties of interestingness measures to determine if support and confidence are increasing functions when contingency tables are definitive or fixed to their margins.

A critical review of criteria used for the evaluation and classification of objective interestingness measures is given in [166].

A list of objective measures following these properties is given, with corresponding references, in Table 35.10. Recent overviews on objective measures of association rule interestingness can be found in [163, 171]. Methods for choosing the adequate measures were also developed to further help the end user [101].

35.4.1.2 *Subjective Measures* End user's view plays a crucial role during the evaluation and interpretation of the extracted association rules. The end users are most often application domain experts having their own views and beliefs that influence their analysis and choice of information. For example, trivial rules or rules depicting well-known relationships are generally uninteresting whereas rules confirming some hypothetical relationships are very relevant from the end user's viewpoint.

Incorporating subjective criteria, such as end user's beliefs and hypotheses or surprisingness and novelty of the rule, for example, to assess the interestingness of extracted association rules has been the subject of many research works. Figure 35.6 shows 13 subjective interestingness measures used in many association rule mining applications. Extensive recent reviews of these subjective interestingness measures can be found in [63, 131].

Comparative evaluation of objective and subjective measures of interestingness for association rules are presented in [102, 121]. A comparison of the strengths and weaknesses of subjective and objective measures, throughout the analysis of 12 association rule interestingness measures, is presented in [203]. A review and practical evaluation of association rule interestingness measure application in the medical domain are given in [132]. These reports conclude that the combination of both types of measures can optimize interestingness evaluation.

35.4.1.3 *Semantic Measures* These interestingness measures aim at describing the importance of semantic behavior and informativeness of patterns. They are for most application context dependent. Among such measures, the utility and the actionability criteria play an important role.

Utility refers to practical measures of rule usefulness in that they can reflect the actual amount of output achieved by applying each rule. In initial works on this topic, a particular rule can have a different utility value depending on how well the rule fits the purpose of the application for which it was extracted. Nevertheless, several recent works were conducted to define a uniform standard for assessing rule interestingness disregarding application context [188, 194]. Several algorithms incorporating utility measures were proposed, some being dedicated to computational biology applications. For instance, in [99, 151], weightage (W-Gain), utility (U-Gain), and diminution (D-sum) measures are introduced in the association rule mining process to generate a score assessing the utility of each rule. Reviews of association rule utility measures can be found in [9, 187].

TABLE 35.10 Interestingness Measures for Individual Association Rules

Sl.	Measure	Reference	Sl.	Measure	Reference
1	Accuracy	[162]	33	J-Measure	[161]
2	Added value	[150]	34	Jaccard	[169]
3	All-confidence/H-confidence	[133, 181]	35	Kappa	[45]
4	Any-confidence	[133]	36	Klosgen	[91]
5	Asymmetric tau	[205]	37	Laplace	[44]
6	Bayes factor	[86]	38	Leverage	[145]
7	Bond	[133]	39	Least contradiction	[13]
8	Brin's conviction	[30]	40	Lift/Interest	[32]
9	Centered confidence	[27]	41	Log-linear analysis	[6]
10	Certainty factor	[91, 160]	42	Loevinger	[111]
11	Chi-square	[31]	43	Mutual information	[98]
12	Confidence/Precision	[3, 137]	44	Normalize mutual	[98]
13	Collective strength	[2]		information	
14	Conviction	[32]	45	Odds ratio	[126]
15	Correlation coefficient	[5]	46	Odd multiplier	[98]
16	Cosine/IS measure	[170]	47	Piatetsky–Shapiro	[145]
17	Coverage/True positive rate	[162]	48	Prevalence	[98]
18	Conditional influence	[41]	49	Probabilistic	[103]
19	Confidence gain	[168]		discriminant index	
20	Confidence factor/	[65]	50	Recall	[189]
	Predictive Accuracy		51	Relative risk	[98]
21	Comprehensibility	[65]	52	Sebag–Schoenauer	[154]
22	Completeness	[162]	53	Specificity	[98]
23	Entropy intensity of	[71]	54	Strength	[56, 91]
	implication		55	Support	[3]
24	Example and Counter	[98]	56	Symmetrical tau	[205]
	example rate		57	Weighting dependency	[72]
25	Ganascia	[59]	58	Yao's one way support	[190]
26	Generality	[190]	59	Yao's two way support	[190]
27	Gini index	[28]	60	Yao's two way support	[190]
28	Goodman–Kruskal	[69]		variance	
29	Implication index	[104]	61	Yule's Q	[195]
30	Implication intensity	[70]	62	Yule's Y	[196]
31	Influence	[41]	63	Zhang	[201]
32	Interestingness	[162]			

Actionability of discovered knowledge patterns aims at evaluating how meaningful these patterns are to support decision-making actions. A rule is said to be *actionable* if the end user can utilize it to make a decision or gain some advantage [148]. Actionability is a major feature for association rules in most applications since actionable rules are the most useful to achieve the application objectives [109]. A two-way significance framework for evaluating actionability, based on both technical interestingness and domain-specific expectations, was proposed in [37]. A description and formalization of actionability-based knowledge discovery according to four types of generic frameworks, namely postanalysis based, unified interestingness based, combined mining based, and multisource combined mining based, are proposed in [35]. Actionability of association rules can also be characterized using the closed-itemset and the δ-free sets [23]. Detailed reviews of actionability measures and techniques and descriptions of trends in actionable knowledge discovery are available in [36, 78]. An application perspective on actionable knowledge discovery and its trends from this viewpoint can be found in [38, 107].

A detailed description of utility- and actionability-based interestingness measures is available in [63].

35.4.2 Interestingness Measures for Association Rule Groups

An association rule group is a set of rules defined on a certain group of itemsets for grouping rules based on common attributes in the antecedent part [87]. Let I be a frequent itemset containing n items $I_1, I_2, \ldots, I_n$ and G be a group of itemsets on I such that, $\forall G_i \in G$, $G_i \subseteq I$. The group of association rules defined on group G is denoted as $\text{GAR} = \{\bigcup R : I_1 \rightarrow I_2 \mid I_1 \in G\}$. Grouping association rules in such a way allows both to identify all rules concerning a particular group of items and to reduce the number of rules concerning a group of itemsets that have a similar behavior in the data set.

Few measures have already been proposed to assess the interestingness of such kinds of group rules, and the adaptation of standard individual interestingness measures to association rule groups is studied in [87]. Table 35.11 summarizes available measures for evaluating the interestingness of group association rules.

The support of frequent itemsets and valid association rules is measured with respect to the total number of objects present in the data set. For these measures, the support of an itemset in a group or an association rule group is measured with respect to the data set objects involved in that particular group. Similarly, all other measures in Table 35.11 are calculated by considering only the data set objects containing the group itemsets. Computing group measures can be less time consuming than classical measures as it needs to scan only those transactions containing the group itemsets instead of the whole data set. However, because of differences between the definitions of support and confidence of itemsets and rules and the group support and confidence, more calculations can be required. For example, some standard measures require to calculate only one probability where two probabilities must be calculated in the case of group measures, such as for the gain measure:

$$\text{gain}(I_1 \rightarrow I_2) = \text{conf}(I_1 \rightarrow I_2) - \text{supp}(I_2)$$
$$= \frac{P(I_1 \cup I_2)}{P(I_1)} - P(I_2)$$
$$\text{gain}_G(I_1 \rightarrow I_2) = \text{conf}_G(I_1 \rightarrow I_2) - \text{supp}_G(I_2)$$
$$= \frac{P(G \cup I_1 | I_2)}{P(G \cup I_1)} - \frac{P(G \cup I_1)}{P(G)}$$

This can make a big difference for measures that require the calculation of a large number of support and confidence values. However, the concept of association rule groups presents several advantages:

- The number of items in rules can be reduced, to make easier their interpretation, by regrouping the common items in their association rule groups.

TABLE 35.11 Interestingness Measures for Association Rule Groups

Sl.	Measure	Notation	Definition
1	Group support (I)	$\text{supp}_G(I)$	$= \dfrac{P(G\mid I)}{P(G)} = \text{conf}(G \to I)$
2	Group support($I_1 \to I_2$)	$\text{supp}_G(I_1 \to I_2)$	$= \dfrac{P(G\mid I_1 \cup I_2)}{P(G)} = \text{conf}(G \to I_1 I_2)$
3	Group confidence	$\text{conf}_G(I_1 \to I_2)$	$= \dfrac{\text{supp}_G(I_1 \to I_2)}{\text{supp}_G(I_1)} = \text{conf}(G I_1 \to I_2)$
4	Group gain	$\text{gain}_G(I_1 \to I_2)$	$= \text{conf}_G(I_1 \to I_2) - \text{supp}_G(I_2)$ $= \text{conf}(G I_1 \to I_2) - \text{conf}(G \to I_2)$
5	Group gain factor	$\text{GGF}_G(I_1 \to I_2)$	$= \dfrac{\text{gain}_G(I_1 \to I_2)}{1 - \text{supp}_G(I_2)} \text{ if } \text{gain}_G(I_1 \to I_2) \geq 0$ $= \dfrac{\text{gain}_G(I_1 \to I_2)}{\text{supp}_G(I_2)} \text{ if } \text{gain}_G(I_1 \to I_2) < 0$
6	Group variation	$\text{variation}_G(I_1 \to I_2)$	$= \dfrac{\text{gain}_G(I_1 \to I_2)}{\text{supp}_G(I_2)}$ $= \dfrac{\text{conf}_G(I_1 \to I_2) - \text{supp}_G(I_2)}{\text{supp}_G(I_2)}$
7	Group impact	$\text{impact}_G(I_1 \to I_2)$	$= \text{supp}(G I_1) * \text{gain}_G(I_1 \to I_2)$
8	Group impact ratio	$\text{GIR}_G(I_1 \to I_2)$	$= \dfrac{\text{impact}_G(I_1 \to I_2)}{\text{supp}(G)}$

- The end users can more easily apprehend information from these rule groups, as they define a subspace of the solution space made up of rules with identical properties and handle huge sets of rules.
- Group measures can rank the groups according to the end user's interest and determine the interestingness of a group of rules instead of each rule independently of others.

Although quite few measures for association rule groups have been proposed actually, almost all types of standard association rule measures can be adapted to the concept of groups of association rules.

35.5 BIOLOGICAL APPLICATIONS

Association rule mining has multifarious applications ranging from market basket data analysis, customer relationship management, Web mining, hardware and network intrusion detection, finance, telecommunication, to biology. Hereabout, we are mainly interested in applications to biology, or more explicitly in the fields of computational biology, computational genomics, molecular biology, medical and biological information processing, pharmaceutical and disease-related research, biotechnology, and bioinformatics.

Association rule applications in these fields aim at characterizing relationships between sets of genes, proteins, or other cell members and the participation of different biological processes to health and diseases of cells. Such information is important for the analysis of diseases and to help in finding cures by the development of new drugs and adapted medical treatments, for instance. This area of biological applications can be divided into three epochs:

Pregenomic Era This involves the highest levels of application in biology, mainly in medical and biological information processing and pharmaceutical and disease-related researches.

Genomic Era Genome analysis involves the operations on gene or DNA, that is, mainly computational genomics. This also involves the manipulation or functioning related research on functional RNA, micro-RNA, and so on.

Postgenomic and Proteomic Era This last era includes protein components and intermediate biological factors between gene/DNA and protein such as different types of acids, RNA, and other biocells in cellular biology.

The most prominent association rule mining applications in biology are presented according to this classification in the following sections.

35.5.1 Applications in Pregenomics

Applications in this area mainly involve the analysis of medical and environmental behaviors in the living body. Analysis of behavioral characteristics and sociodemographic data on healthy and unhealthy patients are important for the analysis of the different diseases and the prediction of risk factors [33, 130]. Some applications in this context are performed under specific drug or environmental conditions. Instead of using behavioral changes in cellular components, like genes or proteins, this background knowledge information, which shows relationships between diseases and circumstances, is highly important for finding disease cures.

Association rule mining in such research analyses includes different medical, pharmaceutical, and behavioral data sets. These data usually contain heterogeneous information about a large number of characteristics, such as historical background of the patient, addiction of the patient in any individuals, and behavioral changes of different parts of the body. Automatic diagnosis of heart disease using association rule mining for different characteristics of the healthy and unhealthy patient was studied in [134]. Analysis of diabetes using association rule mining of the clinical data of different diabetic patients was studied in [164]. Several studies on medical data interpretation for disease diagnosis by association rule mining are presented in [53, 135, 175]. A classical and evolutionary approach for medical data investigation was studied in [97]

35.5.2 Applications in Genomics

Investigation of a genome includes a part of the DNA string being able to be coded known as a gene and also the noncoding part of DNA along with some viral RNA. Application of genomic covers perhaps all genes in an organism. These genes contain the formula for the protein whose application in association rule mining is discussed in the next section.

Genome analysis is important to understanding the behavior of a gene under different biological reactions and aspects. Many high-throughput techniques are available for generating the gene profile which is used to analyze the function of the gene in different applications.

The microarray gene profiling technique generates huge amounts of information called *gene expression data*. These data have been intensively used and studied to investigate and address issues related to genes. Gene expression data contain expression profiles of several genes under different biological conditions. These expression profiles are generated as continuous numerical values but, depending on applications and end-user requirements, they are usually discretized into three classes: overexpressed, highly repressed, and unchanged. Sometimes, the gene expression data also give certain information based on the applications to correctly analyze gene behavior. Genomic databases can have several forms according to the information they contain:

- Temporal gene expression data (T-GED)
- Spatial gene expression data (S-GED)
- Gene expression data with cellular environmental descriptions and ontological and bibliographic annotations
- Gene expression data with transcription factors
- Gene mutation data
- Gene sequence data

Gene mutation data are a peculiar type of gene related data used to identify the cause of gene tumors and diseases [94, 106]. There are several application areas available under this genomic research. They can be classified into four principal categories: gene expression analysis, gene regulatory analysis, functional genomic analysis, and rowwise gene group analysis. Figure 35.7 shows a hierarchical classification of the different areas of association rule mining applications in genome analyses.

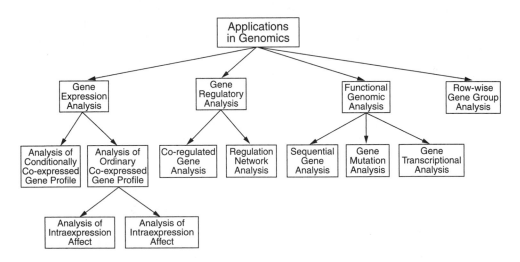

FIGURE 35.7 Categories of association rule mining applications in genomics.

1. *Gene Expression Analysis*   Researches in gene expression analysis mainly include different kinds of microarray gene expression data to understand the mechanism of cellular process under different conditions. Advances in technologies accelerate the growth of huge gene expression data sets that are difficult to manage and costly to process for finding interesting information. Association rule mining is an efficient approach that is well-fitted to the processing of such data sets.

   Gene expression analysis can be divided into two parts according to the nature of the gene expression profiles analyzed. The first part includes the analysis of gene expression to understand the times and conditions of expression of genes that are basically not expressed in healthy samples. This kind of study is known as conditionally expressed gene analysis. The second part analyzes the functional effect of one gene expression profile over another gene expression profile. In this case, two situations arise: Either both genes are of the same group, for example, belong to the same gene regulation network, and it is then called *intraexpression effect analysis*, or genes belong to two different groups, and it is then called *interexpression effect analysis*. Conglomerative research in this field using different of association rule analyse is presented in [62].

2. *Gene Regulatory Analysis*   Gene regulatory analysis involves coregulated gene analysis where genes are regulated under at-least one common transcription factor [8, 191]. This area of investigation also concerns gene regulatory network analysis which aims at understanding the underlying complex genetic regulatory processes [156]. These researches are of importance as they concern several domains, such as the pharmaceutical industry or analysis of complex diseases, that are essential for public health. Several studies pointed out that association rule mining is a particularly relevant approach in the field of gene regulatory analysis [19, 39, 48, 80, 176].

3. *Functional Genomic Analysis*   Functional genomic analysis includes the analysis of different function-related matters inside a cell, such as sequential analysis of genes, gene mutation analysis, or analysis of transcription factors. These analyses use *serial analysis of gene expression* (SAGE) data or gene expression data with different biological sample information. Sometimes, redundant information can be added to the gene sequence data set originating from different sources generating DNA-sequencing information. These redundancies may be due to the absence of cross-referencing of identical sequential information in different databases, to the presence of multiple instances of the same sequence in a database, or to the fact that a sequence can be divided into several parts distributed over the database. Analysis of gene sequences using association rule mining makes it possible to automatically remove such redundancies in data [193].

   Gene mutation analysis is another functional genomic problem that aims at identifying the causes of tumors in genes and the diseases resulting from this kind of abnormal mutation. Association rule mining was successfully applied to the gene mutation databases containing information about mutations, mutagens, diseases, and so on, over each gene [94, 106]. Detailed analyses about the process, mechanism, and controls for transcription factors can be found in [43, 180]. The analysis of transcriptomic data in the context of association rule mining is discussed in [89].

4. *Rowwise Gene Group Analysis*   A quantitative analysis of relationships between coregulation, coexpression, and functional genomes was conducted in [8]. Another study shows the relationships between coexpression and coregulation of gene microarray data [191]. Usually, gene expression data are processed in a columnwise

manner for extracting association rules from the data set and generate the required information for the end user. However, the huge number of attributes in this kind of data can cause important efficiency problems because of the large search space, which is proportional to the number of attribute values, and the large number of association rules generated. To solve this problem, finding association rule groups by analyzing the data set in a rowwise manner is a quite recent trend in genomics [46, 138, 182].

Association rule mining was successfully applied to analyze the relationships between genes in different expression levels and to find conjunctions between gene expressions and biological functions. Almost all types of association rule mining methods have been applied or adapted to discover knowledge from genome-related data. Most of these methods are basically application-type dependent as different techniques are sometimes required for different kinds of applications or data. Some examples of application-dependent works and the different kinds of rule generation methods adapted for the different data types are:

- Distance-based association rule mining [81]
- Heterogeneous association rule mining [9]
- Quantitative association rule mining [64, 89]
- Dynamic association rule mining [62]
- Ant-based association rule mining [77]
- Multiobjective association rule mining [76]
- Fuzzy association rule mining [112]
- Partition-based association rule mining

Recent detailed studies on these approaches can be found in [10, 62].

35.5.3 Applications in Proteomics

After the genomic analysis, understanding the function of a protein is a major challenge for the biologist [177]. Applications in proteomics include the analysis of protein sequences, acid sequences, and sometimes genomic-related sequences [120]. Studies in these fields help to understand the protein interactions in metabolic, the synthesis of *adenosine triphosphate* (ATP), gene replication, and so on. Genetic and biochemical experimentation, such as two-hybrid screenings, generate huge amounts of protein interaction data. Information about the different protein databases can be found in [15, 22] and a detailed analysis of this field of proteomics can be found in [108]. Studies on relationships between gene expression information and protein interaction information are described in [73, 173, 199]. Although some limitations for proteomic analyses have been reported [61], proteomics and system biology applications help to understand system-level functionalities and to analyze the mechanisms behind the working principles [66, 202].

Several application fields of association rule mining can be distinguished in the proteomic domain of research. These proteomic research fields can be classified into three main groups: structural analysis, functional analysis, and protein expression or differential analysis. Figure 35.8 shows a hierarchical classification of the different areas of association rule mining applications in proteomics according to these three groups.

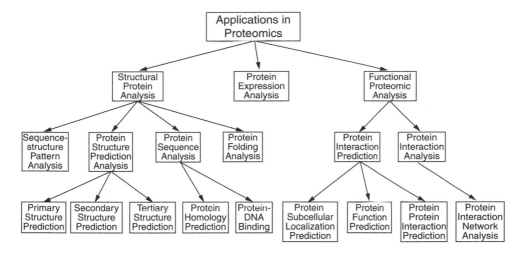

FIGURE 35.8   Categories of association rule mining applications in proteomics.

The following paragraphs present the most prominent applications in each of these areas. Several interesting results have been produced using association rule analysis of proteomic data, but more works are required to understand the relationships between the different components and activities of proteins, and the area of proteomic research still has many open problems in the data-mining domain.

35.5.3.1 *Structural Protein Analysis*

Protein sequences are nonrandom patterns of amino acid molecules. Due to the nonrandom nature of the sequence, finding associations and co-occurrences of amino acids using association rule mining is as efficient as other data-mining methods. A quantitative association rule mining application in this field is presented in [74]. Several protein-sequencing methods generate a huge number of protein sequences, which increases the relationship gap between sequences and structures. Predicting the protein structure and sequence analysis is one of the most important research activities in system biology [173, 185]. This field has an important role in bioinformatics research in association rule mining [206].

Similar to the amino acid sequences, understanding the protein structure is important for pharmaceutical and disease researches. Association rules and rule-based classifiers proved their efficiency for understanding the similarity and differences in protein structures [55, 147]. In protein structure prediction, such as primary- and secondary-structure prediction, association rule mining and association rule–based classification have proved their best. However, few studies have been conducted in this field of research. In [206], an association rule–based classifier is used to analyze secondary-structure sequences to predict a protein secondary structure that is the three-dimensional form of local segments. This also played an important role in the prediction of tertiary structures that correspond to specific atomic positions in three-dimensional space.

An important branch of proteomics is the prediction of homologies between protein sequences in biological information processing. Protein homology prediction is useful for grouping proteins on the basis of functional and structural similarities. In this context, the main objective of protein homology prediction is to predict the value protein sequences. Few works have been done in this field using association rule mining [192]. In [172], a study was conducted by combining an association rule–based classifier with support vector machines.

Binding between protein and DNA plays an important role in transcription, replication, packaging, mutation, and so on [115, 116]. Association rule mining techniques were shown to be very useful for the discovery of protein DNA-binding sequence models as the binding uses the association information between amino acids and nucleotide sequence pairs [105]. A comparative study conducted in the field of predicting protein-DNA interaction is presented in [204].

35.5.3.2   *Protein Expression Analysis*

The area of protein expression analysis or mapping between different protein expression levels is known as differential proteomics. This field of study differentiates the distinct and related proteomes to identify biomarkers of different biological states and diagnose the regulation functions for proteins. Extensive surveys of analyses in the field of differential proteomics are presented in [125, 202]. Data-mining techniques present interesting perspectives to get relevant information from the massive databases related to differential proteomics. In this field of research, data-mining approaches are used for creating efficient databases for query processing, preliminary data analysis, experimental design, and so on [202].

35.5.3.3   *Functional Proteomic Analysis*

Functional proteomics comprises the analysis of protein interactions and the prediction of interactions between different proteins [136]. The prediction part involves protein function prediction, protein–protein interaction prediction, prediction of protein subcellular localizations, and so on. This field also includes determination of protein interactions in a proteome for a specific protein to ascertain the unknown functions.

Protein subcellar localization prediction refers to the problem of predicting the location of a functional protein within a living cell. A machine learning classifier–based approach was proposed in [113] and an association rule mining–based classifier system was proposed in [110] for predicting subcellular localization of proteins.

Understanding the functions of proteins is important to characterize their role in diseases and to discover efficient treatments for these diseases. The unknown functional activities of proteins are predicted from protein–protein interaction data [52], from protein interaction networks [139], via the analysis of interactomes [128], or by analyzing genome sequences [120]. The use of association rule mining in the context of protein function prediction is studied in [139].

Protein–protein interaction network discovery plays a major role in the construction of biological pathways, protein networks, and drug discovery in particular [155]. In the molecular biology field of research, this interaction prediction application is currently the major focus for data-mining applications. Association rule mining methods were successfully applied for discovering and predicting interactions by using association memberships of known and unknown proteins [42, 124]. Other recent research results on protein–protein interaction prediction based on association rule mining and related associative classification can be found in [92, 127, 129, 136].

The analysis of protein interaction networks contributes to the understanding of protein annotation studies [153]. Association rule mining methods play a significant role to discover and identify protein annotation relationships within or between protein–protein interaction networks [136]. In [20] the authors show that differential association rule mining is an efficient solution for the analysis of protein annotations.

35.6 CONCLUSION

Association rule mining is one of the most influential knowledge discovery tasks in data mining. It was adopted in a large number of applications in different domains, from market basket analysis to biological information processing. Recent improvements in biology led to the creation of large data repositories. Using these data requires efficient methods to mine relationships between biological components, such as genes, proteins, amino acids, and RNAs, for example, biological processes and environmental components. Association rules proved to be an efficient method for mining relationships between such heterogeneous classes of elements.

Association rule mining was applied in computational biology for processing information in different types of data sets containing medical, genomic, and proteomic information, interaction and sequence data, and so on. All these applications aim to contribute to the understanding of biological processes and to the conception of efficient protocols to prevent and cure diseases. They can be divided into three groups depending on the type of information processed. The first group includes the processing of medical and pharmaceutical data, which is the upper level of computational biology analyses. These data mostly concern diseases, treatments, and environmental factors. The second group concerns the processing of genome wide information, such as gene expression and sequence data, genomic functional annotations, gene mutation data, gene regulation networks, and so on. These applications aim at understanding structures, activities, evolutions, and functions of genes. The third group involves the system-level or proteomic information, such as protein and amino acid sequences, protein interaction information, protein and gene correspondences, protein biological annotations, and so on.

Application of association rule mining to computational biology is a recent field of research that presents many challenges and open problems still to solve. One of the most promising prospects is the integration of biological knowledge available in the numerous knowledge bases, bio-ontologies, and bibliographic repositories to improve the results of association rule mining from biological data.

REFERENCES

1. H. A. Abbass, R. Sarker, and C. Newton. PDE: A pareto-frontier differential evolution approach for multi-objective optimization problems. In *Proceedings of the 2001 Congress on Evolutionary Computation*, Vol. 2, 2001, pp. 971–978.
2. C. C. Aggarwal and P. S. Yu. A new framework for itemset generation. In *Proceedings of the ACM Symposium on Principles of Database Systems (PODS)*, Issue 2, 1998, pp. 18–24.
3. R. Agrawal, T. Imielinski, and A. N. Swami. Mining association rules between sets of items in large databases. In *Proceedings of ACM International Conference on Management of Data (SIGMOD)*, Vol. 22, Issue: May 1993, pp. 207–216.
4. R. Agrawal and R. Srikant. Fast algorithms for mining association rules in large databases. In *Proceedings of International Conference on Very Large Data Bases (VLDB)*, Vol. 15, Issue 6, September 1994, pp. 487–499.
5. A. Agresti. *Categorical Data Analysis*. Wiley, New York, 1990.
6. A. Agresti. *An Introduction to Categorical Data Analysis*. Wiley, New York, 1996.
7. B. Alatas, E. Akin, and A. Karci. MODENAR: Multi-objective differential evolution algorithm for mining numeric association rules. *Appl. Soft Comput.*, 8:646–656, 2008.

8. D. J Allocco, I. S Kohane, and A. J Butte. Quantifying the relationship between co-expression, co-regulation and gene function. *BMC Bioinformatics*, Volume: 5, Issue: 18, 2004.

9. M. Anandhavalli, M. K. Ghose, and K. Gauthaman. Interestingness measure for mining spatial gene expression data using association rule. *J. Comput.*, 2(1):110–114, 2010.

10. M. Anandhavilli, M. K. Ghose, and K. Gauthaman. Association rule mining in genomics. *Int. J. Comput. Theory Eng.*, 2(2):269–273, 2010.

11. R Angiulli, G. Ianni, and L. Palopoli. On the complexity of mining association rules. *Data Min. Knowl. Discov.*, 2(3):263–281, 1998.

12. W. W. Armstrong. Dependency structures of data base relationships. In *Proceedings of the International Federation for Information Processing Congress (IFIP)*, N-H (Amsterdam), 1974, pp. 580–583.

13. J. Azé and Y. Kodratoff. A study of the effect of noisy data in rule extraction systems. In *Proceedings of the European Meeting on Cybernetics and Systems Research*, Vol. 2, 2002, pp. 781–786.

14. J. L. Balcazar. Redundancy, deduction schemes and minimum-size bases for the association rules. *Logic. Methods Comput. Sci.*, 6(2–3):1–33, 2010.

15. W. C. Barker, J. S. Garavelli, Z. Hou, H. Huang, R. S. Ledley, P. B. McGarvey, H. W. Mewes, B. C. Orcutt, F. Pfeiffer, A. Tsugita, C. R. Vinayaka, C. Xiao, L. S. Yeh, and C. Wu. Protein information resource: A community resource for expert annotation of protein data. *Nucleic Acids Res.*, 29:29–32, 2001.

16. Y. Bastide, N. Pasquier, R. Taouil, G. Stumme, and L. Lakhal. Mining frequent patterns with counting inference. *SIGKDD Explor.*, 2(2):66–75, 2000.

17. Y. Bastide, N. Pasquier, R. Taouil, G. Stumme, and L. Lakhal. Mining minimal non-redundant association rules using frequent closed itemsets. In *Proceedings of the International Conference on Computational Logic (CL)*, Vol. 1861 of *Lecture Notes in Computer Science*, Springer, Heidelberg, 2000, pp. 972–986.

18. R. J. Bayardo and R. Agrawal. Mining the most interesting rules. In *Proceedings of the fifth ACM SIGKDD International Conference on Knowledge Discovery and Data Mining (KDD)*, San Diego, CA, 1999, pp. 145–153.

19. C. Becquet, S. Blachon, B. Jeudy, J.-F. Boulicaut, and O. Gandrillon. Strong-association-rule mining for large-scale gene-expression data analysis: A case study on human sage data. *Genome Biol.*, 3(12), 2002.

20. C. Besemann, A. Denton, A. Yekkirala, R. Hutchison, and M. Anderson. Differential association rule mining for the study of protein-protein interaction networks. In *Proceedings of the forth ACM SIGKDD Workshop on Data Mining in Bioinformatics (BioKDD)*, 2004, pp. 72–80.

21. G. Birkhoff. *Lattice Theory*, 3rd ed., Vol. 25. American Mathematical Society, 1995.

22. B. Boeckmann, A. Bairoch, R. Apweiler, M.-C. Blatter, A. Estreicher, E. Gasteiger, M. J. Martin, K. Michoud, C. O'Donovan, I. Phan, S. Pilbout, and M. Schneider. The SWISS-PROT protein knowledge base and its supplement TrEMBL. *Nucleic Acids Res.*, 31:365–370, 2003.

23. J.-F. Boulicaut and J. Besson. Actionability and formal concepts: A data mining perspective. In *Proceedings of the International Conference on Formal Concept Analysis (ICFCA)*, Vol. 4933 of *Lecture Notes in Computer Science*, Springer, Heidelberg, 2008, pp. 14–31.

24. J.-F. Boulicaut, A. Bykowski, and C. Rigotti. Approximation of frequency queries by means of free-sets. In *Proceedings of the 4th European Conference on Principles of Data Mining and Knowledge Discovery (PKDD)*, Springer-Verlag, London, 2000, pp. 75–85.

25. J.-F. Boulicaut, A. Bykowski, and C. Rigotti. Free-sets: A condensed representation of Boolean data for the approximation of frequency queries. *Data Mining Knowledge Discov.*, 7(1):5–22, 2003.

26. J.-F. Boulicaut and B. Jeudy. Mining free itemsets under constraints. In *Proceedings of the International Database Engineering and Application Symposium (IDEAS)*, 2001, pp. 322–329.

27. Y. Le Bras, P. Lenca, and S. Lallich. Mining interesting rules without support requirement: A general universal existential upward closure property. *Ann. Inform. Syst.*, 8:75–98, 2010.

28. L. Breiman, J. Freidman, R. Olshen, and C. Stone. *Classification and Regression Trees*. Wadsworth and Brooks/Cole Advanced Books, Monterey, CA, 1984.

29. T. Brijs, K. Vanhoof, and G. Wets. Defining interestingness for association rules. *Int. J. Inform. Theor. Appl.*, 10(4):370–376, 2003.

30. S. Brin, R. Motwani, and C. Silverstein. Beyond market baskets: Generalizing association rules to correlations. In *Proceedings of the ACM International Conference on Management of Data (SIGMOD)*, Vol. 26, No. 2, 1997, pp. 265–276.

31. S. Brin, R. Motwani, and C. Silverstein. Beyond market baskets: Generalizing association rules to dependence rules. *Data Mining Knowledge Discov.*, 2(1):39–68, 1998.

32. S. Brin, R. Motwani, J. D. Ullman, and S. Tsur. Dynamic itemset counting and implication rules for market basket data. In *Proceedings of ACM International Conference on Management of Data (SIGMOD)*, 1997, pp. 255–264.

33. L. Brisson, N. Pasquier, C. Hebert, and M. Collard. HASAR: Mining sequential association rules for atherosclerosis risk factor analysis. In *Proceedings of the Discovery Challenge of the International Conference on Principles of Knowledge Discovery in Databases (PKDD)*, October 2004, pp. 14–25.

34. T. Calders, C. Rigotti, and J.-F. Boulicaut. A survey on condensed representations for frequent sets. *Constraint-Based Mining and Inductive Databases*, (3848):64–80, 2005.

35. L. Cao. Flexible frameworks for actionable knowledge discovery. *IEEE Trans. Knowledge Data Eng.*, 22(9):1299–1312, 2010.

36. L. Cao. Actionable knowledge discovery and delivery. *Wiley Interdisciplinary Rev.: Data Mining Knowledge Discov.*, 2(2):149–163, 2012.

37. L. Cao, D. Luo, and C. Zhang. Knowledge actionability: Satisfying technical and business interestingness. *Int. J. Business Intell. Data Mining*, 2(4):496–514, 2007.

38. L. Cao and C. Zhang. Domain-driven actionable knowledge discovery in the real world. In *Advances in Knowledge Discovery and Data Mining*, Vol. 3918 of *Lecture Notes in Computer Science*, 2006, pp. 821–830.

39. P. Carmona-Saez, M. Chagoyen, A. Rodriguez, O. Trelles, J. M. Carazo, and A. Pascual Montano. Integrated analysis of gene expression by association rules discovery. *BMC Bioinformatics*, 7(54), February 2006.

40. A. Ceglar and J. F. Roddick. Association mining. *ACM Comput. Surv.*, 38(2), July 2006.

41. G. Chen, D. Liu, and J. Li. Influence and conditional influence—New interestingness measures in association rule mining. In *Proceedings of the 10th IEEE International Conference on Fuzzy Systems (FUZZ-IEEE)*, Vol. 3, 2001, pp. 1440–1443.

42. H.-W. Chiu and F.-H. Hung. Association rule mining from yeast protein interaction to assist protein-protein interaction prediction. *Biomed. Soft Comput. Human Sci.*, 13(1):3–6, 2008.

43. R. J. Cho, M. J. Campbell, E. A. Winzeler, L. Steinmetz, A. Conway, L. Wodicka, T. G. Wolfsberg, A. E. Gabrielian, D. Landsman, D. J. Lockhart, and R. W. Davis. A genome-wide transcriptional analysis of the mitotic cell cycle. *Mol. Cell*, 2(1):65–73, 1998.

44. P. Clark and R. Boswell. Rule induction with CN2: Some recent improvements. In *Proceedings of the European Working Session on Learning*, Machine Learning—EWSL-91, Springer, Heidelberg, 1991, pp. 151–163.

45. J. Cohen. A coefficient of agreement for nominal scales. *Edu. Psychol. Measur.*, 20:37–46, 1960.

46. G. Cong, A. K. H. Tung, X. Xu, F. Pan, and J. Yang. FARMER: Finding interesting rule groups in microarray datasets. In *Proceedings of the 2004 ACM International Conference on Management of Data (SIGMOD)*, 2004, pp. 143–154.

47. J. Couchet, D. Manrique, J. Rios, and A. Rodriguez-Paton. Crossover and mutation operators for grammar-guided genetic programming. *Soft Comput.*, 11(10):943–955, 2007.

48. C. Creighton and S. Hanash. Mining gene expression databases for association rules. *Bioinformatics*, 19:79–86, 2003.

49. L. Cristofor and D. A. Simovici. Generating an informative cover for association rules. In *Proceedings of the IEEE International Conference on Data Mining (ICDM)*, 2002, pp. 597–600.

50. L. Davis. *Handbook of Genetic Algorithms*. Van Nostrand Reinhold, New York, 1991.

51. S. Dehuri and R. Mall. Mining predictive and comprehensible rules using a multi-objective genetic algorithm. *Knowl. Based Syst.*, 19(6):413–421, 2004.

52. M. Deng, F. Sun, and T. Chen. Assessment of the reliability of protein-protein interactions and protein function prediction. In *Proceedings of the Pacific Symposium on Biocomputing (PSB)*, 2003, pp. 140–151.

53. S. Doddi, A. Marathe, S. S. Ravi, and D. C. Torney. Discovery of association rules in medical data. *Med. Informatics Internet Med.*, 26:25–33, 2001.

54. V. Duquenne and J. L. Guigues. Famille minimale d'implications informatives résultant d'un tableau de donnees binaires. *Mathematiques et Sciences Humaines*, 24(95):5–18, 1986.

55. E. M. F. El-Houby. Mining protein structure class using one database scan. *Int. J. Comput. Internet Manag.*, 18(2):8–16, Aug. 2010.

56. V. Fhar and A. Tuzhilin. Abstract-driven pattern discovery in databases. *IEEE Trans. Knowledge Data Eng.*, 5:926–938, 1993.

57. A. A. Freitas. A survey of evolutionary algorithms for data mining and knowledge discovery. In A. Ghosh and S. Tsutsui (Eds.), *Advances in Evolutionary Computing*, Springer, Heidelberg, 2001, pp. 819–845.

58. K. Y. Fung, C. K. Kwong, K. W. M. Siu, and K. M. Yu. A multi-objective genetic algorithm approach to rule mining for affective product design. *Expert Syst. Appl.*, 39(8):7411–7419, 2012.

59. J. G. Ganascia. Deriving the learning bias from rule properties. *Machine Intell.*, 12:151–167, 1991.

60. B. Ganter, G. Stumme, and R. Wille. Formal concept analysis: Foundations and applications. Vol. 3626 of *Lecture Notes in Computer Science*, Springer, 2005.

61. S. Garbis, G. Lubec, and M. Fountoulakis. Limitations of current proteomics technologies. *J. Chromatogr. A*, 1077:1–18, May 2005.

62. A. Gauthaman. Analysis of DNA microarray data using association rules: A selective study. *World Acad. Sci. Eng. Technol.*, 42:12–16, 2008.

63. L. Geng and H. J. Hamilton. Interestingness measure for data mining: A survey. *ACM Comput. Surv.*, 38(3), September 2006.

64. E. Georgii, L. Richter, U. Ruckert, and S. Kramer. Analyzing microarray data using quantitative association rules. *Bioinformatics*, 21(Suppl 2):ii123–ii129, 2005.

65. A. Ghosh and B. T. Nath. Multi-objective rule mining using genetic algorithms. *Inform. Sci.*, 163:123–133, 2004.

66. E. G. Giannopoulou and S. Kossida. *Data Mining Applications in the Post-Genomic Era*, Data Mining in Medical and Biological Research, Chapter 14, In Tech, Vienna, Austria, December 2008, pp. 237–252.

67. B. Goethals, J. Muhonen, and H. Toivonen. Mining non-derivable association rules. In *Proceedings of the SIAM International Conference on Data Mining (SDM)*, 2005, pp. 239–249.

68. E. Gonzales, K. Taboada, S. Mabu, K. Shimada, and K. Hirasawa. Combination of two evolutionary methods for mining association rules in large and dense databases. *J. Adv. Computat. Intell. Intell. Informatics*, 13(5):561–569, 2009.

69. L. A. Goodman and W. H. Kruskal. Measures of association for cross-classifications. *J. Am. Statist. Assoc.*, 49:732–764, 1968.

70. R. Gras. Contribution de l'étude expérimentale et de l'analyse de certaines acquisitions cognitives et de certains objectifs didactiques en mathématiques. Ph.D. Thesis. Université de Rennes I, 1979.

71. R. Gras, P. Kuntz, R. Couturier, and F. Guillet. Une version entropique de l'intensité d'implication pour les corpus volumineux. In *Actes de la Conference Internationale sur l'Extraction et la Gestion des Connaissances (EGC)*, Vol. 1, No. 1–2, 2001, pp. 69–80.

72. B. Gray and M. E. Orlowska. CCAIIA: Clustering categorical attributes into interesting association rules. In *Proceedings of the Pacific-Asia Conference on Knowledge Discovery and Data Mining (PAKDD)*, Vol. 1394 of *Lecture Notes in Computer Science*, Springer, Heidelberg, 1998, pp. 132–143.

73. A. Grigoriev. A relationship between gene expression and protein interactions on the proteome scale: Analysis of the bacteriophage T7 and the yeas Saccharomyces cerevisiae. *Nucleic Acid Res.*, 29:3513–3519, July 2001.

74. N. Gupta, N. Mangal, K. Tiwari, and P. Mitra. Mining quantitative association rules in protein sequences. In *Proceedings of Australasian Conference on Knowledge Discovery and Data Mining (AUSDM)*, Vol. 3755 of *Lecture Notes in Computer Science*, Springer, Heidelberg, 2006, pp. 273–281.

75. T. Hamrouni, S. Ben Yahia, and E. M. Nguifo. Succinct system of minimal generators: A thorough study, limitations and new definitions. *Concept Lattices and Their Applications*, (4923):80–95, 2008.

76. F. Han and N. Rao. Mining co-regulated genes using association rules combined with hast-tree and genetic algorithms. *IEEE Xplore*, 2009, pp. 858–862.

77. Y. He and S. C. Hui. Exploring ant-based algorithms for gene expression data analysis. *Artif. Intell. Medi.*, 47(2):105–119, 2009.

78. Z. He, X. Xu, and S. Deng. Data mining for actionable knowledge: A survey. Journal *CoRR*, Vol. abs/cs/0501079, 2005.

79. M. L. Hetland and P. Saetrom. Temporal rule discovery using genetic programming and specialized hardware. In *Proceedings of the International Conference on Recent Advances in Soft Computing (RASC)*, 2002, pp. 182–188.

80. Z. Huang, J. Li, H. Su, G. Watts, and H. Chen. Large-scale regulatory network analysis from microarray data: Modified bayesian network learning and association rule mining. *Decision Support Syst.*, 43(4):1207–1225, 2007.

81. A. Icev, C. Ruiz, and E. Ryder. Distance-enhanced association rules for gene expression. In *Proceedings of the 3rd ACM SIGKDD Workshop on Data Mining in Bioinformatics (BIOKDD2003)*. Held in conjunction with the 9th Intl. Conf. on Knowledge Discovery and Data Mining (KDD2003), Washington, DC, August 2003, pp. 34–40.

82. H. Ishibuchi, I. Kuwajima, and Y. Nojima. Multi-objective association rule mining. In *Proceedings of the PPSN Workshop on Multiobjective Problem Solving from Nature*, Reykjavik, Iceland, September 2006, pp. 39–48.

83. H. Ishibuchi, T. Murata, and I. B. Turksen. Single-objective and two-objective genetic algorithms for selecting linguistic rules for pattern classification problems. *Fuzzy Sets Syst.*, 89:135–150, 1997.

84. H. Ishibuchi and Y. Nojima. Accuracy-complexity tradeoff analysis by multiobjective rule selection. In *Proceedings of the 5th ICDM Workshop on Computational Intelligence in Data Mining (CIDM)*, Houston, November 2005, pp. 39–48.

85. H. Ishibuchi and T. Yamamoto. Fuzzy rule selection by multi-objective genetic local search algorithms and rule evaluation measures in data mining. *Fuzzy Sets Syst.*, 141:59–88, 2004.

86. H. Jefreys. Some test of significance treated by theory of probability. In *Proceedings of the Cambridge Philosophical Society*, 1935, pp. 203–222.

87. A. Jimenez, F. Berzal, and J.-C. Cubero. Interestingness measure for association rules within groups. *Knowledge Inform. Syst.*, 80:298–307, 2010.

88. M. Kamber and R. Shinghal. Evaluating the interestingness of characteristic rules. In *Proceedings of the 2nd International Conference on Knowledge Discovery and Data Mining (KDD)*, Portland, Oregon, 1996, pp. 263–266.

89. F. Karel and J. Klema. Quantitative association rule mining in genomics using *a priori* knowledge. In *Proceedings of the ECML/PKDD Workshop on Prior Conceptual Knowledge in Machine Learning and Data Mining*, Warsaw, Department of Cybernetics, Czech Technical University in Prague, September 2007, pp. 53–64.

90. M. Kaya. Multi-objective genetic algorithm based approaches for mining optimized fuzzy association rules. *Soft Comput.*, 10:578–586, 2006.

91. W. Klosgen. Explora: A multi-pattern and multi-strategy discovery assistant. Book chapter in *Advances in Knowledge Discovery and Data Mining*, 1996, pp. 249–271.

92. M. Kotlyar and I. Jurisica. Predicting protein-protein interactions by association mining. *Inform. Syst. Front.*, 8(1):37–47, 2006.

93. S. Kotsiatis and D. Kanellopoulos. Association rule mining: A recent overview. *GESTS Int. Trans. Comput. Sci. Eng.*, 32(1):71–82, 2006.

94. M. Krawczak, E. V. Ball, I. Fenton, P. D. Stenson, S. Abeysinghe, N. Thomas, and D. N. Cooper. Human gene mutation database—A biomedical information and research resource. *Human Mutation*, 15(1):45–51, 2000.

95. M. Kryszkiewicz. Representative association rules and minimum condition maximum consequence association rules. In *Proceedings of ACM International Conference on Knowledge Discovery and Data Mining (KDD)*, Vol. 1510 of *Lecture Notes in Computer Science*, Springer, Heidelberg, 1998, pp. 361–369.

96. M. Kryszkiewicz. Concise representations of association rules. *Pattern Detect. Discov.*, 2447:187–203, 2002.

97. H. Kwasnicka and K. Switalski. Discovery of association rules from medical data—Classical and evolutionary approaches. In *Proceedings of the XXI Autumn Meeting of Polish Information Processing Society (PIPS)*, Department of computer science, Wroclaw University of Technology, Poland, 2005, pp. 163–177.

98. S. Lallich, O. Teytaud, and E. Prudhomme. Association rule interestingness: Measure and statistical validation. *Quality Measures in Data Mining*, 2007, pp. 251–275.

99. P. Laxmi, A. Poongodai, and D. Sujatha. Extended apriori for association rule mining: Diminution based utility weightage measuring approach. *J. Comput. Sci. Technol.*, 11(22):25–30, 2011.

100. P. Lenca, P. Meyer, B. Vaillant, and S. Lallich. A multicriteria decision aid for interestingness measure selection. Technical Report LUSSI-TR-2004-01-EN. GET/ENST, Bretagne, France, 2004.

101. P. Lenca, P. Meyer, B. Vaillant, and S. Lallich. On selecting interestingness measures for association rules: User oriented description and multiple criteria decision aid. *Eur. J. Operational Res.*, 184(2):610–626, 2008.

102. P. Lenca, B. Vaillant, P. Meyer, and S. Lallich. Association rule interestingness measures: Experimental and theoretical studies. In *Quality Measures in Data Mining*, Vol. 43 of *Studies in Computational Intelligence*. Springer, Heidelberg, 2007, pp. 51–76.

103. I. Lerman and J. Aze. Une mesure probabiliste contextuelle discriminante de qualite des règles d'association. In *Actes de la Conférence Internationale sur l'Extraction et la Gestion des Connaissances (EGC)*, Vol. 17 of Revue des Sciences et Technologies de l'Information—série RIA ECA, Hermes Science Publications, 2003, pp. 247–262.

104. I. C. Lerman, R. Gras, and H. Rostam. Elaboration d'un indice d'implication pour les donnees binaires, i et ii. *Mathématiques et Sciences Humaines*, 74(75):5–35, 1981.

105. K.-S. Leung, K.-C. Wong, T.-M. Chan, M.-H. Wong, K.-H. Lee, C.-K. Lau, and S. K. W. Tsui. Discovering protein-DNA binding sequence patterns using association rule mining. *Nucleic Acids Res.*, 38(19):6324–6337, June 2010.

106. P. D. Lewis, J. S. Harvey, E. M. Waters, and J. M. Parry. The mammalian gene mutation database. *Mutagenesis*, 15(5):411–414, 2000.

107. J. Li. A survey on actionable knowledge discovery applications. In *Proceedings of the 2nd International Workshop on Intelligent Systems and Applications (ISA)*, IEEE Wuhan, 2010, pp. 1–3.

108. D. C. Liebler. *Introduction to Proteomics*. Humana Press, 2002.

109. B. Liu, W. Hsu, S. Chen, and Y. Ma. Analyzing subjective interestingness of association rules. *IEEE Intell. Syst.*, 15(5):47–55, 2000.

110. Y. Liu, Z. Guo, X. Ke, and O. R. Zaiane. Protein sub-cellular localization prediction with associative classification and multi-class SVM. In *Proceedings of the 2nd ACM Conference on Bioinformatics*, Computational Biology and Biomedicine, Chicago, Illinois, August 2011, pp. 493–495.

111. J. Loevinger. A systematic approach to the construction and evaluation of tests of ability. *Psychol. Monogr.*, 61(4):i–49, 1947.

112. E. J. Lopez, A. Blanco, F. Garcia, and A. Marin. Extracting biological knowledge by fuzzy association rule mining. IEEE International Fuzzy Systems Conference, FUZZ-IEEE 2007, London, 2007, pp. 1–6.

113. Z. Lu, D. Szafron, R. Greiner, P. Lu, D. S. Wishart, B. Poulin, C. Macdonell, and R. Eisner. Predicting subcellular localization of proteins using machine-learned classifiers. *Bioinformatics*, 20(4):547–556, 2004.

114. J. M. Luna, J. Raul Romero, and S. Ventura. G3PARM: A grammar guided genetic programming algorithm for mining association rules. *Computat. Intell.*, 1(8):18–23, July 2010.

115. N. M. Luscombe, S. E. Austin, H. M. Berman, and J. M. Thornton. An overview of the structures of protein-DNA complexes. *Genome Biol.*, 1(1):1–10, June 2000.

116. N. M. Luscombe and J. M. Thornton. Protein-DNA interactions: Amino acid conservation and the effects of mutations on binding specificity. *J. Mol. Biol.*, 320:991–1009, 2002.

117. M. Luxenburger. Implications partielles dans un contexte. *Mathematiques, Informatique et Sciences Humaines*, 29(113):35–55, 1991.

118. D. Maier. *The Theory of Relational Databases*. Computer Science Press, 1983.

119. H. Mannila and H. Toivonen. Multiple uses of frequent sets and condensed representations. In *Proceedings of ACM International Conference on Knowledge Discovery and Data Mining (KDD)*, AAAI Press, 1996, pp. 189–194.

120. E. M. Marcotte, M. Pellegrini, H. L. Ng, D. W. Rice, T. O. Yeates, and D. Eisenberg. Detecting protein function and protein-protein interactions from genome sequences. *Science*, 285:751–753, 1999.

121. K. McGarry. A survey of interestingness measure for knowledge discovery. *Knowledge Eng. Rev.*, 20(1):39–61, 2005.

122. R. R.F. Mendes, F. de B. Voznika, A. A. Freitas, and J. C. Nievola. Discovering fuzzy classification rules with genetic programming and co-evolution. In *Proceedings of the 5th European Conference on Principles of Data Mining and Knowledge Discovery (PKDD)*, Vol. 2168 of *Lecture Notes in Computer Science*, Springer-Verlag, London, 2001, pp. 314–325.

123. A. Merceron and K. Yacef. Revisiting interestingness of strong symmetric association rules in educational data. In *Proceedings of the International Workshop on Applying Data Mining in e-Learning (ADML)*, 2007, pp. 3–12.

124. K. C. Mondal, N. Pasquier, A. Mukhopadhyay, C. da Costa Pereira, U. Maulik, and A. G. B. Tettamanzi. Prediction of protein interactions on HIV-1-human PPI data using a novel closure-based integrated approach. In *Proceedings of the International Conference on Bioinformatics Models, Methods and Algorithms (BIOINFORMATICS)*, 2012, pp. 164–173.

125. L. Monteoliva and J. P. Albar. Differential proteomics: An overview of gel and non-gel based approaches. *Brief. Funct. Genomics Proteomics*, 3:220–239, 2004.

126. F. Mosteller. Association and estimation in contingency tables. *J. Am. Statist. Assoc.*, 63:1–28, 1968.

127. A. Mukhopadhyay, U. Maulik, S. Bandyopadhyay, and R. Eils. Mining association rules from HIV-human protein interactions. In *Proceedings of International Conference on Systems in Medicine and Biology (ICSMB)*, Dec. 2010, pp. 344–348.

128. E. Nabieva and M. Singh. Protein function prediction via analysis of interactomes. In J. M. Bujnicki (Ed.), *Prediction of Protein Structures, Functions, and Interactions*, Chapter 10. John Wiley & Sons, Hoboken, NJ, 2008, pp. 231–258.

129. Z. Nafar and A. Golshani. Data mining methods for protein-protein interactions. In *Proceedings of the IEEE Canadian Conference on Electrical and Computer Engineering (CCECE)*, 2006, pp. 991–994.

130. J. Nahar. Significant cancer risk factor extraction: An association rule discovery approach. In *Proceedings of the IEEE International Conference on Computer and Information Technology (ICCIT)*, 2008, pp. 108–114.

131. R. Natarajan and B. Shekar. Interestingness of association rules in data mining: Issues relevant to e-commerce. *SADHANA Acad. Proc. Eng. Sci.*, 30:2991–309, 2005.

132. M. Ohsaki, S. Kitaguchi, K. Okamoto, H. Yokoi, and T. Yamaguchi. Evaluation of rule interestingness measures with a clinical dataset on hepatitis. In *Proceedings of the International Conference on Principles of Knowledge Discovery in Databases (PKDD)*, Vol. 3202 of *Lecture Notes in Computer Science*, 2004, pp. 362–373.

133. E. R. Omiecinski. Alternative interest measures for mining associations in databases. *IEEE Trans. Knowledge Data Eng.*, 15(1):57–69, 2003.

134. C. Ordonez, N. Ezquerra, and C. A. Santana. Constraining and summarizing association rules in medical data. *Knowledge Inform. Syst.*, 9(3):259–283, 2006.

135. C. Ordonez, C. Santana, and L. de Braal. Discovering interesting association rules in medical data. In D. Gunopulos and R. Rastogi (Eds.), ACM SIG MOD Workshop on Research Issues in Data Mining and Knowledge Discovery 2000, Dallas, Texas, pp. 78–85, 2000.

136. T. Oyama, K. Kitano, K. Satou, and T. Ito. Extraction of knowledge on protein-protein interaction by association rule discovery. *Bioinformatics*, 18(5):705–714, 2002.

137. G. Pagallo and D. Haussler. Boolean feature discovery in empirical leaning. *Machine Learning*, 5(1):71–99, 1990.

138. F. Pan, G. Cong, and A. K. H. Tung. CARPENTER: Finding closed patterns in long biological datasets. In *Proceedings of the 9th ACM SIGKDD International Conference on Knowledge Discovery and Data Mining (KDD)*. ACM, New York, 2003, pp. 637–642.

139. G. Pandey, M. Steinbach, R. Gupta, T. Garg, and V. Kumar. Association analysis-based transformations for protein interaction networks: A function prediction case study. In *Proceedings of the 13th ACM SIGKDD International Conference on Knowledge Discovery and Data Mining (KDD)*, ACM, New York, 2007, pp. 540–549.

140. N. Pasquier. Frequent closed itemsets based condensed representations for association rules. In *Post-Mining of Association Rules: Techniques for Effective Knowledge Extraction*, Chapter XIII, Information Science Reference, 2009, pp. 248–273.

141. N. Pasquier, Y. Bastide, R. Taouil, and L. Lakhal. Pruning closed itemset lattices for associations rules. In *Proceedings of the 14th BDA international conference on Advanced Databases*, Hammamet, Tunisia, October 1998, pp. 177–196.

142. N. Pasquier, Y. Bastide, R. Taouil, and L. Lakhal. Discovering frequent closed itemsets for association rules. In *Proceedings of the 7th International Conference on Database Theory (ICDT)*, Springer, Heidelberg, 1999, pp. 398–416.

143. N. Pasquier, Y. Bastide, R. Taouil, and L. Lakhal. Efficient mining of association rules using closed itemset lattices. *Inform. Syst.*, 24(1):25–46, 1999.

144. N. Pasquier, R. Taouil, Y. Bastide, G. Stumme, and L. Lakhal. Generating a condensed representation for association rules. *J. Intell. Inform. Syst.*, 24(1):29–60, 2005.

145. G. Piatetsky-Shapiro. Discovery, analysis and presentation of strong rules. In book: *Knowledge Discovery in Databases*, AAAI Press, 1991, pp. 229–248.

146. S. Pramod and O. P. Vyas. Survey on frequent item set mining algorithms. *Int. J. Comput. Appl.*, 1(15):86–91, 2010.

147. N. Rattanakronkul and K. Waiyamai. Combining association rule discovery and data classification for protein structure prediction. In *Proceedings of the International Conference on Bio-informatics (INCOP)*, North-South Network, Bangkok, Thailand, 2002.

148. S. O. Rezende, E. A. Melanda, M. L. Fujimoto, R. A. Sinoara, and V. O. de Carvalho. Combining data-driven and user-driven evaluation measures to identify interesting rules. In Y. Zhao, C. Zhang, and L. Cao (Eds.), *Post-Mining of Association Rules: Techniques for Effective Knowledge Extraction*, Information Science Reference, Chapter 3, IGI Global, Hershey, PA, 2009, pp. 38–55.

149. S. Ruggieri. Frequent regular itemset mining. In *Proceedings of the ACM SIGKDD International Conference on Knowledge Discovery and Data Mining (KDD)*, Washington, DC, July 2010, pp. 263–272.

150. S. Sahar and Y. Mansour. An empirical evaluation of objective interestingness criteria. In *Proceedings of the SPIE Conference on Data Mining and Knowledge Discovery*, Orlando, FL, 1999, pp. 63–74.

151. P. S. Sandhu, D. S. Dhaliwal, and S. N. Panda. Mining utility-oriented association rules: An efficient approach based on profit and quantity. *Int. J. Phys. Sci.*, 6(2):301–307, 2011.

152. R. Sarker and H. A. Abbass. Differential evolution for solving multi-objective optimization problems. *Asia-Pacific J. Oper. Res.*, 21(2):225–240, 2004.

153. B. Schwikowski, P. Uetz, and S. Fields. A network of protein-protein interactions in yeast. *Nature Biotechnol.*, 18(12):1257–1261, 2000.

154. M. Sebag and M. Schoenauer. Generation of rules with certainty and confidence factors from incomplete and incoherent learning bases. In *Proceedings of the European Knowledge Acquisition Workshop (EKAW)*, 1988, pp. 28-1–28-20.

155. E. Segal, H. Wang, and D. Koller. Discovering molecular pathways from protein interaction and gene expression data. *Bioinformatics*, 19(1):i264–i272, 2003.

156. X. Shang, Q. Zhao, and Z. Li. Mining high-correlation association rules for inferring gene regulation networks. *Data Warehousing Knowledge Discov.*, Vol. 5691 of *Lecture Notes in Computer Science*, Springer, Heidelberg, 2009, pp. 244–255.

157. M. Shekofteh. A survey of algorithms in FCIM. In *Proceedings of the International Conference on Data Storage and Data Engineering (DSDE)*, IEEE Computer Society, Washington, DC, February 2010, pp. 29–33.

158. K. Shimada and K. Hirasawa. Exceptional association rule mining using genetic network programming. In *Proceedings of Data Mining (DMIN 2008)*, Vol. 2, Las Vegas, NV, July 2008, pp. 277–283.

159. K. Shimada, K. Hirasawa, and J. Hu. Class association rule mining with chi-squared test using genetic network programming. In *Proceedings of the IEEE Conference on Systems, Man, and Cybernetics (SMC)*, 2006, pp. 5338–5344.

160. E. Shortliffe and B. Buchanan. A model of inexact reasoning in medicine. *Math. Biosci.*, 23:351–379, 1975.

161. P. Smyth and R. M. Goodman. Rule induction using information theory. *Knowledge Discovery Databases (KDD)*, MITPress, 1991, pp. 159–176.

162. M. R. Spruit. Discovery of association rules between syntactic variables. In *Proceedings of the Meeting of Computational Linguistics in the Netherlands (CLIN)*, 2007, pp. 83–98.

163. M. Steinbach, P.-N. Tan, H. Xiong, and V. Kumar. Objective measure for association pattern analysis. *Contemp. Math.*, 443:205–226, 2007.

164. S. Stilou, P. D. Bamidis, N. Maglaveras, and C. Pappas. Mining association rules from clinical databases: An intelligent diagnostic process in healthcare. *Medinfo*, 10:1399–1403, 2001.

165. R. Storn. On the use of differential evolution for function optimization. In Fuzzy Information Processing Society, NAFIPS, Biennial Conference of the North American, IEEE, 1996, pp. 519–523.

166. E. Suzuki. Pitfalls for categorizations of objective interestingness measures for rule discovery. In *Statistical Implicative Analysis*, Vol. 127 of *Studies in Computational Intelligence*. Springer, Heidelberg, 2008, pp. 383–395.

167. K. Taboada, K. Shimada, S. Mabu, K. Hirasawa, and J. Hu. Association rule mining for continuous attributes using genetic network programming. In *Proceedings of the 9th International Conference on Genetic and Evolutionary Computation (GECCO)*, ACM New York, NY, 2007, pp. 1758–1758.

168. R. Tamir and Y. Singer. On a confidence gain measure for association rule discovery and scoring. *VLDB J.*, 15(1):40–52, 2006.

169. P. Tan, V. Kumar, and J. Srivastava. Selecting the right interestingness measure for association pattern. In *Proceedings of the 8th ACMSIGKDD International Conference on Knowledge Discovery and Data Mining (KDD)*, Edmonton, Alberta, Canada, 2002, pp. 32–41.

170. P. N. Tan and V. Kumar. Interestingness measures for association patterns: A perspective. TR00-036, Department of Computer Science, University of Minnesota, 2000.

171. P.-N. Tan, V. Kumar, and J. Srivastava. Selecting the right objective measure for association analysis. *Inform. Syst.*, 29(4):293–313, June 2004.

172. Y. Tang, B. Jin, and Y.-Q. Zhang. Granular support vector machines with association rules mining for protein homology prediction. *Artif. Intell. Med.*, 35:121–134, 2005.

173. J. M. Thorton. From genome to function. *Science*, 292:2095–2097, 2001.

174. H. Toivonen, M. Klemettinen, P. Ronkainen, K. Hatonen, and H. Mannila. Pruning and grouping discovered association rules. In *Proceedings of the ECML MLnet Workshop on Statistics, Machine Learning, and Knowledge Discovery in Databases*, 1995, pp. 47–52.

175. J.-M. Tremeaux and Y. Liu. Mining for association rules in medical data. Technical Report, 2006.

176. A. Tuzhilin and G. Adomavicius. Handling very large numbers of association rules in the analysis of microarray data. In *Proceedings of the ACM SIGKDD International Conference on Knowledge Discovery and Data Mining (KDD)*, 2002, pp. 396–404.

177. M. Tyers and M. Mann. From genomics to proteomics. *Nature*, 422:193–197, Mar. 2003.

178. P. Valtchev, R. Missaoui, and R. Godin. Formal concept analysis for knowledge discovery and data mining: The new challenges. In *Concept Lattices*, Vol. 2961 of *Lecture Notes in Computer Science*, 3901–3901, 2004.

179. P. A. Whigham. Grammatically-based genetic programming. In *Proceedings of the Workshop on Genetic Programming: From Theory to Real-World Applications (GP)*, Vol. 16, No. 3, Morgan Kaufmann, 1995, pp. 33–41.

180. R. White. *Gene Transcription, Mechanisms and Control*. Blackwell Science, 2001.

181. H. Xion, P.-N. Tan, and V. Kumar. Hyperclique pattern discovery. *Data Mining Knowledge Discov.*, 13(2):219–242, 2006.

182. X. Xu, G. Cong, B. C. Ooi, K.-L. Tan, and A. K. H. Tung. Semantic mining and analysis of gene expression data. In *Proceedings of the 30th International Conference on Very Large Data Bases (VLDB)*, Vol. 30, VLDB Endowment, 2004, pp. 1261–1264.

183. Y. Xu, Y. Li, and G. Shaw. A reliable basis for approximate association rules. *IEEE Intell. Inform. Bull.*, 9(1):25–31, 2008.

184. S. B. Yahia, T. Hamrouni, and E. M. Nguifo. Frequent closed itemset based algorithms: A thorough structural and analytical survey. *ACM SIGKDD Explor. Newslett.*, 8(1):93–104, 2006.

185. B. Yang, W. Qu, Y. Xie, and Y. Zhai. Predicting protein second structure using a novel hybrid method. *Expert Syst. Appl.*, 38:11657–11664, 2011.

186. G. Yang, Y. Dang, S. Mabu, K. Shimada, and K. Hirasawa. Searching interesting association rules based on evolutionary computation. In *Proceedings of the PAKDD Workshop on Quality Issues, Measures of Interestingness and Evaluation of Data Mining Models (QIMIE)*, Vol. 7104 in *Lecture Notes in Artificial Intelligence*, 243–253, 2011.

187. H. Yao and H. J. Hamilton. Mining itemset utilities from transaction databases. *Data Knowledge Eng.*, 59(3):603–626, Dec. 2006.

188. H. Yao, H. J. Hamilton, and L. Geng. A unified framework for utility based measures for mining itemsets. In *Proceedings of the ACM SIGKDD Workshop on Utility-Based Data Mining (UBDM)*, 2006, pp. 28–37.

189. Y. Y. Yao. Measuring retrieval performance based on user preference of documents. *J. Am. Soc. Inform. Sci.*, 46(2):133–145, 1995.

190. Y. Y. Yao and N. Zhong. An analysis of quantitative measures associated with rules. In *Proceedings of the 3rd Pacific-Asia Conference on Knowledge Discovery and Data Mining (PAKDD)*, Springer, Heidelberg, 1999, pp. 479–488.

191. K. Y. Yeung, M. Medvedovic, and R. E. Bumgarner. From co-expression to co-regulation: How many microarray experiments do we need? *Genome Biol.*, 5(7):R48.1–R48.11, June 2004.

192. X. Yin and J. Han. CPAR: Classification based on predictive association rules. In *Proceedings of the 3rd SIAM International Conference on Data Mining (SDM)*, Vol. 3, 2003, pp. 331–335.

193. J. L. Y. Koh, M. L. Lee, A. M. Khan, P. T. J. Tan, and V. Brusic. Duplicate detection in biological data using association rule mining. In *Proceedings of the ECML/PKDD European Workshop on Data Mining and Text Mining in Bio-Informatics (DTMBio)*, Locus 501, No. P34180 (2004): S22388, pp. 34–41.

194. G. Yu, K. Li, and S. Shao. Mining high utility itemsets in large high dimensional data. In *Proceedings of the 1st IEEE International Workshop on Knowledge Discovery and Data Mining (WKDD)*, Adelaide, SA, January 2008, pp. 17–20.

195. G. U. Yule. On the association of attributes in statistics. *Philos. Trans. R. Soc. Lond.*, A(194):257–319, 1900.

196. G. U. Yule. On the methods of measuring association between two attributes. *J. R. Statist. Soc.*, 75:579–642, 1912.

197. M. J. Zaki. Generating non-redundant association rules. In *Proceedings of ACM International Conference on Knowledge Discovery and Data Mining (KDD)*, 2000, pp. 34–43.

198. M. J. Zaki. Mining non-redundant association rules. *Data Mining Knowledge Discov.*, 9(3):223–248, 2004.

199. L. V. Zhang, S. L. Wong, O. D. King, and F. P. Roth. Predicting co-complexed protein pairs using genomic and proteomic data integration. *BMC Bioinformatics*, 5(38), 2004.

200. M. Zhang and C. He. Survey on association rules mining algorithms. *Adv. Comput. Commun. Control Manag.*, 56:111–118, 2010.

201. T. Zhang. Association rules. In *Proceedings of the Pacific-Asia Conference on Knowledge Discovery and Data Mining (PAKDD)*, 2000, pp. 245–256.

202. X. Zhang, S. Orcun, M. Ouzzani, and C. Oh. Mass informatics in differential proteomics. In *Encyclopedia of Data Warehousing and Mining*, 2nd ed., John Wang, IGI Global, Chapter 183, 2009, pp. 1176–1181.

203. Y. Zhang, L. Zhang, G. Nie, and Y. Shi. A survey of interestingness measures for association rules. In *Proceedings of the International Conference on Business Intelligence and Financial Engineering (BIFE)*, IEEE, Beijing, July 2009, pp. 460–463.

204. Q. Zhou and J. S. Liu. Extracting sequence features to predict protein-DNA interactions: A comparative study. *Nucleic Acids Res.*, 36:4137–4148, 2008.

205. X. Zhou and T. S. Dillon. A statistical-heuristic feature selection criterion for decision tree induction. *IEEE Trans. Pattern Anal. Machine Intell.*, 13(8):834–841, 1991.

206. Z. Zhou, B. Yang, and W. Hou. Association classification algorithm based on structure sequence in protein secondary structure prediction. *Expert Syst. Appl.*, 37:6381–6389, 2010.

CHAPTER 36

INFERENCE OF GENE REGULATORY NETWORKS BASED ON ASSOCIATION RULES

CRISTIAN ANDRÉS GALLO,[1] JESSICA ANDREA CARBALLIDO,[1] and IGNACIO PONZONI[1,2]

[1]Laboratorio de Investigación y Desarrollo en Computación Científica (LIDeCC), Dept. Computer Science and Engineering, Universidad Nacional del Sur, Bahía Blanca, Argentina
[2]Planta Piloto de Ingeniería Química (PLAPIQUI) CONICET, Bahía Blanca, Argentina

36.1 INTRODUCTION

The most important and widespread mechanism used by cells to regulate molecular functions or biological processes is the coordinate transcriptional and posttranscriptional network of the interacting genes or their products. In this way and under the command of *transcription factors* (TFs), each gene influences the activity of the cell by generating messenger RNA (mRNA) that guides the synthesis of proteins by ribosomes in the cytoplasm. Some of these gene products generated are themselves TFs that return to the nucleus (in eukaryotes) to control the expression of one or several genes. This complicated means of controlling gene expression can be represented as a *gene regulatory network* (GRN). The GRNs are complex interaction maps that describe putative associations among gene products which orchestrate the living organism functions. The reverse engineering of GRNs is a paradigm with great promise for analyzing and constructing biological networks [1–3]; it is an effective way of utilizing experimental data to determine the underlying network of a given model and constitutes an open research problem in bioinformatics.

Gene network modeling uses gene expression profiling data to describe the phenotypic behavior of a system under study. In order to reconstruct such a network, the procedure involves altering the gene network in some way, observing the outcome, and using computational methods to infer the underlying principles of the network. In this context, the data-mining methods configure suitable approaches for performing the reverse engineering of these relational structures and, in particular, these reconstruction strategies can be beneficed from the application of *association rule* (AR) extraction techniques. Basically, an AR establishes a causal link between two or more variables, where the semantics and

Biological Knowledge Discovery Handbook: Preprocessing, Mining, and Postprocessing of Biological Data,
First Edition. Edited by Mourad Elloumi and Albert Y. Zomaya.

the interpretation of the rule depend of the input data and on the mechanisms employed for inferring the association. ARs have been extensively used for discovering interesting relationships between variables in large data sets [4]. In bioinformatics, these methods can be used to reveal biologically relevant associations among genes, at diverse environmental conditions or time point observations, from different microarray samples [5–7].

This chapter focuses on gene regulation and the ways that transcriptome data can be used to unravel the complex relationships between the genes that comprise a GRN. In particular, it describes the main topics that must be considered in the field of AR mining for reverse engineering of GRNs and presents the state-of-the art techniques currently available in the literature. The organization of the chapter is as follows. In Section 36.2 the central concepts about AR mining for GRN reconstruction together with various other relevant issues are presented and discussed. In Section 36.3, different data-mining approaches used for AR inference are reviewed. Finally, in Section 36.4, the conclusions and final remarks are summarized.

36.2 DATA MINING AND INFERENCE OF GRNs BASED ON ARs

A GRN is one kind of causal regulatory network. Others include protein networks and metabolic processes [8]. The GRNs have a messily robust structure as a consequence of evolution [9]. A GRN can be represented as a directed graph [10], in which the set of vertices N represents the genes and the set of edges E describe the regulatory relationships between each pair of genes. The GRNs may also be modeled as undirected graphs [11], although the true underlying regulatory network is better represented as a directed graph. Each edge may also be decorated with additional information, such as the type of regulation (activation or inhibition) and/or the time lag in the regulation, among others. Figure 36.1 shows an example of a GRN represented as a directed graph.

Another common way to represent a GRN is by means of a list of ARs. In this way, each interaction between genes is represented as a rule of the form $g_i \rightarrow g_j$, where $g_i, g_j \in N$, and g_i is the regulator gene whereas g_j is the target gene. Similar to the graph representation, the ARs may contain additional information regarding the interaction between the genes. Even more, given a graph representing a GRN, an equivalent

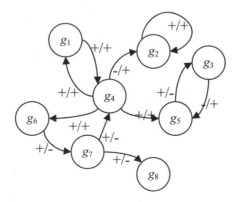

FIGURE 36.1 GRN represented as a directed graph. The direction of the edge indicates the regulatory role (regulator or target) of the genes in each interaction. A $+(-)$ symbol on the left side of the edge label indicates up regulation (down regulation) of the regulator gene, whereas a $+(-)$ symbol on the right side indicates activation (inhibition) of the target gene.

list of ARs can be directly obtained through the edge set of the graph, with an AR for each edge. If the GRN of Figure 36.1 is considered, the following ARs represent the same GRN: $+g_1 \rightarrow +g_4, +g_4 \rightarrow +g_1, -g_4 \rightarrow +g_2, +g_2 \rightarrow +g_2, +g_4 \rightarrow +g_5, +g_5 \rightarrow -g_3, -g_3 \rightarrow +g_5, +g_4 \rightarrow +g_6, +g_6 \rightarrow -g_7, +g_7 \rightarrow -g_4, +g_7 \rightarrow -g_8$. In the rest of this chapter, we will indistinctly refer to edges and ARs, since both represent the same kind of information.

A GRN can be considered as a stochastic system of discrete components. However, modeling a GRN in this way is not tractable in a computational way [12]. For that reason, the stochastic systems are not considered in this chapter, and therefore, the main focus will be put on discrete models of GRNs. In these models, a GRN is a set of genes N and a set of functions F such that there is one function for each gene: $\forall g_i \in N, \exists f_i : f_i \in F$. Each of these functions takes all or a subset of N as parameters, and the output corresponds to a discrete value of a given gene state set. Using this sort of model, the most important features of the regulatory relationships can be inferred and represented.

Data mining can either be used to infer epistasis (determine which genes interact) or to create explanatory models of the network. Epistasis is traditionally identified through synthetic lethality [13–15] and yeast two-hybrid (Y2H) experiments. Data-mining approaches are necessary in these situations because the data are often very noisy, and (as with Per1-3) phenotypic changes may be invisible unless several genes are knocked out. Inferring an explanatory model of the network is often better, with more useful applications to biological understanding, genetic engineering, and pharmaceutical design. In this way, in order to infer an explanatory model of a GRN with a data-mining approach, it is necessary to take into account several considerations. First, a few questions regarding the type of biological data from which the model will be inferred should be answered: What kind of information does it represent? Is it steady-state data or time-series data? Are the data inherently noisy or not? Second, since the whole objective is to infer a GRN with a data-mining approach, the discretization might play an important role in the whole process. Does the algorithm require discretization of data? And if this is true, how many states are necessary to represent the underlying behavior of the genes? How can these estates be obtained? Additionally, there are various other relevant features that should be taken into account: the cardinality pattern of the associations (quantity of genes that can be linked by one rule), the manner in which the temporal behavior is modeled (time delay associations), and how to conciliate rules extracted from multiple data sources. These subjects may affect the computational complexity of the inference algorithm and the biological feasibility of the inferred model. Finally, the biological and statistical validation of the ARs obtained is the more important step in the inference of a GRN, since it determines the biological plausibility of the inferred model. Figure 36.2 summarizes all of these issues, among others, which must be considered in order to infer GRNs with data-mining approaches. In the following sections, all of these topics and other issues will be discussed.

36.2.1 Types of Biological Data Used for GRN Inference

There are few types of biological data available for addressing network modeling in bioinformatics. In this regard, the most widely used data type for data-mining techniques in the reconstruction of GRNs are gene expression data. The gene expression data represent the activity of each gene $g_i \in N$, measured as the concentration of mRNA, since the transcription activity cannot be measured directly. Thus, given that the regulatory or phenotypic protein interaction can consume some mRNA before the regulation of the gene takes place [16], this

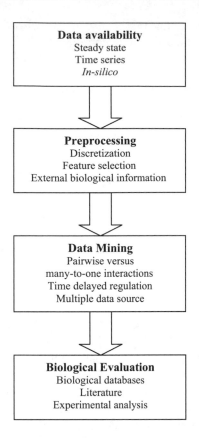

FIGURE 36.2   Summary of several issues that needs to be considered in order to infer GRNs with data-mining approaches.

may seem to be an inaccurate measure of gene activity [17]. Even more, a protein may bind a promoter region without producing any regulatory effect [18]. Additionally, most genes are not involved in most cellular processes [19]. This implies that several of the sampled genes may appear to randomly vary their expression levels. However, if the data set is comprehensible and the only concern is the inference of regulatory relationships, these influences are not important [12]. Increasing the amount of data or performing targeted inference can avoid the problem of irrelevant genes. The nongenetic unmodeled influences are analogous to the hidden intermediate variables in Bayesian networks [18]. An influence like this does not distort the regulatory relationship or the predictive accuracy of the inferred model [12].

36.2.1.1 *Types of Expression Data*

There are two types of gene expression data: equilibrium (steady-state) expression levels that correspond to a static situation and time-series expression levels that are gathered during a phenotypic phase like the cell cycle [20]. The gene expression data are usually obtained employing microarrays or some similar technology. A microarray is a pre-prepared slide divided into cells. Each cell is individually coated with a chemical which fluoresces when it is mixed with the mRNA generated by just one of the genes. The brightness of each cell is used as a measurement of the level of mRNA and therefore of the gene expression level.

Generally, the steady-state expression data are represented by an $N \times M$ matrix A', where the rows represent the N genes sampled and the columns represents the M different experimental conditions (or replicas or both). Different experimental conditions refer to different tissues, temperatures, chemical compounds, or any other condition that may produce different regulatory behavior among the sampled genes. Each element a_{ij} of A' contains the expression value of gene g_i in the sample or experimental condition j. On the other hand, the time series encoded in the gene expression data set are represented by means of a gene expression data matrix, A', where the rows and columns represent genes and time points, respectively. In this case, the time-series data are gathered by using temperature- (or chemical-) sensitive mutants to pause the phenotypic process while a microarray is done on a sample. Thus, the different columns represent the expression values of each sampled gene at different times under the same experimental condition during some phenotypic phase. The sampling intervals at which the genes are sampled are determined by the researcher regarding the nature of the study and are not necessarily taken at the same equidistant interval.

Microarrays can be both biologically noisy [21] and technically noisy [19]. The first one is the biological uncertainty in the form of intrinsic and extrinsic noise. The second one is the experimental noise due to the complex measurement process, ranging from hybridization conditions to microarray image processing techniques. However, the magnitude and impact of the noise are hotly debated issues that depend on the exact technology used to collect samples. Recent research [12, 22] argues that the magnitude and impact of the noise have been "gravely exaggerated."

36.2.2 Gene Expression Discretization

Data discretization, also known as binning, is a frequently used technique in computer science and statistics applied to the biological data analysis. Discretization of real data into a typically small number of finite values is often required by machine learning algorithms [23], Bayesian network applications [24], and any modeling algorithm using discrete-state models. An important advantage of using discrete states is that a significant portion of the noise is absorbed in the process.

Nonetheless, the selection of a reasonable discretization approach is not a trivial task. In general, discretization processes imply loss of information, and different strategies yield to distinct discrete-state models. Therefore, the biological semantics and interpretation of the resulting models differ, even when the subjacent real-valued data are always the same. For this reason, the choice of a discretization method should consider the intrinsic nature of the biological data as well as the particular features of the computational method that will make use of these discretized models.

Several discretization techniques have been proposed in the literature. Binary discretization is the simplest way of discretizing data, used, for instance, for the construction of Boolean network models for GRNs [25, 26]. The expression data are discretized into two qualitative states as either present or absent. An obvious drawback of binary discretization is that labeling the real-valued data according to a present/absent scheme generally causes the loss of a large amount of information. Discrete models and modeling techniques allowing multiple states have been widely developed and studied [27, 28].

36.2.2.1 Discretization Problem   Let A' be an N-row $\times$ M-column gene expression matrix, where a'_{ij} represents the expression level of gene g_i under condition j. The matrix A'

is defined by its set of rows, I, and its set of columns, J. Moreover, let a'_{IJ} denote the average value in the expression matrix A' and a'_{iJ} and a'_{Ij} denote the mean of row i and condition j, respectively. Let H_{IJ} denote the maximum (high) value in the expression matrix A' and H_{iJ} and H_{Ij} denote the maximum value of row i and column j, respectively. In the same way, let M_{IJ} denote the median value in the expression matrix A' and M_{iJ} and M_{Ij} denote the median value of row i and column j, respectively.

A discretized matrix A' is a mapping where each element in A' is mapped to one element of an alphabet Σ, which consists of a set of different symbols representing a distinct activation level. In the simplest case, Σ may contain only two symbols, one symbol used for *regulation* (or *activation*) and another symbol for *no regulation* (or *inhibition*). In this case, the expression matrix is usually transformed into a binary matrix, where 1 means regulation and 0 means no regulation. Another widely used option is to consider a set of three discretization symbols, $\{-1, 1, 0\}$, meaning DownRegulated, UpRegulated, or NoChange. Nevertheless, the values in matrix A' may be discretized to an arbitrary number of symbols. After the discretization process, matrix A' is transformed into matrix A and $a_{ij} \in \Sigma$ represents the discretized value of the expression level of gene g_i under condition j. Several discretization techniques have been used in expression data analysis. According to [29], these techniques can be grouped into two high-level categories:

1. Discretization using expression absolute values
2. Discretization using expression variations between time points

The approaches belonging to the first category can be used in expression data, in general, and they discretize the absolute gene expression values directly using different techniques. The second set of approaches, only applicable to time-series expression data, computes variations between each two consecutive time points and then discretizes these variations. In the following sections the major discretization approaches will be detailed.

36.2.2.2 *Discretization Using Absolute Values*

Discretization Using Average and Standard Deviation A straightforward discretization method discretizes the gene expression matrix A' using the average expression value [30], or the average combined with the standard deviation of the expression values [29, 31, 32]. The limit values among bins can be computed using all the values in the expression matrix, that is, the overall average expression level and its standard deviation. Another possibility is for the average and the standard deviation to be computed for each row or column in the matrix.

When the goal is to discretize the matrix into a binary matrix with two symbols, one for regulation and another one for no regulation (e.g., 1 and 0), the average expression value is usually used alone; the discretization can be computed using all the values in the matrix, by row, or by column, using one of the following expressions:

$$a_{ij} = \begin{cases} 1 & \text{if } a'_{ij} \geq a'_{IJ} \\ 0 & \text{otherwise} \end{cases}$$

$$a_{ij} = \begin{cases} 1 & \text{if } a'_{ij} \geq a'_{iJ} \\ 0 & \text{otherwise} \end{cases}$$

$$a_{ij} = \begin{cases} 1 & \text{if } a'_{ij} \geq a'_{Ij} \\ 0 & \text{otherwise} \end{cases}$$

Another possibility is to discretize the matrix using three symbols (for instance, -1, 0, and 1) meaning down regulated, up regulated, or no change. In this case, the average expression value is usually combined with its standard deviation. Let α be a parameter used to tune the desired deviation from average and σ_{IJ}, σ_{iJ}, and σ_{Ij} be the standard deviations of the overall values in the matrix, row i, and column j, respectively. Then, the discretization can be performed using one of the following equations [29, 31, 32]:

$$a_{ij} = \begin{cases} -1 & \text{if } a'_{ij} < a'_{IJ} - \alpha\sigma_{IJ} \\ 1 & \text{if } a'_{ij} > a'_{IJ} - \alpha\sigma_{IJ} \\ 0 & \text{otherwise} \end{cases}$$

$$a_{ij} = \begin{cases} -1 & \text{if } a'_{ij} < a'_{iJ} - \alpha\sigma_{iJ} \\ 1 & \text{if } a'_{ij} > a'_{iJ} - \alpha\sigma_{iJ} \\ 0 & \text{otherwise} \end{cases}$$

$$a_{ij} = \begin{cases} -1 & \text{if } a'_{ij} < a'_{Ij} - \alpha\sigma_{Ij} \\ 1 & \text{if } a'_{ij} > a'_{Ij} - \alpha\sigma_{Ij} \\ 0 & \text{otherwise} \end{cases}$$

Discretization Based on Equal Frequency Principle   The discretization process based on the equal-frequency principle considers a given number of symbols into which the expression values will be discretized. Then the data points are split in such a way that there exists the same number of data points per symbol, binning the expression values accordingly to the corresponding symbol. This process can be applied to an arbitrary number of symbols. When only two symbols are considered, the process is equivalent to the procedure performed to carry out the discretization of values by means of the median value. As before, the equal-frequency principle can be applied using all the expression values in the matrix, the expression values by row or the expression values by column [33].

Discretization Based on Clustering   Another common discretization technique for the gene expression data matrix A' is based on *clustering* [34]. Generally, a clustering algorithm is applied to each row (gene expression profile) performing the discretization accordingly to the partition returned by the algorithm. Employing clustering for discretization allows the consideration of multiple states in a straightforward manner, although it may introduce additional computational cost depending on the selected clustering technique.

One of the most common clustering algorithms is the *k-means clustering* developed in [35]. The goal of the k-means algorithm is to minimize dissimilarity in the elements within each cluster while maximizing this value among elements in different clusters. The algorithm takes as input a set of points S to be clustered and a fixed integer k. It partitions S into k subsets by choosing a set of k cluster *centroids*. The choice of centroids determines the structure of the partition since each point in S is assigned to the nearest centroid. Then for each cluster the centroids are recomputed based on which elements are contained in the cluster. These steps are repeated until convergence is achieved. Many applications of the k-means clustering, such as the MultiExperiment Viewer [36], start by organizing any random partition into k clusters and computing their centroids. As a consequence, a different clustering of S may be obtained every time the algorithm is run. For the special case when only two states ($k = 2$) are considered in the discretization, the optimal solution can be computed in an optimized manner due to the total ordering of the elements in the gene expression profile [7].

36.2.2.3 Discretization Using Expression Variations between Time Points

Several discretization techniques have been proposed based on the transitions in expression states between successive time points. These techniques usually consider either two or three states, as stated previously. Generally, the discretization of a matrix A' using expression variations between time points produces a discretized matrix A with $J - 1$ samples.

Transitional state discrimination (TSD) [37] is a discretization technique that uses two symbols. After standardizing the expression data A' to z-scores (expression profiles are scaled to zero mean and unit standard deviation), each gene expression profile is discretized using two state transitions:

$$a_{ij} = \begin{cases} 1 & \text{if } a'_{ij} - a'_{i(j-1)} \geq 0 \\ 0 & \text{otherwise} \end{cases}$$

Another discretization technique can be performed by computing variations between successive time instants as before but considering that these variations are significant whenever they exceed a given preset threshold [38, 39]. During the discretization process, the expression matrix is transformed into an $A = N \times (M - 1)$ matrix that reflects the changing tendency of each gene expression value over time. An arbitrary number of changing tendencies may be considered leading to the discretization of the matrix in a set of symbols Σ. When three possible changing tendencies are considered [38, 39], an expression level may increase from time point t_i to t_{i+1}, may decrease, or may remain unchanged. These changing tendencies are then discretized into three symbols (Increase, Decrease, NoChange, respectively). In this case, and with this set of symbols, the discretized matrix A is obtained after two steps. In the first step, the expression matrix A' is transformed into an $A'' = N \times (M - 1)$ matrix of variations such that

$$a''_{ij} = \begin{cases} \dfrac{a'_{i(j-1)} - a'_{ij}}{\left| a'_{ij} \right|} & \text{if } a'_{ij} \neq 0 \\ 1 & \text{if } a'_{ij} = 0 \wedge a'_{i(j-1)} > 0 \\ -1 & \text{if } a'_{ij} = 0 \wedge a'_{i(j-1)} < 0 \\ 0 & \text{if } a'_{ij} = 0 \wedge a'_{i(j-1)} = 0 \end{cases}$$

Once matrix A'' is generated, the final discretized matrix A, also with N rows and $M - 1$ columns, is obtained in a second step by binning the values of the transformed matrix considering a threshold $t > 0$ as follows:

$$a_{ij} = \begin{cases} 1 & \text{if } a''_{ij} \geq t \\ -1 & \text{if } a''_{ij} \leq -t \\ 0 & \text{otherwise} \end{cases}$$

36.2.3 Pairwise versus Many-to-One Associations

The arity of the ARs inferable with data-mining methods have both biological and computational implications. From the biological point of view, the GRN structure appears to be neither random nor rigidly hierarchical but scale free. This means that the probability distribution for the out-degree, k_{out}, follows a power law [40, 41]. In other words, the probability that a gene g_i regulates k other genes is $p(k) \approx k^{\lambda}$, where usually $\lambda \in \{2, 3\}$. In the analysis of [40] regarding the scale-free Boolean networks, it was shown that some very disordered systems spontaneously "crystallize" into a high degree of order, which contributes to GRN's "evolvability" and adaptability [41].

On the computational side, these distributions over k_{out} and k_{in} (the in-degree) means that a number of assumptions have been made in previous research in order to simplify the problem and make it more tractable. For example, the exponential distribution over k_{in} means that most genes are regulated by only a few other genes. Unfortunately, this average is not a maximum. This means that techniques which strictly limit k_{in} to some arbitrary constant [7, 10, 42] might not be able to infer all networks, thus compromising their explanatory power.

36.2.3.1 "One-to-One" Regulatory Functions
The one-to-one regulatory functions refer to a gene g_i (target) that is only regulated by a gene g_j (regulator), that is, a pairwise relationship. In this case, the regulatory function $f_i(j)$ can be roughly lineal, sigmoid, or take any other form. Also, the strength of the effect of g_j over g_i may vary from strong to weak. However, this last feature can only be modeled if several discrete states are considered. Additionally, other nongenetic influences over g_i, denoted by ψ_i, can be considered in the modeling of the regulatory function. In this situation, the regulatory function can be expressed as $g_i' = f_i(g_j, \phi_i)$ (see, e.g., the work of Marnellos and Mjolsness [43]). However, in most situations and for simplicity it is assumed that $\delta f / \delta \varphi = 0$.

The regulatory relationship between gene g_j and gene g_i can be of either activation or inhibition. Even more, gene g_j may both activate the gene g_i when it is upregulated and inhibit g_i when it is downregulated and vice versa. For the case where the opposite regulation applies always (when the regulator is overexpressed or when the regulator is underexpressed), the underground chemical process is not clear. Moreover, in the inferred models of [44] this kind of regulation cannot be biologically verified. In either case, this type of regulation is especially complex and is not evolutionary robust, which means that the occurrence of such a relationship is unlikely in biological terms. Other properties of the organisms also have an influence on the types of regulatory relationships that can be inferred. For example, inhibitory genes are more common in prokaryote than in eukaryote organisms [45].

36.2.3.2 "Many-to-One" Regulatory Functions
A gene g_i may be regulated by several other genes, in which case the regulatory function is usually more complex. In particular, the gene regulation for a eukaryotic organism can be enormously complex [46], in which the regulatory function can be a piecewise threshold function [16, 47, 48]. The complexity arises because of the complex indirect, multilevel and multistage biological process underlying gene regulation. The regulatory process is detailed in works such as [49–51]. Finally, some of the logically possible regulatory relationships appear to be unlikely. For example, it appears that the exclusive-or relationships are biologically and statistically improbable [52].

36.2.4 Inference of GRNs from Multiple Data Sources

Most early researches on automatic learning of transcriptional regulatory networks employ only gene expression data. Recent simulation studies suggest that regulatory networks learned from gene expression data alone can be considerably obscured by the recovery of spurious interactions when the number of observations is small [53]. Integrating findings from multiple data sources (e.g., DNA sequences, gene and protein expression profiles, protein–protein interactions, protein structural information, and protein–DNA binding data) can overcome this drawback [54]. However, there are several problems in integrating diverse genomics data into network models [55]. First, the inference from multiple different data sources can lead to missing interactions that are only present in certain experimental conditions. Also, the genomics data are heterogeneous in their sensitivity and specificity for relationships between genes. For example, experimental methods such as mass spectrometry preferentially observe abundant proteins, while comparative genomics methods apply only to evolutionarily conserved genes. Increasing the sensitivity of detection usually carries out a cost of increasing false-positive identifications. Thus, the systematic bias for each method should be understood and considered during data integration. Additionally, genomics data sets vary widely in their utility for reconstructing gene networks. Thus, robust benchmarking methods that can evaluate each data set and allow comparison of their relative merits are required. Finally, data sets are often correlated, complicating integration, since it can be difficult to measure the correlation because of both data incompleteness (a common problem) and sampling biases.

Two major related approaches have been developed in joint learning transcriptional regulation from multiple data sources. In one approach, various types of data are used to identify sets of genes that interact together in the cell or are coregulated in modules [17, 56]. In the other one, various types of data are used to supplement gene expression data in learning regulatory networks [57, 58]. As regards these last works, Bernard and Hartemink presented a method for jointly learning dynamic models of transcriptional regulatory networks from gene expression data and transcription factor binding data, based on dynamic Bayesian network inference algorithms [58]. Results obtained from analyzing yeast cell cycle data demonstrate that the recovery of dynamic regulatory networks from multiple types of data by this joint learning algorithm is more accurate than that from each data type alone. Imoto et al. proposed a statistical method for estimating a gene network based on Bayesian networks from microarray gene expression data together with biological knowledge, including protein–protein interactions, protein–DNA interactions, transcriptional factor binding information, and existing literature [57]. An advantage of the method is that the balance between microarray information and biological knowledge is optimized automatically by the proposed criterion. Monte Carlo simulations showed the effectiveness of the proposed method in extracting more information from microarray data and estimating the gene network more accurately. Yeang et al. [59] developed a framework for inferring transcriptional regulation. The models they developed, called physical network models, are annotated molecular interaction graphs. The attributes in the model correspond to verifiable properties of the underlying biological system such as the existence of protein–protein and protein–DNA interactions, the directionality of signal transduction in protein–protein interactions, and signs of the immediate effects of these interactions. Possible configurations of these variables are constrained by the available data sources. The application of this algorithm on data sets related to the pheromone response pathway in yeast demonstrated that the derived model was consistent with previous knowledge of the pathway.

36.2.5 Temporal Delayed Associations from Time-Series Data

Another important aspect to be considered when dealing with the reconstruction of GRNs is constituted by the manner in which the temporal patterns of a GRN are captured. As was mentioned in [10, 60], time-delayed gene regulation is a common phenomenon. Thereby, multiple time-delayed gene regulations can be considered the norm, while single time-delayed associations can be considered the exception [54]. This occurs since, within regulation procedures, various events occur at different steps. Usually, the step of transcription (from DNA to mRNA) is fast while the time for translation varies from protein to protein [61]. Besides, the protein–DNA regulation is an accumulation process and the threshold differs for different regulation gene pairs [61]. Suppose g_i regulates g_j, and the change of expression level of g_i may affect the expression level of g_j after a certain time interval. For example, based on the gene expression microarray data set for yeast of Spellman et al. [20], the gene *MCM1* regulates the gene *CLN3*, and each time the expression level of *MCM1* changes, the corresponding expression level of *CLN3* changes about 30 min later. Also, the time delay intervals may vary for different gene regulatory pairs. For example, human *TNF-α* and *iNOS* genes are regulated by AP-1 and NF-κB1. Their delays in expression after the activation of AP-1 and NF-κB1 are 3 and 6 h, respectively [62]. It is further known that there should be an upper limit for the time delay in a gene network since the length of a cell cycle is limited. The regulation of genes can form feedback loops (for example, $g_1 \rightarrow g_2 \rightarrow \cdots \rightarrow g_1$), which exist in many metabolism pathways and are critical in maintaining the stability of a gene network [63].

Variability in the timing of biological processes further complicates the inference of gene association from time-series data. The rate at which similar underlying processes such as the cell cycle unfold can be expected to differ across organisms, genetic variants, and environmental conditions. For instance, Spellman et al. [20] analyze time-series data for the yeast cell cycle in which different methods were used to synchronize the cells. It is clear that the cycle lengths across the different experiments vary considerably and that the series begin and end at different phases of the cell cycle. This complicates the interpretation of the results if several time-series data sets are used in the inference of the interaction among genes [7]. Thus, a method is necessary to align such series so as to make them comparable, such as representing the time-series gene expression profiles as continuous curves, which allows the standardization of the rate at which each sample is considered in each data sets.

36.2.6 Biological and Statistical Validation of Inferred GRNs

Once a GRN is obtained by a data-mining approach, it is crucial to validate it in order to determine the correctness and/or the biological viability of the inferred ARs. The type of validation required depends on the goal of the study that was carried out. First of all, it is necessary to separate those analyses in which the objective is the assessment of the data-mining algorithm from those in which the goal corresponds to the identification of some promising hypothesis of new biological knowledge. In the first case, the analysis also depends on the data type employed in the inference. In silico data allow the use of well-known data-mining metrics, such as *precision*, *sensitivity*, and *specificity*, because the real interactions among genes are known before hand. Thus, it is possible to compare several algorithms and determine which one of them best reconstructs a GRN regarding given in silico data. Although the results cannot be conclusive, since they depend on the approach used in the generation of the in silico data, they may provide insights regarding the behavior of each method.

When real data are employed to assess an algorithm, the real interactions among genes that are present in the data are not known beforehand. In general, only specific curated knowledge regarding the real interactions among genes is available. Even more, those known interactions may not be present in the real data set due to the specific environmental condition employed in the experiment. Thus, the previous mentioned metrics, in general, are not applicable. However, there are other means to assess the algorithm when real data are used. First, there is the rule-by-rule analysis of the biological relevance of the relationships obtained by the method. This is done by means of a search through the literature, looking into known biological interactions for the genes under consideration. This approach is sound when a single method is evaluated; however, it has drawbacks that complicate its application in most scenarios. First, it is only applicable when a small set of rules is evaluated, since the whole process is performed manually. Another disadvantage is that it cannot be used for comparing several methods, because the quality of a rule is biased by the expert that evaluates it, and therefore it is impossible to establish a fair order of merit for the algorithms under consideration. Another approach consists in employing online databases of gene interactions to assess the inferred ARs. As an example, in the case of the yeast organism, there are two well known databases: Kyoto Encyclopedia of Genes and Genomes (KEGG) [64] and Gene Ontology (GO) annotation [65]. The KEGG cell cycle regulation path is a collection of manually drawn pathway maps representing the regulation knowledge on the molecular interaction, and the pathway contains interaction information which is relevant to the cell cycle of yeast. Thus, if an extracted AR is matched with KEGG regulation information, then the rule can be considered as correctly extracted. In the same way, the GO annotation is another source of potential associations for yeast genes. One can consider the gene pairs representing all gene pairs sharing any GO biological process terms between specific levels of a GO annotation and use it as an another benchmarking set. Nonetheless, as stated before, it should be clear that important known interactions will not be found by any data-driven approach if the data sets do not have correlations among the genes involved in such relations.

Independently of the data type employed in the analysis, another common technique to assess the performance of an AR mining algorithm is cross-validation [66–68]. Cross-validation is a technique widely used in data mining for assessing how the results of a statistical analysis will generalize to an independent data set. It is mainly used in the GRN reconstruction to estimate how accurately the predictive model will perform in practice. One round of cross-validation involves partitioning a data set into complementary subsets, performing the analysis on one subset (called *training set*), and validating the analysis on the other subset (called *validation set* or *testing set*). To reduce variability, multiple rounds of cross-validation are performed using different partitions, and the validation results are averaged over the rounds. There are some common types of cross-validation, such as the K-fold cross-validation and the repeated random subsampling validation. The mayor disadvantage of this type of validation in gene AR mining is, in general, the reduced amount of samples available in the data sets. If an inference is performed on a data sets with few samples, the effective amount of samples used in the inference process is even smaller due to the partition into the training and test sets, thus affecting negatively the predictability of the resulting model. Another disadvantage is when time-series data are employed to infer time-delayed rules. The partition into the training and test set cannot be performed because both sets will refer to completely different periods of time, thus becoming incomparable from a biological point of view.

Finally, if the whole goal of the analysis is the inference of new biological knowledge, it is necessary to clarify that the rules inferred by any data-mining approach will always represent confident regulatory associations among genes. That is, the extracting-rules approach can be useful for the identification of some promising hypothesis regarding the nature of the experiments analyzed. However, the corroboration by biological experiments will always be mandatory in order to obtain curated new knowledge.

36.2.7 Advantages and Limitations of Inference of GRNs Based on ARs

Inferring GRNs with AR mining approaches presents several advantages. First of all, the inferred models are highly abstract and hence require less amount of data than continuous models [such as the general *ordinary differential equations* (ODEs)]. This favors its ability to perform inferences, since almost all gene expression data are suitable for extraction of ARs. Additionally, the simplicity of the inferred model allows the inference of larger models with a higher speed of analysis and also facilitates the interpretability of the results.

However, there are also several disadvantages in the inference of ARs. The most important one is that the ARs can display only qualitative dynamic behavior. This could be overcome to some extent if several states for each gene (more than two) were considered. Nonetheless, this also complicates the inference since it requires more data to deduce the interactions, and it also demands more computational resources due to the increased search space. Additionally, as they are highly abstract, the level of detail that can be modeled is very limited. This issue generally affects its faithfulness as regards biological reality, and it also limits its ability to model dynamics.

36.3 TECHNIQUES OF INFERENCE OF GRNs BASED ON AR

36.3.1 Frequent-Itemset-Based Methods

Frequent-itemset-based methods were originally developed to find interesting associations or correlation relationships among data in a large database, such as those of business transaction records. The discovery of interesting ARs derived from the so-called *frequent itemset* is valuable in many business decision-making processes, such as catalog design, cross-marketing, and loss-leader analysis [69]. Following the definitions in [70], let $\Gamma = \{g_1, \ldots, g_N\}$ be a set of distinct literals, called *items*. A set $X \subseteq \Gamma$ with $|X| = k$ is called a *k-itemset* or simply an *itemset*. Let D be a set of *transactions* where each *transaction* T is an itemset. There is a unique identifier associated with each transaction, its *transaction identification* (TID). A transaction T contains or supports an itemset X if $X \subseteq T$. As stated previously, an AR is an expression $X \to Y$, where in this case $X \subseteq \Gamma$, $Y \subseteq \Gamma$, and $X \cap Y = \emptyset$. The itemset X has a *support* x in the transaction database D if $x\%$ of transactions T in D contain X:

$$\text{supp}(X) = \frac{|\{T \mid X \subseteq T, T \in D\}|}{|D|}$$

The rule $X \to Y$ has a support s in the transaction database D if $s\%$ of transactions T in D contain $X \cup Y$, that is,

$$\text{supp}(X \to Y) = \frac{|\{T \mid \{X \cup Y\} \subseteq T, T \in D\}|}{|D|}$$

The rule $X \rightarrow Y$ has a confidence c in the transaction database D if $c\%$ of the transactions T in D that contain X also contain Y, that is,

$$\mathrm{conf}(X \rightarrow Y) = \frac{\mathrm{supp}(X \cup Y)}{\mathrm{supp}(X)}$$

Note the different meanings for the support and confidence measures. While the support of an itemset or a rule indicates the statistical significance of the itemset or the rule, the confidence is a measure of the rule's strength. Generally, only the rules with support and confidence values above certain thresholds (*minsupport* and *minconf*, respectively) are considered.

In this formulation, the problem of rule mining can be decomposed into two steps: frequent-itemset identification and rule generation. The first step entails the identification of all frequent itemsets $F = \{X | \mathrm{supp}(X) \geq \mathrm{minsupp}\}$. Once the set of all frequent itemsets, as well as their supports, is known, the second step involves the derivation of the desired ARs from F. This procedure is very simple: For each $X \in F$, the confidence of all possible rules $X - Y \rightarrow Y$ is checked, where $Y \subset X$ and $Y \neq \emptyset$, and those rules which fall below minconf are excluded.

The main challenge of mining ARs in this way lies in the first step, the identification of frequent itemsets. It is intuitively obvious that a linear increase in $|\Gamma|$ will result in an exponential growth of the number of itemsets to be considered. Fortunately, the itemset support has the *downward-closure property*: All subsets of a frequent itemset must also be frequent [70]. As a result, there is a border in the lattice structure separating the frequent and infrequent itemsets [71], with the frequent itemsets located above the border and the infrequent itemsets located below. The basic principle is to employ this border to prune the search space efficiently.

Most of the proposed itemset mining methods are a variant of the APRIORI algorithm [72]. The APRIORI algorithm adopts a *breath-first-search* approach to the itemset lattice and uses k-itemsets to explore $(k + 1)$-itemsets. The algorithm scans the database in the first round to count the occurrences of each item. It then finds the set of frequent 1-itemset (denote as L_1) with respect to a given threshold minsupp. A subsequent round of the algorithm (e.g., round k) consists of two phases. First, the frequent $(k - 1)$-itemsets L_{k-1} found in the $(k - 1)$th round are used to generate the candidate itemsets C_k. Second, the database is scanned and the k-itemsets in C_k are checked. If a k-itemset X in C_k is not frequent, it is removed from C_k. The remaining k-itemsets in C_k constitute L_k and will be used for the $(k + 1)$th round. These two phases iterate until the set of frequent k-itemsets L_k is empty.

APRIORI-based methods show good performance with sparse data sets such as market-basket data, whre the frequent patterns are very short. However, with dense data sets such as microarrays, where there are many long frequent patterns, these methods scale poorly and are sometimes impractical. This drawback is due to the high computational cost of the evaluation of candidate and test sets used by APRIORI-based approaches. Thus, new methods like FP-GROWTH [73], which simplify the problem of finding long patterns by concatenating small ones, have emerged as a promising strategy. In fact, several methods have been devised on the FP-GROWTH basis [4, 74]. The main idea relies on a compact tree structure called FP-tree, which is searched through recursively in order to enumerate all frequent patterns. The pattern growth is achieved by concatenating the suffix pattern with the frequent pattern generated from a conditional FP-tree (e.g., the patterns with length equal to 1 will be used for generating those with length equal to 2, and so on). Even tree-based methods such as FP-GROWTH may find some difficulties when dealing with high-dimensional data sets. A frequent pattern of size k (number of items) implies the presence of $2^k - 2$ additional frequent patterns as well, each of which is explicitly checked out by such methods. Thus, FPM algorithms that employ sophisticated heuristics for mining long frequent itemsets constitute practical solutions for GAA.

There are currently two alternatives for mining long patterns. The first one is to mine only maximal frequent itemsets, as in MAXMINER [75] and GENMAX [76], which are typically orders of magnitude lower than all frequent patterns. Maximal itemsets are those longest frequent patterns found under a certain support threshold. Despite the fact that maximal patterns help understand the long itemsets in dense domains, they lead to the loss of information; since subset counting is not available, maximal sets are not suitable for generating rules. The second alternative is mining only frequent closed sets as in CLOSE [77], CLOSE+ [78], and CHARM [79]. Closed sets are lossless in the sense that they can be used to uniquely determine the set of all frequent patterns and their exact frequencies. A *closed itemset* is a frequent pattern that fits a support threshold and does not have any other superfrequent pattern set with similar support value covering it. Furthermore, closed-based algorithms can handle pattern redundancy, which is quite common in the application of association mining on high-dimensional databases [4, 74]. However, even by using such a strategy, the high dimensionality of microarrays still poses great challenges for these methods.

It is important to consider that all aforementioned methods employ exponential combination of all the columns (i.e., genes) in the gene expression matrix. Such search space size increases proportionally with the number of genes. Therefore, FPM methods that do not use candidate set generation are usually more efficient. The type of patterns found also plays an important role in the strength or weakness of a FPM method. Thus, closed-itemset strategies are more reliable for the gene AR mining. From such a general discussion, one could expect that CLOSE+ is the most suitable column enumeration approach for gene AR mining. Indeed, the method was not applied to any kind of gene expression data, although it was successfully evaluated against its counterpart by using other high dense data sets [80].

36.3.1.1 *Time-Delayed ARs with Frequent-Itemset Mining*   There are currently two alternatives for mining time-delayed ARs with frequent-itemset methods. The first one is to mine the rules by means of the application of the APRIORI algorithm (or any other itemset mining algorithm) on matrices of *time-delayed gene expression* (TdE) profiles [81], similar to those used in [54]. The TdE captures the regulation among genes in W units of time. It merely consists of an $N \times (W + 1)M$ matrix, in which each row is a time window and the columns contain the W corresponding values for each gene. For example, as Baralis et al. [81] reported, if the discrete matrix in Table 36.1 is considered, the time-delayed

TABLE 36.1   Discrete Matrix

Gene	t_1	t_2	t_3	t_4	$\cdots$	t_M
g_1	0	1	0	0	$\cdots$	1
g_2	1	1	0	0	$\cdots$	0
g_3	0	0	1	1	$\cdots$	0
g_4	1	0	1	0	$\cdots$	1
$\vdots$	$\vdots$	$\vdots$	$\vdots$	$\vdots$	$\ddots$	$\vdots$
g_N	0	0	1	0	$\cdots$	0

TABLE 36.2   Time-Delayed Matrix

Time	$g_1 + 0$	$g_1 + 1$	$g_1 + 2$	$g_2 + 0$	$\cdots$	$g_N + 0$	$g_N + 1$	$g_N + 2$
W_1	0	1	0	1	$\cdots$	0	0	1
W_2	1	0	0	1	$\cdots$	0	1	0
$\vdots$	$\vdots$	$\vdots$	$\vdots$	$\vdots$	$\ddots$	$\vdots$	$\vdots$	$\vdots$
W_M	1	NA	NA	0	$\cdots$	0	NA	NA

matrix in Table 36.2 is obtained in the case of regulations among two time instances (i.e., $W = 2$).

The other alternative is to extend the concepts of itemset mining in order to take into account the time-lagged rules. In this sense, Nam et al. [82] developed a *temporal association rule mining* (TARM) method, based on the APRIORI algorithm, extending the basic concepts as follows: A *temporal item* is an item which has a time stamp. A *temporal itemset* $\ddot{I}$ is a nonempty set of temporal items. Given a temporal itemset $\ddot{I}$, a set T of transactions on $\ddot{I}$, and a positive integer minsupport, $\ddot{I}$ is a temporal frequent itemset with respect to T and minsupport if supp($\ddot{I}$) $\geq$ minsupport. A temporal AR ($X(\Delta) \rightarrow Y$) is a pair of disjoint temporal itemsets where the time stamp of each temporal item in X is ahead of those of all temporal items in Y and where Δ is the interval of two different time stamps.

Figure 36.3 shows an example, reported in [82], of the temporal itemset mining process. Suppose a three-state discretization process as shown in the Figure 36.3a. In order to find temporally associated genes, it is first assumed that all related genes may have various sizes of transcriptional time delays. Therefore, the method searches for associated genes in all possible sets of different time point experiments where the time interval varies from 0 to W (Figure 36.3b). For example, the temporal transaction set $t_0 + t_2 = [+g_{1L}, -g_{2L}, +g_{1R}, +g_{2R}, -g_{3R}]$ consists of up- or down-regulated genes at time stamps t_0 and t_2, with the size of transcriptional time delay $\Delta = 2$. Note that g_1 is up regulated in both cases t_0 and t_2, but it is considered as two different genes: g_{1L} (g_1 on the left-hand side) and g_{1R} (g_1 on the right-hand side). Following, Figure 36.3c indicates the extracted temporal frequent itemsets with support threshold 50%. Finally, two temporal ARs are discovered with confidence threshold 50% as shown in Figure 36.3d. In this way, TARM can find various sizes of transcriptional time delays between associated genes, activation and inhibition relationships, and sets of coregulators for the target genes.

36.3.2 Classification and Regression Tree-Based Approaches

A decision tree is a decision support tool that uses a treelike graph or model of decisions and their possible consequences, including chance event outcomes, resource costs, and utility. Decision trees are commonly used in operations research, specifically in decision analysis, to help identify a strategy most likely to reach a goal. In gene AR mining, a decision tree is a rooted tree in which nonleaf nodes are labeled with explaining genes, the arcs from nonleaf nodes are labeled with possible characteristics of explaining genes, and the leaves of the tree are labeled with the states of the predicted gene. There are two kinds of decision trees: *classification trees* and *regression trees* [83]. The first are those whose outcomes are the classes to which the data belong, whereas the second are those whose outcomes can be considered as real numbers. An example of a decision tree for classification of the yeast gene *CLN2* is shown in Figure 36.4. Each path from the root node to a leaf node in

	t_0	t_1	t_2	t_3	t_4	t_5	t_6
g_1	1	0	1	0	1	0	0
g_2	-1	-1	1	-1	1	0	1
g_3	0	0	-1	-1	0	-1	0

(*a*) Binned time-series data, with three genes and six time points

$$t_0 + t_2 = \{+g_{1L}, -g_{2L}, +g_{1R}, +g_{2R}, -g_{3R}\}$$
$$t_1 + t_3 = \{-g_{2L}, -g_{2R}, -g_{3R}\}$$
$$t_2 + t_4 = \{+g_{1L}, +g_{2L}, -g_{3L}, +g_{1R}, +g_{2R}\}$$
$$t_3 + t_5 = \{-g_{2L}, -g_{3L}, -g_{3R}\}$$
$$t_4 + t_6 = \{+g_{1L}, +g_{2L}, +g_{2R}\}$$

(*b*) Temporal transaction sets, transcriptional time delay $\Delta = 2$

$$\{+g_{1L}\}, \{-g_{2L}\}, \{+g_{2R}\}, \{-g_{3R}\}$$
$$\{+g_{1L}, +g_{2R}\}, \{-g_{2L}, -g_{3R}\}$$

(*c*) Temporal frequent itemsets, support = 50%

$$+g_12 \rightarrow +g_2$$
$$-g_22 \rightarrow -g_3$$

(*d*) Temporal ARs, confidence = 50%

FIGURE 36.3   Temporal AR mining process with transcriptional time delay $\Delta = 2$, support $\geq 50\%$, confidence $\geq 50\%$.

the tree presents a rule that defines a state of the predicted gene via expression levels of explaining genes. It follows that every decision tree is equivalent to a list of decision rules. This method of representation allows the decomposition of decision trees from a complex structure to simple and compactly presented ARs, which can be independently compared to the existing knowledge. Thereby, the decision tree of Figure 36.4 can be

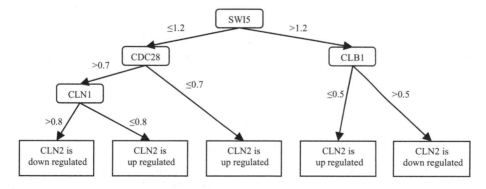

FIGURE 36.4   Possible classification tree for gene *CLN2* of *Saccharomyces cerevisiae*. *CLN2* is the target gene; *SWI5*, *CLB1*, *CDC28*, and *CLN1* are the regulatory genes. Expression thresholds of the respective explaining genes mark all the arcs.

represented by means of the following list of ARs: $-SWI5\hat{}+CDC28\hat{}+CLN1 \rightarrow -CLN2$; $-SWI5\hat{}+CDC28\hat{}-CLN1 \rightarrow +CLN2$; $-SWI5\hat{}-CDC28 \rightarrow +CLN2$; $+SWI5\hat{}-CLB1 \rightarrow +CLN2$; $+SWI5\hat{}+CLB1 \rightarrow -CLN2$, where the symbol $\hat{}$ stands for the logic AND.

In the context of AR mining by means of decision trees, the functions determining states of target genes from data are called *classifiers*, while algorithms building such classifiers on the basis of data with known states are called *inducers*, *induction*, or *ensemble algorithms*. Each expression profile with a known state of a predicted gene is called an *example* or an *instance*. The set of examples used for classifier creation is the training set. If a subset of the examples is separated from the training set and is used for estimation of classification accuracy, it is called a *test set*. Thereby, the inference of a decision tree for AR mining can be considered as a standard classification problem in the following way. Let $Y = \{y_1, \ldots, y_N\}$ be the set of all sample expression profiles and let $Y_{/i} = \{y_{1/i}, \ldots, y_{N/i}\}$ be the set of partial sample expression profiles for a given gene g_i from the matrix A'. Let us define a classifier, C, as a function that maps a vector y to a discrete value s. Sometimes, in the context of classification, the vector y is called a *feature vector*, while s is a *label*. The subset of y vectors with correct labels assigned to them is called a *data set*, D, for a particular classification problem. An induction algorithm I maps a data set D into a classifier C. Thus, in order to solve the problem described above, it is necessary to define the data sets and then choose appropriate induction algorithms. More specifically, let the goal be to predict the state of gene g_i from a matrix A'. An induction algorithm I maps the data set $D_i = (Y_{/i}, s_i)$ into the classifier C_i (the index i for D_i and C_i is used to emphasize that they correspond to the gene g_i). For the given data set D_i, it is necessary to create a classifier that correctly predicts the state of gene g_i, that is, $I(D_i, y_{j/i}) = C_i(y_{j/i}) = s_{ij}$. Thus, for this problem, the predicted gene g_i and the explaining genes belong to the same sample j.

As a part of the classification problem it is necessary to find which genes are relevant to the prediction of a particular gene. This is known as the feature subset selection problem. Two kinds of methods for feature subset selection have been generally presented in the literature: filter and wrapper methods [84, 85]. In the filter approach, the feature set is filtered to find the "most promising" subset by evaluating an objective function before running the induction algorithm. The weak point of this approach is that the properties of a particular induction algorithm are ignored. In the wrapper approach, the selection algorithm uses the induction algorithm itself to evaluate the objective function. The wrapper approach of Kohavi was reported as performing better than the filter approach for many real and artificial data sets [85]. The idea of the wrapper algorithm is to tune parameters of an induction algorithm considering it as a black box in order to optimize some objective function (e.g., the accuracy of a classifier). The set of attributes relevant to the classification may be considered as parameters of an induction algorithm. Selecting the parameters that maximize the objective function gives a list of "good" features. For the details of a selection algorithm see [85]. The classification rules inferred in this way assume that only a limited number of gene regulators are sufficient for accurate predictions.

Soinov et al. [86] were the first authors that approached the task of inferring the ARs by means of decision trees. They used classification algorithms for continuous data, in which the discretization forms part of the algorithm. This allowed them to find abundance thresholds of regulatory genes, which are specific to different gene interactions in the network, and sufficient for the switching of the target gene from one state to the other. In this way, every gene has its own unique discretization threshold for input signals. They used two types of induction algorithms. The first one exploits the wrapper approach for feature subset selection [85]. It is called C4.5, by Quinlan [87], with wrappers by Kohavi [85]. The second one is C4.5 itself. C4.5 is an algorithm that constructs the classification model inductively, generalizing information from examples of correct classification. It has proved to be an algorithm of good performance for a large variety of data sets.

A more recently published example is [88], which employs *regression trees* to solve the problem. The basic idea of this method is to decompose the prediction of a regulatory network between p genes into p different regression problems. In each one of the regression problems, the expression pattern of one of the target genes is predicted from the expression patterns of all the other genes. The difference between this method and Soinov's approach lies in the use of regression trees instead of classification trees. In this way, they compare two tree-based ensemble methods founded on randomization, namely random forests [89] and extra trees [90]. In a random Forests ensemble, each tree is built on a bootstrap sample from the original learning sample and, at each test node, K attributes are selected at random among all candidate attributes before determining the best split. In the extra-trees method, on the other hand, each tree is built from the original learning sample and at each test node the best split is determined among K random splits, and each one is determined by a random selection of an input (without replacement) and a threshold.

36.3.2.1 *Time-Delayed ARs with Decision Trees*

The aforementioned framework for the inference of ARs by means of decision trees does not consider possible delayed interactions. In [86] an extended definition for the problem of single time-delayed interactions was introduced. This formulation is merely the same as before, except that the data set is now $D_i = (Y'_{/i}, s'_i)$, where $Y'_{/i} = \{y_{1/i}, \ldots, y_{N-1/i}\}$ and $s'_i = (s_{i_2}, \ldots, s_{i_N})$. The classifier C_i is said to classify gene g_i for sample j correctly if $C_i(y_{j/i}) = s_{i(j+1)}$. Note that, in the case of this problem, the regulator genes belong to the sample preceding the sample of the target gene g_i. This formulation can be generalized to any time delay in the regulatory effect between the regulator genes and the target gene.

Another approach was proposed by [54]. They introduce a method that allows the expression of a target gene at time $t + 1$ to be interacted with other genes at time frames $\{t, t - 1, \ldots, t - (W - 1)\}$. For each target gene, its time-delayed gene expression profile is constructed. Then, a decision tree is used to discover the time-delayed regulations that modulate the activities of the target gene (see Figure 36.5 for an example).

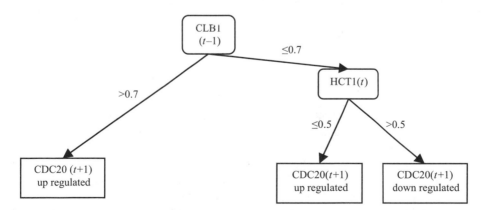

FIGURE 36.5 Possible classification tree for gene *CDC20* of *S. cerevisiae*: *CDC20* is the target gene; *CLB1* and *HTC1* are the regulatory genes. Expression thresholds of the respective explaining genes mark all the arcs.

TABLE 36.3 $D_i = (\text{TdE}, C_i)$ **Matrix for Target Gene** g_i

Gene \ $t+1$	g_1					g_N				C_i
	$t+(W-1)$	$\cdots$	$t-1$	t	$\cdots$	$t+(W-1)$	$\cdots$	$t-1$	t	
$W+1$	d_{11}	$\cdots$	$d_{1(W-1)}$	d_{1W}	$\cdots$	d_{N1}	$\cdots$	$d_{N(W-1)}$	d_{NW}	$C_{i(W+1)}$
$W+2$	d_{12}	$\cdots$	d_{1W}	$d_{1(t+1)}$	$\cdots$	d_{N2}	$\cdots$	d_{NW}	$d_{N(t+1)}$	$C_{i(W+2)}$
$\vdots$	$\vdots$	$\cdots$	$\vdots$	$\vdots$	$\cdots$	$\vdots$	$\cdots$	$\vdots$	$\vdots$	$\vdots$
$W+(M-W)$	$d_{1(M-W)}$	$\cdots$	$d_{1(M-2)}$	$d_{1(M-1)}$	$\cdots$	$d_{N(M-W)}$	$\cdots$	$d_{N(M-2)}$	$d_{N(M-1)}$	C_{iM}

Note: The genes $g_1, \ldots, g_n$ are the putative regulatory genes to be assessed. The d_{kl} values are the temporal transcriptions of these genes, and C_i denotes the phenotype (state) vector for the target gene g_i at the temporal point $(t+1, \ldots, M)$.

A time-delayed gene expression profile (TdE) is an $(M-W) \times (N \times W)$ matrix, where each W-column block in the $N \times W$ columns represents the activities of each of the N (regulating) genes at time points $t, t-1, \ldots, t-(W-1)$ and each row is therefore an $(N \times W)$-dimension vector. As the value of t changes from W to $M-1$ (the time window moves from the first time point to the $M-W$ time point), it produces $M-W$ such vectors or samples. Next, it is necessary to set up the corresponding phenotype (label) for each sample, which was determined by the states of the target gene g_i. Finally, the completed data for the time-delayed gene expression profiles for the target gene is denoted by $D_i = (\text{TdE}, C_i)$, where C_i is a column vector of states for gene g_i. The $D_i = (\text{TdE}, C_i)$ matrix for the target gene g_i is given in Table 36.3.

36.3.3 Bayesian Networks

A Bayesian network is a representation of a joint probability distribution as a *directed acyclic graph* (DAG) [91, 92]. The vertices of a DAG correspond to random variables $[V_1, \ldots, V_N]$ and the edges correspond to parent–child dependencies among variables. The random variables may be either discrete or continuous valued. In the context of GRNs, V_i represents the expression level of gene g_i, and the edges of the DAG represent the relations among genes. Thereby, a Bayesian network can be represented by a list of ARs that correspond to parent–child dependencies among variables. The joint probability distribution can thus be written in the simple product form

$$P[V_1, \ldots, V_N] = \prod_{i-1}^{N} P[V_i \,|\, P_a(V_i)]$$

Bayesian networks have a number of features which make them attractive candidates for modeling gene expression data: They are suitable to handle noisy or missing data, to handle hidden variables such as protein levels which may have an effect on mRNA steady-state levels, to describe locally interacting processes, and to make causal inferences from the derived models. Friedman et al. [92] proposed modeling a gene network as a Bayesian network: Each gene is a vertex and each regulatory relationship is an edge in the Bayesian network. As learning a sparse network is technically difficult, Friedman proposed a two-step algorithm, the *sparse candidate algorithm*, to learn the structure and parameters: For each gene, (1) some candidate parents who are likely to be the parents of the target gene are selected; (2) the Bayesian score for every possible subset of the candidate parent set is computed and the best combination is searched for. In the first step, a general method using pairwise correlation, such as *mutual information* (MI), is applied to find the genes with high dependence with the target genes. However, some dependences cannot be measured by MI. Thus, some weak parents are generated. Weak parents are parents to a target gene but do not have a high dependence with it. *Kullback–Leibler* (KL) divergence is used in the work, which can be improved iteratively using the learned network as the prior knowledge in the iterated learning process, to find better dependence between gene pairs. The second step can be done by some heuristic method such as hill climbing [92]. Friedman showed that the results obtained by the sparse candidate learning algorithm are biologically meaningful by examining them with a set of statistic measurements: robust test, order relation, Markov relation, and so on. Since then, many works based on the Bayesian network frame have been proposed, and biologically relevant results have been obtained. Hartemink et al. [93] extended Friedman's work by adding these annotations to edges: $+$, $-$, or $+/-$, which represent positive, negative, or unknown regulation. Beal et al. [94] proposed including the unmeasured genes as the hidden factors to learn a gene network. They proposed implementing the step by *state-space models* (SSMs). Lee and Lee [95] proposed a modularized learning approach based on the assumption that most genes are likely to be related to other genes in the same biological modules rather than the genes in different modules. They proposed finding overlapping modules in the genes and learning the subnetworks in modules with a Bayesian network. Zhou et al. [96] proposed constructing the probabilistic GRNs that emphasize network topology using a reversible jump Markov chain technique. Rogers and Girolami [97] proposed to infer the regulatory networks by the Bayesian regression approach, which works with continuous variables directly.

Bayesian networks have also the disadvantage of excluding dynamical aspects of gene regulation since they need to be acyclic graphs. To some extent, this can be overcome through generalizations like *dynamical Bayesian networks* (DBNs), which allow feedback relations between genes in a network. A DBN is a Bayesian network which has been temporally "unrolled." Typically, the variables are viewed as entities whose value changes over time. However, if the variables are considered as constant (as in the hidden Markov model), it is possible to represent, for example, g_i at t and g_i at $t + 1$ using two different variables, say g_i^t and g_i^{t+1}. Assuming that the conditional dependencies cannot point backward or "sideways" in time, this means that the graph must be acyclic, even if g_i autoregulates. Also, assuming that the conditional dependencies are constant over time and that the prior joint distribution is the same as the temporal joint distribution [98], the network only needs to be unrolled for one time step. An example is provided in Figure 36.6.

Murphy and Mian [99] and Gransson and Koski [100] used the DBN to model gene networks. In this model, a gene at a time point is regulated by its parent in the previous time point. Thus, the acyclic limitation of the Bayesian network is overcome in the DBN. Murphy et al. gave a thorough report in [99] on the application of the DBN in learning gene networks. Imoto et al. [91] and Kim et al. [101] further extended Bayesian networks and DBNs by integrating nonparametric regression into the models, so that the methods can use continuous gene expression values instead of the discrete values in the general Bayesian network approaches. Their method is capable of capturing the nonlinear relationships among genes. Yu et al. [102] presented an influence score to measure the magnitudes of regulatory strength of the edges. This score is useful for eliminating the false positives as well as for distinguishing the positive or negative regulation of edges. With more and more works using Bayesian networks as the framework to tackle the gene network reconstruction problem [17, 103–105], the Bayesian network is becoming a widely used approach in learning gene networks.

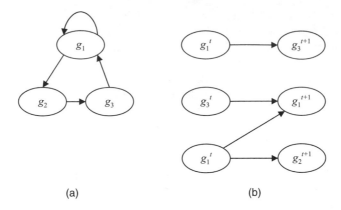

(a)   (b)

FIGURE 36.6   (a) Cyclic Bayesian network impossible to factorize and (b) equivalent acyclic DBN. The prior network [98] is not shown.

An understanding of causal relationships in a network is crucial in the task of determining the impact of interventions at the genetic level and of performing counterfactual reasoning that leads to finding "causes." In general, dependence relations in Bayesian networks do not give unique causal inferences. There are multiple graphs that yield the same joint distribution. Measurements of gene expression, in the absence of interventions, are insufficient to uniquely determine the underlying causal mechanisms. Recently, a few studies provided methods for uniquely inferring causal mechanisms for certain cases of Bayesian networks based on perturbation data [106–108]. However, most researches on reverse engineering of GRNs by either Boolean or differential equation-based models do not take the "causal" aspect of gene connections into consideration. In wet laboratories, learning causal relationships between genes can be done by knocking out all possible subsets of genes of a given set and studying the impact on the other genes in the set. This is not often feasible when the number of genes in the set is more than a handful. An alternative approach is to use time-series gene expression data. Unfortunately, such data can only be obtained for cells of particular organisms such as yeast. For human tissues, high-throughput gene expression data are generally only available for the steady state. Therefore, how to infer causal relationships between genes from steady-state data is an open question for researchers of this field.

Modern variations of Bayesian networks have also added new capabilities to them, particularly fuzzy Bayesian networks. These range from specialized techniques designed to reduce the complexity of *hybrid Bayesian network* (HBN) belief propagation with fuzzy approximations to more general formalizations [53, 109–111]. General formalizations allow variables in Bayesian networks to take fuzzy states, with all of the advantages in robustness, comprehensibility, and dimensionality reduction this provides [98, 112].

36.3.3.1   *Time-Delayed GRNs with Bayesian Networks*   In Tiefei [113], a time-delayed Bayesian network was proposed to model a GRN, which can capture various time-delayed relationships as well as discover directed loops spanning at least one time slice. The time-delayed Bayesian network is defined as follows: Let W be the maximum time delay allowed for each regulation. A time-delayed Bayesian network can be described by $T = <G, \theta, \delta>$, in which $G = <V, E>$ is a directed graph, where $V = \{V_1, V_2, \ldots, V_n\}$ is the set of variables of G and E is the set of directed edges of G. Each variable V_i represents

a gene, and each edge (V_i, V_j) represents the regulation process from V_i to V_j. For every edge $(V_i, V_j) \in E$, $\delta(V_i; V_j)$ represents the unique time delay for the edge (V_i, V_j). Note that $\delta(V_i, V_j)$ is an integer and $0 \leq \delta(V_i, V_j) \leq W$. Assume θ is the parameter set of G that stores the conditional probability distribution $P(V_i | P_a(V_i))$ for every $V_i \in V$, where $P_a(V_i)$ is the parent set of V_i in G. A directed cycle is allowed if at least one of its edges has time delay ≥ 1. Figure 36.7a shows an example of a directed cycle with four genes in a time-delayed Bayesian network.

In order to model the time-delayed Bayesian networks, a relationship between them and the traditional Bayesian network can be established [113]. Given a maximum time delay W, a variable at a time slice can only be affected by variables in the current time slice and the previous W time slices. For each variable V_i, let $V_{i,0}, V_{i,1}, \ldots, V_{i,W-1}, V_{i,W}$ be its states in the previous W time slices and the current time slice. Learning whether the edge (V_j, V_i) has a time delay Δ is equivalent to learning whether $(V_{j,W-\Delta}, V_{i,W})$ is an edge. The formal transformation is described as follows: Given a time-delayed network $T = <G, \theta, \delta>$, where $G = <V, E>$, with the maximum time delay W, T can be represented using a traditional network $U = <H, \theta'>$ such that $H = <V', E'>$, where V' is the vertex set and E' is the edge set. Assume $V' = \{V_{i,t} | V_i \in V, t = 0, 1, \ldots, W\}$. Thus, each vertex $V_i \in V$ is transformed into $W + 1$ vertices $\{V_{i,0}, \ldots, V_{i,W}\}$. Consider a variable $V_i \in V$, with $P_a(V_i) = \{V_{i_1}, \ldots, V_{i_s}\}$ being the parent set of V_i in G. In H, the variable $V_{i,W}$ has parents $V_{i_1,(W-\Delta_1)}, V_{i_2,(W-\Delta_2)}, \ldots, V_{i_s,(W-\Delta_s)}$, where Δ_j is the time delay $\delta(V_i, V_{i_j})$ associated with the edge between V_i and V_{i_j}. In the parameter set θ', the conditional probability distribution $P(V_{i,W} | V_{i_1,(W-\Delta_1)}, V_{i_2,(W-\Delta_2)}, \ldots, V_{i_s,(W-\Delta_s)})$ of U is the same as the conditional probability distribution $P(V_i | V_{i_1}, \ldots, V_{i_s})$ of N.

Figure 36.7 shows an example reported in [113] of the transformation. It can be easily verified that the transformed network U is a directed acyclic graph and that the network U contains all the parameters of T. Once the network U is learned, the parameters of the network T can be easily recovered. Additionally, if the time delay $W = 0$, the time-delayed network is indeed a traditional Bayesian network, and if $W = 1$, the time-delayed network is a dynamic Bayesian network. A work related to this approach is the k-DBN model, where k-DBN was proposed in [114] for finding hidden variables in a network. Though k-DBN was

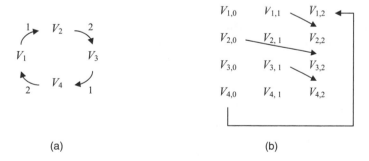

(a)   (b)

FIGURE 36.7 Example of network transformation. (a) The time-delayed network contains 4 variables and 4 edges. The integer on each edge indicates the time delay, and the maximum time delay k is assumed to be 2. This network has one cycle: $V_1 \rightarrow V_2 \rightarrow V_3 \rightarrow V_4 \rightarrow V_1$. (b) The transformed network contains 12 variables and 4 edges. Each variable V_i is transformed into 3 variables: $V_{i,0}, V_{i,1}$ and $V_{i,2}$. The edge (V_i, V_j), with time delay Δ is transformed into edge $(V_{i,W-\Delta}, V_{j,W})$. After the transformation, no cycle exists.

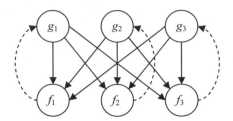

FIGURE 36.8 A Boolean network. For clarity, each $f \in F$ has been put into a node. Normally the functions are implicit in the edges among N; $f_1 = -g_1 \wedge g_2 \wedge g_3$, $f_2 = -g_1 \vee g_2 \wedge g_3$, $f_3 = g_1 \vee g_3$.

not used for learning causal relationships as is the case in a gene network, it can be extended to learn the structure of a gene network, allowing more than one edge with different time delays from gene g_i to gene g_j.

36.3.4 Boolean Networks

Boolean network models, originally introduced by Kauffman [115, 116], can provide useful insights in network dynamics at the coarse level. In a Boolean network, an entity can attain two alternative levels: active (1) or inactive (0). For example, a gene can be described as expressed or not expressed at any time. The level of each entity is updated according to the levels of several entities via a specific Boolean function. The 0–1 vector that describes the levels of all entities is called a *system state* or *global state*. It is assumed to change synchronously such that at every time step the level of each entity is determined according to the levels of its regulators at the previous time step and to the regulation function. Figure 36.8 is an example of a Boolean network. In many cases, the regulatory relationships between network components have not been established and therefore need to be derived from experimental data. For any entity under a Boolean network model, both its regulators and a regulatory function that is consistent with a set of gene expression profiles can be found efficiently provided that the number of regulators of each entity does not exceed a set limit [117].

Boolean networks do not correctly model the dynamics of a transcription factor that down regulates its own expression due to the model's limited level of detail [118]. Another problem is that it is computationally expensive to analyze the dynamics of large networks, as the number of global states is exponential in the number of entities. However, when the number of entities is small and only qualitative knowledge is available, Boolean networks can provide important insights, such as the existence and nature of steady states or network robustness. Furthermore, for modeling large-scale genetic regulatory systems, Boolean networks may represent the only practical alternative [112].

Microarray data exhibit uncertainty on several levels, as stated before. First, there is biological uncertainty in the form of intrinsic and extrinsic noise. Second, there is experimental noise due to the complex measurement process, ranging from hybridization conditions to microarray image processing techniques. Third, there may be interacting latent variables, such as proteins, various environmental conditions, or other genes that are not measured, which are further sources of variability in the measurements. To address the uncertainty, Shmulevich et al. [119] introduced *probabilistic Boolean networks* (PBNs) by associating several predictors with each target gene [119]. If target gene g_i has $l(i)$ associated predictor

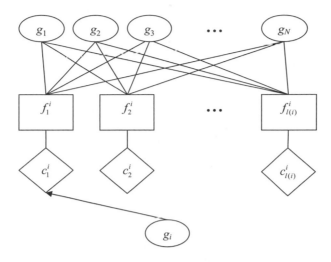

FIGURE 36.9 Basic building block of PBN.

functions, $f_1^{(i)}, f_2^{(i)}, \ldots, f_{l(i)}^{(i)}$, then at each point in time t one of these functions is selected to form the transition rule for g_i at time $t + 1$. Clearly, if $l(i) = 1$ for all $i = 1, 2, \ldots, N$, the PBN simply reduces to a standard Boolean network. The basic building block of a PBN is shown in Figure 36.9. The wiring diagram for the entire PBN consists of N such building blocks. Conceptually, the probabilistic predictor of each target gene can be thought of as a random switch, where at each time point in the network the function $f_k^{(i)}$ is chosen with probability $c_k^{(i)}$ to predict gene g_i. One way to assign these probabilities is to employ the *coefficient of determination* (CoD) [119], normalized in such a way that $\sum_{k=1}^{l(i)} c_k^{(i)} = 1$. That is, $c_k^{(i)} = \theta_k^{(i)} / \sum_{j=1}^{l(i)} \theta_k^{(i)}$, where $\theta_k^{(i)}$ is the CoD for the target gene g_i relative to the genes used as inputs to predictor $f_k^{(i)}$.

Within the context of PBNs, Hashimoto et al. [120] have developed a method to grow a network starting from a smaller number of genes of interest, or seed genes. The proposed algorithm is flexible and permits various designer choices regarding how to proceed, such as the measure of connection strength between genes, search protocol, and stopping conditions. As an example, the CoD [119] can be assigned as the strength-measuring function. Identifying the seed genes of interest is a critical step in this algorithm. The seed genes are usually selected with the aid of prior biological knowledge.

While good at abstracting uncertainty in biological system, the PBN model fails in describing the context-specific determinism of regulatory systems. Context can be defined as a certain condition under which a limited number of genes are tightly regulated by each other for a specific cellular mechanism or a specific task. This specific task can be a different developmental stage, or tissue-specific function, resulting in a specific cell type. The change of this context will result in the change in the set of genes that are highly interactive and probably their connectivity and relationships. Different biological contexts can also correlate with different diseases or might be a reason why certain patients respond to a therapy while others do not. Li et al. [121] developed a *context-sensitive Boolean network* (cBN) model to describe the behavior of cellular systems. A cBN can be considered as a constrained PBN, where the constraint is the way to assign the probability for the model. The rule inference

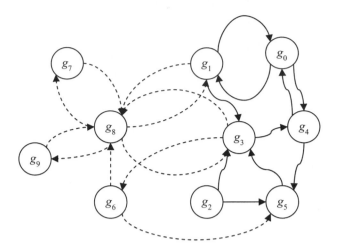

FIGURE 36.10   Example of cBN with two contexts.

is based on the assumption that the inferred rules and the observations are consistent within a (given) context. Figure 36.10 shows an example of cBNs that contain two contexts and 15 genes.

36.3.4.1 *Time-Delayed GRNs with Boolean Networks*   In order to deal with time delay in gene regulation, Silvescu and Honavar [10] proposed an algorithm that uses time-series data to find *temporal Boolean networks* (TBoN). TBoNs were developed to model regulatory delays, which may come about due to missing intermediary genes and spatial or biochemical delays between transcription and regulation, as stated before. An example of a temporal Boolean network is presented in Figure 36.11.

A TBoN is very similar to a regular Boolean network except that the functions $f \in F$ can refer to past gene expression levels. Rather than depending just on N_t to infer N_{t+1}, parameters to f_i can be annotated with an integer temporal delay. For example, $g_3 = f_3(g_1, g_2, g_3) = g_1^0 \vee g_3^{-2}$ means g_3 is expressed at $t + 1$ if g_1 at t is expressed or g_3 was expressed at time $t - 2$. The TBoN can also be reformulated and inferred as a decision tree.

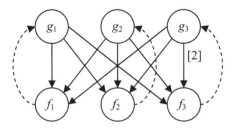

FIGURE 36.11   Temporal Boolean network. Presentation and functions are as in Figure 36.8, but delays are shown in brackets between genes and functions. The default delay if no annotation is present is assumed to be zero.

36.3.5 Other Techniques

Over the past few years, other approaches were proposed that do not correspond to the previous classification. However, these methods can also be used to infer gene ARs from microarray data. These techniques will be briefly described in the following sections.

36.3.5.1 Clustering One of the main problems that hinder research on gene network reconstruction is the dimension problem; that is, there are many genes with a few replicates. A useful approach is to group genes with similar expression patterns into clusters and then infer the regulatory relationship among the clusters [113]. Researchers believe genes with similar expression patterns have similar functions or are involved in the same biological events [122]. Currently, several clustering methods are used for this purpose. Different clustering methods can generate very different results. Each combination of distance measurement and clustering algorithm tends to emphasize a different type of regularity in the data. There is no single criterion for choosing the best clustering method. How to choose the method depends on the particular emphasis.

Given clusters, there are also several methods to find the interactions among them. Chen et al. [123] reduced 3131 yeast genes into 308 clusters by average linkage clustering. Then, they used simulated annealing to optimize a qualitative network based on the timing of peaks in the data. Wahde and Hertz [122] clustered 65 genes from rat spinal cord and hippocampus data sets [124] into four "waves" using the Fitch's hierarchical clustering algorithm [125]. Then, by a genetic algorithm, they built a four-node continuous-time recurrent neural network. Someren et al. [126] reduced 2467 yeast genes into $t - 1$ clusters and represented each cluster by a "prototype" gene calculated from the cluster. A linear model of the prototype genes is then generated by linear regression. Toh and Horimoto [11] proposed averaging the gene expression values of each cluster and then discovered the regulatory relationships by *graphical Gaussian modeling* (GGM). Guthke et al. [127] proposed grouping genes into clusters, and then they found the representative genes for the clusters. The connections among the representative genes are modeled by differential equations.

36.3.5.2 Pairwise Methods Pairwise methods seek to discover the relationships among genes by pairwise comparisons solely. They do not consider interactions where the expression of one gene is achieved by the combined effects of other multiple genes. Arkin et al. [128] proposed *correlation metric construction* (CMC), which computes the magnitude of gene pairs by cross-correlation. A distance matrix is constructed for each gene pair by comparing their similarities to other genes. Then a diagram is constructed to summarize the strength of interaction and predict mechanistic connections between the genes. Chen et al. [123] proposed activation/inhibition networks to find regulation based on whether peaks in one signal precede peaks in another signal, grouping the genes with similar expression profiles. Then a prototype is generated for each group of genes by averaging the expression values of genes in the group. Each prototype represents a group of genes with similar expression patterns and is represented as a series of peaks. The correlations between prototype pairs are calculated to determine the type of regulatory relationships (activation, inhibition, or unmatched) and measure the strength of the regulatory relationship between any two prototypes. Finally, the regulation matrix is generated by the scores. Ponzoni et al. [129] proposed a machine learning algorithm called GRNCOP based on combinatorial optimization that does not assume arbitrary or uniform gene expression value discretizations.

The thresholds are calculated dynamically by applying the same continuous-valued attribute discretization techniques as those used for classification algorithms based on decision trees. Then, each possible pair of genes is evaluates and an AR with a particular accuracy based on an objective function is obtained. Finally, only the rules that achieved an accuracy value over a preselected threshold are reported. Gallo et al. [7] proposed an extension of this approach allowing the inference of ARs with multiple time delays and from multiple data sources.

36.3.5.3 *Support Vector Machine Methods*   *Support vector machine* (SVM) methods have attracted a high interest within the bioinformatics community during the last years due to their good prediction performance for various tasks. They rely on principles from statistical learning theory [130]. The idea is to construct an optimal hyperplane between two classes $+1$ and -1 such that the margin, that is, the distance of the hyperplane to the point closest to it, is maximized. To allow for nonlinear classification, so-called *kernel functions* are employed which can be thought of as special similarity measures. They implicitly map the original data into some high-dimensional feature space in which the optimal hyperplane can be found. As an example, suppose that linear kernels $k(x,x') = \langle x,x' \rangle$ as well as polynomial kernels of degree 2 $k(x,x') = \langle x,x' \rangle^2$ are considered, where x and x' are the expression levels of all genes except for gene g_i in sample j. The polynomial kernel implicitly computes all pairwise products between expression levels of two genes. In this way, not only linear but also nonlinear dependencies between gene expressions can be captured. In addition to a kernel function, a soft margin parameter C has to be fixed. Guyon et al. [131] proposed an algorithm called RFE capable of determining, for each gene g_i, which genes are suited best to predict its state. This algorithm successively eliminates the gene that influences the size of the margin least. The termination of this procedure can be determined by a 10-fold cross-validation.

36.4 CONCLUDING REMARKS

The development of computational methods for GRN modeling is a hot research topic. In this chapter, a specific family of algorithms for extracting ARs among genes is reviewed. The reverse engineering of GRNs from ARs has an important methodological advantage: It allows a model-free reconstruction of the networks. In other words, these techniques do not require, in general, any constraint or previous knowledge about the relationship network structure, nor do they make assumptions related to the physicochemical principles that govern the gene interactions. These methods only need the gene expression information as data source for the inference process.

All of the techniques here reviewed come from diverse data-mining approaches, but most of them share common aspects, like some preprocessing steps. In particular, the discretization of the gene expression data constitutes a central point for these methods, with important semantic implications. As it was described, there are several algorithms for addressing this problem which range from simplistic and straightforward arbitrary discretizations to elaborated adaptive methods. Moreover, additional complex aspects, which emerge as part of this preprocessing step when transitional states are modeled from time-series data, were also presented.

Regarding the inference methodologies, a wide variety of techniques were illustrated here, such as frequent-itemset-based methods, classification and regression trees, Bayesian networks, Boolean networks, SVMs, clustering approaches, and some pairwise algorithms. For most of these data-mining approaches, several algorithms were reviewed, emphasizing the advantages and limitations of these contributions.

Another relevant point is the inference of temporal associations among genes. This point was addressed in a transversal way along the chapter, illustrating how different data-mining methods include these types of time delay rules. Additional topics such as the cardinality model for the rules, statistical and biological validation of the network, or how to extract associations from multiple data sources are also analyzed in detail.

Finally, an important question probably remains in the reader's mind: *How realistic can these discretized regulatory models be?* At this point, as a corollary of this chapter, it is important to remark that in any network modeling methodology there is awareness and acceptance that a model describes only some properties of the real biological system and ignores many others. In other words, a model emphasizes particular aspects of the reality, leaving out details that are not always relevant for the purpose of the study. In this context, the AR inference algorithms constitute a valuable tool for understanding and discovering potential hidden relationships among genes, and the discretization of the gene expression values in states allows the modeler to be focused on the relevant information patterns. Therefore, the discretized view of the data can help to capture the gene behavior in an easier interpretable way. Nevertheless, a realistic reconstruction of the complex regulatory machinery that occurs in the cell will need to attack the problem from different perspectives and with complementary computational approaches. Moreover, the final biological validation of each novel association will always be required in order to obtain a feasible and confident network.

ACKNOWLEDGMENTS

This work was supported by Research Project PIP 112-2009-0100322 founded by the CONICET (National Research Council of Argentina) and by Research Project PGI 24/ZN15 founded by the Universidad Nacional del Sur (Bahía Blanca, Argentina).

REFERENCES

1. H. Kitano. Perspectives on systems biology. *New Generat. Comput.*, 18:199–216, 2000.

2. K. H. Cho, S. M. Choo, S. H. Jung, J. R. Kim, H. S. Choi, and J. Kim. Reverse engineering of gene regulatory networks. *IET Syst. Biol.*, 1:149–63, 2007.

3. M. E. Csete and J. C. Doyle. Reverse engineering of biological complexity. *Science*, 295:1664–1669, 2002.

4. A. Ceglar and J. F. Roddick. Association mining. *ACM Comput. Surv.*, 38:2, 2006.

5. C. Creighton and S. Hanash. Mining gene expression databases for association rules. *Bioinformatics*, 19:79–86, 2003.

6. P. Carmona-Saez, M. Chagoyen, A. Rodriguez, O. Trelles, J. M. Carazo, and A. Pascual-Montano. Integrated analysis of gene expression by association rules discovery. *BMC Bioinformatics*, 7:54, 2006.

7. C. A. Gallo, J. A. Carballido, and I. Ponzoni. Discovering Time-lagged rules from microarray data using gene profile classifiers. *BMC Bioinformatics*, 12(123):1–21, 2011.

8. D. C. McShan, M. Updadhayaya, and I. Shah. Symbolic inference of xenobiotic metabolism. In R. B. Altman, A. K. Dunker, L. Hunter, T. A. Jung, and T. E. Klein (Eds.), *Pacific Symposium Biocomputing*. World Scientific, Hawaii, 2004, pp. 545–556.

9. K. Sterelny and P. E. Griffiths. *Sex and Death: An Introduction to Philosophy of Biology*. Science and Its Conceptual Foundations Series. University of Chicago Press, Chicago, IL, 1999.

10. A. Silvescu and V. Honavar. Temporal Boolean network models of genetic networks and their inference from gene expression time series. *Complex Sys.*, 13:54–70, 2001.

11. H. Toh and K. Horimoto. Inference of A genetic network by a combined approach of cluster analysis and graphical Gaussian modeling. *Bioinformatics*, 18(2):287–297, 2002.

12. C. Fogelberg and V. Palade. Machine Learning and Genetic Regulatory Networks: A Review and a Roadmap. In A. Abraham, A. E. Hassanien, A. Vasilakos, W. Pedrycz, F. Herrera, P. Siarry, A. de Carvalho, and A. P. Engelbrecht (Eds.), *Foundations of Computational Intelligence*. Springer, Heidelberg, 2009, pp. 3–34.

13. G. Giaever et al. Functional profiling of the *Saccharomyces cerevisiae genome. Nature*, 418(6896):387–391, 2002.

14. P. Y. Lum, C. D. Armour, S. B. Stepaniants, G. Cavet, M. K. Wolf, J. S. Butler, J. C. Hinshaw, P. Garnier, G. D. Prestwich, A. Leonardson, P. Garrett-Engele, C. M. Rush, M. Bard, G. Schimmack, J. W. Phillips, C. J. Roberts, and D. D. Shoemaker. Discovering modes of action for therapeutic compounds using a genome-wide screen of yeast heterozygotes. *Cell*, 116(1):121–137, 2004.

15. A. H. Tong, M. Evangelista, A. B. Parsons, H. Xu, G. D. Bader, N. Pagé, M. Robinson, S. Raghibizadeh, C. W. Hogue, H. Bussey, B. Andrews, M. Tyers, and C. Boone. Systematic genetic analysis with ordered arrays of yeast deletion mutants. *Science*, 294(5550):2364–2368, 2001.

16. E. Segal, N. Friedman, N. Kaminski, A. Regev, and D. Koller. From signatures to models: Understanding cancer using microarrays. *Nat. Genetics*, 37:S38–S45, 2005.

17. E. Segal, M. Shapira, A. Regev, D. Pe'er, D. Botstein, D. Koller, and N. Friedman. Module networks: Identifying regulatory modules and their condition-specific regulators from gene expression data. *Nat. Genet.*, 34(2):166–176, 2003.

18. A. J. Hartemink, D. K. Gifford, T. S. Jaakkola, and R. A. Young. Combining location and expression data for principled discovery of genetic regulatory network models. In R. B. Altman, A. K. Dunker, and L. Hunter (Eds.), *Pacific Symposium Biocomputing*. World Scientific, Hawaii, 2002, pp. 437–449.

19. D. Jiang, C. Tang, and A. Zhang. Cluster analysis for gene expression data: A survey. *IEEE Trans. Knowledge Data Eng.*, 16(11):1370–1386, 2004.

20. P. T. Spellman, G. Sherlock, M. Q. Zhang, V. R. Iyer, K. Anders, M. B. Eisen, P. O. Brown, D. Botstein, and B. Futcher. Comprehensive identification of cell cycle-regulated genes of the yeast *Saccharomyces cerevisiae* by microarray hybridization. *Mol. Biol. Cell*, 9(12):3273–3297, 1998.

21. M. Nykter, T. Aho, M. Ahdesmäki, P. Ruusuvuori, A. Lehmussola, and O. Yli-Harja. Simulation of microarray data with realistic characteristics. *Bioinformatics*, 7:349, 2006.

22. L. Klebanov and A. Yakovlev. How high is the level of technical noise in microarray data? *Biol. Direct.*, 2:9, 2007.

23. J. Dougherty, R. Kohavi, and M. Sahami. Supervised and unsupervised discrimination of continuous Features. In A. Prieditis and S. Russell (Eds.), *Machine Learning: Proceedings of the 12th International Conference*, Morgan Kauffman, San Francisco, CA, 1995.

24. N. Friedman and M. Goldszmidt. Discretization of continuous attributes while learning Bayesian networks. In L. Saitta (Ed.), *Proceedings of the 13th International Conference on Machine Learning*. Morgan Kauffman, San Francisco, CA, 1996, pp. 157–165.

25. S. A. Kauffman. Metabolic stability and epigenesist in randomly constructed genetic nets. *J. Theor. Biol.*, 22:437–467, 1969.

26. R. Albert and H. G. Othmer. The topology of the regulatory interactions predics the expression pattern of the segment polarity genes in *Drosophila melanogaster. J. Theor. Biol.*, 223:1–18, 2003.

27. D. Thieffry, R. Thomas. Qualitative analysis of gene networks. In R. B. Altman, A. K. Dunker, L. Hunter, and T. E. Klein (Eds.), *Pacific Symposium Biocomputing*. World Scientific, Singapore, 1997, pp. 77–88.

28. R. Laubenbacher and B. Stigler. A computational algebra approach to the reverse engineering of gene regulatory networks. *J. Theor. Biol.*, 229:523–537, 2004.

29. S. C. Madeira and A. L. Oliveira. An evaluation of discretization methods for non-supervised analysis of time-series gene expression data. Technical Report. INESC-ID, University of Beira Interior, Portugal, 2005.

30. X. Li, S. Rao, W. Jiang, C. Li, Y. Xiao, Z. Guo, Q. Zhang, L. Wang, L. Du, J. Li, L. Li, T. Zhang, and Q. K. Wang. Discovery of time-delayed gene regulatory networks based on temporal gene expression profiling. *BMC Bioinformatics*, 7:26, 2006.

31. M. Koyuturk, W. Szpankowski, and A. Grama. Biclustering gene-feature matrices for statistically significant dense patterns. In *Proceedings of the 8th Annual International Conference on Research in Computational Molecular Biology*, 2004, pp. 480–484.

32. G. Park and W. Szpankowski. Analysis of biclusters with applications to gene expression data. In C. Martinez (Ed.), *2005 International Conference on Analysis of Algorithms*. DMTCS Proceedings, Nancy, 2005, pp. 267–274.

33. S. Lonardi, W. Szpankowski, and Q. Yang. Finding biclusters by random projections. In S. C. Sahinalp, S. Muthukrishnan, and U. Dogrusoz (Eds.), *Combinatorial Pattern Matching*. Springer Berlin, 2004, pp. 102–116.

34. A. Jain and R. Dubes. *Algorithms for Clustering Data*. Prentice Hall, Upper Saddle River, NJ, 1988, pp. 58–89.

35. J. MacQueen. Some methods for classification and analysis of multivariate observations. In *Proceedings of the 5th Berkeley Symposium of Mathematical Statistics and Probability*, Vol. 1, University of California Press, Berkeley, CA, 1967, pp. 281–297.

36. A. Saeed, V. Sharov, J. White, J. Li, W. Liang, N. Bhagabati, J. Braisted, M. Klapa, T. Currier, M. Thiagarajan, A. Sturn, M. Snuffin, A. Rezantsev, D. Popov, A. Ryltsov, E. Kostukovich, I. Borisovsky, Z. Liu, A. Vinsavich, V. Trush, and J. Quackenbush. TM4: A free, open-source system for microarray data management and analysis. *BioTechniques*, 34(2):374–378, 2003.

37. C. Möller-Levet, S. Cho, and O. Wolkenhauer. Microarray data clustering based on temporal variation: Fcv and tsd preclustering. *Appl. Bioinformatics*, 2(1):35–45, 2003.

38. L. Ji and K. Tan. Identifying time-lagged gene clusters using gene expression data. *Bioinformatics*, 21(4):509–516, 2005.

39. L. Ji and K. Tan. Mining gene expression data for positive and negative co-regulated gene clusters. *Bioinformatics*, 20(16):2711–2718, 2004.

40. S. A. Kauffman. Antichaos and adaptation. *Sci. Am.*, 265(2):78–84, 1991.

41. A. L. Barabasi and Z. N. Oltvai. Network biology. Understanding the cell's functional organisation. *Nat. Rev. Genet.*, 5(2):101–113, 2004.

42. J. Tegner, M. K. Yeung, J. Hasty, and J. J. Collins. Reverse engineering gene networks: Integrating genetic perturbations with dynamical modeling. *Proc. Nat. Acad. Sci. USA*, 100(10):5944–5949, 2003.

43. G. Marnellos and E. Mjolsness. A gene network approach to modeling early neurogenesis in drosophila. In R. B. Altman, A. K. Dunker, L. Hunter, and T. E. Klein (Eds.), *Pacific Symposium Biocomputing*. World Scientific, Hawaii, 1998, pp. 30–41.

44. T. J. Perkins1, J. Jaeger, and J. Reinitz. Reverse engineering the gap gene network of drosophila melanogaster. *PLoS Comp. Bio.*, 2(5):e51, 2006.

45. M. J. Herrgård, M. W. Covert, and B. Palsson. Reconciling gene expression data with known genome-scale regulatory network structures. *Genome Res.*, 13(11):2423–2434, 2003.

46. P. C. FitzGerald, D. Sturgill, A. Shyakhtenko, B. Oliver, and C. Vinson. Comparative genomics of drosophila and human core promoters. *Genome Biol.*, 7:R53, 2006.

47. Q. Cui, B. Liu, T. Jiang, and S. Ma. Characterizing the dynamic connectivity between genes by variable parameter regression and Kalman filtering based on temporal gene expression data. *Bioinformatics*, 21(8):1538–1541, 2005.

48. P. Spirtes, C. Glymour, R. Scheines, S. Kauffman, V. Airmale, and F. Wimberly. Constructing Bayesian network models for gene expression networks from microarray data. *Proceedings of the Atlantic Symposium on Computational Biology, Genome Information System and Technology*, 2000. Retrieved from `http://repository.cmu.edu/philosophy/290/`.

49. H. de Jong. Modeling and simulation of genetic regulatory systems: A literature review. *J. Comp. Biol.*, 9(1):67–103, 2002.

50. M. E. Driscoll and T. S. Gardner. Identification and control of gene networks in living organisms via supervised and unsupervised learning. *J. Process Control*, 16(3):303–311, 2006.

51. J. Vohradský. Neural network model of gene expression. *FASEB J.*, 15:846–854, 2001.

52. S. Liang, S. Fuhrman, and R. Somogyi. REVEAL: A general reverse engineering algorithm for inference of genetic network architectures. In R. B. Altman, A. K. Dunker, L. Hunter, and T. E. Klein (Eds.), *Pacific Symposium Biocomputing*. World Scientific, Hawai, 1998, pp. 18–29.

53. D. Husmeier. Sensitivity and specificity of inferring genetic regulatory interactions from microarray experiments with dynamic Bayesian networks. *Bioinformatics*, 19(17):2271–2282, 2003.

54. J. Li, X. Li, H. Su, H. Chen, and D. W. Galbraith. A framework of integrating gene relations from heterogeneous data sources: An experiment on *Arabidopsis thaliana*. *Bioinformatics*, 22:2037–2043, 2006.

55. I. Lee, Z. Li, and E. M. Marcotte. An improved, bias-reduced probabilistic functional gene network of baker's yeast, *Saccharomyces cerevisiae*. *PLoS ONE*, 2(Suppl. 10):e988, 2007.

56. Z. Bar-Joseph, G. K. Gerber, T. I. Lee, N. J. Rinaldi, J. Y. Yoo, F. Robert, D. B. Gordon, E. Fraenkel, T. S. Jaakkola, R. A. Young, and D. K. Gifford. Computational discovery of gene modules and regulatory networks. *Nat. Biotechnol.*, 21:1337–1342, 2003.

57. S. Imoto, T. Higuchi, T. Goto, K. Tashiro, S. Kuhara, and S. Miyano. Combining microarrays and biological knowledge for estimating gene networks via Bayesian networks. *J. Bioinform. Comput. Biol.*, 2:77–98, 2004.

58. A. Bernard and A. J. Hartemink. Informative structure priors: Joint learning of dynamic regulatory networks from multiple types of data. *Pac. Symp. Biocomput.*, 10:459–70, 2005.

59. C. H. Yeang, T. Ideker, and T. Jaakkola. Physical network models. *J. Comput. Biol.*, 11:243–262, 2004.

60. C. H. Yeang and T. Jaakkola. Time series analysis of gene expression and location Data. In *Third IEEE Symposium on BioInformatics and BioEngineering (BIBE'03)*. IEEE, Bethesda, MD, 2003, pp. 305–312.

61. B. Lewin. *Genes*. 7th ed. Oxford University Press, 1999.

62. A. K. Lee, S. H. Sung, Y. C. Kim, and S. G. Kim. Inhibition of lipopolysaccharide-inducible nitric oxide synthase TNF-α and COX-2 expression by Sauchinone effects on NF-κB1 phosphorylation, C/EBP and AP-1 activation. *Br. J. Pharmacol.*, 139:11–20, 2003.

63. O. Cinquin and J. Demongeot. Positive and negative feedback: Striking a balance between necessary antagonists. *J. Theor. Biol.*, 216:229–241, 2002.

64. M. Kanehisa, S. Goto, M. Hattori, K. F. Aoki-Kinoshita, M. Itoh, S. Kawashima, T. Katayama, M. Araki, and M. Hirakawa. From genomics to chemical genomics: New developments in KEGG. *Nucleic Acids Res.*, D354–357, 2006.

65. S. S. Dwight, M. A. Harris, K. Dolinski, C. A. Ball, G. Binkley, K. R. Christie, D. G. Fisk, L. Issel Tarver, M. Schroeder, G. Sherlock, A. Sethuraman, S. Weng, D. Botstein, and J. M. Cherry. Saccharomyces Genome Database (SGD) provides secondary gene annotation using the Gene Ontology (GO). *Nucleic Acids Res.*, 30:69–72, 2002.

66. S. Geisser. *Predictive Inference.* Chapman and Hall, New York, 1993.

67. R. Kohavi. Wrappers for performance enhancement and oblivious decision graphs. Ph.D. Thesis. Stanford University, Computer Science Department, 1995.

68. P. A. Devijver and J. Kittler. *Pattern Recognition: A Statistical Approach*, Prentice-Hall, London, 1982.

69. J. Han and M. Kamber. *Data Mining: Concept and Techniques.* The Morgan Kaufmann Series in Data Management Systems. Morgan Kaufmann, San Francisco, CA, 2000.

70. A. Zhang. *Advanced Analysis of Gene Expression Microarray.* World Scientific, Singapore, 2006.

71. J. Hipp, U. Gntzer, and G. Nakhaeizadeh. Algorithms for association rule mining a general survey and comparison. *ACM SIGKDD Explor.*, 2(Issue 1):58–64, 2000.

72. R. Agrawal, T. Imielinski, and A. Swami. Mining association rules between sets of items in large databases. In *Proceedings of the 1993 ACM-SIGMOD International Conference on Management of Data*, ACM Press, Washington, DC, 1993, pp. 207–216.

73. J. Han, J. Pei, and Y. Yin. Mining frequent patterns without candidate generation. In *Proceedings of the 2000 ACM SIGMOD International Conference on Management of Data.* ACM Press, Dallas, TX, 2000, pp. 1–12.

74. J. Han, H. Cheng, D. Xin, and X. Yan. Frequent pattern mining: Current status and future directions. *Data Min. Knowl. Discov.*, 15:55–86, 2007.

75. R. J. Bayardo. Efficiently mining long patterns from databases. In *Proceedings of the 1998 ACM SIGMOD International Conference on Management of Data.* ACM Press, Seattle, WA, 1998, pp. 88–93.

76. K. Gouda and M. J. Zaki. GenMax: An efficient algorithm for mining maximal frequent itemsets. *Data Min. Knowl. Discov.*, 11:223–242, 2005.

77. N. Pasquier, Y. Bastide, R. Taouil, and L. Lakhal. Efficient mining of association rules using closed itemset lattices. *Inf. Syst.*, 24:25–46, 1999.

78. J. Wang, J. Han, and J. Pei. CLOSET+: Searching for the best strategies for mining frequent closed itemsets. In *Proceedings of the The Ninth ACM SIGKDD International Conference on Knowledge Discovery and Data Mining.* ACM Press, Washington, DC, 2003, pp. 236–245.

79. M. J. Zaki and C. J. Hsiao. CHARM: An efficient algorithm for closed itemset mining. In *Proceedings of the SIAM International Conference on Data Mining.* SIAM Press, Arlington, VA, 2002, pp. 457–73.

80. R. Alves, D. S. Rodriguez-Baena, and J. S. Aguilar-Ruiz. Gene association analysis: A survey of frequent pattern mining from gene expression data. *Brief Bioinformatics*, 11(2):210–224, 2009.

81. E. Baralis, G. Bruno, and E. Ficarra. Temporal association rules for gene regulatory networks. In *Intelligent Systems.* IEEE, Varna, 2008, pp. 2–7.

82. H. Nam, K. Lee, and D. Lee. Identification of temporal association rules from time series microarray data sets. *BMC Bioinformatics*, 10:(Suppl. 3):S6, 2009.

83. L. Breiman, J. H. Friedman, R. A. Olsen, and C. J. Stone. *Classification and Regression Trees.* Chapman & Hall, London, 1984.

84. I. Witten and E. Frank. *Data Mining—Practical Machine Learning Tools and Techniques with JAVA Implementations*. Morgan Kaufmann, San Francisco, CA, 1999.

85. R. Kohavi. A study of cross-validation and bootstrap for accuracy estimation and model selection. *Proc. 14th Int. Joint Conf. Artif. Intell.*, 2(12):1137–1143, 1995.

86. L. A. Soinov, M. A. Krestyaninova, and A. Brazma1. Towards reconstruction of gene networks from expression data by supervised learning. *Genome Biol*, 4(1):R6, 2003.

87. J. R. Quinlan. *C4.5: Programs for Machine Learning*. Morgan Kaufmann, San Francisco, CA, 1992.

88. V. A. Huynh-Thu, A. Irrthum, L. Wehenkel, and P. Geurts. Inferring regulatory networks from expression data using tree-based methods. *PLoS ONE*, 5(9):e12776, 2010.

89. L. Breiman. Random forests. *Machine Learning*, 45:5–32, 2001.

90. P. Geurts, D. Ernst, and L. Wehenkel. Extremely randomized trees. *Machine Learning* 36:3–42, 2006.

91. S. Imoto, T. Goto, and S. Miyano. Estimation of genetic networks and functional structures between genes by using Bayesian networks and nonparametric regression. In R. B. Altman, A. K. Dunker, and L. Hunter (Eds.), *Pacific Symposium Biocomputing*. World Scientific, Hawaii, 2002, pp. 175–186.

92. N. Friedman, M. Linial, I. Nachman, and D. Pe'er. Using Bayesian networks to analyze expression data. *J. Comput. Biol.*, 7:601–620, 2000.

93. A. J. Hartemink, D. K. Gifford, T. S. Jaakkola, and R. A. Young. Using graphical models and genomic expression data to statistically validate models of genetic regulatory networks. In R. B. Altman, K. Lauderdale, A. K. Dunker, L. Hunter, and T. E. Klein (Eds.), *Pacific Symposium Biocomputing*. World Scientific, Hawaii, 2001, pp. 422–433.

94. M. J. Beal, F. Falciani, Z. Ghahramani, C. Rangel, and D. L. Wild. A bayesian approach to reconstructing genetic regulatory networks with hidden factors. *Bioinformatics*, 21(3):349–356, 2005.

95. P. H. Lee and D. Lee. Modularized learning of genetic interaction networks from biological annotations and mRNA expression data. *Bioinformatics*, 21(11):2739–2747, 2005.

96. X. B. Zhou, X. D. Wang, R. Pal, I. Ivanov, M. Bittner, and E. R. Dougherty. A Bayesian connectivity-based approach to constructing probabilistic gene regulatory networks. *Bioinformatics*, 20(17):2918–2927, 2004.

97. S. Rogers and M. Girolami. A Bayesian regression approach to the inference of regulatory networks from gene expression data. *Bioinformatics*, 21(14):3131–3137, 2005.

98. N. Friedman. The Bayesian structure EM algorithm. In G. F. Cooper and S. Moral (Eds), *Uncertainty in Artificial Intelligence*. Morgan Kaufmann Publishers, San Francisco, CA, 1998, pp. 129–138.

99. K. Murphy and S. Mian. Modelling gene expression data using dynamic Bayesian networks. Technical Report. Division of Computer Science, University of California, Berkerley, CA, 1999.

100. L. Gransson and T. Koski. Using a dynamic Bayesian network to learn genetic interactions. Technical Report. Graduate School of Biomedical Research, Linkoping University, 2002.

101. S. Kim, S. Imoto, and S. Miyano. Dynamic Bayesian network and nonparametric regression for nonlinear modeling of gene networks from time series gene expression data. *Biosystems*, 75:57–65, 2004.

102. J. Yu, V. A. Smith, P. P. Wang, A. J. Haremink, and E. D. Jarvis. Advances to Bayesian network inference for generating causal networks from observational biological data. *Bioinformatics*, 20(18):3594–3603, 2004.

103. N. Friedman. Inferring cellular networks using probabilistic graphical models. *Science*, 303(6):799–805, 2004.

104. J. Hasty, D. McMillen, F. Isaacs, and J. J. Collins. Computational studies of gene regulatory networks: In numero molecular biology. *Nat. Rev. Genet.*, 2(4):268–279, 2001.

105. D. Pe'er, A. Regev, G. Elidan, and N. Friedman. Inferring subnetworks from perturbed expression profiles. *Bioinformatics*, 17(Suppl. 1):S215–224, 2001.

106. N. Guelzim, S. Bottani, P. Bourgine, and F. Kepes. Topological and causal structure of the yeast transcriptional regulatory network. *Nat. Genet.*, 31:60–63, 2002.

107. C. Yoo and G. F. Cooper. Discovery of gene-regulation pathways using local causal search. In I. S. Kohane (Ed.), *Proc. AMIA Symp.* Hanley & Belfus, San Antonio, TX, 2002, pp. 914–918.

108. B. Xing and M. J. van der Laan. A causal inference approach for constructing transcriptional regulatory networks. *Bioinformatics*, 21:4007–4013, 2005.

109. T. Akutsu, S. Miyano, and S. Kuhara. Algorithms for inferring qualitative models of biological networks. In R. B. Altman, A. K. Dunker, and L. Hunter (Eds.), *Pacific Symposium Biocomputing*. World Scientific, Hawaii, 2000, pp. 293–304.

110. I. Simon, J. Barnett, N. Hannett, C. T. Harbison, N. J. Rinaldi, T. L. Volkert, J. J. Wyrick, J. Zeitlinger, D. K. Gifford, T. S. Jaakkola, and R. A. Young. Serial regulation of transcriptional regulators in the yeast cell cycle. *Cell*, 106(6):697–708, 2001.

111. K. Sivakumar, R. Chen, and H. Kargupta. Learning Bayesian network structure from distributed data. In *SIAM International Data Mining Conference*. Society for Industrial and Applied Mathematics, San Francisco, CA, 2003, pp. 284–288.

112. P. Smolen, D. A. Baxter, and J. H. Byrne. Modeling transcriptional control in gene networks— methods, recent results and future directions. *Bull. Math. Biol.*, 62:247–292, 2000.

113. L. Tiefei. Learning gene network using Bayesian network framework. Ph.D. Thesis. National University of Singapore, 2005.

114. X. Boyen, N. Friedman, and D. Koller. Discovering the hidden structure of complex dynamic systems. In K. Laskey and H. Prade (Eds.), *Uncertainty in Artificial Intelligence*. Morgan Kaufmann Publishers, San Francisco, CA, 1999, pp. 91–100.

115. S. A. Kauffman. Requirements for evolvability in complex systems: Orderly dynamics and frozen components. *Phys. D*, 42:135–152, 1990.

116. S. A. Kauffman. *The Origins of Order, Self-Organization and Selection in Evolution*. Oxford University Press, New York, NY, 1993.

117. H. Lähdesmäki, I. Shmulevich, and O. Yli-Harja. On learning gene regulatory networks under the Boolean network model. *Machine Learning*, 52:147–167, 2003.

118. S. Kauffman, C. Peterson, B. Samuelsson, and C. Troein. Random Boolean network models and the yeast transcriptional network. *Proc. Natl Acad. Sci. USA*, 100:14796–14799, 2003.

119. I. Shmulevich, E. R. Dougherty, S. Kim, and W. Zhang. Probabilistic Boolean networks: A rule-based uncertainty model for gene regulatory networks. *Bioinformatics*, 18:261–274, 2002.

120. R. Hashimoto, S. Kim, I. Shmulevich, W. Zhang, M. L. Bittner, and E. R. Dougherty. Growing genetic regulatory networks from seed genes. *Bioinformatics*, 20:1241–1247, 2004.

121. H. Li, J. Xuan, Y. Wang, and M. Zhan. Inferring regulatory networks. *Front. Biosci.*, 13:263–275, 2008.

122. M. Wahde and J. Hertz. Coarse-grained reverse engineering of genetic regulatory networks. *Biosystems*, 55:129–136, 2000.

123. T. Chen, V. Filkov, and S. S. Skiena. Identifying gene regulatory networks from exprimental data. In *Research in Computational Molecular Biology*. ACM, Lyon, 1999, pp. 94–103.

124. X. Wen, S. Fuhrman, G. S. Michaels, D. B. Carr, S. Smith, J. L. Barker, and R. Somogyi. Large-scale temporal gene expression mapping of central nervous system development. *Proc. Natl. Acad. Sci.*, 95(1):334–339, 1998.

125. W. M. Fitch and E. Margoliash. Construction of phylogenetic trees. *Science*, 155:279–284, 1967.

126. E. P. V. Someren, L. F. A.Wessels, and M. J. T. Reinders. Linear modeling of genetic networks from experimental data. In R. Altman, T. L. Bailey, P. Bourne, M. Gribskov, T. Leagauer, I. N. Shidyalov, L. F. Ten Eyck, and H. Weissig (Eds.), *International Conference on Intelligent Systems for Molecular Biology*. AAAI Press, La Jolla, CA, 2000, pp. 355–366.

127. R. Guthke, U. Moller, M. Hoffmann, F. Thies, and S. Topfer. Dynamic network reconstruction from gene expression data applied to immune response during bacterial infectioin. *Bioinformatics*, 21(8):1626–1634, 2005.

128. A. Arkin, P. Shen, and J. Ross. A test case of correlation metric construction of a reaction pathway from measurements. *Science*, 277:1275–1279, 1997.

129. I. Ponzoni, F. Azuaje, J. Augusto, and D. Glass. Inferring adaptive regulation thresholds and association rules from gene expression data through combinatorial optimization learning. *IEEE/ACM Trans. Comp. Biol. Bioinformatics*, 4(Suppl. 4):624–634, 2007.

130. B. Schölkopf and A. J. Smola. *Learning with Kernels*. MIT Press, Cambridge, MA, 2002.

131. I. Guyon, J. Weston, S. Barnhill, and V. Vapnik. Gene selection for cancer classification using support vector machines. *Machine Learning*, 46:389–422, 2002.

PART I

TEXT MINING AND APPLICATION
TO BIOLOGICAL DATA

CHAPTER 37

CURRENT METHODOLOGIES FOR BIOMEDICAL NAMED ENTITY RECOGNITION

DAVID CAMPOS, SÉRGIO MATOS, and JOSÉ LUÍS OLIVEIRA

DETI/IEETA, University of Aveiro, Aveiro, Portugal

37.1 INTRODUCTION

With an overwhelming amount of biomedical knowledge recorded in texts, there is high research interest in techniques that can identify, extract, manage, integrate, and exploit this knowledge. *Text mining* (TM) is the field of *data mining* (DM) that deals with those requirements by deriving high-quality information from text. In the past few years, there has been an explosion of research papers on text mining for biomedical literature. The primary goal of text mining is to retrieve knowledge that is hidden in text and to present it in a concise and simple form to the final users. To achieve this objective, two main directions of research can be defined:

- *Information Extraction* (IE)   Extract instances of predefined categories from unstructured data, building a structured and unambiguous representation of the entities and the relations between them [1].
- *Information Retrieval* (IR)   Representation, storage, organization, and access to information items, providing easy access to the information in which the final user is interested [2].

IE and its several methods were introduced by the *message understanding conference* (MUCs), defining the several tasks that need to be performed in order to accomplish the IE idea and goals successfully:

- *Named Entity Recognition* (NER)   Identify chunks of text as specific entity names, such as genes/proteins and diseases.
- *Normalization and Disambiguation*   Associate a unique meaning to a concept (e.g., "June" could refer to a person's name, a calendar month, or a gene).

Biological Knowledge Discovery Handbook: Preprocessing, Mining, and Postprocessing of Biological Data, First Edition. Edited by Mourad Elloumi and Albert Y. Zomaya.

- *Relation Extraction*   Extract relations between concepts (e.g., considering the entities "Barack Obama" and "USA," the relation "President Barack Obama, USA" should be extracted if it is present on text in some manner).
- *Summarization*   Extract and compile main ideas of a text based on a specific goal.
- *Classification*   Identify prime themes of a text (e.g., sports, politics, and arts).

NER is one of the most important tasks, since the following IE steps (e.g., relation extraction) will be performed using the names provided by it. However, biomedical documents (such as articles, books, and reports) present several challenges that make the application of these techniques even harder. The main challenge is related with terminology, due to the complexity of the used terms for biomedical entities and processes [3, 4]:

- *Nonstandardized Naming Convention*   An entity name could be found in various spelling forms (e.g., "*N*-acetylcysteine," "*N*-acetyl-cysteine," and "NAcetylCysteine").
- *Ambiguous Names*   A same name could be related with more than one entity, depending on the text context.
- *Abbreviations*   Biomedical abbreviations are frequently used (e.g., "TCF" may refer to "T cell factor" or to "tissue culture fluid").
- *Descriptive Naming Convention*   Many entity names are descriptive, which makes its recognition a complex task (e.g., "normal thymic epithelial cells").
- *Conjunction and Disjunction*   Two or more entity names sharing one head noun (e.g., "91 and 84 kDa proteins" refers to "91 kDa protein" and "84 kDa protein").
- *Nested Names*   One name may occur within a longer name as well as occur independently (e.g., "T cell" is nested within "nuclear factor of activated T cells family protein").
- *Names of Newly Discovered Entities*   There is an overwhelming growth rate and constant discovery of novel biomedical entities, which takes time to register in curated nomenclatures.

There are several approaches to implement automated NER systems, including rule-based, dictionary-based, machine learning–based, and hybrid approaches. The global work flow of a NER system, presented in Figure 37.1, is composed of the following:

- *Corpus*   Collection of (usually related) texts.
- *Preprocessing*   Perform tasks over natural language texts to simplify the recognition process.
- *NER*   Recognizes specific entity names.
- *Postprocessing*   Refinement of already recognized names, solving problems of the recognition process or extending it to recognize more entity names.
- *Entity Names*   Recognized names from text.

Since the several NER solutions have many steps and/or resources in common, we will describe them first in Section 37.2 in order to better understand the global work flow and the most basic methods. The rest of the chapter is organized as follows. Sections 37.3, 37.4, and 37.5 present the steps necessary to implement solutions using dictionaries and machine

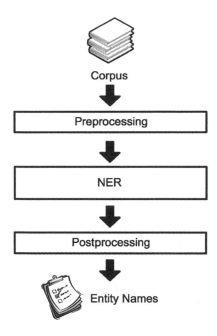

FIGURE 37.1 Global work flow of NER system.

learning and hybrid approaches, respectively. In Section 37.6, we present some practical examples for each approach. Finally, Section 37.7 presents some concluding remarks.

37.2 PRELIMINARIES

37.2.1 Corpora

A *corpus* is a set of text documents that usually contains annotated entity names of one or several categories for use in development and evaluation. The annotation procedure is usually performed by human experts of the entities' domain following specific and detailed guidelines. An annotated corpus allows to obtain performance results, which could be used to compare distinct solutions to the same problem. On the other hand, the annotated names can also be used to train machine learning–based solutions. There are several publicly available corpora that can be used, such as GENETAG [5], GENIA [6], PennBioIE [7], and BioNLP-Corpora [8].

37.2.2 Tokenization

In order for NER tasks to be accomplished by computerized systems in an effective manner, it is necessary to divide natural language texts into meaningful units, called *tokens*. A token is a group of characters that is categorized according to a set of rules. For instance, NUMBER, COMMA, and DOT are examples of token categories. The process of breaking up a text into its constituent tokens is known as *tokenization*. It is one of the most important tasks of the whole NER work flow, since all the following tasks will be based on tokens resulting from this process. Thus, several tokenization solutions were developed for several domains and languages. For instance, OpenNLP [9] has models for biomedical documents in several languages, and SPECIALIST NLP [10] also supports biomedical text.

37.2.3 Word Normalization

In most cases, morphological variants of words have similar semantic interpretations, which can be considered as equivalent. For this reason, several solutions are used to group together the different inflected forms of a word, so they can be analyzed as a single item. During this process, the terms of the natural language texts are represented by headwords rather than the original words. Two distinct approaches to this problem are used, *stemming* and *lemmatization*. The basic idea of *stemming* is to find the prefix that is common to all variations of the term. For example, the words "happy," "happiness," "happier," and "happiest" should be represented by the term "happ," which is called the *stem*. On the other hand, *lemmatization* is a more robust method, because it finds the root term of the variant word. In the previous example, the root word should be "happy," which in this case is called *lemma*.

37.2.4 Stopwords

One of the most used techniques is the deletion of words that are already known to be noninformative to the recognition and normalization processes, reducing the dictionary and corpus sizes. Examples of such words in English are "be," "can," "therefore," and "which" [11].

37.2.5 Evaluation

After the system's development, it is necessary to calculate measures that provide precise and global feedback about the application's behavior. To obtain those measures, the predictions must be classified as follows:

- *True Positive* (TP)   The chunk of text is an entity name and it was predicted as entity name.
- *True Negative* (TN)   The chunk of text is not an entity name and it was not predicted as entity name.
- *False Positive* (FP)   The chunk of text is not an entity name but it was predicted as an entity name.
- *False Negative* (FN)   The chunk of text is an entity name but it was not predicted as an entity name.

After obtaining the numbers of correct and wrong predictions, three measures are commonly used to reflect the system's behavior: *precision*, *recall*, and *F-measure*. These measures can assume values between 0 (worst performance) and 1 (best performance). Precision measures the ability of a system to present only relevant items, and it is formulated as follows:

$$\text{Precision} = \frac{\text{relevant items retrieved}}{\text{total items retrieved}} = \frac{\text{TP}}{\text{TP} + \text{FP}} \qquad (37.1)$$

Recall measures the ability of a system to present all relevant items, and it is formulated as follows:

$$\text{Recall} = \frac{\text{relevant items retrieved}}{\text{relevant items in collection}} = \frac{\text{TP}}{\text{TP} + \text{FN}} \tag{37.2}$$

Finally, the *F*-measure is the harmonic mean of the precision and recall. The balanced *F*-measure is most commonly used and is formulated as follows:

$$F\text{-measure} = 2\frac{\text{precision} \times \text{recall}}{\text{precision} + \text{recall}} \tag{37.3}$$

The several performance measures could be obtained using different matching techniques against the human annotated data in order to consider an annotation as correct with more or less precision. This is useful since some tasks that are performed after NER (e.g., relation extraction) could be performed correctly even if imprecise annotations are provided. Moreover, we can better understand the behavior of the systems regarding its flexibility and output annotations.

At this point, we already understand how algorithms deal with natural language texts as input data and how to evaluate the systems' performance. The following sections describe the existing approaches to develop NER and normalization solutions, presenting and explaining the core techniques accompanied with examples of some existent systems.

37.3 DICTIONARY-BASED APPROACHES

In dictionary-based approaches, it is necessary to perform the matching between the entries of a well-curated and complete dictionary with the chunks of text. Afterward, the successful matches will be precisely related with one or several identifiers, which will give the entity statute to the chunk of text. Figure 37.2 presents the core components and tasks in dictionary-based approaches, illustrating the relations between them:

- *Databases*   Domain knowledge.
- *Dictionary*   A combination of several databases to collect the maximum number of entity names and identifiers as possible.
- *Preprocessing*   Perform tasks on natural language texts and the dictionary to simplify the recognition process.
- *String Searching and Matching*   Perform string matching between dictionary entries and text.
- *Postprocessing*   Refinement of already matched names, resolution of abbreviations, and exploitation of multiple occurrences of the same entity within the text.
- *Entity Names and Identifiers*   Recognized names and respective unique identifiers.

37.3.1 Databases

The dictionary is the core component of these approaches, since the matches with the text are performed using the biomedical names contained on it. The *Unified Medical Language System* (UMLS) is a terminology resource that intends to create a biomedical vocabulary standard [12]. This standard approach works for entities that have well-defined naming

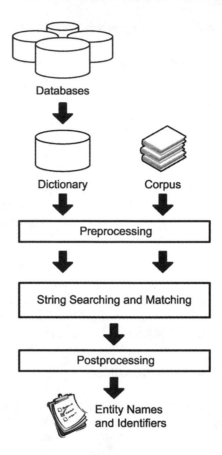

FIGURE 37.2 Global work flow of dictionary-based NER system.

standards (e.g., diseases). However, some entities do not follow strictly defined standards (e.g., genes/proteins and chemicals), which makes the creation of such standards a complex task. Consequently, it is necessary to aggregate various databases on a single resource in order to collect the largest amount of entity names as possible. Several databases already provide information regarding specific entities, for instance, UniProt [13] (proteins), Entrez Gene [14] (genes), KEGG [15] (pathways), PharmGKB [16] (drugs), and OMIM [17] (diseases). The combination of resources is not a trivial task, since each one uses their own identifiers. However, there are various projects that already combine a wide set of databases, such as BioThesaurus [18], LexEBI [19], and GeNS [20].

Despite the wide set of publicly available databases, it is possible to have synonyms that will not be included in the dictionary. Many names are simple orthographic variants of each other [21], and most of these variants can be generated using simple rules, for instance, replacing spaces by hyphens or removing spaces or hyphens [22].

37.3.2 String Matching

The problems encountered on biomedical names demand the usage of sophisticated methods to compare dictionary and text names. Several solutions are used to solve this problem:

exact, *approximate*, and *machine learning (ML)–based matching*. Exact matching tries to find names in text that are exactly the same in the dictionary. Examples of algorithms to perform exact matching efficiently are Aho-Corasick [23], Knuth-Morris-Pratt [24], and Boyer-Moore [25]. On the other hand, approximate matching solutions calculate a value that reflects the similarity between two names (the name in the dictionary and the chunk of text), and then only the matches with a similarity value higher than a predefined threshold will be accepted as names. Examples of approximate solutions are *Levenshtein distance* (also known as *edit distance*) [26], Jaro-Winkler [27], and SoftTFIDF [28]. Finally, ML approaches could be used to induce string similarity from actual examples of string pairs or to combine other string similarity measures.

37.3.3 String Searching

During the matching process, it is necessary to perform a complete match between the entries on the dictionary and the text. Considering a dictionary with thousands of entries and a text with thousands of chunks to be matched, if this process is performed in a brute-force manner, it would take a large amount of time to be processed, becoming completely impracticable. To solve this problem, the basic idea is to organize the several strings on a structure that will streamline the searching process, establishing relations between substrings that are common to specific strings. Thus, to find a specific string, it is necessary to navigate through the several substrings to find the desired object. Trie [29], Suffix Array [30], and PATRICIA Tree [31] are examples of techniques that apply this idea.

37.3.4 Postprocessing

After performing the recognition step using dictionaries, there may remain some entity names that were not recognized with success. For instance, authors of biomedical papers often introduce an abbreviation for an entity by using a format similar to "antilymphocyte globulin (ALG)" or "ALG (antilymphocyte globulin)." Due to the small number of characters, abbreviations are normally discarded during the matching process; otherwise a large amount of false recognitions would appear in the results. Thus, it is common to perform an abbreviation resolution step which can be accomplished using a simple algorithm [32, 33] with high degree of accuracy, which then triggers additional processing to ensure that both mentions are recognized.

During the matching process, it is common that a match associates a name with multiple entity identifiers. This occurs when the dictionary contains very similar names that refer to distinct protein identifiers or even when a unique name is related with multiple identifiers, varying with the context (e.g., different species). To solve this problem, a disambiguation/normalization step is performed to resolve ambiguous names to the correct unique identifiers. There are several approaches to solve this problem. The first and obvious solution is to ignore all ambiguous terms. If a name could be related to more than one unique identifier, it should be ignored, removing any chances of ambiguity. However, the text context of the name could provide useful information to disambiguate the term. Another solution is based in two assumptions [22]: The ambiguous terms are synonyms of other nonambiguous terms, and authors should provide sufficient context for readers to resolve ambiguous terms. The first step of this solution is to collect the concepts that are related with the ambiguous name. Afterward, if any of those concepts appear in the text that contains the name, the ambiguous term is assigned with the identifier of the referred concept. If more than one concept appears on the text, the concept should be chosen randomly from the set of concepts that appear on the context (this is very rare). The third approach is more robust, using external information to detect the protein identifier of the ambiguous name [34–36]. Each gene/protein has a large amount of related information on biomedical resources (e.g., databases and ontologies), such as diseases, functions, tissues, mutations, and domains. For each identifier that is candidate to the ambiguous name, the method will find all such information that is related with the gene/protein in the text and then select the identifier with the highest likelihood.

During the disambiguation process, it is important to keep in mind that one gene could be associated with more than one species. Thus, the disambiguation technique must collect contextual information needed to distinguish between the several species, which is usually performed with external biomedical resources. Another approach to this problem is to develop a system dedicated to resolve species ambiguity. Wang and Matthews [37] present a rule- and ML-based system to resolve species ambiguity in mentions of biomedical named entities. On the other hand, Gerner et al. [38] present a dictionary-based approach to resolve species ambiguity. These solutions confirm the success of this methodology by improving the performance of baseline systems for term identification.

In the end of this process, each extracted name should be related with a unique identifier, creating valuable information from unstructured data.

37.3.5 Related Work

There are several works using the previously described techniques. Peregrine [39] is a gene/protein normalization system that is used in the EU-ADR European Project (FP7-ICT-2007-215847), collecting gene/protein names that are common to a drug–disease pair, in order to detect adverse drug reactions earlier. This solution uses its own dictionary, combining information from five distinct databases: Genew [40], GDB [41], Entrez Gene [14], OMIM [17], and Swiss-Prot [42]. The dictionary is extended through the generation of spelling variations and pruned using filters to remove highly ambiguous terms. It also uses a stemmer and the exact string-matching method.

The system described by Fang et al. [43] uses a dictionary that combines information from the HGNC, Entrez Gene, and Swiss-Prot databases. Ambiguous and noninformative words are removed, and a stemmer is applied to reduce the words representation. In the matching process, the TFIDF approximate string matching is used.

ProMiner [44] is a well-known and complete gene name recognition system. Employing a strict dictionary-based approach, it heavily relies on the (manual) curation and quality of its gene dictionaries. However, because of ProMiner's proprietary nature, many methodological and implementation issues remain hidden.

Finally, Tsuruoka and Tsujii [45] present a system using a dictionary that combines information from GenBank and Swiss-Prot. A variant generator is used to extend the dictionary's names, and noninformative words are not considered during the matching process. The Levenshtein approximate string-matching method is used to map text names with dictionary identifiers.

37.4 ML-BASED APPROACHES

With ML approaches, it is necessary to train a computational model to induce the characteristics of specific entity names. Usually, a supervised ML approach is followed, which

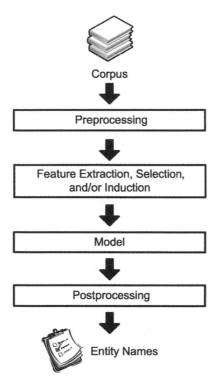

FIGURE 37.3 Global work flow of ML-based NER system.

requires corpora containing annotations of each entity mention. After training the model, the system is prepared to be applied to nonannotated texts, predicting what chunks of text are entity names. Figure 37.3 presents the core components and tasks that are used and performed on ML approaches, illustrating the relations between them:

- *Feature Extraction, Selection, and/or Induction*   Extract, select, and/or induce features from the tokens in order to be used by the model to predict entity names.
- *Model*   A set of rules that describe and distinguish data classes or concepts.
- *Postprocessing*   Refinement of already matched names and resolution of abbreviations.

37.4.1 Class Representation

In ML approaches, the identification of entity mentions is usually based on token-by-token classification that tags the tokens representing each recognized named entity. In order to train the models, it is therefore necessary to identify each token that is part of an entity name. This is achieved by using an encoding method that will give a tag to each word of the text. The simplest encoding is the IO encoding, which tags each token as either being in a particular named entity (tag I) or outside any entity (tag O). This encoding is defective because it cannot represent two entities next to each other, since there is no boundary tag. The BIO encoding is the de facto standard, and it extends the IO encoding solving the

TABLE 37.1   Class Specification of Sentence "Gamma Glutamyl Transpeptidase (GGTP) Activity in the Seminal Fluid"

Sentence	IO	BIO	BMEWO	BMEWO+
Gamma	I	B	B	B_GENE
glutamyl	I	I	M	M_GENE
transpeptidase	I	I	E	E_GENE
(	O	O	O	GENE_O_GENE
GGTP	I	B	W	W_GENE
)	O	O	O	GENE_O
activity	O	O	O	O
in	O	O	O	O
the	O	O	O	O
seminal	O	O	O	O
fluid	O	O	O	O

boundary problem. It subdivides the "in" tags as either being the beginning of the entity (tag B) or the continuation of the entity (tag I). The BMEWO encoding extends the BIO encoding by distinguishing the end of an entity (tag E) tokens from the middle entity tokens (tag M), and adding a new tag (W) for entities with only one token. Finally, the BMEWO+ encoding extends the BMEWO encoding by adding a local contextual behavior. Thus, if a gene/protein name is in the previous or following token, a substring (in this case GENE because only gene/protein names are recognized) should be concatenated to the tag of the current token. Table 37.1 shows an example of the application of the several encoding methods on a sample sentence.

37.4.2   Features

The features are the input of the ML method, which will use them to predict if a specific chunk of text is an entity name or not. In a data-mining problem, some of those features are already submitted as the input of the global work flow. However, in text mining it is necessary to extract these features from text. This process requires special attention, because it demands the definition a wide set of features that will reflect the special phenomena and linguistic characteristics of the naming conventions. In the end, each feature should assume the value 1 if it is present on the current token or 0 if it is not (Table 37.2).

When extracting features, it is crucial to understand how the chosen tokenizer works, because all features will be extracted from the tokens generated by it. This choice will make some features to be useful or not, depending on the information provided by them in the specific context. For instance, if the tokenizer splits words separated by a hyphen

TABLE 37.2   Illustration of Matrix of Features as Input of ML Technique

	Feature 1	Feature 2	$\cdots$	Feature m
Instance 1	1	1	$\cdots$	0
Instance 2	0	1	$\cdots$	0
$\vdots$	$\vdots$	$\vdots$	$\ddots$	$\vdots$
Instance n	0	0	$\cdots$	1

Note: Each vector defines the features present on an instance.

(e.g., tokenization of "nf-kappa" results in three tokens: "nf," "-," and "kappa"), it does not make sense to define a feature that will tag words containing hyphens. The set of extracted features can be divided into three distinct groups:

- *Internal Features*   Extracted from text using heuristics and methods to extract characteristics of the tokens (e.g., feature that describes if a word is capitalized or not).
- *External Features*   Defined using the text and external resources (e.g., matching with an external dictionary).
- *Local Context*   Establish relations between features and/or tokens to model local context.

The most basic internal feature is the token itself. However, in most cases, morphological variants of words have similar semantic interpretations which can be considered as equivalent. For this reason, stemming or lemmatization can be used to group together the different inflected forms of a word so that they can be analyzed as a single item. For instance, the system described in [46] applies lemmatization on its system while in [47] stemming is used.

Part-of-speech (POS) tags can also be used as internal features. POS tagging is the process of marking up the words in a text as corresponding to a particular grammatical category (such as noun, verb, or adjective) based on its definition and context. Example 37.1 presents a POS tagging sample where NN is a singular or mass noun, IN is a preposition or subordinating conjunction, DT is a determiner, and NNP is a singular proper noun.

Example 37.1 *POS Tagging*

> **Sentence**   "Translocation of the NF-kappaB transcription factor."
> **Result:**   [Translocation]/NN [of]/IN [the]/DT [NF-kappaB]/NNP [transcription]/NN [factor]/NN.

The contribution of POS tagging to more accurate systems was already demonstrated [3]. However, it depends on the used tool and corpus [3, 48]. There are several automated NER systems that use POS tags as features [3, 46, 49, 50] in order to better determine the boundaries of entity names. There are several tools to apply POS tags to texts, some of which have been developed and trained for biomedical documents, such as Genia Tagger [51], OpenNLP [9], and LingPipe [52].

In order to extend the POS tagging idea, shallow parsing could be used. It was proposed by Abney [53], and its aim is to divide a text in syntactically correlated parts of words, such as groups of nouns and verbs. This technique is used in several NER systems [47, 54], and its positive impact in the global system's performance has also been demonstrated [54]. Example 37.2 presents a shallow parsing example.

Example 37.2 *Shallow Parsing*

> **Sentence**   "He reckons the current account deficit will narrow to only 1.8billion in September."
> **Result**   [He]/NP [reckons]/VP [the current account deficit]/NP [will narrow]/VP [to]/PP [only 1.8billion]/NP [in]/PP [September]/NP.

TABLE 37.3   List of Most Common Orthographic Features

Feature	Example	Feature	Example	Feature	Example
InitCap	Kappa	SingleDigit	1	Percent	%
EndCap	kappaB	TwoDigit	12	OpenParen	(
AllCaps	DAV	ThreeDigit	123	CloseParen	)
Lowercase	kappa	MoreDigit	12345	Comma	,
LowAndCap	RalGDS	Hyphen	-	Dot	.
DigitsLettersSymbol	MEF-2	BackSlash	/	Apostrophe	'
SingleCap	U	OpenSquare	[	QuotationMark	"
TwoCap	US	CloseSquare	]	Star	*
ThreeCap	USS	Colon	:	Equal	=
MoreCap	USSR	SemiColon	;	Plus	+

Orthographic features are also extracted from text. Their purpose is to capture knowledge about word formation, helping in the detection of entity names. It has been widely used in many automated NER systems [3, 46, 49, 50]. For example, a word that starts with a capitalized character could indicate the existence of an entity name (e.g., in the protein name MyoD, the capitalized M indicates the start of the entity name). Table 37.3 lists the formation patterns that are commonly used [46, 48, 50], in decreasing order of priority.

In order to model common structures and/or subsequences of characters between several entity names, some morphological features can be used. This information is considered very important for terminology identification, and it has been widely used on automated NER systems [3, 48, 55]. To accomplish this goal, three distinct types of morphological features are considered: suffixes and prefixes, char n-grams, and morphological structure. Particular prefixes and suffixes could be used to distinguish entity names. For instance, suffixes like "ase," "ome," and "gen" frequently occur in gene/protein names [33]. If prefixes and suffixes of two, three, and four characters are used, for the token "Alkaline," the resulting prefixes are "Al," "Alk," and "Alka," and the extracted suffixes are "ne," "ine," and "line." A char n-gram is a subsequence of n characters from a given token. This feature type has an identical role to prefixes and suffixes. However, it also finds common subsequences of characters in the middle of tokens. Finally, it is also important to extract the token's structure. Kuo et al. [46] proposed a solution to generate a sequence of characters to reflect how letters and digits are organized in the token. However, this idea could be extended to support symbols too. Thus, three distinct types of structures could be considered:

- *Morphological Type I*   Replace sequence of digits by * (e.g., the structure of Abc1234 is expressed by Abc*).
- *Morphological Type II*   Replace each letter, digit and symbol by a morphological symbol (e.g., the structure of Abc-1234 is expressed by Aaa#1111).
- *Morphological Type III*   Replace each sequence of letters, digits, and symbols by a morphological symbol (e.g., the structure of Abc-1234 is expressed by a#1).

Regarding external features, it is common to use large dictionaries of entity names as features, indicating the presence of such names on tokens. Previous works have already demonstrated the advantage of using this technique (e.g., in the recognition of gene/protein names [55]). The idea is to match the dictionary entries with the natural language text.

However, stopwords must be ignored during this process, because words such as FOR, AT, TO, and OF are gene/protein names and stopwords at the same time. If they are used during the matching process, all the occurrences of those stopwords will be tagged as gene/protein names, which will decrease the matching accuracy dramatically. Example 37.2 illustrates how tokens are tagged as potential entity names.

Example 37.3 *Dictionary Matching*

> **Sentence** "Comparison with alkaline phosphatases and 5-nucleotidase."
>
> **Matches** "alkaline phosphatases" and "5-nucleotidase."
>
> **Result** Comparison with alkaline/DIC-B phosphatases/DIC-I and 5-nucleotidase/DIC-B.

There are specific concepts that co-occur frequently with entity mentions in texts and that could indicate the occurrence of entity names. Thus, it could be important to mark those tokens as relevant concepts to help in the recognition. For instance, during the recognition of gene/protein names, the following concepts can be considered:

- Nucleobase: e.g., "Adenine"
- Nucleoside: e.g., "Adenosine"
- Nucleotide: both long and short forms (e.g., "Adenosine monophosphate" and its short form "AMP")
- Nucleic acid: both long and short forms (e.g., "transfer RNA" and its short form "tRNA")
- Amino acid: both long and short forms (e.g., "Aspartic acid" and its short form "ASP")
- DNA/RNA sequence: e.g., "ACAAGATG"

Some verbs that occur frequently in the *Medical Literature Analysis and Retrieval System Online* (MEDLINE) have proven to be useful in the extraction of interactions between biomedical entities [56, 57]. Thus, those verbs and their derived forms could indicate the presence of entity names in the surrounding tokens. For instance, in the sentence "Selective stimulation of central alpha-autoreceptors," the nominalization "stimulation" points to the presence of the gene "alpha-autoreceptors." In other cases, those verbal forms could also make part of the entity name (e.g., "activation" in the protein name "gamma-interferon activation site"). Those cases demonstrate the importance of tagging those verbs as pointers to entity names. As a verbs resource, BioLexicon [19] could be used, which contains more than two million entries for text mining in the biomedical domain, including information about nouns, verbs, adjectives, and adverbs.

After defining both internal and external features, it is important to define a strategy to establish relations between the tokens and extracted features. To solve this problem, it is common to use a window of features. Thus, when analyzing a token, all the features of the previous and following tokens can be considered. During this process, the predicted classes of the preceding tokens could also be used (Figure 37.4 illustrates this idea). Remember that shallow parsing will also contribute to a better local context definition, establishing relations between the closest tokens that have the same syntactic type. However, it is possible to extend this idea, by linking tokens within a sentence independently of their proximity. This

	Token	Stem	POS	Orthographic	...	Predicted Class
position -2	alkaline	alkalin	JJ	Lowercase	...	B
position -1	phosphatase	phosphatas	NN	Lowercase	...	I
position 0	concentrations	concentr	NNS	Lowercase	...	N/A
position +1	were	were	VBD	Lowercase	...	N/A
position +2	essentially	essenti	RR	Lowercase	...	N/A

FIGURE 37.4 Window of features illustration using sample sentence "...alkaline phosphatase concentrations were essentially...."

is possible using grammatical relations which specify the links between the tokens in the sentence according to the results of a syntactic parsing of the text [58].

After extracting the features from text, usually a very large set of features is obtained, which will affect the speed of training the model and could also make the model overfit the training data. When overfitting occurs, the generated model's performance will drop dramatically when applied to a different data set. To solve this problem, it is important to select only the features that provide useful information for the recognition process, applying a filtering step. This technique is called *feature selection*, and it provides several advantages [59]: (a) avoids overfitting; (b) provides faster and more cost-effective models; and (c) provides a deeper insight into the underlying processes that generated the data. However, the advantages of feature selection come at a certain price, as the search for a subset of relevant features introduces an additional layer of complexity in the modeling task. There are works that already demonstrate the positive effect of feature selection. For instance, Hakenberg et al. [60] showed that, after removing 95% of the features, the prediction quality was practically not affected, and the time necessary to train the model dropped dramatically. Thus, different methodologies to apply feature selection have been proposed. Those techniques can be organized into three categories, depending on how they combine the feature selection search with the construction of the model:

- *Filter* Obtain the features' relevance by looking only at the intrinsic properties of the data. Those techniques treat the problem of finding a good feature subset independently of the model (e.g., information gain and Euclidean distance).
- *Wrapper* The model is used to find the best feature subset by training and testing the subset of features using the specific considered model (e.g., genetic algorithms).
- *Embedded* The search for the optimal subset of features is embedded in the classifier (e.g., decision trees).

The features extracted and selected so far are defined for each token, which already provide a lot of information to recognize entity names. However, it is possible that some informative features were not extracted. To solve this problem, it is possible to automatically extract features that provide useful information, a process called *feature induction*. It works by iteratively considering sets of candidate atomic and conjunction features created from the initially defined set of atomic features. Only candidates that provide useful information are included into the current set of features. As a consequence of this process, feature induction also prevents overfitting by not considering features that do not provide useful information. This technique is deeply related with the used model because the information provided by each feature varies from model to model. At first, an efficient algorithm to search for features was introduced [61] in order to increase the model's performance. This idea was applied to the whole sentence [62], describing it using a conditional exponential model. This idea was extended to *conditional random field* (CRFs) [63] in order to improve the learning efficiency. Later, the same method was applied to *support vector machines* (SVMs) [64]. Regarding NER systems, there are several works that already take advantage of the feature induction technique [46, 50, 65]. Moreover, the positive outcome of using typical feature extraction and induction techniques at the same time was already demonstrated [65].

37.4.3 Model

In ML techniques, a computer algorithm must induce specific patterns or rules from past experiences in order to develop an appropriate response to future data or describe the seen data in some meaningful way. The structure to support this knowledge is known as model, and it could be represented and obtained in several different manners. For a model to successfully learn a concept, it must be (a) descriptive (capture the training data), (b) predictive (generalize to unseen data), and (c) explanatory (provide plausible description of the concept to be learned). Research has demonstrated that it is extremely fruitful to model the behavior of complex systems as some form of a random process. Probabilistic models often show better accuracy and robustness against categorical models. Accordingly, several probabilistic models have turned out to be especially useful for the different tasks in extracting meaning from natural language texts. Those models can be organized in the following manner:

- *Supervised Learning* Generates a function that maps inputs to desired outputs. Examples are hidden Markov models (HMMs), maximum-entropy Markov models (MEMMs), CRF, and SVMs.
- *Semisupervised Learning* Combines both labeled and unlabeled examples to generate an appropriate function.

Along the time, several solutions were created to solve the challenges imposed by supervised learning. Currently, CRF is one of the models with more research interest, because it presents several advantages when compared to other models. At first, CRFs avoid the label bias problem [66], a weakness of MEMMs. On the other hand, CRFs also have advantage over HMMs, namely the fact that independence assumptions considered in HMMs can be relaxed because of the model's conditional nature. CRFs have also been shown to outperform both MEMMs and HMMs on a number of real-world sequence labeling tasks [66]. Regarding SVMs, an in-depth study [67] showed that when the two methods are compared using identical feature functions they do turn out to have quite close peak performance. However, SVMs may take a large amount of time to generate even the simplest models.

To better understand the internal functionality of a ML model, CRFs will be described in detail, since it is widely used and provide-consistent and positive results on NER. CRFs were first introduced by Lafferty et al. [66]. Assuming that we have an input sequence of observations (represented by X) and a state variable that needs to be inferred from the given observations (represented by Y), a CRF is a form of undirected graphical model that defines a single log-linear distribution over label sequences (Y) given a particular observation sequence (X). Figure 37.5 illustrates this idea.

This layout makes it possible to have efficient algorithms to train models in order to learn conditional distributions between Y_j and feature functions from training data. To accomplish

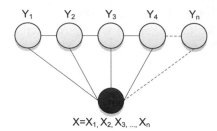

FIGURE 37.5   Graphical structure of CRFs for sequences. The variables corresponding to dark nodes are not generated by the model. Adapted from [68].

this, it is necessary to determine the probability of a given label sequence Y given X and consequently the most likely label. At first, the model assigns a numerical weight to each feature. Then those weights are combined to determine the probability of a certain value for Y_j. This probability is calculated as

$$p(y|x, \lambda) = \frac{1}{Z(x)} \exp \left(\sum_j \lambda_j F_j(y, x) \right) \tag{37.4}$$

where λ_j are parameters to be estimated from training data and indicate the informativeness of the respective feature, $Z(x)$ is a normalization factor, and

$$F_j(y, x) = \sum_{i=1}^{n} f_j(y_{i-1}, y_i, x, i) \tag{37.5}$$

where each $f_j(y_{i-1}, y_i, x, i)$ is either a state function $s(y_{i-1}, y_i, x, i)$ or a transition function $t(y_{i-1}, y_i, x, i)$.

37.4.4   Postprocessing

On ML solutions, it is also necessary to perform postprocessing techniques in order to remove recognition errors and recognize more entity names. Identical to dictionary-based approaches, it also necessary to perform abbreviation resolution, in order to recognize acronyms of entity names. Machine learning recognition generates several errors that could be easily corrected using simple rules or methods:

- Eliminate single punctuation marks (parenthesis, bracket, or quotation mark) on recognized entity names, which are clearly identified as mistakes made by the labeling engine [69].
- Extend incomplete names recognized by the ML procedure (e.g., only "p53" in "p53 mutant" was recognized) [70]. To accomplish this idea, a dictionary lookup solution could be used.
- Remove stopwords, for example, "by" and "or," from the recognized names which have been wrongly recognized as a part of the names [70].
- Other errors identified in the specific problem, which are dependent on the used tokenizer, ML model, and corpus.

37.5 HYBRID APPROACHES

As the number of features for ML systems increases to cover more phenomena in NER, the data sparseness problem becomes more serious. Since the approaches discussed above have their own advantages and limitations, there is a clear need for combining them for better performance and annotations. There are several approaches to harmonize annotations from different NER systems, such as:

- *Union*   Use all the results of the several models.
- *Intersection*   Use only the results that are common to the distinct systems.
- *Machine Learning*   Train a ML model to induce the final class from the results of the several models.

Several research works have already combined distinct types of NER systems to obtain better results. A research work described in [3] uses a HMM as the ML technique and combines it with a set of rules to deal with cascaded entity names (e.g., "⟨RNA⟩⟨DNA⟩CIITA⟨/DNA⟩ mRNA⟨/RNA⟩"). In [33] an ensemble of classifiers with one SVM and two HMMs is used combined with a set of rules to solve some recognition problems and a dictionary matching to increase the system recall. In [71] a system using three SVMs and a dictionary matching step is presented. The results from the four NER tasks are combined using another SVM. Some rules are used to remove inconsistency problems from the corpus and to solve problems from the recognition process. Finally, Campos et al. [72] present a harmonization solution focused on delivering reliable annotation results across various annotated corpora, which is an important contribution toward homogeneous annotation of MEDLINE documents. Such a task is performed through a CRF model that combines annotations from four normalization solutions using domain knowledge provided by annotated data from four heterogeneous and manually annotated corpora.

The solutions presented above confirm the advantages of combining several approaches which should be considered on any NER system that intends to achieve high-performance results.

37.6 USE CASES

To consolidate the knowledge acquired in the previous sections, this section presents one practical example for each approach in order to demonstrate how the several steps could be implemented. The final goal of this experiment is to automatically recognize gene/protein names. To accomplish this, the corpus of the BioCreative II gene mention challenge [73] will be used. This corpus contains contains 20,000 sentences extracted from MEDLINE abstracts divided into 15,000 sentences for training and 5000 for testing. It contains annotations of proteins, DNAs, and RNAs that were performed by experts from biochemistry, genetics, and molecular biology. This corpus is not focused on any specific biomedical domain. The organizers of the challenge also provided an evaluation script in order to obtain measures regarding exact and nested (alternative names provided by human annotators) matching.

The examples presented in this section are illustrated by an implementation in Java.

37.6.1 Dictionary Based

Instead of developing the string *searching* and *matching* algorithms, we decided to use a Java library that already contains stable implementations of those techniques. Lingpipe [52] is a framework that enhances the development of applications in computer linguistics. It allows to perform *exact string matching* using the Aho-Corasick algorithm [23], which is fast and efficient.

The first step in the implementation of any dictionary-based approach (Figure 37.6) is the construction of the dictionary. In this experiment, we used BioThesaurus [18], which aggregates several databases of gene/protein names. To integrate the heterogeneous resources, the developers used the Uniprot [13] identifier to normalize the names. Thus, since the used corpus is focused on human entity names, we can filter the dictionary to this specific goal. Accordingly, we implemented an algorithm to accept only names related with the identifiers of human gene/protein names. Afterward, we specified several orthographic rules (Table 37.4) to generate name variants in order to cover a wider set of names.

After collecting the names and their variants, we need to remove the stopwords from the dictionary. As for gene/protein names, we also need to collect a wide set of noninformative

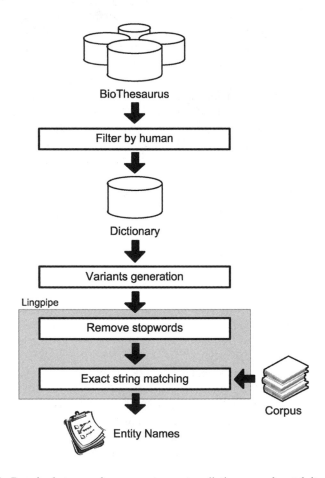

FIGURE 37.6   Required steps and resources to create a dictionary and match it with the corpus.

TABLE 37.4   Rules Used to Generate Orthographic Variants of Gene/Protein Names

Description	Example
Replace spaces by hyphens and vice-versa	A B → A-B
Remove spaces	A B → AB
Remove hyphens	A-B → AB
Insert hyphen between letter–digit sequence	AB12 → AB-12
Replace Roman by Arabic numbers	A IV → A 4
Replace Roman by Arabic numbers using 1 instead of I	A 1V → A 4
Replace Arabic numbers by correspondent Greek letters	A 1 → A alpha
Add prefix h to symbols	AB → hAB
Add suffix p to symbols	AB → ABp

names in order to remove as much false positives as possible. Pubmed provides a list of stopwords [11] for biomedical documents. However, this is not enough to clean our lexicon. After some analysis, we concluded that the dictionary contains some species and biomedical terms which were producing a large amount of incorrect annotations. Consequently, we used BioLexicon [19], a biomedical terminological resource that contains this information, to extend the stopword list. Afterward, the stopwords were ignored from the dictionary during the loading process, following a similar technique such as the exact matching with gene/protein names. This process is presented in the following code snippet, which presents the necessary steps to load a dictionary using Lingpipe [52], ignoring the stopwords through the isStopword method. Both gene/protein names and stopword matching are performed using an ExactDictionaryChunker, which is case insensitive and returns only the larger matched chunk of text:

```
// Load dictionary
MapDictionary<String> dictionary = new MapDictionary<String>();
try {
    BufferedReader br = new BufferedReader(new InputStreamReader(
    new FileInputStream(dictionaryFile)));
    String line;
    while ((line = br.readLine()) != null) {
        ArrayList<String> vars = Variation.getVariations(line);
        vars.add(line);
        for (String v : vars) {
            if (v.length() < 3)
                continue;
            if (!isStopword(v))
                dictionary.addEntry(
                new DictionaryEntry<String>(v, "PRGE", 1.0));
        }
    br.close();
} catch (IOException ex) {
    throw new DictionaryException("There was an error
    reading the dictionary file.", ex);
}
// Initialize exact dictionary matcher
ExactDictionaryChunker dictionaryChunker = new ExactDictionaryChunker(
dictionary, IndoEuropeanTokenizerFactory.INSTANCE, false, false);
```

TABLE 37.5   Results Achieved by Dictionary-Based Approach

TP	FP	FN	Precision	Recall	F-Measure
4255	2182	2076	66.10%	67.20%	66.65%

The matching process and output generation are performed using the dictionary chunker, which returns a list of recognized names. Afterward, we need to get each match and generate the desired output. Such a process is performed using the following code snippet:

```
Chunking chunking = dictionaryChunker.chunk(sentence);
for (Chunk chunk : chunking.chunkSet()) {
  int start = chunk.start();
  int end = chunk.end();
  String type = chunk.type();
  double score = chunk.score();
  String entityName = sentence.substring(start, end);
  // Process name to produce the desired output
  // ...
}
```

In the end, the annotations were exported into a file following the format required by the challenge evaluation script. Considering the simplicity of the presented solution, the dictionary-based approach presents reasonable results (Table 37.5).

37.6.2   Machine Learning Based

The ML based solution was implemented using MALLET [74], a Java frame work for statistical natural language processing. It provides a well-structured workflow that supports the several steps of ML-based applications, such as data processing, feature definition/extraction, models (e.g., CRF), and evaluation. Additionally, it also supports the easy integration of external tools, which is crucial when developing tools focused on the biomedical domain. Our solution is based on CRFs, using a simple set of features and postprocessing module. Figure 37.7 presents the steps and resources required to implement our system. At first, we used the GENIA Tagger tool [51] to perform tokenization, lemmatization, and POS tagging. Afterward, it was necessary to convert the data to a format that can be processed by MALLET. This format follows a CoNNL-like [75] structure, which has one token per line with the correspondent features and label separated by white spaces. In this experiment, the label-tagging process follows the BIO format.

After converting the data, our final CoNNL file contains the label, lemma, and POS tag for each token. The definition of the remaining features is performed using MALLET's feature definition/extraction capabilities. Our final feature set contains orthographic features (Table 37.3), morphological (suffix, prefix, and char n-grams of two, three, and four characters), Greek letter tagging, Roman number tagging, gene/protein dictionary matching, and a $\{-3, 3\}$ window of features. The following code snippet shows some examples of feature definition in MALLET:

```
ArrayList<Pipe> pipe = new ArrayList<Pipe>();
pipe.add(new GeniaSentence2TokenSequence());
pipe.add(new RegexMatches("Hyphen", Pattern.compile("[-]")));
pipe.add(new TokenTextCharNGrams("CHARNGRAM=", new int[]{2, 3, 4}));
```

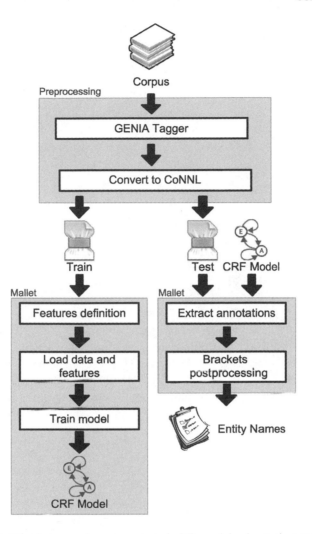

FIGURE 37.7 Required steps and resources to train ML model using train corpus and to extract annotations of test corpus using trained model.

```
pipe.add(new TokenTextCharSuffix("2SUFFIX=", 2));
pipe.add(new FeaturesInWindow("WINDOW\_WORD=", -3, 3,
Pattern.compile("WORD=.*"), true));
pipe.add(new TokenSequence2FeatureVectorSequence(true, true));
Pipe p = new SerialPipes(pipe);
```

With the feature set defined and the data in the desired format, we are able to load the data into MALLET's internal structure. During this process, MALLET considers that each sentence is an instance to train the model. In the following code snippet, we show how to load the data from the CoNNL file:

```
InstanceList trainingData = new InstanceList(p);
GZIPInputStream gzipInputStream = new GZIPInputStream(
new FileInputStream(fileName));
```

```
InputStreamReader reader = new InputStreamReader(gzipInputStream);
LineGroupIterator lgi = new LineGroupIterator(reader,
Pattern.compile("\^\$"), true);
trainingData.addThruPipe(lgi);
```

With the training data (15,000 sentences) and all its features processed and loaded, we can train the CRF model, which could take some time depending on computer characteristics. The following code snippet shows how this task is performed in MALLET:

```
// Initialize CRF
CRF crf = new CRF(trainingData.getPipe(), null);
crf.addFullyConnectedStatesForLabels();
crf.setWeightsDimensionAsIn(trainingData, true);

// Perform training with threads
int numThreads = 4;
CRFTrainerByThreadedLabelLikelihood crfTrainer = new
CRFTrainerByThreadedLabelLikelihood(crf, numThreads);
crfTrainer.train(trainingData);
crfTrainer.shutdown();
// Save model
crf.write(new File(modelFile));
```

At this point, the CRF model is trained and saved into a file, which allows future usage to automatically recognize gene/protein names. Thus, we are able to annotate the testing data (5000 sentences). To accomplish this task, we need to load the trained model, load the testing data, and obtain the predictions for each sentence:

```
// Load Model
CRF crf = CRFBase.loadCRF(modelFile);
// Load Test Data
InstanceList testingData = Corpus.getMalletInstances(crf.getInputPipe(),
connlFile);
// Initialize transducer
NoopTransducerTrainer crfTrainer = new NoopTransducerTrainer(crf);
// Get predictions for test data
for (Instance i : testingData) {
    Sequence input = (Sequence) i.getData();
    Transducer tran = crfTrainer.getTransducer();
    Sequence predOutput = tran.transduce(input);
    //Process predictions to produce the desired output
}
```

Before generating the output based on the provided predictions, we intend to solve some prediction mistakes by implementing a postprocessing module. In this case, we developed a simple script to correct brackets (round, square, and curly):

- *Closing Bracket in Beginning*   Remove bracket.
- *Opening Bracket in End*   Remove bracket.
- *Missing Closing Bracket*   Add closing bracket to the end or before the next opening bracket.
- *Missing Opening Bracket*   Add opening bracket to the beginning or after the previous closing bracket.

TABLE 37.6   Results Achieved by ML-Based Approach

TP	FP	FN	Precision	Recall	F-Measure
5074	740	1257	87.27%	80.15%	83.56%

After exporting the annotations into a file, we can run the evaluation script and obtain the performance results, which are presented in Table 37.6. The ML-based solution presents considerably better results than the dictionary based despite the simple set of features.

37.6.3 Hybrid

Since two different NER approaches were already implemented, we can use them to develop a hybrid solution. Thus, two different methods were defined to combine the annotations provided by the two systems (Figure 37.8):

- *Union*   Collect all the annotations provided by the two NER solutions. When different annotations are provided to the same chunk of text, the one that covers a larger amount of text is chosen, which reflects the union concept.
- *Intersection*   Collect only the annotations provided by the two systems to the same chunk of text. When different annotations are provided to the same chunk of text, the one that covers a smaller amount of text is chosen, which reflects the intersection concept.

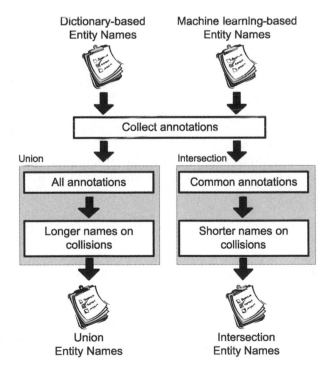

FIGURE 37.8   Required steps to combine two NER solutions using union and intersection.

TABLE 37.7   Results Achieved by Two Hybrid Approaches

	TP	FP	FN	Precision	Recall	F-Measure
Union	5524	2379	807	69.90%	87.25%	77.62%
Intersection	2646	96	3685	96.50%	41.80%	58.33%

Analyzing some state-of-the-art hybrid approaches, we can argue that the successful combination of several NER solutions is dependent on the systems' characteristics and performance:

- The systems should have similar performance between each other.
- The systems should provide heterogeneous annotations.

Both requirements are not fulfilled in our experiment, since the performance results are quite different (66.65% and 83.56% of F-measure), and the annotation heterogeneity is dubious, considering that the lexicon used in the dictionary-based approach is also used as features of the ML-based solution. Nevertheless, the two hybrid solutions provide interesting results (Table 37.7), reflecting the main goal of such approaches. The intersection method presents a very high precision (96.50%), providing only 96 wrong predictions. This high precision is a consequence of the mandatory agreement between the two systems. On the other hand, union presents a very high recall, where only 807 correct annotations were not recognized.

37.7 CONCLUSION

To choose a strategy to implement an NER system, it is important to study the final goal, the context where such a system should be applied, and the available resources. Rule-based solutions require intensive human efforts in order to create the specific rules for each category of entity names. However, the generated rules are too specific, being focused on recognizing entity names on a specific corpus. When these rules are used in a different context, the overall performance falls and fewer entities are correctly recognized. Consequently, rule-based solutions are usually used as pre- or postprocessing tasks of other approaches. This solution does not require any resources, but the required effort and NLP knowledge is not reflected in the achieved results.

Dictionary-based solutions present better results than rule-based approaches but generally worse than ML-based. Such solutions require the construction of a lexicon. Usually, dictionaries are already publicly available. However, if the subdomain is quite new or a different language is used, there are no lexicons available, which could make the implementation of this approach a difficult task. One big advantage of this solution is the direct access to curated identifiers, which confirms the entity by performing normalization at the same time. Nevertheless, this solution has two main problems. The large number of false recognitions caused by entities with short names is a serious drawback. This can be solved by discarding short names from the dictionary, but those entities will never be identified. The other problem is related to the existence of spelling variations, which can be solved using approximate string-matching techniques [76].

ML-based solutions present the best results. However, such solutions are deeply dependent on annotated corpora, which is hard and expensive to obtain. If annotated corpora for such entities is not available, the development of ML solutions is compromised. Nevertheless, this approach tries to solve the dictionary-based problems, recognizing new spelling variations of an entity name. ML solutions do not provide direct ID information of recognized entities from curated resources. This problem can be solved using a dictionary in an extra step in order to link the recognized names to the corresponding entries in the dictionary.

Finally, hybrid approaches are used to collect the annotation heterogeneity provided by different systems. The usability of such solutions is directly dependent on the used systems since the harmonization procedure could be performed using only the output annotation. In the end, if the used systems provide different types of annotations and have similar performance results, hybrid solutions usually present better results.

REFERENCES

1. K. Franzén, G. Eriksson, F. Olsson, L. Asker, P. Lidén, and J. Cöster. Protein names and how to find them. *Int. J. Med. Inform.*, 67:49–61, Dec. 2002.
2. R. Baeza-Yates et al. *Modern Information Retrieval*. Addison-Wesley, Reading, MA, 1999.
3. G. Zhou, J. Zhang, J. Su, D. Shen, and C. Tan. Recognizing names in biomedical texts: A machine learning approach. *Bioinformatics*, 20(7).1178–1190, 2004.
4. S. Ananiadou and J. McNaught. *Text Mining for Biology and Biomedicine*. Artech House, 2006.
5. L. Tanabe, N. Xie, L. Thom, W. Matten, and W. Wilbur. GENETAG: A tagged corpus for gene/protein named entity recognition. *BMC Bioinformatics*, 6(Suppl. 1):S3, 2005.
6. J. Kim, T. Ohta, Y. Tateisi, and J. Tsujii. GENIA corpus—a semantically annotated corpus for bio-textmining. *Bioinformatics-Oxford*, 19(1):180–182, 2003.
7. HLT-NAACL 2004 Workshop: Biolink 2004, Linking Biological Literature, Ontologies and Databases, pp. 61–68. Association for Computational Linguistics.
8. H. Johnson, W. Baumgartner, M. Krallinger, K. Cohen, and L. Hunter. Corpus refactoring: A feasibility study. *J. Biomed. Discov. Collabor.*, 2(1):4, 2007.
9. J. Baldridge, T. Morton, and G. Bierner. openNLP Package, May 2011. http://opennlp.apache.org.
10. A. C. Browne, A. T. McCray, and S. Srinivasan. The SPECIALIST LEXICON. Technical Report. Lister Hill National Center for Biomedical Communications, National Library of Medicine, 2000.
11. Bethesda: National Center for Biotechnology Information. PubMed Help [Internet]. Available: http://www.ncbi.nlm.nih.gov/books/NBK3827/, 2012.
12. O. Bodenreider. The unified medical language system (UMLS): Integrating biomedical terminology. *Nucleic Acids Res.*, 32(Suppl. 1):D267, 2004.
13. A. Bairoch et al. The universal protein resource (uniprot). *Nucleic Acids Res.*, 33(Suppl. 1):D154, 2005.
14. D. Maglott, J. Ostell, K. Pruitt, and T. Tatusova. Entrez gene: Gene-centered information at ncbi. *Nucleic Acids Res.*, 33(Suppl. 1):D54, 2005.
15. M. Kanehisa and S. Goto. Kegg: Kyoto encyclopedia of genes and genomes. *Nucleic Acids Res.*, 28(1):27, 2000.
16. M. Hewett, D. Oliver, D. Rubin, K. Easton, J. Stuart, R. Altman, and T. Klein. Pharmgkb: The pharmacogenetics knowledge base. *Nucleic Acids Res.*, 30(1):163, 2002.

17. A. Hamosh, A. Scott, J. Amberger, C. Bocchini, and V. McKusick. Online mendelian inheritance in man (omim), a knowledgebase of human genes and genetic disorders. *Nucleic Acids Res.*, 33(Suppl. 1):D514, 2005.

18. H. Liu, Z.-Z. Hu, J. Zhang, and C. H. Wu. Biothesaurus: A web-based thesaurus of protein and gene names. *Bioinformatics*, 22(1):103–105, 2006.

19. Y. Sasaki, S. Montemagni, P. Pezik, D. Rebholz-Schuhmann, J. McNaught, and S. Ananiadou. Biolexicon: A lexical resource for the biology domain. In *Proc. of the Third International Symposium on Semantic Mining in Biomedicine (SMBM 2008)*, Vol. 3, 2008.

20. J. Arrais, J. E. Pereira, J. Fernandes, and J. L. Oliveira. Gens: A biological data integration platform. In *World Acad. Sci. Eng. Technol.*, 58:850–855, 2009.

21. A. M. Cohen, W. R. Hersh, C. Dubay, and K. A. Spackman. Using co-occurrence network structure to extract synonymous gene and protein names from medline abstracts. *BMC Bioinformatics*, 6:103, 2005.

22. A. M. Cohen. Unsupervised gene/protein named entity normalization using automatically extracted dictionaries. In *Proceedings of the ACL-ISMB Workshop on Linking Biological Literature, Ontologies and Databases: Mining Biological Semantics*. Association for Computational Linguistics, Morristown, NJ, 2005, pp. 17–24.

23. A. Aho and M. Corasick. Efficient string matching: An aid to bibliographic search. *Commun. ACM*, 18(6):340, 1975.

24. D. Knuth, J. Morris, Jr., and V. Pratt. Fast pattern matching in strings. *SIAM J. Comput.*, 6:323, 1977.

25. R. Boyer and J. Moore. A fast string searching algorithm. *Commun. ACM*, 20(10):762–772, 1977.

26. V. I. Levenshtein. Binary codes capable of correcting deletions, insertions, and reversals. *Soviet Phys. Doklady*, 10(8):707–710, 1966.

27. W. E. Winkler. The state of record linkage and current research problems. *Statist. Med.*, 14:491–498, 1995.

28. W. Cohen, P. Ravikumar, and S. Fienberg. A comparison of string metrics for matching names and records. In *KDD Workshop on Data Cleaning and Object Consolidation*, Vol. 3, 2003.

29. E. Fredkin. Trie memory. *Commun. ACM*, 3(9):490–499, 1960.

30. U. Manber and G. Myers. Suffix arrays: A new method for on-line string searches. In *Proceedings of the First Annual ACM-SIAM Symposium on Discrete Algorithms*. Society for Industrial and Applied Mathematics, 1990, pp. 319–327.

31. D. Morrison. PATRICIA–practical algorithm to retrieve information coded in alphanumeric. *J. ACM (JACM)*, 15(4):514–534, 1968.

32. A. Schwartz and M. Hearst. A simple algorithm for identifying abbreviation definitions in biomedical text. *Pacific Symp. Biocomput.*, 8:451–462, 2003.

33. G. Zhou, D. Shen, J. Zhang, J. Su, and S. Tan. Recognition of protein/gene names from text using an ensemble of classifiers. *BMC Bioinformatics*, 6(Suppl. 1):S7, 2005.

34. J. Hakenberg, C. Plake, R. Leaman, M. Schroeder, and G. Gonzalez. Inter-species normalization of gene mentions with gnat. *Bioinformatics*, 24:i126–132, Aug. 2008.

35. H. Xu, J. Fan, G. Hripcsak, E. Mendonça, M. Markatou, and C. Friedman. Gene symbol disambiguation using knowledge-based profiles. *Bioinformatics*, 23(8):1015, 2007.

36. M. Stevenson, Y. Guo, R. Gaizauskas, and D. Martinez. Disambiguation of biomedical text using diverse sources of information. *BMC Bioinformatics*, 9(Suppl. 11):S7, 2008.

37. X. Wang and M. Matthews. Distinguishing the species of biomedical named entities for term identification. *BMC Bioinformatics*, 9(Suppl. 11):S6, 2008.

38. M. Gerner, G. Nenadic, and C. Bergman. Linnaeus: A species name identification system for biomedical literature. *BMC Bioinformatics*, 11(1):85, 2010.

39. M. J. Schuemie, R. Jelier, and J. A. Kors. Peregrine: Lightweight gene name normalization by dictionary lookup. In *Proceedings of the Biocreative 2 Workshop*, Apr. 2007, pp. 131–140.

40. H. Wain, M. Lush, F. Ducluzeau, and S. Povey. Genew: The human gene nomenclature database. *Nucleic Acids Res.*, 30(1):169, 2002.

41. S. Letovsky, R. Cottingham, C. Porter, and P. Li. Gdb: The human genome database. *Nucleic Acids Res.*, 26(1):94, 1998.

42. B. Boeckmann et al. The swiss-prot protein knowledgebase and its supplement trembl in 2003. *Nucleic Acids Res.*, 31(1):365, 2003.

43. H.-R. Fang, K. Murphy, Y. Jin, J. S. Kim, and P. S. White. Human gene name normalization using text matching with automatically extracted synonym dictionaries. In *Proceedings of the Workshop on Linking Natural Language Processing and Biology (BioNLP '06)*, Association for Computational Linguistics, New York, NY, 2006, pp. 41–48.

44. K. Fundel, D. Hanisch, H.-T. Mevissen, R. Zimmer, and J. Fluck. ProMiner: Rule-based protein and gene entity recognition. *BMC Bioinformatics*, 6:S14, May 2005.

45. Y. Tsuruoka and J. Tsujii. Improving the performance of dictionary-based approaches in protein name recognition. *J. Biomed. Inform.*, 37(6):461–470, 2004.

46. C. Kuo, Y. Chang, H. Huang, K. Lin, B. Yang, Y. Lin, C. Hsu, and I. Chung. Rich feature set, unification of bidirectional parsing and dictionary filtering for high F-score gene mention tagging. In *Proceedings of the Second BioCreative Challenge Evaluation Workshop*, Madrid, Spain, 2007, pp. 105–107.

47. C. Grover, B. Haddow, E. Klein, M. Matthews, L. Nielsen, R. Tobin, and X. Wang. Adapting a relation extraction pipeline for the BioCreAtIvE II task. *Proc. 2nd BioCreative Challenge Eval. Workshop*, 23:273–286, 2007.

48. K. Takeuchi and N. Collier. Bio-medical entity extraction using support vector machines. *Artif. Intell. Med.*, 33(2):125–137, 2005.

49. R. Ando. BioCreative II gene mention tagging system at IBM Watson. In *Proceedings of the Second BioCreative Challenge Evaluation Workshop*, Madrid, Spain, 2007, pp. 101–103.

50. R. Tsai, C. Sung, H. Dai, H. Hung, T. Sung, and W. Hsu. NERBio: Using selected word conjunctions, term normalization, and global patterns to improve biomedical named entity recognition. *BMC Bioinformatics*, 7(Suppl. 5):S11, 2006.

51. Y. Tsuruoka, Y. Tateishi, J. Kim, T. Ohta, J. McNaught, S. Ananiadou, and J. Tsujii. Developing a robust part-of-speech tagger for biomedical text. *Advances in Informatics: 10th Panhellenic Conference on Informatics*, LNCS 3746, 2005, pp. 382–392.

52. I. Alias-i. Lingpipe. Available: http://alias-i.com/lingpipe/index.html, May 2010.

53. S. Abney and S. P. Abney. Parsing by chunks. *Principle-Based Parsing*, Kluwer Academic Publishers, 1991, pp. 257–278.

54. C. Sun, L. Lei, W. Xiaolong, and G. Yi. A study for application of discriminative models in biomedical literature mining. In *Proceedings of the Second BioCreative Challenge Evaluation Workshop*, Madrid, Spain, 2007, pp. 319–321.

55. T. Mitsumori, S. Fation, M. Murata, K. Doi, and H. Doi. Gene/protein name recognition based on support vector machine using dictionary as features. *BMC Bioinformatics*, 6(Suppl. 1):S8, 2005.

56. J. Thomas, D. Milward, C. Ouzounis, S. Pulman, and M. Carroll. Automatic extraction of protein interactions from scientific abstracts. In *Proceedings of the Pacific Symposium on Biocomputing*, Vol. 5, 2000, pp. 538–549.

57. T. Sekimizu, H. Park, and J. Tsujii. Identifying the interaction between genes and gene products based on frequently seen verbs in medline abstracts. In *Genome Informatics.Workshop on Genome Informatics*, Vol. 9, Tokyo, Japan, 1998, pp. 62–71.

58. T. Briscoe and J. Carroll. Robust accurate statistical annotation of general text. In *Proceedings of the 3rd International Conference on Language Resources and Evaluation*, Las Palmas, Canary Islands, Spain, 2002, pp. 1499–1504.

59. Y. Saeys, I. Inza, and P. Larrañaga. A review of feature selection techniques in bioinformatics. *Bioinformatics*, 23(19):2507, 2007.

60. J. Hakenberg, S. Bickel, C. Plake, U. Brefeld, H. Zahn, L. Faulstich, U. Leser, and T. Scheffer. Systematic feature evaluation for gene name recognition. *BMC Bioinformatics*, 6(Suppl. 1):S9, 2005.

61. S. Della Pietra, V. Della Pietra, J. Lafferty, R. Technol, and S. Brook. Inducing features of random fields. *IEEE Trans. Pattern Anal. Machine Intell.*, 19(4):380–393, 1997.

62. R. Rosenfeld, L. Wasserman, C. Cai, and X. Zhu. Interactive feature induction and logistic regression for whole sentence exponential language models. In *Proceedings of the IEEE Workshop on Automatic Speech Recognition and Understanding*, Keystone, CO, Citeseer, 1999, pp. 231–236.

63. A. McCallum. Efficiently inducing features of conditional random fields. In *Proceedings of the Nineteenth Conference on Uncertainty in Artificial Intelligence (UAI-03)*, Acapulco, Mexico, Citeseer, 2003, pp. 403–410.

64. R. Jin and H. Liu. Robust feature induction for support vector machines. In *Proceedings of the Twenty-First International Conference on Machine Learning*. ACM, Banff, Canada, 2004, pp. 57–64.

65. R. McDonald and F. Pereira. Identifying gene and protein mentions in text using conditional random fields. *BMC Bioinformatics*, 6(Suppl. 1):S6, 2005.

66. J. Lafferty, A. McCallum, and F. Pereira. Conditional random fields: Probabilistic models for segmenting and labeling sequence data. In *Proceedings of the Eighteenth International Conference on Machine Learning (ICML-2001)*, Williamstown, MA, 2001, pp. 282–289.

67. S. Keerthi and S. Sundararajan. CRF versus SVM-Struct for sequence labeling. Technical Report. Yahoo Research, 2007.

68. H. Wallach. Conditional random fields: An introduction. Rapport Technique MS-CIS-04-21, Department of Computer and Information Science, University of Pennsylvania, Vol. 50, 2004.

69. R. Leaman and G. Gonzalez. BANNER: An executable survey of advances in biomedical named entity recognition. In *Pacific Symp. Biocomput.*, 13:652–663, 2008.

70. S. Egorov, A. Yuryev, and N. Daraselia. A simple and practical dictionary-based approach for identification of proteins in MEDLINE abstracts. *J. Am. Med. Informat. Assoc.*, 11(3):174–178, 2004.

71. S. Mika and B. Rost. Protein names precisely peeled off free text. *Bioinformatics*, 20(Suppl. 1):i241, 2004.

72. D. Campos, S. Matos, I. Lewin, J. L. Oliveira, and D. Rebholz-Schuhmann. Harmonisation of gene/protein annotations: towards a gold standard medline. *Bioinformatics*, 28(9):1253–1261, 2012.

73. L. Smith et al. Overview of BioCreative II gene mention recognition. *Genome Biol.*, 9(Suppl. 2):S2, 2008.

74. A. K. McCallum. MALLET: A Machine Learning for Language Toolkit. Available: http://mallet.cs.umass.edu, 2002.

75. E. Sang and F. De Meulder. Introduction to the CoNLL-2003 shared task: Language-independent named entity recognition. In *Proceedings of the Seventh Conference on Natural Language Learning (HLT-NAACL 2003)* Vol. 4, Association for Computational Linguistics, 2003, pp. 142–147.

76. G. Navarro. A guided tour to approximate string matching. *ACM Comput. Surv.*, 33(1):31–88, 2001.

CHAPTER 38

AUTOMATED ANNOTATION OF SCIENTIFIC DOCUMENTS: INCREASING ACCESS TO BIOLOGICAL KNOWLEDGE

EVANGELOS PAFILIS,[1] HEIKO HORN,[2] and NIGEL P. BROWN[3]

[1]Institute of Marine Biology Biotechnology and Aquaculture, Hellenic Centre for Marine Research, Heraklion, Crete, Greece
[2]Department of Disease Systems Biology, The Novo Nordisk Foundation Center for Protein Research, Faculty of Health Sciences, University of Copenhagen, Copenhagen, Denmark
[3]BioQuant, University of Heidelberg, Heidelberg, Germany

38.1 INTRODUCTION

Routine tasks of a life sciences researcher include reading the literature, either on the Web or in local files, visiting scientific news portals and topic dedicated websites, and working with text documents or spreadsheets containing experimental data.

Common to all of these cases is that a document may mention several biomedical entities, such as genes, proteins, small chemical molecules, species of organisms, and more. While a reader often knows some things about some of these entities, that may not be enough to understand a biological phenomenon adequately or to explain an observation. The reader is then forced to query multiple databases to obtain more information, a tedious activity that reduces the time they could have spent on other productive tasks. Typical questions posed by various researchers in different fields might include those shown in Table 38.1. Clearly, researchers may have differing though often interrelated knowledge requirements of interest also to interdisciplinary researchers in combination.

If, on the other hand, all these documents were linked to relevant resources offering more information about the mentioned biomedical entities, there would be an improvement in understanding and assimilation of knowledge while saving a great deal of the researcher's time. Table 38.1 lists only a few knowledge sources. In practice, a huge number of biological and biomedical databases exist, holding information on biomedical entities. In the 2011 issue, Galperin and Cochrane [21] reported that the *Nucleic Acids Research* on-line database collection [8] contained 1330 carefully selected databases for just molecular biology alone. Table 38.5 in Section 38.4 lists knowledge sources referenced in this chapter.

Connecting scientific documents with external resources provides researchers with a starting point for the exploration of knowledge behind the document. One way of achieving

Biological Knowledge Discovery Handbook: Preprocessing, Mining, and Postprocessing of Biological Data,
First Edition. Edited by Mourad Elloumi and Albert Y. Zomaya.
© 2014 John Wiley & Sons, Inc. Published 2014 by John Wiley & Sons, Inc.

TABLE 38.1 Typical Questions Posed by Various Researchers with Some Relevant Knowledge Sources

Researchers	Questions	Knowledge Sources	Description
Molecular biologist, structural biologist	What is the function of this protein?	UniProt	Database of protein sequences and functional information
	Has its macromolecular structure been solved?	PDB	Database of solved macromolecular X-ray and NMR structures
	What domains does it contain?	SMART	Database of protein domains
	Are there any other proteins known to be associated with it?	STRING	Database of protein–protein interactions inferred from multiple sources
Chemist, biochemist	What is the formula of this compound?	PubChem	Database of chemical compounds
	Is this chemical compound known under different names?		
Taxonomist	What is known about this species?	Encyclopedia of Life	Encyclopedia of species names, descriptions and related literature
	What is its classification? Is there a comprehensive description available?		
	What are the relevant articles?		

Note: See also Table 38.5 in Section 38.4.

this connectivity would be if content providers, such as journal publishers, offered their material enriched with links to external resources. Some initiatives have already started, such as the *ChemSpider Journal of Chemistry* [3], the *Biochemical Journal* semantic format [1], and the Elsevier *Cell Press Journals* "Article of the Future" format [2]. The state of the art and the future of scientific publishing have been reviewed by Attwood [16] and more recently commented upon in [34].

However, content provider approaches, for example, those involving semantic Web technologies, move forward at a slow pace [28] and lack overall coordination [34]. Moreover, being provider specific, they exclude the possibility of annotation of other publicly available webpages or any local documents of the researcher. Another way of increasing the linkage among scientific databases and biomedical knowledge resources is via client-side tools capable of enriching documents used by the researcher with links to external resources. Through such tools a researcher, instead of being a passive reader, becomes a "power" user having easy access to relevant knowledge.

The ease and utility of this access depend on the client-side tools themselves. Key features are the extent to which these tools complement common user tasks, the intuitiveness and simplicity of their interfaces, the depth of information being offered upon enriching a document, and the breadth of the entity types being annotated. The scientific domains for which various tools provide easy access to knowledge differ. They range from small chemical molecules to proteins, species, as well as cellular components, molecular functions, biological processes, and diseases (Table 38.5). Most of the chapter is devoted to presentation of client-side tools that offer annotation of terms in webpages or local PDF files, together with descriptions of the underlying techniques.

Attaching annotations to terms in a document is tightly bound to text mining. To perform such a task it is required not only to recognize the words in a document but also to associate them with a corresponding entry in a biomedical database. This process is a basic component of text mining known as *named entity recognition* (NER) [24]. Simply enriching documents by cross-linking the term occurrences with relevant database records is useful on its own, besides being a part of larger text-mining systems [24]. Annotations vary in complexity from a simple hyperlink to the relevant record in a biomedical database to powerful concise and interactive summary popups presenting multiple information sources. The latter approach is a very important enhancement of the user experience as an informative summary reduces the likelihood that the reader will have to navigate away to view additional information [28].

The various tools tend to be simple to use and easy to install, requiring, in some cases, as simple a user action as a single mouse click. The complexity of the underlying annotation pipeline is kept hidden from users following the principle of protecting users from technical complexities and allowing them to focus on their research [37]. This requirement is of high importance in the field of text-mining, where one of the pressing issues is the development of interfaces that require little or even no understanding of the underlying text-mining technologies [15]. Tools are based on a set of technologies such as a Web browser or Microsoft Office extensions as well as special-purpose enhanced document readers that allow the enrichment of a document without getting in the user's way.

The rest of the chapter addresses two basic types of reader. Readers only interested in the functionality of such tools and the benefit they may gain by using them can read the survey of tools (Section 38.2). Also in the discussion (Section 38.4) they may find more information, for example, regarding the issues associated with automated document annotation and some of the potential pitfalls. Readers with more information technology background, besides receiving a glimpse of the tool functionality in the survey of tools, will find some basic information on the techniques, technologies, and architectural solutions in the technology section (Section 38.3). All readers are encouraged to refer to the section on future perspectives (Section 38.5) for a brief analysis of how these types of approaches may evolve in the future, along with possible implications for other scientific fields.

38.2 SURVEY OF TOOLS

Modern software technologies (Section 38.3) allow the extension of commonly used applications such as Web browsers, word processors, and spreadsheet programs. Custom tools such as PDF readers and Web services can also be built. With these technologies and tools, common user tasks such as reading a website, a PDF article, or a Microsoft Word document can be tailored to the requirements of life sciences researchers. Rather than try to present a complete review of tools, we have selected an illustrative subset according to the user activity they complement and the document type involved (Web browsing, reading PDF

TABLE 38.2 Tools Associated with User Activities and Types of Documents Enriched for Various Target Audiences

Tool	User Activity and Document Type	Audience	Link	References
Reflect	Browsing Web pages	Molecular biologists, biochemists, chemists, generic (Wikipedia terms)	`http://reflect.ws`	[28, 30]
i-cite	Browsing Web pages	Molecular biologists, biochemists, chemists	`http://i-cite.org`	[19]
NameLink	Browsing Web pages	Biologists, taxonomists	`http://eol.org/ info/namelink`	[32]
Utopia Documents	Reading PDF articles	Molecular biologists, biochemists, structural biologists, journal editors	`http://getutopia. com`	[16, 17]
Ontology Add-in for Word	Reading or writing Word documents	Biomedical ontology researchers, molecular biologists	`http://ucsdbiolit. codeplex.com`	[20]
OnTheFly	Reading text, PDF, Excel, Word documents and batch processing	Molecular biologists, biochemists, chemists	`http://onthefly. embl.de`	[33]

documents, editing Word documents; see Table 38.2). The functionality of each tool is introduced next.

38.2.1 Augmented Web Browsing

Life sciences researchers resort daily to the Web to search the literature and gather information about biological entities [18]. Annotation of webpages allows the reader to enrich an unlimited number of documents. Journal articles, database query result pages, pages focused on specialized biology topics, scientific news portals, fora, and blogs are just some examples of the types of webpages that can be enriched.

The tools in this section take advantage of Web technologies, like the extension of a Web browser's functionality so as to modify the contents and/or the appearance of a webpage in a way that would match the user's requirements. Users employing such tools are making use of *augmented browsing*, the emerging technology that allows them to improve the

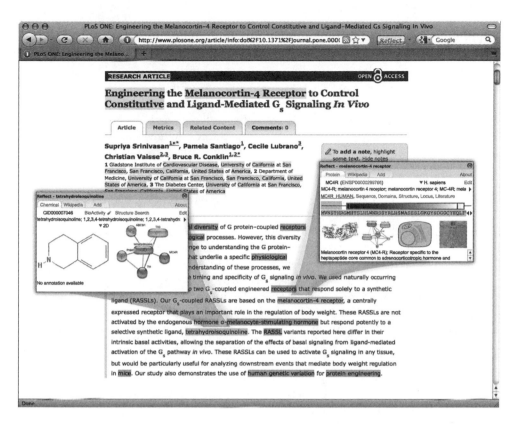

FIGURE 38.1 Reflect annotation of a journal article [36] showing chemical and protein popups. A researcher may click on the Reflect button (upper oval) beside the address bar to annotate the current webpage. Recognized terms (genes, proteins, small chemical molecules) become highlighted. Clicking on a highlighted term displays a compact summary popup with basic information about an entity and links to external resources [28, 30]. The composite view shows summary popups for tetrahydroisoquinoline (left) and the human melanocortin-4 receptor (right).

information on webpages while browsing [28]. Through this technology they may tailor a webpage according to their interests; as described here, they may annotate entities of biomedical importance and gain easy access to relevant knowledge.

Reflect: Annotation of Biological and Biochemical Entities   Reflect is a service [11] that recognizes genes, proteins, small-molecule names, and Wikipedia terms (tested at the time of writing) in webpages, including Web-formatted journal articles [28, 30]. Recognized terms are highlighted and links are generated that provide popups with concise knowledge summaries (Figure 38.1).

There are two standard ways with which one may invoke Reflect. The first is via the project website. The Reflect page allows the user to type in the URL of a webpage which will be retrieved, annotated, and returned to the user. The other, simpler, way is via a Web browser extension (see the Glossary) obtained with a mouse click from the Reflect website and installing automatically. The Reflect extension works with commonly used browsers (tested at the time of writing: Firefox, Internet Explorer, Safari, Chrome) and adds a button that sends the contents of the user's currently displayed webpage to the Reflect server. The Reflect server then annotates the page and returns it to the user (Figure 38.1), as above.

Rather than simply recognizing entity names in the free text of a webpage and adding references to one or other relevant database record, Reflect annotates terms with concise and informative summaries obtained from multiple information sources; compared to the original document, an annotated page contains highlighted terms which link to the Reflect summary popup [28, 30]. Primarily designed for biologists and chemists, these popups (Figure 38.1) are as compact as possible to facilitate access to relevant information.

The protein summary popup (Figure 38.1) provides a preferred name and a database identifier in a reference sequence database (ENSEMBL, UniProt, RefSeq, FlyBase, SGD, depending on organism) and a description, list of synonyms, and the amino acid sequence. Also presented are the domain architecture (SMART) (scrollable and interactively coupled with the sequence), a prediction of subcellular localization, a 3D structure if available (PDB), a network of known interaction partners (STITCH), and an image of the organism from which the protein derives. Other links include relevant MEDLINE abstracts (iHOP) (see Table 38.5 in Section 38.4 for further details of knowledge sources).

Similarly, the chemical summary popup (Figure 38.1) provides a description, synonyms, the 2D or 3D structure of the compound (PubChem), and an image of known interaction partners (STITCH) (see Table 38.5).

The list of synonyms provided in the popup is a quick and convenient way for researchers to identify entities they know under a different name, while the protein sequence can easily be copied and pasted into other tools for further analysis [28]. Finally, as development of Reflect continues, more entity types and knowledge resources are being added. At time of writing [22], Reflect is now capable of recognizing and providing summary information for Wikipedia terms (see Table 38.5).

i-cite: Navigation and Annotation of Life Sciences Literature The i-cite browser extension [6] aims primarily at improving the navigation of life sciences literature by traversal of citation networks [19]. By merging citation information from Google Scholar and CiteXplore (see Table 38.5), i-cite allows users to navigate bidirectionally among related life sciences literature. For example, i-cite enhances a PubMed result page and offers access to articles that cite, or are cited by, any article in the result list. At time of writing i-cite is implemented as a Firefox browser extension.

For automated document annotation, the i-cite system supports the recognition of proteins that are linked to UniProt, Gene Ontology (GO) terms (cellular components, molecular functions, biological processes), diseases listed at HealthCentral.com, and ChEBI chemical terms all of which are obtained via the EBI WhatIzIt text processing system. Chemical structural formulas are separately obtained from the ChemAxon Chemicalize service (see Table 38.5 for details of knowledge sources).

As described in [19], there are two modes of interaction with the system. First, the user may select a portion of text in a webpage and then by right-clicking select it for annotation. In a popup the same text fragment will be shown with entity types like proteins, chemicals, and diseases recognized (Figure 38.2). Any annotated entities will be linked to external resources where the user may seek more information (see Table 38.5). Only one entity type may be recognized at a time.

Using the second mode of interaction, the user may opt to have every page they are browsing annotated for chemicals. The annotation occurs automatically while the page is loading and the whole page is analyzed. A ribbon added at the top of the document presents

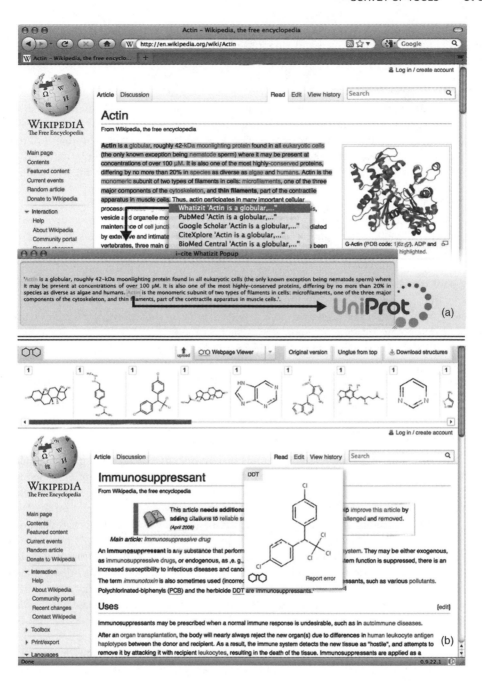

FIGURE 38.2 i-cite annotations of webpages referencing proteins and chemicals. (a) The user may select part of the text in a webpage and have it annotated (right-click menu). In this case the selected paragraph has been annotated for protein names. Clicking on the protein name ("actin") will invoke the corresponding UniProt entry. (b) A webpage annotated for chemicals. A ribbon containing recognized compounds appears at the top of the page. Mousing-over an underlined chemical name in the text will display a popup with its structural formula.

structural formulas of chemicals recognized in the text. The corresponding chemical terms in the document are underlined and, on mousing-over, a popup with the chemical structure is displayed (Figure 38.2).

NameLink: Species Name Recognition   NameLink is a service [7] that recognizes species names in a webpage and links them to appropriate entries in species information/ taxonomy repositories [32]. One way of achieving this is by visiting the NameLink webpage. There a user may type in (or copy–paste) the address of a webpage that will then be retrieved, annotated, and returned to the user. Alternatively, researchers may add the NameLink bookmarklet (see the Glossary) to their browser favorites. Then, with a single click they can have the current webpage annotated.

The NameLink bookmarklet resolves species names to the Encyclopedia of Life (EOL), which is a project aiming at providing researchers with a website for every known species on Earth [31]. Each species page contains a wealth of information, such as images, comprehensive and detailed descriptions, related names, common names and synonyms, taxon distribution maps, and links to relevant resources and literature (Figure 38.3).

NameLink also acts as a front end to the Global Name Index (GNI), which is a collection of scientific biological names (at time of writing, about 17 million name strings in total, deriving from a variety of scientific name repositories [5]). Thus, resolving species names to other taxonomic information repositories such as the Global Biodiversity Information Facility (GBIF) is also possible (see Table 38.5 in Section 38.4 for details of knowledge sources).

At the time of writing, NameLink is, according to the developers, still in prototype stage though the annotation it offers could already be useful to a wide range of biologists.

38.2.2   Reading PDF Documents

The previous section demonstrated how tools that augment webpages can provide readers with easy access to relevant knowledge such as protein sequences and descriptions, chemical compound structures, species information summary pages, and more. Being able to annotate webpages opens new avenues for enrichment of various types of document on the Web. The scientific literature forms only a small part of this but nevertheless includes novel forms of scientific communication such as blogs and wikis. With the tools presented so far, enrichment is limited to webpages and exploits HTML markup, ignoring the fact that PDF is currently the *"de facto* standard format of scientific literature" [38]. Attwood et al. [17] provide a set of reasons why this is true: Publishers are offering their content in this format and researchers are familiar with it. It is convenient since it is a self-contained, offline readable, sharable object with good readability.

An alternative approach has been to design specialist PDF reader software discussed next. Unlike a generic PDF reader, these tools give life sciences researchers new functionality, such as the ability to convert static tables into dynamically generated charts or to view protein structures represented in figures as interactive 3D objects. Some of these more advanced features depend upon the content provider adding appropriate semantic markup to their document that can be recognized by the PDF reader, for example, publisher-added annotation in the *Biochemical Journal* semantic format [1].

Utopia Documents: Linking Literature and Research Data   Utopia Documents is a PDF reader–like desktop application [13] that provides easy access to visualization and

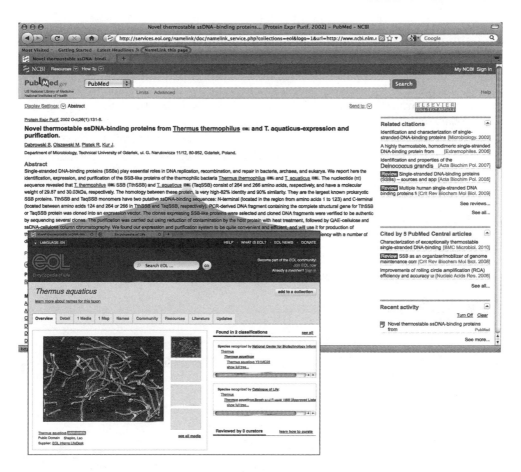

FIGURE 38.3   NameLink annotation of a journal article referencing a species name. The user may click on the NameLink [32] bookmarklet (upper oval) to have the contents of a webpage annotated. Species names are replaced by hyperlinks that point to entries in the EOL. In this case *T. aquaticus* has been annotated on a PubMed abstract and linked to the Thermus aquaticus EOL entry. There, a comprehensive description along with related literature, synonyms, and many more resources are available.

data analysis tools while reading published research articles [16, 17] (see also the online guide [14]). Similar to *augmented browsing* for webpages introduced above, it offers an augmented view of PDF documents.

Instead of reading a static document, researchers can obtain easy access to interactive visualization and analysis tools and, in the context of text mining, automatically added annotations that link terms in the document with external resources [17]. All this complexity is hidden from the users allowing them to work without changing their existing behavior.

Already annotated terms or user text selections can be looked up in various sources, such as Google, Wikipedia, or the NCBI databases (see Table 38.5 in Section 38.4) or simply in a dictionary or thesaurus [14]. Drawing on its plug-in architecture, Utopia Documents may invoke third-party services to extend its functionality. An application of this feature is to invoke NER (Section 38.3.2.3) services that associate annotations with the document. Reflect, GPCRDB text mining, and ACKnowledge Enhancer (see Table 38.5) are three external services (Section 38.3.1.4) that, at the time of writing, may be invoked to annotate the user's document.

- *Reflect Integration*   By employing the Reflect API (Section 38.3.1.4, also see the Glossary), the document contents are sent to the Reflect server (Section 38.2.1). Popups generated by the Reflect server for recognized terms may then be viewed within Utopia Documents. In Utopia Documents the Reflect recognized terms appear underlined rather than highlighted. However, the summary information is identical (Figure 38.4).

- *GPCRDB Integration*   GPCRDB is a resource (see Table 38.5) specializing in G protein–coupled receptor-related information. The GPCRDB-specific plugin [17, 38] communicates with GPCRDB to enrich PDF documents by annotating the proteins, residues, and mutations that are mentioned in the text and for which information is available in the database. The GPCRDB generated annotations are then linked by Utopia Documents to highlighted terms (Figure 38.4) [38].

- *ACKnowledge Enhancer and ConceptWiki Integration*   A third Utopia Documents plugin, as described in [17], invokes the ACKnowledge Enhancer (see AQnowledge

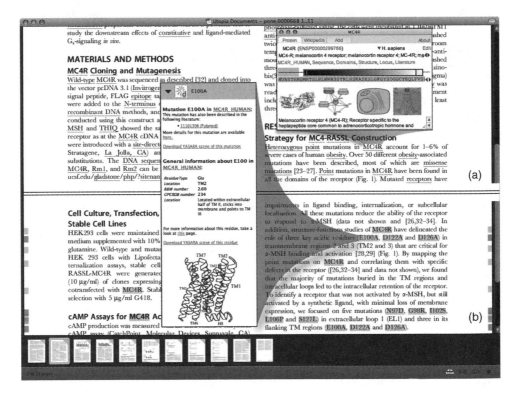

FIGURE 38.4   Utopia Documents annotation functionality showing Reflect and GPCRDB integration [16, 17]. Two views from the same document page [36] are shown stacked one above the other, one for each annotation method. (a) Terms recognized by Reflect appear underlined. Clicking on a term (in this case, MC4R) displays the Reflect summary popup (top) described previously (Figure 38.1). (b) Terms recognized by the GPCRDB text processing module [17, 38] appear highlighted. Clicking on a term displays a relevant information summary. In this example information is shown about the E100A mutation in MC4R_HUMAN (at left).

in Table 38.5). As a result, terms are recognized, highlighted, and linked to entities in ConceptWiki (see Table 38.5). The latter is a community-editable resource that includes two sections, WikiProteins and WikiPeople, holding information about proteins and authors, respectively. At the time of writing, ACKnowledge Enhancer can also recognize and annotate laboratory supplies.

38.2.3 Reading and Writing Microsoft Word Documents

Previous sections described tools that enrich webpages and PDF documents giving users quick and easy access to knowledge while browsing the Web and/or reading a local PDF file. These are typically finished documents and the tools described thus far are not really suitable for annotating a document while it is being written. The biological and biomedical research community makes extensive use of Microsoft Word documents for writing manuscripts and reports. Microsoft Office tools can be customized through add-ins that offer extra functionality.

Ontology Add-in for Word   To assist researchers in associating semantic data with words or phrases in documents not only at the reading but also at the writing step, Fink et al. have developed the Ontology Add-in for Word [20]. This enables the automatic recognition and highlighting of information-rich words and phrases in Word documents, even as they are being written.

Upon opening a document, the text is automatically processed and biological ontology terms (see the Glossary) and database identifiers are recognized. The tool searches the document for matching ontology terms and text patterns that match the syntax of identifiers in widely used biological databases (UniProt, PDB, RefSeq) (see Table 38.5). By hovering over a term and clicking on the relevant icon, users are presented with a set of actions including the semantic annotation of the term. For recognized ontology terms a textual description is given [20]. This functionality is also available while writing a document, that is, in-line highlighting is supported.

A configuration panel allows the user to download and use alternative ontologies of interest from the National Center for Biomedical Ontology (NCBO) (see Table 38.5) as well as to load their own ontology written using an OBO format [9]. At the time of writing, the Ontology Add-in for Word was available for Microsoft Windows and Microsoft Word 2007/2010 users.

38.2.4 Reading Multiple Formats and Batch Processing

The tools presented so far cover a range of common user tasks: browsing and reading and writing of particular formats (HTML, PDF, doc). However, there are other document types used by researchers on a daily basis, such as Microsoft Excel spreadsheets and plain text files. Besides annotating a single document at a time, it is also useful to be able to annotate a collection of files at once.

OnTheFly   OnTheFly is a service [10] that is able to annotate multiple common document formats, including plain text files, PDF files, and Microsoft Word and Excel documents stored as local files [33]. The user submits documents to the OnTheFly server, which converts each target document into HTML and dispatches that to Reflect (Section 38.2.1) to perform the actual annotation (Figure 38.5). It should be noted that the conversion of PDF and Microsoft Office documents into HTML may lose some formatting, leading to slight alterations in the document appearance.

As well as single-document processing, OnTheFly offers multiformat batch document processing, with the added ability to combine the entities across documents for larger projects [33]. This set of entities can then be used to generate a summary of entity descriptions and to generate a STITCH [26] (see Table 38.5) network of known protein–protein and protein–chemical interactions (Figure 38.5) that integrates data from multiple sources (e.g., literature mining, biological databases, experimental results).

38.3   TECHNOLOGIES AND TECHNIQUES

The previous section described how end-user tools apply term annotation to enrich documents in various formats, including HTML pages, PDF, and Microsoft Word documents. Common to most of the tools, except Ontology Add-in for Word, is a client–server model: The user accesses a document in the client, data of some sort are passed to a server, annotated, and returned to the client, which then displays recognized terms using additional markup with links to additional information.

We now describe features of the various clients before describing the annotation process itself, which is usually performed server side. Other details of the server implementations are not discussed and the interested reader is referred to the relevant articles and project websites.

38.3.1   Client Software

The tools we presented earlier (Table 38.2) employ different technologies for the implementation of their user interfaces. Some of the tools (Reflect and NameLink) can be used without installing any additional software; users may annotate public webpages by just copying and pasting the address into an input form on the appropriate project website, in which case the client is simply a standard webpage working within the browser.

While adequate for casual use of the systems, this also offers a simple way by which users may test the annotation offered by either system before deciding to install the local Reflect or NameLink clients on their computer (Section 38.3.1.3). Basic user interactions are briefly presented before covering the implementation of the client tools and the nature of their interaction with the server, if any.

38.3.1.1   *User Interaction*   Regardless of the sophistication of the user interface, all the tools perform document annotation through simple user actions (e.g., mouse clicks), while hiding the complexity away from the user, a feature that is an ongoing area of research [15]. Reflecting the different approaches used to enhance common user tasks (browser extensions, customized PDF reader, office extension; Section 38.3.1.2), the tools presented recruit a variety of interface components and capture different user actions to support document annotation.

- *Simple Annotation*   Invoking the document annotation procedure in some of the tools requires a single click on the corresponding button (Reflect, NameLink) while in others it either occurs automatically (Reflect—continuous mode, i-cite Chemicalize, Ontology Add-in for Word) or upon a mouse click with an appropriate text selection (i-cite WhatIzIt, Utopia Documents).

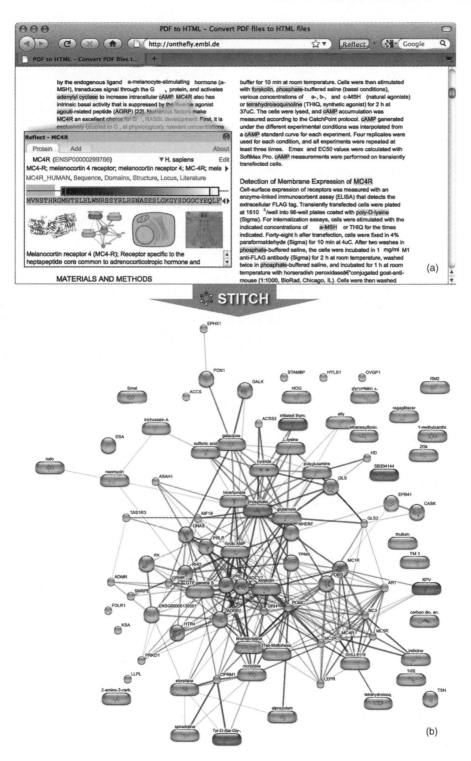

FIGURE 38.5 OnTheFly annotation functionality for a journal article [36] in PDF format showing Reflect and STITCH [26] integration. (a) The annotated article as annotated by Reflect with a popup for the protein MC4R being shown. (b) The STITCH network of known associations between all proteins and chemicals recognized in the article. Line thickness indicates "confidence" in an interaction, while line color indicates the type of interaction: protein–protein, chemical–chemical, or protein–chemical.

Further, Utopia Documents normally only highlights terms on mouse-over of each line, so as to present an uncluttered view of the document. By pressing and holding down the spacebar, the user can see all terms highlighted at once [38].

• *Additional Controls*   Besides the annotated terms, some of the tools employ auxiliary interface elements to support their functionality. Utopia Documents uses a "pager" pane to provide researchers with quick navigation to the different pages. A red mark on the top right indicates the pages in which term annotation is available (Figure 38.4). A sidebar on the right is used for the display of additional information, such as the mutation related information.

User interface components of the Ontology Add-in for Word include a "ribbon" that allows the user to control the add-in behavior and an ontology browser sidebar allowing them to view more information about an ontology term [20].

No annotation mechanism is immune to errors and Reflect allows the user to correct some kinds of error in the document: Improper tagging can be removed, while terms that were missed can be added for future tagging (see Sections 38.4.2.2 and 38.4.3 for more details).

• *Summary Popups*   Most importantly, some of the tools (Reflect, i-cite Chemicalize, Utopia Documents) do not just associate terms with simple links to external database records. Rather, they offer popups with comprehensive information summaries containing links to multiple external knowledge sources (Figures 38.1, 38.2, and 38.4).

Compared to a simple link, a popup has two main advantages. First, its contents can be viewed without having to navigate away to other webpages or tools [28, 30]. Second, the popup content need not necessarily be plain text or static images. Scripting technologies allow dynamic user interaction via the popup.

The Reflect protein popup contains the protein linear sequence and structural domain information, which are tied together and scrollable (Figure 38.1). Further, resolution of ambiguous terms is placed under control of the user via tabs and menu selections (Section 38.4.2.1), and the user can even modify shared annotations for an entity (Section 38.4.3).

38.3.1.2 *Types of Client*   Clients fall into two broad types, those that extend or augment the Web browser and those that are stand-alone applications or extensions to other stand-alone applications conferring network capability and added functionality. Both Reflect and i-cite are implemented as browser extensions (see the Glossary), NameLink is available as a bookmarklet (see the Glossary), Utopia Documents is a PDF reader–like application customized for the life sciences, and Ontology Add-in for Word is a Microsoft Word extension. Moreover the Reflect and NameLink functionality is also accessible via their respective project websites.

• *Web Browser Extensions and Bookmarklets*   Browser extensions and bookmarklet borrow the browser's own machinery (HTML, DOM events, HTTP; see the Glossary) to modify the webpage style and contents. User events (mouse clicks and movement, keyboard presses, etc.) may be captured as usual in HTML pages via DOM events. Using JavaScript, the DOM tree (see the Glossary) of a webpage can be parsed and modified. By combining the above, webpages can be dynamically modified to hold added annotations.

The Reflect browser extension (Figure 38.1) [28, 30], for example, can extract the HTML page content, submit it to the Reflect annotation server, and replace the user's page with an annotated version returned by the server. Any communication to the server occurs via XMLHttpRequest objects (see the Glossary). Similarly, i-cite [19] submits SOAP messages (see the Glossary) to the WhatIzIt annotation service. The messages, besides required parameters such as the dictionary name, include the text selected by the user (Figure 38.2). The returned annotated text is subsequently presented in a popup window.

However, in the case of the ChemAxon Chemicalize annotation service (Figure 38.2) i-cite redirects every page to the Chemicalize server, passing the original page address (URL) as an argument. The functionality of the NameLink bookmarklet [32] is similar, with the original user's page address (URL) being passed to the server. Upon being clicked, the bookmarklet redirects the user to the same page after it has been processed by the NameLink service.

Browser extensions and bookmarklets differ from each other in terms of privileges. Bookmarklets are subjected to the same restrictions as scripts on a webpage and cannot take full advantage of the HTTP protocol. For example, they are not allowed to send HTTP POST requests to servers other than the one where the webpage resides (same origin policy; see the Glossary). On the other hand, browser extensions enjoy the same privileges as the browser itself running on the user's machine.

• *Stand-alone Desktop Applications and Plugins* Utopia Documents is a desktop application that provides users with easy access to additional knowledge resources and analysis tools while they are reading the PDF version of an article [16, 17] (Section 38.2.2). Although a desktop application, it deviates from the monolithic application paradigm by employing services deployed over the Web to complement its functionality. This is enabled through plugins that can access not only client-side libraries, third-party Web services, and other external resources, such as relational databases [17], but also other annotation services such as Reflect, GPCRDB text processing, and ConceptWiki (Section 38.2.2, Figure 38.4).

Utopia Documents attaches annotations to terms without modifying the original PDF document, in contrast to the Web annotation tools (Reflect, i-cite, NameLink) that modify the contents of a webpage. This is achieved by displaying additional information at the stage of rendering the PDF file [17].

Ontology Add-in for Word [20] (Section 38.2.3) is a tool for the annotation of Word documents both while reading and/or writing a document. The tool was implemented using *Microsoft Windows*–specific technology (the .NET platform) and is available for Microsoft Office 2007/2010. The add-in employs the Microsoft Smart Tag (see the Glossary) mechanism for term recognition and annotation [20]. Recognized terms match either ontological terms or regular expression patterns (see the Glossary). This means that once an ontology is loaded, the Ontology Add-in for Word tool operates entirely in the user's computer, in contrast to the rest of the tools presented that all depend on remote servers for annotation.

38.3.1.3 Installation Installation is generally easy. The NameLink bookmarklet may be installed with a simple drag and drop to the bookmark toolbar, while the Reflect browser extension for Firefox, Internet Explorer, Safari, and Chrome (tested at the time of writing) may be installed via a single click from the Reflect website, likewise for i-cite, although the

TABLE 38.3   Selection of Links to API Documentation or Project Websites for Various Annotation Services

Annotation Service	Supported Entity Types	API Documentation or Project Website
Reflect	Genes, proteins, chemicals, generic terms (Wikipedia)	`http://reflect.ws/REST_API.html`
WhatIzIt	Genes, proteins, chemicals, organisms, diseases, GO terms (biological processes, cellular components, molecular functions), drugs	`http://www.ebi.ac.uk/ webservices/ whatizit`
ChemAxon Chemicalize	Chemicals	`http://www.chemicalize.org`
EOL NameLink and NameTag	Organisms	`http://hickory.eol.org: 8081/display/public/ NameLink+Documentation` `http://hickory.eol.org: 8081/display/public/ NameTag+Documentation`
GPCRDB text mining	Proteins (G protein–coupled receptors), mutations, residues	`http://www.gpcr.org/7tm`
Utopia ACKnowledge Enhancer	Proteins, authors, laboratory equipment, and supplies	`http://aqnowledge.com`

supported browser in this case is only Firefox. Utopia Documents and Ontology Add-in for Word may be installed via software installers. Utopia Documents supports a range of operating systems, while Ontology Add-in for Word is Microsoft Windows specific. Moreover the latter may require additional Microsoft.NET runtime libraries, so its installation may not be quite so straightforward.

38.3.1.4 Developer APIs   Developers wishing to write their own client applications or to extend existing ones may make use of some of the annotation services by using a publicly available API (see the Glossary) for that service. Table 38.3 lists known APIs, where available. Some of the tools in this chapter already make use of public APIs to employ other annotation services. For example, Utopia Documents and OnTheFly access Reflect and Utopia Documents accesses the GPCRDB text-mining service.

38.3.2 Document Annotation

The previous sections concentrated on the front-end and design aspects of the presented tools and on the ways that they facilitate user interaction. We now turn to the annotation process that is at the core of every system. As the term is applied here, document annotation refers to establishing mappings between scientific documents and knowledge resources and presenting these as interactive elements for the user.

Key to this process are the parsing of the document, the recognition and tagging of scientific entities mentioned in a document, and the presentation of an appropriate level of information to the user upon inspecting a tagged term [30]. Ideally the system should cover a wide range of entity types and provide a concise, at a glance, and configurable overview of information about the tagged entity. It should also tag terms accurately and offer fast and responsive interaction. In practice, there are limits to the amount and kinds of information that can be displayed and linked in a client tool (Section 38.4.1) as well as to the accuracy of term recognition (Section 38.4.2).

38.3.2.1 Document Parsing

A preliminary step in the tagging of document types other than plain text can be the separation of control codes, tags, and so on, that represent comments and document attributes or govern layout, from the free text of the document itself. As an example, we will consider Reflect's parsing mechanism for HTML markup.

HTML contains many non-free-text elements such as HTML tags, script blocks, and comments. Most of these elements define the structure, appearance, and dynamic functionality of the HTML page. Processing of a page relies on the identification of the free text and, after recognition of biomedical terms to be annotated, replacing the original markup with additional markup for visualization and binding of the terms to knowledge sources.

One way of performing this is to traverse the DOM tree of a Web page to access the free-text snippets. An alternative approach used by Reflect employs a simple lexical analysis to identify non-free-text elements, which are flagged and ignored in subsequent processing. In this way, the original lexical structure of the HTML remains unaltered [29]. Similarly in the case of PDF files, Utopia Documents analyzes the document and constructs a hierarchical semantic model of the layout and content prior to annotation processing and visualization.

38.3.2.2 Term Tagging

Term tagging is a two-step procedure. First, the words of a document have to be scanned for biomedical entity mentions using a process called named entity recognition [24]. In the second step, which we refer to as *resource binding*, the recognized terms are tagged with a visually distinguishing feature (e.g., highlight or underline) and associated with a mechanism that links to knowledge sources. NER and resource binding are discussed further in Sections 38.3.2.3 and 38.3.2.4.

Table 38.4 shows the different tagging approaches used by the tools, which differ in the location of the NER step (client side, server side) and in the richness of the user interaction components (Section 38.3.1.1).

38.3.2.3 Named Entity Recognition

Named entity recognition consists of recognizing terms in a document that refer to entities and cross-matching these terms unambiguously to entries in a knowledge source, such as a model organism sequence database [24].

The simplest of cases is demonstrated by Ontology Add-in for Word. The text is scanned using regular expressions to identify words that match the structure of identifiers and

TABLE 38.4 Term Tagging Architectures That Employ Mainly Server-Side Services to Annotate Terms and Bind Them to Relevant Knowledge Resources

Tool	NER Step	Annotation Service or Technology
Reflect browser extension	Server side	Reflect
OnTheFly	Server side	Reflect
i-cite	Server side	WhatIzIt and ChemAxon Chemicalize
NameLink bookmarklet	Server side	EOL NameLink and NameTag
Utopia Documents	Server side	Reflect, GPCRDB text mining, ACKnowledge Enhancer
Ontology Add-in for Word	Client side	Microsoft Smart Tag

Note: See also Table 38.3 for the services.

accession numbers for common databases (UniProt, PDB, RefSeq), establishing a simple cross-match. However, the situation is not usually so straightforward. For example, gene symbols or names may not be unique to a single organism. Even within the same organism, the same term may refer to more than one entity, and, even worse, it may be spelled or punctuated in different ways.

One can identify entity mentions in a text by cross-matching the words in a document to known names and synonyms in a lexicon or dictionary mined from biomedical databases [25]. Additionally, there are methods to recognize different spelling variants of a name [24]. Usually, more analysis of the text is required, such as relating protein names to organisms using contextual clues. Some solutions are presented in the following sections.

- *Normalization*   Normalization is the process of associating an entity mention to a unique database identifier [38], that is, it is a mapping from known terms to knowledge entities. As an example, the Reflect annotation service uses a dictionary lookup approach to identify terms in the free text of HTML documents that correspond to gene, protein, and chemical names, synonyms, and terms representing other kinds of entity using a precompiled dictionary.

  The Reflect dictionary is based on a lexicon (Reflect lexicon) that has been generated by merging the STRING and STITCH (Table 38.5) database information on names of genes, proteins, and small chemicals, including synonyms, common names, and database identifiers [28]. For the unique association of terms to knowledge entries, Reflect maps terms to identifiers in commonly used resources relevant to an entity. For example, human proteins are mapped to ENSEMBL identifiers, baker's yeast proteins to SGD, and small chemical molecules to PubChem (Table 38.5). A detailed description of the Reflect dictionary, including its structure and examples, can be found in [28].

  Likewise, the GPCRDB text processing module uses a dictionary lookup approach to identify proteins mentioned in the document [38]. The dictionary comprises UniProtKB/Swiss-Prot (Table 38.5) gene and protein identifiers and protein descriptions of the G protein–coupled receptors of GPCRDB.

- *Orthographic Expansion*   While collections of synonyms for entities like gene and protein names and symbols can be used to populate a dictionary, there remains the problem of spelling, letter case, and punctuation variants that are found in published work, even though these might depart from the official terms. For example, official gene symbol synonyms for the protein interleukin-2 are *IL2* and *IL-2*. Nevertheless, an author might write *IL 2* intending to refer to the same entity.

  Alternative spellings and punctuations of terms may be handled by a more flexible dictionary approach termed *orthographic expansion*, which is the process of expanding the names in a dictionary, based on rules that generate name variants that might be encountered.

  Each synonym of an entity in the Reflect lexicon is expanded orthographically to populate the dictionary with plausible variants (e.g., spaces replaced with hyphens, and vice versa). This increases the number of potential matching terms in a document that can be mapped to a known entity [28]. The GPCRDB text processing module also allows some variability in dictionary matching, capturing the different ways a protein name can be written in free text [38].

- *Grounding*   A more complex term-matching method is required to deal with multiple terms that, together, resolve some ambiguity of meaning. A particular example is the recognition of the associated organism when a gene or protein name is matched in a document, so that a dictionary mapping (normalization) can be made to the correct database identifier [38]. *Grounding* [27] resolves ambiguity by considering the co-occurrence of terms (e.g., "mouse" near "interleukin 2") to infer the correct mapping.

Reflect unites organism names with gene and protein names by considering the document as a whole. The Reflect NER uses a two-pass approach: The document is scanned first for organism mentions and then again for the genes/proteins of those organisms [28–30]. Similarly, the GPCRDB text-mining service associates organism names with protein names, as well as residues and amino acid substitutions (found using regular expressions) with the corresponding protein. A word proximity weighting scheme is used for both groundings to rank alternatives [38].

38.3.2.4 Resource Binding   The second stage of the term-tagging process, *resource binding*, is the display in the document of the tagged term and its association with the corresponding entities. The mechanism might be as simple as a single hyperlink through, say, a human protein name to a protein sequence database such as UniProt or more complex, such as a popup (Section 38.3.1.1) presenting summary information about the entity and a collection of links to multiple knowledge sources (Section 38.4.1).

In the case of Reflect, resource binding is accomplished using HTML CSS (see the Glossary) styling to modify the document, changing the appearance of tagged terms, and by injecting JavaScript code to generate and populate the popups with the summary of available knowledge from the Reflect dictionary service [28–30]. For the annotation of a PDF file by Utopia Documents, the annotations from external services (e.g., the GPCRDB text-mining service) are associated at the rendering stage of the PDF without altering it [17].

38.4 DISCUSSION

We now introduce a selection of available knowledge sources and then discuss some issues with the annotation techniques that both users and tool developers should bear in mind. We examine the role of the user community in improving annotation services, and, finally, we consider the uptake of these systems by biomedical researchers and content providers such as journal publishers.

38.4.1 Knowledge Sources

As stated in Section 38.1, different researchers have different information requirements, which can be addressed by connecting their documents to a wide range of specialist as well as general-purpose knowledge sources. Table 38.5 summarizes the breadth of different entity types (approximately 20), supported by the tools we have presented, along with the databases to which these entity types may be mapped in the tagging process.

Such a wide range of entity types could potentially satisfy many types of researchers. However, current tools typically only recognize and tag subsets of these entity types and databases. The table shows the rather sparse scattering of entity types and knowledge sources supported by the various tools. The simultaneous use of more than one tool would alleviate this but obviously requires that the users learn different interfaces as well as offers no scope for combining the results in a common visualization. Tools like Utopia Documents that can make use of external annotation servers though a potentially growing family of plugins may offer a practical solution. In general, there is a need for a greater degree of standardization of tools and services.

TABLE 38.5 Knowledge Sources and Entity Types Used by This Work

Name	Entity Type	Description	Link	Reflect	i-cite	NameLink	Utopia Documents	Ontology Add-in for Word	OnTheFly
AQnowledge	Laboratory equipment and supplies	Commercial laboratory equipment and supplies database	http://aqnowledge.com				○		
BioCyc	Metabolic pathway/genome	SRI International collection of genomes and metabolic pathways for multiple organisms	http://biocyc.org				●		
Catalogue of Life	Organism	Index of species	http://www.catalogueoflife.org			●			
Chemical Entities of Biological Interest (ChEBI)	Chemical	EBI database of chemical compounds	http://www.ebi.ac.uk/chebi		●				
Chemicalize	Chemical	ChemAxon database of chemical structures	http://www.chemicalize.org		●				
ChemSpider	Chemical	RSC database of chemical structures	http://www.chemspider.com						
CiteXplore	Citation	EBI literature search and text mining	http://www.ebi.ac.uk/citexplore		●				
Encyclopedia of Life (EOL)	Organism	EOL database of organism scientific names, species descriptions, and related literature	http://www.eol.org			●			
ENSEMBL	Gene	EBI genome database	http://www.ensembl.org	●			+		+

Resource	Category	Description	URL					
FlyBase	Gene	FlyBase Consortium fruit fly genome database	`http://flybase.org`		+		+	•
Glick glossary	Biomedical glossary	Portland Press glossary of biochemistry and molecular biology by David Glick	`http://www.portlandpress.com/pp/books/online/glick/default.htm`		•			
Global Biodiversity Information Facility (GBIF)	Organism	International collection of biodiversity data	`http://www.gbif.org`			•		
Global Name Index (GNI)	Organism	Collective index of organism scientific names	`http://gni.globalnames.org`			•		
Google	Generic terms	Google search engine	`http://www.google.com`		•			
Google Scholar	Citation	Google Web and literature citation search	`http://scholar.google.com`				•	•
GPCRDB	Protein	CMBI database of G protein–coupled receptor information	`http://www.gpcr.org/7tm`		○			
HealthCentral.com	Disease	Health and illness informational site	`http://healthcentral.com`			•	•	
iHOP	Literature: abstracts	Gene and protein information from journal abstracts	`http://www.ihop-net.org/UniPub/iHOP`		+		+	•
Integrated Taxonomic Information System (ITIS)	Organism	ITIS Organization taxonomic database	`http://www.itis.gov`				•	
NCBO	Ontology: various	National Center for Biomedical Ontology ontologies portal	`http://www.bioontology.org,` `http://bioportal.bioontology.org`	•				

(continued)

TABLE 38.5 *(Continued)*

Name	Entity Type	Description	Link	Reflect	i-cite	NameLink	Utopia Documents	Ontology Add-in for Word	OnTheFly
NCBO	Ontology: various	National Center for Biomedical Ontology ontologies portal	`http://www.bioontology.org`, `http://bioportal.bioontology.org`					●	
PDB	Macromolecular structure	RSCB database of solved macromolecular X-ray and NMR structures	`http://www.pdb.org`	●			●	●	+
PubChem	Chemical	NIH/NCBI database of chemical compounds	`http://pubchem.ncbi.nlm.nih.gov`	●			+		+
PubMed	Literature	NLM/NIH/NCBI database of biomedical literature	`http://www.ncbi.nlm.nih.gov/pubmed`		●		●		
QuickGO	Ontology: Gene Ontology	EBI molecular biology ontology covering cellular components, molecular functions, and biological processes	`http://www.ebi.ac.uk/QuickGO`		●				
Reflect	Annotation service	EMBL/NNF Center for Protein Research document annotation server	`http://reflect.ws`	n/a			○		○
RefSeq	Gene/protein	NCBI Reference Sequence database of genes and proteins	`http://www.ncbi.nlm.nih.gov/RefSeq`	●			+	●	+

Resource	Entity type	Description	URL
SGD	Gene	*Saccaromyces* Genome Database	http://www.yeastgenome.org
SMART	Protein domain	EMBL database of protein domains	http://smart.embl.de
STITCH	Interaction: chemical–protein	EMBL database of chemical–protein interactions inferred from multiple sources	http://stitch.embl.de
STRING	Interaction: protein–protein	EMBL database of protein–protein interactions inferred from multiple sources	http://string.embl.de
uBio Namebank	Organism	Marine Biological Laboratory taxonomic name server	http://www.ubio.org/index.php?pagename=home
UniProt	Protein	UniProt Consortium database of protein sequences and functional information	http://www.uniprot.org
WhatIzIt	Text mining	EBI text processing system	http://www.ebi.ac.uk/webservices/whatizit
Wikipedia	Generic terms	Wikipedia wiki encyclopedia	http://en.wikipedia.org
WikiPeople	Author	ConceptWiki wiki of authors	http://conceptwiki.org/index.php/WikiPeople
WikiProteins	Protein	ConceptWiki wiki of proteins	http://conceptwiki.org/index.php/WikiProteins

Note: Also shown is the breakdown of resource usage by tool: (●) the tool uses the resource, (○) the tool inherits all or many of the entity types of the resource, (+) inherited entity type, (n/a) not applicable.

38.4.2 Annotation Limits

Annotation methods to date are, unfortunately, imperfect. We consider two principal categories of issues: (1) terms that have multiple possible meanings requiring disambiguation and (2) inaccuracies of term recognition, that is, terms that are erroneously tagged or terms that are missed altogether.

38.4.2.1 *Disambiguation of Terms*

Biomedical entity names lack standardization, a crucial issue in NER [24]. In particular, if a term maps to more than one entity, the mapping must be resolved to link to the correct knowledge resource(s). For example, the term IMF could be a synonym *I-MF* for the human gene encoding the MDFI MyoD family inhibitor protein (ENSEMBL peptide record: ENSP00000362142), a chemical (PubChem record: CID005288624, or even conceivably a global organization International Monetary Fund), if linking to entities in Wikipedia.

One solution is to try to infer the intended meaning through algorithmic analysis of textual context, for example, the grounding technique (Section 38.3.2.3) used by the GPCRDB text-mining service to anchor residues and mutations to a nearby protein identifier.

A novel approach is to take advantage of the rich client-side user interface capability and leave the ultimate selection to the user's expertise, since they are better able to recognize the meaning they need. Reflect follows this principle [28] and makes extensive use of the popup interface elements (Section 38.3.1.1), offering alternative tabs and menus that allow the user to set the desired meaning, for example, to change the target organism for an article containing genes and proteins or to select a particular protein from several choices. Utopia Documents also offers different popups when multiple meanings are possible [17].

38.4.2.2 *Tagging Accuracy*

Tagging of biological and biomedical entities is a nontrivial task and there has been extensive research leading to improvements in accuracy in recent years [35]. Nevertheless, errors are inherent in the process, as we now discuss.

False negatives occur when an entity is not tagged but should be. One possible cause is the use in a document of a nonstandard synonym that is missing in the dictionary. Alternatively, the use of a misspelled term or unusual punctuation may prevent exact recognition, in which case orthographic expansion (Section 38.3.2.3) could be effective. Another important reason is the inevitable incompleteness of the dictionaries used in the NER process. A document may contain obsolete identifiers that are no longer maintained or cross-referenced within current knowledge sources. Also, dictionaries lag behind the databases from which they derive, and these in turn lag behind other primary databases and the literature, where novel entities (e.g., gene or protein names) first appear.

False positives, on the other hand, occur when a term is tagged when it should not be. Common examples include datelike information that resembles gene names: *MARCH4* and *Jun* are human gene symbols and might be tagged as such in the wrong context. A more subtle example that we noticed when preparing Figures 38.1 and 38.4 is the adjective *Endogenous* appearing in a section heading (not shown in the figures), which was tagged by Reflect as the mouse protein Endogenous (Fbxo43, ENSEMBL record: ENSMUSP00000054125). The capitalization of that word provides a perfect match to the protein entity, while a lowercased *endogenous* was not matched (the desired result in this particular situation).

Failure to recognize errors (by nonexperts and experts alike) carries the risk of error propagation through the tool chain, so it is important that both users and developers of annotation systems be aware of this [17]. To some extent, problems with both false positives and false negatives may be partially resolved by using more complex NER methods. However, there may be a trade-off between false negatives and false positives, which is influenced by the NER. For example, orthographic expansion, by relaxing term-matching rules, has the capacity to reduce the number of false negatives but can introduce more false positives.

Another way to reduce the number of false positives is to create a blacklist composed of stopwords (see the Glossary) that should never be tagged. Unfortunately, there is again a trade-off, because many biomedical terms (e.g., *the*, *to*, *its*) are common English terms and will then appear as false negatives. Balancing the trade-off requires manual stopword list curation, which is a tedious procedure. A variation is to use a dynamically created stopword list for the document, based on statistical analysis of word frequencies in English language corpora [23].

In general, some degree of natural language processing to resolve semantics through more complex syntactic structure analysis might help. For example, by analyzing the syntactic role of each word within a sentence, it should be possible to discriminate between uses of Endogenous as an adjective or as a noun in the above example. It is not yet clear how effective such methods are at alleviating tagging errors [28], and more complex algorithms may significantly increase the time taken to process a document and decrease the user experience.

38.4.3   Community Editing and Sharing

Most of the tools use a client–server model with powerful client interfaces and server components that can be extended to handle community-added contributions. This opens up two obvious modes of editing and sharing information: (1) the ability to correct tagging errors (false negatives and false positives; Section 38.4.2.2) and (2) extension or modification of annotations associated with existing entities in the dictionary. Two of the tools (Reflect, Utopia Documents) already offer some community editing and/or sharing of changes.

38.4.3.1   Correcting Tagging Errors   Reflect allows the user to correct a false negative by highlighting the requisite term and completing a popup dialogue to connect the new term with entities already known to Reflect. The change is immediately effective in any subsequently served document. A false positive can be removed from a document via a simple menu selection on the term. The change is cached on the server along with any article DOI (see the Glossary) or URL of the webpage and is shared with all subsequent users. Further, if the term is repeatedly struck out five times in different documents, then that term will not be tagged again in any subsequent document served to any user. A user guide to Reflect's dictionary curation is available in [12].

38.4.3.2   Editing Annotations   Reflect also allows users to edit and share descriptions of an entity via a simple editing facility in the popup that extends the attributes of the entity associated with a term [12]. Similarly, Utopia Documents allows registered users to add comments to a document and share them with the rest of the community [14]. These comments are tied to the article in the PDF and can be seen by all researchers reading the same article.

38.4.4   General Technical Issues

The next few sections discuss miscellaneous technical issues: software longevity and maintenance, client- or server-side operation, access to local or remote data, and concomitant issues of confidentiality and security.

38.4.4.1   *Software Longevity and Maintenance*   Reflect, i-cite, NameLink, and Ontology Add-in for Word are not stand-alone applications. The first three extend the functionality of Web browsers, while the last extends the functionality of Microsoft Word. In practice, this means that they gain the advantage of complementing common user tasks at the cost of periodic maintenance and update. As the browser or similar software evolves and new versions appear, the developers of extensions have to comply with the new requirements and changes to the API. Thus, there is a trade-off between simplicity and user friendliness on the one hand and the recurring need for development resources on the other.

Additionally, browser extension implementations differ from browser to browser so that extra effort is required to support and maintain a range of browsers. The use of minimal user interface design along with maximal reuse of code within the different browser extension implementations can help with this issue.

An issue affecting Ontology Add-in for Word is that it has been developed for a specific operating system platform (Microsoft Windows) and only works on recent versions of Microsoft Office that support add-ins and smart tags, both proprietary Microsoft technology. Accordingly, its functionality is simply unavailable to users of other operating systems and word processors or even to users with older versions of Microsoft Office. This also has consequences for developers who must rely on the continued support and stability of features of a proprietary interface.

38.4.4.2   *Client- or Server-Side Annotation*   Most of the systems we have described only work online with a connection between a client application or plugin/extension and a remote server that performs the annotation. A pure client-side approach (e.g., Ontology Add-in for Word) has the simple advantage of being able to work without an Internet connection but may not scale for more sophisticated tools like Utopia Documents or Reflect, because of the sheer volume of the dictionaries on which they rely. That is, a typical user machine will lack sufficient memory and speed to handle more complex annotation processes.

Server-side processing overcomes these scaling restrictions allowing much larger dictionaries that can be used to recognize more entities and more entity types. Larger memory may be sufficient to hold the entire dictionary, which speeds processing. Lastly, server machines are typically more powerful in terms of raw speed, faster memory, and number of cores. Ultimately, when the time to process a document is less than the time required to communicate it to the server, one might say "real-time tagging" has been achieved [28].

38.4.4.3   *Local or Remote Documents*   With server-side annotation, there are two approaches: (1) communicating the contents of a webpage (Reflect), or the user-selected text (i-cite, WhatIzIt), and (2) communicating the URL address of a webpage (i-cite, Chemicalize, NameLink). Each has differences in the range of Web documents that can be annotated.

Communicating whole or partial contents of a webpage to an annotation service means that this functionality is also available for local Web documents (e.g., personal files), although this introduces confidentiality concerns. On the other hand, submitting only a webpage URL to an annotation server offers a different problem, that of right of access. Both of these issues are considered further in the next section.

38.4.4.4   *Confidentiality and Security*   An annotation service that receives whole or partial webpages from the client offers a potential breach of privacy for the user or their organization in that private or confidential material, such as content hidden behind a firewall, may be transmitted over the network to the annotation server. This should be borne in mind or even restricted when using such a service with local files or sensitive site internal pages.

This issue of data privacy has been recognized by the implementers of the Reflect and OnTheFly annotation services [28, 33]. Possible solutions include ensuring that user-supplied data are processed entirely in memory and never written to disk or, if written, automatically wiped after use. Connection privacy between client and server can be enhanced with the use of an HTTPS encrypted connection (see the Glossary). Nevertheless, there will be cases where an in-house annotation service may be necessary, such as in sensitive commercial environments.

A different problem arises for an annotation service that receives the Web address of a page to be annotated. The annotation service is acting as a proxy via which users obtain access to other webpages, so there is an underlying security concern for the provider of the annotation service concerning access rights to the page. To avoid accessing malicious and inappropriate content or subscribed/internal material to which the annotation service provider has access, a set of proactive measures can be taken: URL content filtering (see the Glossary) firewall/network settings as well as Web server usage monitoring tools may be used [29].

38.4.5 Community Response

Although it is not possible to judge the full extent of the community response to all the tools (e.g., the NameLink bookmarklet is still only a prototype), the community adoption of Reflect and Utopia Documents is indicative of the impact such tools may have.

Reflect has attracted considerable interest, as indicated by the high numbers of pages annotated per day and of downloads of the browser extension: according to [28], there were more than 3000 page annotations per day and 30,000 plugin downloads just after initial publication. Reflect was also selected as the winner of the 2009 Elsevier Grand Challenge, a technology contest to find ways to improve the way that scientific information is communicated [4]. As a consequence, readers of Elsevier's *Cell* journal are now able to view online articles annotated using Reflect.

Likewise, Utopia Documents has also been employed by Portland Press in the on-line edition of *Biochemical Journal* [1] and is being used not only for the curation of articles prior to publication but also for the sharing of user-generated comment across the community. A customized version of Utopia Documents was integrated into the Portland Press editorial and document management work flows, allowing permanent markup of articles before publication. This markup, containing definitions and interactive content, is shared with all readers of the document [17].

38.5 FUTURE PERSPECTIVES

In closing, we consider just a few possible future directions. First, we look at how the tools and techniques presented can be combined today to offer greater variety of annotation to researchers. We then comment on how content provider annotation and standardization efforts could contribute to improved interconnections between literature and knowledge sources. Finally, we discuss how such functionality could be extended further to satisfy the growing information requirements of life sciences researchers and beyond.

38.5.1   Tool Combination and Interoperability

A feature that has only been touched upon lightly in the chapter is the interplay of these tools and how they may be combined to increase their overall utility to the user. For example, Utopia Documents makes use of three annotation services and thereby inherits the annotation richness of each. Benefits for the researcher are manifold, ranging from importing the functionality of other services (e.g., offering Reflect functionality while reading PDF documents instead of HTML pages) to the concurrent viewing of input received from different sources (e.g., viewing the Reflect summary along with information from the GPCRDB text-mining service). The latter flexibility provides an easy way to cross-check and validate the added information [17].

We would expect to see more such interplay in the future, permitting more complex levels and choices of knowledge sources to be made available. In such a scenario the user might be able to annotate species mentions using NameLink, then Reflect the page to identify genes, proteins, and small chemical molecules, and finally annotate a paragraph in relation to diseases via i-cite and WhatIzIt.

With most of the annotation functionality based on remote annotation services, then, with suitable APIs and/or by providing plugin capabilities for tool customization, scientific tool developers will be encouraged to employ such services in their own software, leading to a proliferation of annotation-enabled software with common functionality and interface behavior.

38.5.2   Coalescence of Annotation Efforts

There are two kinds of user of information, the producer and the consumer. We have already referred to the ongoing efforts of some publishers to enrich journal articles. In general, content providers, adapting to the semantic Web, can provide annotations in a "top-down" fashion, specifying and enriching their content in machine-readable form. At the same time, there is a reverse engineering approach (as presented in this chapter) already being applied to enrich existing documents in conventional formats, that represents a "bottom-up" movement from the reader community and supported by tool developers.

The tools and techniques presented in this chapter blur the distinction between producer and consumer, since various stakeholders in the community (e.g., journal editors, authors, and the scientific readership) are all able to contribute to and benefit from these new systems. For example, using annotation tools like those described here, content providers will be able to enrich their publications with annotated content, while the community will employ similar tools to contribute further knowledge and feedback and domain experts will steer and curate.

All of these developments will require standardization efforts to specify common annotation protocols, tagging formats, and specialized markup, for which efforts are already underway, for example, the annotation workshop "Beyond the PDF" held at the University of California, San Diego, in January 2011.

38.5.3   Vision for the Community

With expanding adoption of annotation services and stable, user-friendly tools available to publishers, researchers, teachers, and students alike, we would expect to see increased community-based annotation efforts and the formation of more special interest groups establishing and maintaining dedicated knowledge collections across multiple fields.

An important challenge for the scientific community, beyond the issues we have already discussed (improvements in text mining, term-tagging methods, user interfaces), will be the need for a recorded trail connecting displayed content with original sources and all the inference steps and data transformations in between. Associated with this, in many circumstances there will be a need for controlled levels of user access or oversight procedures to prevent malicious editing and copyright violations. These are, of course, the same problems faced by Wikipedia and similar community-curated resources, which are nevertheless highly successful.

Finally, we propose a vision for the future where the community is both producer and consumer of a multiplicity of specialist annotation services ranging from dedicated in-house systems for confidential and commercial material through to a global network of interconnected services spanning research disciplines and knowledge domains that reach far beyond biology.

GLOSSARY

API *Application programming interface*: a specification for the interface between computer programs, or code components such as libraries, that defines the calling conventions, parameters passed, and values returned (http://en.wikipedia.org/wiki/Application_programming_interface).

Bookmarklet An executable URL that looks like a normal bookmark or hyperlink in a user's browser. However, instead of containing a static link to a webpage, it contains a script that is executed upon a single click (http://en.wikipedia.org/wiki/Bookmarklet).

Browser Extension A computer program that extends the default functionality of a Web browser by, for example, adding buttons, menus, or mouse actions with custom functions (http://en.wikipedia.org/wiki/Browser_extension).

CSS *Cascading style sheets*: provide a simple mechanism for adding style (e.g., fonts, colors, spacing) to Web documents (http://www.w3.org/Style/CSS).

DOI *Digital object identifier*: a character string serving as an internationally recognized unique identifier for an object such as an electronic doument (http://en.wikipedia.org/wiki/Digital_object_identifier).

DOM *Document object model*: a language-independent, cross-platform convention for representing and interacting with objects in HTML and related Web documents (http://www.w3.org/DOM, http://en.wikipedia.org/wiki/Document_Object_Model).

DOM Event Allows an event-driven style of programming necessary for a program executing in a browser to interact with the DOM (http://www.w3.org/TR/DOM-Level-2-events, http://en.wikipedia.org/wiki/DOM_events).

DOM Tree The hierarchical arrangement of nodes forming the DOM and representing document data objects.

HTML *Hypertext Markup Language*: used to specify the layout of a webpage (http://en.wikipedia.org/wiki/HTML).

HTTP *Hypertext Transport Protocol*:   the networking protocol for the World Wide Web that forms the basis for communication between a Web browser and server (`http://www.w3.org/Protocols`, `http://en.wikipedia.org/wiki/Http`).

HTTPS *HTTP Secure*:   a variant of HTTP using secure sockets layer (SSL) or its successor transport layer security (TLS) cryptographic protocols to provide an encrypted connection (`http://en.wikipedia.org/wiki/HTTPS`).

HTTP POST request   A data request method from browser to server supported by the HTTP protocol on the World Wide Web (`http://en.wikipedia.org/wiki/POST_(HTTP)`).

JavaScript A scripting language, often implemented in Web browsers, enabling extensions to the browser functionality (`http://en.wikipedia.org/wiki/JavaScript`).

Ontology   In the sense used here, an ontology is a controlled vocabulary of well-defined terms together with their relationships. It provides a standardized description of biological entities and systems (molecules, cellular components, interactions, etc.), in a human- and machine-readable way.

Regular Expression   A means of matching (i.e., specifying and recognizing) strings of text composed of particular characters, patterns of characters, or words (`http://en.wikipedia.org/wiki/Regular_expression`).

Same origin policy   A security policy for Web browser scripting languages, such as JavaScript, that allows scripts to access each other when running in pages served from the same website but prevents such access to scripts on other sites (`http://en.wikipedia.org/wiki/Same_origin_policy`).

SOAP *Simple Object Access Protocol*: a specification based on XML for exchanging structured data in Web services over a computer network via, for example, the HTTP protocol (`http://www.w3.org/TR/soap12`).

Smart Tag   A selection-based search feature in certain Microsoft products by which the application converts the selected text to a hyperlink (`http://en.wikipedia.org/wiki/Smart_tag_(Microsoft)`).

Stopwords   Usually manually curated list of common words that are ignored in a text during text mining (`http://en.wikipedia.org/wiki/Stop_words`).

URL *Uniform or universal resource locator*:   a character string that represents the address of a resource on the Internet, such as a webpage (`http://en.wikipedia.org/wiki/URL`).

URL content filtering   A technique used to allow or block webpages (or other material) based on analysis of content rather than other characteristics, such as the source (`http://en.wikipedia.org/wiki/Content_filtering`).

XML *EXtensible Markup Language*: a specification for exchanging data marked up in machine-readable form (`http://en.wikipedia.org/wiki/XML`).

XMLHttpRequest An API for scripting languages such as JavaScript that is used to send HTTP requests to a Web server and load the returned data back into the script. This allows, among other things, dynamic updating of fragments of a displayed webpage in response to user actions without reloading the entire page every time (`http://www.w3.org/TR/XMLHttpRequest`).

ACKNOWLEDGMENTS

E. P. is funded by the MARBIGEN EU FP7 REGPOT Project (Reference: 264089), H. H. by the Novo Nordisk Foundation Center for Protein Research, and N. P. B. under the German BMBF/FORSYS ViroQuant program. We would like to thank Georgios Pavlopoulos for discussion, comments, and sharing of ideas. E. P. is also grateful to Christos Arvanitidis for support, Sarah Faulwetter for feedback, on taxonomic issues, Christina Pavloudi for user feedback and the rest of the Biodiversity Laboratory at the Institute of Marine Biology and Genetics in the Hellenic Center for Marine research for all their support and patience.

REFERENCES

1. *Biochemical Journal* semantic format, `http://www.biochemj.org/bj/semantic_faq.htm`.
2. *Cell Press Journals* (Elsevier) Article of the Future format, `http://www.elsevier.com/wps/find/authored_newsitem.cws_home/companynews05_01403`.
3. *ChemSpider Journal of Chemistry*, `http://www.chemmantis.com`.
4. Elsevier Grand Challenge, `http://www.elseviergrandchallenge.com`.
5. GNI list of scientific names repositories, `http://gni.globalnames.org/data_sources`.
6. i-cite, `http://i-cite.org`.
7. NameLink, `http://eol.org/info/namelink`.
8. *Nucleic Acids Research* online database collection, `http://www.oxfordjournals.org/nar/database/a`.
9. OBO ontologies, `http://www.obofoundry.org`.
10. OnTheFly, `http://onthefly.embl.de`.
11. Reflect, `http://reflect.ws`.
12. Reflect community editing document, `http://reflect.ws/How_to_Curate_with_Reflect.pdf`.
13. Utopia Documents, `http://getutopia.com/documents`.
14. Utopia Documents guide, `http://getutopia.com/documents/quick_start.php`.
15. R. B. Altman, C. M. Bergman, J. Blake, C. Blaschke, A. Cohen, F. Gannon, L. Grivell, U. Hahn, W. Hersh, L. Hirschman, L. J. Jensen, M. Krallinger, B. Mons, S. I. O'Donoghue, M. C. Peitsch, D. Rebholz-Schuhmann, H. Shatkay, and A. Valencia. Text mining for biology—The way forward: Opinions from leading scientists. *Genome Biol.*, 9(Suppl. 2):S7, 2008. `http://genomebiology.com/supplements/9/S2`.
16. T. K. Attwood, D. B. Kell, P. McDermott, J. Marsh, S. R. Pettifer, and D. Thorne. Calling International Rescue: Knowledge lost in literature and data landslide! *Biochem. J.*, 424(3):317–333, 2009.
17. T. K. Attwood, D. B. Kell, P. McDermott, J. Marsh, S. R. Pettifer, and D. Thorne. Utopia documents: Linking scholarly literature with research data. *Bioinformatics*, 26(18):i568–574, 2010.

18. A. Divoli, M. A. Hearst, and M. A. Wooldridge. Evidence for showing gene/protein name suggestions in bioscience literature search interfaces. *Pac. Symp. Biocomput.*, 568–579, 2008.

19. R. Easty and N. Nikolov. Client-side integration of life science literature resources. *Bioinformatics*, 25(23):3194–3196, 2009.

20. J. L. Fink, P. Fernicola, R. Chandran, S. Parastatidis, A. Wade, O. Naim, G. B. Quinn, and P. E. Bourne. Word add-in for ontology recognition: Semantic enrichment of scientific literature. *BMC Bioinformatics*, 11(1):103, 2010.

21. M. Y. Galperin and G. R. Cochrane. The 2011 nucleic acids research database issue and the online molecular biology database collection. *Nucleic Acids Res.*, 39(Suppl. 1):D1, 2011.

22. H. Horn. NNF Center for Protein Research, University of Copenhagen. Unpublished, 2011.

23. I. Iliopoulos, A. J. Enright, and C. A Ouzounis. Textquest: Document clustering of Medline abstracts for concept discovery in molecular biology. *Pac. Symp. Biocomput.*, 384–395, 2001.

24. L. J. Jensen, J. Saric, and P. Bork. Literature mining for the biologist: From information retrieval to biological discovery. *Nat. Rev. Genet.*, 7(2):119-129, 2006.

25. M. Krallinger and A. Valencia. Text-mining and information-retrieval services for molecular biology. *Genome Biol.*, 6(7):224, 2005.

26. M. Kuhn, C. von Mering, M. Campillos, L. J. Jensen, and P. Bork. STITCH: Interaction networks of chemicals and proteins. *Nucleic Acids Res.*, 36(Database issue):D684–688, 2008.

27. N. Naderi, T. Kappler, C. J. O. Baker, and R. Witte. OrganismTagger: Detection, normalization and grounding of organism entities in biomedical documents. *Bioinformatics*, 27(19):2721–2729, 2011.

28. S. I. O'Donoghue, H. Horn, E. Pafilis, S. Haag, M. Kuhn, V. P. Satagopam, R. Schneider, and L. J. Jensen. Reflect: A practical approach to web semantics. *Web Semantics: Science, Services and Agents on the World Wide Web*, 8(2–3):182–189, 2010.

29. E. Pafilis. Web-based named entity recognition and data integration to accelerate molecular biology research. Ph.D. Thesis. University of Heidelberg, 2009.

30. E. Pafilis, S. I. O'Donoghue, L. J. Jensen, H. Horn, M. Kuhn, N. P. Brown, and R. Schneider. Reflect: Augmented browsing for the life scientist. *Nat. Biotechnol.*, 27(6):508–510, 2009.

31. P. Patterson. Taxonomy: The collector. Paddy Patterson interviewed by Brendan Maher. *Nature*, 449(7158):23, 2007.

32. D. J. Patterson, J. Cooper, P. M. Kirk, R. L. Pyle, and D. P. Remsen. Names are key to the big new biology. *Trends Ecol. Evol.*, 25(12):686–691, 2010.

33. G. A. Pavlopoulos, E. Pafilis, M. Kuhn, S. D. Hooper, and R. Schneider. OnTheFly: A tool for automated document-based text annotation, data linking and network generation. *Bioinformatics*, 25(7):977–978, 2009.

34. A. Rinaldi. For I dipped into the future. *EMBO Reports*, 11(5):345, 2010.

35. L. Smith et al. Overview of BioCreative II gene mention recognition. *Genome Biol.*, 9(Suppl. 2):S2, 2008.

36. S. Srinivasan, P. Santiago, C. Lubrano, C. Vaisse, and B. R. Conklin. Engineering the melanocortin-4 receptor to control constitutive and ligand-mediated Gs signaling *in vivo*. *PloS ONE*, 2(8):e668, 2007.

37. H. Stockinger, T. Attwood, S. N. Chohan, R. Côté, P. Cudré-Mauroux, L. Falquet, P. Fernandes, R. D. Finn, T. Hupponen, E. Korpelainen, A. Labarga, A. Laugraud, T. Lima, E. Pafilis, M. Pagni, S. Pettifer I. Phan, and N. Rahman. Experience using web services for biological sequence analysis. *Brief. Bioinformatics*, 9(6):493, 2008.

38. B. Vroling, D. Thorne, P. McDermott, T. K. Attwood, G. Vriend, and S. Pettifer. Integrating GPCR-specific information with full text articles. *BMC Bioinformatics*, 12(1):362, 2011.

CHAPTER 39

AUGMENTING BIOLOGICAL TEXT MINING WITH SYMBOLIC INFERENCE

JONG C. PARK and HEE-JIN LEE

Department of Computer Science, Korea Advanced Institute of Science and Technology, Daejeon, South Korea

39.1 INTRODUCTION

Current biology is well known for its enormous amount of relevant data, primarily including the biological literature, to which biological text mining focuses on providing efficient computational access for scientists in the field [1]. Biological text mining involves *information extraction* (IE), which purports to recover predefined and interesting pieces of information from a collection of texts [2], with important tasks such as automatically identifying substrings of sentences that denote biological entities, such as genes, proteins, and diseases (*named entity recognition*, NER), and automatically recognizing relations among these entities (*relation extraction*, RE) [3, 4]. The recent advances in NER and RE have made it possible to provide more efficient and diverse access to the information in the literature. In particular, the process of database curation has become much more efficient when human curators are guided by such systems [5, 6], along with many publicly available tools for navigating the literature [7] and for collecting information of interest from the literature [8].

However, there is also a growing recognition that merely collecting information from the literature is no longer sufficient [9]. In particular, this recognition brings up the need for automatic tools to integrate and manage a large collection of biological information and to assist scientists in coming up with novel knowledge from the available collection of information. The need for an automatic aid in knowledge management [10] arises primarily due to the immense volume and high complexity of biological data. The amount of information relevant to a certain biological system, such as the biochemical network of *Escherichia coli*, has become already too large for a single scientist to grasp even with much effort [11], making it nearly impossible for a scientist to understand the full implications of the system, not to mention the difficulty of validating the system without automatic tools. The derivation of new pieces of knowledge often requires putting together only tangentially related subfields of biology as well [12], a task that would consume a lot of time and effort when performed by human experts alone.

Biological Knowledge Discovery Handbook: Preprocessing, Mining, and Postprocessing of Biological Data,
First Edition. Edited by Mourad Elloumi and Albert Y. Zomaya.
© 2014 John Wiley & Sons, Inc. Published 2014 by John Wiley & Sons, Inc.

The growing need for aid in manipulating a large amount of information has spurred the evolution of text-mining tools as well as the development of knowledge integration and management tools. It is necessary for text-mining systems to participate in the knowledge management process, beyond identifying only explicit mentions of the desired information, in order to perform explorative tasks finding "nuggets" from the literature [13]. As a result, current text-mining tools aim not only at extracting explicitly stated information but also at recognizing information *implied* by the text or even proposing *new hypotheses* [1, 14].

In this chapter, we review recent work on such "next-level" text-mining tools. In particular, we focus on the work that uses symbolic inference to augment text-mining, apart from distributional analysis that is based on the co-occurrence of biological terms and statistical methods. By symbolic inference, we refer to the methods of deriving new information from known facts that are represented with nonnumeric symbols to which inference rules are applied deterministically rather than probabilistically. With symbolic inference, the meanings (or semantics) of natural language terms or phrases are determined by human knowledge and represented symbolically. With distributional analysis, the meanings are determined empirically from the distributional characteristics of terms and phrases across a large body of text. While distributional analysis has also been successfully used recently to derive new information from the literature [12, 15–17], the use of symbolic inference retains its own advantages. For instance, the use of symbolic inference does not require a large amount of data for learning, as the inference rules are defined by human experts with their knowledge of the domain. Also, scientific evidence about the inference results can be furnished, which would be quite difficult in distributional analysis. Further details of the advantages and disadvantages of using symbolic inference to augment text mining will be discussed in the subsequent sections.

Researches reviewed in this chapter target one of the two abstract tasks. The first task is to recognize information not explicitly stated but implied in a document, where the targeted information is often scattered across multiple sentences. The second is to propose newly predicted biological knowledge using information gathered from the literature. We review the work that addresses the first task in Section 39.2, and the work that addresses the second in Section 39.3. In Section 39.4, we briefly review text-mining work with distributional analysis to contrast the use of symbolic inference with the use of distributional analysis. We conclude this chapter in Section 39.5.

39.2   IDENTIFYING IMPLIED INFORMATION

For many of the biological IE systems, it is typical to extract only intrasentential information, or information explicitly stated within a single sentence, unless the method is based on the co-occurrence of terms. Although extracting such intrasentential information is itself a complex task that still requires much improvement, we can extend the coverage of the biological IE systems further by augmenting the method to identify intersentential information as well, or information conveyed by multiple sentences. By identifying such intersentential information, the systems would be able to identify a larger amount of target information, ensuring an increased recall, as well as a fuller account of the asserted information, whether implicit or not. The systems would also be able to identify such information with more complex structures to match. In this section, we introduce work that aims to identify information spread over several sentences and to assemble such information into a predefined target structure by using symbolic methods. By putting together fragments of information stated in more than one sentence, the IE systems would also be able to recognize information as implied throughout the whole document.

The IE systems for intersentential information identification first extract the intrasentential information and then put together fragments of such information to produce intersentential information. Generally, the merge process for the fragments of information is guided by several symbolic rules. Applications of the rules are determined by utilizing linguistic knowledge such as coreference and general discourse principles, as illustrated in Section 39.2.1, or by exploiting biological domain knowledge, as illustrated in Section 39.2.2.

39.2.1 Use of Linguistic Knowledge

In this section, we introduce work that exploits linguistic knowledge to identify information spread over multiple sentences. One way in which information stated in more than one sentence can be connected together is through recognizing "anaphora", which is a phenomenon that relates a word or phrase to other text parts, such as the use of a pronoun at some point and an occurrence or occurrences of its antecedent in the preceding context. Known algorithms for anaphora resolution [18] can be used to improve IE systems by connecting information in multiple sentences through the identification of a coreference relation. In particular, a relation extractor for biology can extract the intrasentential relations first and then extend such relations using a coreference relation. That is, when an intrasentential relation between biological entities A and B is identified by the relation extractor and a coreference relation between the terms denoting biological entities B and C is identified by the anaphora resolution algorithm, the intersentential relation between A and C can also be established.

While the exploitation of anaphora may bring performance improvement to IE systems, not all the sentences are explicitly connected through anaphora, even though they might be semantically related. Authors often assume that a certain kind of information, for instance common domain knowledge or information described in the previous context, is already known to the readers, and they may not explicitly state this kind of information when they compose sentences. Human readers have no problem in recovering this omitted information and understanding the intended meaning of such sentences and the text as a whole. IE systems, on the other hand, need an additional mechanism to accomplish this. This additional mechanism becomes more critical when the system targets at information with a more complex structure than a simple binary relation. Complex structures have many slots to be filled, where the necessary pieces of information to fill the slots may not all be stated within a sentence but described across multiple sentences that are not necessarily all connected by anaphora.

In this section, we introduce work by Yoshikawa et al. [19], where coreference relations are utilized for an IE system, and work by Narayanaswamy et al. [20], where a heuristic method with general discourse principles connects sentences that are not connected through anaphora.

Yoshikawa et al. [19] developed a system for event extraction, a task that is divided into three subtasks: identification of event trigger words, classification of event types, and extraction of the relations between events and arguments. They used a pipeline-based *support vector machine* (SVM) classifier for the identification of intersentential event descriptions with a simple pairwise model [21] for coreference resolution. After identifying the intrasentential event–argument relations, their model deterministically attaches, for each intrasentential argument of an event, all antecedents inside and outside the sentence to the same event, implementing the "transitivity" of a coreference relation during a postprocessing step. With this postprocessing step, the F-score of event–argument relation identification is increased by a statistically significant amount (from 52.3 to 53.6).

In this work, Yoshikawa et al. also proposed a joint *Markov logic network* (MLN) model, which is a probabilistic reasoning model that instantiates Markov networks of a repetitive structure with weighted first-order logic formulas [22]. For the MLN model, they used the concept of *salience in discourse*. Following the centering theory [23], the authors argue that as arguments coreferent to something have a higher salience in discourse, they are hence more likely to be arguments of events mentioned in the document. The F-score of event–argument relation identification with the MLN model is also increased when the coreference information is provided to the model, by a degree greater than that of the SVM model. While the authors argue also that the bigger performance increase of the MLN model is due to the use of salience in discourse, a closer assessment is called for to see how exactly the saliency affects the identification of the argument–event relation. In the corpus over which their models are trained and tested, or the GENIA corpus [24], only the coreferring relations between arguments of events are annotated. Such characteristics of the input corpus apparently present a bias towards the concept of salience in discourse.

Narayanaswamy et al. [20] proposed several heuristic rules and a "fusion" operation as a mechanism for recovering omitted information by connecting information from multiple sentences. They developed a system to extract information on phosphorylation and defined the structure of their target information as having three slots to be filled with information about the agent (or the kinase), the theme (or the substrate), and the site (or the residue) of phosphorylation. The authors argue that as it is uncommon to see all the three targeted objects mentioned in the same sentence, a method must be devised to glue information pieces from multiple sentences.

The proposed method starts by matching clause-level patterns to sentences in abstracts of the biological literature. Their patterns are representative of clauses containing verbal and nominal inflected forms of the verb *phosphorylate* and are applied to the text after preprocessing steps including phrase chunking and semantic-type annotation. A sample clause-level pattern from [20] is shown below, where "?" denotes an optional argument and "VG-activate-phosphorylate" denotes a verb group in active form, headed by an inflected form of the verb "phosphorylate". In the pattern below, the positions of the phrases denoting the agent, theme and site information are shown by pairs of angled brackets:

- \<AGENT\> \<VG-activate-phosphorylate\> \<THEME\> (in/at \<SITE\>)?

After matching the patterns, the system inspects the results of the pattern matching to see whether all the three pieces of information to fill the slots are identified or not. When the theme or the site information is not matched, the heuristic rules are activated and the system attempts to identify the corresponding information using them. The rules for recovering theme information are based on the assumption that the missing information is omitted because it is mentioned in the previous context. When a pattern is matched to a sentence without a matching theme, the system takes the previous and closest mention of a substrate protein as a theme. When there are no such substrates available in the abstract, the system examines the title of the abstract and takes the protein name in the title as a theme, regardless of whether the protein is stated as a substrate or not. Such a method of recovering theme information is guided by discourse principles. On the other hand, the rules for recovering site information are less driven by discourse principles but are closer to the co-occurrence-based approaches to IE. When the site information is not identified by the patterns, the system fills site slots with any residue name that is in the sentence. Similar rules are also applied to identify the theme, when the theme protein is not identified despite applications of the heuristic rules above. Such rules, in effect, are designed to make up for the low coverage of the clause-level patterns. The use of heuristic rules drops the precision of the system by a small amount (from 95.1 to 93.2) but increases the recall of the system significantly (from 24.2 to 57.2), thus increasing the overall F-score of the system (from 38.6 to 85.4).

After the rules are applied, the information pieces are combined by an operation called *fusion*. By fusion, information pieces extracted from two different sentences are combined and merged into one if there is some overlapping and no incompatible information. The fusion operation is thus similar to the notion of unification of compatible terms. The use of fusion increases both precision and recall of the system.

Overall, the use of simple rules and the fusion operation is shown to improve the system performance dramatically, in particular regarding the recall. The heuristics rules and fusion seem to be applicable to other IE systems extracting protein *posttranslational modifications* (PTMs) other than phosphorylation. However, their heuristics is apparently suitable only for those articles reporting PTMs as results of low-throughput experiments focusing on a small number of PTM events, making its application to articles of other types quite difficult.

39.2.2 Use of Biological Domain Knowledge

Work discussed in Section 39.2.1 uses linguistic knowledge to connect information from multiple sentences. On the other hand, there are other approaches that use domain knowledge to derive information implied by multiple sentences. In this section, we introduce work by Gaizauskas et al. [25] and work by Kim and Rebholz-Schuhmann [26]. Although the two studies are similar in that both first extract information pieces from individual sentences and then infer implied information with symbolic inference, they are different in the way domain knowledge is represented. The former developed a domain-specific ontology to represent hierarchical relations such as `part_of`, whereas the latter used rules of the form $P \to Q$ to represent biological knowledge on the process of gene regulation. In addition, Kim and Rebholz-Schuhmann provided an in-depth evaluation of the performance of the inference module and showed that symbolic inference can be used for a robust IE system on a real-world task. They also showed that the inference system developed for a particular target information can be easily adapted to the extraction of other semantically similar target information.

Gaizauskas et al. [25] used a limited-domain ontology for an IE system, called *Protein Active Site Template Acquisition* (PASTA), to extract information about the roles of residues in proteins to assist in identifying active sites and binding sites of proteins. Their system aims to identify specific information about individual residue, such as name, number, and function of the residue, and location information of the residue, such as the specific regions or substructure of the protein where the residue resides. Figure 39.1 shows example instances of the target information, or the templates, taken from [25].

After recognizing named entities, such as residue, protein, and species, the system "phrase parses" the sentences to produce a phrase–structure analysis. Using the phrase–structure information, the system derives information about the predicate argument representations. Then, the system goes into the discourse processing phase, where the domain ontology is used. The domain ontology includes inheritable properties and inference rules associated with domain concepts and is used to enhance anaphora resolution and to enrich

```
<RESIDUE-134> :=                        <IN_PROTEIN> :=
    NAME: SERINE                            RESIDUE: <RESIDUE-134>
    NO: 87                                  PROTEIN: <PROTEIN-2>
    SITE/FUNCTION: "catalytic"          <IN_SPECIES> :=
                   "calcium-binding"        PROTEIN: <PROTEIN-2>
                   "active-site"            SPECIES: <SPECIES-5>
    SEC_STRUCT: "helical"               <PROTEIN-2> :=
    QUAT_STRUCT: <not specified>            NAME: "triacylglycerol lipase"
    REGION: "lid"                       <SPECIES-5> :
    INTERACTION: <not specified>            NAME "Pseudomonas cepacia"
```

FIGURE 39.1   Example templates used in PASTA [25].

the discourse model through inference. Table 39.1 shows example sentences from [25] and the predicates added to the discourse model as each of the example sentences is processed. Entities registered to the discourse model are assigned a number and symbolized with the letter "e" followed by the assigned number, as in e1.

After producing predicate argument representations of sentences S1 and S5, the discourse processing module of the system evokes an anaphora resolution scheme to resolve e25 with e1. In doing this, the domain knowledge as defined in the ontology, such as "proteins are molecules", is used for the anaphora resolution. Following the syntactic and semantic processing of S6, the system produces the predicate contain(e52, e61) by identifying the subject and object of the verb *contain*. Based on the domain knowledge, such that "if a region contains a residue then the residue is located in the region", located_in(e61, e52) is derived. Lastly, based on the transitivity of located_in, located_in(e61,e1) is produced, which means that ASP130 is in EndoH.

The discourse processing explained above is a principled approach and includes several schemes to connect information from multiple sentences, such as anaphora resolution and inference based on domain-specific rules. Gaizauskas et al., however, do not explain in detail the structure and size of the domain ontology and do not report any evaluation on the performance of the discourse processing module.

TABLE 39.1   Discourse Processing in PASTA [25]

Sentence	Discourse Model
S1: The three-dimensional structure of Endo H has been determined ...	protein(e1) name(e1,"Endo H")
S5: A shallow curved cleft runs across the surface of the molecule from ...	cleft(e23) molecule(e25) protein(e42) located_in(e23,e42) e42=e25=e1
S6: This cleft contains the putative catalytic residue Asp130 ...	cleft(e52) residue(e61) name(e61,"Asp130") contain(e52,e61) located_in(e61,e52) e23=e52 located_in(e61,e1)

Note: Predicates in the second column are added to the discourse model after the sentence in the first column is processed.

```
<RegulationOfGeneExpression
        hasAgent=?Protein
        hasPatient=?<GeneExpression
                hasPatient=?Gene>>

<RegulationOfTranscription
        hasAgent=?Protein
        hasPatient=<Transcription
                hasPatient=?Gene>>

<BindingOfTFto-TFBindingSiteOfDNA
        hasAgent=?TranscriptionFactor
        hasPatinet=
                <RegulatoryDNARegion
                        hasPatient=?Gene>>
```

FIGURE 39.2 Example templates [26].

Kim and Rebholz-Schuhmann [26] manually compiled domain rules to connect information from multiple sentences and extract target information defined with complex structures. They compiled 28 inference rules in total by consulting their training corpus and a review paper [27] on their target domain.

Their target information is a collection of events in the domain of gene regulation, whose structure is as shown in Figure 39.2. They utilized the concepts defined in the *Gene Regulation Ontology* (GRO) [28], an ontology in the domain of gene regulation, as templates for the target information. The structure of the templates is considered "complex" in that the overall template is the result of the "composition" of "basic events", which are flat-structured and often described with language patterns such as "A regulate B" and "expression of Gene C".

After named entity recognition and parsing, their system produces dependency structures of each sentence. Then the system matches paired patterns of syntax and semantics to the dependency structures to identify mentions of explicit events and to produce corresponding semantic representations. An example pattern is shown below, where the syntactic and semantic patterns, shown in parentheses and angled brackets, respectively, are separated by a solidus. In the syntactic pattern the leftmost item in parentheses is the head of other items. The dependent items are represented with their roles with respect to the head and semantic variables indicating their semantics, where the two are divided by a colon. The system matches the patterns in a bottom-up way. When a pattern is matched, the resulting semantic representation is assigned to the head item of the matched dependency subtree. The assigned semantic representation then instantiates the semantic variable of the head item when the head item is matched as a dependent item of another pattern. In this way, the semantics of multiple phrases are combined into one, compositional structure.

- `(cause_Verb Subject:Agent Object:Patient) / <Regulatory Process hasAgent=Agent hasPatient=Patient>`

The semantic representations produced by pattern matching are then processed by the symbolic inference module. Their inference module is composed of 28 manually developed inference rules, which are in the form of $P \rightarrow Q$ implications. The inference module follows modus ponens. When all of the conditions in P match some of the already identified events, the conclusion Q is instantiated and added to the set of known, identified events. Example rules used in [26] are shown in Table 39.2.

TABLE 39.2   Inference Rules of Kim and Rebholz-Schuhmann [26]

No.	Condition(s) $\Rightarrow$ Conclusion

1	`<RegulatoryProcess hasPolarity=Polarity2`
	    `hasAgent=<RegulatoryProcess`
	       `hasPatient=Patient`
	       `hasPolarity=Polarity1>>`
	`⇒<RegulatoryProcess hasAgent=Patient`
	    `hasPolarity=polarity_sum(Polarity1,Porarity2)`

2	`<RegulatoryProcess hasPolarity=Polarity2`
	    `hasPatient=<RegulatoryProcess`
	       `hasPatient=Patient`
	       `hasPolarity=Polarity1>>`
	`⇒<RegulatoryProcess hasPatient=Patient`
	    `hasPolarity=polarity_sum(Polarity1,Porarity2)>`

3	`<RegulatoryProcess`
	    `hasPatient=GeneExpression>`
	`⇒<RegulationOfGeneExpression`
	    `hasPatient=GeneExpression>`

4	`<RegulationOfGeneExpression`
	    `hasAgent=TranscriptionFactor`
	    `hasPatient=<GeneExpression`
	       `hasPatient=Gene>>`
	`<RegulatoryDNARegion hasAgent=Gene`
	    `hasPart=<TFBS`
	       `hasAgent=TranscriptionFactor>>`
	`⇒<RegulationOfTranscription`
	    `hasAgent=TranscriptionFactor`
	    `hasPatient=<Transcription`
	       `hasPatient=Gene>`
	    `hasPhysicalContact="yes">`

Evaluation of the system on a manually annotated corpus showed that the inference contributed to 53.2% of the correct results and caused no incorrect results. The system was also applied to a real-world task, or the task of populating RegulonDB [29], and showed a performance comparable to that of a state-of-the-art extraction system [30], suggesting the robustness of the proposed inference-based event extraction method. In addition, the authors applied their system to other semantically related events, or the regulation of cell growth and death. For this application, the existing language patterns and inference rules related to the concept of *regulation* were reused, with the addition of 40 patterns related to the concept *growth* and *death*, along with the names of related genes, proteins, and cells. Although the system showed a good performance exhibiting its adaptability, the increase of recall due to the inference module was only 20%, indicating that the inference rules are apparently less effective than the original ones.

The inference rules proposed by Kim and Rebholz-Schuhmann not only connect multiple sentences but also have an effect of modularizing the overall syntactic patterns. While rules 3 and 4 in Table 39.2 can be used jointly to deduce new, implied events from existing, explicit events, rules 1 and 2 in Table 39.2 flatten the compositional structure of semantic representations. With these kinds of inference rules, the authors were able to break down the syntactic patterns into smaller phrases that could later be combined into one compositional structure, not constrained by the complexity of the resulting structures.

39.2.3 Section Summary

So far we discussed some work that used symbolic methods to identify information described across multiple sentences. The methods are either linguistically motivated or motivated by the domain knowledge with the notion of coreference relation, the heuristic rules based on the characteristics of natural language discourse, and the use of a domain ontology and inference rules based on domain knowledge. The methods, composed of only a handful of rules, boost the recall of IE systems to a fairly significant degree, whereas the decrease in the precision is relatively small.

Moreover, when it comes to the identification of information across multiple sentences, the use of such symbolic inference tapping into richer linguistic and domain knowledge is quite likely to become a required part of IE systems. Without the use of such linguistic and domain knowledge, one should annotate each document with every piece of information deducible from the document, which would make it quite difficult, if not impossible, to identify the features responsible for the deduced information. In addition, while other methods such as machine learning require a fairly large amount of data, which may also require much annotation time, inference rules can be constructed in a relatively short time when appropriate help of experts is available. Also, as Kim and Rebholz-Schuhmann [26] have also shown, such rule-based systems can be adapted to other domains quite easily with a minimal amount of work, unlike the common belief that rule-based systems are too specific for a given domain to be applied easily to other domains.

We conclude this section by noting that the identification of information across sentences is a task that should not be overlooked. Kim and Rebholz-Schuhmann [26] evaluated their system once by counting all extracted event instances and again by counting only unique events. They found out that the inference module is used for the extraction of much higher percentage (93.8%) of extracted events in the first case than in the second case (53.2%). They interpreted this as an indication that only a small amount of well-known events are frequently mentioned in concise language forms and that the rest of the events are expressed with more detailed descriptions, which may span multiple sentences. The recent change of attention to extracting information from full-text rather than only from abstracts [31–33] also calls for methods to connect information from multiple sentences effectively. For instance, McIntosh and Curran [34] analyzed 78 full-text articles in biology to find out possible challenges in processing full-text articles and reported that, in order to identify such information from full text, semantic dependencies among information from different sentences should be resolved.

39.3 PREDICTING NEW HYPOTHESES

In 1987, Swanson [35] first showed that information from two disjoint* sets of literature representing different specialties of science can be joined to produce novel and plausible

---

*Two sets of literature are disjoint if they have no articles in common, do not cite or mention each other, and are not cocites [36].

hypothesis in science. Since then, work to uncover "hidden" links between biology and medical concepts using a collection of text, or "literature-based discovery" [37], has been pursued. Although co-occurrence-based statistical analyses [12, 15–17] are well suited to propose a new hypothesis from a collection of the literature, such distributional methods have some limitations as well. The new hypotheses derived with such distributional methods are often in a form that claims the possible existence of an "association" between two concepts, not assigning more specific semantics to the association. Furthermore, it is difficult to provide scientific evidence or explanation for the proposed new hypothesis to the users. On the other hand, by using symbolic inference methods, various semantic information can be assigned to the newly derived hypotheses, and scientific evidence can thus be provided in a human-friendly format.

In this section, we introduce work that employed symbolic inference for literature-based discovery. We first describe the proposals where specific semantics are assigned to the hypothesized binary relations between biology concepts in Section 39.3.1, and then the one where a more complex biology concept than the binary relation, or a biological pathway, is hypothesized in Section 39.3.2.

39.3.1 Hypothesizing Binary Relations

In a typical literature-based discovery methodology, based on simple co-occurrences between concepts, if concepts X and Y co-occur frequently, and if concepts Y and Z co-occur frequently, then concepts X and Z are hypothesized to be in a meaningful relationship. In the process, the semantic types of binary relations are usually not considered. However, we can find some benefits in looking into the semantics of relations. The literature-based discovery system can be focused only on the interested semantic types of relations, not producing hypotheses on binary relations of other semantic types. For instance, the number of spurious hypothetical relations will thus be much reduced, as inference rules based on semantic properties of binary relations can be constrained to prevent such false-positive hypotheses.

The two works we introduce in this section exploit the semantics of binary relations for literature-based discovery. Hristovski et al. [38] showed that semantic properties can be successfully incorporated in the literature-based discovery but did not fully automatize their idea due to scalability and accuracy issues. The more recent work of Tari et al. [39] showed that such issues can be partly addressed to develop a fully automatized system.

To exploit the semantic information for literature-based discovery, Hristovski et al. introduced the notion of *discovery pattern*. A discovery pattern is composed of a set of conditions to be satisfied in order to derive a new hypothesis, where conditions are combinations of relations between concepts that need to be satisfied in order to derive a new hypothesis. Figure 39.3 shows discovery patterns used in [38], where solid lines represent known relations extracted from the literature, while dashed lines indicate a new hypothesis that will be proposed. Their goal was to find out if an existing drug for a disease can be used to treat another disease, which are represented by the `Maybe_Treats1` and `Maybe_Treats2` relations in Figure 39.3.

Based on the proposed discovery pattern, Hristovski et al. succeeded to discover the relation between fish oil and Raynaud's disease, a relation first hypothesized by Swanson [35] with literature-based discovery and later verified experimentally [36]. They also proposed insulin as a new treatment for Huntington disease. However, rather than building a fully automatized system, the authors manually checked if relations extracted from the literature

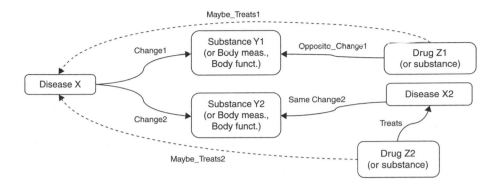

FIGURE 39.3 Discovery pattern from [38]. When Z1 causes "opposite change" to Y1 and the change of Y1 is a characteristic of disease *X*, `Maybe_Treats1` proposes Z1 as a new treatment for disease *X*. When there is a similar disease to *X*, or X2, and drug Z2 is known to treat X2, `Maybe_Treats2` proposes Z2 as a treatment for disease *X*.

using existing natural language processing systems fit their discovery patterns. This is due to scalability and accuracy issues. Processing the whole MEDLINE was a time-consuming task and a small fraction of false positives by IE systems would produce a large number of spurious hypotheses.

Tari et al. [39] employed an approach similar to that of Hristovski et al. [38] discussed above. However, instead of manually checking for new hypotheses, they developed a fully automatized system addressing the scalability and accuracy issues.

Tari et al. targeted at deriving new hypotheses on *drug–drug interactions* (DDIs). DDI refers to the adverse drug reactions that may occur in human bodies when multiple drugs are absorbed simultaneously, as one drug may either increase or decrease the effect of another drug. Identifying such possible DDIs is a vital step in effective drug development. Tari et al. exploited the domain knowledge about the molecular mechanism that causes DDIs. For instance, drug *A* may decrease the effect of drug *B* if drug *A* inhibits a transcription factor that regulates an enzyme which in turn metabolizes drug *B*. Such knowledge about drug metabolism and enzyme regulation is stated as AnsProlog [40, 41] rules, as shown in Table 39.3. In AnsProlog rules, the leftmost predicate before : - is true if the rest of the predicates after : - hold.

Their system first starts by extracting triplets of < actor 1, relation, actor 2 > from the literature. For information extraction, they used a *parse tree database*, which

TABLE 39.3   Inference Rules of Tari et al. [39]

No.	Rules
1	`affects(Dr, level(P, high)):-` `    induces(Dr, P), drug(Dr), protein(P).`

2	`affects(Dr, level(P, high)):-`
	`    affects(Dr, level(TF, high)), protein(P),`
	`    regulates(TF, P), drug(DR), transcription_factor(TF).`

3	`result(Dr1, decreases, Dr2) :-`
	`    affects(Dr1, level(P, high)), enzyme(P),`
	`    metabolized(Dr2, P), drug(Dr1), drug(Dr2).`

stores syntactic structures of sentences from 17 million MEDLINE abstracts along with semantic annotations of sentences, and the *Parse Tree Query Language* (PTQL), a query language designed for extracting various kinds of relations. By preprocessing sentences and storing the resulting syntactic and semantic information in a database, they addressed the scalability issue.

After extracting triplets, a process called *data cleaning* is performed to deal with the accuracy issue. Through semantic verification, some of the false-positive triplets extracted from the literature are removed. For instance, for a triplet < protein 1, regulates, protein 2 > to pass the data-cleaning process and to be used in the subsequent reasoning process, the specific semantic types of protein 1 and protein 2 should be *transcription factor* and *enzyme*, respectively. To specify more detailed semantic types of biology entities, annotations in existing databases and ontologies such as UniProt [42], *Gene Ontology* (GO) [43] and Entrez Gene [44] summary are used. For example, if a protein is annotated under UniProt as having keywords *hydrolase*, *ligase*, *lyase*, or *transferase*, the protein is considered an enzyme. In addition, triplets with negated relations, extracted from sentences with negation words such as *not*, are also utilized to remove false-positive triplets. The whole data-cleaning process incorporating both more detailed semantic typing and negated relations is stated as AnsProlog rules as shown below. In the following example, extr predicates are direct logic translations of the triplets extracted from the literature:

- `metabolized(D, P):- extr(P, metabolizes, D), drug(D),`
  `enzyme(P), not extr(P, not_metabolizes, D).`

The triplets extracted from the literature are handed to an AnsProlog solver. The solver then processes the data-cleaning phase and derives interactions among a given set of drugs. The system produced 5133 new hypothetic DDIs with 17 million MEDLINE abstracts. The authors manually evaluated a small fraction, or 315, of the inferred DDIs and found out that 81.3% of them are correct. Also, most of the incorrectly inferred DDIs were found due to the extraction of incorrect triplets.

39.3.2 Hypothesizing Complex Biology Concepts

By representing biological information symbolically and manipulating the symbolized information with inference rules, biology concepts more complex than binary relations can be dealt with. Although such symbolic methods have been used to represent complex biological processes and to study integrated biological systems [45], symbolic methods for hypothesizing complex biology concepts in literature-based discovery have not been attempted seriously, with the exception of the work by Tari et al. [46], which shows the possibility that literature-based discovery can be extended to handle more complex concepts when augmented with symbolic inference.

In their work, the goal was to build pathways of a drug metabolism. A pathway is essentially a collection of binary relations that can be extracted from the literature. However, a pathway also represents *temporal ordering* between binary relations. Tari et al. utilized the domain knowledge about general properties and behaviors of drug metabolic pathways to assign orderings between binary relations extracted from the literature.

Preconditions and postconditions of binary relations or interactions are specified as AnsProlog rules. In such rules, "time points" are used to specify orderings between binary relations, such that interaction I_1 occurs before interaction I_2 if I_1 is assigned with a time point earlier than that of I_2. Example rules are shown below, where the predicate o is used to represent the occurrence of an event, and the predicate *h* is used to represent a certain state described by some conditions. The first rule states that the action converts(*D*, *M*) occurs at time point *T* in location Loc if drug *D* has been metabolized at time point *T*, and metabolite *M* is known to be a metabolite of *D*, and metabolism of *D* is known to take place in Loc, and it is not known that *D* has been converted into metabolites at a previous time point. The second rule is read similarly.

- o(converts(D, M), Loc, T):- h(metobolized(D), T),
  metabolites(D, M), metabolism(D, Loc),
  not h(converted(D), T).
- h(converted(D), T+1):- o(converts(D, M), Loc, T),
  metabolites(D, M).

They also employed the parse tree database and PTQL to extract triplets representing binary relations. In addition, domain-specific databases and ontologies such as GO and PharmGKB [47] are consulted to collect information about functions or proteins and other additional binary relations. The collected set of information is then used by an answer set solver to produce an *answer set*, which is a model assigning a time point to each binary relation. The produced answer sets correspond to the metabolic pathway of the target drug. Table 39.4 shows an output of the system representing the metabolic pathway of the drug repaglinide.

They produced 20 metabolic pathways and compared the pathways to those available in PharmGKB. While they found that the synthesized pathways were generally consistent with the pathways in PharmGKB, their pathways lack some of the details that the annotated pathways have. For example, the information about which enzyme is responsible for the production of a particular drug metabolite is not incorporated in their pathways.

39.3.3 Section Summary

We have so far discussed symbolic inference–based work that derives new hypotheses from the literature. Unlike proposals that are based on distributional analysis, those that use

TABLE 39.4 Logic Representation of Repaglinide Metabolic Pathway Produced by System of Tari et al. [46]

Timepoint	Events
0	h(is_taken(repaglinide,orally),0).
1	h(is_present(repaglinide,intestine),1). o(transports(repaglinide,intestine),liver,1).
2	-h(is_present(repaglinide,intestine),2). h(is_present(repaglinide,liver),2). o(distributes(slco1b1,repaglinide),liver,2). o(metabolizes(cyp3a4,repaglinide),liver,2). o(metabolizes(cyp2c8,repaglinide),liver,2).
3	h(metabolized(repaglinide,liver),3). o(converts(repaglinide,m1),liver,3). o(converts(repaglinide,m4),liver,3).
4	-h(is_present(repaglinide,liver),4).

Note: The symbol "-" in front of predicate names corresponds to negation.

symbolic inference can provide scientific evidence of the generated hypotheses to the users. For example, in the case of the work by Hristovski et al. [38], a set of binary relations that are used to instantiate the discovery pattern can be used as scientific evidence for the hypothesized disease–drug relation. Also, hypotheses of forms other than binary relations can be made with symbolic inference, as in the work by Tari et al. [46], which automatically predicted drug metabolic pathways.

Rather than using information in the biology databases as in other approaches [48] for knowledge discovery, the systems introduced in this section used information extracted by text-mining systems. By directly incorporating text mining, the literature-based discovery systems can tap into the most up-to-date information in the literature. Furthermore, while the information in a database is in a prespecified format, text-mining systems can be adjusted to extract information in a format that is most suitable for the knowledge discovery task at hand.

However, the imperfect precision of relation extraction systems is still a hindrance to the literature-based discovery systems. False-positive relations produced by relation extraction systems might give rise to low-quality hypotheses with no scientific evidence. Although more research should be made to develop relation extractors with better performance, the imperfection of relation extractors can be addressed by other methods. For instance, only the relations extracted more frequently than a certain threshold can be used to produce new hypotheses or prior biology knowledge can be used to filter out contradicting information, as in the work by Tari et al. [39].

We anticipate more diverse kinds of literature-based discovery systems in the future. In particular, we believe that by utilizing rich semantic aspects of natural language descriptions, such as negation, speculation, and conditionality, newer kinds of hypotheses can be derived. For instance, contradictions among the literature can be found this way [49].

39.4   TEXT MINING WITH DISTRIBUTIONAL ANALYSIS

Work introduced in the earlier sections of this chapter employs symbolic inference methods to recognize implied information from text and to propose new hypotheses. Such tasks can also be performed by employing distributional analysis, in which the semantics of text is empirically determined by its distributional characteristics. Distributional methods are often contrasted with rule-based methods for text-mining systems, including symbolic inference methods. In this section, we briefly review text-mining work that used distributional methods to contrast them with text mining with symbolic inference. Although such distributional analysis is widely accepted in the biology domain to perform various tasks, such as gene clustering [50] and gene function annotation [51], we only introduce work to recognize intersentential relations and to perform literature-based knowledge discovery. The readers who are interested in more diverse uses of distributional analysis for text mining in biology should consult a recent review [52].

As the simplest approach for RE tasks, co-occurrence of terms within a sentence or a document has often been utilized as an indication of the existence of a certain kind of relation between biological concepts represented by the terms. Various statistical or information-theoretic tests are used to find out whether the two terms co-occur more often than by simple chance [53, 54]. Essentially, when the co-occurrence within a document is considered, a text-mining system with such distributional analysis is understood to recognize intersentential relations. However, for RE tasks, such co-occurrence-based methods are considered as producing many false-positive relations to a degree greater than that they increase the recall of the systems. Thus, in current RE work, a distributional method is used as a baseline against which other methods utilizing natural language processing techniques such as parsing are compared [55].

Although distributional analysis is not the most widely accepted method for RE tasks, the use of distributional analysis for explorative tasks such as literature-based discovery is receiving much attention. Various statistical models and spatial models are used to estimate the relatedness of biological concepts across documents. Yetisgen-Yildiz and Pratt represented documents by indexing *medical subject headings* (MeSHs) [56] terms and then weighted co-occurrence of terms by Z-score [17]. Seki et al. adopted an inference network model whose conditional probabilities are estimated from co-occurrences in the literature [16]. Gordon and Dumais proposed the use of *latent semantic indexing* (LSI) [57] and Bruza et al. used *hyperspace analogue to language* (HAL) [58]. Such approaches share the basic assumption: If a biological concept A co-occurs often with biological concept B, and another biological concept C also co-occurs with B, then there may also be a semantic relationship between A and C even though the two concepts do not co-occur often together.

39.5 DISCUSSION AND CONCLUSION

In this chapter we introduced various work that employed symbolic inference to recognize information implied in the text and to propose new hypotheses. The use of symbolic inference is found to increase the recall of the text-mining systems to a meaningful degree. Literature-based discovery systems are enhanced to deal with various types of hypotheses, such as pathways, and to provide scientific evidence of the proposed hypotheses.

The inference rules as discussed in this chapter can be represented as horn clauses, which is a logic clause with at most one positive literal. As horn clause rules have rather simple semantics, stating domain knowledge as a horn clause is not a complex task. Also, there is a logic programming language, Prolog, with an efficient inference engine. However, other logic systems are also looked into. For instance, Kim et al. [59] used an ontology and description logic to deduce implied knowledge from a collection of literature, and Lee and Park [60] used temporal logic in this domain.

We note that for literature-based discovery systems, it is necessary to identify the biological context of information extracted from text. For instance, a spurious hypothesis will be produced if a literature-based discovery system connects two molecular interactions that occur in the normal cells and in the diseased cells, respectively. To incorporate such biological context information into the literature-based discovery system, both text-mining and inference systems should be developed at the same time.

Although symbolic inference is not yet widely employed to enhance text-mined information, it does have unique and good advantages. We expect such symbolic methods to be used more often either alone or in conjunction with other methods for successful biological knowledge discovery.

ACKNOWLEDGMENTS

This work was supported by the Korea Research Foundation Grant funded by the Korean Government (MOEHRD) (KRF-2007-313-D00738) and by the Mid-career Researcher Program through the National Research Foundation (NRF) funded by the Ministry of Education, Science and Technology (MEST) (No. 20110029447).

REFERENCES

1. P. Zweigenbaum, D. Demner-Fushman, H. Yu, and K. B. Cohen. Frontiers of biomedical text mining: Current progress. *Brief. Bioinformatics*, 8(5):358–375, 2007.

2. P. Zweigenbaum and D. Demner-Fushman. Advanced literature-mining tools. In D. Edwardsa, J. Stajich, and D. Hansen (Eds.), *Bioinformatics: Tools and Applications*, Springer, New York, 2009, pp. 347–381.

3. F. Leitner, S. A. Mardis, M. Krallinger, G. Cesareni, L. A. Hirschman, and A. Valencia. An overview of BioCreative II.5. *IEEE/ACM Trans. Computat. Biol. Bioinformatics*, 7:385–399, 2010.

4. M. Krallinger, A. Morgan, L. Smith, F. Leitner, L. Tanabe, J. Wilbur, L. Hirschman, and A. Valencia. Evaluation of text-mining systems for biology: Overview of the second biocreative community challenge. *Genome Biol.*, 9(Suppl. 2):S1, 2008.

5. B. Alex, C. Grover, B. Haddow, M. Kabadjov, E. Klein, and X. Wang. Assisted curation: Does text mining really help. In *Proceedings of Pacific Symposium on Biocomputing*, pp. 556–567, 2008.

6. N. Karamanis, R. Seal, I. Lewin, P. McQuilton, A. Vlachos, C. Gasperin, R. Drysdale, and T. Briscoe. Natural language processing in aid of FlyBase curators. *BMC Bioinformatics*, 9(1):193, 2008.

7. R. Hoffmann and A. Valencia. A gene network for navigating the literature. *Nat. Genet.*, 36:664, 2004.

8. H. Chen and B. Sharp. Content-rich biological network constructed by mining PubMed abstracts. *BMC Bioinformatics*, 5(1):147, 2004.

9. T. Slater, C. Bouton, and E. S. Huang. Beyond data integration. *Drug Discov. Today*, 13(13-14):584–589, 2008.

10. E. Antezana, M. Kuiper, and V. Mironov. Biological knowledge management: The emerging role of the semantic web technologies. *Brief. Bioinformatics*, 10(4):392–407, 2009.

11. P. D. Karp. Pathway databases: A case study in computational symbolic theories. *Science*, 293(5537):2040–2044, 2001.

12. D. R. Swanson and N. R. Smalheiser. An interactive system for finding complementary literatures: A stimulus to scientific discovery. *Artif. Intell.*, 91(2):183–203, 1997.

13. M. A. Hearst. Untangling text data mining. In *Proceedings of the 37th Annual Meeting of the Association for Computational Linguistics*, 1999, pp. 3–10.

14. J. D. Wren. The emerging in-silico scientist: How text-based bioinformatics is bridging biology and artificial intelligence. *IEEE Eng. Med. Biol. Mag.*, 23(2):87–93, 2004.

15. M. Palakal, J. Bright, T. Sebastian, and S. Hartanto. A comparative study of cells in inflammation, EAE and MS using biomedical literature data mining. *J. Biomed. Sci.*, 14(1):67–85, 2007.

16. K. Seiki and J. Mostafa. Discovering implicit associations between genes and hereditary diseases. In *Proceedings of Pacific Symposium on Biocomputing*, Vol. 12, 2007, pp. 316–327.

17. M. Yetisgen-Yildiz and W. Pratt. Using statistical and knowledge-based approaches for literature-based discovery. *J. Biomed. Inform.*, 39(6):600–611, 2006.

18. R. Mitkov. *Anaphora Resolution*. Longman, London, 2002.

19. K. Yoshikawa, S. Riedel, T. Hirao, M. Asahara, and Y. Matsumoto. Coreference based event-argument relation extraction on biomedical text. *J. Biomed. Semantics*, 2(Suppl. 5):S6, 2011.

20. M. Narayanaswamy, K. E. Ravikumar, and K. Vijay-Shanker. Beyond the clause: Extraction of phosphorylation information from MEDLINE abstracts. *Bioinformatics*, 21(Suppl. 1):i319–i327, 2005.

21. W. M. Soon, H. T. Ng, and D. C. Yong Lim. A machine learning approach to coreference resolution of noun phrases. *Computat. Ling.*, 27(4):521–544, 2001.

22. M. Richardson and P. Domingos. Markov logic networks. *Machine Learning*, 62(1):107–136, 2006.

23. B. J. Grosz, S. Weinstein, and A. K. Joshi. Centering: A framework for modeling the local coherence of discourse. *Computat. Ling.*, 21(2):203–225, 1995.

24. J.-D. Kim, T. Ohta, and J. Tsujii. Corpus annotation for mining biomedical events from literature. *BMC Bioinformatics*, 9(1):10, 2008.

25. R. Gaizauskas, G. Demetriou, P. Artymiuk, and P. Willett. Protein structures and information extraction from biological texts: The PASTA system. *Bioinformatics*, 19(1):135–143, 2003.

26. J. J. Kim and D. Rebholz-Schuhmann. Improving the extraction of complex regulatory events from scientific text by using ontology-based inference. *J. Biomed. Semantics*, 2(Suppl. 5):S3, 2011.

27. D. F. Browning and S. J. W. Busby. The regulation of bacterial transcription initiation. *Nat. Rev. Microbiol.*, 2(1):57–65, 2004.

28. E. Beisswanger, V. Lee, J.-J. Kim, D. Rebholz-Schuhmann, A. Splendiani, O. Dameron, S. Schulz, and U. Hahn. Gene Regulation Ontology (GRO): Design principles and use cases. *Studies Health Technol. Informatics*, 136:9–14, 2008.

29. S. Gama-Castro et al. RegulonDB version 7.0: Transcriptional regulation of *Escherichia coli* K-12 integrated within genetic sensory response units (Gensor Units). *Nucleic Acids Res.*, 39(Suppl. 1):D98–D105, 2011.

30. C. Rodriguez-Penagos, H. Salgado, I. Martinez-Flores, and J. Collado-Vides. Automatic reconstruction of a bacterial regulatory network using natural language processing. *BMC Bioinformatics*, 8(1):293, 2007.

31. M. J. Schuemie, M. Weeber, B. J. A. Schijvenaars, E. M. van Mulligen, C. C. van der Eijk, R. Jelier, B. Mons, and J. A. Kors. Distribution of information in biomedical abstracts and full-text publications. *Bioinformatics*, 20(16):2597–2604, 2004.

32. P. Shah, C. Perez-Iratxeta, P. Bork, and M. Andrade. Information extraction from full text scientific articles: Where are the keywords? *BMC Bioinformatics*, 4(1):20, 2003.

33. G. Sinclair and B. Webber. Classification from full text: A comparison of canonical sections of scientific papers. In *Proceedings of JNLPBA at COLING*, 2004, pp. 66–69.

34. T. McIntosh and J. Curran. Challenges for automatically extracting molecular interactions from full-text articles. *BMC Bioinformatics*, 10(1):311, 2009.

35. D. R. Swanson. Two medical literatures that are logically but not bibliographically connected. *J. Am. Soc. Inform. Sci.*, 38(4):228–233, 1987.

36. D. R. Swanson. Complementary structures in disjoint science literatures. In *Proceedings of the 14th Annual International ACM SIGIR Conference on Research and Development in Information Retrieval*, 1991, pp. 280–289.

37. M. Weeber, J. A. Kors, and B. Mons. Online tools to support literature-based discovery in the life sciences. *Brief. Bioinformatics*, 6(3):277–286, 2005.

38. D. Hristovski, C. Friedman, T. C. Rindflesch, and B. Peterlin. Exploiting semantic relations for literature-based discovery. In *Proceedings of AMIA Annual Symposium*, 2006, pp. 349.

39. L. Tari, S. Anwar, S. Liang, J. Cai, and C. Baral. Discovering drug-drug interactions: A text-mining and reasoning approach based on properties of drug metabolism. *Bioinformatics*, 26(18):i547–i553, 2010.

40. C. Baral. *Knowledge Representation, Reasoning and Declarative Problem Solving*. Cambridge University Press, Cambridge, 2003.

41. M. Gelfond. Representing knowledge in A-Prolog. In A. C. Kakas and Fariba Sadri (Eds.), *Computational Logic: Logic Programming and Beyond*, Vol. 2408 of *Lecture Notes in Artificial Intelligence*, Springer Berlin/Heidelberg, 2002, pp. 413–451.

42. UniProt Consortium. The Universal Protein Resource (UniProt). *Nucleic Acids Res.*, 38(Suppl. 1):D142–D148, 2010.

43. M. Ashburner, C. A. Ball, J. A. Blake, D. Botstein, H. Butler, J. M. Cherry, A. P. Davis, K. Dolinski, S. S. Dwight, J. T. Eppig, M. A. Harris, D. P. Hill, L. Issel-Tarver, A. Kasarskis, S. Lewis, J. C. Matese, J. E. Richardson, M. Ringwald, G. M. Rubin, and G. Sherlock. Gene Ontology: Tool for the unification of biology. *Nat. Genet.*, 25(1):25, 2000.

44. D. Maglott, J. Ostell, K. D. Pruitt, and T. Tatusova. Entrez Gene: Gene-centered information at NCBI. *Nucleic Acids Res.*, 35(Suppl. 1):D26–D31, 2007.

45. M. S. Iyengar. *Symbolic Systems Biology: Theory and Methods.* Jones & Bartlett Learning, Sudbury MA, 2011.

46. L. Tari, S. Anwar, S. Liang, J. Hakenberg, and C. Baral. Synthesis of pharmacokinetic pathways through knowledge acquisition and automated reasoning. In *Proceedings of Pacific Symposium on Biocomputing*, Vol. 15, 2010, pp. 465–476.

47. R. B. Altman. Pharmgkb: A logical home for knowledge relating genotype to drug response phenotype. *Nat. Genet.*, 39(4):426–426, 2007.

48. Q. Zhu, Y. Sun, S. Challa, Y. Ding, M Lajiness, and D. Wild. Semantic inference using chemogenomics data for drug discovery. *BMC Bioinformatics*, 12(1):256, 2011.

49. M. Poesio and O. Sanchez-Graillet. Discovering contradicting protein-protein interactions in text. In *Proceedings of BioNLP Workshop at ACL*, 2007, pp. 195–196.

50. P. Glenisson, P. Antal, J. Mathys, Y. Moreau, and B. De Moor. Evaluation of the vector space representation in text-based gene clustering. In *Proceedings of Pacific Symposium of Biocomputing*, 2003, pp. 391–402.

51. M. Aubry, A. Monnier, C. Chicault, M. de Tayrac, M.-D. Galibert, A. Burgun, and J. Mosser. Combining evidence, biomedical literature and statistical dependence: New insights for functional annotation of gene sets. *BMC Bioinformatics*, 7(1):241, 2006.

52. T. Cohen and D. Widdows. Empirical distributional semantics: Methods and biomedical applications. *J. Biomed. Informatics*, 42(2):390–405, 2009.

53. I. Lee, S. V. Date, A. T. Adai, and E. M. Marcotte. A probabilistic functional network of yeast genes. *Science*, 306(5701):1555–1558, 2004.

54. A. Ramani, R. Bunescu, R. Mooney, and E. Marcotte. Consolidating the set of known human protein-protein interactions in preparation for large-scale mapping of the human interactome. *Genome Biol.*, 6(5):R40, 2005.

55. K. Fundel, R. Kuffner, and R. Zimmer. RelEx—Relation extraction using dependency parse trees. *Bioinformatics*, 23(3):365–371, 2007.

56. H. J. Lowe and G. O. Barnett. Understanding and using the Medical Subject Headings (MeSH) vocabulary to perform literature searches. *JAMA*, 271(14):1103, 1994.

57. M. D. Gordon and S. Dumais. Using latent semantic indexing for literature based discovery. *J. Am. Soc. Inform. Sci.*, 49(8):674–685, 1998.

58. R. Cole and P. Bruza. A bare bones approach to literature-based discovery: An analysis of the raynaud/fish-oil and migraine-magnesium discoveries in semantic space. In A. Hoffmann, H. Motoda, and T. Scheffer (Eds.), *Discovery Science*, Vol. 3735 of *Lecture Notes in Computer Science.* Springer Berlin / Heidelberg, 2005, pp. 84–98.

59. J.-D. Kim, S. Kraines, W. Guo, and J. Tsujii. Inference for bio-IE: GENIA meets EKOSS. In *Proceedings of the 3rd International Symposium on Language in Biology and Medicine (LBM2009)*, Hyatt Regency, Seogwipo-si, Jeju Island, South Korea, 2009.

60. H.-J. Lee and J. C. Park. Towards knowledge discovery through automatic inference with text mining in biology and medicine. In *Proceedings of the 3rd International Symposium on Semantic Mining in Biomedicine (SMBM)*, Turku, Finland, September 1–3, 2008.

CHAPTER 40

WEB CONTENT MINING FOR LEARNING GENERIC RELATIONS AND THEIR ASSOCIATIONS FROM TEXTUAL BIOLOGICAL DATA

MUHAMMAD ABULAISH[1,2] and JAHIRUDDIN[2]
[1]Center of Excellence in Information Assurance, King Saud University, Riyadh, Saudi Arabia
[2]Department of Computer Science, Jamia Millia Islamia (A Central University), New Delhi, India

40.1 INTRODUCTION

After sequencing of the human genome, the current bottleneck lies largely in the correct interpretation of the sequences [15]. To facilitate the understanding of the genome, a number of research efforts have been diverted in this direction and biologists are generating reams of biomedical literature. Since molecular biology has been a primary research area for more than the last two decades, the number of text documents disseminating knowledge in this area has gone up manifold and the explosion of literature makes it nearly impossible for a working biologist to keep up with developments in one field. The literature comprises accumulated knowledge in terms of the archival record of biological experiments and their methods, results, and interpretations. The sheer enormity of document collection in this domain necessitates the design of automated content analysis systems without which the assimilation of knowledge from this vast repository is becoming practically impossible [25]. Specialized search engines like PubMed have been designed to access information about these documents over the Web, but most of them use simple pattern matching to answer user queries. Although techniques such as simple pattern matching can highlight relevant text passages from large abstract collection, generating new insights to future research is far more complex.

PubMed [31] is a service of the *National Library of Medicine* [32] (NLM) USA, which includes over 21 million citations for biomedical literatures from MEDLINE, life science journals, and online books. MEDLINE is the NLM's premier bibliographic database and forms the largest component of PubMed containing over 18 million citations dating back to the mid-1960s, covering all fields related to biomedicine [33]. In MEDLINE, the records are indexed with *medical subject headings* [34] (MeSHs)—a NLM's controlled vocabulary

Biological Knowledge Discovery Handbook: Preprocessing, Mining, and Postprocessing of Biological Data,
First Edition. Edited by Mourad Elloumi and Albert Y. Zomaya.

thesaurus containing sets of terms naming descriptors in a hierarchical structure that permits searching at various levels of specificity.

Until now, PubMed is the richest and most updated source of information about biological data despite its unstructured nature [8]. The result of a PubMed search is a list of citations (including authors, title, source, and often an abstract) to journal articles and an indication of free electronic full-text availability. PubMed provides other services, including search filters for clinical queries, links to many other sites providing full-text articles, and other related resources and citation matchers. Given a set of query terms, PubMed can identify research articles containing those terms quite efficiently [14].

In spite of these efforts, there is an increasing demand for intelligent *information retrieval* (IR) that requires analyzing the contextual relationship among query terms and judging the relevance of a document in the perspective of this relationship. For example, a simple query containing the string *Alzheimer* roughly translates to the requirement "list all those documents that contain information about Alzheimer disease" for which a simple pattern-matching technique based on the occurrence of the query terms in a document is sufficient to decide whether it is relevant to the query or not. However, a more complex query in this domain can be expressed as "metabolic ailments cause Alzheimer disease," which translates to the requirement "list all those documents that contain information about the metabolic ailments that cause Alzheimer disease." This is a much more complex query and requires contextual analysis of the query terms. As observed by Bernstein et al. [9], relating the entities in a query with a specific verb restricts the context of the concepts within text to a large extent. Hence, it is important that the relationships among the biomedical entities present in a text are also extracted and interpreted correctly.

Although PubMed does not support contextual queries, it motivates the upsurge of interest in biomedical text mining to facilitate various degrees of automation in analyzing biological literature like *named entity recognition* (NER), document classification, terminology extraction, relationship extraction, and hypothesis generation [8]. Although NER, document classification, and terminology extraction from biomedical text documents have gained reasonable success, reasoning about contents of a text document needs more than identification of the entities present in it. The context of the entities in a document can be inferred from an analysis of the interentity relations present in the document.

Despite the fact that in addition to the development of many biomedical entity recognizers (e.g., ABNER [23], GENIA tagger [27]) a number of approaches have been proposed to identify biological relations from texts [10, 20–22, 26], most of them focus on mining a fixed set of biological relations occurring with a set of predefined tags. Thus, one of the prerequisites for the success of these methods is the availability of tagged corpora in which biological entities are already marked. This is far from the reality, as most of the existing textual databases, including PubMed, do not perform annotations before storing scientific literature. Moreover, each system is tuned to work with a predetermined set of relations and does not address the problem of relation extraction in a generic way. For example, the method of identification of interaction between genes and gene products cannot work for extraction of enzyme interactions from journal articles or for automatic extraction of protein interactions from scientific abstracts. Consider that negation words like *not* and *neither* and morphological variants are also missing from most of the existing biomedical relation-mining systems. In addition, to the best of our knowledge, none of the methods consider the extraction of *validatory entities*, while mining relational verbs and associated entities, whose presence or absence validates a particular biological interaction. For example, in the following PubMed sentence, *regulates* is identified as a relational verb relating the biological entities "Rac1" and "transcription of the APP gene" while "primary hippocampal neurons" can be identified as validatory entity, which restricts the scope of the regulation process mentioned in this sentence: "... Rac1 regulates transcription of the APP gene in primary hippocampal neurons (PMID: 19267423)."

Since free texts are inherently unstructured or semistructured in nature and difficult to interpret by computer programs, there has been increasing interest in the recent past in applying text-mining techniques to facilitate users to quickly perceive knowledge from the Web [2]. In contrast to existing text document processing techniques, which generally convert text documents into term vectors or bags-of-words, the text-mining process involves two subtasks—*text refining* and *knowledge distillation* [1]. The text-refining task focuses on transforming free text into an intermediate machine-processable representation, whereas knowledge distillation analyzes the intermediate representation to deduce patterns or knowledge from it. In line with this approach of the text-mining process, in this chapter, we present the design of a Web content mining system that translates biological text documents into an intermediate representation (conceptual graph) using their syntax trees generated by the parser, which is then analyzed during the knowledge distillation phase to identify information components comprising relational verbs and related constituents. The information components are thereafter analyzed to identifying feasible generic biological relations and their associations. Different categories of variants of a relational verb are recognized by our system. The first category comprises morphological variants of the root verb, which is essentially a modification of the root verb itself. In the English language the word *morphology* is usually categorized into *inflectional* and *derivational* morphology. Inflectional morphology studies the transformation of words for which the root form only changes, keeping the syntactic constraints invariable. For example, the root verb *activate* has three inflectional verb forms—*activates activated*, and *activating*. Derivational morphology, on the other hand, deals with the transformation of the stem of a word to generate other words that retain the same concept but may have different syntactic roles. Thus, *activate* and *activation* refer to the concept of "making active," but one is a verb and the other one a noun. Similarly, *inactivate*, *transactivate*, *deactivate*, and so on, are derived morphological variants created with addition of prefixes.

In the context of biological relations, we also observe that the occurrence of a verb in conjunction with a preposition very often changes the nature of the relation. For example, the focus of the relation "activates" may be quite different from the relation "activates in," in which the verb activates is followed by the preposition *in*. Thus our system also considers a third category of biological relations, which are combinations of root verbs or their morphological variants and prepositions that follow these. Typical examples of biological relations identified in this category include "activated in," "binds to," and "stimulated with." This category of relations can take care of special biological interactions involving substances and sources or localizations. Besides mining relational verbs with accompanying prepositions and associated entities, the entities associated with object entity through conjunctional prepositions are also extracted and termed as *validatory entities*, whose presence or absence validates a particular biological interaction.

The rest of this chapter is structured as follows. Starting with a brief review of the existing state-of-the-art in biological relation mining in Section 40.2, we provide the functional detail of the proposed Web content mining system in Section 40.3. The experimental setup and evaluation results are presented in Section 40.4. Section 40.5 presents the uniqueness of the proposed relation-mining system over existing ones. Finally, we conclude the chapter in Section 40.6 with future directions of work.

40.2   STATE-OF-THE-ART IN BIOLOGICAL RELATION MINING

In this section, we present a brief review of the existing state-of-the-art in biological relation mining. Although, in addition to the development of biological entity recognition systems, a number of research efforts have been directed toward identifying associations between biological entities, most of the researchers have focused on extracting gene–gene, protein–protein, and gene–protein relations. Consequently, a number of relation-mining techniques based on the co-occurrence-based approach, linguistic-based approach, or mixed-mode approach have been proposed by the researchers.

In the co-occurrence-based approach, relations between biological entities are inferred based on the assumption that two entities in the same sentence or abstract are related. Although this approach is very simple to implement and computationally efficient, it provides high recall at the cost of poor precision and negation in sentences is usually ignored. Jenssen et al. [16] collected a set of almost 14,000 gene names from publicly available databases and used them to search MEDLINE abstracts. Two genes were assumed to be linked if they appeared in the same abstract; the relation received a higher weight if the gene pair appeared in multiple abstracts. The biological entity pairs occurring more than four times were assigned a high weight, and it was reported that 71% of such gene pairs were indeed related. However, the primary focus of the work is to extract related gene pairs rather than study the nature of the relations. Albert et al. [6] used dictionaries of protein and interaction terms to retrieve protein–protein interaction from MEDLINE documents. They used tri-occurrences of two proteins and one interaction within a sentence for this purpose. This tri-occurrence extraction method enhances the recall at the cost of the precision. They reported overall precision of 22% only. Wren and Garner [29] identified related biological objects like genes, phenotypes, and chemicals by analyzing the cohesiveness and specificity of the graph structure created by the co-occurrences of the objects within the same MEDLINE records. Mukherjea and Sahay [19] presented a co-occurrence-based technique to automatically discover biomedical relations from the World Wide Web. They first used the Web search engine with manually crafted lexicon-syntactic patterns to retrieve relevant information. Then, they used the extracted information to classify biomedical terms and discover relationships between biomedical entities.

In contrast to the co-occurrence-based approach, which does not exploit the linguistic features of text, the linguistic-based approach usually applies parsing techniques to locate a set of handpicked *verbs* or *nouns*. Rules are specifically developed to extract the surrounding words of the predefined terms and to format them as relations. As with the co-occurrence-based approach, negation in sentences is usually ignored. Sekimizu et al. [22] collected the most frequently occurring verbs in a collection of abstracts and developed partial- and shallow-parsing techniques to find the verb's *subject* and *object*. The estimated precision of inferring relations is about 71%. Thomas et al. [26] modified a preexisting parser based on cascaded finite-state machines to fill templates with information on protein interactions for three verbs—*interact with*, *associate with*, and *bind to*. They calculated precision and recall in four different manners for three samples of abstracts. The precision values ranged from 60 to 81% and the recall values from 24 to 63%. The PASTA system [13] is a more comprehensive system that extracts relations between proteins, species, and residues. It uses type and *parts-of-speech* (POS) tagging along with manually created templates and lexicons assembled from biological databases to extract relationships between amino acid residues and their functions within a protein. This work reports precision of 82% and a recall value of 84% for recognition and classification of the terms and 65% precision and 68% recall for completion of templates. Ono et al. [20] reported a method for extraction of protein–protein interactions based on a combination of syntactic patterns. They employed a dictionary look-up approach to identify proteins in text documents. Sentences that contain at least two proteins were selected and parsed with POS matching rules. The rules were triggered by a set of keywords that are frequently used to name protein interactions (e.g., *associate*, *bind*, etc.). Rinaldi et al. [21] proposed an approach toward automatic extraction of a predefined set of seven relations in the domain of molecular biology based on a complete syntactic analysis of an existing corpus. They extracted relevant relations from a domain corpus based on full parsing of the documents and a set of rules that map syntactic structures into the relevant relations. Friedman et al. [11] developed a natural language processing system, GENIES, for the extraction of molecular pathways from journal articles. GENIES identifies a predefined set of verbs using templates for each one of these, which are encoded as a set of rules. This work reports a precision of 96% for identifying relations between biological molecules from full-text articles. Wattarujeekrit et al. [28] proposed a system, PASBio, to extract a relation between verbs and its arguments by using a *predicate argument structure* (PAS). PASBio is specifically designed for annotating molecular events and defining core arguments that are important for completing the meaning of an event. Presently, PASBio contains the analyzed PAS of over 30 verbs. In [12], the authors proposed a system, RelEx, to extract relations between genes and proteins. For relation extraction, the text documents are first converted into a dependency parse tree using the Stanford lexicalized parser. Thereafter, rules are applied to identify candidate relations from parse trees. Both precision and recall of the proposed system calculated over 1 million MEDLINE abstracts are reported as 80%. Xu et al. [30] proposed a method to extract relationships between genes and diseases from the literature. They used several strategies to filter out the sentences which do not contain relationships, then extracted the relationships between the gene and disease by using the pattern of entities and relationship phrases. They reported the precision, recall, and *F*-score values for their system as 84.6, 77.5, and 80.9%, respectively.

The mixed-mode approach exploits both co-occurrence and linguistic features to identify relations between biological entities. Ciaramita et al. [10] reported an unsupervised learning mechanism for extracting semantic relations between molecular biology concepts from tagged MEDLINE abstracts. For each sentence containing two biological entities, a dependency graph highlighting the dependency between the entities is generated based on linguistic analysis. A relation between two entities is extracted as the shortest path between the pair following the dependency relations. The major emphasis of this work is to determine the role of a concept in a significant relation and enhance biological ontology to include these roles and relations. Sentences containing complex embedded conjunctions/disjunctions or more than 100 words were not used for relation extraction. In the presence of nested tags, the system considers only the innermost tags. Miwa et al. [18] proposed a method to combine kernels based on several syntactic parsers for extracting protein–protein interactions from a given sentence. Their method used *support vector machines* (SVMs) and reported that their method achieves better results than other state-of-the-art *protein–protein interaction* (PPI) systems. Abulaish and Dey proposed an ontology-based *Biological Information Extraction and Query Answering* (BIEQA) System which extracts biological relations from MEDLINE abstracts using a series of natural language processing techniques and co-occurrence-based analysis from tagged documents [5]. Each mined relation is associated to a fuzzy membership value, which is proportional to its frequency of occurrence in the corpus and is termed a fuzzy biological relation. The fuzzy biological relations along with other relevant information components like biological entities occurring within a relation are stored in a database which is integrated with a query processing module. The query processing module has an interface which guides users to formulate biological queries at different levels of specificity.

It can be observed that most of the systems have been developed to extract a predetermined set of relations. The relation set is manually chosen to include a set of frequently occurring relations. Each system is tuned to work with a predetermined set of relations and does not address the problem of relation extraction in a generic way. For example, the method of identification of interaction between genes and gene products cannot work for extraction of enzyme interactions from journal articles or for automatic extraction of protein interactions from scientific abstracts. Although the methods proposed by Ciaramita et al. [10] and Abulaish and Dey [5] consider generic biomedical relation extraction, both of them require annotated text documents in which biomedical entities are already marked.

40.3 PROPOSED BIOLOGICAL RELATION-MINING SYSTEM

In this section, we present the design and functional detail of the proposed biological relation-mining system, which facilitates knowledge curation and relation identification from textual biological data. Figure 40.1 presents the complete architecture of the proposed relation-mining system, in which dotted arrows show data flow, whereas solid arrows are used to represent the interdependence between the modules. The proposed system performs four major tasks to identify biological relations and their associations—*document crawling*, *document preprocessing and parsing*, *information components extraction*, and *feasible biological relations identification*. The functional details of these tasks are presented in the following sections.

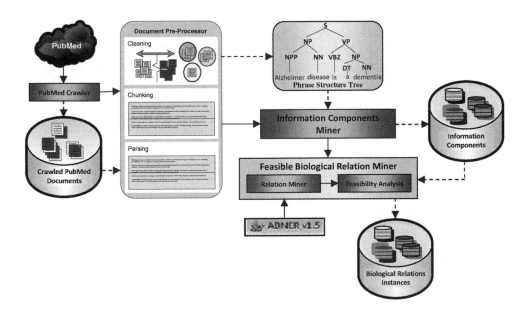

FIGURE 40.1 Architecture of proposed biological relation-mining system.

40.3.1 Document Crawling

The purpose of this module is to download PubMed documents and store them on a local machine for further processing. The crawler is implemented as an interactive module in the Java programming language, which uses PubMed API to fetch documents in Extensible Markup Language (XML) format and store them after parsing into a structured database on a local machine. Biomedical documents stored in the PubMed database are available in XML format in which tags are defined using a *document-type definition* (DTD) file standardized by the *World Wide Web Consortium* (W3C) [35]. The crawler uses DTD file definitions to create database schema to store fetched XML files from the PubMed database into structured format. The fetched XML documents are parsed by the crawler to identify different constituents, such as PMID, title, and abstract, to define the schema of the structured database. There are two types of APIs for parsing XML files: *tree-based document object model* (DOM) and *event-based simple API to XML* (SAX). Our crawler uses the SAX parser as the DOM parser requires that the entire document be read in and stored in main memory prior to writing out any data and this is not possible for a large file that does not fit in the memory. However, the SAX parser receives data through a stream and recognizes the beginning and end of a document, element, or attribute in an event-driven manner. It writes out the data as it proceeds and there is no need to load an entire file in the memory. After parsing XML files *Java database connectivity* (JDBC) is used to store parsed data into a database.

40.3.2 Document Preprocessing and Parsing

The input to this module is the collection of text documents from which information components and biological relations are to be extracted. Initially, the input documents are cleaned through filtering metalanguage tags and unwanted texts such as the authors' names and affiliations and references. A partial list of sample sentences to be filtered out during the cleaning process is shown in Table 40.1. The cleaned documents are tokenized into record-size chunks, boundaries of which are decided heuristically on the basis of the presence of various punctuation marks. Depending on the application, a record-size chunk may contain a sentence, a paragraph, or a complete document. Thereafter, the documents are parsed using a parser that assigns POS tags to every word in a sentence, where a tag reflects the syntactic category of the word [7]. POS analysis plays an important role in text information extraction since the syntactic category of a word determines its role in a sentence to a large extent. The POS tags are useful to identify the grammatical structure of sentences like noun and

TABLE 40.1 Partial List of Texts Associated with PubMed Abstracts That Represent Noise

PMID	Texts Representing Noise
20967920	Copyright ©2010 John Wiley & Sons, Ltd.
20967877	Cancer (Cancer Cytopathol) 2010. ©2010 American Cancer Society.
21221075	Laboratory Investigation advance online publication, 10 January 2011; doi:10.1038/labinvest.2010.199.
21219143	Please see http://www.annualreviews.org/catalog/pubdates.aspx for revised estimates.
21220675	Study Registration clinicalTrials.gov Identifier: NCT00106899.

verb phrases and their interrelationships. For document parsing, we have used the Stanford parser [36], which is a statistical parser. The Stanford parser receives documents as input and works out the grammatical structure of sentences to convert them into an equivalent phrase structure tree. A list of sample sentences and their corresponding phrase structure tree generated by the Stanford parser is shown in Table 40.2.

40.3.3 Information Components Extraction

The concept of the *information component* is introduced to capture and store the semantic structure of text into a structured format which can be used later on to apply association rule mining to identify the list of associated entities and their association strength with respect to a given corpus. Moreover, in line with the generalized association-mining technique proposed by Jiang et al. in [4], the extracted information components can also be used to mine generalized associations of generic biological relations identified by our proposed system. Since the bag-of-words representation of a text document treats each representative term as an independent entity, the semantic relations depicting the conceptual roles are lost; that is, terms lose their semantic relations and texts lose their original meanings [4]. For example, consider the following two sentences, whose bag-of-words representations (i.e., {heart, disease, cause, depression}) are the same, but their meaning is different. The first sentence (S1) represents the facts that "heart disease" causes "depression," whereas the second sentence (S2) expresses an opposite meaning, that is, "depression" causes "heart disease":

Sentence 1 (S1): Heart disease causes depression
Sentence 2 (S2): Heart disease is caused by depression

Therefore, we have designed a set of rules to analyze text semantic structure (phrase structure tree generated by the parser) to identify *noun phrases* (NPs) and *verb phrases* (VPs) and their semantic relationship to generate conceptual graphs and then map them into information components. Since the full conceptual graph standard is complex and could be computationally inefficient for knowledge distillation, we have used simplified conceptual graphs that are used in many existing researches [3, 4]. In conceptual graphs, a node represents a NP or VP, whereas an edge represents a relation between them. In line with [4], three types of relations between the nodes (NP/VP) are identified to map the phrase structure tree of a sentence into a conceptual graph:

(i) $< P$, actor, $Q >$, where P can be a VP and Q can be an NP or VP: In this relation, Q is an actor which performs action P. For example, in Figure 40.2 the relation $<$ activates, actor, NF-Kappa B $>$ is an instance of this type of relation.

(ii) $< P$, theme, $Q >$, where P can be a VP and Q can be an NP or VP: In this relation, Q is a theme of the action P. For example, in Figure 40.2 the relation $<$ activates, theme, HIV promoter $>$ is an instance of this type of relation.

(iii) $< P$, validatedBy, $Q >$, where both P and Q can be an NP or VP: In this relation, P is validated by Q through a proposition. For example, in Figure 40.2 the relation $<$ activates, validatedBy, neurons $>$ is an instance of this type of relation, which represents the fact that the activation is performed in "neurons."

TABLE 40.2   Sample PubMed Sentences Related to Alzheimer Disease and Their Phrase Structure Tree Representations Generated by Stanford Parser

PMID	PubMed Sentence	Phrase Structure Tree Representation
19295912	Transcriptome analysis of synaptoneurosomes identifies neuroplasticity genes overexpressed in incipient Alzheimer's disease.	(ROOT (S (NP (NP (JJ Transcriptome) (NN analysis)) (PP (IN of) (NP (NNS synaptoneurosomes)))) (VP (VBZ identifies) (NP (NP (JJ neuroplasticity) (NNS genes)) (VP (VBN overexpressed) (PP (IN in) (NP (NP (JJ incipient) (NNP Alzheimer) (POS 's)) (NN disease)))))) (. .)))
19295164	Recent studies suggest that bone marrow–derived macrophages can effectively reduce beta-amyloid (Abeta) deposition in the brain.	(ROOT (S (NP (JJ Recent) (NNS studies)) (VP (VBP suggest) (SBAR (IN that) (S (NP (JJ bone) (JJ marrow-derived) (NNS macrophages)) (VP (MD can) (ADVP (RB effectively)) (VP (VB reduce) (NP (NP (JJ beta-amyloid) (PRN (-LRB- -LRB-) (NP (NNP Abeta)) (-RRB- -RRB-)) (NN deposition)) (PP (IN in) (NP (NN brain))))))))) (. .)))
19275635	There is substantial and compelling evidence that aggregation and accumulation of amyloid beta protein (Abeta) plays a pivotal role in the development of Alzheimer's disease (AD).	(ROOT (S (S (NP (EX There)) (VP (VBZ is) (NP (ADJP (JJ substantial) (CC and) (JJ compelling)) (NN evidence)) (SBAR (IN that) (S (NP (NP (NN aggregation) (CC and) (NN accumulation)) (PP (IN of) (NP (NP (JJ amyloid) (JJ beta) (NN protein)) (PRN (-LRB- -LRB-) (NP (NNP Abeta)) (-RRB- -RRB-))))) (VP (VBZ plays) (NP (NP (DT a) (JJ pivotal) (NN role)) (PP (IN in) (NP (NP (DT the) (NN development)) (PP (IN of) (NP (NP (NP (NNP Alzheimer) (POS 's)) (NN disease)) (PRN (-LRB- -LRB-) (NNP AD) (-RRB- -RRB-)))))))))))) (: ;))
19263040	Memory deficits and neurochemical changes induced by C-reactive protein in rats: implication in Alzheimer's disease.	(ROOT (NP (NP (NP (NN Memory) (NNS deficits) (CC and) (NN neurochemical) (NNS changes)) (VP (VBN induced) (PP (IN by) (NP (NP (JJ C-reactive) (NN protein)) (PP (IN in) (NP (NNS rats))))))) (: :) (NP (NP (NN implication)) (PP (IN in) (NP (NP (NNP Alzheimer) (POS 's)) (NN disease)))) (. .)))
19293566	Conclusion: Although flanking SNPs cover the whole gene transcript with strong linkage disequilibrium, our data show that the *CST3* gene is not associated with AD risk in the Finnish population.	(ROOT (NP (NP (NNP Conclusion)) (: :) (S (SBAR (IN Although) (S (VP (VBG flanking) (S (NP (NNP SNP)) (VP (VB cover) (NP (DT the) (JJ whole) (NN gene) (NN transcript)) (PP (IN with) (NP (JJ strong) (JJ linkage) (NN disequilibrium)))))))) (, ,) (NP (PRP$ our) (NNS data)) (VP (VBP show) (SBAR (IN that) (S (NP (DT the) (NNP CST3) (NN gene)) (VP (VBZ is) (RB not) (VP (VBN associated) (PP (IN with) (NP (NNP AD) (NN risk))) (PP (IN in) (NP (DT the) (JJ Finnish) (NN population))))))))) (. .)))

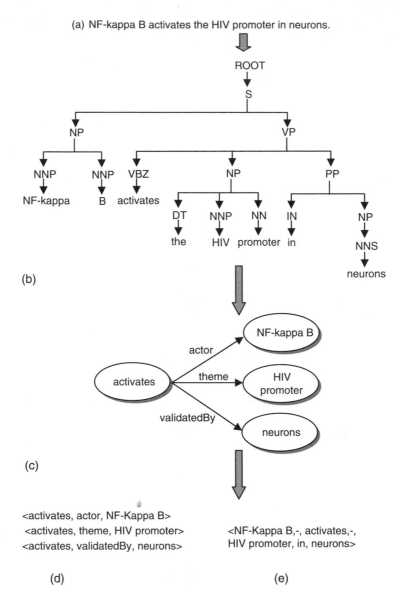

FIGURE 40.2   (a) Sample biological sentence, (b) phrase structure tree generated by parser, (c) conceptual graph to model semantic structure of the text, (d) extracted relation instances from conceptual graph, and (e) generated information component.

As discussed in [4], although a relation can be modeled directly using the template < subject, verb, object >, it fails to model a relation in which either subject or object is missing, especially in the case when a sentence is in the passive form. Once the relations are identified from a conceptual graph, they are clubbed together to create an instance of information component, which is defined in the following paragraph. Individual relations are also stored in a structured repository to mine relation associations. Besides, storing constituents from different relations extracted from a conceptual graph, the information component generation process also contains *adverbs* and *prepositions* to represent negations and states of biological interactions, respectively. Figure 40.2 presents a sample sentence, its phrase structure tree generated by the parser, conceptual graph, identified instances, and information components.

Definition 40.1 *Information Component* An *information component* (IC) is a 7-tuple of the form $< E_i, A, V, P_v, E_j, P_c, E_k >$ where E_i, and E_j are noun phrases associated by V, which is a relational verb; A is adverb; P_v is a verbal preposition associated with V; and E_k is a validatory phrase associated with E_j through the conjunctional preposition P_c.

Semantic tree analysis and the information component extraction process is implemented as a rule-based system as shown in Table 40.3. Dependencies output by the parser are analyzed to identify noun and verb phrases and their semantic relations. Algorithm 40.1, `informationComponentExtraction`, presents the implementation detail of the proposed rule-based system in a formal way. A partial list of information components extracted by this algorithm from PubMed sentences of Table 40.2 is given in Table 40.4.

40.3.4 Feasible Biological Relation Identification

A biomedical relation is usually manifested in a document as a relational verb associating two or more biological entities. The biological actors associated to a relation can be inferred from the entities located in the proximity of the relational verb. At present, we have considered only binary relations. Since relation instances specified at entity levels are rare, while applying mining techniques on them, the support count of many itemsets would be very low. Therefore, the biological entities appearing in information components are marked with a biological entity recognizer that helps in identifying valid biological relations and their associations. For this purpose, our system is integrated with a biological named entity recognizer, ABNER (v1.5) [23], which is a molecular biology text analysis tool. ABNER employs statistical machine learning using linear-chain *conditional random fields* (CRFs) with a variety of orthographic and contextual features and it is trained on both the NLPBA and BioCreative corpora. In order to compile biological relations from information components, we consider only those information components in which either the left-entity or right-entity field has at least one biomedical entity. In this way, a large number of irrelevant verbs are eliminated from being considered as biological relations. Further irrelevant relational verbs are eliminated by applying the following definition of the feasible biological relation.

Definition 40.2 *Feasible Biological Relation* A relational verb V is said to be a *feasible biological relation* with respect to a given corpus if the support count of V in proximity of biological entities is greater than a threshold value θ.

The feasibility analysis helps in eliminating a number of relational verbs which may have chance occurrence in biological domain. These verbs usually represent author biases and their elimination reduces the overall computational load. For example, the verbs *worked with*, *experimented with*, *found*, and so on, may occur in a few technical articles, but not frequent enough to be considered as a significant terms for the biological domain. Since our aim is to identify not just possible relational verbs but also feasible biological relations, we engage in statistical analysis to identify feasible biological relations. To

TABLE 40.3   Rules for Analyzing Phrase Structure Tree to Identify Information Components

Rule No.	Rule Statement
1	$[C(R, E_i) \wedge C(R, VP) \wedge L(VP, E_i) \wedge C_l(VP, V) \wedge S(V, E_j)] \Rightarrow \langle E_i, null, V, null, E_j, null, null \rangle$
2	$[C(R, E_i) \wedge C(R, VP) \wedge C(R, Adv) \wedge L(Adv, E_i) \wedge L(VP, Adv) \wedge C_l(VP, V) \wedge S(V, E_j)] \Rightarrow \langle E_i, Adv, V, null, E_j, null, null \rangle$
3	$[C(R, E_i) \wedge C(R, VP_1) \wedge L(VP_1, E_i) \wedge C(VP_1, VP_2) \wedge C_l(VP_2, V) \wedge S(V, E_j)] \Rightarrow \langle E_i, null, V, null, E_j, null, null \rangle$
4	$[C(R, E_i) \wedge C(R, VP_1) \wedge L(VP_1, E_i) \wedge C(VP_1, Adv) \wedge C(VP_1, VP_2) \wedge L(VP_2, Adv) \wedge C_l(VP_2, V) \wedge S(V, E_j)] \Rightarrow \langle E_i, Adv, V, null, E_j, null, null \rangle$
5	$[C(R, E_i) \wedge C(R, VP_1) \wedge L(VP_1, E_i) \wedge C(VP_1, VP_2) \wedge C(VP_2, VP_3) \wedge C_l(VP_3, V) \wedge S(V, E_j)] \Rightarrow \langle E_i, null, V, null, E_j, null, null \rangle$
6	$[C(R, E_i) \wedge C(R, VP_1) \wedge L(VP_1, E_i) \wedge C(VP_1, VP_2) \wedge C(VP_2, Adv) \wedge C(VP_2, VP_3) \wedge L(VP_3, Adv) \wedge C_l(VP_3, V) \wedge S(V, E_j)] \Rightarrow \langle E_i, Adv, V, null, E_j, null, null \rangle$
7	$[C(R, E_i) \wedge C(R, VP) \wedge L(VP, E_i) \wedge C_l(VP, V) \wedge S(V, PP) \wedge C_l(PP, p) \wedge S(p, E_j)] \Rightarrow \langle E_i, null, V, p, E_j, null, null \rangle$
8	$[C(R, E_i) \wedge C(R, Adv) \wedge C(R, VP) \wedge L(Adv, E_i) \wedge L(VP, Adv) \wedge C_l(VP, V) \wedge S(V, PP) \wedge C_l(PP, p) \wedge S(p, E_j)] \Rightarrow \langle E_i, Adv, V, p, E_j, null, null \rangle$
9	$[C(R, E_i) \wedge C(R, VP_1) \wedge L(VP_1, E_i) \wedge C(VP_1, VP_2) \wedge C_l(VP_2, V) \wedge S(V, PP) \wedge C_l(PP, p) \wedge S(p, E_j)] \Rightarrow \langle E_i, null, V, p, E_j, null, null \rangle$
10	$[C(R, E_i) \wedge C(R, VP_1) \wedge L(VP_1, E_i) \wedge C(VP_1, Adv) \wedge C(VP_1, VP_2) \wedge L(VP_2, Adv) \wedge C_l(VP_2, V) \wedge S(V, PP) \wedge C_l(PP, p) \wedge S(p, E_j)] \Rightarrow \langle E_i, Adv, V, p, E_j, null, null \rangle$
11	$[C(R, E_i) \wedge C(R, VP) \wedge L(VP, E_i) \wedge C_l(VP, V) \wedge S(V, ADVP) \wedge C(ADVP, PP) \wedge C_l(PP, p) \wedge S(p, E_j)] \Rightarrow \langle E_i, null, V, p, E_j, null, null \rangle$
12	$[C(R, E_i) \wedge C(R, Adv) \wedge C(R, VP) \wedge L(Adv, E_i) \wedge L(VP, Adv) \wedge C_l(VP, V) \wedge S(V, ADVP) \wedge C(ADVP, PP) \wedge C_l(PP, p) \wedge S(p, E_j)] \Rightarrow \langle E_i, Adv, V, p, E_j, null, null \rangle$
13	$[C(R, E_i) \wedge C(R, VP) \wedge L(VP, E_i) \wedge C_l(VP, V) \wedge S(V, E_j) \wedge S(V, PP) \wedge L(PP, E_j) \wedge C_l(PP, p) \wedge S(p, E_k)] \Rightarrow \langle E_i, null, V, null, Ej, p, E_k \rangle$
14	$[C(R, E_i) \wedge C(R, VP) \wedge C(R, Adv) \wedge L(Adv, E_i) \wedge L(VP, Adv) \wedge C_l(VP, V) \wedge S(V, E_j) \wedge S(V, PP) \wedge L(PP, E_j) \wedge C_l(PP, p) \wedge S(p, E_k)] \Rightarrow \langle E_i, Adv, V, null, E_j, p, E_k \rangle$
15	$[C(R, E_i) \wedge C(R, VP) \wedge L(VP, E_i) \wedge C_l(VP, V) \wedge S(V, NP) \wedge C(NP, E_j) \wedge C(NP, PP) \wedge L(PP, E_j) \wedge C_l(PP, p) \wedge S(p, E_k)] \Rightarrow \langle E_i, null, V, null, E_j, p, E_k \rangle$
16	$[C(R, E_i) \wedge C(R, VP) \wedge C(R, Adv) \wedge L(Adv, E_i) \wedge L(VP, Adv) \wedge C_l(VP, V) \wedge S(V, NP) \wedge C(NP, E_j) \wedge C(NP, PP) \wedge L(PP, E_j) \wedge C_l(PP, p) \wedge S(p, E_k)] \Rightarrow \langle E_i, Adv, V, null, E_j, p, E_k \rangle$
17	$[C(R, E_i) \wedge C(R, VP_1) \wedge L(VP_1, E_i) \wedge C(VP_1, VP_2) \wedge C_l(VP2, V) \wedge S(V, E_j) \wedge S(V, PP) \wedge L(PP, E_j) \wedge C_l(PP, p) \wedge S(p, E_k)] \Rightarrow \langle E_i, null, V, null, E_j, p, E_k \rangle$
18	$[C(R, E_i) \wedge C(R, VP_1) \wedge L(VP_1, E_i) \wedge C(VP_1, Adv) \wedge C(VP_1, VP_2) \wedge L(VP_2, Adv) \wedge C_l(VP2, V) \wedge S(V, E_j) \wedge S(V, PP) \wedge L(PP, E_j) \wedge C_l(PP, p) \wedge S(p, E_k)] \Rightarrow \langle E_i, Adv, V, null, E_j, p, E_k \rangle$
19	$[C(R, E_i) \wedge C(R, VP_1) \wedge L(VP1, E_i) \wedge C(VP_1, VP_2) \wedge C_l(VP_2, V) \wedge S(V, NP) \wedge C(NP, E_j) \wedge C(NP, PP) \wedge L(PP, E_j) \wedge C_l(PP, p) \wedge S(p, E_k)] \Rightarrow \langle E_i, null, V, null, E_j, p, E_k \rangle$
20	$[C(R, E_i) \wedge C(R, VP_1) \wedge L(VP_1, E_i) \wedge C(VP_1, Adv) \wedge C(VP_1, VP_2) \wedge L(VP_2, Adv) \wedge C_l(VP_2, V) \wedge S(V, NP) \wedge C(NP, E_j) \wedge C(NP, PP) \wedge L(PP, E_j) \wedge C_l(PP, p) \wedge S(p, E_k)] \Rightarrow \langle E_i, Adv, V, null, E_j, p, E_k \rangle$
21	$[C(R, E_i) \wedge C(R, VP_1) \wedge L(VP_1, E_i) \wedge C(VP_1, VP_2) \wedge C(VP_2, VP_3) \wedge C_l(VP_3, V) \wedge S(V, E_j) \wedge S(V, PP) \wedge L(PP, E_j) \wedge C_l(PP, p) \wedge S(p, E_k)] \Rightarrow \langle E_i, null, V, null, E_j, p, E_k \rangle$

TABLE 40.3 (*Continued*)

Rule No.	Rule Statement
22	$[C(R, E_i) \wedge C(R, VP_1) \wedge L(VP_1, E_i) \wedge C(VP_1, VP_2) \wedge C(VP_2, Adv) \wedge$ $C(VP_2, VP_3) \wedge L(VP_3, Adv) \wedge C_l(VP_3, V) \wedge S(V, E_j) \wedge S(V, PP) \wedge L(PP, E_j) \wedge$ $C_l(PP, p) \wedge S(p, E_k)] \Rightarrow \langle E_i, Adv, V, null, E_j, p, E_k \rangle$
23	$[C(R, E_i) \wedge C(R, VP_1) \wedge L(VP_1, E_i) \wedge C(VP_1, VP_2) \wedge C(VP_2, VP_3) \wedge C_l(VP_3, V) \wedge$ $S(V, NP) \wedge C(NP, E_j) \wedge C(NP, PP) \wedge L(PP, E_j) \wedge C_l(PP, p) \wedge S(p, E_k)] \Rightarrow$ $\langle E_i, null, V, null, E_j, p, E_k \rangle$
24	$[C(R, E_i) \wedge C(R, VP_1) \wedge L(VP_1, E_i) \wedge C(VP_1, VP_2) \wedge C(VP_2, Adv) \wedge$ $C(VP_2, VP_3) \wedge L(VP_3, Adv) \wedge C_l(VP_3, V) \wedge S(V, NP) \wedge C(NP, E_j) \wedge$ $C(NP, PP) \wedge L(PP, E_j) \wedge C_l(PP, p) \wedge S(p, E_k)] \Rightarrow \langle E_i, Adv, V, null, E_j, p, E_k \rangle$
25	$[C(R, E_i) \wedge C(R, VP) \wedge L(VP, E_i) \wedge C_l(VP, V) \wedge S(V, PP_1) \wedge S(V, PP_2) \wedge$ $L(PP_2, PP_1) \wedge C_l(PP_1, p_1) \wedge S(p_1, E_j) \wedge C_l(PP_2, p_2) \wedge S(p2, E_k)] \Rightarrow$ $\langle E_i, null, V, p_1, E_j, p_2, E_k \rangle$
26	$[C(R, E_i) \wedge C(R, Adv) \wedge C(R, VP) \wedge L(Adv, E_i) \wedge L(VP, Adv) \wedge C_l(VP, V) \wedge$ $S(V, PP_1) \wedge S(V, PP_2) \wedge L(PP_2, PP_1) \wedge C_l(PP_1, p_1) \wedge S(p_1, E_j) \wedge C_l(PP_2, p_2) \wedge$ $S(p_2, E_k)] \Rightarrow \langle E_i, Adv, V, p_1, E_j, p_2, E_k \rangle$
27	$[C(R, E_i) \wedge C(R, VP) \wedge L(VP, E_i) \wedge C_l(VP, V) \wedge S(V, PP_1) \wedge C_l(PP_1, p_1) \wedge$ $S(p_1, NP) \wedge C(NP, E_j) \wedge C(NP, PP_2) \wedge L(PP_2, E_j) \wedge C_l(PP_2, p_2) \wedge$ $S(p_2, E_k)] \Rightarrow \langle E_i, null, V, p_1, E_j, p_2, E_k \rangle$
28	$[C(R, E_i) \wedge C(R, Adv) \wedge C(R, VP) \wedge L(Adv, E_i) \wedge L(VP, Adv) \wedge C_l(VP, V) \wedge$ $S(V, PP_1) \wedge C_l(PP_1, p_1) \wedge S(p_1, NP) \wedge C(NP, E_j) \wedge C(NP, PP_2) \wedge L(PP2, E_j) \wedge$ $C_l(PP_2, p_2) \wedge S(p_2, E_k)] \Rightarrow \langle E_i, Adv, V, p_1, E_j, p_2, E_k \rangle$
29	$[C(R, E_i) \wedge C(R, VP_1) \wedge L(VP_1, E_i) \wedge C(VP_1, VP_2) \wedge C_l(VP_2, V) \wedge S(V, PP_1) \wedge$ $S(V, PP_2) \wedge L(PP_2, PP_1) \wedge C_l(PP_1, p_1) \wedge S(p_1, E_j) \wedge C_l(PP_2, p_2) \wedge$ $S(p_2, E_k)] \Rightarrow \langle F_i, null, V, p_1, E_j, p_2, E_k \rangle$
30	$[C(R, E_i) \wedge C(R, VP_1) \wedge L(VP_1, E_i) \wedge C(VP_1, Adv) \wedge C(VP_1, VP_2) \wedge$ $L(VP_2, Adv) \wedge C_l(VP_2, V) \wedge S(V, PP_1) \wedge S(V, PP_2) \wedge L(PP_2, PP_1) \wedge$ $C_l(PP_1, p_1) \wedge S(p_1, E_j) \wedge C_l(PP_2, p_2) \wedge S(p_2, E_k)] \Rightarrow \langle E_i, Adv, V, p_1, E_j, p_2, E_k \rangle$
31	$[C(R, E_i) \wedge C(R, VP_1) \wedge L(VP_1, E_i) \wedge C(VP_1, VP_2) \wedge C_l(VP_2, V) \wedge S(V, PP_1) \wedge$ $C_l(PP_1, p_1) \wedge S(p_1, NP) \wedge C(NP, E_j) \wedge C(NP, PP_2) \wedge L(PP_2, E_j) \wedge$ $C_l(PP_2, p_2) \wedge S(p_2, E_k)] \Rightarrow \langle E_i, null, V, p_1, E_j, p_2, E_k \rangle$
32	$[C(R, E_i) \wedge C(R, VP_1) \wedge L(VP_1, E_i) \wedge C(VP_1, Adv) \wedge C(VP_1, VP_2) \wedge$ $L(VP_2, Adv) \wedge C_l(VP_2, V) \wedge S(V, PP_1) \wedge C_l(PP_1, p_1) \wedge S(p_1, NP) \wedge C(NP, E_j) \wedge$ $C(NP, PP_2) \wedge L(PP_2, E_j) \wedge C_l(PP_2, p_2) \wedge S(p_2, E_k)] \Rightarrow$ $\langle E_i, Adv, V, p_1, E_j, p_2, E_k \rangle$
33	$[C(R, E_i) \wedge C(R, VP) \wedge L(VP, E_i) \wedge C_l(VP, V) \wedge S(V, ADVP) \wedge S(V, PP_2) \wedge$ $L(PP_2, ADVP) \wedge C(ADVP, PP_1) \wedge C_l(PP_1, p_1) \wedge S(p_1, E_j) \wedge C_l(PP_2, p_2) \wedge$ $S(p_2, E_k)] \Rightarrow \langle E_i, null, V, p_1, E_j, p_2, E_k \rangle$
34	$[C(R, E_i) \wedge C(R, Adv) \wedge C(R, VP) \wedge L(Adv, E_i) \wedge L(VP, Adv) \wedge C_l(VP, V) \wedge$ $S(V, ADVP) \wedge S(V, PP_2) \wedge L(PP_2, ADVP) \wedge C(ADVP, PP_1) \wedge C_l(PP_1, p_1) \wedge$ $S(p_1, E_j) \wedge C_l(PP_2, p_2) \wedge S(p_2, E_k)] \Rightarrow \langle E_i, Adv, V, p_1, E_j, p_2, E_k \rangle$
35	$[C(R, E_i) \wedge C(R, VP) \wedge L(VP, E_i) \wedge C_l(VP, V) \wedge S(V, ADVP) \wedge C(ADVP, PP_1) \wedge$ $C_l(PP_1, p_1) \wedge S(p_1, NP) \wedge C(NP, E_j) \wedge C(NP, PP_2) \wedge L(PP_2, E_j) \wedge$ $C_l(PP_2, p_2) \wedge S(p_2, E_k)] \Rightarrow \langle E_i, null, V, p_1, E_j, p_2, E_k \rangle$
36	$[C(R, E_i) \wedge C(R, Adv) \wedge C(R, VP) \wedge L(Adv, E_i) \wedge L(VP, Adv) \wedge C_l(VP, V) \wedge$ $S(V, ADVP) \wedge C(ADVP, PP_1) \wedge C_l(PP_1, p_1) \wedge S(p_1, NP) \wedge C(NP, E_j) \wedge$ $C(NP, PP_2) \wedge L(PP_2, E_j) \wedge C_l(PP_2, p_2) \wedge S(p_2, E_k)] \Rightarrow$ $\langle E_i, Adv, V, p_1, E_j, p_2, E_k \rangle$

Legend: E_i, E_j, E_k: entity appearing as noun phrase NP; $L(X,Y)$: Y is left to X; R: root of sub tree of the phrase structure tree; $C(X,Y)$: Y is child of X; $C_l(X,Y)$: Y is left most child of X; $S(X,Y)$: X and Y are sibling consolidate the final list of feasible relations, we take care of two things. First, since various forms of the same verb represent a basic biological relation in different forms, the feasible collection is extracted by considering only the unique root forms after analyzing the complete list of information components. The root verb having support count greater than or equal to a threshold value is retained as root biological relations. Second, information components are again analyzed to identify the morphological variants of the retained root verbs using the partial pattern-matching technique. Algorithm 40.2, `biomedicalRelationExtraction`, defines this process formally. A partial list of feasible biological relations and their morphological variants extracted from a corpus of 500 PubMed abstracts related to *Alzheimer disease* is shown in Table 40.5.

ALGORITHM 40.1 informationComponentExtraction(T)

Input: Phrase structure tree T, created though Stanford parser
Output: A list of Information Components L_{IC}
Steps:
1. $L_{IC} \leftarrow \phi$
2. **for** each node $N \in T$ **do**
3.   **for** each child $\eta_i \in N$ **do**
4. $IC \leftarrow \phi$
5.   **if** $\eta_{i1} = NP$ AND $\eta_{i2} = VP$ AND $i1 < i2$ AND $\alpha_0 \in child[\eta_{i2}] = V$ **then**
6.   **if** $\alpha_j \in child[\eta_{i2}] = NP$ AND $j \neq 0$ **then**
7.   **if** $\alpha_{k1} \in child[\eta_{i2}] = PP$ AND $j < k1$ AND $\beta_0 \in child[\alpha_{k1}] = p$
        AND $\beta_{k2} \in child[\alpha_{k1}] = NP$ AND $k2 \neq 0$ **then**
8. $IC = \langle E(\eta_{i1}), null, V, null, E(\alpha_j), p, E(\beta_{k2}) \rangle$ **// Rule-13 E(x) represent**
                                    // the entity extracted from the subtree rooted at x.
9.   **else if** $\beta_{k1} \in child[\alpha_{k1}] = NP$ AND $\beta_{k2} \in child[\alpha_{k1}] = PP$ AND $k1 < k2$
        AND $\lambda_0 \in child[\beta_{k2}] = p$ AND $\lambda_{k3} \in child[\beta_{k2}] = NP$ AND $k3 \neq 0$ **then**
10. $IC = \langle E(\eta_{i1}), null, V, null, E(\beta_{k1}), p, E(\lambda_{k3}) \rangle$ **// Rule-15**
11.   **else**
12. $IC = \langle E(\eta_{i1}), null, V, null, E(\alpha_j), null, null \rangle$ **// Rule-1**
13.   **end if**
14.   **else if** $\alpha_{j1} \in child[\eta_{i2}] = ADVP$ AND $j1 \neq 0$ AND $\beta_{j2} \in child[\alpha_{j1}] = PP$
      AND $\lambda_0 \in child[\beta_{j2}] = p_1$ AND $\lambda_{j3} \in child[\beta_{j2}] = NP$ AND $j3 \neq 0$ **then**
15.   **if** $\alpha_{k1} \in child[\eta_{i2}] = PP$ AND $j1 < k1$ AND $\beta_0 \in child[\alpha_{k1}] = p_2$
        AND $\beta_{k2} \in child[\alpha_{k1}] = NP$ AND $k2 \neq 0$ **then**
16. $IC = \langle E(\eta_{i1}), null, V, p_1, E(\lambda_{j3}), p_2, E(\beta_{k2}) \rangle$ **// Rule-33**
17.   **else if** $\gamma_{k1} \in child[\lambda_{j3}] = NP$ AND $\gamma_{k2} \in child[\lambda_{j3}] = PP$ AND $k1 < k2$
        AND $\theta_0 \in child[\gamma_{k2}] = p_2$ AND $\theta_{k3} \in child[\gamma_{k2}] = NP$ AND $k3 \neq 0$ **then**
18. $IC = \langle E(\eta_{i1}), null, V, p_1, E(\gamma_{k1}), p_2, E(\theta_{k3}) \rangle$ **// Rule-35**
19.   **else**
20. $IC = \langle E(\eta_{i1}), null, V, p_1, E(\lambda_{j3}), null, null \rangle$ **// Rule-11**
21.   **end if**
22.   **else if** $\alpha_{j1} \in child[\eta_{i2}] = PP$ AND $j1 \neq 0$ AND $\beta_0 \in child[\alpha_{j1}] = p_1$
      AND $\beta_{j2} \in child[\alpha_{j1}] = NP$ AND $j2 \neq 0$ **then**
23.   **if** $\alpha_{k1} \in child[\eta_{i2}] = PP$ AND $j1 < k1$ AND $\beta_0 \in child[\alpha_{k1}] = p_2$
        AND $\beta_{k2} \in child[\alpha_{k1}] = NP$ AND $k2 \neq 0$ **then**
24. $IC = \langle E(\eta_{i1}), null, V, p_1, E(\beta_{j2}), p_2, E(\beta_{k2}) \rangle$ **// Rule-25**
25.   **else if** $\lambda_{k1} \in child[\beta_{j2}] = NP$ AND $\lambda_{k2} \in child[\beta_{j2}] = PP$ AND $k1 < k2$
        AND $\gamma_0 \in child[\lambda_{k2}] = p_2$ AND $\gamma_{k3} \in child[\lambda_{k2}] = NP$ AND $k3 \neq 0$ **then**
26. $IC = \langle E(\eta_{i1}), null, V, p_1, E(\lambda_{k1}), p_2, E(\gamma_{k3}) \rangle$ **// Rule-27**

```
27.      else
28.          IC = ⟨E(η_{i1}), null, V, p_1, E(β_{j2}), null, null⟩              // Rule-7
29.      end if
30.    end if
31.    else if η_{i1} = NP AND η_{i2} = VP AND i1 < i2 AND α_{i3} ∈ child[η_{i2}] = VP
       AND β_0 ∈ child[α_{i3}] = V then
32.      if β_j ∈ child[α_{i3}] = NP AND j ≠ 0 then
33.        if β_{k1} ∈ child[α_{i3}] = PP AND j < k1 AND λ_0 ∈ child[β_{k1}] = p
           AND λ_{k2} ∈ child[β_{k1}] = NP AND k2 ≠ 0 then
34.          IC = ⟨E(η_{i1}), null, V, null, E(β_j), p, E(λ_{k2})⟩              // Rule-17
35.        else if λ_{k1} ∈ child[β_j] = NP AND λ_{k2} ∈ child[β_j] = PP AND k1 < k2
           AND γ_0 ∈ child[λ_{k2}] = p AND γ_{k3} ∈ child[λ_{k2}] = NP AND k3 ≠ 0 then
36.          IC = ⟨E(η_{i1}), null, V, null, E(λ_{k1}), p, E(γ_{k3})⟩           // Rule-19
37.        else
38.          IC = ⟨E(η_{i1}), null, V, null, E(β_j), null, null⟩                // Rule-3
39.        end if
40.      else if β_{j1} ∈ child[α_{i3}] = PP AND j1 ≠ 0 AND λ_0 ∈ child[β_{j1}] = p_1
         AND λ_{j2} ∈ child[β_{j1}] = NP AND j2 ≠ 0 then
41.        if β_{k1} ∈ child[α_{i3}] = PP AND j1 < k1 AND λ_0 ∈ child[β_{k1}] = p_2
           AND λ_{k2} ∈ child[β_{k1}] = NP AND k2 ≠ 0 then
42.          IC = ⟨E(η_{i1}), null, V, p_1, E(λ_{j2}), p_2, E(λ_{k2})⟩           // Rule-29
43.        else if γ_{k1} ∈ child[λ_{j2}] = NP AND γ_{k2} ∈ child[λ_{j2}] = PP AND k1 < k2
           AND θ_0 ∈ child[γ_{k2}] = p_2 AND θ_{k3} ∈ child[γ_{k2}] = NP AND k3 ≠ 0 then
44.          IC = ⟨E(η_{i1}), null, V, p_1, E(γ_{k1}), p_2, E(θ_{k3})⟩          // Rule-31
45.        else
46.          IC = ⟨E(η_{i1}), null, V, p_1, E(λ_{j2}), null, null⟩              // Rule-9
47.        end if
48.      end if
49.    else if η_{i1} = NP AND η_{i2} = VP AND i1 < i2 AND α_{i3} ∈ child[η_{i2}] = VP
       AND β_{i4} ∈ child[α_{i3}] = VP AND λ_0 ∈ child[β_{i4}] = V
       AND λ_{i5} ∈ child[β_{i4}] = NP AND i5 ≠ 0 then
50.      if λ_{j1} ∈ child[β_{i4}] = PP AND i5 < j1 AND γ_0 ∈ child[λ_{j1}] = p
         AND γ_{j2} ∈ child[λ_{j1}] = NP AND j2 ≠ 0 then
51.        IC = ⟨E(η_{i1}), null, V, null, E(λ_{i5}), p, E(γ_{j2})⟩             // Rule-21
52.      else if γ_{j1} ∈ child[λ_{i5}] = NP AND γ_{j2} ∈ child[λ_{i5}] = PP AND j1 < j2
         AND θ_0 ∈ child[γ_{j2}] = p AND θ_{j3} ∈ child[γ_{j2}] = NP AND j3 ≠ 0 then
53.        IC = ⟨E(η_{i1}), null, V, null, E(γ_{j1}), p, E(θ_{j3})⟩             // Rule-23
54.      else
55.        IC = ⟨E(η_{i1}), null, V, null, E(λ_{i5}), null, null⟩               // Rule-5
56.      end if
57.    else if η_{i1} = NP AND η_{i2} = VP AND η_{i3} = Adv AND i1 < i2 < i3
       AND α_0 ∈ child[η_{i2}] = V then
58.      if α_j ∈ child[η_{i2}] = NP AND j ≠ 0 then
59.        if α_{k1} ∈ child[η_{i2}] = PP AND j < k1 AND β_0 ∈ child[α_{k1}] = p
           AND β_{k2} ∈ child[α_{k1}] = NP AND k2 ≠ 0 then
60.          IC = ⟨E(η_{i1}), Adv, V, null, E(α_j), p, E(β_{k2})⟩               // Rule-14
61.        else if β_{k1} ∈ child[α_{k1}] = NP AND β_{k2} ∈ child[α_{k1}] = PP AND k1 < k2
           AND λ_0 ∈ child[β_{k2}] = p AND λ_{k3} ∈ child[β_{k2}] = NP AND k3 ≠ 0 then
62.          IC = ⟨E(η_{i1}), Adv, V, null, E(β_{k1}), p, E(λ_{k3})⟩           // Rule-16
63.        else
64.          IC = ⟨E(η_{i1}), Adv, V, null, E(α_j), null, null⟩                // Rule-2
65.        end if
```

```
66.      else if α_{j1} ∈ child[η_{i2}] = ADVP AND j1 ≠ 0 AND β_{j2} ∈ child[α_{j1}] = PP
         AND λ_0 ∈ child[β_{j2}] = p_1 AND λ_{j3} ∈ child[β_{j2}] = NP AND j3 ≠ 0 then
67.        if α_{k1} ∈ child[η_{i2}] = PP AND j1 < k1 AND β_0 ∈ child[α_{k1}] = p_2
           AND β_{k2} ∈ child[α_{k1}] = NP AND k2 ≠ 0 then
68.          IC = ⟨E(η_{i1}), Adv, V, p_1, E(λ_{j3}), p_2, E(β_{k2})⟩              // Rule-34
69.        else if γ_{k1} ∈ child[λ_{j3}] = NP AND γ_{k2} ∈ child[λ_{j3}] = PP AND k1 < k2
           AND θ_0 ∈ child[γ_{k2}] = p_2 AND θ_{k3} ∈ child[γ_{k2}] = NP AND k3 ≠ 0 then
70.          IC = ⟨E(η_{i1}), Adv, V, p_1, E(γ_{k1}), p_2, E(θ_{k3})⟩              // Rule-36
71.        else
72.          IC = ⟨E(η_{i1}), Adv, V, p_1, E(λ_{j3}), null, null⟩                 // Rule-12
73.        end if
74.      else if α_{j1} ∈ child[η_{i2}] = PP AND j1 ≠ 0 AND β_0 ∈ child[α_{j1}] = p_1
         AND β_{j2} ∈ child[α_{j1}] = NP AND j2 ≠ 0 then
75.        if α_{k1} ∈ child[η_{i2}] = PP AND j1 < k1 AND β_0 ∈ child[α_{k1}] = p_2
           AND β_{k2} ∈ child[α_{k1}] = NP AND k2 ≠ 0 then
76.          IC = ⟨E(η_{i1}), Adv, V, p_1, E(β_{j2}), p_2, E(β_{k2})⟩              // Rule-26
77.        else if λ_{k1} ∈ child[β_{j2}] = NP AND λ_{k2} ∈ child[β_{j2}] = PP AND k1 < k2
           AND γ_0 ∈ child[λ_{k2}] = p_2 AND γ_{k3} ∈ child[λ_{k2}] = NP AND k3 ≠ 0 then
78.          IC = ⟨E(η_{i1}), Adv, V, p_1, E(λ_{k1}), p_2, E(γ_{k3})⟩              // Rule-28
79.        else
80.          IC = ⟨E(η_{i1}), Adv, V, p_1, E(β_{j2}), null, null⟩                 // Rule-8
81.        end if
82.      end if
83.    else if η_{i1} = NP AND η_{i2} = VP AND i1 < i2 AND α_{i3} ∈ child[η_{i2}] = VP
       AND α_{i4} ∈ child[η_{i2}] = Adv AND i4 < i3 AND β_0 ∈ child[α_{i3}] = V then
84.      if β_j ∈ child[α_{i3}] = NP AND j ≠ 0 then
85.        if β_{k1} ∈ child[α_{i3}] = PP AND j < k1 AND λ_0 ∈ child[β_{k1}] = p
           AND λ_{k2} ∈ child[β_{k1}] = NP AND k2 ≠ 0 then
86.          IC = ⟨E(η_{i1}), Adv, V, null, E(β_j), p, E(λ_{k2})⟩                 // Rule-18
87.        else if λ_{k1} ∈ child[β_j] = NP AND λ_{k2} ∈ child[β_j] = PP AND k1 < k2
           AND γ_0 ∈ child[λ_{k2}] = p AND γ_{k3} ∈ child[λ_{k2}] = NP AND k3 ≠ 0 then
88.          IC = ⟨E(η_{i1}), Adv, V, null, E(λ_{k1}), p, E(γ_{k3})⟩              // Rule-20
89.        else
90.          IC = ⟨E(η_{i1}), Adv, V, null, E(β_j), null, null⟩                  // Rule-4
91.        end if
92.      else if β_{j1} ∈ child[α_{i3}] = PP AND j1 ≠ 0 AND λ_0 ∈ child[β_{j1}] = p_1
         AND λ_{j2} ∈ child[β_{j1}] = NP AND j2 ≠ 0 then
93.        if β_{k1} ∈ child[α_{i3}] = PP AND j1 < k1 AND λ_0 ∈ child[β_{k1}] = p_2
           AND λ_{k2} ∈ child[β_{k1}] = NP AND k2 ≠ 0 then
94.          IC = ⟨E(η_{i1}), Adv, V, p_1, E(λ_{j2}), p_2, E(λ_{k2})⟩             // Rule-30
95.        else if γ_{k1} ∈ child[λ_{j2}] = NP AND γ_{k2} ∈ child[λ_{j2}] = PP AND k1 < k2
           AND θ_0 ∈ child[γ_{k2}] = p_2 AND θ_{k3} ∈ child[γ_{k2}] = NP AND k3 ≠ 0 then
96.          IC = ⟨E(η_{i1}), Adv, V, p_1, E(γ_{k1}), p_2, E(θ_{k3})⟩             // Rule-32
97.        else
98.          IC = ⟨E(η_{i1}), Adv, V, p_1, E(λ_{j2}), null, null⟩                // Rule-10
99.        end if
100.     end if
101.   else if η_{i1} = NP AND η_{i2} = VP AND i1 < i2 AND α_{i3} ∈ child[η_{i2}] = VP
       AND β_{i4} ∈ child[α_{i3}] = VP AND β_{i6} ∈ child[α_{i3}] = Adv AND i6 < i4
       AND λ_0 ∈ child[β_{i4}] = V AND λ_{i5} ∈ child[β_{i4}] = NP AND i5 ≠ 0 then
102.     if λ_{j1} ∈ child[β_{i4}] = PP AND i5 < j1 AND γ_0 ∈ child[λ_{j1}] = p
         AND γ_{j2} ∈ child[λ_{j1}] = NP AND j2 ≠ 0 then
```

```
103.        IC = ⟨E(η_{i1}), Adv, V, null, E(λ_{i5}), p, E(γ_{j2})⟩                    // Rule-22
104.        else if  γ_{j1} ∈ child[λ_{i5}] = NP  AND  γ_{j2} ∈ child[λ_{i5}] = PP  AND  j1 < j2
            AND  θ_0 ∈ child[γ_{j2}] = p  AND  θ_{j3} ∈ child[γ_{j2}] = NP  AND  j3 ≠ 0  then
105.        IC = ⟨E(η_{i1}), Adv, V, null, E(γ_{j1}), p, E(θ_{j3})⟩                   // Rule-24
106.        else
107.        IC = ⟨E(η_{i1}), Adv, V, null, E(λ_{i5}), null, null⟩                     // Rule-6
108.        end if
109.      end if
110.      if  IC ≠ φ  then
111.        L_{IC} ← L_{IC} ∪ IC
112.      end if
113.    end for
114.  end for
115.  Return L_{IC}
```

40.4 PERFORMANCE EVALUATION

The performance of the system is analyzed by taking into account the performance of the biological relation extraction process, which aims to identify relevant verbs signifying biological entity interactions from MEDLINE abstracts. We have already explained the extraction process in the previous sections. We now present detailed discussion about how we evaluate the correctness of the extracted biological relations through analyzing the original sentences in which these relational verbs occur. In order to evaluate the correctness of the extraction process, we have randomly selected 10 different feasible biological relations and 100 GENIA abstracts for manual verification. The entity markers were removed from the GENIA abstracts before applying our relation-mining algorithm.

A biological relation is said to be *correctly identified* if its occurrence within a sentence along with its left and right entities is grammatically correct and the system has been able to locate it in the right context. To judge the performance of the system, it is not enough to judge the extracted relations only; it is also required to analyze all the correct relations that were missed by the system. The system is evaluated for its *precision, recall,* and *F-score* values by considering 10 relations: *activate, associate, express, increase, induce, inhibit, modulate, reduce, regulate,* and *stimulate.* For evaluation of the system, an evaluation software was written in Java, which exhaustively checks the corpus for possible occurrences of the required relation. For each relation to be judged, the evaluation software takes the root relation as input and performs partial string matching to extract all possible occurrences of the relation. This ensures that various nuances of English language grammar can also be taken care of. For example, if the root relation used in any query is "activate," all sentences containing *activates, inactivate, activated by, activated in,* and so on, are extracted. Each sentence containing an instance of the pattern is presented to the human evaluator after its appropriate tagging through ABNER. The sentence without ABNER tags is also presented to the evaluator. This makes it easier for the evaluator to judge the grammatical correctness of the relation associated to the concepts or entities around it. Each occurrence of the relation is judged for correctness by the evaluator, and the correct instances are marked. The marked instances are stored by the evaluation software and later used for computing the precision (π), recall (ρ), and *F*-score (F_1) values using Equations (40.1), (40.2), and (40.3), respectively.

TABLE 40.4 Partial List of Information Components Extracted from Sample Sentences Related to Alzheimer Disease of Table 40.2

Left Entity	Adverb	Relational Verb	Verbal Preposition	Right Entity	Conjunctional Preposition	Validatory Entity	PMID
Transcriptome analysis of synaptoneurosomes	—	Identifies	—	Neuroplasticity genes overexpressed in incipient Alzheimer's disease	—	—	19295912
Neuroplasticity genes	—	Overexpressed	In	Incipient Alzheimer's disease	—	—	19295912
Bone marrow–derived macrophages	—	Reduce	—	Beta-amyloid (Abeta) deposition	In	Brain	19295164
Aggregation and accumulation of amyloid beta protein (Abeta)	—	Plays	—	A pivotal role	In	The development of Alzheimer's disease (AD)	19275635
Memory deficits and neurochemical changes	—	Induced	By	C-reactive protein	In	Rats	19263040
CST3 gene	Not	Associated	With	AD risk	In	The Finnish population	19263040

ALGORITHM 40.2 biomedicalRelationExtraction(L_{IC})

Input: L_{IC} - A list of information components
Output: A set R of feasible biological relations and their
            morphological variants
Steps:
1. $L_V \leftarrow \phi, L_{UV} \leftarrow \phi, L_{RV} \leftarrow \phi$
2. **for** all $IC \in L_{IC}$ **do**
3.   **if** $E_i \in IC.leftEntity$ OR $E_i \in IC.rightEntity$ **then**
4. $L_V \leftarrow L_V \cup IC.verb + IC.preposition$ //E_i **is biological entity**
                                                 //**identified by ABNER**
5.   **end if**
6. **end for**
7. $L_{UV} \leftarrow UNIQUE(L_V)$ // **create a list of unique verbs**
8. Filter out verbs from L_{UV} with a prefix as ξ, where $\xi \in$
   {cross-, extra-, hydro-, micro-, milli-, multi-, photo-,
   super-, anti-, down-, half-, hypo-, mono-, omni-, over-,
   poly-, self-, semi-, tele-, dis-, epi-, mis-, non-, pre-,
   sub-, de-, di-, il-, im-, ir-, un-, up- }
9. Filter out verbs from L_{UV} with a suffix as λ, where $\lambda \in$
   {-able, -tion, -ness, -less, -ment, -ally, -ity, -ism, -ous,
   -ing, -er, -or, -al, -ly, -ed, -es, -ts, -gs, -ys, -ds, -ws,
   -ls, -rs, -ks, -en}
10. **for** all $V \in L_{UV}$ **do**
11. $N \leftarrow freqCount(V)$
12.   **if** $N \geq \theta$ **then**   // θ **is a threshold value**
13. $L_{RV} \leftarrow L_{RV} \cup V$
14.   **end if**
15. **end for**
16. $R \leftarrow L_{RV}$
17. **for** all $V_i \in L_{RV}$ **do**   // **identifying morphological variants**
18.   **for** all $V_j \in L_{UV}$ **do**
19.   **if** $V_i \in subString(V_j)$ **then**
20. $R \leftarrow R \cup V_j$
21.   **end if**
22.   **end for**
23. **end for**
24. **Return** R

The precision value of the system reflects its capability to identify a relational verb along with the correct pair of concepts/entities within which it is occurring. The recall value reflects the capability of the system to locate all instances of a relation within the corpus. Table 40.6 summarizes the performance measure values of our relation-mining system in the form of a misclassification matrix for information components centered around 10 different biological relations. On 100 randomly selected documents from the GENIA corpus, the average precision, recall, and F-score values are 92.71, 73.07, and 81.73%, respectively:

$$\text{Precision}(\pi) = \frac{\text{TP}}{\text{TP} + \text{FP}} \tag{40.1}$$

TABLE 40.5 Partial List of Feasible Biological Relations and Their Morphological Variants

Biological Relations	Morphological Variants
Associate	Associate with, associated with, associated to
Increase	Increased, increases, increased in, increased after, increased by, increased over
Induce	Induced, induced by, induces, induced in, induced with
Show	Showed, shown, shown on, show for, shows
Reduce	Reduced, reduces, reduced by, reduced in
Decrease	Decreased in, decreased as, decreased with, decreased across
Regulate	Regulated by, regulates
Affect	Affected, affects, affected in, affected by, affecting
Express	Expressed in, expressing, express as, expresses, expressed from
Attenuate	Attenuated, attenuated by, attenuates, attenuated in
Generate	Generated by, generated from
Enhance	Enhanced in, enhanced by
Activate	Activates, activated
Inhibit	Inhibits, inhibited, inhibited with, inhibition, inhibited by
Modulate	Modulates, modulated, modulated in, modulated by
Stimulate	Stimulates, stimulated, stimulated with, stimulated by

$$\text{Recall}(\rho) = \frac{\text{TP}}{\text{TP} + \text{FN}} \tag{40.2}$$

$$F - \text{score}(F_1) = 2 \times \frac{\pi \times \rho}{\pi + \rho} \tag{40.3}$$

As is observed, the precision of the system is quite high. This indicates that most of the extracted instances are correctly identified. However, the recall value of the system is somewhat low. This indicates that several relevant elements are not extracted from the text. The reason for low recall values is identified as follows. We observed that most misses occur when the parser assigns an incorrect syntactic class to a relational verb. For example, in the following sentence, the relational verb activates and other related constituents could not be identified by the system because activates is marked as a noun by the parser. Similarly, other misses occur when an information component spans over multiple sentences using anaphora: "Increased [Ca2+]i activates Ca2+/calmodulin-dependent kinases including the multifunctional Ca2+/calmodulin-dependent protein kinase II (CaM-K II), as well as calcineurin, a type 2B protein phosphatase [MEDLINE ID: 95173590]."

40.5 UNIQUENESS OF PROPOSED BIOLOGICAL RELATION-MINING SYSTEM

The primary focus of the proposed biological relation-mining system is to locate complex information components embedded within nonannotated biomedical texts, where an information component comprises biological concepts and relations. Though a number of systems have attempted to do the same task, there are certain unique aspects to the proposed approach, which we highlight in this section. The proposed text-mining-based approach unifies natural language processing and pattern-mining techniques to identify all feasible

TABLE 40.6 Evaluation Results of Biological Relation Extraction System

Biomedical Relations	Number of Times IC Is Identified by System	Number of Times IC Is Correctly Identified by System	Number of Times IC Occurs Correctly in Text Corpus	π (%)	ρ (%)	F_1 (%)
Activate	36	35	49	97.22	71.43	82.35
Associate	19	18	22	94.74	81.82	87.80
Express	26	24	35	92.31	68.57	78.69
Increase	19	17	26	89.47	65.38	75.56
Induce	71	67	91	94.37	73.63	82.72
Inhibit	36	34	48	94.44	70.83	80.95
Modulate	6	5	6	83.33	83.33	83.33
Reduce	22	21	30	95.45	70.00	80.77
Regulate	31	28	37	90.32	75.68	82.35
Stimulate	22	21	30	95.45	70.00	80.77
Average				92.71	73.07	81.73

biological relations within a corpus. Unlike most of the related work [20–22, 26] that have described methods for mining a fixed set of biological relations occurring with a set of pre-defined tags, the proposed system identifies all verbs in a document, and then identifies the feasible biological relational verbs using contextual analysis. While mining biological relations the associated prepositions are also considered, which very often changes the nature of the verb. For example, the relation activates in denotes a significant class of biological reactions. Thus, we also consider the biological relations, which are combinations of root verbs, morphological variants, and prepositions that follow these. Typical examples of biological relations identified in this category include *activated in*, *binds to*, and *stimulated with*. Besides mining relational verbs and associated entities, the novelty of the system lies in extracting validatory entities whose presence or absence validates a particular biological interaction. The system also extracts the adverbs associated with relational verbs, which plays a very important role, especially to identify the negation in sentences that are very crucial while answering biomedical queries. Unlike the related work [5], which described a method for mining biological relations from tagged GENIA corpus, the proposed system has been designed to work with a collection of untagged biomedical literature.

40.6 CONCLUSION AND FUTURE WORK

In this chapter, we have presented how text mining can be extended to extract generic biological relations from text corpus. The system uses linguistic and semantic analysis of text to identify NP and VP phrases and their semantic relations to represent texts using conceptual graphs, which are then analyzed to identify relation instances and map them into information components. The information components are centered on domain entities and their relationships, which are extracted using natural language processing techniques and co-occurrence-based analysis. The proposed system employs text-mining principles along with NLP techniques to extract information about the likelihood of various entity–relation occurrences within text documents. Though the system design is fairly generic, the design of the entire system has been validated with experiments conducted over PubMed abstracts. Performance evaluation results show that the precision of the relation extraction process is high. Reliability of the process is established through the fact that all manually identified relational verbs are extracted correctly. The recall value however may be improved with more rigorous analysis of the phrase structure tree generated by the parser. Extracted feasible biological relations along with information components can be used for knowledge visualization and efficient information extraction from text documents to answer biomedical queries posted at different levels of specificity.

An interesting application of the conceptual graphs, generated as an intermediate representation of the texts, is to identify biological relation associations at the generic concept levels rather than at the entity level by using the GP-Close algorithm proposed in [4] to mine frequent generalized association patterns. For this, we may utilize the concept hierarchies defined in existing biological ontologies (e.g., GENIA ontology [17]) to map extracted biological entities from texts over them and then to characterize biological relations at concept levels. Presently, we are enhancing our system to incorporate the GP-Close algorithm to mine frequent generalized associations for the identified generic biological relations. This could be very helpful to enhance existing biological ontologies using generic relations mined from biological text documents.

REFERENCES

1. A.-H. Tan. Text mining: The state of the art and the challenges. In *Proceedings of the Pacific Asia Conference Knowledge Discovery and Data Mining (PAKDD '99) Workshop Knowledge Discovery from Advanced Databases*, 1999, pp. 65–70.

2. J. Dorre, P. Gerstl, and R. Seiffert. Text mining: Finding nuggets in mountains of textual data. In *Proceedings of the International Conference on Knowledge Discovery and Data Mining*, 1999, pp. 398–401.

3. N. Guarino, C. Masolo, and G. Vetere. Ontoseek: Content-based access to the Web. *IEEE Intell. Syst.*, 14(3):70–80, 1999.

4. T. Jiang, A.-H. Tan, and K. Wang. Mining generalized associations of semantic relations from textual Web content. *IEEE Trans. Knowledge Data Eng.*, 19(2), 2007.

5. M. Abulaish and L. Dey. Biological relation extraction and query answering from medline abstracts using ontology-based text mining. *Data Knowledge Eng.*, 61(2):228–262, 2007.

6. S. Albert, S. Gaudan, H. Knigge, A. Raetsch, A. Delgado, B. Huhse, H. Kirsch, M. Albers, D. R. Schuhmann, and M. Koegl. Computer-assisted generation of a protein-interaction database for nuclear receptors. *Mol. Endocrinol.*, 17(8):1555–1567, 2003.

7. J. Allen. *Natural Language Understanding*, 2nd ed. Pearson Education, Singapore, 2004.

8. M. Berardi, D. Malerba, R. Piredda, M. Attimonelli, G. Scioscia, and P. Leo. *Biomedical Literature Mining for Biological Databases Annotation*. I-Tech, Vienna, Austria, 2008, pp. 320–343.

9. A. Bernstein, E. Kaufmann, A. Gohring, and C. Kiefer. Querying ontologies: A controlled English interface for end-users. In *Proceedings of the International Semantic Web Conference*, 2005, pp. 112–126.

10. M. Ciaramita, A. Gangemi, E. Ratsch, J. Saric, and I. Rojas. Unsupervised learning of semantic relations between concepts of a molecular biology ontology. In *Proceedings of the 19th International Joint Conference on Artificial Intelligence (IJCAI'05)*, 2005, pp. 659–664.

11. C. Friedman, P. Kra, H. Yu, M. Krauthammer, and A. Rzhetsky. GENIES: A natural language processing system for the extraction of molecular pathways from journal articles. *Bioinformatics*, 17(1):S74–S82, 2001.

12. K. Fundel, R. Kuffner, and R. Zimmer. Relex—Relation extraction using dependency parse trees. *Bioinformatics*, 23:365–371, 2007.

13. R. Gaizauskas, G. Demetriou, P. J. Artymiuk, and P. Willett. Protein structures and information extraction from biological texts: The pasta system. *Bioinformatics*, 19(1):135–143, 2003.

14. D. Gavrilis, E. Dermatas, and G. Kokkinakis. Automatic extraction of information from molecular biology scientific abstracts. In *Proceedings of the International Workshop on Speech and Computer (SPECOM'03)*, 2003.

15. L. Hirschman, A. Yeh, A. Morgan, and M. Colosimo. Linking biological literature, information, and knowledge. *EDGE-MITRE's Adv. Technol. Newsl.*, 9(1):8–9, 2005.

16. T. K. Jenssen, A. Laegreid, J. Komorowski, and E. Hovig. A literature network of human genes for high-throughput analysis of gene expression. *Nature Genet.*, 28:21–28, 2001.

17. J. D. Kim, T. Ohta, Y. Teteisi, and J. Tsujii. GENIA ontology. Technical Report TR-NLP-UT-2006-2. Tsujii Laboratory, University of Tokyo, 2006.

18. M. Miwa, R. Saetre, Y. Miyao, and J. Tsujii. Protein-protein interaction extraction by leveraging multiple kernels and parsers. *Int. J. Med. Inform.*, 78(12):39–46, 2009.

19. S. Mukherjea and S. Sahay. Discovering biomedical relations utilising the world-wide-web. In *Proceedings of the 11th Pacific Symposium on Biocomputing*, Hawaii, 2006, pp. 164–75.

20. T. Ono, H. Hishigaki, A. Tanigami, and T. Takagi. Automated extraction of information on protein-protein interactions from the biological literature. *Bioinformatics*, 17(2):155–161, 2001.

21. F. Rinaldi, G. Scheidei, C. Andronis, A. Persidis, and O. Konstani. Mining relations in the GENIA corpus. In *Proceedings of the 2nd European Workshop on Data Mining and Text Mining for Bioinformatics*, Pisa, Italy, 2004, pp. 61–68.

22. T. Sekimizu, H. S. Park, and J. Tsujii. Identifying the interaction between genes and genes products based on frequently seen verbs in medline abstract. *Genome Inform*, 9:62–71, 1998.

23. B. Settles. ABNER: An open source tool for automatically tagging genes, proteins and other entity names in text. *Bioinformatics*, 21(14):3191–3192, 2005.

24. P. Srinivasan. Text mining: Generating hypotheses from medline. *J. Am. Soc. Inform. Sci.*, 55(4):396–413, 2004.

25. B. J. Stapley and G. Benoit. Bibliometrics: Information retrieval and visualization from co-occurrence of gene names in medline abstracts. In *Proceedings of the 5th Pacific Symposium on Biocomputing*, Hawaii, 2000, pp. 529–540.

26. J. Thomas, D. Milward, C. Ouzounis, S. Pulman, and M. Carroll. Automatic extraction of protein interactions from scientific abstracts. In *Proceedings of the 5th Pacific Symposium on Biocomputing*, Hawaii, 2000, pp. 538–549.

27. Y. Tsuruoka, Y. Tateishi, J. D. Kim, T. Ohta, J. McNaught, S. Ananiadou, and J. Tsujii. Developing a robust part-of-speech tagger for biomedical text. In *Advances in Informatics—10th Panhellenic Conference on Informatics*, 2005, pp. 382–392.

28. T. Wattarujeekrit, P. K. Shah, and N. Collier. PASBio: Predicate-argument structures for event extraction in molecular biology. *BMC Bioinformatics*, 5:155–174, 2004.

29. J. D. Wren and H. R. Garner. Shared relationship analysis: Ranking set cohesion and commonalities within a literature-derived relationship network. *Bioinformatics*, 20(2):191–198, 2004.

30. Y. Xu, Z. Chang, W. Hu, L. Yu, H. DuanMu, and X. Li. Mining the relationship between gene and disease from literature. In *Proceedings of the 6th International Conference on Fuzzy System and Knowledge Discovery (FSKD'09)*, Tianjin, 2009, pp. 482–486.

31. PubMed, http://www.ncbi.nlm.nih.gov/pubmed.

32. U.S. National Library of Medicine (NLM), `http://www.nlm.nih.gov/`.

33. Medline, `http://www.nlm.nih.gov/pubs/factsheets/medline.html`.

34. MeSH, `http://www.nlm.nih.gov/mesh/`.

35. World Wide Web Consortium, `http://www.w3.org/`.

36. Stanford's Parser, `http://nlp.stanford.edu/downloads/lex-parser.shtml`.

CHAPTER 41

PROTEIN–PROTEIN RELATION EXTRACTION FROM BIOMEDICAL ABSTRACTS

SYED TOUFEEQ AHMED,[1] HASAN DAVULCU,[2] SUKRU TIKVES,[2] RADHIKA NAIR,[2] and CHINTAN PATEL[2]

[1]Vanderbilt University Medical Center, Nashville, Tennessee
[2]Department of Computer Science and Engineering, Ira A. Fulton Engineering, Arizona State University, Tempe, Arizona

41.1 INTRODUCTION

Human genome sequencing marked the beginning of the era of large-scale genomics and proteomics, which in turn led to large amounts of information. Much of that exists (or is generated) as unstructured text of published literature. The first step toward extracting event information, in the biomedical domain, is to recognize the names of proteins [4, 18], genes, drugs, and other molecules. The next step is to recognize the relationship between such entities [5, 19, 30] and then to recognize the biomolecular interaction events with these entities as participants [40, 43]. However, several issues make extracting such interactions and relationships difficult since [38]:

1. The task involves free text and hence there are many ways of stating the same fact.
2. The genre of text is not grammatically simple.
3. The text includes a lot of technical terminology unfamiliar to existing natural language processing systems.
4. Information may need to be combined across several sentences.
5. There are many sentences from which nothing should be extracted.

Information extraction (IE) [9, 17, 23, 34] is the extraction of salient facts about pre-specified types of events, entities [8], or relationships from free text. Information extraction from free text utilizes shallow-parsing techniques [14], part-of-speech tagging [7], noun and verb phrase chunking [27], verb subject and object relationships [14], and learned [9, 13, 38] or hand-built patterns to automate the creation of specialized databases. Manual pattern engineering approaches employ shallow parsing with patterns to extract the interactions.

Biological Knowledge Discovery Handbook: Preprocessing, Mining, and Postprocessing of Biological Data,
First Edition. Edited by Mourad Elloumi and Albert Y. Zomaya.

In the [30] system, sentences are first tagged using a dictionary-based protein name identifier and then processed by a module which extracts interactions directly from complex and compound sentences using regular expressions based on part-of-speech tags. IE systems look for entities, relationships among those entities, or other specific facts within text documents. The success of information extraction depends on the performance of the various subtasks involved. The SUISEKI system of Blaschke [4] also uses regular expressions with probabilities that reflect the experimental accuracy of each pattern to extract interactions into predefined frame structures. GENIES [16] utilizes a grammar-based *natural language processing* (NLP) engine for information extraction. Recently, it has been extended as GeneWays [33], which also provides a Web interface that allows users to search and submit papers of interest for analysis. The BioRAT system [12] uses manually engineered templates that combine lexical and semantic information to identify protein interactions. The GeneScene system [25] extracts interactions using frequent preposition-based templates.

Grammar engineering approaches, on the other hand, use manually generated specialized grammar rules [32] that perform a deep parse of the sentences. Temkin [41] addresses the problem of extracting protein interactions by using an extendable but manually built *context-free grammar* (CFG) that is designed specifically for parsing biological text. The PathwayAssist system uses an NLP system, MedScan [29], for the biomedical domain that tags the entities in text and produces a semantic tree. Slot filler rules are engineered based on the semantic tree representation to extract relationships from text. Recently, extraction systems have also used link grammar [20] to identify interactions between proteins [15]. Their approach relies on various linkage paths between named entities such as gene and protein names. Such manual pattern engineering approaches for information extraction are very hard to scale up to large document collections since they require labor-intensive and skill-dependent pattern engineering. Machine learning approaches have also been used to learn extraction rules from user-tagged training data. These approaches represent the rules learned in various formats such as decision trees [11] or grammar rules [42]. Craven et al. [13] explored an automatic rule-learning approach that uses a combination of FOIL [31] and the naive Bayes classifier to learn extraction rules.

The BioNLP'09 shared task [1] involved recognition of biomolecular events, which appear in the GENIA corpus. We mainly focused on task 1, which was the detection of an event and its participants.

The rest of the chapter is organized as follows. In Section 41.2 we describe the BioEve system, Section 41.3 explains in detail different classification approaches, and event extraction using a dependency parse tree of the sentence is explained in Section 41.4. Section 41.5 describes experiments with classification approaches, event extraction, and evaluation results for the BioNLP'09 shared task 1 [1]. Section 41.6 concludes the chapter.

41.2 BIOEVE: BIOMOLECULAR EVENT EXTRACTOR

A bioevent could be described as a change in the state of a biomolecule or biomolecules. An example of an event is shown in Figure 41.1. The BioEve architecture is shown in Figure 41.2. The biomedical abstracts are first split into sentences, before being sent to the sentence-level classifier. We used the naive Bayes classifier to classify sentences into different event class types. Classification at the sentence level is a difficult task, as sentences have lesser information as compared to the whole document. To help the event extraction

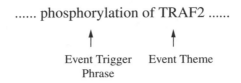

FIGURE 41.1 Example of phosphorylation event.

module, are of these sentences are then semantically labeled with additional keywords. We created a dictionary-based labeler which included trigger words from training data along with the corresponding event type. These labeled sentences are parsed using a dependency parser to identify `argument-predicate` roles. For each event class type, we hand crafted high-coverage extraction rules, similar to Fundel et al. [19], to identity all event participants. For the BioNLP shared task, the event participant output was formatted to GENIA format.

41.2.1 Bioentity Tagging

The first step in extracting bioevents is to identify candidate participants and the classes to which they belong. The intent is to capture entity-type relationships to facilitate queries, which is difficult using simple keyword search. An example could be "What are all genes related to eye disorders?" An abstract may contain the term *conjunctivitis*, which is a type of eye disorder but not the actual term *eye disorders*. Such results would be missed out if we focus on the syntactic term-matching approach. We applied *A Biomedical Named Entity Recognizer* (ABNER) [37], an open-source software tool for molecular biology text

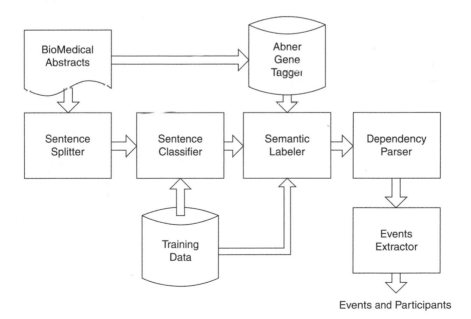

FIGURE 41.2 BioEve system architecture.

mining, to tag different gene types, including protein names, DNA, RNA, cell line, and cell type. Abstracts were also found to contain drugs and chemicals which could also participate in an event. We used *Open Source Chemistry Analysis Routines* (OSCAR3)[35] to identify chemical names and chemical structures. Capturing "ISA" relationships gives a single-level semantic relationship. To capture an ontology relationship, we used the *Unified Medical Language System* (UMLS) [6] MeSH database. A strict matching approach was used to tag valid MeSH terms present in an abstract.

41.2.2 Event Trigger Identification and Classification

A bioevent can be broadly defined as a change in the state of a biomolecule or biomolecules, for example, *phosphorylation of IkB involves a change on the protein IkB*. A relationship generally involves two participants. However, a bioevent can involve one or more participants, where participants could be entities or events. An event is characterized by a trigger word which indicates the presence of an event and extracting the biomedical entities associated with these events. This module is an enhancement of event detection and typing the BioNLP'09 shared task [1]. We applied a dictionary-based semantic labeler for this shared task. Further research on this problem highlighted three different approaches of detecting and typing events at various levels of granularity.

41.3 SENTENCE-LEVEL CLASSIFICATION AND SEMANTIC LABELING

The first step towards bioevent extraction is to identify phrases in biomedical text which indicate the presence of an event. The labeled phrases are classified further into nine event types. The aim of marking such interesting phrases is to avoid looking at the entire text to find participants. The full parsing of the biomedical literature would be very expensive, especially for large volumes of text. We intend to mark phrases in biomedical text which could have a potential event to serve as a starting point for extraction of event participants. The BioEve event extraction module depends on class labels for extraction. To help with this task, we needed to improve sentence labeling with correct class type information. For this, we employed dictionary-based semantic class labeling by identifying trigger (or interaction) words which clearly indicate the presence of a particular event. We used the ABNER [37] gene name recognizer to enrich the sentences with gene mentions. There have been cases in the training data where the same trigger word is associated with more than one event type. To resolve such cases, the trigger words were mapped to the most likely event type based on their occurrence count in the training data. We labeled trigger words in each sentence with their most likely event type. These tagged words served as a starting point for the extraction of event participants. This was done to speed up the extraction process, as the event extraction module now only needs to focus on the parts of the sentences related to these tagged trigger words.

41.3.1 Incremental Approach to Classification Task

For the classification problem at hand, we started with the most popular and simple algorithm first the (the naive Bayes) and incrementally moved to more sophisticated machine classification algorithms. Findings and observations at each level were used to learn improvements at the next level of experiments. Table 41.1 gives an overview of different

TABLE 41.1 Summarization of Classification Approaches

Granularity	Features	Classification Approaches
Single Label, sentence level	Bag-of-words (BOW) BOW + gene names boosted BOW + trigger words boosted BOW + gene names and trigger words boosted	Naive Bayes
Multiple Labels, sentence Level	BOW	Naive Bayes + expectation maximization maximum entropy
Event trigger phrase labeling	BOW + 3gram and 4 gram prefixes and suffixes + orthographic features + trigger phrase dictionary	Conditional random fields (CRF)

classifiers applied at different levels of granularity and the features used by these classifiers. We started with identification of a single label per sentence, advancing to multiple labels per sentence and eventually marking phrases in text and classifying these phrases.

41.3.2 Single-Label, Sentence-Level Classification

This approach was a preliminary attempt to understand the problem at hand and identify features suitable for the classification. We used the naive Bayes classifier as a baseline, since it is known to perform well for text classification and is fast and easy to implement. Bayesian classifiers assign the most likely class to a given example described by its feature vector. Learning such classifiers can be greatly simplified by assuming that features are independent of a given class, that is,

$$P(X|C) = \sum_{i=1}^{n} P(X_i|C)$$

where $X = (X_1, \ldots, X_n)$ is a feature vector and C is a class.

For training the classifier, every sentence in the abstract was treated as a separate instance. The class label for a sentence was based on the most frequent event type occurring in the sentence. If there is a single dominant event in the sentence, the instance is labeled with that event type. If there is more than one event in a training instance, then the first encountered event type is passed to the classifier for that instance. We used WEKA [3], a collection of machine learning algorithms for data-mining tasks, to identify the single-label-per-sentence approach. As WEKA does not support multiple labels for the same instance, we had to include the first encountered label in the case where the instance had multiple labels.

For the feature sets mentioned below, we used the term frequency inverse document frequency (TF-IDF) representation. Each vector was normalized based on vector length. Also, to avoid variations, words/phrases were converted to lowercase. Based on WEKA library token delimiters, features were filtered to include those which had an alphabet as a prefix using regular expressions. For example, features like -300 bp were filtered out, but features like p55, which is a protein name, were retained. We experimented with the list of features described below in order to understand how well each feature suits the corpus under consideration:

- *Bag-of-Words Model*   This model classified sentences based on word distribution.
- *Bag-of-Words with Gene Names Boosted*   The idea was to give more importance to words, which clearly demarcate event types. To start with, we included gene names provided in the training data. Next, we used the ABNER gene tagger to tag gene names, apart from the ones already provided to us. We boosted weights for renamed feature "protein" by 2.0.
- *Bag-of-Words with Event Trigger Words Boosted*   We separately tried boosting event trigger words. The list of trigger words was obtained from training data. This list was cleaned to remove stopwords. Trigger words were ordered in terms of their frequency of occurrence with respect to an event type in order to capture trigger words which are most discriminative.
- *Bag-of-Words with Gene Names and Event Trigger Words Boosted*   The final approach was to boost both gene names and trigger words together. Theoretically, this approach was expected to do better than the previous two feature sets discussed. The combination of the discriminative approach of trigger words and gene name boosting was expected to train the classifier better.

41.3.3 Multiple-Label, Sentence-Level Classification

Based on heuristics, the GENIA corpus data set on average has more than one event per sentence. There were instances in the training data which had a single dominant event. However, in some cases, multiple event types occurred in a training instance with an equal probability. Hence, there is a need to consider multiple labels per sentence. Instead of strictly classifying a sentence under one label, the intent is to determine event-type probability in the sentence. To explain this further, consider the example in Figure 41.3. The phrases italicized indicate trigger phrases, where the terms *blocked* and *prevented* indicate presence of a *negative-regulation* event and *proteolytic degradation* identifies a *protein catabolism* event. Negative regulation is a dominant event type in this sentence. However, the sentence also talks about other event types like protein catabolism, although with a lesser probability. A user looking for content related to protein catabolism could be interested in sentences like Figure 41.3. Based on analysis of PUBMED abstracts, we considered a threshold of 0.2 probability.

We used classification algorithms from the MALLET library [2]. Biomedical abstracts are split into sentences. For training purposes, plain-text sentences are transformed into training instances as required by MALLET. The classifier is trained based on these formatted instances. Test abstracts are converted to instances as well and the trained classifier the predicts the probability of each event type for every sentence. A threshold of 0.2 probability was applied to identify the top event types present in the sentence. Use of the classifiers under MALLET requires data transformation in to formatted training instances. For multiple labels

---

> Furthermore, sodium salicylate *blocked* the LPS-induced *proteolytic degradation* of I kappa B alpha, which *prevented* the nuclear *translocation* of c-Rel/p65 heterodimers.

FIGURE 41.3   Plain-text sentence.

for sentences, we experimented with NaiveBayesEM (the basic naive Bayes classifier, which utilizes *expectation maximization* to facilitate the classification) and the *maximum-entropy* (MaxENT) classifier. Maximum entropy is a probability distribution estimation technique [28], where the underlying principle of maximum entropy is that without external knowledge one should prefer distributions that are uniform [28]. Labeled training data are used to derive a set of constraints for the model that characterize the class-specific expectations for the distribution [28]. The two main aspects of the maximum-entropy classifier are feature selection and parameter estimation. The feature selection part selects the most important features of the loglinear model, and the parameter estimation part assigns a proper weight to each of the feature functions [21]. Maximum-entropy estimation produces a model with the most uniform distribution among all the distributions satisfying the given constraints [21]. The feature set used was the bag-of-words model.

41.3.4 Phrase-Level Labeling

The next level of improvement was to advance from sentence-level to phrase-level labeling. This is more accurate since we are not only identifying event types present in a sentence but also marking their positions in the text. In this approach, we considered event trigger phrase classification as a sequence segmentation problem, where each word is a token in a sequence to be assigned a label [36].

Based on examples from training data, the following were some of the key observations made, which proved to be beneficial while training the phrase-level classifier:

- Not all events are tagged in the GENIA corpus. A set of proteins and certain types of genes were selected and only events related to these selected proteins were tagged. Consider the example in Figure 41.4, where the word *inhibition* is labeled as belonging to the negative-regulation event type. In the second example shown in Figure 41.5, even though it closely resembles the example in Figure 41.4, it was not labeled in the training data, because NF-kappa B was not selected in the list of proteins for abstract ID 8096091.

- Taking context into consideration was important while marking trigger words. Figure 41.6 gives two examples of transcription and phosphorylation event types,

---

··· Cytokine rescue from glucocorticoid induced apoptosis in T cells is mediated through **inhibition** of *IkappaBalpha*. ···

FIGURE 41.4 Selected event annotation (PUBMED abstract ID 9488049).

··· p65 restores intracellular inhibition of NF-kappa B ···

FIGURE 41.5 Valid event not labeled (abstract ID 8096091).

··· leading to NF-kappaB nuclear translocation and **transcription** of E-selectin and IL-8 ···

··· Ligation of CD3 also induces the tyrosine **phosphorylation** of HS1 ···

FIGURE 41.6 Valid event phrases considering context.

> $\cdots$ requires expression of cytokines and chemokines as well as activation of the **transcription** factor nuclear factor (NF)-kappaB
>
> $\cdots$. Protein **phosphorylation** has an important role in the regulation of these two factors $\cdots$

FIGURE 41.7   Invalid event phrases considering context.

respectively, which are valid in the given context. Figure 41.7 indicates examples for the trigger words *transcription* and *phosphorylation*, which are not valid trigger words in the given context.

41.3.5 Conditional Random-Field-Based Classifier

Conditional random fields (CRFs) are undirected statistical graphical models, a special case of which is a linear chain that corresponds to a conditionally trained finite-state machine [36]. CRFs in particular have been shown to be useful in part-of-speech tagging [24], shallow parsing [39], and named entity recognition for news wire data [26]. We customized ABNER [37], which is based on MALLET, to suit our needs. ABNER employs a set of orthographic and semantic features. As an improvement to the approaches discussed so far, we intended to include biomedical domain information while training the classifier. We analyzed the features used by ABNER for protein and gene name recognition.

41.3.6 Feature Selection

We utilized both orthographic and semantic features in training the system. The orthographic features were extracted from the BIONLP-NLPBA 2004 shared task vocabulary, while the semantic features were incorporated through ABNER.

41.3.6.1 Orthographic Features   The default model included the training vocabulary (provided as part of the BIONLP-NLPBA 2004 shared task) in the form of 17 orthographic features based on regular expressions [36]. These include uppercase letters (initial uppercase letter, all uppercase letters, mix of upper- and lowercase letters), digits (special expressions for single and double digits, natural numbers, and real numbers), hyphens (special expressions for hyphens appearing at the beginning and end of a phrase), other punctuation marks, Roman and Greek words, and 3- and 4-gram suffixes and prefixes.

41.3.6.2 Semantic Features   ABNER uses semantic features provided in the form of hand-prepared and database-referenced lexicons. Table 41.2 gives information about the basic lexicon groups used. This information is referenced from [36].

TABLE 41.2   Feature Selection

Lexicon Description	Source	Lexicon Count
Greek letters, amino acids, chemical elements, known viruses, abbreviations of all these	Entered by hand	7
Genes, chromosome locations, proteins, and cell lines	Online public databases	4
Lexicons for CELL_TYPE	Google Web index	30

41.3.7 Trigger Phrase Dictionary

Based on the GENIA training data, a trigger phrase dictionary was created, providing the mapping between a trigger phrase and event type(s). This list was cleaned to remove stopwords. The stopword cleaning was applied for single-word trigger phrases which are included in a stopword list. All possible morphological forms of trigger words were added to the list; for example, for trigger word *upregulation*, terms like *upregulates* and *upregulated* were added as well.

The list was first ordered to identify the discriminating trigger phrases for each event type. An event type was associated with a trigger phrase based on the number of times an event type is associated with that trigger word. Finally, filtered trigger words are ordered such that multiword phrases are tagged in preference to phrases with single word, for example, *gene expression* indicates the presence of a gene expression event as compared to single trigger term *expression*. The dictionary of trigger words was selectively applied based on knowledge about false positives from training data.

41.4 EVENT EXTRACTION USING DEPENDENCY PARSING

The sentences, after being class labeled and tagged, are parsed using a dependency parser (Stanford parser [10]) to identify `argument-predicate` roles. Words in the sentence and the relationships between these words form the dependency parse tree of the sentence. One problem encountered during initial testing stages was due to the gene and protein names. These names are not part of the standard English dictionary and, as a result, the dependency parses of the sentences give unexpected results. To remedy the situation, each mention is substituted by a unique identifier. For example, PU.1 would be substituted by T7, depending on its occurrence in the text. The annotations are not part of the standard English dictionary either, but they do not cause the dependency parser to parse the sentence incorrectly and also searching for them in the dependency tree can be simplified by simple regular expressions. For our system, we used typed-dependency representation output format from the Stanford parser which is a simple tuple, `reln(gov, dep)`, where `reln` is the dependency relation, `gov` is the governor word, and `dep` is the dependent word. Consider the following example sentence:

```
We investigated whether PU.1 binds and activates the
M-CSF receptor promoter.
```

After this sentence is class labeled and tagged:

```
We investigated whether T7 binds/BINDING and
activates/POSITIVE_REGULATION
the T8 promoter.
```

The tagged sentence is parsed to obtain dependency relations as shown below:

```
nsubj(investigated-2, We-1)
complm(binds-5, whether-3)
nsubj(binds-5, T7-4)
ccomp(investigated-2, binds-5)
conj_and(binds-5, activates-7)
```

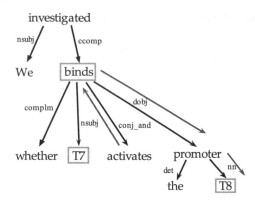

FIGURE 41.8 Dependency parse tree and event binding and its participants.

```
det(promoter-10, the-8)
nn(promoter-10, T8-9)
dobj(binds-5, promoter-10)
```

This sentence mentions two separate events, *binding* and *positive regulation*. Consider extracting the event binding and its participants. Figure 41.8 shows the parse tree representation and the part of the tree that needs to be identified for extracting the event binding.

The rule matching begins from the root node of the dependency parse tree. The module searches the tree in a breadth-first fashion, looking for event trigger words. It does not search for occurrences of protein or gene annotations. On finding a trigger word, it marks the node in the tree and activates the rule matcher for the corresponding event class on that node. The matcher searches the tree for participants of the event and on finding them successfully creates a record in the result set corresponding to the event. For example, in the tree shown in Figure 41.8, *binds* is a trigger word for a binding event. The extraction module fires a signal on detecting its corresponding node in the parse tree. It then marks the node and loads the binding event rule matcher on it. This matcher searches for the participants of the binding event as per the rules created for it. It finds T7 and T8 in the tree and reports them back. This results in the creation of a binding event, with the trigger word "binds" and participants T7 and T8 dereferenced to PU.1 and M-CSF receptor.

41.4.1 One-Pass Extraction

For each event class type, we carefully hand crafted rules, keeping the theme of the event, number of participants, and their interactions into consideration. In an extraction rule, T represents the occurrence of a protein in a sentence. If multiple proteins are involved, then subscripts, T_n, are used to represent this. The rule is triggered when it matches I (for an *interaction word* or *trigger word*) in the sentence. Some dependency relations and rule predicates are explained below.

41.4.1.1 Extraction Algorithm The algorithm to extract events and participants from the abstracts is shown in Figure 41.9. All the abstracts are iterated over once, their text is split into constituent sentences, each sentence is converted to its dependency tree, and the rule matcher then works on the dependency tree to extract an event and its participants.

Input: Abstracts tagged with the interaction words and class labels
Output: Biomolecular events with interation words and the participants
foreach *abstract* **do** Split abstract into sentences

> **foreach** *sentence in current abstract* **do**
>> retrieve all the interation words in current sentence;
>> sort them according to precedence of events;
>> **foreach** *interaction word in the sentence* **do**
>>> extract the participants by applying the corresponding event's rule
>>> to the sentence's dependency parse;
>> **end**
> **end**
end

FIGURE 41.9   One-pass extraction algorithm.

41.4.1.2 *Multiple Events and Nested Events*   A single sentence may contain multiple event mentions and their respective participants. In the case of multiple events per sentence, one of these cases may hold true:

- The sentence mentions multiple and disjoint events.
- The sentence mentions multiple and nested (connected) events.

Multiple, disjoint events involve separate or the same set of proteins or genes. These events do not encapsulate another event within themselves. An example of such an event mention would be the sentence given before: "We investigated whether T7 binds and activates the T8 promoter." In this sentence, "binds" and "activates" are two distinct events, binds represents binding and activates represents positive regulation. They are not nested events, because the participants in both are proteins. One event's result is not the participant for another. Even though both act on the same set of proteins, T7 and T8, they are distinct.

Nested events, on the other hand, have other events or their products as their participants. These kinds of events are difficult to detect. An example of a nested event is: "However, neither TNF or LPS stimulated VCAM-1 expression in HUAECs." The trigger words in the sentence are *stimulated* and *expression*. Stimulated denotes positive regulation and expression denotes gene expression. The gene expression event is catalyzed by the positive-regulation event. This is an example of a nested event.

Extraction of nested events is difficult due to the nature of their parse result. The dependency parse of the sample sentence is given in Table 41.3. The event trigger words stimulated and expression are related to each other. A rule match will be triggered for both

TABLE 41.3   Dependency Parse of Nested Event

advmod(stimulated-7, However-1)
preconj(TNF-4, neither-3)
nsubj(stimulated-7, TNF-4)
conj_or(TNF-4, LPS-6)
nn(expression-9, T9-8)
dobj(stimulated-7, expression-9)
prep_in(stimulated-7, HUAECs-11)

these events and both will result in T9, when the rule for stimulated should produce the trigger word expression and its corresponding event.

41.4.1.3 Sample Parse and Extraction This section uses a sample sentence to demonstrate how BioEve extracts events and their participants from plain text. Consider the following sentence:

> During CD30 signal transduction, we found that binding of TRAF2 to the cytoplasmic domain of CD30 results in the rapid depletion of TRAF2.

The proteins CD30 and TRAF2 are tagged and their occurrences are replaced with proper annotations. The trigger words are also tagged in the sentence. This results in the following form of the sentence:

> During T11 signal transduction, we found that binding/BINDING of T12 to the cytoplasmic domain of T13 results in the rapid depletion/NEGATIVE_REGULATION of T14.

The sentence text that is parsed using the dependency parser is "During T11 signal transduction, we found that binding of T12 to the cytoplasmic domain of T13 results in the rapid depletion of T14." Note that the annotations of the trigger words are removed. This is to prevent the parser from getting confused by the irregular annotation format. Another thing to note is that the event of transduction has not been tagged even though its corresponding participant has been identified. Its dependency parse tree can be visualized as given in Figure 41.10. The extraction procedure will be shown using the tree representation as it is more intuitive.

The extraction module retrieves all the trigger words from the sentence and sorts them as per the event class precedence order. In the sample sentence, *binding* and *depletion* are the

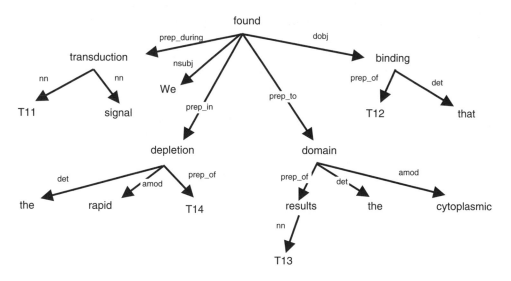

FIGURE 41.10 Dependency parse tree of sample sentence.

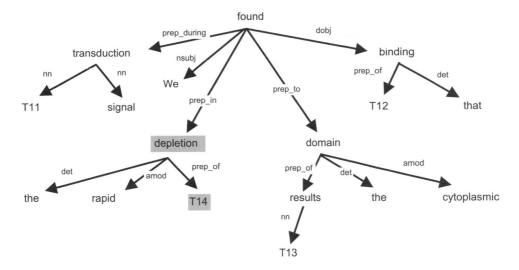

FIGURE 41.11 Extraction of negative-regulation event in given sample sentence. The rule that matches and extracts is prep(T, P), where T represents the trigger word and P is the protein annotation.

trigger words. *Depletion*, which suggests negative regulation, has higher precedence than binding and hence is searched for first. The extraction module starts from the root of the tree and searches for the event trigger word.

Figure 41.11 shows the rule matcher extracting the instance of a negative regulation event. Starting from the root, the module detects depletion at the highlighted node. It knows that this word depicts negative regulation and loads the rules for this event. The first rule for negative regulation is obj(verb/T, P), which means that the trigger word (T) is a verb and the protein (P) is its object. The trigger word here, depletion, is not a verb and hence this rule fails. The module moves to the second rule. This one is prep(T, P), that is, the trigger word and the protein are connected by a preposition. Depletion and T14 are connected by a preposition, the word *of*. Hence, this rule generates a hit and consequently the event and its participant are extracted.

After extracting the negative-regulation event, the module considers the next event in the order. This sentence has just one left, binding. It again starts the search from the root and finds the trigger word as highlighted in Figure 41.12. The first rule to be matched is P_1 (T) P_2, where P_1 and P_2 are the two participant proteins. The rule specifies that the trigger word lies between the nodes for the proteins in the dependency tree. A search for protein annotations on the left tree and right tree of the trigger word node returns a successful match for this rule. The two participant proteins and the trigger word are recorded in the result set as one binding event.

41.4.2 Two-Pass Extraction

Nested events occur as participants for most regulation events. This caused the extraction to give less recall and even lesser precision numbers. To aid this situation, two-pass extraction was used. The precedence order of events is essentially kept the same as one-pass extraction. The difference is that the extraction is done using two passes, the first pass for nonregulation

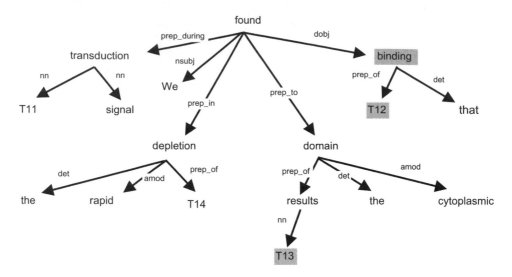

FIGURE 41.12 Extraction of binding event in given sample sentence. The rule that matches and extracts is P_1 (T) P_2.

events and the second pass exclusively for regulation events. At the end of the first pass, the events extracted have their trigger words replaced with event annotations so that they may be extracted as themes in the second pass if a rule matches. The algorithm is given in Figure 41.13.

Input: Abstracts tagged with the interaction words and class labels
Output: Biomolecular events with interation words and the participants
foreach *abstract* **do** Split abstract into sentences
    foreach *sentence in current abstract* **do**
        retrieve all the interation words in current sentence;
        sort them according to precedence of events;
        `First pass, without the regulation events`
        foreach *interaction word in the sentence* **do**
            extract participants for nonregulation events using the extraction rules;
            replace the event trigger words with event annotations;
        end
        `Second pass, for the regulation events`
        foreach *interaction word in the sentence* **do**
            extract the participants, entities or nested events using the rules and the replaced annotations;
        end
    end
end

FIGURE 41.13 Two-pass extraction algorithm to handle nested regulation events separately.

41.4.3 Event Extraction Rules

The BioEve system has been designed to extract events and participants from plain-text abstracts. Dependency parsing generates the dependency graph on which extraction rules are applied. Due to the fact that the extraction relies solely on plain text, the rules reflect the structure of English grammar. Most of the rules are similar in nature, owing to similarities in the style of writing actions being performed on objects or actions being performed by subjects. The binding event is covered in more detail in a separate section, the three types of regulations in another, and the rest of the rules in a third section. Most of the smaller events have common rules which reflect their grammatical representation. Also, these events involved only a single participating protein and hence the rules are also quite simple. Rules for a particular event also have precedence order. They are fired from higher to lower order, a reasoning which is based on the rule's accuracy of extracting events.

41.4.4 Binding

Binding events typically involve two proteins. They may involve more that two participants, but these cases are rare and hence were ignored for the rule set. The first three rules consider a pair of participants. Trigger words for binding are usually in noun or verb form. In noun form, the event will be talking about two object clauses. Searching the object clauses can result in a hit for the proteins. Rule 1 looks for such occurrences. For example, "TRADD was the only protein that interacted with wild-type TES2" has the trigger word *interacted* occurring between two protein occurrences. In another form, the noun trigger word is connected with one protein occurrence with the other protein connected to the first one. Rules 2 and 3 handle this instance of the phrase. As an example, consider the phrases "... binded with TRADD and TES2 ..." and "... binding of TRADD with TES2 ...".

The rules for binding are listed below in order of precedence:

1. $P_1 \ (T) \ P_2$
2. $\text{prep}(T, P_1); \text{prep}(P_1, P_2)$
3. $\text{prep}(T, P_1); \text{conj}(P_1, P_2)$
4. $\text{obj}(\text{verb}/T, P)$
5. $\text{prep}(T, P)$
6. ConnectedRule
7. NearestRule

Rules 4 and 5 are for the instances with only one participant. In such cases, the trigger word is usually a verb with the participant as its direct object or connected with a preposition. The former case is higher in precedence because it is natural to talk about an action occurring over some object in direct speech in English.

41.4.5 Positive, Negative, and Normal Gene Regulation

The three types of gene regulations are considered as separate event types for better classification accuracy and easier extraction. In general, regulation of any type are a collection of processes that are used by cells to transform genes into gene products such as proteins. They involve a single participant. Since they are processes, they appear in written text as verbs, with their participants as direct objects or nouns connected to them with a preposition. The obj and prep rules for positive regulation, negative regulation, and regulation reflect this fact. The regulation events are very likely to have other events as their participants. The initial definition of a biomolecular event applied only to biomolecular entities. To overcome this defect of ignoring nested events, two-pass extraction was used. Two-pass extraction manages to raise the extraction accuracy and volume for the regulation events.

41.4.6 Phosphorylation, Gene Expression, Protein Catabolism, Transcription, and Localization

All of the events in this section are also single-participant events. They are simple events, meaning that they specify certain processes or transformations taking place on the proteins. Hence, they are verbs either connected with their participant with a preposition or occur with the preposition as their direct object.

41.4.7 *ConnectedRule* and *NearestRule*

ConnectedRule and NearestRule are two default rules fired when the rules of an event class' do not produce any participants. They have been used in the system to increase recall without sacrificing precision too much. The rules showed benefits in a few cases where the sentence was too complex, due to which the dependency parse tree caused the rules to fail.

ConnectedRule states that the trigger word and the matching protein should be directly connected with each other, no matter what the dependency relation. The reasoning behind this rule is that if there is a trigger word connected to a protein directly and none of the rules match it, it is either a relation not covered by the rules or a pattern of the event class which is extremely rare. In any case, it is safe to assume that a direct dependency relation implies that the trigger word describes something about its participant.

NearestRule is a catch all. If all the rules fail, including ConnectedRule, the system searches the dependency tree nodes around the trigger word for an occurrence of a participant. The threshold for search is five edge hops.

41.5 EXPERIMENTS AND EVALUATIONS

We evaluated the BioEve system and major modules on the GENIA event corpus made available as part of the BioNLP Shared Task [22]. The training set had 800 abstracts (with 7499 sentences), the development set had 150 abstracts (with 1450 sentences), and the test set had 260 abstracts (with 2447 sentences) in them.

41.5.1 BioEve at BioNLP Shared Task

BioEve shared task evaluation results for task 1 are shown in Table 41.4. Event extraction for classes gene expression, protein catabolism, and phosphorylation performed better comparatively, whereas, for classes transcription, regulation, positive regulation, and negative regulation, it was below par. The reason noticed (in training examples) was that most of the true example sentences of the positive-regulation or negative-regulation class type were misclassified as either phosphorylation or gene expression. This calls for further improvement of sentence classifier accuracy.

TABLE 41.4   BioNLP Shared Task Evaluation: Task 1 Results Using Approximate Span Matching

Event Type	Gold (Match)	Answer (Match)	Recall	Precision	f-Measure
Localization	174 (49)	143 (49)	28.16	34.27	30.91
Binding	347 (60)	190 (60)	17.29	31.58	22.35
Gene expression	722 (323)	803 (323)	44.74	40.22	42.36
Transcription	137 (17)	133 (17)	12.41	12.78	12.59
Protein catabolism	14 (8)	29 (8)	57.14	27.59	37.21
Phosphorylation	135 (72)	107 (72)	53.33	67.29	59.50
EVT-TOTAL	1529 (529)	1405 (529)	34.60	37.65	36.06
Regulation	291 (33)	521 (33)	11.34	6.33	8.13
Positive regulation	983 (113)	1402 (113)	11.50	8.06	9.48
Negative regulation	379 (50)	481 (50)	13.19	10.40	11.63
REG-TOTAL	1653 (196)	2404 (196)	11.86	8.15	9.66
ALL-TOTAL	3182 (725)	3809 (725)	22.78	19.03	20.74

41.5.2   Semantic Classification and Event Phrase Labeling

Employed classifiers were evaluated based on accuracy, precision, and recall. Accuracy of a classifier is the percentage of the test sample correctly classified. Precision indicates the correctness of the system, by measuring the number of samples correctly classified in comparison to the total number of classified sentences. Recall indicates the completeness of the system by calculating the number of results which actually belong to the expected set of results.

Sentence-level single-label classification and sentence-level multilabel classification approaches were evaluated based on how well the classifier labels a given sentence from a test set with one of the nine class labels:

$$\text{Accuracy} = \frac{\text{number of sentences classified correctly}}{\text{total number of sentences}} \tag{41.1}$$

$$\text{Precision}_C = \frac{\text{number of sentences classified correctly under class label } C}{\text{number of sentences classified under class label } C} \tag{41.2}$$

$$\text{Recall}_C = \frac{\text{number of sentences classified correctly under class label } C}{\text{number of sentences which belong to class label } C} \tag{41.3}$$

Document-level classification using the CRF model was evaluated based on how well the model tags trigger phrases. Evaluating this approach involved measuring the extent to which the model identifies that a phrase is a trigger phrase and how well it classifies a tagged trigger phrase under one of the nine predefined event types:

$$\text{Precision} = \frac{\text{number of relevant and retrieved trigger phrases}}{\text{number of retrieved trigger phrases}} \tag{41.4}$$

$$\text{Recall} = \frac{\text{number of relevant and retrieved trigger phrases}}{\text{number of relevant trigger phrases}} \tag{41.5}$$

Retrieved trigger phrases refer to the ones which are identified and classified by the CRF sequence tagger. Relevant trigger phrases are the ones which are expected to be tagged by the model. Retrieved and relevant trigger words refer to the tags which are expected to be classified and which are actually classified by the CRF model. All the classifiers are trained using GENIA training data and tested against GENIA development abstracts.

The average precision and recall for all the approaches is calculated using a weighted average approach, the reason being that test instances are not uniformly distributed. Event types like positive regulation have more test instances as compared to event types like protein catabolism. So a weighted approach gives a more accurate picture than a simple arithmetic average. The weighted average is calculated based on the following equations:

$$\text{Weighted average precision} = \frac{\sum_{i=0}^{9} T_i P_i}{\sum_{i=0}^{9} T_i} \tag{41.6}$$

$$\text{Weighted average recall} = \frac{\sum_{i=0}^{9} T_i R_i}{\sum_{i=0}^{9} T_i} \tag{41.7}$$

where T_i = total number of relevant event phrases for event type i

P_i = precision of event type i

R_i = recall of event type i

41.5.2.1 Test Data Distribution   Table 41.5 gives the total number of test instances for each event type. These counts are used while calculating the weighted average for each approach.

41.5.2.2 Evaluation of Single-Label Sentence-Level Classification   This approach assigns a single label to each sentence. For evaluation purposes, the classifier is tested against GENIA development data. For every sentence, the evaluator process checks if the event type predicted is the most likely event in that sentence. In case a sentence has more than one event with equal occurrence frequency, the classifier predicted label is compared with all these candidate event types. The intent of this approach was to just understand the features suitable for this corpus. The classifier evaluated was the *naive Bayes multinomial* classifier from the WEKA library, a collection of machine learning algorithms for

TABLE 41.5 Event-Type Test Data Distribution

Event Type	Total of Test Instances
Protein_catabolism	17
Gene_expression	200
Localization	39
Phosphorylation	38
Transcription	60
Binding	153
Regulation	90
Positive_regulation	220
Negative_regulation	125
Total	942

TABLE 41.6 Single-Label, Sentence-Level Results

Classifier	Feature Set	Precision (%)
NBC	Bag-of-words	62.39
	Bag-of-words + gene name boosting	50.00
	Bag-of-words + trigger word boosting	49.92
	Bag-of-words + trigger word boosting + Gene name boosting	49.77
	Bag-of-POS tagged words	43.30

data-mining tasks. WEKA contains tools for data preprocessing, classification, regression, clustering, association rules, and visualization. It is also well suited for developing new machine learning schemes (Table 41.6).

41.5.2.3 Evaluation of Multilabel Sentence-Level Classification For maximum-entropy experiments, we used the maxENTTrainer class from the MALLET library. Table 41.7 gives the precision–recall statistics for this classifier.

The multilabel classification shows some improvement over single-label classification. Also, MALLET is dedicated to text classification whereas WEKA has more generalized machine learning algorithms covering other media such as images. The maximum-entropy classifier supersedes the NaiveBayesEM classifier in every event type. One of the main reasons could be because maximum entropy, unlike naive Bayes, does not assume conditional independence among features. Related work [28] shows that even with words as features and word counts as feature weights, maximum entropy was found to perform better than naive Bayes.

41.5.2.4 Evaluation of Phrase-Level Labeling Evaluation of this approach was focused more on the overlap of phrases between the GENIA annotated development and CRF-tagged labels. The reason is that for each abstract in the GENIA corpus, there is generally a set of biomedical entities present in it. For the shared task, only a subset of these entities were considered in the annotations, and accordingly only events concerning these annotated entities were extracted. However, based on the observation of the corpus, there was a probable chance of other events involving entities not selected for the annotations. So,

TABLE 41.7 Multilabel, Sentence-Level Results (Maximum-Entropy Classifier)

Event Type	Precision	Recall	F-Measure
Phosphorylation	0.97	0.73	0.65
Protein catabolism	0.81	0.68	0.83
Gene expression	0.88	0.58	0.74
Localization	0.61	0.69	0.70
Transcription	0.49	0.8	0.61
Binding	0.65	0.62	0.63
Regulation	0.52	0.67	0.59
Positive regulation	0.75	0.25	0.38
Negative regulation	0.54	0.38	0.45
Weighted Average	0.68	0.53	0.57

we focused on coverage, where both the GENIA annotations and CRF annotations agree. The CRF performance was evaluated on two fronts in terms of this overlap:

- *Exact Boundary Matching* This involves exact label matching and exact trigger phrase match.
- *Soft Boundary Matching* This involves exact label matching and partial trigger phrase match, allowing a one-word window on either side of the actual trigger phrase.

A detailed analysis of the results showed that around 3% tags were labeled incorrectly in terms of the event type. There were some cases where it was not certain whether an event should be marked as regulation or positive regulation. Some examples include *the expression of LAL-mRNA*, where *LAL-mRNA* is a gene, specifically a DNA type. As per examples seen in the training data, the template of the form expression of ⟨gene name⟩ generally indicates the presence of a gene expression event. Hence, more analysis may be needed to exactly filter out such annotations as true negatives or deliberately induced false positives.

41.5.2.5 *Comparative Analysis of Classification Approaches*   Table 41.8 gives a comparative view of all approaches. The CRF has a good trade-off as compared to maximum-entropy classifier results. As compared to multiple-label, sentence-level classifiers, it performs better in terms of having a considerably good accuracy for most event types with a good recall. It not only predicts the event types present in the sentence, but also localizes the trigger phrases. There are some entries where ME seems to perform better than CRF; for example in the case of Positive regulation, where the precision is as high as 0.75%. However, in this case the recall is very low (just 25%). The *F*-measure for CRF indicates that, as compared to the other approaches, CRF predicts 80% of the relevant tags and among these predicted tags 65% of them are correct.

41.5.3 Event Extraction Module

The results of the extraction of events from texts selected from the GENIA corpus are shown in Table 41.9. The evaluation measures used are explained below:

$$\text{Precision} = \frac{|\text{correct events} \cap \text{extracted events}|}{|\text{extracted events}|}$$

$$\text{Recall} = \frac{|\text{correct events} \cap \text{extracted events}|}{|\text{correct events}|}$$

$$f\text{-Measure} = \frac{2 \times (\text{precision} \times \text{recall})}{(\text{precision} + \text{recall})}$$

To evaluate the extraction module only, we ran it on the training data, which has all the entities annotated. Table 41.9 shows one-pass extraction results. Event extraction for classes gene expression, protein catabolism, and phosphorylation performed better comparatively, whereas, for transcription, regulation, positive regulation, and negative regulation, it was below par. The reason noticed (in training examples) was that most of the true example sentences of positive-regulation or negative-regulation class type were misclassified as either phosphorylation or gene expression. Improvement in the classification of the semantic labels might help improve the extraction results. On the extraction side, the rules used by the

TABLE 41.8 Summary of Classification Approaches

Event Type	NB + EM			Maximum Entropy			CRF		
	Precision	Recall	F-Measure	Precision	Recall	F-Measure	Precision	Recall	F-Measure
Phosphorylation	0.62	0.42	0.53	0.97	0.73	0.65	0.8	0.83	0.81
Protein catabolism	0.6	0.47	0.53	0.97	0.73	0.83	0.85	0.86	0.85
Gene expression	0.6	0.41	0.48	0.88	0.58	0.74	0.75	0.81	0.78
Localization	0.39	0.47	0.43	0.61	0.69	0.70	0.67	0.79	0.72
Transcription	0.24	0.52	0.33	0.49	0.8	0.61	0.57	0.78	0.66
Binding	0.56	0.63	0.59	0.65	0.62	0.63	0.65	0.81	0.72
Regulation	0.47	0.69	0.55	0.52	0.67	0.59	0.62	0.73	0.67
Positive regulation	0.70	0.27	0.39	0.75	0.25	0.38	0.55	0.74	0.63
Negative regulation	0.42	0.46	0.45	0.54	0.38	0.45	0.68	0.82	0.74
Weighted Average	0.55	0.46	0.47	0.68	0.53	0.57	0.65	0.79	0.71

TABLE 41.9   BioEve Extraction Module Evaluation: One-Pass Extraction

Event Class	Recall	Precision	F-Measure
Localization	61.22	84.29	70.93
Binding	46.14	65.80	54.24
Gene expression	62.20	86.97	72.53
Transcription	62.67	84.35	71.91
Protein catabolism	69.09	85.39	76.38
Phosphorylation	72.73	88.89	80.00
Nonregulation total	59.08	81.58	68.53
Regulation	14.58	21.37	17.34
Positive regulation	19.56	29.26	23.45
Negative regulation	14.88	22.80	18.01
Total	35.58	51.40	42.05

TABLE 41.10   BioEve Extraction Module Evaluation: Two-Pass Extraction

Event Class	Recall	Precision	F-Measure
Localization	69.96	85.98	77.15
Binding	50.00	67.59	57.48
Gene expression	65.25	87.50	74.75
Transcription	67.53	85.31	75.39
Protein catabolism	76.36	86.80	81.16
Phosphorylation	73.33	88.97	80.40
Non regulation total	63.02	82.53	71.47
Regulation	36.15	50.81	42.24
Positive regulation	38.41	55.12	45.27
Negative regulation	36.63	53.21	43.39
Total	48.62	66.93	56.33

system were simple considering the language versatility. Nested events were responsible for the relatively poor numbers for the regulation events. Table 41.10 shows the results for two-pass extraction. Significant improvement was obtained due to two-pass extraction. The numbers for nonregulation events remained relatively constant, whereas the regulation events showed a large improvement.

41.6   CONCLUSIONS

In this chapter, we presented a fully automated system to extract biomolecular events from biomedical abstracts. By semantically classifying each sentence to the class type of the event and then using high-coverage rules, BioEve extracts the participants of that event. We showed significant improvement in the F-measure of our classification and labeling module by 27% by using the CRF-based classifier instead of the naive Bayes classifier. We also improved the F-measure of the event participant extraction module by 14.28%. This experimentation shows that there is great scope for further improvements in all aspects of biomolecular event extraction.

ACKNOWLEDGMENTS

We would like to thank Sheela P. Kanwar and our colleagues for their help with this research.

REFERENCES

1. Bionlp'09 online, http://www-tsujii.is.s.u-tokyo.ac.jp/GENIA/SharedTask/.

2. Mallet online, http://mallet.cs.umass.edu/index.php.

3. Weka online, http://www.cs.waikato.ac.nz/ml/weka/.

4. C. Blaschke, M. A. Andrade, C. Ouzounis, and A. Valencia. Automatic extraction of biological information from scientific text: Protein-protein interaction. In *Proceedings of the AAAI Conference on Intelligent Systems in Molecular Biology*. Vol. 7, AAAI, Washington, DC, 1999, pp. 60–67.

5. C. Blaschke and A. Valencia. The frame-based module of the suiseki information extraction system. *IEEE Intell. Syst.*, 17(2):14–20, 2002.

6. O. Bodenreider. The unified medical language system (UMLS): Integrating biomedical terminology. *Nucleic Acids Res.*, 32(database issue):267–270, 2004.

7. E. Brill. A simple rule-based part-of-speech tagger. In *Proceedings of the Third Conference on Applied Natural Language Processing (ANLP-92)*, Trento, Italy, 1992, Association for Computational Linguistics, Stroudsburg, PA, 1992, pp. 152–155.

8. R. Bunescu, R. Ge, R. J. Kate, E. M. Marcotte, R. J. Mooney, A. K. Ramani, and Y. W. Wong. Comparative experiments on learning information extractors for proteins and their interactions. *Artif. Intell. Med.*, 33(2):139–155, 2005.

9. M. E. Califf and R. J. Mooney. Relational learning of pattern-match rules for information extraction. In *Working Notes of AAAI Spring Symposium on Applying Machine Learning to Discourse Processing*, Menlo Park, CA. AAAI Press, Washington, DC, 1998, pp. 6–11.

10. M. C. De Marneffe, B. Maccartney, and C. D. Manning. Generating typed dependency parses from phrase structure parses. In *Proceedings of LREC*, Vol. 6, 2006, pp. 449–454.

11. J. H. Chiang, H. C. Yu, and H. J. Hsu. GIS: A biomedical text-mining system for gene information discovery, *Bioinformatics*, 20(1):120–121, 2004.

12. D. P. A. Corney, B. F. Buxton, W. B. Langdon, and D. T. Jones. BioRAT: Extracting biological information from full-length papers. *Bioinformatics*, 20(17):3206–3213, 2004.

13. M. Craven and J. Kumlien. Constructing biological knowledge bases by extracting information from text sources. In *Proceedings of the Seventh International Conference on Intelligent Systems for Molecular Biology*, AAAI Press, Washington, DC, 1999, pp. 77–86.

14. W. Daelemans, S. Buchholz, and J. Veenstra. Memory-based shallow parsing. In *Proc. CoNLL*, 99:53–60, 1999.

15. J. Ding, D. Berleant, J. Xu, and A. W. Fulmer. Extracting biochemical interactions from MEDLINE using a link grammar parser. In *Proceedings of the 15th IEEE International Conference on Tools with Artificial Intelligence (ICTAI'03)*, IEEE Computer Society, New York, NY, 2003, p. 467.

16. C. Friedman, P. Kra, H. Yu, M. Krauthammer, and A. Rzhetsky. GENIES: A natural-language processing system for the extraction of molecular pathways from journal articles, *Bioinformatics*, 17:S74–S82, 2001.

17. M. Friedman and D. S. Weld. Efficiently executing information-gathering plans. In *Proceedings of the 15th International Joint Conference on Artificial Intelligence*, Nagoya, Japan, 1997, pp. 785–791.

18. K. Fukuda, A. Tamura, T. Tsunoda, and T. Takagi. Toward information extraction: Identifying protein names from biological papers. *Pac. Symp. Biocomput.*, 707:18, 1998.

19. K. Fundel, R. Küffner, and R. Zimmer. Relex—Relation extraction using dependency parse trees. *Bioinformatics*, 23(3):365–371, 2007.

20. D. Grinberg, J. Lafferty, and D. Sleator. A robust parsing algorithm for LINK grammars. Technical Report CMU-CS-TR-95-125. Carnegie Mellon University, Pittsburgh, PA, 1995.

21. Y. Gu, A. McCallum, and D. Towsley. Detecting anomalies in network traffic using maximum entropy estimation, USENIX Association, 2005, pp. 345–350.

22. J.-D. Kim, T. Ohta, S. Pyysalo, Y. Kano, and J. Tsujii. Overview of BioNLP'09 shared task on event extraction. In *Proceedings of the Workshop on Current Trends in Biomedical Natural Language Processing: Shared Task*, Boulder, Colorado, June 2009. Association for Computational Linguistics, Stroudsburg, PA, 2009, pp. 1–9.

23. N. Kushmerick, D. S. Weld, and R. B. Doorenbos. Wrapper induction for information extraction. In *Proceedings of the International Joint Conference on Artificial Intelligence (IJCAI)*, University of Washington, 1997, pp. 729–737.

24. J. Lafferty, A. McCallum, and F. Pereira. Conditional random fields: Probabilistic models for segmenting and labeling sequence data. In *Proceedings of the 18th International Conference on Machine Learning*, Morgan Kaufmann, San Francisco, CA, 2001, pp. 282–289.

25. G. Leroy, H. Chen, and J. D. Martinez. A shallow parser based on closed-class words to capture relations in biomedical text. *J. Biomed. Informatics*, 36(3):145–158, 2003.

26. A. McCallum and W. Li. Early results for named entity recognition with conditional random fields, feature induction and web-enhanced lexicons. In *Proceedings of the seventh conference on Natural Language Learning (HLT-NAACL 2003)*, Vol. 4, Association for Computational Linguistics, 2003, 188–191.

27. A. Mikheev and S. Finch. A workbench for finding structure in texts. In *Proceedings of the Applied Natural Language Processing (ANLP-97)*, Washington DC, 1997, pp. 372–379.

28. K. Nigam, J. Lafferty, and A. McCallum. Using maximum entropy for text classification. In *IJCAI-99 Workshop on Machine Learning for Information Filtering*, Vol. 1, 1999, pp. 61–67.

29. S. Novichkova, S. Egorov, and N. Daraselia. MedScan, a natural language processing engine for MEDLINE abstracts. *Bioinformatics*, 19(13):1699–1706, 2003.

30. T. Ono, H. Hishigaki, A. Tanigami, and T. Takagi. Automated extraction of information on protein-protein interactions from the biological literature. *Bioinformatics*, 17(2):155–161, 2001.

31. J. R. Quinlan. Learning logical definitions from relations. *Machine Learning*, 5(3):239–266, 1990.

32. F. Rinaldi, G. Schneider, K. Kaljurand, J. Dowdall, C. Andronis, A. Persidis, and O. Konstanti. Mining relations in the GENIA corpus. In *Proceedings of the Second European Workshop on Data Mining and Text Mining for Bioinformatics*, 2004, pp. 61–68.

33. A. Rzhetsky et al. GeneWays: A system for extracting, analyzing, visualizing, and integrating molecular pathway data. *J. Biomed. Informatics*, 37(1):43–53, 2004.

34. L. Schubert. Can we derive general world knowledge from texts? In *Proceedings of the Second International Conference on Human Language Technology Research*, 2002, San Diego, California, Morgan Kaufmann Publishers Inc., San Francisco, CA, 2002, pp. 94–97.

35. B. Settles. Biomedical named entity recognition using conditional random fields and rich feature sets. In *Proceedings of the International Joint Workshop on Natural Language Processing in Biomedicine and Its Applications (NLPBA)*, 2004, pp. 104–107.

36. B. Settles. Biomedical named entity recognition using conditional random fields and rich feature sets. In *Proceedings of the International Joint Workshop on Natural Language Processing in Biomedicine and Its Applications (NLPBA)*, 2004, pp. 104–107.

37. B. Settles. ABNER: An open source tool for automatically tagging genes, proteins and other entity names in text, *Bioinformatics*, 21(14):3191–3192, 2005.

38. K. Seymore, A. McCallum, and R. Rosenfeld. Learning hidden Markov model structure for information extraction. In *AAAI-99 Workshop on Machine Learning for Information Extraction*, Orlando, Florida, July 1999, pp. 37–42.

39. F. Sha and F. C. N. Pereira. Shallow parsing with conditional random fields. In *Proceedings of the 2003 Conference of the North American Chapter of the Association for Computational Linguistics on Human Language Technology*, Vol. 1, Association for Computational Linguistics, 2003, pp. 134–141.

40. Y. Tateisi, T. Ohta, and J. Tsujii. Annotation of predicate-argument structure of molecular biology text. In *JCNLP-04 Workshop on Beyond Shallow Analyses*, 2004.

41. J. M. Temkin and M. R. Gilder. Extraction of protein interaction information from unstructured text using a context-free grammar. *Bioinformatics*, 19(16):2046–2053, 2003.

42. K.-Y. Whang, J. Jeon, K. Shim, and J. Srivastava. Advances in knowledge discovery and data mining, *7th Pacific-Asia Conference (PAKDD 2003)*, Seoul, Korea, April 30–May 2, 2003, Vol. 2637 of *Lecture Notes in Computer Science*, Springer, 2003, pp. 148–158.

43. A. Yakushiji, Y. Tateisi, Y. Miyao, and J. Tsujii. Event extraction from biomedical papers using a full parser. *Pac. Symp. Biocomput.*, 408–419, 2001.

HIGH-PERFORMANCE COMPUTING FOR BIOLOGICAL DATA MINING

CHAPTER 42

ACCELERATING PAIRWISE ALIGNMENT ALGORITHMS BY USING GRAPHICS PROCESSOR UNITS

MOURAD ELLOUMI,[1,2] MOHAMED AL SAYED ISSA,[3] and
AHMED MOKADDEM[1,2]

[1]Laboratory of Technologies of Information and Communication and Electrical Engineering
(LaTICE)
[2]University of Tunis-El Manar, Tunisia
[3]Computers and Systems Department, Faculty of Engineering, Zagazig University, Egypt

42.1 INTRODUCTION

Biological macromolecules, such as *deoxyribonucleic acids* (DNAs), *ribonucleic acids* (RNAs), and proteins are coded by sequences where every character is respectively in {A, T, C; G}, {A, U, C, G}, and {A, C, D, E, F, G, H, I, K, L, M, N, P, Q, R, S, T, V, W, Y}. Among the most studied problems in bioinformatics is the *comparison* of biological sequences. The comparison of biological sequences can be achieved *via aligning* these sequences: It consists in optimizing the number of matches between the characters occurring in the same order in each sequence. We distinguish two main classes of alignments:

 (i) *Pairwise Alignment* Involves the alignment of two sequences.
 (ii) *Multiple Alignment* Involves the alignment of more than two sequences.

In this chapter we are interested in pairwise alignment. We present pairwise alignment algorithms using *graphics processor units* (GPUs).

The rest of the chapter is organized as follows: In Section 42.2, we present the two types of pairwise alignment algorithms. In Section 42.3, we give an overview of GPUs. In Section 42.4, we show how GPUs can be used to accelerate pairwise alignment algorithms. Finally, in the last section, we conclude the chapter.

42.2 PAIRWISE ALIGNMENT ALGORITHMS

There are two types of pairwise alignment algorithms: *pairwise global alignment* algorithms and *pairwise local alignment* ones. Let us begin with pairwise global alignment algorithms.

42.2.1 Pairwise Global Alignment Algorithms

A pairwise global alignment involves the alignment of two entire sequences. There are two main approaches to construct a pairwise global alignment:

(i) *Dynamic Programming Approach* [1, 2] The most used dynamic programming algorithm for pairwise global alignment is the one of Needleman and Wunsch [3]. By using this algorithm, the construction of a pairwise global alignment of two sequences S_1 and S_2 with respective lengths m and n is performed in two steps:

1. In the first step, we construct a matrix M of size mn and we initialize it by using a *substitution matrix*, for example, PAMs (*percent accepted mutations*) [4] and BLOSUM (*blocks substitution matrix*) [5]. Then, we transform matrix M by adding scores line by line, starting with the right lower cell and ending with the left upper one using the equation

$$M[i, j] = \text{se}(i, j) + \max(M[x, y]) \tag{42.1}$$

where $x = i + 1$ and $j < y = n$, or $i < x = m$ and $y = j + 1$, and se is the score between the character at position i in S_1 and the one at position j in S_2. We can also incorporate a gap penalty in the equation. A *gap* is a character (e.g., -) inserted in aligned sequences so that aligned characters are found in front of each other. It is sufficient to subtract from the calculation of every sum a penalty according to their position. So, Equation (42.1) becomes

$$M[i, j] = \text{se}(i, j) + \max \begin{pmatrix} M[i + 1, j + 1] \\ M[x, j + 1] - P \\ M[i + 1, y] - P \end{pmatrix} \tag{42.2}$$

where $i + 2 < x \leq m$ and $j + 2 < y \leq n$ and P is a gap penalty.

The gap penalty P can have several possible forms. Example gap penalties are given in Table 42.1, where k is the number of successive gaps and a, b, and c are constants.

2. In the second step, we establish a path in the matrix, called the *maximum-score path*, which leads to an optimal pairwise global alignment. The construction of this path is achieved by starting from the cell that contains the maximum score in the transformed matrix, which corresponds normally to the leftmost upper cell, and allowing three types of possible movements: (a) *diagonal movement*, which corresponds to the passage from a cell (i, j) to a cell $(i + 1, j + 1)$; (b) *vertical movement*, which corresponds to the passage from a cell (i, j) to a cell $(i + 1, j)$; and (c) *horizontal movement*, which corresponds to the passage from a cell (i, j) to a cell $(i, j + 1)$.

TABLE 42.1 Gap Penalties

Linear gap penalty	$P = ak$
Affine gap penalty	$P = ak + c$
Logarithmic gap penalty	$P = b \log k + c$
Logarithmic–affine gap penalty	$P = ak + b \log k + c$

The time complexity of the Needleman–Wunsch algorithm is $O(mn)$.

Other dynamic programming algorithms for pairwise global alignment exist, such as the one of Huang and Chao [6] and NGILA [7].

(ii) *Anchoring Approach* Pairwise global alignment algorithms that adopt this approach operate as follows: First, they search for identical, or similar, regions in the two sequences by using different techniques such as *suffix trees* [8] and *dot matrices* or a local alignment algorithm such as CHAOS [9]. These regions are called *anchors*. Then, they form the final alignment by chaining the anchors identified in the previous step. Finally, they align the regions situated between the anchors by using a standard dynamic programming algorithm or applying the same procedure by recursive calls or combining both. Compared to the dynamic programming approach, anchoring is economic in memory space, especially when applied on long sequences.

Among the pairwise global alignment algorithms that adopt the anchoring approach, we can cite MUMMER [10]; AVID [11], which uses suffix trees [8] to detect anchors; GLASS [12]; LAGAN [13], which uses the CHAOS algorithm [9]; and ACANA [14].

42.2.2 Pairwise Local Alignment Algorithms

A pairwise local alignment involves the alignment of portions of two sequences. There are two main approaches to construct a pairwise local alignment:

(i) *Dynamic Programming Approach* The most used dynamic programming algorithm for pairwise local alignment is the one of Smith and Waterman [15]. The main difference with the algorithm of Needleman and Wunsch [16] is that any cell of the matrix M can be considered as a starting point for the calculation of the scores and any score which becomes lower than zero stops the progression of the calculation of the scores. The associated cell is then reinitialized to zero and can be considered as a new starting point. That implies that the selected system of scores has negative scores for bad associations which can exist between the characters of the sequences. The equation used for the calculation of each score during the transformation of the initial matrix is the following:

$$M[i, j] = \max \begin{pmatrix} \text{se}(i, j) + M[i + 1, j + 1] \\ \text{se}(i, j) + \max(M[x, j + 1] - P) \\ \text{se}(i, j) + \max(M[i + 1, y] - P) \\ 0 \end{pmatrix} \quad (42.3)$$

where $i + 2 < x \le m$ and $j + 2 < y \le n$, se is the score between the character at position i in S_1 and the one at position j in S_2, and P is a gap penalty, with m and n being respectively the lengths of the sequences S_1 and S_2 to align.

The time complexity of the Smith–Waterman algorithm is $O(mn)$.

(ii) *Seeding Approach* Pairwise local alignment algorithms that adopt this approach use a hashing function to define a seed and use it as a model to detect alignments. A *seed* is a substring that can be made up by characters that can be contiguous or not and defined on a precise alphabet. A seed is characterized by its *extent*, which represents the length of the substrings that can be covered by the seed, and by its *weight*, which represents the number of characters that must appear simultaneously in the seed and in the substrings covered by the seed. These characters are called *matches*. A seed can be represented either by a set $\{i, i, i, \dots\}$, where i is a position of a match, or by a substring defined on alphabets like $\{\#, -\}, \{\#, @, -\}$, or $\{0,1\}$, where # or 1 represents a match, - or 0 a joker character and @ the characters associated with the following substitutions: G with C or A with T.

The seeding approach is based on the notion of *filtering*: It involves, first, the deletion of the zones that have no possibility of participating in the final local alignment and, second, the conservation of the positions that verify the seed.

42.3 GRAPHICS PROCESSOR UNITS

A GPU consists of many *multiprocessors* and a large *dynamic* RAM (DRAM). Each multiprocessor is coupled with a small cache memory and consists of large number of *cores*, that is, *arithmetic logical units* (ALUs), controlled by a control unit.

As shown in Figure 42.1, in contrast to a GPU, a *central processing unit* (CPU) consists of a single *processor* and a large DRAM. The processor is coupled with a single large cache memory and consists of a small number of cores controlled by a single control unit.

GPUs are used in game consoles, embedded systems, mobile phones, and computers. In a computer, a GPU can be found on a video card or on the motherboard. Most of the new desktop and notebook computers have integrated GPUs. Figures 42.2 and 42.3 show the evolution of *floating-point operations per second* (FLOPS) and memory bandwidth for the CPU and GPU.

Figure 42.4 shows *scan* [18, 19] performances on a CPU, a graphics-based GPU using the *Open Graphics Library* (OpenGL) parallel programming language, and a direct-compute GPU using the *Compute Unified Device Architecture* (CUDA). These results were obtained on a GeForce 8800 GTX GPU and an Intel Core2-Duo Extreme 2.93-GHz CPU.

GPUs are well adopted to solve problems with *data-parallel processing*, that is, the same program is executed on many data elements in parallel. Data-parallel processing maps data elements to parallel processing threads. A *thread* is a sequence of instructions that may be executed in parallel with each other. Data-parallel processing is an efficient way to accelerate many algorithms.

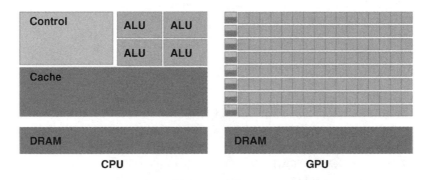

FIGURE 42.1 CPU versus GPU organization [17].

Theoretical GB/s

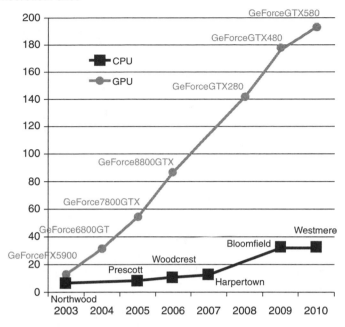

FIGURE 42.2   Memory bandwidth for CPU and GPU [17].

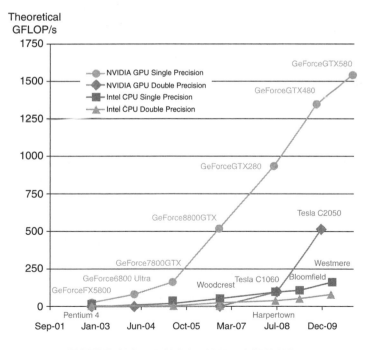

FIGURE 42.3   FLOPS for CPU and GPU [17].

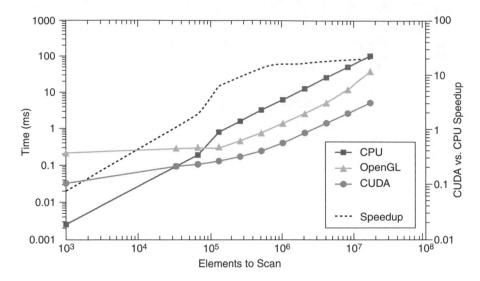

FIGURE 42.4   Scan performances on a CPU, a graphics-based GPU using OpenGL, and a direct-compute GPU using CUDA [19].

GPUs were originally designed to accelerate computer graphics algorithms. However, their high computational capabilities and their highly parallel structure opened them up to a wide range of other fields, for example, scientific computing [20], computational geometry [21], and bioinformatics [22]. In bioinformatics, GPUs were adopted to accelerate, among others, pairwise alignment algorithms.

42.4 ACCELERATING PAIRWISE ALIGNMENT ALGORITHMS

With the new sequencing technologies, the number of biological sequences in databases is increasing exponentially. In addition, the length of one of these sequences is large, hundreds of bases. Hence, comparing, via a pairwise alignment algorithm, a query sequence to the sequences of one of these databases becomes expensive in computing time and memory space. From here comes the need to accelerate pairwise alignment algorithms. In this section, we mainly focus on accelerating the Smith–Waterman (SW) algorithm [15] using GPUs.

GPU programming is based on OpenGL [23] and now on CUDA parallel programming languages [17]. So, we have two types of implementations of SW algorithms on GPUs: using the OpenGL parallel programming language or using CUDA.

42.4.1 Accelerating Smith–Waterman Algorithm Using OpenGL

The first implementations of the SW algorithm on GPUs are described in [24, 25]. These implementations are based on similar approaches and use OpenGL [23]. They operate as follows: First the database and the query sequence are copied to the GPU memory as *textures* [19]. The score matrix is then processed in an antidiagonal way. For each element of the current antidiagonal, a pixel is drawn. Drawing this pixel executes a small program called a *pixel shader* that computes the score for the cell. The results are on a texture, which is then used as input for the next pass.

The implementation of [24] searched 99.8% of the Swiss-Prot database, now merged into the *Universal Protein Resource* (UniProt) database [26] and obtained a maximum speed of 650 *mega cell updates per second* (MCUPS) compared to around 75 for the compared CPU version. The *cell update per second* (CUPS) is defined as

$$\text{CUPS} = \frac{\text{query sequence length} \times \text{database size}}{\text{runtime}} \quad (42.4)$$

The implementation of [25] has two versions, the first with traceback and the second without. Both versions were benchmarked using a Geforce 7800 GTX GPU and executed on a database of just 983 sequences. The version without traceback obtained a maximum speed of 241 MCUPS, compared to 178 with traceback and 120 for the compared CPU version.

42.4.2 Accelerating Smith–Waterman Algorithm Using CUDA

The first implementation of the SW algorithm on a GPU using CUDA is SW-CUDA [3]. This implementation operates as follows: Each GPU thread computes the whole alignment of the query sequence with one database sequence. The threads are grouped in a *grid* of *blocks* during execution. To make the most efficient use of the GPU resources, the computing time of all the threads in the same grid must be as near as possible. That is why it was important to preorder the sequences of the database according to their lengths. So, during execution, the adjacent threads will need to align the query sequence with two database queries having the nearest possible sizes.

SW-CUDA achieves speeds of more than 3.5 GCUPS on a workstation running two GeForce 8800 GTX GPUs. Experimental studies have been done to compare SW-CUDA to BLAST [27] and SSEARCH [28], running on a 3-GHz Intel Pentium IV processor. SW-CUDA was also compared to *single-instruction multiple-data* (SIMD) implementation [29]. The experimental results show that SW-CUDA performs from 2 to 30 times faster than any other previous implementation.

42.4.3 Accelerating Other Pairwise Alignment Algorithms

MUMmerGPU [30] is an implementation on a GPU using CUDA of the MUMmer algorithm [10]. It is targeted at aligning a set of small DNA query sequences with a large reference sequence stored as a suffix tree [8]. MUMmerGPU achieves more than a 10-fold speedup over a serial CPU version of the sequence alignment *kernel* [19]. It outperforms the exact alignment component of MUMmer on a high-end CPU by 3.5-fold when aligning short sequences.

CUDAlign [31] is another pairwise alignment algorithm implemented on a GPU using CUDA. CUDAlign is able to compare megabase biological sequences with an exact SW affine gap variant. CUDAlign was experimented on two GPUs separately. CUDAlign made the alignment of the human chromosome 21 and the chimpanzee chromosome 22 in 21 h on a GeForce GTX 280 GPU, resulting in a peak performance of 20.375 GCUPS.

42.5 CONCLUSION

With the new sequencing technologies, the number of biological sequences in databases is increasing exponentially. Besides, the size of most of these sequences is large. Since the comparison of a query sequence to the sequences of a biological database can mainly be made via pairwise alignment algorithms, accelerating such algorithms becomes a necessity. Graphics processor units are a hardware solution to achieve this task. They enabled to accelerate a number of pairwise alignment algorithms, such as the Smith–Waterman. A number of efforts are in progress to make GPUs even faster.

REFERENCES

1. R. Bellman. *Dynamic Programming*. Princeton University Press, Princeton, NJ, 1957

2. R. Bellman and S. Dreyfus. *Applied Dynamic Programming*. Princeton University Press, Princeton, NJ, 1962.

3. S. A. Manavski and G. Valle. CUDA compatible GPU cards as efficient hardware accelerators for Smith-Waterman sequence alignment. *BMC Bioinformatics*, 9(Suppl. 2):S10, 2008.

4. M. O. Dayhoff, R.M. Schwartz, and B. C. Orcutt, A model of evolutionary change in proteins. In M. O. Dayhoff (Ed.), *Atlas of Protein Sequence and Structure*, National Biomedical Research Foundation, Washington, DC, 1978, pp. 345–358.

5. S. Henikoff and J. G. Henikoff. Amino acid substitution matrices from protein blocks. *Proc. Natl. Acad. Sci. USA*, 89(22):10915–10919, 1992.

6. X. Huang and K. M. Chao. A generalized global alignment algorithm. *Bioinformatics*, 19(2):228–233, 2003.

7. R. A. Cartwright. NGILA: Global pairwise alignments with logarithmic and affine gap costs. *Bioinformatics*, 23(11):1427–1428, 2007.

8. E. Ukkonen. On-line construction of suffix-trees. *Algorithmica*, 14(3):249–260, 1995.

9. M. Brudno, M. Chapman, B. Göttgens, S. Batzoglou, and B. Morgenstern. Fast and sensitive multiple alignment of large genomic sequences. *BMC Bioinformatics*, 4:879–899, 2003.

10. A. L. Delcher, A. Phillippy, J. Carlton, and S. L. Salzberg. Fast algorithms for large-scale genome alignment and comparison. *Nucleic Acids Res.*, 30(11):2478–2483, 2002.

11. N. Bray, I. Dubchak, and L. Pachter. AVID: A global alignment program. *Genome Res.*, 13:97–102, 2003.

12. S. Batzoglou, L. Pachter, J. Mesirov, B. Berger, and E. S. Lander. Human and mouse gene structure: Comparative analysis and application to exon prediction. *Genome Res.* 10:950–958, 2000.

13. M. Brudno, C. Do, G. Cooper, M. Kim, E. Davydov, E. D. Green, A. Sidow, and S. Batzoglou. LAGAN and Multi-LAGAN: Efficient tools for large-scale multiple alignment of genomic DNA. *Genome Res.*, 13:721–731, 2003.

14. W. Huang, D. M. Umbach, and L. Li, Accurate anchoring alignment of divergent sequences. *Bioinformatics*, 22(1):29–34, 2006.

15. T. F. Smith and M. S. Waterman. Identification of common molecular subsequences. *J. Mol. Biol.*, 147:195–197, 1981.

16. S. B Needleman and C. D. Wunsch. A general method applicable to the search for similarities in the amino acid sequence of two proteins. *J. Mol. Biol.*, 48(1):443–453, 1970.

17. Nvidia GPU programming guide, `http://developer.Nvidia.com/Nvidia-gpu-programming-guide`.

18. G. Blelloch. *Vector Models for Data-Parallel Computing*. MIT Press, Cambridge, MA, 1990.

19. J. D. Owens, M. Houston, D. Luebke, S. Green, J. E. Stone, and J. C. Phillips. GPU computing. *Proc. IEEE*, 96(5), May 2008, pp. 879–899.

20. J. Krüger and R. Westermann. Linear algebra operators for GPU implementation of numerical algorithms. *ACM Trans. Graphics (TOG)*, 22(3):908–916, 2003.

21. P. Agarwal, S. Krishnan, N. Mustafa, and S. Venkatasubramanian. Streaming geometric optimization using graphics hardware. In *Proc. 11th Annual European Symposium on Algorithms (ESA'03)*, Budapest, Hungary, September 2003, Vol. 2832 of *Lecture Notes in Computer Science*, Springer, Berlin, 2003, pp. 544–555.

22. M. Charalambous, P. Trancoso, and A. Stamatakis. Initial experiences porting a bioinformatics application to a graphics processor. In *Proc. 10th Panhellenic Conference on Informatics (PCI'05)*, Volos, Greece, *Lecture Notes in Computer Science*, vol. 3746, Springer-Verlag, Berlin, Germany, Nov. 2005, pp. 415–425.

23. D. Shreiner, M. Woo, J. Neider, and T. Davis. *OpenGL Programming Guide*, 5th ed. Addison-Wesley, Reading, MA, Aug. 2005.

24. W. Liu, B. Schmidt, G. Voss, A. Schroder, and W. Muller-Wittig, Bio-sequence database scanning on a GPU. In *Proc. 20th IEEE International Parallel & Distributed Processing Symposium (IPDPS'06), 5th IEEE International Workshop on High Performance Computational Biology Workshop (HICOMB'06)*, Rhode Island, Greece, 2006.

25. Y. Liu, W. Huang, J. Johnson, and S. Vaidya, GPU accelerated Smith-Waterman. In *Proc. Computational Science (ICCS'06), Lecture Notes in Computer Science*, Vol. 3994, Springer-Verlag, Berlin, Germany, 2006, pp. 188–195.

26. UniProt, http://www.uniprot.org/.

27. W. R. Pearson and D. J. Lipman. Improved tools for biological sequence comparison. *Proc. Natl. Acad. Sci. USA*, 85:2444–2448, Apr. 1988.

28. W. R. Pearson. Searching protein sequence libraries: Comparison of the sensitivity and selectivity of the Smith-Waterman and FASTA algorithms. *Genomics*, 11(3):635–650, Nov. 1991.

29. M. Farrar. Striped Smith-Waterman speeds database searches six times over other SIMD implementations. *Bioinformatics*, 23(2):156–161, 2007.

30. M. C. Schatz, C. Trapnell, A. L Delcher, and A. Varshney. High-throughput sequence alignment using graphics processing units. *BMC Bioinformatics*, 8:474, 2007.

31. E. F. O. Sandes and A. C. M. A. de Melo. CUDAlign: Using GPU to accelerate the comparison of megabase genomic sequences. In *Proc. 15th ACM SIGPLAN Symposium on Principles and Practice of parallel programming (PPoPP '10)*, New York, 2010, pp. 137–146.

CHAPTER 43

HIGH-PERFORMANCE COMPUTING IN HIGH-THROUGHPUT SEQUENCING

KAMER KAYA, AYAT HATEM, HATICE GÜLÇIN ÖZER,
KUN HUANG, and ÜMIT V. ÇATALYÜREK
Department of Biomedical Informatics, The Ohio State University, Columbus, Ohio

"If your computer has multiple processors/cores, use -p"

—From *Bowtie* [64] manual.

43.1 INTRODUCTION

In the last five years, sequencing technologies have evolved in a level which forces bioinformatics researchers to think about new ways to cope with the amount of the data they produce. The invention of new high-throughput sequencing devices, such as Roche/454, Illumina/Solexa, and ABI/SOLID, reduced the cost of sequencing a genome from $100 million to $10,000 in 10 years. Nowadays, a megabase of DNA sequence costs only $0.1 [51]. Following the cost reduction, the number of sequencing experiments increased exponentially. As a result, GenBank, a collection of all publicly available DNA sequences, now has 132,067,413,372 base pairs in 144,458,648 entries (as of October 2011), and the number of bases is expected to be doubled approximately every 18 months [6]. So, what do these large number of bases tell us about the DNA? As also stated by Flicek and Birney [40], the answer is "almost nothing." Although the technologies are shiny and game changing, their output is still worthless without a proper analysis by proper tools and algorithms. There has been extensive research on mapping/aligning and assembling this immense amount of data. Several tools have been implemented for this purpose. For a survey of the tools and algorithms, we refer the reader to [16, 41, 67, 93].

High-performance computing (HPC) has been useful in several disciplines and applications including analyzing 15-petabyte data generated by the *large hadron collider* at *Centre Européen de Recherche Nucléaire* (CERN) each year. It is believed that in 2012 the data generated by next-generation sequencing experiments will be more than that [41]. Although there are several tools for analyzing sequence data, the algorithmic techniques used in these tools are not that many. Soon, we may need algorithms which are better and faster than the current state of-the-art. HPC cannot be a replacement for a novel algorithmic technique.

However, considering the advancements in HPC hardware, such as *graphics processing units* (GPUs) and *field-programmable gate arrays* (FPGAs), and recent trends in computing, such as *cloud computing*, using HPC to cope with the sequencing data is a promising solution. It may not be the hero we need, but it is the hero we have.

The rest of the chapter is organized as follows. In Section 43.2, we give an overview of the current active applications for the high-throughput sequencing technology. In Section 43.3, we summarize the current advancement in HPC architectures. Then, in Section 43.4, we present how the different HPC architectures are used in the different high-throughput sequencing applications. Finally, we summarize and conclude in Section 43.5.

43.2   NEXT-GENERATION SEQUENCING APPLICATIONS

Next-generation sequencing (NGS) technology has evolved rapidly, leading to the generation of hundreds of millions of sequences (reads) in a single run. The number of generated reads varies between 1 million for long reads [≈400 base pairs (bp)] generated by Roche 454 Life Sciences sequencers and 2.4 billion for short reads (≈75 bp) generated by Solexa Genome Analyzer from Illumina and SOLiD System from Applied Biosystems. The process of generating and postprocessing the reads can be divided into three stages: primary, secondary, and tertiary. Primary data analysis includes conversion of image data to sequence data and assessment of quality. Generally, this step is performed by the vendor software in real time. Secondary data analysis includes mapping (for known genomes) and assembly (for unknown genomes) algorithms. The mapping is the process of detecting the corresponding genomic position for each read while taking the different DNA properties into consideration, such as the existence of gaps and *single-nucleotide polymorphisms* (SNPs). The assembly is the process of aligning and merging reads to reconstruct the original genomic sequence. In this step, raw sequence reads are transformed into genomic information using an application-specific configuration for further analysis. Since mapping and assembly algorithms are computationally expensive, it is very crucial to complete this step in a fast and accurate manner. Tertiary analysis includes application-specific postprocessing of the data such as identification of variants, identification of differentially expressed regions, peak detection, motif finding, functional annotation, and pathway analysis.

The power of NGS technology allowed researchers to study a wide range of biological problems. Major application areas can be categorized as discussed below.

Genome Assembly   Whole-genome shotgun sequencing is the process of shearing the genome into small fragments and sequencing of these fragments. NGS technologies make it possible to assemble the whole genome by oversampling the shotgun reads, so that reads overlap [82, 93]. Then, genome assembly algorithms can be used to reconstruct the original genome using the reads generated by the sequencer. Longer and paired-end reads result in more accurate assembly.

Assembly is the process of combining and aligning reads to generate continuous portions of DNA called *contigs* based on overlaps and similarity between the reads. There are two genome assembly approaches: *de novo* assembly and *comparative* assembly [93]. De novo assembly is applied to reconstruct genomes that are not previously sequenced. On the other hand, comparative assembly (resequencing) uses a known related genome to guide the assembly process, but sequences that are significantly different from the reference are still needed to be reconstructed by the de novo approach. Since comparative approaches are basically alignment of reads to the reference genome and very limited to a few known genomes, we focus on applications of de novo assembly and discuss their challenges.

The main challenges for the genome assembly process are repeat sequences, sequencing errors, and nonuniform coverage [82]. Assemblers cannot resolve the reads that are coming from a repetitive genomic region that is longer than the read. Spanning the paired reads can help to resolve this problem, but the analysis becomes much more complicated. Existence of sequencing errors makes this problem even harder. Assembly algorithms allow imperfect sequence alignments to take sequencing errors into account. While this tolerance avoids missing true positives, it may result in false-positive discoveries. Another challenge for assembly algorithms is nonuniform coverage of the genome. Variation in coverage can be caused by copy number variation, biases of sequencing technologies, or even by chance. Even when the average coverage of the genome is very high, low coverage of some regions may result in gaps in the final assembly and voids coverage-based statistical tests.

Nevertheless, the most critical factors for improving the assembly quality are the utilization of paired-end experiments and longer reads [24].

Transcriptome Sequencing, RNA-seq   The transcriptome is the complete set of transcripts in a cell. RNA-seq is the process of sequencing cDNA derived from cellular RNA (transcribed portion of the genome) by next-generation sequencing technologies. RNA-seq allows researchers to investigate expression of mRNAs, noncoding RNAs and small RNAs, transcriptional structure of genes and splicing patterns, and other posttranscriptional modifications [111].

The computational challenges for RNA-seq can be categorized as read mapping, transcriptome reconstruction, and expression quantification [42].

The first challenge, the read mapping, can be performed in an unspliced or spliced manner. In the unspliced approach reads are mapped to the reference genome without allowing any large gaps, such as *mapping and assembly with quality* (MAQ) [68] and *Burrows–Wheeler alignment* (BWA) [66] algorithms. This approach is ideal for mapping reads to a reference only for quantification purposes. In the spliced approach, reads are mapped in two step; first all reads are mapped to the reference using an unspliced algorithm, then unmapped reads are split into shorter fragments and mapped independently, such as SpliceMap [14], MapSplice [109], and TopHat [106] algorithms. This approach allows large gaps in the alignment process and enables discovery of novel splice junctions. The specificity of mapping can be increased by using paired-end RNA-seq experiments and longer reads (e.g., 75 bp) [42].

The second challenge, transcriptome reconstruction, is the process of assembling mapped reads into transcripts to identify expressed genes and isoforms. Besides mature mRNA (exons only), there are reads from precursor mRNA (that contain intronic sequences) in RNA-seq samples. Identification of mature transcripts is the first concern for the algorithms [42]. Then, distribution of the reads to different isoforms of the genes is the major difficulty for transcriptome reconstruction algorithms. Basically, these algorithms convert mapped reads into an assembly graph where spliced reads constitute the connections and the rest of the mapped reads constitute the nodes. The most commonly used transcriptome reconstruction algorithms, Cufflinks [108] and Scripture [46] build similar assembly graphs, but the way they parse the graph to determine transcripts is different [42]. Finally, transcript expression levels are estimated using the read counts. The metric of reads/fragments per kilobase of transcript per million mapped reads (RPKM/FPKM) [85, 108] is the most commonly used normalization schema that accounts for both gene length and total number of reads (can be further divided into genome-guided and genome-independent algorithms).

The third challenge, expression quantification, is the analysis of differential expression across samples/conditions. Sequencing depth, expression of the gene, length of the gene, and assumptions on the distribution all affect the differential expression detection [42].

ChIP-seq *Chromatin immunoprecipitation sequencing* (ChIP-seq) is the process of genomewide measurements of protein–DNA interactions to study regulatory and functional elements of the genomes. ChIP-seq experiments integrate chromatin immunoprecipitation and NGS to identify binding sites for a protein of interest, such as transcription factors and other chromatin-associated proteins [55]. In the ChIP step of the experiment, an antibody against the protein of interest is used to pull down cross-linked DNA–protein complexes. Then, purified short DNA fragments are sequenced using next generation sequencing technology.

The computational challenges for ChIP-seq can be categorized as read mapping, peak detection, and motif finding [91]. The main parameters that affect sensitivity and specificity of mapping algorithms are read length, number of allowed mismatches, and the strategy to utilize multireads [91]. After reads are aligned to the genome, enrichment detection algorithms are applied to identify ChIP-seq signals, that is, peaks. Depending on the protein type, peaks might have different expected shapes. These enriched regions are analyzed to determine the most likely position for the DNA–protein cross-linking. Then, motif-finding algorithms are used to identify a genome-wide signature of a binding pattern.

Epigenetics-Methylation and Bisulfite Sequencing Epigenetics is the study of changes in cellular phenotype (e.g., gene expression) that do not involve changes in the DNA sequence. For example, DNA methylation and histone deacetylation do not change DNA sequence but suppress the gene expression. NGS technologies enable detection of such epigenetic modifications at single-base resolution [73]. The methylation pattern of DNA can be determined by using bisulfite treatment. Bisulfite treatment converts unmethylated cytosine residues to uracil and leaves methylated cytosine unaffected. When bisulfite-treated DNA is sequenced using NGS technologies, DNA methylation sites can be determined at single-base resolution [31].

Sequencing reads from bisulfite-treated DNA are mapped to the reference genome. At this step, the mapping algorithm has to differentiate mismatches due to bisulfite conversion and sequencing errors. This issue can be addressed in different ways, such as [73] and [20]. After mapping, methylation levels can be quantified by simply using tag counts [20] as well as using more advanced statistical methods such as [114] and [117].

Metagenomics In the past few decades, microbiologists were only focused on sequencing a single genome by isolating the desired microbe from the environment and growing it in a pure culture. This method suffers from many drawbacks. For instance, most of the microbes resist culturing. In addition, different microbes interact with each other by exchanging chemical signals and nutrients. Hence, by using pure culture techniques, we are preventing these types of interactions and thus limiting our understanding of microbes. Therefore, there was a need for a new method that would help in studying the microbes in their own environment, leading to the evolving of the metagenomics field.

Metagenomics is the field that enables studying uncultured microorganisms by sampling them directly from their environment. This field poses many challenges. For example, the community where the samples are extracted contains a large number of species, e.g., more than 10,000 species. Therefore, it is hard to retrieve the complete genome for each microorganism. Furthermore, the abundance of each organism in the sample is different, thus making it even harder to retrieve the genomes for low abundance organisms. As a result, new fast and accurate computational methods are needed to analyze the generated metagenomics data.

43.3 HIGH-PERFORMANCE COMPUTING ARCHITECTURES: SHORT SUMMARY

Solving a problem with computers requires two types of resources: processing power and memory. We engineer "clever" algorithms to reduce the amount of resources we need. Then, by using these algorithms, we can use our computers or mobile devices to solve the problems in an efficient way. HPC is a way to solve problems with multiple processing units and other resources when a standard computer is not sufficient even with the best known algorithm in the world. HPC distributes the problem over a network of processing units and solves different parts of the problem concurrently. There are several platforms one can use to achieve such concurrency. Here, we briefly describe some of them and in the next section we will survey their use cases for NGS applications.

One can connect several computers over a network and solve the problem by using several computers which are messaging over the network for data/information transfer and synchronization. The *message-passing interface* (MPI) specification is an academic and industry standard for this approach. It is accepted by several institutions and organizations with a variety of implementations. It is highly functional, very portable, and proven to be efficient. Although it is originally proposed for distributed memory architectures, implementations for shared memory and hybrid systems are also available.

The concurrency can also be provided by multiple lightweight program executions, that is, *threads*, on a single machine having more than one processing unit. Such processors with two to eight processing units (cores) have been on the market for a long time and the number of cores on them is increasing. For example, the Intel many integrated core (MIC) architecture is Intel's latest design targeted for processing highly parallel workloads. The current prototype MIC cards, codenamed *Knights Ferry* (KNF), provides up to 32 cores in a single chip with four-way simultaneous multithreading. The first commercial implementation of this design, that includes 61 cores, was announced in Nov 2012 under the name Xeon Phi. Currently, there are multiple ways to have this kind of multiprocessing, but two, POSIX threads (pthreads) and OpenMP, are more prominent than others. pthreads is a library where a thread can use one or more child threads to obtain concurrency (fork model). With pthreads, the control of the execution flow is determined by the programmer and hence it is highly tunable. On the other hand, OpenMP, which is a set of compiler directives, provides an easy way of task parallelism. Recently, it became very popular due to its simplicity and portability.

Graphical processing units have recently evolved for general-purpose computing. NVIDIA's Tesla M 2090 now has 512 cores and 6 GB memory, which makes it a powerful computing environment. General-purpose processors are most effective when the computation's pattern fits well with their design. Without loss of generality, one can claim that a custom design *application-specific integrated circuit* (ASIC) would be more effective than any general-purpose CPU for almost all applications. Unfortunately, it is not feasible to design a new chip for every application. This is where FPGAs fill the gap. FPGAs provide a customizable integrated circuit containing millions of (re)configurable gates while being power efficient. Algorithm development for FPGAs is more involved in comparison to the development of algorithms for general-purpose processors. However, return on investment can be much higher in terms of performance.

Cloud computing is a program execution paradigm which enables execution of applications on virtual machines hosted on commercial computing servers. The applications executed in today's *cloud* can vary from simple to advanced tasks. The users access computing resources in the *cloud* via a vendor and submit their task. Recently, it became popular among the research communities, including bioinformaticians [95, 97].

43.4   HIGH-PERFORMANCE COMPUTING ON NEXT-GENERATION SEQUENCING DATA

Although we mainly focus on genome alignment/mapping and de novo assembly tools, other tools using HPC and algorithms on NGS are also discussed briefly. Let us start with a table (Table 43.1) to summarize the algorithms and tools with respect to the HPC architecture(s) they use.

43.4.1   Sequence Alignment Tools

Although more than 20 short-read alignment tools have been developed in the last two years, they use only three main approaches [16, 41, 67]. The first is based on hashing, the second is based on the suffix trees or the FM-index [39], which uses the *Burrows–Wheeler transform* (BWT) [21], and the last approach is based on merge sorting. As far as we know, only a few tools use merging and they do not use any kind of parallelism. For the details of these algorithms, see [67].

All suffix tree– and BWT-based approaches use the reference genome to build the index. On the other hand, *hash-based* tools either use the reference genome or short reads to build the *hash tables*. This choice depends on the structure of the input and a design rationale. For example, if the *hash index* is built using the reads, its size is usually small. But in this case scanning the index by using the reference genome may be time consuming.

In terms of parallelization, regarding the algorithmic approach, indexing the reference genome is preferable. Note that this approach may not be suitable when the genome is long and the memory is limited. However, employing multithreading with it is much easier, and good speedups can be obtained by executing many threads concurrently. Most of the tools using multithreading in Table 43.1 indexes the reference genome and benefits the power of massive parallelism. Quoting from the manual of a multithreaded aligner segemehl, we can say that "Parallel threads will make matching much faster on machines with multiple cores. Use them!" [48]. Note that parallelism can also be useful while building the index structure. For example, PerM, a hash-based tool, builds the human genome index with 16 CPUs and 15 GB memory in half an hour, which is very good considering the size of the genome [26]. To employ multithreading, most of the tools use pthreads and OpenMP, such as Mosaik [4]. There are also some free and commercial tools, such as MOM [37] and RTG Investigator [10], which are implemented by using Java threads.

Due to exponential increase on sequencing data, several hash-based tools were enhanced and parallelized, and some were even redesigned. A good example for this last case is

TABLE 43.1 Summary of Tools and Algorithms using HPC and Designed Specially for NGS Data

HPC Architecture	Alignment Tools	De novo Assembly Tools	Other Tools
Multithreading	BFAST [49] Bowtie [64] BWA [66] GNUMAP [29, 30] Menon et al. [81] GMAP [115, 116] WHAM [71] MOM [37] Mosaik [4] Novoalign [8] PALMapper [54] PerM [26] mrNA [9] RTG Inv. [10] segemehl [48] SHRiMP2 [33, 94] SOAPaligner [69] SOCS [89] SToRM [87] Zoom [72]	ABySS [103] SOAPdenovo [70] ALLPATHS-LG [44] MIRA3 [27] Graph Const. [3] IDBA [90] Newbler [7] PASHA [77] SSAKE [32] MSR-CA [5] SGA [102] Velvet [119] Meraculous [25] PE-Assembler [13]	SOAPsplice [50] mCUDA-MEME [78] GENIE [28] Myrna [62] Crossbow [63] seqMINER [118] BayesPeak [22] RSEM [65]
MPI	GNUMAP [29, 30] Novoalign mrNA [9] pFANGS [83] Bozdağ et al. [18] Bozdağ et al. [19]	ABySS [103] Forge [2] PASHA [77] YAGA [52] Jackson et al. [53] Kundeti et al. [59] Ray [17]	DecGPU [76] mCUDA-MEME [78] RseqFlow [110]
GPU	SOAP3 [74] PASS [23] (expected) MUMmerGPU [98, 107] GPU-RMAP [11]		CompleteMOTIFs [61] DecGPU [76] CUDA-MEME [75] mCUDA-MEME [78] GENIE [28] Shi et al. [100, 101]
FPGA	Knodel et al. [58]	Graph Const. [3]	
Cloud computing	Menon et al. [81] CloudBurst [96] genome-indexing [81]	Contrail [1]	Myrna [62] Crossbow [63] Quake [56] PeakRanger [38] RUM [45]

SHRiMP2 [33], whose ancestor SHRiMP [94] used the reads to build hash tables. Instead, in SHRiMP2, the developers changed the design and used the reference genome. Hence, genome indexes became reusable, and massive parallelism could be achieved. This new design made SHRiMP2 two to five times faster than BFAST [49], which also uses the genome to build the hash index, on an eight-core 3.0 machine with 16 GB RAM [33]. Note that the first version, SHRiMP, was shown to be much slower than BFAST for some scenarios [49].

Another popular tool, GNUMAP, which uses a probabilistic approach to align short reads, was initially proposed without any concurrency support [30]. One year after its release, Clement et al. proposed a parallel version employing thread-level parallelism via pthreads [29]. GNUMAP uses the genome to build the hash index and the threads are assigned a number of reads. As mentioned above, the major drawback of this approach is the large memory footprint when the genome is large, which is the case for the human genome. This is a general limitation of all tools for obtaining more accurate results. To reduce the memory footprint and further reduce the execution time, Clement et al. used MPI and distributed the genome among the nodes in a network. Since each node indexes its own genome share, the memory requirement per node is reduced significantly. With this hybrid approach, the authors reported a linear speedup on a 32-node cluster having 256 processors in total.

Similar to GNUMAP, there are other tools employing MPI to reduce the memory requirement and distribute the tasks among nodes. The evolution of the tools resemble each other. For example, Novoalign [8], which uses multithreading for parallelism (in its commercial version), now has a version NovoalignMPI, which employs both MPI and multithreading. On the other hand, rNA [9], a multithreaded hash-based alignment tool, recently evolved to mrNA with MPI support. A similar story can be told for the evolution of FANGS [84] to pFANGS [83], but this time with an important difference. Instead of a hybrid solution, to parallelize FANGS, Misra et al. used a pure MPI-based approach. They compared pFANGS with its OpenMP and OpenMP/MPI versions. They reported that the latter versions do not scale well and followed the MPI-based solution. For pFANGS, a 225-fold speedup on 512 processors is reported over the time taken with two processors. Various indexing and data distribution strategies for MPI-based parallelization of short-read alignment algorithms were investigated by Bozdağ et al. [18]. To improve scalability, a cost model valid for each strategy is proposed. Then the most promising strategy is selected by using a novel selection policy. They reported that the policy usually selects the best strategy in practice and if not it selects a good one.

In addition to pthreads, OpenMP, and MPI, other approaches have been used to parallelize hash-based alignment tools. A good example of this is RMAP, a very accurate short-read alignment tool indexing the short reads instead of the genome [104]. Since the hash table is created from the reads, RMAP requires relatively small memory (only 620 MB to align the reads to the hg18 genome) and can be run on a wide range of hardware. Aji et al. proposed the tool GPU-RMAP, which executes RMAP's algorithm on a GPU [11]. They used CUDA to share the reference genome among GPU threads. Note that in this scheme threads can align their shares to the same read in the aligning phase. Aji et al. avoid this race condition by using a synchronization stage during the course of alignment. They tested their approach on the NVIDIA Tesla C1060 GPU and reported 14.5-fold speedup for the alignment process and 9.6-fold speedup for the overall execution over the time required for RMAP.

As a replacement of RMAP in cloud computing, Schatz proposed the tool CloudBurst [96], which uses the Hadoop implementation of MapReduce [35]. On a 24-core system, CloudBurst obtained 2–33-fold speedup over RMAP. Schatz reported that, when the required sensitivity is low, the overhead of shuffling and distributing the data over the network dominates the execution time and for such cases the speedup is low. However, for alignments requiring high sensitivity, a superlinear speedup is obtained. Their experiments in the Amazon EC2 cloud showed that 14 h of execution time of the sequential RMAP can be reduced to 8 min on 96 cores, which means more than 100-fold speedup.

To align the reads more efficiently, instead of a hash index, a suffix tree [113] can be constructed from the reference genome. By using the techniques described above, tools using this approach can be effectively parallelized in a multithreaded setting. For example, a related but smaller data structure suffix array [80] is used by segemehl, which supports thread-level parallelism [48]. MUMmer, which is designed for the exact alignment problem, is the first tool that uses a suffix tree for sequence alignment [60]. Similar to other tool evolutions, to cope with the NGS data, Schatz et al. parallelized MUMmer by using CUDA and developed the tool MUMmerGPU to parallelize exact alignment on the GPUs [98]. Since current GPUs have relatively small memory compared to workstations, a good scaling with CUDA is harder to achieve. To alleviate the memory restriction, Schatz et al. built several smaller but overlapping suffix trees instead of one big tree where the amount of overlap depends on the maximum query length. To improve locality in the small GPU cache, these trees are rearranged into cache blocks. With this approach, they reported a 10-fold speedup for the alignment phase on an NVIDIA GeForce 8800 GTX with 128 processors compared to a sequential execution of MUMmer on the 3.0-GHz dual-core Intel Xeon 5160. For the same experiment, the overall speedup was between 3.47 and 3.79. An interesting observation is the performance difference of MUMmerGPU for short and long queries. Although the proposed tree layout is desirable for short queries, when the queries get longer, there is a dramatic reduction on the speedup due to more cache access time and the divergence of thread loads. In a later work, Trapnell and Schatz observed that these issues came with the proposed data layout strategy. They proposed seven independent data layout heuristics and investigated 128 configurations exhaustively. By choosing the best policy, they obtained speedups of up to 4 over MUMmerGPU on the overall execution time [107].

Another index data structure closely related to suffix trees is the FM-index [39], which is constructed by using the BWT [21]. BWT-based alignment algorithms gained attention in the last three years, and tools such as Bowtie [64], BWA [66], and SOAP2 [69] were proposed for aligning short reads to a reference genome. The BWT index is small: 3 GB memory is sufficient to store the index created from a human genome, whereas a suffix array for the same genome consumes more than 12 GB memory. Since all the algorithms create BWT indexes from the genome, massive parallelism is possible by using pthreads or OpenMP. Actually, when Bowtie was first proposed, it was already more than 30 times faster than most of the non-BWT tools [64]. By using parallelism, Langmead et al. reported a speedup of 3.12, which makes Bowtie able to to align 88.1 million 35-bp reads/hour trimmed from the 1000 genome project on a machine equipped with a four-core 2.4-GHz AMD Opteron processor. It was reported that, by using the BWT index, alignment of the reads in a read set takes 7 min for Bowtie, while SOAP, a hash-based aligner, spends 49 h on the same set. The developers of SOAP used the BWT index in SOAP2 and reported a 23–24-fold speedup on a human reference genome [69]. Recently, a much faster GPU version, SOAP3, has been proposed by Liu et al [74]. They reported that SOAP3 is up to 10 times faster than SOAP2, and it is the first software that can find all 3-mismatch alignments in tens of seconds for one million reads. As far as we know, SOAP3 is the only BWT-based tool developed for GPUs. Cutting-edge graphics cards in the market now have enough memory to store a BWT index constructed from a human genome. Hence, we are expecting to see the new GPU-based alignment tools and/or the GPU-based versions of Bowtie and BWA in the future.

Although the BWT index is very efficient, building it is a time-consuming task. By incorporating an MPI-based approach, Bozdağ et al. investigated the options to parallelize the BWT index construction along with various 2D data and task distribution strategies. They reported a speedup between 2.18 and 10.65 on a 16-node dual 2.4-GHz Opteron cluster. In a more recent work, Menon et al. used cloud computing to distribute the construction of BWT index and suffix array [81]. They followed the MapReduce programming model and implemented a tool called genome indexing. Compared to Bowtie's indexing phase, genome indexing is up to 5.88, 11.09, and 14.93 times faster with 30, 60, and 120 processes, respectively, when executed on Hadoop clusters in the Amazon EC2 cloud.

Several available alignment tools do not support an explicit parallelism, and some of these suggest an implicit parallelization technique. For example, in the manual of mrFAST [12], an assembler which uses a hash-based index, Alkan et al. suggest that the best way to optimize the tool is by splitting the reads into chunks and using MPI to distribute them. Note that this approach is the same as most MPI-based parallelizations described in this section. The only difference is that the tool does not support it explicitly. On the other hand, the manuals of tools with HPC support such as Bowtie say something like "If your computer has multiple processors/cores, use -p." We believe that, regarding the HPC architecture, end-user parallelization should not be harder. The alignment problem is considered embarrassingly parallel and the tools may be used by researchers who are not aware of this kind of parallelism. For the tools, which can be parallelized, one can develop helper tools to automatize the parallelism. For benchmarking purposes, Hatem et al. developed an MPI-based tool pMap, which executes multiple instances of a short-read alignment tool by partitioning the reads among the nodes in a cluster [47]. We refer the reader to [47] for a comparison of speedups obtained by the concurrent executions of these tools.

Other cutting-edge hardware, such as field-programmable gate arrays, are also used for NGS alignment. For example, Knodel et al. implemented the Smith–Waterman local sequence alignment algorithm [105] on a Xilinx Virtex-6 on the ML605 Evaluation board and compared it with short-read mapping algorithms, including Bowtie and SOAP2 [58]. They reported a comparable execution time with Bowtie, where SOAP2 is much faster (14x). They also reported much better quality. Actually, the accuracies of Bowtie and SOAP2 are much less than what was reported in the literature before. Besides, these tools were executed on a personal computer with a 2.66-GHz CPU and 4 GB RAM. Still, the work shows that using FPGAs can be promising on NGS data. Other works in the literature are considering the same problem [57, 88].

43.4.2 De Novo Assemblers

De novo assemblers reconstruct genomes from scratch. That is, no similar genome is available to the assembly process. There are many published and unpublished assembly tools for the NGS data. However, the algorithms they use are not that many. Some components of these algorithms are easily parallelizable, but compared with alignment, the main assembly process is harder to parallelize. For a summary of recent computational challenges in next-generation genome assembly, we refer the reader to [93].

There are two main algorithms employed in current assembly tools: The first approach uses a data structure called are *overlap graph* [86] and the second approach uses the *de Bruijn graph* [34]. In addition to these approaches, some greedy assemblers such as SSAKE [32] and PE-Assembler [13] exist in the literature. For a good algorithmic review of some widely used assembly tools, we refer the reader to [82].

In an overlap graph, nodes and edges represent short reads and overlaps, respectively. In its very simplest form, the assembly problem can be defined as finding a *Hamiltonian path* on the overlap graph [93]. The main challenge on the complexity side is that the Hamiltonian path problem is NP hard [43]. Besides, in practice, there may be some errors and repeats on the reads and genome. The tools MIRA3 [27], Newbler [7], and Forge [2] use a variant of the overlap graph, and SGA [102] further combines it with a suffix array. The second graph structure, the de Bruijn graph, is constructed by using k-mers, a small fixed-length k subsequence. A de Bruijn graph contains a node for each k-mer. An edge between two nodes represents a perfect overlap between the prefix and suffix of the k-mers corresponding to nodes. In its simplest form, the assembly problem can be defined as finding an *Eulerian path* on a de Bruijn graph [93] for which we have polynomial time solutions. The other assembly tools in Table 43.1 use this graph structure, except for greedy SSAKE and PE-Assembler, as well as MSR-CA [5], which uses a combination of de Bruijn and overlap graphs.

Using de Bruijn graphs for the assembly process is proven to be useful and provides accurate solutions for many cases. However, with great accuracy comes great memory requirement. Even though the tools work well for short genomes, their memory footprint is huge when the genome is long. For example, SOAPdenovo [70] requires only 5 GB for bacterial and fungi genomes. However, for human genomes, the memory requirement is approximately 150 GB (2 TB for complex genomes according to [41]). This is due to the large number of nodes in the graph. Since each vertex in the graph represents a unique k-mer, when the genome is long and k is large, there will be many vertices. For example, the number of 27-mers in a de Bruijn graph constructed from the genomic data of the Yoruban male is 7.73 billion [77]. Up to know, constructing de Bruijn graphs in a distributed fashion and/or in a more efficient way is the main HPC research direction for de novo assemblers since this is the bottleneck for the assembly process requiring a vast amount of memory. If one has a supercomputer, a de Bruijn graph can be stored on the shared memory. Recently, ALLPATHS-LG is installed and tested on a SGI build Blacklight supercomputer located at the Pittsburgh Supercomputing Center. The machine has 32 TB memory in total where a 16-TB portion can be used for a shared memory job, which is sufficient to assemble a human genome. If such memory is not available, a distributed memory architecture is an amenable solution. As far as we know, only YAGA and Ray use MPI, and ABySS and PASHA use a hybrid approach employing MPI and a thread-level parallelism. ABySS uses pthreads and OpenMP whereas PASHA uses Intel's *threading building blocks* (TBB) to implement concurrency in shared memory.

In ABySS, the de Bruijn graph is constructed in a distributed fashion [103]. Each k-mer (with its paired end) is assigned to a certain node in the network by using an encoding scheme. The same encoding scheme is also used when a k-mer tries to reach one of its neighbor k-mers. Simpson et al. [103] explain this encoding as follows: Each base is assigned a numerical value and a base-4 representation of a k-mer is computed by using these values, which were then used as input to a hash function. They stated that it is important to distribute the k-mers evenly over the nodes to the extent of this hash function. It is not explained if this encoding scheme helps to assign the neighbor k-mers to the same processor to reduce the amount of communication overhead. Instead, they used a nonblocking communication model in which a node continues to work without waiting for the answer to a message it sends to another processor. Also, to reduce the number of small messages and the latency overhead, they collected the small messages into packets of size 1 kB and then sent the packet at once. Simpson et al. reported a competitive performance with some other assemblers but no speedup or execution time is reported. Boisvert et al. reported a similar performance of Ray with ABySS on a server with 128 GB of memory and 32 AMD Opteron cores [17].

Although different in the algorithm level, YAGA and PASHA follow the approach of ABySS and Ray: They distribute the reads to the cluster nodes and construct/compact the de Bruijn graph in parallel. PASHA distributes the k-mers and obtains linear chains of these k-mers in a parallel fashion. While doing this, it uses an encoding scheme for each k-mer similar to ABySS. To obtain communication–computation overlap, PASHA employs two threads at each cluster node where one thread is responsible for communication and the other for computation. After the chains are obtained, the rest of the assembly process, contig generation and scaffolding, is implemented in a multithreaded shared-memory fashion. Liu et al. reported that PASHA is about 2.25 times faster than ABySS with comparable accuracy when executed on an eight-node (32-core) cluster (for the parallel phase) and 8-core workstation (for the shared memory phase) [77]. Although they did not obtain good speedup on the overall assembly process, they showed that the process gets faster up to 32–64 cores. They reported that, using 256 CPUs on a Blue Gene/L, YAGA takes around 8 min to assemble a bacterial genome. For the same genome, PASHA takes only 5.5 min on a single core. Hence they did not compare PASHA with YAGA extensively. On the other hand, Jackson et al. reported that YAGA obtains very good speedups (e.g., 8.17 on 256 cores) for the overall assembly process where the ideal speedup is 16.02 on the Blue Gene/L [52]. Note that the ideal speedup is not equal to the number of cores since only a portion of the assembly process is parallelized.

YAGA uses a slightly different (bidirectional) de Bruijn graph for genome assembly. A similar data structure is also used and constructed in parallel for the transcriptome assembly problem [53]. Kundeti et al. investigated parallelization options to the construction of this bidirected de Bruijn graph [59]. They also proposed an out-of-core algorithm for the same purpose and compared it with Velvet's [119] graph construction algorithm. They reported that their algorithm survives from cases for which Velvet fails to build a graph on a low-end 32-bit machine with 1 GB RAM due to its memory requirement.

Due to their optimized design for MPI-based parallelism, tools supporting distributing memory architectures may not scale well in shared memory as Ariyaratne and Sung reported that for relatively small genomes [13]. In their experiments, ABySS was two times slower than Velvet, which uses OpenMP for thread-level parallelism. However, they also reported that in their experiment with the hg18 genome Velvet failed due to its high memory usage, and ABySS provided a solution on a four-node distributed memory cluster. Note that Velvet is a widely used fast assembler employing de Bruijn graphs and reported it to be more accurate and 35 times faster than SSAKE [112], which is a popular greedy genome assembler, while assembling a bacterial-size genome [119]. Chapman et al. reported a similar relative performance of ABySS and Velvet on a shared-memory architecture. In their experiments on an eight-core machine, ABySS spent 6 h to assemble a yeast genome where it took 4.6 h for Velvet. They also reported that for the same task SOAPdenovo [70], a multi-threaded de Bruijn assembler, took only 0.7 h. A recent benchmark by Bao et al. also reported that SOAPdenovo is much faster than ABySS (3x) and Velvet (30x–40x) on a shared-memory architecture [16]. On the other hand, Li et al., the developers of SOAPdenovo, noted that ABySS only uses 16 GB of memory for the assembly of a human genome where SOAPdenovo requires 140 GB.

ALLPATHS-LG is another assembler using de Bruijn graphs and supporting thread-level parallelism [44]. It tries to optimize the parallelization by partitioning the graph and assembling each part separately without considering the overlaps. Note that ABySS and PASHA also distribute the graph but k-mers still need to reach their neighbors in different nodes. In ALLPATHS-LG, during the assembly of the parts there is no thread communication to increase the concurrency. These local structures then combined by taking the overlapping regions into account. Experimental evaluations show that ALLPATHS-LG is still slower than SOAPdenovo. Gnerre et al. reported that ALLPATH-LG takes three weeks to assemble a human genome on commodity shared-memory architecture. On the other hand, SOAPdenovo assembles the genome in three days. However, by taking more time, ALLPATHS-LG produces better and high-quality assemblies [44].

To make SSAKE faster, D'Agostino et al. ported its perl code into C and employed advanced data structures [32]. Later, they parallelized two time-consuming stages, k-mer search and sequence deletion, of SSAKE in the thread level. For these stages, 9- and 21.6-fold speedups are obtained, respectively, on a 32-core machine. They reported an overall speedup of 2.82 due to parallelization. Along with the effect of the more advanced C implementation, the new code was 18 times faster on 32 cores.

A scalable assembler, PE-Assembler, is especially designed for optimum parallelism by Ariyaratne and Sung [13]. They showed that the quality of sequences that PE-Assembler obtained is comparable with that of widely used assemblers for some genomes. Furthermore, they reported 4.5-fold (approximately) speedup on eight cores over a serial execution of their algorithm.

In addition to MPI- and thread-based approaches, unpublished cloud- and FPGA-based solutions are publicly or commercially available. Schatz et al. use a cloud to solve the problem in a distributed fashion and proposed the tool Contrail [1]. On the other hand, Convey Computer's hybrid FPGA- and CPU-core-based Graph Constructor [3] is proposed to construct the graph in a more efficient way. We are not aware of a GPU-based solution for this problem (or a GPU-based de novo assembler). This is expected since for complex genomes a de Bruijn graph is huge compared to available memory on a GPU. Besides, the genome assembly problem may not be a suitable problem for the GPU architecture. Still, we believe that it is a challenging open problem.

43.4.3 RNA-Seq Data Analysis

RNA-Seq, also called whole transcriptome shotgun sequencing, is the process of sequencing the transcriptome using high-throughput DNA sequencing methods in order to get information about a sample's RNA content, a technique that quickly became valuable in the study of diseases like cancer [79, 111]. RNA-Seq data analysis depends on having a reference genome and/or transcriptome. Therefore, most of the tools start by building an index for the reference genome or transcriptome and then map the reads and do some further analysis (e.g., [50, 62, 65]. In addition, some of the tools preprocess the reads to facilitate the parallelization of further steps (e.g., [62]).

Most of the RNA-Seq tools use existing read mappers in the intermediate mapping step. Therefore, efficient implementation of read mappers affects the performance of RNA-Seq tools. One of the main mappers used in RNA-Seq analysis is Bowtie [64]. For instance, Myrna [62] uses Bowtie to map the reads to a reference genome, while RUM [65], RESM [45], and RseqFlow [110] use Bowtie to map the reads to both a reference genome and the transcriptome.

Genome indexing facilitates the use of different parallelism techniques. Therefore, RNA-Seq analysis tools use one or more parallelism techniques to speed up the whole process. For instance, Myrna [62] can use either cloud computing or thread-level parallelism to speed up the analysis. It is designed as a work flow with seven stages: preprocess, align, overlap, normalize, statistical analysis, summarize, and postprocess. Some of these stages can be run in parallel, such as preprocess and align, where the input reads can be divided into separate groups that run simultaneously on different nodes. However, other stages, like summarize, do not exploit much parallelism, and therefore a single processor is used to execute these stages. In a cloud computing setting, Myrna's throughput increases from 0.1 to 0.38 experiments per hours when increasing the number of cores from 80 to 150. However, this is less than a linear speedup. The degradation in Myrna performance is due to the load imbalance among the processors in the mapping step, which cannot be avoided in some cases [62].

RUM [65] is another RNA-Seq analysis tool that uses parallelism. Using MPI, it can analyze 94 million reads extracted from the retina in 2 days using 50 processors, in comparison to 16 days for MapSplice [109] and 5 days and 300 processors for GSNAP [115]. In addition, the mass storage required for temporary files is much less than that required by counterpart tools. For example, SpliceMap requires 2.5 TB to store the files while RUM needs only 200 GB for the same data set.

Another MPI-based tool is RseqFlow [110]. However, the parallelism is not achieved explicitly by the tool. Instead, the tool is designed as a work flow of tasks and Pegasus [36], a framework for mapping complex scientific work flows onto distributed systems, is used to manage and execute the work flow. Using Pegasus, RseqFlow was able to achieve 440% improvement in runtime when running on a Linux cluster of 118 nodes with 54 dual hexcore, 24-GB RAM nodes and 64 dual quadcore, 16-GB RAM nodes.

43.4.4 ChIP-Seq Analysis

ChIP-Seq is another important application in which millions of reads need to be processed in a timely manner. Recently, many tools have been developed that exploit different parallelism techniques [38, 75, 118]. Like RNA-Seq analysis, the whole process can be divided into two main steps: mapping the ChIP-Seq reads into a reference genome and analyzing the mapped data.

One of the tools developed to exploit parallelism in handling large amounts of ChIP-Seq data is PeakRanger [38]. The algorithm starts by building an index for the genome. The index is built by dividing the genome into k-mers of a certain length (usually 12). Then the reads are mapped to the index and extended to match the size of the sheared DNA. To achieve parallelism, PeakRanger implements the MapReduce architecture in the top of the Hadoop framework. In this framework, PeakRanger can be expressed as a series of MapReduce subjobs. In the mapping step, each mapper is responsible for building an index for a certain chromosome and independently map the reads to this index. Then, the reduce step comes to analyze the data and performs peak calling. PeakRanger was able to achieve 10x speedup when using cloud computing in comparison to the serial version. However, due to splitting the genome by the number of chromosome, the maximum number of nodes that can be used is 25 (i.e., the number of chromosomes in the genome). Therefore, the genome division method they used does not efficiently make use of the available resources.

In addition to the *cloud*, GPUs were used in three ChIP-Seq tools to achieve parallelism, namely, CompleteMOTIFS [61], CUDA-MEME [75], and mCUDA-MEME [78]. However, CompleteMOTIFS is not implemented in GPU; instead, it is implemented as a pipeline of stages where CUDA-MEME is used as a separate stage to achieve parallelism. Therefore, the parallelism is only achieved in part of the pipeline. Both CUDA-MEME and mCUDA-MEME provide parallelization for a well-known de novo ChIP-Seq motif discovery algorithm called MEME [15]. MEME can detect a large percentage of new motifs [75]. However, the running time is $O(N^2L^2)$, where N is the number of input sequences and L is the length of each sequence. Liu et al. [75] proposed a parallel version CUDA-MEME for GPUs. On a single GPU, CUDA-MEME achieved around 17x speedup in comparison to the sequential algorithm. However, some of the stages were parallelizable on a GPU while others had to be run sequentially on a single CPU, thus reducing the overall running time. Therefore, a second version, mCUDA-MEME, was developed to achieve a further speedup [78]. A hybrid combination of CUDA, OpenMP, and MPI is used for this faster version. The new hybrid combination allowed mCUDA-MEME to run MEME on multiple GPUs, and the use of multithreading makes the sequential stages faster.

43.4.5 Error Correction

NGS machines are not highly accurate; they tend to introduce sequencing errors that increase in frequency at the 3' ends of the read [56]. Sequencing errors complicate the analysis of the reads, especially in applications that require mapping back the reads to a reference genome or performing de novo assembly for the reads. Therefore, minimizing the frequency of errors would help in reducing chimeric contigs in the case of genome assembly and would provide better analysis for the reads (e.g., SNP discovery) in the case of mapping them back to a reference genome.

Considering the above aspect, lately, many error correction tools were developed [92, 99]. However, since the number of reads are increasing exponentially, the error correction is both time and memory consuming. To the best of our knowledge, a few number of tools were developed to overcome this drawback by parallelizing the correction process with multithreading, cloud computing, and GPUs.

Cloud computing is used by Quake [56] on the Hadoop work flow. Each node in the cluster is responsible for processing a batch of reads. This includes the division of the reads into k-mers and counting of the number of occurrences of the different k-mers. The Hadoop work flow is responsible for summing these partial counts. The main purpose behind using cloud computing is the large memory consumption that can reach up to 100 GB when working on the human genome. Counting k-mers is a single stage of Quake which contains five stages: k-mer counting, coverage cutoff, error localization, error probability modeling, and correction search. The other four stages do not require a large amount of memory and therefore can be executed sequentially in a single machine. In addition, to further increase the speedup, multithreading is used in the correction search stage.

For achieving parallelism using GPUs, two main tools were developed: CUDA-EC [100] and DecGPU [76]. DecGPU employs a hybrid CUDA and MPI programming model to maximize the performance by using multiple GPUs at the same time. In addition, it allows the overlapping between the CPU and GPU computations, thus leading to further performance improvement. DecGPU consists of five stages that are executed in a distributed fashion, namely, k-mer spectrum construction, error-free read filtering, erroneous read fixing, fixed read trimming, and an optional iterative stage. On the other hand, CUDA-EC uses a single GPU. In addition, it is designed based on the assumption that the device memory of a single GPU is sufficient to store the k-mer index. Therefore, it is limited to certain genome sizes.

43.5 SUMMARY

To cope with the data generated by NGS devices in bioinformatics, we need efficient approaches. Novel algorithmic techniques are the most important weapons we have against this immense amount of data, yet, as every good thing, they may induce an overhead to the solution or they may be inadequate due to the characteristic of the problem. HPC is an amenable way to overcome some of these issues. Architectures like supercomputers, clusters, and multicore CPUs have their own characteristics and respond to parallelism attempts in unique ways. Although this indeed is a challenge, considering the variety of problems and applications we have, when combined, such differences act as a Swiss army knife.

Everything keeps changing in bioinformatics at a blistering pace. Soon, state-of-the-art sequencing machines will be much faster. That is, the throughput of data generation will change. These machines will generate longer reads. Hence, the structure of the data will change. In metagenomics, we will have reads sequenced from microbial communities with related or unrelated members, and the type of the data will change. So the algorithms and tools should change. Then why do we need such a survey if the techniques described here will be obsolete? Because, we will still continue to borrow algorithms, data structures, and heuristics from the solutions of well-studied bioinformatics problems. Then we will use our experiences on the design and implementation of current tools supporting HPC to make new tools better, faster, and more practical. We believe that we touch most of HPC usage on next-generation sequencing data. We hope that the next generation of researchers will benefit from this survey as today's researchers have done with already existing ones.

REFERENCES

1. Contrail, `http://sourceforge.net/apps/mediawiki/contrail-bio`.

2. Forge, `http://combiol.org/forge`.

3. Graph Constructor, `http://www.conveycomputer.com/`.

4. Mosaik, `http://bioinformatics.bc.edu/marthlab/Mosaik`.

5. MSR-CA, `http://www.genome.umd.edu/SR_CA_MANUAL.htm`.

6. NCBI-GenBank, Distribution Release Notes (Release 186.0). Available: `ftp://ftp.ncbi.nih.gov/genbank/gbrel.txt`.

7. Newbler, `www.454.com`.

8. Novoalign, `http://www.novocraft.com`.

9. rNA, `http://iga-rna.sourceforge.net`.

10. RTG Investigator, `http://www.realtimegenomics.com`.

11. A. M. Aji, Z. Liqing, and W. Feng. GPU-RMAP: Accelerating short-read mapping on graphics processors. In *Proceedings of the 13th IEEE International Conference on Computational Science and Engineering (CSE 2010)*, December 2010, pp. 168–175.

12. C. Alkan, J. M. Kidd, T. Marques-Bonet, G. Aksay, F. Antonacci, F. Hormozdiari, J. O. Kitzman, C. Baker, M. Malig, O. Mutlu, S. C. Şahinalp, R. A. Gibbs, and E. E. Eichler. Personalized copy number and segmental duplication maps using next-generation sequencing. *Nat. Genet.*, 41(10):1061–1067, Oct. 2009.

13. P. N. Ariyaratne and W-K. Sung. PE-Assembler: De novo assembler using short paired-end reads. *Bioinformatics*, 27(2):167–174, Jan. 2011.

14. K. F. Au, H. Jiang, L. Lin, Y. Xing, and W. H. Wong. Detection of splice junctions from paired-end RNA-seq data by SpliceMap. *Nucleic Acids Res.*, 38(18):4570–4578, Oct. 2010.

15. T. L. Bailey and C. Elkan. Unsupervised learning of multiple motifs in biopolymers using expectation maximization. *Machine Learning*, 21:51–83, 1995.

16. S. Bao, R. Jiang, W. Kwan, B. Wang, X. Ma, and Y. Q. Song. Evaluation of next-generation sequencing software in mapping and assembly. *J. Hum. Genet.*, 56(6):406–414, June 2011.

17. S. Boisvert, F. Laviolette, and J. Corbeil. Ray: Simultaneous assembly of reads from a mix of high-throughput sequencing technology. *J. Computat. Biol.*, 17(11):1519–1533, Nov. 2010.

18. D. Bozdağ, C. C. Barbacioru, and Ü. V. Çatalyürek. Parallel short sequence mapping for high throughput genome sequencing. In *Proceedings of the IEEE International Parallel and Distributed Processing Symposium (IPDPS 2009)*, IEEE Computer Society, May 2009.

19. D. Bozdağ, A. Hatem, and Ü. V. Çatalyürek. Exploring parallelism in short sequence mapping using Burrows-Wheeler transform. In *Proceedings of the IEEE International Parallel & Distributed Processing Symposium Workshops (IPDPSW 2010)*. IEEE Computer Society, April 2010.

20. A. L. Brunner, S. W. Kim D. S. Johnson, A. Valouev, T. E. Reddy, N. F. Neff, E. Anton, C. Medina, L. Nguyen, E. Chiao, C. B. Oyolu, G. P. Schroth, D. M. Absher, J. C. Baker, and R. M. Myers. Distinct DNA methylation patterns characterize differentiated human embryonic stem cells and developing human fetal liver. *Genome Res.*, 19(6):1044–1056, June 2009.

21. M. Burrows and D. J. Wheeler. A block-sorting lossless data compression algorithm. Technical Report 124. Digital Systems Research Center, Palo Alto, CA, 1994.

22. J. Cairns, C. Spyrou, R. Stark, M. L. Smith, A. G. Lynch, and S. Tavaré. BayesPeak—An R package for analysing ChIP-seq data. *Bioinformatics*, 27(5):713–718, Mar. 2011.

23. D. Campagna, A. Albiero, A. Bilardi, E. Caniato, C. Forcato, S. Manavski, N. Vitulo, and G. Valle. PASS: A program to align short sequences. *Bioinformatics*, 25(7):967–968, Apr. 2009.

24. M. J. Chaisson, D. Brinza, and P. A. Pevzner. De novo fragment assembly with short mate-paired reads: Does the read length matter? *Genome Res.*, 2(19):1497–1502, Feb. 2009.

25. J. A. Chapman, I. Ho S. Sunkara, S. Luo, G. P. Schroth, and D. S. Rokhsar. Meraculous: De novo genome assembly with short paired-end reads. *PLoS ONE*, 6(8):e23501, Aug. 2011.

26. Y. Chen, T. Souaiaia, and T. Chen. PerM: Efficient mapping of short sequencing reads with periodic full sensitive spaced seeds. *Bioinformatics*, 25(19):2514–2521, Oct. 2009.

27. B. Chevreux, T. Wetterm, and S. Suhai. Genome sequence assembly using trace signals and additional sequence information. In *Proceedings of the German Conference on Bioinformatics (GDB 1999)*, 1999, pp. 45–56.

28. S. Chikkagoudar, K. Wang, and M. Li. GENIE: A Software package for gene-gene interaction analysis in genetic association studies using multiple GPU or CPU cores. *BMC Res. Notes*, 4(1):158, 2011.

29. N. L. Clement, M. J. Clement, Q. Snell, and W. E. Johnson. Parallel mapping approaches for GNUMAP. In *Proceedings of the IEEE International Parallel & Distributed Processing Symposium Workshops (IPDPSW 2011)*, IEEE Computer Society, May 2011, pp. 435–443.

30. N. L. Clement, Q. Snell, M. J. Clement, P. C. Hollenhorst, J. Purwar, B. J. Graves, B. R. Cairns, and W. E. Johnson. The GNUMAP algorithm: Unbiased probabilistic mapping of oligonucleotides from next-generation sequencing. *Bioinformatics*, 26(1):38–45, 2010.

31. S. J. Cokus, S. Feng, X. Zhang, Z. Chen, B. Merriman, C. D. Haudenschild, S. Pradhan, S. F. Nelson, M. Pellegrini, and S. E. Jacobsen. Shotgun bisulphite sequencing of the arabidopsis genome reveals DNA methylation patterning. *Nature*, 452(7184):215–219, Feb. 2008.

32. D. D'Agostino, I. Merelli, R.Warren, A. Guffanti, L. Milanesi, and A. Clematis. Parallelization of the SSAKE genomics application. In *Proceedings of the 19th Euromicro International Conference on Parallel, Distributed and Network-based Processing (PDP 2011)*, IEEE Computer Society, 2011, pp. 326–330.

33. M. David, M. Dzamba, D. Lister, L. Ilie, and M. Brudno. SHRiMP2: Sensitive yet practical short read mapping. *Bioinformatics*, 27(7):1011–1012, 2011.

34. N. G. de Brujin. A combinatorial problem. *Koninklijke Nederlandse Akademie v. Wetenschappen*, 49:758–764, 1946.

35. J. Dean and S. Ghemawat. MapReduce: Simplified data processing on large clusters. *Commun. ACM*, 51(1):107–113, 2008.

36. E. Deelman, G. Singh, M. Su, J. Blythe, Y. Gil, C. Kesselman, G. Mehta, K. Vahi, G. B. Berriman, J. Good, A. Laity, J. C. Jacob, and D. S. Katz. Pegasus: A framework for mapping

complex scientific workflows onto distributed systems. *Sci. Program.*, 13(3):219–237, 2005.

37. H. L. Eaves and Y. Gao. MOM: Maximum oligonucleotide mapping. *Bioinformatics*, 25(7):969–970, Apr. 2009.

38. X. Feng, R. Grossman, and L. Stein. PeakRanger: A cloud-enabled peak caller for ChIP-seq data. *BMC Bioinformatics*, 12(1):139, 2011.

39. P. Ferragina and G. Manzini. Opportunistic data structures with applications. In *Proceedings of 41th Annual Symposium on Foundations of Computer Science (FOCS 2000)*, IEEE Computer Society, 2000, pp. 390–398.

40. P. Flicek. The need for speed. *Genome Biol.*, 10(3):212, 2009.

41. P. Flicek and E. Birney. Sense from sequence reads: Methods for alignment and assembly. *Nat. Methods*, 6(11s):S6–S12, Oct. 2009.

42. M. Garber, M. G. Grabherr, M. Guttman, and C. Trapnell. Computational methods for transcriptome annotation and quantification using RNA-seq. *Nat. Methods*, 8(6):469–477, June 2011.

43. M. R. Garey and D. S. Johnson. *Computers and Intractability: A Guide to the Theory of NP-Completeness*. W. H. Freeman, New York, 1979.

44. S. Gnerre, I. MacCallum, D. Przybylski, F. J. Ribeiro, J. N. Burton, B. J. Walker, T. Sharpe, G. Hall, T. P. Shea, S. Sykes, A. M. Berlin, D. Aird, M. Costello, D. Raza, L. Williams, R. Nicol, A. Gnirke, C. Nusbaum, E. S. Lander, and D. B. Jaffe. High-quality draft assemblies of mammalian genomes from massively parallel sequence data. *Proc. Nat. Acad. Sci. USA*, 108(4):1513–1518, 2011.

45. G. R .Grant, M. H. Farkas, A. D. Pizarro, N. F. Lahens, J. Schug, B. P. Brunk, C. J. Stoeckert, J. B. Hogenesch, and E. A. Pierce. Comparative analysis of RNA-Seq alignment alogrithms and the RNA-Seq unified mapper (RUM). *Bioinformatics*, 27(18):2518–2528, 2011.

46. M. Guttman, M. Garber, J. Z. Levin, J. Donaghey, J. Robinson, X. Adiconis, L. Fan, M. J. Koziol, A. Gnirke, C. Nusbaum, J. L. Rinn, E. S. Lander, and A. Regev. Ab initio reconstruction of cell type-specific transcriptomes in mouse reveals the conserved multi-exonic structure of lincRNAs. *Nat. Biotechnol.*, 28(5):503–510, May 2010.

47. A. Hatem, D. Bozdağ, and Ü. V. Çatalyürek. Benchmarking short sequence mapping tools. Technical Report. The Ohio State University, 2011.

48. S. Hoffmann, C. Otto, S. Kurtz, C. M. Sharma, P. Khaitovich, J. Vogel, P. F. Stadler, and J. Hackermüller. Fast mapping of short sequences with mismatches, insertions and deletions using index structures. *PLoS Computat. Biol.*, 5(9):e1000502+, Sept. 2009.

49. N. Homer, B. Merriman, and S. F. Nelson. BFAST: An alignment tool for large scale genome resequencing. *PLoS ONE*, 4(11):e7767, 2009.

50. S. Huang, J. Zhang, R. Li, W. Zhang, Z. He, T-W. Lam, Z. Peng, and S-M. Yiu. SOAPsplice: Genome-wide ab initio detection of splice junctions from RNA-seq data. *Front. Genet.*, 2(0), 2011.

51. National Human Genome Research Institute, http://www.genome.gov.

52. B. G. Jackson, M. Regennitter, X. Yang, P. S. Schnable, and S. Aluru. Parallel de novo assembly of large genomes from high-throughput short reads. In *Proc. IPDPS 2010*. IEEE Computer Society, Apr. 2010.

53. B. G. Jackson, P. Schnable, and S. Aluru. Parallel short sequence assembly of transcriptomes. *BMC Bioinformatics*, 10(Suppl. 1):S14, 2009.

54. G. Jean, A. Kahles, V. T. Sreedharan, F. De Bona, and G. Raetsch. RNA-Seq read alignments with PALMapper. *Curr. Protocols Bioinformatics*, 32(11):1–11, 2010.

55. D. S. Johnson, A. Mortazavi, R. M. Myers, and B. Wold. Genome-wide mapping of in vivo protein-DNA interactions. *Science*, 316(5830):1497–1502, June 2007.

56. D. Kelley, M. Schatz, and S. Salzberg. Quake: Quality-aware detection and correction of sequencing errors. *Genome Biol.*, 11(11):R116, 2010.

57. M. Kim. Accelerating next-generation genome assembly in FPGAs: Alignment using dynamic programming algorithms. Master's Thesis. Department of Electrical Engineering, University of Washington, 2011.

58. O. Knodel, T. B. Preusser, and R. Spallek.Next-generation massively parallel short-read mapping on FPGAs. In *Proceedings of the IEEE international conference on Application-Specific Systems, Architectures and Processors (ASAP 2011)*, September 2011, pp. 195–201.

59. V. K. Kundeti, S. Rajasekaran, H. Dinh, M. Vaughn, and V. Thapar. Efficient parallel and out of core algorithms for constructing large bi-directed de Bruijn graphs. *BMC Bioinformatics*, 11(1):560+, 2010.

60. S. Kurtz, A. Phillippy, A. Delcher, M. Smoot, M. Shumway, C. Antonescu, and S. Salzberg. Versatile and open software for comparing large genomes. *Genome Biol.*, 5(2):R12, 2004.

61. L. Kuttippurathu, M. Hsing, Y. Liu, B. Schmidt, D. L. Maskell, K. Lee, A. He, W. T. Pu, and S. W. Kong. CompleteMOTIFs: DNA motif discovery platform for transcription factor binding experiments. *Bioinformatics*, 27(5):715–717, 2011.

62. B. Langmead, K. Hansen, and J. Leek. Cloud-scale RNA-sequencing differential expression analysis with Myrna. *Genome Biol.*, 11(8):R83+, Aug. 2010.

63. B. Langmead, M. C. Schatz, J. Lin, M. Pop, and S. L. Salzberg. Searching for SNPs with cloud computing. *Genome Biol.*, 10(11):R134, 2009.

64. B. Langmead, C. Trapnell, M. Pop, and S. L. Salzberg. Ultrafast and memory-efficient alignment of short DNA sequences to the human genome. *Genome Biol.*, 10(3):R25+, 2009.

65. B. Li and C. N. Dewey. RSEM: Accurate transcript quantification from RNA-Seq data with or without a reference genome. *BMC Bioinformatics*, 12:323, Aug. 2011.

66. H. Li and R. Durbin. Fast and accurate short read alignment with Burrows-Wheeler transform. *Bioinformatics*, 25(14):1754–1760, July 2009.

67. H. Li and N. Homer. A survey of sequence alignment algorithms for next-generation sequencing. *Brief. Bioinformatics*, 11(5):473–483, Sept. 2010.

68. H. Li, J. Ruan, and R. Durbin. Mapping short DNA sequencing reads and calling variants using mapping quality scores. *Genome Res.*, 18(11):1851–1858, Nov. 2008.

69. R. Li, C. Yu, Y. Li, T. W. Lam, S. M. Yiu, K. Kristiansen, and J. Wang. SOAP2: An improved ultrafast tool for short read alignment. *Bioinformatics*, 25(15).1966–1967, Aug. 2009.

70. R. Li, H. Zhu, J. Ruan, W. Qian, X. Fang, Z. Shi, Y. Li, S. Li, G. Shan, K. Kristiansen, S. Li, H. Yang, J. Wang, and J. Wang. De novo assembly of human genomes with massively parallel short read sequencing. *Genome Res.*, 20(2):265–272, Feb. 2010.

71. Y. Li, J. M. Patel, and A. Terrell. WHAM: A high-throughput sequence alignment method. *ACM Trans. Database Syst.*, 37(4):28, 2012.

72. H. Lin, Z. Zhang, M. Q. Zhang, B. Ma, and M. Li. ZOOM! zillions of oligos mapped. *Bioinformatics* (Oxford, England), 24(21):2431–2437, Nov. 2008.

73. R. Lister and J. R. Ecker. Finding the fifth base: Genome-wide sequencing of cytosine methylation. *Genome Res.*, 19(6):959–966, June 2009.

74. C.-M. Liu, T-W. Lam, T. Wong, E. Wu, S-M. Yiu, Z. Li, R. Luo, B. Wang, C. Yu, X. Chu, K. Zhao, and R. Li. SOAP3: GPU-based compressed indexing and ultra-fast parallel alignment of short reads. In *Proceedings of the third Workshop on Massive Data Algorithmics (MASSIVE 2011)*, June 2011.

75. Y. Liu, B. Schmidt, W. Liu, and D. L. Maskell. CUDA-MEME: Accelerating motif discovery in biological sequences using CUDA-enabled graphics processing units. *Pattern Recog. Lett.*, 31(14):2170–2177, 2010.

76. Y. Liu, B. Schmidt, and D. L. Maskell. DecGPU: Distributed error correction on massively parallel graphics processing units using CUDA and MPI. *BMC Bioinformatics*, 12:85+, 2011.

77. Y. Liu, B. Schmidt, and D. L. Maskell. Parallelized short read assembly of large genomes using de Bruijn graphs. *BMC Bioinformatics*, 12(1):354+, Aug. 2011.

78. Y. Liu, B. Schmidt, and D. L. Maskell. An ultrafast scalable many-core motif discovery algorithm for multiple GPUs. In *Proc. IPDPSW 2011*, IEEE Computer Society, May 2011, pp. 428–434.

79. C. A. Maher, C. Kumar-Sinha, X. Cao, S. Kalyana-Sundaram, B. Han, X. Jing, L. Sam, T. Barette, N. Palanisamy, and A. M. Chinnaiyan. Transcriptome sequencing to detect gene fusions in cancer. *Nature*, 458(7234):97–101, 2009.

80. U. Manber and G. Myers. Suffix arrays: A new method for on-line string searches. In *Proc. SODA 1990*. Society for Industrial and Applied Mathematics, Philadelphia, PA, 1990, pp. 319–327.

81. R. K. Menon, G. P. Bhat, and M. C. Schatz. Rapid parallel genome indexing with MapReduce. In *Proc. MapReduce 2011*. ACM, 2011, pp. 51–58.

82. J. R. Miller, S. Koren, and G. Sutton. Assembly algorithms for next-generation sequencing data. *Genomics*, 95:315–327, 2010.

83. S. Misra, R. Narayanan, W-K. Liao, A. N. Choudhary, and S. Lin. pFANGS: Parallel high speed sequence mapping for next generation 454-roche sequencing reads. In *Proc. IPDPSW 2010*. IEEE Computer Society, 2010.

84. S. Misra, R. Narayanan, S. Lin, and A. N. Choudhary. FANGS: High speed sequence mapping for next generation sequencers. In *Proc. SAC 2010*. 2010, pp. 1539–1546.

85. A. Mortazavi, B. A. Williams, K. McCue, L. Schaeffer, and B. Wold. Mapping and quantifying mammalian transcriptomes by RNA-seq. *Nat. Methods*, 5(7):621–628, May 2008.

86. E. W. Myer. Toward simplifying and accurately formulating fragment assembly. *J. Computat. Biol.*, 2(2):275–290, 1995.

87. L. Noè, M. Gîrdea, and Kucherova G. Designing efficient spaced seeds for SOLiD read mapping. *Adv. Bioinformatics*, 2010.

88. C. B. Olson. An FPGA acceleration of short read human genome mapping. Master's Thesis. Department of Electrical Engineering, University of Washington, 2011.

89. B. D. Ondov, A. Varadarajan, K. D. Passalacqua, and N. H. Bergman. Efficient mapping of Applied Biosystems SOLiD sequence data to a reference genome for functional genomic applications. *Bioinformatics*, 24(23):2776–2777, Dec. 2008.

90. Y. Peng, H. C. M. Leung, S-M. Yiu, and F. Y. L. Chin. IDBA—A practical iterative de Bruijn graph de novo assembler. In *RECOMB*, 2010, pp. 426–440.

91. S. Pepke, B. Wold, and A. Mortazavi. Computation for ChIP-seq and RNA-seq studies. *Nat. Methods*, 6:S22–S32, 2009.

92. P. A. Pevzner, H. Tang, and M. S. Waterman. An Eulerian path approach to DNA fragment assembly. *PNAS*, 96:9748–9753, 2001.

93. M. Pop. Genome assembly reborn: Recent computational challenges. *Brief. Bioinformatics*, 10(4):354–366, Apr. 2009.

94. S. M. Rumble, P. Lacroute, A. V. Dalca, M. Fiume, A. Sidow, and M. Brudno. SHRiMP: Accurate mapping of short color-space reads. *PLoS Comput. Biol.*, 5(5):e1000386+, May 2009.

95. Clare Sansom. Up in a Cloud? *Nat. Biotechnol.*, 28(1):13–15, 2010.

96. M. C. Schatz. CloudBurst: Highly sensitive read mapping with MapReduce. *Bioinformatics*, 25(11):1363–1369, 2009.

97. M. C. Schatz, B. Langmead, and S. L. Salzberg. Cloud computing and the DNA data race. *Nat. Biotechnol.*, 28(7):691–693, 2010.

98. M. C. Schatz, C. Trapnell, A. L. Delcher, and A. Varshney. High-throughput sequence alignment using graphics processing units. *BMC Bioinformatics*, 8(1):474, 2007.

99. J. Schroder, H. Schroder, S. J. Puglisi, R. Sinha, and B. Schmidt. SHREC: A short-read error correction method. *Bioinformatics*, 25(17):2157–2163, 2009.

100. H. Shi, B. Schmidt, W. Liu, and W. Müller-Wittig. Accelerating error correction in high-throughput short-read DNA sequencing data with CUDA. In *Proc. IPDPSW 2009*. IEEE Computer Society, May 2009.

101. H. Shi, B. Schmidt, W. Liu, and W. Müller-Wittig. Quality-score guided error correction for short-read sequencing data using CUDA. *Procedia Comput. Sci.*, 1(1):1129–1138, 2010.

102. J. T. Simpson and R. Durbin. Efficient construction of an assembly string graph using the FM-index. *Bioinformatics*, 26(12):i367–i373, 2010.

103. J. T. Simpson, K. Wong, S. D. Jackman, J. E. Schein, S. J. M. Jones, and İ. Birol. ABySS: A parallel assembler for short read sequence data. *Genome Res.*, 19(6):1117–1123, 2009.

104. A. D. Smith, Z. Xuan, and M. Q. Zhang. Using quality scores and longer reads improves accuracy of solexa read mapping. *BMC Bioinformatics*, 9(1):128+, Feb. 2008.

105. T. Smith and M. Waterman. Identification of common molecular subsequences. *J. Mol. Biol.*, 147:195–197, 1981.

106. C. Trapnell, L. Pachter, and S. L. Salzberg. TopHat: Discovering splice junctions with RNA-Seq. *Bioinformatics*, 25(9):1105–1111, May 2009.

107. C. Trapnell and M. C. Schatz. Optimizing data intensive GPGPU computations for DNA sequence alignment. *Parallel Comput.*, 35:429–440, Aug. 2009.

108. C. Trapnell, B. A. Williams, G. Pertea, A. Mortazavi, G. Kwan, M. J. van Baren, S. L. Salzberg, B. J. Wold, and L. Pachter. Transcript assembly and quantification by rna-seq reveals unannotated transcripts and isoform switching during cell differentiation. *Nat. Biotechnol.*, 28(5):511–515, May 2010.

109. K. Wang, D. Singh, Z. Zeng, S. J. Coleman, Y. Huang, G. L. Savich, X. He, P. Mieczkowski, S. A. Grimm, C. M. Perou, J. N. MacLcod, D. Y. Chiang, and J. F. Prins. MapSplice: Accurate mapping of RNA-seq reads for splice junction discovery. *Nucliec Acids Res.*, 38(18):e178, 2010.

110. Y. Wang, M. Gaurang, R. Mauani, J. Lu, T. Souaiaia, Y. Chen, A. Clark, H. J. Yoon, L. Wan, O. V. Evgrafov, J. A. Knowles, E. Deelman, and T. Chen. RseqFlow: Workflows for RNA-Seq data analysis. *Bioinformatics*, 27(18):2598–2600, 2011.

111. Z. Wang, M. Gerstein, and M. Snyder. RNA-Seq: A revolutionary tool for transcriptomics. *Nat. Rev. Genet.*, 10(1):57–63, Jan. 2009.

112. R. L. Warren, L. René, G. G. Sutton, S. J. M. Jones, and R. A. Holt. Assembling millions of short DNA sequences using SSAKE. *Bioinformatics*, 23(4):500–501, 2007.

113. P. Weiner. Linear pattern matching algorithms. In *Proceedings of the 14th Annual IEEE Symposium on Switching & Automata Theory (SWAT 2008)*, 2008, pp. 1–11.

114. G. Wu, N. Yi, D. Absher, and D. Zhi. Statistical quantification of methylation levels by next-generation sequencing. *PLoS One*, 6(6):e21034, June 2011.

115. T. D. Wu and S. Nacu. Fast and SNP-tolerant detection of complex variants and splicing in short reads. *Bioinformatics*, 7(26):873–881, 2010.

116. T. D. Wu and C. K. Watanabe. GMAP: A genomic mapping and alignment program for mRNA and EST sequences. *Bioinformatics*, 9(21):1859–1875, 2005.

117. Y. Xin, Y. Ge, and F. G. Haghighi. Methyl-Analyzer—Whole genome DNA methylation profiling. *Bioinformatics*, 27(16):2296–2297, Aug. 2011.

118. T. Ye, A. R. Krebs, M-A. Choukrallah, C. Keime, P. Plewniak, I. Davidson, and L Tora. seqMINER: An integrated ChIP-seq data interpretation platform. *Nucleic Acids Res.*, 39(6):e35, Mar. 2011.

119. D. R. Zerbino and E. Birney. Velvet: Algorithms for de novo short read assembly using de Bruijn graphs. *Genome Res.*, 18(5):821–829, 2008.

CHAPTER 44

LARGE-SCALE CLUSTERING OF SHORT READS FOR METAGENOMICS ON GPUs

THUY DIEM NGUYEN,[1] BERTIL SCHMIDT,[2] ZEJUN ZHENG,[3]
and CHEE KEONG KWOH[1]

[1]School of Computer Engineering, Nanyang Technological University, Singapore
[2]Institut für Informatik, Johannes Gutenberg University, Mainz, Germany
[3]Singapore Institute for Clinical Sciences, Singapore

44.1 INTRODUCTION

Pyrosequencing technologies are frequently used for microbial community studies based on sequencing of hypervariable regions of the 16S rRNA marker gene. Examples include profiling of microbial communities in seawater [21] and human gut [24]. The produced data sets contain reads of average lengths between 200 and 600 base pairs (bp). Typical data set sizes range from a few tens of thousand up to around a million reads. Computational analysis of these data sets can be classified into two approaches: taxonomy dependent and taxonomy independent [8]. The taxonomy-dependent approach compares the input data set against a reference nucleotide or protein database and then assigns each read to an organism based on the reported matches. This approach is both fast and accurate. Notable classifiers include the MEGAN [11], SILVA [19], and RDP classifiers [2]. However, since the vast majority of microbes are still unknown, the incompleteness of most existing reference databases has restricted the usage of taxonomy-dependent tools to only known microbes. Although this approach can differentiate unknown from known species, it cannot categorize novel microorganisms.

On the other hand, the taxonomy-independent approach does not require reference databases for classification. This approach performs hierarchical clustering and then bins input reads into OTUs (*operational taxonomic units*) based on a distance threshold. Clustering is typically computed on a pairwise genetic distance matrix derived from an all-against-all read comparison. Existing OTU clustering tools include CD-HIT [12], UCLUST [5], mothur [20], ESPRIT [23], and ESPRIT-Tree [1]. The advantage of this approach is its ability to characterize novel microbes. However, the all-against-all comparison is highly compute intensive. Furthermore, due to advances in pyrosequencing technologies, the availability and size of input read data sets are increasing rapidly. Thus, finding fast and scalable solutions is of high importance to research in this area.

In this chapter, we present a parallel tool called CRiSPy (*Computing Species Richness in 16S rRNA Pyrosequencing*) based on the pairwise global alignment approach as proposed in the ESPRIT processing pipeline by Sun et al. [23]. CRiSPy contains two different versions to support different hardware configurations: CRiSPy-OpenMP to support parallel processing on CPUs using the *open multiprocessing* (OpenMP) specification and CRiSPy-CUDA to support massively parallel processing on single GPUs and GPU clusters using the *Compute Unified Device Architecture* (CUDA) programming language and the *message-passing interface* (MPI). CRiSPy-OpenMP is more suitable for small and medium metagenomic data sets sized thousands of reads (for more information, please refer to our previous paper [25]). In this work, we focus on using CRiSPy-CUDA for large-scale data sets.

CRiSPy-CUDA is on average a hundred times faster than ESPRIT [23] and two times faster than ESPRIT's successor ESPRIT-Tree [1] while achieving similar accuracy. We attain this acceleration by designing an efficient sorting-based algorithm to compute the pairwise k-mer distances, applying massively parallel algorithms for genetic distance matrix computation based on linear memory banded semiglobal alignment and finally providing a more scalable implementation for complete linkage hierarchical clustering.

The remainder of the chapter is organized as follows. Section 44.2 provides some background information on species richness estimation. Section 44.3 presents the pairwise global alignment approach for clustering OTUs. Section 44.4 reviews several important technologies used for GPU programming in this project. Section 44.5 discusses in detail individual algorithms employed in CRiSPy-CUDA. Section 44.6 reports the runtime and accuracy profiling of CRiSPy-CUDA against other tools such as ESPRIT-Tree and UCLUST. And, finally, Section 44.7 concludes this chapter.

44.2 BACKGROUND

In terms of composition, microbial communities can be divided into two types: those containing a dominant organism and those that do not. For the former type, the dominant population will often contribute to a significant part of the metagenomes sequenced from those samples, thus making it possible to produce the near-complete genome of that governing population. In such cases, the subsequent analyses are similar to conventional genomics. In contrast, for diverse communities without a dominant species, it is nearly impossible to build the genome of any member organisms, and hence the following analyses will focus more on the averaged and combined characteristics of a community such as gene content and abundance.

To select the most suitable sample as well as to estimate the amount of sample and genetic data required for a metagenomic analysis, a pilot study to profile the composition of a community based on marker genes is often carried out. This process is called *species richness estimation*. Presently, the 16S rRNA marker gene is the most popular marker for profiling archaeal and bacterial communities (but not for viruses).

Existing methods for the taxonomy-independent approach to estimate the species richness of a microbial community can be classified into four categories:

1. *Greedy heuristic clustering* (GHC), for example, CD-HIT [12] and UCLUST [5]
2. *Multiple-sequence alignment* (MSA), for example, MUSCLE [4]

3. *Profile-based multiple-sequence alignment* (PMSA), for example, Infernal [16]
4. *Pairwise global alignment* (PGA), for example, ESPRIT [23] and ESPRIT-Tree [1]

Except for GHC, the other three categories refer to the alignment methods to generate a pairwise distance matrix. The distance matrix will later be used for the hierarchical clustering step to bin the 16S rRNA reads into OTUs. Unlike hierarchical clustering, GHC is a flat clustering method which works at a specific distance level at a time. Hence, the GHC approach is often faster than the other approaches which use hierarchical clustering. However, GHC produces clusters which are generally of lower quality than PGA [22]. Furthermore, GHC needs to run multiple times if one is interested in the clustering results at different distance levels.

A number of recent performance evaluations [10, 22] have shown that both the MSA and PMSA approaches often lead to less accurate genetic distance matrix values than the PGA approach. Despite its competitive clustering accuracy, the main drawback of the PGA approach is its high computational complexity and hence is not scalable for large data sets. For an input data set containing n reads of average length l, the time complexity of all optimal global pairwise alignments is $O(n^2 l^2)$.

We address the scalability problem of PGA by designing a fast solution for large-scale clustering of short reads for metagenomics using *graphical processing units* (GPUs) with the CUDA programming language. Recent works on using CUDA for fast biological sequences analysis [14] have motivated the use of CUDA for this project.

44.3 PAIRWISE GLOBAL ALIGNMENT

We consider an input data set $R = \{R_1, \ldots, R_n\}$ consisting of n reads (or sequences) over the DNA alphabet $\Sigma = \{A, C, G, T\}$. Let the length of R_i be denoted as l_i and the average length of all reads be l. The PGA approach consists of three steps:

1. Computation of a symmetric matrix D of size $n \times n$, where $D_{i,j}$ is the genetic distance between two reads R_i and R_j
2. Hierarchical clustering of D
3. Using the dendrogram, group reads into nonoverlapping OTUs at each given distance level d

In the PGA approach, the genetic distance $D_{i,j}$ of the two reads R_i and R_j of length l_i and l_j is usually defined as $D_{i,j} = $ ml/al, where ml denotes the number of mismatches, including gaps (but ignoring end gaps), in the optimal semiglobal alignment of R_i and R_j with respect to a given scoring system and al is the alignment length (ignoring end gaps). The optimal semiglobal alignment of R_i and R_j can be computed with the *dynamic programming* (DP)–based Needleman–Wunsch algorithm [17].

The values of ml and al can be found during the traceback procedure. If all pairwise genetic distances are computed using the Needleman–Wunsch algorithm, the overall amount of DP cells to be calculated is around $3l^2 n^2/2$. Assuming input data sizes of $n = 250,000$ and $l = 400$, as well as a computing power of 10 *giga cell updates per second* (GCUPS), this procedure would take more than 17 days. Furthermore, storing the genetic distance matrix would require 116.4 GB (using 4 bytes per entry) of memory.

ESPRIT [23] uses two techniques to reduce runtime and memory requirements:

1. *Filtration*   Filtration is done by k-mer distance computation. ESPRIT only computes genetic distances for read pairs which have a k-mer distance below a given threshold θ_k. Given two reads R_i and R_j of length l_i and l_j and a positive integer k, their k-mer distance is defined as

$$d_k(R_i, R_j) = 1 - \frac{\sum_{p=1}^{|\Omega|} \min(n_i[p], n_j[p])}{\min(l_i, l_j) - k + 1}$$

   where Ω is the set of all substrings over Σ of length k enumerated in lexicographically sorted order and $n_i(p)$ and $n_j(p)$ are the numbers of occurrences of substring number p in R_i and R_j, respectively. This approach is efficient since computation of all pairwise k-mer distances can be done in time $O(ln^2)$. It also relies on the assumptions that k-mer distance and genetic distance are correlated [4] and that a read pair with a large k-mer distance is usually not grouped into the same OTU. Lower values for θ_k would increase filtration efficiency but decrease sensitivity.

2. *Sparse Matrix Representation*   Filtration typically eliminates the majority of read pairs from further consideration. Thus, the k-mer distance matrix and the genetic distance matrix can both be efficiently stored in a sparse matrix format, which reduces memory requirements. Figure 44.1 shows the processing pipeline of the ESPRIT algorithm.

44.4   GPU PROGRAMMING

In this section, we introduce the CUDA programming and code-profiling techniques for GPUs and GPU clusters.

44.4.1   CUDA Programming for GPUs

CUDA is a parallel programming language extending general programming languages, such as C/C++, with a minimal set of abstractions for expressing parallelism. CUDA enables users to write parallel scalable programs for CUDA-enabled processors using familiar languages [18]. A CUDA program is comprised of two parts: a host program running one or more threads on a host *central processing unit* (CPU) and one or more parallel kernels which are executed on GPU(s) [13].

A *kernel* is a sequential function launched on a set of lightweight concurrent threads. The parallel threads are organized into a grid of thread blocks, where all threads in a thread block can synchronize through barriers and communicate via a high-speed, *per-block shared memory* (PBSM). This hierarchical organization of threads enables coarse-grained parallelism at the block level and fine-grained parallelism at the thread level. Threads from different thread blocks in the same grid are able to cooperate through atomic operations on global memory shared by all threads.

A CUDA-enabled processor is built around a fully programmable scalable processor array organized into a number of *streaming multiprocessors* (SMs). Each SM contains a number of *scalar processors* (SPs) and a small-sized PBSM. For the tesla-based GPU series, the number of SMs per device varies from generation to generation. For example, the state-of-the-art fermi architecture contains 16 SMs with each SM having 32 SPs. Each SM in

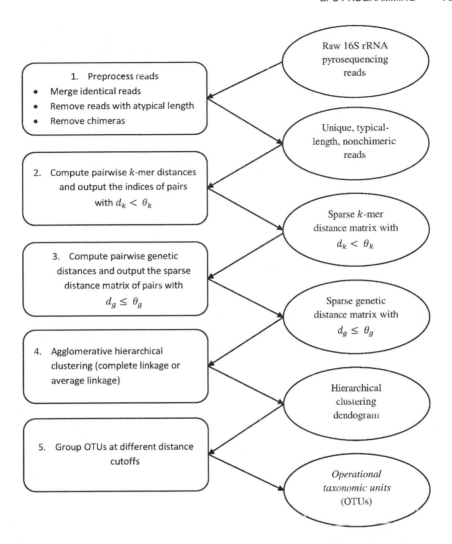

FIGURE 44.1 Processing pipeline of CRiSPy-CUDA based on ESPRIT algorithm (rectangular boxes represent computation and oval boxes denote data).

the *fermi* architecture has a configurable PBSM. This on-chip memory can be configured as 48 kB of PBSM with 16 kB of L1 cache or as 16 kB of PBSM with 48 kB of L1 cache. When executing a thread block, all threads in the thread block split into small groups of 32 parallel threads, called *warps*, which are scheduled in a *single-instruction multiple thread* (SIMT) fashion. Divergence of execution paths is allowed for threads in a warp, but SMs realize full efficiency and performance when all threads in a warp take the same execution path.

44.4.2 Profiling CUDA Codes with NVIDIA Visual Profiler

The NVIDIA Visual Profiler is a profiling tool provided by NVIDIA to help CUDA developers optimize their codes. Due to the use of NVIDIA Visual Profiler and application of

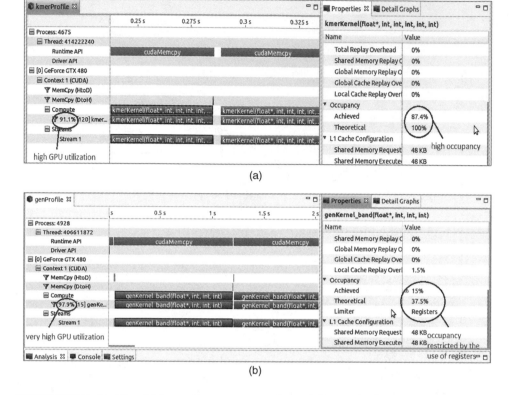

FIGURE 44.2 Profiling (a) k-mer distance computation and (b) genetic distance computation with NVIDIA Visual Profiler.

CUDA optimization techniques, the speed of k-mer distance processing has doubled and that of genetic distance processing has increased by 1.5 times compared to the previous version of CRiSPy-CUDA [25].

Figure 44.2a shows the profiling result for the k-mer distance computation. The achieved occupancy is 85.8% over the theoretical occupancy of 100%. It also achieves a high level of utilization with 91.1% of runtime for computation and only 1.6% for memory transfer. The compute/memory ratio is 58.

Figure 44.2b shows the profiling result for the genetic distance computation. Although it has fully utilized the GPU for computation with 97.9% of wall time, it has an achieved occupancy of 12.4% over the theoretical occupancy of 37.5%. The genetic distance computation is more compute intensive and requires much more memory than the k-mer distance computation. Therefore, its theoretical occupancy is limited by the number of registers required by each thread for computation. The compute/memory ratio is 417, showing that the genetic kernel is compute bound rather than memory bound.

The following practical CUDA optimization guidelines have proven effective in this project:

- Use pinned host memory and minimize the data transfer between host and device. Using pinned host memory, CRiSPy-CUDA achieves an average memory throughput of 5.9 *gigabytes per second* (GBPS) (the maximum host to device bandwidth on

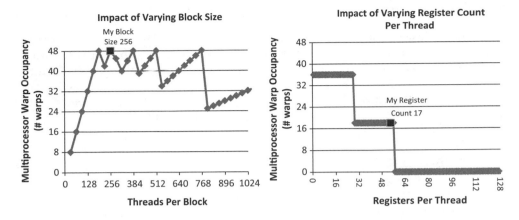

FIGURE 44.3 Occupancy profiling of k-mer distance computation (black squares represent the settings in CRiSPy-CUDA: threads per block $= 16 \times 16$, registers per thread $= 17$).

the PCI Express x16 Gen2 is 8 GBPS) in both k-mer distance and genetic distance modules, which is two times faster than if the nonpinned host memory was used.

- Optimize the use of registers and threads per block. A Fermi-based GPU has 32,768 32-bit registers per SM. Each SM can have maximum of 1024 threads (32 warps $\times$ 32 threads). For the occupancy of 100%, each thread can use up to $32{,}768/1024 = 32$ registers. One can use the CUDA occupancy calculator to help visualize the effects of the number of threads per block and the number of registers per thread to occupancy, as shown in Figures 44.3 and 44.4.

- Maximize the use of shared memory in place of local or global memory.

- Use texture memory for coalesced access of the CUDA two-dimensional array.

- Replace more expensive calculations such as multiplication and division with less expensive ones like addition and subtraction whenever possible.

- Use binary instead of text data files to speed up the file input/output process.

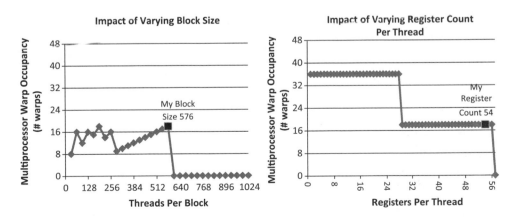

FIGURE 44.4 Occupancy profiling genetic distance computation (black squares represent settings in CRiSPy-CUDA: threads per block $= 576$, registers per thread $= 54$).

44.4.3 MPI and CUDA Programming for GPU Clusters

For the GPU cluster version, we utilize the MPI in addition to CUDA. The sparse matrix of index pairs acquired from the k-mer distance stage is divided equally among the GPUs in the cluster through the host nodes. Each GPU can then perform the pairwise genetic distance computation in parallel since they are independent. The communication between GPU and the controlling CPU threads is via device memory and its own host memory copies while the controlling CPU threads communicate with each other via MPI calls.

44.5 CRISPY-CUDA

In this section, we discuss in detail the algorithms used in CRiSPy-CUDA for k-mer distance computation, genetic distance computation, and on-the-fly complete linkage hierarchical clustering.

44.5.1 Parallel k-Mer Distance Computation

Although the computation of k-mer distances is around two orders of magnitude faster than the computation of genetic distances, it can still require a significant amount of time. Therefore, we have designed a sorting-based k-mer distance calculation method which can be efficiently parallelized with CUDA. Initially, a so-called value array V_i is precomputed for each input read R_i. It consists of all substrings of R_i of length k sorted in lexicographical order. For a pairwise k-mer distance, the two corresponding value arrays are scanned in ascending order. In each step, two elements are compared. If the two compared elements are equal, the indices to both value arrays are incremented and the corresponding counter $\min(n_1(i), n_2(i))$ is increased by one. Otherwise, only the index pointing to the value array of the smaller element is incremented. The pairwise comparison stops when the end of one value array is reached. The sorting-based algorithm is illustrated below. It requires time and space $O(l)$ for two reads of length l each.

ALGORITHM **Sorting-Based k-Mer Distance Calculation for Two Reads R_1 and R_2 of Length l_1, l_2**

```
count ← 0
i ← 0
j ← 0
while i < L₁ − k + 1 and j < L₂ − k + 1 do
   if V₁(i) < V₂(j) then
      i ← i + 1
   else if V₁(i) > V₂(j) then
      j ← j + 1
   else
      count ← count + 1
      i ← i + 1
      j ← j + 1
   end if
end while
distance ← count/(min(L₁, L₂) − k + 1)
```

The pair indices with k-mer distance smaller than a given threshold value are kept in a sparse index matrix for the subsequent processing stage. We use the threshold $\theta_k = 0.5$ as the default setting in CRiSPy-CUDA.

44.5.2 Parallel Genetic Distance Computation

In order to run as many threads as possible on GPUs, we optimize the amount of memory used in each kernel to compute an alignment of two reads. As a result, we derive a linear memory suboptimal formula for semiglobal alignment with affine gap penalty based on the Needleman–Wunsch algorithm [17]. It is suboptimal since we replace three standard scoring matrices M, V, H by one scoring matrix M and three mutually exclusive binary DP matrices U, L, D to store immediate traceback pointers. This replacement results in little effect on the alignment outcomes though it significantly reduces the amount of memory required to store an alignment cell from three integers to one integer and three Booleans (embedded in a char), thus increasing the parallelism level of the CUDA program.

The scoring matrix of the alignment is computed using the following formula:

$$M(p, q) = \max \begin{cases} M(p-1, q-1) + \text{sbt}(R_i[p], R_j[q]) \\ M(p, q-1) + \alpha D(p, q-1) + \beta U(p, q-1) \\ M(p-1, q) + \alpha D(p-1, q) + \beta L(p-1, q) \end{cases}$$

where $D, L,$ and U are binary DP matrices to indicate from which neighbor (diagonal, left, or up) the maximum in cell $M(p, q)$ is derived. Matrices $D, L,$ and U are defined as follows:

$$U(p, q) = 0: \quad L(p, q) = 0, D(p, q) = 1$$
$$\text{if } M(p, q) = M(p-1, q-1) + \text{sbt}(R_i[p], R_j[q])$$
$$U(p, q) = 0: \quad L(p, q) = 1, D(p, q) = 0$$
$$\text{if } M(p, q) = M(p, q-1) + \alpha D(p, q-1) + \beta U(p, q-1)$$
$$U(p, q) = 1: \quad L(p, q) = 0, D(p, q) = 0$$
$$\text{if } M(p, q) = M(p-1, q) + \alpha D(p-1, q) + \beta L(p-1, q)$$

Note that, except for the first row and the first column, $D(p, q) + L(p, q) + U(p, q) = 1$ for $p = 0, \ldots, l_i, q = 0, \ldots, l_j$.

To make the genetic distance calculation more suitable for parallelization, we have designed a traceback-free linear space implementation by merging the ml and al calculation into the DP computation of the optimal global alignment score. To obtain the values ml and al, we introduce two more matrices ML and AL with the recurrent relations as follows:

$$\text{ML}(p, q) = U(p, q)\,\text{ML}(p, q-1) + L(p, q)\,\text{ML}(p-1, q)$$
$$+ D(p, q)\,\text{ML}(p-1, q-1) - m(R_i[p], R_j[q]) + 1$$
$$\text{AL}(p, q) = U(p, q)\,\text{AL}(p, q-1) + L(p, q)\,\text{AL}(p-1, q)$$
$$+ D(p, q)\,\text{AL}(p-1, q-1) + 1$$

where $m(R_i[p], R_j[q]) = 1$ if $R_i[p] = R_j[q]$ and $m(R_i[p], R_j[q]) = 0$ otherwise. Initial conditions are given by $\text{ML}(0, q) = \text{ML}(p, 0) = 0$, $\text{AL}(0, q) = q$, $\text{AL}(p, 0) = p$ for $p = 0, \ldots, l_i, q = 0, \ldots, l_j$.

	-	A	T	G	A	T
-	U L D 0 0 0 / M 0 / ML AL / 0 0	U L D 0 0 0 / M 0 / ML AL / 0 1	U L D 0 0 0 / M 0 / ML AL / 0 2	U L D 0 0 0 / M 0 / ML AL / 0 3	U L D 0 0 0 / M 0 / ML AL / 0 4	U L D 0 0 0 / M 0 / ML AL / 0 5
A	U L D 0 0 0 / M 0 / ML AL / 0 1	U L D 0 0 1 / M 5 / ML AL / 0 1	U L D 0 1 0 / M 0 / ML AL / 1 2	U L D 1 0 0 / M 0 / ML AL / 1 4	U L D 0 0 1 / M 5 / ML AL / 0 4	U L D 0 1 0 / M 0 / ML AL / 1 5
T	U L D 0 0 0 / M 0 / ML AL / 0 2	U L D 0 1 0 / M 0 / ML AL / 1 3	U L D 0 0 1 / M 10 / ML AL / 0 2	U L D 0 1 0 / M 5 / ML AL / 1 3	U L D 1 0 0 / M 0 / ML AL / 1 5	U L D 0 0 1 / M 10 / ML AL / 0 5
T	U L D 0 0 0 / M 0 / ML AL / 0 3	U L D 0 1 0 / M 0 / ML AL / 1 4	U L D 0 0 1 / M 5 / ML AL / 1 4	U L D 0 0 1 / M 6 / ML AL / 1 3	U L D 0 0 1 / M 1 / ML AL / 2 4	U L D 0 0 1 / M 5 / ML AL / 1 6
A	U L D 0 0 0 / M 0 / ML AL / 0 4	U L D 0 0 1 / M 5 / ML AL / 0 4	U L D 0 1 0 / M 0 / ML AL / 1 5	U L D 0 0 1 / M 1 / ML AL / 2 5	U L D 0 0 1 / M 11 / ML AL / 1 4	U L D 0 1 0 / M 6 / ML AL / 2 5
A	U L D 0 0 0 / M 0 / ML AL / 0 5	U L D 0 0 1 / M 5 / ML AL / 0 5	U L D 0 0 1 / M 1 / ML AL / 1 5	U L D 0 0 1 / M -4 / ML AL / 2 6	U L D 0 0 1 / M 6 / ML AL / 2 6	U L D 0 0 1 / M 7 / ML AL / 2 5
T	U L D 0 0 0 / M 0 / ML AL / 0 6	U L D 0 1 0 / M 0 / ML AL / 1 7	U L D 0 0 1 / M 10 / ML AL / 0 6	U L D 0 1 0 / M 5 / ML AL / 1 7	U L D 1 0 0 / M 1 / ML AL / 3 7	U L D 0 0 1 / M 11 / ML AL / 2 7

FIGURE 44.5 DP matrices for two input reads ATGAT and ATTAAT with scoring scheme: $\text{sbt}(x = y) = 5$, $\text{sbt}(x \neq y) = -4$, $\alpha = -10$, $\beta = -5$.

Figure 44.5 illustrates an example for the computation of the DP matrices M, U, D, L, ML and AL. The dark shaded cells and arrows show the semiglobal alignment path from the cell with the largest value in the final row or final column [in this case value 7 in cell(6,5)] to any cell from the first row or the first col [in this example, cell(2,0)]. Note that this is a score-only computation and therefore requires only linear space.

Furthermore, we have employed the banded alignment concept to reduce the number of computed DP matrix cells. In this approach, only cells within a narrow band along the main diagonal are calculated. Even though some of the distance values might change, the pairwise distances can still result in a similar OTU structure after clustering. (See Section 44.6 for more details.)

An overview of the CUDA implementation on a single GPU of the genetic distance computation is shown in Figure 44.6. The pair indices and input reads are transferred to CUDA global memory, whereby reads are represented as binary strings using two bits per base: $A = 00$, $T = 01$, $G = 11$, $C = 10$.

Multiple CUDA threads can calculate the pairwise distances in parallel. During the computation, one row of DP matrix values per pairwise alignment is stored in CUDA global memory which is accessed using coalesced data transfer to reduce transfer time. Moreover, each thread within a thread block computes a DP matrix block of size 4×4

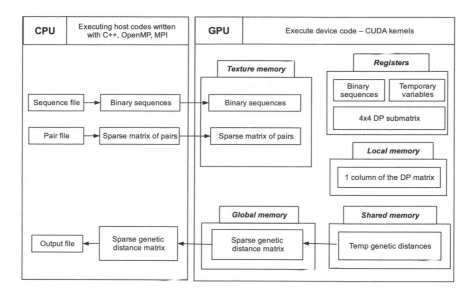

FIGURE 44.6   CUDA implementation on GPU of pairwise genetic distance computation.

using a register—the memory type with fastest access, which reduces the costly accesses to global memory by a factor of 4 and makes the kernel compute bound rather than memory bound. At the end of the computation, each thread returns a distance value to a buffer located in the per-block shared memory. The result buffer is then transferred to CUDA global memory, back to the host memory, and the CPU creates the final sparse genetic distance matrix.

44.5.3 Space-Efficient Hierarchical Clustering

Hierarchical full-linkage clustering is used for binning reads into OTUs from the linkage information provided by the sparse genetic distance matrix. Although the matrix is sparse, it is still of considerable size and often exceeds the amount of available RAM for large-scale data sets. Therefore, we have designed a memory-efficient hierarchical full-linkage clustering implementation which can deal with sparse matrices of several hundred gigabytes in size. To reduce memory, ESPRIT [23] proposed the Hcluster algorithm for complete-linkage hierarchical clustering using an "on-the-fly" strategy. Hcluster sorts the distances first and then shapes clusters by sequentially adding linkages into a linkage table. However, when the sparse matrix is very large, the sorting procedure becomes a bottleneck. We have modified the Hcluster approach to make it faster and more scalable using two techniques:

1. External merge sort to resolve the sorting bottleneck
2. Clustering using the binary tree data structure

Our approach first splits the sparse matrix into a number of smaller chunks and then sorts each chunk separately. Each sorted chunk is then stored into a separate file on the hard disk. The sorting module can be run on either a CPU or a GPU and it requires the Thrust library provided with CUDA 4.0 and above. We then merge the chunks into the complete sparse distance matrix using the queue data structure. Initially each chunk file contributes one value (the smallest value) to the value queue. If the smallest value is removed from the queue, it is replaced by the next value from the corresponding file.

The hierarchical clustering in CRiSPy-CUDA is a procedure of shaping a binary tree, where each leaf node represents a unique read. Pairwise distance values are scanned in ascending order. After a pairwise distance value is read from the file, the top parent nodes of the two corresponding reads are located and the linkage information is added. Linkage information is only stored in the top parent nodes. This approach is memory efficient and achieves a constant search time for the top parent nodes regardless of the sparse matrix size. At the end of the computation, the OTUs with respect to the given genetic distance cutoff as well as the node linkage information are outputted. Unlinked reads and reads with first linkage at high distance level are outputted as outliers.

44.6   EXPERIMENTS

In their benchmark study [22], Sun et al. have compared several popular tools for taxonomy-independent microbial community analysis including mothur [20], UCLUST [5], CD-HIT [12], ESPRIT [23], and ESPRIT's successor, ESPRIT-Tree [1]. ESPRIT-Tree was shown to be the most accurate and UCLUST to be the fastest among the aforementioned tools. Therefore, we chose to benchmark the accuracy performance of CRiSPy-CUDA against ESPRIT-Tree and profile its runtime against both ESPRIT-Tree and UCLUST.

To evaluate the performance of CRiSPy-CUDA, we took the same approach as in the aforementioned benchmark study. We took a real-world human gut data set [24] as the benchmark data set. This data set contains about 1.1 million 16S rRNA reads from V2 hypervariable regions of average length 219 base pairs.

After that, we obtained a bacterial reference data set of 7593 sequences from the RDP database [2]. These types of strain sequences are near full-length, of good quality, and from only individual isolates. We run TaxCollector [7] to annotate each reference sequence with full taxonomic information. Having prepared the reference database, we then acquired the ground-truth taxonomic information by using the UBLAST tool from the USEARCH package [5] to blast the human gut data set against the fully annotated RDP database. After running UBLAST with the stringent criterion of minimum 97% identity over a region of at least 97% of the aligned sequence length, about 400,000 reads are retained.

We have conducted the experiments in this section under the Linux operating system with the following setup. ESPRIT-Tree and UCLUST were executed on a Dell T3500 personal computer (PC) with a quad-core Intel Xeon 2.93-GHz processor and 12 GB RAM. Although CRiSPy-CUDA could run faster on a high-performance general-purpose GPU or a GPU cluster (see our previous work [25]), we chose to run it on the same PC with an attached consumer Fermi-based GPU—the NVIDIA GTX 480—to showcase the usability of CRiSPy-CUDA on common platforms.

We use the following parameters for our experiments: $k = 6, \theta_k = 0.5, \theta_g = 0.2, \mathrm{sbt}(x = y) = 5, \mathrm{sbt}(x \neq y) = -4, \alpha = -10,$ and $\beta = -5$. Please note that CRiSPy-CUDA currently only supports complete-linkage clustering, and the average-linkage clustering module used in these experiments is from the ESPRIT package [23]. Besides, to remove chimeric reads in the preprocessing stage, we use the UCHIME tool [6] from the USEARCH package [5]

We also use the concept of *normalized mutual information* (NMI) [15] as a measure for accuracy among different algorithms, where

$$\text{NMI}(\Omega, C) = \frac{2\text{MI}(\Omega|C)}{H(\Omega) + H(C)}$$

where $\Omega = \omega_1, \omega_2, \ldots, \omega_K$ is the set of ground-truth clusters and $C = c_1, c_2, \ldots, c_J$ is the set of clustering outcomes.

Given a data set of N raw sequences, the *entropies* $H(\Omega)$ and $H(C)$ are computed as

$$H(\Omega) = -\sum \frac{|\omega_k|}{N} \log_2 \frac{|\omega_k|}{N} \quad H(C) = -\sum \frac{|c_j|}{N} \log_2 \frac{|c_j|}{N}$$

where $|\omega_k|$ is the number of sequences in cluster ω_k.

The mutual information $\text{MI}(\Omega|C)$ can be computed as

$$\text{MI}(\Omega|C) = H(\Omega) + H(C) - H(\Omega|C)$$

where $H(\Omega|C)$ is the *conditional entropy* of Ω on C:

$$H(\Omega|C) = -\sum_k \sum_j \frac{|\omega_k \cap c_j|}{N} \log_2 \frac{|\omega_k \cap c_j|}{N}$$

where $|\omega_k \cap c_j|$ denotes the number of sequences that are present in both clusters ω_k and c_j.

For a test of accuracy, we randomly sampled 10 subsets from the annotated large data set, each of which contains of 30,000 reads. Each accuracy-profiling experiment was carried out 10 times on the aforesaid subsets to minimize statistical variations and average outcomes were recorded.

44.6.1   Choosing Bandwidth and Clustering Method

Figures 44.7 and 44.8 show the effect of using different bandwidths in the genetic distance computation module and the effect of different clustering methods on the accuracy of the clustering results, characterized by the NMI scores. From these two figures, we have the following observations.

First, average-linkage clustering gives a consistent performance despite the different bandwidths used for distance computation while the accuracy of complete-linkage clustering results decreases when we reduce the bandwidth for alignment.

This behavior can be explained by the observation that when the bandwidth becomes shorter, the majority of the distance matrix remains unchanged while the other distance elements become larger. The increase of those distance entries in turn affect the clustering outcomes in the case of complete-linkage clustering. At the same distance cutoff, the clusters become more and more compact when the bandwidth gets shorter and shorter, which results in more OTUs. We can see this effect clearly when looking at the number of OTUs at distance cutoff 0.03 in Table 44.1 or at distance cutoff 0.05 in Table 44.2 (under complete-linkage clustering column). Average-linkage clustering, on the other hand, is more tolerable when part of the distance matrix changes due to the bandwidth used for sequence alignment.

Secondly, while average linkage and complete linkage clustering achieve similar peak NMI scores, they peak at different distance levels. As shown in Table 44.1 and Table 44.2, average linkage clustering achieves its best NMI score at 0.05 for species assignments and

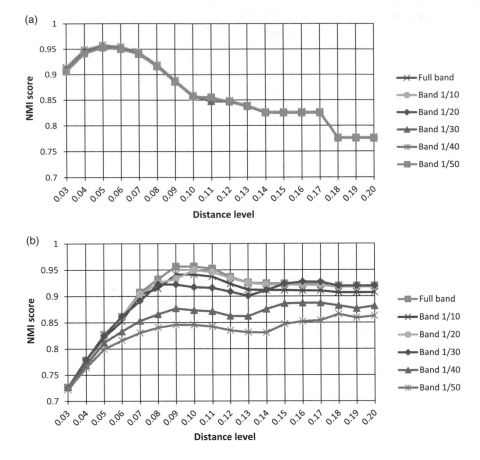

FIGURE 44.7   Accuracy profiling of CRiSPy-CUDA for species assignments: (a) average linkage; (b) complete linkage.

0.14 to 0.17 for genus assignments while the corresponding distance levels for complete linkage clustering are 0.09 to 0.18 and 0.18 to 0.20.

The second observation is consistent with the observations by Huse et al. [10] and Sun et al. [22] that different clustering methods require different distance cutoffs and the conventional cutoffs at 0.03 for species assignments and 0.05 for genus assignments should be considered carefully. Tables 44.1 and 44.2 can further support this argument. At 0.03 and 0.05, the estimated OTUs are much larger than at the distance cutoffs where peak NMI scores occur.

Figure 44.9 shows the effect of the bandwidth for sequence alignment and the chosen clustering method on the runtime of CRiSPy-CUDA. We also include the runtime of ESPRIT-Tree and UCLUST for comparison purpose. CRiSPy-CUDA with complete-linkage clustering is faster than with average-linkage clustering since average-linkage clustering requires recomputation of part of the distance matrix every time two nodes are merged while the other is not. CRiSPy-CUDA is generally faster than ESPRIT-Tree and slower than UCLUST. Please refer to Figure 44.11 for a more detailed comparison of CRiSPy-CUDA processing speed.

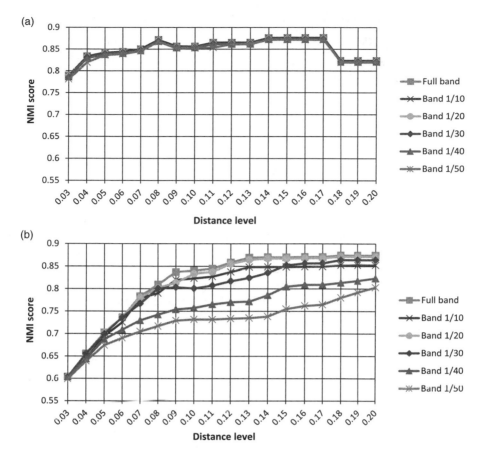

FIGURE 44.8 Accuracy profiling of CRiSPy-CUDA for genus assignments: (a) average linkage; (b) complete linkage.

Combining the above observations, we can see that average-linkage clustering achieves a more consistent performance and a better accuracy compared to complete-linkage clustering. However, since it does not employ online-learning techniques as in HCluster, the whole sparse distance matrix needs to be loaded into memory for processing. Hence, its

TABLE 44.1   Number of OTUs Observed with Species Ground Truth of 133 Species

Band width	Complete-Linkage Clustering		Average-Linkage Clustering	
	At 0.03	At Peak NMI	At 0.03	At Peak NMI
Full band	977	100 ($d = 0.09$)	444	118 ($d = 0.05$)
Band 1/10	982	105 ($d = 0.09$)	441	119 ($d = 0.05$)
Band 1/20	985	106 ($d = 0.10$)	458	129 ($d = 0.05$)
Band 1/30	985	75 ($d = 0.16$)	459	133 ($d = 0.05$)
Band 1/40	989	87 ($d = 0.16$)	462	149 ($d = 0.05$)
Band 1/50	1014	99 ($d = 0.18$)	490	161 ($d = 0.05$)

Note: d denotes distance level at peak NMI.

TABLE 44.2   Number of OTUs Observed with Genus Ground Truth of 58 Genera

Band width	Complete-Linkage Clustering		Average-Linkage Clustering	
	At 0.05	At Peak NMI	At 0.05	At Peak NMI
Full band	303	58 ($d = 0.20$)	118	48 ($d = 0.14$)
Band 1/10	305	63 ($d = 0.18$)	119	49 ($d = 0.15$)
Band 1/20	312	66 ($d = 0.18$)	129	54 ($d = 0.15$)
Band 1/30	318	69 ($d = 0.18$)	133	54 ($d = 0.16$)
Band 1/40	344	81 ($d = 0.20$)	149	57 ($d = 0.17$)
Band 1/50	391	90 ($d = 0.20$)	161	65 ($d = 0.14$)

Note: d denotes distance level at peak NMI.

processing capacity is limited by the RAM capacity. Experiments on our PC with 12 GB RAM show that average-linkage clustering can only process up to a hundred raw reads while complete-linkage clustering can process up to half a million raw reads.

For a reasonable trade-off between accuracy and speed, we recommend the use of 1/20 banded alignment with average-linkage clustering for small and medium data sets and the use of 1/20 banded alignment with complete-linkage clustering for larger data sets.

44.6.2   Assessment of Microbial Richness Estimation Accuracy

Figure 44.10 shows the accuracy profiling of CRiSPy-CUDA with different settings against ESPRIT-Tree. We observe that CRiSPy-CUDA achieves comparable accuracy performance compared to ESPRIT-Tree and hence better than other existing tools, including mothur,

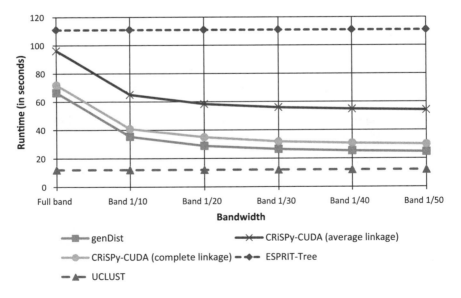

FIGURE 44.9 Runtime profiling of CRiSPy-CUDA with respect to bandwidth employed for alignment.

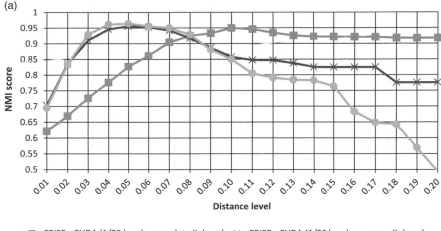

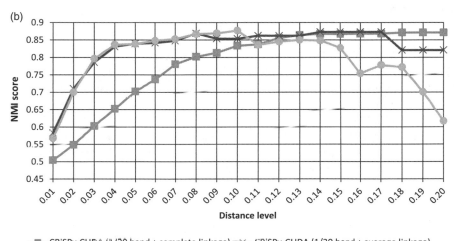

FIGURE 44.10 Accuracy profiling of CRiSPy-CUDA versus ESPRIT-Tree: (a) species assignments; (b) genus assignments.

UCLUST, and CD-HIT. We also note that the suggested setting of 1/20 and complete linkage achieve reasonable accuracy while reducing the processing time for large data sets.

44.6.3 Assessment of Processing Speed

Figure 44.11 reports the runtime of CRiSPy-CUDA, ESPRIT-Tree, and UCLUST applied to the original human gut data sets with the numbers of raw reads ranging from a hundred thousand to half a million reads.

UCLUST employs a flat clustering technique unlike the hierarchical clustering technique in CRiSPy-CUDA and ESPRIT-Tree; that is, UCLUST clusters at one distance level at a

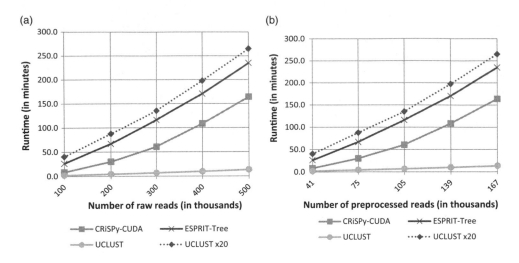

FIGURE 44.11   Runtime profiling of CRiSPy-CUDA versus ESPRIT-Tree and UCLUST: (a) versus number of raw reads; (b) versus number of preprocessed reads.

time (by default 0.03) while CRiSPy-CUDA and ESPRIT-Tree build a hierarchical tree of clusters and output the clustering outcomes at various distance levels (by default 0.01–0.20 with 0.01 step size). Therefore, to compare the relative performance of UCLUST, we have included the estimated UCLUST runtime for 20 distance levels which is annotated as UCLUST × 20 in Figure 44.11 for comparison purpose.

We observe that all three tools achieve quasi-linear time complexity. Although UCLUST is the fastest, ESPRIT-Tree is faster than UCLUST × 20. CRiSPy-CUDA is on average two times faster than ESPRIT-Tree and hence also faster than UCLUST × 20.

44.7   CONCLUSIONS

In this chapter, we presented CRiSPy-CUDA—a scalable tool for taxonomy-independent analysis of large-scale 16S rRNA pyrosequencing data sets running on low-cost hardware. Using a PC with a single CUDA-enabled GPU, CRiSPy can perform species richness estimation of input data sets up to half a million reads. Based on algorithms which are designed for massively parallel CUDA-enabled GPUs, CRiSPy achieves speedup of up to two orders of magnitude over the ESPRIT software. Since large-scale microbial community profiling becomes more accessible to scientists, scalable yet accurate tools like CRiSPy are crucial for research in this area.

Although CRiSPy is designed for microbial studies targeting DNA sequence analysis, the individual k-mer distance and genetic distance modules on GPUs can easily be extended to support protein sequence analysis and be used in general sequence analysis studies such as the usage of k-mer distance for fast, approximate phylogenetic tree construction by Edgar [3] or the utilization of a pairwise genetic distance matrix in other metagenomic processing pipelines such as CROP [9].

CRiSPy is available from the authors upon request.

REFERENCES

1. Y. Cai and Y. Sun. ESPRIT-Tree: Hierarchical clustering analysis of millions of 16S rRNA pyrosequences in quasilinear computational time. *Nucleic Acids Res.*, 39(14):e95, 2011.

2. J. R. Cole, Q. Wang, E. Cardenas, J. Fish, B. Chai, R. J. Farris, A. S. Kulam-Syed-Mohideen, D. M. McGarrell, T. Marsh, G. M. Garrity, and J. M. Tiedje. The Ribosomal Database Project: Improved alignments and new tools for rRNA analysis. *Nucleic Acids Res.*, 37(Database issue):D141–145, 2009.

3. R. C. Edgar. Local homology recognition and distance measures in linear time using compressed amino acid alphabets. *Nucleic Acids Res.*, 32(1):380–385, 2004.

4. R. C. Edgar. MUSCLE: Multiple sequence alignment with high accuracy and high throughput. *Nucleic Acids Res.*, 32(5):1792–1797, 2004.

5. R. C. Edgar. Search and clustering orders of magnitude faster than BLAST. *Bioinformatics*, 26(19):2460–2461, 2010.

6. R. C. Edgar, B. J. Haas, J. C. Clemente, C. Quince, and R. Knight. Uchime improves sensitivity and speed of chimera detection. *Bioinformatics*, 27(16):2194–2200, 2011.

7. A. Giongo, A. G. Davis-Richardson, D. B. Crabb, and E. W. Triplett. TaxCollector: Modifying current 16S rRNA databases for the rapid classification at six taxonomic levels. *Diversity*, 2(7):1015–1025, 2010.

8. M. Hamady and R. Knight. Microbial community profiling for human microbiome projects: Tools, techniques, and challenges. *Genome Res.*, 19(7):1141–1152, 2009.

9. X. Hao, R. Jiang, and T. Chen. Clustering 16S rRNA for OTU prediction: A method of unsupervised Bayesian clustering. *Bioinformatics*, 27(5):611–618, 2011.

10. S. M. Huse, D. M. Welch, H. G. Morrison, and M. L. Sogin. Ironing out the wrinkles in the rare biosphere through improved OTU clustering. *Environ. Microbiol.*, 12(7):1889–1898, 2010.

11. D. H. Huson, A. F. Auch, J. Qi, and S. C. Schuster. MEGAN analysis of metagenomic data. *Genome Res.*, 17(3):377–386, 2007.

12. W. Li and A. Godzik. Cd-hit: A fast program for clustering and comparing large sets of protein or nucleotide sequences. *Bioinformatics*, 22(13):1658–1659, 2006.

13. E. Lindholm, J. Nickolls, S. Oberman, and J. Montrym. NVIDIA Tesla: A unified graphics and computing architecture. *Micro. IEEE*, 28(2):39–55, 2008.

14. Y. Liu, B. Schmidt, and D. L. Maskell. CUDASW++2.0: Enhanced Smith-Waterman protein database search on CUDA-enabled GPUs based on SIMT and virtualized SIMD abstractions. *BMC Res. Notes*, 3:93, 2010.

15. C. D. Manning, P. Raghavan, and H. Schutze. *Introduction to Information Retrieval*. Cambridge University Press, New York, NY, 2008.

16. E. P. Nawrocki, D. L. Kolbe, and S. R. Eddy. Infernal 1.0: Inference of RNA alignments. *Bioinformatics*, 25(10):1335–1337, 2009.

17. S. B. Needleman and C. D. Wunsch. A general method applicable to the search for similarities in the amino acid sequence of two proteins. *J. Mol. Biol.*, 48(3):443–453, 1970.

18. J. Nickolls, I. Buck, M. Garland, and K. Skadron. Scalable parallel programming with CUDA. *Queue*, 6(2):40–53, 2008.

19. E. Pruesse, C. Quast, K. Knittel, B. M. Fuchs, W. Ludwig, J. Peplies, and F. O. Glckner. SILVA a comprehensive online resource for quality checked and aligned ribosomal RNA sequence data compatible with ARB. *Nucleic Acids Res.*, 35(21):7188–7196, 2007.

20. P. D. Schloss, S. L. Westcott, T. Ryabin, J. R. Hall, M. Hartmann, E. B. Hollister, R. A. Lesniewski, B. B. Oakley, D. H. Parks, C. J. Robinson, J. W. Sahl, B. Stres, G. G. Thallinger, D. J. V. Horn, and C. F. Weber. Introducing mothur: Open-source platform-independent

community-supported software for describing and comparing microbial communities. *Appl. Environ. Microbiol.*, 75(23):7537–7541, 2009.

21. M. L. Sogin, H. G. Morrison, J. A. Huber, D. M. Welch, S. M. Huse, P. R. Neal, J. M. Arrieta, and G. J. Herndl. Microbial diversity in the deep sea and the underexplored rare biosphere. *Proc. Nat. Acad. Sci. USA*, 103(32):12115–12120, 2006.

22. Y. Sun, Y. Cai, S. M. Huse, R. Knight, W. G. Farmerie, X. Wang, and V. Mai. A large-scale benchmark study of existing algorithms for taxonomy-independent microbial community analysis. *Brief. Bioinformatics*, 13(1):107–121, 2011.

23. Y. Sun, Y. Cai, L. Liu, F. Yu, M. L. Farrell, W. McKendree, and W. Farmerie. ESPRIT: Estimating species richness using large collections of 16S rRNA pyrosequences. *Nucleic Acids Res.*, 37(10):e76, 2009.

24. P. J. Turnbaugh, M. Hamady, T. Yatsunenko, B. L. Cantarel, A. Duncan, R. E. Ley, M. L. Sogin, W. J. Jones, B. A. Roe, J. P. Affourtit, M. Egholm, B. Henrissat, A. C. Heath, R. Knight, and J. I. Gordon. A core gut microbiome in obese and lean twins. *Nature*, 457(7228):480–484, 2009.

25. Z. Zheng, T. D. Nguyen, and B. Schmidt. CRiSPy-CUDA: Computing species richness in 16S rRNA pyrosequencing datasets with CUDA. *Pattern Recog. Bioinformatics*, 7036:37–49, 2011.

SECTION III

BIOLOGICAL DATA POSTPROCESSING

PART K

BIOLOGICAL KNOWLEDGE INTEGRATION AND VISUALIZATION

CHAPTER 45

INTEGRATION OF METABOLIC KNOWLEDGE FOR GENOME-SCALE METABOLIC RECONSTRUCTION

ALI MASOUDI-NEJAD, ALI SALEHZADEH-YAZDI, SHIVA AKBARI-BIRGANI, and YAZDAN ASGARI

Laboratory of Systems Biology and Bioinformatics, Institute of Biochemistry and Biophysics, University of Tehran, Tehran, Iran

45.1 INTRODUCTION

Genome-scale metabolic reconstruction is the ultimate goal of system biologists for finding out the genotype–phenotype relationship. For achieving this purpose, we need enough knowledge about the metabolic pathways and genome annotation. During the present study, we aim to describe the foundational concepts, central to omics data, model formulation, history, method, and applications of metabolic network reconstruction as well as some related sources. In Section 45.2, we describe omics data and high-throughput technologies for gaining these data. In section 45.3, we present different ways for metabolic network modeling. In section 45.4, we summarize the history of genome-scale modeling as one of the most important methods for metabolic network modeling. In sections 45.5 and 45.6, we elucidate how genome-scale metabolic models could be generated and what their applications are. Finally, in section 45.7, we review biochemical pathways and genome annotation databases.

45.2 OMICs ERA

Innovative *omics* technologies such as genomics, transcriptomics, proteomics, and metabolomics facilitate a strategy toward the simultaneous analysis of the large number of genes, transcripts, proteins, and metabolites. Therefore, a huge volume of data has generated about the make-up of cells and their behavior at various cellular levels and different environmental conditions, which enable us to reconstruct genome-scale *biomolecular networks* (e.g., transcriptional regulatory networks, interactomic networks, and metabolic networks)

Biological Knowledge Discovery Handbook: Preprocessing, Mining, and Postprocessing of Biological Data, First Edition. Edited by Mourad Elloumi and Albert Y. Zomaya.
© 2014 John Wiley & Sons, Inc. Published 2014 by John Wiley & Sons, Inc.

to perform deeper biological analyses. Furthermore, along with omic data generation, in order to compile the biomolecular networks, analytical platforms are being developed that can mathematically process raw data, integrate and curate various data types in a biologically meaningful way, and finally interpret them in a system context to properly describe cellular functions [1, 2].

As a result of these recent technological advances, our view of molecular biology has been changed so that we consider each component as a part of a complex network, not as a single entity. Moreover, to have a more accurate look at the cell biology, it has been recommended to integrate *omic data* (e.g., genome sequence, transcriptome, proteome, and metabolome) and gain a global insight into cellular behavior because it results from the action and interplay between the distinct networks in a complex web of hierarchical, multileveled and regulated dynamic processes [3]. According to Linus Pauling, "Life is a relationship among molecules and not a property of any molecule."

45.2.1 High-Throughput Technologies to Omic Data

Introduction of high-throughput technologies has provided possibility to high-content screening and analysis of cells so that over the past few decades it has become a major and indispensable tool in gaining a better understanding of cell function, disease study, and drug discovery. Moreover, their development has been accelerated in the postgenomic era since technologies such as DNA sequencing, from its first application in the early 1970s using backbreaking methods based on two-dimensional chromatography to date, has evolved dramatically, and nowadays this technology, due to the development of dye-based sequencing methods with automated analysis, has become easier and highly faster [4, 5]. As a result of this significant progress, biological research has been accelerated in the field of omics, as described in Figure 45.1, which shows an intensive increase in the number of sequenced genomes belonging to various organisms [6].

Afterward, the global methods were developed to reconstruct networks based on direct sequencing and expression array approaches, which measure changes in gene expression on a genomewide basis or at the RNA level, upon mutation or in response to environmental changes. Emerging *chromatin immunoprecipitation* (ChIp) assays analyzing genomewide location of mammalian transcription factors and ChIP-on-chip technologies, combining ChIP assays with DNA microarray, and ChIP-sequencing have provided complex and detailed information about transcriptional networks [7]. Two distinct powerful proteomic technologies, *yeast two-hybrid* (Y2H) systems and *mass spectrometry* (MS)

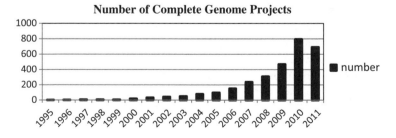

FIGURE 45.1 Progress of genome sequencing of various organisms (archeal, bacterial, and eukaryotes) from 1995 to 2011 (www.genomesonline.org).

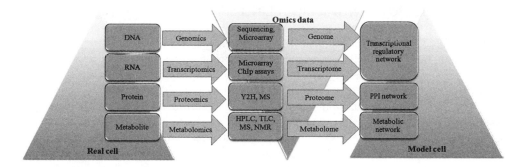

FIGURE 45.2 Schematic representation of developing a model cell from a real cell using high-throughput omics technologies.

technologies, give direct evidence of protein–protein and protein–DNA interactions in cells and identify proteins that co-*affinity purify* (co-AP) with a bait protein [8, 9]. Integration of the genomics, transcriptomics, and proteomics knowledge has allowed the assessment of the activities, regulation, and interactions of proteins in response to internal and external stimuli.

In addition, the metabolomic technologies—*two-dimensional thin-layer chromatography* (2D TLC), *high-performance liquid chromatography* (HPLC), *nuclear magnetic resonance* (NMR) spectroscopy, and MS—have provided unique opportunities for studying metabolic pathways and their response to drugs, environmental changes, and disease processes [10–13].

On the whole, these high-throughput technologies have provided a framework for understanding observations at the cell, phenotypic, or physiological level. They are also helping us to unravel the complex relationships between genes, gene products, and cellular and biological functions to develop novel therapeutic, diagnostic, and prognostic agents (Figure 45.2).

45.2.2 Metabolomics

Metabolomics is a branch of systems biology analyzing the global metabolism in the metabolite level. Indeed, metabolomics is the characterization, identification, and quantitation of metabolites resulting from a wide range of biochemical processes in metabolic pathways of living systems [14]. Today's metabolic pathways are evolved from traditional pathways, including *glycolysis*, the *pentose phosphate pathway*, and the *tricarboxylic acid* (TCA) cycle, with modern and advanced biochemical techniques such as TLC, HPLC, NMR, and MS, detecting more than hundred metabolites simultaneously [10–13].

There are some advantages to study metabolomics. First, it is simpler than transcriptomics and proteomics because of its fewer metabolite types. Second, unlike genome and proteome data, it is accompanied with more certainty. Third, some environmental perturbations or genetic manipulations have just mirrored metabolomics. It is noteworthy to mention however that it has many applications; the real power of metabolomics lies in its integration with other omic data. Now, metabolomics is considered as an emerging new tool for functional genomics and proteomic methodologies that contributes to raise our understanding of the complex molecular interactions in biological systems [15, 16].

45.3 METABOLIC NETWORK MODELING

There are three key phenomena occurring in a cell: *metabolism*, *transcription*, and *translation*. Metabolism is a well-known characterization of all the biomolecular interaction networks in biology and phenotypes, influenced at least by the biochemical reactions catalyzed by several enzymes thermodynamically: Living organisms are open systems that obey the nonequilibrium thermodynamics and self-organizational properties of complex systems and continuously exchange energy and materials with their surrounding environment. This kind of cellular uptake of energy and materials leads to a series of conversions called metabolism. Metabolism is divided into two categories: *catabolism*, in which nutrients and macromolecules break down to smaller units and high-energy compounds, and *anabolism*, in which new macromolecules and cell components are produced by simple precursors in an energy-dependent process. Metabolism is a dynamic process that allows all organisms to maintain their lives in different situations and environmental perturbations by metabolic homeostasis, robustness, and stability of biological systems, and these metabolic activities are controlled by feedback regulation mechanisms [17].

Modeling is a mathematical representation employed to define the natural system. According to Richard Feynman, "what I cannot create, I do not understand," so it seems necessary to use the modeling process to identify the variables and study the relationships among them. Modeling of metabolic systems provides a better understanding of the genotype–phenotype relationship or the physiology of the cell. Understanding metabolic diseases, application of medicines, genetic knockout, metabolic engineering, biotechnology, and the production of some essential metabolites in organisms (e.g., drugs) are the major applications of metabolic modeling. Regarding the intricate cellular processes, we cannot use comprehensive mathematical models to exactly explain metabolic processes in a cell, so different kinds of models can be used for topological description and stoichiometric and kinetic analyses [18].

Since metabolic information grew and traditional biology as well as high-throughput technologies produced enough metabolic data, system-level analysis shows that this is the time to integrate metabolic knowledge for modeling, simulation, prediction, and ultimately understanding the systemic behavior of a cell.

Kinetic modeling is used for the analysis of dynamic properties of metabolic networks that refer to a system of *ordinary differential equations* (ODEs) and *partial differential equations* (PDEs). This kind of modeling examines evolution at the time of metabolic concentrations from one state to another. Many computational tools and an extensive number of models have evolved, but the lack of enough knowledge on kinetic parameters, rate laws, rate constants, and initial concentrations leads to limitations of the kinetic models [19].

Structural modeling has a further advantage and needs less information than kinetic modeling to build the model. Structural modeling consists of two distinct analyses, *topological analysis* and *flux balance analysis* (FBA), as stated in Figure 45.3.

For the topological analysis of metabolic networks, we need a branch of discrete mathematics named *graph theory*, in which a metabolic network model is represented as a *graph*. In these graphs, vertices and edges represent the metabolites and enzymatic reaction, respectively. Many computational tools are available for analyzing global and local properties of this network, such as finding the essential nodes of a network. All the information we need in this modeling is a list of biochemical reactions [20].

Genome-scale metabolic models have emerged as valuable tools for illustrating whole-cell function, based on a complete set of reactions of biochemical networks. These models

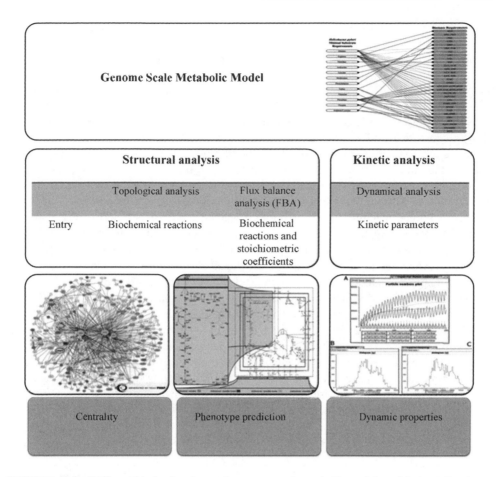

FIGURE 45.3 Different kinds of analyses of reconstructed metabolic models and their applications.

are used for the prediction of an organism's behavior. All the information we need in this modeling is a list of biochemical reactions and their stoichiometry [21, 22].

45.4 HISTORY OF GENOME-SCALE MODELS

Following the introduction of the omic era and the accumulation of comprehensive biological knowledge about individual cell types and cellular processes, the next challenge is to use the available detailed information about organisms in conjunction with modeling techniques to enhance our insight of biological systems to answer important questions in this regards. A well-established approach to this goal is the reconstruction of a genome-scale metabolic network with predictive and functional capabilities. This new approach has properly paved the way for investigating molecular processes. In 2000, the first model organism, *Haemophilus influenza,* was represented by Schilling and Palsson [23], reconstructed from 461 reactions operating on 367 intracellular and 84 extracellular metabolites. To date, due to the growing number of sequenced organisms, many predictive genome-scale metabolic models are compiled for numerous organisms, including bacterial species, yeast, fungi, and mammalian cells. Table 45.1 provides a list of existing reconstructed models for different organisms (http://gcrg.ucsd.edu/In_Silico_Organisms) [21].

In 2007, the first multispecies stoichiometric metabolic model, composed of the two strains *Desulfovibrio vulgaris* and *Methanococcus maripaludis*, with the aim of examining the mutual interactions between sulfate-reducing bacteria and methanogens, was developed by Stolyar et al. [83]. Recently, several large-scale human metabolic networks have been reconstructed for specific cell types and organelles of mammals. In 2006 Vo and Palsson [118] used the myocardial metabolic network, composed of 257 reactions and 240 metabolites, to study the perfused mouse heart. In 2008 Shlomi et al. [121] integrated a genome-scale metabolic network with tissue-specific gene and protein expression data to predict the metabolic behavior of 10 human tissues. Two years later, in 2010, Jerby et al. [116] developed a new algorithm for the rapid reconstruction of tissue-specific genome-scale models of human metabolism. The algorithm generates a tissue-specific model from the generic model of human by integrating a variety of tissue-specific molecular data sources, including literature-based knowledge, transcriptomic, proteomic, metabolomic, and phenotypic data. Applying the algorithm, they constructed the first genome-scale stoichiometric model of hepatic metabolism. Recently, in 2011, Folger et al. [114] reconstructed the first genome-scale network model for cancer metabolism, validated by correctly identifying genes essential for cellular proliferation in cancer cell lines.

Fortunately, in the near future, by sequencing more and more genomes from different organism species, the possibility of developing a large number of models and improving them will be increased. Therefore, we expect that the list of modeled organisms and cell types will continuously grow, which will be helpful in studying the genotype–phenotype relationship and cellular processes and investigating genetic metabolic disorders.

TABLE 45.1   Genome-Scale Metabolic Models of Bacteria, Achaea, and Eukaryote

Organism	Reference
Acinetobacter baumannii	[24]
Acinetobacter baylyi	[25]
Bacillus subtilis	[26, 27]
Buchnera aphidicola	[28]
Burkholderia cenocepacia	[29]
Chromohalobacter salexigens	[30]
Clostridium acetobutylicum	[31, 32]
Clostridium thermocellum	[33]
Corynebacterium glutamicum	[34, 35]
Escherichia coli	[36–39]
Francisella tularensis	[40]
Geobacter metallireducens	[41, 42]
Haemophilus influenza	[23, 43]
Helicobacter pylori	[44, 45]
Klebsiella pneumonia	[46]
Lactobacillus plantarum	[47]
Lactococcus lactis	[48]
Mannheimia succiniciproducens	[49, 50]
Mycobacterium tuberculosis	[51–53]
Mycoplasma genitalium	[54]

TABLE 45.1 (*Continued*)

Organism	Reference
Neisseria meningitidis	[55]
Porphyromonas gingivalis	[56]
Pseudomonas aeruginosa	[57]
Pseudomonas putida	[58–60]
Rhizobium etli	[61]
Rhodobacter sphaeroides	[62]
Rhodoferax ferrireducens	[63]
Salmonella typhimurium	[64–66]
Shewanella oneidensis	[67]
Staphylococcus aureus	[68–70]
Streptococcus thermophilus	[71]
Streptomyces coelicolor	[72, 73]
Synechocystis sp. PCC6803	[74]
Thermotoga maritima	[75]
Trypanosoma cruzi	[76]
Vibrio vulnificus	[77]
Yersinia pestis	[78]
Zymomonas mobilis	[79, 80]
Methanosarcina acetivorans	[81]
Methanosarcina barkeri	[82]
Desulfovibrio vulgaris/Methanococcus maripaludis	[83]
Natronomonas pharaonis	[84]
Arabidopsis thaliana	[85, 86]
Aspergillus nidulans	[87]
Aspergillus niger	[88, 89]
Aspergillus oryzae	[90]
Chlamydomonas rheinhardtii	[91, 92]
Cryptosporidium hominis	[93]
Homo sapiens	[94]
Human mitochondria	[95]
Leishmania major	[96]
Mus musculus	[97–100]
Pichia pastoris	[101–103]
Plasmodium falciparum	[104]
Saccharomyces cerevisiae	[105–110]
Synechocystis sp PCC 6803	[49, 111]
Zea mays	[112]
Zymomonas mobilis	[113]
Human cancer cell line	[114]
Human cholinergic neuron	[115]
Human GABAergic neuron	[115]
Human glutamatergic neuron	[115]
Human hepatocyte	[116, 117]
Mouse cardiomyocyte	[118]
Human alveolar macrophage and *M. tuburculosis*	[119]
Mesophyll and bundle sheath cells in C4 plants	[120]
Human brain cells	[115]

Note: References from `http://gcrg.ucsd.edu/In_Silico_Organisms` [21].

45.5   HOW GENOME-SCALE METABOLIC MODELS CAN BE GENERATED

The reconstruction process for genome-scale metabolic networks is well developed but labor intensive. The best protocol in this area of research was published by Thiele and Palsson [122]. The protocol consists of five stages:

1. Creation of draft reconstruction according to genome annotation databases of a particular organism and biochemical databases: This draft could be generated as manual curation, semiautomated or automated reconstruction and is a collection of genome-encoded metabolic functions. Drafts reconstructed by tool-based pathways (e.g., metabolic tools [123] and metaSHARK [124]) are not acceptable in comparison with manual curation. Genome annotation defines the *open reading frames* (ORFs) of an organisms' DNA sequence and its properties with respect to the genome itself. Clearly, the quality and trustworthiness of the genome annotation databases are critical to the reconstruction. In this stage, a list of metabolites that is connected by enzymatic reactions is extracted. This list will not necessarily be inclusive and comprehensive.

2. The whole draft reconstruction should be reassessed and refined. In this part, the metabolic reactions need reannotation of genes by the organism-specific literature. It is recommended that refinement should start from a canonical pathway. Some missing data can be fixed from phylogenetically closed organisms. Heteromeric enzymes, multifunctional enzymes, and isozymes must be determined for better verification and refinement. Reversibility or irreversibility of a reaction is determined by the Gibbs free energy. Metabolites must be considered in their protonation state, consistent with the pH of interest, and then a balance is necessary between every element and charges on both sides of the reaction. Incorrect representation of reaction localization can lead to additional gaps in the metabolic network and misunderstanding of network properties. Metabolite identifiers should be extracted from metabolomic and fluxomic data. Intracellular transport reactions must be considered in the case of multicompartment networks. Identification of missing functions is another part of the refinement process. The biomass composition may be different for each system and different conditions. So, it should be done with proper care. In addition, *growth-associated ATP maintenance* (GAM) reactions, NGAM (non-GAM) reactions, and demand (unbalanced reactions, which lead to the accumulation of a compound that is not allowed in the steady state) and sink (similar to demand reactions but reversible) reactions should be considered in the refinement section. Finally, requirements for the growth medium, that is, all information about the medium, such as medium composition and the presence of specific metabolites, should be considered. The more carefully this step is done, the better the model constructed and the fewer problems are confronted.

3. Mathematical representation of a metabolic reconstructing network: This step could be done automatically using different kinds of software [125]. In addition, system boundaries are defined and some constraints are simulated.

4. Network verification, evaluation, and validation: To make the model more realistic, the following points should be considered: finding the metabolic dead end (gaps) and trying to use some candidate reactions for filling them (some computational methods have been developed to predict these missing reactions or genes to fill these knowledge

gaps [126]); looking for type III–extreme pathways, which are also called *stoichio-metrically balanced cycles* (SBCs); finding reactions which could not carry any flux in all conditions (blocked reactions); and, finally, testing the ability of the model to produce each individual biomass production. The model should also be tested to determine its abilities and incapabilities to simulate different conditions. Some deletions in the model, such as single-gene-deletion, could help in understanding whether the model works well or not. Comparison of predicted physiological properties, which is done with the help of the model, with known properties is another option for testing the model. Using these tests, steps 2 and 3 should be repeated until anticipated results are obtained.

5. After obtaining the desired capability of the model, it should be used for the simulation of different conditions and getting qualitative or quantitative results.

45.6 APPLICATIONS

Since the publishing of the first *genome-scale metabolic reconstruction* (GSMR) about a decade ago [43], this field has expanded rapidly. Previous works have shown that GSMR provides an excellent scaffold for integrating data into single, coherent models. Although most models have been focused on *E. coli*, many other organisms have been studied even though there is a lack of plant metabolic reconstruction. Today, there have been more than 50 GSMRs. As a result, the application of GSMRs is very important and it is time to use these models to answer biological questions. Generally, the GSMR is used for the prediction of various phenotypes. These include the growth rates of organisms, extracellular secretion rates of the products, and the uptake rates of nutrients in addition to exploring the active routes in metabolic networks under certain growth conditions. Therefore, method development has now been substituted by application development. In this section, some GSMR applications are introduced.

As a bottom-up model, GSMR can be used to organize, classify, and make correlations between the sets of high-throughput data. For example, by using the data of gene microarrays, we can get insight into changes occurring in metabolic activity [121] since there is no obvious relationship between gene expression and protein expression [127, 128]. It could also propose some ideas about the pathways that change specifically under certain conditions [129]. The conjunction of genetic expression data and GSMR of *S. cerevisiae* leads to a better and deeper understanding of the occurrence of certain changes in gene expression under different conditions [109, 129–131]. GSMR is also considered as a framework for interpreting metabolic concentration data [132].

By definition, metabolic engineering is used for selective changes in the cellular metabolism in order to improve a specific cellular function [133]. Another application of GSMR is in metabolic engineering called *systems metabolic engineering*, which includes a network and overall look instead of a superficial insight [134]. In *S. cerevisiae*, some changes have been done to increase the production of intermediates in the TCA cycle such as malic acid and succinic acid [49, 50, 135, 136]. Usage of knockout analysis to increase a certain product is another application of GSMR [137].

Increasing the biological data leads to the introduction of different hypotheses that need to test their accuracy. Since performing experiments for different hypotheses is not practically accessible, use of GSMRs seems helpful to test them. A number of studies have been performed in this area and some led to discoveries [57, 87, 138–140].

Comparison of different organisms and finding similarities among them are other applications of GSMR [44, 70, 83, 95, 141–145]. Based on complex systems theory, a holistic approach helps better understand some network properties which are not accessible in the reduction procedure. GSMRs give an opportunity to explore these properties, such as existence of loops [146, 147], optimal pathway usage [148], metabolic connectivity [149–151], and pathway redundancy [152, 153]. Understanding the evolutionary relationships is another application of GSMRs, a new aspect of this approach and there are only a small number of papers in this field [154–156].

The growth of GSMRs will increase diversity of their applications. However, the final goal of GSMR is the development of mechanistic and predictive models which could contain whole cells [157]. In other words, it tries to link the genotype and phenotype through a mechanistic model. Here, we summarized some important applications of GSMRs. The study of Oberhardt et al. [158] explains the same approach in which the applications of GSMRs are classified into five major categories. The applications of GSMRs are focused mainly on *E. coli* [159].

45.7 BIOCHEMICAL PATHWAYS AND GENOME ANNOTATION DATABASES

As mentioned before, the literature and biochemical integration of metabolites, individual compounds, enzymes, and reactions provide the main source for knowledge needed to reconstruct the metabolic pathways. Today, with the revolution in omic data generation and ability to sequence and annotate whole genomes, the reconstruction of a genome-scale metabolic network requires knowledge and data about metabolomics, fluxomics, genome annotation, and biochemical pathways. These databases are heterogeneous and differ in their schemes, software architecture, query capabilities, user interface, and the content of information stored in terms of reactions and pathways [160]. Along with the increasing metabolomic information, many metabolomic databases have been designed that can be classified into two major groups according to their data content:

1. *Reference metabolite profile databases*, including the spectral databases/library, species-specific metabolite profile databases, compound databases, and pathway databases
2. The metabolomic *Laboratory Information Management System* (LIMS), which stores the experimental work flows [14]

This section has represented a review of some general and specific databases that are needed for the integration of metabolic knowledge to perform metabolic reconstruction (Figure 45.4).

Metabolic network reconstruction often integrates many knowledge data sets representing different facets of metabolic networks (i.e., biochemical knowledge, metabolomics, genome annotation, fluxomic knowledge, etc.). Public data are available via the literature or collections of high-throughput databases. Here we list a series of useful databases for genome-scale metabolic reconstruction:

- **KEGG** *Kyoto Encyclopedia of Genes and Genomes* is a knowledge database for systematic analysis of gene functions in terms of the networks of genes and molecules (http://www.genome.jp/kegg).

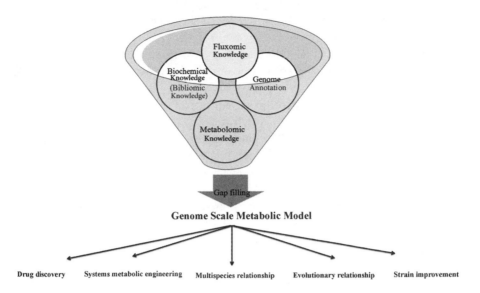

FIGURE 45.4   Integration of metabolic knowledge for genome-scale metabolic reconstruction.

- *EcoCyc*   A database for the bacterium *E. coli* K-12 MG1655 that performs literature-based curation of the entire genome, transcriptional regulation, transporters, and metabolic pathways (`http://ecocyc.org`).
- *BioCyc*   Each database in the BioCyc collection describes the genome and metabolic pathways of a single organism (`http://biocyc.org`).
- **BRENDA**   A comprehensive enzyme information system (`http://www.brenda-enzymes.org`).
- **UMBBD**   Lists and describes microbial pathways for the enzymatic degradation of numerous synthetic compounds (`http://umbbd.msi.umn.edu`).
- *BioCarta*   Developer, supplier, and distributor of uniquely sourced and characterized reagents (`http://www.biocarta.com`).
- *Reactome*   A curated pathway database encompassing many areas of human biology (`http://www.genomeknowledge.org`).
- **BiGG**   A knowledge base of biochemically, genetically, and genomically structured genome-scale metabolic network reconstructions. Integrates several published genome-scale metabolic networks into one resource with standard nomenclature, which allows components to be compared across different organisms (`http://bigg.ucsd.edu`).
- **CycADS**   Cyc Annotation Database System is an automated annotation management system that allows the seamless integration of the latest sequence information into metabolic network reconstruction (`http://www.cycadsys.org`).
- **OMMBID**   The Online Metabolic and Molecular Basis of Inherited Diseases (`http://www.ommbid.com`).
- **HPD**   Integrated human pathway database providing comprehensive and combined view connecting human proteins, genes, RNAs, enzymes, signaling, metabolic reactions, and gene regulatory events (`http://discern.uits.iu.edu:8340/HPD`).

- *BioSilico*   Allows users to efficiently retrieve the relevant information on enzymes, biochemical compounds, and reactions (http://biosilico.kaist.ac.kr).

- **ENZYME**   A repository of information relative to the nomenclature of enzymes and describes each type of characterized enzyme for which an EC number has been provided (http://enzyme.expasy.org).

- *PathCase*   All applications store, query, and visualize metabolic pathways in addition to their specialized tasks (http://nashua.case.edu/pathwaysweb).

- *Metabolic Disease Database*   The tumor expression metabolome that takes into account the fact that different tissues with totally different basic metabolism, such as liver and brain, generally shift to the same metabolic phenotype during tumorigenesis (http://www.metabolic-database.com).

- **GMD**   The *Golm Metabolome Database* provides public access to custom mass spectra libraries, metabolite profiling experiments, and other necessary information related to the field of metabolomics (http://csbdb.mpimp-golm.mpg.de).

- **HMDB**   Human Metabolomic Database is designed for three kinds of data related to *Homo sapiens*: (1) chemical, (2) clinical, and (3) molecular biology/biochemistry data (http://www.hmdb.ca).

- **MMCD**   Madison Metabolomic Consortium Database is a resource for metabolomics research based on NMR spectroscopy and MS (http://mmcd.nmrfam.wisc.edu).

- **PMN**   A central feature of the PMN is PlantCyc, a comprehensive plant biochemical pathway database containing curated information from the literature and computational analyses about the genes, enzymes, compounds, reactions, and pathways involved in primary and secondary metabolism (http://plantcyc.org).

- *MetaCyc*   A database of nonredundant, experimentally elucidated metabolic pathways involved in both primary and secondary metabolism as well as the associated compounds, enzymes, and genes (http://www.metacyc.org).

- *PlantGDB*   Plant Genome Database provides genome browsers with a display of current gene structure models and transcript evidence from spliced alignments of EST and cDNA sequences (http://www.plantgdb.org).

- *MetaCrop*   A database that summarizes diverse information about metabolic pathways in crop plants and allows automatic export of information for the creation of detailed metabolic models (metacrop.ipk-gatersleben.de).

- *Entrez Genome Database Search*   Organizes information on genomes, including maps, chromosomes, assemblies, and annotations (http://www.ncbi.nlm.nih.gov).

- *Ensembl Genome Browser*   Produces genome databases for vertebrates and other eukaryotic species (http://www.ensembl.org).

- *Animal Genome Size Database*   A comprehensive catalogue of animal genome size data (http://www.genomesize.com).

- *Vertebrate Genome Annotation*   A central repository for high-quality manual annotation of a complete vertebrate genome sequence (http://vega.sanger.ac.uk).

- *Organism Database*   Includes the genome database of several organisms (http://saf.bio.caltech.edu).

- **IMG** Integrated Microbial Genomes serves as a community resource for comparative analysis and annotation of all publicly available genomes from three domains of life (`http://img.jgi.doe.gov`).
- *G-compass* A comparative genome browser. It visualizes evolutionarily conserved genomic regions between human and 12 other vertebrates (`http://www.h-invitational.jp`).
- **H-InvDB** An Integrated Database of Annotated Human Genes and transcripts (`http://www.h-invitational.jp`).
- *euGenes* A genomic information database for eukaryotic organisms (`http://eugenes.org`).
- **GOLD** *Genome On-line Database* is a comprehensive resource that provides information on genome and metagenome projects (`http://genomesonline.org`).
- **Genome Reviews** A database that provides an up-to-date, standardized, and comprehensively annotated view of the genomic sequence of organisms with completely deciphered genomes (`http://www.ebi.ac.uk/GenomeReviews`).

In addition to these databases, there are repositories that store the full metabolic reconstructed networks, such as BiGG, CycSim (`www.genoscope.cns.fr/cycsim`), CellML (`http://www.cellml.org`), E-Cell (`http://www.e-cell.org`), and Biomodels (`http://www.ebi.ac.uk/biomodels-main`).

45.8 CONCLUSION

Since the advent of systems biology and the omic era, a wealth of metabolic knowledge has been generated and its application for reconstructing genome-scale metabolic models.

Although the first reconstructed genome-scale metabolic model dates back to 2000, to date more than 100 models have been introduced.

Today the major challenge of the biological sciences and medicine is in finding the molecular basis of disorders to design and target the most efficient drugs. To this goal, genome-scale metabolic reconstruction can help to develop mechanistic and predictive models with the aim of answering biological questions, unraveling the genotype–phenotype relationship, and gaining a better knowledge of cell behavior in light of the systems biology approach.

REFERENCES

1. M. W. Covert et al. Metabolic modeling of microbial strains in silico. *Trends Biochem. Sci.*, 26:179–186, 2001.
2. B. Palsson and K. Zengler. The challenges of integrating multi-omic data sets. *Nat. Chem. Biol.*, 6:787–789, 2010.
3. S. C. De Keersmaecker, I. M. Thijs, J. Vanderleyden, and K. Marchal. Integration of omics data: How well does it work for bacteria? *Mol. Microbiol.*, 62:1239–1250, 2006.
4. E. Pettersson, J. Lundeberg, and A. Ahmadian. Generations of sequencing technologies. *Genomics*, 93:105–111, 2009.

5. O. Olsvik et al. Use of automated sequencing of polymerase chain reaction-generated amplicons to identify three types of cholera toxin subunit B in Vibrio cholerae O1 strains. *J. Clin. Microbiol.*, 31:22–25, 1993.

6. I. Pagani et al. The Genomes OnLine Database (GOLD) v.4: Status of genomic and metagenomic projects and their associated metadata. *Nucleic Acids Res.* 40:D571–579, 2012.

7. B. Ren and B. D. Dynlacht. Use of chromatin immunoprecipitation assays in genome-wide location analysis of mammalian transcription factors. *Methods Enzymol.*, 376:304–315, 2004.

8. K. H. Young. Yeast two-hybrid: So many interactions, (in) so little time. *Biol. Reprod.*, 58:302–311, 1998.

9. A. Pandey and M. Mann. Proteomics to study genes and genomes. *Nature*, 405:837–846, 2000.

10. J. A. Papin, N. D. Price, S. J. Wiback, D. A. Fell, and B. O. Palsson. Metabolic pathways in the post-genome era. *Trends Biochem. Sci.*, 28:250–258, 2003.

11. R. P. Maharjan and T. Ferenci. Global metabolite analysis: The influence of extraction methodology on metabolome profiles of *Escherichia coli*. *Anal. Biochem.*, 313:145–154, 2003.

12. J. Zaldivar et al. Fermentation performance and intracellular metabolite patterns in laboratory and industrial xylose-fermenting *Saccharomyces cerevisiae*. *Appl. Microbiol. Biotechnol.*, 59:436–442, 2002.

13. J. I. Castrillo, A. Hayes, S. Mohammed, S. J. Gaskell, and S. G. Oliver. An optimized protocol for metabolome analysis in yeast using direct infusion electrospray mass spectrometry. *Phytochemistry*, 62:929–937, 2003.

14. E. P. Go. Database resources in metabolomics: An overview. *J. Neuroimmune Pharmacol*, 5:18–30, 2009.

15. Q. Z. Wang, C. Y. Wu, T. Chen, X. Chen, and X. M. Zhao. Integrating metabolomics into a systems biology framework to exploit metabolic complexity: Strategies and applications in microorganisms. *Appl. Microbiol. Biotechnol.*, 70:151–161, 2006.

16. A. Lafaye et al. Combined proteome and metabolite-profiling analyses reveal surprising insights into yeast sulfur metabolism. *J. Biol. Chem.*, 280:24723–24730, 2005.

17. M. Jeremy and J. L. T. Berg. *Biochemistry*. W. H. Freeman, New York, 2002.

18. O. Wolkenhauer. Mathematical modelling in the post-genome era: Understanding genome expression and regulation—A system theoretic approach. *Biosystems*, 65:1–18, 2002.

19. S. Hoops et al. COPASI—A COmplex PAthway SImulator. *Bioinformatics*, 22:3067–3074, 2006.

20. A. L. Barabasi and Z. N. Oltvai. Network biology: Understanding the cell's functional organization. *Nat. Rev. Genet.*, 5:101–113, 2004.

21. A. M. Feist, M. J. Herrgard, I. Thiele, J. L. Reed, and B. O. Palsson. Reconstruction of biochemical networks in microorganisms. *Nat. Rev. Microbiol.*, 7:129–143, 2009.

22. M. G. Poolman, B. K. Bonde, A. Gevorgyan, H. H. Patel, and D. A. Fell. Challenges to be faced in the reconstruction of metabolic networks from public databases. *Syst. Biol. (Stevenage)*, 153:379–384, 2006.

23. C. H. Schilling and B. O. Palsson. Assessment of the metabolic capabilities of *Haemophilus influenzae* Rd through a genome-scale pathway analysis. *J. Theor. Biol.*, 203:249–283, 2000.

24. H. U. Kim, T. Y. Kim, and S. Y. Lee. Genome-scale metabolic network analysis and drug targeting of multi-drug resistant pathogen *Acinetobacter baumannii* AYE. *Mol. Biosyst.*, 6:339–348, 2010.

25. M. Durot et al. Iterative reconstruction of a global metabolic model of *Acinetobacter baylyi* ADP1 using high-throughput growth phenotype and gene essentiality data. *BMC Syst. Biol.*, 2:85, 2008.

26. Y. K. Oh, B. O. Palsson, S. M. Park, C. H. Schilling, and R. Mahadevan. Genome-scale reconstruction of metabolic network in *Bacillus subtilis* based on high-throughput phenotyping and gene essentiality data. *J. Biol. Chem.*, 282:28791–28799, 2007.

27. C. S. Henry, J. F. Zinner, M. P. Cohoon, and R. L. Stevens. iBsu1103: A new genome-scale metabolic model of *Bacillus subtilis* based on SEED annotations. *Genome Biol.*, 10:R69, 2009.

28. G. H. Thomas et al. A fragile metabolic network adapted for cooperation in the symbiotic bacterium *Buchnera aphidicola. BMC Syst. Biol.*, 3:24, 2009.

29. K. Fang et al. Exploring the metabolic network of the epidemic pathogen *Burkholderia cenocepacia* J2315 via genome-scale reconstruction. *BMC Syst. Biol.*, 5:83, 2011.

30. O. Ates, E. T. Oner, and K. Y. Arga. Genome-scale reconstruction of metabolic network for a halophilic extremophile, *Chromohalobacter salexigens* DSM 3043. *BMC Syst. Biol.*, 5:12, 2011.

31. R. S. Senger and E. T. Papoutsakis. Genome-scale model for *Clostridium acetobutylicum*: Part II. Development of specific proton flux states and numerically determined sub-systems. *Biotechnol Bioeng.*, 101:1053–1071, 2008.

32. J. Lee, H. Yun, A. M. Feist, B. O. Palsson, and S. Y. Lee. Genome-scale reconstruction and in silico analysis of the *Clostridium acetobutylicum* ATCC 824 metabolic network. *Appl. Microbiol. Biotechnol.*, 80:849–862, 2008.

33. S. B. Roberts, C. M. Gowen, J. P. Brooks, and S. S. Fong. Genome-scale metabolic analysis of *Clostridium thermocellum* for bioethanol production. *BMC Syst. Biol.*, 4:31, 2010.

34. K. R. Kjeldsen and J. Nielsen. In silico genome-scale reconstruction and validation of the *Corynebacterium glutamicum* metabolic network. *Biotechnol. Bioeng.*, 102:583–597, 2009.

35. Y. Shinfuku et al. Development and experimental verification of a genome-scale metabolic model for *Corynebacterium glutamicum. Microb. Cell. Fact*, 8:43, 2009.

36. J. S. Edwards and B. O. Palsson. The *Escherichia coli* MG1655 in silico metabolic genotype: Its definition, characteristics, and capabilities. *Proc. Natl. Acad. Sci. USA*, 97:5528–5533, 2000.

37. J. L. Reed, T. D. Vo, C. H. Schilling, and B. O. Palsson. An expanded genome-scale model of *Escherichia coli* K-12 (iJR904 GSM/GPR). *Genome Biol.*, 4:R54, 2003.

38. A. M. Feist et al. A genome-scale metabolic reconstruction for *Escherichia coli* K-12 MG1655 that accounts for 1260 ORFs and thermodynamic information. *Mol. Syst. Biol.*, 3:121, 2007.

39. J. D. Orth et al. A comprehensive genome-scale reconstruction of *Escherichia coli* metabolism. *Mol. Syst. Biol.*, 7.535, 2011.

40. A. Raghunathan, S. Shin, and S. Daefler. Systems approach to investigating host-pathogen interactions in infections with the biothreat agent *Francisella*. Constraints-based model of *Francisella tularensis. BMC Syst. Biol.*, 4:118, 2010.

41. J. Sun et al. Genome-scale constraint-based modeling of *Geobacter metallireducens. BMC Syst. Biol.*, 3:15, 2009.

42. R. Mahadevan, B. O. Palsson, and D. R. Lovley. In situ to in silico and back: Elucidating the physiology and ecology of *Geobacter* spp. using genome-scale modelling. *Nat. Rev. Microbiol.*, 9:39–50, 2010.

43. J. S. Edwards and B. O. Palsson. Systems properties of the *Haemophilus influenzae* Rd metabolic genotype. *J. Biol. Chem.*, 274:17410–17416, 1999.

44. C. H. Schilling et al. Genome-scale metabolic model of *Helicobacter pylori* 26695. *J. Bacteriol.*, 184:4582–4593, 2002.

45. I. Thiele, T. D. Vo, N. D. Price, and B. O. Palsson. Expanded metabolic reconstruction of *Helicobacter pylori* (iIT341 GSM/GPR): An in silico genome-scale characterization of single- and double-deletion mutants. *J. Bacteriol.*, 187:5818–5830, 2005.

46. Y. C. Liao et al. An experimentally validated genome-scale metabolic reconstruction of *Klebsiella pneumoniae* MGH 78578, iYL1228. *J. Bacteriol.*, 193:1710–1717, 2011.

47. B. Teusink et al. In silico reconstruction of the metabolic pathways of *Lactobacillus plantarum*: Comparing predictions of nutrient requirements with those from growth experiments. *Appl. Environ. Microbiol.*, 71:7253–7262, 2005.

48. A. P. Oliveira, J. Nielsen, and J. Forster. Modeling *Lactococcus lactis* using a genome-scale flux model. *BMC Microbiol.*, 5:39, 2005.

49. S. H. Hong et al. The genome sequence of the capnophilic rumen bacterium *Mannheimia succiniciproducens*. *Nat. Biotechnol.*, 22:1275–1281, 2004.

50. T. Y. Kim et al. Genome-scale analysis of *Mannheimia succiniciproducens* metabolism. *Biotechnol. Bioeng.*, 97:657–671, 2007.

51. N. Jamshidi and B. O. Palsson. Investigating the metabolic capabilities of *Mycobacterium tuberculosis* H37Rv using the in silico strain iNJ661 and proposing alternative drug targets. *BMC Syst. Biol.*, 1:26, 2007.

52. D. J. Beste et al. GSMN-TB: A web-based genome-scale network model of *Mycobacterium tuberculosis* metabolism. *Genome Biol.*, 8:R89, 2007.

53. X. Fang, A. Wallqvist, and J. Reifman. Development and analysis of an in vivo-compatible metabolic network of *Mycobacterium tuberculosis*. *BMC Syst. Biol.*, 4:160, 2010.

54. P. F. Suthers et al. A genome-scale metabolic reconstruction of *Mycoplasma genitalium*, iPS189. *PLoS Comput. Biol.*, 5:e1000285, 2009.

55. G. J. Baart et al. Modeling *Neisseria meningitidis* metabolism: From genome to metabolic fluxes. *Genome Biol.*, 8:R136, 2007.

56. V. Mazumdar, E. S. Snitkin, S. Amar, and D. Segre. Metabolic network model of a human oral pathogen. *J. Bacteriol.*, 191:74–90, 2009.

57. M. A. Oberhardt, J. Puchalka, K. E. Fryer, V. A. Martins dos Santos, and J. A. Papin. Genome-scale metabolic network analysis of the opportunistic pathogen *Pseudomonas aeruginosa* PAO1. *J. Bacteriol.*, 190:2790–2803, 2008.

58. J. Nogales, B. O. Palsson, and I. Thiele. A genome-scale metabolic reconstruction of *Pseudomonas putida* KT2440: iJN746 as a cell factory. *BMC Syst. Biol.*, 2:79, 2008.

59. J. Puchalka et al. Genome-scale reconstruction and analysis of the *Pseudomonas putida* KT2440 metabolic network facilitates applications in biotechnology. *PLoS Comput. Biol.*, 4:e1000210, 2008.

60. S. B. Sohn, T. Y. Kim, J. M. Park, and S. Y. Lee. In silico genome-scale metabolic analysis of *Pseudomonas putida* KT2440 for polyhydroxyalkanoate synthesis, degradation of aromatics and anaerobic survival. *Biotechnol. J.*, 5:739–750, 2010.

61. O. Resendis-Antonio, J. L. Reed, S. Encarnacion, J. Collado-Vides, and B. O. Palsson. Metabolic reconstruction and modeling of nitrogen fixation in *Rhizobium etli*. *PLoS Comput. Biol.*, 3:1887–1895, 2007.

62. S. Imam et al. iRsp1095: A genome-scale reconstruction of the *Rhodobacter sphaeroides* metabolic network. *BMC Syst. Biol.*, 5:116, 2011.

63. C. Risso et al. Genome-scale comparison and constraint-based metabolic reconstruction of the facultative anaerobic Fe(III)-reducer *Rhodoferax ferrireducens*. *BMC Genomics*, 10:447, 2009.

64. A. Raghunathan, J. Reed, S. Shin, B. Palsson, and S. Daefler. Constraint-based analysis of metabolic capacity of *Salmonella typhimurium* during host-pathogen interaction. *BMC Syst. Biol.*, 3:38, 2009.

65. M. AbuOun et al. Genome scale reconstruction of a *Salmonella* metabolic model: Comparison of similarity and differences with a commensal *Escherichia coli* strain. *J. Biol. Chem.*, 284:29480–29488, 2009.

66. I. Thiele et al. A community effort towards a knowledge-base and mathematical model of the human pathogen *Salmonella Typhimurium* LT2. *BMC Syst. Biol.*, 5:8, 2011.

67. G. E. Pinchuk et al. Constraint-based model of *Shewanella oneidensis* MR-1 metabolism: A tool for data analysis and hypothesis generation. *PLoS Comput. Biol.*, 6:e1000822, 2010.

68. S. A. Becker and B. O. Palsson. Genome-scale reconstruction of the metabolic network in *Staphylococcus aureus* N315: An initial draft to the two-dimensional annotation. *BMC Microbiol.*, 5:8, 2005.

69. M. Heinemann, A. Kummel, R. Ruinatscha, and S. Panke. In silico genome-scale reconstruction and validation of the *Staphylococcus aureus* metabolic network. *Biotechnol. Bioeng.*, 92:850–864, 2005.

70. D. S. Lee et al. Comparative genome-scale metabolic reconstruction and flux balance analysis of multiple *Staphylococcus aureus* genomes identify novel antimicrobial drug targets. *J. Bacteriol.*, 191:4015–4024, 2009.

71. M. I. Pastink et al. Genome-scale model of *Streptococcus thermophilus* LMG18311 for metabolic comparison of lactic acid bacteria. *Appl. Environ. Microbiol.*, 75:3627–3633, 2009.

72. I. Borodina, P. Krabben, and J. Nielsen. Genome-scale analysis of *Streptomyces coelicolor* A3(2) metabolism. *Genome Res.*, 15:820–829, 2005.

73. M. T. Alam et al. Metabolic modeling and analysis of the metabolic switch in *Streptomyces coelicolor*. *BMC Genomics*, 11:202, 2010.

74. A. Montagud et al. Flux coupling and transcriptional regulation within the metabolic network of the photosynthetic bacterium *Synechocystis* sp. PCC6803. *Biotechnol. J.*, 6:330–342, 2011.

75. Y. Zhang et al. Three-dimensional structural view of the central metabolic network of *Thermotoga maritima*. *Science*, 325:1544–1549, 2009.

76. S. B. Roberts et al. Proteomic and network analysis characterize stage-specific metabolism in *Trypanosoma cruzi*. *BMC Syst. Biol.*, 3:52, 2009.

77. H. U. Kim et al. Integrative genome-scale metabolic analysis of *Vibrio vulnificus* for drug targeting and discovery. *Mol. Syst. Biol.*, 7:460, 2011.

78. A. Navid and E. Almaas. Genome-scale reconstruction of the metabolic network in *Yersinia pestis*, strain 91001. *Mol. Biosyst.*, 5:368–375, 2009.

79. K. Y. Lee, J. M. Park, T. Y. Kim, H. Yun, and S. Y. Lee. The genome-scale metabolic network analysis of *Zymomonas mobilis* ZM4 explains physiological features and suggests ethanol and succinic acid production strategies. *Microb. Cell. Fact*, 9:94, 2010.

80. H. Widiastuti et al. Genome-scale modeling and in silico analysis of ethanologenic bacteria *Zymomonas mobilis*. *Biotechnol. Bioeng.*, 108:655–665, 2010.

81. V. Satish Kumar, J. G. Ferry, and C. D. Maranas. Metabolic reconstruction of the archaeon methanogen *Methanosarcina acetivorans*. *BMC Syst. Biol.*, 5:28, 2011.

82. A. M. Feist, J. C. Scholten, B. O. Palsson, F. J. Brockman, and T. Ideker. Modeling methanogenesis with a genome-scale metabolic reconstruction of *Methanosarcina barkeri*. *Mol. Syst. Biol.*, 2:2006.0004, 2006.

83. S. Stolyar et al. Metabolic modeling of a mutualistic microbial community. *Mol. Syst. Biol.*, 3:92, 2007.

84. O. Gonzalez et al. Characterization of growth and metabolism of the haloalkaliphile *Natronomonas pharaonis*. *PLoS Comput. Biol.*, 6:e1000799, 2010.

85. C. G. de Oliveira Dal'Molin, L. E. Quek, R. W. Palfreyman, S. M. Brumbley, and L. K. Nielsen. AraGEM, a genome-scale reconstruction of the primary metabolic network in *Arabidopsis*. *Plant Physiol.*, 152:579–589, 2010.

86. D. Saha et al. In silico analysis of the lateral organ junction (LOJ) gene and promoter of *Arabidopsis thaliana*. *In Silico. Biol.*, 7:7–19, 2007.

87. H. David, I. S. Ozcelik, G. Hofmann, and J. Nielsen. Analysis of *Aspergillus nidulans* metabolism at the genome-scale. *BMC Genomics*, 9:163, 2008.

88. M. R. Andersen, M. L. Nielsen, and J. Nielsen. Metabolic model integration of the bibliome, genome, metabolome and reactome of *Aspergillus niger*. *Mol. Syst. Biol.*, 4:178, 2008.

89. H. David, M. Akesson, and J. Nielsen. Reconstruction of the central carbon metabolism of *Aspergillus niger*. *Eur. J. Biochem.*, 270:4243–4253, 2003.

90. W. Vongsangnak, P. Olsen, K. Hansen, S. Krogsgaard, and J. Nielsen. Improved annotation through genome-scale metabolic modeling of *Aspergillus oryzae*. *BMC Genomics*, 9:245, 2008.

91. R. L. Chang et al. Metabolic network reconstruction of *Chlamydomonas* offers insight into light-driven algal metabolism. *Mol. Syst. Biol.*, 7:518, 2011.

92. N. R. Boyle and J. A. Morgan. Flux balance analysis of primary metabolism in *Chlamydomonas reinhardtii*. *BMC Syst. Biol.*, 3:4, 2009.

93. N. Vanee, S. B. Roberts, S. S. Fong, P. Manque, and G. A. Buck. A genome-scale metabolic model of *Cryptosporidium hominis*. *Chem. Biodivers.*, 7:1026–1039, 2010.

94. N. C. Duarte et al. Global reconstruction of the human metabolic network based on genomic and bibliomic data. *Proc. Natl. Acad. Sci. USA*, 104:1777–1782, 2007.

95. T. D. Vo, W. N. Paul Lee, and B. O. Palsson. Systems analysis of energy metabolism elucidates the affected respiratory chain complex in Leigh's syndrome. *Mol. Genet. Metab.*, 91:15–22, 2007.

96. A. K. Chavali, J. D. Whittemore, J. A. Eddy, K. T. Williams, and J. A. Papin. Systems analysis of metabolism in the pathogenic trypanosomatid *Leishmania major*. *Mol. Syst. Biol.*, 4:177, 2008.

97. K. Sheikh, J. Forster, and L. K. Nielsen. Modeling hybridoma cell metabolism using a generic genome-scale metabolic model of *Mus musculus*. *Biotechnol. Prog.*, 21:112–121, 2005.

98. L. E. Quek and L. K. Nielsen. On the reconstruction of the *Mus musculus* genome-scale metabolic network model. *Genome Inform.*, 21:89–100, 2008.

99. M. I. Sigurdsson, N. Jamshidi, E. Steingrimsson, I. Thiele, and B. O. Palsson. A detailed genome-wide reconstruction of mouse metabolism based on human Recon 1. *BMC Syst. Biol.*, 4:140, 2010.

100. S. Selvarasu, I. A. Karimi, G. H. Ghim, and D. Y. Lee. Genome-scale modeling and in silico analysis of mouse cell metabolic network. *Mol. Biosyst.*, 6:152–161, 2009.

101. S. B. Sohn et al. Genome-scale metabolic model of methylotrophic yeast *Pichia pastoris* and its use for in silico analysis of heterologous protein production. *Biotechnol. J.*, 5:705–715, 2010.

102. B. K. Chung et al. Genome-scale metabolic reconstruction and in silico analysis of methylotrophic yeast *Pichia pastoris* for strain improvement. *Microb. Cell. Fact*, 9:50, 2010.

103. M. Tortajada, F. Llaneras, and J. Pico. Validation of a constraint-based model of *Pichia pastoris* metabolism under data scarcity. *BMC Syst. Biol.*, 4:115, 2010.

104. C. Huthmacher, A. Hoppe, S. Bulik, and H. G. Holzhutter. Antimalarial drug targets in *Plasmodium falciparum* predicted by stage-specific metabolic network analysis. *BMC Syst. Biol.*, 4:120, 2010.

105. G. Plata, T. L. Hsiao, K. L. Olszewski, M. Llinas, and D. Vitkup. Reconstruction and flux-balance analysis of the *Plasmodium falciparum* metabolic network. *Mol. Syst. Biol.*, 6:408, 2010.

106. N. C. Duarte, M. J. Herrgard, and B. O. Palsson. Reconstruction and validation of *Saccharomyces cerevisiae* iND750, a fully compartmentalized genome-scale metabolic model. *Genome Res.*, 14:1298–1309, 2004.

107. L. Kuepfer, U. Sauer, and L. M. Blank. Metabolic functions of duplicate genes in *Saccharomyces cerevisiae*. *Genome Res.*, 15:1421–1430, 2005.

108. I. Nookaew, R. Olivares-Hernandez, S. Bhumiratana, and J. Nielsen. Genome-scale metabolic models of *Saccharomyces cerevisiae*. *Methods Mol. Biol.*, 759:445–463, 2011.

109. M. J. Herrgard, B. S. Lee, V. Portnoy, and B. O. Palsson. Integrated analysis of regulatory and metabolic networks reveals novel regulatory mechanisms in *Saccharomyces cerevisiae*. *Genome Res.*, 16:627–635, 2006.

110. M. L. Mo, B. O. Palsson, and M. J. Herrgard. Connecting extracellular metabolomic measurements to intracellular flux states in yeast. *BMC Syst. Biol.*, 3:37, 2009.

111. A. Shastri and J. Morgan. Calculation of theoretical yields in metabolic networks. *Biochem. Mol. Biol. Edu.*, 32:314–318, 2004.

112. R. Saha, P. F. Suthers, and C. D. Maranas. *Zea mays* iRS1563: A comprehensive genome-scale metabolic reconstruction of maize metabolism. *PLoS One*, 6:e21784, 2011.

113. I. C. Tsantili, M. N. Karim, and M. I. Klapa. Quantifying the metabolic capabilities of engineered *Zymomonas mobilis* using linear programming analysis. *Microb. Cell. Fact*, 6:8, 2007.

114. O. Folger et al. Predicting selective drug targets in cancer through metabolic networks. *Mol. Syst. Biol.*, 7:501, 2011.

115. N. E. Lewis et al. Large-scale in silico modeling of metabolic interactions between cell types in the human brain. *Nat. Biotechnol.*, 28:1279–1285, 2010.

116. L. Jerby, T. Shlomi, and E. Ruppin. Computational reconstruction of tissue-specific metabolic models: Application to human liver metabolism. *Mol. Syst. Biol.*, 6:401, 2010.

117. C. Gille et al. HepatoNet1: A comprehensive metabolic reconstruction of the human hepatocyte for the analysis of liver physiology. *Mol. Syst. Biol.*, 6:411, 2010.

118. T. D. Vo and B. O. Palsson. Isotopomer analysis of myocardial substrate metabolism: A systems biology approach. *Biotechnol. Bioeng.*, 95:972–983, 2006.

119. A. Bordbar, N. E. Lewis, J. Schellenberger, B. O. Palsson, and N. Jamshidi. Insight into human alveolar macrophage and *M. tuberculosis* interactions via metabolic reconstructions. *Mol. Syst. Biol.*, 6:422, 2010.

120. C. G. Dal'Molin, L. E. Quek, R. W. Palfreyman, S. M. Brumbley, and L. K. Nielsen. C4GEM, a genome-scale metabolic model to study C4 plant metabolism. *Plant Physiol.*, 154:1871–1885, 2010.

121. T. Shlomi, M. N. Cabili, M. J. Herrgard, B. O. Palsson, and E. Ruppin. Network-based prediction of human tissue-specific metabolism. *Nat. Biotechnol.*, 26:1003–1010, 2008.

122. I. Thiele and B. O. Palsson. A protocol for generating a high-quality genome-scale metabolic reconstruction. *Nat. Protoc.*, 5:93–121, 2010.

123. P. Grosu, J. P. Townsend, D. L. Hartl, and D. Cavalieri. Pathway Processor: A tool for integrating whole-genome expression results into metabolic networks. *Genome Res.*, 12:1121–1126, 2002.

124. C. Hyland, J. W. Pinney, G. A. McConkey, and D. R. Westhead. metaSHARK: A WWW platform for interactive exploration of metabolic networks. *Nucleic Acids Res.*, 34:W725–728, 2006.

125. A. Reyes-Palomares et al. Systems biology metabolic modeling assistant: An ontology-based tool for the integration of metabolic data in kinetic modeling. *Bioinformatics*, 25:834–835, 2009.

126. J. D. Orth and B. O. Palsson. Systematizing the generation of missing metabolic knowledge. *Biotechnol. Bioeng.*, 107:403–412, 2010.

127. G. Chechik et al. Activity motifs reveal principles of timing in transcriptional control of the yeast metabolic network. *Nat. Biotechnol.*, 26:1251–1259, 2008.

128. T. Ideker et al. Integrated genomic and proteomic analyses of a systematically perturbed metabolic network. *Science*, 292:929–934, 2001.

129. R. Usaite, K. R. Patil, T. Grotkjaer, J. Nielsen, and B. Regenberg. Global transcriptional and physiological responses of *Saccharomyces cerevisiae* to ammonium, L-alanine, or L-glutamine limitation. *Appl. Environ. Microbiol.*, 72:6194–6203, 2006.

130. R. A. Notebaart, B. Teusink, R. J. Siezen, and B. Papp. Co-regulation of metabolic genes is better explained by flux coupling than by network distance. *PLoS Comput. Biol.*, 4:e26, 2008.

131. P. Daran-Lapujade et al. Role of transcriptional regulation in controlling fluxes in central carbon metabolism of *Saccharomyces cerevisiae*. A chemostat culture study. *J. Biol. Chem.*, 279:9125–9138, 2004.

132. T. Cakir et al. Integration of metabolome data with metabolic networks reveals reporter reactions. *Mol. Syst. Biol.*, 2:50, 2006.

133. J. E. Bailey, S. Birnbaum, J. L. Galazzo, C. Khosla, and J. V. Shanks. Strategies and challenges in metabolic engineering. *Ann. N Y Acad. Sci.*, 589:1–15, 1990.

134. J. H. Park and S. Y. Lee. Towards systems metabolic engineering of microorganisms for amino acid production. *Curr. Opin. Biotechnol.*, 19:454–460, 2008.

135. S. Y. Lee et al. From genome sequence to integrated bioprocess for succinic acid production by *Mannheimia succiniciproducens*. *Appl. Microbiol. Biotechnol.*, 79:11–22, 2008.

136. R. M. Zelle et al. Malic acid production by *Saccharomyces cerevisiae*: Engineering of pyruvate carboxylation, oxaloacetate reduction, and malate export. *Appl. Environ. Microbiol.*, 74:2766–2777, 2008.

137. M. Izallalen et al. *Geobacter sulfurreducens* strain engineered for increased rates of respiration. *Metab. Eng.*, 10:267–275, 2008.

138. D. Segura, R. Mahadevan, K. Juarez, and D. R. Lovley. Computational and experimental analysis of redundancy in the central metabolism of *Geobacter sulfurreducens*. *PLoS Comput. Biol.*, 4:e36, 2008.

139. C. Risso, S. J. Van Dien, A. Orloff, D. R. Lovley, and M. V. Coppi. Elucidation of an alternate isoleucine biosynthesis pathway in *Geobacter sulfurreducens*. *J. Bacteriol.*, 190:2266–2274, 2008.

140. K. R. Patil and J. Nielsen. Uncovering transcriptional regulation of metabolism by using metabolic network topology. *Proc. Natl. Acad Sci. USA*, 102:2685–2689, 2005.

141. J. Forster, I. Famili, P. Fu, B. O. Palsson, and J. Nielsen. Genome-scale reconstruction of the *Saccharomyces cerevisiae* metabolic network. *Genome Res.*, 13:244–253, 2003.

142. M. Falb et al. Metabolism of halophilic archaea. *Extremophiles*, 12:177–196, 2008.

143. O. Gonzalez et al. Reconstruction, modeling & analysis of *Halobacterium salinarum* R-1 metabolism. *Mol. Biosyst.*, 4:148–159, 2008.

144. E. Borenstein, M. Kupiec, M. W. Feldman, and E. Ruppin. Large-scale reconstruction and phylogenetic analysis of metabolic environments. *Proc. Natl. Acad. Sci. USA*, 105:14482–14487, 2008.

145. K. D. Verkhedkar, K. Raman, N. R. Chandra, S. Vishveshwara. Metabolome based reaction graphs of *M. tuberculosis* and *M. leprae*: A comparative network analysis. *PLoS One*, 2:e881, 2007.

146. J. Wright and A. Wagner. Exhaustive identification of steady state cycles in large stoichiometric networks. *BMC Syst. Biol.*, 2:61, 2008.

147. A. Kun, B. Papp, and E. Szathmary. Computational identification of obligatorily autocatalytic replicators embedded in metabolic networks. *Genome Biol.*, 9:R51, 2008.

148. T. Nishikawa, N. Gulbahce, and A. E. Motter. Spontaneous reaction silencing in metabolic optimization. *PLoS Comput. Biol.*, 4:e1000236, 2008.

149. S. A. Becker, N. D. Price, and B. O. Palsson. Metabolite coupling in genome-scale metabolic networks. *BMC Bioinformatics*, 7:111, 2006.

150. A. Samal et al. Low degree metabolites explain essential reactions and enhance modularity in biological networks. *BMC Bioinformatics*, 7:118, 2006.

151. R. Guimera, M. Sales-Pardo, and L. A. Amaral. A network-based method for target selection in metabolic networks. *Bioinformatics*, 23:1616–1622, 2007.

152. J. A. Papin, N. D. Price, and B. O. Palsson. Extreme pathway lengths and reaction participation in genome-scale metabolic networks. *Genome Res.*, 12:1889–1900, 2002.

153. R. Mahadevan and D. R. Lovley. The degree of redundancy in metabolic genes is linked to mode of metabolism. *Biophys. J.*, 94:1216–1220, 2008.

154. B. Papp, B. Teusink, and R. A. Notebaart. A critical view of metabolic network adaptations. *HFSP J.*, 3:24–35, 2009.

155. S. S. Fong et al. In silico design and adaptive evolution of *Escherichia coli* for production of lactic acid. *Biotechnol. Bioeng.*, 91:643–648, 2005.

156. S. S. Fong and B. O. Palsson. Metabolic gene-deletion strains of *Escherichia coli* evolve to computationally predicted growth phenotypes. *Nat. Genet.*, 36:1056–1058, 2004.

157. J. M. Lee, E. P. Gianchandani, J. A. Eddy, and J. A. Papin. Dynamic analysis of integrated signaling, metabolic, and regulatory networks. *PLoS Comput. Biol.*, 4:e1000086, 2008.

158. M. A. Oberhardt, B. O. Palsson, and J. A. Papin. Applications of genome-scale metabolic reconstructions. *Mol. Syst. Biol.*, 5:320, 2009.

159. A. M. Feist and B. O. Palsson. The growing scope of applications of genome-scale metabolic reconstructions using *Escherichia coli*. *Nat. Biotechnol.*, 26:659–667, 2008.

160. S. Tsoka and C. A. Ouzounis. Metabolic database systems for the analysis of genome-wide function. *Biotechnol. Bioeng.*, 84:750–755, 2003.

CHAPTER 46

INFERRING AND POSTPROCESSING HUGE PHYLOGENIES

STEPHEN A. SMITH[1] and ALEXANDROS STAMATAKIS[2]
[1]Department of Ecology and Evolutionary Biology, University of Michigan, Ann Arbor, Michigan
[2]Scientific Computing Group, Heidelberg Institute for Theoretical Studies, Heidelberg, Germany

46.1 INTRODUCTION

Biology experienced a revolution when Darwin presented the theory of natural selection that helped explain how the diversity of life was generated. Many early biologists found that this diversity could be represented as a tree, and in fact the only figure in *The Origin of Species* is of a tree of related organisms [7]. The fields of evolutionary biology and systematics devote a great deal of effort toward determining how organisms are related and building phylogenetic trees. They construct phylogenetic trees using information from the genomes and morphological characteristics of species. Although many scientists work specifically on reconstructing the Tree of Life, all of biology has been affected by the incorporation of phylogenetic information. The fields of ecology and environmental studies use information on how species are related to better interpret how communities form. The medical fields use phylogenetics to better understand how infections and diseases respond and react. Because of the importance of the Tree of Life to the biological sciences, phylogenetic inference methods and data set construction techniques have been the focus of much development for many years, attracting the interests of not only biologists but also computer scientists.

In this chapter, we examine the recent developments in the effort to construct large phylogenetic trees. The first paper discussing a parametric method for calculating the likelihood of a phylogenetic tree was published in 1981 [18]. Since then, methods have been developed that estimate phylogenetic trees with more than 100,000 species. In order to accomplish this, many computational and conceptual challenges have to be overcome. Here, we discuss many of those challenges facing data set assembly and phylogenetic reconstruction.

The rest of this chapter is organized as follows. In Section 46.2 we discuss some of the recent advances in data set assembly, phylogenetic inference, and the postprocessing of phylogenetic trees. In Section 46.3 we present an example of the growth of data in the *rbc*L gene region in seed plants. Finally, in Section 46.4 we discuss some challenges

Biological Knowledge Discovery Handbook: Preprocessing, Mining, and Postprocessing of Biological Data,
First Edition. Edited by Mourad Elloumi and Albert Y. Zomaya.
© 2014 John Wiley & Sons, Inc. Published 2014 by John Wiley & Sons, Inc.

and limitations of phylogenetic inference as well as postprocessing and we conclude in Section 46.5.

46.2   RECENT ADVANCES

The field of phylogenetics has experienced a number of computational and methodological advances in aspects of data set assembly and phylogenetic reconstruction.

46.2.1   Data Set Assembly

Before a phylogeny can be constructed, the data used to build the phylogeny must be assembled into an aligned matrix (a multiple-sequence alignment). For at least the first few decades of phylogenetic research, phylogenetic data sets, with few exceptions, consisted of fewer than 100 species. Often sampling and data collection reflected the relatively narrow taxonomic interests of a laboratory or working group. These data sets typically included morphological data and relatively little molecular data until the widespread adoption of rapid molecular wet-laboratory techniques for isolation, amplification, and sequencing. With the increased availability of molecular data in public databases and the continued improvement of computational tools and systems, the field has seen the creation of ever-growing synthetic data sets with broad groups of organisms. More recently, next-generation methods for sequencing have allowed for the rapid collection of many more gene regions and fragments than traditional sequencing techniques.

Data set assembly strategies for large phylogenetic analyses have been categorized many times before. It has been difficult to place these methods into well-formed groups in large part because the methods are relatively new and still in continuous development. Some strategies of large-data-set assembly include the alignment of whole genomes across a set of organisms [17] and is sometimes deemed phylogenomics (this term has come to mean many things). Matrices can also be constructed using more of an informatics approach where an entire sequence database, typically of a particular clade of organisms, is processed to discover orthologous gene regions, or those gene regions arising from a common ancestor, across a set of taxa. These gene regions can then be combined into a supermatrix or, less frequently, gene trees can be made of each of the orthologous sets and reconciled into a species tree. These types of data sets represent some of the first attempts to construct phylogenetic data sets of thousands of species [34]. Finally, data sets can be constructed with a few orthologous gene regions determined a priori to be well represented for the question at hand. With this approach, some of the methods used to determine orthologous sequences, like clustering, can be simplified by seeding the sequence similarity analyses with sequences known to represent the gene regions of interest. This can greatly reduce the computational burden of clustering and all sequences versus all sequences BLAST analyses.

Given the subject of this chapter, we will discuss data set construction methods that produce matrices with large numbers of taxa for which there are a variety of computational challenges that have to be overcome.

Plant phylogenies containing more than 1000 species began to receive more attention after the publication of McMahon and Sanderson [34]. The two alignment matrices illustrated in that study contained 1794 and 2228 taxa and were constructed using a computational approach where the entire database of papilionoid legume sequences was analyzed to discover orthologous clusters. These were then combined into a supermatrix (a concatenated matrix of the orthologous regions) and analyzed with parsimony reconstruction methods [22, 62]. Larger phylogenies were constructed with a seed approach and only a few orthologous regions [15, 16, 46–48]. These phylogenies were not only larger but were also reconstructed with maximum-likelihood techniques. The largest multigene phylogeny constructed to date consists of 73,060 eukaryotic taxa [21]. This phylogeny also includes just a few orthologous gene regions and is the largest phylogeny to include morphological as well as molecular data. As improved methods for data set assembly and analysis have increasingly become available, phylogenies consisting of thousands of taxa are becoming more common.

There are a number of important steps in the construction of these matrices that can generally be separated into issues of homology assessment and sequence alignment.

46.2.1.1 Homology Assessment
Homologous sequences are those sequences that share common ancestry due to either a gene duplication event (paralogues) or a speciation event (orthologues). Homology assessment in the context of phylogenetic data set construction is a difficult problem. Furthermore, for large phylogenies, we are typically only interested in including orthologous sequences, as we are often constructing phylogenies meant to show how species are related.

Two major approaches are commonly used to determine homologous gene regions and sequences for large phylogenies. The first, called the *seed approach*, involves specifying a priori gene regions of interest and determining which sequences in the database are identified as being one of these gene regions. The other approach, called the *clustering approach*, involves a set of analyses on all the available sequences (typically stored in a database of sequences) and discovers homologous sets of sequences in the entire database.

Seed Approach This approach is quite simple and one implementation thereof is described in more detail by Smith et al. [47]. Essentially, gene regions of interest are determined before beginning analyses. These gene regions are often of interest to particular wide sets of organisms (e.g., *rbc*L in plants, *cyt*B in animals, 18S across life) and preferably have fewer incidences of paralogy than other gene regions. Also, such target gene regions are more helpful when they are sampled broadly and evenly across the taxonomic group under study. Once these regions are identified, seed sequences that represent the breadth of diversity of the gene region are identified and the full database of sequences is compared to those seed sequences. The sequences in the database that are found to significantly match the seed sequences are retained and those that do not match are removed. This procedure also allows for the correction of problems such as reverse complements. Because the procedure dramatically reduces the set of sequences to be compared, it is very fast and straightforward to parallelize.

Clustering Approach This approach actually encompasses many diverse approaches each of which has been described in more detail elsewhere [13, 34, 49]. Although there are details that differ between individual instances of this approach, there are many common elements. Typically, a database of sequences is identified and created that is limited to a particular group of interest. This can be a large portion of a public database or it can be a set of transcriptomes, genomes, and/or other sequences. These sequences are then compared, often using a sequence comparison tool such as pairwise alignment in BLAST or the Smith–Waterman algorithm [50]. This step can be particularly computationally intensive as it requires $O(n^2)$ comparisons, where n is the number of sequences, but is easily parallelizable. The results of these analyses (i.e., the similarity of the sequences in the database) are then typically fed into one of a number of clustering tools (e.g., Markov clusting tool, [10]). The clustering analysis represents the first step in the determination of homology. Once clusters have been identified, there are many possible routes for sets of sequences. Often, orthology will be determined by one of a number of different ways. For example, clusters containing paralogues may be completely discarded. Given the number of clusters resulting from these analyses, this may be done while still obtaining large final matrices. Unlike the seed approach, the clustering approach requires an additional step to determine which gene region to include in the final matrix. This additional step, because of the complicated nature of missing data [42], may consist of a quasi-biclique analysis [65] or other analysis [13, 24, 49] where the acceptable amount of missing data is determined. Although there has been considerable work in this area (see previous citations), there is plenty to still be explored in regard to optimal clustering data set contruction, especially considering the continued growth of sequence data. Alternatively, clusters may be aligned to reconstruct phylogenies from which paralogous gene sets can then be removed and analyzed independently [24, 49].

Generally speaking, the seed and clustering approaches often, but not always, yield vastly different types of data matrices. The most obvious difference between the resulting matrices of these two approaches is the shape. For the former approach there are often many species but very few gene regions, and for the latter approach there can be many species but typically many more gene regions. Another difference between these two types of matrices is the degree to which homology analyses affect matrix construction. For deeper analyses that span hundreds of millions of years, a seeded approach can drastically limit the available homologous gene set that can be identified a priori [21]. Therefore, an approach that finds clusters of homologous gene regions may be favored [13, 24, 49]. Also, once sequences have been determined to be homologous in the seed approach, matrix construction consists of analyzing the individual gene regions or concatenating the gene regions. For the cluster approach, an additional step is required to determine which gene regions and which sequences to actually include in a data matrix.

Regardless of which method is used to determine homology, once homologous sets of sequences have been identified, these sets of sequences must be aligned into a multiple sequence alignment.

46.2.1.2 Multiple-Sequence Alignment
For most phylogenetic analyses of any size, a multiple-sequence alignment is required (but see for alignment-free methods [26]). These consist of many individual sites of homologous amino acids or nucleotides and can consist of individual or concatenated gene regions. Concatenated matrices are constructed by combining individual gene regions with the intention of simultaneous analysis and the potential to apply independent models of evolution to each gene regions. So the relevant discussion on multiple-sequence alignment is equally pertinent to both individual and concatenated alignments.

Multiple-sequence alignment algorithms and implementations have experienced many advances recently, including parallelization, ability to handle extremely large data sets, and incorporation of dedicated evolutionary models [14, 29, 32]. Specific methods, comparisons, and benchmarks have been reviewed elsewhere [30, 63]. However, their relevance to data set assembly for large phylogeny reconstruction will be discussed here.

There are two major uses pertaining to multiple-sequence alignment in large phylogeny reconstruction. The first is as part of the procedure to determine homology among a set of sequences in the clustering approach to data set assembly (see above). The second is in the construction of a multiple-sequence alignment once homologous sequences have been identified. For some approaches, these two uses are identical and no particular approach to multiple-sequence alignment need be taken other than to use the most accurate method available. As mentioned above, specific benchmarks and performance characteristics will not be discussed at length here, but due to their ability to handle large numbers of sequences, MUSCLE [14] or MAFFT [29] often are used.

For some large data set assembly problems, traditional alignment procedures fail to accommodate the challenges faced. For example, many alignment methods first build an initial phylogeny based on sequence similarity to guide the construction of the final alignment. If the sequences evolve at a high rate, this tree will be highly inaccurate and may be positively misleading [31, 47]. Some of these problems have been theoretically addressed with newer methods that allow for evolutionary reconstructions to be part of the algorithm, as in PRANK [32], but for large alignments where these methods are not efficient, other techniques must be used. Because of this challenge, some have developed methods that deploy profile alignments where alignments are aligned to each other. Profile alignments can be used to design *divide-and-conquer* approaches to constructing large alignments of divergent sequences. Implementations of this approach, such as SATE [31] and PHLAWD [47], attempt to use hierarchical information to construct better alignments for extremely large and divergent gene regions. In both cases larger alignments or sequence sets are broken into smaller sequence sets that are then aligned individually, and those alignments are then aligned together. In SATE, the hierarchical information that is used to break down the data set is an initial set of trees, and in PHLAWD the information that is used is available taxonomic information or an input phylogeny. In either case, the approach is meant to alleviate the problems associated with aligning extremely large and/or divergent sequence sets.

As a result of the advances in multiple-sequence alignment methods and hybrid approaches like SATE and PHLAWD, it is now possible to construct multiple-sequence alignments reasonably well with many tens of thousands of sequences [16, 46–48]. However, there is plenty of room for improvement in methods for multiple-sequence alignment as it relates to large phylogeny reconstruction. Foremost are potential problems caused by outlier sequence detection and individual sequences or small numbers of sequences that are misaligned. Such outliers and errors can bias alignment or tree building. Most automated data set assembly methods, including PHLAWD and those described by McMahon and Sanderson [34], attempt to automate the detection of these sequences, but this can still be very challenging.

46.2.2 Phylogenetic Inference

As a result of the molecular data explosion, phylogenetic inference is progressively becoming a computational science. It is facing similar computational challenges as well-established supercomputing application areas tackled more than 20 years ago in the fields of astrophysics and fluid mechanics. Because of the quite distinct nature of the computational problems involved, one needs to differentiate between large-scale phylogenetic analyses for tens of thousands of taxa and a few genes and large-scale phylogenomic data sets with 100 to at most 1000 taxa that contain the entire transcriptome or genome of each taxon. Initially we will focus on phylogenomic data sets.

46.2.2.1 *Crunching Phylogenomic Data Sets*   An emerging issue is how to obtain the necessary computational resources for conducting large-scale phylogenetic analyses that can easily require more than one million *central processing unit* (CPU) hours [24]. An

advantage of *maximum-likelihood* [18] inferences is that they exhibit an intrinsic source of fine-grain parallelism [58, 59] that can be exploited with *POSIX Threads* (PThreads) or the *message-passing interface* (MPI).

The scalability of the codes mainly depends on the alignment length, that is, the longer the alignment, the more cores can be deployed to simultaneously compute the likelihood on a single tree. Thus, this type of fine-grain approach is particularly well-suited for whole-genome or whole-transcriptome data analyses. Moreover, because this parallelization approach requires a high-bandwidth and, more importantly, low-latency interconnect network, it will be comparatively easy to obtain a large CPU time allocation at scientific supercomputing centers that are always looking for new applications. However, using MPI-parallelized codes for phylogenetic inference requires several code changes/adaptations to fit the operating model and typical queue configurations of supercomputers. First, the capability to checkpoint and restart such analyses is required because of limited run times for large parallel jobs (typically 24 or 48 h). The checkpointing mechanism needs to be lightweight in the sense that the checkpoint files that are written are as small as possible and the time spent for writing checkpoints is as small as possible. Checkpointing ML-based inference codes is more difficult than saving the state of "classic" supercomputing applications that typically deploy iterative numerical solvers. For such applications simply storing the state of the matrix or grid on which computations are conducted is sufficient for checkpointing.

In ML-based phylogenetics, heuristic *hill-climbing* algorithms [23, 54] are used that can be in different states (fast initial search, model parameter optimization, slow final search). Therefore, restarting is challenging because, in the case of *randomized axelerated maximum likelihood* (RAxML [54]), one needs to restore the state and local variables of the specific search algorithm phase at restart. Nonetheless, the complexity of implementing lightweight checkpointing mechanisms is highly program dependent. Bayesian phylogenetic inference programs are easier to checkpoint, because they only need to store *Markov chain Monte Carlo* (MCMC) states at every nth proposal, where n can be tuned to obtain the desired checkpoint granularity. The ML-based code GARLI [67] is also more straightforward to checkpoint because of the genetic search algorithm that is deployed; that is, similar to Bayesian programs, GARLI relies on states and randomized state transitions. Most Bayesian and ML-based inference codes have by now been parallelized using *Open Multi-Processing* (OpenMP) for multicore platforms. Hence, the codes do not scale beyond one node, which can become problematic for large data sets.

We have recently developed a lightweight version of RAxML, called RAxML-Light, for supercomputers. While not yet published, the code is already available for download and actively developed under GNU GPL at [61]. The code offers simple ML-based tree searches under the standard models of statistical sequence evolution for DNA and protein input data. Moreover, it offers a production-level fine-grain MPI and PThreads parallelization of the likelihood function as well as a lightweight checkpointing mechanism. To illustrate the need for such codes, we generated a simulated DNA alignment using SeqGen [39] with 1481 taxa and 20,000,000 sites. This corresponds roughly to the sequence data of 1481 full genomes, and we are aware of several ongoing large-scale sequencing projects that will generate such a large amount of data in the course of the next two years. The simulated alignment file already has a size of 27 gigabytes (GB) and the memory requirements for computing the likelihood on this data set under a simple model of sequence evolution without the more memory-intensive Γ model of rate heterogeneity [66] already amount to 1 terabyte (TB). To test RAxML-Light on this data set, we used our cluster at the Heidelberg Institute for Theoretical Studies, which is equipped with 42 AMD Magny-Cours nodes. Each node has

48 cores and 128 GB or 256 GB RAM, respectively. The nodes are connected via a Qlogic low-latency, high-bandwidth Infiniband interconnect. RAxML-Light was started on 672 cores (14 nodes) and required less than 48 h to complete the tree search. Hence, analyzing such large data sets is feasible.

An issue that needs to be further addressed is that of reading in the alignment file, in particular with respect to Amdahl's law. Typically, phylogeny programs have an initial sequential phase for parsing the input alignment and compressing identical site patterns which can become time consuming (considering an input file of 27 GB). This sequential part can substantially decrease parallel efficiency. To alleviate this problem for the time being, we implemented a file-parsing and compression option in RAxML-Light that needs to be executed sequentially and only once on a less powerful computer. The output is a binary file that contains the compressed alignment information and can be read quickly by the MPI master process. While this significantly improved parallel efficiency, further improvements are possible by using parallel input/output such that all processes can concurrently read in their fraction of the alignment at program initialization. Ideally, the community should come up with a standardized binary alignment file format.

46.2.2.2 Crunching Many-Taxon Data Sets
Obtaining resources for many-taxon/few-genes data sets is more complicated because of the limited parallel scalability of the codes. Typically, on a representative data set with, for instance, 55,000 taxa and 8 genes, the scalability will be limited to a single multicore node and the expected execution time will amount to about 100 CPU hours. While the long run-time requirements can be accommodated via the checkpointing mechanism, assuming that a cluster queue limit of 24 or 48 h is imposed, it will be difficult to obtain supercomputer access because of limited scalability. Essentially, an expensive high-performance internode interconnect will not be required and hence supercomputer usage cannot be properly justified. Nonetheless, many independent searches can be submitted independently and simultaneously to a queue. Another problem may be the memory consumption of the inference, that is, for such large data sets (we are currently analyzing 75,000 and 100,000 taxon data sets with a couple of genes) "fat" multicore nodes with at least 64 GB of RAM will be required (but see Section 46.2.2.4). Finally, data sets with thousands of taxa generate a new category of problems associated to the numerical stability of the codes, in particular with respect to the Γ model of rate heterogeneity. The key problem is that for such comprehensive trees the double-precision number range may not be sufficient to represent the range of possible values in ancestral probability vectors. While numerical scaling mechanisms for avoiding numerical underflow are already implemented in most likelihood-based phylogeny programs, they cannot solve the aforementioned problem. These numerical issues are discussed in more detail in [20].

46.2.2.3 Using x86 Vector Intrinsics
Another issue we have recently addressed is deploying 256-bit-wide AVX vector instructions as available on the new Intel i7 processor generation and the future AMD Bulldozer systems. All RAxML versions are already fully vectorized by means of SSE3 intrinsics [3] and we also achieved performance improvements of more than one order of magnitude for the maximum-parsimony function (as implemented in standard RAxML and Parsimonator available at [60]).

Currently, we have identified two problems with respect to AVX intrinsics: First, using AVX intrinsics puts a larger pressure on the memory subsystem because more data are needed per cycle and RAxML performance is already mostly memory bound. Second, the performance of current AVX auto-vectorization mechanisms in the Intel and gcc compilers is still suboptimal. When vectorizing a RAxML function using AVX intrinsics that accounts for approximately 65% of overall execution time, we initially observed a slowdown. A detailed analysis indicated that, while the function that had been vectorized using AVX intrinsics was indeed executing faster, the rest of the code had been slowed down by the AVX auto-vectorization (-mavx switch) so dramatically that we obtained an overall slowdown. As vector units become longer and thus automatic vectorization more complex, explicit vectorization via intrinsics will need to be considered as an alternative. We solved the problem in RAxML-Light by just compiling an additional source file that only contains the vectorized likelihood functions with AVX intrinsics with the -mavx flag, thus preventing the compiler from auto-vectorizing any other parts of the code.

We tested the AVX vectorization of RAxML-Light with a DNA data set comprising 150 taxa and 1130 site patterns on an Intel i7-2620M CPU running at 2.7 GHz. Under the CAT model of rate heterogeneity [53] the execution times were 73.92 s for the SSE3 version and 63.30 s for the AVX version. Under the Γ model of rate heterogeneity the SSE3 version required 205.39 s while the AVX version required 166.92 s. We also tested performance for the protein model likelihood implementation under the CAT model of rate heterogeneity on an amino acid data set with 40 taxa and 958 site patterns. The SSE3 version required 84.59 s while the AVX version required 49.74 s. Clearly, the speedups increase as the data access to computation ratios become more favorable (speedups: DNA CAT 1.17, DNA GAMMA 1.23, Protein CAT 1.70).

We also tested the performance of Parsimonator on the same CPU on a DNA data set with 125 taxa and 29,149 sites. The unvectorized version required 4.77 s, the SSE3 version 1.54 s, and the AVX version 0.95 s.

46.2.2.4 Reducing Memory Footprints For computing large phylogenies there exist two limiting factors: CPU time and memory requirements. As pointed out above, memory requirements can be as high as 1 TB for large whole-genome data sets that do not exhibit a large fraction of missing data. For many-taxon data sets, at present, the proportion of missing data is still relatively high (between 80 and 90%), but it is hard to predict if future data sets will have less missing data. Two basic algorithmic techniques can be deployed to reduce both memory footprints and potentially the number of required floating-point operations on such large data sets with missing taxa. The first technique, the mesh-based approach [55, 58], exhibits a high degree of code complexity and is only applicable to partitioned analyses with per-partition branch-length estimates. Because of the code complexity and somewhat limited applicability, the mesh-based approach is currently only available as a proof-of-concept implementation but has given rise to theoretical work on tree searches on data sets with missing taxa [44]. The second approach to reduce memory footprints on phylogenomic data sets with missing data is less complex from the software engineering point of view and more generally applicable. However, the savings in computing time are smaller than for the mesh-based approach. Here, we reintroduced the old idea of *subtree equality vectors* (SEVs) for accelerating the phylogenetic likelihood function [57] and adapted it to gappy data sets (for details see [20]). The memory savings are analogous to the mesh-based approach (proportional to the fraction of missing data) and we have implemented this technique at the production level in RAxML-Light. The SEV technique allowed us to reduce the memory footprints of a phylogenetic inference (a data set with 10 genes and almost 120,000 taxa with 90% missing data) from 70 to 19 GB and thereby also use multicore nodes for this production run that were equipped with only 32 GB RAM.

The increase in memory efficiency of the mesh-based and SEV-based techniques depends on the fraction of missing data in the respective input data sets. For large, densely sampled, whole-genome data sets without missing data these methods can therefore not be deployed for reducing memory footprints.

Future phylogenomic data sets will therefore require different techniques for reducing memory footprints. Initially, we experimented with out-of-core (also called *external memory algorithm*) approaches [27]. The performance of the out-of-core implementation was substantially better than relying on the operating system to swap pages (in the stress case when not enough RAM is available). However, the overall slowdown incurred by moving data to and from the disk was too large to be of any practical use. While developing the out-of-core approach, we observed that there exists a high data locality (in terms of the number of accessed ancestral probability vectors at the inner nodes of the tree) during the tree search. Hence, we started exploring trading memory space for additional (re-)computations of ancestral probability vectors. According to our experiments, this approach allows for reducing the used RAM by a factor of 10 while only inducing a run time increase of approximately 40%. Moreover, this memory–execution time trade-off can be tuned by a simple command line parameter. For details please refer to [28]. This recomputation approach will soon be fully integrated into RAxML-Light and represents a viable approach for analyzing dense phylogenomic alignments under RAM restrictions.

Finally, we should note that all of the above algorithmic techniques for saving memory and partially also computations are sufficiently generic as to be applied to all likelihood-based (ML and Bayesian) inference programs.

46.2.3 Postprocessing Phylogenetic Trees

The term *phylogenetic postprocessing* refers to summarizing or downstream processing of the information contained in one or more phylogenetic trees. The tree or trees that have been computed can, for instance, be used to infer divergence times by using dated fossils or to map certain organismal traits to the trees. Initially, we will focus on discrete operations on tree collections, that is, computing topological distances between trees and building consensus trees from a collection of plausible trees.

46.2.3.1 Bipartition Concept   Algorithmically, the most important concepts to postprocessing trees are the nontrivial bipartitions of a tree. A nontrivial bipartition describes the disjoint set of leaf labels obtained by splitting/cutting a tree at one of its inner branches. An inner branch connects two inner node of the tree. An unrooted binary tree with n taxa has $2n - 3$ branches and $n - 3$ inner branches because the remaining n branches lead to the n leaves. Therefore, an unrooted binary tree has a total of $n - 3$ nontrivial bipartitions. A list of all $n - 3$ nontrivial bipartitions suffices to fully characterize an unrooted binary tree. In other words, a binary tree and a complete (nontrivial) bipartition list are identical representations of the same mathematical object. Bipartitions are usually stored as bit vectors of length n. The bits representing the taxa in one part of the split (induced by cutting the branch) are set to 1 and the bits representing the other part of the split are set to 0. Bipartition lists are typically stored in hash tables. Such bipartition data objects (bit vectors of length n) in a hash table are also used to store additional information, such as in which tree of the tree collection they were present.

46.2.3.2 Computing Distances between Trees   With this basic concept at hand, it is now straightforward to define and understand the *Robinson–Foulds* (RF) topological distance [40] between two tree topologies. When comparing two trees, the RF distance simply corresponds to the sum of the number of bipartitions that are contained in one of the two trees but *not* in both. This count can be normalized by the maximum possible RF value which is $2(n - 3)$. In this case the two trees do not share a single bipartition and each tree has $n - 3$ unique bipartitions. RAxML [54] and MrsRF [33] offer efficient implementations for computing the pairwise RF distance on collections of many large trees.

There also exist other distance measures such as the *quartet distance* [5] or the *subtree prune-and-regraft* (SPR) distance between trees that are less frequently used. Note that computing the SPR distance between two unrooted binary trees is NP hard [25].

46.2.3.3 *Computing Consensus Trees*

The other important discrete postprocessing task is building *consensus trees*. The three main flavors are strict, *majority-rule* (MR), and *majority-rule extended* (MRE) consensus trees. Given a tree collection whose bipartitions have been stored in a hash table, building a *strict consensus tree* is straightforward. One just needs to traverse the hash table once and collect those bipartitions that appear in every tree. These bipartitions can then be used to build a potentially multifurcating unresolved strict consensus tree. Reconstructing a majority-rule consensus tree is also straightforward, since, in this case, all bipartitions that appear in more than half of the trees are used to build a potentially unresolved majority-rule consensus tree. Finally, MRE trees are substantially harder to reconstruct. The problem is that bipartitions that are contained in half, or less than half of the trees, shall also be included in the consensus. Adding bipartitions supported by $\leq 50\%$ of the trees requires $O(n^2)$ time (where n is the number of taxa) for a compatibility check. For each bipartition supported by $\leq 50\%$ of the trees we need to check if it is compatible with the bipartitions that already form part of the consensus. Moreover, the problem of optimally adding bipartitions with $\leq 50\%$ support to the MRE consensus is NP hard [8]. Algorithms for all three consensus methods using standard greedy heuristics for MRE are available in RAxML [1].

Finally, identifying so-called *rogue taxa*, that is, taxa that assume highly variable phylogenetic positions in a tree collection and can thereby substantially reduce the resolution of consensus trees, also represents an important current postprocessing problem.

46.2.3.4 *Divergence–Time Analyses*

There are a number of analyses that are conducted on the resulting maximum-likelihood phylogenies and postprocessed consensus trees, including divergence–time estimation. Divergence–time analyses typically involve either adjusting branch lengths based on relaxed clock estimates or estimating the phylogeny while accommodating for rates of molecular evolution and fossil information. There has been considerable development in these areas, including the development of *nonparametric rate smoothing* (NPRS) [45], Bayesian autocorrelated methods (as implemented in multidivtime) [64], *penalized likelihood* (PL) [43], uncorrelated Bayesian methods (as implemented in BEAST) [11, 12], and path length methods (as implemented in PATHD8) [4]. Despite the development of these sophisticated methods, the nature of the large data sets makes only a few of these methods useful for huge phylogenies. Specifically, both the NPRS and PL methods suffer from problems of optimization caused by the complex likelihood surfaces. The likelihood surface grows even more complex when additional constraints are induced by fossil placement and time calibrations. With large phylogenies, the optimization algorithms often fail to converge, or at least fail to converge in a reasonable amount of time. Because uncorrelated Bayesian methods (as implemented in BEAST) reestimate both the phylogenetic relationships as well as the divergence–times, these methods suffer from run times that are quite long and difficult convergence assessment due to complex parametrization. BEAST must overcome the problems of large phylogeny estimation as described above and the problem of divergence–time estimation. So, while the benefits of estimating the posterior probability of a phylogenetic data set may be great, it is practically very difficult. Essentially, only PATHD8 has the ability to handle data sets on the order of hundreds of thousands of taxa. There is plenty of room for the development of methods that can handle larger trees in this context. Before those methods are developed, phylogenetics would benefit from the additional optimization of existing methods.

46.3 DATA AVALANCHE: EXAMPLE WITH RBCL

The chloroplast gene region *ribulose-biphosphate carboxylase large* (*rbc*L) subunit encodes the large subunit of ribulose 1,5-bisphosphate carboxylase/oxygenase (RUBISCO) and is a very well studied gene region often used to resolve deep relationships. It has been sequenced by plant biologists for decades (beginning in 1990 [9, 51]) and has been extensively used to resolve relationships among the major groups in the plant Tree of Life. Because of its relative ease of isolation and amplification, due in part to its rate of evolution, it has remained popular among plant systematists, and some of the largest molecular phylogenetics data sets consist of *rbc*L sequences from broad samples of species throughout plants (e.g., [47]). One of the first such analyses was conducted by Chase et al. [6] and reported in a seminal paper not only for the plant Tree of Life but also for the limits of phylogenetic analyses at the time. Two data sets of 475 and 499 species were constructed of seed plants, and the authors conducted parsimony analyses with extensive discussion of the caveats concerning large data sets and phylogenetic analyses. Automated alignment techniques and software of high quality would not exist for many years to come, and so the multiple-sequence alignments were often adjusted and corrected extensively by eye. Biologists have continued to examine *rbc*L and have, in many cases, combined the information from other gene regions to construct more complete pictures of the evolution of plants. We exemplify the growth of phylogenetic information and the challenges faced in analyzing real data set(s) by the green plants and the *rbc*L gene.

46.3.1 Phylogenetic Inference

We illustrate the increase in the number of species and diversity of sampling across plants for the last 15 years with *rbc*L for green plants (Viridiplantae) looking across four time periods: 1996, 2001, 2006, and 2011. The data sets were assembled with PHLAWD [47] using default parameters and sequences for the Viridiplantae (green plant) clade. PHLAWD, as described above, collects the genetic data deposited in the *National Center for Biotechnology Information* (NCBI) repository GenBank for a particular gene region, in this case *rbc*L. PHLAWD then attempts to construct the best alignment for these samples using a *divide-and-conquer* algorithm for gene regions with high rates of evolution. It also chooses the best sequence per species (several sequences for the same gene from different specimen may be available) so that only one sequence per species is represented. PHLAWD may also remove outlying sequences that were misaligned. Runs were parallelized with pthreads in PHLAWD and run times ranged from 5 min to a few hours. Data sets were constructed with only sequences from the time period in question and these dates were based on the submission dates in the respective database entries. So the 1996 data set includes only sequences that were time stamped by NCBI to be deposited by

1996. When sequences have been replaced by the original author, they receive a new time stamp. For example, although a *rbc*L sequence for *Amborella* was deposited for Chase et al. [6], it was replaced in 2003 and so it will be represented in the 2006 data set. However, these situations are rare.

The four data sets contained 540 species for 1996, 2571 for 2001, 10,180 for 2006, and 21,955 for 2011. The alignment width was roughly equivalent for each time period with alignment lengths ranging between 1376 and 1443 sites. For 1996, 2001, and 2006, full bootstraps [19], with at least 200 replicates, and maximum-likelihood analyses were performed. For the 2011 sample, bootstraps, with more than 900 replicates, and maximum-likelihood analyses were performed, though final branch lengths were not estimated in part because the estimates of branch lengths with a data set of that size and dimension are not reliable.

46.3.2 Phylogenetic Postanalysis

There are a number of interesting points regarding the distribution of data. The dramatic increase in number of unique sequence names (species names or uniquely identified names) can be seen mostly from 2006 to 2011 (Figure 46.1). Although it is not ideal to summarize the taxonomic information by family because the definitions of the families are not specifically phylogenetic, we can see that the representation of families in green plants becomes asymptotic at 2006 and 2011. We might conclude from this that all the major groups have mostly been represented at this point. The data deposition has also not been particularly evenly distributed throughout each time slice. For example, from 1996 to 2001 there was a major increase in the mosses and monocots as well as others (Figure 46.2). In general, as also illustrated by the increase in the number of families represented, between 1996 and 2001 there was considerable increase in sampling for deep clades. Between 2001 and 2006, there was a dramatic increase in the number of species sampled, but it was mostly for more derived groups. In general, the deep clades were all fairly well represented. This pattern is even more dramatic with the increase in sampling from 2006 to 2011 where only derived groups have species added.

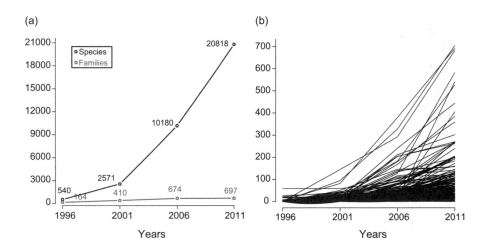

FIGURE 46.1 Plots of numbers of species for *rbc*L data sets: (a) number of species for entire datasets (gray are number of unique families represented); (b) number of species in each family.

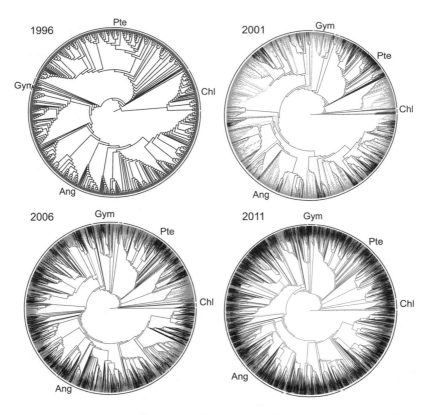

FIGURE 46.2 Plot of new species in each *rbc*L analysis. Gray branches are new, black are retained from previous analyses. Dominant members of major clades are marked: *angiosperms* (Ang), *gymnosperms* (Gym), *pteridophyta* (Pte), and *chlorophyta* (Chl). Because of the size of the tree, not only do these marked areas include species within the clades but also the names reflect the dominant members.

Other interesting patterns emerge from the increase in the number of species. One particularly interesting observation can be extracted from the distribution of bootstrap support for each data set. One way to examine this is by visually inspecting whether there are hierarchical patterns of bootstrap support (e.g., whether more nested subtrees or more ancestral edges are better supported). If we color where support is high versus low in each of these data sets, there is a notable pattern (Figure 46.3). Specifically, there is no clear pattern to the support. Certainly, especially in the data sets made with more recent data, there is a noticeable lack of support in many of the deeper angiosperm clades. We can also examine just the distribution of support values outside of the hierarchy of the phylogeny. The mean tendency of the distribution of support values decreases with the increase in the size of the data set with the values 72, 66, 60, and 56. The first quantiles also follow this trend (50, 41, 33, and 29). Previous results based on simulation suggest that accuracy (not necessarily support) increases with increased taxon sampling [38, 68]. Because we cannot compare these results to the "known" phylogeny, we cannot easily assess how accurate the results are. However, we can compare to other estimated phylogenies of plants.

The most recent multigene angiosperm phylogeny included 17 genes and 640 taxa [52]. Although we cannot compare the *rbc*L trees to a "known" phylogeny, we can begin to

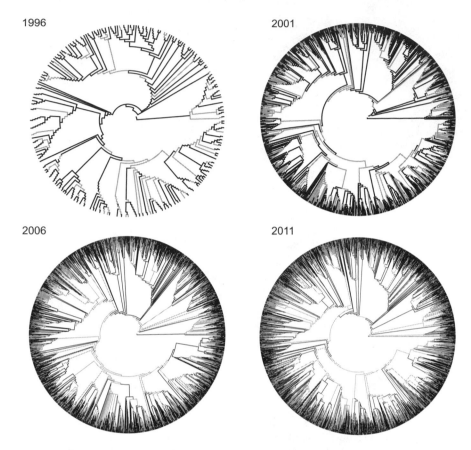

FIGURE 46.3 Plot of support for each branch in *rbc*L analyses. Gray branches are branches with less than 50% support and black branches have more than 50% support. The trees are in the same orientation as in Figure 46.2.

compare the *rbc*L trees to those trees presented in Soltis et al. [52]. Some of the taxa that were included in the Soltis et al. [52] study were newly sampled species and so may not be included in the sampling of these trees. In order to compare the trees generated for this chapter and those generated in the Soltis et al. [52] study, we took only the intersection of taxa between the two. Probably the most direct comparison that can be made between the trees is where there is agreement in particular clades: the number of clades that agree and the placement of those clades. The Soltis et al. [52] trees have genera as the taxonomic units and the trees presented here have species, or something analogous, as the taxonomic units. We sink these to just the generic names for comparison. For each clade in the Soltis et al. [52] trees, we extract the genera present and search through each of the *rbc*L trees for matching clades (of course, only considering the intersection of taxa). We then report the number of matches over the number of clades that have taxa and are well supported (greater than 50% support) in the Soltis et al. [52] study.

There is a general trend in the number of clades that are found in both the Soltis et al. [52], combined analyses and the *rbc*L trees. There is an increase in the number of supported clades as the trees grow, with the exception of the 2011 tree: 48% for 1996, 62% for 2001, 70% for

2006, and 66% for 2011. The number of branches colored in the figure would suggest lower numbers of correspondence, but many nodes have species that are not present in the Soltis et al. study and therefore cannot be determined to be congruent or not and are therefore colored gray. Initially, the trend would suggest perhaps empirical evidence for the hypothesis, based mostly on simulations, that increased taxon sampling increases accuracy [38, 68]. However, the 2011 results suggest that something else is going on. Perhaps the tree size and data set dimensions (few sites versus species) are such that the likelihood surface is more difficult to explore. It has been shown in simulations that more alignment sites are required to accurately reconstruct trees with more taxa [36]. Hence, the 2011 data set may just not have enough sites for a more accurate phylogenetic reconstruction. Alignment problems may also occur as the alignment grows in size which causes conflicts in the phylogenetic analyses. Therefore, the maximum-likelihood estimates are not as optimal. Despite this trend, generally, the accuracy of the tree as measured in comparison to the Soltis et al. [52] tree increases.

The other aspect of this comparison that can be explored is the phylogenetic location or placement of the agreement between the Soltis et al. [52] study and the *rbc*L trees. We can see the distribution of support for particular clades in Figure 46.4. Keeping in mind

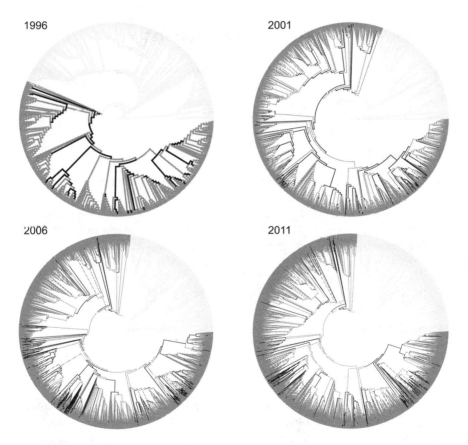

FIGURE 46.4   Plot of support for branches in *rbc*L analyses that agree with Soltis et al. [52] analyses. The trees are in the same orientation as in Figure 46.2.

that the Soltis et al. [52] study only considered seed plants (so the bottom part of the *rbc*L phylogenies would not be considered), there is a tendency for support for many of the deep relationships. In the flowering plants in both the 2006 and 2011 trees, there is less support for deeper relationships. These nodes are precisely where support is lost from the bootstrap analyses and likely reflect the same lack of information.

There are important conclusions to be made by generating and comparing the *rbc*L trees. First, data are being generated and added to increase species sampling, but for plants many of the major clades have been sampled. This is not the case for many other organisms where major groups remain unsampled [13, 49]. Also, as species sampling increases, we can expect that support will decrease in general, especially when the number of alignment sites remains constant. This does not necessarily mean that the trees are less accurate. Quite the contrary. The trees should more accurately reflect the "known" phylogeny. We may have overestimated support when fewer taxa were sampled. Of course, some overcome this by adding more gene regions, which can help (either in the form of gene trees or gene regions for combined analyses). However, it is also important to better represent species. The 2011 analysis stands out as an example where perhaps having more species takes away from our ability to explore tree space. The fact that it has fewer nodes that support the Soltis et al. [52] tree may reflect this issue.

46.4 FUTURE CHALLENGES AND OPPORTUNITIES

Despite the technological developments that have facilitated the rapid growth of phylogenetic trees, there are challenges that need to be overcome to take full advantage of ongoing rapid data generation. With many of these challenges, there are opportunities for substantial methodological development and advances.

46.4.1 Computational Limits of Phylogenetic Inference

Some of the current computational limits have already been addressed in Section 46.2.2. From the growth in data set sizes it is clear that phylogenetic inference is becoming a computational science with all the associated, well-known problems. One major problem is verifiability of results, that is, if a phylogenetic analysis requires one million CPU hours, it will not be possible for reviewers to repeat the computations for result verification. Other issues are archiving and result verification requirements as imposed, for instance, by the *German Science Foundation* (DFG), which requires not only that all scientific data be archived for 10 years but also that all experiments be reproducible for 10 years. Given the rapid development of computer architectures, software, and compilers it will almost certainly not be possible to exactly reconstruct large-scale supercomputer analyses after some years. Moreover, researchers frequently tend to forget the caveats of parallel reduction operations, that is, that simply using a different number of processors may yield slightly different numerical results. Hence phylogenetics may be heading toward becoming a nonverifiable scientific discipline.

Another major problem is the development of complex analysis pipelines that entail steps such as sequence assembly, orthology assignment, multiple-sequence alignment, phylogeny reconstruction, and finally postanalysis in the tree. The potential and danger for introducing program bugs in such large pipelines that frequently involve several multidisciplinary teams will increase with the complexity of the pipelines and the number of computational resources used. Some examples of program bugs and their impact on phylogenetics are discussed in [56].

At the technical level, we see three major challenges: (i) numerical stability on many-taxon data sets, (ii) increasing vector unit sizes, and (iii) memory bandwidth.

The problem of numerical stability, especially regarding the Γ model of rate heterogeneity, is that the Γ model seems to be required to directly compare the likelihood scores of competing phylogenetic tree topologies. The CAT approximation of rate heterogeneity, which is numerically more stable (see [20]), seems to be difficult to deploy for likelihood-based tree comparisons because the per-site rate estimates appear to depend more strongly on the topology at hand [35]. Also, it is not guaranteed that analogous numerical problems as observed for Γ on data sets with 20,000 taxa or more will not start appearing with CAT on data sets with say 200,000 taxa. One option may be to deploy arbitrary precision libraries such as implemented in the GNU Scientific Library. However, their use should be limited as far as possible because of the substantial execution time penalties. Overall, a more detailed analysis of numerical issues is required and a better statistical understanding of per-site rate heterogeneity models has become necessary because they can at least help to alleviate some numerical issues.

With respect to computer architectures, there seems to be a trend for vector units on general-purpose CPUs to increase in length with Intel already working on 512-bit vector units. Inversely, small general-purpose processors are being integrated with GPUs, such as the ARM CPUs that form part of the Nvidia Tegra system. From an abstract point of view, general-purpose processors (x86, ARM) that can steer computations, parse input files, and so on, are coupled with a narrow (AVX) or wide (GPU) vector processing unit onto which floating-point intensive computations can be offloaded. One major challenge will thus consist in adapting commonly used likelihood function implementations to vector architectures. For instance, certain computational shortcuts (e.g., the SEV technique) and memory-saving tricks that work well on x86 architectures may not be directly applicable to wide vector units, especially when they entail irregular data access patterns. For instance, storing tip vectors as raw DNA sequences and using probability look-up tables indexed by these raw sequences or the indexing scheme required for the CAT model of rate heterogeneity may prove difficult to map to wide vector units. A transition toward x86 512-bit vector intrinsics would already require a substantial redesign of RAxML.

Since likelihood function implementation performance is already memory bandwidth bound at present, it may well be that the performance of wider vectors unit cannot be exploited due to memory bandwidth limitations. We may reach the point where recomputing data, rather than retrieving it from memory, will represent the more efficient implementation alternative.

Another major challenge will consist in integrating more complex statistical models that account, for instance, for heterotachy (different statistical models of evolution in different parts of the tree) or for explicit insertion/deletion events into the existing codes.

Given the prolegomena, phylogenetic inference will be limited by the computational resources (also taking into account the energy costs for building phylogenies), the ability of evolutionary biologists to use these resources, and the number of software engineers that understand the application domain and at the same time have the programming skills to handle ever more complex parallel computing environments.

Finally, one limit that one should never forget about is that phylogenetic inference under maximum likelihood is NP hard [41].

46.4.2 Computational Limits of Phylogenetic Postprocessing

In addition to the computational limits in constructing large phylogenetic trees, there are limits to the analyses that can be performed on the trees that are generated.

46.4.2.1 *Discrete Postanalysis*

RF distances and strict as well as majority-rule consensus trees can easily be computed on very large trees and tree collections provided that a sufficient amount of RAM is available for storing the hash table that contains the bipartitions. However, because of the extremely time-consuming compatibility test, the computation of MRE trees is limited to about 50,000 taxa at present. Of course, the scalability of these algorithms also depends on the number of trees in the tree collection. Another problem is that in particular the MRE algorithm is hard to parallelize on multicore systems because it requires frequent and irregular data accesses [1] leading to well-known problems such as pointer chasing in hast tables on distributed shared memory systems.

Some recently developed methods for rogue taxon identification are limited by either memory requirements [37] or excessive inference times [2]. Because the algorithms developed by Pattengale and Aberer [37] also operate on hash tables of bipartitions, the parallelization of rogue taxon identification methods is equally difficult as for the MRE case. One major challenge will therefore consist in analyzing, optimizing, and parallelizing hash table operations on multicore architectures.

46.4.2.2 *Divergence–Time Estimation and Comparative Methods*

Divergence–time estimation is central to many questions addressed in biology. Despite the recent improvements to the theoretical development of the field, relatively few of these methods are available for large phylogenies. In particular, Bayesian methods for autocorrelated and uncorrelated relaxed clock estimation of divergence–times are not currently computationally efficient for large data sets. There is a great need for the optimization of those methods or the development of new methods that can accommodate large phylogenies.

In addition to divergence–time analysis, biologists often conduct comparative analyses including but not limited to ancestral state calculations, diversification rate estimation, biogeographic reconstructions, and estimation of evolutionary models throughout the phylogeny. As with divergence–time estimation, with some exceptions, few of these methods can handle huge phylogenies. There is the need for further optimization and development of methods to accommodate huge phylogenies.

Because the scope and scale of comprehensive phylogenies can bring new insights into the discovery of biological patterns, in addition to the further development of existing methods, new methods should be developed that take advantage of the increased information.

46.4.3 Data Limits

Large phylogenetic data sets will always be limited by the availability of data. Molecular data in public databases continue to grow at an ever more rapid rate and the limitations posed by the available data should continue to be less important. In fact, the biological world is currently experiencing an exciting revolution in the speed at which molecular data can be gathered. However, despite this rapid increase in available data, there are still limitations posed by the public databases. Basically, the construction of large phylogenetic data sets is currently limited by the number of available species and available sequences.

New species continue to be added to public databases, though for some groups of organisms this is faster than others. For example, as demonstrated with the *rbc*L plant data set presented here, the number of species rapidly increased over the last few years. Also, most of the families have at least one representative. However, for some groups such as insects, there is still extremely poor representation.

In addition to the number of species, there is a limitation in the representation of sequences per species. Although there is a dichotomy between data sets that have large numbers of species and few gene regions and those that have large numbers of gene regions and few species, this is not a biological dichotomy. Preferably, as more sequences become available, we will be able to construct large data sets of species and sequences. This is becoming a reality with the introduction of next-generation sequencing technologies. However, despite the availability of new technologies, until their widespread adoption by the systematics community, representation of nonmodel organisms will be limited.

46.5 CONCLUSION

In this chapter we have presented an overview of some computational methods that allow for the reconstruction and downstream analysis of phylogenetic trees with thousands of species. In some cases, as the example with *rbc*L demonstrates, data are available for single gene regions that can be used to infer reasonable trees for broad portions of the tree of life. These data continue to grow and more data are being produced at an increasingly rapid pace, including data generated from next-generation sequencing techniques.

As the field of phylogenetics looks forward, it will be important to continue to develop computational techniques that keep pace with the rate of data acquisition. We expect numerical scalability of analytical methods as well as parallel scalability to hundreds or thousands of cores in conjunction with architecture-specific optimizations to become increasingly important.

In fact, we view phylogenetics as an emerging computational science. Hence, a closer interaction between the phylogenetics and *high-performance computing* (HPC) communities will be required to advance the field. One possible approach is to establish dedicated thematic computing centers (e.g., similar to, by now, well-established climate computing centers) for biodiversity informatics that can address the special requirements and capture the application domain knowledge of our community.

ACKNOWLEDGMENT

This research was supported in part by a grant from the National Science Foundation iPlant Collaborative (No. 0735191).

REFERENCES

1. A. J. Aberer, N. D. Pattengale, and A. Stamatakis. Parallel computation of phylogenetic consensus trees. *Procedia Comput. Sci.*, 1(1):1059–1067, 2010.

2. A. J. Aberer and A. Stamatakis. A simple and accurate method for rogue taxon identification. In *Proceedings of IEEE International Conference on Bioinformatics and Biomedicine*, Atlanta, GA, 2011, pp. 118–122.

3. S. A. Berger and A. Stamatakis. Accuracy and performance of single versus double precision arithmetics for maximum likelihood phylogeny reconstruction. In *Proceedings of PBC09, Parallel-Biocomputing Workshop*. Vol. 6068 of *Lecture Notes in Computer Science*, Springer, Heidelberg, 2010, pp. 270–279.

4. T. Britton, C. L. Anderson, D. Jacquet, S. Lundqvist, and K. Bremer. Estimating divergence times in large phylogenetic trees. *Syst. Biol.*, 56(5):741–752, 2007.

5. D. Bryant, J. Tsang, P. Kearney, and M. Li. Computing the quartet distance between evolutionary trees. In *Proceedings of the Eleventh Annual ACM-SIAM Symposium on Discrete Algorithms*. Society for Industrial and Applied Mathematics, ACM Press, NY, 2000, pp. 285–286.

6. M. W. Chase et al. Phylogenetics of seed plants: An analysis of nucleotide sequences from the plastid gene rbcL. *Ann. Missouri Botan. Garden*, 80:528–580, 1993.

7. C. Darwin. *On the Origin of the Species by Means of Natural Selection: or, The Preservation of Favoured Races in the Struggle for Life.* John Murray, London, 1859.

8. W. H. E. Day and D. Sankoff. Computational complexity of inferring phylogenies by compatibility. *Syst. Biol.*, 35(2):224, 1986.

9. J. Doebley, M. Durbin, E. M. Golenberg, M. T. Clegg, and D. P. Ma. Evolutionary analysis of the large subunit of carboxylase (rbcl) nucleotide sequence among the grasses (gramineae). *Evolution*, 44(4):1097–1108, 1990.

10. S. Dongen. A cluster algorithm for graphs. Technical Report. CWI, Amsterdam, The Netherlands, 2000.

11. A. J. Drummond and A. Rambaut. BEAST: Bayesian evolutionary analysis by sampling trees. *BMC Evol. Biol.*, 7(214):1471–2148, 2007.

12. A. J Drummond, S. Y. W. Ho, M. J. Phillips, and A. Rambaut. Relaxed phylogenetics and dating with confidence. *PLoS Biol.*, 4(5):e88, 2006.

13. C. W. Dunn et al. Broad phylogenomic sampling improves resolution of the animal tree of life. *Nature*, 452(7188):745–749, 2008.

14. R. C. Edgar. Muscle: Multiple sequence alignment with high accuracy and high throughput. *Nucleic Acids Res.*, 32(5):1792–1797, 2004.

15. E. J. Edwards, C. P. Osborne, C. A. E. Strömberg, S. A. Smith, and C 4 Grasses Consortium. The origins of c4 grasslands: Integrating evolutionary and ecosystem science. *Science*, 328(5978):587–591, 2010.

16. E. J. Edwards and S. A. Smith. Phylogenetic analyses reveal the shady history of c4 grasses. *Proc. Natl. Acad. Sci.*, 107:2532–2537, 2010.

17. J. A. Eisen and C. M. Fraser. Phylogenomics: Intersection of evolution and genomics. *Science*, 300(5626):1706–1707, 2003.

18. J. Felsenstein. Evolutionary trees from DNA sequences: A maximum likelihood approach. *J. Mol. Evol.*, 17:368–376, 1981.

19. J. Felsenstein. Confidence limits on phylogenies: An approach using the bootstrap. *Evolution*, 39(4):783–791, 1985.

20. F. Izquierdo-Carrasco, S. A. Smith, and A. Stamatakis. Algorithms, data structures, and numerics for likelihood-based phylogenetic inference of huge trees. Technical Report. Heidelberg Institute for Theoretical Studies, 2011.

21. P. A. Goloboff, S. A. Catalano, J. M. Mirande, C. A. Szumik, J. S. Arias, M. Källersjö, and J. S. Farris. Phylogenetic analysis of 73060 taxa corroborates major eukaryotic groups. *Cladistics*, 25:1–20, 2009.

22. P. A. Goloboff, J. S. Farris, and K. Nixon. TNT: Tree analysis using new technology. *Program and Documentation*, Version 1, 2000. Available: http://www.cladistics.com/aboutTNT.html.

23. S. Guindon and O. Gascuel. A simple, fast, and accurate algorithm to estimate large phylogenies by maximum likelihood. *Syst. Biol.*, 52(5):696–704, 2003.

24. A. Hejnol et al. Rooting the bilaterian tree with scalable phylogenomic and supercomputing tools. *Proc. R. Soc. B*, 276:4261–4270, 2009.

25. G. Hickey, F. Dehne, A. Rau-Chaplin, and C. Blouin. Spr distance computation for unrooted trees. *Evol. Bioinformatics Online*, 4:17, 2008.

26. M. Höhl and M. A. Ragan. Is multiple sequence alignment required for accurate inference of phylogeny? *Syst. Biol.*, 56(2):206–221, 2007.

27. F. Izquierdo-Carrasco and A. Stamatakis. Computing the phylogenetic likelihood function out-of-core. In *Proceedings of IPDPS 2011 (HICOMB Workshop)*, IEEE, NY, 2011, pp. 444–451.

28. F. Izquierdo-Carrasco, J. Gagneur, and A. Stamatakis. Trading memory for running time in phylogenetic likelihood computations. Technical Report. Heidelberg Institute for Theoretical Studies, 2011.

29. K. Katoh, K. Kuma, H. Toh, and T. Miyata. Mafft version 5: Improvement in accuracy of multiple sequence alignment. *Nucleic Acids Res.*, 33:511–518, 2005.

30. K. Katoh and H. Toh. Recent developments in the mafft multiple sequence alignment program. *Brief. Bioinformatics*, 9(4):286–298, 2008.

31. K. Liu, S. Raghavan, S. Nelesen, C. R. Linder, and T. Warnow. Rapid and accurate large-scale coestimation of sequence alignments and phylogenetic trees. *Science*, 324(5934):1561–1564, 2009.

32. A. Löytynoja and N. Goldman. Phylogeny-aware gap placement prevents errors in sequence alignment and evolutionary analysis. *Science*, 320(5883):1632–1635, 2008.

33. S. Matthews and T. Williams. Mrsrf: An efficient mapreduce algorithm for analyzing large collections of evolutionary trees. *BMC Bioinformatics*, 11(Suppl. 1):S15, 2010.

34. M. M. McMahon and M. J. Sanderson. Phylogenetic supermatrix analysis of genbank sequences from 2228 papilionoid legumes. *Syst. Biol.*, 55(5):818–836, 2006.

35. S. Meyer and A. V. Haeseler. Identifying site-specific substitution rates. *Mol. Biol. Evol.*, 20:182–189, 2003.

36. B. M. E. Moret, U. Roshan, and T. Warnow. Sequence-length requirements for phylogenetic methods. *Lecture Notes Comput. Sci.*, 2452:343–356, 2002.

37. N. Pattengale, A. Aberer, K. Swenson, A. Stamatakis, and B. Moret. Uncovering hidden phylogenetic consensus in large datasets. *Trans. Computat. Biol. Bioinformatics, IEEE/ACM*, 4(8):902–911, 2011.

38. D. D. Pollock, D. J. Zwickl, J. A. McGuire, and D. M. Hillis. Increased taxon sampling is advantageous for phylogenetic inference. *Syst. Biol.*, 51(4):664–671, 2002.

39. A. Rambaut and N. C. Grass. Seq-Gen: An application for the Monte Carlo simulation of DNA sequence evolution along phylogenetic trees. *Bioinformatics*, 13(3):235–238, 1997.

40. D. F. Robinson and L. R. Foulds. Comparison of phylogenetic trees. *Math. Biosci*, 53(1–2):131–147, 1981.

41. S. Roch. A short proof that phylogenetic tree reconstruction by maximum likelihood is hard. *IEEE/ACM Trans. Computat. Biol. Bioinformatics*, 3:92–94, 2006.

42. M. Sanderson, M. McMahon, and M. Steel. Phylogenomics with incomplete taxon coverage: The limits to inference. *BMC Evol. Biol.*, 10(1):155, 2010.

43. M. J. Sanderson. Estimating absolute rates of molecular evolution and divergence times: A penalized likelihood approach. *Mol. Biol. Evol.*, 19(1):101–109, 2002.

44. M. J. Sanderson, M. M. McMahon, and M. Steel. Terraces in phylogenetic tree space. *Science*, 333(6041):448–450, 2011.

45. M. J. Sanderson. A nonparametric approach to estimating divergence times in the absence of rate constancy. *Mol. Biol. Evol.*, 14(12):1218, 1997.

46. S. A. Smith and M. J. Donoghue. Rates of molecular evolution are linked to life history in flowering plants. *Science*, 322(5898):86–89, 2008.

47. S. Smith, J. Beaulieu, and M. Donoghue. Mega-phylogeny approach for comparative biology: An alternative to supertree and supermatrix approaches. *BMC Evol. Biol.*, 9(1):37, 2009.

48. S. A. Smith, J. M. Beaulieu, A. Stamatakis, and M. J. Donoghue. Understanding angiosperm diversification using small and large phylogenetic trees. *Am. J. Bot.*, 98(3):404–414, 2011.

49. S. A. Smith, N. G. Wilson, F. Goetz, C. Feehery, S. Andrade, G. Rouse, G. Giribet, and C. W. Dunn. Resolving the evolutionary relationships of molluscs with phylogenomic tools. *Nature*, 480:364–367, 2011.

50. T. F. Smith and M. S. Waterman. Identification of common molecular subsequences. *J. Mol. Biol.*, 147(1):195–197, 1981.

51. D. E. Soltis, P. S. Soltis, M. T. Clegg, and M. Durbin. rbcl sequence divergence and phylogenetic relationships in saxifragaceae sensu lato. *Proc. Natl. Acad. Sci.*, 87(12):4640–4644, 1990.

52. D. E. Soltis et al. Angiosperm phylogeny: 17 genes, 640 taxa. *Am. J. Bot.*, 98(4):704–730, 2011.

53. A. Stamatakis. Phylogenetic models of rate heterogeneity: A high performance computing perspective. In *Proc. of IPDPS2006 (HICOMB Workshop)*, Proceedings on CD, IEEE, NY, April 2006, pp. 1–8.

54. A. Stamatakis. RAxML-VI-HPC: Maximum likelihood-based phylogenetic analyses with thousands of taxa and mixed models. *Bioinformatics*, 22(21):2688–2690, 2006.

55. A. Stamatakis and N. Alachiotis. Time and memory efficient likelihood-based tree searches on phylogenomic alignments with missing data. *Bioinformatics*, 26(12):i132, 2010.

56. A. Stamatakis and F. Izquierdo-Carrasco. Result verification, code verification and computation of support values in phylogenetics. *Brief. Bioinformatics*, 12(3):270, 2011.

57. A. Stamatakis, T. Ludwig, H. Meier, and M. J. Wolf. AxML: A fast program for sequential and parallel phylogenetic tree calculations based on the maximum likelihood method. In *Proceedings of 1st IEEE Computer Society Bioinformatics Conference (CSB2002)*, IEEE, NY, 2002, pp. 21–28.

58. A. Stamatakis and M. Ott. Efficient computation of the phylogenetic likelihood function on multigene alignments and multi-core architectures. *Phil. Trans. R. Soc. Ser. B Biol. Sci.*, 363:3977–3984, 2008.

59. A. Stamatakis and M. Ott. Exploiting fine-grained parallelism in the phylogenetic likelihood function with MPI, Pthreads, and OpenMP: A performance study. In M. Chetty, A. Ngom, and S. Ahmad (Eds.), *PRIB*, Vol. 5265 of *Lecture Notes in Computer Science*, Springer, Berlin, 2008, pp. 424–435.

60. A. Stamatakis. Parsimonator source code. Available: `https://github.com/stamatak/Parsimonator-1.0`.

61. A. Stamatakis. RAxML-Light source code. Available: `https://github.com/stamatak/RAxML-Light-1.0.5`.

62. D. L. Swofford. PAUP*: Phylogenetic Analysis Using Parsimony (*and OtherMethods), Version 4.0b10. Sinauer Associates, MA, 2002.

63. J. D. Thompson, B. Linard, O. Lecompte, and O. Poch. A comprehensive benchmark study of multiple sequence alignment methods: Current challenges and future perspectives. *PLoS ONE*, 6(3):e18093, 2011.

64. J. L. Thorne, H. Kishino, and I. S. Painter. Estimating the rate of evolution of the rate of molecular evolution. *Mol. Biol. Evol.*, 15(12):1647–1657, 1998.

65. C. Yan, J. G. Burleigh, and O. Eulenstein. Identifying optimal incomplete phylogenetic data sets from sequence databases. *Mol. Phylogenet. Evol.*, 35(3):528–535, 2005.

66. Z. Yang. Maximum likelihood phylogenetic estimation from DNA sequences with variable rates over sites. *J. Mol. Evol.*, 39:306–314, 1994.

67. D. Zwickl. Genetic algorithm approaches for the phylogenetic analysis of large biological sequence datasets under the maximum likelihood criterion. Ph.D. Thesis. University of Texas at Austin, Apr. 2006.

68. D. J. Zwickl and D. M. Hillis. Increased taxon sampling greatly reduces phylogenetic error. *Syst. Biol.*, 51(4):588–598, 2002.

CHAPTER 47

BIOLOGICAL KNOWLEDGE VISUALIZATION

RODRIGO SANTAMARÍA

Department of Computer Science and Automation, University of Salamanca, Salamanca, Spain

47.1 INTRODUCTION

Since the Human Genome Project [1], technology in life sciences, at least from the genomics point of view, has rapidly evolved. From the polymerase chain reaction to microarray chips to new-generation sequencing, technology is providing vast amounts of biological data. During the last decade, information technology has been able to deal with the data produced by life sciences technology, producing databases, repositories, ontologies, and standards. But even the basic infrastructure to deal with biological data (storage, classification, and transference) is becoming a challenge. Just as an example, the cost of sequencing a base pair is already cheaper than the cost for its storage [2].

Considering this, higher layers of data manipulation (representation and analysis) have become a real issue, giving way to thousands of computational techniques, tools, and publications. Biological knowledge visualization has become the best companion of computational methods in order to find structure in these complex, high-dimensional sets of data, helping to reduce analysis times and boost the detection of patterns.

In this chapter we make a humble review of these issues and the state-of-the-art solutions. The next section briefly introduces the concepts of information visualization and visual analytics, which guide us beyond simple, static representations of data. The third section discusses the characteristics of biological data that most affect its useful visualization. The following sections compile the most relevant methods and tools developed for different types of biological data (sequence data, functional and relational data, expression data, and molecular structure data). The last section sums up the review and presents future challenges for biological knowledge visualization.

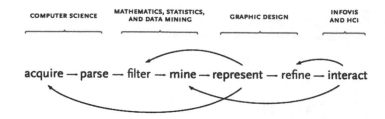

FIGURE 47.1   Computational information design [5].

47.2   INFORMATION VISUALIZATION AND VISUAL ANALYTICS

Information visualization is the use of interactive visual representations of abstract data to amplify cognition [3]. Interaction is possibly the word that better distinguish information visualization from mere representation. The more complex data are, the more difficult it is to represent them all on a static view, and the more important it is to support abstract data with interactive representations.

Typically, patterns and structure in biological data are found by means of numerical analysis, but numerical analysis only exploits our abstract (logical, mathematical) intelligence. In order to maximize our understanding of a given problem, we should make use of other kinds of intelligence, especially verbal and visual intelligence.[*] In particular, information visualization exploits visual intelligence in order to help abstract intelligence.

Visual analytics goes one step beyond information visualization, integrating visual representation into the thinking process [4] so visualization becomes a relevant factor within the whole thinking discourse, empowering our analytical capabilities. Therefore, visual analytics aims at producing visualizations that help the user to reason, synthesize data, and discover patterns.

Both disciplines (information visualization and visual analytics) are very closely related and are sometimes considered the same, although information visualization focuses more on interaction and visual analytics does on the contribution of visual representation to the reasoning process. In either case, the design of visual solutions must take into account the reasoning process, our visual capabilities, the interaction between human and computer, and the problem under study. Figure 47.1, from Ben Fry's master thesis [5], defines a comprehensive schema of the main tasks and fields that are involved in a visual thinking process. Note how computer science, mathematics, statistics, graphic design, and visualization are intermingled in a highly iterative thinking process, where the inspection of representations and results can lead us to repeat or redesign our analysis.

Keim et al. [6] provide a more formal schema, introducing an important element: the problem at hand. They define visual analytics as an integration of data, visualizations, and hypotheses that lead to insight about the problem, the interaction and feedback among these four entities being key to the thinking process.

47.3   BIOLOGICAL DATA TYPES

Biological knowledge comes from different sources, both biological and technological. We will use the following classification in order to discuss their characteristics and review visualization approaches.

---

[*]Howard Gardner developed the psychological theory of multiple intelligences, published in 1983.

47.3.1 Sequence Data

DNA sequences contain all the genetic information about living organisms. DNA sequences develop into other kinds of sequences, from mRNA to amino acids. In between, there is a myriad of sequence types [e.g., expressed sequence tags (ESTs), miRNA, shiRNA, piRNA, microsatellites] and sequence sizes (e.g., genome, chromosome, gene, shotgun sequence). However, they share some characteristics: (1) a limited alphabet composed of a small number of characters; (2) are defined by a typically long, one-dimensional vector of characters from that alphabet; and (3) have location relationships between sequences, either at the same level (proximity of one gene to another) or among levels (location of a gene on a chromosome or genome).

Sequence data analysis has two major goals: to characterize and detect patterns (e.g., determine GC content or search for candidate genes on a new genome) and to compare sequences, more known as *sequence alignment*.

47.3.2 Expression Data

DNA sequence data, following the central dogma of molecular biology, expresses into several copies of mRNA and proteins. The accounting of the number of copies by means of different technologies (microarray chips, tiling arrays, RNA-seq) links an expression level to each expressed sequence. When measuring expression levels under several experimental conditions, the result is a numerical matrix to be analyzed: (1) by detecting differentially expressed genes and (2) by searching for sequences and/or experimental conditions with similar expression patterns. The two most important expression data repositories are GEO [7] and ArrayExpress [8].

47.3.3 Relational Data

As a result of the analysis of sequence and expression data and of wet-laboratory experiments, conclusions have been reached about how sequences relate to each other. Those relationships are recorded as networks, where nodes represent biological entities (raw sequences, genes, gene products, or even organisms) and edges linking them represent relationships, which can be quantitative (e.g., correlation networks), qualitative (e.g., regulatory or metabolic networks), or topological (e.g., protein–protein interactions). Pathways may also be incorporated to the analysis, typically by mapping candidate genes to already known pathways, which gives us insight on how biological processes occur by following expression flows on a pathway (for a compilation of pathway analysis techniques, see [9]). There are several resources that store relational information, maybe the best known being KEGG [10].

47.3.4 Functional Data

As we discover new relations among genes or gene products, we also discover new functions related to them. As in the case of relational data, these functional annotations are both the result of analyses and income for newer analyses, typically to validate or guide them. For example, *gene set enrichment analysis* [11] tries to find which sets of genes (each set is a group of genes annotated with the same function) are differentially expressed on a given experiment, instead of searching for single genes. These kinds of techniques are useful because they give "biological sense" to the results, but as a drawback they can bias the analysis toward already known sets.

Functional annotations are recorded into ontologies, which are dictionaries of functions with controlled, hierarchical vocabularies, in order to make them standard and comparable. The most widespread ontology is Gene Ontology [12], which covers molecular functions, biological processes, and cellular components.

47.3.5 Structure Data

DNA, RNA, and protein sequences fold into 3D structures that interact with the surroundings. The sequence influences the resulting 3D structure, and understanding the 3D structure is key to understand how it interacts (binds) to other compounds, that is, proteins, DNA, small ligands, or drugs.

Protein structure is divided into four levels: (1) *primary structure* refers to the 2D amino acid sequence, (2) *secondary structure* determines if the highly regular substructures are alpha helixes or beta strands, (3) *tertiary structure* is the 3D representation of secondary structure, and (4) *quaternary structure* assembles a larger number of small subunits.

Structure data are available for about 1% of all proteins, stored by the public versions of the worldwide *Protein Data Bank* (PDB) [13], especially the RSCB PDB [14] and the PDBe [15]. Of the remaining protein structures 40–50% are significantly similar to one in the PDB [16].

47.4 BIOLOGICAL DATA VISUALIZATION ISSUES

Biological data present some issues from the point of view of visualization. Several of them are also relevant for numerical/statistical analyses. Some of these issues are common to all types of biological data, while others affect more to a given type of data.

47.4.1 Complexity

Complexity is common ground to biological data because of the diversity of species, the length of genomes, and the several layers found in molecular biology. As of today, technology is capable of measuring almost every detail of this complex world.

Visualizing all this is computationally complicated, if not unfeasible (e.g., we do not have enough pixels in the screen to visualize every base pair in the human genome), and it is often perceptually useless.

Therefore, different simplification techniques are implemented, typically the use of biological layers (not to represent the whole genome but only the exome or divide it into chromosomes) and mathematical/statistical filters (e.g., select only genes differentially expressed).

Visualization provides the user with two additional tools for reducing complexity: zooming and filtering. Filtering gives the option to remove information that is irrelevant at a given moment of the analysis. Zooming techniques allow starting with general representations of data and getting deeper into details for small portions, as analysis develops.* There are two

---

*This is sometimes called semantic zoom, as opposed to normal zoom, where information is only magnified but no additional details are added with zoom changes.

very important characteristics to consider when implementing visual zoom and filters: Do not lose context (to know at every moment where we are in the general "map of data") and do not lose track of the analysis (filter back or zoom out, so we can reach any previous point of the analysis). These two characteristics are key in order to support visual analysis and to some extent refer to the "feedback loops" that appear in visual analytics models (e.g., Figure 47.1).

47.4.2 Dimensionality

A problem related to complexity is dimensionality. Biological data usually present several dimensions, while digital displays have only two. Complexity reduction visual methods such as zooming and filtering can be applied, but there are specific numerical methods for dimensionality reduction. *Principal-component analysis* (PCA) [17] is a commonly used numerical technique to reduce complexity by calculating the most relevant vectors that separate data, but as a drawback they lose detail and may oversimplify the available information. 3D graphics is another popular visual solution, although it is not actual 3D representation (it is still displayed on a 2D surface) and, except for natural 3D data such as molecular structures, is not enough when we handle dozens or hundreds of dimensions.

47.4.3 Asymmetry

Biological data are often not only complex but also asymmetric. Single sequences are long one-dimensional vectors. Sequence alignments consider a few sequences of hundreds of nucleotides or amino acids. Expression matrices usually have thousands of rows (genes, probes) and only some columns (one for experiment or replicate). Phylogenetic trees have several leafs but only one root.

These asymmetries give way to different visualization issues, three being the most frequent: navigation overuse, loss of context and waste of screen space. These effects can be minimized with different visual approaches, for example to use different scaling factors for width and height (although this could lead to unaesthetic or unreadable solutions), persistent labels (e.g., to keep the context of the row names at the left when scrolling right), and zooming. However, asymmetry is an intrinsic characteristic of data that is hard to overcome completely.

Some computational techniques to reduce complexity can be used also to reduce asymmetry, such as probe summarization into genes on microarray experiments or the conversion of nucleotides into amino acids on sequences.

Waste of space is a lesser issue but in the case of hierarchies can easily affect one-third of the representation area. Some authors have adopted radial visualizations to minimize it (see Section 47.5.1). Tree maps [18] are another visualization approach to cover space in hierarchical structures such as ontologies or phylogenies.

47.4.4 Diversity

Living organisms are diverse, and so is the information we get from them. Diversity may come in at least three different ways: (1) diversity on complexity levels, (2) diversity on biological points of view, and (3) diversity on data sources. For a single gene, we may have information about its chromosome, organism, and individual (different complexity levels); we can also have information about its sequence, expression level under different experiments, relations with other genes, and functional annotations (diversity on biological points of view); this information may come from different databases, each with different standards and formats (diversity on data sources.)

Biology, especially systems biology [19], makes use of different points of view to provide integrative explanations to biological problems. Information visualization, but especially visual analytics, considers integration as a key feature to improve visual understanding. The major strategy toward integration is visualization linkage. For example, the selection of a group of differentially expressed genes provokes the selection of the same genes on a linked biological network, which happens to be closely related, automatically uncovering a relationship pattern to the analyst.

Linkage between two visualizations is a relatively easy strategy to implement, if both visualizations represent the same biological entities. However, the technique becomes more complex if we deal with visualizations at different biological levels (a gene may map to different isoforms, several genes map to the same chromosome, etc.) An even more complicated issue is the fact that information is distributed among a large number of heterogeneous, usually noncompatible, databases and repositories. Standards like Entrez [20] or UniProt [21] identifiers significantly help on this task, but there remains a high degree of heterogeneity* that hinders integration.

47.5 SEQUENCE DATA VISUALIZATION

Sequence visualization is probably the most developed visualization in the postgenomic era. The most basic sequence representation is an array of characters representing nucleotides or amino acids following a standard code. This initial representation is useful for a handful of elements, but for larger numbers we are more interested in the general structure of the sequence rather than in the identity of the bases.

Roughly speaking, there are two major patterns of structure we can detect on a sequence: patterns due to inherent characteristics and patterns due to abundance. Inherent characteristics of sequence elements usually refer to physicochemical properties (e.g., amino acids can be classified as hydrophobic or hydrophilic). Visually speaking, we can color sequence elements differently for each type, so sections of the sequence with a predominant color will rise up (Figure 47.2, top) and help on the understanding of the sequence.

Visualizing abundance for each sequence element is also a way of detecting patterns. Cumulative abundance accounts for the amount of a given property from the beginning of the sequence to a given point or on a window around the point. For example, GC content is a typical cumulative abundance metric,[†] determining the percentage of guanine and cytosine around each point of the sequence. Abundance is usually represented by histograms, so a change in the abundance is conveyed by a change in the bar's heights or the line's slope (Figure 47.2, bottom).

These techniques, along with generic techniques such as scrolling, zooming, or filtering, are the basis for visualizing more complex sequence data in either the "horizontal" dimension (genomes) or the "vertical" dimension (multiple sequence alignments.)

---

*And will probably continue existing, since it is an intrinsic characteristic of biological data.

[†] Used, for example, for classifying bacterias. It can also be related to some selective processes.

MAAPSRTTLMPPPFRLQLRLLILPILLLLRHDAVHAEPYSGGFGSSAVSSGGLGSVGIHIPGGGVGVITEARCPRVCSCTGLNVDCSHRGLTSVPRKISAD
VERLELQGNNLTVIYETDFQRLTKLRMLQLTDNQIHTIERNSFQDLVSLERLRLNNNRLKAIPENFVTSSASLLRLDISNNVITTVGRRVFKGAQSLRSLQ
LDNNQITCLDEHAFKGLVELEILTLNNNNLTSLPHNIFGGLGRLRALRLSDNPFACDCHLSWLSRPLRSATRLAPYTRCQSPSQLKGQNVADLHDQEFKCS
GLTEHAPMECGAENSCPHPCRCADGIVDCREKSLTSVPVTLPDDTTDVRLLEQNFITELPPKSFSSFRRLRRIDLSNNNISRIAHDALSGLKQLTTLVLYGN
KIKDLPSGVFKGLGSLQLLLLNANEISCIRKDAFRDLHSLSLLSLYDNNIQSLANGTFDAMKSIKTVHLAKNPFICDCNLRWLLADYLLHKNPIETSGARCES
PKRMHRRRIESLREEKFKCSWDELRMKLSGECRMDSDCPAMCHCEGTTVDCTGRGLKEIPRDIPLHTTELLLNDNELGRISSDGLFGRLRPHLVKLELLKRNQ
LTGIEPNAFECAGHIQELDLGENKIKEISNKMFGLHQLKTLNLYDNQISCVMPGSFEHLNSLTSLNLASNPFNCNCHLLAWFAEWLRKKSLNGGAARCGAP
SKVRDVQIKDLPHSEFKCSSENSEGCLGDGYCPPSCTCTGTVVRCSRNQLKEIPRGIPAETSELLYLESNEIEQIHYERIRHLRSLTRLDLSNNQITILSNY
TFANLTKLSTLIISYNKLQCLQRHALSGLNNLRVLSLHGNRISMLPEGSFEDLKSLTHIALGSNPLYCDCGLKWFSDWIKLDYVEPGIARCAEPEQMKDKL
ILSTPSSSFVCRGRVRNDILAKCNACFEQPCQNQAQCVALPQREYQCLCQPGYHGKHCEFMIDACYGNPCRNNATCTVLEEGRFSCQCAPGYTGARCETNI
DDCLGEIKCQNNATCIDGVESYKCECQPGFSGEFCDTKIQFCSPEFNPCANGAKCMDHFTHYSCDCQAGFHGTNCTDNIDDCQNHMCQNGGTCVDGINDYQ
CRCPDDYTGKYCEGHNMISMMYPQTSPCQNHECKHGVCFQPNAQGSDYLCRCHPGYTGKWCEYLTSISFVHNNSFVELEPLRTRPEANVTIVFSSAEQNGI
LMYDGQDAHLAVELFNGRIRVSYDVGNHPVSTMYSFEMVADGKYHAVELIAIKKNFTLRVDRGLARSIINEGSNDYLKLTTPMFLLGGLPVDPAQQAYKNWQ
IRNLTSFKGCMKEVWINHKLVDFGNAQRQQKITPGCALLEGEQQEEDDEQDFMDETPHIKEEPVDPCLLENKCRRGSRCVPNSNARDGYQCKCKHGQRGRY
CDQGEGSTEPPTVTAASTCRKEQVREYYTENDCRSRQPLRYAKCVGGCGNQCCAAKIVRRRKVRMVCSNNRKYIKNLDIVRKCGCTKKCY

FIGURE 47.2 Leucines (highlighted with black background) in SLIT protein sequence from *Drosophila melanogaster* (top), revealing leucine-rich regions (e.g., at first third of first line). Histogram representing the number of leucines on a 20-amino-acid window scrolled along the sequence. Four major leucine-rich areas appear plus a peak at the very beginning and a possible fifth area near the end (bottom).

47.5.1 Genome Data Visualization

Genomes are, in the end, very large sequences. This increase in complexity and asymmetry is, by itself, enough to pose a great challenge in visualization. However, genomes are also a great source of information, especially because it is the ground where lower level sequences locate (chromosomes, genes, exons, etc.) and several genetic events occur (deletions, insertions, single-point mutations, etc.). *Next-generation sequencing* (NGS) technologies [22] are considerably lowering the cost of sequencing entire genomes, so previously not sequenced species and population studies are now (and will be) more and more common. Following Nielsen et al. classification [23], we will divide genome analysis into three major categories: (1) genome assembly, (2) genome browsing, and (3) genome comparison.

Genome assembly is the main task when inspecting de novo genomes. This analysis aims at merging sequence reads into full genomes, maximizing consensus and coverage. It shares several visual actions with other genome visualizations, especially genome navigation and zoom. Tools for genome assembly are probably the ones with higher storage and performance needs, since they must consider every read for a sequenced genome. This was a challenge with Sanger sequencing [24] but is even more demanding with NGS.

Genome navigation and computer efficiency are the basis for assembly inspection, that is, to manually inspect the whole genome to solve contig areas with low consensus or not solved by automatic assembly. Consed [25], although designed for Sanger sequencing, has adapted to NGS and is still one of the most complete suits for genome assembly. Broadly speaking, it presents three linked views, contig, aligned reads, and consensus, so the analyzer starts inspecting contigs, with color coding highlighting bad quality areas, that can be further analyzed on the aligned reads and consensus visualization. It also implements some options

TABLE 47.1 Selected Tools for Genome Visualization

Name	Description	Reference
Hawkeye	Visual analytics tool for genome assemblies designed to aid at detecting and correcting assembly errors.	[26]
Consed	Integrative tool with linked visualizations of different degrees of detail to assist manual assembly of genomes	[25]
ABySS-Explorer	Visual solution encoding several useful characteristics for manual genome assembly	[27]
GBrowse	Stand-alone classical genome visualization with online version (WebGBrowse)	[28]
IGB	Very flexible stand-alone browser for any kind of genome-scale data sets	[29]
IGV[a]	Integrative genomics viewer which includes several different sequence-related tracks (expression, copy number, insertion-deletion, etc.) on highly interactive framework	[30]
UCSC[a] Browser	Most popular Web-based genome browser to date with several track options	[31]
Ensembl	EBI online browser, similar to UCSC Browser	[32]
MapViewer	NCBI browser, uses a vertical track display rather than horizontal	[33]
GenoMap	First circular genome viewer	[34]
CGView	Circular genome viewer, mostly static representation	[35]
Circos[a]	Static circular genome displays, several options and high level of details	[36]
MizBee	Highly interactive circular genome visualization with focus on comparison	[37]

[a]Our recommendations.

to speed up the assembly process, such as to jump to the next low-consensus area. Hawkeye [26] updates the concepts in Consed from a visual analytics point of view.

Some more recent tools (see Table 47.1) introduce new techniques to visually encode sequence read properties that are especially useful for analysts. For example, ABySS-Explorer [27] implements de Bruijin graph (a technique to represent overlapping sequences) with special encodings to visualize assemblies and relevant characteristics such as DNA direction (edge polarity), contig size (wave shapes), and assembly inconsistencies (color).

Once a genome is assembled (and while assembling it), genome browsing is the most basic action to do. Browsing implies to travel along the genome to explore different sections. The browsers from public institutions are the most popular ones: the University of California, Santa Cruz (UCSC) Browser [31], the Ensembl Genome Browser [32], and the NCBI MapViewer [33]. All are Web-based browsers, and especially the UCSC Browser is widely used by the scientific community. The UCSC Browser starts with several search options (clade, organism, assembly version, gene, or locus) that serve as an initial filter to explore a genomic region in particular. The resulting visualization is a group of horizontal annotation tracks showing different aspects of the genomic region at hand (see Figure 47.3).

The most important track is the gene track, which represents coding DNA as rectangles. Color and other shapes might be used to represent secondary data about genes (for example, exons and introns). There are two other types of track visualization modes that sometimes

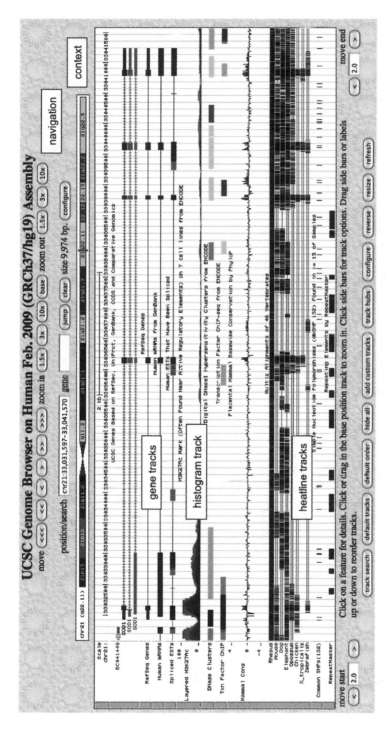

FIGURE 47.3 UCSC Genome Browser. Top buttons and text boxes allow navigation along genome and bar below them contextualizes our position inside chromosome. Stacked tracks form main section of visualization: gene tracks (top) for location of genes and other elements; histogram tracks (middle) convey quantitative measures on sequence (in this case level of enrichment of histone mark detected by ChiP-seq experiment); and heatlines (near bottom) use gray scale to represent match scores with other species.

are represented along with gene tracks. The first are histogram tracks, which use bar or line heights to represent some quantitative measure, such as coverage, expression level, or conservation level. The second are heatmap tracks, in this context better called heatline tracks. Similar to gene tracks, heatline tracks use color scales to convey some quantitative measure, typically expression (as in expression heatmaps) but also, for example, the matching level with sequences from other organisms (as in Figure 47.3).

To keep the context and allow relocation, a chromosome bar is usually visualized, marking our current position on it. Navigation options cover zooming/scaling and displacement plus searches for annotations or locations. Genome visualizations also allow to add or to remove tracks, an option especially wide in the UCSC Browser.

The way interaction works in online genome browsers is especially important. A query for a new location or track is sent to the server, which performs the search, produces a static image, and returns it to the client. The size of the data sets and the number of different tracks, along with the computational costs of the searches, make this interaction mode very convenient, but not totally desirable, because interaction is not immediate and always implies communication with the server.

GBrowse [28], IGV [30], and IGB [29] are stand-alone browsers that avoid this issue, but at the cost of burdening the analyst with the management of sequence and annotation files and formats, storage, and computation. This is convenient for some researchers, but the Web-based options are more broadly used.[*]

Finally, circular genome visualization has been recently introduced and, if not genuine browsers, are able to represent the whole genome at a moderate detail level, including additional tracks (see Circos in Figure 47.4).

Sequence comparison is possibly the most typical analysis in bioinformatics, helping to identify similarities among species, to define phylogenies, to assemble genomes, and so on. For smaller sequences (genes, proteins), alignment algorithms position sequences to optimize their comparison and will be reviewed in the next section.

Regarding the genome or large-scale sequence comparisons, the major visualization option to link corresponding fragments is a line joining them. This type of visualization has evolved from straight lines joining horizontally arranged genomic sequences to curved bundles of edges joining cocircular genomes. Straight lines often get cluttered when several correspondences are found between two sequences, something that can be accepted on short sequences but definitely not in complete genomes. Hierarchical edge bundles [38] was a revolution in the way of displaying large number of edges by stacking together edge sections while their directions are very similar. Besides, asymmetry makes straight line lengths overgrow if joining distant sections.

GenoMap [34] was the first circular genome visualizer, being rapidly improved by other tools such as CGView [35], MizBee [37], and Circos [36]. On circular genomes (Figure 47.4) chromosomes appear as sectors, and further annotations (expression levels, coverage, etc.) can be stacked as concentric rings.

When comparing two genomes, the second genome is displayed adjacent or opposed to the first one. Circos uses this approach, generating information-rich but noninteractive genome comparisons. Circos' strength relies in its adaptation to different needs on the contexts of comparison and annotation, its ability to generate bitmap and vector images, and the possibility to integrate the image generation in data analysis and reporting pipelines. On the

---

[*]In fact, GBrowse launched a Web server version, WebGBrowse, for online visualization of local GFF files.

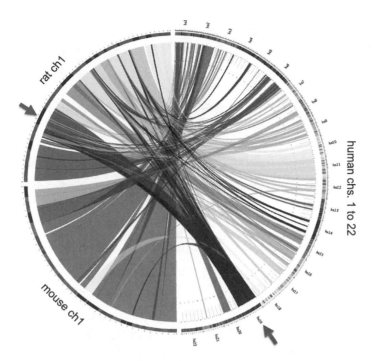

FIGURE 47.4 Circos visualization of human genome chromosomes (right half) against chromosome 1 from mouse (bottom left quarter) and rat (top left quarter) as provided in example data of the tool. Colored bundles (in gray hues) represent sequence matches. There is, for example, an outstanding relationship between chromosome 19 and rat chromosome 1 (arrows). The outside heatline track conveys coverage.

other hand, MizBee is more based on information visualization principles, implementing three interactive layers of detail: genome, chromosome, and blocks (the latter displays the exact matching sequences between the genomes). It also implements filtering by chromosome or block, so navigation through whole genomes is easy. Therefore, MizBee perfectly implements information visualization principles, especially interaction, but the lack of analysis options (especially synteny detection algorithms) and concrete sequence details limits its visual analysis power. It must be said that these kinds of algorithms and the storage of full sequences can be time and space consuming for desktop applications, which points to the need for more efficient ways to perform these tasks or maybe to integrate interactive client-based tools with sever analyses. Circos has been better accepted than MizBee by the scientific community, suggesting that the ability of quick reporting and integration in the analysis pipeline (in the end, visual analysis requirements) is more interesting than interaction alone.

47.5.2 Alignment Data Visualization

Sequence alignment deals with the correct colocation of sequences in order to perform precise comparisons. Alignments (and thus sequence comparisons) can be pairwise or multiple. The most popular software for pairwise sequence alignment is BLAST. BLAST searches for highly similar pairwise alignments (hits) between a query sequence and sequences from

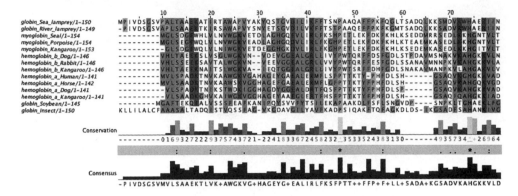

FIGURE 47.5 EBI ClustalW multiple alignment and visualization of 13 globins from different species. Coloring (here as gray hues) allows to identify highly conserved areas and in combination with gaps (−) enhances detection of patterns (e.g., beginning sequence in lampreys or the five-residue gap after position 60 in alpha hemoglobins). The conservation, residue, and consensus tracks are visualized below, respectively.

a database. Although it may give hundreds of hits, which makes the inspection of results hard, there are few approaches to visualize them, being the most popular one provided by the NCBI BLAST. It represents the original sequence as a horizontal line, and matching sequences as additional horizontal lines shifted (and maybe split) to the position of the original sequence where they align. These additional lines are sorted by their similarity to the original sequence and colored based on their matching statistic. By clicking on a line we are redirected to details about its sequence and alignment.

Only two commercial tools provide other alignment visualizations, as reviewed by [39]. VectorNTI integrates three linked representations: an NCBI-like visualization with a histogram representing the number of sequence hits for each residue; a resume of the major conserved regions; and a traditional multiple-alignment visualization (as in Figure 47.5). Geneious [40] builds a tree using the hits as leaf nodes and clades as intermediate nodes, with cells grayed out for clades with hits below a user defined threshold.

Multiple-sequence alignment (MSA) algorithms go a step further: Instead of comparing sequences two by two, they compare several sequences at once. The result is a matrix in which each row is an aligned sequence and each column is the equivalent position across all sequences (it might be a gap), usually called *residues*. Color helps to determine the residue conservation, that is, the amount of sequences that share the same residue or residues with similar physicochemical properties. The conservation track is a histogram with the number of sequences that share the most conserved amino acid on each column. The residue track encodes that information in a simpler way, for example Clustal2X [41] uses characters to summarize the degree of conservation of residues: mostly conserved (·), conserved (:) and identical (∗). Finally, the consensus track represents the sequence with the most conserved amino acids (it can be a gap, or an unsolved residue, represented with a plus sign).

Residue conservation leads to the concept of consensus sequence: the sequence that better represents the alignment. In order to quantify and visualize consensus, a concept borrowed from information theory, the Shannon entropy[*] [42], is commonly used. It is a

---

[*]Although commonly called entropy, it is actually a measure of uncertainty.

(a)

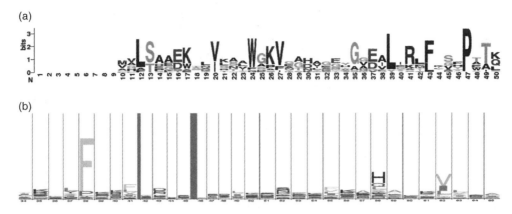

(b)

FIGURE 47.6 (a) Consensus logo generated by Weblogo [44] for the first 50 residues of MSA in Figure 47.5. (b) HMM-logos introduce insertion probabilities, this one generated by Logomat-P [43].

measure of how much uncertainty there is in predicting the residue at each position, so it turns to zero if every sequence has the same element at the position (no uncertainty) and grows with variability.

A consensus logo (see Figure 47.6) visualizes the consensus sequence of a multiple alignment. For each residue, the logo stacks all the possible letters of the amino acids or nucleotides, with the consensus sequence always on top and letter heights scaled depending on their probability to be at that position (usually computed as the inverse of Shannon uncertainty). *HMM logos* [43] are protein consensus logos in which the contribution of each amino acid is calculated by a *hidden Markov model* (HMM), which models residues as states, with transition probabilities between them. Intermediate insertion states are also considered in the model, and the probability of inserts is visualized by the separation width between vertical lines.

MSA and logo visualization tools (Table 47.2) usually provide low interaction, limited to selection and filtering of rows and columns, in order to generate static images ready for sharing or publication. Integration with alignment algorithms is very common and permits some degree of visual analysis flow, such as to realign sequences with different methods, although differences must be compared by hand. MEGA5 [45] is probably one of the best examples of this integration of computational methods and the standard lowly interactive visualization.

As far as we know, no alternative approaches to the standard MSA visualization have been proposed, and issues like asymmetry, usual on sequences of moderate length, remain mostly unaddressed. Weblogo, on its third version, minimizes it by "chopping" the sequence in chunks of the same size and displaying them one below the previous one.

47.6 RELATIONAL AND FUNCTIONAL DATA VISUALIZATION

To know which genes collaborate with a given gene in order to perform a biological process or to know which functions a gene is related to is key in several types of analyses, especially if the focus is on understanding the biology of the problem as a whole system. These types of analyses rely on large repositories that contain up-to-date knowledge of gene functions

1086 BIOLOGICAL KNOWLEDGE VISUALIZATION

TABLE 47.2 Selected Tools for Multiple Sequence Alignment Visualization

Name	Description	Reference
MEGA5[a]	MSA computation and visualization of alignment, integrating phylogenetic tree computation and visualization, along with other evolutionary analyses	[45]
ClustalX2	ClustalW MSA alignment and visualization of alignment and consensus tracks	[41]
Jalview[a]	Integrative tool including multiple and pairwise alignment and other alignment analyses and visualizations, molecular structures, PCA, and trees	[46]
PFAAT	Integrative software of MSA, phylogeny, and structure visualization, with moderate level of linkage and interaction	[47]
Logomat-P	HMM logo visualization; allows to visualize alignments between HMM consensus logos of two protein families	[43]
Weblogo	Online sequence logo generator from user-supplied multiple-sequence alignment	[44]

[a]Our recommendations.

and relations. Although there is controversy about the suitability and confidence of these types of repositories, a large part of the community uses them in everyday work. These are some of the largest data sources to be visualized and fringe into scaling issues that are still to be satisfactorily solved. In this section we will review the major visualization techniques and tools available nowadays.

47.6.1 Biological Networks

Genes and gene products collaborate in order to achieve different biological functions. There are various types of relationships (see Section 47.3.3), but from the point of view of visualization all of them can be summarized as nodes representing genes or gene products, with edges linking nodes to represent relations. The visualization problem often arises from the complexity of these relationships.

Some biological processes (e.g., metabolic processes or immune cascades) have been summarized on well-known, small networks of connections, usually called *pathways*. In these cases, complexity is not a big problem and the focus can be set on adding information about cell topology. KEGG [10], BioCarta [48], and Reactome [49] are the three most popular repositories for these kinds of networks and their visualization (see Figure 47.7). KEGG displays pathway nodes (genes or compounds) and their connections but also curated topographic elements such as cell walls, molecule wrappers, nucleus areas, and ancillary labels. Interaction is enabled with zooming, scaling, and inspection of element details. A last remarkable characteristic of KEGG pathways is the ability to map nodes with colors in order to complement pathway analysis of gene expression, for example, as in [50]. BioCarta presents more colorful and compact biological maps but in essence deals with the same network complexity and interaction options than KEGG. Reactome may be the least aesthetically attractive option, but it implements better navigation methods and allows browsing the pathways hierarchy when available.

Other networks, usually built from relationship databases or inferred from genomic data, for example, coregulation networks computed from expression levels, have a higher complexity (larger numbers of nodes and edges) so they are much more difficult to visualize.

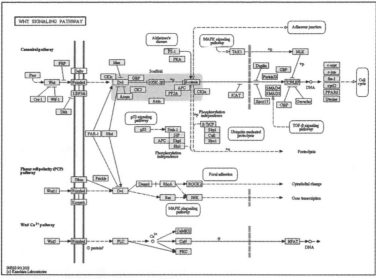

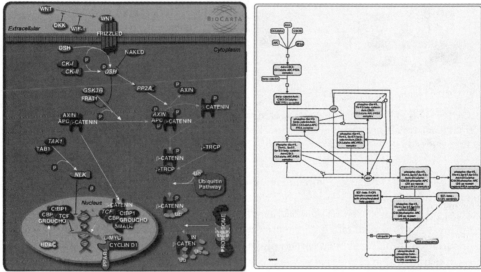

FIGURE 47.7 Visualization of Wnt signaling pathway by KEGG (top), BioCarta (bottom left), and Reactome (bottom right).

Typically, for moderately large networks (about a hundred nodes), force-directed layouts are a good option that is implemented on mostly every network visualization tool (see Figure 47.8, top). A force-directed layout simulates gravitational and spring forces in order to separate unconnected nodes and keep close connected ones.

There are several other options for network drawing, such as circular layouts, hierarchical layouts, or grid layouts, but they are almost always outperformed by force-directed layouts (see Table 47.3 for some selected tools). Cytoscape [51] is the most popular resource for network visualization. It provides a basic framework for network representation and navigation (zoom, scrolling), and part of its success resides on its integrative plug-in structure,

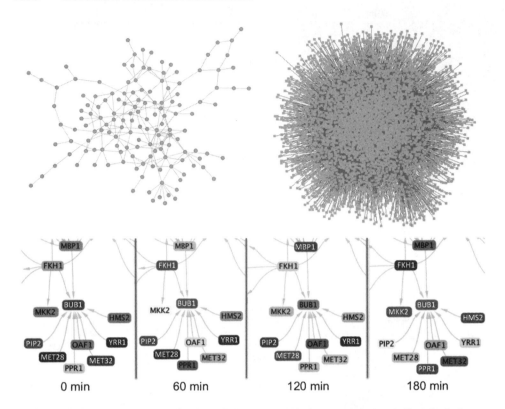

FIGURE 47.8   Cytoscape visualization of kinase transcription network (top left) and whole transcription network (top right) of *S. cerevisiae*. Detail of yeast expression level mapping to color (here as gray hues) on kinase transcription network along four time points of stress response.

which allows third parties to implement new functionalities over it. Plug-ins for functional annotation analysis [52–54], omics analysis [55, 56], and expression analysis [57], among several others, have been developed. Another useful characteristic of Cytoscape is node coloring based on qualitative or quantitative measures, typically expression levels. This helps to identify network areas predominantly underexpressed or overexpressed for a single experiment, one of the major visual supports for pathway analysis. Expression levels from several experiments have been mapped on networks in a number of ways: Histograms [58], profile plots [59], linear heatmaps [60], and circular heatmaps [61] have all been embedded or displayed along with the corresponding nodes on the network. Another option is to use animation, changing the color of nodes as time goes by (see Figure 47.8, bottom), which better conveys the overall reaction of the network to a series of experiments, especially in the case of time experiments.

A still open question is the visualization of larger networks (thousands of nodes). Due to the complex nature of biological data, such networks are naturally generated from analysis (e.g., coregulation networks) and compiled in databases (e.g., the protein interaction network or the chaperone network). The number of links is so high that force-directed layouts are unable to disentangle the network, and resulting visualizations become unreadable[*]

---

[*]Martin Krzywinski calls these networks "hairballs."

TABLE 47.3 Selected Tools for Network Visualization

Name	Description	Reference
KEGG[a]	Pathway database with pathway-curated images; programmatic access to pathways and color mapping	[10]
BioCarta	Pathway database with pathway-curated images, maybe more simplified and aesthetic than KEGG	[48]
Reactome	Pathway database with pathway-curated images, maybe more detailed and hierarchically sorted than KEGG	[49]
Cytoscape[a]	Most popular tool for network visualization and mapping, with large collection of plug-ins	[51]
Osprey	Cytoscape-like tool for visualization of networks, includes option for radial multicoloring of nodes	[62]
Pajek	Generic, widely used tool for network visualization and analysis	[63]
Biological Networks	Integrative visualization tool with collaborative projects that link networks to other data such as abundance or molecular structure	[64]
ProViz	Visualization of protein–protein interaction networks, allows filtering based on ontologies	[65]
GENeVis	Dynamic force-directed layout networks to visualize relative concentrations of regulatory proteins	[58]
LGL	Introduces an algorithm to visualize very large biological networks in 2D or 3D, based on a force-directed layout	[66]
Linnet	Linear visualization of very large networks using parallel coordinate-like solution	[67]

[a]Our recommendations.

(see Figure 47.8, top right). Several approaches (relying on force-directed layouts) have been proposed, but none of them is fully satisfying. For example, color and size rendering can be of help on large but not highly connected networks [68, 69]. 3D force-directed layouts have also been applied to biological networks [70], but another dimension is not usually enough to disentangle the networks and adds up 3D-related problems, such as node occlusion and computational performance.

Lately, a novel visualization technique called Linnet [67] proposes a parallel coordinates–like display (see Section 47.7), with nodes assigned to radial axes depending on, for example, node type or edge degree, and in-axis location based on some other property (node connectivity, expression level, etc.) The success of the visualization relies on the fixed position of nodes (which avoids cluttering) and the mathematical meaningfulness of node location in the axes. To visualize different properties, several displays can be generated and compared. The technique is mostly static, and parameters should be modified previously to the generation of the images.

47.6.2 Phylogenetic Trees

Multiple-alignment output can be seen as a hierarchy of similarity among the aligned sequences. When applied to whole organisms, we can talk of traditional phylogenies, but phylogenetic trees have been extended to represent protein or gene families, making phylogenetic tree visualizations ubiquitous.

TABLE 47.4   Selected Tools for Phylogenetic Tree Visualization

Name	Description	Reference
TreeView	Most popular tree visualizer, generates simple, static dendrograms	[71]
MEGA5[a]	Multiple-sequence alignment tool that offers representations of resulting trees and evolutionary analyses	[45]
Dendroscope	Complete software for traditional visualization of trees, includes rerooting, collapsing coloring, image export, etc.	[72]
ARB	Analysis environment that integrates phylogenetic tree visualization (allows collapsing branches) with MSA and secondary-structure visualization and edition	[73]
Archaeopterix	Software tool for visualization and analysis of large trees, especially strong in annotation editing and labelling, and very flexible about tree formats	[74]
iTOL[a]	Online and very complete tool for visualization of large-scale circular trees	[75]
Treevolution	Highly interactive tool for visual analysis of large-scale circular trees	[76]

[a]Our recommendations.

Tree visualization is a simplification of network visualization, because there is only one upward connection for each node. Usually, just a low number of sequences or species are compared, so cluttering and other visualization issues are not a problem.

The most traditional way of representing trees is by a linear dendrogram (see Figure 47.9, left), which is usually generated by alignment tools (see Table 47.4) or by tools fed by alignment data (possibly the most popular one is TreeView [71], but there are several others). Usually, phylogeny representations are not very interactive, as they are one of the final outcomes of an alignment analysis, so most of the tools are focused on the generation of reports and figures ready to publish.

An online tool designed to generate large tree visualizations is iTOL [75], which offers lots of options to customize phylogenetic trees and generates high-resolution images that can be browsed online. These tools for visualization of large trees use circular dendrograms, which make the most of the screen space, maximizing the number of leaf nodes that can be represented without cluttering (see Figure 47.9, right). Another tool that focuses on the visual analysis of large phylogenetic trees is Treevolution [76], which implements several interaction options, such as bifocal and fisheye distortion/zoom, filtering by node name or clade, or cluster coloring.

Finally, trees can be visualized with *tree maps* [18], a technique that reserves an area to each leaf node, and parent nodes are represented as wrappers of their child areas. An application of a type of tree map, the *Voronoi map*, to the visualization of the tree of life is available in Involv [77], producing a nested tessellation of convex polygons for each taxa.

47.6.3   Annotations

Functional knowledge is usually summarized as gene or protein annotations from a controlled vocabulary or ontology. These annotations can be used to give an idea of what functional processes are more active on our experiment and put into context differentially expressed genes. It can even guide our analysis, as in the case of GSEA [11].

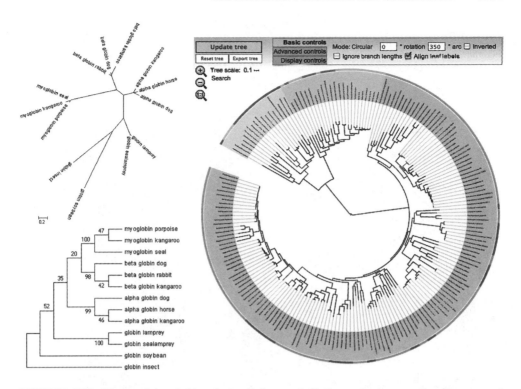

FIGURE 47.9 Unrooted (top left) and rooted (bottom left) linear dendrogram for alignment of 13 globins (produced with MEGA5, rooted tree numbers are bootstrap values representing confidence of branch). iTOL visualization (right) of tree of life (about 200 species) and navigation interface.

However, because functional annotations are simply natural language words from a controlled vocabulary, functional annotation visualization has been out of the scope for most researchers. From the point of view of a single entity (gene or protein), there is little to visualize, apart from displaying its functional annotations as plain text. But in the case of whole hierarchies such as the whole *Gene Ontology* (GO) or the case of annotations from several entities, visualization can be of great help.

Visualization of ontology hierarchies is a common place for different fields, not only biology. Mostly every visualization technique designed for visualization of hierarchical data has been applied [78]: indented lists, *directed acyclic graphs* (DAGs), dendrograms, 3D trees, tree maps, and so on. Focusing on bioinformatics, GOTM [79] provides DAGs, trees, and indented lists to visualize significantly enriched terms displayed on a set of webpages. What can be displayed is not only the enriched terms but also the hierarchy of GO terms that contain the enriched term, providing a context for the enrichment. Blast2GO [80] integrates annotation, statistics, and visualization of GO DAGs using color for node relevance (either in number of annotations or in statistical significance). BinGO [54] provides DAG visualizations similar to Blast2GO, but as a Cytoscape plugin. GOrilla [81] provides an updated version of similar visual functionalities.

Apart from visualization approaches focused on hierarchy, novel techniques allow to represent annotation abundance. For example, BicOverlapper [83] visualizes the GO terms related to a set of genes as a *tag cloud*, where size indicates the number of genes sharing the

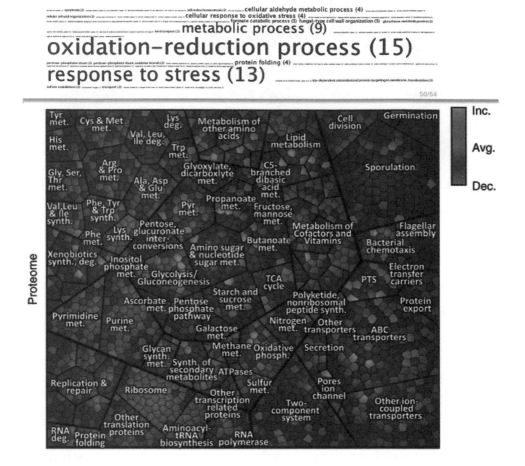

FIGURE 47.10   Tag cloud generated by BicOverlapper from the GO terms related to group of differentially expressed genes on stress experiment (top). Voronoi map generated by OntologyMaps for KEGG ontology; map is colored (gray hues) by relative protein amount (bottom, figure reproduced from [82]).

term or the *p*-value of the most relevant terms (see Figure 47.10, top). OntologyMaps [84] uses *Voronoi diagrams* to map expression into whole ontologies, keeping hierarchy context (Figure 47.10, bottom). Each term in the ontology is represented by a cell, which is inside the cells of its parents (as in a tree map) and is colored by the average expression of every gene annotated with the term.

47.7   EXPRESSION DATA VISUALIZATION

Apart from sequencing, expression measuring is the other most important technology developed during the last decade. If sequence visualization focuses on the identification of patterns in one or more sequences, expression visualization focuses on the identification of patterns in abundance levels linked to these sequences (usually at the level of genes or proteins).

Until recently,[*] due to technical limitations, microarray technologies only covered the expression of small sections of genes (probe sequences), effectively losing the full gene sequence-expression match. Therefore, most expression data visualizations focus solely on expression abundance, usually from microarray experiments.

We will first review the basic visualization techniques used for expression visualization (either in single and multiple experiments) and then explore the existing options for visualization of groups in the context of gene expression.

47.7.1 Visualization of Expression Data from One or Two Conditions

A condition usually relates to a run of an expression-measuring technology.[†] Although most of the expression analyses are based on comparing several experimental conditions (e.g., what is the difference in behavior for genes in cancer conditions with respect to normal conditions? What is the evolution of expression along several time points?), the first visualizations were designed to inspect expression levels from just one or two conditions, especially for checking technology errors or biases. The most usual way to visualize expression from two conditions is to use *scatter plots* (Figure 47.11), where genes are represented as points, and its position is determined by the expression level of the conditions (one on each axis). *MA plots* are a variation in which the y axis represents the log ratio (M) between the two conditions (usually, one of them is a control condition) and the x axis represents the mean intensity on both samples (A). In both cases a regression line can be drawn to see if the points follow a linear model or not, which is very useful in order to detect biases due to imperfections on the technology or methodology (Figure 47.11, bottom). *Volcano plots* visualize statistical significance along with differential expression: The x axis represents (log) fold expression change and the y axis represents the statistical significance (typically p-values.)

Other representations of summarized expression behavior are *boxplots* and *histograms*, used along with scatter plots in order to detect biases or imperfections in the experiments. All these representations are mostly static, with no or little interaction or integration with other visualizations or analysis methods.

47.7.2 Visualization of Expression Data from Several Conditions

Heatmaps are possibly the most popular way of visualizing expression data from several conditions, since its successful application by Eisen et al. [86]. A heatmap is a matrix in which rows represent biological elements (genes, probes, etc.) and columns represent experimental conditions. Each cell in the matrix represents the expression level of an element for a given condition, which is coded in a color scale. This matrix alone is not very useful, but patterns will arise if rows and columns are sorted based on some grouping criteria. In the original work of Eisen et al., the sorting criterion was hierarchical clustering, represented by row (and/or condition) dendrograms (see Figure 47.12, right).

---

[*]Novel techniques, such as RNA-Seq, and their analysis methods are now more clearly linking sequences with their corresponding transcripts because of, for example, splicing events.

[†]Typically microarray technologies, but this is rapidly evolving into RNA-Seq.

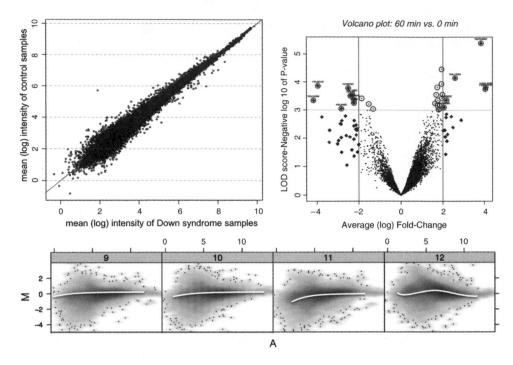

FIGURE 47.11 Scatter plots comparing mean expression of seven Down syndrome samples versus seven control samples (GEO experiment with accession GSE1000) following overall linear behavior (top left). Volcano plot comparing the expression level of yeast after 60 min of stress against 0 min. Genes differentially expressed are drawn as diamonds and significantly expressed genes are encircled (top right). MA plots for four samples against the same control sample generated with BioConductor package ArrayQualityMetrics [85]. Nonoutlier points have been substituted by a density cloud, and the white regression lines highlight a possible problem with condition 12 (bottom).

The technique evolved in order to improve navigation, browsing, and filtering [83, 87–89]. Some of the interactions implemented are *focus + context navigations* [90], *dendrogram browsing* techniques such as *branch pruning* or *collapsing* [88], and *bifocal distortion* techniques [91].

Further than the visualization of expression levels from multiple conditions in a single experiment, the *gene expression atlas* [92] represents genes differentially up/down regulated on multiple conditions and experiments by dividing each heatmap cell into two triangles (for up and down regulation) and printing a number to indicate the number of experiments in which the corresponding gene is differentially expressed for the given condition (Figure 47.12, top right).

The second most popular technique to visualize gene expression is *parallel coordinates*. In parallel coordinates, a vertical axis is displayed for each experimental condition, and each gene expression profile is represented by a polyline that joins expression-level points at every axis (Figure 47.12, bottom right). Like heatmaps, the representation of lots of gene profiles is uninformative, but patterns arise when just a few profiles filtered by some criterion are selected. In fact, the ability of the human eye to detect changes in line slopes is better than to detect changes in color. However, scientific standards leaned toward heatmaps, and parallel coordinates research and interaction have been largely out of the scope, with

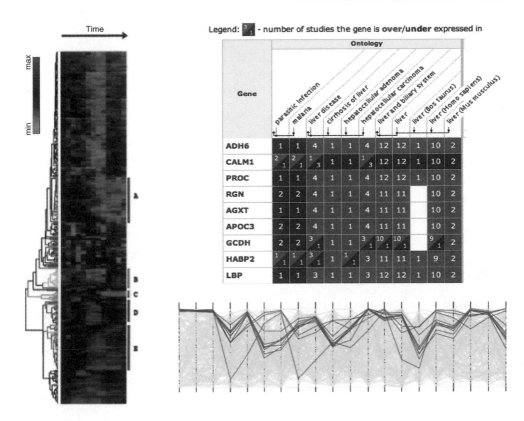

FIGURE 47.12 Heatmap sorted by hierarchical row clustering represented as dendrogram; some groups are marked with letters; columns are sorted by time (left, reproduced from [86]). ArrayExpress Atlas heatmap for different liver conditions (top right). Parallel coordinates with 20 conditions and 10 highlighted gene profiles. A pattern of overexpression can be seen for the first three conditions (bottom right).

some tools generating gene profiles, but in a static way [89, 93]. GGobi [94] implements minor parallel interactions based on case identification and coloring, while HCE [95] has possibly the best implementation, including brushing (i.e. filtering of gene profiles) based on expression levels and/or slopes (changes in expression). Dendrograms and sorting are an easy way to represent several, nonoverlapping groups on heatmaps, but there is no such solution on parallel coordinates. Some partial solutions have been given by the use of 3D and color/transparency [96].

Expression visualization tools (see Table 47.5 for a small selection) are among the most complete biology visualization tools from the point of view of information visualization and visual analysis, implementing a high degree of interaction, integration with databases and numerical methods, and linkage among views. HCE is possibly the best example of it, integrating computational analysis (array normalization, clustering algorithms) with linked views (heatmap, parallel coordinates, scatter plots) on a highly interactive framework. BicOverlapper [83] provides a similar framework for biclustering analysis, integrating these numerical methods with linked parallel coordinates, heatmaps, and a novel visualization technique to represent intersecting groups. It also links available information in the form of GO term annotations and user-provided biological networks. BicAT [89], EXpander

TABLE 47.5 Selected Tools for Gene Expression Visualization

Name	Description	Reference
BicOverlapper	Integrates biclustering algorithms with visualizations of gene expression, overlapping groups, and functional and relational data	[83]
EXpander	Integrates clustering analysis with some mostly static gene expression visualizations and group listings	[87]
BicAT	Integrates biclustering algorithms with mostly static visualizations of gene expression (heatmaps and parallel coordinates)	[89]
HCE[a]	Highly interactive tool that integrates hierarchical clustering with gene expression visualization (heatmaps, parallel coordinates, and scatter plots)	[18]
gCLUTO	Visualization of gene expression and hierarchical clustering with options to prune dendrograms, and a 3D PCA visualization of clusters	[88]
Java TreeView	Java implementation of original TreeView [86], visualization of heatmaps and dendrograms	[90]
BiGGEsTS	Tool for biclustering analysis of time series with visual module including parallel coordinates, heatmaps, dendrograms, and ontology graphs mapped to expression	[97]
Spotfire	Commercial, highly interactive and integrative tool	[98]
GeneSpring	Commercial, highly interactive and integrative tool	[99]
OntologyMaps	Commercial visual mapping of gene expression to ontologies based on Voronoi diagrams	[84]

[a]Our recommendations.

[87], gCLUTO [88], Java TreeView [90], and BIGEsTS [97] are other examples with different levels of interaction and integration. GeneSpring GX [99] and Spotfire [98] are two commercial analysis suites with many linked visualization and exploration tools.

47.7.3 Visualization of Groups and Expression Data

When we analyze an expression matrix, we search for groups of genes that behave similarly and differently from the average. There are several computational techniques to do this, hierarchical clustering being the most spread one. This method builds a hierarchy of similarity among genes (or conditions) based on some distance metric. The hierarchy is then "cut" at some level, and the branches at that level are considered as separate groups of genes with similar profiles. This process is visualized by a dendrogram representing the hierarchy, which attaches to and sorts the heatmap rows (see Figure 47.12, left). Two major interaction techniques have been traditionally implemented on this schema. The first one is a threshold line that can be dragged to set the level at which the groups are selected [100]. The second one is the ability to merge all the elements of one branch, visualizing the average expression profile for the branch [88].

Other grouping techniques such as *biclustering* [101] produce intersecting groups that are harder to visualize. A common option is to offer the list of all groups and visualize them one by one [89], but other options visualize all of them with a 2D projection [88], a Venn-like diagram [91], or a replication of rows and columns on the heatmap [102].

With the increase in biological knowledge we can, instead of searching for gene groups that behave differentially, start by groups already known, such as the ones from a given ontology (e.g., genes involved in metabolism, cell division, immune response) and determine which groups are enriched (i.e., the group has several genes that are differentially expressed in our experiment). From a visualization point of view, the problem is similar, but additionally these groups can follow an inclusion hierarchy. On some cases, the elements can be identified directly by the group name, so there is no need to represent them individually, simplifying the visualization. For example, Bernhardt et al. [84] developed a layout method to visualize ontologies by means of Voronoi maps, where each ontology term is represented by a small polygon colored by the average expression of the genes annotated with the term (Figure 47.10, bottom).

An intermediate option is to perform a blind data analysis and then visualize the data in the context of available biological information. For example, Lukk et al. [103] perform a principal-component analysis of thousands of expression experiments and then visualize the projection, colored by experiment information (source, malignancy, etc.). The result is a partially separated colored set of elements which both supports the validity of the grouping method and gives insight on the biological sense of the separation.

47.8 STRUCTURE DATA VISUALIZATION

Structure data are primarily 3D and come from post-DNA entities, fundamentally proteins, but also others (such as RNA). Posttranslational properties depend to a great extent of 3D structure. For example, two proteins coming from very different DNA sequences can have similar, or partially similar, 3D structures which make them capable of binding to the same given drug. This is also important in some transcriptional events such as in the case of how the 3D structure of polymerase binds to DNA sites in order to start transcription.

Therefore, most of the visualizations of structure data are 3D, implementing most of the typical 3D browsing techniques: pan and zoom, rotation, fixation of the point of view, and so on. It is important to note that a proper 3D visualization is not possible on a 2D display, which is the typical visualization device,[*] and it would be more correct to talk of 2D graphical projections of 3D objects, or 2.5D visualizations. This limitation implies some issues that must be addressed by the interactive browsing, such as occlusion.

There are two major applications of molecular structure visualization: structure inspection and binding site analysis [104]. We will focus on these two applications for the remainder of the section.

47.8.1 Structure Inspection

The view, comparison, and combination of protein structures help to understand how protein domains, chemical properties, exon sequences, *single-nucleotide polymorphisms* (SNPs), binding sites, and so on, relate to the final 3D structure. There are several visual tools to achieve this, usually Web based and fed by a PDB instance. 3D interaction is more or less standard across these tools, so they vary on the visual conventions used to represent

---

[*]There are some approaches to visualize 3D structures in other devices, such as virtual reality or 3D screens, but we will focus on 2D displays.

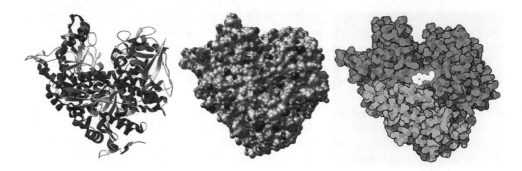

FIGURE 47.13 Different visualizations of aconitase (PDB entry 2B3Y) protein structure. Ribbon-like representation shows tertiary structure: alpha helices in dark gray and beta strands in light gray (left, generated with Jmol). A surface-filling rendering made by PMV and colored by hydrophobicity (in gray scale, center). Non-photorealistic simplification of surface, highlighting its two molecular domains in gray hues and its active site wrapped inside (right, image reproduced from RCSB PDB).

structure. There are five major visual conventions to represent proteins: *wirelike* representation, *ribbonlike* representation, *surface-filling* rendering, *non-photorealistic* rendering, and *superimposition* (see Figure 47.13). Each of these representations gives a different point of view of the protein: ribbonlike representation conveys tertiary structure; surface-filling techniques are used to detect cavities and represent physicochemical properties such as hydrophobicity or polar charge; wirelike representations are mostly used to visualize additional structures such as DNA strands, ligands, or active sites; and non-photorealistic renderings generate simplified surfaces that are optimal to get an overall idea of the molecule shape and active sites.

Representation styles combine with coloring in order to provide useful visualizations. Some of the characteristics most often colored are the type of secondary structure, the protein subunits, the protein chains, and the physicochemical properties.

These combinations of color and representation give a first impression of the protein (shape and form) and may lead to identify interesting properties, such as protein-binding sites (usually flat, large surfaces) or hydrophobic pockets.

There are several tools that produce 3D representations of PDB molecules (see Table 47.6) but probably the most popular one is Jmol [105]. Jmol provides an intuitive and powerful 3D navigation interface, permits several combinations of color and representation schemes, and is fast and integrated on several Web resources such as RSCB PDB and FirstGlance [106]. Although very good for first impressions and educational purposes, Jmol lacks of complicated molecular analyses and visualizations. Jmol is actually a simplification of RasMol [107], which offers a wider range of coloring and representation options, as do other also widely used stand-alone tools such as WMD [108] or PMV [109].

In order not to lose sequence context in 3D structure analysis, more recent tools such as SRS 3D [117] or Chimera [114] offer integrated 2D sequence visualizations and selection and coloring by sequence characteristics such as exons, SNPs, or sequence conservation. Furthermore, in the case of RNA structure visualization, it is useful to visualize multiple-sequence alignments along with 2D and 3D structures, because secondary structure can be related to them. S2S [110] visualizes RNA multiple alignments and 2D structures (see Figure 47.14), implementing links to other tools (Chimera, PyMOL) for visualization of 3D structures. Assemble [112] visualizes 2D and 3D structures and can also integrate with S2S.

TABLE 47.6 Selected Tools for Molecular Structure Visualization

Name	Description	Reference
Jmol[a]	Java applet for basic but interactive visualization of molecular structures; widely used on Web resources (PDB, Rfam, etc.); a simplified version of RasMol	[105]
RasMol[a]	Stand-alone application rich in commands for 3D structure visualization	[107]
PMV	Stand-alone application for molecule visualizations, with lots of options for visualization and structural analysis	[109]
VMD	Stand-alone application for molecule visualizations, with lots of options for visualization and structural analysis; can also make tubular representations of NMR structures	[108]
S2S	RNA 2D structure visualization; integration with multiple alignments and links to 3D renderers (PyMOL, Chimera)	[110]
ConSurf	Web service to compute multiple-sequence alignments, map conservation to protein structure, and visualize it via Jmol	[111]
Assemble	Secondary and tertiary visualization tool.	[112]
PyMOL	High-quality, widely used 3D renderer (not free)	[113]
Chimera	Stand-alone tool of 3D structure and sequence visualization	[114]
FirstGlance	Online visualization of PDB structures via Jmol	[106]
PDBe	European PDB	[15]
RSCB[a] PDB	NCBI version of PDB with curated reports and non-photorealistic views for several proteins; integrates Jmol	[14]
PoseView	Online service for simplified 2D visualizaiton of ligand–protein bindings	[115]
STITCH 2	Database of ligand-protein networks, based on chemical, biological and evidence significance	[116]

[a]Our recommendations.

ConSurf [111] maps alignment consensus (conservation) to amino acids on 3D structure visualizations.

Most of the 3D protein structures are determined by X-ray crystallography, but some of them are inferred from *nuclear magnetic resonance* (NMR), which produces several similar 3D measures of the structure. The final 3D structure is reconstructed from the consensus of these measures, and the precision and accuracy of the NMR are determined by their degree of superimposition. Wirelike and tubular representations are used to represent such structures, conveying accuracy by the bundling of wires or the tube width. MOLMOL [118] and VMD [108] are two popular tools for NMR structure visualization.

47.8.2 Binding Analysis

The second major application of structure visualization is the inspection of ligand binding sites. While protein–protein binding sites usually occur on large, flat surfaces, the interaction with ligands usually happens in buried active sites. Wirelike representations are useful to visualize these kinds of interactions, because they avoid occlusion of these small molecules located in protein cavities (see Figure 47.15, left). Many graphic tools that support binding site analysis implement different variations of wirelike representations (PMV, PyMOL, VMD, RSCB PDB ligand explorer, etc.)

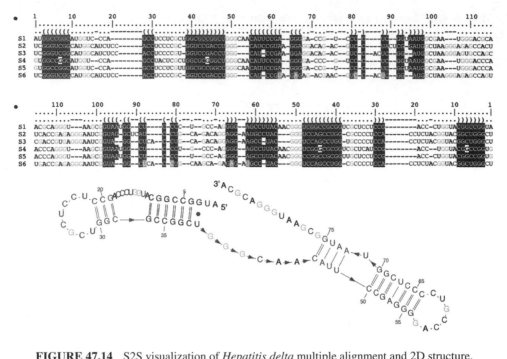

FIGURE 47.14 S2S visualization of *Hepatitis delta* multiple alignment and 2D structure.

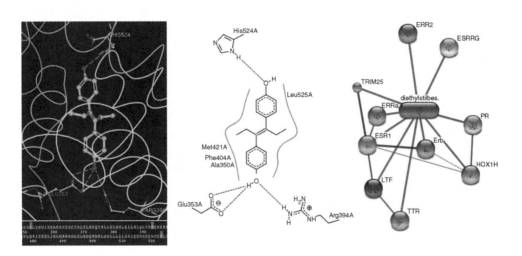

FIGURE 47.15 DES ligand (ball-and-stick representation) and estrogen receptor alpha ERRa (wirelike representation), with hydrogen bonds (dashed lines). Contact amino acids are also highlighted with gray boxes in chain sequence below. The figure was generated with RSCB Ligand Explorer (left). Simplified 2D view produced with PoseView; hydrogen bonds are represented by dashed lines and hydrophobic contacts are represented by splines indicating its amino acids (middle). Associated proteins to ligand DES (rounded rectangle), among them ERRa (right, generated with STITCH-2).

Another simplified visualization is the 2D representation of binding sites, with special visual conventions, such as "eyelashes" to convey unbounded contacts [119] or as different line types to represent hydrogen bonds and hydrophobic contacts [115], as shown in Figure 47.15 (middle).

Finally, another approach (specially from the point of view of drug design) is to search for proteins likely to bind to a given ligand or the other way round. In this case, the relevant aspect is the significance, chemical, biological, or by experimental evidences. For example, STITCH 2 [116] is an interaction database that allows searches for evidence-based ligand–protein interactions and visualizes them as a force-directed network (Figure 47.15, right).

47.9 CONCLUSION AND FUTURE PERSPECTIVES

Each biology field has a large set of good visualization techniques and tools. Some of these visualization techniques have become standards because of their simplicity and capability of conveying information and discovering patterns, such as heatmaps in gene expression or logos in sequence alignments.

Two challenges are important and will be important in the near term (and possibly forever): the development of novel visualization techniques to get better data representations and the improvement of current visualization techniques to improve interaction, integration, and usability. On an evolutionary simile, novel visualization techniques represent successful evolutionary mutations to adapt to data and our cognitive capabilities, and the usability, interaction and integration improvements represent specialization of such techniques.

Integration has a great challenge in diversity, in both data sources and analysis techniques. Some tools, such as Circos, rely on subordinating the visualization to the analysis work flow, which provides more adaptation but possibly reduces the interaction. Scientific community has accepted this kind of model very quickly. The inverse solution is to integrate numerical analysis on the visual tool, maybe providing an easy way to integrate new analysis techniques (such as plug-ins in Cytoscape). In this case format problems may arise from the very different sources of input data and algorithm interfaces, but this option can offer a more visual solution. This second case leads to another definition of integration: as an accumulation of features. Several approaches, especially systems biology, talks about the usefulness of watching several points of view of the problem: sequence, expression, product, relations, functions, and so on. Taking all this into account boosts the capability to find patterns or relevant features and, at least in part, is quite common in the reviewed tools.

Interaction must enhance our ability to roll back, undo, redo, change parameters in the analysis, navigate through visualizations and link analysis and visualization, and visualizations among them. Especially this last characteristic must be enhanced in forthcoming solutions, because it speeds up analysis (one click modifies several views) and boosts pattern recognition (a relevant feature may arise on one visualization but not in others). The HCE is a good example of it.

The above characteristics will not work if the solutions are not usable. Availability, installation issues, nonstandard interaction options, cryptic analysis methods, and lack of tutorials are some of the typical defects of some visualization tools that lead to the misuse or refusal by the final user. A good example of how biological analysis can become attractive is Foldit [120].

Novel visualization techniques arise everyday, some of them so impressive that they might become standards quickly. For instance, hierarchical bundling [38] is becoming common in genome comparisons. Linnet, OntologyMaps, and ABySS-Explorer present promising techniques in relational, functional, and assembly data visualizations, respectively.

Besides, advances in technology will also require new visualization techniques. On the one hand, information technologies introduce new devices, such as tactile or 3D screens, that can be exploited from a visualization point of view. On the other hand, biotechnology advances also require novel visualization techniques. For example, RNA-Seq measurements will require effective ways of representing gene splice variants in the context of expression visualization and probably a stronger relationship with sequence visualizations.

To conclude, it is worth saying that, although visualization by itself will not provide the solution to the big questions that biology faces, it will definitely help in our coliving with the large amounts of data that we generate, providing an excellent breeding ground from which inspiration eventually pops out.

REFERENCES

1. F. S. Collins, M. Morgan, and A. Patrinos. The Human Genome Project: Lessons from large-scale biology. *Science*, 300:286–290, 2003.

2. L. D. Stein. The case for cloud computing in genome informatics. *Genome Biol.*, 11:1–7, 2010.

3. C. Ware. Information visualization: Perception for design, S. Card and J. Grudin (Eds.), The Morgan Kaufmann Series in Interactive Technologies, 2004.

4. J. J. Thomas and K. A. Cook. Illuminating the path: The research and development agenda for visual analytics, 2005. Available: `http://vis.pnnl.gov/pdf/RD_Agenda_VisualAnalytics.pdf`.

5. B. Fry. Computational information design, 2004. Available: `http://benfry.com/phd/`.

6. D. Keim, F. Mansmann, and J. Schneidewind. Visual analytics: Scope and challenges. *Visual Data Mining*, Vol. 4044 of *Lecture Notes in Computer Science*, 2008, pp. 1–15.

7. T. Barrett et al. NCBI GEO: Mining tens of millions of expression profiles—Database and tools update. *Nucleic Acids Res.*, 35:D760–D765, 2007.

8. H. Parkinson et al. ArrayExpress update—From an archive of functional genomics experiments to the atlas of gene expression. *Nucleic Acids Res.*, 37:D868–D872, 2009.

9. T. Werner. Bioinformatics applications for pathway analysis of microarray data. *Curr. Opin. Biotechnol.*, 19:50–54, 2008.

10. M. Kanehisa. KEGG: Kyoto Encyclopedia of Genes and Genomes. *Nucleic Acids Res.*, 28(1): 27–30, 2000.

11. A. Subramanian, P. Tamayo, V. K. Mootha, and E. Al. Gene set enrichment analysis: A knowledge-based approach for interpreting genome-wide expression profiles. *PNAS*, 102:1–6, 2005.

12. M. Ashburner, C. A. Ball, J. A. Blake, and D. Botstein. Gene Ontology: Tool for the unification of biology. *Nat. Genet.*, 25(1):25–29, 2000.

13. H. Berman, K. Henrick, and H. Nakamura. The worldwide Protein Data Bank (wwPDB): Ensuring a single, uniform archive of PDB data. *Nucleic Acids Res.*, 35:D301–D303, 2007.

14. A. Kouranov et al. The RCSB PDB information portal for structural genomics. *Nucleic Acids Res.*, 34:D302–D305, 2006.

15. S. Velankar, C. Best, and B. Beuth. PDBe: Protein Data Bank in Europe. *Nucleic Acids Res.*, 38:D308–D317, 2010.

16. K. Arnold, F. Kiefer, J. Kopp, and J. N. D. Battey. The protein model portal. *J. Struct. Funct. Genomics*, 10:1–8, 2009.

17. K. Pearson. On lines and planes of closest fit to systems of points in space. *Philos. Mag.*, 2:559–572, 1901.

18. B. Shneiderman. Treemaps for space-constrained visualization of hierarchies. *ACM Trans. Graphics (TOG)*, 1998. Available: `http://www.ifs.tuwien.ac.at/~silvia/ wien/vu-infovis/articles/shneiderman_treemap-history_1998-2009 .pdf`.

19. H. Kitano. Computational systems biology. *Nature*, 420:206–210, 2002.

20. D. Maglott, J. Ostell, and K. D. Pruitt. Entrez Gene: Gene-centered information at NCBI. *Nucleic Acids Res.*, 1(33):D54–D58, 2005.

21. A. Bairoch et al. The universal protein resource (UniProt). *Nucleic Acids Res.*, 33:D154–D159, 2005.

22. J. Shendure and H. Ji. Next-generation DNA sequencing. *Nat. Biotechnol.*, 26:1135–1145, 2008.

23. C. B. Nielsen, M. Cantor, I. Dubchak, D. Gordon, and T. Wang. Visualizing genomes: Techniques and challenges. *Nat. Methods*, 7:S5–S15, 2010.

24. F. Sanger and A. R. Coulson. A rapid method for determining sequences in DNA by primed synthesis with DNA polymerase. *J. Mol. Biol.*, 94:441–448, 1975.

25. D. Gordon, C. Abajian, and P. Green. Consed: A graphical tool for sequence finishing. *Genome Res.*, 8:195–202, 1998.

26. M. C. Schatz, A. M. Phillippy, B. Shneiderman, and S. L. Salzberg. Hawkeye: An interactive visual analytics tool for genome assemblies. *Genome Biol.*, 8:R34, 2007.

27. C. B. Nielsen, S. D. Jackman, I. Birol, and S. J. M. Jones. ABySS-Explorer: Visualizing genome sequence assemblies. *IEEE Trans. Vis. Comput. Graphics*, 15:881–888, 2009.

28. L. D. Stein, C. Mungall, S. Q. Shu, and M. Caudy. The generic genome browser: A building block for a model organism system database. *Genome Res.*, 12:1599–1610, 2002.

29. J. W. Nicol, G. A. Helt, S. G. Blanchard, and A. Raja. The Integrated Genome Browser: Free software for distribution and exploration of genome-scale datasets. *Bioinformatics*, 25:2730–2731, 2009.

30. J. T. Robinson et al. Integrative genomics viewer. *Nat. Biotechnol.*, 29:24–26, 2011.

31. W. J. Kent, C. W. Sugnet, T. S. Furey, and K. M. Roskin. The human genome browser at UCSC. *Genome Res.*, 12:996–1006, 2002.

32. J. Stalker, B. Gibbins, P. Meidl, and J. Smith. The Ensembl Web site: Mechanics of a genome browser. *Genome Res.*, 14:951–955, 2004.

33. D. L. Wheeler, T. Barrett, and D. A. Benson. Database resources of the national center for biotechnology information. *Nucleic Acids Res.*, 35:D5–D12, 2007.

34. N. Sato and S. Ehira. GenoMap, a circular genome data viewer. *Bioinformatics*, 19:1583–1584, 2003.

35. P. Stothard and D. S. Wishart. Circular genome visualization and exploration using CGView. *Bioinformatics*, 21:537–539, 2005.

36. M. Krzywinski et al. Circos: An information aesthetic for comparative genomics. *Genome Res.*, 19:1639–1645, 2009.

37. M. Meyer and T. Munzner. MizBee: A multiscale synteny browser. *IEEE Trans. Vis. Comput. Graphics*, 15:897–904, 2009.

38. D. Holten. Hierarchical edge bundles: Visualization of adjacency relations in hierarchical data. *IEEE Trans. Vis. Comput. Graphics*, 12:741–748, 2006.

39. J. B. Procter et al. Visualization of multiple alignments, phylogenies and gene family evolution. *Nat. Methods*, 7:S16–S25, 2010.

40. http://www.geneious.com (n.d.).

41. M. A. Larkin et al. Clustal W and Clustal X version 2.0. *Bioinformatics (Oxford, England)*, 23:2947–2948, 2007.

42. C. E. Shannon. A mathematical theory of communication. *Bell Syst. Tech. J.* 27:379–423, 1948.

43. B. Schuster-Böckler and A. Bateman. Visualizing profile-profile alignment: Pairwise HMM logos. *Bioinformatics* (Oxford, England), 21:2912–2913, 2005.

44. G. E. Crooks, G. Hon, and J. M. Chandonia. WebLogo: A sequence logo generator. *Genome Res.*, 14:1188–1190, 2004.

45. K. Tamura et al. MEGA5: Molecular evolutionary genetics analysis using maximum likelihood, evolutionary distance, and maximum parsimony methods. *Mol. Biol. Evol.*, 2011.

46. A. M. Waterhouse, J. B. Procter, D. M. A. Martin, M. Clamp, and G. J. Barton. Jalview Version 2—A multiple sequence alignment editor and analysis workbench. *Bioinformatics (Oxford, England)*, 25:1189–1191, 2009.

47. D. R. Caffrey et al. PFAAT version 2.0: A tool for editing, annotating, and analyzing multiple sequence alignments. *BMC Bioinformatics*, 8:381, 2007.

48. D. Nishimura. BioCarta. *Biotech Software & Internet Report*, 2:117–120, 2001.

49. L. Matthews, G. Gopinath, and M. Gillespie. Reactome knowledgebase of human biological pathways and processes. *Nucleic Acids Res.*, 37:D619–D622, 2009.

50. C. E. Wheelock et al. Systems biology approaches and pathway tools for investigating cardio-vascular disease. *Mol. BioSyst.*, 5:588, 2009.

51. P. Shannon, A. Markiel, O. Ozier, and N. S. Baliga. Cytoscape: A software environment for integrated models of biomolecular interaction networks. *Genome Res.*, 13:2498–2504, 2003.

52. G. Bindea, B. Mlecnik, and H. Hackl. ClueGO: A Cytoscape plug-in to decipher functionally grouped gene ontology and pathway annotation networks. *Bioinformatics*, 25:1091–1093, 2009.

53. O. Garcia, C. Saveanu, and M. Cline. GOlorize: A Cytoscape plug-in for network visualization with Gene Ontology-based layout and coloring. *Bioinformatics*, 23:394–396, 2007.

54. S. Maere and K. Heymans. BiNGO: A Cytoscape plugin to assess overrepresentation of gene ontology categories in biological networks. *Bioinformatics*, 21(16):3448–3449, 2005.

55. T. Xia and J. A. Dickerson. OmicsViz: Cytoscape plug-in for visualizing omics data across species. *Bioinformatics*, 24:2557–2558, 2008.

56. T. Xia and J. V. Hemert. OmicsAnalyzer: A Cytoscape plug-in suite for modeling omics data. *Bioinformatics*, 26(23):2995–2996, 2010.

57. M. Clément-Ziza et al. Genoscape: A Cytoscape plug-in to automate the retrieval and integration of gene expression data and molecular networks. *Bioinformatics* (Oxford, England), 25:2617–2618, 2009.

58. C. A. H. Baker, M. S. T. Carpendale, P. Prusinkiewicz, and M. G. Surette. GeneVis: Visualization tools for genetic regulatory network dynamics. In *VIS '02: Proceedings of the Conference on Visualization*. IEEE Computer Society, New York, 2002, pp. 243–250.

59. Z. Hu, J. Mellor, J. Wu, and C. DeLisi. VisANT: An online visualization and analysis tool for biological interaction data. *BMC bioinformatics*, 5:17, 2004.

60. H. Neuweger, M. Persicke, and S. Albaum. Visualizing post genomics datasets on customized pathway maps by ProMeTra—Aeration-dependent gene expression and metabolism of *Corynebacterium glutamicun* as an example. *BMC Syst. Biol.*, 3(1):82, 2009.

61. D. Hwang et al. A systems approach to prion disease. *Mol. Syst. Biol.*, 5, 2009. DOI: 10.1038/msb.2009.10.

62. B. J. Breitkreutz and C. Stark. Osprey: A network visualization system. *Genome Biol.*, 4, 2003. Available: http://www.ncbi.nlm.nih.gov/pmc/articles/PMC153462/.

63. V. Batagelj and A. Mrvar. Pajek—Program for large network analysis, 1999. Available: `http://vlado.fmf.uni-lj.si/pub/networks/pajek/`.

64. S. Kozhenkov et al. BiologicalNetworks—Tools enabling the integration of multi-scale data for the host-pathogen studies. *BMC Syst. Biol.*, 5:7, 2011.

65. F. Iragne, M. Nikolski, B. Mathieu, D. Auber, and D. Sherman. ProViz: Protein interaction visualization and exploration. *Bioinformatics* (Oxford, England), 21:272–274, 2005.

66. A. T. Adai, S. V. Date, S. Wieland, and E. M. Marcotte. LGL: Creating a map of protein function with an algorithm for visualizing very large biological networks. *J. Mol. Biol.*, 340:179–190, 2004.

67. M. Krzywinski. Linear layout for visualization of networks. *Genome Informatics*. Available: `http://mkweb.bcgs.ca/linnet`, 2010.

68. K. I. Goh et al. The human disease network. *Proc. Nat. Acad. Sci.*, 104:8685–8690, 2007.

69. The New York Times. Mapping the human diseasome. Available: `http://www.nytimes.com/interactive/2008/05/05/science/20080506_DISEASE.html`, 2008.

70. G. A. Pavlopoulos, A.-L. Wegener, and R. Schneider. A survey of visualization tools for biological network analysis. *BioData Mining*, 1:12, 2008.

71. R. D. M. Page. Tree View: An application to display phylogenetic trees on personal computers. *Comput. Appl. Biosci.*, 12(4):357–358, 1996.

72. D. H. Huson et al. Dendroscope: An interactive viewer for large phylogenetic trees. *BMC Bioinformatics*, 8:460, 2007.

73. W. Ludwig et al. ARB: A software environment for sequence data. *Nucleic Acids Res.*, 32:1363–1371, 2004.

74. M. V. Han and C. M. Zmasek. phyloXML: XML for evolutionary biology and comparative genomics. *BMC Bioinformatics*, 10:356, 2009.

75. I. Letunic and P. Bork. Interactive Tree Of Life (iTOL): An online tool for phylogenetic tree display and annotation. *Bioinformatics*, 23:127–128, 2006.

76. R. Santamaría and R. Therón. Treevolution: Visual analysis of phylogenetic trees. *Bioinformatics* (Oxford, England), 25:1970–1971, 2009.

77. M. S. Horn, M. Tobiasz, and C. Shen. Visualizing biodiversity with voronoi treemaps. Paper presented at the 6th Intl. Symposium on Voronoi Diagrams, Copenhagen, Denmark, 2009, pp. 265–270.

78. A. Katifori, C. Halatsis, and G. Lepouras. Ontology visualization methods—A survey. *ACM Comput. Surv.*, 39:10, 2007.

79. B. Zhang, D. Schmoyer, and S. Kirov. GOTree Machine (GOTM): A web-based platform for interpreting sets of interesting genes using Gene Ontology hierarchies. *BMC Bioinformatics*, 2004. Available: `http://www.biomedcentral.com/1471-2105/5/16/`.

80. A. Conesa et al. Blast2GO: A universal tool for annotation, visualization and analysis in functional genomics research. *Bioinformatics* (Oxford, England), 21:3674–3676, 2005.

81. E. Eden, R. Navon, I. Steinfeld, D. Lipson, and Z. Yakhini. GOrilla: A tool for discovery and visualization of enriched GO terms in ranked gene lists. *BMC Bioinformatics*, 10:48, 2009.

82. A. Otto et al. Systems-wide temporal proteomic profiling in glucose-starved *Bacillus subtilis*. *Nat. Commun.*, 1:137, 2010.

83. R. Santamaría, R. Therón, and L. Quintales. BicOverlapper: A tool for bicluster visualization. *Bioinformatics*, 24:1212–1213, 2008.

84. J. Bernhardt, S. Funke, and M. Hecker. Visualizing gene expression data via Voronoi treemaps. Paper presented at the International Symposium on Voronoi Diagrams, Copenhagen, Denmark, 2009.

85. A. Kauffmann, R. Gentleman, and W. Huber. arrayQualityMetrics—A bioconductor package for quality assessment of microarray data. *Bioinformatics* (Oxford, England), 25:415–416, 2009.

86. M. Eisen, P. Spellman, P. Brown, and D. Botstein. Cluster analysis and display of genome-wide expression patterns. *Proc. Nat. Acad. Sci.*, 95:1–6, 1998.

87. R. Sharan, A. Maron-Katz, and R. Shamir. CLICK and EXPANDER: A system for clustering and visualizing gene expression data. *Bioinformatics*, 19:1787–1799, 2003.

88. M. Rasmussen and G. Karypis. gCLUTO—An interactive clustering, visualization, and analysis system, 2004. Available: http://www.cs.umn.edu/tech_reports_upload/tr2004/04-021.pdf.

89. S. Barkow, S. Bleuler, A. Prelic, P. Zimmermann, and E. Zitzler. BicAT: A biclustering analysis toolbox. *Bioinformatics*, 22:1282–1283, 2006.

90. A. J. Saldanha. Java Treeview—Extensible visualization of microarray data. *Bioinformatics*, 20:3246–3248, 2004.

91. R. Santamaría, R. Therón, and L. Quintales. A visual analytics approach for understanding biclustering results from microarray data. *BMC Bioinformatics*, 9:247, 2008.

92. M. Kapushesky et al. Gene expression atlas at the European bioinformatics institute. *Nucleic Acids Res.*, 38:D690–D698, 2010.

93. K. O. Cheng, N. F. Law, W. C. Siu, T. H. Lau. BiVisu: Software tool for bicluster detection and visualization. *Bioinformatics* (Oxford, England), 23:2342–2344, 2007.

94. D. F. Swayne, D. T. Lang, and A. Buja. GGobi: Evolving from XGobi into an extensible framework for interactive data visualization. *Computat. Statist. Data Anal.*, 43:423–444, 2003.

95. J. Seo and B. Shneiderman. Interactively exploring hierarchical clustering results. *Computer*, 35:80–86, 2002.

96. O. Rübel, G. H. Weber, S. V. E. Keränen, and C. C. Fowlkes. PointCloudXplore: Visual analysis of 3D gene expression data using physical views and parallel coordinates. In *IEEE-VGTC Symposium on Data Visualization*, Boston, MA, 2006, pp. 203–206.

97. J. P. Gonçalves, S. C. Madeira, and A. L. Oliveira. BiGGEsTS: Integrated environment for biclustering analysis of time series gene expression data. *BMC Research Notes*, 2:124, 2009.

98. Tibco. Spotfire. Available: http://www. spotfire.tibco.com.

99. Agilent. GeneSpring GX. Available: http://www.chem.agilent.com.

100. J. Seo, H. Gordish-Dressman, and E. P. Hoffman. An interactive power analysis tool for microarray hypothesis testing and generation. *Bioinformatics*, 22:808–814, 2006.

101. S. C. Madeira and A. L. Oliveira. Biclustering algorithms for biological data analysis: A survey. *IEEE Trans. Computat. Biol. Bioinformatics*, 1:24–45, 2004.

102. G. A. Grothaus, A. Mufti, and T. M. Murali. Automatic layout and visualization of biclusters. *Algorithms Mol. Biol.*, 1:15, 2006.

103. M. Lukk et al. A global map of human gene expression. *Nat. Biotechnol.*, 28:322–324, 2010.

104. S. I. O'Donoghue et al. Visualization of macromolecular structures. *Nat. Methods*, 7:S42–S55, 2010.

105. A. Herráez. Biomolecules in the computer: Jmol to the rescue. *Biochemistry and Molecular Biology Education: A Bimonthly Publication of the International Union of Biochemistry and Molecular Biology*, 34:255–261, 2006.

106. E. Martz. FirstGlance. Available: http://firstglance.jmol.org, 2005.

107. R. A. Sayle, E. J. Milner-White. RASMOL: Biomolecular graphics for all. *Trends Biochem. Sci.*, 20:374, 1995.

108. W. Humphrey. VMD: Visual molecular dynamics. *J. Mol. Graphics*, 14:33–38, 1996.

109. M. F. Sanner, B. S. Duncan, C. J. Carrillo, and A. J. Olson. Integrating computation and visualization for biomolecular analysis: An example using Python and AVS. In *Pacific Symposium on Biocomputing*, Mauna Lani, HI, 1999, pp. 401–412.

110. F. Jossinet and E. Westhof. Sequence to Structure (S2S): Display, manipulate and interconnect RNA data from sequence to structure. *Bioinformatics* (Oxford, England), 21:3320–3321, 2005.

111. M. Landau et al. ConSurf 2005: The projection of evolutionary conservation scores of residues on protein structures. *Nucleic Acids Res.*, 33:W299–W302, 2005.

112. F. Jossinet, T. E. Ludwig, and E. Westhof. Assemble: An interactive graphical tool to analyze and build RNA architectures at the 2D and 3D levels. *Bioinformatics* (Oxford, England), 26:2057–2059, 2010.

113. L. Schrödinger. The PyMOL Molecular Graphics System. Available: `http://www.pymol.org`, accessed Oct. 5, 2011.

114. E. F. Pettersen et al. UCSF Chimera—A visualization system for exploratory research and analysis. *J. Computat. Chem.*, 25:1605–1612, 2004.

115. K. Stierand, P. C. Maass, and M. Rarey. Molecular complexes at a glance: Automated generation of two-dimensional complex diagrams. *Bioinformatics* (Oxford, England), 22:1710–1716, 2006.

116. M. Kuhn et al. STITCH 2: An interaction network database for small molecules and proteins. *Nucleic Acids Res.*, 38:D552–D556, 2010.

117. S. I. O'Donoghue, J. E. W. Meyer, A. Schafferhans, and K. Fries. The SRS 3D module: Integrating structures, sequences and features. *Bioinformatics* (Oxford, England), 20:2476–2478, 2004.

118. R. Koradi. MOLMOL: A program for display and analysis of macromolecular structures. *J. Mol. Graphics*, 14:51–55, 1996.

119. A. C. Wallace, R. A. Laskowski, and J. M. Thornton. LIGPLOT: A program to generate schematic diagrams of protein-ligand interactions. *Protein Eng. Design Selection*, 8:127–134, 1995.

120. S. Cooper et al. Analysis of social gameplay macros in the Foldit Cookbook. In *Proceedings of the 6th International Conference on Foundations of Digital Games*, Bordeaux, France, 2011, pp. 9–14.

CHAPTER 48

VISUALIZATION OF BIOLOGICAL KNOWLEDGE BASED ON MULTIMODAL BIOLOGICAL DATA

HENDRIK ROHN[1] and FALK SCHREIBER[1,2]

[1]Leibniz Institute of Plant Genetics and Crop Plant Research (IPK), Gatersleben, Germany
[2]Institute of Computer Science, Martin Luther University Halle-Wittenberg, Halle, Germany

48.1 INTRODUCTION

Biology-related sciences such as biotechnology, biochemistry, genetics, and molecular biology are becoming increasingly important. The development and production of pharmaceutical product, food, and feed as well as different materials are based on the scientific progress achieved in these fields. This also demands growing effort for the analysis and understanding of biological data. Especially systems-oriented approaches using high-throughput methods gather enormous collections of various types of data on different levels of resolution from various sources. Such complex data enable not only to focus on singular phenomena but also to catch complex cause-and-effect chains. These finally lead to the discovery of biological knowledge which can be published and spread throughout the community. The focus of this chapter deals with how to discover biological knowledge from such multimodal biological data using visualization. The rest of the chapter is organized as follows. In Section 48.2, we describe multimodal biological data and how to structure a data model. Section 48.3 gives an overview of other approaches for knowledge discovery from multimodal biological data. Section 48.4 describes how the data are integrated, mapped, and visualized based on a visualization pipeline concept. Finally, we present a number of implemented integration views which enable the extraction of knowledge from multimodal biological data.

48.2 MULTIMODAL BIOLOGICAL DATA

Biological knowledge is distributed and stored in various forms: papers and books (textual form), databases and spreadsheets (values), schemata (diagrams, conceptual drawings), verbal (communication, talks), and many more. This knowledge is gathered by mining different data acquired mainly in experiment-based laborious work. Knowledge again may

Biological Knowledge Discovery Handbook: Preprocessing, Mining, and Postprocessing of Biological Data,
First Edition. Edited by Mourad Elloumi and Albert Y. Zomaya.
© 2014 John Wiley & Sons, Inc. Published 2014 by John Wiley & Sons, Inc.

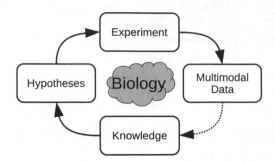

FIGURE 48.1   Cycle of biological knowledge accumulation (adapted from [15]). Based on the existing knowledge, experiments are planned, leading to multimodal biological data. The data have to be transferred into new biological knowledge. The dashed arrow indicates the focus of this chapter.

be used to generate further hypotheses about organisms, leading to new experiments and therefore closing the cycle of knowledge accumulation (compare Figure 48.1).

All experiments performed in this cycle result in large data sets from different data domains. Important multimodal biological data types are structural or functional 2D and 3D images, for example, volumetric nuclear magnetic resonance (NMR) data sets, histological cross sections, and phenotypic photographs. Graph-based modeling approaches support the understanding of biological processes such as metabolism and gene regulation. Gene expression and metabolite concentrations are numerical data measured to describe organisms at the cellular level. These data types include large portions of multimodal biological data gathered in experiments (some instances can be seen in Figure 48.2).

An important attribute of such data is the modality. Multimodal biological data usually have some time resolution, either developmental or experimental stages. Also the species, environmental influences, and genetic background are of great importance. Furthermore there is a high complexity in the structure and organization of organisms. Additionally, different types of data are usually gathered at different resolution: Spatial information (e.g., images and volumes) is usually measured at the tissue or organ level, because it gets technically difficult and laborious to measure spatial information at higher resolution. Numerical data, such as gene expression and metabolite concentration, on the other hand, are in most instances measured at the cellular level but usually lack spatial information. Finally, such multimodal biological data are gathered from different groups around the world in increasing quantity and quality.

To transform multimodal data into biological knowledge, preprocessing steps have to be applied. These include the removal of methodological artifacts by denoising but also important are the normalization and removal of outliers. Further processing consists of enrichment by biological knowledge (e.g., for segmentation information). Here a segmentation step is usually carried out to assign each pixel of the image to a structure, for example, the tissue to which it belongs. Another example of processing is the clustering of gene expression values into small groups of similar-behaving genes.

The analysis and visualization of such preprocessed data already enable to discover biological knowledge, especially when considering different visualization approaches. Having said that, multimodal biological data should always be viewed in the context of surrounding information, because all data gathered from one organism are in context of each other.

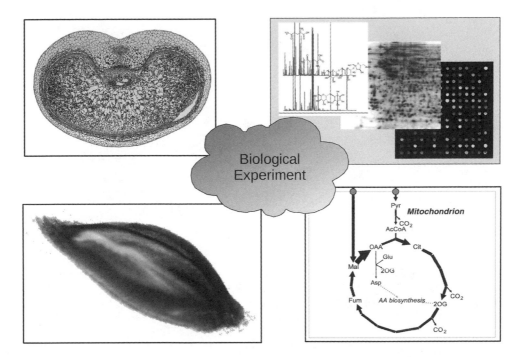

FIGURE 48.2 Illustration of important types of multimodal biological data derived from experiments. Top left: Histological cross section. Top right: Genomics, proteomics, and metabolomics data. Lower right: Flux distribution in metabolic network. Lower left: Volume model.

Therefore data integration may provide a more complete view on the organism, facilitating knowledge beyond the intended results of single experiments [2]. Consequently there is need for an integrated view on several biological data domains to analyze manifold cause-and-effect chains. It already could be shown that the combination of networks and numerical data is useful and leads to novel insight into data and organisms [9]. We will expand such approaches by considering additional spatial data in order to be able to account for the aforementioned modalities.

48.3 APPROACHES TO DISCOVER KNOWLEDGE FROM MULTIMODAL BIOLOGICAL DATA

There are a large number of approaches and tools to visualize single types of multimodal biological data separately. On the other hand, until now there are only a smaller number of tools enabling the combination of data of different types together, which would assist scientists in relating and visualizing multimodal data and ease discovery of biological knowledge.

Numerous database-oriented approaches to integrate multimodal biological data were established (see [34]), but the main focus usually is data storage and the structured query of large quantities of data. Biological users usually are overwhelmed by the sheer number of biological databases, exponentially increasing data quantity and unhandy Web interfaces

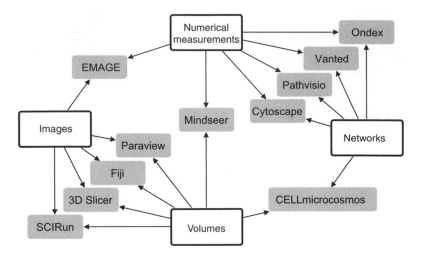

FIGURE 48.3   Illustration of four multimodal biological data domains (white rectangles) and selection of tools (gray rectangles) which are able to combine data of two or more domains (depicted by arrows). The number of tools for 2D and 3D combination, respectively numerical and network data, are selected from a larger set of available tools.

to access data. Until now it is even laborious work to annotate one's own data correctly and upload it to databases [2]. Consequentially, the field of available tools is substantially reduced.

A considerable number of tools exist for the combination of numerical data with networks (for an overview see [9]). The combination of 2D images or 3D data with numerical data is typically popular in neuroscience [10, 21, 24]. The combination of 2D and 3D data is again covered by a larger number of tools (see, e.g., [1, 3, 19, 22, 23, 33]). The integration of networks with 2D or 3D data is sparse [32]. Some of these representative tools are illustrated in Figure 48.3. Apparent is the accumulation of tools for 2D and 3D data combination, as well as tools for network and numerical data combination. There are no tools able to flexibly combine more than two data types in order to discover biological knowledge. A detailed analysis in Table 48.1 shows that mainly the network-focused tools are easy to use and provide sufficient support for metadata. Mindseer [21], EMAGE [24], and CELLmicrocosmos [32] are primarily tools for data display rather than knowledge discovery, as they lack advanced interaction capabilities. Although most tools support add-ons, only few (high-quality) ones are available in most cases. A positive aspect of most tools is the availability of the source code as well as platform independence and easy installation procedure.

48.4   NOVEL APPROACH FOR VISUALIZATION AND DISCOVERY OF BIOLOGICAL KNOWLEDGE BASED ON MULTIMODAL BIOLOGICAL DATA

We present a novel approach based on a visualization pipeline for visualization and discovery of biological knowledge based on multimodal data. All parts of this pipeline are explained in detail in the following sections.

TABLE 48.1 Detailed Comparison of Tools Illustrated in Figure 48.3

Tool	Vanted [12]	Ondex [17]	Cytoscape [30]	PathVisio [36]	Mindseer [21]	EMAGE [24]	Fiji [1, 28]	MBAT [3]	ParaView [19]	SCIRun [22]	3D Slicer [23]	Amira [33]	CELLmicrocosmos [32]
Numerical measurements	***	**	*	***	*	*	—	—	—	—	—	—	—
Images	—	—	—	—	—	***	***	**	**	***	**	***	—
Volumes	—	—	—	—	***	—	***	***	***	***	***	***	***
Networks	***	***	***	***	—	—	—	*	—	—	—	—	**
Interaction	***	***	***	**	*	*	***	**	***	***	***	***	*
Combination	***	***	***	**	*	*	**	**	***	***	*	***	**
Metadata support	**	***	*	*	*	*	—	***	—	—	—	—	**
Resources[a]	***	***	***	**	*	**	*	***	*	*	**	—	**
Extendability	**	**	***	**	*	—	***	**	**	*	*	**	—
Usability	***	***	***	***	***	***	***	**	**	**	***	**	**
Licence	OS[b]	OS	OS	OS	OS	NC[c]	OS	NC	OS	OS	OS	$	—
Operating system	Java[d]	Java	Java	Java	Java	Java	Java	Java	WLM[e]	WLM	WLM	WLM	Java

Note: The more stars, the better the support for the feature (—, not at all; *, barely; **, moderate; ***, good).

[a]E.g., access to databases and example data.
[b]Open source.
[c]Noncommercial use free.
[d]Where Java is available.
[e]Windows, Linux, Mac.

1113

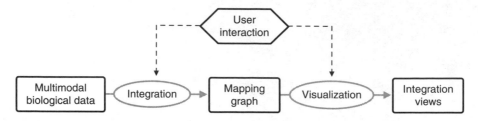

FIGURE 48.4 Visualization pipeline for visualization and discovery of biological knowledge adapted from [29]. Multimodal biological data are integrated into a mapping graph and mappings are created by applying mapping functions. Such integrated and combined data can be transformed by visualization functions into integration view s, representing a special view onto the multimodal biological data. Each transformation can be manipulated by the user in order to alter downstream steps.

48.4.1 Visualization Pipeline

The generation of visualizations is usually structured in the form of a visualization pipeline, guiding the user from the data to the visualization in different steps. The structure of this reference model changes according to the use case, resulting in a number of available pipelines for different tasks [6].

In Figure 48.4 the visualization pipeline to discover biological knowledge is shown. It consists of three parts: Multimodal biological data are split into measurements and accompanying metadata during the integration step. The mapping graph is a graph structure consisting of a number of mappings, which are created by applying mapping functions. The mappings can be transformed by the visualization step using visualization functions to create integration views. These integration views finally make it possible to discover knowledge from the multimodal biological data. Each transformation integration and visualization can be manipulated and parameterized by the user in order to create an adapted pipeline instance for a certain biological question.

48.4.2 Multimodal Biological Data

The multimodal biological data which are transformed by the pipeline in several steps and finally used to discover and visualize biological knowledge have been already described in detail in Section 48.2.

48.4.3 Integration

The multimodal biological data are split during the integration step into two parts: the measurements itself (e.g., numerical values, images) and the metadata accompanying these measurements.

48.4.3.1 Measurements   During the integration several data types are mapped to four distinct measurement types:

1. Gene expression values, protein activity values, metabolic concentrations, flux measurement, and similar values values can be modeled using a float number and hence belong to the type of *numerical measurements*.

2. Metabolic pathways, gene regulatory networks, protein interaction networks, and similar networks can be represented as graphs and hence belong to the type of *networks*; additionally, stoichiometric and kinetic models belong to this type, as they can be represented as graphs with information about stoichiometry and kinetic laws.

3. Microscopic images, histological cross-sections, in situ hybridization images, phenotypic photographs, and similar images are two-dimensional information and hence belong to the type of *images*.

4. Computer tomography scans, NMR imaging data, magnetic resonance tomography volumes, and similar volumes are usually three-dimensional information and hence belong to the type of *volumes*; also other three-dimensional data such as surface models can be implicitly modeled as volumes.

It should be noted that this separation is not always strictly possible. In such situations user interaction may be required. For example, a number of images may be seen as a number of separate images but also as a stack of images converted into a volumetric representation.

48.4.3.2 *Metadata*   The recently described measurements can be enriched by biological knowledge already during integration, such as segmentation information, knowledge about the biological object, experimental conditions, and so on. Such information is called *metadata* and represents descriptive information of data. It is important for search and selection of specific measurements, for example, search all measurements from one species or with a certain environmental influence such as drought stress. Metadata can also be important to be able to bring multimodal biological data of different experiments together, for example, the normalization approach for gene expression values may differ from experiment to experiment and hence has to be specified as metadata. The metadata are specified during the integration process and consider five types:

1. *Species Name (e.g., Arabidopsis thaliana)*   Describes the taxonomic name of the species.

2. *Genotype (e.g., Wild Type, SXD1-14)*   Describes the genetic background of the organisms, as mutants may have favorable characteristics.

3. *Environment (e.g., Cold Stress, Exposition to Perchloric Acid)*   Describes important environmental influences, such as special treatment which may have substantial impact on the performance of an organism.

4. *Time (e.g., Day 7 after Flowering)*   Describes temporal properties such as developmental stages or experiment-specific temporal attributes such as exposition time.

5. *Substance (e.g., Fructose-6-phosphate, LEC1)*   Describes the substance (gene, metabolite, etc.), which is represented by the measurement value.

The user specifies the metadata during integration as uncontrolled strings and has to take care of the equality or nonequality of names.

It is apparent that only a part of the experiment work flow is modeled by the metadata. Otherwise it would be essential to include experiment description, design and setup, normalization methods, annotation methods, data standards, and more. Instead the focus is on already processed, filtered, and normalized experimental data, which is required for visualization and analysis. This is in contrast to the one used in the MIAME standard [5] (microarray data), PEDRo database [35] (proteomics data), or ArMet framework [26] (metabolomics

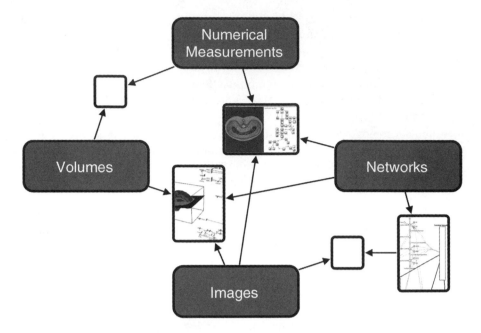

FIGURE 48.5   Mapping graph containing initial MI nodes (gray nodes) and mapping nodes (other nodes, some with exemplary screenshots). Integrated measurements are split and integrated into four MI nodes. Mapping functions combine these measurements and measurements from other mappings into a new mapping, indicated by edges between nodes.

data) but shows some advantages such as enhanced comprehensibility, easier extendability, and short specification period during integration.

48.4.4   Mapping Graph

Based on the previous steps the multimodal biological data get integrated into a structure called a *mapping graph* (compare Figure 48.5). It consists of four initial nodes called *measurement import nodes* (MI-nodes). All measurements are split by type and integrated into the corresponding MI-nodes, which represent a collection of all measurements of one measurement type. An arbitrary number of such measurements can be selected and used as an input for a mapping function. These mapping functions transform the input collection of measurements into a new collection, which may contain any number of (copied) input measurements, but also newly generated measurements. The new measurement collection is called a *mapping* and is represented as an additional node in the mapping graph. Thus, mappings represent novel combinations of measurements. Edges in the mapping graph represent the measurement flow, pointing from the source of input measurements to the new mapping node. Therefore MI-nodes have only outgoing edges, as they serve only as sources of measurements. Mappings can be created by mapping functions under use of any number of mapping nodes and MI-nodes, but the input measurement collection is not allowed to be empty. Consequently, mappings can be mapped again and measurements, which were integrated into the mapping graph, may get mapped over and over again, thereby participating in various mappings.

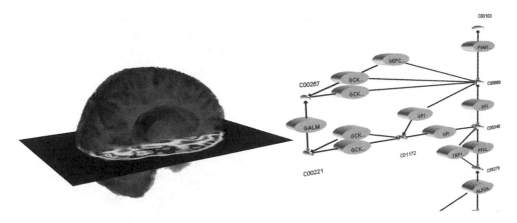

FIGURE 48.6   Screenshot of 3D visualization showing human brain MRT volume, two-dimensional PET image of brain, and representation of human glycolysis pathway.

48.4.5 Visualization

To be able to explore and visualize combined measurements, different visualization functions can be applied to mappings in order to achieve specific views or graphical representations. This is achieved by projecting the measurements into Euclidean space and providing interaction possibilities in order to manipulate view properties. It is possible that a mapping can be transformed by more than one visualization function, for example, a network can be visualized in two dimensions with nodes represented as rectangles and edges represented as arrows. It may also be visualized in three dimensions with nodes as cuboids and edges as cylinders or even as static images as in the KEGG database [14].

48.4.5.1 3D Visualization   The three-dimensional (3D) visualization makes it possible to visualize all four measurement types in 3D space (compare Figure 48.6). All measurement representations may be rotated and translated in three dimensions.

The computationally most demanding visualization part is to render typical volumetric data sets, which is achieved based on a slice-based volume renderer [20]: The rendering algorithm generates a stack of planes through the volume in three orthogonal directions and aligns these planes in the space. Transparency effects are applied to the planes and can be changed using sliders. Besides the general plane transparency, single planes may be highlighted and model cutoffs realized. Some planes may be skipped to achieve higher frame rates or stretched to implement nonisotropic voxels. In case of a gray-value volume, a set of color maps enable to highlight interesting regions or to generate an appealing appearance. Segmented volumes are also supported by highlighting or hiding segments based on user input. These segments may serve as a backbone for spatial navigation, for example, selecting a tissue to trigger the visualization of the corresponding tissue-specific pathway.

Images are visualized by applying the image data onto a textured plane. They may be resized on user request and texture transparency data can be applied similar to volumes. Segmented images work the same way as for volumes, by selecting and highlighting or deleting segments.

Networks are also represented in the 3D visualization. Nodes are implemented as spheres, cuboids, or cylinders, whereas edges are represented either by a cone and a cylinder or as a primitive line. Network elements support transparency and alteration of colors. Beside the structure of networks, also the visualization of omics data can be achieved similar to the diagrams in the graph visualization. These diagrams are rendered as images and applied to the nodes as textures.

48.4.5.2 *Network Visualization*   The network visualization projects data of the types network and numerical measurement into two dimensions (see Figure 48.7). Nodes and edges are represented as graphic primitives: Nodes are represented by a rectangle or circle, whereas edges are represented as arrows. It is possible to directly manipulate the network structure and hence construct, edit, and layout networks manually. The visualization of experimental data within the network context is implemented by embedding

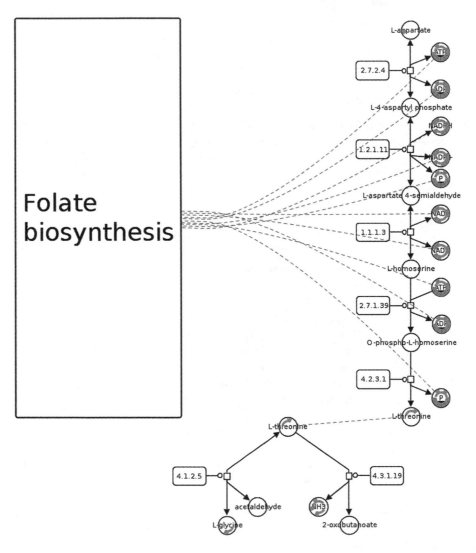

FIGURE 48.7   Screenshot of network visualization showing three networks (one collapsed) in two dimensions. If networks are interconnected, edge bundling is applied to provide better overview.

diagrams inside network nodes or onto network edges. The drawing style of these diagrams can be interactively modified, for example, alter coloration, display of range, or category labels and line widths. Besides standard networks, the view is able to visualize experiment data as hierarchies by relating them to functional categories such as *Gene Ontology* (see, e.g., [31]). Networks may be exported as interactive explorable websites. These comprise diagrams and clickable network elements (linking to Web entries in databases) in order to provide a convenient way to spread biological knowledge throughout the scientific community.

The network visualization supports the interaction technique network collapsing, similar to the one described in [16]. There, the KEGG pathways may be collapsed into a pathway overview node. All edges to and from such collapsed nodes then point to the overview node, instead of single graph elements. These nodes then may be relocated and expanded again. Such expansion results in the replacement of the node by the pathway's graph elements and reset of edges to the correct elements. In the network visualization all edges between two networks are bundled together to improve lucidity (similar to [11]). This edge-bundling facilitates visual tracking of single edges but in addition maintains a good overview of general network interconnections.

48.4.5.3 *Image Visualization*   The image visualization is able to visualize multimodal biological data of the types volumes and images in two dimensions. Images are displayed as usual by drawing the pixels in a scaled manner onto the screen. Segmentation information is displayed by utilizing a blending effect between the source image and the labelfield image. The user can adapt the blending factor in order to check the segmentation quality or to look up the corresponding segment for single pixels. The image visualization further is able to handle a stack of images by providing a slider, determining the actually displayed image of the stack (similar to [1]). If a number of images share a spatial or temporal relation, dragging the slider helps to catch these relations during the interaction. Volumetric data are represented as a stack of images, generated by traversing the volume in an orthogonal direction.

An interaction technique is the graphical triggering of spatial queries based on segmentation information (similar to [7]). The user selects a spatial region of the image by painting directly onto the image. All segments covered by this operation are extracted and used to trigger a query in a large collection of integrated numerical measurements. A result of such a query could be a smaller collection of measurements gathered in this segment.

48.4.5.4 *Brushing Visualization*   This visualization enables users to utilize the interaction technique brushing [8] in order to explore spatial-related experimental data sets (see Figure 48.8). It is divided into two parts: The first part visualizes a segmented image, serving as the navigational backbone for the brushing operation. The other part comprises a network visualization, showing a network and associated numerical measurements, which were measured in different segments. The user is able to hover the mouse over the image segments of interest. The network visualization reacts to this event by highlighting or displaying only data which were measured in the corresponding segment. A biological use case for this view is to investigate two-dimensional distribution of metabolic measurements in an interactive way: If biologists are interested in the state of the metabolism during the exposition in different oxygenic environments, the two-dimensional oxygen distribution may serve as navigational backbone for highlighting the corresponding data.

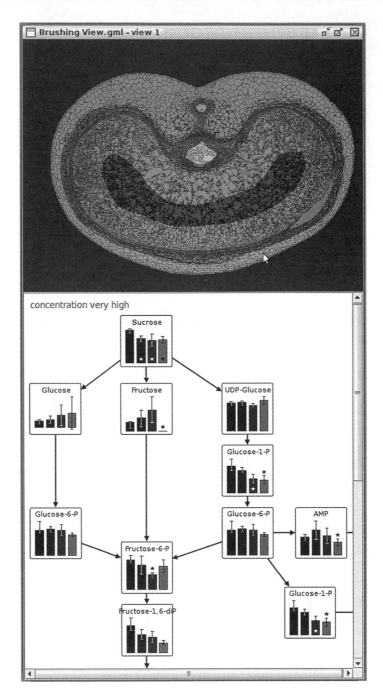

FIGURE 48.8   Screenshot of brushing visualization showing segmented cross section and network with associated numerical measurements. The user selects segments by hovering the mouse over the image and automatically highlighting segment-specific measurement data in network (bright bars).

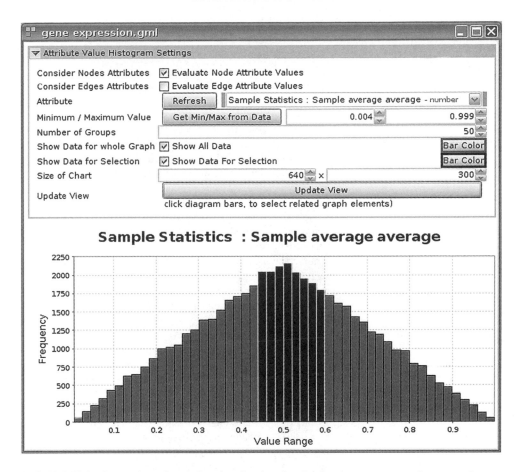

FIGURE 48.9 Screenshot of statistics visualization showing human gene expression rate values as histogram. The user is able to select parts of the data (dark bars) to, for example, remove the data. If the data are mapped onto a network, such actions will also be applied to the underlying network.

48.4.5.5 *Scatterplot Visualization* This visualization enables users to observe potentially correlated substances. A matrix is built up by adding all numerical measurements of pairwise substances to each element of the matrix. The elements are displayed by plotting points for pairwise measurement values.

48.4.5.6 *Statistics Visualization* Statistics visualization shows the distribution of network element attribute values as a histogram (see Figure 48.9). It can be used to visually inspect network properties or experimental data. An example is the investigation of comprehensive gene expression data sets to perform a quality check by recognizing the distribution of the multimodal biological data or by selecting and removing outlier values.

48.4.6 Integration Views

The abstract step of visualizing the model or parts of it results in a view or graphical representation. Here, if mappings are visualized using visualization functions, *integration*

TABLE 48.2 Overview of Some Integration Views Generated by Presented Visualization Pipeline

Integration View	Description
Image stacking	Several images are aligned in 3D space according to their position in organism
Network stacking	Several networks are aligned based on node labels in 3D space allowing visual comparison of network structure [4]
Image omics brushing	Enables to highlight numerical measurements from segments by brushing with segmented image as navigational backbone, enabling the exploration of numerical data in the context of networks
Omics query by graphical selection	Enables users to select a spatial region of a segmented image by painting and thereby triggering a query in numerical measurements acquired in this segment in order to visualize or further map these data (compare [24])
Omics network context	Shows numerical measurements as diagrams in their biological context, such as metabolic or gene regulatory networks [12]
Linked pathway integration	Generates an overview network [16], where each node represents a collapsed network, enabling navigation through all linked networks
Network comparison	Generates a new network, consisting of all elements of the input networks, colored according to the frequent occurrence in the input networks
Advanced network navigation	Enables to explore a number of related or interconnected networks by the advanced navigation developed in [13]
Condition log ratio	Compares the data of two species/genotypes/environments according to their substance concentrations as $\log_2$ ratio
Substance ratio matrix	Creates a matrix displaying pairwise ratio of substances as bar charts
Substance scatter matrix	Correlates numerical measurements of pairwise substances in scatter plot matrix
Gradient on image	Visualizes tuple of numerical measurements (e.g., gradient) in context of image-based structural properties (see, e.g, [25])
Multimodal alignment	Registers 2D images into 3D volumes to be able to compare information of different resolution and measurement techniques [27]
Volume registration	Registers two or more 3D volumes onto each other to be able to compare differences in spatial substance distribution or bring functional information into structural context
Volumetric reconstruction	Reconstructs 3D structure of organism from rotation images using space carving, similar to [18]

views are generated: A user selects a mapping node in the mapping graph and chooses a suitable visualization function, which projects these measurements into Euclidean space. Thus, an integration view is a tuple consisting of a mapping and a visualization function. In Table 48.2 a number of such combinations are explained in detail. As integration views may also visualize more than two types of measurements, they can be quite complex and depend on the requirements of biologists for special problems and are often strongly use-case oriented.

Integration views realize interactive and explorative work with combined multimodal biological data as well as aid in generating publication-ready visualizations. Integration views are the final step of the pipeline, to discover biological knowledge from integrated data. They promote understanding of multimodal biological data and the data context by providing interaction and exploration capabilities, as described in Section 48.4.5.

48.5 CONCLUSION

In this chapter we presented a way of how knowledge can be attained and visualized by transforming multimodal biological data in human-perceptible ways.

Biological data may consist of various data modalities, which have all to be taken into account to understand intrinsic properties from a systemwide perspective. Although there are a large number of advanced approaches able to handle and visualize single measurement types, for most combinations of data types there are only few, if any at all, available that accomplish this task. Based on the reference model of a visualization pipeline we showed how these multimodal biological data can be transformed into views from multiple directions onto combined data of different data domains Here visualization helps in discovering and presenting biological knowledge.

REFERENCES

1. M. D. Abramoff, P. J. Magelhaes, and S. J. Ram. Image processing with Image. *J. Biophoton. Int.*, 11:36–42, 2004.

2. C. A. Ball, G. Sherlock, and A. Brazma. Funding high-throughput data sharing. *Nat. Biotechnol.*, 22(9):1179–1183, 2004.

3. J. Boline, A. MacKenzie-Graham, D. Shattuck, H. Yuan, S. Anderson, D. Sforza, R. Williams, W. Wong, M. Martone, I. Zaslavsky, and A. Toga. A digital atlas and neuroinformatics framework for query and display of disparate data. In *Society for Neuroscience Conference*, 2006. Available: www.ccb.ucla.edu/twiki/pub/MouseBIRN/MouseSFN2006Presentations/ MBAT_2006.pdf.

4. U. Brandes, T. Dwyer, and F. Schreiber. Visual triangulation of network-based phylogenetic trees. In *Proceedings of Joint Eurographics—IEEE TCVG Symposium on Visualization*, Vol. 2912 of *Lecture Notes in Computer Science*, 2004, pp. 75–84.

5. A. Brazma, P. Hingamp, J. Quackenbush, G. Sherlock, P. Spellman, C. Stoeckert, J. Aach, W. Ansorge, C. A. Ball, H. C. Causton, T. Gaasterland, P. Glenisson, F. C. Holstege, I. F. Kim, V. Markowitz, J. C. Matese, H. Parkinson, A. Robinson, U. Sarkans, S. Schulze-Kremer, J. Stewart, R. Taylor, J. Vilo, and M. Vingron. Minimum information about a microarray experiment (MIAME)—Toward standards for microarray data. *Nat. Genet.*, 29(4):365–371, 2001.

6. N. Churcher and W. Irwin. Informing the design of pipeline-based software visualisations. In *Proceedings of Asia-Pacific Symposium on Information Visualisation*, Vol. 45, Australian Computer Society, Inc. Darlinghurst, Australia, Australia, 2005, pp. 59–68.

7. D. Davidson, J. Bard, R. Brune, A. Burgerc, C. Dubreuil, W. Hill, M. Kaufman, J. Quinn, M. Stark, and R. Baldock. The mouse atlas and graphical gene-expression database. *Semin. Cell Devel. Biol.*, 8(5):509–517, 1997.

8. S. G. Eick and G. J. Wills. High interaction graphics. *Eur. J. Oper. Res.*, 81(3):445–459, 1995.

9. N. Gehlenborg, S. I. O'Donoghue, N. S. Baliga, A. Goesmann, M. A. Hibbs, H. Kitano, O. Kohlbacher, H. Neuweger, R. Schneider, D. Tenenbaum, and A.-C. Gavin. Visualization of omics data for systems biology. *Nat. Methods*, 7:S56–S68, 2010.

10. T. Hjornevik, T. B. Leergaard, D. Darine, A. M. Moldestad, O. Dale, F. Willoch, and J. G. Bjaalie. Three-dimensional atlas system for mouse and rat brain imaging data. *Front. Neuroinform.*, 1:1–12, 2007.

11. D. Holten and J. J. Van Wijk. Force-directed edge bundling for graph visualization. *Comput. Graphics Forum*, 28(3):983–990, 2009.

12. B. H. Junker, C. Klukas, and F. Schreiber. VANTED: A system for advanced data analysis and visualization in the context of biological networks. *BMC Bioinformatics*, 7:109. 1–13, 2006.

13. I. Jusufi, C. Klukas, A. Kerren, and F. Schreiber. Guiding the interactive exploration of metabolic pathway interconnections. *Inform. Visual.*, 11(2):136–150, 2012.

14. M. Kanehisa and S. Goto. KEGG: Kyoto encyclopedia of genes and genomes. *Nucleic Acids Res.*, 28(1):27–30, 2000.

15. H. Kitano. Systems biology: A brief overview. *Science*, 295:1662–1664, 2002.

16. C. Klukas and F. Schreiber. Dynamic exploration and editing of KEGG pathway diagrams. *Bioinformatics*, 23(3):344–350, 2007.

17. J. Köhler, J. Baumbach, J. Taubert, M. Specht, A. Skusa, A. Ruegg, C. Rawlings, P. Verrier, and S. Philippi. Graph-based analysis and visualization of experimental results with ONDEX. *Bioinformatics*, 22(11):1383–1390, 2006.

18. K. N. Kutulakos and S. M. Seitz. A theory of shape by space carving. *Int. J. Comput. Vision*, 38(3):199–218, 2000.

19. C. C. Law, A. Henderson, and J. Ahrens. An application architecture for large data visualization: A case study. In *IEEE Symposium on Parallel and Large-Data Visualization and Graphics*, IEEE Press Piscataway, NJ, 2001, pp. 125–128. Available: `http://dl.acm.org/citation.cfm?id=502149`.

20. J. McGonigle. Java and 3D interactive image display. Master's Thesis. University of Aberdeen, 2006.

21. E. B. Moore, A. V. Poliakov, P. Lincoln, and J. F. Brinkley. Mindseer: A portable and extensible tool for visualization of structural and functional neuroimaging data. *BMC Bioinformatics*, 8:389. 1–12, 2007.

22. S. G. Parker and C. R. Johnson. SCIRun:A scientific programming environment for computational steering. In *Proceedings of the 1995 ACM/IEEE Conference on Supercomputing*, ACM New York, NY, 1995, pp. 2–19. Available: `http://dl.acm.org/citation.cfm?id=224354`.

23. S. Pieper, M. Halle, and R. Kikinis. 3D slicer. In *Proceedings of the 2004 IEEE International Symposium on Biomedical Imaging: From Nano to Macro*, Arlington, VA, April 15–18, 2004, pp. 632–635.

24. L. Richardson, S. Venkataraman, P. Stevenson, Y. Yang, N. Burton, J. Rao, M. Fisher, R. A. Baldock, D. R. Davidson, and J. H. Christiansen. EMAGE mouse embryo spatial gene expression database: 2010 update. *Nucleic Acids Res.*, 38(1):D703–D709, 2010.

25. H. Rolletschek, W. Weschke, H. Weber, U. Wobus, and L. Borisjuk. Energy state and its control on seed development: Starch accumulation is associated with high ATP and steep oxygen gradients within barley grains. *J. Exper. Botany*, 55(401):1351–1359, 2004.

26. D. V. Rubtsov, H. Jenkins, C. Ludwig, J. Easton, M. R. Viant, U. Günther, J. L. Griffin, and N. Hardy. Proposed reporting requirements for the description of NMR-based metabolomics experiments. *Metabolomics*, 3(3):223–229, 2007.

27. M. Scharfe, R. Pielot, and F. Schreiber. Fast multi-core based multimodal registration of 2D cross-sections and 3D datasets. *BMC Bioinformatics*, 11:20, 2010.

28. B. Schmid, J. Schindelin, A. Cardona, M. Longair, and M. Heisenberg. A high-level 3d visualization API for java and ImageJ. *BMC Bioninformatics*, 11(1):274.1–7, 2010.

29. F. Schreiber. Visual analysis of biological networks. Postdoctoral Thesis. Universität Passau, Fakultät für Mathematik und Informatik, 2006.

30. P. Shannon, A. Markiel, O. Ozier, N. S. Baliga, J. T. Wang, D. Ramage, N. Amin, B. Schwikowski, and T. Ideker. Cytoscape: A software environment for integrated models of biomolecular interaction networks. *Genome Res.*, 13(11):2498–2504, 2003.

31. T. F. Sharbel, M. L. Voigt, J. M. Corral, G. Galla, J. Kumlehn, C. Klukas, F. Schreiber, H. Vogel, and B. Rotter. Apomictic and sexual ovules of Boechera display heterochronic global gene expression patterns. *Plant Cell*, 22(3):655–671, 2010.

32. B. Sommer, J. Künsemöller, N. Sand, A. Husemann, M. Rumming, and B. Kormeier. CELLmicrocosmos 4.1: An interactive approach to integrating spatially localized metabolic networks into a virtual 3D cell environment. In A. L. N. Fred, J. Filipe, and H. Gamboa (Eds.), *BIOINFORMATICS 2010: Proceedings of the First International Conference on Bioinformatics*, INSTICC Press, Valencia, Spain, January 20–23, 2010, pp. 90–95.

33. D. Stalling, M. Westerhoff, and H.-C. Hege. Amira: A highly interactive system for visual data analysis. In *The Visualization Handbook*. Academic, Orlando, FL, 2005, pp. 749–767.

34. W. Sujansky. Heterogeneous database integration in biomedicine. *J. Biomed. Informatics*, 34(4):285–298, 2001.

35. C. F. Taylor, N. W. Paton, K. L. Garwood, P. D. Kirby, D. A. Stead, Z. Yin, E. W. Deutsch, L. Selway, J. Walker, I. Riba-Garcia, S. Mohammed, M. J. Deery, J. A. Howard, T. Dunkley, R. Aebersold, D. B. Kell, K. S. Lilley, P. Roepstorff, J. R. Yates, A. Brass, A. J. Brown, P. Cash, S. J. Gaskell, S. J. Hubbard, and S. G. Oliver. A systematic approach to modeling, capturing, and disseminating proteomics experimental data. *Nat. Biotechnol.*, 21(3):247–254, 2003.

36. M. van Iersel, T. Kelder, A. Pico, K. Hanspers, S. Coort, B. Conklin, and C. Evelo. Presenting and exploring biological pathways with PathVisio. *BMC Bioinformatics*, 9:399.1–9, 2008.

INDEX

Biological Knowledge Discovery Handbook: Preprocessing, Mining, and Postprocessing of Biological Data,
First Edition. Edited by Mourad Elloumi and Albert Y. Zomaya.
© 2014 John Wiley & Sons, Inc. Published 2014 by John Wiley & Sons, Inc.

Wiley Series on

Bioinformatics: Computational Techniques and Engineering

Bioinformatics and computational biology involve the comprehensive application of mathematics, statistics, science, and computer science to the understanding of living systems. Research and development in these areas require cooperation among specialists from the fields of biology, computer science, mathematics, statistics, physics, and related sciences. The objective of this book series is to provide timely treatments of the different aspects of bioinformatics spanning theory, new and established techniques, technologies and tools, and application domains. This series emphasizes algorithmic, mathematical, statistical, and computational methods that are central in bioinformatics and computational biology.

Series Editors: **Professor Yi Pan** and **Professor Albert Y. Zomaya**
pan@cs.gsu.edu   albert.zomaya@sydney.edu.au